Assessing Adolescent and Adult Intelligence

Alan S. Kaufman

THE UNIVERSITY OF ALABAMA

Allyn and Bacon, Inc.
Boston London Sydney Toronto

Series editor: John-Paul Lenney
Managing Editor: Mylan Jaixen
Production: The Book Company
Design: The Book Company
In-house production coordinator: Peter Petraitis
Cover coordinator: Linda Dickinson
Composition buyer: Bill Alberti
Manufacturing buyer: Linda Cox

Library of Congress Cataloging-in-Publication Data

Kaufman, Alan S.
    Assessing adolescent and adult intelligence / Alan S. Kaufman.
        p.   cm.
    Includes bibliographical references.
    ISBN 0-205-12390-2
    1. Wechsler Adult Intelligence Scale. 2. Intelligence tests. 3. Teenagers—Intelligence testing. I. Title.
BF432.5.W4K38   1990
153.9′3—dc20   90-30448
                                                    CIP

Printed in the United States of America
10 9 8 7 6 5 4 3 2 1   95 94 93 92 91 90

Credits:

Selected quotes from A. S. Kaufman, *Intelligent Testing with the WISC-R,* copyright © 1979, John Wiley & Sons, Inc., and from B. B. Wolman (Ed.), *Handbook of Intelligence,* copyright © 1985, John Wiley & Sons, Inc. Reprinted by permission of John Wiley & Sons, Inc.

Selected quotes from D. Wechsler, *Measurement and Appraisal of Adult Intelligence* (4th ed.), 1958; from J. D. Matarazzo, *Wechsler's Measurement and Appraisal of Adult Intelligence* (5th ed.), 1972; and from M. Lezak, *Neuropsychological Assessment* (2nd ed.), 1983. Reprinted by permission of Oxford University Press.

Selected quotes from R. S. Dean: Adapted and reproduced by special permission of the publisher, Psychological Assessment Resources, Inc., from the Reports of Individual Evaluation for the WAIS/WAIS-R by Raymond S. Dean. Copyright 1983 by Psychological Assessment Resources, Inc. All rights reserved.

Selected quotes from *NASP Communique,* Volume 17, No. 4 (December, 1988). Reprinted with the permission of Alex Thomas.

Selected quotes from M. D. Lezak (1988). IQ: R.I.P. *Journal of Clinical and Experimental Neuropsychology, 10* (No. 3), 351–361. Reprinted with the permission of the author, M. D. Lezak, and the publisher, Swets & Zeitlinger.

Selected quotes from test reviews appearing in the *Ninth Mental Measurements Yearbook* (1985) are reprinted with permission of the publisher, the Buros Institute of Mental Measurements, University of Nebraska Press.

Table 1.3 is adapted from a table in P. L. Harrison et al. (1988), A survey of tests used for adult assessment, *Journal of Psychoeducational Assessment, 6* (No. 3), 188–198. Appreciation is expressed to the *Journal of Psychoeducational Assessment* for permitting use of this table.

Figure 2.1 appeared in *Education Week*'s Special Report, "Here They Come, Ready or Not." Reprinted with permission of *Education Week,* May 14, 1986.

Figure 5.1 appeared in R. A. Zachary, *Shipley Institute of Living Scale: Revised Manual* (1986). Copyright © 1939 by The Institute of Living, The Neuro-Psychiatric Institute of the Hartford Retreat. Copyright © renewed 1967 by Barbara Shipley Boyle. Reprinted by permission of the publisher, Western Psychological Services, 12031 Wilshire Boulevard, Los Angeles, California 90025, USA.

Tables 6.1, 6.4, 6.9, 6.11, and 6.12 were adapted from tables that appeared in C. R. Reynolds et al. (1987), Demographic characteristics and IQ among adults: Analysis of the WAIS-R standardization sample as a function of the stratification variables. *Journal of School Psychology, 25* (No. 4), 323–342. Reprinted by permission of the publisher, Pergamon Press plc.

Table 7.7 and Figures 7.1, 7.2, and 7.3 appeared in A. S. Kaufman et al. (1989), Age and WAIS-R intelligence in a national sample of adults in the 20- to 74-year age range: A cross-sectional analysis with education level controlled. *Intelligence, 13,* 235–253. They are reprinted with the permission of the publisher, Ablex Publishing Corporation.

Figure 7.10 is adapted from a figure appearing in J. L. Horn's chapter in L. R. Goulet & P. Baltes (Eds.) (1970), *Lifespan Developmental Psychology: Research and Theory.* It is reproduced with the permission of J. L. Horn and the publisher, Academic Press.

Figure 16.2 appeared in the *Manual for the K-TEA Comprehensive Form.* It is reproduced with permission of American Guidance Service, Publishers' Building, Circle Pines, MN 55014. *Kaufman Test of Educational Achievement* (K-TEA) by Alan S. Kaufman and Nadeen L. Kaufman. Copyright 1985. All rights reserved.

Numerous tables in this text appeared or will appear in *Journal of Clinical Psychology* articles coauthored by J. E. McLean, C. R. Reynolds, and A. S. Kaufman. They are reprinted with the permission of the authors, who retain the copyright.

For Nadeen,
for her inspiration, insight, loyalty, and love,
forever

and

For the memory of David Wechsler,
mentor, friend, pioneer,
with undying respect

CONTENTS

P R E F A C E

Assessing Adolescent and Adult Intelligence presents comprehensive coverage of the clinical and neuropsychological assessment of intelligence, particularly as measured by the Wechsler Adult Intelligence Scale—Revised (WAIS-R). The text focuses on ages 16 to 74 years, the WAIS-R age range, but also addresses research and assessment issues for adolescents aged 12 to 15 years and adults in their 80s. It is intended as the primary textbook for graduate-level courses in intellectual assessment, whether a beginning course or an advanced practicum, and whether the focus of the course is on theory, research, or practice. It is also designed to serve as a handbook for interns and professionals who routinely or occasionally evaluate adolescents and adults. The book is oriented toward practitioners, researchers, and academicians in the fields of clinical psychology, school psychology, neuropsychology, and educational psychology; but it is equally relevant for graduate courses and professionals in the related fields of psychiatry, special education, counseling, medical psychology, developmental psychology, gerontology, and psychometrics.

Because the WAIS-R is the instrument of choice for adolescent and adult intellectual assessment, this text focuses on the WAIS-R throughout its 17 chapters. The history of the clinical evaluation of adult intelligence virtually begins with David Wechsler's innovations and insights, culminating in the Wechsler-Bellevue;

present-day assessment of brain damage, retardation, psychopathology, dementia, and learning disabilities in adolescents and adults likewise begins with Wechsler's contributions. The main question faced by most examiners is not whether to give the WAIS-R, but what instruments should be used to supplement the WAIS-R. Memory tests? Other cognitive tasks? Achievement batteries? Adaptive behavior inventories? Tests of creativity? Thorough neuropsychological batteries? Tests in all of these areas are covered in some depth in *Assessing Adolescent and Adult Intelligence* (especially in Part IV); virtually every important test for the 12+ age range that was designed to measure intelligence or closely related skill areas is described and evaluated. Coverage of instruments includes tests that have recently been published (e.g., the Wechsler Memory Scale—Revised) and some that just became available as this book went to press (the Peabody Individual Achievement Test—Revised and the Woodcock-Johnson Psycho-Educational Battery—Revised). Evaluations are direct, sometimes hard hitting, and nearly always based on a blend of the empirical, the clinical, the practical, and the theoretical.

Indeed, the entire approach to assessment presented throughout the text represents a dynamic integration of the following ingredients: (a) over 1,000 clinical and neuropsychological research investigations on adolescent and adult intelligence, many on the WAIS-R or its predecessors; (b) an empirical approach to WAIS-R Verbal–Performance and subtest profile interpretation that can be applied at a sophisticated level by the psychometrically oriented professional, or via simple rules of thumb by the mathematically insecure; (c) a clinical, neuropsychological, and psychoeducational approach to intelligence tests that facilitates interpretation of significant profile fluctuations; (d) the application of theories of intelligence (e.g., Cattell-Horn, cerebral specialization) whenever the theories are clinically or neuropsychologically relevant; and (e) adherence to the *intelligent testing* philosophy, which elevates clinicians above the tests they use and places less emphasis on the IQs than on the peaks and valleys in the total test profile.

Throughout *Assessing Adolescent and Adult Intelligence,* the emotion-laden IQ concept is treated in a societal context. Controversies surrounding the IQ construct and challenges to intelligence tests are dealt with in a straightforward, rational, research-supported manner that often involves new syntheses of the existing literature. Many questions of interest to professionals and laypeople alike regarding the IQ and its clinical applications are addressed—for example: Is the IQ a valid construct, or should intelligence tests be abandoned? What portion of IQ is genetic, and is the black–white difference due to heredity? Are the Japanese smarter than Americans, and how does the U.S. compare with numerous other nations regarding changes in intelligence over the past few generations? Do adults evidence dramatic declines in their intelligence with increasing age? Is there a characteristic WAIS-R profile to aid in the diagnosis of Alzheimer's disease? Is either the Stanford-Binet IV or the Woodcock-Johnson—Revised a formidable competitor for the WAIS-R? Are the brief, commonly used Slosson and Shipley-Hartford tests suitable replacements for the WAIS-R when testing time is at a premium, and is the WRAT-R a worthy WAIS-R supplement?

I needed help with some questions and issues on key topics that extend beyond intelligence testing and enlisted experts on adaptive behavior inventories and neuropsychological batteries to write guest chapters. I am extremely grateful to Dr. Patti L. Harrison of the University of Alabama for her chapter on mental retardation, adaptive behavior, and giftedness (chapter 15); and to Dr. George Hynd and Ms. Margaret Semrud-Clikeman of the University of Georgia for their chapter on neuropsychological assessment (chapter 17). Their excellent contributions have enhanced greatly both the coverage and quality of this text.

In addition, I would like to acknowledge numerous individuals for other valuable contributions to *Assessing Adolescent and Adult Intelligence.* Dr. Cecil Reynolds graciously shared his WAIS-R data tape with me and my colleague, Dr. James McLean, allowing the three of us to conduct numerous investigations on topics that were essential to fill gaps in the literature and to facilitate WAIS-R profile interpretation (e.g., aging and IQ decline, factor analysis by gender and race, relationship of subtests to background variables). Cecil and Jim, along with Patti Harrison, George Hynd, and my wife Nadeen, merit my special appreciation for their professional competence and advice, and for their consistent friendship; each has left his or her mark on my personal and professional growth, and on the quality of this text.

Dr. Tom Oakland accepted the yeoman task of reviewing the entire 17 chapters composing this text. He spent countless hours carefully digesting each sentence, and made numerous valuable, insightful, and probing comments and criticisms. I tried to heed virtually all of his suggestions, and am grateful for his diligence and considerable expertise. Dr. Donald Kausler, an expert in the methodology and interpretation of research on aging, reviewed chapter 7 on age and IQ across the adult lifespan. I wanted an extra reviewer for this key topic, partly because of the controversial nature of the relevant research, and partly because of a new longitudinal study of Wechsler intelligence that appears for the first time in this text. I am extremely grateful to Dr. Kausler for his excellent suggestions for improving the chapter (and for giving his "blessing" to my new study!). Dr. Kevin McGrew also merits thanks for reviewing carefully about 100 manuscript pages devoted to interpretation and evaluation of the Woodcock-Johnson. Unfortunately, nearly all of these pages are excluded from the text (winding up in the waste basket); they became obsolete when Woodcock announced in the summer of 1988 that a thoroughly expanded, revised, and restandardized Woodcock-Johnson battery was forthcoming.

I am grateful to several graduate students, all but one from the University of Alabama, for helping me locate and xerox literally thousands of research articles on adolescent and adult assessment: Toshinori (Toshi) Ishikuma, Richard Ittenbach, Valerie Okun, Marcia O'Neal, and Carol Schmitt. Toshi and his wife Harue have been especially vital in my effort to complete this text on time without sacrificing quality. They performed countless mathematical computations and generated numerous formulas for the tables in chapters 13 and 14, and contributed greatly to this text in many other ways as well. Toshi, my teaching assistant, has been an inspiration to me, an invaluable professional colleague and friend.

The University of Alabama merits my special, sincere thanks for its unflagging support of my research and writing. I am grateful for so many reasons to Dr. Joab Thomas (former President), Dr. E. Roger Sayres (President), Dr. Rod Roth (Dean of the College of Education), Dr. James McLean (Chairman of the Area of Behavioral Studies), Dr. Patti Harrison (Head of School of Psychology), and Brenda Spencer (typist).

I appreciate the numerous psychologists, including many former students and colleagues, who sent me copies of their case reports on adolescents and adults. In addition to selecting several reports that were written by graduate students in my assessment courses at the University of Alabama, I selected two reports from Dr. Judith Ivins for inclusion in the text; I'd like to give a special thanks to Judy and to these former students (who are listed by name at the end of each pertinent report). I am indebted to Dr. Joanne Callan, Dr. Sidney Smith, and others at CSPP–San Diego for teaching me much about clinical assessment when Nadeen and I were on their core faculty. Also, I appreciate the kindness of Drs. Gary Robertson and Elizabeth Rengel of American Guidance Service for sending me a copy of the PIAT-R test and manual prior to publication, and of Drs. Robert Zachary and Marc Daniel of The Psychological Corporation for sending me a Differential Abilities Scales standardization kit along with prepublication information about this forthcoming test.

Allyn & Bacon has given me excellent support during the course of this arduous project. I am especially grateful to Bill Barke, Mylan Jaixen, John-Paul Lenney, Susan Brody, Wendy Calmenson, and Steven Hiatt for their extreme competence and kind cooperation.

My family plays a very important and special part in my life, and has provided continued, much needed support during the writing of this text. I would like to thank my daughter Jennie for her daily encouragement; my son David for his long-distance interest in my writing; my son James for teaching me how to word process on "his" Macintosh; my granddaughter Nicole for helping me to maintain perspective; and my wife Nadeen for everything.

I was fortunate to have had the privilege of working closely with David Wechsler from 1970 to 1974. I learned much from this brilliant innovator, a wise and compassionate man. I have also learned much from my lifelong colleague and companion, Nadeen.

Alan S. Kaufman
January, 1990

CHAPTER 1

IQ Tests: Their History, Use, Validity, and Intelligent Interpretation

INTRODUCTION

The field of intelligence, particularly of adolescent and adult mental development, has dominated the psychological literature for decades, and now encompasses a diversity of domains within cognitive psychology, clinical psychology, psychobiology, behavioral genetics, education, school psychology, sociology, neuropsychology, and everyday life. Excellent 1,000-page handbooks are available with chapters written by experts in many aspects of intellectual theory, measurement, and development (Sternberg, 1982, 1988; Wolman, 1985), and even these texts cover only a portion of the territory and quickly become outdated. Consequently, in writing this text on the assessment of adolescent and adult intelligence, I have had to make several decisions about which areas to include and how thoroughly to cover each topic.

First, this book focuses on the clinical assessment of intelligence, and every topic must bear, either directly or indirectly, on the clinical aspect of mental measurement. Since clinical assessment within the fields of neuropsychology, special education, and clinical, school, and counseling psychology involves individual evaluations, research on group-administered tests is subordinated to the more pertinent research on individual intelligence tests.

For example, the monumental efforts of Schaie and his colleagues to understand the development of adult intelligence (e.g., Schaie, 1983; Schaie & Strother, 1968; Schaie & Hertzog, 1983) have been based on the group-administered Primary Mental Abilities Test. The key findings from these innovative cross-sequential studies are of interest to psychology in general, but have limited applicability to the work of clinical and neuropsychological practitioners. Consequently, investigations by Schaie will be discussed in the context of aging studies on more pertinent instruments—the Wechsler Adult Intelligence Scale (WAIS; Wechsler, 1955) and its revision (WAIS-R; Wechsler, 1981) (Birren

& Morrison, 1961; Kaufman, Reynolds, & McLean, 1989; Parker, 1986).

Wechsler's Scales

Even a casual observer of the clinical or neuro-psychological assessment scene is aware that Wechsler's scales are uncontested as measures of adolescent and adult intelligence. Individuals in their teens and adults of all ages are invariably administered the Wechsler Intelligence Scale for Children—Revised (WISC-R; Wechsler, 1974) or the WAIS-R when they are referred to a competent professional for a thorough assessment of their intellectual abilities, usually as part of a clinical, vocational, neuropsychological, or psychoeducational evaluation. The WISC-R is used for adolescents as old as 16 years, while the WAIS-R is used for individuals aged 16 to 74.

I have elsewhere discussed the WISC-R as a clinical and psychometric tool (Kaufman, 1979b) and, in any case, the WISC-R will soon be superseded by an updated version. (The standardization of the WISC-III was under way as this book went to press.) For practical purposes, then, this book is primarily devoted to the WAIS-R, child of the WAIS and grandchild of the Wechsler-Bellevue Form I (Wechsler, 1939). This test battery has so far outdistanced its competition that any other test for adolescents and adults can reasonably be thought of as either a supplement or an alternative to the WAIS-R.

Clinical Relevance of Theory

To be included in this book in any depth, a topic needs to contribute to a psychologist's understanding of intelligence in the clinical arena, not in the laboratory. For example, Horn and Cattell's (1966) theory of fluid and crystallized intelligence, including Horn's (1985) refinements of it, is treated throughout the book because it is instrumental in explaining changes in verbal and nonverbal abilities with advancing age, and it underlies three new tests of adolescent and adult intelligence: the Woodcock-Johnson Psycho-Educational Battery—Revised (WJ) (Woodcock & Johnson, 1989a), the Stanford-Binet Intelligence Scale, Form IV (Thorndike, Hagen, & Sattler, 1986a), and the Kaufman Adolescent and Adult Intelligence Test (KAIT; Kaufman and Kaufman, in press *a*). In contrast, Sternberg's (1985) three-pronged triarchic theory of intelligence, though popular and widely discussed, is ignored because of its limited application to clinical assessment and the interpretation of the WAIS-R and other individual intelligence tests. Perhaps this theory will become valuable outside the laboratory once the Sternberg Multidimensional Abilities Test (cited by Cohen, Montague, Nathanson, & Swerdlik, 1988, pp. 239–240) becomes available, if the test author is successful in translating laboratory principles to the domain of the clinical psychologist, neuroclinician, and psychoeducational diagnostician.

Reaction-Time and EEG Studies

Also excluded from this text, apart from the summary presented here, is the provocative laboratory research conducted on reaction time and evoked potentials. Jensen's (1985b) reaction-time investigations, which explore the relationships of psychometric intelligence scores to simple and complex reaction time (measured to the nearest millisecond), reflect a return to the similar techniques used by Sir Francis Galton and James McKeen Cattell in their anthropometric laboratories established before 1900. Eysenck and Barrett's (1985) use of electroencephalographs (EEGs) to assess IQ objectively takes advantage of modern technology and seems more like futuristic science fiction than a return to the sensorimotor "intelligence" tests of the pre-Binet era.

Yet the Jensen and Eysenck approaches share common elements: Both use machines requiring simple motor responses like pushing a button; both are content-free measures of intelligence; and both seek to measure intelligence validly and objectively with high-tech instrumentation that may revolutionize contemporary standards of reliability. Reaction-time studies have produced correlations with IQ typically in the .35 range (actually - .35, reflecting the finding that shorter response times are associated with higher IQs). When several reaction-time tasks are combined into a battery, however, considerably higher coefficients are possible, perhaps in the .70 range (Vernon, 1983). Reaction-time tests discriminate among groups differing in intelligence, with the brighter subjects earning the lowest mean reaction-time scores (Jensen, 1982; Vernon, Nador, & Kantor, 1985). In addition, speed of response in reaction-time investigations correlates about equally well with IQ whether it is measured under timed or untimed conditions (Vernon & Kantor, 1986).

EEG studies have produced even more impressive statistical findings than the Jensen/Vernon reaction-time investigations, although cross-validation of the evoked potential research has been inconsistent (Brody, 1985). For example, research conducted in the early 1980s by D. E. and A. E. Hendrickson, based on a complex theoretical model and utilizing different methodologies than those used by Ertl (1971) in his pioneering research, yielded correlations between average evoked potential (AEP) and WAIS IQs in the .72 to .83 range (Eysenck & Barrett, 1985, Table 2). Ertl obtained coefficients that averaged about .30 (Chalke & Ertl, 1965; Ertl, 1971; Ertl & Schafer, 1969), while others have reported strictly negative results (e.g., Davis, 1971). Focusing on the positive results by the Hendricksons and others, Eysenck (1982) has argued that the EEG is a better measure of **g** than are the WAIS subtests.

Like computerized testing, the measurement of intelligence with binary response consoles and other types of chronoscopes to record reaction time—or with EEGs to permit measurement of the "string" and "variance" of the AEPs—may become the procedure of choice in the twenty-first century. But as the twentieth century enters its final decade, these methodologies are still laboratory based and remain controversial (for criticisms, see Engel & Henderson, 1973; Longstreth, 1984; and Ruchalla, Schalt, & Vogel, 1985). These approaches have yet to have an impact on the clinical assessment of adolescents and adults referred for psychological or neuropsychological evaluation.

OUTLINE OF THE BOOK

Assessing Adolescent and Adult Intelligence has four parts:

  I. Introduction to the Assessment of Adolescent and Adult Intelligence (three chapters)
 II. Integration and Application of WAIS-R Research (five chapters)
III. Interpretation of the WAIS-R V-P Discrepancy and Subtest Profile (six chapters)
 IV. Clinical and Neuropsychological Assessment with the WAIS-R and Other Instruments (three chapters)

Part I includes chapter 1, which discusses pertinent historical information, issues regarding validation of the IQ construct, and my philosophy of intelligent testing; chapter 2, which discusses pressing issues and challenges to the IQ concept (e.g., heritability of the IQ and the differences in intelligence among 14 nations); and chapter 3, which provides the rationale for the 11 subtests for adolescents and adults and traces the empirical and logical continuity from the Wechsler-Bellevue to the WAIS to the WAIS-R.

Part II presents research on the WAIS-R in five chapters, each one dealing with essential information about the interpretation of the IQ for adolescents and adults, and the understanding of important psychological issues regarding intelligence, like race differences and the impact of aging on test performance: Administration, scoring, and stability (chapter 4); WAIS-R short forms, including two popular substitutes for the WAIS-R—the Shipley Institute of Living Scale (Shipley-Hartford; Zachary, 1986) and the Slosson Intelligence Test (Jensen & Armstrong, 1985) (chapter 5); IQ and the stratification variables (chapter 6); aging (chapter 7); and factor analysis (chapter 8).

Part III comprises three chapters on the interpretation of WAIS-R Verbal-Performance IQ discrepancies (9, 10, and 11), with a special focus on neuropsychological research involving patients with lateralized lesions; and three chapters (12, 13, and 14) dealing with the empirical and clinical interpretation of WAIS-R subtest profiles.

Part IV discusses a number of supplementary tests for adolescent and adult assessment and integrates them with the WAIS-R, focusing on clinical and neuropsychological assessment. Chapter 16 discusses and evaluates numerous supplements to the WAIS-R. These tests include the new Wechsler Memory Scale—Revised (Wechsler, 1987) and five individual achievement tests: Wide Range Achievement Test—Revised (WRAT-R; Jastak & Wilkinson, 1984); Woodcock-Johnson—Revised, Achievement portion (Woodcock & Johnson, 1989b); Kaufman Test of Educational Achievement (K-TEA; Kaufman & Kaufman, 1985a, 1985b), Brief and Comprehensive Forms; Peabody Individual Achievement Test—Revised (PIAT-R; Markwardt, 1989); and Woodcock Reading Mastery Test—Revised (Woodcock, 1987). In addition to the memory and achievement batteries, which are common supplements to the WAIS-R, are the homogeneous, quick Peabody Picture Vocabulary Test—Revised (PPVT-R; Dunn & Dunn, 1981) and three comprehensive intelligence tests that are best used to supplement the WAIS-R rather than serve as the main measure of mental ability:

the Woodcock-Johnson—Revised, Cognitive portion (Woodcock & Johnson, 1989a); the Stanford-Binet IV (Thorndike et al., 1986a); and the Detroit Tests of Learning Aptitude (DTLA-2; Hammill, 1985). The Detroit and new Binet, both standardized in the mid-1980s, have psychometric limitations (especially their norms), and they were not standardized across the whole adult range. The new Woodcock-Johnson, though psychometrically excellent and normed through old age, adheres to a theoretical model that seems to lack clinical pertinence. Nonetheless, each battery includes clever subtests that help augment the information provided by the WAIS-R, particularly for following up hypotheses generated during a psychoeducational or neuropsychological evaluation.

Part IV also contains two chapters guest-written by experts in their fields. Chapter 15, on the assessment of mental retardation, adaptive behavior, and giftedness, was written by Dr. Patti Harrison; chapter 17, on neuropsychological assessment, was written by Dr. George Hynd with his colleague, Margaret Semrud-Clikeman. A variety of WAIS-R supplements are treated in some depth in chapters 15 and 17: The Vineland Adaptive Behavior Scales (Sparrow, Balla, & Cicchetti, 1984), along with several other adaptive behavior tools are covered in chapter 15; and the Halstead-Reitan (Reitan & Wolfson, 1985) and Luria-Nebraska (Golden, Hammeke, & Purisch, 1980) are treated in chapter 17.

A variety of psychometric tools are thus evaluated in Part IV, but the WAIS-R, like the WAIS and Wechsler-Bellevue before it, remains the key tool for clinical and neuropsychological evaluation of adolescents and adults and, hence, the focus of all sections of the book. For who interprets the Halstead-Reitan in the absence of Reitan's ever-present Wechsler-Bellevue or the more modern WAIS-R? Who gives a Vineland without relating the results to Wechsler's global IQs? The chapters on clinical applications of intelligence tests, along with the previous parts of the book, place the focus of this text squarely on the WAIS-R.

The ubiquity of the WAIS-R struck me while I was taking time out from writing this text by relaxing with the February 1, 1988, copy of *The Sporting News*. I suddenly read that a dispute between a basketball coach and player about their relative mental prowess ought to be settled by having the principals "placed in glass-enclosed booths and scribble furiously as they plow through the Wechsler Adult Intelligence Scale."

Never mind that the sports columnist thought the WAIS was a self-administered paper-and-pencil test. Or that he didn't know it had been revised. I was impressed!

A SHORT HISTORY OF IQ TESTS

The history of intellectual assessment is largely a history of the measurement of the intelligence of children or retarded adults. Sir Francis Galton (1869, 1883) studied adults and was interested in giftedness when he developed what is often considered the first comprehensive individual test of intelligence (Kaufman, 1983b). But despite Galton's role as the father of the testing movement (Shouksmith, 1970), he did not succeed in constructing a true intelligence test. His measures of simple reaction time, strength of squeeze, or keenness of sight proved to assess sensory and motor abilities, skills that relate poorly to mental ability, and that are far removed from the type of tasks that constitute contemporary intelligence tests.

The Binet-Simon Scales

Alfred Binet and his colleagues (Binet & Henri, 1895; Binet & Simon, 1905, 1908) developed the tasks that survive to the present day in most tests of intelligence for children and adults. Binet (1890a, 1890b) mainly studied children; beginning with systematic developmental observations of his two young daughters, Madeleine and Alice, he concluded that simple tasks like those used by Galton did not discriminate between children and adults. In 1904, the Minister of Public Instruction in Paris appointed Binet to a committee to find a way to distinguish normal from retarded children. But 15 years of qualitative and quantitative investigation of individual differences in children—along with considerable theorizing about mental organization and the development of a specific set of complex, high-level tests to investigate these differences—preceded the "sudden" emergence of the landmark 1905 Binet-Simon intelligence scale (Murphy, 1968).

The 1908 scale was the first to include age levels, spanning the range from III to XIII. This important modification stemmed from Binet and Simon's unexpected discovery that their 1905 scale was useful for much more than classifying a child at one of the three levels of retardation: moron, imbecile, idiot (Matarazzo, 1972). Assessment of older adolescents and adults, however, was not built into the Binet-Simon system until the 1911 revision. That scale was extended to age level XV and included five ungraded adult tests (Kite, 1916). This extension was not conducted with the rigor that characterized the construction of tests for children, and the primary applications of the scale were for use with school-age children (Binet, 1911).

Measuring the intelligence of adults, except those known to be mentally retarded, was almost an afterthought. But the increased applicability of the Binet-Simon tests for various child assessment purposes dawned on Binet just prior to his untimely death in 1911: "By 1911 Binet began to foresee numerous uses for his method in child development, in education, in medicine, and in longitudinal studies predicting different occupational histories for children of different intellectual potential" (Matarazzo, 1972, p. 42).

Terman's Stanford-Binet

Lewis Terman was one of several Americans who translated and adapted the Binet-Simon scale for use in the United States, publishing a "tentative" revision (Terman & Childs, 1912) 4 years before releasing his painstakingly developed and carefully standardized Stanford Revision and Extension of the Binet-Simon Intelligence Scale (Terman, 1916). This landmark test, soon known simply as the Stanford-Binet, squashed competing tests developed earlier by Goddard, Kuhlmann, Wallin, and Yerkes. Terman's success was undoubtedly due in part to heeding the advice of practitioners whose demand "for more and more accurate diagnoses . . . raised the whole question of the accurate placing of tests in the scale and the accurate evaluation of the responses made by the child" (Pintner & Patterson, 1925, p. 11).

But like Binet, Terman (1916) saw intelligence tests useful primarily for the detection of mental deficiency or superiority in children and for the identification of "feeblemindedness" in adults. He cited numerous studies of delinquent adolescents and adult criminals, all of which pointed to the high percentage of mentally deficient juvenile delinquents, prisoners, or prostitutes, and concluded that "there is no investigator who denies the fearful role played by mental deficiency in the production of vice, crime, and delinquency" (p. 9). Terman also saw the potential for using intelligence tests with adults for determining "vocational fitness"; but again, he emphasized employing "a psychologist . . . to weed out the unfit" or to "determine the minimum 'intelligence quotient' necessary for success in each leading occupation" (p. 17).

Perhaps because of this emphasis on the assessment of children or concern with the lower end of the intelligence distribution, Terman (1916) did not use a rigorous methodology for constructing his adult-level tasks. Tests below the 14-year level were administered to a fairly representative sample of about 1,000 children and early adolescents. To extend the scale above that level, data were obtained from 30 businessmen, 50 high school students, 150 adolescent delinquents, and 150 migrating unemployed men. Based on a frequency distribution of the mental ages of a mere 62 adults (the 30 businessmen and 32 of the high school students above age 16), Terman partitioned the graph into the following MA categories: 13–15 (inferior adults), 15–17 (average adults), and above 17 (superior adults).

The World War I Tests

The infant field of adult assessment grew rapidly with the onset of World War I, particularly after U.S. entry into the war in 1917 (Anastasi, 1988; Vane & Motta, 1984). Psychologists saw with increasing clarity the applications of intelligence tests for selecting officers and placing enlisted men in different types of service, apart from their generation-old use for identifying the mentally unfit. Under the leadership of Robert Yerkes and the American Psychological Association, the most innovative psychologists of the day helped translate Binet's tests to a group format. Arthur Otis, Terman's student, was instrumental in leading the creative team that developed the Army Alpha, essentially a group-administered Stanford-Binet, and the Army Beta, a novel group test composed of nonverbal tasks.

Yerkes (1917) opposed Binet's age-scale approach and favored a point-scale methodology, one that advocates selection of tests of specified, important functions rather than a set of tasks that fluctuates greatly with age level and developmental stage. The Army group tests reflect a blend of Yerkes's point-scale approach and Binet's notions of the kind of skills that should be measured when assessing mental ability. The Army Alpha included the Binet-like tests of Directions or Commands, Practical Judgment,

Arithmetical Problems, Synonym-Antonym, Dissarranged Sentences, Analogies, and Information. Even the Army Beta had subtests resembling Stanford-Binet tasks: Maze, Cube Analysis, Pictorial Completion, and Geometrical Construction. The Beta also included novel measures like Digit Symbol, Number Checking, and X-O Series (Yoakum & Yerkes, 1920).

Never before or since have tests been normed and validated on samples so large; 1,726,966 men were tested (Vane & Motta, 1984)! Point-scores on the Army Alpha or Army Beta were converted to letter grades ranging from A to D− (the Beta was given only to illiterate and non–English-speaking candidates). Validity was demonstrated by examining the percent of A's obtained by a variety of Army ranks, for example, recruits (7.4%), corporals (16.1%), sergeants (24.0%), and majors (64.4%). In perhaps the first empirical demonstration of the Peter Principle in action, second lieutenants (59.4% A's) outperformed their direct superiors—first lieutenants (51.7%) and captains (53.4%)—while those with ranks above major performed slightly worse than majors (Yoakum & Yerkes, 1920, Table 1). Can there be any more compelling affirmation of the validity of the Army intelligence tests?

Another intelligence scale was developed during the war, one that became an alternative for those who could not be tested validly by either the Alpha or Beta. This was the Army Performance Scale Examination, composed of tasks that would become the tools-of-trade for clinical psychologists, school psychologists, and neuropsychologists into the twenty-first century: Picture Completion, Picture Arrangement, Digit Symbol, and Manikin and Feature Profile (Object Assembly). Except for Block Design (developed by Kohs in 1923), Wechsler's influential Performance Scale was added to the Army battery, "[t]o prove conclusively that a man was weakminded and not merely indifferent or malingering" (Yoakum & Yerkes, 1920, p. 10).

Wechsler's Creativity

David Wechsler assembled a test battery in the mid-1930s that comprised subtests developed primarily by Binet and World War I psychologists. His Verbal Scale was essentially a Yerkes point-scale adaptation of Stanford-Binet tasks; his Performance Scale, like other similar nonverbal batteries of the 1920s and 1930s (Cornell & Coxe, 1934; Pintner & Patterson, 1925), was a near replica of the tasks and items making up the individually administered Army Performance Scale Examination.

In essence, Wechsler took advantage of tasks developed by others for nonclinical purposes to develop a clinical test battery. He paired verbal tests that were fine-tuned to discriminate among children of different ages with nonverbal tests that were created for adult males who had flunked both the Alpha and Beta exams—nonverbal tests that were intended to distinguish between the nonmotivated and the hopelessly deficient. Like Terman, Wechsler had the same access to the available tests as did other psychologists; like Terman and Binet before him, Wechsler succeeded because he was a visionary, a man able to anticipate the needs of practitioners in the field.

While others hoped intelligence tests would be psychometric tools to subdivide retarded individuals into whatever number of categories was currently in vogue, Wechsler saw the tests as dynamic clinical instruments. While others looked concretely at intelligence tests as predictors of school success or guides to occupational choice, Wechsler looked abstractly at the tests as a mirror to the hidden personality. With the Great War over, many psychologists returned to a focus on IQ testing as a means of childhood assessment; Wechsler (1939), however, developed the first form of the Wechsler-Bellevue exclusively for adolescents and adults.

Most psychologists saw little need for nonverbal tests when assessing English-speaking individuals other than illiterates. How could it be worth 2 or 3 minutes to administer a single puzzle or block-design item when 10 or 15 verbal items can be given in the same time? Some test developers (e.g., Cornell & Coxe, 1934) felt that Performance scales might be useful for normal, English-speaking people to provide "more varied situations than are provided by verbal tests" (p. 9), and to "test the hypothesis that there is a group factor underlying general concrete ability, which is of importance in the concept of general intelligence" (p. 10).

Wechsler was less inclined to wait a generation for data to accumulate. He followed his clinical instincts and not only advocated the administration of a standard battery of nonverbal tests to everyone but placed the Performance Scale on an equal footing with the more respected Verbal Scale. *Both* scales would constitute a complete Wechsler-Bellevue battery, and each would contribute equally to the overall intelligence score.

Wechsler also had the courage to challenge the Stanford-Binet monopoly, a boldness not unlike Binet's when the French scientist created his own forum (the journal *L'Année Psychologique*) to challenge the preferred but simplistic Galton sensorimotor approach to intelligence (Kaufman, 1983b). Wechsler met the same type of resistance as Binet, who had had to wait until the French Ministry of Public Instruction "published" his Binet-Simon Scale. When Wechsler's initial efforts to find a publisher for his two-pronged intelligence test met failure, he had no cabinet minister to turn to, so he took matters into his own hands. With a small team of colleagues, he standardized Form I of the Wechsler-Bellevue by himself. Realizing that stratification on socioeconomic background was more crucial than obtaining regional representation, he managed to secure a well-stratified sample from Brooklyn, New York.

The Psychological Corporation agreed to publish Wechsler's battery once it had been standardized, and the rest is history. Although

an alternative form of the Wechsler-Bellevue (Wechsler, 1946) was no more successful than Terman and Merrill's (1937) ill-fated Form M, a subsequent downward extension of Form II of the Wechsler-Bellevue (to cover the age range 5 to 15 instead of 10 to 59) produced the wildly successful WISC (Wechsler, 1949). Although the Wechsler scales did not initially surpass the Stanford-Binet in popularity, serving an apprenticeship to the master in the 1940s and 1950s, the WISC and the subsequent revision of the Wechsler-Bellevue, Form I (WAIS; Wechsler, 1955) triumphed in the 1960s. "With the increasing stress on the psychoeducational assessment of learning disabilities in the 1960s, and on neuropsychological evaluation in the 1970s, the Verbal-Performance (V-P) IQ discrepancies and subtest profiles yielded by Wechsler's scales were waiting and ready to overtake the one-score Binet" (Kaufman, 1983b, p. 107).

Irony runs throughout the history of testing. Galton developed statistics to study relationships between variables—statistics that proved to be forerunners of the coefficient of correlation, later perfected by his friend Karl Pearson (DuBois, 1970). The ultimate downfall of Galton's system of testing can be traced directly to coefficients of correlation, which were too low in some crucial (but, ironically, poorly designed) studies of the relationships among intellectual variables (Sharp, 1898–99; Wissler, 1901). Similarly, Terman succeeded with the Stanford-Binet while the Goddard-Binet (Goddard, 1911), the Herring-Binet (Herring, 1922), and other Binet-Simon adaptations failed because he was sensitive to practitioners' needs. He patiently withheld a final version of his Stanford revision until he was certain that each task was appropriately placed at an age level consistent with the typical functioning of representative samples of American children.

Terman continued his careful test development and standardization techniques with the first revised version of the Stanford-Binet (Terman & Merrill, 1937). But 4 years after his death in 1956, his legacy was devalued when the next revision of the Stanford-Binet comprised a merger of Forms L and M, *without a standardization* of the newly formed battery (Terman & Merrill, 1960). The following version saw a restandardization of the instrument, but without a revision of the placement of tasks at each age level (Terman & Merrill, 1973). Unfortunately for the Binet, the abilities of children and adolescents had changed fairly dramatically in the course of a generation, so the 5-year level of tasks (for example) was now passed by the average 4½-year-old!

Terman's methods had been ignored by his successors. The ironic outcome was that Wechsler's approach to assessment triumphed, at least in part because the editions of the Stanford-Binet in the 1960s and 1970s were beset by the same type of flaws as Terman's competitors in the 1910s. The newest Stanford-Binet (Thorndike, Hagen, & Sattler, 1986a, 1986b) attempted to correct these problems and even adopted Wechsler's multisubtest, multi-scale format. However, these changes in the Fourth Edition of the Binet were too little and too late to be much threat to the popularity of the Wechsler scales, to offer much contribution to the field of intelligence testing, or to merit the linkage with the Binet tradition (see pages 608–614).

A SURVEY OF TEST USAGE FOR ADULTS

Surveys of test use in the United States appear occasionally in the literature, usually based on data from clinical agencies and hospitals (Lubin, Larsen, & Matarazzo, 1984), school systems (Goh, Teslow, & Fuller, 1981), industry (Swenson & Lindgren, 1952), military settings (Lubin, Larsen, Matarazzo, & Seever, 1986), and private practitioners (Lubin et al., 1986). Apart from the latter study, the questionnaires are typically mailed to institutions and thus exclude psy-

chologists who assess clients in private practice. Other than Brown and McGuire's (1976) survey of mental health centers, researchers have failed to distinguish between test usage for children versus adults or to distinguish between intelligence tests, personality measures, and other instruments when constructing the questionnaires. They have also tallied the frequency of use of each instrument without assessing user satisfaction, and they have not delineated the purposes for which intelligence tests are administered.

To address these issues, my colleagues and I conducted a survey by mailing questionnaires in mid-1985 to 1,315 members of four clinically oriented APA divisions and to 480 directors of APA-accredited programs (Harrison, Kaufman, Hickman, & Kaufman, 1988). The main goals of the investigation were: (a) to confine questions to adult assessment, and organize tests by type (intelligence, achievement, personality, adaptive behavior, vocational interest); (b) to survey the professionals who do the assessments, rather than institutions, to produce a more representative cross-section of test users; (c) to discover characteristics (age, ability level) of adults who are assessed; (d) to find out how important test users perceive the information that they obtain from the tests; and (e) to determine why examiners administer intelligence tests to adults.

The Respondents

Of 1,315 questionnaires mailed out, 402 were returned, a response rate of 22.4%. Of the respondents, 313 indicated that they currently assess adults or had done so in the past 10 years; this group became the subjects for the study. The low response rate may be related to the focus on adult assessment; many recipients of the survey may have failed to respond because they test only children (or because they do not conduct test evaluations at all). In addition, some undoubtedly failed to respond because they perceived the questionnaire as a marketing survey, since it inquired about the respondents' assessment needs (T. Oakland, personal communication, 1989). Nonetheless, the sample of 313 is representative of employment settings, is distributed fairly equally across the four geographic regions of the country, and had much relevant work experience (over 90% had worked at least 6 years in pertinent jobs). Interestingly, 75% reported spending less than one-quarter of their total job in assessing adult functioning, while less than 10% reported spending at least half of their time in that capacity (Harrison et al., 1988).

What Kinds of Adults Are Assessed?

The respondents estimated that on the average about three-quarters of the adults that they test are below age 45 and less than 1% are elderly. The distributions of the median percentages assessed in each of four age ranges are shown in Figure 1.1, based on the values obtained from the responses of the 299 respondents who answered this question. Whereas the mean (as opposed to median) percentage who test the elderly is a more respectable 6.8 (Harrison et al., 1988), older clients are clearly not the norm. The relatively few adults aged 65 and above who are assessed is contrary to the trend of greater interest in geriatric psychology and in the changing nature of intelligence during the aging process (Wolman, 1985). The median value of <1% indicates that most respondents test no elderly clients at all. It is conceivable, however, that these percentages will grow steadily during the 1990s.

Figure 1.2 presents distributions of the estimated intelligence of the adults they assess. Median percentages follow a surprisingly normal distribution, although there is an inflated left "tail," indicating that the number of retarded adults tested exceeds their proportion in the population at large. The mean percentages are similar to the median values except for IQs below 70 (mean = 12.3%), again indicating the

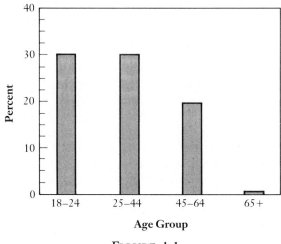

FIGURE 1.1

Relative proportions of adults assessed in each of four age groups, as estimated by clinicians who evaluate adult clients (data from Harrison et al., 1988; median values are shown).

disproportionate number of low-functioning individuals who are referred for evaluation. The latter result is axiomatic; more unexpected is the finding that half the adults tested by clinicians on individual tests are estimated to be of average intelligence (that is, within a standard deviation of the mean).

How Frequently Is the WAIS-R Used With Adults?

Clinicians who test adults almost always use the WAIS-R (or WAIS). Of the 300 respondents who answered the question regarding the instruments given during an adult evaluation, 290 (97%) listed the WAIS or WAIS-R among the measures of intelligence that they commonly use. The old Binet was a distant second (25%), followed by the Peabody Picture Vocabulary Test or its 1981 revision (the PPVT-R), the Bender-Gestalt, and the Shipley Institute of Living Scale (Shipley-Hartford) (see Figure 1.3). Table 1.1 details the number of respondents

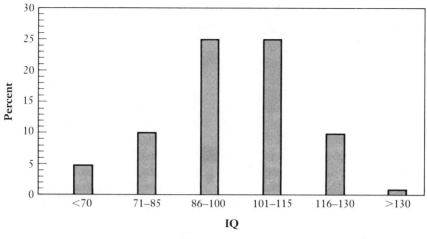

FIGURE 1.2

Relative proportions of adults assessed in each of six ability classifications, as estimated by clinicians who evaluate adult clients (data from Harrison et al., 1988; median values are shown).

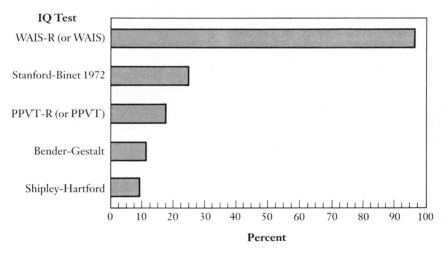

FIGURE 1.3

Prevalence of use of the five most popular intelligence tests for adults (data from Harrison et al., 1988).

selecting each intelligence test as well as instruments in other categories. This table was excluded from Harrison et al.'s (1988) article on the survey because of space limitations.

Of the Wechsler scale users, 75% listed the WAIS-R, 9% listed the WAIS, and 16% listed both tests. The survey was conducted 4 years following the release of the WAIS-R, so clinicians who still give the outdated instrument may simply resist change. Even though the WAIS-R is sometimes referred to as the WAIS, these percentages are probably accurate because

TABLE 1.1   Frequency of use with adults of various intelligence, achievement, adaptive behavior, personality, and vocational interest tests (*N*=300)

Test	Number Who Commonly Use Test	Test	Number Who Commonly Use Test
Intelligence		**Personality**	
WAIS-R or WAIS	290	MMPI	200
Stanford-Binet (1972)	75	Rorschach	196
PPVT-R or PPVT	52	TAT	168
Bender-Gestalt	35	Sentence Completion	108
Shipley-Hartford	27	Draw-A-Person	77
Raven's Progressive Matrices	25	Bender-Gestalt	66
WISC-R	24	House-Tree-Person	54
Slosson	18	16 PF	19
Leiter	13	Millon Clinical Multiaxial Inventory	18
Quick Test	10	Self concept Inventories	13
Achievement		CPI	11
WRAT-R or WRAT	175	Beck Depression Inventory	10
PIAT	59	**Vocational Interest**	
Woodcock-Johnson	29	Strong-Campbell	111
Adaptive Behavior		Kuder General Interest Survey	28
Vineland Adaptive Behavior Scales (Vineland Revision) or Vineland Social Maturity Scale	101	Career Assessment Inventory	12
AAMD Adaptive Behavior Scale	41	Kuder Occupational Interest Survey	11
		Minnesota Vocational Interest Inventory	10
		Holland Self-Directed Search	9

NOTE: Tests are included in this table only if they were listed as commonly used by at least nine respondents (3% of sample).

respondents were specifically told to specify the WAIS or WAIS-R if they gave the Wechsler adult test. Such resistance to change is not surprising; some esteemed psychologists like Ralph Reitan still prefer the Wechsler-Bellevue to either subsequent adult battery (Herring & Reitan, 1986), and other clinicians persist in administering the Wechsler-Bellevue (Lubin et al., 1984; Lubin et al., 1986).

I discussed this topic in 1983 with a respected colleague, Dr. Sidney Smith, now with the Menninger Clinic. He insisted that the redrawing of the pictures for numerous Performance items, especially Picture Arrangement, took away the ambiguity from many Wechsler-Bellevue stimuli and robbed the items of some of their clinical value. My empirical and psychometric sides win out in such discussions (see pp. 363–365), but I am reminded of David Wechsler's frequent admonition to me when I worked with him in the development of the WISC-R: "Do not forget that the WISC is first and foremost a clinical test."

Of the 290 clinicians who reported in the survey that they commonly use the WAIS-R (or WAIS), about half indicated that they use other intelligence tests as well (this includes the group that gives both Wechsler adult tests). Nonetheless, they choose the WAIS-R more often than the other tests for most evaluations. For example, two out of five of the clinicians who use the WAIS-R along with other intelligence tests give the WAIS-R in 90% or more of their evaluations. In contrast, only two respondents to the survey (<1%) use the 1972 Stanford-Binet for more than half of their adult evaluations (Harrison et al., 1988).

The popularity of Wechsler's scales for adult assessment has not diminished since Brown and McGuire's (1976) survey, which found the WAIS to be the most popular intelligence test for individuals aged 18 and above. In that survey, the WAIS was followed by the Bender-Gestalt, Binet, Slosson, and Wide Range Achievement Test (WRAT). Those researchers asked professionals to list the three instruments

used most frequently by their agencies for intellectual assessment and for personality assessment for each of seven age levels. In the more recent Harrison et al. (1988) study, the Bender and Binet remained in the top five, but the Slosson dropped to eighth place (only 6% of respondents used it), and the WRAT was categorized only as a measure of achievement.

The fact that tests of design copying (Bender), receptive vocabulary (PPVT-R), and achievement (WRAT) could rank in the top five in the Brown and McGuire (1976) or Harrison et al. (1988) studies—along with the poorly normed and brief Slosson and Shipley-Hartford—attests to the lack of well-normed and validated intelligence tests for adults other than the WAIS-R. The only comprehensive non-Wechsler intelligence test with adequate adult norms available at the time of the 1988 survey was the 1977 edition of the WJ, Cognitive portion. But this test is not used frequently by psychologists, especially for adult assessments. Even though nearly 10% of the clinicians in the Harrison et al. (1988) survey use the WJ Achievement battery with adults, the Cognitive portion was listed by only 4 respondents (1%).

Consequently, the WAIS-R is the focus of this text. Discussions of the other instruments mentioned here, and/or their revisions, appear in the following chapters: Chapter 5 discusses short forms of the WAIS-R (Shipley-Hartford, Slosson); chapter 16 covers supplements to the WAIS-R (PPVT-R, Stanford-Binet IV, WJ); and chapter 17 gives brief coverage to the Bender-Gestalt.

How Frequently Are Tests From Other Domains Used for Adults?

As Table 1.1 shows, the WRAT-R (or WRAT) dominated the achievement test category, appearing on the lists of 175 respondents (58%), with the Peabody Individual Achievement Test (PIAT) a distant second (20%). (In Table 1 of the Harrison et al. article, the PIAT and WJ appear to be tied for second place with 29 responses apiece. However, the value for the PIAT is a typo; it should be 59.) Among measures of adaptive behavior, the Vineland Adaptive Behavior Scales or its predecessor (the Vineland Social Maturity Scale) ranked as a decisive number one, although its usage rate of 34% indicates that most respondents do not assess adaptive behavior in their clinical evaluations. The AAMD Adaptive Behavior Scale ranked second with 14%. Similarly, the Strong-Campbell (37%) far outdistanced the Kuder General Interest Survey (9%), but clinicians do not seem to emphasize interest inventories (see Table 1.1).

Unlike the other assessment areas, personality measurement produced stiff competition between the Minnesota Multiphasic Personality Inventory (MMPI; 67%), Rorschach (65%), and Thematic Apperception Test (TAT; 56%). Various sentence completion tests (36%) and the Draw-A-Person (26%) rounded out the top five, showing remarkable consistency with survey results from the mid-1970s. Brown and McGuire (1976) reported the same five personality measures as the top five tests for adults, with the only difference in ranking concerning the reversal of sentence completion and Draw-A-Person (Harrison et al., 1988).

When the popularity of tests is considered apart from the type of instrument, the WAIS-R (or WAIS) emerges as the single most used test by the clinicians who responded to Harrison et al.'s questionnaire. The top 10 tests are listed below, along with the percentage (out of a sample of 300) who commonly use it. (For the Bender-Gestalt, the percentage is based on the number of respondents listing it on their survey form, whether as an intelligence test, a personality test, a visual-motor test, or some combination of these.)

TEST	PERCENT
1. WAIS-R or WAIS	97
2. MMPI	67
3. Rorschach	65
4. WRAT-R or WRAT	58
5. TAT	56
6. Strong-Campbell	37
7. Sentence Completion	36
8. Vineland	34
9. Bender-Gestalt	29
10. Draw-A-Person	26

Of these 10 most administered tests in the 1980s, the WAIS-R is the only one that is truly an intelligence test.

Among the various high-ranking tests in areas other than intelligence, the WRAT-R and revised PIAT are discussed in chapter 16 of this text on supplements to the WAIS-R, and the revised Vineland is treated in depth in chapter 15 on the assessment of mental retardation, adaptive behavior, and giftedness.

How Important Is the Information Yielded by Intelligence Tests?

Respondents were asked to "list all the tests you commonly use in the assessment of adults and rate them on a scale from 1 (limited importance) to 5 (great importance) in relation to the information they provide." Harrison et al. (1988) constructed an "Importance Index" by subtracting the percentage who said a given test yielded information of limited importance (rankings of 1 or 2) from the percentage rating the information provided as being of high importance (rankings of 4 or 5).

The WAIS-R or WAIS earned an Importance Index of +89.7, with 92.1% of Wechsler users perceiving the information yielded to be of great importance. In contrast, the other commonly used intelligence tests, the 1972 Stanford-Binet (+18.7), Bender-Gestalt (+8.5), and PPVT or PPVT-R (−5.7), had unimpressive Importance Indexes.

Indeed, the WAIS-R was perceived by the survey respondents as providing the most important information of any instrument, regardless of category. Only the MMPI came close (+81.0), and just five other tests had indexes above 40: the WJ Achievement battery (+69.0), the Rorschach (+66.8), the Strong-Campbell (+53.2), the WRAT-R or WRAT (+44.5), and the TAT (+43.4). Those respondents who specifically indicated the Vineland Adaptive Behavior Scales gave this recent instrument a respectable Importance Index of +52.2, but the low index for the old Vineland (+4.6) lowered the overall Importance Index for this adaptive behavior scale. In fact, indexes for other revised tests were also higher than corresponding values for the superseded version of the test (WAIS-R versus WAIS, PPVT-R versus PPVT).

The low Importance Indexes for three measures of intelligence, the Binet, Bender, and PPVT, rank these tests among the bottom six in perceived importance when considering all measures, regardless of test type; they are joined by Draw-A-Person, House-Tree-Person, and the Kuder General Interest Survey.

The WAIS-R was thus both the most commonly used test and the one perceived as yielding the information of the greatest importance. The 7 most popular tests were among the 10 most important tests, and a significant rank-order correlation of .64 was obtained between popularity and importance (Harrison et al., 1988). Generally, clinicians seem satisfied with the tests they commonly use, although the Draw-A-Person test is a notable exception. This tenth most popular instrument was nonetheless perceived as providing information of limited importance—perhaps because it is often used as an ice breaker that aids in establishing rapport (Lubin et al., 1984).

For What Purposes Are Adults Given Intelligence Tests?

Harrison et al. (1988) presented a list of seven purposes for which adults might be administered intelligence tests, and asked the respondents to (a) indicate all the reasons that applied to them, and (b) rank order the reasons they checked from most important to least important. Respondents were allowed to write in alternative reasons, but these were generally special cases of one of the seven reasons and were recategorized accordingly.

Table 1.2 lists the purposes, the percentage who assess adults for each purpose, and the percentage who consider each purpose very important (i.e., the first or second most important reason why they give intelligence tests to adults). As shown, 85% of the respondents use intelligence tests as both a *psychometric* tool (to measure potential) and a *clinical* one (to obtain clinically relevant information). About three-quarters give intelligence tests for reasons pertaining to brain functioning, but less than half measure intelligence as an aid in making educational or vocational decisions. The tests, in general, are used a bit more frequently for decisions regarding placement (whether educational or vocational) than intervention.

Table 1.2 shows that the frequency with which each purpose was chosen corresponds almost exactly to how important the respondents perceived this purpose to be. Yet the two columns in the table provide complementary information. Even though nearly every examiner administers intelligence tests for both psychometric and clinical reasons, only a little more than half the sample considered either the obtained scores or the supplementary clinical information as the primary reason for giving the test in the first place. Similarly, 40% to 50% of the respondents use intelligence tests for educational or vocational purposes, but the actual decisions regarding placement or intervention tend *not* to be the main reasons for assessing IQ. In fact, using intelligence tests for placing adults in educational or vocational programs was of prime importance to only about 15% of the respondents, and using test results for developing intervention strategies headed the lists of only 5% to 10%.

Since the respondents to Harrison et al.'s survey so overwhelmingly chose the WAIS-R or WAIS as the intelligence test of choice, the results shown in Table 1.2 for intelligence tests in general may be applied specifically to Wechsler's adult scales.

What Are the Main Strengths and Weaknesses of IQ Tests?

Ten attributes of intelligence tests were listed by Harrison et al. (1988), and respondents were asked to rate each on a scale from 1 (significant weakness) to 5 (significant strength). For this question, the attributes were specifically intended for intelligence tests administered to adolescents and adults, so the results are undoubtedly pertinent to the WISC-R as well as the WAIS-R and WAIS.

Table 1.3 lists the attributes in order of perception from most positive to most negative concerning contemporary IQ tests for adolescents and adults. The table shows the percentage of respondents rating each attribute as a strength and the percentage rating the same attribute as a weakness. Using the difference between these two percentages as an informal index of the strength-weakness continuum reveals that the two most positive features of Wechsler's scales are the representativeness of his consistently excellent standardization samples and the soundness with which he developed his batteries from theory. In contrast, the biggest weaknesses were the Wechsler scales' inability to measure real-life problem-solving situations or to relate meaningfully to vocational interests and decision making.

Overall, the strengths of the tests are related to their internal properties and the interpretability of the obtained scores; their weaknesses involve real-world, everyday applications of standardized IQ tests. In a survey conducted by Snyderman and Rothman (1987), the respondents (661 experts in intelligence testing) likewise cited the inadequate measurement of "adaptation to one's environment" as one of the main weaknesses of intelligence tests. Frederiksen (1986), in his plea for a broader conception of human intelligence, stressed the need to supplement traditional IQ tests with "realistic simulations of real-life problem situations" (p. 451).

TABLE 1.2   Purposes for using intelligence tests when assessing adults

Purpose	% Who Assess Adults for This Purpose	% Who Rank This Purpose as Very Important
1. Measure potential or capacity	85.2	58.5
2. Obtain clinically relevant information	85.2	53.1
3. Assess functional integrity of brain	77.6	43.3
4. Determine educational placement	48.4	17.0
5. Determine vocational placement	45.5	12.3
6. Develop educational interventions	44.0	10.8
7. Develop vocational interventions	39.4	5.8

NOTE: Data are from Harrison et al. (1988) based on 277 respondents asked to list all the purposes for which "you generally use a standardized intelligence test in your assessment battery" and "then rank the ones you checked in order of their importance, with 1 as the most important." The "% who rank this purpose as very important" equals the percentage of the total group of 277 who assigned each purpose a ranking of 1 or 2.

TABLE 1.3   Perceived strong and weak attributes of commonly used intelligence tests for adolescents and adults

Attribute	% Rating Attribute a Strength	% Rating Attribute a Weakness	Difference in Percent
1. Representative standardization sample	67.1	7.4	+59.7
2. Development based on sound theoretical principles	62.2	12.4	+49.8
3. Guidance in how to interpret the results	47.3	18.7	+28.6
4. Relevant content for adults	36.7	15.9	+20.8
5. Interest to adults	32.9	18.0	+14.9
6. Guidance in how to make meaningful recommendations based on test results	35.7	22.3	+13.4
7. Interpreted in the context of life-span developmental psychology	21.2	35.7	−14.5
8. Measurement of mature decision-making capacities	21.9	37.1	−15.2
9. Relationship to vocational interests and career choice	14.8	40.6	−25.8
10. Real-life problem-solving situations	17.0	43.8	−26.8

NOTE: Data are from Harrison et al. (1988) based on 283 respondents asked to "rate the following attributes of the intelligence tests you most frequently use for adolescents and adults on a continuum from 1 (significant weakness) to 5 (significant strength)." In this table, "strength" corresponds to ratings of 4 or 5, and "weakness" to ratings of 1 or 2.

The questionnaire in the Harrison et al. (1988) study included two questions, one open ended, that explored the perceived need for new tests. About one-quarter of the respondents felt that new intelligence tests were needed. Interestingly, those who chose to expand on their perceptions consistently cited the need for intelligence tests that assess practical, social, everyday functioning; that deal more effectively with ethnic-cultural issues; and that assess a broader scope of functions, e.g., creativity. Inadequate assessment of creativity was also a prime criticism of intelligence tests in Snyder-

man and Rothman's (1987) survey of experts. Frederiksen (1986) argued that "the structure of intellect of the future will include a much broader spectrum of intelligent behaviors. Furthermore, it will not be a static model but will be one that recognizes the interactions involving test formats, subject characteristics, and the settings in which the problems are encountered" (p. 451).

But intelligence testing was not seen by Harrison et al.'s (1988) sample as the main need for the assessment field; that honor went to tests of neuropsychological functioning and adaptive behavior, each named by nearly half of the respondents as requiring better instruments. They wanted neuropsychological tests that are brief, simple, and easy to give and score, that have excellent norms, and that serve a screening function. New adaptive behavior measures should embody the characteristics suggested for both tests of intelligence and neuropsychological functioning: brevity, simplicity, ease of administration and scoring, excellent psychometric properties, more adult orientation, relevance to real-life problems and living skills, and geared for the whole ability spectrum, not just retarded individuals.

Conclusions

The Harrison et al. (1988) survey results indicate that the WAIS-R is king among assessment tools used to assess adult functioning in numerous domains, and has no peer in the intelligence domain. The importance attributed to the information yielded by the WAIS-R, the fact that a majority of respondents (74%) saw no need for new intelligence tests, and the consensus that the norms and theoretical soundness of the Wechsler scales are major strengths show that the WAIS-R is both well used and highly regarded. If the Wechsler batteries have a fault, it is their failure to measure responses to everyday, real-life problems and to tie in better with vocational choice.

VALIDITY OF THE IQ CONSTRUCT FOR ADOLESCENTS AND ADULTS

Matarazzo (1972, chapters 6, 7, and 12) devoted most of three chapters to support the validity of the IQ construct, Jensen (1980) addressed the issue from both theoretical and empirical perspectives (his chapters 6 and 8, respectively), and Brody (1985) published a thought-provoking chapter on "The Validity of Tests of Intelligence." These three esteemed psychologists concluded, in essence, that the IQ construct, as measured by contemporary intelligence tests, is valid when defined within the societal context and when the IQ's limitations are kept fully in mind. Although the validity of the IQ construct and the tests purported to assess it are important to this text, I treat it cursorily here because it has been thoroughly discussed elsewhere.

Prediction of Academic Achievement

The age-old IQ criterion of prediction of school achievement has been explored in thousands of studies across the age range, and "the conclusion seems to [Matarazzo, 1972] well-documented that there is a correlation of approximately .50 between measured intelligence (IQ) and performance in school" (p. 285). Coefficients are typically a bit higher in elementary school and lower in college (Brody, 1985). The overall value of .50 is high enough to support the validity of the IQ for the purpose that Binet originally intended it, but low enough to indicate that about 75% of the variance in school achievement is accounted by factors other than IQ.

For the WAIS-R, the correlation has been between .45 to .70 (averaging in the low .60s) based on the following illustrative coefficients obtained between Full Scale IQ and the WRAT or WRAT-R Reading, Spelling, and Arithmetic subtests: (a) .50 to .71 for 45 clients (62% female, 71% black), average age = 24, referred to a college clinic (Spruill & Beck, 1986); (b) .60 to .76 for 60 patients (97% male), average age = 38, at a Veterans Administration Medical Center referred for psychological evaluation (Ryan & Rosenberg, 1983); and (c) .44 to .72 for two samples each composed of about 120 patients at a medical center (51% male), average age = 36½, referred for neuropsychological evaluation (Warner, Ernst, Townes, Peel, & Preston, 1987).

Coefficients for Wechsler's Verbal IQ are consistently higher than for Performance IQ; in the Spruill and Ryan studies cited above, the mean coefficient was .65 for V and .54 for P. In two WAIS studies cited by Matarazzo (1972, p. 284) V-IQ correlated higher than P-IQ with high school rank (.63 versus .43) and college grade point average (GPA) (.47 versus .24). Based on numerous WISC-R investigations summarized by Sattler (1988, p. 125), mean coefficients with scores on various standardized achievement tests are .61 for V-IQ and .41 for P-IQ.

In general, the use of the WAIS-R for predicting college achievement is likely to produce coefficients lower than the values in the .60s observed for patient populations, where standardized achievement tests are the criteria. The values may be even lower than the overall value of .50 that typifies predictive validity studies (Jensen, 1980; Matarazzo, 1972). Matarazzo (1972, p. 284), for example, cited a coefficient of .44 between WAIS FS-IQ and GPA for 335 college students with a mean IQ of 115. And Jensen (1980, p. 330) reported a median correlation of .40 between the General Intelligence test of the General Aptitude Test Battery (GATB) and college grades in 48 different samples (comprising 5,561 students). These results generalize directly to the WAIS-R since the WAIS and GATB General Intelligence test reportedly correlate .89 (Jensen, 1980).

Strong evidence exists that prediction of college grades consistently produces higher coefficients for females than males (Jensen, 1980), and some evidence suggests that WAIS-R prediction of GPA may be biased against Chicano high school students relative to white students (Armstrong, 1982).

Even if correlation coefficients involving the WAIS or WAIS-R account for only 15% to 20% of the variability in college students' grades (compared to 25% for the typical predictive validity study or 50% for the occasional study in the literature), such values nonetheless strongly support the Wechsler scales' validity for educational purposes. Correlations for college students are attenuated substantially—having nothing to do with the quality of the instrument—because of (a) the restricted range of IQs found in highly selected samples, (b) the questionable nature of the GPA criterion (it, too, is restricted to a 5-point scale from A to F, and college grading systems fluctuate notoriously from instructor to instructor), and (c) the role played by nonintellective factors such as motivation and study habits.

Relationship of IQ to Education

For a children's intelligence test, correlations between IQ and school achievement are among the best evidences of validity, but those coefficients are less valuable for adult tests. The best arguments for the validity of an adult test are the relationships between IQ and formal education and between IQ and occupational level (a variable that correlates substantially with years of schooling; see Gottfredson & Brown, 1981). Success in school is a key task of children and adolescents; life accomplishments are the goals of an adult.

Logically, people who score higher on a so-called intelligence test should advance higher within the formal education hierarchy and should assume positions within the more prestigious occupations. Which is cause and which is effect is not relevant to this point. Perhaps individuals score higher on IQ tests because of what they learn in school; perhaps they proceed to higher levels of education because they are smart to begin with; or perhaps these two variables combine in some way. In any case, a strong relationship between education and IQ supports the construct that underlies tests that purport to measure intelligence.

This relationship is explored in depth for the WAIS-R in chapter 6 (pp. 172–179), and again in chapter 10 (pp. 337–342) regarding

V-P differences and brain damage. The present discussion gives only an overview of the relationship between years of schooling and WAIS-R scores in order to illustrate the over-whelming validity support for the WAIS-R when educational attainment is the criterion. Data for Full Scale IQ are from Reynolds, Chastain, Kaufman, & McLean (1987); data for Information and Block Design are weighted means for ages 20–34 and 35–54 (Kaufman, McLean, & Reynolds, 1988).

Mean Full Scale IQs for 16- to 74-year-olds with different formal education levels are as follows:

Years of Schooling	Mean Full Scale IQ
16+ (College graduate)	115.2
13–15 (Some college)	107.3
12 (High school graduate)	100.0
9–11 (Some high school)	96.4
8 (Elementary school graduate)	90.8
0–7 (Some elementary school)	82.5

The two extreme groups differ by nearly 33 points, more than two standard deviations! These differences tend to be larger for Verbal than Performance subtests, but they are nonetheless substantial even for tasks like Block Design or Digit Symbol that are not specifically taught in the classroom. The mean scaled score for ages 20 to 54 on two selected WAIS-R subtests, one closely related to the specific content taught in school (Information) and one unrelated to curriculum (Block Design), are shown in Table 1.4 for five different education levels. The age range was restricted to young adults and middle-aged adults to avoid contamination due to incomplete educational attainment (ages 16–19) or the differential impact of aging on Verbal and Performance test scores (ages 55–74; see chapter 7).

These data show that relatively uneducated people perform about equally poorly on school-related and school-unrelated tasks, and that both types of tests are substantially related to formal education. Highly educated adults, however, have a greater advantage on crystallized than on fluid tasks (i.e., on Information than on Block Design). Data from the Fels Longitudinal Study (McCall, 1977) reveal that childhood IQs correlate about .50 (±.10) with both adult educational and occupational attainment, stabilizing at that relatively high level at ages 7 to 8 for males and females.

The strong relationship between IQ and formal education should not obscure the considerable *variability* of IQs earned by individuals with the same educational attainment. Fluctuations in IQ by education level are shown in Table 6–10 (see page 170), based on data compiled (but not published) by Reynolds et al. (1987). These results indicate that each level of educational attainment is accompanied by a wide range of Full Scale IQs. For example, individuals with some college education have a higher mean IQ by about 11 points than those with some high school, but their IQ ranges are fairly similar: 76–139 for those with 13–15 years of schooling compared to 59–146 for those with 9–11 years of schooling.

TABLE 1.4   Mean scaled score for ages 20–54 on two selected WAIS-R subtests

Years of Schooling	Mean Score on Information (School-Related)	Mean Score on Block Design (Not School-Related)
16+	12.7	11.0
13–15	10.8	10.3
12	9.8	9.4
9–11	8.2	8.3
0–8	6.5	6.1

IQ and Occupation

For ages 20 to 54, WAIS-R data provide additional validation evidence for Wechsler's IQs by examining mean scores earned by adults actively engaged in different levels of occupation (Reynolds et al., 1987). Adolescents have been eliminated from consideration because occupational data are based on their parents' occupation, and the 55–74 year olds have been eliminated because two-thirds are categorized as "Not in Labor Force."

Occupational data are treated in depth in chapter 6 (pp. 166–172), and are summarized here to illustrate the validity of the IQ construct. Mean Full Scale IQs are shown for five categories of occupation, listed in order of the average educational level (from high to low) that typifies each category.

Occupational Group	Mean Full Scale IQ
1. Professional and technical	112.4
2. Managers and administrators, clerical workers, and sales workers	103.6
3. Skilled workers (craftsmen and foremen)	100.7
4. Semiskilled workers (operatives, service workers—including private household—farmers, and farm managers)	92.3
5. Unskilled workers (laborers, farm laborers, farm foremen)	87.1

The 25-point difference between professionals and unskilled workers combined with the educational data gives strong support to the construct underlying WAIS-R Full Scale IQs; occupational and educational data presented in chapter 6 give substantial validity support for the separate Verbal and Performance IQs as well.

When IQs are provided for specific jobs instead of general categories, even wider discrepancies emerge between diverse occupations. For example, Matarazzo (1972, pp. 178–180) cites numerous studies and his own considerable clinical experience to show that physicians, medical students, dentists, university professors, psychiatrists, executives in industry, scientists, and attorneys have consistently averaged IQs of 125 on the Wechsler-Bellevue and WAIS. In a recent study of 35 medical students, Mitchell, Grandy, and Lupo (1986) reported mean Full Scale IQs in the same range on both the WAIS (124.5) and WAIS-R (120.8).

The wide range of mean scores by people in different occupations is further illustrated by a comprehensive ($N = 39,600$) 1970 U.S. Department of Labor study cited by Jensen (1980, pp. 341–342). Mean IQs on the GATB General Intelligence scale were provided for 444 specific occupations, and ranged from 55 for Tomato Peeler to 143 for Mathematician. Although the GATB General Intelligence score correlates .89 with the WAIS (as indicated on page 19), the two scales have different standard deviations. When the GATB scores for Tomato Peelers and Mathematicians are converted to the Wechsler metric, the means become 66 and 132, respectively. This discrepancy is not as impressive as the 88-point difference on the GATB scale (mean of 100, SD of 20), but it nonetheless provides additional evidence of the IQ construct's validity.

Figure 1.4, adapted from Matarazzo (1972, p. 178) and Jensen (1980, p. 113) and modified based on WAIS-R data cited in this chapter, presents graphically the educational or occupational referents of different IQ levels. However, these values are just the averages for different jobs or educational accomplishments. As Matarazzo (1972) and Jensen (1980) stress, adults in each occupation or educational category vary considerably in IQ range. Table 6-10 (see

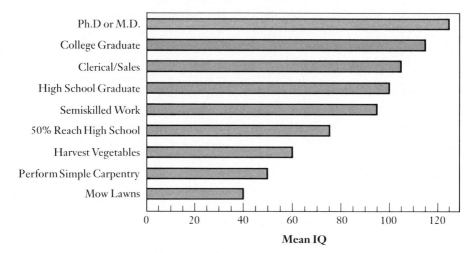

FIGURE 1.4

Mean Wechsler adult IQs that correspond to different educational and occupational accomplishments (based on data in Table 7–3 of Matarazzo, 1972, p. 178; data in Table 4.5 in Jensen, 1980, p. 113; WAIS-R standardization data reported on pages 166–179 of this text).

p. 170), discussed previously regarding educational attainment and IQ range, also presents pertinent data that reveal the fairly wide range of IQs for individuals from the same occupational category. For occupational groups, the range is relatively small for people employed in routine, menial jobs usually reserved for the mentally retarded, but substantial IQ ranges characterize members in jobs as diverse as physicians or policemen or even unskilled construction workers.

One of the most frequently cited series of studies in support of the IQ's validity is Terman's (1925; Terman & Oden, 1959) longitudinal study of 1,528 gifted children (average IQ of 152), a group that generally achieved remarkable success in life. Over 85% entered professional occupations or became high-ranking executives in education or business; only about 3% were employed as farmers or semi-skilled laborers. Interestingly, though, data obtained in a 50-year follow-up of the males in Terman's original sample (Sears, 1977) re-

vealed that, "the objective facts of life—the high-level preparation, the success and status and financial rewards received—appear to have had negligible importance in determining final satisfaction with the occupational side of life" (p. 123).

The strong relationship depicted here between IQ and occupation may be an artifact of the even stronger relationship described previously between IQ and educational attainment. Occupation and education correlate substantially, particularly since advanced formal education is frequently a prerequisite for many high-prestige occupations. Gottfredson and Brown (1981) observed an interesting age-related finding in the occupation-education relationship in their large-scale longitudinal study. Occupational status correlated a modest .17–.20 with years of schooling at ages 18–20 years, but increased at age 22 (.45) and age 24 (.60) before plateauing in the mid-.60s for 26- and 28-year-olds. Gottfredson and Brown interpreted these age-related findings as a function of the facts that (a) the later entrants into the work force are brighter and better educated, and (b) among those already employed, the smarter and more educated adults advance from low-level to high-level positions.

Regardless, years of schooling "is the single most important determinant of occupational status in United States society" (Brody, 1985, p. 361). Brody states further that the results of path analysis in several studies indicate that IQ has "a large influence on educational attainment and *relatively little indirect influence on occupational status*" (pp. 361–362, italics mine)—that is, separate from the IQ-education relationship.

Prediction of Job Performance

Average correlations between general intelligence and job proficiency are traditionally in the .20s (Ghiselli, 1966, 1973). However, because the predictors and criteria are typically restricted in variability due to selection factors and other practical limitations of test validation in industrial settings, some have argued that such coefficients require statistical correction to reflect more accurately the "true" relationship between IQ and job success (Hunter & Hunter, 1984). For the purposes here (i.e., to determine the validity of the *theoretical* construct underlying intelligence tests), the corrected values seem more appropriate.

In an ambitious meta-analysis of hundreds of studies relating intelligence to job performance, Hunter (1986) concluded that "general cognitive ability has high validity predicting performance ratings and training success in all jobs" (p. 359). He organized data from three major sources, correcting coefficients for restriction of range in all cases, and for attenuation (imperfect test reliability) in the first two sets of studies: (a) Ghiselli's lifework, involving several summaries of a quarter-century's worth of validity studies in industry on the prediction of job proficiency and success in training programs; (b) 515 validation studies conducted by

the U.S. Employment Service with the GATB, 425 on job proficiency ($N = 32,124$) and 90 on training success ($N = 6,496$); and (c) U.S. military studies of training success in mechanical, clerical, electronic, and general technical fields (828 studies totalling 472,539 subjects).

Coefficients of correlation between intelligence and job proficiency (performance ratings) were consistently higher for complex jobs than for those demanding less complexity. The Ghiselli studies produced substantial corrected correlations for the complex jobs of manager (.53), clerk (.54), and salesperson (.61). Coefficients in the mid-.40s were obtained for jobs of medium complexity (e.g., crafts and trades), while values in the high .20s and .30s were typical of low complexity jobs like vehicle operator. Similar averages emerged when Hunter (1986) grouped the U.S. Employment Service studies by complexity: high complexity ($r = .58$), medium (.51), and low (.40).

Intelligence correlated even more impressively with success in training than it did with job performance. Further, the coefficients obtained for various training programs were about equally good, regardless of job complexity. The average corrected coefficient for the 828 studies of training success conducted by the U.S. military was .62, with values hovering around that overall value for each of the four job families (i.e., mechanical, clerical, electronic, and general technical). Coefficients from the Ghiselli summaries ranged from .37 (vehicle operator) to .87 (protective professions) with a median correlation of .65 across seven categories of jobs. The 90 training studies carried out by the U.S. Employment Service yielded average values of .50 to .65 (median = .56) for jobs grouped into four categories.

Hunter showed further that validity coefficients are even higher when objective work samples of job performance are used instead of subjective supervisor ratings. Based on a handful of particularly well-designed investigations that used objective criteria to evaluate job proficiency, corrected correlations were .75 in civilian data and .53 in military data.

Jensen's (1980) analysis of some of the same data summarized by Hunter in 1986 presents a sobering view of the ability of intelligence tests to predict job performance and training success. Coefficients reported by Hunter were corrected for restriction of range and, usually, for attenuation as well; these corrections inflate the correlations by estimating their magnitude in "what if" situations. The correction for attenuation (test unreliability) is particularly questionable, however, since by definition tests are not perfectly reliable. Jensen (pp. 347–350) notes that Ghiselli's actual coefficients were in the .20 to .25 range, on the average, and that the median coefficient for the GATB General Intelligence score for 537 U.S. Employment Service studies was .27.

Similarly, Jensen demonstrates that correlations are greater for more complex jobs but that the values for jobs with high complexity are in the .35 to .47 range. Jensen also notes that the average correlation between IQ and success in training programs is close to .50, not the values of about .60 reported by Hunter.

Data from both Hunter (1986) and Jensen (1980) support the IQ construct as reasonably valid in its role as predictor of job success, although the claims made by Hunter may be exaggerated by his incautious and perhaps overzealous correction of obtained coefficients. From a theoretical perspective, Hunter's data give excellent support of the construct validity of IQ in vocational settings. In a practical sense, however, the obtained correlations are often the most pertinent. In all instances, readers are wise to heed the cautions of two expert statisticians and psychometricians, Lloyd Humphreys and Robert Linn, regarding Hunter's correction procedures. Humphreys (1986), in his commentary on Hunter's article (and other papers as well) in a special issue of the *Journal of Vocational Behavior*, wrote, "Given the heterogeneity among the many studies to be aggregated, corrections for measurement error and restriction of range

of talent are rough estimates at best" (p. 427). In a similar commentary, Linn (1986) asserted that "adjustments for range restriction and attenuation are nontrivial[;] . . . correlations that are changed dramatically by adjustments should always be viewed with caution" (pp. 440–441).

THE INTELLIGENT TESTING PHILOSOPHY

I became enamored with the term *intelligent* (as opposed to *stupid*) testing when I read Wesman's (1968) article "Intelligent Testing" in the *American Psychologist*, although I subsequently refined and modified the concept to represent an approach, indeed a philosophy, toward the interpretation of individually administered clinical tests (Kaufman, 1979b). This approach has been spelled out in detail for the WISC-R (Kaufman, 1979b) and applied to the K-ABC (Kamphaus & Reynolds, 1987) and to a variety of other clinical and neuropsychological instruments as well (Reynolds & Fletcher-Janzen, 1989). Consequently, my goal here is only to summarize the assumptions underlying the approach and the basic methodology that characterizes it. The essential method is the same, whether applied to tests for children, adolescents, or adults. Intelligent testing rests on several assumptions, which are discussed in the sections below.

The Focus of Any Assessment Is the PERSON Being Assessed, Not the Test

Many psychological reports stress what the scales or subtests measure instead of what aspects of the person are particularly well developed or in need of improvement; many reports are so number oriented that the reader loses sight of the person's uniqueness. The WAIS-R and other fine psychometric tools are primarily *clinical* tests, administered to uncover vital aspects of the person's total personality; mental functioning is just one facet of the personality structure. The behavioral observations section of a case report is often more revealing, and ultimately of more value, than the section that systematically reports and interprets the IQs and scaled scores.

The content of the responses and the person's style of responding to various types of tasks can be more important as a determiner of developmental level and intellectual maturity than the scores assigned to the items or tasks (a principle that Jean Piaget learned many years ago while working in Simon's testing laboratory, and that David Wechsler was well aware of, even while studying in England with the ardent empiricist Karl Pearson).

The Goal of Any Examiner Is to Be Better Than the Tests He or She Uses

Individual intelligence tests typically are administered by professionals with rigorous training in the content areas of psychology and extensive supervision of their clinical skills. An intelligence test is a static set of stimuli designed to yield scores derived from a single model of intelligence—the test author's. The WAIS-R yields 3 IQs and 11 scaled scores; the subtests are preclassified as Verbal or Performance, and the resultant IQs reflect Wechsler's adherence to the V-P dichotomy and to the concept of global intelligence. For some individuals, this model works, and works quite well. But what does one do when the scales are replete with scatter and the V-P distinction seems like a weak reduction of the data at best? Then the skilled examiner should call upon his or her training as a theoretician, researcher, and clinician to find a new synthesis of the test data; to group and regroup the subtests into a totality that reflects sophisticated understanding of relevant theory and research, coupled with clinical sensitivity to the person's individuality; in sum, to be *better* than the test.

Intelligence Tests Measure What the Individual Has Learned

This concept comes directly from Wesman's (1968) introduction of the intelligent testing approach. The content of all tasks, whether verbal or nonverbal, is learned within a culture. The learning may take place formally in the school, casually in the home, or incidentally through everyday life. As a measure of past learning, the IQ test is best thought of as a kind of achievement test, not as a simple measure of aptitude. Like the SAT, IQ tests assess *"developed abilities, . . .* broadly applicable intellectual skills and knowledge that develop slowly over time through the individual's experiences both in and out of school . . . [that are] is not tied to the content of any specific course or field of study" (Anastasi, 1988, p. 330).

The interaction between learning potential and availability of learning experiences is too complex to ponder for any given person, making the whole genetics-environment issue of theoretical value, but impractical and irrelevant for the interpretation of that person's test profile. Even the sophisticated scientific challenges to the IQ construct issued by Lezak (1988) and Flynn (1987), or the emotional, less informed indictments of IQ tests handed out by members of the public, become almost a side issue when the tests are viewed and interpreted simply as measures of accomplishment. The term *achievement* implies a societal responsibility to upgrade the level of those who have not attained it; the term *aptitude* implies something inborn and personal and can justify a withdrawal of educational resources (Flaugher, 1978).

Issues of heredity versus environment and the validity of the IQ construct are meaningful for understanding the multifaceted intelligence construct; the accumulating research helps test developers, practitioners, and theoreticians appreciate the foundation of the tests used to measure intelligence; and the IQ tests, as vehicles for the research, are essential sources of group data for use in scientific study of these topics. But all of the controversy loses meaning for each specific person referred for evaluation, when the clinician administers an IQ test to study and interpret just what the person has or has not learned and to help answer the practical referral questions.

The Tasks Composing Intelligence Tests Are Illustrative Samples of Behavior and Are Not Meant to Be Exhaustive

The 10 or 11 or 12 Wechsler subtests do not reflect the essential ingredients of intelligence whose mastery implies some type of ultimate life achievement. They, like tasks developed by Binet and other test constructors, are more or less arbitrary samples of behavior. Teaching people how to solve similarities, assemble blocks to match abstract designs, or repeat digits backward will not make them smarter in any broad or generalizable way. What we are able to infer from the person's success on the tasks and style of responding to them is important; the specific, unique aspect of intellect that each subtest measures is of minimal consequence.

Limitations in the selection of tasks necessarily means that one should be cautious in generalizing the results to circumstances that are removed from the one-on-one assessment of a finite number of skills and processing strategies. Intelligence tests should therefore be routinely supplemented by other formal and informal measures of cognitive, clinical, and neuropsychological functioning to facilitate the assessment of mental functioning as part of psychodiagnosis. The global IQ on any test, no matter how comprehensive, does not equal a person's total capacity for intellectual accomplishment.

Intelligence Tests Assess Mental Functioning Under Fixed Experimental Conditions

Standardized administration and scoring means conducting an experiment with $N = 1$ every

time an examiner tests someone on an intelligence test. For the results of this experiment to be meaningful, the experimenter-examiner must adhere precisely to the wording in the manual, give appropriate probes as defined in the instructions, time each relevant response diligently, and score each item exactly the way comparable responses were scored during the normative procedure. Following these rules prevents examiners from applying a flexible clinical investigatory procedure during the administration (like Piaget's semistructured *methode clinique*), from teaching the task or giving feedback to a person who urgently desires this intervention, or from cleverly dislodging from the crevices of a person's brain his or her maximum response to each test item.

It is necessary to be an exceptional clinician to establish and maintain rapport and to weave the standardized administration into a natural, pleasant interchange between examiner and subject. Clinical skills are also essential when observing and interpreting a person's myriad behaviors during the examination and during interpretation of all available information and data when interpreting the profile of test scores. But it is vital for an examiner to follow the standardized procedures to the letter while administering the test; otherwise, the standard scores yielded for the person will be invalid and meaningless. To violate the rules is to negate the value of the meticulous set of norms obtained under experimental conditions by most major test-publishing companies for their tests.

The testing situation has a certain built-in artificiality by virtue of the stopwatch, the precise words to be spoken, and the recording of almost everything spoken by the examinee. A person with excellent visual-spatial and manipulative skills might perform slowly and ineffectively on Object Assembly because of anxiety caused by the time pressure; or a person with an impressive store of general knowledge and a good commonsense understanding of social situations may fail several Information and Comprehension items because of failure to understand some of the questions. It is tempting to give credit to a puzzle solved "just 2 or 3 seconds over-time" or to simplify the wording of a question that the person "certainly knows the answer to." But the good examiner will resist these temptations, knowing that the people in the reference group did not receive such help. Testing the limits on a subtest can often give valuable insight into the reasons for failure or confusion, so long as this flexible, supplemental testing occurs *after* the score has been recorded under appropriate conditions.

In an experiment, the empirical results are of limited value until they are interpreted and discussed in the context of pertinent research and theory by a knowledgeable researcher. By the same token, the empirical outcomes of an IQ test are often meaningless until put into context by the examiner. That is the time for a clinician's acumen and flexibility to be displayed.

Tests Like the WAIS-R Are Not Just Administered Individually; They Must Also Be INTERPRETED Individually by a Shrewd and Flexible Detective

Test score profiles are optimally meaningful when interpreted in the context of known background information, observed behaviors, and approach to each problem-solving task. Virtually any examiner can deduce that Verbal IQ is not a very good measure of the verbal intelligence of a person raised in a foreign culture, a person who understands Spanish or Vietnamese far better than English, or a person with a hearing impairment; and that Performance IQ does not measure nonverbal intelligence very well for a person with crippling arthritis or a visual handicap. The goal of the intelligent tester is to deduce when one or more subtests may be an invalid measure of a person's intellectual functioning for more subtle reasons: distractibility, minimal brain dysfunction, poor arithmetic achievement in school, subcultural differences in language or custom, emotional content of the

items, suspected or known lesions in specific regions of the brain, fatigue, boredom, extreme shyness, bizarre thought processes, inconsistent effort, and the like.

As I have noted elsewhere (Kaufman, 1979b), "The value of the scores increases when the examiner . . . tries to determine why the [person] earned the particular profile revealed on the record form; the IQs become harmful when they are unquestionably interpreted as valid indicators of intellectual functioning" (p. 13). Being a great detective, able to follow up leads and hunches about peaks and valleys in a profile, is the hallmark of an intelligent tester.

Intelligence Tests Are Best Used to Generate Hypotheses of Potential HELP to the Person; They Are Misused When the Results Lead to a Harmful Outcome

The primary goal of intellectual assessment is often to reorganize the person's test profile to achieve dynamic understanding of his or her strengths and weaknesses—not to label or categorize. When a person is referred for psychological evaluation there is typically a problem, sometimes a serious one; the examiner's job is to help solve it or at least ameliorate its negative effects. Systematic profile attack, both empirical and clinical, may render Wechsler's division of tasks into verbal and nonverbal components meaningless for a given individual. *Identifying* strengths and weaknesses requires the use of empirical guidelines; *interpreting* the peaks and valleys requires clinical inference and a broad research and theoretical base.

The empirical identification of substantial scatter is merely the first step in profile interpretation. The more important second step is discovering a new synthesis of the test results that is optimally, perhaps uniquely, meaningful for the particular person. Strong areas need to be unified based on their commonalities, as do the weaker areas, to form working hypotheses about the person's cognitive structure; the goal is to unveil a valid and clinically meaningful reorganization of the person's test scores, preferably one with theoretical or research-based support. Ideally, the examiner will be able to infer from this individualized interpretive approach some helpful and practical recommendations regarding referral issues.

Obviously, test scores will often be used to help make diagnostic and placement decisions, such as the diagnosis of mental retardation or neurological dysfunction, or placement in a sheltered workshop. When such decisions are made based on a comprehensive test battery that includes an intelligence test, then the intelligent testing philosophy urges the examiner *not* to be forced to use rigid, blind applications of guidelines or empirical cut-off points. If the diagnostic or placement decision is sensible and consistent with an appropriate clinical interpretation of the test scores, then there is no problem. However, when clinical sense and inference tell an examiner that the global IQs misrepresent the person's intellectual functioning, and that the state-mandated placement is wrong and potentially harmful, then the examiner needs to martial the evidence and articulate it cogently to secure the best possible outcome for the individual.

When several tests are administered to a person (intelligence, language, achievement, personality, visual-motor), the results must be integrated from one test battery to the other. Intelligent testing does not apply only to the interpretation of intelligence tests. Why is the inability to copy abstract designs with paper and pencil on the Bender-Gestalt often attributed to visual-perceptual or visual-motor integration problems, but the inability for the same person to copy abstract designs with cubes on WAIS-R Block Design attributed to poor nonverbal intelligence? Why are problems with general information or arithmetic on the Peabody Individual Achievement Test (PIAT or PIAT-R) considered poor school achievement, while the same difficulties on the WAIS-R reflect low verbal intelligence? Integration of test scores from all component tests in a comprehensive battery is the key. This type of integration extends to measures of personality as well. A case report might discuss an individual's severe figure-ground difficulties on a perceptual test and later diagnose a thought disorder partly because of off-the-wall responses to several cards on the Thematic Apperception Test. Intelligent testing demands that these two findings be integrated to determine if the perceptual problem, and not a thought disorder, is responsible for the misinterpreted pictures.

This integrative, flexible, clinical-empirical methodology and philosophy, as outlined in the preceding tenets of the faith, represents the approach taken in this book for the interpretation of the WAIS-R and other tests for adolescents and adults. The guidelines for interpreting WAIS-R V-P IQ discrepancies (chapters 9–11) and profile fluctuations (chapters 12–14), and the illustrative case reports throughout this book rest solidly on the intelligent testing framework.

CHAPTER 1 SUMMARY

This chapter first delineates the goal of this book to serve as a text on individual, clinical assessment of intelligence and then outlines the four sections that make up the book: (a) introduction to adolescent and adult intellectual assessment, (b) integration and application of WAIS-R research, (c) WAIS-R scale and subtest profile interpretation, and (d) clinical and neuropsychological applications. Topics like the interesting laboratory findings on the relationship between reaction time and the EEG to IQ are deemphasized in favor of topics of more direct pertinence to individual mental assessment. The remainder of the chapter sketches a brief history of the IQ, gives a survey of test usage, presents evidence for the validity of the IQ construct, and introduces the intelligent testing philosophy.

Alfred Binet was truly the pioneer of IQ testing. His concepts and approach dominated the field for years to come, and Terman's adaptation, the Stanford-Binet, became the criterion of intelligence in the U.S. The nonverbal Performance tests developed during World War I to assess non–English-speaking recruits, low-functioning individuals, and suspected malingerers joined with the verbal-oriented Binet tradition to pave the way for David Wechsler's creative contribution of a dual Verbal and Performance approach to intellectual assessment. Wechsler went on to become a proponent of clinical, not just psychometric, assessment. The need for multiscore measurement that accompanied the learning disabilities movement in the 1960s catapulted the Wechsler series of scales ahead of the Binet as the most popular intelligence test.

A survey of test usage for adults revealed that about three-quarters of the adult clients tested are below age 45 and that very few are elderly. A disproportionate number of clients are retarded, but about half the individuals assessed are of average intelligence. The WAIS-R (or WAIS) is by far the most widely used intelligence test for adults, with the old Binet finishing a distant second. Similarly, the WRAT-R (or WRAT) dominated the achievement test category, the Vineland (either the original test or its revision) was the most commonly used measure of adaptive behavior, and the Strong-Campbell was the number one interest inventory. Competition among personality tests was evident with the MMPI more popular than the Rorschach and TAT. The five most popular tests, regardless of type, were the WAIS-R (or WAIS), MMPI, Rorschach, WRAT-R (or WRAT), and TAT.

The survey requested answers about the value of the information yielded by the tests that the respondents use, and the WAIS-R (or WAIS) ranked as the test yielding the most important information. The remainder of the top five in terms of importance of information were the MMPI, Woodcock-Johnson (Achievement portion), Rorschach, and Strong-Campbell. Respondents also indicated that they give intelligence tests primarily to measure potential and secure clinically relevant information; the use of IQ tests for educational and vocational purposes, especially intervention, is less common. Finally, respondents indicated that the main advantages of intelligence tests concern their internal properties and the interpretability of the scores they yield; the main weaknesses involve their real-world, everyday applications.

The validity of the IQ construct was explored for adolescents and adults. Empirical evidence supports the IQ as a good predictor of academic achievement for college students and clinical referrals, and as a strong correlate of educational attainment; IQ also relates substantially to the status of an occupation and correlates significantly with job performance, especially with success in training programs. In general, validity evidence is provided for both verbal and nonverbal measures of intelligence.

The intelligent testing philosophy, which considers the clinician's expertise and training to be more important an aspect of the assessment process than the specific instruments administered or the scores obtained, embodies the following principles: (a) focusing on the person being assessed, not on the test scores; (b) training clinicians to be better than the tests they use; (c) interpreting intelligence tests as measures of what the individual has learned; (d) treating the tasks in IQ tests as illustrative samples of behavior; (e) regarding the assessment of intelligence as an analog of a controlled experiment; (f) serving as a flexible and shrewd detective to uncover test interpretations that are truly "individual"; and (g) using intelligence tests to generate hypotheses that will ultimately help the person referred for evaluation.

Heritability and Malleability of IQ and Attacks on the IQ Construct

Chapter 1 presented evidence for the validity of the IQ construct, particularly for adolescents and adults. This chapter treats topics that are generally controversial and that relate either directly or indirectly to the utility and validity of the IQ construct. The topics of heredity, environment, and IQ malleability are discussed, exploring questions such as "How important are genetics and environment in determining a person's IQ?" and "Do genetic differences explain some or all of the mean IQ difference between blacks and whites?" Questions arising from cross-cultural investigations of intelligence are then examined, including Flynn's (1987) analysis of the intelligence of people from 14 nations: "Do Japanese people have substantially higher IQs than Americans?"; "Do nations differ in their IQ gains from generation to generation?"; and "Do IQ tests measure something other than intelligence?" Flynn's challenge to the IQ construct is discussed and rebutted, as is another attack by Lezak (1988a), who deliv-

ered a eulogy for the IQ before the International Neuropsychological Society.

THE HERITABILITY AND MALLEABILITY OF IQ

Heritability

Although laypeople and professionals alike have long argued whether IQ is determined almost exclusively by genetics or by environment, and whether IQ tests are fair or hopelessly biased, the scientific issues involved are complex and the answers are not simple. Excellent technical, empirical, logical, and objective treatments of the genetic question appear as chapters in three comprehensive handbooks of intelligence (Sternberg, 1982, 1988; Wolman, 1985), written by respected leaders in the field of behavioral genetics (Plomin, 1988; Scarr & Carter-

Saltzman, 1982; Vandenberg & Vogler, 1985). In this section, the major points in these summaries are featured and integrated with additional research to show that (a) the evidence for a strong genetic influence on IQ is striking, (b) the evidence that this genetic component explains the observed black–white difference is virtually nonexistent, and (c) the key question to consider is *not* genetics versus environment but genetics versus *malleability* of the IQ (Angoff, 1988).

Evidence for the Roles of Both Genes and the Environment

Different types of evidence bear on the association between genetics and IQ, such as the characteristic intellectual profiles displayed by individuals with single gene abnormalities (e.g., PKU, Tay Sachs disease) or an abnormal number of either nonsex chromosomes (Down's syndrome) or sex chromosomes (Klinefelter's or Turner's syndrome) (Vandenberg & Vogler, 1985). In addition, McKusick (1986) reports the identification of more than 100 rare single-gene mutations involving intellectual retardation. In fact, the recessive gene that causes the chromosomal condition of fragile X syndrome (Madison, George, & Moeschler, 1986) appears, according to Plomin (1989), "to be a major reason for the excess of mild mental retardation in males" (p. 106). Although this line of research is provocative, this section focuses on the accumulated evidence obtained from studies of normal individuals, specifically the correlations between the IQs earned by people who differ in their degree of genetic similarity. Identical twins have the same genetic makeup, whereas fraternal twins are no more similar genetically than any two siblings born at different times.

Table 2.1 summarizes pertinent coefficients from a plethora of studies conducted for more than half a century by investigators throughout the world. As indicated, the average correlation for identical twins reared together is .86, not very different from the test-retest reliability coefficient of .95 for the WISC-R or WAIS-R for the same person tested twice over about a 1-month interval. Since many of the IQ tests used in these diverse studies do not match the stability coefficients of Wechsler's revised batteries, the correlation for identical twins probably closely approximates the coefficient that would have been obtained if either twin had been tested twice. In contrast, the coefficient for fraternal twins—though a substantial .60—is not as high as the correlation obtained for identical twins reared apart (.72).

Further, the high coefficient for identical twins has been resistant to change over time. In contrast, Plomin and DeFries (1980) have shown convincingly that coefficients for various degrees of genetic relationship have changed substantially when comparing "older" data (obtained prior to 1963) to "newer" data (obtained in the late 1970s). For example, the IQs of a parent and child living together correlated .50 (older data) versus .35 (newer data). Coefficients for fraternal twins changed in the opposite direction: .53 in the old data compared to .62 in the new data. Interestingly, coefficients were exactly the same whether the fraternal twins were the same sex or different sexes; this finding held for both the old and new data (Plomin & DeFries, 1980).

Results from a 21-year longitudinal investigation of aging in twins aged 60 and above (Jarvik & Bank, 1983) add a fascinating complication to research on the relationship between genetics and IQ over the life span. Based on data from several Wechsler-Bellevue subtests and the Binet Vocabulary task, Jarvik and Bank observed that the intelligence scores of fraternal twins were no more disparate than the scores of identical twins: "[T]he genetically identical MZ [monozygotic] twins tended to show increasing dissimilarities over the years. Possibly, the additional years . . . allowed environmental factors to play an increasing role in determining intellectual change" (p. 46).

TABLE 2.1   Average correlations, from numerous studies, between the IQs of people differing in their degree of genetic relationship

Nature of Relationship	Number (pairs)	Average Correlation
Same person tested twice	422	.95
Monozygotic (identical) twins: reared together	4,672	.86
Monozygotic (identical) twins: reared apart	65	.72
Dizygotic (fraternal) twins: reared together	5,546	.60
Siblings: reared together	26,473	.47
Siblings: reared apart	203	.24
Unrelated siblings: reared together (adopted/natural or adopted/adopted)	714	.32
Half-siblings	200	.31
Cousins	1,176	.15
Parent–child: living together	8,433	.42
Parent–child: living apart	814	.22
Adoptive parent–child: living together	1,397	.19
Midparent–child: living together	992	.50
Mid-adoptive parent–child: living together	758	.24
Unrelated persons: reared apart	15,086	−.01

NOTE: Most data in this table are from Vandenberg and Vogler (1985, Figure 7), based on data originally summarized by T. J. Bouchard and M. McGue in 1981. Test–retest data are for the WISC-R (Wechsler, 1974, Table 11) and WAIS-R (Wechsler, 1981, Table 11) for three groups of children and two groups of adults (ranging from age 6½ to 54 years) tested twice within a span of 2–7 weeks. Data for unrelated persons reared apart are from Plomin and DeFries (1980, Table 1).

Apart from the increased role that environment may play over time, further important evidence for the genetic basis of intelligence is evident in Table 2.1: (a) correlations between one or both parents living with their child are substantially higher for natural than adoptive parents; (b) when siblings are reared together, the correlation between their IQs is much higher for those who are biologically related (.47) than for those who are unrelated due to adoption (.32).

The essential impact of a person's environment is also revealed by the patterns of correlation summarized in Table 2.1. The coefficient for fraternal twins (.60), who share a more similar environment than siblings of different ages, is considerably higher than the correlation for natural siblings in general. In addition, correlations for identical twins and for siblings drop substantially when they are raised in different homes; the difference is especially noteworthy for siblings (.47 versus .24). The coefficient of .32 for unrelated siblings (two adopted children, or one adopted child compared to one natural child) is about the same as the correlation for half-siblings (.31), and is higher than the value of .24 for biological siblings who are reared apart. Finally, the relationship between the IQs of a parent and his or her natural child is fairly close if they are living together (.42), but not if they are living apart (.22).

Adoption studies have contributed much to our understanding of the relative roles of genetics and environment (Scarr & Carter-Saltzman, 1982). Interestingly, one adoption study conducted by Scarr and Weinberg (1976) has been widely interpreted as supporting the importance of environment on IQ, whereas a second adoption study by the same investigators (Scarr & Weinberg, 1978) supports the role of heredity. The 1976 investigation, which shows the relatively high IQs earned by black children raised by advantaged white adoptive parents, is discussed in detail on pages 41–42.

The 1978 study examined the role of environmental variables in predicting adolescents' IQs in 120 biological and 104 adoptive families (average age at adoption was 2.6 months). Parents and children were given a four-subtest short form of the WAIS. Variables like parental education and income produced a much higher multiple correlation for biological families (.33) than adoptive families (.14). The IQ of the mother rearing the adolescent increased the correlation substantially *only* for the biological families. In fact, the one variable that raised the multiple correlation most for the adoptive families was the *natural* mother's educational attainment.

The broad heritability of a trait such as intelligence corresponds to "the proportion of the total variance that is due to heredity" (Vandenberg & Vogler, 1985, p. 14). Falconer's (1960) formula for estimating broad heritability is fairly simple (the difference between intraclass correlations for identical versus fraternal twins, times 2), and is widely used (Horn, 1985; Vandenberg & Vogler, 1985). The formula makes some untenable assumptions, but the heritability estimates obtained by Falconer's formula are, nonetheless, quite close to values yielded by more complex formulas (Plomin & DeFries, 1980). As Scarr and Carter-Saltzman (1982)

remind us, however, the heritability estimate "is a *population statistic,* not a property of the trait" since estimates of heritability "differ from population to population as genetic and environmental variances change as proportions of the total variance" (p. 820).

Table 2.2 provides broad heritability estimates for a variety of variables, mostly cognitive in nature, obtained from diverse investigations. This table, while not exhaustive, shows which variables have been studied and presents the coefficients for identical and fraternal twins, along with the estimates of the percentage of total variance due to heredity. The first two variables in the table, though noncognitive, are presented for comparison purposes, since we have a good sense of the degree to which height and weight have genetic components. Probably most people would consider height largely genetic, but would perceive weight as having a strong environmental component as well. Data in Table 2.2 reveal those perceptions to be correct. Identical twins correlate above .90 for both height and weight, but fraternal twins show a greater disparity in the coefficients. The net result is that height has a broad heritability estimate of 80% versus 48% for weight in one investigation that explored those variables (Garfinkle, 1982).

General intelligence has an estimated broad heritability index of 52%, indicating that about half of the variability in IQ scores is due to genetic factors. This value is lower than Jensen's (1969, 1980) estimates of 70% to 80%, and is very much in line with the current estimates of most experts in the field: Vandenberg and Vogler's (1985) estimate is 30% to 40%; Plomin's (1986) estimate is 40% to 60%; and Scarr and Weinberg's (1978) estimate is 40% to 70%. The high estimates that Jensen and others made in the past were sensible in view of Plomin and DeFries's (1980) comparisons of data obtained from older and newer studies, as discussed previously. These experts concluded from a review of studies involving twins, nontwin siblings, and parent–offspring relationships that the more recent data "indicate that the heritability of IQ is closer to .50 than to .70" (p. 21).

Interestingly, a survey of experts in the field of intelligence testing gave similar estimates of the heritability of IQ (Snyderman & Robinson, 1987). Limiting responses to those experts who believed that sufficient evidence exists to reasonably estimate heritability, these authors obtained mean estimates of 60% for whites and 57% for blacks. Scientists have thus moved from a strongly environmentalist position in which it was unfashionable to even mention genetics as a determinant of IQ or behavior to a position that acknowledges the key role played by genes (Plomin, 1989). Ironically, this acceptance of the role of heredity has come at a time when behavior genetics research indicates lower heritability estimates for IQ than the values formerly obtained.

Heritability is not built into a test, but is instead a population parameter. Hence, real changes in the relative contributions of environment and heredity to the total IQ variance may have occurred over the past generation. Plomin and DeFries (1980) agree that the role of environment may have increased substantially over time, but they also warn that "differences in sample size and methodological differences are also likely hypotheses" (p. 21). Ongoing investigations of both identical and fraternal twins reared apart (Bouchard, 1984; Pederson, McClearn, Plomin, & Friberg, 1985) have greatly increased the data base in this area and reflect state-of-the-art methodology. Preliminary results support previous findings "implicating substantial genetic influence on IQ scores" (Plomin, 1989, p. 106). Further, longitudinal twin studies of cognitive abilities (Plomin, Pederson, McClearn, Nesselroade, & Bergeman, 1988;

TABLE 2.2   Broad heritability estimates for numerous variables based on correlations for identical versus fraternal twins

Variable	r for Identical Twins	r for Fraternal Twins	Broad Heritability Estimate[a]
Height[b]	.94	.54	80%
Weight[b]	.91	.67	48%
General intelligence (various IQ tests)[c]	.86	.60	52%
Crystallized intelligence tasks[d]	.76	.58	37%
Fluid intelligence tasks[d]	.67	.49	36%
Specific abilities[e]			
Reasoning	.74	.50	48%
Spatial visualization	.65	.41	46%
Clerical speed and accuracy	.70	.47	46%
Verbal comprehension	.78	.59	38%
Number	.78	.59	38%
Memory	.52	.36	32%
Verbal fluency	.67	.52	30%
Divergent thinking (creativity)	.61	.50	22%
Specific areas of achievement[e]			
Social studies	.85	.61	48%
Language	.81	.58	46%
Natural science	.79	.64	30%

TABLE 2.2   (Continued)

Variable	r for Identical Twins	r for Fraternal Twins	Broad Heritability Estimate[a]
Specific tests			
1949 WISC (with 8-year-olds)[f]			
Full Scale IQ	.82	.45	74%
Verbal IQ	.79	.41	76%
Performance IQ	.67	.41	52%
V–P discrepancy	.49	.27	44%
Norwegian WAIS[g]			
Full Scale IQ	.88	.47	82%
Verbal IQ	.88	.42	92%
Performance IQ	.79	.51	56%
Distractibility factor	.77	.41	72%
Peabody Picture Vocabulary Test (PPVT)[b]	.69	.52	34%
Raven's Progressive Matrices[b]	.49	.39	20%

[a]The broad heritability estimate equals the correlation for identical twins minus the correlation for fraternal twins, multiplied by 2 (Falconer, 1960). In this table, the decimal is expressed as a percentage that equals the *estimated* percentage of variability attributable to heredity. Some values differ slightly from the aforementioned formula because of rounding.

[b]Data are from Vandenberg and Vogler (1985, Table 15), based on a 1982 study by A. S. Garfinkle of 137 identical and 72 fraternal pairs of twins.

[c]Data are from Vandenberg and Vogler (1985, Figure 7), based on data originally summarized by T. J. Bouchard and M. McGue in 1981. The values shown were weighted means of 34 correlation coefficients for identical twins reared together ($N = 4,672$ pairs) and 41 coefficients for fraternal twins reared together ($N = 5,546$ pairs).

[d]Data are from Horn (1985, Table 5). The values shown are averages of mean intraclass correlations obtained by Nichols (1978) for a variety of ability and achievement tests reported in the literature for numerous samples. Horn selected from Nichols's summary only those tasks that he considered to be marker tests for either crystallized or fluid intelligence.

[e]Data are mean intraclass correlations from Nichols (1978, Table 1); see footnote d.

[f]Data are from Scarr and Carter-Saltzman (1982, Table 13.5), which summarized data reported in 1977 by R. S. Wilson for 71 identical and 86 fraternal pairs of twins.

[g]Data are from Tambs, Sundet, and Magnus's (1984) Norwegian study of 40 identical and 40 fraternal pairs of twins tested on the Norwegian WAIS (renormed in 1978) at ages 30 to 57.

Wilson, 1983) indicate that the role of genetics on IQ *increases* considerably during childhood; Plomin et al.'s (1988) data suggest a high correlation of "genetic effects on IQ during early childhood . . . with genetic effects on adult IQ" (Plomin, 1989, p. 106).

Table 2.2 also shows heritability estimates for numerous specific abilities and standardized tests. The lowest values (20%–32%) are shown for Raven's Progressive Matrices, divergent thinking (creativity), achievement in natural sci-

ence, verbal fluency, and memory. The highest values reported (74%–92%) are for Verbal and Full Scale IQs on the Norwegian WAIS and 1949 WISC. No differences in heritability were found for measures of fluid or crystallized intelligence, refuting the notion that differences observed in the two types of intelligence relate to different contributions to each of genetic and environmental influences (Horn, 1985). An overview of studies on a diversity of specific cognitive skills, derived from a large data base, reveals a substantial genetic component throughout the life span, almost as high as the component for global IQ (Plomin, 1988).

Indeed, all values for cognitive variables in Table 2.2 correspond to the range of .30 to .70 (with an average of about .50) that experts consider to be the heritability of intelligence. The principal outlier to the range, data obtained in Norway on an adapted WAIS, point clearly to heritability being a population statistic rather than a quality of any particular test.

Concerning the lower heritability estimates from recent versus older investigations, Plomin and DeFries (1980) state:

> *Although we conclude that the new mental test data point to less genetic influence on IQ than do the older data, the new data nonetheless implicate genes as the major systematic force influencing the development of individual differences in IQ. In fact, we know of no specific environmental influences nor combinations of them that account for as much as 10 percent of the variance in IQ. (pp. 21–22)*

The latter assertion agrees with Bouchard and Segal's (1985) conclusions based on an exhaustive review of a plethora of environmental variables (anoxia, malnutrition, family income, family configuration, and many more): "The principal finding in this review of environmental effects on IQ is that no single environmental factor appears to have a large influence on IQ. Variables widely believed to be important are usually weak" (p. 452). Table 2.3 was developed from Bouchard and Segal's (1985) chapter to provide a concise summary of the relationship of numerous environmental variables to IQ.

Environmental contributions are complex, varying from culture to culture and within heterogeneous cultures as well. Despite disappointing results in their evaluation of the impact of environmental variables on IQ when taken one at a time, Bouchard and Segal (1985) were not discouraged by the findings, recognizing "that environmental effects are multifactorial and largely unrelated to each other" (p. 452). When the impact of aggregated (but unspecified) cultural or environmental influences on IQ are

evaluated (Vandenberg & Vogler, 1985, Table 6), the estimates vary more than do heritability estimates, but they "are usually of similar magnitude" (p. 34). Further, it is conceivable (Bouchard & Segal, 1985)—perhaps even likely (Scarr & Grajek, 1982)—that the correlation between genotype and environment is considerably larger than usually believed. For example, siblings may be treated significantly differently by their parents.

In addition, the cross-cultural research on IQ changes from generation to generation conducted by Flynn (1987), discussed later in this chapter, attests to the vital impact of environmental factors on IQ, coupled with the difficulty of apportioning the variance among specific variables. Flynn (1987) points out that "the fact that the factors are unknown does not mean that when identified, they will prove exotic or unfamiliar" (p. 189).

Is the Black–White IQ Difference Primarily Genetic?

Within the population as a whole, white children and adults outscore blacks by about 15 IQ points on major intelligence tests and on minor ones as well, whether the test is administered in a group or individually by a trained clinician (Jensen, 1980; Kaufman & Doppelt, 1976; Reynolds et al., 1987). When the races are matched on background variables such as socioeconomic status, the difference favoring whites reduces to 10 points (Kaufman, 1973a; Shuey, 1966). Occasional findings of smaller differences have surfaced for children on the Kaufman Assessment Battery for Children (K-ABC; Kaufman & Kaufman, 1983b) and McCarthy Scales of Children's Abilities (Kaufman & Kaufman, 1977), but the standard deviation difference in adult IQs has been a robust finding (see pages 158–163).

These differences have been attributed to a variety of causes, with many attributions depending on the analyst's point of view. For example, suggested causative factors include differences in genetic endowment, differences in

TABLE 2.3   Summary of relationships between environmental variables and IQ, based on Bouchard and Segal's (1985) review

Prenatal and Early Developmental Influences

Variable	*General Results of Investigations*
Birth weight	Correlates about $+.10 \pm .05$ with later IQ for blacks & whites; *very low* weights may impair IQ substantially
Anoxia	Lowers later IQ by about 5 points
Childhood illness	No relationship of following illnesses to later IQ: measles, pertussis, rubella, mumps, scarlet fever
Lead poisoning	Relationships to IQ are inconsistent & controversial
Overview	Effects of perinatal stress on IQ are small

Malnutrition and Famine

Variable	*General Results of Investigations*
Malnutrition	May impair later IQ by about 4 points if it occurs at ages 0–2; doesn't impair IQ if it occurs in adulthood
Famine	No association with scores on Raven Progressive Matrices
Overview	As experienced in developed countries, seems not to have substantial impact on retardation or IQ distribution

Family Background (Global Indexes)

Variable	*General Results of Investigations*
Parental education	Correlates with IQ (on the average) .30 for biological families and .21 for adoptive families
Father's occupation	Correlates with IQ (on the average) .28 for biological families and .15 for adoptive families
Income	Correlates with IQ (on the average) .22 for biological families and .09 for adoptive families
Overview	Correlations for biological families are significant, but are much more modest for adoptive families; therefore, much of the variance between family variables and children's IQ is genetic for biological families

(Continues)

TABLE 2.3   (Continued)

Home Environmental Factors (Specific Variables)

Variable	*General Results of Investigations*
Press for achievement (e.g., intellectual expectations for child); press for language development (e.g., quality of language models); provisions for general learning (e.g., availability of books)	Combinations of a diversity of these specific variables (assessed by home interviews and direct observation) have consistently produced substantial multiple correlations with children's IQs of about .65 to .75
Overview	High multiple correlations are confounded with genetic variance, and may reflect aspects of the child rather than the environment (e.g., bright children may elicit from parents a greater press for achievement and language development than do slow children)

Family Configuration

Variable	*General Results of Investigations*
Birth order, family size, interval between births	Data aggregated across families show substantial effects (e.g., mean IQs may decrease by about 3 points from 1st born to 2nd born, from 2nd born to 3rd born, etc.); data obtained within families show less impressive differences
Overview	The key family configuration variables in Zajonc's (1983) confluence model, an environmental theory purporting to explain individual differences in IQ, account for very little IQ variance when social class variables are controlled. Though not refuted, Zajonc's theory is strongly challenged

Schooling

Variable	*General Results of Investigations*
Inequality of schooling	Most IQ differences between groups of children (e.g., social class groupings) appear *before* formal schooling; several large-scale studies in the U. S. and Europe, including the well-known Coleman report, attribute between 2% and 10% of the IQ variance to school quality

TABLE 2.3   (Continued)

Schooling (Continued)

Variable	General Results of Investigations
Amount of schooling	Correlations are high (about .70) between years of schooling and WAIS IQ, but one cannot easily distinguish cause from effect in the relationship; best guess is that each extra year of schooling boosts adult IQ by 1 point
Preschool enrichment programs	Jensen's (1969) controversial conclusion that compensatory education has failed seems to have held up; significant gains (3–5 IQ points) may exist even after 4 years, but the gains disappear over time
Overview	The magnitude of the education factor on IQ is less substantial than one might expect

NOTE: This table has been constructed entirely based on Bouchard and Segal's (1985) impressive, insightful, and comprehensive review of pertinent variables in their chapter "Environment and IQ."

environmental opportunity, cultural disadvantages, subcultural differences, linguistic differences, linguistic deficiency, the middle-class orientation of schools, the quality of formal schooling available to whites versus blacks, and the middle-class bias of intelligence tests. Controversies surrounding these factors are heated and intense, and positions run the gamut from damning the IQ tests as biased and genocidal (Williams, 1974) to encouraging scientific investigation of genetic differences (Jensen, 1969), while hypothesizing that 50%–75% of the race difference is genetic in origin (Jensen, 1973).

Unfortunately, extremist positions have dominated the headlines, with each camp proposing legislation and social policies that range from slanderous and overly pessimistic to unreasonably optimistic: "At their extreme, hereditarian arguments have been used both to defend notions of racial inferiority and supremacy in the domain of intellectual ability and to attack intervention programs . . . as naive, untenable exploitations of federal funds. 'Pure' environ-

mentalists have offered a rationale for developing specific intervention and enrichment programs and social policies that would guarantee the permanent 'raising of intelligence' " (Weinberg, 1989, p. 101).

Although most empirical, objective studies of bias in IQ tests have found that the IQ and other general cognitive scores are nonbiased (Reynolds, 1982), the definition of bias is complex and not always objectifiable. Answers to pressing practical and socio-legal questions are thus rarely simple or intuitive (Flaugher, 1978; Oakland & Parmelee, 1985). Nonetheless, the IQ gap is accompanied by a corresponding *achievement* gap, as evidenced by scores on the Scholastic Aptitude Test (SAT) Verbal and Math sections (Walton, 1987). Data for whites and various minority groups on the SAT Verbal and Math sections between 1975 and 1984 are shown in Figure 2.1, with whites surpassing blacks by more than one *SD* (100 points) on both the verbal (including reading) and mathematics sections of the SAT. The performance of Mexican-

Americans, Puerto Ricans, and American Indians fell between these two extremes. Asian Americans outperformed whites on the Math section but not the Verbal.

The reasons for these group differences are multiple and interactive. However, Walton (1987) presents interesting and provocative data to accompany the SAT scores regarding level of poverty. At ages 15 to 21, a little less than 14% of white adolescents were living in poverty in 1983; for adolescents of Spanish origin, about 31%, and for blacks about 41%. Yet poverty is certainly not the entire explanation for race differences in IQ or achievement: "Twin studies of academic-achievement test scores show substantial genetic influence, about the same as for specific cognitive abilities" (Plomin, 1989, p. 106).

One needs to accept the role of genes in helping to shape IQ, along with a multitude of

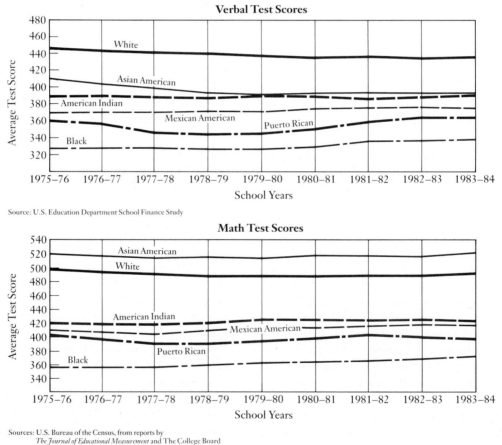

FIGURE 2.1

Average standard scores on the Verbal and Math Scholastic Aptitude Tests earned by American Indians, Asian Americans, blacks, Mexican Americans, Puerto Ricans, and whites between 1975–1976 and 1983–1984. (Reprinted with permission of *Education Week,* May 14, 1986)

environmental and "organic" factors (such as a mother's taking drugs or exposure to excessive radiation during pregnancy), such that acceptance of our "genetic heritage . . . need not be pessimistic nor bode evil for social and educational policy" (Weinberg, 1989, p. 102). At the same time, Plomin (1989) wisely cautions: "As the pendulum swings from environmentalism, it is important that the pendulum be caught midswing before its momentum carries it to biological determinism" (p. 110).

This section addresses only one aspect of the complex issue concerning black–white differences and IQ: Does the evidence presented previously of the IQ's strong genetic component also imply a genetic explanation of the well-known difference in favor of whites on IQ tests? At present, there are insufficient data to answer this question definitively, although available evidence, highlighted here, suggests that the best answer seems to be "No."

1. One cannot infer heritability *between* groups from studies that have provided evidence of the IQ's heritability *within* groups. Even if IQ is equally heritable within the black and white races separately, that does not prove that the IQ differences between the races are genetic in origin. Scarr-Salapatek's (1971, p. 1226) simple example explains this point well: Plant two randomly drawn samples of seeds from a genetically heterogeneous population in two types of soil—good conditions versus poor conditions—and compare the heights of the fully grown plants. *Within* each type of soil, individual variations in the heights are genetically determined; but the average difference in height *between* the two samples is solely a function of environment.

2. Despite the large number of studies of the heritability of IQ, very few have involved populations of blacks or populations containing equal numbers of whites and blacks (Angoff, 1988). In Snyderman and Rothman's (1987) survey of experts in intelligence testing, about twice as many believed that suf-

ficient evidence exists to make a reasonable estimate of the heritability of IQ for whites (39%) as for blacks (20%).

3. One would anticipate considerably smaller heritabilities in heterogeneous environments like the United States than in homogeneous environments. An example of the latter is Norway, which produced phenomenally high heritability estimates of 80%–90% (see Table 2.2) for the Norwegian WAIS Verbal and Full Scale IQs (Tambs et al., 1984). Recent estimates for U.S. samples are considerably smaller (Plomin & DeFries, 1980).

4. Some studies do not address the black–white issue directly but are relevant to it. Fischbein (1980), in a study of twins, divided his samples into three groups categorized by social class. He found that heritability estimates increased with increasing social class. The estimate of broad heritability from the intraclass correlations for identical and fraternal twins was 78% for the highest social class, but only 30% for the lowest. Since blacks in U. S. society tend to be lower in social class than whites, it is conceivable that the heritability of IQ is likewise lower for blacks than whites. In addition, Scarr and Carter-Saltzman (1980, Figure 13.12) demonstrate substantial differences among three ethnic groups in the relationships between the cognitive scores obtained by children and their parents. Regressions of midchild on midparent for verbal, spatial, perceptual speed, and visual memory factors averaged about .70 for Koreans, .50 for Americans of European ancestry living in Hawaii, and .35 for Americans of Japanese ancestry living in Hawaii. Again, these results suggest that racial differences in heritability estimates are to be expected.

5. Scarr and her colleagues conducted studies that bear directly on the question at hand, and these "three investigations of the possible genetic origins of racial differences in performance on school and IQ tests have

rejected the hypothesis of genetic differences as the major source of intellectual differences between the races" (Scarr & Carter-Saltzman, 1982, p. 863). Predictions from genetic theories simply cannot account for the findings from these three studies:

- Black and interracial children ($N = 130$) adopted at an average age of 18 months by socially advantaged white families in Minnesota earned an average global IQ of 106.3 on the 1949 WISC, 1972 Stanford-Binet, or WAIS, about 20 points higher than the typical mean IQ earned by blacks, and about 1 *SD* above the mean earned by black children from the North Central region of the U.S. (Scarr & Weinberg, 1976).

- Scores on cognitive tests were totally unrelated to the degree of African (compared to European) ancestry within a black population, where estimates of the proportions of African to European ancestry were made objectively using blood groups (Scarr, Pakstis, Katz, & Barker, 1977).

- Black twins scored lower than white twins (aged 10–16, in Philadelphia) by ½ to 1 standard deviation on all cognitive tests, but the difference was *not* primarily due to genetic differences because (a) black twins performed poorest on the most culture-loaded tests, (b) whites had considerably higher heritability estimates than did blacks, and (c) family differences account for more of the variability in the cognitive scores of blacks than whites (Scarr & Barker, 1981).

The evidence opposing a primarily genetic explanation of the black–white difference in IQ is compelling, but it is not beyond criticism. A devil's advocate could marshal counterarguments against most or all of the points above. For example, the Scarr and Weinberg (1976) adoption study is frequently cited (e.g., Brody, 1985) as showing the black children to score "above the white mean" (p. 382) and as supporting "the hypothesis that the black–white difference

in intelligence is substantially attributable to the environmental conditions surrounding the experience of being reared within the black subculture of the United States" (p. 382).

Yet the black children's mean IQ of 106.3 was inflated to some extent by the outdatedness of the WISC and WAIS norms (only the 1972 Binet had been recently normed) and thus may be equal to, not above, the so-called "white mean." Also, influences attributed to the "black subculture" are unwarranted because Scarr and Weinberg (1976) did not study that milieu. Further, the natural children of the adoptive parents earned a weighted mean IQ of 116.6, about 10 points higher than the adopted black children; this is the exact black–white difference found in numerous studies of race comparisons for children matched on pertinent background variables (Shuey, 1966). White adopted children in Scarr and Weinberg's (1976) study had an average IQ of 111.5; and black children with one white parent outscored black children with two black parents 109.0 to 96.8.

These counterarguments have their own weaknesses. For example, Scarr and Weinberg (1976) showed that the 12-point discrepancy in favor of black adoptees with one white parent can largely be accounted for by differences between the two subsamples in their placement histories and in the natural mother's education. The point is that the issues involved are complex and multifaceted, and that neither proponents of the environmental position (Scarr & Carter-Saltzman, 1982) or the genetic approach (Jensen, 1980) have incontrovertible arguments.

Because of the richness of the research in this area, Jensen's (1968) plea for scientists to systematically study the genetics of race differences is justified—but not his premature conclusions (Jensen, 1973, 1980) about the vital role played by heredity in explaining the observed race differences in IQ. As indicated previously, more recent and thorough genetic investigations indicate that about half the variance in IQ is due to genetics with an equal amount left over for environmental and organic influences. From a practitioner's standpoint, it is important to be abreast of current research so that low scores earned by blacks are not quickly attributed to genetics or dismissed as simply a function of poor environment. From the perspective of the intelligent testing philosophy, regarding intelligence tests as measures of what individuals have learned reduces the whole genetics-environment issue to a scientific debate (pp. 25–26), albeit a very important one. Rather than concentrating on apportioning IQ variance into its component parts, clinicians should be aware of the practical finding that blacks and whites do, in fact, differ in their mean IQs; this difference averages about 1 standard deviation within the population, and reduces to about 10 points when the racial groups are matched on socioeconomic status. Whereas this black–white discrepancy is smaller in magnitude than the IQ differences observed for different educational and occupational groups (see chapters 1 and 6), it is a large enough difference to take fully into account when interpreting a black individual's test profile (see pp. 162–163).

Malleability

Angoff (1988) has argued that the wrong question has continually been asked by those trying to determine the relative influences of heredity and environment on IQ variability. Researchers have insisted that "genetic does not mean immutable" (Plomin, 1983, p. 253), and have deplored the fact that "[t]he myth of heritability limiting malleability seems to die hard" (Scarr, 1981, p. 53). Yet Angoff argues that intelligence is "thought by many to be largely innate . . . and to a considerable extent inherited, and *therefore* unchangeable both within a given lifetime and across generations" (p. 713).

To Angoff, *"The real issue is whether intelligence can be changed, an issue that does not at all go hand in hand with the issue of heritability"* (p. 713, emphasis in original). "Whatever the 'true' heritability coefficient for intelligence is

. . ., whether it is high or low . . ., the essential point is that in the context of group differences and what these differences connote, its numerical value is irrelevant. What is relevant is whether these group differences can be changed, with what means, and with what effect" (p. 716).

Angoff (1988) uses a simple but powerful illustration to show that a variable with unusually high heritability (see Table 2.2) can and does change markedly from generation to generation. Adolescents in the U.S. and Great Britain gained about 6 inches in average height in the course of a century (Tanner, 1962). Within Japan, Angoff notes, the average height of young adult males increased by 3 to 4 inches from the mid-1940s to the early 1980s, a change that is "not inconsiderable by anyone's standards" (p. 714). As further evidence of the powerful role played by environment in modifying a trait with very high heritability, Angoff cites a 1957 study by Greulich showing that American-born Japanese children were taller, heavier, and more advanced in skeletal development than their contemporaries in Japan.

In fact, Angoff did not have to go so far afield to bring his point home. The average *intelligence* of the Japanese people has reportedly increased at the impressive rate of 8 IQ points per decade since World War II (Flynn, 1987; Lynn & Hampson, 1986a), based on large samples of data from numerous sources. Flynn interprets the results of the studies from Japan more cautiously than do Lynn and Hampson, but both sets of investigators agree that the rise of IQ in postwar Japan has been substantial. Closer to home, the average IQ of white Americans rose at the rate of 3 points per decade between 1932 and 1978 (Flynn, 1984). These results are not as impressive as the Japanese gains (or the gains in most other developed countries; see pp. 48–52), but they outstrip the 2-point-per-decade increase in Great Britain (Flynn, 1987; Lynn & Hampson, 1986a).

Among Flynn's (1984) numerous data sources for the U.S. (73 studies composed of nearly

7,500 subjects aged 2 to 48 years) were the Binet data from the early 1930s to the early 1970s and Wechsler data from the late 1940s to the late 1970s. Comparisons of the scores yielded by the older versus the revised batteries consistently show the newer test to yield substantially *lower* IQs than the test it replaced for individuals given both versions of the test. This paradoxical effect occurs because the newer reference groups (normative samples) do better on the same test questions than did the previous standardization samples. Consequently, the older test has "soft" norms because the reference group was less able; it will produce spuriously high IQs. The newer test has "steep" norms, but norms that accurately portray the intelligence of the current generation of children and adults. The net result is that the "brighter" people of today will obtain lower scores on any restandardized test (on which they are compared to their contemporaries) than on the outdated test (on which they are compared to a less able normative sample).

Likely explanations for the increases in U.S. IQs from the 1930s and 1940s to the late 1970s are the advent of television, the increasing reach of the mass media in general, changing attitudes toward parenting (including better understanding of stimulation in infancy), and so forth. The changes are clearly related to cultural factors, not to modifications in specific test items or subtests or administration procedures. For example, the large differences in IQs yielded by a test and its successor occurred even when the test had not been revised, such as the 1972 Binet (Thorndike, 1975) and most of the studies from other countries (Flynn, 1987), and when analyses of the WISC and WISC-R IQ differences were based only on the core of items that was common to both batteries (Doppelt & Kaufman, 1977; Kaufman, 1979b).

These IQ gains are certainly due to environment, not heredity. Flynn (1987) states: "Massive IQ gains cannot be due to genetic factors. Reproductive differentials between social classes would have to be impossibly large to raise the mean IQ even 1 point in a single generation (Flynn, 1986; Vining, 1986)" (p. 188). When evaluating the 20-point Dutch gain in a generation (about 7 points per decade), Flynn (1987) was able to conduct further analyses of this exceptional data set to apportion the 20 points into specific environmental components. He was able to attribute 1 point of the increase to formal education, 3 points to socioeconomic status (estimated by father's occupation), and 2 points to test sophistication. Overall, he estimated that 5 of the 20-point Dutch IQ gain from the 1950s to the 1980s was accounted for by the three variables indicated previously (he did not simply add the 1+3+2 points per variable because of confounding), leaving 75% of the difference due to unknown environmental variables. The potency of environmental variables, despite the difficulty in identifying the contributions of each one separately, echoes the problem of the relationship of environment to IQ.

Within Japan, the rapid industrialization of "a relatively undeveloped country in the 1930s . . . [one that] suffered considerable disruption and deprivation in and immediately after World War II" (Lynn & Hampson, 1986a, p. 31) should logically lead to great improvement in the people's intelligence. As might be predicted, the gains in Japan were more rapid just after the war (10–11 points per decade) and decelerated to about 5 points per decade since 1960.

Interestingly, U.S. gains in IQ have not decelerated but have remained at an apparent constant 3 points per decade into the 1980s. The 6½-point lower IQs on the WAIS-R than WAIS (see pp. 90–93) conform to Flynn's (1984) rule of thumb. So do the mean "IQs" produced by the K-ABC and Stanford-Binet IV, both normed in the 1980s, which are lower than those produced by the WISC-R, normed in the 1970s: 3.1 points for 182 normal children on the K-ABC (Kaufman & Kaufman, 1983b, Table 4.19), and 2.8 points for 205 normal children on the new Binet (Thorndike, Hagen, & Sattler, 1986b, Table 6.7). By contrast, the new Binet and K-ABC produced virtually identical mean scores for 175 normal children (Thorndike et al., 1986b, Table 6.10).

Lynn and Hampson's (1986a) and Flynn's (1984) data support the concept of the malleability of intelligence for whole cultures and confirm the fact that the level of intelligence seems to be in continual flux; this topic is addressed later in this chapter regarding Flynn's (1987) expanded study of the intelligence of 14 nations. A similar malleability is shown by several studies from the 1940s (e.g., Tuddenham, 1948) that Angoff (1988) cited regarding the issue of the IQ's changeability. But studies attempting specific interventions, usually in the early years of life and sometimes with the treatments spanning several years, have generally been unsuccessful. Studies to raise the IQs of retarded children (Spitz, 1986) generate "the dismal conclusion that they have been uniformly failures" (Angoff, 1988, p. 718). Some investigations have produced positive results (e.g., Honzik, Macfarlane, & Allen, 1948; Ramey & Haskins, 1981a, 1981b), but most—including one of Feuerstein's (1979) well-publicized training studies—suggest the conclusion that "there is little evidence that short-term interventions will lead to enduring changes in intelligence" (Brody, 1985, p. 371). Furthermore, like Sir Cyril Burt's questionable or fraudulent heritability data (Hearnshaw, 1979), the most dramatic findings reported for any intervention study (Heber & Garber, 1970) have been under a cloud of suspicion (Sommer & Sommer, 1983) and must be discounted.

Unfortunately, the headline stories received more publicity than the subsequent criticism of the work. According to Reynolds (1987b), "Following the indictment of Heber for misuse of the project funds and the exposure not only of the failure to produce the actual data of the project (believed by many now to be nonexistent) but of considerable fraudulence as well, the Milwaukee Project continues to be cited, in introductory textbooks in psychology, . . . as evidence of the malleability of intelligence and the ease of environmental manipulation" (p. 311). Reynolds (1987b) offered other illus-

trations of exaggerations and unsubstantiated claims and concluded that the "entire history of the raising of intelligence is permeated with bad science, foolishness, and outright fraud (just as is the radical hereditarian view of intelligence!)" (p. 311).

To Brody (1985), the relative constancy of the IQ from early childhood through adulthood (Conley, 1984; Pinneau, 1961) and the failure of most intervention studies to demonstrate a malleable IQ "suggest that intelligence tests are valid measures of the construct intelligence" and are "congruent with our ordinary intuitions about the meaning of the construct" (p. 371). He is probably right in that sense. The stability data do support the validity of the IQ construct. For example, IQs at age 5 have been shown to correlate .50–.60 with IQ at age 40, and IQs at age 9 to correlate about .70 (McCall, 1977); the average of children's IQs at ages 10 through 12 have been shown to predict average IQ at ages 17 and 18 to the tune of .96 (Pinneau, 1961); and 101 retarded children tested four times on Form L-M of the Binet, with 1-year intervals between assessments, obtained rather constant IQs, producing a median correlation of .85 (Silverstein, 1982d).

But these are group data, which obscure individual differences. As Anastasi (1988) points out, "Studies of individuals . . . reveal large upward or downward shifts in IQ" (p. 339). She also cites research suggesting that one can improve prediction of a person's future intellectual status by combining current IQ with "measures of the individual's emotional and motivational characteristics and of his or her environment" (p. 341). Additionally, the group data presented by researchers studying intelligence across generations (Flynn, 1984, 1987; Lynn & Hampson, 1986a) demonstrate that IQ is indeed malleable based on environmental changes, despite the stability of the rank ordering of people over time or the substantial heritability coefficient for the trait of intelligence.

Research conducted systematically on different cultures over time (or retrospectively) may help isolate specific sets of environmental variables that are most associated with the largest gains in intelligence. Because the average intelligence of Americans seems to be increasing at a steady, measurable, and rather substantial rate, researchers can investigate possible answers to these pressing questions—answers that might be a precursor for developing successful interventions to reduce group differences between races and across social classes. Similar intervention strategies may be developed based on research on motivation and emotional stability, as well as environmental variables "that can effectively alter the course of intellectual development in the desired directions" (Anastasi, 1988, p. 341).

Angoff has argued that researchers and other professionals should focus more on the IQ's changeability than on dividing its variance into genetic and environmental components. As he pointed out, the prevalent focus has led to controversy, unscientific arguments and assertions about a scientific issue, name-calling, and claims that intelligence tests are invalid or useless. A shift in focus is a step toward reducing the difference in the IQs of groups of whites and blacks. To close the IQ gap, "such an effort will have to be buttressed by a broad program of educational, psychological, cultural, and economic types of interventions targeted not only at the child but also at the child's parents, his or her extended family, and indeed, the entire community" (Angoff, 1988, p. 719).

JAPANESE IQ AND THE INTELLIGENCE OF 14 NATIONS

Cross-cultural research holds the promise of a broader understanding of the intelligence construct and its measurement, but there are many inherent difficulties with this type of research that force investigators to interpret the findings cautiously. A good illustration of the difficulties of this type of research comes from investigations of Japanese intelligence relative to that of Americans.

Japanese Versus American IQ

Lynn's (1982) analysis of data from the standardization sample of the Japanese WISC-R made national news when he reported an 11-point IQ superiority for Japanese versus American children. He based his conclusions on five Performance subtests that remained virtually unchanged when the WISC-R was adapted for Japan. No publicity accompanied articles by other researchers that pointed out flaws—some logical, some statistical—in Lynn's research:

Some of his analyses assumed equal variability in the two cultures, although data show smaller standard deviations for IQ in homogeneous Japan (Vining, 1983).

The appropriate comparison for Japanese IQs is 102.3 (the mean for whites), not the grand mean of 100 (Flynn, 1983).

Contrary to Lynn's (1982) claim, the Japanese WISC-R normative sample was *not* stratified by the variable of socioeconomic status (Stevenson & Azuma, 1983).

Lynn should not have excluded Arithmetic and Digit Span from his calculations, since these two subtests were essentially unchanged in the American and Japanese WISC-Rs (Flynn, 1983).

The Japanese sample was tested 3 years after the American sample, necessitating an adjustment of 1 point to account for generational shifts in IQ (Flynn, 1983).

The Japanese sample excluded rural children (Stevenson & Azuma, 1983).

Lynn (1983) generally conceded most of these points to the critics and concluded that the Japanese superiority should be reduced from 11 to 4½ points. Then he conducted a subsequent study that incorporated all WISC-R subtests except Vocabulary, reasoning that the modifications on the tasks were too minor to be of much concern (Lynn & Hampson, 1986c). Using 11 of the 12 WISC-R tasks, Lynn and Hampson concluded that the Japanese children enjoyed a statistically significant, but small, Full Scale IQ advantage over their American counterparts: 2½ points—quite a difference from the initial claim of 11 points. Interestingly, Japanese children outscored Americans by 8 points on the Performance Scale, but trailed Americans by 3 points in V-IQ. This finding has led Lynn and other researchers (including me and my colleagues) to focus more on profile differences between the cultures than on their relative levels of performance.

Research indicates that Japanese children and adolescents perform better on nonverbal-simultaneous problem-solving tasks than on verbal-sequential ones (Ishikuma, Moon, & Kaufman, 1988; Kaufman, McLean, Ishikuma, & Moon, in press; Lynn & Hampson, 1986b, 1986c; Stevenson et al., 1985). This type of research is especially intriguing because of its implications for differences in brain functioning and cognitive styles that may characterize people of different nationalities. Lynn (1987) has articulated a theory comprising evolutionary, empirical, and neurological components that he applies to peoples of the "Mongoloid" race: genetically programmed superiority in general intelligence and in visual-spatial abilities, coupled with relatively low verbal ability.

However, the results of Lynn's studies of Japanese children do not accord well the results of other so-called Mongoloid nationalities—for example, the Koreans and Chinese. Moon (1988) has shown that Korean children and preadolescents have a High Sequential–Low Simultaneous profile on the Korean K-ABC, a profile that is the opposite of the profiles Lynn reported for the Japanese. Korean youngsters displayed a remarkable serial memory for digits (scoring, on the average, at about the 98th percentile compared to American norms). Chinese first and fifth graders from Taiwan also performed exceptionally well on a test of serial memory for numbers in Stevenson et al.'s (1985) comparison of the intelligence of Japanese, Chinese,

and American children. On the other nine subtests in Stevenson's cognitive battery, the three nationalities scored within a range of 0–4 raw score points. On the number memory task, Chinese first graders averaged 36, compared to 21 for Americans and 15 for the Japanese; at fifth grade, the means were 42, 30, and 26, respectively. The Chinese first graders far surpassed the performance of Japanese and American fifth graders.

Neither Korean children (Moon, 1988) nor Chinese children (Stevenson et al., 1985) in these studies displayed a high visual-spatial, low verbal profile, even though this profile has indeed characterized Japanese children and adolescents in numerous investigations. Consequently, Lynn's (1987) theory does not seem to generalize to Asians in general, which must cast doubt on its validity even for the Japanese.

Occasionally, cross-cultural investigators provide valuable data on the comparative intelligence of different cultures. Stevenson et al. (1985), for example, went through great pains to develop cognitive and achievement tests that were comparable for three cultures, and controlled for SES, size of city, and cultural relevance of test content. These researchers produced the provocative finding that the Japanese, Chinese, and American children performed about *equally* well on their 10-subtest cognitive battery. But despite this intellectual equality, the American children performed significantly more poorly than (a) the Chinese children in reading achievement and (b) both the Chinese and Japanese children in mathematics achievement.

Most comparisons of cultures, however, are derived from available tests that have been translated and adapted from one culture to another, and have then been normed by different techniques in each culture. Some of the difficulties in such studies have been enumerated previously regarding the illustration of the Japanese-American investigations by Lynn. Yet even these studies have been beset by new problems. Recently, my colleague Toshinori Ishikuma carefully read the Manual for the Japanese

WISC-R (Kodama, Shimagawa, & Motegi, 1978) and discovered that in the Japanese adaptation of the WISC-R the time limit for Coding had been inexplicably reduced from 120 to 90 seconds (Kaufman et al., 1989). Lynn (1982, 1983) and Flynn (1983) were unaware of this huge difference in the Coding subtest and treated it as the same task in both the American and Japanese WISC-Rs. Hence, all of the data, including Lynn and Hampson's (1986c) most recent analysis, are somewhat distorted.

The studies of profile differences between nationalities may provide fruitful cross-cultural hypotheses, but they also share the same potential problems as the simple comparison of the general intellectual levels of various nationalities. Probably more practical are cross-cultural investigations conducted *within* each country for the purpose of examining generational changes in IQs for each separate culture. Lynn and Hampson (1986a) conducted one such study, and Flynn (1984, 1987) has applied an impressive psychometric rigor in his comprehensive treatment of changes in IQ over time within various countries. This line of research was discussed earlier regarding the malleability of IQ (pp. 43–46), and is covered in depth in the next section.

Flynn's Study of IQ Gains in 14 Nations

In an ambitious undertaking to study IQ gains by different countries over time, Flynn (1987) contacted 165 scholars in 35 countries who were known to be interested in IQ trends. To assess changes in IQ within each country from one generation to the next, he set up unusually stringent standards, applying four criteria (derived from Jensen's suggestions) to each data set he received:

- Were the samples comprehensive (e.g., composed of draft registrants), to eliminate sampling bias?

- Were the tests unaltered from one generation to the next, and was it possible to estimate trends based on *raw* score differences?

- Were at least some of the available data based on culturally reduced tests like Raven's Matrices, which provide more valuable information than tests of acquired knowledge composed of items that might be specifically learned?

- Are the data at least partially based on mature subjects, those who have reached their "peak" raw score performance?

Flynn used the first two criteria (the quality of the samples and the continuity of the tests) to categorize each data set into four statuses:
Status 1 = verified evidence of IQ gains
Status 2 = probable evidence
Status 3 = tentative evidence
Status 4 = speculative evidence.
He used the last two criteria in his discussions of the implications of the results he obtained. These criteria are rigorous, as supported by the statuses he assigned to data that he previously reported from 73 studies (sample size of nearly 7,500) in the United States (Flynn, 1984) and by the statuses that he assigned to Lynn and Hampson (1986a) impressive data sets in Japan and Great Britain. Flynn (1987) assigned status 2 to his American data for subjects aged 2–18 and status 3 to a set of American data for adolescents and adults; he assigned status 3 to the British data and status 3/4 to the Japanese data.

Flynn applied sophisticated logical and empirical treatment of the data to determine the number of IQ points that each country has gained per year, focusing on the generation from about 1950 to 1980. His results are presented in the following sections.

Gains in IQ From One Generation to the Next

Figure 2.2 summarizes data that are included in Flynn's (1987) Table 15. He presented the

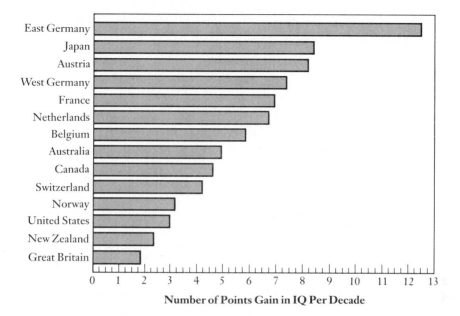

FIGURE 2.2

Gains in IQ per decade by 14 nations (Flynn, 1987, Table 15). Flynn categorized data from each country by its status: 1= verified, 2= probable, 3= tentative, 4= speculative. For each country, the status of the data is given below in parentheses, along with the measures used. When data were available from more than one type of test (verbal, nonverbal, mixed), the different rates of IQ gain were averaged. If data differing in status were available for the same nation, only the highest-status data were included in the figure. Whenever possible, verbal and nonverbal measures were weighed equally. The tests used, and status of the data, are as follows: East Germany (Raven, status 3/2), Japan (Wechsler, status 3/4), Austria (Wechsler, status 4), West Germany (Wechsler, status 3/4), France (Raven + Verbal−math, status 3), Netherlands (Raven, status 1), Belgium (Raven, shapes and Verbal−math, status 1), Australia (Jenkins Nonverbal, status 3), Canada (Raven + CTMM, status 1), Switzerland (Wechsler, status 4), Norway (Matrices + Verbal−math, status 1), United States (Wechsler-Binet, status 2), New Zealand (Otis, status 1), and Great Britain (Raven, status 3).

amount of gain per year and per generation (30 years), but I have converted his results to IQ gain per decade. He also presented his results grouped by type of test (nonverbal, verbal, or both), and he kept samples separate if they differed in age range or geographic location within the country. I took averages across samples to provide data for each country as a whole. When data sets for a given country differed in status, I used only the data with the highest status; for example, I preferred not to risk contaminating the verified (status 1) data for Canada from Edmonton with the probable/tentative (status 2/3) data from Saskatchewan.

Figure 2.2 indicates that each of the 14 nations showed gains in IQ from the previous to the present generation, and in some countries these gains have been quite large. Japan joins six Western European countries (East Germany, Austria, West Germany, France, Netherlands,

Belgium) in gaining more than 5 points per decade (more than a standard deviation per generation!). Of the 14 nations listed in the figure, only data from the following countries are status 1, or verified evidence of generational IQ gains: Netherlands (6.7 points), Belgium (5.8), Canada (4.6), Norway (3.2), and New Zealand (2.4). Consequently, all evidence of *extreme* gains in Figure 2.2 (half a standard deviation or more) is either tentative or speculative.

As impressive as the 3-point gain per decade for Americans has seemed to readers of Flynn's (1984) article, the United States has outgained only two of the nations studied by Flynn (1987). In addition, the U.S. has been outgained by four nations with verified data—the Netherlands, Belgium, Norway (barely), and neighboring Canada. However, such comparisons must remain highly speculative because the data presented in the figure are not directly comparable. They have different statuses as scientific evidence, different tests were generally used in different countries, the samples were not comparable in age or background from one country to the next, and so forth.

Gains on Verbal
Versus Nonverbal Tests

As Flynn (1987) points out, gains on tests of fluid intelligence like Raven's Progressive Matrices have more theoretical meaning than gains on crystallized tests like Wechsler's Information subtest. Gains on the former imply true improvement in abstract problem-solving ability; gains on the latter may merely reflect greater mastery of the specific content of the items (i.e., improved achievement, not cognitive ability). As Flynn reminds us, "[t]he average person today would outscore Aristotle or Archimedes on general information, but this hardly shows greater intelligence" (p. 184).

In fact, Flynn (1987) showed fairly consistently that gains were greater on fluid tests than on crystallized tests, indicating a true increase in problem-solving ability. For all nations stud-

ied by Flynn, the median gain on the Raven and related tests was 5.9 points per decade, compared to 3.7 points per decade on verbal tests (either the Otis or tests of verbal and math ability). A value about midway between these extremes (5.2) was obtained by taking the median of the gains on tests with both verbal and nonverbal content (invariably a Wechsler scale), using data from Flynn's (1987) Table 15, which included nine samples representing seven nations. Separate gains are shown in Table 2.4 for the countries in Figure 2.2 whose gains were averaged from fluid and crystallized tests.

Of the countries using the Wechsler scales for which separate data were available for the Verbal and Performance Scales, a similar pattern emerged for the post-1950 generation (table adapted from Flynn, 1987, Table 17) shown in Table 2.5.

Table 2.6 supplements Figure 2.2 by showing the gains in IQ per decade by various nations on tests of nonverbal, usually fluid, ability, and also on verbal tests. The median gain on nonverbal tests was 7.0, compared to a median of 4.0 on tests of verbal and mathematical ability. The following nations scored at or above the median gain on *both* verbal and nonverbal measures: Japan, Austria, Belgium, West Germany. The U.S. earned gains well below the median on both types of tests. France showed a striking difference in gains on the nonverbal Raven test (10.0) and on the verbal-math test (3.7). An extremely similar finding was also reported for France from the "speculative" Wechsler data cited previously, offering good cross-validation of the results for that country.

Persistence of
Gains Through Adulthood

The IQ gains across generations, to be truly meaningful, must persist into adulthood until adults reach their full mental maturity. If these gains are like most of the gains from Head Start programs—temporary and short-lived— they would only show that citizens of a par-

TABLE 2.4 Separate nonverbal and verbal gains for countries in Figure 2.2

Nation	Gain in IQ points per decade		
	Nonverbal	*Verbal*	*Overall*
France (status 3)	10.0	3.7	6.9
Belgium (status 1)	7.6	4.1	5.8
Norway (status 1)	4.2	2.2	3.2
Mean	7.3	3.3	5.3

TABLE 2.5 Separate performance and verbal gains on the Wechsler scales for countries after 1950

Nation	Gain in IQ points per decade		
	Performance	*Verbal*	*Full Scale*
Japan (status 3/4)	7.3	6.7	8.4
Austria (status 4)	9.3	6.7	8.2
West Germany (status 3/4)	9.3	4.0	7.4
France (status 4)[a]	6.3	1.0	3.7
United States (status 2)[b]	3.3	2.7	3.0
Mean	7.1	4.2	6.1

[a]Data for France do not match the data in Figure 2.2; these Wechsler data are status 4 data that were excluded from that figure.
[b]Data for the U.S. are just WISC vs. WISC-R in order to hold generation (post-1950) constant.

ticular nation reached peak ability at an earlier age but did not raise their ultimate level of performance.

For this analysis, Flynn (1987) focused on tests of fluid intelligence, whose growth, according to Jensen (1980), "is steady but relatively rapid and reaches a maximum in the late teens or early twenties, after which it shows a gradual decline; the decline becomes more accelerated after 55 or 60 years of age. Such a curve of growth and decline closely parallels measures of physical strength, air capacity of the lungs . . ., and brain weight" (p. 235). Crystallized intelligence, by contrast, does not peak until the 50s or 60s, preventing Flynn (1987) from applying his extensive data sets to the important theoretical question that he raised.

Flynn's data suggest that IQ gains are not temporary, but instead persist to maturity. His status 1, or verified data, on tests of fluid intelligence for Belgium, Netherlands, and Norway reveal unequivocally that the IQ gains persist to full mental maturity. In the U. S., the adult data were based on different instruments (WAIS and WAIS-R), and hence classified by Flynn (1987) as status 3, or tentative, data. Focusing on Wechsler Full Scale IQ analyses (it is unclear why Flynn did not use P-IQ, which more closely resembles fluid ability), Flynn showed that gains per decade in the U. S. were 1.85 points for adults below age 35, and 3.4 points for adults ages 35–75. When contrasted to the rate of 3 points per decade for school children, Flynn (1987) concluded from these

TABLE 2.6 Gains in IQ per decade by 14 nations, based either on verbal or nonverbal tests

Nation	Gains on Nonverbal Tests	Nation	Gains on Verbal Tests
East Germany (Leipzig)	12.5	Japan	6.7
France	10.0	Austria (Vienna)	6.7
Austria (Vienna)	9.3	Canada (Saskatchewan)	4.9
West Germany	9.3	Belgium	4.1
Belgium	7.6	West Germany	4.0
Japan	7.3	France	3.7
Netherlands	6.7	United States	2.7
Australia	4.9	New Zealand	2.4
Norway	4.2	Norway	2.2
Canada (Edmonton)	4.0		
United States	3.3		
Great Britain	1.85		

NOTE: Data are from Flynn (1987, Tables 15 & 17). Nonverbal tests are the Raven for East Germany, France, the Netherlands, Canada (Edmonton), and Great Britain; the Raven and a Shapes test for Belgium; an adapted Raven for Norway; matrices and other "fluid" tests for Australia; and Wechsler's P-IQ for Japan, Austria, West Germany, and the U.S. Verbal tests are Verbal-math tests for Norway, Belgium, and France; the Otis for New Zealand and Canada (Saskatchewan); and Wechsler's V-IQ for Japan, Austria, West Germany, and the U.S. Data for Canada (Saskatchewan) are status 2/3 that were excluded from Figure 2.2 in favor of the status 1 data from Edmonton. Status 4 Wechsler data are excluded from this table.

results that "American gains on Wechsler tests appear to persist into late adulthood" (p. 186). Additional support for his tentative conclusion comes from Parker's (1986) research findings that the peak raw-score performance of Americans on Wechsler's subtests has risen from age 22 in the mid- to late-1930s to age 30 in the late 1970s (see p. 186).

ATTACKS ON THE IQ CONSTRUCT

Flynn's (1987) cross-cultural findings are provocative and are open to numerous interpretations and speculations. Flynn's personal response has been to question what intelligence

tests actually measure. His research-based attack on the IQ construct is joined by other attempts to discredit intelligence tests, most notably the clinically based challenge issued by Lezak (1988a) as a result of her practical experience as a neuropsychologist. Both of these anti-IQ approaches are described and rebutted in the sections that follow.

Flynn's Challenge

Flynn (1987) was disheartened that the current generation of adults has not exhibited greater creativity as a *de facto* validation of their greater intelligence than adults of previous generations. If IQ tests really measure intelligence, Flynn reasoned, the increasing number of geniuses throughout the world should have made their mark by registering an unprecedented number of patents and making mathematical and scientific discoveries. Flynn saw no evidence of such worldwide genius and concluded: "The Ravens Progressive Matrices Test does not measure intelligence but rather a correlate with a weak causal link to intelligence; the same may apply to all IQ tests" (p. 187).

Flynn (1987) proposes that abstract problem-solving ability (APSA), not intelligence, increases with time, and that "psychologists should stop saying that IQ tests measure intelligence" (p. 188). He sees the interpretation of IQ as a measure of APSA as a means of reconciling the IQ gains with the well-documented losses on the Scholastic Aptitude Tests in the United States (Donlon, 1984; Turnbull, 1985). Flynn considers the Wechsler or Binet to require elementary academic skills, in contrast to the advanced academic skills required by the SAT. Decreasing SAT scores over the 14-year period from 1963 to 1977 (SAT Verbal fell from a mean of 478 to 429; SAT Math fell from 502 to 470) indicate a clear decline in high school students' advanced academic skills.

Flynn (1987) reasoned: "[H]ow could more intelligent students be getting so much less education? . . . The hypothesis that Wechsler-Binet tests are like the Ravens test, that they measure APSA rather than intelligence, makes everything fall into place" (p. 189).

Flynn has provided ample evidence for a worldwide trend toward massive generational gains in IQ, gains that are real and persist into adulthood. His data are among the more potent arguments for the environmental impact on IQ (see pp. 43–46), because no genetic explanation can account for IQ shifts of the magnitude observed for any of the 14 nations. Even Great Britain's gain of "only" 1.85 points per decade translates to a gain of 5 to 6 points over a generation.

His conclusion that IQ measures the euphemistic APSA rather than the ubiquitous construct of intelligence is debatable, however. Flynn

seems to confuse group data with individual scores. His evidence comes from large samples, not from clinical study of specific cases. Yet he criticized the IQ as a measure of intelligence because specific members of society have not created masterpieces or made key discoveries. These criteria are questionable, and it is unclear whether gains in various countries are uniform at all IQ levels or are perhaps more prevalent at the low or average ranges of intelligence. A group perspective is therefore preferable. If the generation of the late 1970s and early 1980s is more intelligent than the generation of the 1950s, society as a whole should have benefitted from these intellectual gains.

Advances in Technology

In 1950, television was a new luxury and space exploration just a dream. A generation later, technology has advanced so rapidly and so steadily that microcomputers are in many homes, laser surgery has become routine, video cassette recorder and compact disc machinery becomes outdated every year or two, the realities of space travel sometimes exceed even the imaginations of science fiction writers of the 1930s and 1940s, and every aspect of society from medical diagnosis and treatment to instant replays during televised football games bears the imprint of high technology. The days of associating one person with one invention (like Marconi and the radio or Bell and the telephone) are mostly over. (Who discovered the TV or the microwave oven?) Flynn's search for "the number of patents granted" (p. 187) in the Netherlands obscures the group efforts necessary to keep pace with modern technology. For example, many teams of researchers around the world have advanced our knowledge about the brain to a remarkable and unprecedented level over the past 5 years. The so-called increase in intelligence over the past generation is entirely compatible with the tangible evidence of a society that has developed sophisticated technological advances and that shows no sign of plateauing.

In addition, advances in computer technology and other electronics-related fields reflect the kinds of visual-spatial and fluid abilities measured by nonverbal tests—precisely the abilities that have shown the greatest advances. In contrast, the much slower rate of improvement in crystallized intelligence may relate to Flynn's (1987) concern that "no one has remarked on the superiority of contemporary schoolchildren" (p. 187). It is well known that verbal, crystallized tests are far better at predicting conventional school achievement than the fluid tasks that are generally included in Raven's Progressive Matrices or Wechsler's Performance Scale. The lower predictive value of fluid tests in the classroom may also be part of the answer to Flynn's question why more intelligent students do not learn more in school.

Another aspect of the answer may relate to the discontinuity between the skills needed for success in school and those required for career success, a topic discussed thoroughly and cogently by Resnick (1987). She pointed out that school learning: (a) emphasizes *individual* accomplishment, although learning in real-world contexts tends to be cooperative and group-oriented; (b) rewards pure thought, whereas the external world emphasizes tool-assisted learning; (c) focuses on symbol manipulation, rather than on the reasoning with objects and events that characterizes learning outside of school; and (d) stresses generalization, compared to the situation-specific learning that is often essential for job success.

Resnick noted that, "a major part of the core activity of schooling is designed as individual work" (p. 13); outside of school, however, "each person's ability to function successfully depends on what others do and how several individuals' mental and physical performances mesh" (p. 13). She further stressed that the use of tools is "a way of enhancing the capacity of highly educated people well beyond what they could do independently" (p. 14). In sum, more intelligent

people will not necessarily excel within the school arena or contribute to society on an individual basis. However, a more intelligent group of adults will conceivably work together in cooperative fashion, taking advantage of newer and better tools (some of which they have either invented or improved upon) to upgrade technology.

Schooling and the Decline in SAT Scores

Naturally, the decline from 1963 to 1977 in the advanced academic skills measured by the SAT would not be predicted by the apparent gain of 3 points per decade in Wechsler-Binet IQ in the U.S. But Flynn's simple explanation that IQ measures APSA instead of intelligence, no matter how convenient, is not necessarily the answer. First, the variable of the quality of formal education, as elaborated by Resnick (1987) and others (e.g., Turnbull, 1985), is an issue that is separate from the intelligence level of the students; so is achievement motivation. Stevenson et al.'s (1985) provocative cross-cultural study showed that American students were surpassed by a substantial amount in mathematics achievement by Chinese and Japanese students (and in reading achievement by Chinese children), despite performing comparably—in some instances better—on tests of cognitive ability. Perhaps American schools have not improved in proportion to the increase in the average student's intelligence.

Second, individual intelligence tests like the Wechsler or Binet tap verbal, crystallized skills in a way quite different from the group-administered SAT. The Wechsler and Binet demand virtually no reading, and the arithmetic items focus on reasoning via simple computations. The SAT measures *"developed abilities"* (Anastasi, 1988, p. 330) and are thus achievement measures that call on high-level reading comprehension and arithmetical computation skills. Computer and video technology encourage a more visual approach to learning, which may enhance success on nonverbal, visual-spatial tasks; unfortunately, it also discourages students from spending leisure time by reading. Similarly, reliance on calculators and deemphasis on rote learning of mathematical facts in many schools may result in poorer computational skills. These societal changes would predict lower scores on the Verbal and Mathematics tests on the SAT, but not on the individually administered Wechsler scales or on the old or new Binets.

A special panel commissioned 38 studies by experts in various areas (Anastasi, 1988) to help determine the causes of the 14-year decline in SAT scores. (Current studies have tried to understand the slow but steady increases in SAT scores since 1980; e.g., Wainer, 1988). The experts attributed the decline in the first 7 years largely to a change in the composition of the groups taking the SAT. Changes in the second 7 years are more complex, Anastasi points out: "Among the many factors cited as probably significant . . . were a diminished emphasis on academic standards; grade inflation and automatic promotions; reduced homework assignment; increased school absenteeism; diminished attention to mastery of skills and knowledge; excessive TV watching; and the social upheavals of the period, which competed for attention in the lives of students" (p. 354).

Turnbull (1985) posits an indirect cause-effect relationship between the change in the population of high school students taking the SAT (which occurred in the first 7 years of the decline) and the educational variables that might have contributed to the continued decline in the second 7 years. The students remaining in high school and applying for college included a substantially larger portion of less able students. As a response, high schools may have adopted simplified textbooks, reduced homework, and otherwise adapted to the needs of the less able students. Consistent with Turnbull's hypothesis is the rise in SAT scores beginning in the late 1970s, which coincided with "evidence of a turning point in the academic demand level of the schools" (Anastasi, 1988, pp. 354–355).

Therefore, the answer to Flynn's (1987) question about why more intelligent students show a decline in advanced school skills is far more complex than the simple issue of what IQ tests measure. According to Flynn, students as a whole had higher IQs in the late 1970s than in the early 1960s. According to Turnbull, high schools also had an increasing number of relatively poor students with college aspirations. The schools might have adapted their curriculum and methods to accommodate the higher IQ students; instead, Turnbull (1985) showed that accommodations were made in the opposite direction—to meet the needs of the poorer students. These analyses indicate the need for educational reform—perhaps incorporating some of the methods Resnick (1987) has proposed to bridge the gap between intelligence in school and intelligence in the outside world.

Thus, there is little evidence for Flynn's argument that the IQ must be branded a measure of APSA rather than intelligence. The IQ has much construct validation support as a group concept. As a score for any given individual, however, it often serves a different function, one that forms the starting point of the intelligent testing approach to assessment.

Lezak's Eulogy

Muriel Lezak announced to the professional world that the IQ concept was dead in an address to the International Neuropsychological Society in January 1988, which she subsequently published as "IQ: R. I. P." in the *Journal of Clinical and Experimental Neuropsychology* (Lezak, 1988a). However, she delivered a funeral oration for a corpse that has been dead for at least 10 to 15 years (Kaufman, 1988; Reynolds, 1988), thus demonstrating that some leaders in the field of neuropsychology may be oblivious to the research and philosophy that characterize the related fields of clinical and school psychology together with special education.

Because of Lezak's (1983) deserved influence on the clinical assessment scene, the provocativeness of the comments in her eulogy, the relevance of the topic for any text on intellectual assessment, and the fact that her criticisms echo those of many others in the field (including those of Naglieri, 1988a, who was invited to comment on her paper, presumably as a rebuttal!), I have treated the issues in some depth. First, I summarize the key points of her funeral oration; after each point, I respond from the vantage point of the intelligent testing philosophy (described in chapter 1) and research base that have typified my approach, and that of others in the field, to the interpretation of diverse instruments (Kamphaus & Reynolds, 1987; Kaufman, 1979b; Kaufman & Kaufman, 1977, 1983b). The rebuttal arguments include many of the points raised by Dean (1988), Hynd (1988), Reynolds (1988), and me (Kaufman, 1988) in our invited responses to Lezak's paper that appeared in a special section of the *NASP Communique* organized by Telzrow (1988).

Lezak (1988a) eulogized "a concept that, when young, served psychology well by giving it a metric basis that made it less of a speculative philosophy and more like a science. . . . [But the] IQ—as concept and as score—has long ceased to be a useful scientific construct for organizing and describing our increasingly complex and sensitive behavioral observations. . . . "[T]he IQ became senescent soon after its brilliant adolescence, and should have been put to rest by now" (pp. 351–352).

Basically, Lezak's specific criticisms can be grouped into two general categories: the meaninglessness and impurity of global IQs, and the misuse and abuse that commonly accompany psychologists' interpretation of IQs.

The Global IQs Are Impure and Meaningless

CRITIQUE Lezak (1988a): "When the many and various neuropsychological observations elicited by so-called 'intelligence' tests are lumped and leveled into a single IQ-score—or even three—the product of this unholy conversion is a number that, in referring to everything, represents nothing" (p. 352).

REBUTTAL Worship or overinterpretation of global IQs has not existed among the mainstream of clinical and school psychologists for at least a decade, probably longer. For clinical purposes, IQs exist as midpoints of the person's overall performance, providing reference points for *ipsative* profile interpretation. Practitioners have become accustomed to following the interpretive strategy that psychologists and trainers (e.g., Kaufman, 1979b) have urged: "[T]he Full Scale IQ serves as a target at which the examiner will take careful aim. . . . Large V-P differences, numerous fluctuations in the scaled-score profile, or inferred relationships between test scores and extraneous variables (e.g., fatigue, anxiety, subcultural background) greatly diminish the importance of the Full Scale IQ as an index of the [person's] level of intelligence" (p. 21).

Global IQs are useful summaries and provide a concrete starting point for profile interpretation. When the search for strengths and weaknesses proves fruitless, as it sometimes does, *then* the V-P IQ discrepancy or even the "unholy conversion" into the FS-IQ becomes quite meaningful. In those instances, the empirical validation of the IQ construct based on data obtained for *groups* (presented in chapter 1) comes into play, enabling the clinician to interpret the scores with meaning. Even a multiscore professional like myself can appreciate the extensive empirical support for the *g* construct (e.g., Jensen, 1980, pp. 213–239), which justifies the combination of diverse mental abilities into one, two, or three global ability scales.

Indeed, the V and P IQs provide an exceptional summary of abilities for many individuals, and the difference between them may have important diagnostic or remedial implications. Lezak (1988a) seemed to acknowledge this benefit herself when she noted that "as we all know, persons with left hemisphere damage tend to have relatively lowered scores on the more verbally demanding subtests compared to their better scores on several of the less verbally dependent subtests" (p. 358). (Ironically, this generalization does not hold up very well; see the discussion in chapters 9 through 11.)

For *individuals*, global IQs are frequently nothing more than overviews of a person's total ability spectrum that mask substantial variability among the subtest scores; but for *groups*, the summative scores have abundant meaning. How can one summarily dismiss a construct that produces discrepancies of 33 points between college graduates and individuals who failed to graduate from elementary school (see p. 20)? Yet, nowhere in her funeral oration does Lezak make the important distinction between the IQ construct for individuals and for groups.

Lezak (1988a) also seems to believe that wide profile fluctuations reside within the domain of neuropsychology, "where most examinations are conducted on persons whose mental functioning is only partially impaired" (p. 352). Much research shows emphatically that the Wechsler profiles of normal, intact individuals are characterized by a striking amount of inter- and intra-scale variability (Kaufman, 1976a, 1976b; Matarazzo & Herman, 1985). Competent clinical and school psychologists are aware of this normal scatter; as Reynolds (1988) notes, "Lezak has set-up the IQ in an archaic, once used manner that has been antithetical to good practice for at least a decade" (p. 6).

CRITIQUE Lezak (1988a): "Perhaps Wechsler's VIQ and PIQ concepts would have had a greater chance for independent survival if they had been not only theoretically attractive but psychologically sound. However, hundreds of factor analytic studies . . . have repeatedly and consistently demonstrated that not all Verbal Scale subtests measure verbal functions, that one Performance Scale subtest has a considerable Verbal loading, and that other important aspects of cognitive behavior—particularly attention and

concentration, mental tracking, and response speed—contribute variously to both Wechsler's VIQ and PIQ scores without being recognized or measured in their own right" (p. 355).

REBUTTAL Lezak is correct that the Wechsler subtests do not always behave in a predictable manner, but she is off the mark in labeling the Verbal and Performance Scales as psychometrically unsound. Probably nowhere in the psychometric literature has there been *more* support than for the constructs underlying Wechsler's V and P IQs. Although Wechsler developed the scales from an armchair, the empirical validity of the Verbal Comprehension and Perceptual Organization dimensions has been affirmed by factor analysis for a multitude of samples, between the ages of 3 and 74 years, differing in gender, ethnic group, and presence and type of exceptionality.

When two factors are rotated, the match of the rotated factors to Wechsler's V and P scales borders on the astonishing. Table 8.1 (page 240) and Table 8.2 (page 241) give an overview of the WAIS-R data for several samples; the support is just as impressive for the WISC-R (Kaufman, Harrison, & Ittenbach, in press), and for other Wechsler scales as well (Silverstein, 1968; Wechsler, 1989, Tables 17 and 18). But even when three factors are rotated, the support for Wechsler's V and P IQs is still overwhelming.

Lezak's criticism that noncognitive variables affect test scores represents a strength of the tests, not a weakness. Wechsler did not consciously develop a neuropsychological test or even a psychometric test; he constructed a clinical test intended to measure an aspect of the total personality structure. The assessment of what Wechsler (1950) terms "conative" or nonintellective factors, "necessary ingredients of intelligent behavior" (Wechsler, 1974, p. 6), is essential because general intelligence is simply a multifaceted construct. Wechsler (1974) states that "such traits as persistence, zest, impulse control, and goal awareness[,] . . . [l]ike enzymes, . . . serve to direct and to enhance (sometimes also to demean) the utilization of other capacities" (p. 6). To criticize the role of personality traits on mental measurement is, in effect, to blame Binet for having the vision to go beyond Galton's psychophysical tests of intelligence.

When Lezak states that these nonintellective factors are neither "recognized nor measured in their own right," she is only partly correct. They certainly are *recognized* by any clinical or school psychologist who has completed even a halfway decent training program, and are incorporated completely into the *interpretation* of the person's profile. They are not specifically measured because there are no empirical criteria for determining which subtest scores are depressed due to anxiety or inattention. Even if identifiable, will those particular subtests be subject to the influences of distractibility (or impulsivity, or anxiety, or shyness, and so forth) for each person tested? Some people interpret the *third* Wechsler factor as a behavioral dimension (Freedom from Distractibility, Freedom from Disruptive Anxiety), but how reasonable is it to believe that distractible or anxious people will perform poorly on Arithmetic, Digit Span, and perhaps Coding/Digit Symbol primarily or exclusively because of these behavioral variables?

In sum, Lezak's criticisms of the failure of IQ tests to specifically measure behavioral traits is both impractical and antithetical to the clinical interpretation of test profiles.

CRITIQUE Lezak (1988a): "Not surprisingly, IQ scores do not do a very good job at predicting success in real life" (p. 356).

REBUTTAL What does?

CRITIQUE Lezak (1988a): "One major problem that from its inception has dogged the IQ, whether score or concept, is its questionable conceptual basis" (p. 356).

REBUTTAL This is a valid criticism, one that has impelled Nadeen and me to develop the K-ABC from a sequential versus simultaneous processing model and to base the forthcoming KAIT on the Cattell-Horn distinction between fluid and crystallized intelligence. It also led Thorndike et al. (1986a) to apply a modified Cattell-Horn crystallized versus fluid intelligence model to the revamped Stanford-Binet Form IV and was the impetus for Woodcock (1988) to apply Horn's ability model to the revised Woodcock-Johnson Psycho-Educational Battery. But the criticism does not mitigate the value of Wechsler's scales for clinical, neuropsychological, or educational assessment; nor does it diminish the value or meaning of the global IQs yielded by his scales. The K-ABC, KAIT, Binet IV, and WJ-R may stand beside Wechsler's batteries and provide useful alternatives to them, but no test already in existence or likely to be developed in the foreseeable future will replace them.

Despite a list of definitions for intelligence that exceeded 90 in the early 1960s (Lezak, 1988a) and that has perhaps "doubled in the last quarter century" (p. 357), the Wechsler system is not threatened by an unclear theoretical model underlying Wechsler's batteries, by an inadequate conceptual framework for the construct of intelligence, or by a lack of unanimity in its definition. The validity evidence from thousands of research investigations indicates the practical and clinical utility of the tests and the scores they yield.

CRITIQUE Lezak (1988a): "[N]europsychological studies have repeatedly failed to identify neuroanatomic or neurophysiologic correlates of IQ" (p. 357).

REBUTTAL The call for a search for neuroanatomic correlates for a construct so deliberately multifaceted and complex as a global IQ scale seems naive coming from an expert in the specificity of neuropsychological function. In any case, I do not see the necessity for an intelligence test to have a clear-cut neurophysiological correlate. However, perhaps Lezak should study the reaction time and evoked potential research (Eysenck & Barrett, 1985; Jensen, 1985; see pp. 2–3) and reconsider her position on the neurophysiology of IQ.

CRITIQUE   Lezak (1988a): "IQ scores and all their conceptual trappings have been built on the unstable sands of arbitrary and shifting item selection" (p. 357).

REBUTTAL   Lezak bases this statement on research (including a study she conducted) showing that the WAIS-R yields lower scores than the WAIS by about a half a standard deviation. She attributes the lower IQs to the "effects of relatively small changes in the tests" (p. 357). But here she is simply wrong. As discussed previously in this chapter, Flynn's (1984) research has shown *real* changes in the abilities of children and adults from generation to generation at the quantifiable rate of 3 points per decade within the U.S. These shifts in the norms occur even when *no* items are modified (as in 1972, when the 1960 Binet was restandardized but not revised) and have nothing to do either with the specific items that are included or excluded, or with the arbitrary choice of "tasks chosen or devised by test makers according to their notions of what is intelligent behavior" (Lezak, 1988a, p. 357).

Misinterpretation of What IQ Measures

CRITIQUE   Lezak (1988a): "[P]sychometricians have dug their own grave by misusing mental ability tests and thereby limiting children's opportunities for objective evaluation of their ability potential" (p. 358).

REBUTTAL   In reaching this conclusion, Lezak (1988a) referred specifically to the *Larry P.* case and to the increase in the plaintiff's IQ by 38 points when retested by a black examiner. She

is evidently unaware of decisions in similar cases or in the absurdity of taking the 38-point gain at face value. As Reynolds (1988) states: "The *Larry P.* decision is a judicial anomaly. Related cases have been decided in just the opposite direction, the most prominent, and more recent, at the Federal level being *PASE* v. *Hannon* and *Marshall* v. *Georgia*" (p. 6). He continues: "The 'black examiner' example of 38-point IQ gains is simply ludicrous. Examination of the *Larry P.* transcript indicates that wholly inappropriate answers were given credit in an attempt to increase the IQ of the so-called Larry P. Furthermore, the extant research literature demonstrates that white examiners do not impede the performance of black children (e.g., Sattler & Gwynne, 1982)" (p. 6).

Elliott (1987), in a thorough and insightful treatment of IQ tests in the courtroom, showed how West, the examiner of Darryl L. ("Larry P."), violated standard testing procedures: "He accepted 'acting bad' as the definition of 'nonsense'. . . . When West asked Darryl why criminals should be locked up, Darryl seemed not to understand the question, so he rephrased it, identifying criminals as people who sometimes break the law" (p. 33). Elliott further described how Judge Peckham of the *Larry P.* case differed from Judge Grady of Chicago's *PASE* decision regarding the alleged bias of test items, even though the "tests and testimony were much the same" (p. 148). "One very significant difference in these two trials was in the willingness of the judges to accept a broad range of social science data. Judge Peckham . . . adopted the strategy of other government agencies . . . confronting test differences that threaten opportunities for minorities: He particularized the validation requirements so much . . . that the large quantity of data available generally on the prediction of black school achievement became almost irrelevant . . . Judge Grady, on the other hand, pleaded with both sides to give him any and everything they had on race differences in item passing rates" (p. 187).

In his summation, Elliott indicated that the impetus for his book "was the outcome in *Larry P.*, which violated the scientific consensus, and the contrary outcome in *PASE*, which added inconsistency to perversity in the adjudication of a scientific issue in psychology" (p. 194).

CRITIQUE   Lezak (1988a): "[T]oday, most psychologists, psychiatrists, educators, judges, the United States Social Security Administration, among others, think, write, talk, and make decisions as if an IQ score represented something real and essentially immutable with a locus somewhere in the cranium" (p. 356).

REBUTTAL   Not since 1961, when J. McV. Hunt published his landmark book *Intelligence and Experience,* has any self-respecting psychologist regarded the IQ as fixed, immutable, or imprinted indelibly somewhere beneath the dura mater in the cerebral cortex. Lezak can legitimately criticize judges or federal agencies or members of the Mensa Society or state departments of education or medically trained professionals. She would also be justified in criticizing those neuropsychologists who still administer the obsolete Wechsler-Bellevue, who ignore the available base-rate data on the magnitude of V-P IQ discrepancies (see pp. 265–270), or who conduct study after study on patients with lateralized brain damage without reporting their subtest scores. Perhaps, as Hynd (1988) states, "clinical-psychometric-legal issues that have so impacted on school psychologists are just now beginning to impact on the perspectives employed in clinical neuropsychology" (p. 4). But Lezak is wrong to criticize the clinical and school psychologists who administer and interpret the tests, or the educators who apply the test results in a practical setting, for reasons that Dean (1988), Hynd (1988a), Reynolds (1988), and I have all echoed in our rebuttals to Lezak.

For example, I stated (Kaufman, 1988): "Rigidly interpreted IQs for individuals referred for assessment have been embalmed for nearly a generation by psychologists and educators who realized in the early 1960s that one, two, or three summative scores are far less useful for psychodiagnosis than a profile of abilities. . . . Is Dr. Lezak aware of the strong focus on intra-individual differences that accompanied the rise of the learning disabilities movement in the 1960s (Bannatyne, 1971)? Or of the legal responsibilities of psychologists, educators, and other multi-disciplinary team members who endeavor to meet the stipulations of PL 94-142, which *prohibits* overemphasis on global IQs? . . . Does Lezak understand the 'intelligent testing' approach that many clinical psychologists, school psychologists, and special educators apply in their psychological or psychoeducational evaluations and teach to their students in graduate programs?" (p. 5).

To her credit, Lezak (1988b) candidly admitted that "I have little acquaintance with the literature and current teaching in school psychology and special education" (p. 6). I wish that those members of several state departments of education who still insist on using only the FS-IQ to determine student placement in classes for the learning disabled would be equally as candid.

CRITIQUE   Lezak (1988a): "Psychologists who take IQ scores at face value without taking account of the patient's status or subtest variations, tend to interpret an IQ score that has been lowered by virtue of some specific neurologic deficit to be an indicator of the patient's overall ability level" (p. 358).

REBUTTAL   The intelligent testing approach is specifically designed to put the global scores aside if neurological, behavioral, or other factors suggest that one or more subtests do not validly assess a person's intelligence. This technique has been available to clinicians for 10 to 15 years (Kaufman, 1979b; Sattler, 1974) and has been studied by numerous clinicians around the world (Anastasi, 1988, chapter 16; Strein, 1987).

Some of the basic tenets of the intelligent testing approach (Kaufman, 1979b), summarized in chapter 1, are repeated here to emphasize that this philosophy is not new: "Global scores are deemphasized, flexibility and insight on the part of the examiner are demanded, and the test is perceived as a dynamic helping agent rather than as an instrument for placement, labeling, or other types of academic oppression (p. 1). . . . The burden is on test users to be 'better' than the tests they use (p. 11). . . . The value of the scores increases when the examiner functions as a true experimenter and tries to determine why the [person] earned the particular profile revealed on the record form; the IQs become harmful when they are unquestionably interpreted as valid indicators of intellectual functioning and are misconstrued as evidence of the [person's] maximum or even typical performance (p. 13).

In addition: "It is during the process of clinical interpretation of the test profile of any given individual referred for evaluation—someone who may have depressed scores on one or more subtests due to sensory, motor, emotional, attentional, neurological, motivational, or cultural factors—that the global IQs have, for many years, resided in a coffin six feet below the foundations of schools and clinics throughout the country" (Kaufman, 1988, p. 5).

Lezak's Proposed Alternative to the IQ

Lezak (1988a): "Rather than equating mental abilities with intelligence and thinking of them as aspects of a unitary phenomenon that can be summed up in an IQ score, we need to conceptualize them in all their multivariate complexity and report our examination findings in a profile of test scores" (p. 359).

Lezak wants examiners to treat the results of an intelligence test as a multiplicity of scores representing an enchanting array of disparate abilities. Eliminate "IQ" from one's vocabulary, and study the peaks and valleys in the scaled-score profile. The good part of her suggestion is that she is able to damn the IQ concept without cavalierly discarding the instruments altogether. The bad part is that her suggestion, if followed assiduously, represents a return to a clinical interpretation approach that was once popular but is now out of favor. That approach treated each subtest as a discrete entity, with each task a measure of a long string of traits and abilities. Books typifying that approach often devoted a separate chapter to each of Wechsler's subtests, with few chapters devoted to their integration (e.g., Glasser & Zimmerman, 1967; Zimmerman & Woo-Sam, 1973).

Such books were quite informative, but they often encouraged young professionals to interpret the Wechsler scales one subtest at a time, thus losing the global perspective. For example, a person scoring low in Picture Completion was typically reported to be deficient in visual alertness and in distinguishing essential from nonessential details. That same person may well have earned a high score in Picture Arrangement (which also requires close attention to visual detail), but the examiner is not likely to have integrated the data across subtests. Why? Because too much focus on the uniqueness of each subtest in a profile (including its unique neurological correlates) can work against a more integrated treatment of the total picture. And despite Lezak's arguments to the contrary, the global IQs, as well as the results of factor analysis, are just as much a part of the totality of test interpretation as the profile of 10 or 11 or 12 Wechsler subtests. As Dean (1988) notes, "the aggregate IQ offers the psychologist a stable baseline from which to consider profile points" (p. 4).

I agree with Lezak's focus on the subtest profile and on the potential neuropsychological (not to mention clinical, subcultural, educational, behavioral) impact on selected subtests for a given individual—whether that person has an intact brain or not; I've spent most of my professional life arguing for that type of flexibility in test interpretation. I have at the same time opposed methods of interpretation that fragment intelligence tests into their component parts, ignoring the empirical or rational foundations that the test authors used, either implicitly or explicitly, when they developed their tests. Such approaches lead to interpretation of findings in isolation; they lead to the use of pairwise comparisons (do Object Assembly and Similarities differ significantly from each other?) instead of a systematic, empirically defensible method of determining strengths and weaknesses; and they often lead examiners to ignore statistical significance to focus on what seem like high or low scores in the profile. ("Her 13 on Block Design is her best performance, indicating well developed spatial visualization and visual-constructive ability. In contrast, her lowest score, a 9 on Information, indicates a relatively poor range of general knowledge.")

I prefer to take into account profile fluctuations—but in sequence, going from the most global (i.e., most reliable) scores to the most specific (generally, the least reliable) scores. First, start with the Full Scale IQ, which, despite its conceptual and practical shortcomings, serves as a useful overview of the person's own "performance midpoint" on a Wechsler scale. Second, examine the V–P IQ discrepancy for statistical significance. Third, determine whether significant subtest strengths and weaknesses emerge in the separate Verbal and Performance profiles, and whether the degree of scatter is sufficient to declare one, two, or all three global IQs meaningless. Fourth, study the profile of strong and weak cognitive areas and try to regroup the scores by a different model (e.g., the three factors that emerge from factor analysis, Bannatyne's regrouping of subtests into four categories, processing models derived from neuropsychological research, clinically derived groupings). Fifth, integrate the reorganized subtest profile with all background and behavioral information about the individual, i.e., neurological, medical, subcultural, educational, psychopathological.

Ultimately, I agree with Lezak's eulogy of the IQ concept, except that she missed the funeral, which was held more than 10 years ago by clinical and school psychologists. I disagree with her dismissal of IQs altogether, and her failure to distinguish between their different types of value for group versus individual interpretation. I disagree with many of her arguments regarding intelligence tests and their use/abuse by the professionals who are trained to administer them. And I see her proposal to return to the multisubtest profile in place of the IQs as a regressive suggestion, one that will be no more helpful for neuropsychology than for clinical, school, or educational psychology.

CHAPTER 2 SUMMARY

This chapter discusses the heredity, environment, and malleability of the IQ; cross-cultural studies of IQ, including Flynn's analysis of the intelligence of 14 nations; and attacks on the IQ construct by Flynn and Lezak. A variety of investigations, especially studies of twins, indicate that the role of genes in determining intelligence is considerable. These same studies also highlight the role of environment, although studies of specific aspects of environmental differences (e.g., malnutrition and famine, poor schooling) typically do not account for large proportions of IQ variance. Environment presents a complex interaction of factors that together are likely to account for an amount of IQ variance that equals that of IQ. Research during the past 25 years indicates that about 50% of the variation in IQ is genetic while estimates from older data are usually closer to 70%. Despite the increasing role attributed to environment by more recent studies in behavior genetics, the substantial impact of genes has finally been recognized by a scientific community that previously tended to focus on environmental factors.

Evidence suggests that the higher IQs earned by whites versus blacks is *not* due to genetic factors. It is inappropriate to infer intergroup heritability from intragroup investigations. In addition, other research such as investigations of adopted children yield data that are inconsistent with predictions from genetic theories. Angoff has argued that the *malleability* of the IQ is more important than the issue of heredity versus environment. Studies of specific intervention strategies designed to improve intelligence have produced disappointing results. Many of the investigations that have produced sizable increments must be discounted because of alleged fraud. Nonetheless, the IQ seems quite malleable to environmental influences based on studies that have shown substantial generational gains in the intelligence of Americans and of individuals in other countries such as Japan.

Interesting cross-cultural research has been conducted on intelligence that potentially enriches our understanding of the construct; however, such research is fraught with problems. For example, the study of Japanese intelligence produced an initial finding of an 11-point advantage for Japanese versus American individuals. Yet flaws in the analysis revealed by subsequent investigators show that the "true" difference is probably closer to 2–3 points. Further, different cultures seem to process information differently, a distinction that is masked by focusing on the global IQ.

Flynn conducted an investigation of IQ generational changes within 14 countries. He discovered that intelligence has been improving at a steady rate throughout the civilized world, although countries differ in their rate of IQ increase. For example, the gain of about 3 points per decade in the U.S. is far less than gains of 6–7 points in Belgium and the Netherlands. Evidence indicates that gains are greater on fluid/nonverbal tests than on verbal/achievement tasks, and that these gains persist into adulthood.

Flynn challenged the generality of the IQ construct, suggesting that it reflects nothing more than abstract problem solving ability. He argued that if people around the world have truly become more intelligent, there should have been a concomitant increase in patents and other indicators of individual creativity; and that increased intelligence is inconsistent with the declining SAT scores observed in the U.S. However, Flynn's arguments seem specious since he has avoided consideration of group (rather than individual) contributions to a society that has advanced technologically at a dramatic pace during the past generation. Further, SAT declines observed between 1963 and 1977 have been attributed by experts partly to changes in the composition of groups taking the SAT, and partly to a variety of school-related and societal changes.

Lezak eulogized the IQ construct, arguing that it has outlived its usefulness and should be buried. Her main criticisms concern the meaninglessness and impurity of global IQs and the misuse and abuse that have accompanied psychologists' interpretation of them. Major arguments against Lezak's position include: (a) the fact that worship of the global IQ gave way to an intelligent testing model of profile interpretation 10 to 15 years ago within the fields of clinical and school psychology; (b) IQs for *groups* have considerable validation; (c) the impact of nonintellectual factors on obtained IQs is a strength, not a weakness, of intelligence tests; (d) her citation of the *Larry P.* case ignores other, contradictory evidence as well as testing errors made by "Larry P.'s" examiner; (e) the learning disabilities movement begun in the 1960s, and pertinent legislation since that time, have elevated the interpretation of profiles above the rigid treatment of precise IQ scores; and (f) Lezak's proposals to focus exclusively on the separate subtests represents a return to an older, less sensible, approach to Wechsler interpretation.

From the Wechsler-Bellevue I to the WAIS to the WAIS-R

The WAIS-R is the most popular test for assessing adult intelligence (Harrison, Kaufman, Hickman, & Kaufman, 1988) and, as discussed in chapter 1, it is used in most clinical, educational, and vocational evaluations of individuals aged 16 through old age; as of 1989 it was without serious competition. The WAIS-R is basically a slight modification of the 1955 WAIS (Kaufman, 1985), a cosmetized WAIS with a new standardization sample. The WAIS was in turn a modified and restandardized version of the 1939 Wechsler-Bellevue, Form I (W-B I), so the evolution of the WAIS-R from the W-B I through the WAIS is direct and of importance to present-day clinicians. This importance is not merely historical, although the history of intellectual assessment, and of David Wechsler's role in it, is both fascinating and illuminating. Rather, the value of studying the W-B I and the WAIS, even though the former is virtually a historical relic and the latter is about to become one, concerns interpretation of the WAIS-R.

Thousands of research investigations have been conducted during the past half-century on the WAIS-R's predecessors. These studies have ranged from the banal and repetitive to the ingenious and vital; the better endeavors have revealed much about intellectual development, mental functioning, and neuropsychological processing of different types of information. But how many of these insights are test-specific, valid for the W-B I or WAIS, but not necessarily for the WAIS-R? The answer lies in the continuity of measurement from one test battery to another. The degree of change in test content, in reliability coefficients, in standardization samples, and in underlying constructs all bears on the question of continuity. Major changes from one revision to another, especially in the construct validity of the respective batteries, would greatly limit generalization of research findings from the W-B I or WAIS to the present-day adult battery; empirical evidence of similarity, however, would argue for the direct application of many previous research findings to the WAIS-R.

This chapter compares the W-B I, WAIS, and WAIS-R and attempts to answer the theoretical question of continuity of measurement and the practical question of generalizability of W-B I and/or WAIS findings to the WAIS-R.

Selection of the 11 Subtests

Wechsler selected tasks for the Wechsler-Bellevue from among the numerous tests available in the 1930s, many of which were developed to meet the assessment needs of World War I. Although Wechsler chose not to develop new subtests for his intelligence battery, his selection process incorporated a blend of clinical, practical, and empirical factors. His rationale for each of the 11 well-known subtests is discussed in the sections that follow.

Verbal Scale

Information

Wechsler (1958) included a subtest designed to tap a subject's range of general information, despite "the obvious objection that the amount of knowledge which a person possesses depends in no small degree upon his [or her] education and cultural opportunities" (p. 65). Wechsler had noted the surprising finding that the fact-oriented information test in the Army Alpha group examination had among the highest correlations with various estimates of intelligence: "It correlated . . . much better with the total score than did the Arithmetical Reasoning, the test of Disarranged Sentences, and even the Analogies Test, all of which had generally been considered much better tests of intelligence. . . . The fact is, all objections considered, the range of a [person's] knowledge is generally a very good indication of his [or her] intellectual capacity" (p. 65). Wechsler was also struck by a variety of psychometric properties of the Army Alpha Information Test compared to other tasks (excellent distribution curve, small percentage of zero scores, lack of pile-up of maximum scores), and the long history of similar factual information tests being "the stock in trade of mental examinations, and . . . widely used by psychiatrists in estimating the intellectual level of patients" (p. 65).

Always the astute clinician, Wechsler was aware that the choice of items determined the value of the information subtest as an effective measure of intelligence. Items must not be chosen whimsically or arbitrarily, but must be developed with several important principles in mind, the most essential being that generally, "the items should call for the sort of knowledge that an average individual with average opportunity may be able to acquire for himself" (p. 65). He usually tried to avoid specialized and academic knowledge, historical dates, and names of famous individuals, "[b]ut there are many exceptions to the rule, and in the long run each item must be tried out separately" (p. 66). Thus, he preferred an item like "What is the height of the average American woman?" to ones like "What is iambic tetrameter?" or "In what year was George Washington born?", but occasionally items of the latter type appeared in his information subtest. Wechsler was especially impressed with the exceptional psychometric properties of the Army Alpha Information Test "in view of the fact that the individual items on [it] left much to be desired" (p. 65).

Although Wechsler (1958) agreed with the criticism that factual information tests depended heavily on educational and cultural opportunities, he felt that the problem "need not necessarily be a fatal or even a serious one" (p. 65). Similarly, he recognized that certain items would vary in difficulty in different locales or when administered to people of different nationalities: "Thus, 'What is the capital of Italy?' is passed almost universally by persons of Italian origin irrespective of their intellectual ability" (p. 66). Yet, he was extremely fond of information, considering it "one of the most satisfactory in the battery" (p. 67).

Digit Span

Memory Span for Digits (renamed Digit Span) combines in a single subtest two skills that subsequent research has shown to be distinct in many ways (Costa, 1975; Jensen & Figueroa, 1976): repetition of digits in the same order as they are spoken by the examiner, and repetition of digits in the reverse order. Wechsler (1958) combined these two tasks for pragmatic reasons, however, not theoretical ones: Each task alone had too limited a range of possible raw scores, and treating each set of items as a separate subtest would have given short-term memory too much weight in determining a person's IQ— 1/6 instead of 1/11.

Wechsler was especially concerned about overweighing memory because Digit Span proved to be a relatively weak measure of general intelligence (*g*). He gave serious consideration to dropping the task altogether, but decided to retain it for two reasons. First, Digit Span is particularly useful at the lower ranges of intelligence; adults who cannot recall 5 digits forward and 3 backward are mentally retarded or emotionally disturbed "in 9 cases out of 10" (p. 71), except in cases of neurological impairment (Wechsler, 1958). Second, poor performance on Digit Span is of unusual diagnostic significance, according to Wechsler, particularly for suspected brain dysfunction or concern about mental deterioration across the life span.

Digit Span also has several other advantages that may account for Wechsler's (1958) assertion that "[p]erhaps no test has been so widely used in scales of intelligence as that of Memory Span for Digits" (p. 70): It is simple to administer and score, measures a rather specific ability, and is clinically valuable because of its unusual susceptibility to anxiety, inattention, distractibility, and lack of concentration. Wechsler noted that repetition of digits back-

ward is especially impaired in individuals who have difficulty sustaining concentrated effort during problem solving. The test has been popularly "used for a long time by psychiatrists as a test of retentiveness and by psychologists in all sorts of psychological studies" (p. 70). Because Wechsler retained Digit Span as a regularly administered subtest on the WAIS-R but treated it as supplementary on the WISC-R, it is evident that he saw its measurement as a more vital aspect of adult than of child assessment.

Vocabulary

"Contrary to lay opinion, the size of a [person's] vocabulary is not only an index of his schooling, but also an excellent measure of his general intelligence. Its excellence as a test of intelligence may stem from the fact that the number of words a [person] knows is at once a measure of his learning ability, his fund of verbal information and of the general range of his ideas" (Wechsler, 1958, p. 84). The Vocabulary subtest formed an essential component of Binet's scales and the WAIS but, surprisingly, this task, which has become prototypical of Wechsler's definition of verbal intelligence, was not a regular W-B I subtest. In deference to the objection that word *knowledge* "is necessarily influenced by . . . educational and cultural opportunities" (p. 84), Wechsler included Vocabulary only as an alternative test during the early stages of W-B I standardization. Consequently, the W-B I was at first a 10-subtest battery and Vocabulary was excluded from analyses of W-B I standardization data such as factor analyses and correlations between subtest score and total score. Based on Wechsler's (1941) reconsideration of the value of Vocabulary and concomitant urging of examiners to administer it routinely, Vocabulary soon became a regular W-B I component. When the W-B II was developed, 33 of the 42 W-B I words were included in that battery's Vocabulary subtest. Since many W-B I words were therefore included in the WISC when the W-B II was revised and restandardized to become the Wechsler children's scale in 1949, Wechsler (1955) decided to include an all-new Vocabulary subtest when the W-B I was converted to the WAIS.

This lack of overlap between the W-B I Vocabulary subtest and the task of the same name on the WAIS and WAIS-R is of some concern regarding the continuity of measurement from the W-B I to its successors. Wechsler himself (1958) noted, "The WAIS list contains a larger percentage of action words (verbs). The only thing that can be said so far about this difference is that while responses given to verbs are easier to score, those elicited by substantives are frequently more significant diagnostically" (pp. 84–85). This difference in diagnostic significance is potentially important because Wechsler (1958) found Vocabulary so valuable, in part because of its qualitative aspects: "The type of word on which a subject passes or fails is always of some significance" (p. 85), yielding information about reasoning ability, degree of abstraction, cultural milieu, educational background, coherence of thought processes, and the like.

Nonetheless, Wechsler was careful to ensure that the various qualitative aspects of Vocabulary performance had a minimal impact on quantitative score. "What counts is the number of words that he knows. Any recognized meaning is acceptable, and there is no penalty for inelegance of language. So long as the subject shows that he knows what a word means, he is credited with a passing score" (1958, p. 85).

Arithmetic

Wechsler (1958) included a test of arithmetical reasoning in an adult intelligence battery because such tests correlate highly with general intelligence; are easily created and standardized; are deemed by most adults as "worthy of a grownup" (p. 69); have been "used as a rough and ready measure of intelligence" (p. 69) prior to the advent of psychometrics; and have "long been recognized as a sign of mental alertness" (p.

69). Such tests are flawed by the impact on test scores of attention span, temporary emotional reactions, and of educational and occupational attainment. As Wechsler notes: "Clerks, engineers and businessmen usually do well on arithmetic tests, while housewives, day laborers, and illiterates are often penalized by them" (p. 69). However, he believed that the advantages of an arithmetical reasoning test far outweighed the negative aspects. He pointed out that adults "may be embarrassed by their inability to do certain problems, but they almost never look upon the questions as unfair or inconsequential" (p. 69). He took much care in developing the specific set of items for the W-B I and the WAIS and believed that his particular approach to constructing the Arithmetic subtest was instrumental in the task's appeal to adults. Wechsler constructed items dealing with everyday, practical situations such that the solutions generally require computational skills taught in grade school or acquired "in the course of day-to-day transactions" (p. 70), and the responses avoid "verbalization or reading difficulties" (p. 69). Whereas the WISC-R and W-B I involve the reading of a few problems by the subject, all items on the WAIS and WAIS-R are read aloud by the examiner. Bonus points for quick, perfect performance are not given to children on the WISC-R, but Wechsler considered the ability to respond rapidly to relatively difficult arithmetic problems to be a pertinent aspect of adult intelligence; bonus points are given to two items on the W-B I Arithmetic subtest, to four items on the WAIS task, and to five items on WAIS-R Arithmetic.

Comprehension

Measures of general comprehension were plentiful in tests prior to the W-B I, appearing in the original Binet scale and its revisions, and in group examinations like the Army Alpha and the National Intelligence Test. However, the test in multiple choice format, though still valuable, does not approach the contribution of the task when subjects have to compose their own responses. "Indeed, one of the most gratifying things about the general comprehension test, when given orally, is the rich clinical data which it furnishes about the subject. It is frequently of value in diagnosing psychopathic personalities, sometimes suggests the presence of schizophrenic trends (as revealed by perverse and bizarre responses) and almost always tells us something about the subject's social and cultural background" (Wechsler, 1958, p. 67).

In selecting questions for the W-B I Comprehension subtest, Wechsler (1958) borrowed some material from the Army Alpha and the Army Memoirs and included a few questions that were also on the old Stanford-Binet, "probably because they were borrowed from the same source" (p. 68). He was not bothered by overlap because of what he perceived to be a very small practice effect for Comprehension: "It is curious how frequently subjects persist in their original responses, even after other replies are suggested to them" (p. 68).

The WAIS Comprehension subtest was modified from its predecessor by adding two very easy items to prevent a pile-up of zero-scores and by adding three proverb items "because of their reported effectiveness in eliciting paralogical and concretistic thinking" (p. 68). Wechsler found that the proverbs did not contribute to the subtest exactly what he had hoped; they were useful for mentally disturbed individuals, "but 'poor' answers were also common in normal subjects . . . [and] even superior subjects found the proverbs difficult. A possible reason for this is that proverbs generally express ideas so concisely that any attempt to explain them further is more likely to subtract than add to their clarity" (1958, p. 68). Despite the shortcomings of proverbs items, particularly the fact that they seem to measure skills that differ from prototypical general comprehension items (Kaufman, 1985), Wechsler (1981) retained the three proverbs items in the WAIS-R Comprehension subtest. Since these three items are relatively difficult (they are among the last five

in the sequence), they are instrumental in distinguishing among the most superior adults regarding the abilities measured by WAIS-R Comprehension.

According to Wechsler (1958), Comprehension was termed a test of common sense on the Army Alpha, and successful performance "seemingly depends on the possession of a certain amount of practical information and a general ability to evaluate past experience. The questions included are of a sort that the average adult may have had occasion to answer for himself at some time, or heard discussed in one form or another. They are for the most part stereotypes with a broad common base" (pp. 68–69). Wechsler was also careful to include no questions with unusual words "so that individuals of even limited education generally have little difficulty in understanding their content" (p. 69). Comprehension scores are, however, dependent on the ability to express one's thoughts verbally.

Similarities

Unlike the other subtests in Wechsler's Verbal Scale, "similarities questions have been used very sparingly in the construction of previous scales . . . [despite being] one of the most reliable measures of intellectual ability" (1958, p. 72). Wechsler felt that this omission was probably due to the belief that language and vocabulary were necessarily too crucial in determining successful performance. However, "while a certain degree of verbal comprehension is necessary for even minimal performance, sheer word knowledge need only be a minor factor. More important is the individual's ability to perceive the common elements of the terms he is asked to compare and, at higher levels, his ability to bring them under a single concept" (p. 73). A glance at the most difficult items on the W-B I, WAIS, and WAIS-R Similarities subtests (fly-tree, praise-punishment), makes it evident that Wechsler was successful in his goal of increasing "the difficulty of test items without resorting to esoteric or unfamiliar words" (p. 73).

Wechsler (1958) saw several merits in the Similarities subtest: it is easy to administer, has an interest appeal for adults, has a high g loading, sheds light on the logical nature of the person's thinking processes, and provides other qualitative information as well. Regarding the latter point, he stressed the "obvious difference both as to maturity and as to level of thinking between the individual who says that a banana and an orange are alike because they both have a skin, and the individual who says that they are both fruit. . . . But it is remarkable how large a percentage of adults never get beyond the superficial type of response" (p. 73). Consequently, Wechsler (1958) considered his 0-1-2 scoring system to be an important innovation to allow simple discrimination between high-level and low-level responses to the same item. He also found his multipoint system helpful in providing insight into the evenness of a person's intellectual development. Whereas some individuals earn almost all 1's, others earn a mixture of 0, 1, and 2 scores. "The former are likely to bespeak individuals of consistent ability, but of a type from which no high grade of intellectual work may be expected; the latter, while erratic, have many more possibilities" (p. 74).

Performance Scale

Picture Completion

This subtest was commonly included in group-administered tests such as the Army Beta. A variant of this task known as Healy Picture Completion II, which involves placing a missing piece into an uncompleted picture, was given individually in various performance scales, including the Army Performance Scale Examination; however, individual administration of Picture Completion, though conducted with the Binet scale for an identical task named Mutilated Pictures, was less common. Wechsler (1958) was unimpressed with the group-administered versions of Picture Completion because the subject had to draw in (instead of name or point to) the missing part, too few items were used, unsatisfactory items were included, and items were chosen haphazardly (such that a typical set of items incorporated many that were much too easy and others that were unusually difficult).

Wechsler nonetheless believed that the test's "popularity is fully deserved" (1958, p. 77); he tried to select an appropriate set of items while recognizing the difficulty of that task. "If one chooses familiar subjects, the test becomes much too easy; if one turns to unfamiliar ones, the test ceases to be a good measure of intelligence because one unavoidably calls upon specialized knowledge" (p. 77). He thought that the W-B I set of items was generally successful, although he had to increase the subtest length by 40% when developing WAIS Picture Completion to avoid a fairly restricted range of obtained scores. Although Wechsler was critical of the group-administered Picture Completion tasks, it is still noteworthy that four of the W-B I and WAIS items were taken directly from the Army Beta test, and an additional four items were clear adaptations of Beta items (using the same pictures, with a different part missing, or the same concept).

The subtest has several psychometric assets, according to Wechsler (1958), including brief administration time, minimal practice effect even after short intervals, and good ability to assess intelligence for low-functioning individuals. Two of these claims are true, but the inconsequential practice effect is refuted by data in the WAIS-R *Manual* (Wechsler, 1981), which shows test-retest gains for Picture Completion over a 2- to 7-week interval to be about 1 scaled-score point for 25–34 and 45–54-year-olds; this gain was typical of all Performance subtests, leading to a practice effect of about 8–9 points for P-IQ (compared to only 3 points for V-IQ). Limitations of the task are that subjects must be familiar with the object in order to have a fair opportunity to detect what is missing, and the susceptibility of specific items to sex differences. Wechsler (1958) notes that women did better in finding the missing eyebrow in the girl's profile and that men did better in detecting the missing thread on the electric light bulb. Similarly, on the WISC-R, about two-thirds of the boys but only about one-third of the girls across the entire 6–16 age range were able to find the missing "slit" in the screw; in contrast, many more girls than boys detected the sock missing from the girl who is running.

Because a person must first have the basic perceptual and conceptual abilities to recognize and be familiar with the object pictured in each item, Wechsler (1958) saw Picture Completion as measuring "the ability of the individual to differentiate essential from non-essential details" (p. 78) and "to appreciate that the missing part is in some way essential either to the form or to the function of the object or picture" (p. 78). But because of the total dependence of the assessment of this skill on the person's easy familiarity with the content of the item, "[u]nfamiliar, specialized and esoteric subject matter must therefore be sedulously avoided when pictures are chosen for this test" (p. 78).

Picture Arrangement

Tests requiring the examinee to arrange a set of pictures presented in mixed-up order so that they tell a sensible story were first used in France by DeCroly (1914). Similar items were developed for the Army Beta group examination but were found inadequate before a different set of items emerged as a component of the individually administered Army Performance Scale Examination (Wechsler, 1958). Yet this task was not used much by the Army and was not popular in the United States except for its inclusion on the Cornell-Coxe Performance Ability Scale (Cornell & Coxe, 1934). Wechsler believed that its relative unpopularity was due to difficulty in scoring the items (because of

numerous alternative solutions that are conceivably worthy of full or part credit) and in finding good sequences. However, "[c]artoons appear to have an international language of their own" (p. 75), and the task has some positive features: "[I]t effectively measures a subject's ability to comprehend and size up a total situation . . . [and] . . . the subject matter of the test nearly always involves some human or practical situation" (p. 75).

Consequently, Wechsler considered it worthwhile to develop a Picture Arrangement subtest for the W-B I despite unavoidable limitations inherent in the test itself. He borrowed three items from the ill-fated Army group-administered version of the task and added four new items taken from Soglow's "Little King" series of cartoons (Wechsler, 1958). For the WAIS, he dropped one W-B I item and added two by new cartoonists. He selected items based on "interest of content, probable appeal to subjects, ease of scoring and discriminating value" (p. 75). Yet Wechsler was never satisfied with the result, noting that "the final selection leaves much to be desired" (p. 75). He spent much time and statistical analysis trying to discern which alternative responses deserved credit and even called in a team of four judges—yet, the final system for assigning credit for alternative arrangements "turned out to be more or less arbitrary" (p. 76).

The problems with Picture Arrangement concern the important role that content must play for each item, which introduces variables regarding cultural background, urban versus rural upbringing, sex differences, interests, and so forth. Yet this limitation is also the subtest's greatest asset, since it is the unique content of each item that gives the task its clinical power. Although Wechsler (1958) did not believe in social intelligence (considering it merely the application of general intelligence to social situations), he conceded that comprehension of the Picture Arrangement items "more nearly corresponds to what other writers have referred to as 'social intelligence'" (p. 75). When individuals perform well on Picture Arrangement, despite poor performance on other tasks, they "seldom turn out to be mental defectives" (p. 76). Furthermore, Wechsler stressed the clinical information obtainable from listening to the subject explain the story behind his or her arrangement, whether the sequence is correct, arguably correct, or plain wrong. "Consistently bizarre explanations are suggestive of some peculiar mental orientation or even psychotic trend" (p. 76). Wechsler considered the explanations given to various arrangements to be "[m]ore interesting than the question of credits allowed" (p. 76) and recommended that examiners routinely ask for verbal explanations of their arrangements when time permits. To avoid violating the norms, these explanations should not be elicited until the entire subtest is completed; then the items of interest can be placed in front of the subject in the order that they gave.

The emphasis on speed changed from the W-B I to the WAIS to the WAIS-R. Bonus points for quick, perfect performance were allotted for more items on the WAIS than the W-B I, increasing the range of possible subtest scores and enhancing the role played by speed of performance on the obtained score. However, Wechsler (1981) reversed this trend for the WAIS-R and deemphasized speed greatly by not allowing bonus points for any of the Picture Arrangement items.

Block Design

Kohs (1923) developed the Block Design test, which used blocks and designs that were red, white, blue, and yellow. His test was included in numerous other tests of intelligence and neuropsychological functioning before Wechsler adapted it for the W-B I. Wechsler (1958) shortened the test substantially, used designs having only two colors (although the W-B I blocks included all four colors, unlike the red and white WAIS and WAIS-R blocks), and

altered the patterns that the examinee had to copy. Block Design has been shown to correlate well with various criterion measures, to be a good measure of *g*, and to be quite amenable to qualitative analysis (Wechsler, 1958). It intrigued Wechsler that those who do very well on this subtest are not necessarily the ones who treat the pattern as a gestalt, but are more often the individuals who are able to break up the pattern into its component parts.

Wechsler (1958) believed that observation of individuals while they solve the problems, such as their following the entire pattern versus breaking it into small parts, provided qualitative, clinical information about the subject's problem-solving approach, attitude, and emotional reaction that is potentially more valuable than the obtained scores. "One can often distinguish the hasty and impulsive individual from the deliberate and careful type, a subject who gives up easily or becomes disgusted, from the one who persists and keeps on working even after his time is up" (p. 80). He also felt that the Block Design subtest is most important diagnostically, particularly for persons with dementia or other types of neurological impairment. From Goldstein's (1948) perspective, those with brain damage perform poorly on Block Design because of loss of the "abstract approach," although Wechsler preferred to think that most "low scores on Block Design are due to difficulty in visual-motor organization" (1958, p. 80).

Object Assembly

Two of the three W-B I Object Assembly puzzles (Manikin and Feature Profile) are slight adaptations of items developed by Pintner and first used in the Army Performance Scale Examination before appearing in performance tests devised by Pintner and Patterson (1925) and by Cornell and Coxe (1934); Wechsler developed the third W-B I item (Hand) and the new item added to the WAIS (Elephant). Wechsler (1958) was dissatisfied with the popular form-board tests, especially for assessing adults, but he "wanted at least one test which required putting things together into a familiar configuration" (pp. 82–83). He included Object Assembly, but only "after much hesitation" (p. 82) because of its known liabilities: (a) relatively low reliability and predictive value, (b) large practice effects, and (c) low correlations with other subtests.

The assets of Object Assembly that impelled Wechsler (1958) to include it in the battery despite its considerable shortcomings were partly psychometric (it contributed something unique to the total score), but mostly clinical and qualitative. Observing individuals solve the puzzles offers great insight into their thinking and work habits and allows the examiner to view several different approaches to the task—"an immediate perception of the whole, accompanied by a critical understanding of the relation of the individual parts[;] . . . rapid recognition of the whole but with imperfect understanding of the relations between the parts [; . . . or a response] which may begin with complete failure to take in the total situation, but which after a certain amount of trial and error manifestation leads to a sudden though often belated appreciation of the figure" (p. 83).

The special clinical value of Object Assembly, according to Wechsler, therefore derives from the examiner's opportunity to observe firsthand "the subject's mode of perception, the degree to which he relies on trial and error methods and his manner of reaction to mistakes" (1958, p. 84).

Digit Symbol

"The Digit Symbol or Substitution Test is one of the oldest and best established of all psychological tests. It is to be found in a large variety of intelligence scales, and its wide popularity is fully merited" (Wechsler, 1958, p. 81). The W-B I Digit Symbol subtest was taken from the Army Beta, the only change being the reduction in response time from 2 minutes to 1½ minutes to avoid a pile-up of perfect scores.

For the WAIS, the number of symbols to be copied was increased by about one-third, although the response time remained unchanged.

Wechsler's (1958) main concern regarding the use of Digit Symbol for assessing adult intelligence involved its potential dependency on visual acuity, motor coordination, and speed. He discounted the first two variables, except for people with specific visual or motor disabilities but gave much consideration to the impact of speed on test performance. He was well aware that Digit Symbol performance drops dramatically with increasing age and is especially deficient for older individuals, who "do not write or handle objects as fast as younger persons, and what is perhaps equally important, they are not as easily motivated to do so. The problem, however, from the point of view of global functioning, is not merely whether the older persons are slower, but whether or not they are also 'slowed up' " (p. 81). Since correlations between Digit Symbol performance and total score remain high (or at least consistent) from age 16 through old age, Wechsler concluded that older people deserve the penalty for speed, "since resulting reduction in test performance is on the whole proportional to the subject's over-all capacity at the time he is tested" (p. 81). Although neurotic individuals also have been shown to perform relatively poorly on Digit Symbol, Wechsler attributed that decrement to difficulty in concentrating and applying persistent effort, i.e., "a lessened mental efficiency rather than an impairment of intellectual ability" (p. 82).

Compared to earlier Digit Symbol or Substitution tests, Wechsler saw particular advantages to the task he borrowed from the Army Beta and included on his scales: It includes sample items to ensure that examinees understand the task, and it requires copying the unfamiliar symbols, not the numbers, lessening "the advantage which individuals having facility with numbers would otherwise have" (1958, p. 82).

Item Content Changes From the W-B I to the WAIS to the WAIS-R

Table 3.1 presents a summary of changes in the item content of the 11 subtests when the W-B I was first revised to produce the WAIS, and the WAIS was revised a generation later to become the WAIS-R. This table was constructed from helpful tables in the WAIS and WAIS-R manuals (Wechsler, 1955, 1981), and

also from examination of the actual items on all three batteries to determine how much of the W-B I is still evident in the present-day WAIS-R. A glance at the first three columns shows that the number of items was increased for 9 of the 11 subtests when the W-B I was revised; however, when the WAIS was revised the overall number of items remained about constant, as increases in four subtests were offset by reductions in the length of three subtests. Overall, Vocabulary has become progressively shorter, whereas Comprehension, Simi-

TABLE 3.1   Changes in the item content from the Wechsler-Bellevue I to the WAIS to the WAIS-R

Subtest	Number of Items on			Percent of W-B I Items Retained on		Percent of WAIS Items Retained on WAIS-R	Percent of New Items Written for	
	W-B I	WAIS	WAIS-R	WAIS	WAIS-R	WAIS-R	WAIS	WAIS-R
Verbal								
I	26	29	29	61.5	34.6	69.0	44.8	31.0
DSp	14	14	14	100.0	100.0	100.0	0.0	0.0
V	42	40	35	0.0	0.0	82.5	100.0	5.7
A	10	14	14	50.0	40.0	85.7	64.3	14.3
C	12	14	16	66.7	58.3	85.7	42.9	25.0
S	12	13	14	83.3	66.7	76.9	23.0	28.6
Performance								
PC	15	21	20	73.3	40.0	66.7	47.6	30.0
PA	7	8	10	85.7	57.1	75.0	25.0	40.0
BD	9	10	9	77.7	66.7	90.0	30.0	0.0
OA	3	4	4	100.0	100.0	100.0	25.0	0.0
DSy	67	90	93	100.0	100.0	100.0	25.6	3.2
Total								
Verbal	116	124	122	46.5	36.2	81.4	57.3	17.2
Performance	101	133	136	93.1	85.1	92.5	29.3	9.6
Full Scale	217	257	258	67.7	59.0	87.2	42.8	13.2

NOTE: The percent of items retained from the Wechsler-Bellevue I or WAIS includes items that were modified slightly by rewording, redrawing, or reduction in size. In addition, the blocks used for Block Design were red, white, blue, and yellow for the W-B I, but were just red and white for the WAIS and WAIS-R. The new items written for the WAIS are expressed as a percentage of the number of items on the WAIS, and the new items written for the WAIS-R are expressed as a percentage of the number of items on the WAIS-R.

larities, Picture Arrangement, and Digit Symbol have increased in length.

The development of an entirely new set of Vocabulary items when the WAIS was developed, discussed previously, represents the biggest change in the item content across the two revisions. In general, however, there has been a rather substantial turnover in the Verbal items from the W-B I to its successors as only 46.5% of the W-B I Verbal items were retained in the WAIS, and only 36.2% are still in the WAIS-R. Excluding Vocabulary and Digit Span (which have not changed at all), the remaining four WAIS Verbal subtests include an average of about two-thirds of the W-B I items, and the four WAIS-R tasks include an average of about one-half of the W-B I items. For the Performance Scale the changes have been more modest, as 93.1% of W-B I items are on the WAIS and 85.1% are on the WAIS-R. However, those percentages are inflated by Digit Symbol; content changes for Picture Completion, Picture Arrangement, and Block Design resemble closely the changes characterizing the Verbal subtests.

Across all subtests, about two-thirds of 217 W-B I items were on the WAIS and nearly three-fifths remain on the WAIS-R. In contrast, item changes from the WAIS to the WAIS-R are generally minor; 81.4% of the WAIS Verbal items and 92.5% of the WAIS Performance items (87.2% overall) appear on the WAIS-R. Only four WAIS-R subtests include less than 80% of the WAIS items: Information, Similarities, Picture Completion, and Picture Arrangement. The similarity in content between the WAIS and its successor is also evident from the percentage of WAIS-R items that are totally new—13.2—a far cry from the 42.8% of the WAIS items that were written expressly for that battery.

Thus, relatively major content changes occurred when the W-B I was revised to become the WAIS, and fairly minor content changes accompanied the metamorphosis of the WAIS into the WAIS-R. Modifications in the W-B I were made by Wechsler (1955) primarily be-

cause "[r]estriction of range of item difficulty was the principal inadequacy . . . [leading to] less than the desired reliability for some of the single tests" (p. 1), and because some items were ambiguous. Content changes were made from the WAIS to the WAIS-R (Wechsler, 1981) primarily to remove or modify dated or ambiguous items, to include more Verbal and Performance items relevant to women and minority group members, and to eliminate very easy items. In addition, administration and scoring changes were made to conform more closely to WISC-R procedures—for example, alternating the administration of Verbal and Performance subtests instead of giving all Verbal tasks first, giving both trials of Digit Span to everyone, asking for a second reason on Comprehension when more than one idea is required for full credit. Yet the fact that more than half of the W-B I items are still administered to adults evaluated in the last decade of the twentieth century, despite sweeping cultural and technological changes, illustrates the continuity of the W-B I through its most recently revised and restandardized edition, the WAIS-R.

RELIABILITY COMPARISONS OF THE W-B I, WAIS, AND WAIS-R

Reliability of a scale is directly related to the number of items in that scale (holding other variables constant), such that longer versions of tests tend to be more reliable than shorter versions of those same tests. Based on the increased test length of most W-B I subtests when the WAIS was constructed, one would logically assume that the reliability of the WAIS would outstrip that of its predecessor.

Table 3.2 presents the best reliability estimates available for the W-B I, WAIS, and WAIS-R. Although the same psychometric procedures were not applied uniformly to the three

TABLE 3.2 Reliability coefficients for the Wechsler-Bellevue I, WAIS, and WAIS-R

Subtest/IQ	W-B I (Test-Retest)	WAIS (Split-Half)	WAIS-R (Split-Half)	WAIS-R (Test-Retest)
Verbal				
Information	.86	.91	.89	.91
Digit Span	.67	.68	.83	.86
Vocabulary	.88	.95	.96	.92
Arithmetic	.62	.82	.84	.85
Comprehension	.74	.78	.84	.81
Similarities	.71	.86	.84	.84
Performance				
Picture Completion	.83	.83	.81	.88
Picture Arrangement	.64	.67	.74	.73
Block Design	.84	.84	.87	.86
Object Assembly	.69	.68	.68	.70
Digit Symbol	.80	.92	.82	.84
Verbal IQ	.84	.96	.97	.96
Performance IQ	.86	.93	.93	.90
Full Scale IQ	.90	.97	.97	.96

NOTE: Data for the Wechsler-Bellevue I are from a test–retest study conducted by Derner, Aborn, and Cantor (1950) with 158 normals. Wechsler (1958, p. 102) and Matarazzo (1972, p. 239) feature these data, apparently considering them as the best estimates of W-B I reliability. Data for the WAIS are the means of the values provided in the WAIS Manual (Wechsler, 1955, Table 6) for ages 18–19 (N=200), 25–34 (N=300), and 45–54 (N=300). The value for WAIS Digit Symbol was based on a test–retest study of 59 female nursing applicants aged 18–19, who were tested on the WAIS and W-B I Digit Symbol subtests. Split-half data for the WAIS-R are the means provided in the WAIS-R Manual (Wechsler, 1981, Table 10) for the nine age groups between ages 16 and 74. The values for WAIS-R Digit Symbol and Digit Span are test–retest coefficients based on four age groups (Ns of 48–80). Test–retest data for the WAIS-R are the means of the values for the two groups presented in the WAIS-R Manual (Wechsler, 1981, Table 11) at ages 25–34 (N=71) and 45–54 (N=48).

When mean split-half values for the WAIS-R are based only on ages 18–19, 25–34, and 45–54 to make them directly comparable to the mean split-half values for the WAIS, the results are highly similar to the WAIS-R split-half means based on all nine age groups; values for the three IQs are identical, and values for the subtests are within .03 of each other.

batteries, preventing simple or direct comparisons from test to test, the table reveals that the WAIS is indeed more reliable than the W-B I. As Wechsler had intended when he lengthened the W-B I, the reliabilities of V- and P-IQs rose from the mid-80s on the W-B I to the mid-90s on the WAIS; the coefficient for Full Scale likewise jumped from 90 to 97. Two of the three subtests that were most lengthened when the WAIS was developed (Arithmetic, Digit Symbol) showed the biggest jumps in reliability. Surprisingly, Picture Completion evidenced the same coefficient on the W-B I and WAIS, even though it was increased from 15 to 21 items; nonetheless, the increase served the useful function of raising the maximum scaled score obtainable on Picture Completion from 15 on the W-B I to 18 on the WAIS.

Reliability coefficients for the WAIS and WAIS-R are similar, especially for the IQs. Digit Span's reliability increased the most, probably because of the administrative change noted in the previous section requiring examiners to give both trials to all individuals, even if they pass the first trial. This difference from WAIS and W-B I procedures, which required second trials only for those who failed the first time, effectively increases the number of items in the WAIS-R subtest, even though technically each battery contains the same 14 items. The WAIS-R subtests that were lengthened most are Comprehension (from 14 to 16 items) and Picture Arrangement (from 8 to 10 items); these tasks also showed the largest gains in reliability (aside from Digit Span), increasing by .06 and .07, respectively, from the WAIS to the WAIS-R.

Overall, the reliability coefficients for the three batteries show improvement with each revision and restandardization, implying that Wechsler was successful in one of the key psychometric goals that accompanies updating a test. Yet the values of the reliability coefficients are sufficiently similar for the three batteries on both the global scales and separate subtests to support the continuity of consistent measurement from the W-B I to the WAIS to the WAIS-R.

STANDARDIZATION OF THE W-B I, WAIS, AND WAIS-R

The standardization samples of the Wechsler adult batteries have improved significantly with each successive norming program. The initial standardization of the W-B I was conducted by Wechsler and his colleagues before he received financial backing from a test publisher, so a nationwide norming was not feasible; consequently the W-B I was standardized on a population that was "mostly urban from the City and State of New York" (Wechsler, 1958, p. 92). The W-B I normative sample was also all white, excluding blacks and other nonwhite groups "because it was felt at the time that norms derived from a mixed population could not be interpreted without special provisos and reservations . . . [which] appears now to have been an unnecessary concern" (Wechsler, 1958, p. 90).

Although the W-B I sample (which ranged from ages 7 to 70) included males and females, it was not systematically stratified by gender. The W-B I adult normative population was roughly stratified by education level, but not occupational group. Hence, the W-B I was stratified by age and education, but not on variables that today are considered essential for an intelligence test: gender, race, geographic region, occupation, and urban versus rural residence. Yet, the stratification on age was an important contribution to psychometrics, because "the practice for a long time was to treat all individuals over 16 years as constituting a single age group" (Wechsler, 1958, p. 86). In addition, the choice of education as a rough stratification variable was a good one because of its correlations in the .50s to low .70s with IQ (Matarazzo, 1972; Reynolds, Chastain, Kaufman, & McLean, 1987).

The WAIS was normed on a nationwide sample of blacks and whites and was systematically stratified for ages 16 to 64 on the variables of age, gender, race, geographic region, urban versus rural residence, educational attainment, and occupational group. This sample was far superior to the W-B I sample, but it did not include a stratified sample of older individuals. Norms for ages 65–69, 70–74, and 75 and over were derived from 359 individuals included in a sample of 475 elderly Kansas City residents. Although this elderly sample was carefully selected using probability sampling techniques, it was not stratified on the major variables used to stratify the WAIS for all other age groups and is therefore not ideal. In contrast, the WAIS-R was stratified on all of the same key variables as the WAIS through age 74, and thus represents the ultimate in adult norming of a Wechsler battery.

The W-B I sample included 50 to 70 children at each year of age between 7 and 14, and 100 children at age 15. Sample sizes for the individuals aged 16 and above ($N = 1181$) are as depicted in Table 3.3. (Wechsler, 1958).

TABLE 3.3   Sample sizes for individuals aged 16 and above in the W-B I standardization sample ($N = 1181$)

Age Group	Number of Cases	Age Group	Number of Cases
16	100	40–44	91
17–19	100	45–49	70
20–24	160	50–54	55
25–29	195	55–59	50
30–34	140	60–70	85
35–39	135		

Clearly, the younger half of the age range (16–39, $N = 830$) is far better represented than the older half (40–70, $N = 351$).

In the WAIS and WAIS-R these unusual disproportions were eliminated. The WAIS included 200 individuals aged 16–17, 18–19, 20–24, and 55–64, and 300 subjects aged 25–34, 35–44, and 45–54; the sample of 1700 included exactly equal numbers of males and females at each of the seven age groups. The WAIS-R sample included 1880 individuals spread across nine age levels between 16 and 74, as shown in Table 3.4 (each group included equal numbers of males and females).

TABLE 3.4   WAIS-R standardization sample spread across nine age levels ($N = 1880$)

Age Group	Number of Cases	Age Group	Number of Cases
16–17	200	45–54	250
18–19	200	55–64	160
20–24	200	65–69	160
25–34	300	70–74	160
35–44	250		

Wechsler (1955, 1981) does not provide a rationale for having larger samples at the younger ages or for having narrower age bands at the extremes of the age range (16–24 and 65–74 years). Presumably, the age bands are narrower for the younger and older ages because of the more rapid intellectual development (whether increasing or declining) associated with adolescence and old age. The larger samples of younger than older subjects probably reflects the relative ease or difficulty of obtaining volunteers for testing from the different age groups.

One interesting difference between the WAIS and WAIS-R samples is the inclusion of one male and one female institutionalized mentally retarded individual at each of the seven WAIS age groups (Wechsler, 1955), although the sample did not include any other "known hospital or mentally disturbed subjects" (Wechsler, 1958, p. 92); for the WAIS-R, the normative sample excluded "institutionalized mental defectives, individuals with known brain damage or severe behavioral or emotional problems, or individuals with physical defects which would restrict their ability to respond to test items" (Wechsler, 1981, p. 18). However, this difference in the two samples involves too few individuals to be of much practical consequence.

Since the W-B I, WAIS, and WAIS-R standardization samples were each stratified on education level, this variable is a good way of comparing the three samples. Table 3.5 presents the proportion of the subjects in each sample attaining different levels of education. The total sample for the W-B I matched the best available Census data for the 1930s reasonably well, and the total samples for the WAIS and WAIS-R matched best estimates of Census data for the 1950s and 1970s, respectively. Hence, differences in proportions of the samples for each educational level reflect real differences in the population as a whole at the time of each standardization.

Overall, the data in Table 3.5 reveal that each level of educational attainment was appropriately represented in all three standardization samples. In view of the importance of this

TABLE 3.5 Comparison of education levels characterizing the total standardization samples of the W-B I, WAIS, and WAIS-R

Education Level (Years of School Completed)	Percent in W-B I Sample	Percent in WAIS Sample	Percent in WAIS-R Sample
16 or more (college graduate)	5.10	4.86	11.38
13–15 (some college)	3.77	8.57	13.35
12 (high school graduate)	10.81	23.28	34.68
9–11 (some high school)	18.76	27.78	25.11
8 or less	61.57	35.49	15.48

NOTE: Data for the W-B I and WAIS are from Wechsler (1958, Tables 9 and 10). Data for the WAIS-R are based on sample sizes for the total standardization group provided in Table 1 by Reynolds et al. (1987). The group listed as "8 or less" for the W-B I is actually a combination of percentages provided for elementary school graduates, those with some elementary school, and illiterates.

variable in terms of its impact on IQ compared to most other variables (Reynolds et al., 1987), the state of the art regarding the psychometrics underlying test standardization in the 1930s versus the 1950s and 1970s, and the cultural influences of the time (which would have made it understandable to omit nonwhites from the W-B I sample), it is reasonable to conclude that the standardization samples of the three adult Wechsler batteries are appropriately comparable.

COMPARISON OF THE CONSTRUCT VALIDITY OF THE W-B I, WAIS, AND WAIS-R

Construct validity, which determines the degree to which a test measures the traits or constructs it was developed to measure, is considered by Messick (1980) to be the only real type of validity. More than a comparison of reliability

coefficients, content changes, or standardization samples, a comparison of the constructs underlying the three adult Wechsler test batteries is instrumental in deciding whether the bulk of research obtained on the W-B I and WAIS is legitimately generalizable to the WAIS-R. Three of the types of acceptable evidence in support of a test's construct validity (Anastasi, 1988) will be examined for the W-B I, WAIS, and WAIS-R: internal consistency (correlations between each subtest and total score on the battery), factor analysis, and developmental changes (progression of mean Verbal, Performance, and Full Scale scores across the age range).

Internal Consistency

Table 3.6 presents correlations between subtest scores and total scores on each of the three test batteries based on age groups that are roughly comparable, after correction for contamination due to the subtest's overlap with total score. These coefficients are good estimates of the

TABLE 3.6   Coefficients of correlation between the subtests and Full Scale score on the W-B I, WAIS, and WAIS-R

Subtest	W-B I (Ages 20–34)	WAIS (Ages 25–34)	WAIS-R (Ages 25–34)
Verbal			
Information	.67	.84	.79
Digit Span	.51	.56	.57
Vocabulary	(.75)	.84	.82
Arithmetic	.63	.66	.72
Comprehension	.66	.71	.74
Similarities	.73	.74	.72
Performance			
Picture Completion	.61	.72	.72
Picture Arrangement	.57	.69	.65
Block Design	.71	.79	.74
Object Assembly	.48	.58	.59
Digit Symbol	.67	.63	.52
MEAN Verbal	.66	.72	.73
MEAN Performance	.61	.68	.64
MEAN Full Scale	.64	.70	.69

NOTE: The coefficients for the Wechsler-Bellevue I are between each subtest and total score minus the particular subtest, based on $N=355$. The value for Vocabulary was estimated by Wechsler (1958, p. 84–85) from studies conducted subsequent to the W-B I standardization, since correlations with Full Scale score were not computed for Vocabulary, an alternative test in the early stages of the W-B I standardization. The coefficients for the WAIS ($N=300$) and the WAIS-R ($N=300$) are between each subtest and total score corrected for contamination due to overlap. Data for the W-B I and WAIS are from Wechsler (1956, Table 17); data for the WAIS-R are from Wechsler (1981, Table 15).

internal consistency of each battery. (The value for W-B I Vocabulary had to be estimated by Wechsler, 1958, from research conducted after standardization because Vocabulary was merely an alternative test during the early standardization testing.) Overall, the coefficients for the 11 W-B I subtests ranged from .48 to .75, slightly lower than the ranges of .56 to .84 for the WAIS and .52 to .82 for the WAIS-R. The mean coefficient for all W-B I subtests was .64,

compared to a mean of about .70 for the WAIS and WAIS-R. Since all validity coefficients are a function of reliability, it is likely that the slightly attenuated W-B I values are merely a reflection of the lower reliability of most subtests and all IQ scales of that battery.

For each test battery, Vocabulary, Information, and Block Design were among the highest correlates of Full Scale, while Object Assembly and Digit Span were among the lowest correlates. When the task-total correlations are rank ordered from high to low for each of the three batteries, the following rank-order correlations are obtained: W-B I with WAIS, rho = .78 (p<.02); W-B I with WAIS-R, rho = .63 (p<.05); and WAIS with WAIS-R, rho = .90 (p<.01). These results attest to the similar construct validity of the W-B I, WAIS, and WAIS-R—especially the latter two—when applying the internal consistency criterion.

Factor Analysis

Factor-analytic investigators of Wechsler's adult scales do not agree on the number of meaningful factors or constructs underlying the batteries. Silverstein (1982) frequently has argued for two, corresponding fairly closely to the intended constructs of verbal and nonverbal intelligence, while others have opted for factor solutions that interpret three or more meaningful dimensions (Berger, Bernstein, Klein, Cohen, & Lucas, 1964; Matarazzo, 1972; Wechsler, 1958). The issue of the number of meaningful WAIS-R factors is treated at length in chapter 8. For now, the most meaningful generalization regarding the factor structure of the W-B I, WAIS, and WAIS-R is that there are three dimensions that emerge for each test battery for a wide variety of normal and special samples using an even greater variety of psychometric techniques; the two main, omnipresent factors are Verbal Comprehension and Perceptual Organization, and the third, smaller dimension has been assigned labels like Freedom from Distractibility, Memory, Sequential Ability, and Number Ability.

When two factors are rotated, the six Verbal subtests tend to load highly on the first or Verbal Comprehension factor, and the five Performance subtests primarily define the Perceptual Organization dimension (a factor more accurately described as Visual Organization). Digit Span, Digit Symbol, and Arithmetic (which together often constitute the third or distractibility factor) occasionally deviate from the expected pattern. Table 3.7 presents the Verbal Comprehension and Perceptual Organization factors for the W-B I, WAIS, and WAIS-R. These results are taken from two-factor solutions for the latter two test batteries, based on the entire standardization samples; for the W-B I, the best available data were the first two factors from three-factor solutions of abnormal populations.

Despite these differences in samples and procedures (including the fact that correlated factors were obtained for the W-B I, whereas independent factors were extracted for the WAIS and WAIS-R), the three Verbal factors are quite similar to each other, as are the three Performance dimensions. Table 3.7 shows the rankings of each subtest on each factor (where 1 denotes the highest loading and 11 signifies the lowest), as well as the precise factor loadings.

For each adult Wechsler battery, the best measures of Verbal Comprehension are Vocabulary, Information, Comprehension, and Similarities, and the best measures of Perceptual Organization are Block Design, Object Assembly, and Picture Completion. The note to Table 3.7 gives the rank-order correlations between pairs of factors assigned the same name on the three test batteries. These values are statistically significant, averaging .86 for the Verbal factors and .87 for the Performance factors.

Also of interest is a comparison of the nature of the relationships between the Verbal and Performance factors on the W-B I, WAIS, and WAIS-R. Using correlations between Verbal and Performance IQs to quantify these relationships, the following V-P IQ correlations from available standardization data are observed (Wechsler, 1958, 1981): W-B I (r = .71 for ages 20–25); WAIS (r = .78, mean of ages 18–19, 25–34, and 45–54); WAIS-R (r = .74 for the total sample ages 16–74). These three values are similar to each other, again affirming the comparability of the two major constructs underlying the three adult Wechsler batteries. "These correlations are fairly high but not sufficiently high that substantial differences in the separate IQ's obtained by any individual may not occur" (Wechsler, 1958, p. 102).

TABLE 3.7 Comparison of the Verbal Comprehension (VC) and Perceptual Organization (PO) factors of the W-BI, WAIS, and WAIS-R

| | Rotated factor loadings | | | | | | Rank order of factor loadings | | | | | |
| | W-BI | | WAIS | | WAIS-R | | Verbal Comprehension | | | Perceptual Organization | | |
Subtest	VC	PO	VC	PO	VC	PO	W-BI	WAIS	WAIS-R	W-BI	WAIS	WAIS-R
Verbal												
I	63*	-02	79*	42*	79*	31	1	2	2	9	6	11
DSp	-02	-03	52*	34	47*	37	10	7	6	10	11	8
V	61*	-08	83*	35	84*	32	2	1	1	11	9.5	10
A	27	04	61*	40*	58*	47*	6	5	5	6.5	7	4
C	55*	00	70*	35	73*	34	3	4	3	8	9.5	9
S	54*	04	71*	38	69*	39	4	3	4	6.5	8	7
Performance												
PC	34	43*	48*	63*	44*	55*	5	8.5	8	3	3	3
PA	18	42*	48*	57*	45*	45*	7	8.5	7	4	4	6
BD	02	59*	35	72*	33	72*	8	10	10	2	1	1
OA	-08	73*	28	70*	22	69*	11	11	11	1	2	2
DSy	01	23	54*	44*	39	46*	9	6	9	5	5	5

NOTE: Decimal points are omitted. Loadings of .40 and above are asterisked. Data for the Wechsler-Bellevue I are the means of the oblique rotated loadings from three-factor solutions reported by Cohen (1952) for three neuropsychiatric groups, each composed of 100 hospitalized male veterans between the ages of 20 and 40: psychoneurotic, schizophrenic, brain-damaged. The data for the WAIS and WAIS-R are the means of the varimax rotated loadings from two-factor solutions reported by Silverstein (1982) for the standardization samples of each instrument. For the WAIS, means are based on three age groups (18–19, 25–34, 45–54) comprising a total of 800 subjects; for the WAIS-R, means are based on all nine age groups between 16 and 74, comprising 1880 subjects. Rank-order correlations of subtest ranks between pairs of Verbal Comprehension (VC) factors are as follows: W-BI and WAIS, rho = .81; W-BI and WAIS-R, rho = .85; WAIS and WAIS-R, rho = .93. Rank-order correlations for Perceptual Organization (PO) factors are: W-BI and WAIS, rho = .91; W-BI and WAIS-R, rho = .91; WAIS and WAIS-R, rho = .78. All values are significant at the .01 level, except for the .78, which is significant at the .02 level.

TABLE 3.8   Comparison of the Freedom from Distractibility (FD) factors of the W-B I, WAIS, and WAIS-R

| | ROTATED FACTOR LOADINGS | | | RANK ORDER OF FACTOR LOADINGS | | |
| | | | | Freedom from Distractibility | | |
Subtest	W-B I FD	WAIS FD	WAIS-R FD	W-B I	WAIS	WAIS-R
Verbal						
I	03	07	30	6	7	6
DSp	55*	71*	64*	1	1	1
V	01	12	34	8	4	4
A	30	32	55*	3	2	2
C	00	−06	27	9.5	10	7.5
S	06	10	27	5	5	7.5
Performance						
PC	−09	−07	17	11	11	10.5
PA	02	08	23	7	6	9
BD	18	04	33	4	7	5
OA	00	03	17	9.5	8	10.5
DSy	37	24	36	2	3	3

NOTE: Decimal points are omitted. Loadings of .40 and above are asterisked. Data for the Wechsler-Bellevue I are the means of the oblique rotated loadings from three-factor solutions reported by Cohen (1952) for the three groups described in the note to Table 3.7. Data for the WAIS are oblique rotated loadings from three-factor solutions reported by Fowler, Richards, & Boll (1980) based on the mean intercorrelation matrix for the three standardization age groups in the WAIS *Manual* (ages 18–19, 25–34, 45–54). Data for the WAIS-R are the means of the varimax rotated loadings reported by Parker (1983) for the nine standardization groups, ages 16–74; three-factor solutions were used for seven age groups, but four-factor solutions had to be used to obtain the desired three factors for ages 18–19 and 45–54.

Rank-order correlations of subtest ranks between pairs of Freedom from Distractibility (FD) factors are as follows: W-B I and WAIS, rho = .86; W-B I and WAIS-R, rho = 84; WAIS and WAIS-R, rho = .85. All values are significant at the .01 level.

Table 3.8 presents data on the third factor extracted from three-factor solutions of the W-B I, WAIS, and WAIS-R, and again the similarity from battery to battery is remarkable. The prototypical triad of distractibility subtests had the highest loadings on each of the dimensions, and the average rank-order correlation between pairs of factors, shown in the note to Table 3.8, is .85.

The constructs that underlie the W-B I, WAIS, and WAIS-R, as defined by the em-

pirical technique of factor analysis, are the same. The similarity between the WAIS and WAIS-R constructs was shown definitively in a study by Warner, Ernst, and Townes (1986), who tested 474 consecutive right-handed neuropsychiatric patients referred for evaluation on the WAIS (N = 198, tested 1976–1981) or WAIS-R (N = 276, tested 1981–1983). Factor analyses of the WAIS and WAIS-R for these highly similar patient samples produced extremely congruent factor structures. For the

WAIS-R and its predecessor, the Verbal Comprehension factors were defined by loadings of .59 to .91 by the four subtests associated with this dimension; the Perceptual Organization factors were defined by loadings of .62 to .81 by the five Performance subtests; and the Freedom from Distractibility dimension had its two highest loadings by Arithmetic and Digit Span.

Developmental Trends

Since scaled scores for each of the three adult batteries are based on a reference group of individuals aged 20–34 (an unfortunate decision that is discussed on pages 423–425), an examination of sums of scaled scores (not IQs, which are adjusted for age) allows comparisons of the relative ability level of separate age groups. Data for the W-B I are incomplete, as mean scores are only available through age 59 for the Verbal and Full Scales, and through age 49 for the Performance Scale (Wechsler, 1958, Table 13). In view of the small sample sizes for the older half of the W-B I sample, one cannot have too much confidence in the generalizability of the developmental trends across the entire age range. Nevertheless, mean scaled scores were computed for W-B I age groups having 150 or more cases to permit some comparison to the WAIS and WAIS-R. (Mean scaled scores allow direct comparison because the W-B I sums of scaled scores are based on only 10 subtests, not 11—because Vocabulary was excluded.) These mean scaled scores are shown in Table 3.9.

As is evident in these data, individuals aged 16–19 performed not quite as well as those aged 20–24; verbal scores began to decline after age 29, and nonverbal scores began to descend after age 24. Table 3.10 presents similar data for the WAIS and WAIS-R for seven age groups within the 16- to 64-year range. Again, mean scaled scores are used, not just to allow comparison to the W-B I but also to permit comparison of the Verbal (six subtests) and Performance (five subtests) Scales of the WAIS and WAIS-R.

TABLE 3.9   Mean scaled scores computed for W-B I age groups having 150 or more cases

Age Group	Verbal	Performance	Full Scale
16–19	9.3	10.2	9.7
20–24	9.4	10.2	9.8
25–29	9.4	9.7	9.5
30–39	9.2	8.8	9.0
40–49	8.8	7.7	8.3

The data in Table 3.10 are quite revealing. On the WAIS, Verbal scores increase gradually from ages 16 through 34 and don't really begin to decline until after age 44. Performance scores likewise increase gradually, but only through age 24 before plunging after age 34. A comparison of the WAIS to the W-B I (see Table 3.9) suggests similarities in age-related changes: Increases in scores are slight but fairly steady from the upper end of the teen-age years through the early 20s; 16- to 19-year-olds scored about as well on the Performance Scale as those in their 20s. Verbal scores begin to decline slightly during the 30s and more rapidly in the 40s, and Performance scores begin an early decline on both the W-B I and the WAIS during the mid-20s.

Note that the changes in mean scores with age cannot be interpreted as meaningful developmental fluctuations because the various cross-sectional age groups differ on other key variables such as educational attainment. This topic is addressed in detail in chapter 7.

Problems With WAIS-R Adolescent Data

The data on the WAIS-R, however, are only in accord with the W-B I and WAIS data for adults aged 20 and above. Indeed, the mean scaled scores for the WAIS and WAIS-R Full Scales are virtually identical—within one-tenth of a point of each other—for each of the five adult age groups between 20–24 and 55–64, and the WAIS versus WAIS-R means for the

TABLE 3.10   Mean scaled scores on the Verbal, Performance, and Full Scales of the WAIS and WAIS-R earned by different age groups across the 16–64 year range

Age Group	VERBAL		PERFORMANCE		FULL SCALE	
	WAIS	WAIS-R	WAIS	WAIS-R	WAIS	WAIS-R
16–17	9.1	8.5	9.8	9.5	9.4	8.9
18–19	9.6	8.6	9.9	9.4	9.7	9.0
20–24	9.9	9.8	10.1	10.2	10.0	10.0
25–34	10.1	10.2	9.9	10.0	10.0	10.1
35–44	10.0	9.6	9.2	9.1	9.4	9.3
45–54	9.7	9.7	8.2	8.4	9.0	9.1
55–64	9.3	9.3	7.4	7.6	8.4	8.5

NOTE: Data for the WAIS and WAIS-R were computed from data provided in the test manuals by Wechsler (1955, Table 10; 1981, Table 7).

separate Verbal and Performance Scales are similar for the five adult groups (see Table 3.10). The data for ages 16–19, however, do not correspond at all, a point raised previously (Kaufman, 1985a; Gregory, 1987).

The older adolescents in the WAIS-R sample performed very poorly compared to their age-mates in previous standardization samples, scoring strikingly lower on the Verbal and Full Scales and substantially lower on the Performance Scale. Even more inexplicable is the failure of 18- and 19-year-olds to outperform the 16- and 17-year-olds on the WAIS-R even though they have more education.

Based on data in Table 5 of the WAIS-R *Manual* (Wechsler, 1981), 48.5% of 18- and 19-year-olds had completed high school, and an additional 12.0% had some college; the contrasting Census-based figures for 16- and 17-year-olds are 3.0% and 0.0%, respectively. The lack of a gradual increase in intellectual skills for older adolescents on the WAIS-R leads to an enormous jump in the norms between ages 18–19 and 20–24.

On the W-B I, 16-year-olds averaged 9.6 on the 10 regular subtests, compared to a mean of 9.8 for both 17–19 and 20–24-year-olds (means computed from data appearing in Wechsler, 1958, Table 13). On the WAIS, the means on

all 11 subtests for 16–17, 18–19, and 20–24-year-olds increased systematically from 9.4 to 9.7 to 10.0. Yet the WAIS-R, with the most modern and sophisticated norms, shows mean scaled scores of 8.9, 9.0, and 10.0 for the three youngest age groups in the standardization sample.

Also of great concern regarding the norms for ages 16 to 19 are the low standard deviations for these standardization age groups compared to most other age groups (Wechsler, 1981, Table 7). This inconsistency in standard deviations from age group to age group on the WAIS-R did not occur for the W-B I or WAIS (Lindemann & Matarazzo, 1984), thereby reflecting a potentially important difference among the three adult Wechsler scales and creating problems in the interpretation of the IQs earned by individuals who are tested more than once.

Possible Explanations of Questionable WAIS-R Adolescent Norms

Has the development of intelligence changed for the present generation, or is there some error in the norms? The former explanation makes no sense. How can the far better-educated 18- and 19-year-olds perform comparably to 16- and 17-year-olds? How can both groups do so much worse than contemporary 20–24-year-olds or 16–19-year-olds from past generations? How can one reconcile a *loss* of intelligence by older adolescents when Flynn (1987) has shown decisively that people around the world have increased their IQs over the past generation? The only sensible conclusion is that the WAIS-R norms for ages 16–19 include some type of unknown, systematic bias that limits their value.

Different procedures were used to select 16–19-year-olds and 20–74-year-olds for the WAIS-R standardization sample. For the older adolescents, occupation of the subject's head of household was used to stratify the sample; for the adults, their own occupation was used. Additionally, all age groups matched Census proportions on years of school completed, based on divisions into the following educational categories: 8 years or less, 9–11 years, 12 years, 13–15 years, and 16 or more years.

The categories of 9–11 years of education and high school graduate (12 years) are quite different for adolescents and adults. For adults, those categories usually reflect a person's ultimate educational attainment, whereas for 16–19-year-olds they may just be intermediate points in their education. Paradoxically, the stratification difference resulting from the variable of education should have produced a bias that was opposite to the one that apparently occurred; that is, individuals with 9–11 years of education who are destined to go on to college should perform better than those who will never graduate from high school.

Thus, the explanation of the problem is not simple or obvious. Yet, there certainly seems to be some connection to the occupational and educational variables, as evidenced by the relationships of IQ to these socioeconomic variables at ages 16–19 (see chapter 6 for further discussion). For example, educational attainment correlated at only .19 with Full Scale IQ at ages 16–17, compared with coefficients of .50–.67 for other age groups, suggesting a problem with the sampling at ages 16–17.

However, the fact that the stratification variables of occupational group and educational attainment operated differently for 16–19 versus 20–74-year-olds may well be related to the seemingly wrong norms for the youngest two age groups in the WAIS-R sample. Further, the lack of a clear-cut explanation does not vitiate the severity of the problem.

Clinical Implications of the WAIS-R Norms at Ages 16–19

Simply put, the WAIS-R norms for 16–19-year-olds are suspect and examiners should interpret the obtained scaled scores with extreme caution. The norms for 16–19-year-olds are "soft" or "easy" because the reference group performed more poorly than 16-to-19-year-olds really perform. The surprising result is that the IQs of 16- through 19-year-olds tested on the WAIS-R will be spuriously high by 3 to 5 points, if the WAIS sums of scaled scores for older adolescents are still roughly accurate for today's 16- to 19-year-olds. The scaled scores on the separate subtests are not affected, however, because they are computed relative to the norms for 20–34-year-olds.

Overview of Developmental Trends

The present discussion supports the construct validity of the W-B I and WAIS inasmuch as the developmental trends observed for these instruments conform to what research has shown to characterize adolescent and adult intellectual development when no effort is made to control for cohort differences (see chapter 7). The construct validity of the WAIS-R is supported for the adult age range but *not* for 16–19-year-olds. Consequently, the W-B I, WAIS, and WAIS-R are sufficiently comparable in the constructs they measure across the adult age ranges, when developmental changes are used as the criterion, but the WAIS-R is *not* comparable to its two predecessors for the groups of 16–17- and 18–19-year-olds.

Correlations Between the W-B I and WAIS and Between the WAIS and WAIS-R

The various construct validation approaches described previously are instrumental in determining whether research findings on the W-B I and WAIS can be applied to the WAIS-R. Just as valuable as these theoretically based approaches is a simple, pragmatic procedure: correlations between the scores yielded by one test battery and the test battery that was developed to replace it.

Relationship of the W-B I and WAIS

Zimmerman and Woo-Sam (1973, Table 2-1) and Matarazzo (1972, Table 10.21) present data summarizing the relationships between W-B I and WAIS IQs found in diverse studies published from 1956 to 1964. In five of these studies, both instruments were administered to groups ranging in size from 28 college students (Duncan & Barrett, 1961) to 179 brain-damaged patients (Fitzhugh & Fitzhugh, 1964a); the total number of subjects in the five studies was 356.

Correlations between the W-B I and WAIS Verbal IQs ranged from .72 to .95 with a mean value of .83. Performance IQ correlations ranged from .25 to .84 with a mean of .48, and Full Scale coefficients ranged from .46 to .87 with a mean of .72. These values, however, are attenuated greatly by an unusual degree of range restriction in the obtained IQs of three of the four groups; standard deviations in the 8 to 12 range were found for the IQs of the two samples of college students, and standard deviations of 6 to 9 points were obtained for a group of Air Force psychiatric patients. When variability of the IQs is far less than the designated standard deviation of 15, lower correlations are the predictable result. Hence, the observed correlations, particularly for the Verbal and the Full Scale IQs, are large enough to support the continuity of measurement from the W-B I to its successor.

Fitzhugh and Fitzhugh (1964a) assessed the one group that had normal-sized standard deviations and that also produced the highest correlations between the W-B I and WAIS IQs (.84 to .95). Yet they were skeptical about the comparability of the two instruments because their group of 179 brain-damaged patients displayed different V-P IQ discrepancies on the W-B I and WAIS. Their caution is sensible, but because about 2 years had elapsed between the administrations of the W-B I and the WAIS, it is possible that changes occurred in the verbal and nonverbal abilities of those patients.

In reviewing a number of different types of studies pertaining to this issue, Matarazzo concluded "that in a very general and gross sense, the Verbal versus Performance differential on the WAIS has as much potential to differentiate left from right hemisphere lesions as does such a differential on the W-B I. . . . Nevertheless, . . . [the] Verbal versus Performance differences which the practitioner obtains with an individual patient might be a function of the Wechsler Scale employed, rather than reflecting an underlying brain dysfunction in such a patient" (1972, p. 398).

Matarazzo therefore agreed that W-B I research is generalizable to the WAIS, but he cautioned that for any given client or case, the clinician must be alert to the influences of precisely which battery was administered. This issue becomes particularly important when comparing the results of Wechsler Bellevue studies of brain-damaged individuals with similar studies that used the WAIS or WAIS-R (see chapters 9, 10 and 11).

Relationship of the WAIS to WAIS-R

In the WAIS-R Manual, Wechsler (1981, Table 17) provided correlations between the WAIS and WAIS-R for 72 adults aged 35–44, tested on both instruments in a counterbalanced order with an interval of 3 to 6 weeks between administrations. He reported WAIS versus WAIS-R coefficients of .91 for the Verbal Scale, .79 for the Performance Scale, and .88 for the Full Scale.

Ryan, Nowak, and Geisser (1987, Table 2) summarized the results of eight groups, including the one cited by Wechsler (1981), that were tested on both the WAIS and WAIS-R. These samples ranged in size from 29 mildly and moderately retarded adults (Simon & Clopton, 1984) and 29 medical and psychiatric patients (Warner, 1983) to 88 college students (Mishra & Brown, 1983). Table 3.11 summarizes the correlations between IQ scales and subtests of the same name on the WAIS and WAIS-R based on the results of these eight samples, which totaled 420 individuals. Median coeffi-

cients are reported, rather than means, because of several uncharacteristically low values reported by R. S. Smith (1983) for 70 college students. Mean test-retest reliability coefficients for the WAIS-R, obtained from data on two samples provided by Wechsler (1981, Table 11), are also shown in Table 3.11 to serve as a reference point for evaluating the WAIS/WAIS-R coefficients.

Overall, the corresponding WAIS and WAIS-R IQs correlated quite substantially (.84 to .92) and not much lower than the respective WAIS-R IQs correlated with each other in a test-retest situation (.90 to .96). The correlation of .87 between V-IQ on the W-B I and

TABLE 3.11   Summary of correlations between WAIS and WAIS-R IQs and scaled scores for eight samples tested on both instruments

Subtest or Scale	Range of Correlations	Median Correlation	Mean WAIS-R Stability Coefficient
Verbal			
Information	.47 to .94	.88	.91
Digit Span	.66 to .86	.76	.86
Vocabulary	.26 to .95	.92	.92
Arithmetic	.27 to .88	.80	.85
Comprehension	.51 to .85	.72	.80
Similarities	.33 to .90	.82	.84
Performance			
Picture Completion	.30 to .83	.68	.88
Picture Arrangement	.15 to .80	.58	.72
Block Design	.74 to .89	.82	.86
Object Assembly	.14 to .80	.60	.70
Digit Symbol	.29 to .94	.78	.84
IQ Scales Verbal	.73 to .96	.92	.96
Performance	.76 to .89	.84	.90
Full Scale	.85 to .94	.92	.96

NOTE: Data for the WAIS/WAIS-R comparisons are based on Table 2 in a summary article by Ryan et al. (1987). Mean WAIS-R stability coefficients, provided for comparison purposes, are computed from data provided by Wechsler (1981, Table 11) for 71 people aged 25–34 and 48 individuals aged 45–54.

WAIS-R, reported by Stewart (1981) for 44 normal white, middle-class adults (median age = 31.5), is wholly consistent with the coefficients observed for the W-B I and WAIS and for the WAIS and WAIS-R.

Five of the 11 subtests on the WAIS and WAIS-R correlated about as high with each other as one could reasonably expect in view of WAIS-R stability coefficients: Information, Vocabulary, Arithmetic, Similarities, and Block Design each correlated within .05 of the test-retest coefficient. If .10 is selected as an arbitrary "allowable" discrepancy between WAIS/WAIS-R correlation and WAIS-R stability coefficient, then only two subtests, Picture Completion and Picture Arrangement, show an inadequate relationship. The WAIS and WAIS-R Picture Completion subtests correlated .68, well below its WAIS-R stability coefficient. The two Picture Arrangement tasks correlated a moderate .58, not nearly as high as its test-retest coefficient of .72 on the WAIS-R.

The three IQs yielded by the WAIS and WAIS-R correlated so well that their comparability is axiomatic. Nine of the 11 subtests also correlated sufficiently well to support their comparability on the WAIS and WAIS-R. However, the two Picture Completion and the two Picture Arrangement subtests do not relate well enough to support their continuity of measurement from the WAIS to the WAIS-R. Not coincidentally, these two subtests were modified substantially when the WAIS was revised (Wechsler, 1981). They retained only 60% to 70% of the WAIS items; among other subtests, only Information rivaled that percentage (see Table 3.1).

COMPARISON OF SYSTEMS FOR CLASSIFYING INTELLIGENCE ON THE W-B I, WAIS, AND WAIS-R

Although the classification systems used to describe IQs do not relate to the comparability of the instruments, it is still worthwhile to examine the changes in the system espoused by Wechsler for his adult intelligence tests. These systems and their modifications are indicated in Table 3.12.

Note that the IQ ranges for the W-B I differ a bit from the more familiar ranges used for the WAIS and WAIS-R; the differences are relatively sizable for the Mentally Retarded and Borderline categories, as a cutoff for retardation of 65 (rather than the more familiar 69) was used for the W-B I. Examination of Table 3.12 reveals that the IQ ranges were modified when the W-B I was revised, and the labels applied to some IQ ranges were altered when the WAIS was revised.

The lesson here is that classification systems are necessarily arbitrary and can change at the whim of test authors, government bodies, or professional organizations. They are statistical concepts and do not correspond in any real sense to the specific capabilities of any particular person with a given IQ. The classification systems provide descriptive labels that may be useful for communication purposes in a case report or conference, and nothing more.

COMPARISON OF IQs YIELDED BY THE W-B I, WAIS, AND WAIS-R

W-B I Versus WAIS

Zimmerman and Woo-Sam (1973, Table 2-1) summarized the results of four counterbalanced studies involving the W-B I and WAIS. In all four studies the mean Verbal IQ was essentially the same on the W-B I and WAIS. However, two studies with college students produced Performance IQs that were 6 to 7 points higher on the WAIS and Full Scale IQs that were 3 points higher on the WAIS. In contrast, two studies with clinical samples (college counseling cases, Air Force psychiatric patients) produced Performance IQs that were 5 points lower on the WAIS, and Full Scale IQs that were 3

TABLE 3.12   Classification systems used for W-B I, WAIS, and WAIS-R IQs

WAIS-R Classification	CORRESPONDING IQ RANGE			Theoretical %	Actual % WAIS-R
	W-B I	WAIS	WAIS-R		
Very Superior	128+	130+	130+	2.2	2.6
Superior	120–127	120–129	120–129	6.7	6.9
High Average (Bright-normal on W-B I & WAIS)	111–119	110–119	110–119	16.1	16.6
Average	91–110	90–109	90–109	50.0	49.1
Low Average (Dull-normal on W-B I & WAIS)	80–90	80–89	80–89	16.1	16.1
Borderline	66–79	70–79	70–79	6.7	6.4
Mentally Retarded (Defective on W-B I & WAIS	65 & below	69 & below	69 & below	2.2	2.3

NOTE: The classification systems for the W-B I and WAIS are from Wechsler (1958, Tables 2 and 3); the system for the WAIS-R and the theoretical and actual percentages are from Wechsler (1981, Table 9). The theoretical percentages correspond to the IQ ranges for the WAIS and WAIS-R but not the W-B I ranges.

points lower. The net effect of the four studies was to show no mean differences on any of the IQ scales on the W-B I and WAIS. More important, the size and direction of the IQ differences seem to vary as a function of the characteristics of the specific group tested on the two predecessors of the WAIS-R.

Based on extensive cross-generational analyses conducted by Flynn (1984), one would expect a restandardized test to yield mean scores lower than the scores yielded by the original test because norms become steeper with time; people apparently perform better in the present than did those in the past on the same test items, perhaps due to the greater impact of mass media, increased urbanization of the society, and so forth. If on the average a whole generation does better on a test than the preceding generation, harder norms for the revised test battery result. The paradoxical outcome of a

society doing better on an intelligence test is for the revised test to produce lower scores than its predecessor. In essence, the older test yields scores that are spuriously high because its norms are outdated, and the norms for the newly revised test correct this inequity (see pp. 43–44).

According to Flynn (1984), American norms become outdated at the rate of about 3 points per decade. Hence, one would have anticipated lower scores on the WAIS than the W-B I by 4 to 5 points in view of the approximately 15 years between their standardizations. This discrepancy did not occur, perhaps because the W-B I standardization was inadequate in many ways; for example, it was not truly representative of the U.S. population in the 1930s because it lacked stratification on the variables of geographic region, urban-rural residence, sex, race, or occupational group.

Another possible explanation is the small number of individuals included in each of the four previously mentioned studies (sample sizes of 28 to 52). Two studies with larger samples were also cited by Zimmerman and Woo-Sam (1973, Table 2-1). One comprised 179 brain-damaged patients who were tested on the W-B I about 2 years prior to the WAIS administration (Fitzhugh & Fitzhugh, 1964a), and the other included two groups of psychiatric patients (Goolishian & Ramsay, 1956), one tested only on the W-B I ($N = 395$) and one given only the WAIS ($N = 154$). In these studies the WAIS produced Verbal IQs that were 1 to 2 points lower than the W-B I, Performance IQs that were 6 to 7 points lower, and Full Scale IQs that were 3 to 4 points lower. These findings are closely in accord with Flynn's (1984) estimates of the changes that take place from generation to generation.

WAIS Versus WAIS-R

Ryan et al. (1987) summarized an enormous number of studies that were specifically designed to compare the IQs yielded by the WAIS and WAIS-R. They grouped the investigations according to the three different methodologies that were employed by various investigators: counterbalanced test-retest administration of the WAIS and WAIS-R; administration of either a complete WAIS or WAIS-R, with the unique items from the other battery added (combined administration); and administration of either a WAIS or WAIS-R to groups considered to be equivalent. Table 3.13 summarizes the data from these three types of studies, including some excluded from Ryan et al.'s (1987) overview, to answer the question of the mean differences in the IQs provided by the WAIS and its successor.

Across 20 samples, the median difference in IQs ranged from 5.9 to 6.5 points, with the WAIS producing higher IQs for the Verbal, Performance, and Full Scales. In each study, except for Simon and Clopton's (1984) with

mentally retarded individuals, the WAIS-R consistently yielded lower IQs than its predecessor. For retarded adolescents and adults, the WAIS-R produced higher Verbal and Full Scale IQs, by 3.9 and 2.1 points, respectively. This aberration is not surprising because norms for individuals at the extremes of the normal curve are based on so few cases in each standardization that the actual IQ values are often extrapolated or "guesstimated"; hence, norms for retarded or gifted people tend to be on less firm empirical ground than norms for the average functioning individual.

Atypical Discrepancies for Atypical Samples

In Table 3.13, smaller than usual discrepancies between WAIS-R and WAIS IQs were also found for Malone's (1985) EMH sample and for the two samples of subjects that earned mean Full Scale IQs above 120 on both batteries: Edwards and Klein's (1984) group of Mensa Society members, and Michell, Grandy, and Lupo's (1986) population of medical students. For these groups, WAIS/WAIS-R Full Scale IQ discrepancies were only 3.1 and 3.7 points, respectively.

The difference in WAIS versus WAIS-R IQs for extreme and average samples was predicted by Lindemann and Matarazzo (1984), who warned: "On the WAIS-R, unlike its predecessors, the standard deviations of the sums of scaled scores varied among the nine age groups of the standardization population, and some of the differences between standard deviations reached significance. . . . [This problem] may be significant . . . in comparing WAIS and WAIS-R scores at various age and intelligence levels" (pp. 82–83). The discrepancy in standard deviations is also of concern when comparing WAIS-R scores obtained by the same individual at different times (Lindemann & Matarazzo, 1984). The standard deviations are especially low at the extreme ages (for ages 16–17, 18–19, and 70–74 the values for the Full Scale sum of

TABLE 3.13   Mean WAIS/WAIS-R IQ differences based on the results of diverse well-designed investigations

Authors	Types of Subjects	Size of Sample	MEAN DIFFERENCE IN		
			V–IQ	P–IQ	FS–IQ
Counterbalanced Designs					
Wechsler (1981)	Normal	72	+6.9	+8.0	+7.5
Edwards & Klein (1984)	Mensa Society	38	+5.7	+2.9	+3.1
Mishra & Brown (1983)	College Students	88	+5.8	+4.8	+4.7
R. S. Smith (1983)	College Students	70	+5.5	+2.4	+3.7
Urbina et al. (1982)	Normals & Psychiatric Patients	68	+5.4	+5.3	+5.3
Prifitera & Ryan (1983)	Psychiatric & Vocational Counseling	32	+7.6	+7.0	+7.8
Warner (1983)	Alcoholics	32	+8.4	+9.5	+9.8
Warner (1983)	Medical & Psychiatric Patients	29	+6.8	+10.2	+8.9
Simon & Clopton (1984)	Mildly & Moderately Retarded	29	−3.9	+1.4	−2.1
Malone (1985)	EMH High School Students	32	+2.0	+8.4	+4.5
Combined Administrations					
Whitworth & Gibbons (1986)	Black, White, & Hispanic College Students	75	+6.5	+4.4	+5.8
Lippold & Claiborn (1983)	Neuropsych. Referrals	30	+7.6	+8.6	+8.4
Raybourn (1983)	Counseling Clients	52	+6.2	+7.6	+6.7
Mitchell et al. (1986)	Medical Students	35	+4.8	+5.8	+3.7
Field & Sisley (1986)	New Zealand Normals (N=25) and Neurolog. Referrals (N=17)	42	+5.3	+6.8	+5.9
Equivalent Groups					
Lewis & Johnson (1985)	College Students	39 WAIS 35 WAIS-R	+7.9	+12.5	+10.4
Rogers & Osborn (1984)	Psychiatric and Neurolog. Patients	89 WAIS 87 WAIS-R	+8.2	+8.4	+8.9
Ryan, Rosenberg, & Heilbronner (1984)	Psychiatric and Neurolog. Patients	60 WAIS 60 WAIS-R	+6.9	+5.2	+6.8
Kelley et al. (1984)	Brain-damaged Patients	55 WAIS 59 WAIS-R	+6.4	+3.5	+5.8
Zarantonello (1988)	Psychiatric & Neurolog. Patients	75 WAIS 105 WAIS-R	+4.8	+6.2	+5.9
MEDIAN DIFFERENCE (20 Studies)			+6.3	+6.5	+5.9

NOTE: Mean difference in IQs equals WAIS IQ minus WAIS-R IQ.

scaled scores equals 20–21 compared to values typically in the 24–26 range); hence, IQs obtained by older adolescents and the elderly may differ considerably from IQs earned by these same individuals at other times in their lives. This problem at ages 16–19, in particular, underscores the questionable WAIS-R norms for older adolescents.

Practical Implications of WAIS/WAIS-R IQ Differences

The overall differences of about 6 to 6½ points between the WAIS and WAIS-R IQs are consistent with Flynn's (1984) expected discrepancies between tests normed about 25 years apart. The WAIS was standardized in 1953–1954 and the WAIS-R in 1976–1980, so one would predict that the WAIS-R would yield IQs that are about 7½ points lower than the WAIS IQs. If the four groups with extremely low or high IQs are excluded from the computation of typical discrepancies, the median values for the 16 remaining samples are 6.6 for Verbal IQ, 6.9 for Performance IQ, and 6.8 for Full Scale IQ—almost precisely what Flynn would have predicted. WAIS/WAIS-R IQ differences of about ½ standard deviation characterize a wide variety of normal and clinical samples (see Table 3.13) as well as college students from three different ethnic groups—whites, blacks, and Mexican Americans (Whitworth & Gibbons, 1986).

The IQ discrepancy findings affirm the similarity between the WAIS and WAIS-R standardization samples. The only differences between them are the predictable, "real" differences in intellectual performance that characterize successive generations in the United States. They are *not* due to changes in the items from the WAIS to the WAIS-R, as Lezak (1988a) inferred. These lawful findings reinforce the continuity from the WAIS to the revised test that replaced it.

Nonetheless, the differences in the IQs yielded by the two test batteries have practical consequences for examiners. Those who still cling to the WAIS for some or all of their evaluations (Harrison, Kaufman, Hickman, & Kaufman, 1988) should recognize that the WAIS IQs are very out of date and therefore incorrect. As Gregory (1987) has stressed, "the failure to use the modern test and norms can throw the IQ score off by as much as 8 points. In selected cases, 8 points could make the difference between recommending a college instead of a technical school or placing an individual in a group home instead of in an institution" (p. 140).

Clinicians who give the WAIS-R to adults who have previously been tested on the WAIS should anticipate substantially lower WAIS-R scores (except, perhaps, for retarded or gifted individuals). Even discrepancies of about 1 standard deviation between them (i.e., about twice the expected difference between WAIS and WAIS-R IQs) may not indicate loss of intellectual function. Such determinations are especially crucial in instances of brain damage or dementia; examiners should guard against making inferences about deterioration when the decrease in IQ accompanies a switch from the WAIS to the WAIS-R. Supplementary support for a loss of function is necessary in such circumstances.

Zarantanello (1988) has shown that the WAIS-WAIS-R discrepancy for neuropsychiatric patients is comparable despite the patients' level of neuropsychological impairment (nonimpaired, mild, moderate, severe). Nonetheless, the difference in WAIS and WAIS-R IQs affects prediction of a patient's neuropsychological functioning, such as performance on the Halstead Category Test (Ryan, Rosenberg, & Prifitera, 1983). Ryan and his colleagues warn: "Failure to recognize the situation could lead to erroneous clinical decisions which may underestimate the precarious nature of a patient's cognitive status or degree of his deterioration" (p. 134).

GENERALIZATION FROM THE W-B I AND WAIS TO THE WAIS-R

The preceding sections have typically supported the continuity of measurement from the W-B I to the WAIS to the WAIS-R. In general, research findings on the older Wechsler adult batteries must be considered fairly applicable to the current instrument. There are, however, some qualifications and these are discussed in the following sections.

Studies at Ages 16–19 Years

The lack of construct validity for the 16–19-year-olds based on the developmental change criterion is the finding of greatest concern. This problem with the adolescent norms on the WAIS-R may invalidate the use of the WAIS-R for 16- to 19-year-olds in general and calls into question attempts to generalize any research findings from the W-B I or WAIS to the WAIS-R when the samples are composed exclusively or primarily of older adolescents.

Studies Focusing on Picture Completion or Picture Arrangement

The item content changes from the WAIS to the WAIS-R affected the continuity of the Picture Completion and Picture Arrangement subtests. Research investigations on the W-B I or WAIS that were devoted to one or both of these subtests should therefore be generalized to the WAIS-R with considerable caution. For example, Fogel (1965) found WAIS Picture Arrangement to be a better discriminator of "organics" than five other WAIS subtests, including Block Design; introverts scored significantly lower on Picture Arrangement than did extraverts, as selected by the MMPI Social Isolation scale (Schill, 1966); and Blatt and his colleagues concluded that WAIS Picture Arrangement was a measure of anticipation and planning by relating subtest performance to criteria like punctuality versus procrastination or subscores on the Thematic Apperception Test (Blatt & Quinlan, 1967; Dickstein & Blatt, 1967). Because of the content changes in Picture Arrangement, it is dubious whether findings such as these with WAIS Picture Arrangement are generalizable to the WAIS-R.

Factor Analysis Studies

Because of strong similarities in the factor structures for the three adult Wechsler batteries, it is usually reasonable to generalize from W-B I or WAIS investigations of the two or three constructs that underlie the test batteries. Since Verbal and Performance IQs denote the two major factors, any studies that explored V-P IQ differences on the W-B I or WAIS for diverse samples, such as those with known brain damage (Matarazzo & Herman, 1985; see chapters 9–11), are generalizable to the WAIS-R. Similarly, studies using the WAIS Freedom from Distractibility factor are generalizable to the WAIS-R—for example, Roszkowski's (1983), which correlated factor scores with a measure of adaptive behavior and concluded that the factor probably taps a cognitive rather than behavioral dimension.

Typical results of factor analysis of the W-B I and WAIS on diverse clinical and normal samples are applicable to the WAIS-R, but not the specific nuances of the loadings of particular subtests. Thus, Fowler, Richards, and Boll's (1980) factor analysis of the WAIS for epileptic adults produced the three familiar factors for this exceptional sample. It is reasonable to conclude from that analysis that epileptics also display the same three factors on the WAIS-R. However, it would be inappropriate to conclude that the Perceptual Organization factor for epileptics is composed only of Block Design and Object Assembly because the other three Performance subtests loaded below .40 on that factor.

The specific loadings of any given subtest are subject to the influences of variables such as sample size, geographic location of the subject pool, and simple chance error, as well as variables having to do with modifications in the test battery itself. Hence, when generalizing research findings from the W-B I or WAIS to the WAIS-R, it is better to focus on key results dealing with the two or three global constructs or with the general factor underlying overall performance (e.g., Full Scale IQ) than to dwell on subsidiary results or relatively minor details.

Short Form Studies

Short form studies on the W-B I or WAIS should *not* be generalized to the WAIS-R. These studies usually capitalize on chance relationships between pairs of subtests and total score in selecting the best dyads (or triads, or tetrads, etc.). The best Verbal dyad on the WAIS may be the tenth best WAIS-R dyad owing to myriad factors related to sample selection, content changes in the subtests, differences in reliability coefficients, differences in the correlation matrices, and chance error. Techniques such as the Satz-Mogel split-half approach (Satz & Mogel, 1962) fare no better because they face many of the same problems and have other limitations of their own. (See chapter 5 for a discussion of WAIS-R short forms.)

Correlational Studies

The numerous correlational studies involving the WAIS and other instruments are generally applicable to the WAIS-R—but only if the cor-

relations involving the IQs are examined and if the other instrument has not also been revised. However, correlations involving the W-B I are invariably with older tests, and therefore of little current relevance.

In no instance should mean differences between WAIS IQs and the overall scores on the "other" test be generalized to the WAIS-R. The differences in the IQs yielded by the WAIS and WAIS-R are nearly half a standard deviation, and the WAIS-R (but not the WAIS) standard deviations for sums of scaled scores differ significantly from each other (Lindemann & Matarazzo, 1984). Obviously the difference in the IQs produced by the WAIS and any other instrument will not characterize the differences between the WAIS-R and that test. Hence, the correlations between the WAIS and another measure are likely to generalize to the WAIS-R, but not the differences in the global scores they yield.

Group Versus Individual Interpretation

The studies and variables discussed in this chapter address the issue of comparability to discern whether the body of research accumulated on the W-B I and WAIS is applicable to the most recent version, the WAIS-R. As indicated, the answer to this question is generally yes. However, this continuity concerns the generalizability of group data obtained on one instrument to group data on another instrument.

In the case of specific individuals, one would not immediately assume, for example, that a person with a significant V-P IQ difference on the WAIS when evaluated 5 or 10 years ago will necessarily have that same significant difference when tested again on the WAIS-R. Test scores for an individual are too variable, and are much less stable than group data. Any given person's ability spectrum may have changed over time, or chance factors may have been operating; he or she may not have displayed a significant

V-P difference if retested 6 months later on the same instrument (the WAIS).

Thus, one cannot make predictions about a specific person's obtained scores on any of the adult Wechsler scales. But one can be reasonably assured, based on the literature review analyzed in this chapter, that, apart from the exceptions noted, a clinician who gives the WAIS-R to anyone will be measuring the same constructs that Wechsler intended to measure when he first developed the W-B I, and that he continued to measure with the WAIS.

Conclusions

Most comparisons and analyses discussed in this chapter support the comparability and continuity of the W-B I, WAIS, and WAIS-R. Comparisons of item content revealed that a core of items from the W-B I is retained in the present-day WAIS-R, but that modification in content during the WAIS and WAIS-R revisions was the rule rather than the exception. These content changes, however, did not usually affect the constructs underlying the test batteries. Reliability, construct validity, and correlational analyses generally revealed similarities in the values observed for the three adult Wechsler scales; any changes typically reflected refinement and improvement in the revision and restandardization process. The constructs forming the foundation of the three test batteries seem particularly robust to the changes in item content.

CHAPTER 3 SUMMARY

The goal of this chapter was to relate the WAIS-R to its predecessors, the WAIS and Wechsler-Bellevue I, primarily to determine the degree to which W-B I and WAIS research results are generalizable to the current battery. First, Wechsler's rationale was explored for selecting each of the 11 subtests for the original W-B I; the three Wechsler adult scales were

then compared on their test content, reliability coefficients, standardization samples, and construct validity.

Wechsler selected his tasks from other available tests of the day, especially the series of instruments developed by the U.S. Army during World War I. He chose Information despite its obvious relationship to education, because similar tasks displayed excellent psychometric properties and correlated exceptionally well with various measures of intelligence. Digit Span, despite being a weak measure of g, was included because of its value with low-functioning individuals and its diagnostic significance. Vocabulary was originally a W-B I alternate (Wechsler's concession to its educational and cultural dependency); however, its great clinical value and excellence as a measure of g led to its ultimate inclusion on the regular W-B I and core membership on subsequent Wechsler batteries. Arithmetic shares many of the pros and cons of Information and Vocabulary, but is subject to the influences of attention span and temporary emotional states; nonetheless, such tasks are easily created and are perceived as face valid by adults. Comprehension, though heavily dependent on verbal expression, invariably contributes rich clinical information (especially concerning the diagnosis of psychopathology). Similarities is the only verbal subtest to have appeared sparingly in previous tests; Wechsler selected it primarily for its ease of administration and interest to adults, and for providing insight into a person's logical thinking process.

Wechsler selected Picture Completion for the Performance Scale, despite the difficulty in constructing hard items that are not too specialized, because it is both short and easy to administer and is effective for measuring the intelligence of low-functioning individuals. He included Picture Arrangement because of its interpersonal content and enormous clinical value despite nearly insurmountable obstacles in developing unambiguous items. Block Design affords examiners direct observation of a person's problem-solving strategy and has important neurological implications; Wechsler found little to criticize with this task, unlike the other subtests. In contrast, Object Assembly was included in spite of difficulties regarding reliability and low correlations with other measures because of its clinical value and its use of familiar stimuli. Digit Symbol, though perhaps too reliant on motor coordination and speed, was one of Wechsler's favorites as a good, quick measure of nonverbal intelligence.

Major item content changes occurred when the W-B I was revised to become the WAIS, including the lengthening of numerous subtests and the development of a new set of Vocabulary words. Changes from the WAIS to the WAIS-R, by contrast, were relatively minor as 87% of the WAIS items were retained. In general, more item changes have characterized the Verbal than Performance subtests. Nonetheless, continuity of content is supported from the old W-B I to the present day WAIS-R by virtue of the inclusion, in the current battery, of more than half the original W-B I items.

One of Wechsler's key goals in revising the W-B I was to obtain better score distributions and greater reliability for most subtests, and the substantial increase in reliability from the W-B I to the WAIS demonstrates his success. In general, reliability has improved with each revision, although the magnitudes of the coefficients for the three batteries are similar enough to support the continuity of consistent measurement from one scale to the other.

Like the reliability coefficients, Wechsler aimed to improve the quality of the standardization samples with each successive revision. The W-B I sample (ages 7–70 years) was composed mostly of white, urban New Yorkers; it was roughly stratified on education, but not on gender, race, or occupational level. In contrast, the WAIS (ages 16–64 years) and WAIS-R (ages 16–74 years) were carefully stratified on many important variables. Old age norms for the WAIS were developed from a nonrepresentative sample; the key improvement in the WAIS-R norms was the inclusion of a stratified elderly population. Each of the standardization samples matched Census proportions on the crucial variable of educational attainment; in addition, each sample represented the state of the art for its era. Consequently, the samples are reasonably comparable.

The continuity of the constructs measured by the W-B I, WAIS, and WAIS-R has been documented amply by the techniques of internal consistency, factor analysis, and correlational analysis. The method of inferring construct validity from developmental changes in mean scores, however, suggested the continuity of constructs only for adults aged 20 and above. Construct validity was *not* supported on the WAIS-R for ages 16–19 years, strongly suggesting a major flaw in the WAIS-R norms for adolescents. This flaw has vital practical and clinical implications and demands extremely cautious interpretation of WAIS-R profiles for 16- to 19-year-olds.

WAIS and WAIS-R IQs correlate extremely highly with each other, indicating excellent continuity of measurement of Wechsler's major constructs; further, WAIS/WAIS-R correlations are adequate for 9 of the 11 subtests—all but Picture Completion and Picture Arrangement. Wechsler modified his system for classifying IQs on the W-B I, WAIS, and WAIS-R, although such changes do not affect the continuity of measurement from one battery to another.

The IQs yielded by the WAIS-R are consistently about 6 to 6½ points lower than the corresponding values on the WAIS. This finding is quite consistent across 20 separate investigations and seems to reflect real changes in the ability levels of the generations, with present-day individuals scoring better than adults in the past (hence, producing "steep" WAIS-R norms). These IQ changes indicate the need to restandardize tests fairly frequently but they do *not* imply a lack of consistency in the constructs measured by the WAIS and WAIS-R.

Overall, these comparisons support the continuity of measurement from the W-B I to the WAIS to the WAIS-R. Hence, in general, one may legitimately generalize research results from the older scales to the WAIS-R. There are important exceptions, however (e.g., development of short forms), and clinicians need to understand the distinction between generalizations made for groups versus those made for individuals.

WAIS-R Research on Administration, Scoring, and Stability Over Time

The previous chapter compared the W-B I and WAIS to the WAIS-R to determine whether the findings from research investigations conducted with previous editions of the Wechsler adult battery could be generalized to the WAIS-R. With some reservations, the answer was yes. However, applying research results from the Wechsler-Bellevue or WAIS to the WAIS-R is not a substitute for conducting a variety of new psychometric investigations with the WAIS-R to better understand the properties of the revised and restandardized battery. Furthermore, some types of research do not generalize very well from the old tests to the current edition. Stability of the test scores must be determined directly with the WAIS-R, as must any estimates of reliability, because changes in item content and test length are directly related to the consistency of the scores yielded by that scale.

The overall factor structure of the WAIS-R is similar to that of the W-B I and WAIS (see Tables 3.7 and 3.8), but the nuances of the factor loadings on the two or three factors for normal and clinical samples likewise depend on subtle content changes or administration modifications (e.g., asking for a "second reason" on some Comprehension items); consequently, factor analyses of the WAIS-R are necessary to fully understand the nature of the Verbal Comprehension, Perceptual Organization, and Freedom from Distractibility factors. In addition, differences in intelligence test scores due to gender, race, residence, and so forth need to be evaluated directly on the WAIS-R to be meaningful. Not only are such differences potentially related to changes in content or administration procedures, but they are conceivably a function of updated norms and changes in society. Comparable data on the W-B I or WAIS are of more limited value, even if they were obtained today, because of their outdated norms and outmoded content of numerous items; even items that were modified only slightly (and are therefore treated as the "same" from the vantage point of Table 3.1, which summarized content changes from battery to battery) were changed to reflect current prices or customs. If, however, the data were gathered years ago, then societal changes such as greater educational and occupational opportunities for minorities and women would relegate individual differences data to nothing more than a historical footnote.

Psychometric investigations of the WAIS-R are treated in chapters 4 through 8. This chapter discusses studies on the following topics: administration time, scoring errors, stability of scores over time, reliability of difference scores, and a special case of alternate forms reliability (the relationship of the WAIS-R to its cousin, the WISC-R). The remaining chapters in this section of the book likewise treat WAIS-R research on important clinical and theoretical topics, each forming part of the foundation of WAIS-R interpretation that highlights Part III of this text.

Chapter 5 reviews the short-form literature; chapter 6 explores individual differences on the stratification variables; chapter 7 integrates intriguing findings of changes in WAIS-R scores with increasing age—both with and without a control for education—with the body of literature on changes in intellectual functioning across the lifespan; and chapter 8 summarizes studies on factor analysis of the WAIS-R (including the related topics of the *g* factor and subtest specificity).

At the end of chapter 8, which concludes the WAIS-R research foundation, the pros and cons of the WAIS-R will be presented, based on major reviews of the test battery.

ADMINISTRATION AND SCORING

Prior to the interpretation of any test battery, the intricacies of administration and scoring must be mastered. Without correct techniques for obtaining the data, any interpretation of test profiles is meaningless. This section integrates

WAIS-R research with the topics of administration time and scoring errors.

Administration Time

Wechsler (1981) estimated that typically "the eleven tests of the WAIS-R require from 60 to 90 minutes to administer" (p. 52). Ryan and Rosenberg (1984a) obtained systematic data on administration time, subtest by subtest, for a clinical population of 50 male neurological and psychiatric patients at a Veterans Administration Medical Center. This group was composed of 36 whites and 14 blacks with a variety of diagnoses, averaging 42.5 years of age (*SD* = 11.5), a WAIS-R Full Scale IQ of 90.7 (*SD* = 13.0), and 13.3 years of schooling (*SD* = 1.9). The group's average age was near the middle of the WAIS-R age range, the education level was a bit higher than average, and the IQ was at the low end of average. Hence, the obtained data were probably not too different from data that would be obtained for a group of normal individuals.

The data provided by Ryan and Rosenberg (1984a) should generalize nicely to the typical types of subjects who are referred for evaluation on the WAIS-R. Table 4.1 shows the administration time data for Ryan and Rosenberg's (1984a) sample of clinical patients. Overall testing time averaged about 1½ hours, which is at the upper end of Wechsler's estimate; the Verbal Scale took 7 minutes longer to give than the Performance Scale, although each scale took about 45 minutes to administer. Four subtests required an average administration time in excess of 10 minutes: Vocabulary, Comprehension, Picture Arrangement, Block Design. In contrast, Digit Span, Arithmetic, Similarities, Picture Completion, and Digit Symbol each took less than 6 minutes to administer. The range of testing time for each subtest and scale was rather large. Using a range of plus or minus 2 *SD*s from the mean administration time, the

TABLE 4.1   Average WAIS-R administration time as determined by Ryan and Rosenberg (1984a) for 50 clinical patients, and by Ward et al. (1987) for 60 low-functioning clients

Subtest/Scale	RYAN & ROSENBERG (1984A) TIME (IN MIN. AND SEC.)			WARD ET AL. (1987) TIME (IN MIN.)		
	Mean	SD	Range	Mean	SD	Rank
Vocabulary	13:20	4:21	6:00–26:10	6.65	2.99	5
Block Design	12:42	3:43	6:00–20:00	9.85	2.84	1
Comprehension	12:00	4:22	2:20–23:51	7.18	3.06	4
Picture Arrangement	11:45	3:29	5:38–21:00	9.20	3.42	2
Object Assembly	9:03	2:43	4:02–14:54	9.00	2.71	3
Information	7:51	2:27	2:12–13:05	5.62	2.66	7
Similarities	5:33	1:52	2:00–10:30	4.15	2.03	9
Arithmetic	5:28	1:59	2:00–12:00	4.65	2.19	8
Picture Completion	5:04	1:29	2:00–10:00	5.93	2.52	6
Digit Span	4:59	1:43	2:55–10:00	3:45	1.32	10
Digit Symbol	3:46	2:03	2:00–15:00	3.17	0.96	11
Verbal Scale	49:09	9:45	30:00–79:40	31.70	—	—
Performance Scale	42:15	8:06	26:49–69:00	37.15	—	—
Full Scale	91:24	14:15	61:00–133:00	68.85	—	—

NOTE: Subtests are listed in the order of their mean administration time (longest to shortest) in the Ryan and Rosenberg (1984a) study. The column labeled "rank" in the Ward et al. (1987) study refers to a ranking of administration times in which 1 equals the longest subtest to administer and 11 equals the shortest. Note that Ryan and Rosenberg reported their data in minutes and seconds, whereas Ward et al. reported theirs in minutes. Hence, the value of 9.85 minutes observed by Ward et al. for Block Design corresponds to 9 minutes, 51 seconds.

complete WAIS-R legitimately takes between 1 and 2 hours to give to patients who are of about average intelligence. This empirically determined administration time represents a better estimate of WAIS-R testing time than Wechsler's (1981) estimate of 60 to 90 minutes.

A similar administration time study (Ward, Selby, & Clark, 1987) used 30 patients at a Veterans Administration Hospital (70% white, 97% male) and 30 private practice "Social Security evaluation" clients (37% white, 50% male). Since these groups were comparable in age (early to mid-40s) and ability level (FS-IQs in the mid to upper 70s), data for both subsamples are combined in Table 4.1 to show the mean

administration times for 60 low-functioning individuals whose average ages are almost identical to those of Ryan and Rosenberg's sample of clinical patients.

There are some similarities in the time it takes to administer the WAIS-R subtests to low-functioning and average patients. For both groups, the five longest subtests to give are identical (although they do not appear in the same order), and the two subtests with the shortest administration time are Digit Symbol and Digit Span. However, the WAIS-R is clearly a shorter test to give to low-functioning patients than to those with average intelligence, with the largest discrepancy occurring on the Verbal

Scale (see Table 4.1). The three longest subtests to administer to low-functioning patients are all on the Performance Scale (Block Design, Picture Arrangement, Object Assembly, each with an administration time of 9 to 10 minutes); in contrast, Vocabulary and Comprehension are two of the three longest tasks to give to patients of average intelligence.

On the average, the WAIS-R took nearly 70 minutes to administer to Ward et al.'s (1987) sample of low-functioning private practice clients and hospitalized patients. The mean administration time was 22½ minutes longer for Ryan and Rosenberg's (1984a) group, with most of the difference (17½ minutes) accounted for by the Verbal Scale. Conceivably, the WAIS-R is shorter to give to people with low IQ than those with average IQ. Thompson, Howard, and Anderson (1986) tested 90 psychiatric patients on the WAIS-R whose average Full Scale IQ was 86.5. Not only was this group's Low Average mean IQ in between the average IQs of the samples tested by Ward et al. (1987) and Ryan and Rosenberg (1984a), but so too was their average administration time for the complete WAIS-R (76.9 minutes). Thompson et al. did not, unfortunately, report times for the separate subtests or scales.

Despite the evidence, one must be hesitant before concluding that the differences between the administration time data in the three studies are primarily a function of the ability levels of the respective samples. Individual examiners differ substantially in their rates of test administration, the degree of questioning verbal responses, and the like. Possibly the data from the three studies differ in part because of examiner variables. This hypothesis has some support if one examines Ward et al.'s (1987) administration time data separately for the examiner who conducted the Social Security evaluations and the examiner who tested the patients at the Veterans Administration Hospital. Total average administration time for the former examiner was 77 minutes (Verbal = 36, Performance = 41), while for the latter examiner it was 61

minutes (Verbal = 28, Performance = 33). Note, however, that even the slower examiner was considerably quicker than the six examiners used by Ryan and Rosenberg (1984a) to test patients with average ability. Also, both of Ward et al.'s (1987) examiners took about 5 minutes longer to give the Performance than the Verbal Scale, whereas the examiners in Ryan and Rosenberg's (1984a) investigation took 7 minutes longer to administer the Verbal Scale.

Scoring Errors

A number of studies have demonstrated that experienced and inexperienced examiners alike make clerical and other errors when scoring Wechsler protocols (Sattler, 1988). Two investigations of scoring accuracy have been conducted with the WAIS-R. Ryan, Prifitera, and Powers (1983) conducted a prototypical study of the different scores obtained when the same record forms are scored by numerous subjects who vary in their level of experience, and Jaffe (1983) conducted an innovative study that tried to determine the source of scoring errors that appear repeatedly on the three subjectively scored Verbal subtests.

The Nature of WAIS-R Scoring Errors

Ryan et al. (1983) compared the scoring accuracy of 19 Ph.D. psychologists averaging 7.3 years experience with that of 20 psychology graduate students. Each subject was asked to score two actual test protocols, one of a male and one of a female middle-aged vocational counseling client. The record forms were unchanged and therefore did not include an unusual number of ambiguous responses. Nonetheless, both groups of subjects made errors in scoring that produced a large degree of variability in the obtained IQs, which are summarized in Table 4.2. Although the mean IQs for each protocol were almost identical to the actual IQs earned by the clients, the ranges of the IQs were huge, reflecting an abominable

TABLE 4.2   The mean and range of the IQs assigned to two actual WAIS-R protocols by experienced and inexperienced examiners

Experience Level of Examiners	Verbal IQ		Performance IQ		Full Scale IQ	
	Mean	(Range)	Mean	(Range)	Mean	(Range)
Protocol 1						
Experienced (19 Ph.D.'s)	99.4	(96–105)	122.5	(119–129)	110.1	(107–115)
Inexperienced (20 Students)	99.1	(97–105)	122.2	(122–126)	109.9	(108–117)
Combined (N = 39)	99.2	(96–105)	122.3	(119–129)	110.0	(107–117)
Actual IQs	99		122		110	
Protocol 2						
Experienced (19 Ph.D.'s)	108.5	(104–116)	98.5	(88–105)	103.8	(101–108)
Inexperienced (20 Students)	107.2	(98–116)	99.2	(98–102)	103.2	(98–110)
Combined (N = 39)	107.8	(98–116)	98.8	(88–105)	103.5	(98–110)
Actual IQs	108		99		103	

NOTE: Data are from Ryan et al. (1983).

number of scoring errors. According to Ryan et al., examination of the separately scored protocols "revealed that IQ variability resulted from mechanical errors in scoring, such as incorrectly converting scaled scores to IQs, giving incorrect credit to individual items, and calculation errors in adding raw scores of subtests" (p. 149). Although this result is consistent with previous research (Sattler, 1988), it is nevertheless disheartening that the experienced examiners performed just as miserably in this scoring exercise as did the novices; there were no significant group differences for any IQ or scaled score for either protocol, when focusing on mean values. However, mean scores are less important than the variability in the scores in a study like this one, and Ryan et al. (1983) reported that the experienced examiners had greater variability than did the novices in the Performance

IQs of both protocols; hence, the Ph.D. psychologists were *more* likely to make errors in computing Performance IQs than were the graduate students. This greater degree of variability is evident in Table 4.2; the experienced examiners ranged from 119 to 129 in their computations of Performance IQ of protocol 1 and from 88 to 105 for protocol 2; this carelessness far exceeded that of the graduate students, who produced corresponding "reasonable" ranges of 122–126 and 98–102, respectively.

Across both protocols, the percentages of perfect agreement with the actual IQs are shown in Table 4.3. When both levels of examiners are combined, the percentages of subjects who computed IQs within 1 standard error of measurement of the actual IQs were 89% for Verbal IQ, 95% for Performance IQ, and 83% for Full Scale IQ. Yet, how encouraging is it to find

TABLE 4.3 Percentage of perfect agreement with actual IQs in Ryan et al.'s (1983) investigation of WAIS-R scoring accuracy

	Verbal IQ	*Performance IQ*	*Full Scale IQ*
Experienced	40%	69%	32%
Inexperienced	38%	88%	35%

out that trained professionals can usually compute a score within 1 SE_M of the actual score? The standard error of measurement doesn't even include examiner variability as anything more than a minor source of error because during standardizations the test protocols are scored and rescored by statistical clerks who check each other's accuracy. In that sense, scoring errors constitute fluctuations in the IQs that are not fully taken into account by the SE_M, and therefore represent *additional* errors over and above the known or "built-in" chance errors.

The degree of error found in the Ryan et al. (1983) study of the WAIS-R is of the same order of magnitude as the scoring errors found in previous studies of other Wechsler scales (Sattler, 1988), including the WAIS (Franklin, Stillman, Burpeau, & Sabers, 1982), but that fact provides little comfort. If 39 subjects in a study that is obviously concerned with scoring accuracy (including about half with considerable clinical experience) come up with a Verbal IQ ranging from 98 to 116 for a person having a V-IQ of 108, and with a Performance IQ ranging from 88 to 105 for a person having a P-IQ of 99, what type of accuracy can one expect when the pressure to be careful is not present? Someone may argue that examiners are more careful with their own cases that "count." However, my personal examination of files of "official" cases given by highly trained examiners has revealed many careless (often striking) errors; clerical accuracy does not seem to correlate highly with clinical ability, and errors seem to be an unfortunate, built-in aspect of individual assessment that is often resistant to training or spontaneous improvement.

Professors who teach graduate-level assessment courses should strongly consider adopting the comprehensive and well-thought-out automated package for training clinicians and students to administer and score the WAIS-R (Blakey, Fantuzzo, Gorsuch, & Moon, 1987; Blakey, Fantuzzo, & Moon, 1985; Moon, Fantuzzo, & Gorsuch, 1986). Blakey et al. (1985), for example, showed that 11 hours of systematic training and just two test administrations led to striking improvement in their subjects' WAIS-R administration and scoring accuracy (pretest error rate of 62% versus posttest error rate of 94%).

Slate and Hunnicutt (1988), in an intelligent and persuasive article on the sources of examiner errors, make a strong case for the inadequate training of psychological examiners. Lack of quality graduate-level instruction, a problem that may be more pervasive in clinical psychology than in school psychology training programs (Oakland & Zimmerman, 1986), may produce examiners who lack knowledge of the specifics in the manual, fail to appreciate the need for applying rigorous standardized procedures, and dislike testing—often because they failed to administer enough tests during the training process. Slate and Hunnicutt cite several surveys in the literature that find clinical psychology graduate students and interns to have deficient assessment and diagnostic skills due to a combination of factors: (a) superficial teaching; (b) disparaging, critical, condemning attitude about standardized testing by clinical faculty; (c) lack of knowledge of psychometric procedures; and (d) poor supervision during internships.

Most of the other sources of examiner error cited by Slate and Hunnicutt (1988)—ambiguity in test manuals, carelessness, examiner–examinee relationships (e.g., "halo" effect, coldness or warmth of examiner), and job concerns (e.g., examiners trying to deal with excessive caseloads)—are probably reduceable to the initial inadequacy of the examiners' training in psychodiagnostics.

The Sources of WAIS-R Scoring Errors

Jaffe (1983) explored possible reasons for examiner error when scoring the WAIS-R Similarities, Vocabulary, and Comprehension subtests, free response tasks "which according to Wechsler (1955) demand 'considerable judgment by the examiner,' a caveat reduced to 'some judgment' in the recent [WAIS-R] manual (Wechsler, 1981)" (p. 1). Unlike Ryan et al. (1983), who used actual protocols as stimuli, Jaffe used ambiguous responses to assess scoring errors. Consequently, Jaffe's results are not typical or directly generalizable to everyday clinical occurrences, but they are nonetheless revealing. He examined four variables that potentially contribute to examiner error: ambiguity of scoring criteria, specific instructions given to the examiner regarding the most efficient way to score the responses, the level of the examiner, and the personality attributes of the examiner. In this regard, Jaffe (1983) was investigating systematically several of the inferred sources of error enumerated by Slate and Hunnicutt (1988).

Jaffe's (1983) study included 63 subjects organized into three groups, each with about an equal number of males and females: 20 with "low experience" (graduate students having classroom, but no clinical, experience with the WAIS or WAIS-R), 26 with "medium experience" (graduate students with at least 1 year of clinical experience administering the WAIS or WAIS-R on a regular basis), and 17 with "high experience" (licensed clinical psychologists who regularly administer at least 12 tests per year). Jaffe felt it was important to establish specific criteria for level of experience, since previous studies evaluating this variable have differed markedly in their definitions of *experienced*.

Subjects were asked to score two responses to each of 42 items: all 14 Similarities items, 14 of the 16 Comprehension items (excluding numbers 3 and 4, which require two separate ideas for full credit), and 14 randomly selected Vocabulary items. For each item, one response was verbatim from the scoring system provided by Wechsler (1981), and one was from clinical test results. All responses required judgment to score, based on the opinions of a six-member panel. Wechsler's (1981) specific scoring guidelines for the 42 items were given to each subject, along with the general scoring guidelines for each subtest; the only modification in Wechsler's list of specific illustrative responses was exclusion of one response per item, taken from the sample responses, that the subject was asked to score.

Subjects were randomly assigned to two groups. One experimental group was given a cover sheet explaining precisely what they had to do, i.e., score the two responses to each of 42 items using the general and specific scoring criteria that were provided. The second group was given additional information in the cover sheet advising them of the possible ambiguity of responses and the need for referring to the general rules for each subtest; they were told that the study was concerned with scoring difficulties and they were to minimize guessing. The self-report Eysenck Personality Inventory was administered to all subjects to explore the relationships between scoring errors and two personality dimensions: introversion/extraversion and neuroticism/stability. Jaffe computed two types of error scores, total error and bias error. Total error was simply the sum of all errors, regardless of whether the errors were due to leniency (giving more credit than was legitimately earned) or strictness (assigning a lower score than was deserved); bias error allowed lenient and strict errors to cancel each other out, and equaled the net error rate, the degree to which all errors combined to lower or raise the "person's" total score on the items. The latter error score was included because of research findings (e.g., Sattler & Winget, 1970) showing that examiners' errors tend to reflect a "halo" effect rather than occurring randomly.

Jaffe (1983) obtained the following results:

1. Subjects made numerous errors, both on the manual responses and the clinical responses. Across all subtests and items, subjects made errors on an average of nearly *half* the responses.

2. The three subtests were differentially susceptible to scoring errors, with significantly more errors occurring on Vocabulary than on Similarities or Comprehension.

3. Bias errors were in the direction of leniency for all subtests, with Comprehension producing the strongest halo effect.

4. Experimental subjects who were given extra precautions to be aware of ambiguities in the responses, to check the general scoring guidelines, and so forth, generally did *not* differ significantly in their scoring accuracy from subjects who did not receive a special instructional set. The only significant finding was that subjects given the precautions made fewer bias errors.

5. The subjects' level of experience was unrelated to scoring accuracy. This finding reinforces similar results from other studies (Kasper, Throne, & Schulman, 1968; Slate & Hunnicutt, 1988).

6. Contrary to Jaffe's (1983) hypothesis, high neuroticism subjects made more scoring errors than low neuroticism subjects.

7. Males with high extraversion scores made fewer total errors, whereas females with high extraversion scores made more total errors.

Ryan et al.'s and Jaffe's studies of scoring error on the WAIS-R reinforce numerous previous findings with Wechsler's scales showing that it is very common for examiners to make scoring errors, and that level of experience is unrelated to scoring accuracy. Jaffe has given some evidence that an examiner's personality is related to his or her scoring accuracy, and that it may be quite difficult to teach or urge examiners to be more careful, unless trainers adopt comprehensive, systematic programs for teaching the WAIS-R and similar tests (Blakey et al., 1987; Fantuzzo, Sisemore, & Spradlin, 1983).

STABILITY OF WECHSLER SCORES FOR ADOLESCENTS AND ADULTS

This section treats three major research topics: test-retest reliability of the WAIS and WAIS-R, reliability of the differences between scores, and alternate forms reliability between the WISC-R and WAIS-R (including longitudinal investigations). The latter topic also concerns the practical question of whether to select the WISC-R or WAIS-R at the age (16 years) where the two tests overlap.

Test-Retest Reliability

Practice effects on Wechsler's scales tend to be profound, particularly on the Performance Scale, although many examiners ignore this fact when interpreting profiles. Matarazzo and his colleagues have studied this variable extensively for the WAIS (Matarazzo, Carmody & Jacobs, 1980) and now the WAIS-R (Matarazzo & Herman, 1984a), stressing the importance of understanding the predictable retest gains in IQs when interpreting clinical data; they have applied the practice effect to research as well, showing how consideration of normal or base rate data on retesting forces reevaluation of the supposed gains in intelligence that accompany surgical removal of placque from the carotid artery (Matarazzo, Matarazzo, Gallo, & Wiens, 1979).

Stability of the WAIS

With the WAIS, Matarazzo et al. (1980) reviewed 11 retest studies with intervals ranging from 1 week to 13 years, sample sizes ranging from 10 to 120, and mean ages ranging from 19 to 70. Across this heterogeneous group of studies, the authors found Verbal, Performance, and Full Scale IQs to have median stability coefficients of .89, .85, and .90, respectively. Average gains were 2 points for V-IQ, 8 points for P-IQ, and 5 points for FS-IQ. Catron (1978; Catron & Thompson, 1979) explored the relationship of WAIS retest gains to the interval between test administrations for college undergraduates and found a smaller retest effect for Performance and Full Scale IQs as the interval was increased. Gain scores ranged from 1 to 5 points on the Verbal Scale; the practice effect was only 2 points after 1 or 2 months, and less than 1 point after 4 months. On the Performance Scale, however, a gain of about 1 standard deviation was observed when the second testing immediately followed the first administration (no interval), and a difference of about ½ of a standard deviation was still evident after a 4-month interval. The gradual decline in the P-IQ practice effect is shown in Table 4.4. For Full Scale IQ, the gain gradually reduced from 8 points with no interval to 4 points for a 4-month interval.

Matarazzo stressed that all these findings are for groups, and are therefore important to internalize, but that information of perhaps equal value to clinicians are the distributions of test-retest changes for specific individuals within the various groups. Whereas his detailed analyses of individual and group retest differences for the WAIS (Matarazzo et al., 1979, 1980) are of interest, these data do not necessarily generalize to the WAIS-R. However, his presentation of data for the WAIS-R (Matarazzo & Herman, 1984a; Wechsler, 1981) is quite pertinent, and will be elaborated upon in the sections that follow.

Stability of the WAIS-R

Wechsler (1981, Table 11) presented WAIS-R stability data for 71 adults aged 25–34 and 48 adults aged 45–54; both groups of normal individuals were retested after intervals ranging from 2 to 7 weeks. Test-retest reliability coefficients averaged .95–.96 for Verbal and Full Scale IQs and .89–.90 for Performance IQ. Gain scores were 3 points on the Verbal Scale, 8 to 9 points on the Performance Scale, and about 6 points on the Full Scale. The gain scores are quite similar to the values reported previously for the WAIS, and to the average values of 3 to 4 points (V), 9 to 10 points (P), and 7 points (FS) that characterize the WISC-R (Wechsler, 1974, Table 11). The WAIS-R stability coefficients are higher than the ones reported for the WAIS by about .05, but are comparable to the WISC-R correlations. This finding is probably due to the similar retest interval employed in the WISC-R study, compared to the very long intervals that characterized many of the WAIS studies summarized by Matarazzo et al. (1980).

Matarazzo and Herman (1984a) combined the two WAIS-R stability samples into a single group of 119 normal adults to study the distributions of changes in IQ upon retesting; they

TABLE 4.4   Gradual decline in the P-IQ practice effect based on data from Catron's studies

Interval	None	1 week	1 month	2 months	4 months
P-IQ Gain	14	11	10	9	8

merged the samples because "inspection of the different frequencies of gains and losses between the younger and older of these two subsamples revealed no discernible effects due to their age difference" (p. 353). Table 4.5 presents the proportions of adults aged 25 to 54 that they found to show gains or losses upon retesting about a month later. The largest losses for anyone in the sample were 12 points on each IQ scale; largest gains were 15 points in V-IQ, 28 points in P-IQ, and 20 points in FS-IQ. A summary of the point-by-point distribution presented by Matarazzo and Herman (1984a) is shown in Table 4.6, which was constructed from the vantage point of the standard errors of measurement of about 3 points that characterize the WAIS-R IQs (V-IQ averages 2¾ points, P-IQ averages 4 points, and FS-IQ averages 2½ points; see Wechsler, 1981, Table 12).

Table 4.6 shows that meaningful losses in IQ upon retesting are rare, occurring less than 10% of the time for Verbal IQ and less than 5% of the time for Performance and Full Scale IQs. Indeed, the practice effect on WAIS-R IQs is so profound that nearly half the adults tested twice improved notably (i.e., more than the error of measurement) on the Verbal Scale, and almost three-quarters of the sample improved substantially on the Performance and Full Scales. Whereas gains in Verbal IQ tend to be modest, improvement on the Performance Scale is typically large and is sometimes dramatic.

The differential between the two scales is certainly related to the lower reliability of most Performance than most Verbal subtests (a topic treated in more detail on p. 112) and the concomitant lower reliability of the Performance than Verbal IQ; the less stable a score, the greater the changes from test to retest. However, the fact that the changes in Performance IQ from test to retest tend to be gains far more often than losses is undoubtedly due to the relative unfamiliarity of the Performance items. Verbal tasks tend to be similar to the kinds of problems presented in school or magazines such as *Readers Digest,* and even for adults who are far removed from school such verbal-oriented items will be familiar. In contrast, Performance items are far less related to the real world and everyday situations and require a little getting used to. This orientation to the task and learning what is expected occurs during the first testing session; an additional habituation period is not needed on a retest, allowing examinees to proceed more quickly (always a benefit on the Wechsler Performance Scales) and with more assurance (a benefit on any test). In the case of Object Assembly, improvement may be related as well to recall of specific puzzles.

Clinical and Research Implications of Practice Effects

The impact of retesting on test performance, whether using the WAIS-R, other Wechsler scales, or similar tests, needs to be internalized by researchers and clinicians alike. Researchers should be aware of the routine and expected gains of about 3 points in V-IQ, 8½ points in P-IQ, and 6 points in FS-IQ that accompany

TABLE 4.5 Porportions of adults aged 25 to 54 showing gains or losses upon retesting ($N = 119$)

	Verbal IQ	Performance IQ	Full Scale IQ
Loss of 1 or more point	20.2%	8.4%	6.7%
No change in IQ	5.9%	2.5%	4.2%
Gain of 1 or more point	73.9%	89.1%	89.1%

TABLE 4.6 Frequency distribution of the different magnitudes of gains or losses from initial WAIS-R to retest WAIS-R over a 2–7 week interval for 119 adults tested twice

Gain or Loss	Verbal IQ %	Performance IQ %	Full Scale IQ %
Loss			
10–12 points	1.7	0.8	0.8
7–9 points	0.0	0.8	0.0
4–6 points	5.0	2.5	2.5
Total of Losses			
> 3 points	6.7	4.2	3.4
No Meaningful Change			
−3 to +3 points (within about 1 SE_M)	46.2	23.5	24.4
Gain			
4–6 points	19.3	16.8	23.5
7–9 points	21.0	11.8	23.5
10–12 points	4.2	12.6	16.8
13–15 points	2.5	16.0	5.0
16–18 points	0.0	5.9	1.7
19–21 points	0.0	5.0	1.7
22 + points	0.0	4.2	0.0
Total of Gains			
> 3 points	47.1	72.3	72.3
> 6 points	27.7	55.5	48.7
> 9 points	6.7	43.7	25.2
> 12 points	2.5	31.1	8.4

NOTE: Data are from Matarazzo and Herman (1984a, Table 1).

readministration of the WAIS-R. These values should always be used as base-rate or control statistics, whenever a suitable control group is unavailable for comparisons in a study employing a test–retest paradigm.

Gains in intelligence that are sometimes attributed to recovery from an illness or operation or to any intervention designed to improve cognitive abilities may be nothing more than a demonstration of the Wechsler practice effect. The most notable instance of such an occur-

rence concerns patients who had undergone carotid endarterectomy, surgery for the removal of arteriosclerotic deposits that partially block blood flow in the artery leading from the heart to the brain. Several investigators (e.g., King, Gideon, Haynes, Dempsey, & Jenkins, 1977) interpreted pre- to post-surgery gains on the WAIS as clear-cut evidence of cognitive improvement following the surgery. As optimistic as such a finding would be, Matarazzo et al. (1979) argued that the gains demonstrated by the surgical patients on the retest were not appreciably different from the gains shown by nonpatients. Although Shatz (1981) called the conclusion of no discernible intellectual gains following surgery premature because of uncontrolled variables in the available test-retest studies, a subsequent well-controlled investigation by Parker, Granberg, Nichols, Jones, & Hewett (1983) concluded that gains in test scores of surgical patients after a 6-month interval were not significantly greater than gains displayed by the control groups.

Clinicians must keep these average gains in mind for assessment purposes, along with the distributions of base-rate data, because of the frequency with which psychiatric, medical, and neurological patients are retested in the course of treatment. The possible loss of function over time by an Alzheimer's patient, or gain in cognitive function by a recovering stroke patient, has to be inferred to make important medical, legal, educational, or vocational decisions. The base rates of the WAIS-R practice effect must always be considered when making determinations about a relative change in function.

Determining an Abnormal Loss or Gain on a WAIS-R Retest

Probably the most sensible way to use the base-rate data is to determine how unusual or abnormal any particular loss or gain is, and to conclude that an individual's change in IQ over time is significant if it occurs infrequently within the normal population. There is no specific rule to define *unusual,* so Table 4.7 has been constructed from the data presented by Matarazzo and Herman (1984a) to allow clinicians to select the degree of abnormality that makes the most sense to them. This table shows the size of the losses and gains in IQ that occur less than 10%, 5%, 2%, and 1% of the time.

The top portion of Table 4.7 shows how large an IQ loss is needed to infer a significant loss in function when a person is retested on the WAIS-R. For Verbal IQ, a loss of 4 or more points occurs less than 10% of the time,

a loss of 5 or more points occurs less than 5% of the time, and so forth. Probably 5% is an appropriate definition of *unusual* for most clinical purposes. If we use that level of abnormality to infer a meaningful or significant loss in function, Table 4.7 tells us that the following minimum decreases in IQ from test to retest are required: 5 points in V-IQ, and 4 points on both P-IQ and FS-IQ.

The bottom portion of Table 4.7 shows analogous data for determining whether a person shows a significant gain in cognitive function from test to retest. If the 5% criterion of abnormality is again used, a meaningful gain in intellectual functioning may be inferred from increases in IQ of at least 12 points on the Verbal Scale, 23 points on the Performance Scale, and 15 points on the Full Scale. The huge gain required in Performance IQ again reinforces the large practice effect that characterizes Wechsler's nonverbal tasks.

WAIS-R Stability for Clinical Patients

WAIS-R stability data for 21 psychiatric and neurological patients (retest intervals ranging from 2 to 144 weeks with a mean of 38 weeks), revealed test-retest coefficients that were lower than the values for the normals tested by Wechsler (1981), but that were nonetheless substantial in magnitude: .79 for V-IQ, .88 for P-IQ, and .86 for FS-IQ (Ryan, Georgemiller, Geisser, & Randall, 1985). The practice effect was 3 points for the Verbal Scale, 4½ points for the Performance Scale, and about 4 points for the Full Scale.

Since Ryan et al. (1985) provided IQs on both administrations of the WAIS-R for each subject, it is possible to determine which patients showed "abnormal" changes in IQ from the first to second testing. Using the values in Table 4.7 for the 5% level as the criterion of abnormality, only two of the patients (one diagnosed as a substance abuser, the other with possible Alzheimer's) manifested an unusual loss in Full Scale IQ, and just one patient (a schizophrenic) demonstrated an unusual gain in Full

TABLE 4-7   The magnitudes of losses or gains in IQ on a WAIS-R retest that correspond to different degrees of unusualness or abnormality

Loss of Function

	SIZE OF LOSS IN IQ FROM INITIAL TEST TO RETEST OCCURRING LESS THAN:			
WAIS-R IQ Scale	*10% of the time*	*5% of the time*	*2% of the time*	*1% of the time*
Verbal	4	5	10	12
Performance	1	4	8	12
Full Scale	1	4	5	12

Gain in Function

	SIZE OF GAIN IN IQ FROM INITIAL TEST TO RETEST OCCURRING LESS THAN:			
WAIS-R IQ Scale	*10% of the time*	*5% of the time*	*2% of the time*	*1% of the time*
Verbal	10	12	14	15
Performance	19	23	27	28
Full Scale	13	15	18	20

NOTE: Data are from Matarazzo and Herman (1984a).

Scale IQ. No one demonstrated an abnormally large gain in Performance IQ, although two patients (including the one with possible Alzheimer's) evidenced an unusual loss in P-IQ. On the Verbal Scale, the schizophrenic patient and one other showed an unusually large gain, and two other patients lost more than 5 points in V-IQ. In isolation, the abnormal changes made by these patients are limited in value; with behavioral, cognitive, or neuropsychological corroboration, however, such changes become clinically meaningful (Matarazzo et al., 1980; Matarazzo & Herman, 1984a).

Overview of Matarazzo's Research

The following rules of thumb can be deduced from the important work done by Matarazzo and his associates:

1. Decreases in IQ are very unusual when a person is retested on the WAIS-R. Any decrease in IQs from test to retest is cause for some concern, and a loss of just 5 points is significant.

2. Substantial increases in WAIS-R IQ from test to retest are common. An increase of at least 1 standard deviation (15 points) in Full Scale IQ is usually necessary to justify inferring a significant improvement in general intelligence. Matarazzo et al. (1980) suggest using this 15-point rule of thumb for each of the three IQs, but the present analyses suggest that 15 points is fine for Full Scale IQ and even Verbal IQ, but that a 20- to 25-point gain is needed for Performance IQ.

3. The practice effect is much stronger for the Performance than the Verbal Scale. Increases

in Performance IQ will typically be about twice as large as increases in Verbal IQ.

4. Changes in IQs by themselves are only of potential clinical importance, even if such changes are unusually large. Matarazzo et al. (1980) warn that "unless other corollary clinical or behavioral evidence *also* is available to corroborate that patient's change in WAIS [-R] score(s) . . ., the burden of proof that the change is mirroring a clinically significant effect quite likely has not been met" (p. 103). Matarazzo and Herman (1984a) expand this appropriately conservative position by stressing that if a large IQ change from test to retest "is a truly meaningful finding, it typically also will be corroborated in one or more of the other neuropsychological tests which were administered to this patient" (p. 359).

Generalization of Matarazzo's Findings

Examiners must be careful *not* to apply the data in Table 4.7 or the above rules of thumb to instances where the WAIS was administered first, followed by the WAIS-R. The data and rules hold only when *both* the test and retest use the WAIS-R. The WAIS norms are long out-of-date, and they do not produce IQs that are comparable to WAIS-R IQs (as discussed at length in chapter 3). WAIS-R IQs are known to be about 6 to 6½ points lower than WAIS IQs. Consequently, increases due to the practice effect are negated to a large extent by the steeper WAIS-R norms when a person who was tested on the WAIS is retested on the WAIS-R.

It is not known precisely how the practice effect relates to intervals of different lengths or to individuals of different ages. The data provided by Matarazzo and Herman (1984a) and summarized here are most generalizable to retest intervals of 1 or 2 months and to adults aged 25–34 and 45–54. With the WAIS, a substantial practice effect was still in evidence for intervals as long as 4 months (Catron & Thompson,

1979) or longer, and for individuals across virtually the entire WAIS age range (Matarazzo et al., 1980).

But once the intervals reach 1 year or longer, the practice effect is far less pronounced or even nil, especially with older subjects (Shatz, 1981). As a general rule, retest intervals should not be much longer than *6 months* in order to apply the present stability findings. However, we need much additional data on the WAIS-R before we can infer the degree to which the data discussed here are applicable to a broad spectrum of ages and retest intervals. Other variables may be relevant as well. Ryan et al. (1985) found that gain or loss for their 21 clinical patients was not significantly related to age at initial testing, initial intelligence level, days between tests, or diagnosis (brain damage versus psychiatric disorder); however, these investigators found a significant correlation ($r = .55$) between gain score and years of education.

Shatz's and Seidenberg's Cautions

Seidenberg et al. (1981) and Shatz (1981) believe that practice effects based on largely or exclusively normal subjects are not particularly generalizable to neurological patients. But if the WAIS-R norms (which systematically excluded brain-damaged patients) are considered applicable to neurological patients, "norms" regarding the WAIS-R practice effect must also be applicable. Norms are just that: reference points for comparison to determine whether something abnormal exists.

If neurological patients truly have smaller practice effects than normal, as Shatz (1981) contends based on a review of pertinent studies, that finding is made possible only by the existence of test-retest norms for a random group of adults. However, the finding that a neurological patient has made significant gains in IQ compared to other patients is not impressive. That patient's IQs were computed from norms derived from normal individuals, not brain-damaged patients; consequently, any significant change in that patient's IQs should be relative to the expected gains made by normal individuals.

Seidenberg et al. (1981) seem to present especially specious arguments regarding the "significant" gains made by epileptic patients. They divided the WAIS gains made by the patients into three categories: no gain, little gain, and high gain. Those with high gains also made significant gains on the Halstead-Reitan (the other two groups did not), but this may simply indicate that those individuals who are able to benefit from practice can do so on more than one test. The authors emphasize the "significant" finding that the "high gain" group had larger WAIS gains than the typical gain demonstrated by Matarazzo's controls. But the high gain group was identified solely by the magnitude of their WAIS gains. Naturally, that group will have a larger than normal practice effect. So will any group that is retested—normal, epileptic, or otherwise—if they are selected based on the size of their retest gain!

Nonetheless, Seidenberg et al. (1981) did have one provocative finding when they divided their epileptic sample into two subgroups, one that had improved in their seizure activity, and one that had not improved. The group that had improved in seizure activity showed significantly larger test-retest gains in Verbal and Full Scale IQ (not Performance IQ) than the group showing no improvement in seizure activity. This result is consistent with Matarazzo's mandate to support substantial IQ gains with external validating evidence before attributing meaningfulness to the apparently large gains. However, the result is also consistent with the finding that substantial gains in Performance IQ are normal and expectable and not necessarily a function of meaningful variables such as improvement in an epileptic's seizure activity.

Test-Retest Findings for the Separate Subtests

Matarazzo and Herman (1984a) also provided test-retest information for the 11 separate WAIS-R subtests. Table 4.8 was prepared from Matarazzo and Herman's (1984a) Table 2 to show at a glance which subtests are the most subject to the influence of practice. The average SE_M of 1 point that characterizes most WAIS-R subtests (Wechsler, 1981, Table 12) was applied in developing this table.

The three WAIS-R subtests producing the largest gains from test to retest are Object Assembly, Picture Arrangement, and Picture Completion, all of which are on the Performance Scale. However, the subtest data do not conform to a simple V–P split; the tasks showing the next largest gains are Verbal subtests (Similarities, Arithmetic), and Block Design demonstrated one of the smallest practice effects. In actuality, the rank ordering of the subtests in Table 4.8 from the most to least retest gains conforms in almost one-to-one inverse fashion to the average split-half reliability coefficients of the subtests (Wechsler, 1981, Table 10). (Split-half coefficients, rather than test-retest coefficients, are used here to avoid contamination with the differential impact of the practice effect.) The three WAIS-R subtests with the largest practice effects have the lowest average reliability coefficients (.68, .74, and .81, respectively). In contrast, the three subtests with the smallest practice effects have the highest average reliabilities: Vocabulary (.96), Information (.89), and Block Design (.87). The five subtests with medium-sized practice effects all have average reliability coefficients in the .82 to .84 range.

That the reliability of a subtest is inversely proportional to the amount of change from test to retest is sensible in view of the greater error of measurement that accompanies low reliability; however, there is no psychometric reason that would impel these large changes to be predominantly *gains*, rather than an equal mixture of gains and losses. Consequently, I believe that the relative unreliability of most Performance subtests allows sizable changes to occur; but it is the novel nature of these tasks that converts most of the observed changes to substantial retest gains (see p. 107).

TABLE 4.8 Gains and losses on the 11 separate subtests for 119 adults tested twice on the WAIS-R

Subtest	Percent Losing 2 or More Pts.	Percent Showing No Change (± 1 pt.)	Percent Gaining 2 or More Points
Object Assembly	5.0	41.2	53.8
Picture Arrangement	7.5	51.3	41.2
Picture Completion	4.2	58.0	37.8
Similarities	3.3	63.9	32.8
Arithmetic	10.9	60.5	28.6
Digit Symbol	5.0	67.2	27.8
Digit Span	10.9	64.7	24.4
Comprehension	13.4	64.7	21.9
Block Design	6.7	72.3	21.0
Information	3.4	79.8	16.8
Vocabulary	6.7	80.7	12.6

NOTE: Data are from Matarazzo and Herman (1984a, Table 2). WAIS-R subtests are listed in order of the percentage gaining 2 or more points.

Reliability of Scores and the Differences Between Them

Wechsler (1981, Tables 10, 11, and 12) has amply documented the reliability, stability, and standard error of measurement of the WAIS-R global scales and the separate subtests. In this section, the main focus is on the reliability of the differences between scores.

Reliability of WAIS-R Scores for Normal Individuals

Reliability coefficients for the WAIS-R were summarized in chapter 3 (see Table 3.2) and are in the mid-90s for the three IQ scales; all subtests except Object Assembly (mean = .68) and Picture Arrangement (mean = .74) have a mean coefficient above .80. At ages 16–17, six subtests have reliability coefficients below .75, and Object Assembly dips to a very unsatisfactory .52. At ages 18–19, five subtests have average coefficients below .75, although the values for ages 20 and above are exemplary.

The SE_Ms range from about 2½ to 3¾ points for Verbal IQ across the age range (mean = 2¾); from about 3¾ to 5 points for Performance IQ (mean = 4); and from about 2¼ to 3 points for Full Scale IQ (mean = 2½). For the subtests, the mean SE_M is approximately 1 point for Information, Vocabulary, and Block Design—easily the most reliable WAIS-R subtests. The average SE_M is about 1¼ points for the remaining Verbal subtests and for Picture Completion and Digit Symbol and reaches 1½ points for Picture Arrangement and Object Assembly.

WAIS-R Reliability for Clinical Patients

WAIS-R split-half reliability coefficients and SE_Ms for a sample of 50 psychiatric and neurologic patients who had an average age of 38 and had completed an average of 12 years of education were statistically comparable to values reported for the normative sample at ages 35–44 (Ryan, Prifitera, & Larsen, 1982). Ryan et al. (1982) found only one subtest, Arithmetic, that differed significantly from normative reliability coefficients; they attributed the lower value for the patients to probable difficulties in concentration. However, Ryan et al. failed to correct their computations for the numerous multiple comparisons that were conducted. When appropriate corrections are made, the z value for Arithmetic is no longer significant; it is chance, not concentration difficulties, that best explains the "finding" for Arithmetic.

Feingold's Research on Reliability of Differences

The separate reliability coefficients for the WAIS-R IQs and subtests are important, but clinicians usually do not interpret any particular score in isolation. More commonly, they compare the Verbal IQ to Performance IQ, scores on various pairs of subtests to each other, or the score on a particular subtest to the global score on which that subtest is included. The *size* of the differences required for statistical significance for each type of comparison is a practical and clinical issue, and is discussed in chapter 9 (V-P IQ comparison) and chapter 13 (subtest comparisons) along with other rules and guidelines for interpreting an individual's profile of WAIS-R scores.

However, the *reliability* of those differences is more of a theoretical and psychometric consideration. To compute the reliability of the difference between any pair of scores, one must consider the reliability (and SE_M) of each component of the pair as well as the correlation between them. Since the reliability of the difference between any two scores is a function of the reliability coefficient of *both* scores in the comparison, that reliability is necessarily less than the reliability of each score taken singly.

Feingold (1984) computed the reliability of the differences between Verbal and Performance IQ, between all possible pairs of subtests, and between a subtest and each global IQ; he provided this information for the WAIS, WISC-R, and WAIS-R. The reliability of the difference between V-IQ and P-IQ averaged

.81 for the WAIS-R. This coefficient is higher than the values for the WISC-R (.76) and WAIS (.76) but is less than one might anticipate from the phenomenally high reliabilities of the separate WAIS-R IQ scales. Nonetheless, .81 is a very respectable reliability for a difference score, and it justifies interpretation of a person's WAIS-R V-P IQ discrepancy (as if clinicians needed permission!).

The interpretive procedure advocated for the WAIS-R in this book (and for the WISC-R in Kaufman, 1979b) depends not only on the V–P discrepancy, but also on a comparison of each separate WAIS-R subtest with the scale (either Verbal or Performance) on which it is included. Frequently, this comparison involves the difference between an individual's scaled score on each Verbal subtest with that individual's mean scaled score on all six Verbal subtests, and the difference between that person's scaled score on each Performance task and his or her mean score on the five Performance subtests.

Feingold (1984) has provided a table of the reliability of the difference between each subtest and each IQ for the entire WAIS-R and WISC-R standardization samples, and for the WAIS at ages 25–34. Differences between each Verbal subtest and Verbal IQ, and between each Performance subtest and Performance IQ, are directly germane to the interpretive approach that I advocate. These values for the WAIS-R are taken from Feingold (1984, Table 2) and are presented in Table 4.9 along with corresponding values for the WISC-R and WAIS. Since it is sometimes wise to compare each subtest to the mean of all Wechsler subtests, rather than to the separate Verbal and Performance means (see p. 428), Feingold's (1984) data for the reliability of the difference between each subtest and Full Scale IQ are also presented in Table 4.9.

Clinical Implications of Feingold's Research

The reliabilities of the difference between subtests and the scales on which they are included

TABLE 4.9 Reliability coefficients of the difference between WAIS-R, WAIS, and WISC-R scaled scores on the separate subtests and the global scales on which they are included

Subtest	WAIS-R			WAIS			WISC-R		
	V-IQ	P-IQ	FS-IQ	V-IQ	P-IQ	FS-IQ	V-IQ	P-IQ	FS-IQ
Verbal									
I	.50	—	.63	.41	—	.54	.34	—	.59
DSp	.68	—	.71	.39	—	.49	.75	—	.77
V	.65	—	.77	.59	—	.71	.23	—	.55
A	.52	—	.57	.48	—	.59	.46	—	.59
C	.41	—	.55	.32	—	.43	.28	—	.48
S	.44	—	.52	.44	—	.57	.26	—	.48
Performance									
PC	—	.38	.59	—	.42	.59	—	.41	.60
PA	—	.39	.55	—	.00	.07	—	.36	.56
BD	—	.44	.69	—	.29	.58	—	.31	.62
OA	—	.15	.51	—	.07	.50	—	.13	.50
DSy (Cod)	—	.58	.70	—	.71	.81	—	.57	.68
Mean	.53	.39	.62	.44	.30	.53	.39	.36	.58

NOTE: Data are from Feingold (1984, Table 2).

are not impressive. The low values are largely a result of the high correlations between the subtests and their member scales. Obviously the same rules for acceptable reliabilities of separate subtests or IQ scales do not apply to the reliabilities of difference scores. How high is *high* for a difference score? There are no unequivocal answers, although the notion that reliability limits validity comes into play here. One needs at least some reliability to permit substantial validity coefficients to occur. The highest validity coefficient obtainable with a variable equals the square root of its reliability coefficient; thus, even a reliability coefficient of .50 permits validity coefficients of about .70.

For argument's sake, consider .50 an adequate (if not impressive) minimum for the reliability of the difference between a subtest and a global IQ. For the WAIS-R, then, only four Verbal subtests (Information, Digit Span, Vocabulary, Arithmetic) are reliably different from Verbal IQ, and only Digit Symbol is reliably different from Performance IQ. All the WAIS-R tasks, however, differ reliably from Full Scale IQ, and only Object Assembly (with an absurdly low value of .15) has an unacceptable reliability of the difference when compared to the Verbal and Performance Scales. In addition, the WAIS-R has markedly better coefficients than the WAIS, averaging .09 higher than its predecessor for all three scales. The WAIS-R also exceeds the WISC-R in its reliability of the difference coefficients. Only Digit Span on the Verbal Scale and Coding on the Performance Scale have a coefficient of .50 or greater.

The formulas for determining the size of a significant difference when comparing a *single* subtest score to the individual's own mean score on all subtests in the scale fully take into account the reliability of the difference between each subtest and its scale. Consequently, Feingold's (1984) psychometric findings do not invalidate the method that Silverstein (1982d), Sattler (1988), or I propose for interpreting WAIS-R or WISC-R profiles.

Nonetheless, the low reliabilities of the difference scores for most comparisons should impel examiners (1) *not* to interpret as meaningful any observed differences in scores that fall short of the values required for statistical significance, (2) to be cautious in making strong clinical inferences about the meaning of any particular subtest that deviates significantly from its respective IQ scale, (3) to try to integrate the findings from two or more subtests when reaching clinical hypotheses rather than focusing on the tasks one at a time, and (4) to have relatively little confidence in the meaningfulness of the findings when subtests producing very low reliability of the difference scores (such as WAIS-R Object Assembly or WISC-R Object Assembly, Vocabulary, Comprehension, and Similarities) are among the only subtests that deviate significantly from their respective scales.

Comparisons of Verbal subtests to Performance IQ, and vice versa, are not presented in Table 4.9, even though Feingold (1984) presents these data, because they are not germane to the interpretive approach that I advocate. However, these reliability of the difference coefficients tend to be far more substantial in magnitude than the values shown in Table 4.9 because of the comparatively low intercorrelations between Wechsler subtests and the scale on which they are *not* included. For the WAIS-R, the values for Verbal subtests, when compared to Performance IQ, range from .68 (Similarities) to .84 (Vocabulary); values for the Performance subtests, versus Verbal IQ, range from .66 (Picture Arrangement and Object Assembly) to .79 (Block Design). For the WISC-R and WAIS, corresponding reliability of the difference coefficients are also typically in the .60s and .70s. Thus, examiners who choose to compare a person's

score on a single subtest to his or her IQ on the opposite scale are able to do so with confidence because of the relatively high reliability of the difference coefficients that support such comparisons.

I do not advocate an approach to subtest interpretation that focuses on pair-wise comparisons of subtests (see chapter 13). However, such comparisons are psychometrically acceptable when two conditions are met: They are few in number—no more than five—and they are specified in advance, rather than decided upon at the whim of the examiner after first scrutinizing the subtest profile.

Feingold (1984) has also presented reliability of the difference data for all possible pairs of subtests on the WAIS-R, WISC-R, and WAIS. The values reported for these comparisons are generally much more favorable than the coefficients shown in Table 4.9. For the WAIS-R, all coefficients exceed the arbitrary minimum value of .50 except for Object Assembly versus Block Design (.39) and Object Assembly versus Picture Completion (.47). The most reliable contrast is between Vocabulary and Block Design (.82), a potentially important comparison because each is the best measure of *g* on its respective scale, and because some researchers (e.g., Silverstein, 1982a) recommend the use of the Vocabulary-Block Design dyad as a WAIS-R short form.

Other very reliable WAIS-R contrasts (coefficient of .75 or greater) are Vocabulary-Digit Span, Information-Block Design, and Vocabulary-Digit Symbol. WAIS coefficients are not nearly as impressive as values for the WAIS-R; 14 pair-wise coefficients are below .50, including nearly every contrast involving Picture Arrangement. For the WISC-R, four coefficients are less than .50: Vocabulary-Comprehension (.46), Similarities-Comprehension (.49), Object Assembly-Picture Completion (.49), and Object Assembly-Block Design (.44). The highest reliability of the difference between a pair of WISC-R subtests is the value of .73 obtained for Digit Span versus Block Design; the coefficient for Vocabulary-Block Design is .72.

Alternate Forms Reliability and Stability: WAIS-R Versus WISC-R

Wechsler used three separate test batteries to cover the age span from 3 to 74 years: the WPPSI-R (ages 3 to 7), the WISC-R (ages 6 to 16, soon to be replaced by the WISC III), and the WAIS-R (ages 16 to 74). At the ages of overlap, the Wechsler Scales are, in effect, alternate forms, and their correlations should be treated as alternate forms reliability coefficients. This section assesses the magnitude of the coefficients between the WISC-R and WAIS-R at age 16 to determine the alternate forms reliability of Wechsler's batteries. In addition, stability of the test scores over time is examined, since typically the WAIS-R is given to young adults or older teenagers who previously were tested on the WISC-R as 2 young adolescents, perhaps at age 13 or 14. The stability of the scores, and the difference in the means yielded by the two instruments, are of practical importance; the continuity of measurement is likely to have a vital impact on placement decisions—for example, of retarded adolescents who were identified with the WISC-R and are reevaluated with the WAIS-R.

The major practical issue addressed in this section, however, is whether an examiner would be wiser to select the WAIS-R or WISC-R (or ultimately the WISC III) when testing individuals at the age of overlap: 16 years 0 months through 16 years 11 months. When the WISC III becomes available for use during the 1990s, presuming that its upper range is still age 16, it will assuredly become the test of choice because of its newer set of norms. (The WAIS-R norms for adolescents will not only be older, but they are beset with unexplained problems, as documented in chapter 3.)

The studies cited in this section and the discussion of the relative merits of the WISC-R and WAIS-R for 16-year-olds should also help examiners evaluate the numerous studies that will relate the WAIS-R to the WISC III when the latter battery becomes available. The extreme similarity in the factor structures of the WAIS-R and WISC-R is discussed in chapter 8 (see Table 8.10). Indeed, the WAIS-R is a descendant of Form I of the Wechsler-Bellevue, and the WISC-R is the offspring of its alternate form, the Wechsler-Bellevue II. One would therefore anticipate comparable underlying structures for the two tests; a simple examination of the items composing each of the 11 subtests that the WAIS-R and WISC-R share (all but Mazes) reveals that each set of items comes from essentially a common item pool. The next sections evaluate the statistical comparability of the WAIS-R and WISC-R by studying the relationships between the scores yielded by their respective IQ scales and subtests.

Wechsler's Counterbalanced Study of a Normal Sample

Wechsler (1981, Table 18) presented data from a carefully counterbalanced study of eighty 16-year-olds of average intelligence who were administered the WAIS-R and WISC-R with a time interval of 1 to 6 weeks. Correlations between Verbal IQs were .89, Performance IQs .76, and Full Scale IQs .88. Mean Verbal IQs were virtually identical, with the WAIS-R producing mean Performance and Full Scale IQs that were slightly lower than WISC-R IQs, by 1½ and 1 point, respectively. Since the WAIS-R was standardized about 5 to 6 years later than the WISC-R, one would have predicted lower WAIS-R IQs by about 1½ points, based on Flynn's (1984) analyses of changes in intelligence test performance across generations. That prediction was approximately borne out, although there is still great concern about the accuracy of the WAIS-R norms for older adolescents. Possibly, the WAIS-R normative data are more accurate for age 16 than for ages 17–19.

Whereas the WAIS-R and WISC-R IQ scales correlated substantially, the equivalence for the separate subtests was less obvious. Correlations between the Information ($r = .83$) and Vocabulary (.86) subtests were substantial and the coefficients for Digit Span, Block Design, and Digit Symbol/Coding (.70–.72) were barely adequate; however, the "alternate form" reliability coefficients were unacceptably low for Picture Arrangement (.39), Object Assembly (.47), and the remaining four tasks (.60–.67).

Counterbalanced Studies of Exceptional Samples

Sandoval, Sassenrath, and Penaloza (1988) conducted a similar counterbalanced study of the WISC-R and WAIS-R, although they used a small sample ($N = 30$; 15 males, 15 females; 18 whites, 12 Hispanics) of learning-disabled 16-year-olds with Full Scale IQs between 87 and 116. WISC-R IQs were higher than WAIS-R IQs by about 1 point on the Full Scale and nearly 3 points on the Performance Scale; WAIS-R V-IQ was about 1 point higher than the corresponding WISC-R IQ. None of these differences reached significance at the .05 level. The Verbal and Full Scale IQs each correlated .96 and the Performance Scale correlated .82, mirroring the pattern of correlations found by Wechsler (1981) for normal adolescents.

As was true for normals, the learning-disabled adolescents tested by Sandoval et al. (1988) manifested high correlations for some subtests (the four Verbal Comprehension subtests on the WAIS-R correlated .82–.93 with their WISC-R counterparts) and abysmally low coefficients for other subtests (Arithmetic, Picture Completion, Block Design, and Object Assembly produced correlations of only .28–.54). These results may not necessarily generalize to other samples because of a substantial $P > V$ profile of 11 points on the WAIS-R (15 points on the WISC-R). This nonverbal superiority is likely

a combination of the nature of the group's exceptionality (learning disabled; see pp. 285–286) and ethnic background (40% were Hispanics; see pp. 281–284).

Other researchers have also conducted carefully counterbalanced investigations of small samples of exceptional 16-year-olds—for example, 37 hearing-impaired residential students (Meacham, 1985), 30 low-functioning males enrolled in special education programs (Sisemore, 1985), and 30 males in gifted programs (Sisemore, 1985). Mean Performance IQs of the hearing-impaired sample did not differ significantly for the two instruments, with the WAIS-R producing a higher value than the WISC-R by 1⅓ point (Meacham, 1985). Similarly, the mean WAIS-R and WISC-R IQs for the special education and gifted students did not differ significantly, except for the 4.4-point advantage in favor of the WAIS-R Verbal IQ for low-functioning 16-year-olds (Sisemore, 1985).

Grace (1986) administered the WAIS-R ($N = 30$) or WISC-R ($N = 25$) randomly to 16-year-old male delinquents. The two groups were well matched on age, race (each group was composed of approximately equal numbers of blacks and whites), and prior exposure to the tests. Overall, the subjects earned about equal FS-IQs on both tests (WAIS-R mean was ½ point higher). Otherwise, the results of the study were quite unusual and inexplicable: (a) WAIS-R produced a 4-point higher V-IQ but a 5-point *lower* P-IQ; (b) WAIS-R Full Scale IQ was 9½ points higher for whites, but 5½ points *lower* for blacks; and (c) as detailed on pp. 286–288 regarding P>V profiles for delinquent populations, a substantial characteristic profile emerged for both blacks and whites on the WISC-R, but for *neither* race on the WAIS-R.

Longitudinal Relationship of WISC-R to WAIS-R

Studies conducted with experimental rigor, using normal subjects of average intelligence and diverse exceptional populations, are essential to understand the equivalence (or lack of it) for two instruments that overlap and that are intended to provide continuous measurement across the life span. However, in real life the WISC-R is administered first and the WAIS-R is later given to exceptional populations who must be reevaluated by law, to clinical patients who have outgrown the WISC-R, and so forth. Table 4.10 summarizes several studies that examined the longitudinal relationship of the WISC-R and WAIS-R for clinical samples of deaf and low-functioning adolescents.

The intervals between the WISC-R and WAIS-R administrations were 3 to 4 years for all studies listed in Table 4.10, long enough to minimize or negate the impact of any practice

effect. Coefficients of correlation between the three WISC-R and WAIS-R IQs were quite substantial, despite the lengthy interval between testings. The median values of .78 for V-IQ, .82 for P-IQ, and .84 for FS-IQ compare favorably to coefficients obtained for children with school learning problems tested twice on the WISC-R with a 3-year interval: correlations of .78–.85 for 367 Anglo, black, and Mexican American children (Elliott et al., 1985); and correlations of .70–.74 for 150 students (Oakman & Wilson, 1988). In Elliott et al.'s (1985) study, coefficients were significantly higher for Anglos (.83–.90) than for either blacks (.61–.70) or Mexican Americans (.66–.81).

Neither study of exceptional children tested twice on the WISC-R produced meaningful

TABLE 4.10   Longitudinal comparison of WISC-R and WAIS-R IQs for clinical populations

Authors	Nature of Sample	N	Mean Age WISC-R	Mean Age WAIS-R	Mean IQ WISC-R	Mean IQ WAIS-R	Difference	r
Sattler et al. (1984)	In LD or MR Classes	30	13.8	17.5	V 81.0	81.3	+0.3	.76
					P 84.7	86.5	+1.8	.82
					FS 81.1	82.7	+1.6	.86
Zimmerman et al. (1986)	Special Ed. Referrals (white)	50	13.7	17.9	V 75.8	81.2	+5.4	.84
					P 79.7	83.3	+3.6	.85
					FS 75.9	81.2	+5.2	.88
	Special Ed. Referrals (black)	40	13+ (est.)	16.8	V 70.6	75.3	+4.7	.57
					P 72.6	72.3	−0.3	.75
					FS 69.6	73.0	+3.4	.70
Rubin et al. (1985)	TMR & EMR (residential)	41	15.1	18.3	V 58.8	70.0	+11.2	.80
					P 60.7	65.5	+4.8	.82
					FS 55.8	66.9	+11.1	.83
Vance et al. (1987)	Special Ed. Students	28	14.2	17.0	V 72.4	77.9	+5.5	—
					P 77.2	79.5	+2.3	—
					FS 72.4	77.5	+5.1	—
Braden & Paquin (1985)	Deaf (residential)	32	14.7	18.1	P 94.9	97.2	+2.3	.74
Median Values			14.0	17.7	V		+5.4	.78
					P		+2.3	.82
					FS		+5.1	.84

NOTE: Difference equals WAIS-R IQ minus WISC-R IQ.

differences in mean IQs. Oakman and Wilson (1988) found a 1½-point gain on the second testing, while Elliott et al. (1985) obtained identical mean WISC-R Full Scale IQs of 77 on each administration; Anglos, blacks, and Mexican Americans earned virtually identical IQs on both the test and retest. In marked contrast, each WISC-R/WAIS-R study listed in Table 4.10 produced higher IQs on the WAIS-R, although the differences failed to reach significance in the studies by Sattler, Polifka, Polifka, and Hilsen (1984) and Braden and Paquin (1985). The WAIS-R produced higher Verbal IQs than the WISC-R by an average of 5.4 points (range of 0.3 to 11.2); higher Performance IQs by an average of 2.3 points (range of -0.3 to 4.8), and higher Full Scale IQs by an average of 5.1 points (range of 1.6 to 11.1).

These discrepancies are *opposite* in direction to what one would anticipate, inasmuch as tests normed more recently invariably produce *lower* mean scores than their predecessors (Flynn, 1984). Although regression to the mean will tend to increase IQs for the low IQ adolescents who are retested on the WAIS-R, the differences of 5 to 5½ points for the Verbal and Full Scale IQs are larger than one would expect from a simple regression effect. These findings accord with similar results of nearly a dozen WISC/WAIS or WISC-R/WAIS investigations in the literature (Carvajal, Lane, & Gay, 1984).

The difference in the scores yielded by the WAIS-R and WISC-R may be primarily due to the problems cited previously with the WAIS-R norms at ages 16–19, to the instability of norms for low IQ levels because of the few individuals at those levels who are included in the standardization samples, to the lack of "bottom" for several WAIS-R subtests (a serious problem discussed in the next section), to a real gain in intelligence for retarded individuals over time, or some other reason. Since the identical results occurred with the 1955 WAIS, the problem is not likely to be the problematical WAIS-R adolescent norms.

The possibility of the gain truly reflecting improved ability was given some support by Carvajal et al.'s (1984) WISC/WAIS study. They analyzed data for 66 retarded individuals tested on the WISC at an average age of 11 years, 9 months and on the WAIS at 17 years, 6 months. The group gained 9½ points in FS-IQ on the retest. But Carvajal et al. were able to retest 21 subjects on the WAIS at a mean age of 28 years, 6 months. This subsample showed a gain in mean IQ from 64 on the WISC at time 1 to 73 on the WAIS at time 2 to 79½ on the WAIS at time 3; the gain from older adolescence to adulthood for this retarded sample held the instrument constant. However, the sample was small and contained only those willing to be tested; conclusions are tentative and not generalizable. The only conclusion is that the WAIS-R (like the WAIS before it) tends to yield higher IQs than the WISC-R, especially on the Verbal and Full Scales, for low-functioning individuals who are retested on the WAIS-R after several years.

WAIS-R Versus WISC-R for Retarded Individuals

When Zimmerman, Covin, and Woo-Sam (1986) combined data from their two subsamples of referrals, they found that the discrepancies in favor of WAIS-R were largest for mentally retarded individuals and virtually disappeared for subjects with average or near-average IQs. Based on WISC-R Full Scale IQ, they found the following discrepancies with WAIS-R IQ by IQ level:

IQ LEVEL	N	MEAN DIFFERENCE
40–59	11	+14.4
60–69	23	+ 5.5
70–79	32	+ 2.7
80–89	15	+ 1.1
90 and above	9	+ 1.3

These results are highly similar to the results

reported by Zimmerman et al. (1986) for the separate Verbal and Performance Scales.

Rubin, Goldman, and Rosenfeld (1985) divided their institutionalized retarded sample into subgroups of trainable mentally retarded ($N = 21$) and educable mentally retarded ($N = 20$), using a WISC-R Full Scale IQ of 55 as the cutoff. Like Zimmerman et al. (1986), Rubin et al. (1985) found the difference in Full Scale IQs for the group with lower IQs to be larger than the WAIS-R/WISC-R discrepancy for the EMRs (14 versus 7 points). Also, Carvajal et al. (1984) found slightly larger gains from WISC to WAIS over a 6-year interval for retarded people with IQs below 70 (10½ points) than for those with IQs of 70 and above (8 points). Again, the *direction* of the relationship between the size of the IQ discrepancy and level of intelligence is predictable based on the known impact of the phenomenon of regression to the mean; however, the *magnitude* of the relationship is more than one would anticipate from the statistical artifact.

The consequence of the higher WAIS-R than WISC-R IQs for low IQ individuals is a different intelligence classification upon reevaluation, which occurred frequently in Zimmerman et al.'s (1986) study, and dramatically in the investigation by Rubin et al. (1985). The former group of researchers state: "Such dramatic changes in classification may have ominous repercussions for school personnel" (p. 150). Rubin et al. add that the reclassification in their study of nearly all TMRs as EMRs based on the WAIS-R IQs "could shift placement from one type of class or school to another, with a totally different educational plan and available resources, and perhaps also even present a major shift in funding base" (p. 395).

These concerns are legitimate. However, such consequences are primarily a function of rigid federal, state, and local guidelines that emphasize the specific IQs earned by an individual, and that adhere rigidly to specific IQ cutoff points. The differences in the norms of any two instruments at the extremes of the IQ distribution,

even two instruments that are intended to be comparable, are expectable in view of the state of the art of test development. The main problem for clinicians is to try to coordinate their sophisticated knowledge of psychometrics and the intelligence construct with rigid, unsophisticated decision-making guidelines.

Interestingly, results for learning-disabled (LD) individuals also suggest potential classification differences upon a retest, but these results are *opposite* to the findings for retarded adolescents and adults. McQuaid and Spreen (1989) followed up a group of learning-disabled individuals over a 15-year period; a sample of 81 was tested on the old WISC at age 10 and on the WAIS-R at age 24. These LD adults obtained significantly *lower* IQs on the WAIS-R than WISC, even after the investigators included a control for the outdated WISC norms. Approximately equal decrements were noted for all three IQs; however, the largest IQ decreases on all scales were found for LD individuals without soft or hard neurological signs when assessed as children. In contrast, the smallest decrements resulted for those who evidenced hard signs in a childhood neurological examination (McQuaid & Spreen, 1989; Spreen, 1987).

Selecting the WAIS-R or WISC-R at Age 16

Ordinarily, there would be no contest between a new instrument and an old one; logic dictates giving the test with the more recent norms. But the WAIS-R standardization is suspect for older adolescents (see pages 83–85), offering clinicians little confidence in the profile of obtained scores.

The WAIS-R also has relatively low subtest reliability for 16- and 17-year-olds, yielding split-half coefficients of .52 for Object Assembly, .66 for Picture Arrangement, and .70–.73 for Digit Span, Arithmetic, Picture Completion, and Digit Symbol. The WISC-R subtests are better in this respect for 16-year-olds, but not appreciably so; Arithmetic, Picture Completion, Picture Arrangement, and Object Assembly produced reliability coefficients in the .70 to .75 range. (The optional WISC-R Mazes task had a value of .57, but there is little justification for administering this subtest to subjects aged 12 or above.) The mean split-half coefficient on the 11 WAIS-R subtests equaled .76 for ages 16–17, compared with a mean of .80 for the 10 regular WISC-R tasks at age 16.

The WISC-R does not have adequate "top" for 16-year-olds for Arithmetic, Picture Completion, and Mazes (each subtest yields a maximum scaled score of 16 or 17). The WAIS-R fares better in this regard when clinicians interpret the scaled scores developed directly for 16- and 17-year-olds (as opposed to the age 20–34 norms used to calculate scaled scores for everyone for IQ computation). Only Picture Completion and Picture Arrangement (which offer a maximum score of 18) fail to yield scores of 19, the highest possible scaled scores on Wechsler's subtests.

However, the WISC-R has a much more ample "bottom" than the WAIS-R for 16-year-olds. Taking advantage of the numerous easy items on the WISC-R subtests, which are included to permit assessment of children as young as 6, it is possible for 16-year-olds to earn scaled scores of 1 on every subtest. In fact, adolescents of 16 must earn at least 6 raw score points (most tasks require at least 10 raw score points) to earn a scaled score of 2 on any WISC-R subtest. Contrast this excellent bottom to the WAIS-R at ages 16–17. A raw score of *zero* translates to a scaled score of 2 for three subtests, and raw scores of just 1 point yield scaled scores of 3 for Similarities, Picture Arrangement, and Block Design.

Both the WISC-R and WAIS-R have the flaws that accompany the extreme ages for which a test battery is normed. The WISC-R was developed for ages 6–16 and fails to accommodate very bright 16-year-olds. The WAIS-R was developed for 16–74 years olds and is inefficient for assessing low-functioning

16-year-olds. Indeed, the WAIS-R has an inadequate floor on several subtests for all adults. When examining the norms for the reference group of 20- to 34-year-olds, raw scores of 1 point earn a scaled score of 2 for four subtests; and raw scores of only 2 points translate to scaled scores of 3 or 4 for three subtests.

Carvajal et al.'s (1984) study, discussed on pages 119–120, suggests that retarded individuals may truly gain in general intelligence over time. Nonetheless, the serious problem with the WAIS-R's "bottom" is also a conceivable explanation for the higher IQs yielded for the WAIS-R than the WISC-R when retarded individuals are retested on the WAIS-R after a 3- or 4-year interval.

Frequently, retarded individuals simply do not understand what is expected of them on Wechsler subtests like Similarities or Picture Arrangement and will earn a raw score of zero, or perhaps 1 or 2. On Picture Arrangement, for example, examinees can earn 2 points on the WISC-R, and 1 point on the WAIS-R, by simply copying the examiner's response (even if they fail to grasp the time concepts involved). On the WAIS-R, the "bottom" for Picture Arrangement was actually made worse when the WAIS was revised. One of the simple three-card items (Nest) was eliminated "because it was extremely easy" (Wechsler, 1981, p. 14). Now the examinee must proceed from a single easy arrangement (House) to a fairly complex five-card item (Flirt) that often baffles retarded individuals. The additional "extremely easy" item is sorely missed by low-functioning subjects.

Suppose that a retarded 16-year-old girl barely understands any of Wechsler's tasks and earns (for the sake of comparison) 2 raw score points on every subtest. She will earn the lowest possible sums of scaled scores on the WISC-R: 5 on Verbal (IQ < 45), 5 on Performance (IQ < 45), and 10 on Full Scale (IQ < 40). On the WAIS-R, her raw scores of 2 on each subtest yield a Verbal sum of scaled scores of 10 (IQ = 58), a Performance sum of 11 (IQ = 55), and a Full Scale sum of 21 (IQ = 54).

The retarded girl earns WAIS-R IQs in the mid-50s, compared to WISC-R IQs that are less than 45, based on essentially the same lack of knowledge. As noted previously, the poor floor on the WAIS-R for retarded individuals may be the real culprit in the research findings summarized in Table 4.10 that show higher WAIS-R than WISC-R IQs for retarded adolescents tested twice over an interval of 3 or 4 years. This hypothesis would predict that the WAIS-R's IQs are the most discrepant with WISC-R IQs for retarded individuals the lower their functioning. That is precisely what Zimmerman et al. (1986) found in their study, discussed in the previous section: The WAIS-R was higher by 14½ points for individuals with IQs of 40 to 59, compared to 5½ points for those with IQs of 60–69 and only 2½ points for people scoring 70–79.

Since the 1955 WAIS was beset with the same problem with floors as its successor, one would anticipate that the WAIS yielded higher IQs than the WISC for low-functioning adolescents. This is exactly what happened in previous Wechsler investigations of low-functioning boys, slow learners, black mentally retarded adolescents, and white mentally retarded adolescents (Zimmerman & Woo-Sam, 1973, Table 2–3). The WAIS was higher than the WISC by 7 to 11 points in each of six pertinent studies summarized by Zimmerman and Woo-Sam. When separate IQs were reported by the investigators, differences favored WAIS over WISC about equally on the Verbal and Performance Scales. In addition, the same discrepancies occurred whether the tests were given to the low-functioning adolescents concurrently in counterbalanced order, or with 3 years separating the WISC and WAIS administrations.

One conclusion is clear regarding the choice of instrument for 16-year-olds: *Use the WISC-R in preference to the WAIS-R whenever assessing someone known or suspected of low intellectual functioning (IQs of about 80 or below).* This recommendation holds even when the person has previously been tested on the WISC-R, since the practice effect is likely to occur regardless of which Wechsler battery is used for the retest.

In view of the very questionable WAIS-R norms for ages 16–19 and the low subtest reliability for ages 16–17 it is probably better to give a WISC-R instead of the WAIS-R to a 16-year-old of any ability level. For example, Spruill (1984) noted, "When testing sixteen-year-olds it is recommended that the WISC-R be used unless there is some specific reason to use the WAIS-R" (p. 734). I agree with her, but the only specific reason I can think of is that you've misplaced your WISC-R kit. Or, when it comes out, your WISC III kit.

CHAPTER 4 SUMMARY

This chapter reviews research studies pertaining to WAIS-R administration time, scoring errors, reliability and stability of IQs and scaled scores, reliability of V–P IQ differences, and "alternate forms" reliability of the WAIS-R with the WISC-R. Studies of administration time for clinical samples suggest that groups of average intelligence require about 90 minutes of testing time, with shorter administration times (about 75 minutes) observed for low-functioning samples. Block Design is the longest subtest to administer (10 to 12 minutes), while Digit Span and Digit Symbol are the shortest (3 to 4½ minutes).

Scoring errors due to mechanical mistakes and other types of carelessness are just as common for the WAIS-R as they have been for other Wechsler batteries. Huge numbers of errors are made by examiners regardless of their scoring experience, and inadequate training in individual assessment may be the chief problem. A well-designed study of scoring errors on the three WAIS-R Verbal subtests with subjective scoring systems yielded the following results:

- Subjects made errors on nearly half the ambiguous responses they had to score, whether these responses were taken from the manual or from clinical cases.

- More errors were made on Vocabulary than on Comprehension or Similarities.
- Errors tended to be biased toward leniency for all three tasks.
- Neither specific cautions to be careful nor the experience level of the examiner was related to scoring accuracy.
- An examiner's personality was significantly related to accuracy.

WAIS and WAIS-R stability has been thoroughly reviewed and investigated by Matarazzo and his colleagues, leading to the following conclusions about practice effects when the two administrations surround an interval of 1 or a few months:

- V-, P-, and FS-IQs increase by an average of about 3 points, 8½ points, and 6 points, respectively.
- Decreases in IQ upon a retest are quite rare.
- FS-IQ gains of at least 15 points are necessary to infer a meaningful gain in general intelligence, with gains of 20–25 points needed for P-IQ.
- Any changes in IQ are meaningful only if interpreted in the context of base-rate data concerning the practice effect, along with clinical and behavioral inferences.

Some researchers have applied strong cautions regarding generalizations from Matarazzo's work, but his findings seem to have serious implications for the interpretation of both clinical and research data.

Among separate WAIS-R subtests, the largest practice effect was observed for Object Assembly and Picture Arrangement; the smallest was noted for Vocabulary and Information. Subtest reliabilities are similar for normal and clinical samples. Reliability of the difference between V- and P-IQs is larger for the WAIS-R (.81) than for the WAIS or WISC-R (.76). Whereas these values are adequate, the individual subtests do not differ reliably from the scales on which they are included. However, the formulas used in this book and advocated elsewhere regarding subtest profile interpretation are not adversely affected by the relatively low subtest versus scale reliability.

WAIS-R and WISC-R IQs correlate substantially for normal and clinical samples, although the corresponding subtests on the two batteries often do not. When 16-year-olds are tested on both tests, mean IQs have been quite similar in magnitude. Longitudinal investigations of the WISC-R and WAIS-R, administered in that order about 3 to 4 years apart, show substantial correlations between the IQs yielded by the two Wechsler batteries. Typically, the WAIS-R IQs earned on the retest have averaged about 5 FS-IQ points higher than the WISC-R IQs for the various samples, most of which were composed of low-functioning subjects. Some evidence suggests a real gain in intelligence over time for retarded individuals, but the results are speculative; other evidence suggests that WAIS-R IQ gains over time are larger the lower the mean IQ of the retarded sample. These gains, whatever their cause, have important practical implications for clinicians regarding changes in classification from test to retest.

For 16-year-olds, use the WISC-R or its forthcoming replacement, the WISC III. The WAIS-R norms are suspect for adolescents, and the battery has an insufficient "bottom" for low-functioning 16-year-olds. Although the WISC-R lacks a "top" on several tasks and has older norms, its subtests are more reliable and have many more easy items for low-functioning adolescents. Avoid the WAIS-R for 16-year-olds.

CHAPTER 5

Short Forms of the WAIS-R

Examiners want to save time. Many clinicians want to measure a child's or adult's IQ quickly, without devoting too much time to psychometric evaluations. They want to obtain a reliable and valid estimate of the person's intelligence but prefer to spend their valuable time on therapy or personality assessment, not on the standardized administration of a comprehensive test battery, which, they erroneously believe, gives you just a few IQ scores. Some of these examiners are content to obtain IQ estimates from a quick-and-dirty measure—never mind the psychometric stuff—that can be given by their receptionist or secretary. Most clinicians, however, see the value of a thorough battery and use brief tests only under circumstances that justify them.

In many cases administration of a short test may be wise because the time with an individual may be limited and a short IQ test may help optimize how that time is spent. Time limita-

tions are especially pervasive in institutional settings (Klett, Watson, & Hoffman, 1986). Terman and Merrill (1937) recognized this need more than a half-century ago when they identified four tasks at each level to be given as an abbreviated form of the Stanford-Binet, "[w]hen limitations of time make it necessary" (p. 31). Their proposed short form saved the examiner about one-third of the testing time and yielded an IQ that "is still reliable enough for most purposes" (p. 31). Terman and Merrill developed the shortened Binet with care and sophistication: "The . . . tests have been selected so as to be as representative of the entire scale as possible with respect to variety, difficulty, interest to subject, sex differences, and validity as measured by correlation with total score" (pp. 31–32). Unfortunately, many developers of brief intelligence tests have not heeded this lesson. Several have tried to meet clinicians' needs for brief intelligence tests, but their products have often been inferior; some test developers believed that the word "brief" was supposed to apply to the test construction efforts as well as the administration time.

BRIEF ALTERNATIVES TO THE COMPLETE WAIS-R

This chapter presents and evaluates the best methods available to clinicians for quickly obtaining IQs when administration of the WAIS-R is a luxury. For all ages, the current best method is to administer a well-chosen short form derived from a standardized, individually administered intelligence test with excellent norms. For adolescents and adults, that means a WAIS-R short form. In the early 1990s, another option will be the Kaufman Brief Intelligence Test (K-BIT; Kaufman & Kaufman, in press b), standardized for ages 4 to 75+ years; although still in standardization as this book went to press, preliminary analyses suggest that the K-BIT has promise as a reliable, valid, and well-normed brief tool for clinicians. The four-subtest Quick Screening Battery that is part of the Fourth Edition of the Stanford-Binet Intelligence Scale (Thorndike, Hagen, & Sattler, 1986a) does not hold such promise: It is only suitable for use with subjects 23 years old or less, and it has the same psychometric flaws that characterize the new Binet as a whole (see pp. 608–614).

Although this chapter focuses on short forms of the WAIS-R, it includes discussions of two brief tests that are not technically WAIS-R short forms but are used as such in a practical sense: the Slosson Intelligence Test (Jensen & Armstrong, 1985) and the Shipley Institute of Living Scale (Shipley-Hartford; Zachary, 1986). Another brief test, the Peabody Picture Vocabulary Test—Revised (PPVT-R; Dunn & Dunn, 1981), is excluded from this chapter because it measures a homogeneous cognitive skill; it is included instead in chapter 16 along with other tests that supplement the WAIS-R. The Shipley and PPVT-R ranked in the top 5 in terms of use with adult populations (see Figure 1.3 on page 11), and the Slosson ranked in the top 10 (Harrison et al., 1988).

The Bender-Gestalt, the fourth most-used test of intelligence for adults (Harrison et al., 1988), is better suited to assess visual-motor integration, the cognitive style of impulsivity/reflectivity (Oas, 1984), or even personality, than IQ. Data do not typically support its use as a valid measure of intelligence, and certainly not for adults (e.g., Armentrout, 1976). Hynd and Semrud-Clikeman dismiss the Bender-Gestalt for neuropsychological assessment because it is usually interpreted from the erroneous conception of neurological impairment as a unidimensional phenomenon (see chapter 17). Nonetheless, the Bender-Gestalt, primarily as a measure of visual-motor functioning, is integrated into case reports at the end of several chapters in Part III and Part IV of this book.

This chapter does not include several group-administered tests, despite the body of research showing that tests like the Henmon-Nelson (Klett & Watson, 1986; Watson et al., 1981), Revised Beta (Hiltonsmith, Hayman, & Kleinman, 1984; Hiltonsmith, Hayman, & Ursprung, 1982), or Wonderlic Personnel Test (Edinger, Shipley, Watkins, & Hammett, 1985) generally provide good prediction of WAIS or WAIS-R IQs (mid .40s for the nonverbal Beta, high .70s for the more verbal group tests). But even if these group tests are given individually, sometimes to serve as short forms of the WAIS-R, the examiner learns little by watching someone solve multiple-choice, paper-and-pencil items. A good clinician can learn much from observing an individual respond to verbal and manipulative items, however, even in only 10 or 20 minutes of testing time. Similarly, rich clinical information is obtainable from the self-administered Shipley-Hartford by evaluating the patient's written responses to the Abstraction subtest (see Figure 5.1 on page 146).

WHEN TO ADMINISTER SHORT FORMS OR OTHER BRIEF TESTS

When assessing adolescents and adults, clinicians sometimes have legitimate reasons to spend a half hour or less on an intellectual evaluation. Perhaps the individual was referred for a psychiatric disturbance, and only a global estimate of IQ is needed in the context of a complete personality evaluation. Or the person was given a thorough clinical or neuropsychological evaluation within the past several years, and a quick check of current intellectual status is desired. Perhaps large groups of individuals need to be screened for potential educational or neurological impairment to determine which areas need a thorough follow-up. Or the time spent with a client is limited by practical constraints, and intelligence is but one of several areas (vocational interests, educational achievement, adaptive behavior, special abilities, personality development) requiring evaluation. Or any similar circumstances in which the clinicians' goals are *not:* (a) to categorize the individual's intelligence into a specific level of functioning such as retarded, gifted, or (in the case of learning disabilities assessment) "normal"; (b) to make neuropsychological or clinical inferences about the person's ability profile; or (c) to diagnose cognitive disorders. Brief tests are also ideal for use in research investigations, where an individual's precise score is less important than group performance. But King and King (1982) far overstate the case when they argue that "perhaps the most valuable and only justifiable use of short forms is for research purposes" (p. 436).

When brief intellectual assessment is called for, some clinicians, perhaps naively, administer short tests with imaginary psychometric properties; as noted, some examiners even use the Bender-Gestalt to assess IQ, while others have for years relied on the IQs generated by the Slosson Intelligence Test. Reynolds, Willson, and Clark (1983) admonish clinicians who select tests like the Slosson in situations where brief intellectual assessment is appropriate: "Short forms of major intelligence scales are clearly superior to such measures: they are typically better normed, more reliable, [and] have greater depth and breadth of research backing" (p. 111).

Reynolds et al. (1983) rightly suggest that a short form of a major test battery be used. For adolescents and adults, WAIS-R short forms are the best available tools to meet this need. However, it is desirable for examiners to have access to brief tests that were developed from the outset to provide psychometrically sound estimates of IQ based on a short administration time. The forthcoming K-BIT may fill such a need, as may other well-designed instruments of the future.

Short forms of the WAIS-R are, by definition, after-the-fact tests whose psychometric properties are derived from data on complete WAIS-R administrations. Indeed, virtually all short form research is based on abbreviated scores extrapolated from the whole battery; rarely are groups of individuals administered just a short form. When short forms are administered to research subjects, as in Scarr and Weinberg's (1976) landmark adoption study of black children by white parents (see p. 42), the IQ estimates are simply treated as IQs. No effort is usually expended to study the psychometric properties of the abbreviated test.

CONVENTIONAL WAIS-R SHORT FORMS

Aside from factor analysis, the abbreviation of Wechsler's multitask batteries has received the most attention from psychometric researchers, even as far away as South Africa (Pieters & Sieberhagen, 1986) and Denmark (Kandel et al., 1988). Indeed, articles on short forms by Silverstein (1982a) and Reynolds et al. (1983)

appeared in print before most clinicians were aware that the WAIS-R was available for use! Nonetheless, the proliferation of examiners who use brief tests with poor norms is reason enough to be thankful to the Wechsler short form researchers.

I, too, have always had an interest in developing short forms, starting with the WPPSI nearly 20 years ago (Kaufman, 1972) and extending to the present day with the K-ABC and WAIS-R (Kaufman & Applegate, 1988; Kaufman & Ishikuma, 1989). I once attended a meeting in the 1970s to determine the fate of a would-be publication. I suggested that we publish only four of the six subscales of the proposed battery, believing that two of the subscales assessed maturational development, not intelligence. I was quickly admonished facetiously by Dr. Alexander Wesman to "please wait until *after* we publish the test before developing a short form for it."

Current Trends in WAIS-R Short Form Development

There has been a subtle change in the predominant type of short form research conducted on the 1955 WAIS and the revised battery. Many WAIS short form articles involved efforts to discover the "best" brief battery for specialized populations such as psychiatric inpatients (Robertson, Steinmeyer, & Goff, 1980; Stricker, Merbaum, & Tangeman, 1969). That approach was flawed because short forms developed for a specific, atypical population do not generalize well to other specific populations, even ones with the same "label" but from a different part of the country or spanning a different age range. WAIS-R researchers have tended to validate with special populations specific brief tests with known psychometric properties, selected by conscientious researchers (Reynolds et al., 1983; Silverstein, 1982a) from data on the large, normal standardization sample.

The sections that follow examine research on several of these well-known brief

WAIS-Rs and also treat contemporary issues in short form development—for example, the use of "split-half" abbreviated batteries. In addition, I present data on three new *very* brief WAIS-R short forms that I developed with a colleague (Kaufman & Ishikuma, 1989): a dyad, triad, and tetrad, each of which takes less than 20 minutes to administer.

Silverstein's Two-Subtest and Four-Subtest WAIS-R Short Forms

Probably the most prodigious and innovative researcher in this field is Arthur Silverstein, who has developed Wechsler short forms for more than 20 years and has been instrumental in advancing psychometric technology in this area (Silverstein, 1971, 1984a, 1984b, 1985b). He has proposed the use of two different abbreviated WAIS-Rs (Silverstein, 1982a), both of which have rich clinical histories based on previous Wechsler scales.

The first is the Vocabulary-Block Design dyad, composed of the one Verbal and one Performance subtest that is generally the most reliable task, and the best measure of *g*, on its respective scale. This very abbreviated Wechsler battery has been used in numerous large-scale investigations conducted by the Public Health Service (e.g., Sells, 1966) and was investigated for the WISC and WAIS by Silverstein (1967a, 1967b).

The second of Silverstein's WAIS-R short forms adds one Verbal and one Performance subtest to the popular dyad to maintain the equality of verbal and nonverbal skills in the assessment of intelligence: Vocabulary-Arithmetic-Block Design-Picture Arrangement. This particular combination of four subtests is identical to the tetrad selected by Doppelt (1956) for the 1955 WAIS, and by me for the WISC-R (Kaufman, 1976a).

V-BD had the highest correlation of any dyad with WAIS-R Full Scale (.91) and had an excellent split-half reliability coefficient of .94 (Silverstein, 1982a). The V-A-BD-PA tetrad had the same .94 reliability coefficient as the dyad, but was more valid (.95). Silverstein (1982a) noted that his chosen four-subtest short form did not even rank among the top 10 tetrads, but he selected it anyway because of its clinical, practical, historical, and empirical virtues. In the past, many researchers have selected a short form simply because it was the very highest correlate of Full Scale IQ, even if that combination of tasks was a clinical hodgepodge (composed, for example, of one Performance and three Verbal tasks). Silverstein (1982a) pointed out that the validity of V-A-BD-PA trailed the coefficient of the very best tetrad by less than .01, a difference of no practical consequence.

In a subsequent paper, Silverstein (1985b) applied some complex formulas to allow for differences among the nine age groups and then examined the psychometric properties of his short forms of the WAIS-R for each age group separately. Validities ranged from .89 to .93 for the dyad and from .93 to .96 for the tetrad. Reliability coefficients for both abbreviated batteries were in the .93 to .95 range for virtually every age group. These analyses supported the use of V-BD and V-A-BD-PA for all normal individuals within the WAIS-R's 16–74 age range. However, the advisability of administering V-BD to black individuals is open to question (see pp. 162–163).

Cross-Validation of Silverstein's Short Forms

The validity of these short forms has been explored for abnormal populations as well. Some illustrative studies from the burgeoning literature have compared the validity of Silverstein's (1982a) two-subtest and four-subtest short forms using samples of low-functioning adults (Haynes, 1985), elderly patients referred for suspected dementia (Margolis, Taylor, & Greenlief, 1986), vocational rehabilitation clients (Banken & Ban-

ken, 1987; Clayton, Sapp, O'Sullivan, & Hall, 1986), psychiatric patients (Thompson, Howard, & Anderson, 1986), and brain-impaired patients (Roth, Hughes, Monkowski, & Crossen, 1984).

These investigations, as well as studies of just the V-BD dyad (Haynes, 1983; Ryan, 1983) or just V-A-BD-PA (Ryan, Georgemiller, & McKinney, 1984), have come to the same general conclusion: Both short forms are valid for abnormal populations (correlations with Full Scale of about .90 or higher) but they *misclassify* the IQ level of substantial percentages of individuals and should be used *only* for screening purposes.

The four-subtest brief WAIS-R is typically more valid than V-BD, but it too misclassifies about 15% to 40% of mentally retarded, emotionally disturbed, physically handicapped, psychiatric, or elderly patients (e.g., Clayton et al., 1986; Margolis et al., 1986). Probably clinicians and researchers place too much weight on the "misclassification index," because so-called errors in classifying a person's level of intelligence can occur even if the short form IQ estimate is only 1 point away from the actual IQ (e.g., 69 versus 70).

Such "errors" occur as a simple consequence of the errors of measurement in *any* test—even one as reliable as the complete WAIS-R. Many misclassifications of a person's intelligence level would occur from one administration of the complete WAIS-R to the second administration of the whole battery, even if the person was tested twice over a short time interval and could, magically, be spared the impact of practice, fatigue, or boredom.

Silverstein (1985a) discredits the three criteria used to evaluate short forms that Resnick and Entin formally proposed in 1971: (1) high validity coefficients; (2) similar mean IQs yielded by short form and complete test; and (3) few misclassifications. He argues cogently that the first criterion is easily met by selecting the short form in the first place; that the second criterion is irrelevant and easily correctable (by adding or subtracting a few points to a person's estimated IQ whenever the small differences in mean IQs reach statistical significance); and that the misclassification criterion *must* be failed whenever a perfect 1.0 correlation is reduced, even to .95.

Silverstein's arguments are persuasive. Nevertheless, research using rigorous criteria to evaluate Wechsler short forms is valuable. Although misclassifications must be a statistical given of every abbreviated scale, it is important for clinicians to keep reading this fact throughout the literature to help ensure that short forms are not used arbitrarily or carelessly as the measure of intelligence in a diagnostic battery. The percentage of misclassifications is a practical reminder to examiners to use WAIS-R short forms for screening purposes and not to overvalue the obtained IQ estimate.

Thompson's Key Investigation of Silverstein's Brief WAIS-Rs

Thompson (1987) and his colleagues (Thompson et al., 1986) have contributed greatly to the validation of Silverstein's (1982a) short forms and delineated the range of their usefulness by conducting a long-needed study that needs replication but that still has dramatic implications for clinicians. Researchers have long conducted short form research after the fact. Rather than administer just the two or four subtests constituting the brief battery to a fresh sample, the investigators (myself included) have analyzed data from samples administered a complete test in the usual order. The various possible short forms are then evaluated against the criterion of the whole battery, but always on a "what if" basis: What if only the V-BD dyad had been given? What if a particular tetrad had been given?

But Thompson was the first to carefully research the question of what might happen differently if *just* the short form is given. Will the subject have a different level of motivation when taking only a few subtests than when

tested for an hour and a half? What about the ability to sustain attention and concentration for a short period of time compared to a long testing session? Exactly how much time is saved when particular short forms are given? These are precisely the questions that Thompson et al. (1986) addressed when they compared the validity of Silverstein's (1982a) two- and four-subtest short forms with a psychiatric sample of 90 inpatients.

Thompson and his colleagues divided their sample of 45 males and 45 females into three subsamples of 30 patients each. To one subsample, they administered V-BD as the first two subtests, followed by the remaining nine WAIS-R subtests in standard order; to a second subsample, they gave V-A-BD-PA as the first four tasks, followed by the rest of the WAIS-R; and to the third subsample they administered a standard WAIS-R. They found that the patients who were given V-BD as the first two subtests obtained significantly overestimated short form IQs when compared to their actual Full Scale IQs. There was some overestimation, but significantly less, when Vocabulary and Block Design were embedded in the total WAIS-R (i.e., given in the standard order as the fifth and sixth subtests, respectively).

Thompson et al. inferred from these results that the patients were more motivated and attended better to the task at hand when given just the two short form subtests. However, when V-BD were given in the standard format, precisely in the middle of the 11-subtest WAIS-R, their attention, concentration, and perhaps motivation lagged to some extent. If these results are replicated, then the V-BD dyad—when given alone as an abbreviated WAIS-R—will yield uncharacteristically high estimated IQs. This overestimate may be especially large for groups who are known to fatigue easily or have difficulty sustaining attention, such as elderly people or those with brain damage (Thompson, 1987).

Interestingly, this bias due to order of administration was *not* found by Thompson et al.

(1986) for Silverstein's (1982a) four-subtest WAIS-R short form. However, V-A-BD-PA overestimated IQ significantly more for males (4 points) than females (1 point). Thompson's separate validation of the WAIS-R short forms for females and males was another important contribution inasmuch as most previous WAIS-R studies (often conducted in VA hospitals) included a preponderance of men.

These investigators found significantly fewer intelligence level misclassifications for females (27%) than males (53%) with V-A-BD-PA, but suggested that the difference was due to the female patients' lower IQs (82 versus 91 for male patients). Haynes (1985) observed that only 15% of his low-functioning clients (mean IQ=66) were misclassified by Silverstein's four-subtest WAIS-R, a much better rate of agreement than has been reported by most other investigators for samples with higher IQs.

Administration Time of Silverstein's Short Forms

Thompson and his colleagues (1986) reported an average administration time for their Low Average sample (mean IQ=86.5) of 19 minutes for V-BD, 35 minutes for V-A-BD-PA, and 77 minutes for the complete battery. However, the administration time of a Wechsler battery seems to be a function of the intelligence level of the subjects (see pages 100–101). Ward, Selby, and Clark (1987) reported a mean WAIS-R administration time of 69 minutes for their low-functioning clinical sample (mean IQ=76.9), whereas Ryan and Rosenberg (1984a) found an average testing time of 91 minutes for their neurological and psychiatric patients with an average IQ of 90.7.

Since Ryan and Rosenberg (1984a) and Ward et al. (1987) also reported mean administration times for each separate WAIS-R subtest (see Table 4.1), I have computed the estimated administration times for both of Silverstein's short forms based on data from these three diverse clinical samples. These results are pre-sented in Table 5.1, along with administration times for four additional brief versions of the WAIS-R that are discussed later in this chapter.

As shown in Table 5.1, Silverstein's (1982a) WAIS-R dyad saved about an hour of administration time in each study, representing about a 75% savings of total WAIS-R administration time. His tetrad saved about 40 to 45 minutes of testing, effectively halving administration time. Note that even though total WAIS-R administration time varied substantially from study to study, the percentage of time actually saved was a virtual constant for each specific short form, regardless of the nature of the sample.

Reynolds' Four-Subtest WAIS-R Short Form

Reynolds et al. (1983) were sensitive to administration time when they developed their four-subtest WAIS-R short form. They followed the guidelines for short form selection that I recommended when constructing brief versions of the WPPSI and WISC-R (Kaufman, 1972, 1976a): Select two Verbal and two Performance subtests that (a) correlate highly with their respective scales (V or P), (b) measure a variety of mental processes, (c) are quick to administer and score, and (d) form a clinically interesting unit. They chose the Verbal dyad of Information–Arithmetic and the Performance dyad of Picture Completion–Block Design to constitute their short form of the WAIS-R.

Empirically, Vocabulary–Arithmetic was superior to Reynolds et al.'s chosen Verbal dyad, but they felt that I-A met the guidelines for short forms more completely. They rejected Vocabulary because of its long administration time and difficult scoring. Similarly, they chose Picture Completion–Block Design over the equally strong Picture Arrangement–Block Design dyad because of the long administration time of both PA and BD. They also found PC appealing because its lack of a motor component made it a good complement to BD.

Reynolds et al.'s (1983) arguments are sound, and their four-subtest WAIS-R is quite appealing.In retrospect, I didn't follow my own guidelines well when I chose the V-A-BD-PA tetrad for the WISC-R short form (Kaufman, 1976a)! Similarly, that same tetrad for the WAIS-R, although chosen systematically by Silverstein (1982a) and validated extensively by him and other investigators, falls far short of Reynolds's short form as an effective screening device. There is no good reason to include three of the

longest subtests in the WAIS-R as part of a four-subtest "short" form, or to include a task that takes as long to score as Vocabulary.

The Reynolds short form is reported to have reliability and validity coefficients of .85 to .90 across the 16- to 74-year age range (mean = .88 for both), values substantially less than the coefficients in the mid-.90s for Silverstein's (1982a, 1985b) tetrad (mean reliability = .94; mean validity = .95). Differences of that magnitude made no sense, so my colleague (Ish-

TABLE 5.1   Administration times for selected WAIS-R short forms based on data from three clinical samples

WAIS-R Short-Form	MEAN ADMINISTRATION TIME (IN MINUTES)			
	Ward et al. (1987) IQ = 77	Thompson et al. (1986) IQ = 86	Ryan & Rosenberg (1984a) IQ = 91	Mean
Silverstein's				
V-BD	16.5	18.8	26.0	20.4
V-A-BD-PA	30.4	34.6	43.2	36.1
Reynolds's				
I-A-PC-BD	26.0	—	31.1	28.6
Kaufman's				
I-PC	11.6	—	12.9	12.2
I-PC-DSp	15.0	—	16.9	16.0
S-A-PC-DSy	17.9	—	19.8	18.8
Time for Total WAIS-R:	68.8	76.9	91.4	79.0
Percent Time Reduction				
Silverstein's				
V-BD	76.0%	75.6%	71.6%	74.4%
V-A-BD-PA	55.8%	55.0%	52.7%	54.5%
Reynolds's				
I-A-PC-BD	62.2%	—	66.0%	64.1%
Kaufman's				
I-PC	83.1%	—	85.9%	84.5%
I-PC-DSp	78.2%	—	81.5%	79.8%
S-A-PC-DSy	74.0%	—	78.3%	76.2%

NOTE: Thompson et al. reported mean times only for Silverstein's short forms and the total battery.

ikuma, personal communication, 1988) recomputed the reliabilities and validities presented by Reynolds et al. (1983) and found the values reported in the article to be too low. Applying the same formulas used by Silverstein (1985b) for his tetrad, Ishikuma found the reliability and validity coefficients for Reynolds's I-A-PC-BD short form (average values of .94 for each) to be quite similar in magnitude to the values observed for Silverstein's V-A-BD-PA. According to Willson (personal communication, 1988), the low values reported in their article may have been due to a column being inadvertently omitted from their table, and/or their use of a different formula than the conventional one used by Silverstein.

Despite these problems, the Silverstein and Reynolds tetrads are empirically comparable when the same formulas are applied to both. Although Silverstein's four-subtest WAIS-R has been validated far more extensively than has Reynolds's, Ryan (1985) found strong validation for the Reynolds tetrad (83% correct classifications, .94 validity coefficient) for 70 male neurology inpatients. He also reported substantial correlations between short form IQ and several neuropsychological tests (e.g., the Halstead Category Test), coefficients that were at least as impressive as the values obtained for the Full Scale.

Table 5.1 reveals that the Reynolds short form takes about 25 to 30 minutes to administer, compared to about 30 to 45 for Silverstein's four-subtest WAIS-R. Reynolds's abbreviated battery reflects a savings of approximately 65% in administration time, compared to a 55% savings for the historically relevant—but perhaps less practical—Silverstein tetrad of V-A-BD-PA.

Amazingly Short Forms of the WAIS-R

Few clinicians or researchers would dispute the contention that WAIS-R short forms are primarily useful as screening instruments, regardless of how high into the .90s their validities and reliabilities may be. They are intended neither for diagnostic purposes nor to assess thoroughly the range and breadth of a person's intellectual functioning. Given the goals of short form administration, it seems counterproductive to select subtests that have subjective scoring systems or numerous timed items of 1 to 2 minutes apiece.

If an examiner must sharply reduce testing time to the extent that he or she can give only two subtests, it seems unwise to pick Vocabulary and Block Design, tasks with built-in headaches. Why select subtests that Thompson (1987; Thompson et al., 1986) has shown overestimate IQ when given alone—under conditions of optimum attention and motivation—rather than embedded in the full battery? Even though, as Silverstein (1985a) has noted, it is simple to subtract a few points from a person's estimated IQ if a short form is shown consistently to overpredict intelligence, why start with a brief test with known biases? Further, individuals differ in the degree to which their motivation and concentration fluctuate as a function of when in the test sequence a particular subtest is administered. Such differences are not addressed by subtracting a constant value from all estimated IQs.

Because of these concerns, I and a colleague (Kaufman & Ishikuma, 1989) developed some WAIS-R short forms that were extremely short. The available data on subtest administration time (Ryan & Rosenberg, 1984a; Ward et al., 1987) allowed us to determine objectively which tasks take the least time and to select subtests accordingly. For our dyad, we placed the added constraint that both tasks be given at or near the beginning of the test battery to reduce the impact of motivation and attention on the estimated IQs. This factor was also considered when choosing a triad, but not a tetrad; Thompson et al. (1986) showed that it did not affect the magnitude of the estimated IQs whether the Silverstein four-subtest brief form was given first, or embedded in the standard order of administration.

In choosing these brief WAIS-Rs, we tried to meet the criteria that I have advocated for short form development. We simply placed the greatest premium on the criterion that stipulates selection of subtests that can be administered and scored quickly. Data from Ryan and Rosenberg's (1984) and Ward et al.'s (1987) administration time studies identified two subsets of WAIS-R tasks: five that were consistently long to administer, requiring an average time (across both investigations) of 9 to 11 minutes; and six that were relatively short to give, averaging 3½ to 6½ minutes of administration time (see Table 4.1).

The long subtests—Vocabulary, Comprehension, Block Design, Picture Arrangement, Object Assembly—were virtually eliminated from consideration when we selected short forms. Instead, we focused on the four Verbal and two Performance tasks that are quick to give: Information, Digit Span, Similarities, Arithmetic, Picture Completion, and Digit Symbol (Kaufman & Ishikuma, 1989). Similarities was retained, despite its 2-1-0 scoring system, because the items are generally easy to score objectively, unlike many Comprehension and Vocabulary items.

The Quick Dyad: Information–Picture Completion

We selected the first two WAIS-R subtests administered for our dyad, Information and Picture Completion. This brief form is almost as valid as the popular V-BD short form (average correlation with Full Scale of .88 for the standardization sample, compared to .91 for V-BD). Although no combination of one Verbal and one Performance subtest can match the astonishing .94 reliability of the V-BD dyad, I-PC is nonetheless adequately reliable. Each subtest alone has an average split-half coefficient above .80 (Wechsler, 1981, Table 10), and together the I-PC dyad has a good average reliability coefficient of .90. The value is below .90 for

ages 16 to 24, but equals .90–.93 for ages 25 and above. The coefficients range from .86 at ages 16–17 to .93 for 65- to 69-year-olds.

The psychometric properties for the I-PC dyad are quite good, especially for a screening test that has an average administration time of only about 12 minutes, representing a savings of about 85% of the time it takes to give a complete WAIS-R (see Table 5.1). In addition, concerns regarding optimal motivation and concentration, stemming from Thompson et al.'s (1986) data on Silverstein's V-BD dyad, do not apply to I-PC. These are the first two subtests given whenever the complete WAIS-R is administered.

To use the I-PC dyad, simply administer these subtests under standard conditions. Then compute the *age-corrected* scaled scores for each subtest, using the supplementary norms tables in Appendix D of the WAIS-R Manual (Wechsler, 1981, Table 20). Finally, enter Table 5.2 (taken from Kaufman & Ishikuma, 1989) with the adolescent's or adult's sum of scaled scores on the two subtests to determine the estimated Full Scale IQ. This obtained value has an average standard error of measurement of 4.7 points and an average standard error of estimate of 7.4 points. (The standard error of estimate reflects the accuracy of the estimated IQ as a predictor of actual IQ.)

The Quick Triad: Information–Picture Completion–Digit Span

I have usually advocated equal numbers of Verbal and Performance subtests in Wechsler short forms, even for the WAIS-R, which includes one more V than P subtest. However, clinicians who emphasize the factor structure of Wechsler's tests, rather than his dichotomous division of intelligence, might find it useful to administer a short form that represents each of the three factors that repeatedly occur for Wechsler's scales in analyses of normal or abnormal individuals. Consequently, we developed a very brief triad of the WAIS-R composed of Information,

Picture Completion, and Digit Span (Kaufman & Ishikuma, 1989).

These are the first three subtests given during the standard WAIS-R administration, so the impact of motivation and attention-concentration will not adversely affect estimated IQs for the triad, just as they did not for the I-PC dyad. Each subtest chosen for the brief triad is an excellent measure of one Wechsler factor across the 16- to 74-year span (see Table 8.7): Verbal Comprehension (Information), Perceptual Organization (Picture Completion), and Freedom from Distractibility (Digit Span).

The addition of a third WAIS-R subtest reflects a slight improvement in the reliability found for the dyad, yielding a mean coefficient of .91 for the triad, and an average standard error of measurement of 4.4 points (compared to values of .88 and 4.7 for the dyad). The validity increases by a substantial amount, from .88 to .92 on the average (Kaufman & Ishikuma, 1989). The improved reliability and validity of the triad, compared to that of the I-PC dyad, seem to offset the additional 3½ to 4 minutes of administration time (see Table 5.1) for examiners who prefer the three-factor approach over Wechsler's two-scale system.

Overall, the triad takes an average of 16 minutes to give, saving 80% of the administration time for the complete battery. The estimated Full Scale WAIS-R IQs may be obtained by entering Table 5.2 with the sum of a person's three *age-corrected* scaled scores (Wechsler, 1981, Table 20). This obtained short-form IQ has an average standard error of estimate of 6.4 points (Kaufman & Ishikuma, 1989).

The Quick Tetrad: Similarities-Arithmetic-Picture Completion-Digit Symbol

In choosing a tetrad, the order of administration of the subtests was not a factor since Thompson et al. (1986) did not find Silverstein's (1982a) tetrad to be influenced significantly by motivational or attentional variables. Consequently, we used Reynolds et al.'s (1983) table showing the correlations of each Verbal dyad and each

Performance dyad with their respective IQs. One goal of our tetrad, in addition to quick administration time, was to select a Verbal dyad that correlated substantially with V-IQ, and a Performance dyad that was an excellent measure of P-IQ (Kaufman & Ishikuma, 1989). It was unnecessary to consider the correlation of various tetrads with Full Scale IQ when selecting the short form; Silverstein (1982b) has shown that even a randomly selected WAIS-R tetrad will correlate quite well (.93) with the Full Scale.

Only two Performance tasks can be administered briefly, and fortunately this dyad correlated .68, on the average, with P-IQ; the only dyads with a better prediction of P-IQ were PC-BD (.70) and the lengthy BD-PA (.69). Hence, Picture Completion–Digit Symbol is not only a quick dyad, but it satisfied one of our most important empirical criteria. Had it been a poor predictor of P-IQ, we would have selected the same PC-BD Performance dyad chosen by Reynolds et al. (1986), despite Block Design's long administration time.

Of the six possible verbal dyads (taking the four short Verbal subtests two at a time), two (A-DSp and S-DSp) were poor predictors of Verbal IQ. The remaining four dyads were comparable in their relationship to V-IQ (correlations of .82–.84). We selected Similarities–Arithmetic mostly for clinical reasons concerning the mental processes assessed (especially reasoning ability) and its "fit" with the PC-DSy dyad as a cohesive unit (Kaufman & Ishikuma, 1989). The I-A and I-S dyads were also appealing, but were rejected primarily because Information takes close to 7 minutes to give versus 5-minute administration times for Similarities and Arithmetic.

S-A-PC-DSy requires an average of about 19 minutes to give, about a 75% savings of time (see Table 5.1). It has an average reliability coefficient of .93 and validity coefficient of .95, excellent values that are entirely comparable to the coefficients obtained by Silverstein (1982a) and Reynolds et al. (1983) for their longer

TABLE 5.2   Estimated WAIS-R Full Scale IQ equivalents of sums of scaled scores on three very short forms of the WAIS-R

Sum of Scaled Scores	ESTIMATED FULL SCALE IQ			Sum of Scaled Scores	ESTIMATED FULL SCALE IQ		
	2-Test[a]	3-Test[b]	4-Test[c]		2-Test[a]	3-Test[b]	4-Test[c]
2	48			34	141	108	90
3	51	43		35	144	111	92
4	54	45	42	36	146	113	94
5	57	48	44	37	149	115	95
6	59	50	46	38	152	117	97
7	62	52	47	39	155	119	98
8	65	54	49	40	158	121	100
9	68	56	50	41		123	102
10	71	58	52	42		125	103
11	74	60	54	43		127	105
12	77	62	55	44		129	106
13	80	64	57	45		132	108
14	83	66	58	46		134	110
15	86	69	60	47		136	111
16	88	71	62	48		138	113
17	91	73	63	49		140	114
18	94	75	65	50		142	116
19	97	77	66	51		144	118
20	100	79	68	52		146	119
21	103	81	70	53		148	121
22	106	83	71	54		150	122
23	109	85	73	55		153	124
24	112	87	74	56		155	126
25	115	90	76	57		157	127
26	117	92	78	58			129
27	120	94	79	59			130
28	123	96	81	60			132
29	126	98	82	61			134
30	129	100	84	62			135
31	132	102	86	63			137
32	135	104	87	64			138
33	138	106	89	65			140

TABLE 5.2   (Continued)

Sum of Scaled Scores	Estimated Full Scale IQ			Sum of Scaled Scores	Estimated Full Scale IQ		
	2-Test[a]	3-Test[b]	4-Test[c]		2-Test[a]	3-Test[b]	4-Test[c]
66			142	72			151
67			143	73			153
68			145	74			154
69			146	75			156
70			148	76			158
71			150				

[a]Information + Picture Completion
[b]Information + Digit Span + Picture Completion
[c]Arithmetic + Similarities + Picture Completion + Digit Symbol
NOTE: Enter this table only with *age-corrected* scaled scores. When the estimated IQ is less than 45 or more than 150, report it as "Less than 45" or "More than 150," respectively. This table is from Kaufman and Ishikuma (1989).

WAIS-R tetrads. Out proposed four-subtest short form takes a shorter time to give than Silverstein's *dyad,* and takes about half the administration time of his tetrad; it saves about 10 minutes when compared to Reynolds et al.'s brief WAIS-R. Hence, S-A-PC-DSy is a strong alternative to the more popular abbreviated WAIS-Rs whenever testing time is really at a premium—for example, when many individuals need to be assessed by a good measure of intelligence, but psychodiagnosis is not at issue. In such instances, even the 12-minute I-PC short form might be a reasonable choice. Note that all three of the very brief WAIS-Rs take less than 20 minutes to administer (see Table 5.1).

Table 5.2 allows computation of estimated WAIS-R Full Scale IQs from the short tetrad when entered with the sum of the person's *age-corrected* scaled scores on S, A, PC, and DSy (Wechsler, 1981, Table 20). The short form IQ thus obtained has an average standard error of measurement of 4.0 points and a standard error of estimate of 5.5 points (Kaufman & Ishikuma, 1989).

ALTERNATE APPROACHES AND ISSUES REGARDING WAIS-R SHORT FORMS

Several additional lines of research have occupied much journal space and are discussed here briefly: Feingold's proposed dyad of Information and Vocabulary; Cyr and Brooker's emphasis on short form reliability; Satz and Mogel's split-half short forms; Cella's "modified" WAIS-R; and Silverstein's correction of validity coefficients.

Feingold's Information–Vocabulary Dyad

Feingold (1982, 1983a, 1983b) was impressed by the high reliabilities of the WAIS Information and Vocabulary subtests and compared the criterion-related validity of these subtests (alone and in tandem) to Verbal IQ, Full Scale IQ, and measures of college aptitude. He consistently found that the WAIS I-V dyad correlated about as high as (and sometimes higher than) various global scales, including WAIS FS-IQ. The pair of subtests together was better than either one alone, but adding a third subtest did not improve prediction. Feingold (1983a, 1983b) considered his findings probably generalizable to the WAIS-R, and cautiously proposed that the I-V dyad be used in college settings by guidance counselors or psychologists to obtain a quick estimate of academic ability. His suggestion is sensible for white college students, but will unfairly penalize black, Hispanic, Asian American or other minority adolescents and young adults.

In addition, the WAIS-R I-V dyad is useful *only* when the goal is predicting a white, middle-class person's likely success in a formal educational setting. Alternative uses of short forms mandate representation of both the Verbal and Performance Scales in the abbreviated battery and reliance on at least some tasks that are not saturated with cultural and achievement variables. Otherwise, the estimate of the person's intelligence will be inaccurate, and will not reflect Wechsler's approach to mental assessment.

An extreme instance of biased intellectual assessment is the contention that the complete Verbal Scale should be used as a WAIS or WAIS-R short form (Gibson, 1981; Ryan & Rosenberg, 1984b; Wildman & Wildman, 1977). This suggestion makes sense for patients with "marked visual difficulties and/or severe motor dysfunction of the upper extremities" (Ryan & Rosenberg, 1984b, p. 306), but for no one with the physical ability to take some or all of the Performance subtests. Yet, in the case of visually or motor-impaired individuals, it is axiomatic that a clinician give only the Verbal Scale. Why bother with short form research, especially with samples of psychiatric patients with adequate visual-motor skills? Is it necessary to conduct short form research with the Performance Scale to support its use for hearing-impaired individuals?

This line of research neglects important clinical and psychological factors and misuses statistics—namely the well-known fact that Verbal IQ correlates in the mid-.90s with Full Scale IQ.

Cyr and Brooker's Stress on Short Form Reliability

Cyr and Brooker (1984) have pointed out that many short form researchers have focused on the validity of brief tests and have ignored the reliability of the abbreviated battery. Cyr and Brooker therefore used formulas that took into account both the validity and reliability of various dyads, triads, and tetrads of WAIS-R subtests when selecting their short forms (Cyr and Brooker, 1984) and when developing appropriate conversion tables (Brooker & Cyr, 1986).

Certainly attending closely to reliability was wise; I have also used reliability and validity data conjointly to select short forms of the K-ABC (Kaufman & Applegate, 1988). Further, Mittenberg and Ryan (1984) offered an interesting analysis of what happens to WAIS-R Full Scale reliability when various numbers of subtests are omitted from the battery.

But Brooker and Cyr, by attending so closely to reliability and validity when choosing the very best combinations of WAIS-R subtests, seemed to forget clinical and common sense. Their triad comprised Information, Vocabulary, and Block Design—a group of subtests that overlaps greatly in assessing mental processes (I and V both measure a person's fund of information, long-term memory, and acquired knowledge), and that includes no measure of the distractibility factor. Brooker and Cyr's tetrad (V-A-S-BD) is three-quarters verbal. So much for the rigid use of formulas!

Satz-Mogel Abbreviations of the WAIS-R

Satz and Mogel (1962) abbreviated the WAIS by administering Digit Span and Digit Symbol in their entirety, while giving every third item on Information, Picture Completion, and Vocabulary and every second item on the remaining six subtests. This approach to short form development has been commonly researched (Dinning & Craft, 1983; Evans, 1985; Nelson, Edinger, & Wallace, 1978) and has probably been used fairly widely in clinical practice (Cella, Jacobsen, & Hymowitz, 1985). Unlike the method of selecting several subtests for a short form, the Satz-Mogel approach yields estimated V-, P-, and FS-IQs and a complete profile of scaled scores.

Silverstein (1982c) reported correlations of .95 between estimated and actual WAIS-R Full Scale IQs for the standardization sample when using the Satz-Mogel short form, along with .94 and .89 correlations for the V- and P-IQs, respectively. He reported similar values for the 1955 WAIS. Evans (1985) found virtually the identical correlations for a sample of 81 normal adults tested by graduate students in an assessment course, and also reported coefficients between the curtailed and complete subtests. These values ranged from .66 to .88 (median = .80). Coefficients were lowest for Picture Arrangement (.66) and Similarities (.74).

The Satz-Mogel method of abbreviating Wechsler's tests is questionable, a point I have discussed elsewhere regarding Yudin's (1966) similar abbreviation of the WISC-R (Kaufman, 1979b, pp. 206–207). It is highly unlikely that norms obtained on a complete administration of a Wechsler battery are applicable to scores produced by administering every second or third item of a subtest. Thompson et al. (1986) showed that subjects do better on the V-BD dyad when these subtests are given first rather than in their usual position midway through the WAIS-R. They speculated that motivation and attention are more nearly optimal when the short form is given alone than when it is embedded in the complete battery. In effect, they are suggesting that the WAIS-R norms for Vocabulary and Block Design are valid for these tasks when they are given as part of the long, complete battery but not when the dyad is given in isolation.

Perhaps the norms for several Wechsler subtests are likewise invalid when only one-half or one-third of the relevant items are given. But instead of being too "soft," like the V and BD norms when these tasks are administered first, the norms for the shortened subtests are probably too "steep." Some Wechsler subtests function as "learning" tasks during a test administration. Practice on easy items facilitates performance on harder items. Progressing gradually from easy to hard items helps ensure success on each more difficult item. This learning takes place most clearly on subtests that do not emphasize knowledge of facts, but instead require the examinee to learn how to solve different types of items. The best examples are Similarities, Picture Arrangement, Block Design, Picture Completion, and Digit Span. All but Digit Span are abbreviated in the Satz-Mogel short form.

Thus, examinees who are administered every third Picture Completion item or every second Block Design item may not do as well when they come to the harder items as they would have if they were shaped gradually to learn the response set by taking every item. This question is answerable by a good research design, but no studies have focused on administration of only a Satz-Mogel short form to subjects; as with the dyad or tetrad methodology, research on the split-half short forms of the WAIS or WAIS-R invariably analyzes data obtained on complete test batteries.

I did come across some informal support for my contention when I conducted a WISC-R study with a colleague. We were trying to identify a common core of items from the 1949 WISC that were retained intact in the WISC-R in order to compare how the WISC and WISC-R standardization samples performed on identical items (Doppelt & Kaufman, 1977). This methodology helped us determine the magnitude of WISC/WISC-R IQ differences. However, we found that Similarities items could not be included in this common core, even though numerous items were retained in the WISC-R (e.g., Beer–Wine). This was because some items were much more difficult on the WISC than WISC-R due to their place in the administration sequence. For example, consider the item Cat–Mouse. On the 1949 WISC, this was the *second* item of its type (i.e., In what way are _____ and _____ alike?) to be administered. On the WISC-R, it was the *seventh* item given (because several new, easy items in the same format were added to provide a "bottom" for the WISC-R Similarities subtest). Cat–Mouse was a much easier item on the WISC-R because it appeared after the individual had "practiced" six times with comparable items.

Because of this probable practice effect on several Wechsler subtests, the validity of Satz-Mogel short forms is doubtful when their psychometric properties and estimated scores are based on data obtained for the complete battery. In addition, the split-half methodology fosters interpretation of V–P IQ discrepancies and subtest fluctuations although the correlations between the short form and long form IQs and scaled scores do *not* support profile analysis of any sort.

Evans (1985) warned that "with the exception of only a few subtests (such as Arithmetic and Vocabulary), Satz-Mogel estimates of individual subtests do not appear to yield the accuracy needed to discuss them interpretively in a psychological report" (p. 103). That is not a particularly stern warning, and Evans didn't even address the issue of interpreting V–P discrepancies—also an inadvisable practice in view of the data. But if IQ and scaled-score profiles are derived and then reported based on a Satz-Mogel administration, examiners will interpret them. (I have never understood what "cautious interpretation" means, and doubt that it means much in practice.)

In sum, if examiners need a brief WAIS-R, it is preferable to use a dyad, triad, or tetrad rather than split-half short form. These preferred abbreviated batteries produce only a single IQ; if an examiner chooses to interpret the separate scaled scores or the scatter among the subtests, he or she is at least using scores from

tasks that have been administered in their entirety, under standard conditions, without a loss of reliability or validity.

Cella's "Modified" WAIS-R

Vincent (1979) suggested a different type of abbreviation for the WAIS, recommending that the examiner save 15 to 20 minutes of testing time by adjusting the starting points of five subtests. If a person answers the first 10 Information items correctly, the examiner is instructed to begin Comprehension at Item 6, Arithmetic at Item 10, Vocabulary at Item 13, Block Design at Item 4, and Picture Arrangement at Item 3. This modified WAIS spurred other adjustments to Vincent's method (Himelstein, 1983) to enable clinicians to further shorten the WAIS. (Why save time only with examinees who can respond correctly to the first 10 Information items?)

These articles generated validation research—for example, with patients at a medical center (Jeffrey & Jeffrey, 1984) and elderly war veterans referred for psychological evaluation (Cargnello & Gurekas, 1987). All studies showed high correlations (.99+) between IQs obtained on the modified and regular WAISs. And, naturally, all studies, including Vincent's (1979), were ex post facto research designs—rescoring WAIS protocols from the files to see what would have happened if. . . . Has anyone ever actually administered a modified WAIS to a real person?

Cella (1984) integrated Vincent's and Himelstein's methods and applied them to the WAIS-R. Further, he added Similarities and Picture Completion to Vincent's list of five subtests so that in Cella's approach a total of seven WAIS-R tasks are truncated based on a person's success on Information. Following Himelstein's (1983) lead, the clinician administers Information under standard conditions and determines an examinee's scaled score. If a person obtains an Information scaled score of 7, for example, then the examiner starts that person on Item 8 for Picture Completion, Item 6 for Similarities, and so forth.

All modified starting points correspond to the Information scaled score earned by the person—in this case, 7. Examinees who answer the starting item correctly for any subtest are given full credit for all earlier items; those who fail it are administered items in reverse order until two perfect scores are obtained. This procedure permits modification of the seven WAIS-R subtests for anyone who earns a scaled score of 4 or above on Information. Cella (1984) reported correlations of .995 to .998 between the modified and actual IQs earned by 50 psychiatric patients *who were given the WAIS-R under standard conditions.* Naturally.

All of the concerns expressed about the use of Satz-Mogel short forms apply to the modified WAIS-R, and with even greater emphasis. Learning sets are built up for the subtests; if the clinician starts Comprehension at Item 9 or Picture Arrangement at Item 4, examinees are unlikely to catch on right away without the benefit of success on easy items. Further, how can one expect individuals who earn a scaled score of 6 or 8 on Information to earn at least that scaled score on six other subtests, including some on the Performance Scale? Research on scatter suggests otherwise (Kaufman, 1976b; McLean, Kaufman, & Reynolds, in press).

Why would any examiner with clinical sense start a low-functioning individual with an advanced item, depriving him or her of the confidence that comes from experiencing success? The rule allowing the administration of easier items if the starting item is failed does not help enough. Confidence may erode when an examinee fails the first item given in a new subtest, leading to possible disrupted performance on easier items. Going back to Item 1 might have been more acceptable, but administering items in reverse order may totally destroy a person's confidence before they ever reach the "confidence-building" items.

If Cella or others who advocate saving time by modifying WAIS-R starting points insist on continuing in this line of research, I implore them to start *administering* the modified WAIS-R to determine empirically how this altered administration compares to the standard administration in the scores yielded. With even greater fervor, I implore clinicians not to use the *modified* WAIS-R.

Silverstein's Correction of Validity Coefficients

Silverstein has published numerous articles on sophisticated statistical techniques concerning short form development—for example, linear equating to obtain norms and computing standard errors (Silverstein, 1984a, 1984b). One set of articles has provoked mild controversy, namely the correction of short form validity coefficients for the spuriousness that enters into the coefficients when the short form scores are derived from a complete administration of a Wechsler battery (Kaufman, 1977; McNemar, 1974; Silverstein, 1971, 1975).

Correlations between short form and full scale, when obtained from a single administration of the battery, violate a basic assumption underlying computation of the coefficients—that the respective error variances are uncorrelated. Silverstein's (1971) formula corrects for the slight spuriousness. Silverstein (1977b) concurs with my proposed resolution to the question of whether short form validity coefficients should be corrected (Kaufman, 1977): They should be adjusted when the short form is used as a replacement for the total battery (when administered in research studies, for example), but *not* when the brief version is used for screening purposes such that individuals "flagged" by the short form are likely to be given the remaining Wechsler subtests.

The preceding sections, have discussed only the *uncorrected* coefficients because most clinicians who use a WAIS-R short form do so for clinical or screening purposes and give the complete battery if the short form score (or scatter among the component subtests, or clinical observations during the brief administration) arouse any concern. In such instances, the uncorrected coefficients are the relevant indices of validity.

If, however, examiners use short forms with no intention of giving the remainder of the battery, the validity coefficients presented previously are a bit high. For Silverstein's (1982a, 1985b) dyad and tetrad, the correction is only .01; for less reliable brief WAIS-Rs, the correction is likely to be about .02 to .03. The correction is thus slight, but is something more psychometrically oriented examiners should know.

THE SLOSSON AND SHIPLEY-HARTFORD AS WAIS-R SHORT FORMS

The Slosson Intelligence Test (Jensen & Armstrong, 1985; Slosson, 1982) and Shipley Institute of Living Scales (Shipley-Hartford; Shipley, 1940; Zachary, 1986) are among the eight most commonly used tests for assessing adults (Harrison, Kaufman, Hickman, & Kaufman, 1988). Although both trailed the WAIS-R by a wide margin in popularity (see chapter 1), these two brief tests are used often enough in clinical assessment to warrant discussion. Since examiners who select either measure are bypassing the WAIS-R to opt for an IQ in just 15 to 20 minutes of testing time, these tests are, in effect, WAIS-R short forms or "potential WAIS-R surrogates" (Klett, Watson, & Hoffman, 1986, p. 344). Indeed, the Shipley norms have been so entwined with the WAIS and WAIS-R norms in their conception and development that this brief verbal and abstract thinking test is truly a WAIS-R short form.

The Slosson Intelligence Test

The Slosson, often referred to as the SIT, is organized in an old Binet age-by-age format, containing levels ranging from two *weeks* (". . . will grasp handle of spoon, rattle or like object . . .") to 27 *years* (understanding the word *anthropophagite*). The item types are straight from the old Binet and Gesell Developmental Schedules. The Slosson may be dropping in popularity as a measure of adult intelligence; it ranked as the fifth most popular test in the 1970s (Brown & McGuire, 1976) and as the eighth most popular in the 1980s (Harrison et al., 1988). The Slosson was actually developed as a short form of the old Stanford-Binet and its most recent norms (gathered from 1968 to 1977, referred to as the "1981 norms," and "expanded" in 1985) represent an attempt to equate the Slosson with the 1972 Binet. But the old Binet is no more, so users of the Slosson for adolescents and adults should evaluate the brief test in terms of its effectiveness as a short form of the WAIS-R.

The 1963 version of the Slosson was quite popular despite its use of the outmoded ratio IQ; the restandardized, but not revised, 1981 norms edition continued to offer this psychometric dinosaur, although tables of standard scores became available subsequent to Richard Slosson's death (Jensen & Armstrong, 1985). The test includes a variety of item types, mostly verbal, such as knowledge of facts (how many feet in a mile, age 15-2), arithmetical reasoning (area of 9- × 12-foot room, age 15-6), short-term memory (repeating 6 digits backward, age 18-3), and vocabulary (defining *prognosticate*, age 20-6).

Psychometric Properties

The reliability is reported only as a test-retest coefficient, based on 139 individuals aged 4 to 50 years tested over a 2-month interval. The reported coefficient of .97 is meaningless; it is inflated because of the absurdly heterogeneous age range of the sample and the unusually large standard deviations for Slosson ratio IQs (estimated at 25 by Reynolds, 1979). The manual reports little evidence of validity for the 1981 norms edition, relying mostly on correlational studies involving the first edition. The few studies with the renormed version have small sample sizes (10–15 cases); like most Slosson research, studies with children predominate. Differences between mean IQs on the 1981 Slosson and 1955 WAIS are about 3 points. A similar difference was found by Klett et al. (1986) between the new Slosson and the WAIS-R for 90 male patients (mean age = 41.5) at a VA Hospital (103.7 on the Slosson, 101.7 on the WAIS-R Full Scale).

Klett et al. (1986) obtained correlations between Slosson and WAIS-R IQs of .83 (Verbal), .51 (Performance), and .78 (Full Scale). The higher relationship with V-IQ is expected in view of the heavy verbal loading of the Slosson, and is consistent with findings in the literature. Also consistent is the general magnitude of the obtained coefficients with other Wechsler scales, usually the WISC or WISC-R (Sattler & Covin, 1986; Stewart & Jones, 1976).

The 1981 norms for the Slosson are based on 1,109 people between the ages of 2 years 3 months and 18 years 0 months. The sample was tested on the Slosson and Form L-M of the Binet in counterbalanced order. Subjects "were not selected at random. . . . They were persons in the northeastern part of the United States, specifically New England" (Jensen & Armstrong, 1985, p. 133). Data are not provided for the sample on key variables like gender, race, socioeconomic status, or urban versus rural residence. Even the age breakdowns are in wide groupings, i.e., 6 years 6 months and below (N = 123), 6 years 7 months to 10 years 6 months (N = 439), 10 years 7 months to 13 years 6 months (N = 316), and 13 years 7 months to 18 years 0 months (N = 231). Although Jensen and Armstrong (1985) are correct that the normative sample "was large, heterogeneous, and representative of all levels of ability and age" (p. 134), the Slosson sample had a pile-up of

cases with below-average ability. For example, within the older adolescent sample, 37% had IQs below 84; 48% had IQs within 1 standard deviation of 100; and 15% had IQs above 117. The theoretical percentages are approximately 16, 68, and 16, respectively.

The technique of equipercentile equating with the 1972 Binet was used to develop norms, a method that Jensen and Armstrong (1985) consider impervious to the failure of Slossen to draw a sample "at random from the population at large" (p. 134). The correlations with Binet IQ for the four age groups indicated above were .93 to .96, impressive at first glance. However, these values are meaningless as validity data because of the heterogeneous age groups and the large standard deviations characterizing both the Binet and Slosson IQs (20–22) of the normative sample (Jensen & Armstrong, 1985). When individuals with IQs above 116 are considered separately, correlations with the Binet drop to the .60s and .70s (Jensen & Armstrong, 1985, p. 141).

Evaluation

Unfortunately, the Slosson seems to have gotten by on its brevity, not its merit. Oakland (1985), in his Buros review, assailed it as having a standardization sample that "is meager, narrow, and unrepresentative of the U.S." (p. 1403), and as including numerous "statements in the test manual and norm tables [that] are misleading or incorrect" (p. 1402). A second Buros reviewer (Reynolds, 1985) stated flatly that the Slosson "remains a psychometrically poor measure of general intelligence. . . . [T]he extant problems still inherent in this test . . . [are] cause for ethical concern regarding its utilization beyond a limited application as a preliminary screening measure" (p. 1404).

I concur with these reviewers. Jensen and Armstrong (1985) are not wrong to emphasize the power of the equipercentile equating technique as a norming method; indeed a representative sample is not necessary to secure norms via this empirical approach. But part of the goal in obtaining a heterogeneous sample for the equating process is to include people who differ on crucial variables like gender, race, and socioeconomic status. Perhaps the sample did provide a good representation of minority group members, children of unskilled laborers, and so forth. But there is no excuse for Slosson or Jensen and Armstrong to fail to present these data for the test user's evaluation.

Also, the Slosson has been equated to a historical relic in the 1972 Binet; further, the sample was tested mostly in the decade of the 1970s, and was about half a generation out-of-date before Jensen and Armstrong (1985) even published their expanded norms tables to allow examiners to compute standard score IQs for the Slosson instead of the MA/CA ratio IQs. An additional problem with the Slosson for adolescent and adult assessment concerns the type of items included to distinguish among the more intelligent individuals; the harder items invariably assess esoteric bits of trivial word knowledge (e.g., *uxoricide,* and *amenuensis*). I can't think of any reason to use the Slosson in preference to a WAIS-R short form.

The Shipley Institute of Living Scale (Shipley-Hartford)

For a brief test, the Shipley-Hartford has a history of long names: It was christened the Shipley-Hartford Retreat Scale for Measuring Intellectual Impairment and later renamed the Shipley Institute of Living Scale for Measuring Intellectual Impairment. Although originally developed to assess impaired mental functioning, the Shipley has attained popular use, especially in institutions, as a brief measure of IQ for adolescents and adults. Ironically, despite these origins, Zachary (1986) noted that the Shipley "is not appropriate for use with individuals who have suspected mental retardation or have suffered profound cognitive deterioration due to neurological or severe psychological disturbances. Rather, [it] is intended as a screening device for the broad band of near-average intelligence" (p. 2).

The Shipley is intended for adolescent and adult populations, ages 14 and older. It comprises two self-administered subtests, each with a 10-minute time limit that includes the time it takes to read the instructions: Vocabulary, composed of 40 multiple-choice items; and Abstraction, containing 20 series completion items that require subjects to fill in the blanks. Figure 5.1 shows a filled-out record form of both parts of the Shipley for a patient having an acute psychotic episode. This figure not only shows all items in the Shipley but demonstrates the potential clinical value of the subjects' free responses to the Abstraction items. Zachary (1986) sees the Shipley as especially useful for "personal selection, vocational guidance, and intellectual screening of psychiatric patients" (p. 1).

The Shipley was developed to detect impaired intellectual functioning, based on clinical observations and research findings that skills are differentially "susceptible to cognitive deterioration associated with organic brain dysfunction, mental disorder, or the normal aging process" (Zachary, 1986, p. 43). In particular, complex mental skills like the series completion items on the Abstraction subtest deteriorate far more rapidly than the acquired knowledge measured by the Vocabulary subtest. Consequently, Shipley (1940, 1953) focused on a mental age–based ratio of a person's Abstraction and Vocabulary performance (multiplied by 100), known as the Conceptual Quotient (CQ). Shipley (1940) assigned to low quotients labels like "Very Suspicious" (70–75) or "Probably Pathological" (<70). This approach closely resembles Wechsler's (1958, pp. 211–213) Deterioration Quotient method based on "Hold" versus "Don't Hold" subtests.

The mean scores on the two Shipley subtests change with chronological age in very different ways, and in ways that are consistent with the body of literature on aging and intelligence (see chapter 7). The mean raw scores presented in Table 5.3 are based on data provided by Tamkin

SHIPLEY INSTITUTE OF LIVING SCALE
Administration Form
Walter C. Shipley, Ph.D.

Published by

wps WESTERN PSYCHOLOGICAL SERVICES
Publishers and Distributors
12031 Wilshire Boulevard
Los Angeles, California 90025

Name: _Mr. K._ Sex: (M) F Age: _18_

Education: _10 years_ Usual Occupation: _Unemployed_ Today's Date: _7-12-83_

Part I

Instructions: In the test below, the first word in each line is printed in capital letters. Opposite it are four other words. Circle the *one word* which means the *same thing*, or most nearly the same thing, as the first word. If you don't know, guess. Be sure to circle the *one word* in each line that means the same thing as the first word.

EXAMPLE:

LARGE　　　red　　　(big)　　　silent　　　wet

(1) TALK	draw	eat	speak	sleep
(2) PERMIT	allow	sew	cut	drive
(3) PARDON	forgive	pound	divide	tell
(4) COUCH	pin	eraser	(sofa)	glass
(5) REMEMBER	swim	(recall)	number	defy
(6) TUMBLE	drink	dress	(fall)	think
(7) HIDEOUS	(silvery)	tilted	young	dreadful
(8) CORDIAL	swift	muddy	(leafy)	hearty
(9) EVIDENT	green	obvious	skeptical	(afraid)
(10) IMPOSTOR	conductor	(officer)	book	pretender
(11) MERIT	(deserve)	distrust	fight	separate
(12) FASCINATE	welcome	fix	stir	(enchant)
(13) INDICATE	defy	(excite)	signify	bicker
(14) IGNORANT	red	sharp	(uninformed)	precise
(15) FORTIFY	submerge	(strengthen)	vent	deaden
(16) RENOWN	length	head	(fame)	loyalty
(17) NARRATE	yield	buy	associate	(tell)
(18) MASSIVE	bright	(large)	speedy	low
(19) HILARITY	(laughter)	speed	grace	malice
(20) SMIRCHED	(stolen)	pointed	remade	soiled
(21) SQUANDER	tease	(belittle)	cut	waste
(22) CAPTION	drum	ballast	heading	(ape)
(23) FACILITATE	(help)	turn	strip	bewilder
(24) JOCOSE	(humorous)	paltry	fervid	plain
(25) APPRISE	(reduce)	strew	inform	delight
(26) RUE	eat	lament	(dominate)	cure
(27) DENIZEN	senator	inhabitant	fish	(atom)
(28) DIVEST	(dispossess)	intrude	rally	pledge
(29) AMULET	(charm)	orphan	dingo	pond
(30) INEXORABLE	(untidy)	involatile	rigid	sparse
(31) SERRATED	dried	(notched)	armed	blunt
(32) LISSOM	(moldy)	loose	supple	convex
(33) MOLLIFY	mitigate	(direct)	pertain	abuse
(34) PLAGIARIZE	(appropriate)	intend	revoke	maintain
(35) ORIFICE	brush	(hole)	building	lute
(36) QUERULOUS	maniacal	(curious)	devout	complaining
(37) PARIAH	(outcast)	priest	lentil	locker
(38) ABET	(waken)	ensue	incite	placate
(39) TEMERITY	rashness	timidity	desire	(kindness)
(40) PRISTINE	vain	(sound)	first	level

Turn over this sheet and continue with Part II when instructed to do so.

19
0
19

Vocabulary raw score _19_

DO NOT WRITE IN THIS AREA

FIGURE 5.1

Shipley-Hartford test protocol for an 18-year-old-male experiencing an acute psychotic episode (Reprinted with permission).

Part II

> **Instructions:** Complete the following by filling in either a number or a letter for each dash (_____). Do the items in order, but don't spend too much time on any one item.
>
> **EXAMPLE:** A B C D _E_

(1) 1 2 3 4 5 _6_

(2) white black short long down _4 P_

(3) AB BC CD D _C_ _⚡⚡_ _Electricity!!_

(4) Z Y X W V U _A_

(5) 1 2 3 2 1   2 3 4 3 2   3 4 5 4 3   4 5 6 _5 4_

(6) NE/SW SE/NW E/W N/ _⌐_

(7) escape scape cape _e s c_

(8) oh ho rat tar mood _o m d o_

(9) A Z B Y C X D _C_

(10) tot tot bard drab 537 _d i e_

(11) mist is wasp as pint in tone _m o_

(12) 57326 73265 32657 26573 _7 7 7 7 7_

(13) knit in spud up both to stay _u P_

(14) Scotland landscape scapegoat _s h eep_ ee

(15) surgeon 1234567 snore 17635 rogue _c u I u p_

(16) tam tan rib rid rat raw hip _r i P_

(17) tar pitch throw saloon bar rod fee tip end plank _d r i n K_ meals

(18) 3124 82 73 154 46 13 _2_

(19) lag leg pen pin big bog rob _r a p e_

(20) two w four r one o three _3_

Summary Scores

V: Raw _19_ T _37_   A: Raw _6_ T _32_   Total: Raw _25_ T _32_

CQ: _72_ AQ: _85_ Est. IQ: _65_

Abstraction raw score _3_ / _6_

FIGURE 5.1 (Continued)

Shipley-Hartford test protocol for an 18-year-old-male experiencing an acute psychotic episode (Reprinted with permission).

TABLE 5.3 Mean raw scores on the Shipley-Hartford Vocabulary and Abstraction subtests for 486 male inpatients categorized by age

Age Group	N	Vocabulary	Abstraction
20–29	88	25.0	21.1
30–39	121	25.1	19.3
40–49	85	25.4	15.2
50–59	95	24.2	12.9
60–79	97	22.2	9.2

NOTE: Data are from Tamkin and Jacobsen (1987, Table 1).

and Jacobsen (1987) for 486 male inpatients at a VA hospital. Scores stay fairly constant across the broad age range for Vocabulary, rising slightly until ages 40–49 before dropping slightly; as Shipley (1940) predicted, Abstraction scores drop dramatically with increasing age.

However, a body of literature has accumulated regarding the impact of cohort effects and the difficulties in interpreting cross-sectional data for different age groups (see chapter 7); also, generational changes (Flynn, 1987; see chapter 2) impact differently on skills that are more fluid (like Abstraction) than on those that are more crystallized (like Vocabulary). Therefore, the occurrence of mean differences from age to age does not automatically translate into deterioration of abilities, and the changes for Vocabulary and Abstraction are not necessarily directly comparable.

Furthermore, Shipley's CQ is based on a naive neuropsychological framework, one that interprets brain damage as a simple, homogeneous condition rather than as a complex phenomenon intimately related to location of the lesion (see chapters 9–11). Hence, Wechsler's Deterioration Quotient has not stood up to research scrutiny (Matarazzo, 1972, pp. 429–430).

Nonetheless, the Shipley offers *T*-scores (mean=50, *SD*=10) for the separate subtests

along with the following aggregate scores, based either on self-administration with paper-and-pencil (individual or group administration), or via microcomputer: a Total score (Vocabulary + Abstraction raw score, converted to a *T*-score); a Conceptual quotient (CQ) or impairment index; an Abstraction Quotient (AQ), which is the CQ adjusted for age and education; and an estimated Full Scale IQ based on either the WAIS or WAIS-R.

The tie-in with Wechsler's scales is long-standing and goes back to the Wechsler-Bellevue. Researchers have continually converted Shipley scores to WAIS or WAIS-R IQs using a wide variety of empirical techniques (Bartz & Loy, 1970; Paulson & Lin, 1970), with the more recent approaches reflecting incredible statistical sophistication (Zachary, Crumpton, & Spiegel, 1985; Zachary, Paulsen, & Gorsuch, 1985). Thus, the evaluation of the Shipley as a WAIS-R short form is quite relevant to its use, development, and clinical history.

Psychometric Properties

Because of the Shipley's speeded nature, reliability techniques such as Cronbach's coefficient alpha or split-half are not appropriate for it. Test-retest reliability is pertinent, but the values reported in the manual (Zachary, 1986, Table 13) for eight small samples (*N*s of 17 to 56), mostly of female student nurses, are unimpressive. Weighted mean coefficients for the 231 adults, tested over an average interval of 10 months, are .62 for Vocabulary, .65 for Abstraction, and .73 for Total Score. These values are too low to merit all of the scores for which norms are provided. Examiners would be unwise to interpret the separate scores on the two subtests, the "unusualness" of a person's *difference* between the subtest scores, despite the empirical sophistication of the formulas derived for that purpose (Silverstein, 1987b; Zachary & Huba, 1985), or either the CQ or the AQ. The difference score and the quotients will necessarily be unstable because they are computed from two subtest scores that are each unreliable; the net result of comparing two unstable scores (by either subtraction or division) is a score that is even more unreliable than its component parts.

The only score that is sufficiently stable (barely) to warrant interpretation is a combination of the two subtests. The Total score is obtained by summing raw scores, a questionable procedure in view of their quite different distributions; the *T*-scores of the separate subtests should have been combined, not their raw scores, before converting the Total to its own *T*-score. Nonetheless, the one score worth interpreting based on a Shipley administration is the estimated WAIS-R Full Scale IQ. An impressive empirical procedure known as "continuous norming," which builds in a correction for age differences (Zachary, Crumpton, & Spiegel, 1985), is used to convert Total raw scores to a Wechsler IQ metric having a mean of 100 and *SD* of 15 (Zachary, 1986, Table D-2).

Zachary and his colleagues showed that the estimated IQs from a Shipley administration correlated substantially with the WAIS ($r = .74$; Zachary, Paulson, & Gorsuch, 1985), and with the WAIS-R ($r = .85$; Zachary, Crumpton, & Spiegel, 1985), when applying the continuous norming procedure to cross-validation samples of psychiatric inpatients. The IQ estimates from the Shipley closely approximated the actual Wechsler IQs, in contrast to the overprediction that presented a serious problem when other formulas have been applied (Fowles & Tunick, 1986; Heinemann, Harper, Friedman, & Whitney, 1985). However, studies by other researchers have not replicated the high Shipley–WAIS-R coefficient found by Zachary: Dalton, Pederson, and McEntyre (1987) found a coefficient of .73 with actual WAIS-R FS-IQ for male patients; and Retzlaff, Slicner, & Gibirtini (1986) produced a correlation of only .46 for their sample of normal medical patients with orthopedic injuries. The latter sample, however, was extremely restricted in their range of IQs, serving to attenuate validity coefficients. In fact, coefficients in the high .70s are typical of nu-

merous investigations over the years between the Shipley and various Wechsler adult scales (Zachary, 1986, Table 17).

The evidence thus suggests adequate validity for the Shipley as a short form of the WAIS-R; coefficients in the high .70s or low .80s do not match the values for actual short forms (typically in the low .90s), but the Shipley does not have the advantage of being embedded in the WAIS-R Full Scale. However, there is one strikingly serious problem with the Shipley that cannot be solved by all of the statistical sophistication and psychometric applications of Zachary and his colleagues: The Shipley has a terrible norms group, one that makes the Slosson standardization sample seem adequate by comparison.

For some reason, the Shipley was *not* renormed by Zachary (1986) when he applied his advanced statistical technology to the Shipley data to generate WAIS and WAIS-R IQ estimates. Instead, the "restandardization" involved taking data already in existence from Paulson and Lin's (1970) investigation of a mixed sample of 290 psychiatric patients. This sample included equal numbers of males and females; comprised 28 to 80 patients at each of six age groups between 16–17 and 45+; and was composed of adolescents and adults from lower-, middle-, and upper-class backgrounds (Zachary, 1986, pp. 45–48). No mention is made of the racial composition of the sample.

Zachary (1986) stated: "While not 'normative' in the usual sense, this sample was chosen because it is fairly typical of the kind of clinical population for which the *Shipley* is most often used" (p. 45). That is a weak argument. It is a good justification for a *validation* sample, which it originally was, but not for a normative sample, which by its very name implies a population of *normal* individuals to serve as a reference group. A clinical sample can be used to produce *specialized* norms intended to supplement national norms; such an atypical sample cannot, however, substitute for a normal, representative standardization population. The Shipley is a quick test to give, and it can easily be administered to groups. How can anyone justify the decision *not* to test a fresh sample of normal adolescents and adults for standardization purposes? A portion of that sample could have been given a WAIS-R (even a four-subtest short form) for the estimation study.

Evaluation

Zachary (1986) has written a manual for the Shipley that is among the best I have seen. The introduction includes an unusual number of practical, clinical, and ethical cautions about proper test use; the rest of the manual is written with statistical acumen, clinical insight, and research expertise that blend to form a systematic and thorough approach to profile interpretation. The illustrative case studies and computerized reports enhance the whole process.

Unfortunately, this palace has been built on a swamp. The norms are not only unrepresentative but are based on an abnormal sample tested at least 20 years ago. Test–retest reliability is weak, and even the reliability coefficient for the total score is unimpressive; it doesn't compare to the reliability of the PPVT-R (see pp. 605–608), which takes less than the 20 minutes required to administer the Shipley.

Yet the item types are appealing, especially the enjoyable, clever items that compose the Abstraction subtest. The combination of one verbal and one conceptual test makes a nice package of skills, and item difficulty is attained without resorting to Slosson-like trivia (although Zachary, 1986, warns that the Shipley has a low ceiling that prevents discrimination among high-IQ individuals).

When time is at a premium but nonetheless permits the individual administration of an intelligence test by a qualified professional, the Shipley should *not* be used. A short form of the WAIS-R is a far better choice because of its excellent standardization sample, reliability, and validity. Further, Dalton et al. (1987) obtained better prediction from one or two WAIS-R subtests than from the Shipley, in about half the time that it takes to administer the Shipley.

If time and/or qualified personnel are so limited that use of a WAIS-R short form is not feasible, the Shipley is a reasonable choice because of the strong points that I have noted, along with its self-administration and computerized administration capabilities. However, one should interpret *only* the estimated WAIS-R IQ, not the separate subtest scores or any of the quotients derived from Vocabulary and Abstraction. I would opt for the Shipley over the Slosson, although neither is attractive in a psychometric sense.

Chapter 5 Summary

This chapter reviews literature pertaining to WAIS-R short forms and various other modifications of the WAIS-R made to save administration time; it also evaluates two brief tests that are commonly used to obtain estimates of an adolescent's or adult's intellectual functioning—the Slosson and the Shipley-Hartford. The use of brief intelligence tests is justified under certain conditions—for example, for screening, so long as the scores are not used for categorization, diagnosis, or drawing neuropsychological inferences. The most popular WAIS-R short forms are the two- and four-subtest abbreviations developed by Silverstein and validated by numerous other investigators. His Vocabulary–Block Design (V-BD) dyad has excellent psychometric properties, while the statistical characteristics of his tetrad (V-BD + Arithmetic and Picture Arrangement) are exceptional. Nonetheless, misclassifications of ability level are still prevalent with outstanding short forms, limiting their primary use to screening.

Research by Thompson has explored the impact of estimated IQs obtained just from administration of Silverstein's short form, versus the IQs estimated from these same brief tests embedded in the complete WAIS-R. Such studies are sorely needed because virtually all short form research has come from after-the-fact studies of complete intelligence tests, not from separate administrations of the abbreviated batteries. Silverstein's dyad was found by Thompson to yield overestimates of IQ when administered in isolation; another aspect of his research indicated that administration times for Silverstein's tetrad were relatively long (about 35 minutes).

A good alternative to Silverstein's WAIS-R short forms is the one developed by Reynolds and his colleagues (Information-Arithmetic-Picture Completion-Block Design). This tetrad takes about 5 to 10 minutes less to give than Silverstein's four-subtest brief test. Although it has not been validated as extensively as Silverstein's test, the Reynolds abbreviation has excellent psychometric properties. So do three brief versions of the WAIS-R that I developed with a colleague, Toshinori Ishikuma. These short forms contain only the shortest subtests (e.g., Digit Span, Picture Completion), and are truly quick to administer (less than 20 minutes); they also avoid the pitfalls that led Thompson to find overestimated Full Scale IQs for Silverstein's dyad. Although these very short forms (a dyad, triad, and tetrad) lack external validation with clinical samples, they demonstrate excellent psychometric properties.

Feingold suggested a brief form composed of the Information-Vocabulary dyad, citing its high reliability and validity. However, this brief, verbal-dominated version of the WAIS-R seems to have little use apart from predicting a white, middle-class person's academic success. Cyr and Brooker stressed the need to select short forms based on *both* the reliability and the validity of the battery, but they forgot to use clinical common sense when choosing their test. Satz-Mogel split-half abbreviations of Wechsler's tests have been common research topics, but it is highly questionable whether norms based on a complete administration of the WAIS-R are applicable to IQs obtained when every second or third item is administered. Cella's "modified" WAIS-R, which adjusts the starting points of numerous subtests to save administration time, has flaws similar to the Satz-Mogel procedure. Depending on the purposes of administering a short form, it is sometimes advisable to apply Silverstein's "correction" to validity coefficients; this correction, however, is of more theoretical than practical interest.

The Slosson Intelligence Test, a brief, mostly verbal test organized in the format of the old Binet, has been commonly used for decades. Unfortunately, the Slosson has largely unknown psychometric properties and a poor standardization sample, and was equated to a test (the 1972 Binet) that is outmoded. Because of these problems, the Slosson should not be used, period. The Shipley-Hartford, one of the top five most common tests administered to adolescents and adults, especially in hospital settings, is a self-administered test that contains two subtests, Vocabulary and Abstraction. It comes equipped with an outstanding manual, yet has a thoroughly inadequate normative sample and unimpressive reliability and stability data. The item types are appealing, but the test should not be given when a qualified examiner is available. The self-administered format and other positive features make administration of the Shipley-Hartford an occasionally useful option.

Individual Differences on the WAIS-R Stratification Variables

Large, nationwide, carefully stratified standardization samples almost always represent the best sample ever obtained at one point in time on that test. Such samples serve the vital function of providing a representative normative group for determining an individual's accurate profile of IQs and scaled scores, but they can also serve the equally important function of understanding individual differences on key background variables like occupational group, urban versus rural residence, and race. Subsequent studies with new samples can also address these issues (and occasionally do), but such investigations are usually conducted with nonrandom samples of individuals who are referred for intellectual assessment for diverse reasons, or with essentially random samples of normal subjects who are typically small in number and who reside in the same geographic region.

The sections that follow explore IQ and scaled-score differences for people who differ on the WAIS-R stratification variables of gender, race, geographic region, urban versus rural residence, occupational group, and education level. The standardization sample of 1,880 in-

dividuals aged 16 to 74 provided the data source, and the results are usually presented for four large age groups, representing a merger of two or three adjacent standardization age groups: ages 16–19 (N=400), ages 20–34 (N=500), ages 35–54 (N=500), and ages 55–74 (N=480). Data for WAIS-R IQs are taken primarily from Reynolds, Chastain, Kaufman, and McLean (1987), and data for WAIS-R scaled scores are from Kaufman, McLean, and Reynolds (1988). Whenever relevant, data for the adolescent and adult sample (ages 12–23) tested during the recent standardization of the Stanford-Binet IV are compared to the WAIS-R results.

OVERVIEW OF RELATIONSHIPS OF VARIABLES TO WAIS-R SCORES

Table 6.1 presents an overview of the IQ differences on each variable for the total sample (Reynolds et al., 1987, Table 1). IQ differences due to gender, geographic region, and urban–

TABLE 6.1   Means on Verbal, Performance, and Full Scale IQs for the entire WAIS-R standardization sample, by background variable

Variable	N	V-IQ	P-IQ	FS-IQ
Gender				
Male	940	100.9	100.5	100.9
Female	940	98.7	99.1	98.7
Race				
White	1664	101.2	101.3	101.4
Black	192	87.9	87.3	86.9
Others	24	94.2	96.5	94.0
Region				
Northeast	464	101.6	101.4	101.6
North Central	497	98.6	100.0	99.0
South	576	98.6	97.0	98.0
West	343	101.0	101.9	101.5
Residence				
Urban	1421	100.4	100.0	100.3
Rural	459	98.0	99.2	98.4
Education				
16+ years (coll. grad.)	214	115.7	111.0	115.2
13–15 years	251	107.7	105.4	107.3
12 years (H. S. grad.)	652	100.1	100.2	100.0
9–11 years	472	96.1	97.7	96.4
8 years	158	90.2	93.0	90.8
0–7 years	133	82.2	84.5	82.5
Occupation				
Professional and Technical	206	111.3	108.2	111.0
Managerial, Clerical, Sales	409	104.3	103.3	104.1
Skilled Workers	213	98.4	101.2	99.5
Semiskilled Workers	404	92.7	94.5	93.1
Unskilled Workers	68	88.9	90.8	89.1
Not in Labor Force	580	99.2	98.5	98.8

NOTE: Data are from Reynolds et al. (1987, Table 1). Standard deviations are included in Reynolds et al.'s table but are excluded here. Standard deviations tended to be about 14–15 for males, females, whites, people from all four regions and both type of residences, and for the following occupational categories: semiskilled workers, unskilled workers, not in labor force. Standard deviations were typically in the 12–13 range for blacks and other nonwhites, for each separate education level, and for the occupational groups of professional and technical, managerial/clerical/sales, and skilled workers.

rural residence were small in magnitude, ranging from about 1 to 3 points. In contrast, differences due to race, education level, and occupational group were considerably larger.

With such large sample sizes, even differences of 2 points, such as the differences in IQ favoring males over females, are likely to be statistically significant when each variable is treated separately. However, such small differences are not of practical significance. Partly to ensure that unimportant differences would not emerge as statistically significant, Reynolds et al. analyzed five stratification variables at once, conducting separate analyses of variance (ANOVAs) for Verbal, Performance, and Full Scale IQs; main effects were gender, race, region, residence, and education level.

Although occupational differences were substantial, Reynolds et al. (1987) excluded this variable from the analyses because it is highly correlated with education level, a large portion of the sample (nearly one-third) was not in the labor force, and the occupational groupings were composed of those actually in the labor force (ages 20–74) and those whose head of household was employed (ages 16–19). To avoid numerous empty cells in the design matrix, the 24 individuals from "other" nonwhite races were likewise excluded.

The results of the ANOVAs were the same for the separate analyses of Verbal, Performance, and Full Scale IQs: The variables of race and education level produced significant differences ($p < .001$), but the variables of gender, region, and residence failed to reach significance at the .05 level. Each variable is discussed in turn below, although Table 6.1 offers a quick summary of the basic findings.

GENDER DIFFERENCES ON THE WAIS-R

As shown in Table 6.1, males earned IQs that were slightly, but not significantly, higher than the IQs earned by females; they scored higher by about 2 points on V-IQ, 1½ points on P-IQ, and 2 points on FS-IQ. These results are remarkably similar to the findings for the WISC (Seashore, Wesman, & Doppelt, 1950) and WISC-R (Kaufman & Doppelt, 1976), as boys outscored girls on both children's tests by 2½ points on the Verbal Scale, ½ point on the Performance Scale, and 1¾ point on the Full Scale.

Data for the WAIS were analyzed for mean sums of scaled scores instead of IQs (Matarazzo, 1972); if one enters the relevant IQ tables for the WAIS, males are found to outscore females on the WAIS Verbal and Full Scale IQs by about 1 point, with no Performance IQ discrepancy evident. In another large-scale study of gender differences on the WAIS (Turner & Willerman, 1977), involving 264 male and 257 female adoptive parents (mean ages of 40.3 and 37.4, respectively), males outperformed females on the Full Scale by 2.6 points (114.8 versus 112.2). The overall trend on the WISC and WAIS and their respective revisions is for males consistently to score slightly higher than females on the IQ scales, but for these gender differences to be of no practical consequence.

Data for the new, fourth edition of the Stanford-Binet (Thorndike, Hagen, & Sattler, 1986a) also produced trivial gender differences, but did not reveal any trends indicating male superiority. At ages 2 to 6 years and 7 to 11 years, females scored 1 to 1½ points higher than males on the Composite standard score. At ages 12 to 23 (the oldest Binet norms group is 18 to 23 years), the 800 males and 926 females earned almost identical mean Composite standard scores (99.1 versus 99.4, respectively).

Gender Differences by Age and Education

Table 6.2 summarizes WAIS-R gender differences for four broad age groups. The differences are largest for the middle two age groups, spanning the 20- to 54-year age range; males scored higher by about 2½ points on V- and P-IQs and by approximately 3 points on FS-IQ. Gen-

TABLE 6.2   Gender differences on the WAIS-R IQs for four age groups

| Age Group | VERBAL IQ | | | PERFORMANCE IQ | | | FULL SCALE IQ | | |
	Male	Female	Diff.	Male	Female	Diff.	Male	Female	Diff.
16–19 (N = 200/sex)	99.6	98.5	+1.1	99.1	99.1	0.0	99.4	98.6	+0.8
20–34 (N = 250/sex)	101.3	98.7	+2.6	101.3	99.1	+2.2	101.5	98.7	+2.8
35–54 (N = 250/sex)	101.2	98.5	+2.7	101.3	98.6	+2.7	101.5	98.3	+3.2
55–74 (N = 240/sex)	101.2	99.0	+2.2	100.0	99.5	+0.5	101.0	99.3	+1.7

NOTE: Diff. = Difference. Differences are equal to mean IQ for males minus mean IQ for females.

der differences at the older adolescent years were almost nonexistent, and the Performance IQs of elderly individuals (ages 55–74) were about equal for males and females. When gender differences are evaluated for males and females at different educational levels (Reynolds et al., 1987), males were found to outscore females within each educational category by 1½ to 3½ points; differences in favor of males on all three IQs were largest for the most educated category (13 or more years of schooling).

Gender Differences on the WAIS-R Subtests

Gender differences on the separate WAIS-R subtests were examined for all 11 subtests simultaneously, using multivariate analyses of variance (MANOVAs) (Kaufman et al., 1988). Four MANOVAs were conducted, one for each of the four broad WAIS-R age groups; independent variables were gender, race, region, residence, and education, and the 11 WAIS-R subtests constituted the dependent variables. The independent variable of gender produced a significant main effect ($p < .001$) for all four age groups, indicating that males and females did not perform equivalently on the 11 subtests.

To determine which of the subtests yielded significant gender differences, the MANOVA was followed by 11 univariate ANOVAs at each of the four age levels. The mean difference between males and females on each subtest, by age, appears in Table 6.3, along with an indication of whether that difference reached statistical significance in the univariate ANOVAs. A plus sign indicates that males scored higher, and a minus sign indicates better performance by females.

Overall, males significantly and consistently outperformed females on Information, Arithmetic, and Block Design, while females were far superior on Digit Symbol. Males demonstrated less consistent, occasionally significant, superiority on Comprehension, Picture Completion, Picture Arrangement, and Object Assembly. Digit Span, Vocabulary, and Similarities produced no significant gender differences for any age group.

Gender differences on subtests virtually did not occur for the 16- to 19-year-old group, mirroring the lack of such differences on the IQ scales for older adolescents; only two WAIS-R subtests produced significant gender differences for older adolescents, Block Design in favor of males and Digit Symbol in favor of

TABLE 6.3   Differences in the mean scores earned by males and females on the 11 separate WAIS-R subtests for four age groups

Subtest	Ages 16–19	Ages 20–34	Ages 35–54	Ages 55–74
Verbal				
Information	+0.44	+1.04***	+0.91***	+0.91***
Digit Span	+0.01	+0.03	−0.13	−0.18
Vocabulary	+0.01	+0.20	+0.17	+0.22
Arithmetic	+0.42	+1.13***	+1.35***	+0.90***
Comprehension	−0.22	+0.17	+0.54*	+0.52*
Similarities	+0.36	−0.05	−0.01	−0.12
Performance				
Picture Completion	+0.45	+0.26	+0.64*	+0.62*
Picture Arrangement	+0.06	+0.53*	+0.82**	+0.23
Block Design	+0.85***	+0.98***	+0.83***	+0.31
Object Assembly	+0.14	+0.60*	+0.55*	−0.16
Digit Symbol	−1.29***	−0.85***	−0.82***	−0.72***

*$p < .05$; **$p < .01$; ***$p < .001$

NOTE: Data are from Kaufman et al. (1988, Tables 2 and 3). Differences equal the mean for males minus the mean for females.

females, which counterbalanced each other. Data for the Stanford-Binet, fourth edition (Thorndike, Hagen, & Sattler, 1986b) likewise showed virtually no gender differences for ages 12–23 on the four area scores. (Differences ranged from a 1-point male superiority in Verbal Reasoning to a 2-point female advantage in Short-Term Memory.) In contrast to the WAIS-R (and Binet) data for adolescents and young adults, 8 of the 11 WAIS-R tasks yielded significant gender differences at ages 35–54, with seven of the differences favoring males.

Female superiority on Digit Symbol and male superiority on the Information-Arithmetic-Block Design triad mirror the results of gender difference analyses on the WISC-R and WAIS (Jensen & Reynolds, 1983; Turner & Willerman, 1977; Wechsler, 1958). On the WAIS and WISC-R, males did better on Information and Block Design while females performed better on Digit Symbol/Coding (Jensen & Reynolds, 1983; Wechsler, 1958). Although meaningful gender differences were not observed on WISC-R Arithmetic (Jensen & Reynolds, 1983), WAIS Arithmetic produced a larger difference in favor of males (about ⅓ SD) than did any other WAIS subtest (Wechsler, 1958, Table 39), and it produced four specific items that consistently yielded significantly higher scores for males than females (Turner & Willerman, 1977).

Female superiority on Coding, Digit Symbol, and symbol-digit substitution tasks (rapidly copying the digit rather than the symbol) is well documented in the literature, although the reason for this female advantage is less apparent; numerous experimental psychologists have systematically explored explanations for this persistent gender difference. Estes (1974) hypothesized that females outperform males on these psychomotor tasks because of a greater ability to verbally encode the abstract symbols. This hypothesis has received support from Royer (1978), who devised three forms of the symbol-digit substitution task. One form used the easily encoded WAIS symbols, while the others used symbols of greater spatial and orientational complexity (ones not readily encoded verbally). Females outperformed males significantly on the WAIS symbols, as expected, but males significantly outscored females on the most complex symbol set. Additional support for the Estes verbal encoding hypothesis comes from Majeres's (1983) experiment indicating female superiority on matching and symbol-digit tasks that utilize verbal material, contrasted with male superiority on symbol-digit substitution tasks employing spatial stimuli.

However, arguments against the Estes hypothesis persist. Delaney, Norman, and Miller (1981) also used symbol sets that varied in their degree of verbal encodability and concluded that the female advantage seems due to a perceptual speed superiority rather than a verbal encoding strength. Laux and Lynn (1985) also challenged the encoding hypothesis, but unlike the previous investigations, Laux and Lynn's correlational and componential analyses and experimental design did not provide a direct test of the pertinent question.

There is evidence that the female superiority in the skill underlying Digit Symbol may be diminishing over the years. Standardization data for the Differential Aptitude Tests (DAT) were analyzed for four samples tested between 1947 and 1980 (Feingold, 1988). Females consistently outperformed males on the Clerical Speed and Accuracy subtest, a DAT analog of Digit Symbol, but "[b]y 1980, boys had . . . cut in half the difference in Clerical Speed and Accuracy" (Feingold, 1988, p. 101).

Gender Differences and Manual Dexterity

Chastain and Joe (1987) performed a canonical correlation analysis using data from the entire WAIS-R standardization sample. They entered the 11 subtests and a variety of background variables into the analysis, interpreting as meaningful the following three canonical factors: General Intelligence, Age-Related Performance, and Manual Dexterity. Gender was substantially associated with only one of these factors, Manual Dexterity (.72 loading; males were coded as 1, females as zero). Block Design (.49) and being in a skilled occupation like carpentry (.38) also related substantially to this dimension; other tasks with moderate loadings were Picture Completion, Object Assembly, Picture Arrangement, and Arithmetic. This canonical factor, defined primarily by "maleness," reiterates other findings of men generally outperforming women on visual-spatial, visual-motor, and mathematical tasks.

Clinical Implications of Gender Differences on Mental Tasks

The results of gender differences on major intelligence tests are of limited generalizability regarding a theoretical understanding of male versus female intellectual functions. The results are contaminated because test developers have consistently tried to avoid gender bias during the test development phase, both in the selection of subtests for the batteries and in the choice of items for each subtest. Matarazzo (1972) pointed out: "From the very beginning developers of the best known individual intelligence scales (Binet, Terman, and Wechsler) took great care to *counterbalance* or *eliminate* from their final scale any items or subtests which *empirically* were found to result in a higher score for one sex over the other" (p. 352; Matarazzo's italics). According to Wechsler (1958), "[t]he principal reason for adopting such a procedure is that it avoids the necessity of separate norms for men and women" (p. 144).

Thus, the mean gender differences in global IQs are undoubtedly an artifact of the specific subtests included in the WAIS-R and, to some extent, of the specific items chosen for each subtest. However, it is possible to reach some hypotheses about "true" male–female differences on some of the subtests (Kaufman et al., 1988). It is hard to imagine how any Block Design or Digit Symbol items could have been eliminated due to gender bias (or any other kind of bias) because of the abstract, nonmeaningful nature of the stimuli; similarly, Arithmetic items are far more dependent on the computational process than on the verbal content, and therefore are not reasonably subject to the potential impact of bias.

In contrast, item selection on the Information, Comprehension, Picture Completion, Picture Arrangement, and Object Assembly subtests may have been instrumental in unwittingly producing the small, but occasionally significant, differences favoring males. Thus, it seems reasonable to conclude that adult males are superior to adult females in the skills assessed by Block Design and Arithmetic, and that adult females clearly outstrip adult males in the ability measured by Digit Symbol.

Relationship to Other Studies of Gender Differences

The WAIS-R findings are consistent with the results of other investigations of gender differences, utilizing different instruments (Maccoby & Jacklin, 1974). As mentioned previously, the female advantage in Digit Symbol and other tests of clerical speed has emerged in numerous other investigations, although the size of the discrepancy has fallen substantially over the past 40 years (Feingold, 1988). Males have consistently outperformed females in quantitative ability and visual-spatial ability. The quantitative superiority does not emerge until early adolescence, about age 12 or 13 (Hyde, 1981; Maccoby & Jacklin, 1974), which may account for the significant gender difference on WAIS-R Arithmetic, but not on its WISC-R counterpart. Also, the mathematical advantage enjoyed by males tends to be greatest and most resistant to change "at the highest levels of performance on high school mathematics" (Feingold, 1988, p. 101). Whereas some investigators (Benbow & Stanley, 1980, 1982, 1983) have implicated

biological factors as causing the gender differences in mathematics, Jacklin (1989) cites the lack of evidence for biological causation; she focuses instead on a series of investigations indicating "that math anxiety, gender-stereotyped beliefs of parents, and the perceived value of math to the student account for the major portion of sex differences in mathematical achievement" (p. 127). Regardless of causation, gender differences in mathematics have not declined over the years (Feingold, 1988).

The results of studies on verbal skills are different. Much past research has revealed better performance by females than males on verbal and language tasks (Maccoby & Jacklin, 1974), but more recent research does not (Hyde & Linn, 1988); females still outperform males on the DAT Spelling and Language tests, but the differences have fallen steadily between 1947 and 1980 (Feingold, 1988). The lack of gender differences on Verbal Comprehension subtests for the WAIS-R (or WAIS or WISC-R), though, is conceivably due to the preselection factors that operated in choosing tasks and items for the Wechsler-Bellevue and subsequent batteries. An additional consideration may be the small amount of variation in verbal ability that is attributable to gender differences; this amount is only about 1%, the same as the percentage for quantitative ability but less than the value of about 4% for visual-spatial abilities (Hyde, 1981).

Gender differences on verbal, language, visual-spatial, clerical, and mechanical tasks have clearly declined over the past 20 to 40 years (Feingold, 1988; Rosenthal & Ruben, 1982). Although the narrowing of the gap between males and females on verbal tasks as well as on other intellectual tasks cannot be attributed to clear-cut causes, Rosenthal and Ruben (1982) concluded that "females appear to be gaining in cognitive skill relative to males rather faster than the gene can travel!" (p. 711).

According to Deaux (1984), similar small effect sizes for the variable of gender have been identified for noncognitive factors as well, such as aggression and social influence. She states that "although additional evidence remains to be gathered, 5% may approximate the upper boundary for the explanatory power of subject-sex main effects in specific social and cognitive behaviors" (p. 108). Hyde's (1981) meta-analysis of the studies treated by Maccoby and Jacklin (1974) in their often-cited book on gender differences leads her to the conclusions that "well established" gender differences in cognitive functioning are nonetheless quite small in magnitude, and that far better methodologies regarding sampling procedures and hypothesis testing are needed to understand more fully the magnitude of the gender differences.

More recently, Jacklin (1989) noted: "Although gender issues have been central to the study of intellectual abilities in the past, they should no longer have this emphasis, given the current findings of a lack of gender differences" (p. 131). This statement is perhaps too strong, as is her proclamation that "gender is not an important variable in the measurement of intellectual abilities" (Jacklin, 1989, p. 131). The differences in some areas are diminishing, but they have not disappeared. The subtest differences between males and females on the WAIS-R are *not* trivial, even though their net effect on IQ gender differences is minor. The differences in favor of males on DAT Mechanical Reasoning remain striking, even though the discrepancies in 1980 were considerably smaller than in 1947 (Feingold, 1988). In addition, male superiority in Scholastic Aptitude Test Mathematics has remained large in the 1980s, as does the female advantage in DAT Spelling, Language, and Clerical Speed and Accuracy. Fruitful and potentially important research hypotheses have addressed the genetic, environmental, clinical, or neuropsychological reasons for these substantial—albeit declining—gender differences. The exciting line of research in neuropsychology that has uncovered probable gender differences in the V–P discrepancies observed in patients with lateralized lesions (see discussion in chapter 10) may well be related to the "minor" task differences that continue

to emerge for males and females. From a clinical neuropsychological vantage point, the termination of studies of gender differences would be a backward step.

RACE DIFFERENCES ON THE WAIS-R

The difference of about 1 standard deviation in the IQs earned by whites and blacks, identified for numerous samples with a wide variety of tests (Jensen, 1980; Reynolds & Brown, 1984) and seemingly impervious to time, also characterizes the WAIS-R. For the total sample (see Table 6.1), whites outscored blacks by about 13½ points on V-IQ, 14 points on P-IQ, and 14½ points on FS-IQ. Table 6.4 presents race differences by age, gender, education, and occupation. The differences are a virtual constant across age groups and for males and females, as blacks consistently earned mean V-, P-, and FS-IQs between 86½ and 88½.

Thorndike, Hagen, and Sattler (1986b) reported data for blacks and whites in the new Binet's standardization sample, and observed similar race differences for their adolescent and adult sample (ages 12–23) to the ones found for the WAIS-R. Whites outscored blacks by 17.4 points on the Composite (means of 103.5 and 86.1 based on standard scores having a mean of 100 and SD of 16), and demonstrated a comparable discrepancy on the Verbal Reasoning, Abstract/Visual Reasoning, and Quantitative Reasoning Area scores; blacks earned mean standard scores of 85.4 to 87.7 on these three area scores. In Short-Term Memory, whites scored about 11 points higher, 102.1 versus 91.2.

Black–White Differences and Education and Occupation

For education level, unlike for the variables of age and gender, the WAIS-R IQs of blacks varied by about 1 standard deviation, ranging

TABLE 6.4   Differences in the mean WAIS-R IQs earned by whites and blacks, by age, gender, education, and occupation

Variable	Verbal IQ			Performance IQ			Full Scale IQ		
	Whites	Blacks	Diff.	Whites	Blacks	Diff.	Whites	Blacks	Diff.
Age									
16–19	100.7	88.0	+12.7	100.7	87.2	+13.5	100.8	86.9	+13.9
20–34	101.5	88.4	+13.1	101.9	87.5	+14.4	101.8	87.0	+14.8
35–54	101.3	87.2	+14.1	101.4	87.2	+14.2	101.4	86.6	+14.8
55–74	101.3	87.8	+13.5	101.0	87.3	+13.7	101.4	87.0	+14.4
Gender									
Male	102.3	88.2	+14.1	101.9	87.9	+14.0	102.4	87.3	+15.1
Female	100.2	87.6	+12.6	100.6	86.8	+13.8	100.3	86.4	+13.9
Education									
0–8 Years	87.9	80.9	+7.0	91.0	81.0	+10.0	88.6	80.2	+8.4
9–11 Years	97.4	87.8	+9.6	99.5	86.4	+13.1	98.0	86.3	+11.7
12 Years	101.1	91.9	+9.2	101.2	90.9	+10.3	101.1	90.7	+10.4
13+ Years	112.1	95.8	+16.3	108.4	97.5	+10.9	111.6	95.8	+15.8
Occupation									
Prof./Tech./Mgr./ Cler./Sales/Skilled	105.2	94.9	+10.3	104.7	93.1	+11.6	105.4	93.5	+11.9
Semiskilled and Unskilled	93.9	84.8	+9.1	96.0	85.3	+10.7	94.4	84.2	+10.2
Not in Labor Force	100.8	86.5	+14.3	100.0	85.6	+14.4	100.5	85.3	+15.2

NOTE: Diff. = Difference. Difference scores equal the mean earned by whites minus the mean earned by blacks. Data are from Reynolds et al. (1987).

from a low of 80–81 for those with less than 9 years of education to 96–97 for those with at least some college experience. White–black differences were smallest for individuals with 0–8 years of schooling (7 to 10 points), and only reached the traditional 1 standard deviation discrepancy for the most educated group. However, the data for individuals with 13 or more years of education are tentative at best because the entire sample of blacks totaled only 20. (No

other cell in Table 6.4 is based on a sample size of less than 41.)

To investigate occupation differences by race, several of the occupational categories listed in Table 6.1 had to be combined to avoid small cell sizes. The results of race difference analyses in Table 6.4 indicate that within middle-class occupations whites outscored blacks by about 10 to 12 points, and they outscored blacks by about 9 to 11 points within working-class occupations. It is only for the group of adults not in the labor force that the familiar 15-point difference emerged. When one looks at occupational group IQ differences *within* each race, the middle-class workers outscored the working-class subjects by about 9 to 11 points for whites, and by about 8 to 10 points for black adolescents and adults. Thus, the impact of occupational group on IQ is comparable for both races. However, as Reynolds et al. (1987) have pointed out, the mean IQs for black middle-class individuals are of the same order of magnitude as the mean IQs of white working-class people.

The reduced black–white IQ discrepancies for the groups that were essentially matched for educational level or occupational group are about as large as racial differences that have been found in a wide variety of studies that have employed some type of control for socioeconomic background (Shuey, 1966).

Race Differences by Urban–Rural Residence and by Region

Data are not presented in Table 6.4 for race differences by region or residence because of small sample sizes for rural blacks ($N=25$) and for blacks from the North Central region ($N = 26$) and the West ($N = 12$). Reynolds et al. (1987) have reported, however, that the mean IQs for the small sample of rural blacks were trivially lower than the means for urban blacks (1 point on the Full Scale). Similarly, whites outscored blacks by 13½ points in the South and West, 14 points in the Northeast, and 18 points in the North Central region (Reynolds et al., 1987), but the small samples of blacks from the North Central and Western regions of the United States preclude interpretation of race differences from those two areas.

Race Differences on the 11 Separate Subtests

The MANOVAs conducted on the 11 WAIS-R subtests by Kaufman et al. (1988) produced significant main effects for race ($p<.001$) for each of the four age groups. The follow-up univariate ANOVAs indicated that whites significantly outscored blacks on each of the 11 subtests for all age groups; of the 44 contrasts, 43 were significant at the .001 level, with Picture Arrangement significant at the .01 level for ages 16–19. Since all differences were highly significant, Table 6.5 was developed by Kaufman et al. (1988) to allow comparisons of race differences from subtest to subtest.

All race differences are converted to a common metric, proportions of a standard deviation, using a computational method advocated by Jensen and Reynolds (1982, 1983) for the WISC-R. This procedure divides the mean scaled-score difference between whites and blacks by a function of the *SD*s obtained for each race. The resultant proportions of a *SD* allow direct comparison of the racial differences on each subtest; the larger the value, the greater the difference in subtest performance between whites and blacks.

Table 6.5 shows that WAIS-R Block Design and Vocabulary produced the most substantial differences between the races, with "effect sizes" of about 1.0; smallest effect sizes, of about 0.50, were yielded for Digit Span and Picture Arrangement. The results were similar for each of the age groups, and are summarized in Table 6.6.

Each of these categories includes both Verbal and Performance subtests, and the category encompassing the tasks producing the smallest black–white differences comprises one requiring much abstract, high-level reasoning (Picture Arrangement, a Level II task to Jensen) and one requiring rote memory (Digit Span, a Level I task). Interestingly, when the general ability factor is eliminated from consideration (in effect, by matching blacks and whites on Full Scale IQ), whites still significantly outscore blacks on Block Design (Kaiser, 1986).

WISC-R race differences (Jensen & Reynolds, 1982) were also relatively large for Block Design (.93 *SD*) and Vocabulary (.88 *SD*) and moderate for Digit Span (.31 *SD*) and Coding

TABLE 6.5 Differences between the mean scores earned by whites and blacks on the 11 WAIS-R subtests, for four broad age groups, expressed in proportions of a standard deviation

Subtest	Ages 16–19	Ages 20–34	Ages 35–54	Ages 55–74	Mean
Verbal					
Information	.68	.83*	.80*	.83*	.78*
Digit Span	.52	.45	.58	.50	.51
Vocabulary	.83*	1.00**	.96**	.82*	.90**
Arithmetic	.84*	.77*	.89**	.89**	.84*
Comprehension	.85**	.72*	.86**	.84*	.82*
Similarities	.72*	.69	.81*	.68	.72*
Performance					
Picture Completion	.65	.89**	.71*	.70*	.74*
Picture Arrangement	.41	.55	.62	.51	.52
Block Design	1.04**	1.16**	.95**	1.00**	1.04**
Object Assembly	.69	.71*	.82*	.75*	.74*
Digit Symbol	.59	.44	.67	.71*	.60

**Very Strong Racial Difference (.85+)
*Strong Racial Difference (.70–.84)
NOTE: Positive values denote differences favoring whites over blacks. All differences are statistically significant, virtually all at the .001 level. The values in this table were computed by subtracting the mean for blacks from the mean for whites on each subtest for each age group, and dividing the obtained discrepancy score by the weighted average standard deviation for blacks and whites. Data are from Kaufman et al. (1988), who also report the formula used for the computations.

TABLE 6.6 Summary of results in Table 6.5

Very Strong Black–White Discrepancy	Strong Black–White Discrepancy	Moderate Black–White Discrepancy
Block Design Vocabulary	Comprehension Information Arithmetic Object Assembly Picture Completion Similarities	Digit Symbol Picture Arrangement Digit Span

(.47 *SD*). However, black–white discrepancies for children and adults deviated to some extent (Kaufman et al., 1988):

- Comprehension produced the largest effect size (.94 *SD*) for children.

- Arithmetic produced strong race differences for adults but moderate differences for children (.61 *SD*).
- Picture Arrangement produced moderate race differences for adults but strong differences (.77 *SD*) for children.

WAIS-R Race-Difference Data and the Spearman Hypothesis

Jensen (1984, 1985b) has argued that the size of black–white differences is proportional to the test's *g* loading, a hypothesis first proposed by Spearman (1927). Jensen (1985b) presented data from 11 comprehensive studies of race differences on preschool, children's, and adult intelligence tests, and found substantial, significant correlations between the magnitude of black-white differences and *g* loadings; Jensen found support for Spearman's hypothesis across all studies and within each of the 11 studies.

The present data for the WAIS-R are certainly generally in accord with the Spearman hypothesis, as are the WISC-R data studied by Jensen and Reynolds (1982). For the WAIS-R, the subtests producing very large black–white discrepancies are both good measures of *g* (see Table 8.11), whereas the three subtests yielding moderate race differences are all fair measures of *g*. Mean *g* loadings for the total WAIS-R sample equal .79 for the "very strong" discriminators between blacks and whites, .74 for the "strong" discriminators, and .61 for the "moderate" discriminators.

Kaiser's (1986) analysis of WAIS-R standardization data revealed that the general factor extracted from hierarchical factor analysis conducted separately by race accounted for most of the variance between blacks and whites, when compared to the variance attributable to group factors or subtest specificity. In addition, general ability, defined by Kaiser (1986) in a different analysis as Full Scale IQ, contributed to racial discrimination (the size of white–black differences) more than four times the amount contributed by variability in the subtest profile.

However, the portion of the total variance attributed to general ability in Kaiser's (1986) analyses was relatively small. Further, the rank-order correlation between the mean size of the black–white difference (Table 6.5) and mean *g* loading (Table 8.11) for the 11 WAIS-R subtests equals .61. This value is of the same general order of magnitude as the relationships reported

by Jensen (1985b) and reaches significance at the .05 level, using a one-tail test. But more than 60% of the variance in the size of race differences on WAIS-R subtests is left unaccounted for by the *g* loadings of the tasks.

Furthermore, based on Kaiser's (1986) data on separate *g* factors for blacks and whites, discussed on pages 254–255, Block Design is only a *fair* measure of *g* for blacks (*g* loading = .67), whereas Picture Arrangement, only a moderate discriminator between the two races, is a *good* (indeed excellent) measure of *g* for blacks (.80 *g* loading). Thus, even though the Spearman hypothesis is obviously at work to some extent in explaining the size of the WAIS-R black–white differences, evidently other factors are involved as well. In addition, even if Jensen is correct that the Spearman hypothesis accounts for the size of race differences in various cognitive tasks, the mass of evidence presented in chapter 2 argued against the general notion of Jensen and others that genetics explains much of the observed black–white difference in IQ.

Clinical Implications of WAIS-R Race Differences

The extremely large differences between whites and blacks on Vocabulary and Block Design have two important implications. First, these two tasks are opposites in terms of the fluid intelligence–crystallized intelligence dimension. Block Design is almost a prototypical measure of fluid intelligence, requiring the ability to be flexible and adaptive when faced with a novel problem-solving situation; Vocabulary is equally prototypical as a measure of crystallized thinking, dependent on formal school training and other learning experiences such as reading and cultural interests. Block Design is perhaps the least culture-loaded task on the WAIS-R, and Vocabulary is often considered one of the most culture-loaded measures.

The fact that both tasks produced about equally large racial differences—while a socially and culturally saturated task like Picture Arrangement produced much smaller racial differences—argues against those (e.g., Hilliard, 1979; Williams, 1974) who attribute racial differences to the white, middle-class orientation of certain items or subtests.

The second implication of the findings regarding Vocabulary and Block Design is more practical and concerns the selection of short forms for clinical screening or other situations for which brief measures of intelligence are sufficient. The Vocabulary-Block Design dyad is a popular short form that is reliable and valid; it is often proposed for clinical use (Sattler, 1988; Silverstein, 1982a). When this two-subtest short form of the WAIS-R or WISC-R is used with blacks, it will consistently underestimate their Full Scale IQs because it emphasizes their areas of greatest weakness. Consequently, I strongly advise using other short forms (discussed in chapter 5) when assessing black children, adolescents, or adults.

REGIONAL DIFFERENCES ON THE WAIS-R

IQ differences due to geographic region are trivial and nonsignificant for the Verbal, Performance, and Full Scales (see Table 6.1 for data on the total sample). Overall, the Northeast and West averaged 101–102, the North Central region averaged 99–100, and the South averaged 97–98. The mean Verbal IQs spanned only a 3-point range, compared to a 5-point range for Performance IQ and a 3½-point range for Full Scale IQ. Because of the small, nonsignificant nature of these differences in the analyses of variance conducted by Reynolds et al. (1987), no other regional IQ data are presented here.

Of interest, however, is the finding that the 2-point superiority on the Full Scale displayed by males over females for the total sample was reflected precisely in the data for each of the four regions as well (Reynolds et al., 1987). The WAIS-R data for the four regions of the

United States are quite consistent with similar data obtained from the standardization samples of the WISC-R (Kaufman & Doppelt, 1976) and WPPSI (Kaufman, 1973). For the WISC-R, the IQ range for the four regions was about 6 points for each IQ scale, and the range was 6–7 points for the WPPSI. For all three of the Wechsler scales, WAIS-R included, individuals from the Northeast and West scored highest and those from the South earned the lowest mean IQs. However, as Reynolds et al. (1987) reiterate, the regional differences are too small to be of any practical significance regarding clinical or psychometric interpretation of test scores.

Regional Differences on the 11 Separate Subtests

Despite the nonsignificant findings relating region to IQ, the MANOVAs conducted by Kaufman et al. (1988) to determine regional differences on the 11 separate WAIS-R subtests yielded significant main effects for region at ages 16–19 ($p < .001$), 35–54 ($p < .05$), and 55–74 ($p < .001$), failing to produce significance only for 20- to 34-year-olds. Consequently, univariate ANOVAs were conducted within each age group to understand which of the 11 subtests yielded significant regional differences, and to try to make sense of these differences. Table 6.7 presents the range for each subtest by age, computed by subtracting the lowest regional mean from the highest regional mean. The region scoring highest and lowest on each task is identified in the table, as are the differences reaching statistical significance.

Why so many subtests should have produced significant regional differences is a mystery, especially in view of the nonsignificant IQ discrepancies for the four regions. Residing in any of the four regions was also completely unrelated to each of the three canonical factors interpreted by Chastain and Joe (1987) in their analysis of the 11 WAIS-R subtests in conjunction with a variety of background variables.

TABLE 6.7   Mean scaled-score differences between the highest and lowest scoring regions on the 11 WAIS-R subtests, by age

Subtest	Ages 16–19	Ages 20–34	Ages 35–54	Ages 55–74
Verbal				
I	1.0 NE/W**	0.6 NE & W/NC	0.9 NE/NC*	1.5 W/NC***
DSp	1.1 NE/W**	0.7 NE/NC	1.0 NE/S*	0.8 NE/S
V	0.4 NE/W	0.6 W/NC	1.0 W/NC*	1.3 W/S**
A	0.9 NC/S*	0.6 NE/NC	0.9 NE/NC	1.2 W/S*
C	0.7 NC/S	0.5 S/NC	1.0 W/NC	1.2 W/NC*
S	0.5 NE/S	0.8 S/NC*	0.9 W/S	1.4 W/S**
Performance				
PC	0.7 W/S	0.7 W/NE	1.0 W/S	1.5 W/S**
PA	0.7 W/S	0.4 W/NC	1.0 NE/NC & S*	1.1 NE/NC**
BD	1.6 NC/S**	1.1 W/S*	1.1 NE/S	1.5 W/S***
OA	0.8 NC/S	1.1 W/NC*	1.1 W/S	1.0 W/S
DSy	1.7 NC/S***	0.4 NC/W	1.1 NE/S*	0.9 NE/S

***$p < .001$; **$p < .01$; *$p < .05$

NOTE: NE = Northeast, NC = North Central, S = South, W = West. The region earning the highest scaled score on each subtest, by age level, appears directly following the difference score; then comes a slash followed by the region earning the lowest scaled score. Discrepancies emerging as significant in the univariate ANOVAs are asterisked. Data are from Kaufman et al. (1988).

In Table 6.7, five subtests produced significant differences for ages 16–19; on these tasks, people from the Northeast and North Central regions tended to perform best and those from the West and South did the worst. The five tasks included Block Design and the four subtests that form the "ACID profile," the set of tasks on which learning-disabled individuals have the most difficulty: Arithmetic, Digit Symbol (Coding on the WISC-R, hence the "C" in ACID), Information, and Digit Span. The ACID grouping also includes the so-called "distractibility" triad. Do the geographic regions differ in the degree to which they perform on the Freedom from Distractibility factor? In the degree to which they conform to the subtest pattern of learning-disabled individuals? In their ability to handle abstract symbols? I have included Table 6.7 in case readers have useful hypotheses.

The three significant regional differences identified for ages 20–34 should be treated as chance findings because the overall regional main effect in the MANOVA for the 11 subtests failed to reach significance. At ages 35–54 and 55–74, however, the MANOVA did produce significant main effects. At those two age groups, the West or Northeast scored highest on all subtests, and the North Central and South scored lowest; this finding held true whether or not the tasks produced significant differences. At ages 35–54, all ranges between the highest and lowest scoring regions were virtually identical, spanning 0.9–1.1. About half these differences reached significance at the .05 level, and about half did not.

Since the regions scoring best and worst on all 11 subtests at ages 35–74 mirror the small, but nonsignificant, IQ differences among the regions, there does not seem to be any special significance to the results. The reason that the IQ data yielded no statistical significance, while the scaled-score data yielded significance, is probably an artifact of the methodologies employed in the two research studies (ANOVA by Reynolds et al., 1987, and MANOVA by Kaufman et al., 1988).

Consequently, only the data at ages 16–19 are of potential interpretive interest because (a) they do not mimic the overall patterns found for the IQs, and (b) the pattern of subtests producing statistical differences are theoretically related to each other.

URBAN–RURAL RESIDENCE DIFFERENCES ON THE WAIS-R

Table 6.1 summarized urban versus rural residence differences on the WAIS-R IQs for the total sample, and revealed these differences to be small and nonsignificant: Urban residents outscored their rural counterparts by a trivial 2½ points on V-IQ, less than 1 point on P-IQ, and 2 points on FS-IQ. For males, urban–rural IQ differences on the Verbal, Performance, and Full Scales were 2, 0, and 1½ points, respectively; for females, urban residents scored higher by 3 points, 2 points, and 2½ points. Residence differences were nonsignificant for males and females, and the interaction between gender and residence was nonsignificant as well, as were the interactions between residence and all other stratification variables examined by Reynolds et al. (1987). Consequently, no further urban–rural IQ data are presented here.

Further, urban versus rural residence had loadings of approximately zero on all three canonical factors rotated by Chastain and Joe (1987), derived from an analysis of the WAIS-R sub-

tests and pertinent background variables. Therefore, coming from an urban or rural background was independent of a person's general intelligence, nonverbal ability, and manual dexterity.

Generational Changes in Urban–Rural Differences

Urban versus rural residence IQ discrepancies have gradually declined in the past half-century; the urban superiority on the old Stanford-Binet at ages 2–18 years ranged from 6 to 12 points for different age groups tested in the 1930s (McNemar, 1942). For children aged 5 to 15 tested on the WISC in the late 1940s, the urban advantage was 4 to 6 IQ points (Seashore et al., 1950), and for preschool and primary grade children tested on the WPPSI in the mid-1960s the difference was only 3½ points.

Urban children, adolescents, and adults still retained a slight advantage over rural individuals into the 1970s, scoring 1½ to 2 points higher on the WISC-R (Kaufman & Doppelt, 1976), normed in the early 1970s, and on the WAIS-R, normed in the mid- to late-1970s. However, as noted, the WAIS-R difference did not reach statistical significance, and it is conceivable that even the 2-point urban advantage on the WISC-R and WAIS-R would disappear if other variables were controlled. The reduction to zero of the urban–rural difference on WPPSI is precisely what occurred when urban and rural children were matched carefully on age, gender, race, region, and father's occupation (Kaufman, 1973).

Data for the new Stanford-Binet (Thorndike, Hagen, & Sattler, 1986a, 1986b) are consistent with the trend of reduced urban superiority. Thorndike et al. (1986b) presented data for rural individuals and for people from cities of various sizes. At ages 2 to 6 years, urban children (those living in cities with populations of 2,500+) outscored rural youngsters by 2.6 points; at ages 7 to 11 and 12 to 23, however, rural individuals earned higher mean Composite scores on the new Binet by 1.1 and 3.2 points, respectively.

The elimination of the urban superiority from earlier years is obvious, but the Binet urban–rural data are undoubtedly contaminated by the socioeconomic variable, which was poorly stratified in the Binet norming program.

The best explanation of the steady reduction, and perhaps elimination, of residence differences over the past 50 years is the impact of mass media on people living anywhere in the United States. Television and other means of communication, along with improved educational facilities and opportunities, have ended the relative isolation of people living in rural areas, making the kinds of facts and problems assessed by intelligence tests readily accessible to almost everyone.

Residence Differences on the WAIS-R Subtests

Urban–rural residence differences on the 11 separate WAIS-R subtests were nonsignificant at ages 16–19, 20–34, and 35–54 in the MANOVAs conducted by Kaufman et al. (1988), but reached significance at the .01 level for the 55- to 74-year-olds. Table 6.8 shows the mean scaled scores on the 11 WAIS-R subtests earned by urban and rural adults aged 55–74 and indicates the four tasks that reached statistical significance, all favoring urban elderly adults: Information, Digit Span, Vocabulary, and Arithmetic.

As Kaufman et al. (1988) point out, three of these subtests (not Digit Span) measure what Bannatyne (1968) has termed Acquired Knowledge—school-related, crystallized abilities. The implication is that those individuals who were born from the early 1900s to the mid-1920s (and were therefore 55 to 74 years old when the WAIS-R was normed), and who were raised in rural areas, did not have the opportunity to benefit from improved education and more accessible mass media; hence they did not perform as well on school-related tasks as did their urban contemporaries.

One would anticipate that growing up in a rural environment in the first quarter of the twentieth century would not adversely affect success on nonverbal subtests, and that is precisely what is revealed in Table 6.8. Hence, urban–rural residence is probably not a meaningful variable for elderly people per se, but just for those individuals who grew up before World War II. If this interpretation of the interaction between age group and residence found in the WAIS-R subtest data is correct, future standardizations of the WAIS-R or other tests for adults will *not* reveal a significant urban superiority among elderly individuals on verbal-achievement tasks—just as no urban advantage was evidenced by adolescents, young adults, and middle-aged adults tested in the late 1970s as part of the WAIS-R standardization.

OCCUPATIONAL DIFFERENCES ON THE WAIS-R

In Table 6.1, occupation differences are provided for the total WAIS-R sample, revealing a steady decline in mean IQs from professional and technical workers through unskilled laborers. The IQ ranges for these extreme occupational groups are from 17½ to 22½ points, with the Verbal Scale producing the largest discrepancies. Examination of occupation differences for different age groups within the WAIS-R age range is essential because of the changing nature of this background variable: For ages 16–19, occupational group corresponds to the adolescent's head of household, but for ages 20 and above it relates to the person's own job. The group labeled "not in labor force" becomes quite substantial (67% of the sample) for ages 55–74. To conduct an occupational group by age analysis, the four broad age groups had to be reduced to three (by merging ages 20–34 with ages 35–54) so that no mean IQs would be based on a sample size smaller than 20 (Reynolds et al., 1987). The results of this analysis appear in Table 6.9.

TABLE 6.8 Mean scaled scores on the WAIS-R subtests earned by urban and rural adults aged 55–74

Subtest	Urban Mean	Rural Mean	Difference
Verbal			
Information	9.5	8.7	+0.8*
Digit Span	9.0	8.0	+1.0*
Vocabulary	9.6	8.4	+1.2**
Arithmetic	9.2	8.3	+0.9*
Comprehension	9.3	9.1	+0.2
Similarities	8.1	7.5	+0.6
Performance			
Picture Completion	7.4	7.0	+0.4
Picture Arrangement	6.9	6.7	+0.2
Block Design	7.0	7.1	−0.1
Object Assembly	7.1	7.4	−0.3
Digit Symbol	5.9	5.8	+0.1

**p < .01; *p < .05
NOTE: Difference equals urban mean minus rural mean. Data are only presented for adults aged 55–74 because this is the only age group for which a significant main effect for residence was obtained in the MANOVAs investigating urban–rural differences on the 11 subtests (Kaufman et al., 1988).

Best Estimate of IQ Differences for Adults in Different Occupations

Since the 16- to 19-year-old group included occupations of the head of household, and the 55- to 74-year-olds included less than 60 adults per occupational group (except for the huge unemployed or retired sample), the data for ages 20–54 are the most representative and typical for generalizing about IQ differences by occupational category. The following mean IQ range seems to best exemplify workers in the five different occupational categories used by Wechsler (1981) to stratify the WAIS-R standardization sample.

OCCUPATIONAL CATEGORY	IQ LEVEL
Professional and Technical	110–112
Managers, Clerical, Sales	103–104
Skilled Workers	100–102
Semiskilled Workers	92–94
Unskilled Workers	87–89

The difference in the mean IQs for the two extreme occupational groups at ages 20–54 equals 26 points for Verbal IQ, 20 points for Performance IQ, and 25 points for Full Scale IQ. This discrepancy is huge, approaching 2 standard deviations for the Verbal and Full Scales, and is far greater than the IQ discrepancy in favor of whites over blacks discussed previously. As noted on pages 159–160, the mean difference in IQs between those in middle-class occupations and those in working-class occupations is comparable in magnitude for whites and blacks. The impact of a person's occupational group on intelligence test scores is a consideration that clinicians need to keep in mind during the WAIS-R interpretive process.

The IQ ranges of 20 to 26 points between professionals and unskilled workers found for 20- to 54-year-olds actively engaged in occupations are considerably larger than the ranges of 13–15 IQ points for the 16- to 19-year-olds whose father or mother was employed. Comparable analyses with the 6- to 16-year-old WISC-R sample (Kaufman & Doppelt, 1976) produced ranges across the occupational groups of 21 points on the Verbal Scale, 17 points on the Performance Scale, and 21 points on the Full Scale. These values for the WISC-R are based on the occupation of the head of household, as are the values computed for the 16- to 19-year-olds on the WAIS-R, yet the WISC-R occupational IQ ranges of 17–21 are substantially higher than the ranges of only 13 to 15 points found for the 16- to 19-year-olds. Indeed, the values of slightly less than 1 standard deviation are a bit small when compared with similar data from numerous other investigations (Anastasi, 1958), and with data obtained on the parents of preschool children: IQ ranges between extreme occupational groups equaled 15 to 18 points for the WPPSI (Kaufman, 1973), and the McCarthy General Cognitive Index range equaled 16½ points (Kaufman & Kaufman, 1975).

Occupational Data for Adolescents and Elderly Adults

The atypical occupational IQ data obtained for 16- to 19-year-olds on the WAIS-R, most notably when compared to data for 20- to 54-year-olds, is of concern (see Table 6.9). The different results reinforce the lack of comparability of samples selected on the basis of pa-

rental occupation versus the person's actual occupation. This lack of congruence in sample selection for adolescents compared to adults may be related to the unusual growth curves noted for the WAIS-R from ages 16–17 to 18–19, and for 18–19 to 20–24; as discussed on pages 83–85, these unanticipated developmental changes lead to speculation of some problem with the normative data for ages 16–19. The results of occupational group analyses endorse that speculation.

Even the data for ages 55–74 differed markedly from data for 16- to 19-year-olds. Because of an insufficient sample size of elderly unskilled workers, an IQ range could not be computed for the 55- to 74-year-olds. However, the range in mean Full Scale IQ between professionals and semiskilled workers equaled 19 points for ages 55–74; this difference is closer in magnitude to the corresponding range of 20 points for 20- to 54-year-olds than to the value of 14 points at ages 16–19 (see Table 6.9).

Reynolds et al. (1987) point out the importance of the finding that the group of individuals not in the labor force earned mean IQs of about 100 for ages 20–54 (means of 98–99 with SDs of 16) and ages 55–74 (means of 99 with SDs of 15); they also earned normative values of 100 and 15 when data were analyzed separately for males and females, and whites and blacks not in the labor force earned means and SDs close in magnitude to the values obtained for each total racial group (Reynolds et al., 1987). The unemployed or retired members of the WAIS-R standardization sample are thus incredibly representative of adults in general, a fact that inspires confidence in the WAIS-R norms for adults.

Had the group not in the labor force been obtained unsystematically or without extreme care (e.g., by testing an overabundance of former professionals, a group that is often easier to get to volunteer for standardization testing), the mean IQs of that group would have been skewed and a biased set of norms, especially for elderly people, would have resulted. However, the obtained data suggest that the group labeled "Not

TABLE 6.9   Mean IQs earned by different occupational groups for three broad age groups

Occupational Group	Ages 16–19			Ages 20–54			Ages 55–74		
	V	P	FS	V	P	FS	V	P	FS
Professional and Technical	108	105	107	113	110	112	115	109	114
Managers, Clerical, Sales	103	103	103	104	103	104	110	106	109
Skilled Workers	97	99	98	99	103	101	99	102	100
Semiskilled Workers	93	95	93	92	94	92	94	96	95
Unskilled Workers	93	92	92	87	90	87	—	—	—
Not in Labor Force	—	—	—	99	98	99	99	99	99

NOTE: V = Verbal, P = Performance, FS = Full Scale. Data are from Reynolds et al. (1987). Means are not provided for samples with fewer than 20 subjects ($N = 0$ for 16- to 19-year-olds whose head of household is Not in Labor Force; $N = 9$ for Unskilled Workers aged 55–74). For ages 16–19, sample sizes ranged from 24 (Unskilled Workers) to 120 (Semiskilled Workers); for ages 20–54, sample sizes for the five occupational groups ranged from 35 (Unskilled Workers) to 248 (Managers, Clerical, Sales), and for ages 55–74, sample sizes ranged from 20 (Professional and Technical) to 59 (Semiskilled). At ages 20–54, the Not in Labor Force category comprised 265 people; for ages 55–74 this group was composed of 315 subjects.

in Labor Force" was probably employed previously in occupational groups in proportions closely similar to U.S. Census proportions (Reynolds et al., 1987).

IQ Variability Within Occupational Groups

The sizable differences in mean IQs corresponding to different occupational levels should not be used to mask the considerable range of IQs earned by individuals *within* the same occupational category. Fluctuations in IQ by occupational category (and also by education level) are shown in Table 6.10, and also in Figure 6.1, based on data compiled (but not published) by Reynolds et al. (1987).

Table 6.10 shows the *range* of Full Scale IQs for adults (ages 20–74) in the WAIS-R standardization sample from each of six occupational groupings. Also presented are the FS-IQs corresponding to the *bottom 5%* and *top 5%* for each category. Figure 6.1 presents a bar

graph depicting the IQ range of the *middle 50%* (semi-interquartile range) of adults in different occupational groups.

Despite the substantial differences in mean IQs already noted for the occupational categories, the wide variability within each level is quite evident in both the table and the figure. In Table 6.10, the ranges (both the lowest and the highest scores) tend to increase steadily with occupational status, although the overlap in IQ distributions is still enormous. Some professionals score in the low 80s; some white-collar workers (managers, clerks, salespersons) score in the low 70s; and a number of semiskilled workers (e.g., factory workers, truck drivers, domestics) earn IQs in the superior and gifted ranges. Figure 6.1 shows differences as well as similarities in the distributions of the "middle 50%." The average unskilled worker, for example, falls within a "middle 50%" IQ range that is completely below the range for white-collar workers and professionals.

Additionally, Matarazzo (1972, pages 175–181) presents distributions of scores earned by

TABLE 6.10   Range of intelligence (Full Scale IQs) corresponding to different levels of educational attainment and occupational category

	Sample Size	WAIS-R FULL SCALE IQs		
		Range	5th %ile	95th %ile
Education (Years of Schooling)				
16+ (college graduate)	214	87–148	96	136
13–15 (some college)	227	76–139	89	124
12 (high school graduate)	549	63–141	81	121
9–11 (some high school)	224	59–146	72	117
8 (elem. school graduate)	140	65–125	76	111
0–7 (some elem. school)	126	53–139	59	106
Occupational Group				
Professional and Technical	144	81–148	92	136
Manager, Clerical, and Sales	301	73–137	86	125
Skilled Workers	127	72–131	81	119
Semiskilled Workers	284	56–135	70	117
Unskilled Workers	44	53–126	65	115
Not in labor force	580	55–146	75	124

NOTE: These data are based on adults (ages 20–74) in the WAIS-R standardization sample from data compiled, but not published, by Reynolds et al. (1987). Adolescents (ages 16–19) were eliminated because (a) data were only available for their parents' occupations, and (b) many had not yet completed their formal educations.

several diverse groups who demonstrated the following range of Full Scale IQs on the WAIS: (a) 243 police and firemen applicants (86 to 130, median = 113); (b) 80 medical students at the University of Oregon (111 to 149, median = 125.5); and (c) 148 faculty members at the University of Cambridge (110 to 141, mean = 126.5).

As Table 6.10, Figure 6.1, and Matarazzo's (1972) distributions show, however, even the lowest scoring individuals in professions requiring much advanced education are still well above the average of adults in general. The lowest scores among professors (110) and med-

ical students (111) correspond to percentile ranks of 75 and 77, respectively. More generally, people are found at all levels of the IQ distribution in low-level occupations, but the reverse does not hold; low IQ individuals are rarely members of high-status occupations (Gottfredson, 1984), a generalization supported from the WAIS-R standardization data summarized in Table 6.10 and Figure 6.1. Brody (1985) concluded from this relationship that "intelligence test score acts as a threshold variable for occupational success. Individuals with low scores have a low probability of being found in prestige occupations" (p. 362).

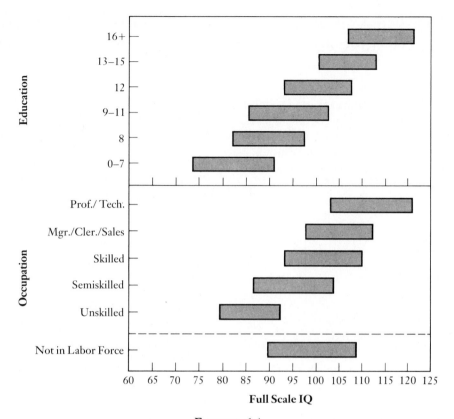

FIGURE 6.1

WAIS-R Full Scale IQs earned by the middle 50% of adults (aged 20–74) in the WAIS-R standardization sample, categorized by educational attainment and occupational category (data compiled by Reynolds et al., 1987, but not published).

Occupational Status and Canonical Factors

No data have been published to examine mean scaled-score differences on the 11 separate WAIS-R subtests for individuals in different occupational groups. However, Chastain and Joe (1987) included membership in each of the five occupational categories as variables, along with the 11 subtests and a variety of other background factors, in their canonical correlation analysis of the WAIS-R standardization sample. Being in a professional occupation such as engineering was associated with the General In-

telligence canonical factor (.37 loading); so was *not* being in a semiskilled job like driving a taxi cab or bus (−.33 loading). However, neither of these occupational variables was nearly as related to the general factor as years of education or success on the Vocabulary or Information subtests (loadings of .80+).

Holding a job as an electrician or being in other skilled occupations was meaningfully related to the Manual Dexterity dimension; the "skilled worker" variable helped define this canonical factor, as did two other variables with high loadings: being a male (see p. 156) and performing well on Block Design.

EDUCATIONAL ATTAINMENT AND WAIS-R IQS

In Table 6.1, huge IQ differences are evident for the total WAIS-R standardization sample when individuals are grouped by education level, defined as years of school completed. Across the broad 16- to 74-year range, the following mean Full Scale IQs typify people who differ in their educational attainment (Reynolds et al., 1987):

16+ (college graduate)	115
13–15 (some college)	107
12 (high school graduate)	100
9–11 (some high school)	96
8 (elementary school graduate)	91
0–7 (minimal formal education)	82

The 33-point difference in Full Scale IQ for those who graduated college versus those with minimal formal education exceeds 2 standard deviations, and is a larger range, by far, than was found for any other stratification variable. The corresponding ranges for Verbal IQ and Performance IQ equaled 34 points and 27 points, respectively.

Consequently, the relationship between education and IQ is monstrous in magnitude. Although the relationship is stronger for verbal than nonverbal intelligence, the steady, huge drop in Performance IQ with decreasing educational attainment makes it clear that the strong education–IQ correlation is not merely a direct function of being formally taught specific facts and school-related skills (see page 20 for a comparison of Information and Block Design). For each of the WAIS-R IQs, Reynolds et al. (1987) showed statistically that all six educational categories differed significantly from every other one, with a single, minor exception: Performance IQ for those with 12 versus those with 9–11 years of education.

Education and IQ Across the Age Range

Table 6.11 presents mean IQs for individuals differing in education level for the six age groups for which Reynolds et al. (1987) provided data. Matarazzo and Herman (1984b) also analyzed the standardization data to understand the relationship between education level and IQ. I use the data presented by Reynolds et al. (1987) for this discussion because Matarazzo and Herman (1984b) merged data for the 16- to 19-year-olds (who had not finished their formal education) with data for young adults aged 20–24, and presented mean IQs only for three very broad age ranges. Reynolds et al. (1987) reduced the number of educational levels to four by merging 0–7 years with 8 years and by merging 13–15 years with 16+ years to ensure that no cell included less than 20 individuals.

The data in Table 6.11 reveal that a substantial relationship exists between educational attainment and WAIS-R IQs for each of the six age groups studied. The difference in mean IQs for those with 13 or more years of education versus those with 0 to 8 years equals 26–33 points on the Verbal Scale, 15–27 points on the Performance Scale, and 24–33 points on the Full Scale. In only one instance was there a lack of increase in mean IQ with increasing education level: At ages 16–19 the average Performance IQ equaled 99 for older adolescents with 9–11 years of schooling and for those with 12 years of schooling.

These two groups of older adolescents barely differed in Full Scale IQ (2-point discrepancy), again raising doubts about the validity of the norms for 16- to 19-year-olds. Using educational level as a stratification variable for older adolescents is quite different from using education to stratify groups of adults. For adults, an educational level of 9–11 means that the person did not graduate from high school, and 12 years of education means that the person did not attend college. For older adolescents,

TABLE 6.11   Mean IQs earned by individuals differing in educational level for six age groups

	VERBAL IQ YEARS EDUCATION				PERFORMANCE IQ YEARS EDUCATION				FULL SCALE IQ YEARS EDUCATION			
Age Group	13+	12	9–11	0–8	13+	12	9–11	0–8	13+	12	9–11	0–8
16–19	114	101	98	83	111	99	99	88	114	100	98	84
20–34	109	96	91	76	107	97	94	80	109	96	91	76
35–44	110	99	88	80	108	101	91	84	110	100	88	81
45–54	113	102	94	86	108	102	98	86	112	102	95	85
55–64	113	104	97	87	108	105	98	87	112	105	97	86
65–74	117	105	99	90	109	102	101	94	115	105	100	91

NOTE: Data are from Reynolds et al. (1987). The sample sizes ranged from 24 (13+ yrs.) to 248 (9–11 yrs.) for ages 16–19; from 23 (0–8 yrs.) to 210 (13+ yrs.) for ages 20–34; from 26 (0–8 yrs.) to 106 (12 yrs.) for ages 35–44; from 40 (0–8 yrs.) to 100 (12 yrs.) for ages 45–54; from 26 (9–11 yrs.) to 59 (12 yrs.) for ages 55–64; and from 51 (9–11 yrs.) to 133 (0–8 yrs.) for ages 65–74.

especially at ages 16 through 18 years, an individual with 9–11 years of education will conceivably graduate from high school shortly and may subsequently go on to college; a person who has completed 12 years of education may have already been accepted by a college.

Table 6.11 shows some interesting age-related trends that were masked in Matarazzo and Herman's (1984b) exploration of education–IQ relationships within three broad age groups. If data for 16- to 19-year-olds are ignored because many adolescents in this group have not completed their education, and only adults aged 20 and above are considered, there is a steady increase in mean IQ with increasing age *within* each educational level. This trend is more pronounced for the Verbal and Full Scales than the Performance Scale, and for adults with 0–8 years of education than for any other educational category. For this low education category, mean V- and FS-IQ is only 76 for ages 20–34 but rises steadily to 90–91 at ages 65–74.

The explanation for this trend is probably related to the fact that a single table (derived from norms for ages 20–34) is used to compute scaled scores on the 11 subtests, but separate tables for each age group are used to compute

IQs. Adults within each educational category earn about the same mean Verbal sum of scaled scores regardless of their age group (Kaufman et al., 1989). However, the same sum of scaled scores yields very different Verbal IQs for different age groups, with the highest Verbal IQs obtained for the older samples. Thus, the higher IQs earned by older than younger adults within each educational category give the illusion that if education is held constant, older individuals will score higher than younger individuals. Actually, they perform about the same when compared on a common yardstick (the reference group of 20- to 34-year-olds used to determine scaled scores). This explanation also accounts for the relatively high IQs earned by 16- to 19-year-olds within each educational category, since their IQ norms (like those of older adults) are much "softer" than the norms for the 20- to 34-year-old reference group.

The other age-related trend for adults evident from Table 6.11 is that in comparing the most to the least educated samples the size of the differences in mean IQs gets smaller with increasing age. For ages 20–34, the range is 27 points for the Performance Scale and 33 points for the Verbal and Full Scales; for ages 65–74, the range is only 15 points for P-IQ and about 25 points for V- and FS-IQ. These age-related changes are also probably an indirect function of the use of a single reference group for computing scaled scores versus the use of separate age groups for determining IQs.

The interrelationships of age, education, and intellectual development are treated more thoroughly in chapter 7, including the finding, cited above, that adults matched on educational attainment perform about equally well on the Verbal sum of scaled scores regardless of their age. This topic is included here for only one reason: to show that apparent developmental trends in WAIS-R data are always potentially artifacts of the different procedures used to obtain an individual's scaled scores and IQs.

IQ Variability
Within Educational Groups

IQ and education are closely related, but there is still considerable variability in the IQs earned by individuals with the same educational attainment. Fluctuations in IQ by education level are shown in Table 6.10, and also in Figure 6.1, based on data compiled (but not published) by Reynolds et al. (1987). This table and figure have already been discussed regarding the variability of IQs within occupational categories.

Table 6.10 presents the range of Full Scale IQs for adults (ages 20–74) in the WAIS-R standardization sample, categorized by educational attainment; also shown are IQs corresponding to the bottom 5% and top 5% for each level. Figure 6.1 depicts the IQ range of the middle 50% of adults completing varying numbers of years of education.

Despite the substantial differences in mean IQs already noted for education levels, there is nonetheless wide variability within each level. College graduates, for example, ranged in FS-IQ from 87 to 148, while high school graduates ranged from 63 to 141. The ranges for the four lowest educational levels do not differ very much from each other; the ranges for the highest

levels differ only at the low end, as no college graduate scored more than 1 standard error of measurement below the Average category, and no one with some college scored below 75.

If the values of FS-IQ corresponding to the 5th and 95th percentiles are thought of as a range, they cut off the middle 90% of adults achieving each education level. All of these ranges overlap substantially. The top 5% of people with 7 years of education or less outscore considerably the bottom 5% of college graduates. Figure 6.1 depicts the IQ ranges for each educational group corresponding to the *middle 50%* (the semi-interquartile range). Again, the substantial degree of overlap from level to level is evident. However, Figure 6.1 also reveals, for example, that the IQs of the middle 50% of adults who failed to graduate from elementary school do not overlap at all with the IQs earned by the middle group of adults with at least a high school education.

Correlations Between
Educational Attainment and IQ

Table 6.12 uses a different approach to relate educational level to intelligence, namely correlation coefficients between years of education (actually the six categories used to code educational attainment) and IQ. These data are taken from Reynolds et al. (1987) and are presented for each of the nine separate normative age groups and for divisions of the sample by gender and race. As shown, the correlations are substantial in magnitude for all separate age groups between 18–19 and 70–74, but are quite small for ages 16–17. The values of .10 to .23 for the youngest age group indicate that only about 1% to 5% of the variability in the IQs for 16- to 17-year-olds can be attributed to education level.

Although the range of the educational variable for this age group is restricted (no one has 13 or more years of education), the amount of shared variance between education and IQ is still unusually low. There is also some range restriction for ages 18–19, yet education and IQ share 17% to 28% of the variance for that group. These results again cast doubt on the accuracy of the norms for older adolescents, this time pinpointing the culprit as inadequate sample selection of 16- to 17-year-olds on the crucial stratification variable of educational attainment.

Because of the questionable nature of the education data for the youngest norms group, data for males versus females, for blacks versus whites, and for the total group were based on only the sample of 18- to 74-year-olds (Reynolds et al., 1987). In Table 6.12, the overall relationships between education and IQ are .60

for the Verbal Scale, .44 for the Performance Scale, and .57 for the Full Scale. Correlations for Verbal IQ and education and for Full Scale IQ and education are highest for ages 25 to 74, averaging .68 and .64, respectively. The mean correlation is .54 with Verbal IQ and .53 with Full Scale IQ for ages 18–24, a group that includes a number of individuals still completing their education. Although the correlations with Performance IQ fluctuate from a low of .40 (ages 70–74) to a high of .57 (ages 55–64), no developmental trends are evident.

Relationships between education and IQ are stronger for whites than blacks on the Verbal and Full Scales, but not on the Performance

TABLE 6.12 Coefficients of correlation between educational level and WAIS-R IQ by age, gender, and race

Group	Sample Size	Verbal IQ	Performance IQ	Full Scale IQ
Age				
16–17	200	.23	.10	.19
18–19	200	.58	.42	.56
20–24	200	.49	.41	.50
25–34	300	.69	.51	.66
35–44	250	.67	.51	.64
45–54	250	.65	.48	.62
55–64	160	.68	.57	.67
65–69	160	.68	.46	.60
70–74	160	.68	.40	.63
Race				
Whites	1492	.60	.42	.56
Blacks	166	.44	.43	.45
Gender				
Males	840	.63	.47	.59
Females	840	.57	.42	.54
Total	1680	.60	.44	.57

NOTE: Data are from Reynolds et al. (1987). Correlations by race and gender, and for the total sample, are based only on individuals aged 18–74.

Scale; correlations were about .05 higher for males than females on each IQ scale. Nonetheless, with the exception of the coefficients for ages 16–17, the data in Table 6.12 support the strong relationship between obtained WAIS-R IQs and educational attainment, regardless of age, gender, or race.

Correlations between education and IQ were higher for the WAIS than the WAIS-R. Wechsler (1958, p. 251) reported coefficients between years of schooling and WAIS sums of scaled scores for ages 18–19, 25–34, and 45–54; he found correlations of .66–.73 for the Verbal Scale, .57–.61 for the Performance Scale, and .66–.72 for the Full Scale. Matarazzo's (1972) statement that a correlation of .70 best summarizes the relationship between IQ and education, though applicable to the WAIS, is too high for the WAIS-R. However, Matarazzo and Herman's (1984b) obtained values of .56 (V-IQ), .41 (P-IQ), and .54 (FS-IQ) for the WAIS-R are a bit low because they included 16- to 17-year-olds in the computations.

The value of .57 between education and Full Scale IQ, reported by Reynolds et al. (1987) for 18- to 74-year-olds and presented as a summary statistic in Table 6.12, is the best current estimate of the relationship between education level and general intelligence. Thus, education accounts for about *one-third* of the variance in WAIS-R Full Scale IQ, substantially less than the 49% value for WAIS Full Scale IQ. I have no explanation for the change, although in view of the great similarity in the constructs measured by the WAIS and WAIS-R (see chapter 3), I feel confident that the change is related to generational differences rather than modifications in the test battery.

Interestingly, the correlation of .57 between education and WAIS-R FS-IQ is about the same as the correlation of .58 between IQ at age 12 and subsequent educational attainment obtained by Bajema (1968) from retrospective interviews of 437 adults who were 45 years old. In addition, correlations between educational attainment and IQ were similar in magnitude for 157 workers from Mexico City who were referred for psychological or psychiatric evaluation and administered the Spanish WAIS, or Escuela de Inteligencia para Adultos (Kunce & Schmidt de Vales, 1986). For this clinical sample of men and women, which had a mean age of 38.5, a mean educational level of 10.0, and mean IQs of 93–94, years of schooling correlated .66 with V-IQ, .51 with P-IQ, and .61 with FS-IQ. Also, Thompson, Howard, and Anderson (1986) found a .52 coefficient between Full Scale IQ and highest grade completed for an American clinical sample of 45 male and 45 female psychiatric inpatients (mean age = 29.2, mean educational attainment = 9.7, mean FS-IQ = 86.5).

Finally, education was also found to correlate in the .50s and .60s with achievement, as measured by the Wide Range Achievement Test (WRAT) and Peabody Individual Achievement Test (PIAT). The WRAT was administered to two separate samples of 115 or more neuropsychological referrals (Warner, Ernst, Townes, Peel, & Preston, 1987). Coefficients were .57 with Arithmetic for each sample, and ranged from .46 to .52 for Reading and Spelling. In addition, WRAT Reading and Spelling each correlated about .65 with education level for 55 adults (mean age = 62.2 years, mean education = 10.1 years) admitted to the hospital with carotid artery disease (Bornstein, 1983b).

The PIAT was given to 162 patients with lateralized lesions (left = 86, right = 76) and 100 normal control subjects (Heaton, Schmitz, Avitable, & Lehman, 1987). The groups averaged 35–40 years of age and 13 to 13½ years of education. Correlations with education for both groups ranged from .45 to .53 for Spelling and Reading Comprehension. Coefficients with Reading Recognition (oral reading) were .52 (brain damaged) and .68 (normals).

Educational Attainment and the 11 WAIS-R Subtests

Kaufman et al. (1988) analyzed the relationships of scores on the 11 WAIS-R subtests to educational attainment, reporting mean differences in IQs for five educational categories for each of four broad age groups. Their MANOVAs produced significant education main effects ($p < .001$) for each age group; the follow-up univariate ANOVAs yielded significant relationships for years of education to scores on each of the 11 subtests. All scaled-score differences due to education level reached significance at the .001 level except for two comparisons at ages 16–19: Object Assembly ($p < .01$) and Digit Symbol ($p < .05$).

Mean scaled scores on each subtest, by age and education level, are presented by Kaufman et al. (1988), but are not shown here. However, the correlations computed by those investigators between years of education and subtest scores for four age groups are presented in Table 6.13. All correlations reached statistical significance at the .001 level except for Object Assembly at ages 16–19 ($p < .01$). The coefficients in Table 6.13 are therefore highlighted based on

the proportion of variance accounted for, and subtests are listed in order of their median coefficient.

Correlations are substantial in magnitude for all age groups except for 16- to 19-year-olds, a group for which none of the tasks accounted for as much as 15% of the variance. Most likely these correlations were attenuated primarily by the subsample of 16- to 17-year-olds, inasmuch as IQs for that age range correlated so poorly with educational attainment. Also leading to depressed coefficients within the sample of 16- to 19-year-olds was the restriction of range in the measure of educational attainment because many of the adolescents were still in the middle of their formal education, and none was old enough to have graduated from college.

For the three samples of adults, correlations were in the .50s and .60s for the four Verbal Comprehension subtests, in the .40s and .50s for Freedom from Distractibility subtests, and

TABLE 6.13   Coefficients of correlation between educational attainment (years of school completed) and scaled scores on the 11 WAIS-R subtests for four broad age groups

Subtest	Ages 16–19 (N = 400)	Ages 20–34 (N = 500)	Ages 35–54 (N = 500)	Ages 55–74 (N = 480)	Median Correlation
Vocabulary	.37	.58**	.61**	.65**	.60**
Information	.38	.55**	.61**	.62**	.58**
Comprehension	.36	.55**	.53**	.60**	.54**
Similarities	.32	.49*	.55**	.56**	.52**
Arithmetic	.29	.49*	.52**	.55**	.50**
Digit Symbol	.25	.45*	.49*	.44*	.44*
Digit Span	.24	.42*	.48*	.42*	.42*
Block Design	.17	.37	.46*	.44*	.40*
Picture Completion	.18	.37	.38	.41*	.38
Picture Arrangement	.19	.39*	.39*	.36	.38
Object Assembly	.14	.26	.34	.30	.28

**Accounts for 25% or more of variance
*Accounts for 15%–24% of variance
NOTE: Data are from Kaufman et al. (1988). Subtests are listed in order of their median correlation with educational attainment.

in the .30s and .40s for the Perceptual Organization subtests.

Median coefficients (computed in preference to means because of the atypical nature of the values for 16- to 19-year-olds) are highest for two very school-related, achievement-oriented tasks (Vocabulary and Information) and lowest for three Performance tasks (Object Assembly, Picture Completion, and Picture Arrangement). Picture Arrangement was also one of the WAIS-R subtests least related to race. Overall, education accounted for more than 25% of the variance in subtest performance for all Verbal tasks except for Digit Span, but only accounted for as much as 15%–20% of the variance in two Performance subtests: Block Design (which makes sense in view of its high g loading) and Digit Symbol (which makes no sense at all). The rank order of subtests from the most education related to the least education related, as indicated in Table 6.13, is virtually identical for each of the four age groups, including the maverick sample of 16- to 19-year-olds.

Birren and Morrison (1961) presented correlations between educational attainment and WAIS subtest scores for a sample of 933 native-born white males and females spanning the wide 25- to 64-year age range. They obtained coefficients that are quite consistent with the median values shown in Table 6.13 for the WAIS-R: correlations in the .60s for Information and Vocabulary, and in the .50s for Digit Symbol, Similarities, and Comprehension; the lowest value reported by Birren and Morrison (1961) was .40 for Object Assembly.

Kunce and Schmidt de Vales (1986), in their study of 157 clinical referrals tested on the Spanish WAIS in Mexico City, found that educational attainment correlated highest with Information (.60) and lowest with Object Assembly (.29). In addition, Bornstein (1983) reported essentially the same findings for 55 elderly patients with carotid artery disease: WAIS Information correlated highest (.56) with years of formal education, while Object Assembly correlated lowest (.05). Hence, the relationship of subtest performance to years of education is rather comparable for the WAIS and WAIS-R, and even generalizes to medical patients in the U.S. and to psychological and psychiatric referrals in Mexico.

The subtest data mirror the IQ data regarding the relationship of intelligence to education. Based on IQ analyses and logic, one would anticipate that Verbal Comprehension subtests would emerge as the WAIS-R tasks most related to years of education; unexpected was the finding that distractibility subtests were more related than Perceptual Organization subtests to educational attainment.

Educational Attainment and the General Factor

Perhaps no study demonstrates so dramatically the strong relationship between formal education and general intelligence as the canonical correlational analysis performed by Chastain and Joe (1987). They extracted a large first canonical factor that included loadings of .42 to .85 by the 11 WAIS-R subtests; highest loadings were by the traditional g tasks of Vocabulary (.85), Information (.80), and Comprehension (.77). The very best measure of the g factor, however, was years of education (.86).

Clinical Implications of WAIS-R Educational Data

The strong impact of education on intelligence test performance must be kept in mind when interpreting WAIS-R profiles. As Reynolds et al. (1987) have noted, a Full Scale IQ of 110 has quite a different meaning for individuals from varying educational backgrounds. Using the data for the total sample in Table 6.1 (along with the standard deviations provided by Reynolds et al., 1987), we can compute that a Full Scale IQ of 110 corresponds to the 97th percentile for individuals with only 0–7 years of education, to the 79th percentile for a high school graduate, and to the 34th percentile for a college graduate!

The high correlations between WAIS-R scores and education should not be used to infer causality. Clearly, a decisive relationship exists between the two variables, but the direction of the relationship is unclear. Do people score higher on intelligence tests because of their long years of education? Or do people stay in school longer because they are smarter to begin with? Unquestionably, the answer to both questions is yes, but the relative variance attributed to each aspect of the education–IQ entanglement is unknown, and "surprisingly few studies have attempted to distinguish between these two possibilities" (Bouchard & Segal, 1985, p. 448). Of the investigations that have attempted to answer the questions posed here, one found that additional education did not enhance IQ (Bradway, Thompson, & Cravens, 1958), but four other investigations reached opposite conclusions (Harnqvist, 1968; Husen, 1951; Lorge, 1945; Newman, Freeman, & Holzinger, 1937).

Certainly, formal education should logically facilitate performance on Information and Vocabulary, and these two tasks correlated highest with educational attainment. Yet the highly significant correlations between education and nonacademic tasks like Digit Symbol, Digit Span, and Block Design argue that it is not just educational experience per se that leads to high IQs. In addition to the studies cited previously suggesting that additional years of education enhance IQ is an often cited study by Dillon (1949) that is consistent with the reciprocal notion that intelligence level limits educational attainment.

Dillon investigated 2,600 seventh grade students and found seventh grade IQ to be an excellent predictor of when students dropped out of school. For example, only 16.5% of the 400 students with IQs below 85 entered grade 11 and only 3.5% graduated from high school. The corresponding percentages for IQs of about 100 are 75.8% and 63.4%; 92.2% of those with

IQs of 115 and above entered eleventh grade and 86.0% graduated from high school.

Naturally, even Dillon's study does not prove causality because education prior to seventh grade may have had a vital impact on the children's IQs. Further, that study involved IQs obtained during childhood on group-administered tests; the results may not be generalizable to individually administered tests or to IQs measured during adulthood. But Dillon's results do reinforce current WAIS-R data and findings from numerous other studies suggesting a powerful relationship between educational attainment and intelligence.

An overview of the education–IQ relationship, based on Jencks et al.'s (1972) review of pertinent investigations, is the generalization "that each extra year of education boosts an individual's adult IQ score about 1 point above the expected level" (p. 88). Although Jencks's estimate is not based on systematic or recent research designed specifically to define the impact of each year of formal education on adult IQ, it "is a reasonable estimate" (Bouchard & Segal, 1985, p. 449).

CHAPTER 6 SUMMARY

This chapter examines individual differences on the variables used to stratify the WAIS-R standardization sample (gender, race, geographic region, urban–rural residence, and educational attainment); it then relates these differences to comparable findings in the literature. Males scored 1–2 points higher than females on the three IQs, a finding consistent with the results of previous Wechsler studies but of no practical consequence. Across the age range, males consistently outperformed females on Information, Arithmetic, and Block Design; females were far superior on Digit Symbol. The mathematical and visual-spatial advantage of males, and the psychomotor speed advantage of females, conform to a wide array of prior investigations; however, researchers disagree on the explanations of these gender differences. In addition, the gender differences in numerous skill areas have been diminishing over the past four decades, impelling some investigators to minimize the important of research in this area.

The persistent finding that whites outperform blacks by about 1 standard deviation on intelligence tests occurred for the WAIS-R standardization sample. V-, P-, and FS-IQ differences of about 13 to 15 points were observed for each age group studied and for males and females. Within each educational category, race differences reduced to about 8–12 points, except for the most educated sample (13+ years of education), which produced the same standard deviation advantage for whites. When the standardization sample was divided by occupational group, race differences were about 10–11 points for subjects in both white-collar and blue-collar jobs. Whites and blacks differed most on Block Design and Vocabulary and least on Digit Span and Picture Arrangement. The results of these analyses of WAIS-R data by race conform fairly well to previous findings and are generally in accord with the Spearman hypothesis that Jensen has researched.

IQ differences for adolescents and adults living in different geographic regions are trivial. Several subtests, however, produced significant regional differences that defy explanation. Urban individuals outscored those living in rural areas by about 2 points, a small difference that reflects a trend toward less urban–rural difference over the years. The urban advantage was substantial in the 1930s, but has virtually disappeared since then. Subtest differences were significant only for the oldest sample (ages 55–74) and primarily on tasks of school-related learning; this finding is related to generational change, since elderly rural individuals were born in the first quarter of the twentieth century.

Mean WAIS-R IQs earned by members of different occupational categories differ strikingly, ranging from about 87–89 for unskilled workers to 110–112 for professional and technical workers; however, there is considerable variability within each of the five categories studied, and much overlap in the distributions. Even larger IQ differences were observed for educational category (a mean of about 115 for college graduates versus 82 for elementary school dropouts), although variability within each of the six educational groups was substantial. Age-related trends were found for the IQ–education relationship; small relationships were noted for the adolescent sample, again underscoring some questionable aspects of the normative sample of 16- to 19-year-olds. The difference between the most educated and least educated samples declined with increasing age, but this finding may be an artifact of the method of obtaining scaled scores.

Overall, educational attainment correlated about .60 with V- and FS-IQ and about .45 with P-IQ. These results occurred for each age group (except 16–17 years), for whites, and for males and females. Coefficients for blacks were .43–.45 regardless of IQ scale. These overall results reflect a drop in the correlation of close to .70 that was observed between WAIS IQ and education. Consistent with much previous research, however, is the finding that the best correlates of educational attainment were Vocabulary and Information, while the worst was Object Assembly. The substantial race, occupational, and educational differences found for the WAIS-R are important, and must be fully taken into account by clinicians when they interpret IQ and subtest profiles.

CHAPTER 7

Age and IQ
Across the
Adult Lifespan

Research on the relationships between aging and intelligence had its inception nearly 100 years ago in comparisons between adults and children (Kirkpatrick, 1903). The topic has captivated researchers in theoretical and clinical disciplines for over half a century (Jones & Conrad, 1933; Lorge, 1936; Miles & Miles, 1932; Willoughby, 1927). Whether intelligence declines with increasing age has been debated by experts in the field (Baltes & Schaie, 1976; Botwinick, 1977; Horn & Donaldson, 1976), and numerous studies have been conducted to determine the nature of the complex relationship between aging and changes in intellectual functioning (see Birren & Schaie, 1985; Kausler, 1982; and Poon, 1980 for reviews). The issue of aging and IQ change is of prime concern to clinicians who test clients across a wide age span, inasmuch as proper WAIS-R interpretation demands understanding of normal, or expected, differential fluctuations in a person's ability spectrum from late adolescence and young adulthood to old age. Distinguishing between

normal and pathological development is often the essence of competent diagnosis in clinical and neuropsychological assessment.

Probably the most comprehensive and cleverly conceived set of studies has been the life's work of K. Warner Schaie (e.g., 1958, 1983b) in collaboration with numerous colleagues (e.g., Hertzog & Schaie, 1988; Schaie & Labouvie-Vief, 1974; Schaie & Strother, 1968). His results have transformed the preconceptions of professionals throughout the world regarding the inevitability of declines in mental functioning along the path to old age. Although some of Schaie's findings remain controversial (Horn, 1977), it is incontestable that his clever sequential combination of cross-sectional and longitudinal research designs has shown the importance of considering cohort (generational) effects when conducting research on aging. Further, Schaie's research program suggests that when declines in intelligence do occur with age, they do so at far later ages than was formerly believed.

But Schaie has consistently used the group-administered, speeded Primary Ability Tests (PMA; Thurstone & Thurstone, 1949), based on Thurstone's theory of intelligence. As valuable as his findings are, they cannot replace research results based directly on the WAIS-R or its predecessors in helping clinicians understand the kinds of changes to anticipate during clinical, neuropsychological, or psychoeducational assessment. Evaluation of adolescents and adults depends on the WAIS-R as its primary or exclusive measure of intellectual functioning. Age changes on the PMA, Army Alpha (Yoakum & Yerkes, 1920), or other group instruments do not necessarily generalize to the profile changes to anticipate when testing the same person several times during his or her lifetime, or when comparing the subtest profiles of individuals or groups who differ in chronological age.

For these reasons, the studies conducted on the WAIS-R (Kaufman, Reynolds, & McLean, 1989; McLean, Kaufman, & Reynolds, 1988b; Parker, 1986), along with other investigations involving the WAIS (Birren & Morrison, 1961; Botwinick, 1967, 1977; Doppelt & Wallace, 1955; Eisdorfer & Wilkie, 1973; Green, 1969) provide the most valuable research findings for the clinical interpretation of aging and intelligence. Even though the WAIS-R data base is cross-sectional and is subject to the impact of unpredictable cohort effects, one of the most important generational differences contributing to cohort effects and the most substantial correlate of IQ—educational level—can be controlled statistically to allow comparison of adults at different age groups on the WAIS-R. This background information was obtained reliably from each member of the standardization sample; indeed it had to be verified carefully because educational attainment was a key variable for the WAIS-R standardization.

In addition, the WAIS and WAIS-R standardization samples are comparable, permitting the longitudinal analysis of specific cohorts over a 25-year period. Later in this chapter (pp. 212–219) I present a new longitudinal investigation using the two standardization samples to explore alleged declines in intelligence, especially nonverbal ability, during the aging process. I believe that these studies on the WAIS and WAIS-R—both the longitudinal analysis and the cross-sectional analysis with education level controlled (Kaufman et al., 1989; McLean et al., 1988b)—provide some of the most important data on aging available to aid clinical assessment. I focus on these data in this chapter and integrate them with other research and clinical findings, including those emerging from Schaie's (1983b) landmark 21-year cohort-sequential Seattle longitudinal study.

The WAIS-R data have a number of advantages in addition to the ones already mentioned:

- *The WAIS-R is the criterion of adult intelligence;* it has an excellent standardization and outstanding psychometric properties (e.g., reliability).

- *The WAIS-R is individually administered.* Data obtained on group-administered instruments like the PMA are subject to individual differences in test-taking behaviors, such as motivation level, attention span, and so forth; these variables are often important in testing elderly individuals. All WAIS-R data were obtained by well-trained psychologists who ensured the maintenance of rapport throughout the testing session.

- *The different adult age groups in the WAIS-R normative group are matched on the Census data—and to each other—for the key variables of gender, race, and geographic region.* The groups also are closely similar on the variable of urban–rural residence and were matched on educational level as part of Kaufman et al.'s (1989) and McLean et al.'s (1988b) educational design. Where else can one obtain such comparable age groups of substantial size (each of the seven age groups between 20–24 and 70–74 comprised 160 to 300 adults) on so many pertinent variables? Also, the excellent WAIS normative group, comparable to the WAIS-R sample on key variables, allows interpretation of IQ changes over the course of a generation.

- *The factor structure of the WAIS-R is virtually identical for all WAIS-R age groups* (Parker, 1983; see chapter 8), supporting the construct validity of the battery from ages 16 through 74; the WAIS-R's factor pattern converges as well with the structure of its predecessors, the Wechsler-Bellevue I and WAIS (see chapter 3). Schaie and Hertzog (1985) have stressed the importance of showing that a test's structure is the same for different versions of a test across the age range, admitting that the PMA does not always satisfy this psychometric criterion. Nonetheless, recent evidence for the PMA shows that this test too has an invariant factor structure across the adult lifespan (Hertzog & Schaie, 1988; Schaie & Hertzog, 1986).

Do WAIS-R IQs Decline With Advancing Age?

Inferring developmental changes from cross-sectional data is a risky business. Groups that differ in chronological age necessarily differ on other variables that may confound apparent age-related differences. A child growing up in the 1920s had different educational and cultural opportunities from one growing up in the 1950s. When tested in the late 1970s as part of the WAIS-R standardization sample, the former child was in the 45- to 54-year-old category, while the latter individual was a member of the 25- to 34-year-old group. Differences in their test performance may be partially a function of their chronological ages during the 1970s, and partially a function of the generational or cohort differences that characterized their respective periods of growth from childhood to adulthood.

Cohort differences, even seemingly obvious ones like the greater number of years of education enjoyed by adults born in more recent years, were mostly ignored by clinicians and researchers through the 1950s and even the 1960s. Wechsler (1958) himself inferred an early and rapid decline in intelligence by uncritically accepting changing mean scores across the adult age range as evidence of a developmental trend: "What is definitely established is . . . that the abilities by which intelligence is measured do in fact decline with age; and . . . that this decline is systematic and after age 30 more or less linear" (p. 142). Although such interpretations were prevalent a generation ago, most researchers are now thoroughly familiar with the impact of cultural change and cohort differences, including educational attainment, on apparent declines in intelligence with age, and have greatly revised the pessimism of Wechsler's conclusions. (An exception is Sattler's, 1982, interpretation of declining mean scaled scores on the WAIS-R as clear evidence of a steep age-related decline in fluid ability.) Based on the bulk of research that has been conducted via cross-sectional (Botwinick, 1977), longitudinal (Schaie, 1983a), and sequential (Schaie, 1983b) methodologies, the most sensible conclusions about the changes in intelligence with age are that fluid abilities do decline more rapidly with age than crystallized abilities (which continue to *grow* well into middle age), but that the declines begin far later in life than was formerly believed.

Horn and Cattell's Viewpoint

The distinction in the adult development of fluid versus crystallized abilities (roughly analogous to Wechsler's Performance and Verbal Scales; see pages 382–383) was first made by Horn and Cattell (1966, 1967) in the 1960s and remains a viable theoretical model for understanding the aging process (Dixon, Kramer, & Baltes, 1985; Horn, 1985). Fluid intelligence (G_f), manifested by the ability to solve novel problems, is presumed to increase with neurological maturation during childhood and adolescence and to decline throughout adulthood concomitantly with neurological degeneration. In contrast, crystallized intelligence $(G_c,$ knowledge and skills dependent on education and experience) is expected to continue to increase during one's life, reflecting cultural assimilation (Horn & Cattell, 1966, 1967).

Applications of this theory have been at the center of the debates on intelligence and aging (Baltes & Schaie, 1976; Horn & Donaldson, 1976). Horn, Donaldson, and Engstrom (1981) have conceded that "the evidence of direct relationships between alterations of physiological systems and decline of G_f is too scant to permit anything more than reasonable conjecture" (p. 41); nonetheless, they assert that considerable evidence supports the conclusion that "[r]elative to the G_c abilities, the G_f abilities decline first, decline over the longest period of adult development, and decline most" (p. 39). Indeed, support for that statement has been substantial (Cunningham, Clayton, & Overton, 1975; Hayslip & Sterns, 1979; Horn, 1982; McLean, Kaufman, & Reynolds, 1988b). Even if one disputes the neurological aspects of intellectual decline and whether the decline in fluid ability begins in young adulthood or late in life, Horn and Cattell's contributions to gerontology have been enormous. Excellent reviews of the burgeoning literature on changes in intelligence with increasing age are readily available in superior textbooks (Kausler, 1982) and handbooks (Dixon et al., 1985; Labouvie-Vief, 1985).

Cross-Sectional Analysis of Wechsler's Tests at Ages 20 to 75+

Before considering the impact of educational attainment on the age–IQ relationship, let us examine the mean IQs earned by adults of different ages on the Wechsler-Bellevue I, WAIS, and WAIS-R. Typically, researchers present tables or graphs of sums of scaled scores on Wechsler's batteries, since these are the values that reveal increases or decreases in mean performance from age to age. IQs are derived separately for each adult age group, so, by definition the mean V-, P-, and FS-IQs equal 100 for each age level. However, I prefer to work

directly with IQs rather than sums of scaled scores for two reasons: (a) IQs are familiar, practical units to clinicians, whereas scaled score sums are nothing but intermediary raw scores; and (b) the mean sums of scaled scores are not comparable from scale to scale because the WAIS and WAIS-R Verbal Scale has 6 subtests, the Performance Scale has 5 subtests, and the Full Scale has 11 subtests (in contrast, IQs are comparable from scale to scale).

The conversion of mean sums of scaled scores to mean IQs is a simple procedure. First, I selected the IQ conversion table for a single adult age group to serve as a reference group for comparing all age groups. Any age might have been selected, but I chose ages 25–34 because this age group comes closest to the reference group that Wechsler selected (ages 20–34) for computing everyone's subtest scaled scores. Next, I entered the 25–34 age group's IQ table with the mean sums of scaled scores earned by every age group and interpolated to compute their mean V-, P-, and FS-IQs based on the performance of 25- to 34-year-olds. This procedure, also followed in the WAIS-R research that I conducted with my colleagues (Kaufman et al., 1989; McLean et al., 1988b), allows a simple comparison of mean IQ differences on the three IQ scales for all age groups.

I applied these simple procedures to the Wechsler-Bellevue I (using the midpoint of the norms tables for ages 25–29 and 30–34) and to the WAIS. For the WAIS, I used data for the standardization sample at ages 20–64 and data for the separate Kansas City old-age sample (Doppelt & Wallace, 1955) at ages 65 to 75+. (See the note to Table 7.1 for more information.) Although the old-age sample was not stratified on Census variables, there is evidence that the 60- to 64-year-olds in the Kansas City sample were reasonably comparable to the adults of the same age in the stratified normative sample in terms of mean performance levels (Wechsler, 1955, Table 16). For all of these analyses, I have excluded individuals below age 20. Most of these adolescents had not yet finished their formal educations, making it impossible to control for their educational attainment in direct comparisons to adult age groups. Also, the WAIS-R data for ages 16–19 are tainted by an unknown bias (see pp. 83–85), precluding generalization to older adolescents in general.

Mean IQ Differences on Wechsler's Adult Tests Across the Adult Lifespan

Table 7.1 presents mean IQs for the different age groups in the Wechsler-Bellevue I, WAIS, and WAIS-R standardization samples (including the elderly adults in the WAIS old-age sample). For the Wechsler-Bellevue, the oldest group was 55–59 years, compared to 75+ for the WAIS, and 70–74 for the WAIS-R. For all three instruments, the mean scores tended to decrease with increasing age, with the most dramatic changes evident on the Performance

Scale. The sharp drop in P-IQ evidenced through age 59 on the W-B I was instrumental in Wechsler's (1939, 1946) decision *not* to permit computation of P-IQ above age 49. He did not even provide sums of scaled scores for ages 50 and above, although these values could be estimated from the Verbal and Full Scale sums (Matarazzo, 1972, Table 10.3).

Overall, the striking apparent age-related changes in intelligence from the 20s through old age, especially in P-IQ, are so overwhelming (and depressing, if taken at face value) that it is easy to understand why Wechsler and others concluded that the path to old age is paved by a steady, unrelenting loss of intellectual function. Also intriguing in Table 7.1 is the incredible similarity in the cross-sectional data for the three adult Wechsler batteries that were normed in 1937, 1953, and 1978. In particular, the mean P-IQs (relative to the reference group of 25- to 34-year-olds) for the WAIS and

TABLE 7.1   Mean IQs (based on norms for ages 25–34) across the adult lifespan on the Wechsler-Bellevue I, WAIS, and WAIS-R

Age Group	VERBAL IQ			PERFORMANCE IQ			FULL SCALE IQ		
	W-B I	*WAIS*	*WAIS-R*	*W-B I*	*WAIS*	*WAIS-R*	*W-B I*	*WAIS*	*WAIS-R*
20–24	100.5	98.5	95.6	105.2	101.6	101.1	103.1	99.8	97.2
25–34	100.2	99.8	98.4	100.2	100.1	98.9	100.2	99.9	98.2
35–44	98.1	99.2	94.5	93.0	95.1	93.3	95.4	97.5	93.5
45–54	95.4	97.0	95.1	86.4	89.0	89.2	90.6	93.4	91.8
55–64[a]	93.0	94.8	92.6	82.8	84.1	84.2	87.6	89.6	87.6
65–69	—	90.9	91.0	—	79.7	78.8	—	85.5	84.4
70–74	—	85.0	89.5	—	72.3	75.6	—	78.5	81.7
75+	—	80.2	—	—	66.1	—	—	72.9	—

[a]W-B I data listed for ages 55–64 are based only on adults ages 55–59.
NOTE: Data for the W-B I were obtained by entering mean sums of scaled scores (Matarazzo, 1972, p. 232) into the W-B I IQ conversion table for ages 25–29 and 30–34. Mean Performance sums of scaled scores for the two oldest W-B I groups were computed by subtracting the Verbal sum from the Full sum. Data for the WAIS were obtained by entering mean sums of scaled scores into the WAIS IQ conversion table for ages 25–34. Mean sums for ages 20–24 through 55–64 are from Wechsler (1955, p. 19); mean sums for ages 65–69 through 75+ were computed from mean scaled scores on the 11 WAIS subtests obtained by the old-age sample, as reported by Doppelt and Wallace (1955, pp. 318–319). WAIS-R data are from Kaufman, Reynolds, and McLean (1989).

WAIS-R are uncannily similar for each age group between 20–24 and 70–74, never differing by more than 2.3 IQ points. Considering that the two standardization samples differed substantially in educational attainment (a point that will be discussed in the next section), and that each corresponding age group in the WAIS and WAIS-R samples was subject to huge generation or cohort effects, the similarities in the cross-sectional data seem quite remarkable. (Forty-year-olds in the WAIS sample, for example, were born just before World War I, while their age contemporaries in the WAIS-R sample were born just prior to World War II.)

Peak Performance on the Wechsler-Bellevue, WAIS, and WAIS-R

Table 7.1 shows that peak performance shifted slightly from Wechsler battery to battery: Ages 20–24 performed best on the Wechsler-Bellevue FS-IQ; ages 20–24 and 25–34 performed about equally well on the WAIS FS-IQ; and ages 25–34 earned the highest WAIS-R FS-IQ. Matarazzo (1972, Tables 10.3 and 10.4) presented mean sums of scaled scores on the Wechsler-Bellevue I and WAIS for more homogeneous adult groups (5- instead of 10-year intervals), and for adolescent samples, yielding the results shown in Table 7.2 regarding peak performance. (WAIS-R data were available only for the more heterogeneous normative age groups. Only the midpoint of each "peak" age interval is shown.)

These results show that intelligence, as measured on Wechsler's adult scales (especially Verbal and overall ability), tends to reach a peak later in life with each succeeding generation. Parker (1986) studied this "peak" phenomenon for global intelligence using as his data sources the three Wechsler standardizations plus three additional fairly representative samples tested between 1916 and 1931: Terman (1916), Jones and Conrad (1933), and Miles and Miles (1932). Including the Wechsler data, Parker (1986) observed the following ages of peak global performance on IQ tests:

Year tested	Peak age
1916	16
1926	20
1931	18.5
1937	22
1953	27
1978	30

The steady increase in the peak performance of adolescents and adults between 1916 and 1978 reinforces findings by Flynn (1984, 1987) that scores on intelligence tests are increasing in the United States at the rate of 3 points per decade (see chapter 2).

TABLE 7.2   Peak intellectual performance on Wechsler's adult scales

Test	Approximate Year Normed	Peak Performance on		
		Verbal	Performance	Full Scale
W-B I	1937	age 24.5	age 18	age 22
WAIS	1953	age 27	age 27	age 27
WAIS-R	1978	age 29.5	age 22	age 29.5

Education Differences for Wechsler's Standardization Age Groups

Table 7.3 reveals the folly of interpreting changes in mean scores from age to age as evidence of developmental change. Good standardization samples match the U.S. Census proportions on key background variables, and some variables, like educational attainment, differ widely from age group to age group. With each passing decade, an increasing proportion of adults stay longer in elementary and high school, and more and more people attend college. Consequently, the younger adult age groups will be relatively more educated than the older adult age groups. Similarly, any age group tested in the early 1950s on the WAIS will be considerably less educated than that same age group tested in the late 1970s on the WAIS-R. These facts are quite evident in Table 7.3; comparable data for the Wechsler-Bellevue I were not available, although the lower level of education for the *total* adolescent and adult W-B I sample (Matarazzo,

1972, Table 9.3) was evident from the low percentage of high school graduates (10.8).

Table 7.3 shows the tremendous change in the proportion of adults in the WAIS-R sample with 11 or fewer years of education (17% for ages 20–24 versus 60% for ages 70–74), as well as the sizable change in the percentage of individuals within each age group who have at least 1 year of college. Similarly, 40% of the 45- to 54-year-olds in the WAIS-R sample graduated from high school, compared to only 15.5% of the 45- to 54-year-olds in the WAIS sample. These discrepancies from age to age and from test to test reflect the true meaning of cohort differences. Since education level correlated about .70 with WAIS FS-IQ and about .60 with WAIS-R FS-IQ, producing mean FS-IQ differences of *over 2 standard deviations* between the most and least educated individuals (see chapter 6), no meaningful comparison of age and intelligence can take place without exerting some control over each age group's educational attainment. Several such investigations

TABLE 7.3   Comparison of educational attainment for different adult age groups in the WAIS and WAIS-R standardization samples

	Percentage of Adults with					
	11 or Less Years of Education		*12 Years (High School Graduate)*		*One or More Years of College*	
Age Group	*WAIS*	*WAIS-R*	*WAIS*	*WAIS-R*	*WAIS*	*WAIS-R*
20–24	44.0	17.0	36.0	43.5	20.0	39.5
25–34	48.0	17.0	32.5	39.5	19.5	43.5
35–44	59.5	26.0	22.5	42.5	18.0	31.5
45–54	70.5	34.5	15.5	40.0	14.0	25.5
55–64	77.5	43.5	11.5	37.0	11.0	19.5
65–69	—	55.0	—	25.5	—	19.5
70–74	—	60.0	—	24.0	—	16.0

NOTE: All values are rounded to the nearest half-point. Data for the WAIS are from Wechsler (1955, Table 5); data for the WAIS-R are from Wechsler (1981, Table 5). Age-by-education data were unavailable for the WAIS old-age sample or for the Wechsler-Bellevue I standardization sample.

were conducted with the WAIS (Birren & Morrison, 1961; Green, 1969; Heaton, Grant, & Matthews, 1986); they will be discussed after complete results of the WAIS-R age-education study are presented.

Age–IQ Relationships on the WAIS-R With Education Controlled

Taken together, Tables 7.1 and 7.3 present an interesting picture of three variables correlating together in a way that obscures the relationship between any two of them. As age increases IQs decrease; but a similar, steady decrease occurs as well in years of education. Table 7.4 depicts this triple relationship for the WAIS-R, using FS-IQ data from Table 7.1 and the percentage of adults with at least some college experience from Table 7.3.

Overview of the WAIS-R Research Investigations

These relationships demanded systematic investigation to determine whether the decline in intelligence scores with increasing age was more a function of aging or of limited education. My colleagues and I set out to answer this important question (Kaufman, Reynolds, & McLean, 1989; McLean, Kaufman, & Reynolds, 1988b; Rey-

nolds had available the WAIS-R standardization data tape from The Psychological Corporation). We conducted this research with complete awareness of the limitations of cross-sectional studies, mainly the intrusion of cohort effects. We were satisfied that controlling for education level ruled out (to the degree possible in post hoc research) the impact of probably the single most confounding cohort variable, indeed the variable that shows the strongest relationship to IQ *within* any cohort. Further, we were pleased to have access to data from seven large, carefully selected adult age groups that matched Census data *and each other* on gender, race, geographic region, and urban versus rural residence. By matching these age groups on educational attainment, we were able to analyze recent, well-stratified data on an excellent test across a wide age span (20–74 years).

We applied two different statistical procedures to answer the same question about relationships between age and IQ with a control for education: (a) multiple regression analysis, to determine whether age added significantly and substantially to the prediction of IQ obtainable from education alone; and (b) an equating technique, whereby each age group was equated on educational attainment by weighting their scores in proportion to the percentage of adults in each educational category that char-

TABLE 7.4   The relationship between age, WAIS-R FS-IQ, and education

Age Group	Mean WAIS-R Full Scale IQ	Percentage with 1 or More Years of College
20–24	97.2	39.5
25–34	98.2	43.5
35–44	93.5	31.5
45–54	91.8	25.5
55–64	87.6	19.5
65–69	84.4	19.5
70–74	81.7	16.0

acterized a reference group (ages 25–34 years). Both analyses were reported and interpreted by Kaufman et al. (1989) and McLean et al. (1988b); however, the first source emphasizes the multiple regression analysis, while the second one features the equating technique.

Both analyses were applied to WAIS-R data for the three IQs as well as the 11 subtests. These results are summarized in the sections that follow. In subsequent parts of the chapter, these findings are integrated with previous research, including longitudinal and Schaie's cross-sequential investigations, and they are interpreted from the Horn-Cattell theoretical model.

Results of the Multiple Regression Analysis

Striking relationships between educational attainment and intelligence were demonstrated in chapter 6 for WAIS-R IQs and scaled scores. Consequently, entering educational attainment into regression equations as the first predictor of WAIS-R IQs (actually, sums of scaled scores) and scaled scores should account for a substantial proportion of variance. (The education variable was years of education, grouped into six categories ranging from 0–7 years to 16 or more years of formal education.) This is precisely what occurred for the 1,480 adults in the WAIS-R standardization sample, ages 20–74, as shown in Table 7.5 (adapted from Kaufman et al., 1989, Table 2). Education accounted for nearly half the variability in V-IQ and FS-IQ, and about one-third of the variance in P-IQ; this crucial variable also accounted for about one-third of the variance of Verbal Comprehension subtests, one-fourth of the variance in the distractibility triad (Digit Span, Arithmetic, Digit Symbol), and about 15% of the variance in the Perceptual Organization subtests (all Performance tasks except Digit Symbol).

The strong relationships of education to IQ were never at issue; instead, the key was whether chronological age would add substantially to the prediction of intelligence when entered as the second predictor in the regression equations.

We defined *substantial* as meeting two requirements: statistical significance at the .01 level, and accounting for an additional 2% or more of the total variance. Significance was not enough, because a sample size of nearly 1,500 yields significance with very small increments; the increment had to be of practical, not just statistical, significance.

Adding age as a predictor led to a striking increment of nearly 13% for P-IQ but only a trivial increase of 0.3% for V-IQ (see Table 7.5). Age increased prediction of FS-IQ by the requisite amount, but barely (exactly 2%). None of the increments for the Verbal subtests reached the 2% criterion, whereas each of the Performance subtests easily met the requirement. Age improved the prediction of scaled score by at least 5% for every Performance task, ranging from 5.6% for Picture Completion to 14.4% for Digit Symbol; the latter task has long been recognized as producing substantially lower scores with increasing age (Kausler, 1982).

These results support Botwinick's (1977) classical aging pattern: Age was shown to be a substantial correlate of intelligence, over and above the contribution of educational attainment, for the timed Performance subtests and for P-IQ, but not for the nontimed components (Arithmetic is an exception) of the Verbal Scale.

Table 7.5 reveals the interesting finding that the *combination* of education and age accounts for almost the precise amount of variance in V-IQ (45.4%) as in P-IQ (45.6%). However, the relative contributions of each variable are quite different when age and education are treated separately, as shown in Table 7.6 (additional data from Kaufman et al., 1989).

The WAIS-R Equating Study: Verbal, Performance, and Full Scale IQ

The first step in equating the seven adult age groups on educational attainment was to identify a reference group to use as the standard or "target" against which to match all other groups. The logical group was ages 25–34, the age

TABLE 7.5   Multiple regression analysis, using education and age as predictors of WAIS-R scores: the amount of variance accounted for by age over and above the contribution of education

WAIS-R Criterion	PERCENTAGE OF VARIANCE ACCOUNTED FOR BY		
	Education Alone	Education and Age Combined	Increment Due to Age
Sum of Scaled Scores			
Verbal	45.1	45.4	0.3%*
Performance	32.9	45.6	12.7%**
Full Scale	45.5	47.5	2.0%**
Verbal Scaled Score			
Information	34.7	35.8	1.1%**
Digit Span	21.4	21.5	0.1%
Vocabulary	37.0	38.6	1.6%**
Arithmetic	27.9	28.2	0.3%
Comprehension	31.0	31.8	0.8%**
Similarities	33.0	33.6	0.6%**
Performance Scaled Score			
Picture Completion	21.2	26.8	5.6%**
Picture Arrangement	20.7	28.6	7.9%**
Block Design	24.3	31.2	6.9%**
Object Assembly	15.2	23.8	8.6%**
Digit Symbol	28.9	43.3	14.4%**

*$p < .01$; **$p < .001$
NOTE: Table is adapted from Kaufman et al. (1989, Table 2).

TABLE 7.6   Relative contributions of age and education to WAIS-R IQs

Criterion	Amount of Variance Accounted for by	
	Age Alone	Education Alone
Verbal IQ	3.1%	45.1%
Performance IQ	28.2%	32.9%
Full Scale IQ	13.4%	45.5%

NOTE: Data are from Kaufman et al. (1989).

category that earned the highest sum of scaled scores on the WAIS-R Full Scale (Wechsler, 1981, Table 7), and the group that overlaps most with the reference group used by Wechsler to determine everyone's scaled scores. We selected this group, and then weighted each of the other six age groups' V, P, and FS sums of scaled scores by the proportions of adults in each educational category at ages 25–34.

The mean sums of scaled scores for each separate educational category were computed for each of the seven adult age groups. This age-by-education breakdown is shown in Table 7.7. Within each age group, these means were weighted by the following percentages, corresponding to the proportion of 25- to 34-year-old adults in each educational category: 0–8 years of education (5.3%), 9–11 years (11.7%), 12 years (39.3%), 13–15 years (20.0%), and 16+ years (23.7%). Using this weighting technique, the variable of educational attainment was controlled across the age range from 20 to 74; every age group was made comparable to the reference group (and hence to each other) in terms of its proportion of adults in each of the five educational categories.

Table 7.7 includes some interesting findings, all of which are entirely consistent with the results of the multiple regression analysis.

- Regardless of chronological age (and, hence, *when* people were educated), adults with the same amount of formal education earned about the same mean sum of scaled scores on the Verbal Scale. Adults with 0–8 years of education earned Verbal sums of about 40; those with 9–11 years scored about 50; high school graduates scored 55–60; adults with some college earned means of approximately 65; and college graduates scored in the 70–75 range. This relationship maintained whether the adult was 25, 50, or 65, and whether he or she was educated in the 1910s, 1930s, or 1950s.
- Unlike Verbal sums, Performance sums *decreased steadily* within each educational cat-

egory, although the decrements were relatively small for the least educated samples.

- The weighted (education-controlled) verbal means for each of the seven age groups were all approximately 60 to 62. The seven means did *not* differ significantly based on an analysis of variance, although the unweighted means produced significance at the .001 level (Kaufman et al., 1989). This equality of weighted means did not hold for either the Performance or Full Scales, which each yielded significant F values ($p < .001$) both before and after weighting.

We entered each of the weighted means into the WAIS-R IQ norms table for ages 25–34 to permit comparisons of the seven age groups using the more familiar IQ units rather than sums of scaled scores (as was done for the Wechsler-Bellevue, WAIS, and WAIS-R cross-sectional data in Table 7.1). After controlling for education, the decline in Verbal IQ disappeared, but the declines in P-IQ and FS-IQ remained substantial.

The overall results of this WAIS-R study are depicted in Figures 7.1, 7.2, and 7.3, which show the mean IQs for seven adult age groups, both with and without a control for education. These findings join with the alternate (multiple regression) analysis to give clear-cut support to Botwinick's (1977) classic intellectual aging pattern. The results also support Horn's (1985) interpretation of the classic pattern from the fluid/crystallized theory of intelligence: Crystallized abilities remain stable through old age, while fluid abilities decline steadily and rapidly, starting in young adulthood. Although Botwinick's view of the aging pattern in terms of the speed factor (maintenance of performance on nontimed tasks, decline on timed tasks) may seem as plausible as Horn's fluid versus crystallized approach, the evidence presented on pages 222–231 provides strong support for Horn's interpretation.

On the Verbal Scale, the peak IQ (99.8) occurred for ages 55–64 after equating for ed-

TABLE 7.7   Mean WAIS-R Verbal, Performance, and Full Scale sums of scaled scores for adults completing different numbers of years of education, by age

Years of Education	AGE GROUP						
	20–24	25–34	35–44	45–54	55–64	65–69	70–74
Verbal Scale							
0–8	41.6	31.9	37.3	41.8	42.3	42.4	43.0
9–11	51.1	50.8	45.8	51.4	52.7	52.2	51.1
12	55.5	57.6	58.2	60.0	59.9	59.4	55.6
13–15	65.0	67.7	63.6	65.4	65.0	62.2	66.0
16+	69.5	74.3	72.8	74.2	75.3	73.8	72.9
Weighted mean	59.5	61.4	60.2	62.4	62.8	61.6	60.6
Performance Scale							
0–8	37.0	33.1	31.9	31.0	28.9	28.3	27.7
9–11	47.7	44.0	38.0	40.2	37.6	35.8	30.8
12	49.5	47.6	46.1	43.8	42.1	36.0	31.7
13–15	54.3	53.6	50.0	44.4	42.6	37.4	35.9
16+	58.7	57.2	53.7	50.2	47.9	41.8	38.0
Weighted mean	51.8	49.9	47.0	44.4	42.4	37.2	33.7
Full Scale							
0–8	78.6	65.0	69.2	72.8	71.2	70.7	70.7
9–11	98.8	94.8	83.7	91.6	90.3	88.0	81.8
12	105.0	105.3	104.4	103.8	101.9	95.5	87.3
13–15	119.2	121.2	113.5	109.8	107.7	99.6	101.9
16+	128.2	131.5	126.5	124.4	123.2	115.6	110.9
Weighted mean	112.2	111.3	107.2	106.8	105.1	98.9	94.3

NOTE: Weighted means were obtained by using as weights the proportions of adults in each educational category at ages 25–34 years. Data are from Kaufman et al. (1989).

ucation level; even at ages 70–74, the weighted mean V-IQ was nearly 98. In contrast, education-controlled means in P-IQ dipped below 90 at ages 55–64, and below 80 for 70- to 74-year-olds. For the latter sample of elderly individuals, the mean FS-IQ was only 87.9 despite the control for educational attainment.

The WAIS-R Equating Study: The 11 Separate Subtests

Equating for education has also been applied to the 11 separate subtests (McLean et al., 1988b) as well as to the three IQs. Mean scaled scores on each subtest were determined *within* each

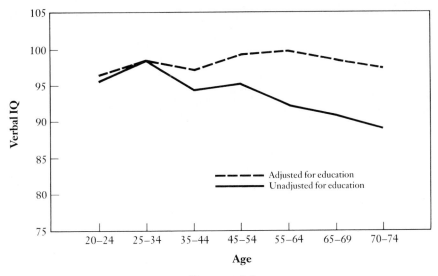

FIGURE 7.1

Change in WAIS-R Verbal IQ across the 20- to 74-year age range, both with and without a control for education; IQs were based on norms for ages 25–34 (data from Kaufman, Reynolds, & McLean, 1989).

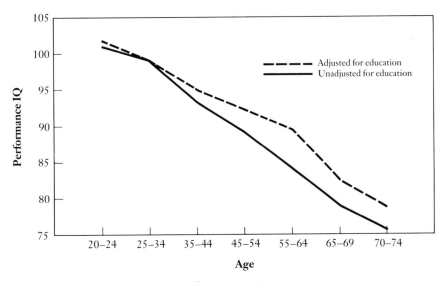

FIGURE 7.2

Change in WAIS-R Performance IQ across the 20- to 74-year age range, both with and without a control for education; IQs were based on norms for ages 25–34 (data from Kaufman, Reynolds, & McLean, 1989).

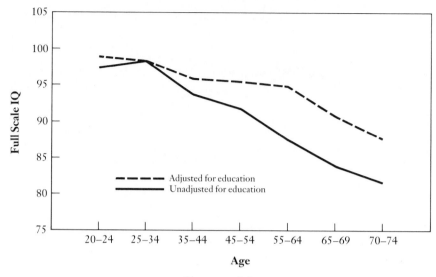

FIGURE 7.3

Change in WAIS-R Full Scale IQ across the 20- to 74-year age range, both with and without a control for education; IQs were based on norms for ages 25–34 (data from Kaufman, Reynolds, & McLean, 1989).

age group for the five educational categories, and these means were then weighted by the proportions of 25- to 34-year-olds in each category. Unlike the sums of scaled scores that require conversion to IQs, scaled scores need no such conversion; these units were already derived from a reference group of 20- to 34-year-olds, and they are quite familiar to clinicians.

Before weighting the scaled scores at each age for education level, the mean values for each age group (given by Wechsler, 1981, Table 15) show a general downward trend. Verbal subtests peaked at ages 25–34 before beginning a fairly steady decline through old age. Ages 70–74 performed poorest on all subtests, although the means for Similarities (7.3) and Digit Span (8.4) were lower than the values of about 9 for the other four tasks. Performance subtests also displayed similar patterns. Peak scores were observed at ages 20–24 (tied by ages 25–34 for the two "Picture" subtests) followed by a steady, rapid decline after age 34. The group of adults in their early 70s averaged about 6 to 6 ½ on

all Performance subtests except Digit Symbol, which plunged to 4.9.

After equating for education, the declines in Verbal means disappeared and were replaced by gradual increments into the mid- to late 60s for Information, Vocabulary, and Comprehension. Arithmetic produced nearly equal weighted means (9.9–10.4) for *each* of the seven age groups. Only Digit Span and Similarities showed a declining trend (in the mid-50s), but it was small in magnitude.

In contrast, each Performance subtest (like the total Performance Scale), continued to reveal striking decrements in mean scaled scores, even after balancing the groups on education. With the control, however, performance was maintained at a respectable level for some nonverbal subtests. Picture Completion and Picture Arrangement, for example, produced weighted means of approximately 9.0 through age 64 before dropping substantially to the 7–8 level.

Table 7.8 presents peak and low performance on each WAIS-R subtest, based on the edu-

TABLE 7.8 "Peak" and "low" ages of performance on the 11 WAIS-R subtests for age groups controlled for educational attainment

Subtest	Peak Age[a]	Low Age[a]	MEAN EDUCATION-ADJUSTED SCALED SCORE		
			Highest Age Group	Lowest Age Group	Scaled-Score Range[b]
Verbal					
Information	62	22	10.9	9.9	1.0
Digit Span	22/49.5	69.5	10.1	9.4	0.7
Vocabulary	72	22	11.1	9.7	1.4
Arithmetic	54.5	22	10.4	9.9	0.5
Comprehension	62	22	11.0	9.9	1.1
Similarities	29.5	72	10.2	9.0	1.2
Performance					
Picture Completion	22	72	10.3	7.4	2.9
Picture Arrangement	22	72	10.2	6.6	3.6
Block Design	22	72	10.3	7.2	3.1
Object Assembly	22	72	10.3	7.1	3.2
Digit Symbol	22	72	10.5	5.5	5.0

[a]Peak age and low age equal the *midpoint* of the age group, or adjacent age groups, having the highest (or lowest) mean scaled score on each WAIS-R subtest after the scaled scores were adjusted for educational attainment.

[b]Scaled-score range equals the difference between the highest and lowest mean scaled scores (adjusted for educational attainment) earned by the seven separate age groups between 20–24 and 70–74.

NOTE: These data are based on McLean et al.'s (1988b) Table 6.

cation-balanced mean scores. Peak ages for all Verbal subtests except Similarities and Digit Span were above 50. These two maverick subtests each produced their lowest performance by elderly subjects, whereas the "low age" for the other Verbal subtests was 22. Each Performance task revealed its peak at 22 and its bottom score at age 72. The ranges of the mean weighted scaled scores (high minus low mean for the seven age groups, also shown in Table 7.8) were substantial for the Performance tasks, averaging 3 to 5 points. The Verbal ranges were much smaller, only about 1 point. Thus, even though Similarities and Digit Span resembled the Performance tasks in their peak and

low ages (manifesting similar *trends*), the magnitude of the changes with age were quite small, resembling the other Verbal subtests.

Figure 7.4 (Verbal) and Figure 7.5 (Performance) show pictorially the changes in mean scaled scores on the WAIS-R subtests, both with and without a control for educational attainment. The precise mean weighted (for education) scaled scores earned by each age group are given in chapter 12 in the subtest-by-subtest analysis of each WAIS-R task. All of these figures and tables, including the peak ages and scaled-score ranges in Table 7.8, suggest the same conclusion: After controlling for education level, scores on Verbal subtests tend to maintain,

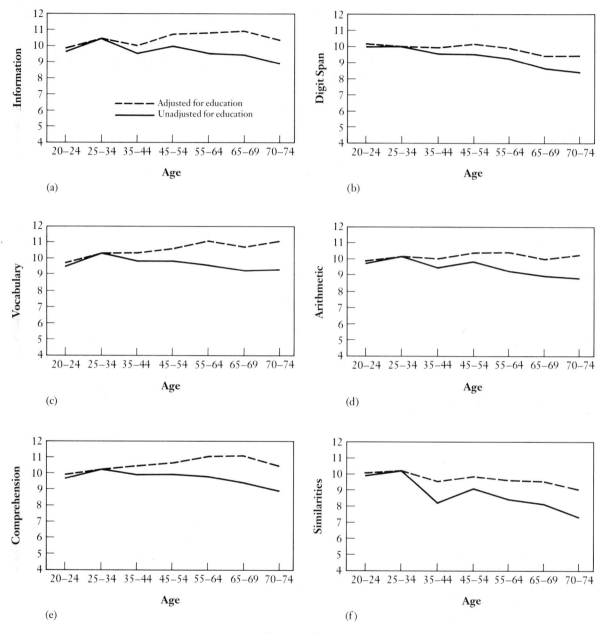

FIGURE 7.4

Change in WAIS-R Verbal subtest scaled scores across the 20- to 74-year age range, both with and without a control for education (data from McLean, Kaufman, and Reynolds, 1988b).

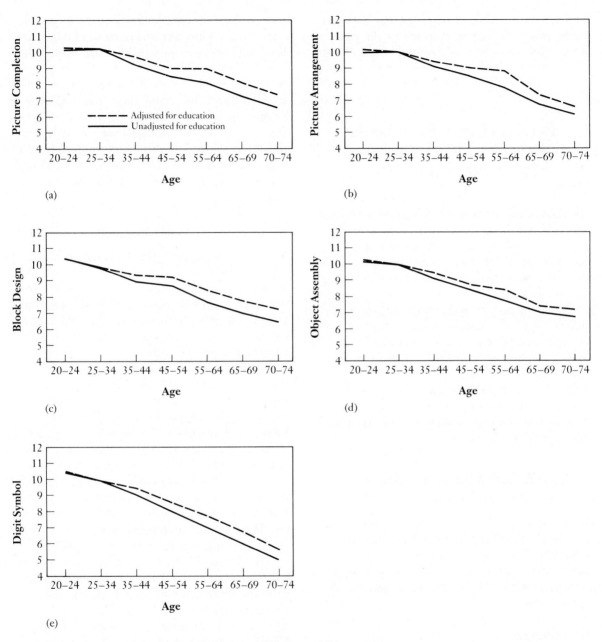

FIGURE 7.5

Change in WAIS-R Performance subtest scaled scores across the 20- to 74-year age range, both with and without a control for education (data from McLean, Kaufman and Reynolds, 1988b).

or improve slightly, through the late 60s and, occasionally, the early 70s; scores on Performance subtests show a clear-cut decline with age, beginning in the mid-30s but not becoming pronounced until the 50s or 60s.

INTEGRATION OF WAIS-R RESULTS WITH CROSS-SECTIONAL RESEARCH

The aim of this section is to integrate the results of the WAIS-R cross-sectional study, controlled for educational attainment (Kaufman et al., 1989; McLean et al., 1988b), with previous well-designed cross-sectional investigations of aging and intelligence.

Three cross-sectional WAIS investigations deserve special attention because of their systematic treatment of the variables of chronological age and educational level in attempts to determine the relative contributions of each. Each of these studies (Birren & Morrison, 1961; Green, 1969; Heaton et al., 1986) included excellent samples of at least 500 adults spread across a wide age range.

Birren and Morrison's Study of White Adults on the WAIS

Birren and Morrison (1961) controlled education level statistically by partialling out years of education from the correlation of each WAIS subtest with chronological age, using standardization data for 933 white males and females aged 25–64.

Key Findings

Scores on each of the 11 subtests initially correlated negatively with age, with all Performance subtests correlating more negatively (−.28 to −.46) than did the Verbal tasks (−.02 to −.19). After statistically removing the influence of educational attainment from the correlations, four of the six Verbal subtests produced *positive* correlations. However, the removal of education level did *not* erase the negative correlations with the Performance subtests; partial correlations were only slightly lower (about .10) than the original coefficients, and they remained statistically significant. Although Birren and Morrison (1961) did not conduct these analyses with the three IQ scales, their study did show the decrease in mean V-IQ with age—but *not* the decrement in P-IQ—to be an artifact of education level.

Relationship to WAIS-R Results

Birren and Morrison's (1961) WAIS results are strikingly similar to our WAIS-R findings. All WAIS subtests correlated negatively with age, just as all WAIS-R subtests revealed decreasing scaled scores with increasing age when education was left unchecked. When Birren and Morrison removed education level from the correlations, the coefficients remained negative for Similarities (−.04) and Digit Span (−.08)—the same two WAIS-R Verbal tasks that evidenced slight age-related score decreases after balancing the samples on education. Of the four WAIS Verbal subtests with positive partial correlations, indicating slight increments in scaled scores with increasing age, the highest coefficients were obtained for Vocabulary (.22) and Information (.17), two of the three subtests on the WAIS-R (Comprehension was the other) evidencing apparent growth into the 60s.

The Birren-Morrison data for the WAIS Performance Scale revealed strong negative correlations, even after removing education level, for Digit Symbol (−.38) and Picture Arrangement (−.27). As evident in Table 7.8, these WAIS-R subtests produced the two largest decreases in test scores between early adulthood and old age. More moderate, but still significant, negative partial correlations (−.16 to −.22) emerged for the three remaining WAIS Performance subtests, further corroborating the findings with the WAIS-R. The results of Kaufman et al.'s (1989) multiple correlation analysis (see Table 7.5) indicated that age added substantially to the prediction of all five WAIS-R Performance subtests, over and above the prediction by education alone; by far the largest increment was observed for Digit Symbol, with Picture Arrangement ranking third.

Comparison to the Doppelt-Wallace Data

Birren and Morrison (1961) used WAIS standardization data for white males and females between 25 and 64 years of age. Doppelt and Wallace (1955) analyzed data for the total WAIS standardization sample (including nonwhites and adults below age 25) and for the special old-age sample aged 60–75+. Although these authors did not attempt to control for education level, they did graph the mean V, P, and FS sums of scaled scores obtained by each age group between 17 and 79.5 years, as well as their mean scaled scores on all 11 subtests (Doppelt & Wallace, 1955, Figures 1, 2, and 3). When the portions of their graphs corresponding to ages 20–74 are compared to the cross-sectional data for the WAIS-R IQs and subtests that are *uncorrected* for education (see Figures 7.1 through 7.5), the similarities in the WAIS and WAIS-R curves for each corresponding IQ scale and subtest appear quite high. These virtual cross-sectional identities maintained despite the passage of about 25 years between data collection.

Green's Spanish WAIS Study for Education-Balanced Groups

Green (1969) approached the problem differently in his analysis of the Puerto Rican standardization data for the Spanish WAIS. He added and subtracted subjects from each of four age groups (25–29, 35–39, 45–49, and 55–64) until they were balanced on educational attainment. Each of the education-balanced samples comprised about 135 adults (total sample = 539), with mean years of education ranging from 7.6 to 7.8.

Key Findings

Green's equated samples demonstrated an increase in Verbal sums of scaled scores and only a slight decrement in Performance scores, as shown in Table 7.9. (The mean values have been adjusted for education level and urban–rural residence, and are from Green's Table 4.)

Before balancing for education, Verbal scores increased through the early 40s and then began a slight decline; Performance scores started to decrease in the 20s, with a more dramatic decline beginning during the 40s. The unbalanced samples differed widely in education level, but even the youngest sample averaged only about 8 years of education (the oldest averaged a *third* grade education). Green (1969) concluded from his analyses that "intelligence as measured by the WAIS does not decline in the Puerto Rican population before about age 65. . . . [T]he same conclusion is almost certainly true for the United States" (p. 626). Despite Birren and Morrison's (1961) contradictory finding with the WAIS Performance Scale, Green's assertions seem to have been tacitly accepted by writers (e.g., Labouvie-Vief, 1985) who usually cite his findings without pointing out the limited generalizability of his results. Whether the increment in V-IQ with age, coupled with the apparent lack of a sizable decrement in P-IQ, generalizes to samples that are higher in education is surely not intuitive; Green's (1969, Tables 1 and 2) groups averaged less than 8 years of education, with 43% having between 0 and 5 years of formal education.

Disagreement With Green's Findings

Green's (1969) results were *not* supported by the WAIS-R data. Green observed increments in Verbal scores and only trivial decrements in Performance scores for his education-balanced age groups in Puerto Rico. The key to the discrepancy may reside in the low education level of the Puerto Rican education-balanced samples. Table 7.7 reports the mean sums of

TABLE 7.9   Mean verbal and Performance scores earned by Green's education-balanced samples on the Spanish WAIS

	Ages 25–29	Ages 35–39	Ages 45–49	Ages 55–64
Verbal Sum	56.0	61.9	64.7	65.7
Performance Sum	45.9	47.1	44.7	43.4

scaled scores on the WAIS-R, across the age range, earned by adults in each separate educational category. For adults with 0–8 years of education, the category closest to Green's sample, WAIS-R Verbal sums of scaled scores rose steadily and substantially between ages 25–34 and 55–64 (the ages most resembling Green's youngest and oldest samples); WAIS-R Performance scores dropped only trivially between these ages for the least educated group. *These results parallel Green's (1969) findings almost identically.* However, these relationships do not maintain on the WAIS-R for more educated samples: Within each age category between 9–11 and 16+ years of education, Verbal sums of scaled scores are approximately equal regardless of age, and Performance sums decrease substantially between ages 25–34 and 55–64.

This distinction between Green's and Kaufman et al.'s results is depicted in Table 7.10, which shows the differences between the mean sums of scaled scores earned by Green's oldest and youngest samples on the Spanish WAIS Verbal, Performance, and Full Scales. Comparable discrepancies are then shown for the WAIS-R, separately by education category. WAIS-R data for adults with 0–8 years of education show identical patterns to Green's relatively uneducated sample; WAIS-R data for all other education categories are quite different from Green's results, with the biggest differences occurring for the most educated samples, the ones with one or more years of college.

As Kaufman et al. (1989) point out, differences between the results of the two studies may also be a function of cohort differences

(1960s versus 1970s), instrument differences (WAIS versus WAIS-R), language differences (Spanish versus English), and cultural differences (Puerto Rico versus the U.S.). Yet the education hypothesis remains a viable and strong explanation (or partial explanation) for the discrepancies observed. Kausler (1982) correctly states that Green's study has high internal validity, but low external validity. Hence, one can generalize the causative role played by education to other samples, but "the age differences found for his balanced groups no longer estimate accurately the age differences extant for the entire population of adults living in Puerto Rico" (p. 73). Kausler might have added that one ought to be cautious in generalizing Green's results to more educated samples, a caution that has been lacking as well in most of the numerous other citations of Green's work—for example: the "most careful study thus far of education-related effects on patterns of intellectual aging" (Labouvie-Vief, 1985, p. 515).

Can Education Be Equated?

Matarazzo (1972) was cautious in interpreting Green's findings, but primarily because he wondered whether years of formal education is "a variable with identical meaning across generations" (p. 115). Matarazzo's question obviously has no definitive answer, although his criticism is refuted to some extent by the provocative data in Table 7.7. Certainly Verbal skills are closely related to formal education, both in their correlation with years of education (chapter 6) and the logical correspondence between edu-

TABLE 7.10 Comparison of Green's (1969) Spanish WAIS data with Kaufman et al.'s (1989) WAIS-R data for education-balanced groups

Sample	DIFFERENCE IN MEAN SCORE EARNED BY AGES 55–64 AND BY AGES 25–34[a]		
	Verbal Sum	Performance Sum	Full Scale Sum
Green's (1969) Puerto Rican sample (mean education level = 7.7 years); Spanish WAIS	**+ 9.7**	**−2.5**	**+ 7.6**
Kaufman et al.'s (1989) U.S. sample; WAIS-R:			
0–8 years of schooling	**+10.4**	**−4.2**	**+6.2**
9–11 years of schooling	+ 1.9	−6.4	−4.5
12 years of schooling	+ 2.3	−5.5	−3.4
13–15 years of schooling	− 2.7	−11.0	−13.5
16+ years of schooling	+ 1.0	−9.3	−8.3

[a]Ages 25–29 for Green's (1969) sample

NOTE: Difference scores appear in bold print for Green's sample and for the Kaufman et al. sample that is closest in educational attainment to Green's sample. Data for Green's sample are adjusted values, covarying education and urban–rural residence.

cation and success on tests of general information, word meaning, and arithmetic ability. Table 7.7 shows that regardless of age, and with only mild aberrations, individuals with a comparable amount of education earned similar scores on the WAIS-R Verbal Scale.

Heaton's WAIS Investigation With Neuropsychological Controls

Heaton et al. (1986) considered the impact of both age and education on test scores in their WAIS investigation of 553 adults (64% male), ages 15–81 years (mean = 39.3) who were tested as normal controls at several neuropsychological laboratories. The groups were divided by age (<40, 40–59, 60+) and education (<12, 12–15, 16+), although as a group they

were a highly educated sample (mean years of education = 13.3).

Key Findings

All 11 subtests showed significant main effects for education, but only seven evidenced significant *age* main effects: Similarities, Digit Span, and the five Performance tasks. The largest age effects were observed for Digit Symbol and Picture Arrangement. These findings conform closely to the WAIS-R subtest analysis.

Significant age x education interactions emerged in Heaton's investigation for four WAIS tasks: Comprehension, Picture Completion, Picture Arrangement, Block Design. These investigators graphed the changes in mean scaled score with age *within* each of the three education categories for two of these tasks, Picture Arrangement and Block Design. For both WAIS Performance subtests, the most educated groups (college graduates) maintained or improved their mean score through age 59, followed by a dramatic drop in the mean earned by the oldest (60+) sample. The least educated groups (< 12 years) showed a striking decrease in mean Picture Arrangement score for the "< 40" versus the middle-aged (40–59) samples; the changes in mean scores on Block Design, however, revealed more modest decreases for the least educated sample.

These findings do *not* match the WAIS-R results for the total Performance Scale (see Table 7.7), which reveal a steady decrease in mean score from age to age, starting at ages 35–44 for adults with 16+ years of schooling. In addition, the two WAIS-R education groups that together correspond to Heaton et al.'s least educated group (0–8 and 9–11 years of education) each showed very small decrements in mean scores from age to age through the 60s. The large, early decrease reported by Heaton for Picture Arrangement contradicts the WAIS-R finding, although the results for Block Design are reasonably consistent with the WAIS-R pattern. Heaton et al. (1986) concluded from their WAIS data that, compared to the more educated samples, the sample "at the lowest education level (mean, 9 years) gave evidence of greater cognitive decline between the young and middle-age periods" (p. 117). This result certainly is at odds with Green's (1969) findings with the Spanish WAIS and with the WAIS-R results reported by Kaufman et al. (1989) and McLean et al. (1988b). In view of the greater representativeness of the WAIS-R sample, Heaton's conclusions should be given less weight than the more recent results.

Age–Education Gradients

Heaton et al. (1986) also computed an age–education gradient for each WAIS subtest by subtracting the amount of variance accounted for by education from the amount accounted for by age; positive values denote the more age-related subtests, while negative values indicate the tasks more heavily dependent on education.

Heaton's gradient showed Picture Arrangement, followed closely by Digit Symbol and Object Assembly (each with values in the +5 to +10 range) as the most age-related WAIS tasks; in contrast, Vocabulary and then Information (with values close to −40) were the most education related. For comparison, I computed this gradient for WAIS-R subtests, using data provided by Kaufman et al. (1989, Table 2). I have added Heaton et al.'s ranks in parentheses, where 1 equals the most age-dependent subtest and 11 equals the most education-dependent.

WAIS-R Subtest	AGE VARIANCE MINUS EDUCATION VARIANCE
Object Assembly	+ 1.5 (3)
Digit Symbol	+ 0.3 (2)
Picture Arrangement	− 3.2 (1)
Picture Completion	− 6.8 (5)
Block Design	− 7.1 (4)
Digit Span	−18.2 (6)
Similarities	−25.8 (8)
Arithmetic	−26.2 (7)
Comprehension	−29.9 (9)
Information	−33.7 (10)
Vocabulary	−36.2 (11)

The rank-order correlation between the WAIS and WAIS-R ranks equals .945 ($p < .01$), indicating striking agreement between the Heaton et al. and Kaufman et al. results. Once again, the WAIS-R findings show Digit Span and Similarities to be the Verbal subtests that behave most like the Performance subtests in their relationship to chronological age and the Vocabulary-Information dyad to be the tasks least related to adult aging.

Overview

Overall, data from all studies cited support Botwinick's (1977) classic intellectual aging pattern, which posits maintenance of performance on nontimed tasks, even through old age, versus a much earlier decline in timed tests; however, as noted previously, Horn's interpretation of the pattern as stable crystallized abilities compared to declining fluid abilities is more defensible than a timed/nontimed approach (see pp. 222–231 for a careful analysis of this issue). Kaufman et al.'s (1989) and Birren and Morrison's (1961) results offer strong support for the classic aging pattern, while Green's (1969) findings for an educationally homogeneous group of Puerto Ricans affords mild support. The studies by Doppelt and Wallace (1955) and Heaton et al. (1986) also broadly agree with the Botwinick pattern, although their age-by-age comparisons of mean scores did not include simultaneous controls for education. In total, the cross-sectional results of WAIS-R analyses, both with and without a control for education, demonstrate strong consistency with WAIS findings.

Cohort and Time-of-Measurement Effects

Regardless of consistency across studies and Wechsler instruments, inferences from cross-sectional studies about developmental (ontogenetic) changes in intelligence are speculative at best. As long as different individuals compose the separate age samples, one can only guess at the nature of the age-related changes in intelligence in the same individuals over time. When education level is controlled, one aspect of cohort differences is eliminated to some extent. However, numerous other nonage and noneducation variables associated with growing up at a given period of time are either unknown, unmeasured, or unquantifiable. Yet such variables as motivation level, historical events, social customs and mores, the availability of television and personal computers, child-rearing techniques, and the impact of mass media will affect apparent age-related changes in scores on mental tests.

In addition, time-of-measurement effects interact with performance on intelligence tests.

Real changes either in mental ability or in test-taking ability could affect how every group of adults (regardless of cohort) performs on a given test. These sweeping cultural changes could affect individuals aging from 25 to 35 in much the same way that they affect others who age from 40 to 50 during the same time frame. For example, in the early 1900s tests were uncommon for everyone, and scores would likely be relatively low for a person of 20 or 40 or 60 tested on unfamiliar items like verbal or figure analogies; people of the same ages tested in the 1960s or 1970s would likely score relatively higher on these same tests because such tests had become a familiar part of American culture. This type of control for cultural change was used by Owens (1966) in his landmark longitudinal study (discussed on pages 207–208).

Not all cultural changes relate to test-taking ability, however, as Flynn (1984, 1987) has made abundantly clear (see chapter 2). Indeed, Flynn has probably come as close as anyone to quantifying these cultural or time-of-measurement effects by using cross-sectional data to show systematic IQ gains across generations. That these gains differ dramatically from country to country stresses their cultural-environmental origin. Because differences in IQs earned in different eras by individuals of the same age reflect *both* time-of-measurement and cohort effects, Kausler (1982) prefers to use the term *time lag* to denote these changes in intelligence scores.

Internal and External Validity

By controlling for education level in various WAIS and WAIS-R studies, the investigators have conducted studies high in *internal* validity, permitting both the identification of causative factors and the generalization of these causative factors to other samples (Kausler, 1982). Thus, apparent age-related declines in verbal intelligence may be attributed to educational attainment; declines with age in mean Performance scores are due partly to education, but mostly to age differences plus an unknown proportion of cohort variation. The downside of the high internal validity of the WAIS and WAIS-R age–education studies is low *external* validity, meaning poor generalization of the "adjusted" age differences to the population at large; in fact, in the real world, older individuals *are* less well educated than younger adults. Consequently, the actual, unadjusted values validly describe true differences in the mean scores of different age groups. However, they cannot be used to infer causality of the differences, and they have limited value for implying developmental change. But education-balanced groups, according to Kausler (1982), "give a truer picture of ontogenetic change than our previous contrasts between educationally imbalanced age groups that were, nevertheless, representative of their respective populations" (p. 67).

INTEGRATION OF WAIS-R RESULTS WITH LONGITUDINAL RESEARCH

Inferring developmental trends from cross-sectional data is risky, partly because of cohort effects and partly because of the failure to test the same individuals more than once. Longitudinal investigations of aging and intelligence solve both problems by holding constant cohort variance (each individual is, in effect, his or her own cohort control), and by observing developmental changes within the same person over time. In fact, longitudinal investigations of the Wechsler-Bellevue (Berkowitz & Green, 1963) and WAIS (Eisdorfer & Wilkie, 1973) have generally shown little age-related decline in ability, far less than has been revealed by cross-sectional analysis, with or without an education control. Unfortunately, longitudinal studies of intelligence and aging are beset by problems—different from the disadvantages of cross-sectional studies but nonetheless potentially debilitating.

In the next sections I discuss some of these pitfalls, especially in studies using Wechsler's adult tests, and then treat two of the best designed and most influential longitudinal studies: Owens's (1953, 1966) Army Alpha investigation of adults tested originally in 1919 as Iowa State freshmen; and Schaie's (1983b) 21-year Seattle longitudinal study with the PMA that utilized sophisticated cohort-sequential methodology.

Problems in Investigating Aging Longitudinally

Ideally, the alleged early and rapid decline in P-IQ with increasing age could be verified or disproved by the continual retesting of the same individuals. Some excellent longitudinal investigations using the WAIS, or a portion of it, have been conducted (Schaie, 1983a), but the results have not answered the question. The main difficulty lies less with the research studies than with the WAIS itself.

Practice Effects and Progressive Error on Wechsler's Performance Scale

With all tests, the effects of using the same instrument repeatedly introduce unwanted error into the analysis, a confounding known as *progressive error* (Kausler, 1982). This type of error is important for any studies involving Wechsler's Performance Scale because of the nature of the items and the enormous practice effect associated with them. Adults who are retested on the WAIS or WAIS-R after about a month will gain only about 2 to 3 points on the Verbal Scale, versus 8 to 9 points on the Performance Scale (see chapter 4). This profound practice effect on P-IQ extends for at least 4 months (Catron & Thompson, 1979). Even if the practice effect dissipates after a year or two and does not impede the results of the first retest in a longitudinal study, it surely will not disappear by the third, fourth, or fifth retest.

In the first of two Duke longitudinal studies, comprising an initial sample of 267 adult volunteers between the ages of 59 and 94 from North Carolina (who matched the age, sex, race, and socioeconomic characteristics of the community), 42 "survivors" were tested up to 11 times on the WAIS between 1955 and 1976 (Siegler, 1983)! The second Duke study involved a four-subtest WAIS short form administered to an initial sample of 502 adults, aged 46–70, from the same general area; the 331 survivors were given the short form four times between 1970 and 1976 (Siegler, 1983). The two Duke longitudinal investigations were exceptional studies, uncovering fascinating relationships among the cognitive, memory, personality, sensory, and motor variables administered repeatedly to the subjects. But it is impossible to make inferences about changes in P-IQ over time for samples that are so overexposed to the five Performance subtests. Wilkie and Eisdorfer (1973), for example, found decrements of 3.2 points on the Verbal sums of scaled scores, and a similar 4.4 points on the Performance sum, for 50 of the Duke subjects in the first study who were tested in both the first wave in the late 1950s and the seventh wave in 1972. The Verbal data are reasonably interpretable because of the small practice effect for V-IQ, but the Performance data are meaningless for individuals tested five, or six, or seven times over a 15-year span.

The Performance tasks are generally considered measures of fluid ability—tests that assess a person's adaptability and flexibility when faced with *new* problem-solving situations. These tasks are new the first time they are given, but the novelty wears off quickly. College students tested back-to-back on the WAIS with no time interval at all improved their P-IQ by 14.2 points, versus a 3.1-point gain on V-IQ (Catron, 1978). A different retest sample found little novelty in the Performance tasks after a 4-month interval, showing an 8-point gain (compared to less than a 1-point gain in V-IQ). When people are retested after a few weeks or months, they seem to remember only a few specific nonverbal items; even if they recall many of the puzzles or pictures, no feedback for correctness is given either during or after the test. What people do tend to remember is the *type* of items they faced and the kinds of *strategies* and attack modes that seemed successful. When individuals are tested repeatedly on Wechsler's Performance tasks, the five well-known subtests no longer measure fluid intelligence in the true sense, and it becomes questionable whether they measure intelligence as opposed to a combination of mental ability, long-term memory, and the ability to apply learning sets.

The progressive error from the practice effect could have been neutralized to some extent by testing fresh samples during each "wave" of the study (matched on age and other relevant variables to the longitudinal sample at each point in time) to provide "base-line" data. But this type of control was not included in the Duke design. Similarly, the design of the excellent Bonn longitudinal study, utilizing the Hamburg-Wechsler (German WAIS) did not permit identification of the impact of practice on the successive Performance scores of adults tested as many as six times between 1965 and 1980 (Schmitz-Scherzer & Thomae, 1983). The investigators tested two cohorts simultaneously, initially composed of 222 men and women aged 60–65 (1900–1905 cohort) or aged 70–75 (1890–1895 cohort).

Schmitz-Scherzer and Thomae (1983) presented mean Hamburg-Wechsler sums of scaled scores on the Verbal and Performance Scales for each cohort tested in 1965, 1967, 1969, 1972, and 1976–1977. The younger cohort performed fairly constantly on the Verbal Scale over the 12-year period, while the older cohort dropped significantly (almost five weighted score points) as they aged from the 70s to mid-80s. On the Performance Scale, both cohorts either maintained or improved their scores between the 1965 and 1972 testings (four administrations) before showing a sizable drop in 1976–1977. The Verbal changes are consistent with the results of other cross-sectional and longitudinal investigations, including the decrement by the older cohort during their late 70s and early 80s (Botwinick, 1977; Jarvik & Bank, 1983). The Performance changes imply virtually no loss of function for the older cohort between the ages of about 72 to 79, and small gains in Performance scores for the younger cohort between ages 62 and 66. However, such interpretations of Performance abilities are fanciful, based on the considerable practice effect inherent in the separate nonverbal subtests.

Botwinick (1977) showed how failure to consider the differential practice effect can confound studies based on a single retest. He criticized the faulty conclusions reached by Rhudick and Gordon (1973), who retested an initial sample of 58- to 88-year-old men and women using intervals of 1 to 8 years. They concluded that the adults showed improvement in their V, P, and FS scores over 1- to 8-year intervals. Yet when the authors divided their samples by length of interval, "Full and Verbal scale scores were found unchanged, but the Performance scores changed in a way to emphasize the importance of the length of the test–retest interval. The interval of 2 or less years showed a significant *age-increase* while the interval of 6–8 years showed a significant *age-decrease*" (Botwinick, 1977, pp. 595–596). Botwinick explored explanations for this "paradoxical pattern," opposite to the classical aging pattern, but he missed the most obvious (and probable) explanation: the powerful effect of practice on P-IQ.

The practice effect undoubtedly colored the results of a fascinating study of twins, aged 60 and above, over a 20-year span (Feingold, 1950; Jarvik & Bank, 1983). Selected Wechsler-Bellevue subtests were administered along with Binet Vocabulary and a motor test in 1947–1949 to an initial sample of 134 pairs of twins. Consistent with other longitudinal results, Vocabulary and W-B Similarities scores maintained into old age, contrasting with notable declines in Block Design and Digit Symbol. However, even performance on the latter two tasks failed

to show a significant decrement when the elderly twins (mean age = 67.5) were retested the first time less than 1 year later at the age of 68.4 (Jarvik, Kallmann, & Falek, 1962). Jarvik and Bank (1983) indicate that "given an elderly non-test-wise group of subjects, one would expect artificially low initial scores and substantial practice effects on subsequent retests" (p. 44). These authors were apparently unaware, however, of the practice differential for verbal versus nonverbal tests.

Selective Attrition

A second major problem of longitudinal aging research is *selective attrition of subjects*. When using volunteer subjects, "at all ages in adulthood, those who do not volunteer initially and those who do not show up in retesting tend to be lower scorers on ability tests than those who do cooperate" (Horn & Donaldson, 1976, p. 717). The Duke longitudinal study was especially valuable in generating research to help quantify this effect. Analysis of data from the first 10 years of the first Duke study (Eisdorfer & Wilkie, 1973) revealed "a substantial loss of Ss, with the lowest IQ group sustaining a loss of 72 percent; the middle IQ group, a loss of 51.4 percent; and the high IQ group, a loss of only 36.8 percent" (p. 28). Even more dramatic evidence of the selective attrition factor came from Siegler and Botwinick's (1979) analysis of data from all 11 "waves" of the first Duke study. Individuals who continue to be retested over time are more intelligent than those who drop out early. Among 60- to 74-year-olds in the Duke study, the relationship is nearly linear between IQ at the initial assessment and the number of times the person returned to be tested, as depicted in Figure 7.6. Of the 179 individuals tested on the WAIS in the first wave, only 18 returned to be tested at all 10 subsequent assessments. Overall, the 60- to 74-year-olds who came once or twice earned mean sums of scaled scores on the Full Scale of 85 to 90,

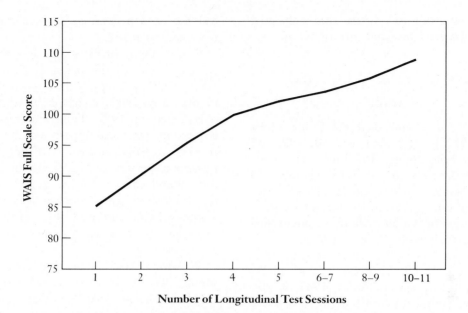

FIGURE 7.6

Mean WAIS Full Scale scores earned by adults (aged 60–74 years) on the initial assessment, shown as a function of the number of longitudinal test sessions in which the subjects participated. (Data points, based on samples ranging in size from 43 to 179, are weighted means for ages 60–64 and 65–75, obtained from Table 1 and Figure 1 in Siegler and Botwinick, 1979.)

compared to means of close to 110 for those who came to be tested 10 or all 11 times!

Obviously some of the elderly subjects died or were too ill to be tested, but many simply chose not to be retested for whatever reason; the selective attrition factor occurs as well for younger adults, although the effect seems to increase with age (Horn & Donaldson, 1976). Research has been divided over the level of initial intelligence and the rate of IQ decline over time, with some investigators showing no significant interaction (e.g., Owens, 1959), and others (including Siegler and Botwinick, 1979) finding different patterns of decline for the more and less able subjects. Nonetheless, all such analyses are based on people who return at least once to be tested. Those who drop out very early in a study (and whose IQ changes are

never evaluated) may be a breed apart from the low IQ subjects who keep coming back. Hence, generalizations from longitudinal studies must be made quite cautiously because of the considerable selective attrition factor. At the very least, it is essential for researchers to partly compensate for this problem by following Eisdorfer and Wilkie's (1973) advice: "The appropriate analysis of longitudinal data should use data only from the same subjects across time, whether Ss are lost secondary to death or drop out" (p. 28).

Other potential difficulties with longitudinal research, and with cross-sectional research, have been treated in depth by experts on aging (e.g., Kausler, 1982; Nesselroade & Labouvie, 1985); the reader is referred to these sources for a more thorough and technical treatment of the topic. I now turn to two of the most influential and well-designed investigations of IQ and aging.

The Iowa State Army Alpha Study

Owens (1953) administered the Army Alpha test in 1950 to 127 men, age 50, who had previously been among 363 Iowa State University freshmen who had been administered the same test in 1919 at age 19. These initial results "were important in stimulating a critical reexamination of the inevitability of intellectual decline in adulthood" (Schaie, 1983c, pp. 13, 15); the study "ushered in an era of new ideas in research on adult development and intelligence" (Cunningham & Owens, 1983, p. 20). The study continued in 1961 when 96 of these men were tested once more, at age 61 (Owens, 1966); Owens also tested a random sample of 19-year-old Iowa State freshmen on the Army Alpha in 1961–1962 to permit a time-lag comparison, thereby estimating the impact of cultural change on the obtained test scores.

Key Findings

The Army Alpha, one of Wechsler's primary sources for selecting Verbal subtests, comprises eight tasks, including tests of Information, Practical Judgment (Comprehension), Arithmetical Problems, and Synonyms–Antonyms (Vocabulary). For simplicity of interpretation, Owens (1966) focused on age changes in the three factors that Guilford (1954) identified for the Army Alpha: Verbal, Numerical, and Relations (or Reasoning). Results of the Iowa State longitudinal investigation for the 96 men tested three times on the Army Alpha reveal improvement in Verbal and Total scores between ages 19 and 50, followed by a slight decline from age 50 to 61. Reasoning displayed small increments from one testing occasion to the next, while Numerical evidenced the opposite profile. The most noteworthy changes were the improvement in Verbal scores from age 19 to 50

and the sudden decrease in Numerical scores from age 50 to 61.

Owens then corrected the data for cultural change, based on the better performance (especially in Reasoning) by the 19-year-olds tested in the early 1960s compared to the 19-year-olds tested in 1919. Following this time-lag correction, what had appeared to be slight *increments* in Reasoning were actually steady *decrements* in performance. Despite the correction for cultural change, Verbal factor scores continued to show gains between ages 19 and 61; Numerical scores showed a loss across this same age span, but a smaller loss than was observed for Reasoning.

Botwinick (1977) concluded that the Reasoning "factor score was based more on the speeded test items than the other factor scores: in this way it was more similar to the WAIS Performance subtests than the Verbal" (p. 593). Cunningham and Owens's (1983) overall conclusion from the Iowa State study: "The results suggest peak performance and the beginning of declines of overall intellectual functioning roughly in the decade of the 50s for this elite sample. The losses appear to be small and probably are not of much practical significance until at least age 60" (p. 34).

Relationship to WAIS-R Results

All eight subtests of the group-administered Army Alpha involve verbal and/or numerical ability. Even the Reasoning factor, although interpreted by Owens (1966) as a measure of fluid ability, is defined by verbal tests like Analogies (e.g., "fear" is to "anticipation" as "regret" is to ?). Thus, the findings from Owens's longitudinal investigation and Cunningham and Owens's overall conclusions are quite consistent with the WAIS-R cross-sectional study holding education constant. Both sets of data indicate verbal skills that increase slightly with age during adulthood and that are still strong into the 60s.

Schaie's 21-Year Seattle Cohort-Sequential Study

Schaie's (1983b) sophisticated combination of cross-sectional and longitudinal designs was predicated on the contributions of three variables to the scores obtained by adults on intelligence tests: chronological age, cohort (year of birth), and time-of-measurement (the year the tests were administered). He conducted four independent cross-sectional studies with the group-administered Primary Mental Abilities (PMA) test, starting with his 1956 sample of 500 adults. This group was divided into seven ages, with means ranging from 25 to 67 (cohorts 1889–1931); subsequent independent samples were tested in 1963 ($N = 996$, ages 25–74, cohorts 1889–1938), 1970 ($N = 705$, ages 25–81, cohorts 1889–1945), and 1977 ($N = 609$, ages 25–81, cohorts 1896–1952). All samples comprised approximately equal numbers of men and women, with the groups tending to be relatively educated (about 50% with one or more years of college).

Coinciding with the last three cross-sectional studies were longitudinal investigations ranging from 7 to 21 years. Three 7-year studies included the retesting of as many subjects as possible from the 1956 ($N = 303$), 1963 ($N = 420$), and 1970 ($N = 340$) cross-sectional investigations. In addition, two 14-year studies included 162 adults followed from 1956 to 1970, and 337 individuals tested in 1963 and 1977; finally, one sample of 130 was followed for the 21-year interval between 1956 and 1977. These rigorous cross-sequential, cohort-sequential, and longitudinal designs permitted Schaie and his colleagues to identify cohort and time-of-measurement variation in an attempt to understand "true" intelligence differences due to aging.

Key Findings

His 1968 investigation (Schaie & Strother, 1968) was widely publicized in popular texts (Cronbach, 1970; Matarazzo, 1972) because it showed dramatic differences in the aging–IQ growth curve from cross-sectional data alone (his 1956 sample of 500) and the curve obtained from his first 7-year longitudinal study (the 303 members of the 1956 sample retested in 1963). The cross-sectional data for ages 20–70 revealed the same type of plunge in abilities with age that characterized the WAIS-R Full Scale IQ *prior* to an adjustment for education (see Figure 7.3); the mix of cross-sectional and longitudinal data for the smaller sample (a *sequential* analysis) demonstrated growth curves showing *virtually no decline* across the age range, not unlike the education-corrected WAIS-R Verbal IQs shown in Figure 7.1. These findings applied to the separate components of the PMA, whether measuring verbal ability (Verbal Meaning, a multiple-choice vocabulary test) or skills akin to Wechsler's Perceptual Organization (Space, a match-to-sample spatial orientation test).

Relationship to WAIS-R Results

These data became the subject of controversy, with Horn and Donaldson (1976) and Botwinick (1977), for example, citing variables such as selective attrition to account for the apparent maintenance of both fluid and crystallized abilities through old age. Regardless of the arguments and counterarguments (Baltes & Schaie, 1976; Horn, 1977), the early Schaie data show both consistency and inconsistency with WAIS-R results. In Schaie's findings, scores on the nonverbal, fluid tasks (Space, along with a measure of inductive reasoning) clearly began a decline much later in life than was found for Wechsler's Performance subtests. Yet, like the WAIS-R findings, scores on Space and Reasoning peaked far earlier than the more crystallized PMA subtests (Verbal Meaning and Number).

Subsequent analyses (e.g., Schaie & Hertzog, 1983) revealed Schaie's responsiveness to the criticisms and the concomitant efforts by his research team to refine their methodologies and analyses. Schaie and Hertzog (1983) admitted that their original cross-sequential design was ill-suited to evaluate age changes; further, the results of the two 14-year longitudinal studies they reported indicated earlier declines in intelligence (i.e., prior to age 60) than were previously observed in Schaie's laboratory. In Schaie and Hertzog's (1983) analysis, however, the pattern of decline for the 14-year longitudinal samples was quite similar for both verbal and nonverbal PMA subtests. Schaie and Labouvie-Vief's (1974) generalization about aging and intelligence, that "most of the adult life span is characterized by an absence of decisive intellectual decrements" (p. 15), summarizes well the overall results of their many PMA studies.

The best integration of the numerous analyses appears in Schaie's (1983b) thorough treatment of the 21-year Seattle project. Among other syntheses of the data, he organized the findings of the three 7-year longitudinal studies into two tables, each comparing the performance of every age group to age 25; the average score was set at 100. The first table showed these comparisons without correction for potentially confounding variables, while the second one corrected all values for time-of-measurement effects, attrition, and cohort differences (Schaie, 1983b, Tables 4.17 and 4.18). Figure 7.7 depicts Schaie's results for Verbal Meaning, Space, and Reasoning, where these values are corrected for the three variables noted previously. For these three tasks, the uncorrected and corrected values were quite similar for each age, usually disagreeing by only 1 to 3 points.

In Figure 7.7, Verbal Meaning increases steadily until age 53, with a notable decline occurring between ages 67 and 74. Space peaks earlier than Verbal Meaning (age 46), but has its first sizable decline between the same 67- to 74-year period. Nonetheless, its decline is more dramatic than that of the vocabulary test. Reasoning declines substantially after age 60, plunging to 73 by age 81. These results are basically in agreement with the differential WAIS-R results for V-IQ and P-IQ, although, in contrast to Wechsler's visual-motor Performance tasks, adults maintained their ability on the PMA Space and Reasoning subtests into the decade of the 60s. Unlike the popular interpretations of the initial findings reported by Schaie and his colleagues, intelligence does indeed decline with chronological age, and that decline becomes precipitous; however, the use of longitudinal data juxtaposed with cross-sectional results on the PMA indicate that the decrements do not begin until relatively late in life.

Should Corrections Be Made for Cohort Effects?

I have excluded Number from Figure 7.7, despite its similarity to Wechsler's Arithmetic subtest, because its corrected and uncorrected values were so disparate. Prior to correction, peak performance on Number was at age 32 (a score of 111), with scores declining to 91 at age 60 and 55 at age 81. After correction, peak performance on Number was an astonishing 126 at age 60, and 74-year-olds outperformed 32-year-olds. I have difficulty accepting the validity of corrected results when the changes are so dramatic (rather like seeing a correlation of .15 jump to .70 after correcting it for range restriction). In general, I am not totally in agreement with the idea of correcting IQs for cohort differences, which may be the main culprit in the Number data. Selective attrition certainly requires correction to the degree possible, and so do time-lag effects, so long as these effects can be shown to apply to virtually every group of adults living at the time. If an entire group of people responds to cultural changes by performing differently at time 1 and time 2 (perhaps because of some type of generic change in society that affects nearly everyone), then correction makes sense. How can one attribute developmental significance to a change that occurs for everyone within that same time frame, even if some part of the change is due to cohort effects? If variables like familiarity with standardized tests or the availability of television tend to improve each person's score (on average) between 1940 and 1980, it would be foolish to attribute the gain to "mental growth."

But specific cohort effects are different. These variables are assumed to affect intelligence *differently* for people born in different years. Adults who were raised in a time of parental enlightenment about infant stimulation are likely to outscore those who were born at other times. Children reared during the Depression or the world wars might not develop their intellect at the same rate as children born during other historical periods. However, I'm not sure that it always makes sense to correct IQs for such factors. At what point do chronological age and the time one is reared become separable? I certainly favor controlling for educational attainment when exploring age differences in IQ. Since education is a cohort-related variable, I can see some value in keeping cohort factors out of the developmental picture. But education is separate from most other cohort effects. Its

impact on IQs is known, quantifiable, and profound. It is commonly a variable that is considered along with intelligence for vocational selection and placement, and in other real-life situations associated with intellectual assessment. As Reese and Rodeheaver (1985) have noted: "Performance on cognitive tasks is often correlated more highly with education than with age. . . . The issue of education is critical in assessing adult age differences in problem solving" (p. 479).

The specific attitudes toward child-rearing and the social and historical environment associated with any particular group of years are intrinsically interwoven with the person's chronological age such that separation can become artificial; indeed, "cohort and age are inseparable" (Botwinick, 1977, p. 583). For gerontological research, I grant that the identification and quantification of the impact of cohort effects on intelligence is crucial; one

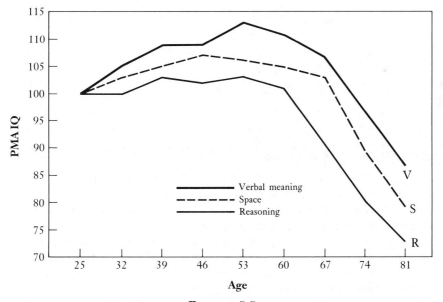

FIGURE 7.7

Performance on three Primary Mental Abilities (PMA) subtests at ages 25–81 as a proportion of age 25 performance (set at 100), corrected for time-of-measurement, attrition, and cohort effects (from Schaie, 1983b, Table 4.18, based on 7-year longitudinal data).

must try to separate ontogenetic factors from cohort variables as causations of age differences in IQ to understand lifespan development of intelligence. From a practical standpoint, however, most cohort differences closely resemble the kinds of differences that characterize one subculture versus another or one family versus another within a single cohort. Yet we do not ordinarily adjust a person's IQ because of a disadvantaged home life or other deprivations, or for growing up within the different cultures associated with the United States. As clinicians, such factors enter into test interpretation, but we do not infer that the person should have a few points added to his or her score to be "fair." Nor do intelligence tests provide separate norms for individuals based on race, social class, region, residence, or income level; supplementary norms are sometimes provided (Kaufman & Kaufman, 1983a), but the global intelligence scores are necessarily derived from representative national norms.

In the extreme, the view that cohort differences are of vital concern and must be controlled to truly measure intelligence implies that norms for any intelligence test are not generalizable to other cohorts. The WAIS-R norms, for example, might be viewed as suitable for 65- to 69-year-olds born in the 1910s, but not the early 1920s. Restandardizations would be needed every 5 years or so, a nice ideal but not a very practical one. Schaie and Schaie (1977), using Wechsler's adult tests as examples, have even suggested that "tests which have been constructed for a given cohort . . . may not be valid for successive cohorts" (p. 695). For the most part, I agree with Botwinick's (1977) view of cohort effects: "In the world outside the laboratory where abstractions differentiating between cohort and age do not exist, age and cohort are one. Age is not synonymous with biology, nor is cohort synonymous with sociocultural influences" (p. 583).

Schaie's research has been quite valuable in helping us understand intelligence and aging and

in stimulating research. Surely the simple cross-sectional data do not have important ontogenetic implications, and declining intelligence for a given person undoubtedly occurs far later in the lifespan than ever conceptualized prior to Schaie's and Owens's series of studies. Yet it is unclear to what degree findings with group tests generalize to the Wechsler scales; and it is at least arguable whether correction for all variance attributable to cohort effects is justifiable, except as a basis for enhancing our theoretical understanding of intellectual development across the lifespan.

A New Longitudinal Study of the Alleged Performance IQ Decline

Schaie's research "substantiated the position that cohort differences exert profound effects in observed patterns of intellectual development in adulthood" (Dixon, Kramer, & Baltes, 1985, p. 318). Perhaps IQs earned by different cohorts should be adjusted for these effects—and perhaps not. But the key question that remains unanswered is whether the rapid decline in Wechsler's Performance IQ, even after control for the cohort effects attributable to years of formal education, is an artifact of other unknown cohort variables. Do the descending mean P-IQs evident in Figure 7.2 apply only to different age groups at a fixed point in time, or do these results have at least some implications for ontogenetic changes? Are Schaie and Labouvie-Vief (1974) correct to assert that "[i]n times of rapid cultural and technological change it is primarily in relation to younger populations that the aged can be described as deficient" (p. 15)? Would Schaie and his colleagues have found maintenance of P-IQ through the 60s before decline began had they used the WAIS instead of the PMA?

Previous Results

Certainly the evidence necessary to answer this question was not available in the existing Wechsler literature. Most longitudinal studies of the Wechsler-Bellevue or WAIS focused on older subjects, even at the initial assessment, and none of these studies adequately handled the issue of practice effects on the Performance subtests (see pp. 204–206). Botwinick (1977) considered the classic aging pattern "one of the best replicated results for normal aging populations" (p. 584). Eisdorfer, Busse, and Cohen (1959) observed this pattern in their North Carolina sample of elderly patients, as 82% had V-IQ > P-IQ; this differential was observed for males and females, blacks and whites, different levels of socioeconomic status, and whether the adult was institutionalized. Yet none of these results addresses the degree to which Schaie's PMA results generalize to the Wechsler scales.

Cross-sectional data from Schaie's investigations offer conflicting answers to the question. Based on evidence from his four comprehensive studies (Schaie, 1983b, Table 4.5), scores on the PMA subtests closest to Wechsler's Performance subtests—Space and Reasoning—do not typically start their decline until age 32 or 39, compared to the early 20s for the WAIS-R Performance subtests. However, the decrease in cross-sectional means from the mid-20s to the mid-70s for these two subtests is just as profound (1½ to 2 standard deviations) as the dramatic age-to-age changes revealed for the WAIS-R Performance subtests in Figure 7.2.

While writing this chapter, I was troubled by the lack of an answer to this important question and conducted a study that was inspired by the methodologies of Owens (1966), Schaie (1983b), and Parker (1986), and by Kausler's (1982) detailed discussions of the pros and cons of diverse methodologies. The design and re-sults of this investigation are discussed in the next few sections.

Methodology for a WAIS/ WAIS-R Longitudinal Analysis

Parker (1986) had the clever idea of examining the comparative performance of year-of-birth cohorts by equating the standardization samples of the Wechsler-Bellevue I, WAIS, and WAIS-R. However, he encountered methodological flaws by: (a) including the Wechsler-Bellevue data in his analysis, because that standardization sample was not nearly comparable to the representative WAIS and WAIS-R samples; and (b) equating the three samples on the basis for norms at ages 16–19, in view of the very questionable WAIS-R norms for older adolescents. Further, he focused solely on the Full Scale IQ, when it is the separate V- and P-IQs that are of the greatest theoretical interest for analyses of aging.

But Parker's article made me realize the analogy between the WAIS and WAIS-R standardization samples and Schaie's repeated cross-sectional analyses between 1956 and 1977. In fact, the WAIS standardization sample, tested in 1953–1954, and the WAIS-R sample, tested between 1976 and 1980, correspond closely to the dates of Schaie's first and fourth cross-sectional analyses. Although data analogous to Schaie's longitudinal analyses were not possible (the same individuals were not tested twice for the WAIS and WAIS-R standardizations), the two Wechsler standardization samples were quite comparable, allowing longitudinal interpretation of data obtained by *independent* samples from the *same cohort*. Schaie (1983b) also conducted several longitudinal analyses based on comparable independent samples, in part to answer criticisms of the selective attrition associated with conventional longitudinal analysis, and concluded that the results were "generally quite comparable" (p. 106), particularly for the 7-year and 21-year longitudinal data.

Identifying the Same Cohorts in Both the WAIS and WAIS-R Samples

The WAIS and WAIS-R standardization samples are indeed quite similar to each other, each matching relevant Census data on numerous key variables. They differ in that the data were collected 25 years apart, in approximately 1953 and 1978. Thus, several cohorts in the WAIS sample are also represented in the WAIS-R sample. For example, adults born in the 1909–1913 cohort were tested at ages 40–44 in 1953 (on the WAIS), and again at ages 65–69 in 1978 (on the WAIS-R). To the degree that the two samples are comparable, a comparison of the test performance of 40- to 44-year-olds on the WAIS with that of the 65- to 69-year-olds 25 years later on the WAIS-R represents a *longitudinal comparison of adults from the same cohort.* The use of independent samples or "cohort substitution" (Kausler, 1982), if they are truly comparable and random, makes it "possible to compute age-change estimates that are controlled for the effects of testing and experimental mortality" (Schaie, 1983b, p. 106).

Other computations are necessary to make the analyses feasible. WAIS-R scores must be converted to WAIS scores to ensure continuity of measurement from one assessment to the next. This is easily accomplished because of the numerous studies that reveal the high correlations between IQs yielded by the two Wechsler batteries and that also chronicle the magnitude of the differences in their respective IQs (see

chapter 3). In addition, it is important to correct the IQs earned in 1978 for time-lag effects or cultural change, as Owens (1966) did when he retested the former Iowa State freshmen at age 61. This analysis, too, is easily performed, as will be described in a later section.

There are four adult cohorts represented within both the WAIS and WAIS-R standardization samples, as shown in Table 7.11.

Mean sums of scaled scores were available for each 5-year age interval for the WAIS (Matarazzo, 1972, Table 10.4), but only for the larger age bands (45–54, 55–64) for the WAIS-R. This limiting factor necessitated using two 10-year cohorts (1924–1933 and 1914–1923) instead of the more desirable 5-year cohorts. It would have been possible to use an additional cohort (1934–1937), ages 16–19 on the WAIS and ages 41–44 on the WAIS-R, but I chose to eliminate that cohort because of the questionable WAIS-R norms for ages 16–19 (data that would have been needed for the time-lag analysis).

In essence, the present analysis follows each of four cohorts longitudinally from 1953 to 1978 to see if individuals born in the same era gained or lost IQ points over the course of a generation. A time-lag correction must be applied to control for cultural change during the 25-year span, just as Owens (1966) did in his Iowa State study.

Owens' precise procedure was applied to each cohort in the WAIS/WAIS-R study; in effect, I replicated Owens' longitudinal study

TABLE 7.11   The four adult age cohorts represented in the WAIS and WAIS-R standardization samples

Cohort (Year of Birth)	Age in 1953 (WAIS Standardization)	Age in 1978 (WAIS-R Standardization)
1924–1933	20–29	45–54
1914–1923	30–39	55–64
1909–1913	40–44	65–69
1904–1908	45–49	70–74

four times. The main differences were that the analysis used cohort substitution instead of testing the same individuals twice, and the WAIS (or WAIS-R) was studied instead of the Army Alpha. The availability of data from the two WAIS samples tested 25 years apart permitted a variety of analyses (cross-sequential, time-sequential, cohort-sequential; see Kausler, 1982, chapter 4). However, the lack of access to the case-by-case WAIS data made some of these analyses unfeasible. The Owens (1966) replication for four cohorts, though less sophisticated than the sequential designs elaborated by Kausler, will answer an important question: Do individuals from the same cohort drop in intelligence over time, especially on Wechsler's Performance Scale? Although the data from the study cannot legitimately be used to form a developmental age-IQ gradient, they will provide longitudinal—rather than cross-sectional—answers to the question of whether P-IQs decrease with advancing age, and whether these decreases appear in the youngest cohort.

Comparability of the Samples

First, the comparability of the samples must be demonstrated. Table 7.12 compares the edu-cational attainment of the WAIS and WAIS-R standardization samples for each cohort. The data show excellent agreement between the educational level of each cohort in 1953 and 1978. For each cohort, there is an increase from 1953 to 1978 in the percentage of high school graduates and a concomitant decrease in the percentage with 11 or less years of education. This consistent change for each cohort is in the logical direction, probably reflecting the proportion of adults who went back to complete their high school education or earned a high school equivalency certificate. The percentage of adults with 1 or more years of college stayed remarkably similar for each cohort from 1953 to 1978. The only group to show a notable increase in this category is the sensible choice, the cohort aged 20–29 years in 1953.

Both standardization samples included proportional representation of nonwhites and were distributed fairly similarly across the four geographic regions. The WAIS-R sample reflected the increased urbanization of society, having an urban–rural ratio of 77:23 for the adult groups compared to a 67:33 ratio for the WAIS sample. Overall, the independent samples were extremely well matched and comparable within each of the four cohorts.

TABLE 7.12 Comparison of the education level of independent samples from the same four cohorts tested in 1953 (WAIS standardization) and in 1978 (WAIS-R standardization)

	PERCENTAGE OF ADULTS WITH					
Cohort (Year of Birth)	11 or Less Years of Education		12 Years (High School Graduate)		One or More Years of College	
	1953 Sample	1978 Sample	1953 Sample	1978 Sample	1953 Sample	1978 Sample
1924–1933	45.3	34.5	34.8	40.0	19.9	25.5
1914–1923	53.8	43.5	27.5	37.0	18.8	19.5
1909–1913	62.2	55.0	20.8	25.5	17.0	19.5
1904–1908	67.8	60.0	17.2	24.0	15.0	16.0

NOTE: Values for the WAIS were obtained by interpolation, based on the values for somewhat different age groups reported by Wechsler (1955, Table 5). Values for the WAIS-R are from Wechsler (1981, Table 5).

Conversion of WAIS-R IQs to WAIS IQs

Previous longitudinal investigations have used the same instrument during each retest, whether the test is the PMA, Army Alpha, WAIS, or Wechsler-Bellevue. The present investigation changed from the WAIS to the WAIS-R in midstream. However, the two batteries are extremely similar in item content and factor structure (see chapter 3). The WAIS Verbal and Full Scale IQs correlated .92, on average, with the corresponding WAIS-R IQ, while the P-IQs correlated .84 (see Table 3.11). These relationships compare favorably to the test–retest coefficients of both the WAIS and WAIS-R, indicating clear-cut continuity of measurement.

Psychometrically, the tests are interchangeable for the analysis of group data. The only major difference is the scores they yield, with the WAIS-R producing lower IQs by 6 to 6½ points. Twenty studies of IQ differences on the WAIS and WAIS-R, encompassing over 1,300 subjects, were summarized in Table 3.13. A data source of that magnitude provides reliable evidence of the differences in the IQs yielded by the two Wechsler batteries. I used the median values from the 20 studies as "corrections" for the WAIS-R IQs. Although the differences in the IQs yielded by the WAIS and WAIS-R provide a gross estimate of cultural change over the generation that separated the standardizations, for the present purpose these discrepancies serve better as excellent answers to the question: "How many IQ points higher would adults have scored had they been administered the WAIS instead of the WAIS-R in 1978?" Cultural change, for this study, must be estimated separately and more specifically for each cohort.

In the computations, I first obtained the Verbal, Performance, and Full Scale sums of scaled scores for each cohort on the WAIS (from Matarazzo, 1972, Table 10.4) and the WAIS-R (Wechsler, 1981, Table 7). Next, I converted each sum of scaled scores to an IQ by entering the IQ conversion table for ages 25–34, the same reference group used by Kaufman et al. (1989) in the WAIS-R cross-sectional study of age differences. I used the WAIS conversion table for WAIS sums and the WAIS-R conversion table for WAIS-R sums. Finally, I converted all WAIS-R IQs to "estimated" WAIS IQs by adding the median differences between them, as reported in Table 3.13: +6.3 points to V-IQ, +6.5 points to P-IQ, and +5.9 points to FS-IQ.

For example, consider Verbal IQ for the 1909–1913 cohort. In 1953, this group ranged in age from 40 to 44; according to Matarazzo's table, this group earned a mean Verbal sum of 59.2. Entering this value into the WAIS IQ table for the reference group (ages 25–34) produces a WAIS Verbal IQ of 98.2. In 1978 the same cohort was 65–69 years, a sample that earned a mean Verbal sum on the WAIS-R of 53.5; this sum translates to a WAIS-R V-IQ of 91.0, based on the sample for 25- to 34-year-olds. This value must be "corrected" by adding the constant +6.3, producing an estimated WAIS V-IQ of 97.3 on the 1978 retest.

Thus, the 1909–1913 cohort earned a mean WAIS IQ of 98.2 in 1953 and a mean of 97.3 in 1978, reflecting a loss of about 1 IQ point. However, this difference should be adjusted for time-lag effects, or cultural change, to be considered a "true" developmental change.

Before discussing the time-lag correction, the choice of a reference group for computing IQs merits mention. In studies of age change on the Wechsler scales, the sums of scaled scores, *not* the IQs per se, are evaluated for assessing change. These scaled score sums represent a common yardstick for evaluating change because they are derived from the same reference group of 20- to 34-year-olds. Consequently, when converting sums of scaled scores to IQs, a similar common yardstick must also be used (in this case, the IQ norms for ages 25–34). In fact, I could have dealt only with sums of scaled scores for the WAIS and WAIS-R (it would have been just as easy to convert WAIS-R scaled score sums to their WAIS equivalents as it was to convert IQs). My preference, however, is to deal with IQs, a language spoken fluently by clinicians of every persuasion.

Correction for Time Lag

Adjustment for time lag, or cultural change, requires a comparison of the IQs earned by each cohort in 1953 with the IQs earned by adults of the same *age* in 1978. The 1909–1913 cohort, for example, was 40 to 44 years old in 1953. This group must be compared to adults aged 40–44 in 1978 to determine how cultural changes have affected test scores for this age group. Similar time-lag comparisons must be conducted for each of the other three cohorts who, in 1953, were ages 20–29, 30–39, and 45–49. Table 7.13 shows these computations for each of the four cohorts. WAIS-R sums of scaled scores were not available for these precise age ranges, so values for the midpoint of each range (24.5, 34.5, 42, and 47) were interpolated from the mean sums provided by Wechsler for the standardization age groups. These values were then converted to WAIS-R IQs using the

table for the reference group of 25- to 34-year-olds, and finally they were translated to estimated WAIS IQs by adding constants of about 6 to 6½.

Table 7.13 shows that cultural change affected each of the four cohorts about equally. The time-lag effect produced about a 3-point IQ gain on the Verbal and Full Scales and about a 5½-point gain on the Performance Scale, presumably due to some type of culture-related change between 1953 and 1978 that affected all adults who were between the ages of 20 and 49 in 1953. The larger gain in P-IQ than in V-IQ over the 25-year period is entirely consistent with Flynn's (1987) investigation of IQ changes over time in 14 nations, which showed about twice as large a gain in fluid as in crystallized abilities. Yet the change of 3 points in 25 years, or 1.2 points per decade, is less than the 3-point per decade gain he reported for the U.S. as a whole. Closer inspection of Flynn's (1987, p. 186) results, however, reveals an American per decade gain of 3.0 points for schoolchildren, 1.8 points for adults aged 35 years or less, and 3.4 points for adults aged

TABLE 7.13 Time-lag effects, as determined by comparing the mean WAIS IQs earned by the four cohorts in 1953 with the mean estimated WAIS IQs earned in 1978 by adults matched with each cohort on chronological age

Age Group	VERBAL IQ			PERFORMANCE IQ			FULL SCALE IQ		
	1953 Mean	1978 Mean	Time-Lag Effect	1953 Mean	1978 Mean	Time-Lag Effect	1953 Mean	1978 Mean	Time-Lag Effect
20–29	99.9	102.8	+2.9	101.9	106.9	+5.0	100.9	103.4	+2.5
30–39	99.2	102.7	+3.5	97.8	102.6	+4.8	98.7	101.7	+3.0
40–44	98.2	100.9	+2.7	92.8	98.8	+6.0	95.8	99.0	+3.2
45–49	98.3	101.3	+3.0	90.2	96.1	+5.9	94.7	98.1	+3.4
Mean Effect			+3.0			+5.4			+3.0

NOTE: All IQs are based on ages 25–34 as a reference group. Sums of scaled scores used to compute WAIS IQs for each 5- or 10-year interval are from Matarazzo (1972, Table 10.4). Sums of scaled scores used to compute WAIS-R IQs for each 5- to 10-year interval are interpolated from the data for the age groups provided by Wechsler (1981, Table 7). WAIS-R IQs earned in 1978 have been converted to WAIS IQs by adding constants (see text).

35–75. In the present time-lag analysis, the samples studied represented the younger half of the WAIS and WAIS-R standardization samples, and the norms for ages 25–34 were used as the reference group for computing all IQs.

The estimated WAIS IQs earned by each cohort in 1978 should be adjusted for these time-lag effects to remove the influence of cultural change. Consequently, I subtracted 3 points from each estimated WAIS V-IQ and FS-IQ, and 5.4 points from each estimated WAIS P-IQ. I used the average values, rather than the separate values obtained for each cohort, partly because the values were so similar from group to group, and partly because Schaie (1983b) provided evidence that, "the least biased estimates of period effects will be the average time-lag difference between successive occasions across all available cohorts equating for age" (p. 103).

WAIS IQ Changes Over a 25-Year Period

Table 7.14 takes all previously mentioned variables into account to show the changes in WAIS IQ from 1953 to 1978 for four cohorts tested twice via the cohort-substitution technique. When corrected for time-lag effects, all cohorts earned lower IQs in 1978 than they did in 1953. The decrements became slightly larger with increasing age, but these cohort differences were mild, only 2 to 4 IQ points. The most striking finding in the data is the difference between the Verbal and Performance Scales. Decrements in V-IQ were small for each cohort, reaching as high as 5.5 points for the 1904–1908 cohort (the average decrease was 3.5 points or .23 *SD*). In contrast, P-IQ decrements were large for each cohort, ranging from 11.6 to 13.5 IQ points (an average decrease of 12.6 points or .84 *SD*). Large decreases in P-IQ occurred for each cohort whether they advanced in age from 24.5 to 49.5 (on the average) or from 47 to 72. These results support the findings from the cross-sectional analyses

of the WAIS and WAIS-R, with or without a control for education. Decreases in FS-IQ averaged 8.2 points (.55 *SD*), but these results are far less compelling than the separate findings for the Verbal and Performance Scales.

Comparison of Longitudinal and Cross-Sectional Wechsler Data

Technically, it is methodologically incorrect to construct age gradients from a combination of longitudinal and cross-sectional data, a procedure used by Schaie and Strother (1968); "the use of cross-sequential results to evaluate age changes [is] ill considered" (Schaie & Hertzog, 1983, p. 532). Nonetheless, I believe that the best way to show relationships between the WAIS/WAIS-R longitudinal and WAIS-R cross-sectional data is to graph the age gradients from each study simultaneously, which I have done for the V-IQ (Figure 7.8) and P-IQ (Figure 7.9). The data graphed for the longitudinal analysis represent two data points for each of the four cohorts, the WAIS IQs earned in 1953, and the estimated WAIS IQs (adjusted for time lag) earned in 1978. Cross-sectional data are the same education-adjusted values shown in Figures 7.1 and 7.2.

The V-IQs from both analyses follow a similar pattern, although the longitudinal values show an earlier decline than the cross-sectional values. However, the P-IQs from each study form nearly identical curves, emphasizing the consistency of the dramatic decrease in mean Performance IQ with increasing age, starting early in adult life. Neither curve can rightfully be considered a growth curve, and ontogenetic changes should either be inferred with caution or not at all. Yet the fact that adults within each of the four cohorts showed sizable decrements across a 25-year period reinforces the notion that adults do decline in nonverbal intelligence with advancing age, and this decline begins far earlier on Wechsler's scales than on the Army Alpha or PMA. The shape of the precise growth curve remains elusive, but lon-

TABLE 7.14   Mean WAIS and estimated WAIS IQs earned by each of four cohorts at two points in time (1953 and 1978), using independent samples and controlling for instrument and time-log effects

WAIS IQ	COHORT				
	1924–1933 *(Ages 20–29* *and 45–54)*	*1914–1923* *(Ages 30–39* *and 55–64)*	*1909–1913* *(Ages 40–44* *and 65–69)*	*1904–1908* *(Ages 45–49* *and 70–74)*	*Mean*
Verbal					
1953	99.9	99.2	98.2	98.3	98.9
1978	101.4	98.9	97.3	95.8	98.4
Change	+1.5	−0.3	−0.9	−2.5	−0.5
Correction for time lag	−1.5	−3.3	−3.9	−5.5	−3.5
Performance					
1953	101.9	97.8	92.8	90.2	95.7
1978	95.7	90.7	85.3	82.1	88.5
Change	−6.2	−7.1	−7.5	−8.1	−7.2
Correction for time lag	−11.6	−12.5	−12.9	−13.5	−12.6
Full Scale					
1953	100.9	98.7	95.8	94.7	97.5
1978	97.7	93.5	90.3	87.6	92.3
Change	−3.2	−5.2	−5.5	−7.1	−5.2
Correction for time lag	−6.2	−8.2	−8.5	−10.1	−8.2

gitudinal analysis suggests that the lower P-IQs for successive age groups is not just a cross-sectional phenomenon.

One problem with correcting for time-lag effects is that the adjustment fails to distinguish between time-of-measurement effects and cohort effects. When comparing, for example, 20- to 29-year-olds tested in 1953 and in 1978 to determine time-lag effects, one is comparing the performance of two different cohorts: 1924–1933 and 1949–1958. Any observed dif-

ferences may be due to cohort effects, not just time-of-measurement effects. Kausler (1982, p. 93) considers adjustments for the latter variable sensible, but not for the portion of the variance due to cohort effects. Certainly, differences in education between the cohorts representing a given age group would be sizable, and would contribute to the 3- to 5 1/2-point cultural change observed in Table 7.13.

Nonetheless, I believe that the adjustment for the total time lag is appropriate. First, the values

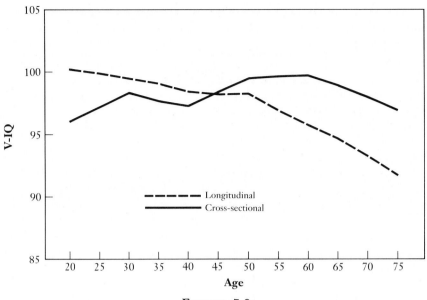

FIGURE 7.8

Changes in Wechsler Verbal IQ with chronological age using two different experimental designs: cross-sectional (controlling for education) and longitudinal (controlling for instrument and time-lag effects).

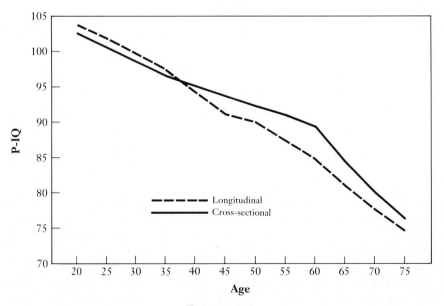

FIGURE 7.9

Changes in Wechsler Performance IQ with chronological age using two different experimental designs: cross-sectional (controlling for education) and longitudinal (controlling for instrument and time-lag effects).

for each of the four cohorts are similar, arguing in favor of a cultural change that affected all adults born between 1904 and 1933 about equally rather than cohort-specific effects that would have had a differential impact on the diverse samples. Second, when education was controlled in the WAIS-R cross-sectional study (Kaufman et al., 1989; McLean et al., 1988b), it showed a minimal effect on P-IQ, the variable of most interest in the longitudinal analysis; consequently, there is no strong evidence to imply that very much of the time-lag adjustment was due to differential cohort effects. Finally, the use of a common reference group of 25- to 34-year-olds for all computations probably reduces the impact of specific cohort differences; these effects would be more in evidence if IQs were derived from age-specific norms. Flynn's (1987) larger estimates of cultural change within the U.S. were based on IQs computed on separate groups of individuals aged 35–44, 45–54, and so forth.

When *no* adjustment is made for time lag, the changes in WAIS IQs over 25 years for the four cohorts were negligible for V-IQ, but were still substantial for P-IQ (see Table 7.14). Thus, even without the time-lag adjustment, there is a marked Verbal–Performance differential; V-IQ stayed virtually the same over time, while P-IQ declined about 1/2 standard deviation for each cohort.

Comparison of Wechsler and PMA Results

The WAIS longitudinal study suggests that declines in P-IQ with age start early, as the change in P-IQ for the youngest cohort in 1953 was a striking 11.6-point drop between ages 20–29 and 45–54. In this respect, the Wechsler longitudinal data differ from Schaie's PMA data, which indicated a decline much later in life. Of the various analyses reported by Schaie and his colleagues, the one that most resembles the 25-year longitudinal WAIS study is his analysis of data for a 21-year span, based on scores earned by independent samples from the same cohorts (Schaie, 1983b, Table 4.14). The initial data point was 1956 and the final data point was 1977, closely resembling the dates for the WAIS and WAIS-R standardizations.

I have converted the 21-year changes (reported by Schaie in *T*-score units) to units corresponding to Wechsler's *SD* of 15. I have also averaged data for the PMA Verbal Meaning and Number subtests, offering an analog to Wechsler's V-IQ, and I have similarly averaged data for Space and Reasoning, the best P-IQ counterpart. Each of the four cohorts listed showed decrements across the 21-year span on each subtest. (Data for a group that aged from 60 to 81 is excluded because no comparable WAIS sample is available; data for two of Schaie's cohorts were merged—32/53 and 39/60—to enable the PMA cohorts to match the WAIS cohorts on a one-to-one basis). The pattern of decline for the verbal and nonverbal combinations is shown in Table 7.15.

The PMA trends do not resemble the WAIS findings. Declines on the PMA verbal and nonverbal tasks are similar to each other: small for the youngest cohort and increasing steadily until reaching .81 *SD* (verbal) and .64 *SD* (nonverbal). The decline is approximately one-half of a standard deviation for the cohort aged 46 years in 1956, and this sizable decrement occurs at that time for *both* verbal and nonverbal tasks. There is some PMA evidence that the nonverbal decline is larger for the two younger cohorts, but this finding is offset by a reverse trend for the two older cohorts. At its peak (ages 53 to 74), the nonverbal PMA decline is smaller than all of the longitudinal declines observed for WAIS P-IQ (see Table 7.14), and is also smaller than the PMA verbal decrement for the age 53 cohort. Schaie's data were uncorrected for time-lag and cohort effects, but these adjustments to his data invariably reduce declines, not increase them.

The comparisons between WAIS and PMA longitudinal data suggest that (a) the same striking differential V-IQ/P-IQ pattern observed on the WAIS is *not* observed for the PMA tasks; (b) the large, early decline in P-IQ does *not* occur for the PMA; and (c) if Schaie had used the WAIS instead of the PMA in his research, it is unlikely—regardless of his adjustments to the data—that P-IQ would have maintained itself into the 50s or 60s before declining substantially.

The reasons for the difference in the relationships of age to P-IQ and the PMA nonverbal tests may relate to the visual-motor components of Wechsler's tasks and the cognitive complexity that defines virtually each Performance subtest. This complexity, which makes Wechsler's nonverbal subtests so sensitive to brain damage and psychiatric disorders (see chapter 9) as well as aging, is explained nicely by Zarit, Eiler, and Hassinger's (1985) statement that Digit Symbol "requires the integration of left-hemisphere verbal skills in understanding instructions, frontal lobe planning of motor activity, primary occipital visual ability, right-parietal-lobe perceptual abilities, left-hemisphere motor performance in right-handed individuals, and memory for digit-symbol pairs after practice" (p. 729).

INTERPRETATION OF THE P-IQ DECLINE: SPEED OR FLUID ABILITY?

The combination of WAIS-R cross-sectional data with an education control and the longitudinal WAIS/WAIS-R study support the classic intellectual aging pattern, and the notion that the P-IQ decline starts in young adulthood at a rapid rate and continues steadily toward old age. Botwinick (1977) interpreted the pattern as part of a timed-nontimed framework, alleging that adults maintain their performance on nontimed tests, but drop rapidly on timed tests. Numerous investigators have interpreted the classical pattern from Botwinick's perspective—for example, Jarvik and Bank (1983) in their longitudinal analysis of aging among elderly twins. However, considerable evidence also supports Horn's (1985) insistence that the classic pattern reflects maintenance of crystallized abilities (school-like tasks often associated with formal training) versus the early decline of fluid abilities (novel problem solving that demands adaptability and flexibility for success). In the sections that follow, I present evidence that the early, severe decline in P-IQ with age is the

TABLE 7.15 Decline in PMA verbal and nonverbal scores across a 21-year span for independent samples included in Schaire's Seattle Longitudinal Study

Age in 1956	Age in 1977	Change in PMA Verbal Standard Score (Verbal Meaning, Number)	Change in PMA Nonverbal Standard Score (Space, Reasoning)
25	46	− 0.7	−3.2
35.5	56.5	− 1.8	−5.7
46	67	− 7.9	−7.0
53	74	−12.2	−9.6

NOTE: Change equals standard score in 1956 minus standard score in 1977. Standard scores have a standard deviation equal to 15.

result of a decline in fluid abilities rather than a generalized difficulty with timed tasks.

The Case Against Botwinick's Speed Hypothesis

The decline in speed with advancing age is a fact. This slowing "is not only an acknowledged laboratory result but also of considerable practical importance. . . .[A]ge-related slowness is evident in tasks of daily living such as zipping a garment, dialing a telephone, picking up coins, unwrapping a band-aid, cutting with a knife, and even putting on a shirt" (Salthouse, 1985, p. 400). Research has shown that healthy adults (especially in cardiovascular functions) have quicker reaction times than less healthy adults, yet even data for healthy and physically fit samples suggest "that the age deficiencies, although possibly attenuated, are nevertheless present" (Salthouse, 1985, p. 404).

Wechsler's Arithmetic Subtest

Nonetheless, decrements in P-IQ with age do not seem to be simply a function of speed. When vocal answers are required rather than motor responses, the relationship between speed and aging no longer holds (Salthouse, 1985). This consistent research finding was supported by the age trends for the WAIS-R Arithmetic subtest in McLean et al.'s (1988b) investigation. When education was controlled, each adult age group between 20–24 and 70–74 earned a mean scaled score of about 10 (see Figure 7.4). Yet all Arithmetic items are timed (the first nine items allow only 15–30 seconds apiece) and the last five items award 1 bonus point apiece for quick, perfect performance. Clearly, older adults do not score low on Wechsler's Performance Scale simply because they are slow.

Speed of Motor Coordination

Is motor speed the problem? Digit Symbol produces the most dramatic age declines, and this task is a strong measure of psychomotor speed. However, cognitive research suggests that poor Digit Symbol performance is not just a function of speed of responding. Storandt (1976) tested the pure motor speed of young and elderly adults by simply having them copy symbols as rapidly as possible without the matched pairs. Younger adults far outstripped the elderly in this task. However, when these groups were also given the standard Digit Symbol subtest, a clear-cut cognitive differential was evident as well; the superior performance by the younger subjects could not be explained by the speed differential alone. In fact, the cognitive and speed components contributed about equally to the differential.

Doppelt and Wallace (1955) administered Arithmetic and all Performance subtests to the WAIS old-age sample under standard conditions and also under "irregular" conditions, where they were allowed to solve each item with unlimited time (bonus points were not considered in their analysis). The subjects aged 60 and above improved their scores only trivially on all tasks except Block Design, which yielded raw score increases of about 2½ points (amounting to less than one-third of a SD). Storandt (1977), in a similar investigation with 40 young and 40 elderly adults matched on verbal ability, supported Doppelt and Wallace's results. The elderly group improved their raw scores significantly on only one of the five WAIS subtests, this time Picture Arrangement. Interestingly, the younger subjects (ages 20–30) failed to improve their scores significantly on any of the tasks.

Storandt (1977) studied bonus points as well and discovered that the young earned more bonuses than the elderly on all tasks, with the mean difference relatively small on Arithmetic (1.7 versus 1.2), and striking on Block Design (3.5/0.6) and Object Assembly (7.0/2.2). That analysis might implicate speed as the culprit, except that "even when this advantage in favor of the young is eliminated, the old still exhibit poorer performance than the young" (Storandt, 1977, p. 177). Furthermore, the bonus-point argument has little support from McLean et al.'s (1988b) WAIS-R study. Figure 7.5 indicates that excluding Digit Symbol, the four Performance subtests evidence highly similar decreases in mean scaled scores with increasing age. This comparability is evident for both sets of data, regular scaled scores and the values adjusted for education. However, WAIS-R Picture Completion and Picture Arrangement do *not* allot bonus points for quick performance, while much of the Block Design and Object Assembly variance is due to bonus points. Picture Completion is not even a highly speeded task. There is a time limit of 20 seconds per item, but that limit is obviously quite adequate since neither the subjects in Doppelt and Wallace's nor Storandt's investigations improved their Picture Completion raw scores significantly with unlimited time. In fact, trivial gains of less than a half point were observed for all subsamples in the two studies.

Taken together, all of these data relegate motor speed to second place behind some type of cognitive deficit. This conclusion is consistent with Salthouse's (1985) review of numerous studies exploring the roles of input (sensory) and output (motor) on speed of performance, showing that sensory and motor factors "can account for only a small part of the slower behavior of older adults" (p. 409). He notes further that "the evidence is very convincing that central factors are involved" (p. 421). Salthouse (1984) hypothesizes that age-related intellectual decline, often evident during the decade of the 30s, is "an intrinsic, maturational-based alteration in the central nervous system, which results in a slowing down of the processing of nearly all types of information" (p. 19).

Noncognitive (Behavioral and Health-Related) Variables

Some writers have summarized research on noncognitive variables such as cautiousness and avoidance of risk-taking (Okun, 1976), low motivation (Kausler, 1982), or poor self-esteem (Bengtson, Reedy, & Gordon, 1985) as the causes of the slower and less efficient test performance of elderly individuals. Older adults do

show evidence of cautiousness and low risk-taking, for example, by making more errors of *omission* than younger adults who, in turn, make more errors of *commission* (Okun, Siegler, & George, 1978); however, no evidence implicates cautiousness as a major cause of the P-IQ decline. Research does suggest that elderly adults do not suffer from low self-esteem (Bengtson et al., 1985), and it does not "seem likely that age differences in motivational level account for a great deal of the age differences in performance found on a wide range of psychological tasks" (p. 124). Nonetheless, Reese and Rodeheaver (1985) emphasize that despite the burgeoning literature showing that younger adults easily outstrip the elderly on conceptual tasks— older adults use more primitive and inefficient strategies, are less likely to change strategies, commit more errors, and are less likely to achieve correct solutions—"[d]ifferences in performance cannot be definitively interpreted as deficits in competence . . . [and] few significant steps have been taken toward understanding the nature of the differences" (pp. 495–496).

Diminished attention span in elderly individuals has been implicated as an explanation for the fluid intelligence decline with increasing age (Stankov, 1988). In an analysis of the WAIS-R and numerous variables purported to measure attention, Stankov showed that the correlation between age and fluid intelligence reduced to approximately zero when various attentional factors were partialed out of the coefficient. However, this alleged dependency of fluid intelligence on "age-related changes in attentional processes" (Stankov, 1988, p. 72) is speculative at best for a number of reasons, the first two of which were mentioned by Stankov:

- One cannot infer causality from a correlation—diminished attention can cause low test performance, *or* low intelligence can impair attention span.

- A third variable, perhaps physiological in nature, may cause both depressed attention span and lowered fluid intelligence in elderly people.

- The sample was composed of only 100 Australians, ages 20–70, not nearly a large enough group to support Stankov's factor analysis of 36 variables (the ratio of less than three subjects per variable falls far short of the 10:1 ratio that is usually recommended for factor analysis).

- The small samples of 20 adults per age group were not matched on key variables from age to age, and they were atypical, composed of three-quarters women, averaging 12.4 years of education, and earning a mean WAIS-R FS-IQ of 115.

- Block Design, the most reliable Performance task and often considered the best measure of fluid intelligence on the Wechsler scales, was eliminated from the analyses because of a statistical technicality.

Another noncognitive variable that might affect an age-related intellectual decline is physical health. Elderly individuals tend to have more health problems, such as cardiovascular disease, than younger adults (Abrahams, 1976), and these problems may lead to lower test scores. Whereas even mild hearing loss by older people can lower IQs substantially (Granick, Kleban, & Weiss, 1976), most studies on the relationship between physical ailments and intelligence have not established a direct causal link between the illness and depressed intelligence.

Cardiovascular disease was found to be associated with dropping out from longitudinal research, and also was significantly related to performance on PMA subtests in a study by Hertzog, Schaie, and Gribbin (1978); however, the data were not wholly consistent with a causal relationship, and other alternative explanations were feasible. Also, WAIS scores for two age groups (21–39, 45–65) tended not to relate significantly to hypertension (Schultz, Dineen, Elias, Pentz, & Wood, 1979). Verbal decrements were associated with high blood pressure for the younger, but not the older, sample, and

Performance scores were *unrelated* to hypertension for both age groups. In a longitudinal investigation that included some of the subjects from the Schultz et al. (1979) study, hypertensives experienced no significant decline in WAIS verbal intelligence over the 5- to 6-year test interval, while those with normal blood pressure ("normotensives") displayed small but significant gains (Schultz, Elias, Robbins, Streeten, & Blakeman, 1986). Importantly, in view of the age-related decline on timed nonverbal subtests, neither sample evidenced decline on the WAIS Performance subtests. The results of this longitudinal investigation are consistent with the findings from most investigations of high blood pressure in elderly people: "[M]ean differences between hypertensive and normotensive groups have been relatively small and clinically insignificant and . . . many factors other than hypertensive disease processes or medication may contribute to them" (Schultz et al., 1986, p. 173).

Field, Schaie, and Leino (1988) assessed health via self-reports from interviews and related this variable to the WAIS IQs earned at two points in time (mean ages of 69 and 83) by individuals included in the Berkeley Older Generation Study. There was some evidence that health was more related to intellectual functioning for the oldest individuals, and that self-reported health related more strongly to Performance than to Verbal scores. However, most relationships between health status and either present or future intelligence test performance were not significant; Field et al. (1988) concluded that "[s]elf-assessed health was not found to be as strong a correlate of cognitive functioning as was anticipated" (p. 390).

Overall, health problems contribute only a small amount of variance toward declining intelligence once socioeconomic status, cohort effects, and other pertinent variables are controlled (Willis, 1985)—and even this small relationship may be due to other causes such as limited stimulation or activity following disease (Schaie & Willis, 1986). Just as behavioral variables do not seem to explain the decline in test scores with advancing age on Wechsler's timed nonverbal subtests, neither do health variables. However, research on the relationship between health and IQ has revealed some fascinating findings, including great *individual* variation in the relationship between physical health and mental test performance. This work supports the view that the "stereotype of inevitable frailty in old age . . . is yielding in the face of evidence from longitudinal studies" (Field et al., 1988, p. 390).

Are the Performance Subtests Measures of Intelligence for Elderly People?

If speed is the main reason for the P-IQ decline with age, due to coordination difficulties, cautiousness, low risk-taking, slow reaction time, poor motivation, inattention, hypertension, or any other combination of noncognitive variables, then one prediction follows logically: Wechsler's Performance subtests should be poor measures of the *g* factor for older adults. In fact, age changes in *g* loadings for Wechsler's subtests show just the *opposite* trend, as evidenced in Table 8.11 in the next chapter. Across all subtests, the mean *g* loading for WISC-R subtests is .64 versus .71 for the WAIS-R. For the WAIS-R alone, *g* loadings tend to increase with age (.68 for ages 16–19 and .73 for ages 55–74). On the WISC-R, Performance subtests (excluding Mazes) averaged *g* loadings of .59 for ages 6–16 years; on the WAIS-R corresponding mean *g* loadings are shown here (based on Table 8.11 and Parker's, 1983, data for separate age groups):

AGE GROUP	MEAN *g* LOADING FOR PERFORMANCE SUBTESTS
16–19	.58
20–34	.64
35–54	.70
55–64	.66
65–69	.72
70–74	.63

Quite clearly, the Performance subtests measure general intelligence just as well or better for old adults as they do for young adults, children, and adolescents. Even the *g* loadings for the oldest age group, though lower than the values for ages 65–69, are approximately the same as the values for 20- to 34-year-olds. These results strongly suggest that Wechsler's Performance subtests are primarily measures of cognitive, not noncognitive, factors for adults of all ages within the 20- to 74-year range. The *g* loadings for adults fluctuated between the mid .60s and low .70s with no apparent age trend in evidence; these findings neither support nor disconfirm the controversial *dedifferentiation hypothesis* (Balinsky, 1941; Reinert, 1970), which posits that the elderly "are expected to revert cognitively to the structure of intelligence characteristic of childhood" (Kausler, 1982, p. 583).

Data from a different set of nonverbal intelligence subtests are entirely in agreement with the findings reported here for the WAIS-R. Three of the subtests in the first edition of the Woodcock-Johnson Psycho-Educational Battery (Woodcock & Johnson, 1977) are nonverbal: Spatial Relations, Analysis-Synthesis, and Concept Formation. The mean *g* loading on these three tasks was .59 for adolescents in grades 8 and 12, .62 for adults aged 20–39, .68 for ages 40–64, and .62 for ages 65 and above (Kaufman & O'Neal, 1988a).

Conclusion

The evidence is strongly against the hypothesis that the P-IQ decline is primarily a result of the fact that the Wechsler Performance tasks are timed. In fact, had a speed hypothesis been given support, one would have to wonder how Schaie and his colleagues have obtained such consistent findings of the maintenance of test performance on a diversity of abilities across the lifespan, with declines occurring quite late in life, based on the highly speeded subtests of the PMA.

The Case for a Decline in Fluid Intelligence

Horn (1985) has advanced far beyond a two-pronged fluid–crystallized approach to the assessment of human abilities, but the Cattell-Horn distinction between these two types of general intelligence factors has been a commonly proposed explanation of Botwinick's hypothesis for the differential changes with aging that characterize Wechsler's Verbal and Performance Scales (Dixon, Kramer, & Baltes, 1985). This theory predicts increase and stability across the lifespan in crystallized intelligence because of its dependence on accumulated knowledge from a culture. In contrast, fluid intelligence, because of its dependency on physiological functioning and neurological integrity, is expected to peak in late adolescence and decline steadily throughout adulthood concomitant with neurological degeneration (Horn & Cattell, 1966; Horn, 1978). The theory has its detractors (e.g., Guilford, 1980), but predictions from the theory seem to accord quite well with the observed aging pattern associated with the WAIS and WAIS-R in education-controlled and longitudinal investigations: maintenance of the verbal or crystallized abilities throughout the lifespan, coupled with an early and striking decline in the performance or fluid abilities.

Based on reviews of numerous studies, mostly cross-sectional and including a diversity of fluid and crystallized tests (including a number of untimed fluid tests), Horn and his associates (Horn, 1982, 1985; Horn & Donaldson, 1980; Horn, Donaldson, & Engstrom, 1981) have found broad-based support for a decline throughout adulthood in fluid intelligence. Horn's best estimates of the rate of decline is 5 IQ points per decade, with the largest loss occurring between ages 30 and 60 years. WAIS and WAIS-R data for P-IQ across the age range (see Figure 7.9) show a decrease of about 25

IQ points between the early 20s and early 70s (5 points per decade), with about half of the decrement occurring between ages 30 and 60. The agreement with Horn's predictions may be coincidental, but the findings are nonetheless compelling. Figure 7.10 shows Horn's (1970) hypothetical growth curves for crystallized intelligence (G_c) and fluid intelligence (G_f), alongside theoretical curves for other neurological, cognitive, or environmental variables. Note the extreme similarity in the curve for G_c and for WAIS-R Verbal IQ with education controlled (Figure 7.1); and for G_f and Performance IQ, controlling for education (Figure 7.2).

Supportive Evidence

Other sources of support for an interpretation of the Wechsler classic aging pattern from a fluid–crystallized model rather than a timed–nontimed approach are listed briefly below:

- Most of the evidence listed previously against a speed interpretation of the aging pattern offers indirect support for a decline in fluid intelligence. For example, all Performance subtests except Digit Symbol are considered measures of fluid intelligence (Horn, 1985). Declines on Picture Completion and Picture Arrangement—two tasks with no bonus points and generally ample time limits—parallel closely the age-related decrements in the highly speeded Block Design and Object Assembly tasks. The most sensible explanation is a decline in whatever underlying ability these tasks have in common.

- Two Verbal subtests have fluid components, differentiating them from the remainder of the Verbal Scale: Digit Span and Similarities (Horn, 1985; see pp. 382–383). These are also the precise WAIS or WAIS-R Verbal subtests that consistently behave differently from the other four more achievement-oriented tasks in cross-sectional studies (Birren & Morrison, 1961; Doppelt & Wallace, 1955; Heaton et al., 1986; McLean et al., 1988b). With education controlled, these were the

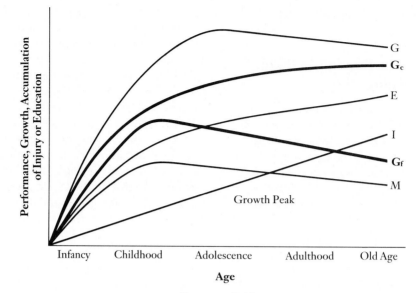

FIGURE 7.10

Hypothetical age changes, from infancy to old age, of crystallized intelligence (G_c), fluid intelligence (G_f), maturational growth and decline of neural structures (M), accumulation of injury to neural structures (I), accumulation of educational exposures (E), and overall ability (G). Curves for G_c and G_f appear in bold. (Adapted from J. L. Horn, 1970. Copyright 1970 by Academic Press. Reprinted by permission.)

only two Verbal tasks in Birren and Morrison's investigation that did not change the sign of their correlation with age from negative to positive; in Heaton's study, these were the only two Verbal subtests to produce a significant age main effect. And in McLean et al.'s (1988) study, Digit Span and Similarities alone among the Verbal tasks showed a decline in mean scaled score after age 54 (see Figure 7.4), even when controlling for education. The decreases in mean scores occurred at older ages for these two tasks than for the Performance subtests, and the decrements were relatively small, but the pattern is consistent with the fluid hypothesis.

• Studies of aging and memory indicate small or no age differences on measures of sensory memory (identification of briefly presented stimuli), primary memory (tasks like Digit Span), and tertiary (remote) memory, but large differences between young and old adults occur repeatedly for tests of *secondary* memory like paired associates (Poon, 1985). These tasks require the acquisition and retrieval of newly acquired information from secondary memory. Poon's (1985) conclusion from numerous studies supports the hypothesized decline in fluid ability with age: "Age decrements are found when the memory task requires spontaneous organizational and elaborative processes" (p. 437).

• Creative contributions of men and women provide indirect support for the early decline in fluid ability. Table 7.16 presents the average ages when people in diverse fields made their greatest innovations (adapted from Matarazzo, 1972, Table 7.4, based on Lehman, 1953, 1954). Virtually all of these creative works, the products primarily of fluid intelligence, were contributed by men and women in their 20s and 30s. The only field in which the most creative works were developed by people in their 40s was literature (when authors wrote their "best" books); this endeavor seems to relate to crystallized intelligence more so than writing poetry, coming up with practical inventions, or making discoveries in science and mathematics.

- Elderly adults often perform more poorly on Piagetian conservation tasks than do adolescents and adults, although the findings tend to be inconsistent (Reese & Rodeheaver, 1985). Papalia (1972), for example, found approximately the same proportions of elderly people (mean age = 74.8) and young children (mean age = 6.7) to conserve substance, weight, and volume; in contrast, individuals aged 18–64 conserved to a much

greater degree. Rubin, Attewell, Tierney, and Tumolo (1973) also found old adults (76.3 years) to be poorer conservers than samples of adults aged 21 and 44, but some other researchers have found no differences in conservation ability between young adults and elderly individuals (Chance, Overcast, & Dollinger, 1978). In general, however, in comparisons of different adult age groups on conservation, [W]orse performance has been reported for the older adults compared to younger adults" (Muhs, Hooper, & Papalia-Finlay, 1979–1980, p. 312). An apparent age-related decline has been observed on Piagetian formal operations tasks as well (Reese & Rodeheaver, 1985), although results with college-educated elderly adults have been mixed (Blackburn, 1984; Hooper, Hooper, & Colbert, 1985).

- The Piagetian tasks employed in these studies are mostly nonverbal or combinations of nonverbal judgments and verbal explanations. The skills seem to reflect fluid problem solving, and the apparent regression during the aging

TABLE 7.16 Average ages of men and women in diverse fields when they contributed their most creative works

Late 20s	Early 30s	Mid 30s	Late 30s	Early 40s
Literature (poetry)	Mathematics	Literature (fiction)	Geology	Literature (best books)
Baseball	Physics	Genetics	Bacteriology	
Boxing	Electronics	Entomology	Astronomy	
Racing	Practical inventions	Psychology	Physiology	
Chemistry	Botany	Surgical techniques	Pathology	
	Classical descriptions of disease		Medical discoveries	
			Philosophy	

NOTE: Adapted from Table 7.4 in Matarazzo (1972, p. 186), based on work by H. C. Lehman (1953, 1954).

process may reflect declining fluid intelligence (Hooper, Fitzgerald, & Papalia, 1971). In addition, there has been some empirical support for a significant relationship between formal operational reasoning and "marker" tests of fluid thinking (Hooper et al., 1985; Reese & Rodeheaver, 1985).

Overview

The evidence supports a decline in fluid intelligence with increasing age, starting early in adult life. The cause may be neurological, consistent with Cattell-Horn theorizing. Wechsler subtest patterns observed in normal aging are extremely similar to the patterns observed for patients with damage to the right cerebral hemisphere (Schaie & Schaie, 1977), but there is little neuroanatomic support for right hemisphere dysfunction within the elderly population (Zarit et al., 1985). (See chapters 9–11 for a thorough discussion of V–P IQ discrepancies and damage to the left and right hemispheres.) Albert and Kaplan (1980) attributed the decrement to frontal lobe function, citing the consistency of this hypothesis with age changes in attention and arousal and with neuroanatomic observations. In view of the mutual interactions among neurological changes, observed behaviors (such as attention), and test scores, it is extremely difficult to determine whether the fluid intelligence decline is due more to neurological dysfunction or to noncognitive variables that may characterize elderly people apart from brain-related changes. Horn et al. (1981) conceded from their investigation of the specific causes of fluid intelligence decline (e.g., organizing information, holding information in working memory, persistence) that the results suggest "that the aging losses of fluid intelligence mainly relate to decline in capacities, but the possibility that the losses are due to disinclinations to exercise effort cannot be entirely ruled out" (p. 74).

Knowledge of behavioral differences in elderly individuals is essential for competent clinical evaluation. Zarit et al. (1985) have made the following useful hints for assessing older adults:

- Be sensitive to sensory or motor weaknesses, and be aware that medication and health status may affect mood, attention span, and test scores.

- Distinguish between a patient's age and the age of onset of the disorder, since a person whose first problem appeared in old age may have numerous competencies and resources.

- Be knowledgeable about treatable "pseudo-dementia" disorders (e.g., depression, metabolic disorder, bacterial infection, accidental hypothermia) to avoid misdiagnosing a person as having irreversible dementia.

Evidence does exist that life-style is related to decline in intellectual functioning. One cannot attribute causality to these relationships because they tend to be reciprocal, but people who pursue much environmental stimulation and who continue their formal and informal educations throughout their lifespans tend to maintain strong mental functioning in later years (Gribbin, Schaie, & Parham, 1980). Being involved in a stimulating *early* work experience has also been associated with IQ maintenance (Willis, 1985). In contrast, the largest declines tend to be shown by older adults (most notably by intelligent females) who have faced family dissolution or personal disengagement (Willis, 1985). Whereas education is closely related to current mental ability, the simple number of years of education does not predict the rate of cognitive decline; and although health problems such as heart disease contribute a small amount of variance toward declining intelligence (see pp. 224–225), "[C]ardiovascular disease may only be a mediator of decline" (Schaie & Willis, 1986, p. 223). That is to say, the adverse lifestyles leading up to disease may be the true culprit in declining IQ.

There is, nonetheless, evidence that the decline in fluid intelligence can be reversed. Elderly people can be trained to improve their fluid skills, such as the abilities measured by the PMA Space and Reasoning subtests (e. g., Schaie & Willis, 1986). Reviews of the bulk of literature in this area show "rather overwhelmingly that significant performance gains can be affected, often with minor interventions" (Labouvie-Vief, 1985). The results are interesting, and do indeed suggest the need for an educational psychology of the older adult learner (Willis, 1985). Whether the ability to reverse a decline casts "grave doubts" on the "irreversible decrement models that assume normative patterns of intellectual decline" (Schaie & Willis, 1986, p. 224) is another matter. I don't believe that norms make any such assumption of irreversibility. They describe what is, not what might be under different circumstances. Fluid intelligence implies the ability to solve *new* problems in adaptive, flexible ways. Once training intervenes, these problems are no longer new. Transfer of training has been supported (Baltes & Willis, 1982), but such studies do not imply a universal gain in fluid intelligence.

Further, young adults also show improvement when trained on fluid ability tasks (Denney, 1982), and "the few studies in which elderly adults have been compared with younger adults [indicate] that there is a *decrease* in plasticity with increasing age" (p. 817, italics mine). Very recent research in this area by Nancy Denney and Bert Hayslip has nicely demonstrated the ease in training young adults, as well as alternative explanations of training effects (D. H. Kausler, personal communication, 1989). The key question is thus whether individuals who are trained on tasks like the PMA fluid subtests will improve substantially on the WAIS-R Performance Scale 6 months after the training (controlling for a Wechsler practice effect). I doubt it, but that is the type of research result that would make me share the optimism of investigators like Schaie and Willis (1986) regarding the importance of the training studies.

CHAPTER 7 SUMMARY

The relationship between aging and intelligence is reviewed in this chapter, with the key question being the nature of the decline in IQ with increasing age. Although Schaie and his colleagues have conducted the most exhaustive and excellent investigations of this topic, their general conclusion of small declines occurring relatively late in life were based on the group-administered, highly speeded, and old Primary Mental Abilities Test. Consequently, the degree to which their findings are generalizable to a clinical test like the WAIS-R is uncertain. Schaie's controversial research has, however, shown the power of cohort (generational) effects to affect the mean intelligence test scores earned by different age groups.

Mean scores earned by different adult age groups on the Wechsler-Bellevue, WAIS, and WAIS-R across the lifespan show declines in V-, P-, and FS-IQs between young adulthood and old age, with the declines in Performance IQ particularly striking. The age of peak performance on the Full Scale has increased through the years, rising from age 22 in 1937 to age 27 in 1953 to age 29.5 in 1978. The apparently declining Wechsler IQs are accompanied by a decline in the educational attainment of successive age groups. Thus, older age groups not only earn lower mean IQs than younger age groups but are also less educated. To control for this potentially contaminating variable on the WAIS-R, research was conducted in which each age group between 20 and 74 was equated on educational attainment. The decline in V-IQ disappeared following the statistical control, but the decisive decline in P-IQ remained. Declines on the separate Verbal subtests likewise tended to disappear following the control for education, although a small decrement was still noted for Similarities and Digit Span. Decreases on Performance subtests continued to be dramatic following the education control, with the largest decline observed for Digit Symbol.

Previous cross-sectional investigations of aging using the WAIS and incorporating education as a key variable found results closely similar to the WAIS-R findings. Green's widely cited study of the Spanish WAIS found discrepant results, as age-related decrements on P-IQ virtually disappeared for samples balanced on educational attainment. However, Green's age groups had limited education (averaging less than eight years), so these results may not generalize to more educated samples. Data from the WAIS-R investigation suggest that Green's findings may indeed be a function of low education level; individuals with less than 8 years of formal education showed very small age decrements in WAIS-R P-IQ after education was controlled, whereas more educated samples displayed large decrements.

Longitudinal investigations of the relationship between aging and IQ have occasionally been conducted with Wechsler's scales, but the findings are difficult to interpret because of the highly selective attrition that accompanies any longitudinal investigation and the practice effect that differentially influences scores on the Verbal and Performance Scales (with gains in P-IQ being far more substantial) when the same individuals are tested over and over again. Owens's longitudinal investigation of the Army Alpha, which resembles Wechsler's Verbal Scale, provided interesting data. Initial findings generally suggested improved test performance between age 19 and 50. However, when a portion of the group was retested at age 61 and a control for time lag (cultural change) was incorporated, what had first seemed like gains in Reasoning were, in fact, slight decrements. Overall findings from Owens's study are in agreement with the results of the WAIS and WAIS-R studies.

The comprehensive series of studies conducted by Schaie and his colleagues both agree and disagree with the Wechsler results. The PMA subtests that are the most "fluid" (like Wechsler's Performance tasks) show earlier declines than the more "crystallized" tasks. However, unlike the Wechsler findings, sizable decrements with age begin relatively late in life (the decade of the 60s). Part of the difference between Schaie's and the WAIS-R findings may result from the control for cohort effects that Schaie traditionally applies, a control that is arguable.

To determine whether the Wechsler results and PMA results would be similar if the experimental designs were similar, a new longitudinal research study was conducted that followed the same four cohorts over a 25-year span. The WAIS and WAIS-R standardization samples served as the data sources. Because of their comparability, it was possible to identify independent samples from the same set of cohorts and to trace the growth of these cohorts' intelligence between 1953 and 1978. Statistical corrections were used to equate for the different instrument administered (WAIS versus WAIS-R) and to control for cultural change, using a technique analogous to the one used by Owens. Results showed that all four cohorts evidenced small declines in V-IQ over the 25-year interval, in contrast to substantial (12–13 point) declines in P-IQ. Even the youngest cohort (ages 20–29 in 1953) dropped strikingly in P-IQ over this interval. These findings strongly agree with the cross-sectional data obtained for the WAIS-R that employed a control for education level; the results disagree with Schaie's PMA data indicating a decline in nonverbal/fluid abilities relatively late in life.

The existence of an age-related decline on Wechsler's Performance, but not Verbal, Scale is a well-validated finding that constitutes Botwinick's classic intellectual aging pattern. Botwinick's explanation of the pattern from a speeded/nonspeeded perspective, however, differs from Horn's interpretation of the same pattern from a fluid–crystallized model. Botwinick's hypothesis that the age-related decline occurs on speeded tasks is opposed by a lack of decrement on the speeded Arithmetic subtest, the failure of elderly people to improve their scores on most of Wechsler's Performance subtests when they are allotted unlimited time, and by other empirical results that argue against the hypothesis that speeded tasks are unduly influenced by noncognitive factors for elderly individuals.

Horn's fluid–crystallized hypothesis is supported by data from a variety of sources: (a) Horn's own research findings with a different set of fluid and crystallized measures; (b) similar age changes in mean scores for Wechsler's tests of fluid ability, whether the tasks are highly speeded or not; (c) declines with age for the two Verbal subtests with decided fluid components (Digit Span, Similarities); (d) the results of aging studies on memory that show striking decrements in secondary memory, a skill related to fluid ability; and (e) poor performance by the elderly on Piagetian conservation and formal operations tasks, both of which resemble fluid tests. The decline in fluid intelligence with age may be related to neurological factors, as Horn hypothesized. Regardless of cause, clinicians need to be sensitive about elderly individuals' possible sensory and motor weaknesses and aware of normal aging patterns if they are to perform a competent diagnosis.

In addition, research has shown that intellectual declines with age do not affect everyone equally. For example, people who continue their education throughout life show relatively small decrements, while larger declines are observed for people who have suffered family dissolution. A growing body of research has supported the finding that elderly adults can be taught to substantially improve their fluid intelligence via direct intervention.

Factor Analysis
of the WAIS-R

There seems to be nothing more irresistible to a psychometric researcher than factor analysis of a Wechsler battery—except, possibly, developing or validating short forms. The passion for factor analysis reached its height with the WISC-R, but the WAIS-R seems to be generating an enormous number of investigations as well (Leckliter, Matarazzo, & Silverstein, 1986). This chapter addresses WAIS-R psychometric research related to factor analysis; the concepts of the *g* factor and subtest specificity, both dependent on factor analysis, are also covered.

Chapter 3 presented the basic three-factor structure of the WAIS-R to show the similarities with the factor structures of its predecessors, the Wechsler-Bellevue I and the WAIS. As noted, the Verbal Comprehension, Perceptual Organization, and so-called Freedom from Distractibility factors were highly similar for each adult Wechsler scale, reinforcing the continuity of the constructs measured by the original adult battery and its two subsequent revisions. In this chapter, the factor structure of

the WAIS-R is reexamined to aid interpretation of the test. This discussion is primarily limited to techniques such as principal factor analysis followed by orthogonal or oblique rotations, rather than empirical procedures like hierarchical factor analysis that produce large general dimensions (Blaha & Wallbrown, 1982; Silverstein, 1987c).

As the last of the five chapters in Part II that are devoted to the integration and application of WAIS-R research, this chapter concludes with a systematic treatment of the strengths and weaknesses of the instrument, based on the comments of reviewers.

THE WAIS-R AS A ONE-FACTOR TEST

How many factors underlie the WAIS-R? O'Grady (1983) attempted to answer that key question with confirmatory maximum likelihood factor analysis, a sophisticated empirical approach that pits various possible factor solutions against each other to see which one emerges victorious. He considered the following alternative solutions: (a) one-factor, hypothesizing that the WAIS-R is primarily a measure of Spearman's *g*; (b) two-factor, corresponding precisely to Wechsler's armchair division of the battery into six Verbal and five Performance tasks; (c) three-factor, reflecting the results of numerous previous analyses of Wechsler batteries and adding the distractibility triad of Arithmetic, Digit Span, and Digit Symbol to the verbal and performance dimensions; (d) three-factor, assuming that the relevant dimensions are a general factor plus verbal and performance factors; and (e) four-factor, speculating that a general factor might accompany the verbal, performance, and distractibility factors.

O'Grady found that none of these models produced a statistically acceptable fit to the data. He rejected as unacceptable the models that postulated the coexistence of a general factor with two or three other factors, but found about equal acceptability for the one-factor solution and both the two- and three-factor oblique solutions. Statistically, O'Grady noted that the two-factor oblique solution (Verbal and Performance factors) produced an "improvement in fit" over the one-factor or *g* model, and that the three-factor oblique solution fit the data even better than the two-factor result. However, he concluded that in a practical sense the "fits" of the two- or three-factor solutions were only marginally better. O'Grady does not reject the notion that multiple factors underlie the WAIS-R, but he seems most comfortable in concluding from his analyses that the one-factor solution is the most parsimonious result. Certainly, he argues against the importance of the V–P dichotomy because of his focus on *g*: "Thus, in contrast to Blaha and Wallbrown's (1982, p. 652) assertion that their findings 'support the validity of maintaining separate Verbal and Performance IQs,' the results of this study clearly argue otherwise" (p. 830). Further, O'Grady (1983) downplays the role of multiple common ability factors, stressing that "none of

these other common ability factors account for anything other than a small measure of intellectual ability (as reflected in the WAIS-R), and thus it is difficult to consider them important in either understanding or explaining WAIS-R performance" (p. 831).

In short, based on practical and empirical considerations, O'Grady regards the WAIS-R as a one-factor test.

THE WAIS-R AS A TWO-FACTOR TEST

Silverstein (1982e) applied two empirical procedures to determine the number of WAIS-R factors: (a) Kaiser's criterion, which considers as significant all factors with latent roots, or eigenvalues, equal to or greater than 1.0, when unities are placed in the diagonal; and (b) the Montanelli-Humphreys parallel analysis criterion, which compares the latent roots of the correlation matrix with the latent roots of random-data matrices. The Kaiser criterion yielded two factors for five standardization age groups and only one factor for the remaining four age groups. The parallel-analysis criterion, by contrast, indicated that the WAIS-R was either a two-factor test (six age groups) or a three-factor test (three age groups).

Silverstein (1982e) examined the three-factor solutions for the three age groups (ages 16–24) for which more than two factors were suggested by the Montanelli-Humphreys criterion and found inconsistency. He expected to find clear-cut Freedom from Distractibility factors, but in fact they emerged only for ages 16–17 and 20–24; at ages 18–19, the third factor represented a splitting apart of the Perceptual Organization dimension. Because of this inconsistency and on empirical support from both criteria for two factors at a majority of age levels, Silverstein advocated the interpretation of two significant WAIS-R factors.

Gutkin, Reynolds, and Galvin (1984) also applied the Kaiser eigenvalue > 1.0 criterion, and like Silverstein (1982e) concluded that there are only two meaningful WAIS-R factors. They rejected the possibility of three significant factors, noting that the average eigenvalue for the third factor was only .82 when the Kaiser criterion indicated two significant factors. Gutkin et al. (1984) likewise rejected the possibility of only one meaningful factor by pointing out that whenever only one factor emerged with an eigenvalue of 1.0 or greater, the second factor's eigenvalue generally "hovered just below 1.0, with the average value being .94" (p. 86). Consequently, Silverstein (1982e) and Gutkin et al. (1984) concluded that the WAIS-R is a two-factor test.

THE WAIS-R AS A THREE-FACTOR TEST

Parker (1983) relied less than did the previous authors on empirical guidelines for addressing the issue of the appropriate number of factors; instead, he preferred to give more credence to the voluminous body of literature supporting "the consistency and frequency of studies reporting three and more factors in Wechsler tests" (p. 303). Hence, he examined the two-, three-, and four-factor solutions for each age group, searching for dimensions that have become familiar to Wechsler clinicians over the years. In doing so, he adopted the procedure that I had applied to the WISC-R nearly a decade before (Kaufman, 1975).

When examining the three-factor solutions, Parker (1983) easily identified the well-known Verbal Comprehension, Perceptual Organization, and Freedom from Distractibility dimensions for seven of the nine age groups. Even for the two maverick age levels (18–19, as Silverstein, 1982e, discovered, and also 45–54), the four-factor solutions included the three readily identifiable factors. Parker believed that the clinical familiarity of the three factors attested to their meaningfulness and "reality" and

was unconcerned that the three dimensions failed to emerge in a neat and clean manner or without overwhelming empirical support. Thus, Parker concluded that the WAIS-R is a three-factor test.

HOW MANY FACTORS UNDERLIE THE WAIS-R?

Researchers and clinicians using the WAIS tended to interpret many factors when trying to explain adult intellectual performance. Cohen typically interpreted as meaningful four or five WAIS factors for various normal and clinical samples (Berger, Bernstein, Klein, Cohen, & Lucas, 1964; Cohen, 1957a, 1957b). Wechsler (1958) delighted in finding clinical interpretations of small, exotic factors. For example, he interpreted Cohen's Factor D, defined by Picture Completion and little else, as a dimension of "relevance": "By relevance we mean appropriateness of response. This is perhaps illustrated by instances when appropriateness is lacking. For example, many schizophrenics and other subjects, instead of noting the called for and essential missing part of a picture, respond with an irrelevant detail" (p. 126).

Cohen's statistical sophistication was vitally necessary during the 1950s to impose some psychometric order on the clinical "art" of profile interpretation, and Wechsler's clinical genius is axiomatic. In retrospect, however, Cohen grossly overfactored in most of his landmark factor-analytic studies of Wechsler's scales, and Wechsler attempted to assign clinical meaning to statistical artifacts.

Is there any justification for interpreting four or five WAIS-R factors? Certainly not five. Naglieri and Kaufman (1983) examined the number of significant factors based on six different empirical criteria. The most stringent criterion (Cattell's scree test) suggested only one factor at each standardization age group, and the most liberal criterion (accounting for

75% of the total variance) indicated four factors for eight age groups and three factors for one group. The fourth factor was defined by generally substantial loadings by Picture Completion and Picture Arrangement for all groups, and is thus reminiscent of Wechsler's "relevance" factor or of Rapaport, Gill, and Schafer's (1945–1946) "visual organization without essential motor activity." However, the factor was inconsistent from age to age: Sometimes it was joined by Digit Symbol; sometimes it was joined by Similarities; sometimes it was defined by just one subtest (e.g., at ages 16–17, only Picture Arrangement loaded .30 or greater); and sometimes five factors had to be extracted in order for it to emerge. There is simply no empirical or logical support for interpreting more than three WAIS-R factors.

But which is it—one, two, or three? Not one. Cattell's scree test says one, and O'Grady (1983) used the empirical defense of confirmatory factor analysis to argue for one factor. Even canonical research that I have conducted with my colleagues (McLean, Kaufman, & Reynolds, 1988a) revealed great redundancy between the Verbal and Performance Scales, suggesting a single WAIS-R factor of intelligence. But where do such conclusions lead? Not very far, at least in the real world, and not towards the future. A one-factor interpretation of the WAIS-R is as progressive as a return to Spearman's *g* theory and to the original Binet scale, and is as clinically relevant as the rigid use of cut-off scores. O'Grady's plea for parsimony and his consequent rejection of the value of the V–P IQ discrepancy and other multiple common factors such as the distractibility dimension treat the WAIS-R as purely a psychometric instrument, to be used in a psychological vacuum or, at best, for research purposes.

But Wechsler was a consummate clinician who developed the Wechsler-Bellevue as a clinical tool to be used for measuring cognition within the broader domain of personality. Reducing the WAIS-R to a one-score instrument and cautioning clinicians to beware of the sep-

arate Verbal and Performance IQs because of their statistical overlap, which makes it "not surprising that both researchers . . . and practitioners . . . have been unable to employ a Verbal–Performance discrepancy index with any degree of power as a diagnostic tool" (O'Grady, 1983, p. 830), effectively cripples clinical artistry. As Leckliter et al. (1986) stress, the main reason for factor-analyzing a Wechsler battery is "to provide the basis for hypothesis testing by the examiner" (p. 341). With that as a rationale, the real issue is whether the WAIS-R is best interpreted as a two- or a three-factor test battery.

TWO VERSUS THREE WAIS-R FACTORS

In the case of the WISC-R, the choice between two or three factors was fairly easy. The Kaiser eigenvalue greater than 1.0 criterion produced *three* significant factors for 5 of the 11 age groups; even when this criterion suggested only two factors, the eigenvalue for the third dimension was within 0.1 of the cut-off (Kaufman, 1975). Readily interpretable distractibility factors were found for each age group. The consistency of the composition of the distractibility triad from age to age, along with the fairly solid empirical support, made it clear that the WISC-R was a three-factor test battery.

For the WAIS-R, the Kaiser criterion did not yield three factors for any group, and actually produced only *one* significant factor for the four age groups between ages 25 and 64. Further, the eigenvalues of the third factor were only close to 1.0 for the three youngest age groups (the values ranged from .85 to .97 for ages 16–24); for the six oldest age groups, eigenvalues were only about .70 (Naglieri & Kaufman, 1983). Yet, as Parker (1983) stressed, clear-cut distractibility factors emerged for each of the nine age groups.

Silverstein (1985c) attempted to resolve the discrepancy between Parker's acceptance of three factors and Silverstein's (1982e) own acceptance of only two factors by applying a different methodology, namely a hierarchical cluster analysis. Based on this procedure, Silverstein reversed his initial position when he found that three major clusters emerged for almost all standardization age groups:

- Verbal Comprehension (composed of Information, Vocabulary, Comprehension, and Similarities for all nine age groups; all six Verbal tasks formed the cluster for only four groups).
- Perceptual Organization (composed of just Block Design and Object Assembly for eight age groups, which were joined by Picture Completion for four groups).
- Freedom from Distractibility (composed of Digit Span and Arithmetic for seven of the nine groups; Digit Symbol joined the cluster for only one group).

In addition to the cluster analysis, two of the six statistical criteria evaluated by Naglieri and Kaufman (1983) endorsed three or four meaningful factors. Yet the remaining four criteria proposed only one or two factors.

To resolve this problem, one must examine the reasons for using empirical criteria in the first place. Basically, empirical criteria are necessary to prevent the interpretation of statistical artifacts that creep into data due to chance errors in the correlation matrix, idiosyncrasies of a particular sample, and so forth. Can anyone reasonably conclude that a cluster or factor defined by Digit Span and Arithmetic—with or without Digit Symbol—is artifactual or sample dependent? The history of Wechsler factor analyses argues strongly to the contrary, as does the consistency of the factor patterns for each of the 11 WISC-R and the 9 WAIS-R age groups. If a factor has emerged for the Wechsler-Bellevue, WISC, WAIS, WISC-R, and WAIS-R for every age group between 6 years and 70–74 years and if it comprises the same two or three tasks, it is surely not an artifact. Even the technique of hierarchical factor analysis, which first extracts a large g factor before yielding smaller group factors, has identified Verbal Comprehension, Perceptual Organization, and Freedom from Distractibility factors on both the WAIS-R and WISC-R for learning-disabled populations (Blaha, Mandes, & Swisher, 1987; Blaha & Vance, 1979).

The evidence for the third factor is not "scanty," despite Hill, Reddon, and Jackson's (1985) assertions. Consequently, logic and history outweigh rigid empiricism in justifying the conclusion that the WAIS-R is a *three-factor* test battery.

Leckliter et al.'s (1986) reminder that factor analysis is conducted to facilitate hypothesis testing provides more support for a three-factor approach. After all, so much of clinical hypothesis testing centers on the third factor because of the presumed behavioral component of the dimension (interpreted variously as distractibility, attention–concentration, or anxiety), and because low scores on the third-factor triad of subtests are frequently associated with individuals with reading problems and learning disabilities (Rugel, 1974) and with other special populations such as alcoholics, the brain-injured, and those with Huntington's disease (Leckliter et al., 1986). Indeed, the nonintellective components of the third factor are such that "three-factor solutions may provide the applied investigator with a potentially richer source of hypotheses" (Leckliter et al., 1986, p. 341).

Thus, clinicians have reason to interpret three constructs as underlying WAIS-R performance. The three factors emerge repeatedly for groups of individuals at the ages of 16 through 74, whether these groups are composed of normal individuals, psychiatric inpatients, medical patients, or learning-disabled adolescents and adults (Leckliter et al., 1986; Snow, Koller, & Roberts, 1987). However, findings with group data do not always translate to each individual assessed, especially when the third factor has been shown (particularly for the WAIS-R) to be small in size and not as robust as one would like a major dimension to be. Hence, the results of cluster and factor analysis suggest that three factors *may* be interpreted for a person, but it is also plausible that only two factors will be necessary to explain the WAIS-R performance of some individuals. In essence, the preceding discussion *allows* the interpretation of the potentially valuable third factor, but it does not *mandate* it.

When should examiners interpret the WAIS-R as a two-factor or three-factor test? The answer depends on the fluctuations in a person's subtest profile, as Naglieri and Kaufman (1983) have advised. The key question is whether the third factor represents a distinct entity for a given individual. Do Digit Span and/or Arithmetic deviate significantly from the person's scores on other Verbal subtests? Is Digit Symbol much higher or lower than other Performance tasks (for those ages where Digit Symbol may be considered as part of the factor)?

Did the person perform at about the same general level on all subtests composing the third factor? If the individual performed *differently* on the distractibility dyad or triad from his or her performance on one or both other factors, and if the individual performed *consistently* on the component subtests, the distractibility factor measures a distinct and unitary trait for that person and merits interpretation. Otherwise, the WAIS-R is probably best thought of as a two-factor test for that examinee.

Empirical guidelines for determining when to interpret the third factor are treated briefly in chapter 13, as are clinical suggestions for deciding how to interpret the dimension, i.e., as a behavioral measure of anxiety, distractibility, or limited attention span, or as a cognitive measure of memory, sequential processing, symbolic manipulation, or automatic processing. For a more thorough discussion of this topic, see Kaufman (1979b, Chapter 3).

TWO-FACTOR SOLUTIONS OF THE WAIS-R

When only two factors are rotated for the WAIS-R, the results do not quite correspond to Wechsler's division of subtests into the Verbal and Performance Scales, although the fit is adequate. Table 8.1 presents varimax rotated two-factor solutions of the WAIS-R for the normal standardization sample and for several homogeneous samples, mostly of exceptional groups. Table 8.2 offers two-factor solutions for adolescents and adults grouped by gender and race (Kaufman, McLean, & Reynolds, in press *a*); and Table 8.3 shows similar solutions for four different age groups of normal individuals, based on data provided by Gutkin et al. (1984). Tables 8.4 through 8.7 present three-factor solutions for some of these same samples and for a few different ones. Most examiners presented data for *both* the two- and three-factor solutions, although some chose to interpret only a single factor pattern.

Patterns for Various Normal and Clinical Populations

Table 8.1 reveals that for the total normative sample and for six cross-validation samples all Verbal subtests loaded more highly on the Verbal Comprehension than the Perceptual Organization factor (the single exception being Digit Span for the incarcerated population). However, Digit Span and Arithmetic generally show strong secondary loadings on the Performance factor, and their loadings on the Verbal dimension are not as consistently strong as the loadings for the other four Verbal subtests. Thus, just as Silverstein (1985c) found in his cluster analysis, the Verbal Comprehension dimension is composed primarily of Information, Vocabulary, Comprehension, and Similarities. Nonetheless, the pattern of factor loadings for all six Verbal subtests is sufficiently clean to offer strong sup-

TABLE 8.1 Varimax rotated two-factor solutions of the WAIS-R for a variety of samples

Subtest	Normal Standardization Sample (N=1880)		Vocational Rehabilitation Sample (N=206)		Incarcerated Population (N=234)		Psychiatric Inpatients (N=385)		Medical Patients (N=200)		Neurologically Impaired (N=100)		Neuropsychiatric Patients (N=276)	
	VC	PO	VC	PO	VC	PO	VC	PO	VC	PO	VC	PO	VC	PO
Verbal														
I	79*	31	75*	16	93*	08	82*	29	82*	18	85*	19	85*	16
DSp	47*	37	42*	16	15	58*	64*	35	52*	40*	62*	31	51*	30
V	84*	32	70*	27	73*	45*	89*	28	85*	29	90*	12	88*	18
A	58*	47*	65*	14	85*	03	69*	41*	67*	39	72*	37	65*	36
C	73*	34	68*	19	67*	46*	74*	40*	75*	38	81*	27	76*	21
S	69*	39	57*	48*	66*	50*	70*	50*	65*	53*	74*	43*	69*	36
Performance														
PC	44*	55*	38	55*	28	68*	40*	71*	38	72*	43*	74*	34	75*
PA	45*	45*	20	47*	35	69*	48*	67*	34	76*	29	75*	31	66*
BD	33	72*	23	62*	03	84*	34	78*	28	78*	25	85*	24	83*
OA	22	69*	06	70*	25	67*	22	77*	20	77*	10	88*	10	78*
DSy	39	46*	22	38	09	67*	38	60*	40*	64*	31	66*	25	63*

NOTE: VC = Verbal Comprehension, PO = Perceptual Organization. Decimal points are omitted. Loadings of .40 or above are asterisked. This table is partially based on a summary table presented by Leckliter et al. (1986). Data for the normal standardization sample are the means reported by Silverstein (1982e) for the nine standardization age groups. Data for the vocational rehabilitation sample are the means of the loadings reported for two samples of adults seeking vocational rehabilitation services: N = 121 (Fraboni, Sattstone, Baines, & Cooper, 1988), and N = 85 (Ryan, Rosenberg, & DeWolfe, 1984). Data for the incarcerated population are from Faulstich et al. (1986). Data for the psychiatric inpatients are the means of the loadings reported for two samples of psychiatric inpatients: N=271 (Beck, Horwitz, Seidenberg, Parker, & Frank, 1985), and N=114 (Atkinson & Cyr, 1984). Data for medical patients are from Beck et al. (1985), data for the neurologically impaired sample are from Doherty in a 1985 personal communication to Leckliter et al. (1986), and data for the neuropsychiatric patients are from Warner et al. (1986).

TABLE 8.2   Varimax rotated two-factor solutions of the WAIS-R for groups categorized by gender and race

	GENDER NORMAL STANDARDIZATION SAMPLE (AGES 16–74)				RACE NORMAL STANDARDIZATION SAMPLE (AGES 16–74)			
	Male (N=940)		Female (N=940)		White (N=1,664)		Black (N=192)	
Subtest	VC	PO	VC	PO	VC	PO	VC	PO
Verbal								
I	81*	28	83*	27	81*	26	85*	23
DSp	46*	39	48*	40*	46*	38	53*	41*
V	90*	25	89*	26	90*	23	90*	23
A	63*	39	60*	46*	60*	40*	60*	52*
C	75*	27	76*	33	75*	28	74*	37
S	62*	49*	70*	44*	64*	45*	70*	48*
Performance								
PC	34	67*	41*	66*	36	66*	47*	61*
PA	33	63*	40*	57*	36	59*	45*	66*
BD	28	80*	29	79*	27	80*	20	73*
OA	21	76*	21	69*	19	73*	21	71*
DSy	27	65*	24	65*	24	61*	29	68*

NOTE: Decimal points are omitted. Loadings of .40 or above are asterisked. Data are from Kaufman, McLean, and Reynolds (in press *a*). The number of whites and blacks totals 1,856 rather than 1,880 because 24 individuals in the standardization sample whose race was classified as "other" (e.g., American Indian, Asian American) were excluded from the race analysis.

port to the construct validity of Wechsler's WAIS-R Verbal IQ.

Also evident in Table 8.1 is the finding that each of the five Performance subtests loaded more highly on the Perceptual Organization than the Verbal Comprehension factor for the total standardization sample and for the various supplementary groups. (Again, there was one exception as Picture Arrangement loaded equally on both factors for the normative group.) Picture Completion and Digit Symbol also had substantial Verbal Comprehension loadings for the normal sample of 16- to 74-year-olds, loading just a bit more highly on the Perceptual Organization factor. However, the double loadings for three of the five Performance subtests for the standardization sample did not generally hold for the six cross-validation populations

shown in Table 8.1. Even though each of the three subtests in question had substantial Verbal Comprehension loadings for one or more of the supplementary groups, they consistently loaded much higher on their own factor (i.e., Perceptual Organization).

The factor analyses producing two factors therefore provide very good construct validity support for Wechsler's WAIS-R Performance IQ, especially for exceptional populations.

Differences Due to Gender and Race

Table 8.2 summarizes data presented by Kaufman, McLean, and Reynolds (in press *a*) affirming the construct validity of the WAIS-R for males and females and also for whites and

TABLE 8.3   Varimax rotated loadings on the WAIS-R Verbal Comprehension and Perceptual Organization factors for four age groups

Subtest	VERBAL COMPREHENSION				PERCEPTUAL ORGANIZATION			
	Ages 16–19	Ages 20–34	Ages 35–54	Ages 55–74	Ages 16–19	Ages 20–34	Ages 35–54	Ages 55–74
Verbal								
I	82*	80*	77*	81*	25	29	37	27
DSp	43*	47*	56*	47*	34	32	32	41*
V	86*	86*	88*	86*	31	30	29	31
A	61*	58*	57*	60*	44*	45*	51*	44*
C	72*	73*	75*	76*	33	33	29	33
S	74*	67*	72*	68*	31	38	36	45*
Performance								
PC	41*	45*	53*	45*	44*	58*	51*	58*
PA	42*	51*	55*	42*	30	40*	43*	52*
BD	26	34	36	34	82*	72*	78*	76*
OA	22	24	25	18	60*	74*	78*	74*
DSy	41*	34	48*	39	43*	35	40*	53*

NOTE: Decimal points are omitted. Loadings of .40 or above are asterisked. Data are from Gutkin et al. (1984), based on two-factor solutions for each of the nine standardization age groups.

blacks. Extremely congruent factor patterns emerged for separate groups of males and females and for separate groups of white and black individuals. For all samples, the six Verbal subtests were primarily associated with the Verbal Comprehension factor, whereas the five Performance tasks loaded highest on the Perceptual Organization dimension. Secondary loadings on the "wrong" factor occurred for all samples for Similarities, Arithmetic, and Digit Span. Picture Completion and Picture Arrangement had secondary Verbal loadings only for females and blacks.

The verbal component of some Performance subtests for females and blacks is a particularly important result because it may partially explain crucial gender-related and race-related neuropsychological findings regarding V–P IQ discrepancies and the location of a person's brain lesion (see chapter 10).

Age-Related Findings

Table 8.3 permits an age-related interpretation of the factor patterns for normal adolescents and adults by providing data separately for four different age levels: 16–19, 20–34, 35–54, and 55–74. All Verbal subtests loaded substantially on the Verbal Comprehension factor for each age group, and Arithmetic consistently had a secondary nonverbal loading in the .44–.51 range. Only one age-related trend of note was observed for the six Verbal tasks: Digit Span and Similarities joined Arithmetic with secondary loadings on the Perceptual Organization factor at ages 55–74. However, factor analyses conducted by gender (Kaufman, McLean, & Reynolds, in press *a*), presented in chapter 10 (Table 10.6), revealed that the nonverbal loadings for these three Verbal subtests occurred for elderly *women*, but not for men in the 55- to 74-year range;

in addition, women aged 35–54, to a greater degree than middle-aged men, also applied nonverbal processing strategies to verbal tasks (Kaufman et al., in press *a*).

The age-by-age analysis of Performance subtests affirms the findings for the total sample, as only Object Assembly and Block Design are reasonably "pure" measures of Perceptual Organization ability across the entire age range. Picture Completion and Digit Symbol load about equally well on each factor for most age groups, and Picture Arrangement shows the only clear-cut age-related trend: It is primarily a Verbal test for the three younger age groups and does not load more highly on the Perceptual Organization factor until ages 55–74. Thus, Picture Arrangement joins Digit Span and Similarities as tasks that are primarily verbal in nature for ages 16–54, but that have a clear-cut nonverbal (or simultaneous processing) component for older individuals, again implying age-related changes in the way people process information. Despite the apparent relationship of the findings to age level, the fact that the different age samples are from different cohorts makes any inferences about *developmental* changes tenuous at best (see chapter 7).

Kaufman et al.'s (in press *a*) study of the factor structure for men and women at different ages helps clarify these patterns: (a) Picture Completion is processed similarly by men and women within each age level; (b) Picture Arrangement is primarily a nonverbal test for men, but a *verbal* test for women, at ages 16–34; and (c) Digit Symbol, at ages 35–54, is a distinctly verbal test for men but a nonverbal test for women (see Table 10.6 on p. 315).

Overview of the Composition of the Two Factors

I propose that examiners who choose to interpret two WAIS-R factors use the obtained V- and P-IQs as the factor scores. Even though separate analyses by age and gender indicate differences in the way various subgroups process some of the component subtests, data for diverse

clinical groups (see Table 8.1) strongly affirm Wechsler's (1981) scale assignment of the six Verbal and five Performance subtests; so do the data for males versus females and blacks versus whites when all ages are combined (see Table 8.2).

Despite Gutkin et al.'s (1984) interpretation of a four-subtest Verbal Comprehension factor (excluding Arithmetic and Digit Span) and a two-subtest Perceptual Organization factor (Block Design, Object Assembly)—and despite empirical support from confirmatory factor analysis for Gutkin's approach compared to Wechsler's (Plake, Gutkin, Wise, & Kroeten, 1987)—I see no reason to depart from Wechsler's two comprehensive scales when interpreting WAIS-R profiles. There is ample evidence to support Wechsler's approach, and a two-subtest Performance factor may be psychometrically pure, but it is clinically barren. Nonetheless, examiners should be aware of Plake et al.'s (1987) research, and of the processing differences by age and gender for several subtests, when interpreting WAIS-R profiles.

Three-Factor Solutions of the WAIS-R

Table 8.4 shows three-factor varimax rotated solutions for the WAIS-R for a variety of normal and exceptional samples. Table 8.5 presents the three emergent dimensions for samples categorized by gender and race; Table 8.6 presents these data for Spanish-speaking populations; and Table 8.7 reveals the three-factor WAIS-R pattern for four different age groups.

Patterns for Various Normal and Clinical Populations

For the normal standardization sample, the Verbal Comprehension factor is defined by loadings of .67 to .81 by the familiar quartet: Information, Vocabulary, Comprehension, Similari-

TABLE 8.4   Varimax rotated three-factor solutions of the WAIS-R for a variety of samples

Subtest	Normal Standardization Sample (N=1,880)			Psychiatric Inpatients (N=385)			Medical Patients (N=200)			Learning-Disabled Sample (N=115)			Brain-Damaged Patients (N=100)			Neuro-psychiatric Patients (N=276)			Vocational Rehabilitation Sample (N=121)		
	VC	PO	FD	VC	PO	FD	VC	PO	FD	VC	PO	FD	VC	PO	FD	VC	PO	FD	VC	PO	FD
Verbal																					
I	75*	27	30	80*	29	22	83*	20	08	85*	12	-05	71*	21	17	78*	16	30	70*	12	06
DSp	30	22	64*	53*	26	48*	42*	34	47*	14	-20	81*	16	16	59*	38	26	44*	45*	07	29
V	81*	26	34	88*	28	19	85*	30	15	87*	13	02	96*	09	13	84*	18	24	57*	22	19
A	44*	34	55*	59*	34	48*	60*	35	36	60*	08	53*	21	24	71*	48*	30	67*	68*	15	06
C	71*	30	27	71*	36	25	70*	36	30	82*	08	-01	66*	33	29	79*	23	10	68*	10	-01
S	67*	36	27	67*	49*	24	62*	53*	22	68*	25	16	57*	56*	21	67*	37	20	50*	41*	23
Performance																					
PC	44*	56*	17	38	69*	22	34	70*	24	10	69*	19	23	77*	18	32	76*	13	49*	42*	04
PA	42*	42*	23	40*	61*	41*	32	76*	17	21	64*	-09	21	81*	18	29	66*	13	25	32	-12
BD	27	69*	33	30	74*	25	25	77*	18	16	74*	28	12	83*	26	17	81*	24	24	54*	10
OA	19	73*	17	21	82*	08	19	78*	06	06	81*	-20	29*	79*	07	08	78*	08	-04	64*	11
DSy	32	38	36	29	53*	42*	34	62*	28	-09	21	49*	13	69*	35	20	62*	17	12	11	85*

NOTE: VC = Verbal Comprehension, PO = Perceptual Organization, FD = Freedom from Distractibility. Decimal points are omitted. Loadings of .40 or above are asterisked. Data for the normal standardization sample are reported by Parker (1983) for the entire group of individuals aged 16 to 74. Data for psychiatric inpatients are the means obtained for two samples, as computed by Leckliter, Matarazzo, and Silverstein (1986), based on analyses conducted by Beck, Norwitz, Seidenberg, Parker, and Frank (1985) with 271 inpatients and by Atkinson and Cyr (1984) with 114 inpatients. Data for medical patients are from Beck et al. (1985); data for the learning-disabled sample are from Snow, Koller, and Roberts (1987), based on a group of learning-disabled adolescents and adults (mean age = 20.5); data for the brain-damaged patients are from Ryan and Schneider (1986); data for the neuropsychiatric patients are from Warner et al. (1986); and data for the vocational rehabilitation sample are from Fraboni et al. (1988).

TABLE 8.5 Varimax rotated three-factor solutions of the WAIS-R for groups categorized by gender and race

Subtest	GENDER NORMAL STANDARDIZATION SAMPLE (AGES 16–74)						RACE NORMAL STANDARDIZATION SAMPLE (AGES 16–74)					
	Male (N=940)			Female (N=940)			White (N=1,664)			Black (N=192)		
	VC	PO	FD	VC	PO	FD	VC	PO	FD	VC	PO	FD
Verbal												
I	78*	27	23	80*	25	24	78*	25	24	84*	22	16
DSp	33	30	57*	37	32	50*	33	30	52*	45*	32	54*
V	87*	24	24	85*	24	26	86*	22	25	87*	22	23
A	52*	31	52*	48*	37	57*	49*	32	54*	53*	46*	42*
C	72*	27	21	75*	33	19	73*	28	19	71*	35	23
S	61*	49*	16	67*	43*	22	63*	45*	18	70*	48*	15
Performance												
PC	35	70*	08	40*	68*	12	36	68*	09	50*	66*	–03
PA	31	63*	15	38	56*	19	34	59*	16	43*	65*	17
BD	22	76*	29	24	75*	29	21	76*	29	14	69*	33
OA	19	75*	17	20	69*	11	17	72*	14	20	71*	11
DSy	21	62*	29	19	61*	26	19	58*	24	26	65*	23

NOTE: Decimal points are omitted. Loadings of .40 or above are asterisked. Data are from Kaufman, McLean, and Reynolds (in press *a*). The number of whites and blacks totals 1,856 rather than 1,880 because 24 individuals in the standardization sample whose race was classified as "other" (e.g., American Indian, Asian American) were excluded from the race analysis.

ties. The Perceptual Organization dimension is composed of high loadings in the .56–.73 range by Picture Completion, Block Design, and Object Assembly, the triad that Bannatyne (1971) terms Spatial and that is associated with the cognitive style of field-independence/field-dependence. Freedom from Distractibility on the WAIS-R is constituted by a dyad, Digit Span and Arithmetic. Of the two Performance subtests unaccounted for in the three-factor pattern for normal adolescents and adults, Picture Arrangement loads equally well on both the verbal and nonverbal dimensions; and Digit Symbol loads everywhere and nowhere, achieving loadings in the netherlands of the .30s on each factor.

When three-factor solutions are examined for the six clinical samples shown in Table 8.4 and the normal group already discussed, the picture becomes more clouded. On the bright side, Picture Arrangement takes its place alongside the Spatial triad as a member of the Perceptual factor, and Picture Completion appears even more strongly nonverbal than it did for the normal sample alone. On the dim side, Arithmetic and Digit Span—the backbone of the distractibility factor—take on strong verbal overtones, especially for the medical patients; and Digit Symbol, unobtrusive in the analyses of normals, is either a measure of Perceptual Organization (for medical, brain-damaged, and neuropsychiatric patients), Freedom from Dis-

TABLE 8.6   Rotated three-factor solutions for Hispanics tested in Spanish on the WAIS or adapted WAIS-R

Subtest	NORMAL ARGENTINE ADOLESCENTS TESTED ON TRANSLATED AND ADAPTED WAIS-R (N=100)			MIDDLE-AGED MEXICAN PSYCHIATRIC REFERRALS TESTED ON SPANISH TRANSLATION OF WAIS (N=157)		
	VC	PO	FD	VC	PO	FD
Verbal						
I	65*	−13	00	71*	24	28
DSp	−05	−03	50*	09	15	82*
V	61*	05	00	82*	18	18
A	30	01	31	48*	13	64*
C	64*	07	−20	81*	18	−04
S	53*	11	−04	77*	23	27
Performance						
PC	34	11	09	39	55*	33
PA	41*	01	12	30	56*	44*
BD	11	52*	00	26	66*	37
OA	−10	66*	−04	20	83*	−17
DSy	11	16	36	07	60*	42*

NOTE: Decimal points are omitted. Loadings of .40 or above are asterisked. The Argentine analysis represents an *oblique* promax rotation; the Mexican analysis is varimax. Data for Argentines are for 15- to 19-year-olds who constituted part of the norms for the Argentine adaptation and Spanish translation of the WAIS-R (Insua, 1983). Data for Mexicans are for adults (mean age = 38.5) referred for clinical evaluation in Mexico City and administered the direct Spanish translation of the 1955 WAIS as part of a larger battery (Kunce & Schmidt de Vales, 1986).

tractibility (for the learning-disabled and the vocational rehabilitation sample), or of both factors (psychiatric inpatients).

It is noteworthy that the familiar distractibility triad of Digit Span, Arithmetic, and Digit Symbol emerged decisively for only one group, the sample of learning-disabled individuals. This is the one exceptional group that routinely performs poorly on the three subtests constituting the distractibility triad (Rugel, 1974); in fact, the 115 learning-disabled adolescents and adults in the sample analyzed in Table 8.4 earned a mean scaled score of 7.4 on the distractibility subtests compared to a mean of 8.2 on the remaining eight tasks (Snow, Koller, & Roberts, 1987).

Differences Due to Gender and Ethnicity

The three WAIS-R factors for males versus females and for whites versus blacks are shown in Table 8.5 (data from Kaufman et al., in press *a*). The factor patterns obtained in analyses of Hispanics, based on an Argentine translation and adaptation of the WAIS-R administered to normal 15- to 19-year-olds (Insua, 1983) and on a Spanish translation of the 1955 WAIS

TABLE 8.7 Varimax rotated factor loadings on the three WAIS-R factors for four age groups

Subtest	VERBAL COMPREHENSION				PERCEPTUAL ORGANIZATION				FREEDOM FROM DISTRACTIBILITY			
	Ages 16–19	*Ages 20–34*	*Ages 35–54*	*Ages 55–74*	*Ages 16–19*	*Ages 20–34*	*Ages 35–54*	*Ages 55–74*	*Ages 16–19*	*Ages 20–34*	*Ages 35–54*	*Ages 55–74*
Verbal												
I	76*	72*	69*	76*	19	24	33	26	32	35	33	27
DSp	25	32	33	31	19	15	19	31	63*	58*	67*	58*
V	80*	80*	83*	81*	25	24	24	26	29	35	35	36
A	48*	42*	42*	44*	32	29	43*	34	52*	63*	48*	60*
C	69*	70*	69*	73*	28	29	24	31	20	29	29	26
S	72*	64*	65*	67*	27	34	30	44*	23	25	30	21
Performance												
PC	33	46*	42*	41*	34	61*	43*	58*	16	15	26	20
PA	32	50*	37	37	20	39	31	50*	24	20	35	24
BD	23	24	29	28	79*	67*	70*	74*	26	41*	30	27
OA	20	23	22	15	58*	73*	81*	72*	10	20	17	19
DSy	32	27	33	35	33	25	34	50*	40*	38	42*	23

NOTE: Decimal points are omitted. Loadings of .40 or above are asterisked. Data are from Parker (1983), based on three-factor solutions for seven age groups and on four-factor solutions for ages 18–19 and 45–54.

administered to psychiatric referrals in Mexico City, are shown in Table 8.6.

As was true for the two-factor solutions, there is much convergence in the three WAIS-R factors for males versus females and for blacks versus whites. The similarities in the underlying WAIS-R structure for separate samples of males and females are striking. Both sexes reveal a Verbal Comprehension factor that is closely associated with all Verbal subtests except Digit Span and a Perceptual Organization factor that has high loadings by every Performance subtest. Coefficients of congruence between factors assigned the same name for males and females exceeded .99 for all three dimensions (Kaufman et al., in press *a*).

The large samples of males and females each produced a two-subtest Freedom from Distractibility factor, identified by Digit Span and Arithmetic. For both sexes, Digit Span had its only high loading (mid-.50s) on the distractibility factor; Arithmetic was about equally associated (mid-.50s) with the Verbal and distractibility factors; and Digit Symbol, usually a member of the distractibility triad, consistently loaded below .30 on the third dimension. Although the distractibility dyads were congruent from group to group, the third dimension for the WAIS-R tends to be so small in magnitude that most empirical criteria do not support it as a significant factor (Gutkin, Reynolds, & Galvin, 1984; Kaufman et al., in press *a*).

Whereas the samples of males and females span a wide age range (16–74), thereby effectively masking the age-related trends discussed in the next section, the factor patterns are nonetheless quite stable because of the huge number of males and females (940 per sex). Consequently, the same three dimensions of intellect define males and females when they are faced with the tasks constituting the WAIS-R.

For blacks and whites, the convergence in WAIS-R factor solutions is also exceptional (congruence coefficients above .98; Kaufman et al., in press *a*). The familiar same three dimensions were identified for both races, but

two important differences nonetheless emerged: (a) *Verbal* ability was an important component of solving Picture Completion and Picture Arrangement items for blacks, but not whites; and (b) *Nonverbal* ability was an essential component of solving Arithmetic items for blacks (not whites). Again, Kaufman et al. (in press *a*) recommended two factors as the most meaningful for analyses of black–white performance.

The factor analyses for Hispanics with the Spanish WAIS (Mexican referrals) and a Spanish adaptation of the WAIS-R for Argentines administered to normal adolescents, shown in Table 8.6, generally support the cross-cultural construct validity of Wechsler's adult tests. The familiar three dimensions emerged for both Hispanic groups (neither set of researchers presented two-factor solutions), but the support was far greater for the Mexicans than the Argentines.

In the Mexican analysis, Kunce and Schmidt de Vales (1986) identified almost classical factors. Insua (1983) found a traditional distractibility factor for Argentines, but her Perceptual Organization dimension was defined by only the two constructional tasks, Block Design and Object Assembly. Picture Completion and Picture Arrangement loaded only on Verbal Comprehension, while Digit Symbol was associated solely with Freedom from Distractibility.

Conceivably, the factor pattern for normal adolescents in Argentina is different from the conventional pattern in the United States. The same nonverbal problems may be processed differently because of cultural differences. However, there are other possible explanations. Insua (1983) used an oblique rotational procedure, which produces correlated factors, as opposed to the varimax approach used in all other analyses cited in this chapter. Since the varimax rotation yields uncorrelated or independent factors, the small Perceptual Organization dimension for Argentine adolescents may be a function of methodology. Also, the Spanish WAIS-R used in Argentina was adapted substantially from the American version, so the different factor structure may be partly due to item differences.

Neither of these alternative explanations seems too potent. Insua (1983) used the same oblique procedure with data for 18- to 19-year-olds from the American standardization sample to allow U.S.–Argentine comparisons. Despite the correlated factors for the American sample, Picture Completion was primarily associated with the hypothesized Perceptual Organization factor, while Picture Arrangement was a weak measure of all factors. In addition, the only subtests that were modified in the Argentine adaptation of the WAIS-R were Vocabulary (extensively), Information (moderately), and Comprehension (slightly); each of these subtests was associated strongly with the Verbal Comprehension dimension in both the Argentine and American analyses. The best explanation of the structural differences in the WAIS-R across cultures is that Argentine adolescents tend to use verbal processing more than do Americans for solving nonverbal problems.

Age-Related Findings

The age-related analysis of the factors that is possible from the data presented in Table 8.7 adds meaningfully to the previous discussion. The six Verbal subtests behave similarly for all four age groups: The four traditional Verbal Comprehension subtests load .64 or above at each age level; Digit Span loads meaningfully on the distractibility factor, and only that factor, for each group; and Arithmetic has dual Verbal Comprehension/Freedom from Distractibility loadings for every age group but consistently loads higher on the latter factor.

On the Performance Scale, only Block Design and Object Assembly behave in a lawful manner, achieving loadings in the .58–.81 range for all age groups. Picture Completion is associated with the Perceptual Organization factor for adults (ages 20–74) but not adolescents (ages 16–19); however, it also has decided secondary verbal loadings for adults. Picture Arrangement is a verbal task for ages 20–34 and a nonverbal task for ages 55–74, but relates meaningfully to *no* factor for the other two age groups; hence, the "equal" loadings on the two major WAIS-R factors for the total sample are really misleading.

Also misleading are the nebulous loadings for Digit Symbol for the entire normative group. As is evident in Table 8.7, there is a clear-cut age-related trend as Digit Symbol is indeed meaningfully associated with the Freedom from Distractibility factor for ages 16–54, but is a measure of Perceptual Organization for ages 55–74. The switchover for the elderly may be related to the likelihood that their diminished motor coordination and ability to work rapidly change the nature of Digit Symbol from a measure of attention-concentration, memory, and/or sequential processing ability to primarily a measure of visual-motor coordination and clerical speed and accuracy. (However, the inability to control for cohort differences in cross-sectional analyses of several age groups renders any developmental interpretation speculative; see chapter 7.) When analyses were conducted for each gender separately at the four age groups, Digit Symbol was a clear-cut distractibility subtest for both men and women at ages 16–34, but *not* at ages 35–54 or for the elderly (Kaufman et al., in press *a*). The inconsistency of Digit Symbol's relationship to the distractibility factor is revealed in Table 8.8, which presents the third factor isolated by Kaufman et al. (in press *a*) for males and females grouped by age.

Related to the aging pattern associated with Digit Symbol is another important age-related trend evident in Table 8.7: The Perceptual Organization factor gets larger with increasing age. At ages 16–19, the nonverbal dimension comprises only Block Design and Object Assembly; at ages 20–54, Picture Completion joins those two tasks to form a Performance triad; and for ages 55–74, the Perceptual Organization factor comprises all five Performance Scale subtests.

TABLE 8.8   Varimax rotated loadings on the third (Freedom from Distractibility) factor for males and females at four age levels

Subtest	AGE LEVEL							
	16–19		20–34		35–54		55–74	
	M	F	M	F	M	F	M	F
Verbal								
I	32	46*	34	27	44*	29	22	27
DSp	51*	57*	71*	48*	58*	63*	63*	71*
V	34	36	30	33	53*	28	30	40*
A	64*	62*	54*	70*	71*	53*	56*	48*
C	25	21	28	35	39	28	32	18
S	30	35	20	34	31	33	27	19
Performance								
PC	18	19	14	26	15	27	15	23
PA	22	22	16	26	18	40*	31	12
BD	44*	35	36	43*	38	35	23	35
OA	20	07	17	17	24	13	14	30
DSy	59*	45*	41*	45*	30	46*	29	20

NOTE: M = Male; F = Female. Decimal points are omitted. Loadings of .40 and above are asterisked. Data are from Kaufman et al. (in press a).

Data for separate groups of men and women across the age range (see Table 8.8) reveal that Digit Span and Arithmetic tended to have high loadings on the distractibility factor for each sex at each of the four age groups studied.

Overview of the Composition of the Three Factors

Table 8.9 represents the best synthesis of the composition of the three constructs underlying WAIS-R performance, based on the various factor analysis and cluster analysis investigations summarized in this chapter. (Note that Picture Arrangement and Digit Symbol are excluded from the factor pattern because of the inconsistency in what they measure.)

Although some might argue that the most defensible Perceptual Organization grouping is simply the Block Design–Object Assembly dyad

(Gutkin et al., 1984; Plake et al., 1987), inclusion of Picture Completion has ample empirical and clinical support. Clinically, the proposed dyad measures a narrow skill—visual construction ability, expressed in as quick a response time as possible. With Picture Completion, the perceptual dimension assesses a considerably broader aspect of mental functioning, because this task measures visual-spatial ability without motor coordination or bonus points.

COMPARISON OF WAIS-R AND WISC-R FACTORS

Just as it was important to establish the continuity between the WAIS-R constructs and the constructs defining its predecessors, the Wechsler-Bellevue I and WAIS, so too is it necessary

TABLE 8.9 Composition of the three constructs underlying WAIS-R performance

Verbal Comprehension	Perceptual Organization	Freedom from Distractibility
Information	Picture Completion	Digit Span
Vocabulary	Block Design	Arithmetic
Comprehension	Object Assembly	
Similarities		

to evaluate the continuity between the WAIS-R factors and the WISC-R factors because the two tests are intended for essentially adjacent age ranges. Examiners who test children and adolescents within the 6- to 16-year age range on the WISC-R may conceivably assess these same individuals on the WAIS-R when they are too old for the children's battery. Rather than assuming that the two batteries measure identical constructs, which is done implicitly whenever a clinician compares a person's WISC-R scores to his or her subsequent WAIS-R scores to detect either growth or decline, it is essential to demonstrate empirically that the constructs are the same.

Table 8.10 presents factor-analytic data for both the WAIS-R and the WISC-R, showing three-factor solutions for the total standardization samples of each battery. Although the age-related trends in the WAIS-R factor structure are reasonably pronounced (unlike the WISC-R, which produced quite similar patterns across the 6- to 16-year range), it still seemed most efficient to compare the factor structures obtained for the entire normative groups. It would have been feasible to compare the WISC-R factor pattern to that of the WAIS-R at ages 16–19, the age group that is adjacent to the upper end of the WISC-R range, but that procedure would not have addressed the question at hand; a child tested at any age on the WISC-R may well be tested at any age as an older adolescent or adult on the WAIS-R. Hence, Table 8.10 examines the continuity of WISC-R and WAIS-R constructs in a global fashion.

From the table, it is easily inferred that the WAIS-R and WISC-R measure highly similar constructs across their respective age ranges. The three familiar factorial dimensions are defined by the same set of subtests. As indicated in the note to the table, the coefficients between factors given the same verbal label are quite high, ranging from .82 to .95. Interestingly, it is the factor that is least robust and most often maligned or ignored (Freedom from Distractibility) that produced the highest coefficient. Despite the similarity in constructs measured by the WAIS-R and WISC-R, the differences in the IQs that the two instruments yield for low IQ adolescents create interpretive and other practical difficulties for clinicians and educators (see chapter 4).

THE GENERAL FACTOR (g)

The unrotated first factor of principal factor analyses is commonly used as an estimate of the g factor that presumably underlies cognitive functioning. The loadings of the different subtests on this large, unrotated dimension reveal the degree to which the tasks are related to g. By convention, g loadings of .70 and above denote subtests that are *good* measures of g; loadings of .51 to .69 characterize *fair* measures of g; and loadings of .50 and below are typical of *poor* measures of g (Kaufman, 1975).

TABLE 8.10   Comparison of WAIS-R and WISC-R three-factor varimax rotated solutions for their respective total standardization samples

Subtest	VERBAL COMPREHENSION		PERCEPTUAL ORGANIZATION		FREEDOM FROM DISTRACTIBILITY	
	WAIS-R	WISC-R	WAIS-R	WISC-R	WAIS-R	WISC-R
Verbal						
Information	75*	63*	27	25	30	41*
Digit Span	30	18	22	12	64*	56*
Vocabulary	81*	72*	26	24	34	33
Arithmetic	44*	37	34	20	55*	58*
Comprehension	71*	64*	30	30	27	24
Similarities	67*	64*	36	34	27	28
Performance						
Picture Completion	44*	35	56*	57*	17	11
Picture Arrangement	42*	33	42*	41*	23	12
Block Design	27	27	69*	66*	33	28
Object Assembly	19	21	73*	65*	17	12
Digit Symbol (Coding)	32	15	38	20	36	42*
Mazes	—	12	—	47*	—	22

NOTE: Decimal points are omitted. Loadings of .40 or above are asterisked. Data for the WAIS-R are from the three-factor solutions reported by Parker (1983) for the entire WAIS-R standardization sample ages 16–74 ($N = 1,880$). Data for the WISC-R are the median factor loadings for 11 WISC-R standardization age groups between ages 6 and 16 (total $N = 2,200$) reported by Kaufman (1975).

Rank-order correlations of subtest ranks between factors assigned the same name on both the WAIS-R and WISC-R are as follows: Verbal Comprehension, rho = .89; Perceptual Organization, rho = .82; Freedom from Distractibility, rho = .95. All coefficients are significant at the .01 level. WISC-R Mazes was excluded from the computations.

Table 8.11 presents *g* loadings for the WAIS-R for four age groups, and also for the WISC-R for children (ages 6½–11½) and adolescents (ages 12½–16½), to permit comparison among age groups. Overall the following WAIS-R subtests (listed in order of their median *g* loadings) are good measures of *g*: Vocabulary, Information, Similarities, Comprehension, Arithmetic, Block Design, and Picture Completion. The remaining four subtests are all fair measures of *g*, having mean loadings of about .60, as no WAIS-R tasks came close to being poor measures of general ability.

On the WISC-R, the four Verbal Comprehension subtests are the only good measures of *g*, and three subtests emerged as poor measures of *g*: Digit Span, Coding, and Mazes. Differences between the magnitude of the WAIS-R and WISC-R *g* loadings occurred virtually across the board as all subtests except Block Design and Object Assembly loaded higher on the WAIS-R than WISC-R; the differences were substantial (.10 or more, on the average) for Digit Span, Arithmetic, and Digit Symbol/Coding. Nonetheless, the general factors for children and adults were quite comparable, as evi-

TABLE 8.11 Loadings on the general factor (*g*) for the WISC-R and WAIS-R across the 6- to 74-year age range

| Subtest | WISC-R | | WAIS-R | | | | OVERALL VALUES | |
	Ages 6–11	Ages 12–16	Ages 16–19	Ages 20–34	Ages 35–54	Ages 55–74	WISC-R	WAIS-R
Verbal								
I	74*	77*	81*	80*	83*	79*	75*	81*
DSp	46	48	57	58	65	64	47	62
V	76*	83*	87*	86*	87*	86*	79*	86*
A	63	65	75*	74*	76*	76*	64	75*
C	68	73*	78*	78*	77*	79*	70*	78*
S	73*	78*	78*	76*	79*	81*	75*	79*
Performance								
PC	59	63	60	72*	74*	72*	61	70*
PA	61	55	52	65	70*	65	58	63
BD	72*	74*	68	72*	75*	74*	73*	72*
OA	65	57	53	64	67	61	61	61
DSy/Cd	41	43	59	49	62	64	42	59
Mazes	49	43	—	—	—	—	46	—
Mean (Excluding Mazes)	63	65	68	70*	74*	73*	64	71*

NOTE: Decimal points are omitted. Unrotated loadings of .70 or above are asterisked. Mean values reported in this table were obtained from data reported by Kaufman (1979b) for the WISC-R and by Parker (1983) for the WAIS-R. Overall values are the means of the 11 WISC-R standardization age groups (Kaufman, 1979b) and the medians of the 9 WAIS-R standardization age groups (Parker, 1983). The rank-order correlation between the *g* coefficients for the total WISC-R and WAIS-R standardization samples is .93 (*p* < .01).

denced by a .93 rank-order correlation between the subtest *g* loadings for the WISC-R and WAIS-R.

The generally higher *g* loadings for the WAIS-R than the WISC-R represent an age-related trend wherein the same Wechsler task seems to be more dependent on general intellectual ability for adults than for children and adolescents. This tendency was also noted on the 1977 edition of the Woodcock-Johnson Cognitive Battery (Kaufman & O'Neal, 1988a) and the Stanford-Binet, Fourth Edition (Reynolds, Kamphaus, & Rosenthal, 1988), suggest-

ing that the constructs influencing test performance change systematically during the aging process. The finding was much more pronounced for Verbal Comprehension and Freedom from Distractibility subtests than for Perceptual Organization tasks on the Wechsler scales, a result that was reinforced by Woodcock-Johnson analyses; the latter battery is composed largely of tasks that are verbal or sequential in nature, with no tasks comparable to the prototypical Wechsler Performance subtests such as Block Design.

The high *g* loadings by WAIS-R subtests are a primary reason for the small (in terms of variance accounted for) factors in the WAIS-R factor analyses; the outcome was generally low eigenvalues in the principal components analysis and legitimate debate over whether or not it is feasible to interpret three significant WAIS-R factors. Simply put, when a subtest is heavily dependent on general ability, it will be less dependent on smaller group factors.

When Table 8.11 is examined for age-related trends across virtually the entire 6- to 74-year age range, fairly systematic increments in *g* loading with age are noted for Information, Digit Span, Similarities, and Digit Symbol/Coding. Vocabulary, Arithmetic, and Comprehension have increasing *g* loadings through age 19 before plateauing, and Picture Completion suddenly changes from a decidedly fair measure of *g* to a good measure of *g* between ages 19 and 20.

The Best Measures of *g* on the WAIS-R

For the purpose of WAIS-R interpretation, all subtests are at least fair measures of *g* across the 16–74 age range (the poor .49 *g* loading of Digit Symbol at ages 20–34 is best treated as an aberration), and most subtests are good measures of general ability. If the .68 loading of Block Design at ages 16–19 and the .70 loading of Picture Arrangement at ages 35–54 are considered statistical artifacts, the WAIS-R subtests listed below emerge as good measures of *g* for older adolescents and adults:

Good Measures of *g* on the WAIS-R

AGES 16–19	AGES 20–74
Information	Information
Vocabulary	Vocabulary
Arithmetic	Arithmetic
Comprehension	Comprehension
Similarities	Similarities
Block Design	Block Design
	Picture Completion

Measures of *g* for Blacks and Whites

Kaiser (1986) conducted a factor analysis of the WAIS-R using separate groups of blacks and whites from the total standardization sample. The *g* loadings on the unrotated first factor (*g*) were as follows for the two races:

BLACKS	WHITES
Similarities (.86)	Vocabulary (.81)
Vocabulary (.82)	Similarities (.80)
Arithmetic (.82)	Information (.78)
Comprehension (.81)	Comprehension (.76)
Picture Arrangement (.79)	Arithmetic (.75)
Information (.79)	Block Design (.75)
Picture Completion (.79)	Picture Completion (.74)
Digit Span (.71)	Picture Arrangement (.71)
Digit Symbol (.70)	Object Assembly (.66)
Block Design (.67)	Digit Span (.65)
Object Assembly (.66)	Digit Symbol (.63)
Mean *g* Loading = .77	Mean *g* Loading = .73

These data show that the average *g* loading is higher for blacks than for whites, and that Block Design, almost always found to be a good measure of *g*, is only a fair measure for blacks. The rank-order correlation between the *g* loadings for whites and blacks equals .70, which is statistically significant ($p < .05$), but of an order of magnitude that indicates that the *g* loadings for blacks and whites have considerable uniqueness.

SUBTEST SPECIFICITY

For half a century clinicians have interpreted the specific abilities or traits believed to be measured by the separate Wechsler subtests.

Case reports are typically filled with an individual's strength or weakness in commonsense understanding of social situations or the ability to distinguish essential from nonessential details or psychomotor speed or attention span, based on strong or weak performance on a single subtest. Yet implicit in the interpretation of a person's score on any particular subtest is the presumption that the task in question has an adequate amount of *reliable specific variance,* which Cohen (1952b) has termed *subtest specificity.*

Definition of Subtest Specificity

Basically, a subtest has three types of variance: common variance, which is the portion that is shared with other subtests in the battery (e.g., each Verbal subtest shares variance with the other Verbal subtests, as evidenced by robust Verbal Comprehension factors); specific variance, which is the portion that is both reliable and unique to that subtest (a subtest's unique contribution to a Wechsler battery); and error variance (which equals 1 minus the reliability coefficient).

In order to legitimately interpret the abilities supposedly measured by any subtest, that task must have a reasonable amount of reliable specific variance (subtest specificity), and the specificity should exceed the subtest's error variance. How large is reasonable? Clearly, the median of 14% that characterized WAIS subtests (Cohen, 1957b) does not qualify. Cohen states: "Thus, on the average, only one-seventh of the subtests' variance is not attributable to common factors and error. Under these circumstances, the attribution of specific measurement functions to the subtests as has been done by such clinicians as Rapaport [1945] in connection with the Wechsler-Bellevue, is clearly unjustified" (p. 289). However, the results with the WISC were a bit more promising (Cohen, 1959), and Cohen seemed to treat 25% as the amount of specific variance that is large enough (as long as it exceeds error variance) to warrant subtest-specific interpretation.

The application of Cohen's (1959) informal rules to the WISC-R showed that subtest-specific interpretation is feasible for nearly every subtest across the age range (Kaufman, 1979b, Table 4.2). Only Similarities (at ages 9½–16½) and Object Assembly have inadequate specificity; three other subtests have marginally adequate specificity (Vocabulary, Comprehension, and, at ages 9½–16½, Picture Completion); and all other subtests have ample specificity. Adequate, as opposed to ample, specificity occurs when a subtest comes close to meeting Cohen's empirical criteria but doesn't quite make it: (a) the specific variance exceeds error variance but is consistently less than 25%; or (b) the specific variance is at least 25% but the error variance tends to be a bit more.

Computation of subtest specificity is easy. The reliability coefficient equals the percentage of reliable variance for a subtest (no, it does *not* have to be squared, as some psychologists have tried to insist at my workshops). Subtract from the reliability coefficient the best estimate of common or shared variance, and the remainder is the subtest specificity. Cohen (1957b, 1959) used the communality from factor analysis as the best estimate of common variance, but Silverstein (1977a) has argued in favor of the multiple squared correlation between a subtest and all remaining subtests. Silverstein's arguments are sensible; he points out that the communality varies as a function of the number of factors that are extracted, but R^2 is totally determined by the correlation matrix.

Subtest Specificity of WAIS-R Subtests

Parker's (1983) values for WAIS-R subtest specificity are used here instead of the specific variances reported by Gutkin, Reynolds, and Galvin (1984) because Parker employed R^2 as the estimate of shared variance, whereas Gutkin et al. used the communality from the two-factor solution. Table 8.12 presents subtest specificities for the 11 WAIS-R subtests for four broad age ranges. These values were computed by taking the mean of data for adjacent age groups provided by Parker (1983, Table 5). Table 8.12 also presents the error variance for the subtests at the four age groups; these values were obtained by computing the mean reliability coefficient for adjacent age groups (Wechsler, 1981,Table 10) and subtracting that value from 1.0.

To illustrate, consider the WAIS-R Information subtest for ages 20–34. For these ages, Information has a reliability coefficient of .90 (Wechsler, 1981, Table 10), indicating that 90% of Information's variance is *reliable* (only 10%, therefore, is due to error). Using the multiple squared correlation of Information with the remaining 10 WAIS-R subtests as the best estimate of *common* variance yields a value of .70, or 70% for Information at ages 20–34. (R^2 was computed with a computer program that conducts principal factor analysis.) Subtract the estimate of common variance (70%) from the reliable variance (90%), and the specificity for Information at ages 20–34 equals .20 or 20% (see Table 8.12). This amount of specific variance exceeds the error variance (10%), but it falls short of Cohen's suggested value of 25%. Consequently, Information has an adequate amount of subtest specificity, but not enough to be labeled *ample*.

The subtest specificity values for WAIS-R subtests average 30%, compared to an average error variance of only 17%; these results are far more impressive than corresponding values

TABLE 8.12 Subtest specificities and error variances for WAIS-R subtests at four age levels and for the total sample

Subtest	Ages 16–19		Ages 20–34		Ages 35–54		Ages 55–74		Total Sample	
	Spec.	Error	Spec.	Error	Spec.	Error	Spec.	Error	Spec.	Error
Verbal										
I	20*	10	20*	10	17*	12	20*	10	20*	11
DSp	36*	30	52*	11	40*	16	38*	18	45*	17
V	20*	04	20*	05	18*	04	18*	04	19*	04
A	21	23	30*	16	28*	14	30*	13	30*	16
C	18	21	20	20	24*	14	22*	14	23*	16
S	21*	18	24*	20	24*	15	21*	14	24*	16
Performance										
PC	35*	28	28*	20	30*	17	33*	15	34*	19
PA	40*	32	30*	28	32*	20	28*	26	35*	26
BD	36*	13	33*	12	24*	14	24*	15	32*	13
OA	24	38	20	30	18	28	18	33	23	32
DSy	36*	27	58*	14	44*	17	38*	18	48*	18
Mean	28*	22	30*	17	27*	16	26*	16	30*	17

NOTE: Spec. = specific variance. Error = error variance. Decimal points are omitted. Specific variances are asterisked if they exceed their respective error variances.

for the WAIS (Cohen, 1957b), and they are quite comparable to the findings for the WISC-R (mean specificity for 11 subtests, excluding Mazes, equals 32%, and mean error variance equals 22%; Kaufman, 1979b, Table 4.2). Nearly half of the variance for WAIS-R Digit Span and Digit Symbol is subtest specific, and about one-third is subtest specific for Picture Completion, Picture Arrangement, and Block Design.

Table 8.13 groups the subtests into categories based on the data in Table 8.12. Although the error variance is slightly greater than the specific variance for Arithmetic and Comprehension at ages 16–19, these tasks are still deemed to have adequate specificity for that age group.

These empirical findings justify clinicians in continuing their half-century-old practice of interpreting the specific abilities or traits presumed to be measured by each WAIS-R subtest, with the exception of Object Assembly. Object Assembly should be treated primarily as a measure of Perceptual Organization; it has an insufficient amount of specificity, compared to its large dose of error variance, to permit interpretation of any presumed unique abilities or traits. To understand the distinction between interpretation of subtests with ample versus adequate specificity, as well as instances where even Object Assembly's unique variance is interpretable, see pages 484–485.

EVALUATION OF THE WAIS-R

To help evaluate the WAIS-R, Table 8.14 summarizes the advantages and disadvantages of the instrument as extrapolated from three major WAIS-R reviews: two in Buros's *Ninth Mental Measurements Yearbook* (Kaufman, 1985; Matarazzo, 1985), and Spruill's (1984) review in Volume 1 of Test Corporation of America's *Test Critiques*.

Conclusions of Reviewers

Kaufman (1985)

"Intelligence tests and the IQ concept are social phenomena. . . . Tests coming out in the 1980s cannot isolate themselves from these social, legal, practical, and theoretical issues. The WAIS-R is *the* criterion of adult intelligence, and no other instrument is even close. It embodies the genius of David Wechsler, has impressive ancestors in the WAIS and Wechsler-Bellevue, and was constructed with excellence

TABLE 8.13 WAIS-R subtests grouped by specificity category

Ample Specificity	Adequate Specificity	Inadequate Specificity
Digit Span	Information	Object Assembly
Arithmetic (ages 20–74)	Arithmetic (ages 16–19)	
Picture Completion	Vocabulary	
Picture Arrangement	Comprehension	
Block Design	Similarities	
Digit Symbol		

TABLE 8.14   Summary of the advantages and disadvantages of the WAIS-R based on three comprehensive reviews (K = Kaufman, 1985; M = Matarazzo, 1985; S = Spruill, 1984)

Area	Advantage	Disadvantage
Test Development	1. Most poor items eliminated; new items are generally updated & less ambiguous, & show sensitivity to blacks and women (K, M, S)	1. Some outdated items were retained (K) 2. "Proverbs" were retained in Comprehension, but don't measure social intelligence (K) 3. Easy items in Picture Arrangement & Block Design were eliminated from the WAIS, when new easy items should have been added (K)
Administration and Scoring	1. Administration & scoring rules of WAIS-R made more uniform with WISC-R rules, facilitating transfer (K) 2. Expanded scoring criteria for most Verbal items with subjective scoring systems (K, S) 3. Placement on separate lines of all words spoken by examiner (K) 4. Directions for administration and scoring are uniformly of high quality (M, S); care was taken to reduce ambiguities in items and scoring rules (M) 5. Alternation of Verbal and Performance subtests reduces examinee boredom and fatigue (M, S) 6. Modifications in administration procedures are an improvement over WAIS (S) 7. Record form is designed well for recording responses, and now includes discontinue criteria (S) 8. Manual is clear, easily read, and gives good scoring directions (S)	1. Record form leaves little room for recording the subject's test behaviors (S) 2. Scoring some subtests is not simple and often requires judgment, especially when ambiguous responses are given (S)
Standardization	1. Sample selection was done with precision and meticulousness, leading to a well-stratified sample on all stratification variables (K, M, S) 2. Inclusion of stratified samples at ages 65–69 and 70–74, unlike the	1. Data for total sample excluded from tables (K) 2. Apparent systematic bias in selection of 16- to 19-year-olds, leading to very questionable teenage norms (K)

TABLE 8.14 (Continued)

Area	Advantage	Disadvantage
	WAIS's unstratified "old-age" sample (K) 3. Great care taken to ensure that standardization examiners were experienced and qualified (M, S) 4. Manual gives good description of sample and procedures used to derive scores and IQ tables (S)	3. Hispanics not systematically included in sample; no mention of how Hispanics were categorized, if any were tested (K) 4. Equal numbers of males & females tested at each age, so "sex" was not truly stratified (S) 5. Lack of *homogeneity* in standard deviations around mean of sums of scaled scores; yet rescaling was done anyway via "smoothing" and "adjusting" (M) 6. Range of IQs, from 46 to 150, is not sufficient (S) 7. Nonuniformity of range of scaled scores for different subtests; ceilings are reached earlier on some subtests than others (S)
Reliability and Validity	1. Split-half reliability coefficients and standard errors of measurement for Verbal and Full Scale IQs are truly outstanding, and values for Performance IQ are excellent (K, M, S) 2. Split-half reliability coefficients for separate subtests are excellent at ages 18 and above (K, M) 3. Test–retest reliability coefficients are excellent for all IQs and most subtests (K, M) 4. Excellent counterbalanced WAIS/WAIS-R study at ages 35–44 (K, M) 5. Well-designed counterbalanced WISC-R/WAIS-R study (K)	1. Split-half reliability coefficients for separate subtests are below .75 for 6 of 11 tasks at ages 16–17, and for two tasks across the age range: Picture Arrangement and Object Assembly (K) 2. Test–retest reliability coefficients are not exceptional for Picture Arrangement and Object Assembly (K) 3. Publisher should have obtained larger test–retest samples and longer intervals (M) 4. Practice effects are pronounced over a 1-month interval, especially on Performance Scale (K, M) 5. WISC-R/WAIS-R comparison necessary for low IQ, not just normal, individuals (S) 6. Validity data for the revised WAIS are virtually lacking in the Manual (K, M)

(Continues)

TABLE 8.14   (Continued)

Area	Advantage	Disadvantage
Test Interpretation	1. Elicits and yields personality information and other data over and above IQ (M, S)	1. Manual shows limited awareness of clinicians' practical needs (K, M)
	2. Separate Verbal and Performance Scales permit use of the test with visually, motor, or verbally handicapped individuals (S)	2. Manual includes little pertinent research on aging and IQ, minority assessment, or other pressing topics (K, M)
	3. Valuable aid in vocational settings for predicting whether individual has appropriate IQ for different occupations (S)	3. Several subtests have insufficient "floors" for adequate assessment of retarded individuals: Picture Arrangement, Arithmetic, Similarities, Picture Completion, Block Design (K)
		4. WAIS/WAIS-R study at ages 35–44 doesn't generalize to ages 16–19 because of poor teenage norms (K)
		5. WAIS is less than adequate alternate form for WAIS-R because of mean IQ discrepancies (M)
		6. Comparison of WAIS-R scores to those obtained on WAIS and WISC-R must be done cautiously because studies in Manual are only generalizable to normal individuals (S)
		7. WISC-R is generally preferable to WAIS-R for testing 16-year-olds (S)
		8. Retaining the WAIS's indefensible method of using a reference group (ages 20–34) to determine *everyone's* scaled scores impairs profile interpretation below age 20 and above 34 (K)
		9. Separate scaled-score tables by age group in the Appendix invite clerical errors and confusion in case reports (K)
		10. Profile interpretation is impaired at ages 16–17 because of low subtest reliability (K)

TABLE 8.14 (Continued)

Area	Advantage	Disadvantage
		11. Manual fails to provide appropriate empirical guidelines for profile interpretation (K, M)
		12. Possible noncomparability of WAIS-R scaled scores from one age to another, or to other Wechsler Scales, because of the "smoothing" and "adjusting" of norms; a potential problem for clinicians and neuropsychologists who retest the same person (M)
		13. Difficult to assess moderately retarded or extremely gifted because of limited IQ range (S)
		14. Hard-to-use profile analysis for very gifted individuals because subtests differ in highest possible scaled score—e.g., 19 for Vocabulary, 17 for Arithmetic (S)
		15. Data on size of V–P difference required for statistical significance are misleading when presented in Manual without data on frequency of occurrence in normal population (S)

and considerable psychometric expertise. Yet the substance of the WAIS-R Manual could just as well have been written 20 years ago."

Matarazzo (1985)

"It is my opinion that the WAIS-R is probably the best standardized test designed for individual administration which the science and profession of psychology has produced to date. . . . [T]he WAIS-R is a completely updated, renormed, and partly revised test which examiners will find to be superior to the test it replaces. No other test currently extant, or which is likely to be published in the foreseeable future, is as reliable, valid, or clinically useful for assessing

the measureable aspects of adult intelligence as is this latest edition of the Wechsler Scales."

Spruill (1984)

"The WAIS-R is the standard against which all other measures of adult ability are compared. The paragon of intelligence tests, it is used in a wide variety of settings requiring an accurate assessment of a person's abilities. . . . The major limitations of the WAIS-R, which were also true of the WAIS, are its limited floor and ceiling and the nonuniformity of scaled scores. . . . In summary, the WAIS-R has very little competition in the measurement of adult intelligence and will likely be as well received as was the WAIS. The principal contribution of the WAIS-R is its standardization and updating of some of the subtest items."

Chapter 8 Summary

This chapter reviews factor analysis of the WAIS-R for the normal standardization sample, a variety of clinical populations, for males and females, and for different age and ethnic groups across the 16- to 74-year range. Since this chapter is the final one in the section on WAIS-R research, a table at the end summarizes the advantages and disadvantages of the WAIS-R, as delineated in three major reviews of the battery.

Investigators have disagreed on the appropriate number of factors underlying the WAIS-R, and empirical techniques have also yielded different factor solutions depending on the criterion employed. Some researchers have argued that the WAIS-R is just a one-factor test, while other investigators, using diverse techniques, have insisted on either two or three significant factors. A one-factor solution is fairly meaningless for clinical assessment; two- or three-factor solutions are each defensible as the best reduction of WAIS-R data. Examiners may choose to interpret either two or three factors, depending on the profile obtained by any given individual (i.e., the decision should rest on whether the small third dimension is interpretable for a given person).

Two-factor solutions of the WAIS-R offer outstanding support of the construct validity of the WAIS-R for normal and clinical samples, for males and females, for blacks and whites, and for different age groups spanning adolescence and old age. The Verbal Comprehension dimension is defined by all six Verbal subtests, although the loadings for Digit Span are not as decisive as the loadings for the other five tasks. Similarly, Perceptual Organization is defined by the five Performance subtests. Two Perfor-

mance subtests (Picture Completion and Picture Arrangement) have substantial loadings on the Verbal factor as well, but this tendency is stronger for the normal standardization sample than for the diverse clinical groups.

A third factor, usually labeled Freedom from Distractibility but sometimes called Sequential Ability, Short-term Memory, Number Ability, or Attention/Concentration, was identified for various abnormal samples and for normal groups differing in gender, ethnic background (blacks, whites, Hispanics), and age. This third factor is composed of two WAIS-R subtests: Digit Span and Arithmetic. Although Digit Symbol (Coding) is associated with the third factor for the WISC-R, there is only weak and inconsistent support for its inclusion on the third WAIS-R factor. When three WAIS-R factors are rotated, Verbal Comprehension is defined by four subtests (all but the two "distractibility" tasks), and Perceptual Organization is defined by three: Block Design, Object Assembly, and Picture Completion. Neither Picture Arrangement nor Digit Symbol is consistently associated with any of the three factors, although both evidence interesting age-related trends for males and females.

The factor analyses also provide data pertaining to each subtest's relationship to the g factor and to the degree of subtest specificity (reliable unique variance) that each task possesses. The best measures of g are Vocabulary and Information; lowest g loadings are consistently obtained by Object Assembly and Digit Symbol. For blacks, the pattern of g loadings differs to some extent from the pattern for whites. For example, Block Design is a better measure of g for whites than blacks. All WAIS-R subtests have adequate or ample specificity, except for Object Assembly, permitting examiners to make subtest-specific interpretations for nearly all tasks. The subtests that share the least variance with other WAIS-R tasks and that have the highest subtest specificities are Digit Symbol and Digit Span.

CHAPTER 9

Verbal–Performance IQ Discrepancies: Base Rates, Lateralized Brain Damage, and Diverse Correlates

Wechsler (1939) published the first edition of the Wechsler-Bellevue about a half-century ago, and clinical interest in Verbal–Performance IQ discrepancies probably surfaced a few minutes after publication. Just as Wechsler researchers enjoy nothing more than factor analyzing or abbreviating a battery, Wechsler clinicians have a difficult time satisfying their craving for interpreting V–P IQ discrepancies and relating such differences to neurological impairment, psychopathology, and diverse variables encompassing nearly every aspect of human behavior. Because of the extensive literature on group differences in verbal and nonverbal functioning and the clinical value of Wechsler's dichotomy for any particular individual, this book treats the topic of V–P IQ differences in three chapters.

Chapter 9 deals with five major areas: (a) psychometric issues like statistical *significance,* statistical *abnormality,* and the distinction between the two; (b) an overview of V–P studies of neurological patients having damage confined to the left or right hemisphere; (c) a discussion of variables sometimes associated with P > V profiles (bilingualism, autism, learning disabilities or illiteracy, delinquency or psychopathic behavior, mental retardation, blue-collar occupations); (d) a discussion of variables sometimes associated with V > P profiles (psychiatric disorders, motor coordination problems, Alzheimer's-type dementia, Full Scale IQs of 110 or above, professional and technical occupations); and (e) illustrations of instances when V–P IQ discrepancies are meaningless.

Chapters 10 and 11 dissect, integrate, and apply findings from the wealth of research investigations on V–P differences in patients with unilateral brain damage; the chapters are an expansion and elaboration of the summative findings on this topic presented in chapter 9. Chapter 10 investigates patient variables such as gender and race that interact with the V–P discrepancies; chapter 11 treats findings relevant to the subtest profiles, the Inglis/Lawson Laterality Index, and clinical issues regarding V–P interpretation for patients with lateralized lesions.

PSYCHOMETRIC CONSIDERATIONS REGARDING V–P IQ DISCREPANCIES

Chapters 3 and 8 presented empirical support for the reality of the dimensions underlying the Verbal and Performance Scales for children, adolescents, and adults; this support exists for Wechsler's original scales and for his various revisions of them. Factor analysis provides ample validation of the constructs that each scale (Verbal and Performance) assesses, and this validation has been documented even when three factors are extracted. As demonstrated in Tables 8.1 through 8.7, the WAIS-R Verbal Comprehension factor is consistently defined by Information, Vocabulary, Comprehension, and Similarities; and the WAIS-R Perceptual Organization factor typically includes substantial factor loadings by Picture Completion, Block Design, and Object Assembly.

Although Wechsler's assignment of subtests to the Verbal and Performance Scales does not match exactly with each subtest's primary factor loading on Verbal Comprehension or Perceptual Organization, the match is sufficiently close to conclude that Wechsler's Verbal and Performance IQs have construct validity. Consequently, exploring the interpretation of the difference between the two IQs is empirically defensible and psychologically meaningful. Further, the difference between the two IQs was shown by Feingold (1984) to be reliable with coefficients ranging from .76 (WAIS, WISC-R) to .81 (WAIS-R).

As noted in previous discussions of these empirical results, the research findings give clinicians "psychometric permission" to interpret the differences between Wechsler's Verbal and Performance IQs—a fortunate outcome since, quite obviously, the examination of V–P IQ

discrepancies will proceed with or without such permission.

Statistically Significant V–P IQ Differences

Before attempting to interpret V–P IQ discrepancies, it is necessary to determine the size of the V–P difference required for statistical significance: How large must a discrepancy be to be "real" or repeatable and, hence, worthy of comment? Wechsler (1981) provided the values that are significant for each WAIS-R age group at the 15% and 5% levels of significance, and Naglieri (1982) augmented Wechsler's data by providing the values significant at the 10% and 1% levels. Data from these two sources are pooled to construct Table 9.1, which shows the size of the differences required for statistical significance at various levels of confidence when comparing a person's WAIS-R Verbal and Performance IQs.

For most assessment purposes, 95% confidence (.05 level of significance) is ample. Table

TABLE 9.1 Difference between WAIS-R Verbal and Performance IQs (in either direction) required for statistical significance

Age Group	LEVEL OF CONFIDENCE			
	85%	90%	95%	99%
16–17	9	10	12	16
18–19	8	9	11	14
20–24	7	8	10	13
25–34	7	8	9	12
35–44	7	8	9	12
45–54	6	7	9	12
55–64	7	8	9	12
65–69	7	8	9	12
70–74	7	8	9	12
Total	7	8	10	13

NOTE: Data are from Wechsler (1981, Table 14) and Naglieri (1982, Table 2).

9.1 shows that 9 points are required for significance at the .05 level for most of the adult age range, i.e., 25–74 years. On the WISC-R, 12 points are required for significance at the 95% level of confidence across the 6- to 16-year age range (Kaufman, 1979b); 12 points are also required on the WAIS-R at ages 16–17, with the difference required for significance gradually declining to 9 points by age 25. This summary of the magnitude of V–P IQ discrepancies required for significance at the 5% level is shown in Table 9.2.

Base Rates of Verbal–Performance Discrepancies

Interpretation of a V–P IQ discrepancy begins with a determination of the significance or meaningfulness of the difference. If an apparent discrepancy proves to be nonsignificant, e.g., V > P by 8 points, the difference may just as well be zero in most cases; lack of significance means a chance or meaningless discrepancy that precludes interpretation (for exceptions to this rule, see pp. 295–299). If the V–P difference is large enough to be statistically significant, the next question should be, "How unusual or abnormal is the difference among the normal population?" To answer that question, it is necessary to have data from the large, representative standardization sample regarding the frequency of occurrence of V–P IQ discrepancies of different magnitudes.

Grossman (1983) and Knight (1983) estimated the frequencies of V–P differences of various magnitudes based on correlations presented in the WAIS-R Manual between the Verbal and Performance Scales. Matarazzo and Herman (1984a, 1985) actually computed the frequencies of different V–P discrepancies by using data on the specific cases constituting the normative population. Consistent with the duplication that seems to accompany research in this area, both Silverstein (1985d) and Grossman, Herman, and Matarazzo (1985) compared the estimated frequencies of V–P IQ discrepancies with the actual observed values and found only minor differences.

Matarazzo and his colleagues found that the magnitude of V–P IQ discrepancies was not a function of an adult's age (Matarazzo & Herman, 1984a, 1985) or biological sex (Matarazzo, Bornstein, McDermott, & Noonan, 1986), but it was decidedly related to his or her Full Scale IQ (Matarazzo & Herman, 1984a, 1985). Consequently, Table 9.3 was developed from data provided by Matarazzo and Herman (1985, Table 4) to show the actual frequencies of V–P IQ differences earned by adolescents and adults in the WAIS-R standardization sample, grouped by Full Scale IQ. In this table, data are combined for all males and females within the age range of 16 to 74.

Table 9.3 provides the *base rates* of V–P IQ discrepancies that characterize normal adolescents and adults tested on the WAIS-R. The

TABLE 9.2 Summary of differences between V- and P-IQs required for statistical significance at the 95% level of confidence on the WISC-R and WAIS-R

WISC-R/WAIS-R Age Group	Size of Significant V–P IQ Discrepancy (5% level of significance)
6–17	12
18–19	11
20–24	10
25–74	9

table deals only with the *absolute value* of the V–P difference, ignoring the direction. For the population at large, the number of individuals with substantial V > P discrepancies is approximately equal to the number demonstrating P > V profiles (Matarazzo & Herman, 1984a). For example, among the 15.5% of individuals in the standardization sample who displayed differences of 16 or more points between

the Verbal and Performance Scales (see Table 9.3), virtually the same proportion exhibited V > P as P > V profiles (Matarazzo & Herman, 1984a, Table 4). Consequently, for the purpose of developing Table 9.3 and, hence, for determining whether a person's V–P IQ discrepancy is abnormally large when compared to a baseline of normal V–P differences, the direction of the discrepancy is ignored.

TABLE 9.3 Base rate V–P IQ discrepancy table: percentage of normal adolescents and adults in the WAIS-R standardization sample obtaining Verbal–Performance IQ discrepancies of a given magnitude or greater, by Full Scale IQ

	WAIS-R FULL SCALE IQ					
Size of V–P Discrepancy (Regardless of Direction)	≤79 (N=165)	80–89 (N=302)	90–109 (N=924)	110–119 (N=312)	≥120 (N=177)	*Total Sample (N=1880)*
6	47.3	53.0	60.7	66.7	67.2	59.4
7	41.8	45.7	54.9	59.3	63.8	53.3
8	26.7	39.4	49.5	55.1	55.9	47.4
9	20.6	33.1	45.5	49.0	50.8	42.4
10	15.8	27.8	40.9	44.6	47.5	37.8
11	10.9	24.2	36.4	39.4	43.5	33.4
12	9.1	20.2	30.5	35.9	37.9	28.6
13	6.7	16.9	25.4	31.4	34.5	24.3
14	3.6	13.9	22.0	28.8	29.9	21.0
15	2.4	9.6	19.2	24.7	25.4	17.7
16	1.2	8.3	17.0	21.5	22.6	15.5
17	1.2	6.6	14.6	19.6	18.6	13.4
18	1.2	6.0	13.1	16.7	18.1	12.0
19	1.2	5.0	11.7	14.7	14.7	10.5
20	0.6	3.6	9.8	12.8	13.0	8.8
21	0.0	2.6	8.5	9.9	11.9	7.4
22	0.0	1.3	7.3	6.7	9.6	5.8
23–25	0.0	0.7	5.7	5.4	7.9	4.6
26–29	0.0	0.3	2.2	3.8	5.6	2.3
30+	0.0	0.0	1.3	1.0	2.8	1.1

NOTE: Data are adapted from Table 4 of Matarazzo and Herman (1985, pp. 920–921).

Table 9.3 tells how frequently in the normal standardization sample V–P IQ discrepancies of different magnitudes occurred. The first row of the table indicates the percentage of normal individuals who displayed a V–P difference of 6 points or greater. Entering the column labeled "Total Sample," one reads the number 59.4 in the row denoting a V–P IQ discrepancy of 6 points; interpret this value to mean that 59.4% of normal adolescents and adults (about 3 out of 5 people) obtained V > P or P > V of at least 6 points. However, the percentages are quite related to Full Scale IQ level, as Matarazzo and Herman (1984a, 1985) reported; less than half the people with IQs of 79 or less had V–P differences of 6 or more points, whereas about two-thirds of those with IQs of 110 and above displayed V–P discrepancies of at least 6 points.

Discrepancies of 9 or more points are statistically significant at the 5% level for adults aged 25–74, and V–P differences of 12 or more points are significant for those adults at the 1% level (see Table 9.1). From Table 9.3, it is evident that 42.4% of normal individuals in the total WAIS-R standardization sample had significant differences (95% confidence) of 9 or more points, and 28.6% had significant discrepancies at the 99% confidence level (12 or more points). Again, these results are quite related to Full Scale IQ level. About half the people with IQs of 110 or greater had 9+ points separating their V- and P-IQs, compared to one-third or less of those individuals with IQs below 90.

These results indicate that it is a normal, common phenomenon for adolescents and adults to demonstrate significant differences on the two major scales assessed by the WAIS-R. The same finding emerged for children and adolescents on the WISC-R (Kaufman, 1976b, 1979b) and, in fact, the V–P IQ discrepancy distributions for the WAIS-R and WISC-R are incredibly similar. The results also indicate that the base rate of normal V–P differences is considerably lower for people with low Full

Scale IQs than for those with relatively high IQs. On the WISC-R, the same type of relationship was evidenced between V–P discrepancy and IQ, although I chose to provide separate V–P baseline data for five different socioeconomic groups, as determined by parental occupation (Kaufman, 1979b, Table 2.1). Large V–P IQ discrepancies are more common for individuals from higher than lower socioeconomic categories, mirroring the results for the IQ categories.

It is important for clinicians to use a relevant comparison group when determining whether a person's significant V–P discrepancy is large enough to be considered abnormal. An unusual or abnormal discrepancy for a person with low Full Scale IQ (or from a low socioeconomic category) may not be large enough to be considered abnormal for someone with a high Full Scale IQ (or from a high socioeconomic group).

Table 9.4 was developed to facilitate the easy determination of whether an individual's V–P IQ difference is large enough to be abnormal and, therefore, of potential concern and diagnostic value. Based on Table 9.3 and the more specific distributions presented by Matarazzo and Herman (1985), it was possible to compute the size of the V–P IQ discrepancy required to be considered abnormal or atypical at several different levels of frequency of occurrence. Four levels of abnormality were selected to correspond to the levels typically used to determine the statistical significance of the difference between the V- and P-IQs. For the total sample, V–P differences of 17 or more points occurred less than 15% of the time in the normal population; differences of 20 points or more occurred less than 10% of the time, and discrepancies of 23 or more points occurred less than 5% of the time. To achieve an abnormality level of "<1%," huge differences of more than 30 points are required.

When using Table 9.4, enter with the precise size of the person's V–P IQ discrepancy and determine whether it is large enough to be unusual. If the value is smaller than the magnitude needed for abnormality based on the most liberal criterion (<15%), the V–P discrepancy is not unusually or abnormally large. If the discrepancy exceeds the value for "<15%," determine exactly how unusual its magnitude is from Table 9.4 and record the information (e.g., <15%, <5%) on the front page of the individual's WAIS-R record form. This specific result should be included in the person's case report to supplement and amplify the meaning of a statistically significant V–P difference.

But just how unusual must a difference be to be considered abnormal? Is the <15% criterion too liberal? Is the <1% criterion too stringent? There are no absolute answers. The definition of abnormality is partly a function of the clinician's personality, and partly a function of the reason for assessment. If an important goal of the assessment process is to draw a conclusive diagnosis, the stricter <1% or <5% criteria are preferable. However, for reevaluations, screening, vocational evaluations, and many other testing purposes, even the liberal <15% criterion yields valuable clinical data.

Some examiners may choose a level of abnormality in advance, such as <10% or <5%, and apply that level fairly uniformly to each person they assess, regardless of the reason for referral. Thus, if an individual's profile reveals a discrepancy that occurs, say, less than 5% of the time in the normal population, that person has an abnormal difference; if it occurs more than 5% of the time, it reflects normal variability. If the 5% criterion is selected, V–P IQ differences of at least 23 points, on the average, are needed to be considered abnormal or rare. However, this average value masks the fact that only 14 or more points are required for abnormality for adolescents and adults with Full Scale IQs below 80, whereas discrepancies nearly twice that large (27+ points) are needed before inferring an abnormal V–P difference in the profiles of individuals with IQs of 120 and above.

The formula-based estimates of the frequencies of individuals in the WAIS-R normative sample having V–P IQ discrepancies of various magnitudes (Grossman, 1983; Knight, 1983) are fairly similar to the actual observed frequencies (Grossman et al., 1985; Silverstein, 1985d). However, since the actual frequencies are available, thanks to Matarazzo and Herman (1984a, 1985), the data summarized here in Tables 9.3

TABLE 9.4   Size of WAIS-R V–P IQ discrepancy (regardless of direction) required to be abnormal at various levels of occurrence, by IQ category

Frequency of Occurrence in Normal Population	FULL SCALE IQ					
	≤79	80–89	90–109	110–119	≥120	Total
<15%	11	14	17	19	19	17
<10%	12	15	20	21	22	20
<05%	14	20	24	24	27	23
<01%	20	24	30+	30+	30+	30+

NOTE: These values are based on frequency distributions provided in Table 4 by Matarazzo and Herman (1985, pp. 920–921). Some of the values in this table are estimated because exact frequencies were not provided by Matarazzo and Herman for each specific discrepancy.

and 9.4 are clearly preferable to any estimates of these data provided by other researchers.

Statistical Significance Versus Abnormality

Tables 9.1 and 9.2 present values that determine whether a person's Verbal and Performance IQs are significantly different, and Tables 9.3 and 9.4 provide empirical guidelines for determining whether the V–P discrepancies are abnormal. Taking the values from these tables for the total standardization sample produces the comparison figures in Table 9.5. For each level, the size of the discrepancy required to denote an abnormal difference is more than twice the value required for statistical significance.

The determination of statistical significance assesses only one aspect of a V–P IQ discrepancy. Is it a chance fluctuation, or is it large enough to be meaningful ("real")? The levels of significance serve only to tell the clinician how confident to be in the reality or meaningfulness of the discrepancy. A V > P difference that is statistically significant at the 5% level means that the examiner can have 95% confidence that the observed discrepancy in favor of Verbal IQ is real and not due to chance. The 1% level of significance has an analogous interpretation. A person earning P > V, for example, at the 1% level is highly likely (99% confidence) to have a real or meaningful discrepancy be-

tween the two IQs. The latter individual is simply better at expressing his or her intelligence nonverbally than verbally. This fact has nothing to do with how often people evidence similar discrepancies; it just doesn't address the issue of frequency of occurrence or abnormality.

The magnitudes of V–P differences required to indicate abnormally large discrepancies are unrelated to formulas or conventional notions of statistical significance. These values simply reflect the proportion of the individuals in the standardization sample who actually obtained V–P IQ discrepancies of a given size or greater—statements of fact, not of statistical probability. Hence, for adults aged 25–74, 9 points defines a *statistically significant* difference at the 5% level of significance but, in fact, 42.4% of normal individuals obtained discrepancies of 9 or more points (see Table 9.3). Similarly, for most adults, 12 points equals a significant V–P difference at the 1% level, but 28.6% of normal people displayed discrepancies of 12 or more points.

These findings show that V–P differences of 9 and 12 points are *statistically* meaningful (they are real), but they are not *abnormal* because they occur too frequently (in about 40% and 30% of the normal population, respectively) to be of any concern. In order to determine whether a V–P discrepancy is truly abnormal, one must enter Tables 9.3 or 9.4 to find out which differences occurred rarely among the members of the standardization sample. The fact that so many people have differences of 9 or more points between their V- and P-IQs underscores the fact that it is normal for people to differ significantly in how well they manifest their intelligence via verbal comprehension and expression versus the manipulation of concrete, nonverbal materials. This finding also characterized the children and adolescents in the WISC-R normative group (Kaufman, 1976b, 1979b).

When interpreting a person's V–P IQ difference, the first thing to do is determine whether it is statistically significant, using the values

TABLE 9.5 Statistically significant and abnormal differences between V–IQ and P–IQ (regardless of direction)

Level	Statistically Significant	Abnormal
<15%	7	17
<10%	8	20
<05%	10	23
<01%	13	30+

shown in Tables 9.1 or 9.2. If it is not significant, and there are no compelling clinical or empirical reasons to bypass the conventional statistical procedures (see pp. 295–299), one should infer that the person displays his or her intelligence about equally well verbally and nonverbally. One should not speak of an "almost" significant difference or a "slight" preference for verbal or nonverbal thinking. If the difference is due to chance, then for all practical purposes, it should be thought of as being zero.

If the difference is large enough to be significant (unless it is misleading, see pp. 295–299), the examiner should conclude that the adolescent or adult has a real preference for verbal or nonverbal expression of intelligence. This difference may relate to the best way to teach new material to a person, or to remediate that person (e.g., a learning-disabled high school or college student); it may relate to recommendations regarding a person's occupational choice, or it may be pertinent to any decision about the person's clinical treatment that is affected by whether the person is more adept verbally or nonverbally. But it does *not*, by itself, have any diagnostic implications. To be potentially important diagnostically, the difference must be *abnormal*. It makes no sense to diagnose a person as having an abnormality based primarily on a WAIS-R V–P IQ discrepancy unless that discrepancy is of a magnitude that is likewise abnormal.

Consequently, after finding a statistically significant V–P difference, clinicians should routinely assess the abnormality of that meaningful discrepancy. They may use Table 9.4 to determine whether the magnitude of the discrepancy denotes an unusual V > P or P > V profile, or they may find Table 9.3 more useful for descriptive purposes.

Suppose a 35-year-old female obtained a Verbal IQ of 76, a Performance IQ of 93, and a Full Scale IQ of 83. The P > V difference of 17 points is significant at the 1% level (see Table 9.1). Entering Table 9.3 in the column denoting Full Scale IQs of 80–89 with the value

of 17 points, one discovers that 6.6% of the normal population of individuals with Full Scale IQs in the Low Average range obtained V–P IQ discrepancies of 17 or more points. That empirical fact might be reported in the woman's case report to indicate the precise frequency of occurrence of her V–P difference. Or, enter Table 9.4 with the value of 17, using the column for Full Scale IQs of 80–89. Such discrepancies occur "<10%" of the time in the normal population, and that fact might be included in her case report.

It is not important whether a clinician uses Table 9.3 or 9.4, but it *is* important that he or she uses some base-rate table. For a V–P difference to be of potential diagnostic significance, that difference must be *both* statistically significant *and* reasonably abnormal. The determination of abnormality should always be derived from the normal base-rate tables presented here or from similar types of tables provided by Matarazzo and Herman (1984a, 1985). The decision about the unusualness of a particular Wechsler profile is an empirical issue, not a clinical one. Clinical acumen becomes important in selecting the most appropriate criterion of abnormality for a given assessment purpose in trying to interpret the meaning of the abnormal difference, and in deciding what to do about it.

Matarazzo and Herman (1985) noted: "Data regarding the *statistical significance* (relative to a 'true' difference from zero) of an obtained VIQ versus PIQ difference have at times been misunderstood to reflect the actuarial *abnormality* of the difference. Too often the result has been conclusions about an examinee that are clinically unsound" (p. 925). They added: "[A] VIQ versus PIQ difference of 15 points is merely the *initial* datum that should stimulate the clinician to search for corroborating, extra-test evidence from the *clinical or social history* that such a difference of 15 points is associated with a potentially significant diagnostic finding" (p. 928).

V–P Discrepancies and Brain Damage

Research in neuropsychology has consistently supported the notion that lesions in the left cerebral hemisphere are associated with diminished verbal and language abilities, whereas lesions in the right cerebral hemisphere are accompanied by visual-spatial deficits (Reitan, 1955c). Consequently, a logical hypothesis is that people with left-brain lesions will demonstrate P > V profiles, and those with documented right-brain lesions will show V > P discrepancies. This hypothesis has been tested in dozens of research investigations with the Wechsler-Bellevue, WAIS, and WAIS-R, and the results of these many studies are summarized and integrated in this section. Chapter 10 treats numerous issues regarding the literature on brain damage, such as the controversial topic of gender differences in the relationship between localization of lesion and V–P differences; chapter 11 discusses additional topics regarding patients with lateralized lesions, e.g., subtest profiles and the utility of the Inglis-Lawson Laterality Index.

Right- Versus Left-Brain Lesions

The predicted interaction between the nature of a brain-damaged patient's V–P IQ discrepancy and the location of his or her lesion has been investigated with a diversity of samples, for example, those with head injuries (Uzzell, Zimmerman, Dolinskas, & Obrist, 1979), those wounded by a missile (Black, 1973, 1976), epileptics undergoing temporal lobectomies (Ivnik, Sharbrough, & Laws, 1987; Meier & French, 1966), and patients with strokes or tumors (Haaland & Delaney, 1981). Most samples, however, are heterogeneous regarding the cause of the brain damage and are best labeled "mixed" (Matarazzo & Herman, 1985).

Table 9.6 summarizes pertinent studies with the Wechsler-Bellevue, and Table 9.7 summa-rizes the numerous WAIS studies along with the few WAIS-R studies; many of these references were compiled by Matarazzo and Herman (1985, pp. 902–905) and Inglis and Lawson (1982), although I tracked down the original source for every study in both tables. Reading the original articles impelled me to eliminate Kløve and Reitan's (1958) study from Table 9.6, even though this investigation has often been cited as evidence for the predicted relationship between V–P discrepancies and localization of brain lesion in the left or right hemisphere (Inglis & Lawson, 1982; Matarazzo, 1972; Matarazzo & Herman, 1985). In fact, Kløve and Reitan (1958) formed their groups based on a patient's inability to copy a Greek cross (a skill that overlaps with Wechsler's perceptual organization ability), evidence of dysphasia, or both: "No attempt was made in this study to select patients with respect to such variables as localization, extent, or type of brain lesion" (Kløve & Reitan, 1958, p. 708).

Table 9.6 and 9.7 also include studies that have previously been excluded from past summaries because the investigators failed to provide Verbal and Performance IQs for the brain-damaged samples. These include studies that provided just the V–P IQ discrepancy, but not the actual V- and P-IQs (Goldstein & Shelly, 1973; Lansdell, 1968; Reitan & Fitzhugh, 1971), as well as investigations that provided just the subtest scaled scores (Reitan, 1955c) or weighted sums of scaled scores (Smith, 1966b, 1966c) for the brain-damaged patients. Since several of these studies have been widely cited in the literature (especially Reitan, 1955c, and Smith, 1966b), it seemed important to include their data in the computations to determine the relationship between V–P discrepancies and location of brain lesion.

For Reitan's (1955c) and Smith's (1966b, 1966c) studies, it was necessary to determine the best estimate of the Wechsler-Bellevue IQs for the brain-damaged samples. For his samples, Smith (1966b, 1966c) provided the weighted sums of Verbal scores (excluding Vocabulary)

TABLE 9.6 V–P IQ discrepancies on the Wechsler-Bellevue I or II for adult patients with lesions localized in the left or right hemisphere of the brain

Authors	Total N	% Males	Mean Age	Mean Educ.	MEAN V-IQ MINUS MEAN P-IQ (SAMPLE SIZE IN PARENTHESES)	
					Left Lesions	Right Lesions
Reitan (1955)	31	—	40	11	−17.0 (14)	+6.5 (17)
Meyer & Jones (1957) Temporal lobe epileptics (postoper.)						
Males	16	100	30	—	−10.8 (11)	+3.2 (5)
Females	15	0	24	—	−1.9 (9)	+7.0 (6)
Kløve (1959)	79	84	36	10	−10.0 (42)	+11.9 (37)
Doehring et al. (1961)	38	—	38	11	−9.0 (19)	+17.0 (19)
Fitzhugh et al. (1962)						
Recent	43	84	38	8	−9.1 (18)	+15.0 (25)
Chronic	45	42	32	5.5	−3.9 (20)	+2.1 (25)
Dennerll (1964) Temporal lobe epileptics	60	55	21	8	−10.3 (29)	+12.5 (31)
Meier & French (1966) Temporal lobe epileptics (postoper.) Sample I	30	60	28	—	−8.7 (14)	+2.7 (16)
Smith (1966b) Tumor (Generalized)	99	—	46	10.5	0.0 (48)	+6.8 (51)
Smith (1966c) Tumor (Frontal lobe)	41	59	46	10.5	−1.4 (18)	+3.8 (23)
Lansdell (1968) Temporal lobe epileptics (postoper.)						
Males	24	100	33	—	−8.8 (11)	+2.2 (13)
Females	28	0	33	—	−4.9 (8)	−3.4 (20)
Reitan & Fitzhugh (1971) Stroke	30	100	51	10.5	−19.8 (15)	+10.8 (15)
Leli & Filskov (1981a)	71	—	53	12	−4.4 (38)	+12.1 (33)

TABLE 9.6 (Continued)

Authors	Total N	% Males	Mean Age	Mean Educ.	MEAN V-IQ MINUS MEAN P-IQ (SAMPLE SIZE IN PARENTHESES)	
					Left Lesions	Right Lesions
Reitan (1985)	56	—	30	11.5	−10.1 (25)	+7.8 (31)
Herring & Reitan (1986) Tumor (2/3) & Stroke (1/3)						
Males	48	100	46	11	−8.0 (24)	+8.8 (24)
Females	48	0	46	11	−4.1 (24)	+3.2 (24)
Weighted Mean					**−7.5 (369)**	**+8.1 (392)**

NOTE: Mean V–P IQ differences for several samples are estimated from graphs presented in the articles (Doehring et. al., 1961; Herring & Reitan, 1986) or from weighted sums of scaled scores (Reitan, 1955c; Smith, 1966b). For Reitan's sample, weighted sums were computed from graphs of scaled scores on each subtest (excluding Vocabulary). Dennerll (1964) used one of four Wechsler scales: Wechsler-Bellevue, Form I or II, WAIS, WISC. Data for Smith's (1966c) sample with frontal lobe tumors are excluded from the computations of mean V–P IQ discrepancies because 31 of the 41 patients were also included in Smith's (1966b) sample of 99 tumor patients.

TABLE 9.7 V–P IQ discrepancies on the WAIS and WAIS-R for adult patients with lesions localized in the left or right hemisphere of the brain

Authors	Total N	% Males	Mean Age	Mean Education	MEAN V-IQ MINUS MEAN P-IQ (SAMPLE SIZE IN PARENTHESES)	
					Left Lesions	Right Lesions
WAIS Studies						
Fitzhugh & Fitzhugh (1964b)						
Chronic seizure activity	52	48	37	5.5	-4.8 (28)	+4.5 (24)
Meier & French (1966)						
Temporal lobe epileptics (postoper.) Sample II	40	55	30	—	-3.7 (15)	+8.4 (25)
Satz (1966)	30	—	43	—	-10.3 (12)	+7.5 (18)
Satz et al. (1967)	47	—	—	—	-12.6 (23)	+10.5 (24)
Warrington & James (1967)	65	58	44	—	-6.0 (29)	+13.0 (36)
Parsons et al. (1969)	49	—	48	9.5	-7.5 (24)	+10.4 (25)
Zimmerman et al. (1970)	54	100	40	—	-1.0 (23)	+5.4 (31)
Simpson & Vega (1971)	44	—	48	10	-3.6 (21)	+12.8 (23)
Black (1973)						
Missile wounds	40	100	21	12	-1.8 (20)	+3.5 (20)
Goldstein & Shelly (1973)	48	—	45	11.5	+5.9 (26)	+7.9 (22)
Black (1974a)						
Missile wounds	60	100	21	12	-6.0 (30)	+7.4 (30)
Black (1974b)						
Missile wounds	86	100	21	12	-3.4 (50)	+4.5 (36)
Buffery (1974)						
Temporal lobe epileptics (postoper.)	30	73	24	—	-4.6 (13)	+7.4 (17)
Landsdell & Smith (1975)						
Mostly missile wounds & closed head injuries	150	100	24	—	+0.3 (76)	+10.9 (74)
Black (1976)						
Missile wounds to frontal lobes	44	100	21	11.5	-3.3 (28)	-1.1 (16)

TABLE 9.7 (Continued)

Authors	Total N	% Males	Mean Age	Mean Education	MEAN V-IQ minus MEAN P-IQ (sample size in parentheses)	
					Left Lesions	Right Lesions
Munder (1976)						
Blacks	50	100	—	—	+5.7 (25)	+10.4 (25)
Whites	50	100	—	—	−5.2 (25)	+15.1 (25)
Todd et al. (1977)	114	63	38	12	+6.0 (68)	+7.7 (46)
McGlone (1978)						
Stroke (2/3) & tumor (1/3)						
Males	40	100	48	11	−11.2 (23)	+13.5 (17)
Females	37	0	48	11	−0.1 (20)	+4.2 (17)
Uzzell et al. (1979)						
Head injury	21	95	30	11	−8.7 (8)	+17.5 (13)
Haaland & Delaney (1981)						
Tumor	29	—	46	11.5	0.0 (14)	+3.0 (15)
Stroke	43	—	56	12	−7.0 (26)	+12.0 (17)
Inglis et al. (1982)						
Stroke						
Males	40	100	67	10	−15.3 (20)	+19.6 (20)
Females	40	0	71	10	+0.2 (20)	+4.5 (20)
Snow & Sheese (1985)						
Stroke						
Males	28	100	63	11.5	+13.9 (14)	+19.8 (14)
Females	17	0	66	10.5	+8.0 (5)	+22.7 (12)
Ivnik et al. (1987)						
Temporal lobe epileptics (postoper.)	63	54	28	13	−7.6 (28)	+1.9 (35)
Whelan & Walker (1988)						
Tumors (anterior or posterior)						
Males	34	100	47	10.5	+2.7 (13)	+10.5 (21)
Females	30	0	47	11.5	+0.8 (16)	+13.9 (14)
Weighted Mean of WAIS studies					**−2.2 (665)**	**+9.7 (666)**

(Continues)

TABLE 9.7 (Continued)

Authors	Total N	% Males	Mean Age	Mean Education	Mean V-IQ minus mean P-IQ (sample size in parentheses)	
					Left Lesions	Right Lesions
WAIS-R Studies						
Bornstein (1983)	44	—	39	11	-4.9 (20)	+10.7 (24)
Bornstein (1984)						
Males	33	100	37	11.5	-4.9 (17)	+10.6 (16)
Females	30	0	39	11	-5.5 (15)	+11.1 (15)
Weighted Mean of WAIS-R studies					**-5.1 (52)**	**+10.8 (55)**
Weighted Mean of WAIS & WAIS-R studies					**-2.4 (717)**	**+9.8 (721)**

NOTE: Unless otherwise indicated, the brain-damaged samples are "mixed," composed of a variety of etiologies. Buffery (1974) presumably administered the WAIS to most of his sample of temporal lobe epileptics, tested 1964–1967 at Montreal Neurological Institute. His sample, ranging in age from 13 to 51 years preoperatively, were tested "using the appropriate Wechsler Intelligence Scale throughout" (Buffery, 1974, p. 214). Black's several samples were not completely independent (Bornstein & Matarazzo, 1982), so only the data from his largest sample (Black, 1974b) were used for the computations of mean WAIS V–P IQ discrepancies. Also, McGlone's (1977, 1978) samples were "largely overlapping" (Bornstein & Matarazzo, 1984, p. 707), so only her 1978 sample was included in this table. Lansdell and Smith's (1975) sample of 150 included only 119 (79%) with clearly lateralized lesions. However, their data are included here because they noted that the "[r]esults with the 119 patients with the localized damage were similar" (p. 923) to the data for the overall group of 150.

and Performance scores. I entered these sums into the Wechsler-Bellevue IQ conversion table, using the mean age of each sample to determine the appropriate column to enter (i.e., the column for ages 45–49 for 46- and 47-year-olds; the midpoint of the columns for ages 40–44 and 45–49 for his 45-year-olds). Reitan (1955c) provided a graph of scaled scores on the separate subtests. To estimate V- and P-IQs, I determined the scaled score on each subtest (excluding Vocabulary) from his graph; computed the weighted Verbal and Performance sums; and entered these weighted sums into the Wechsler-Bellevue IQ conversion tables, using the midpoint of the values in the columns for ages 35–39 and 40–44 (the average age of subjects in his samples was 40 years).

I did not believe that these estimates introduced any substantial error into the magnitude of the mean V–P IQ discrepancies for Reitan's or Smith's samples. To check out this hunch, I followed the same procedure for data provided by Kløve (1959) and Kløve and Reitan (1958). Since these investigators gave the mean IQs *and* the mean weighted sums for their samples, I was able to see how close the estimated V- and P-IQs were (i.e., the values obtained by entering the mean weighted sums into the columns for the average age of each sample) to the actual, reported IQs for the various samples. For Kløve and Reitan's (1959) three samples and Kløve's (1959) four samples, the estimated Verbal IQs were within 1 point of the actual values for each of the seven groups. Estimated Performance IQs were within 1 point of actual Performance IQs for three samples and were within 3 points for all seven groups of brain-damaged patients. Consequently, I feel confident in my estimates of the V–P IQ differences for Reitan's and Smith's samples summarized in Table 9.6. I would have liked to have followed similar estimation procedures for Andersen's (1951) samples of brain-damaged groups, since Andersen (1950, 1951) was truly the pioneer of the type of Wechsler research presented in Tables 9.6 and 9.7. Unfortunately, his findings cannot

be included because of the peculiar nature of the subtest scores he used.

Wechsler-Bellevue Studies

The results presented in Table 9.6 generally conform to the predictions from neuropsychology, where patients with left-brain lesions had higher mean P- than V-IQs in all but one Wechsler-Bellevue study, and patients with right hemisphere lesions likewise had mean V > P profiles for 17 of the 18 samples. Overall on the Wechsler-Bellevue, left–brain-damaged adults had an average P > V superiority of 7.5 points, and right–brain-damaged had a mean V > P advantage of 8.1 points. By contrast, patients with diffuse brain damage (spanning both hemispheres) had a mean V–P IQ discrepancy of approximately zero (−0.1 points) with values ranging from −5.2 to +3.5, based on data included in five of the studies cited by Matarazzo and Herman (1985, Table 1); in two of Reitan's studies not included in their table (Reitan, 1985, Reitan & Fitzhugh, 1971); and in studies by Reitan (1955c) and Smith (1966b), which required estimation of V- and P-IQs.

WAIS and WAIS-R Studies

The results with the WAIS and WAIS-R, shown in Table 9.7, are not nearly as decisive as the Wechsler-Bellevue data. Of the 33 samples (30 WAIS and 3 WAIS-R) summarized in Table 9.7, 21 (or 64%) displayed *both* the characteristic V > P pattern for right-brain lesions and P > V pattern for left-brain lesions, using a mean V–P IQ discrepancy of ± 1 point or more as necessary for satisfying the criterion. However, if one insists on a 6-point difference between mean V- and P-IQs in the predicted directions, only 9 of the 33 samples (27%) behaved as predicted. For the 18 Wechsler-Bellevue samples summarized in Table 9.6, 16 (89%) showed the predicted V–P patterns using the liberal ± 1 criterion, and 8 samples (44%) displayed the hypothesized pattern applying the more stringent ± 6 criterion. These percentages are higher than the corresponding values for the WAIS and WAIS-R, but not substantially higher in the case of the more conservative criterion.

Overlapping Samples of Patients

Several of the samples summarized in Tables 9.6 and 9.7 are not independent but used some of the same patients in more than one study. About three-fourths of Smith's (1966c) group of patients with frontal lobe lesions were included in his larger group of patients with generalized lesions (see Table 9.6). Overlap also characterized the WAIS research conducted by McGlone (1977, 1978) and Black (1973, 1974a, 1974b, 1976), reported in Table 9.7. Whereas Smith (1966c) noted the overlap with his previous study (Smith, 1966b), Black and McGlone, unfortunately, did not make readers aware of the contamination in their respective samples until they evidently were contacted for clarification by Bornstein and Matarazzo (1982, 1984).

Data from Vega and Parsons (1969) for groups with minimal and maximal sensory-motor deficit have typically been included in summaries of WAIS brain lesion studies (Matarazzo & Herman, 1985). However, Vega and Parsons (1969) reported that their total sample was essentially identical to the sample used by Parsons, Vega, and Burn (1969), so only the Parson et al. data are included in the table. Similarly, because McGlone's (1977, 1978) samples were "largely overlapping" (Bornstein & Matarazzo, 1984, p. 707), only data from her 1978 sample are included in Table 9.7. (Bornstein and Matarazzo, 1984, used only data from McGlone's, 1977, larger sample. They were evidently unaware that McGlone provided mean Verbal and Performance IQs for *different* samples in her 1977 article. Verbal IQs were given just for *nonaphasic* patients; Performance IQs were presented for *all* left-lesion and right-lesion patients.)

Data from all of Black's studies are included in Table 9.7, however, because the amount of overlap from sample to sample is unclear. Nonetheless, as indicated in the notes to Tables 9.6 and 9.7, the *known* contamination in the brain-damaged samples listed in each table is accounted for in the procedure used to compute the mean V–P discrepancies. Hence, the overall values shown for the Wechsler-Bellevue and WAIS P > V and V > P discrepancies are presumably corrected for the overlap in samples.

Comparison of Results for Wechsler-Bellevue vs. WAIS/WAIS-R

The mean P > V discrepancy for patients with left lesions is only 2.2 points on the WAIS and 5.1 points for the WAIS-R (the weighted mean for the WAIS and WAIS-R combined is 2.4). These values are quite a bit lower than the comparable value of 7.5 found for the Wechsler-Bellevue. However, the mean values of V > P on the WAIS (9.7 points) and WAIS-R (10.8) for those with right-brain damage are higher than the mean of 8.1 obtained for the Wechsler-Bellevue (the overall mean for WAIS/WAIS-R studies equals 9.8).

Hence, the failure of most studies summarized in Table 9.7 to display characteristic P > V and V > P profiles by 6 or more points is apparently a function of the insensitivity of the WAIS/WAIS-R V–P IQ discrepancy to *left-*hemisphere lesions. Examination of Table 9.7 confirms that suspicion. Of 33 samples (some overlapping) in the table, 24 of the patient samples with right-brain damage had V > P discrepancies of 6 or more points (73%), versus only 10 of the left-brain damaged samples having mean P > V discrepancies of 6 or more points (30%). For the Wechsler-Bellevue (see Table 9.6), the comparable value is 61% for *both* categories of brain-damaged samples. Hence, the V–P discrepancy is sensitive to lesions of the right hemisphere for all adult Wechsler scales, but only the data for the old Wechsler-Bellevue suggest sensitivity to left hemisphere lesions.

Todd, Coolidge, and Satz's Large-Scale Study With the WAIS

Most of the groups shown in Table 9.7 include relatively small numbers of patients with localized brain damage in the left or right hemispheres. Todd, Coolidge, and Satz (1977) published the only study with more than 100 patients having a well-defined lesion in either the left ($N = 68$) or right ($N = 46$) hemisphere. (Lansdell and Smith, 1975, had a larger sample, but included some patients with bilateral lesions; see the note to Table 9.7.) These researchers found V > P profiles for patients having lesions in *either* hemisphere, as well as for additional samples of adults having diffuse brain damage localized in both hemispheres ($N = 69$), nonspecific brain damage evidencing no clear-cut localization ($N = 74$), or psychiatric problems with no known brain involvement ($N = 78$). These five groups showed the following mean V–P IQ differences:

Left Damage	+6.0
Right Damage	+7.7
Diffuse Damage	+7.6
Nonspecific Damage	+4.6
Psychiatric Controls	+4.5

Smith's Large-Scale Investigations Using the Wechsler-Bellevue

Smith (1966a, 1966b) also found results contrary to the predicted patterns. In his large-scale study of 92 left brain–damaged and 99 right brain–damaged adults using the Wechsler-Bellevue, Smith (1966a) reported that V > P IQs characterized *both* groups; only about one-third of the left brain-damaged patients he studied at several medical centers had the predicted P > V profile. Although Smith's (1966a) sample was criticized for varying "dramatically in the type and the duration of their brain damage" (Todd et al., 1977, p. 450), he obtained similar results for a segment of his larger sample, a rather homogeneous group of 99 patients with

acute tumors lateralized to the left ($N = 48$) or right ($N = 51$) hemisphere; less than half of the left hemisphere patients (43.8%) demonstrated the predicted P > V profile (Smith, 1966b). Smith's (1966a, 1966b) results were considered not too generalizable to most types of brain damage (e.g., Reitan & Fitzhugh, 1971), or applicable only to chronic (as opposed to acute) lesions (Russell, 1972).

The controversies surrounding Smith's negative findings, and to methodological issues in general, were among the reasons why Todd et al. (1977) conducted their large-scale study. As indicated, Todd and his colleagues duplicated Smith's (1966a, 1966b) results of V > P profiles, but this time with samples that were carefully defined on key variables. Todd et al. (1977) not only failed to find a relationship between V–P IQ discrepancy and left–right lateralization of brain lesions, but found no significant relationship between V–P difference and acuteness versus chronicity of the lesions, or even between V–P discrepancy and the presence or absence of brain damage. As evident from the preceding discussion, Todd et al.'s (1977) psychiatric controls and the four brain-damaged groups were not distinguishable on the basis of their V–P profiles.

Smith's (1966a, 1966b) studies included large samples, but his data have been excluded from tables summarizing V–P/localization studies (e.g., Matarazzo, 1972; Matarazzo & Herman, 1985) because he failed to present mean Verbal and Performance IQs for his brain-damaged groups, as discussed previously.

Like Todd et al.'s (1977) findings, and the general results of WAIS and WAIS-R studies summarized in Table 9.7, Smith's data *do* support lowered Performance IQ for patients with brain damage to the right hemisphere. Only 18.2% of his heterogeneous sample of right-damaged adults and 23.5% of his homogeneous group of patients with acute brain tumors had P > V IQ. Again, like the bulk of previous research, his results do not reveal a consistent P > V profile for adult patients with damage to the left hemisphere. I have included Smith's (1966b) study in Table 9.6 because I was able to estimate mean V- and P-IQs for that sample. Unfortunately, this procedure could not be followed for his larger, more heterogeneous sample of 191 adults with lateralized lesions (Smith 1966a) because he did not supply the requisite raw data.

Bilateral Brain Damage

As indicated, Todd et al. (1977) identified a V > P profile on the WAIS for patients having lesions in both cerebral hemispheres. Smith 1966a) also found V > P patterns on the Wechsler-Bellevue for 55 patients with bilateral damage; only 27.3% had P > V patterns. In fact, the nine studies cited by Matarazzo and Herman (1985, Table 2) that included patients with diffuse brain damage spanning both cerebral hemispheres produced a WAIS V > P profile by an average of 6.2 points (range = −1.8 to 13.4). Munder (1976) found WAIS V > P profiles of similar magnitude for both of her samples with diffuse brain damage, 25 black patients (+4.5 points) and 25 white patients (+6.3).

Bornstein (1983a) included a group with bilateral lesions in one of his WAIS-R studies, and similar to the results of the WAIS investigations of brain-damaged adults, this diffuse brain-damaged group (N = 45) had a mean V > P difference of 7.8 points. This V–P pattern for patients with bilateral lesions on the WAIS or WAIS-R differs from the discrepancy of close to zero points for the Wechsler-Bellevue, cited previously (although Smith's, 1966a, data for 55 patients with diffuse lesions were excluded from that analysis because of insufficient raw data).

The V > P pattern on the WAIS and WAIS-R for patients with bilateral damage conforms to Wechsler's (1958) original clinical observation that patients with "organic brain disease" usually display depressed Performance IQs. In this regard, the V–P IQ discrepancy

on the WAIS or WAIS-R for *groups* of adults may be more sensitive than the Wechsler-Bellevue V–P difference for distinguishing between normal samples and samples having diffuse brain damage. This greater sensitivity may be a trade-off for the Wechsler-Bellevue's apparent edge in sensitivity regarding left-hemisphere lesions. Also, the Wechsler-Bellevue may be better than the WAIS or WAIS-R at distinguishing between patients with right-hemisphere versus bilateral damage.

General Conclusions Regarding Studies of Brain Damage

Two general conclusions seem warranted based on the numerous WAIS/WAIS-R studies of patients having left-, right-, and bilateral hemisphere disease:

1. Patients with damage to the *right* hemisphere, whether the damage is unilateral or accompanied by damage to the left hemisphere as well, are very likely to manifest a substantial V > P profile.
2. Patients with unilateral damage to the *left* hemisphere *may* show a slight P > V profile, but not of a magnitude that is large enough or displayed consistently enough to be of much diagnostic benefit; indeed, they are almost as likely to show V > P or no V–P discrepancy.

For the present, let's ignore the subtleties of the study-to-study differences in the brain-damaged samples, or in the neuropsychological procedure employed, and combine data from *all* relevant investigations. In the absence of ideal, well-controlled studies using large numbers of patients with unilateral brain damage, a compilation of data from the existing literature with the Wechsler-Bellevue, WAIS, and WAIS-R provides the best guess at the relationship between V–P IQ difference and lateralized brain lesions. This overview of over 2,000 adult patients (combining data from Tables 9.6 and 9.7) is as follows:

LEFT LESION (N = 1,086)	RIGHT LESION (N = 1,113)
P > V = 4.1	V > P = 9.2

The interacting effects of other variables on the relationship between V–P IQ discrepancy and location of a brain lesion—for example, of acuteness versus chronicity of lesion, age of onset, gender, race, and the role played by each separate subtest—are discussed in chapters 10 and 11.

CORRELATES OF HIGH PERFORMANCE IQ

The previous sections of this chapter have stressed the impact of unilateral brain damage on differential performance on the two subscales of the Wechsler batteries for adolescents and adults, focusing on the cognitive specialization attributed to each cerebral hemisphere. In this section, several variables that are believed to relate systematically to P > V discrepancies are treated apart from the specific issue of known lateralized lesions.

Although education level is related to V–P difference, particularly for college graduates, who typically earn V > P profiles, that topic is not included here. Instead, educational attainment (already discussed in chapter 6) is related to V–P discrepancies in chapter 10 (see pp. 337–342) for both normal individuals and brain-damaged patients.

Individuals who obtain substantially higher Performance than Verbal IQs may do so because of a strength in fluid intelligence compared to crystallized intelligence (Horn, 1985; Horn & Cattell, 1967); strong Perceptual Organization skills in comparison with Verbal Comprehension abilities; a field-independent cognitive style

(Goodenough & Karp, 1961); better developed simultaneous-holistic than analytic-sequential processing; or for a number of other reasons.

Some adolescent and adult groups who characteristically obtain P > V profiles, or who are generally believed to do so, are those who are bilingual, autistic, learning disabled or illiterate, delinquent or psychopathic, mentally retarded, and those engaged in skilled, semiskilled, or unskilled occupations. These variables are treated in the sections that follow.

Bilingualism

An enormous number of investigations with bilingual children convincingly support the notion that Hispanics and American Indians obtain substantially higher Performance than Verbal IQs on the WPPSI, WISC, and WISC-R (Kaufman, 1979b; McCullough, Walker, & Diessner, 1985; McShane & Cook, 1985; McShane & Plas, 1984a).

Age- and Instrument-Related Findings

For children, Hispanics typically score about 10–15 points higher on the Performance than Verbal Scale (McShane & Cook, 1985); for American Indians, the discrepancies are often monstrously large. Navajo children tend to score about 30 points (2 standard deviations!) higher on the Performance Scale; other tribes, such as Cree, Sioux, Tlingit, and Ojibwa (Chippewa), tend to have large P > V patterns, but the differences are usually in the 10- to 20-point range (Connelly, 1983; Kaufman & Kaufman, 1983b, Table 4.19; McCullough et al., 1985, Table 1). The differences of 2 standard deviations between the P- and V-IQs of Navajo children and adolescents have been found to hold for separate groups of learning-disabled, educationally disadvantaged, and nonhandicapped individuals (Teeter, Moore, & Peterson, 1982).

WAIS studies with adolescents and adults have been much less common. The results have generally been similar (Crandall, 1969), although the differences in favor of Performance IQ for American Indians have not been as dramatic for the WAIS as was sometimes found for Wechsler's children's scales. McCullough et al. (1985) studied 75 adolescent American Indians from the Pacific Northwest (mostly Yakima), ages 12–19, attending a private junior and senior high school. Those administered the WISC-R ($N = 42$) scored 19 points higher on the Performance Scale (99 versus 80); the 33 adolescents given the WAIS showed a 15-point difference (P-IQ = 106, V-IQ = 91).

Even Navajo 16- and 17-year-olds ($N = 100$) had a relatively moderate P > V difference of 10 points on the WAIS (Howell, Evans, & Downing, 1958), when compared to the 30-point differences typically identified for samples of Navajo children. The slightly smaller P > V pattern on the WAIS than WISC-R in McCullough et al.'s (1985) study, and the different magnitude of discrepancies for Navajo children versus adults are consistent with WISC results reported by St. John, Krichev, and Bauman (1976) for 100 Cree and Ojibwa children and adolescents aged 7–15 years: The magnitude of P > V decreased with increasing age.

However, the evidence regarding the magnitude of V–P discrepancies for different age groups is not clear-cut (McShane & Plas, 1984a). Connelly (1983) detected the *opposite* pattern in his samples of Tlinget Indian children aged 6–10 versus Tlinget adolescents aged 11–16: The younger sample had P > V of 10.2 points, while the older sample had P > V of 17.5 points.

An interesting finding in one of the few WAIS studies of American Indians is that the P > V profile may not reflect just diminished verbal ability; Howell et al. (1958) found that his group of older adolescent Navajos had elevated scores on Block Design and Object Assembly compared to the normative sample.

McShane and Cook (1985) identified only a single WAIS study with Hispanics in their thorough review of transcultural intellectual assessment with the Wechsler scales (Murray, Waites, Veldman, & Heatly, 1973), and I have found one additional investigation (Whitworth & Gibbons, 1986). Murray et al. (1973) tested nearly 2,500 delinquent students aged 10–19, of whom 663 were Mexican American. The portion of these Mexican Americans below age 16 were given the WISC; they earned a mean V-IQ of 76, 12 points lower than their mean P-IQ of 87. On the WAIS, the Mexican American delinquents in the 16- to 19-year age range scored 8 points lower on the Verbal than Performance Scales (V-IQ = 83, P-IQ = 91).

The smaller Hispanic discrepancy on the WAIS than WISC is the same as the age-related finding for American Indians, but it is unclear to what degree it is reasonable to generalize from data obtained from delinquents, a group that is also known to display the P > V profile (Kaufman, 1979b). Nonetheless, the Mexican Americans were the only group of 16- to 19-year-old delinquents who displayed the P > V pattern on the WAIS in Murray et al.'s (1973) sample; blacks earned equal V- and P-IQs, and whites had only a 2-point Performance IQ advantage.

Whitworth and Gibbons (1986) tested 25 white, 25 black, and 25 Mexican American college students on the WAIS and WAIS-R using a combined administration technique (see p. 90). The Mexican Americans obtained a P > V discrepancy of nearly 7 points on the WAIS and 9 points on the WAIS-R. The whites and blacks each evidenced small (1-point) P > V profiles on the WAIS and 3½-point P > V discrepancies on the WAIS-R.

Curiously, all three ethnic groups displayed about a 2-point increase in P > V when comparing the WAIS to the WAIS-R. As with delinquents, however, generalization from college students is tenuous. Certainly, though, the results with the WAIS and WAIS-R reported by Murray et al. (1973) and Whitworth and Gibbons (1986) are consistent with the large body of data obtained for Hispanic children with the WISC and WISC-R (McShane & Cook, 1985).

Proposed Explanations of the P > V Profile for Hispanics

Explanations for the P > V pattern are varied because a multiplicity of factors undoubtedly contribute to the discrepancy. Language variables are important, particularly for individuals who learned English as a second language, but they are not nearly the whole explanation; Hispanic children who speak English extremely well frequently display P > V profiles, as do those who are tested directly in Spanish (Kaufman, 1979b). Linguistic variables are joined by cultural and subcultural differences in influencing V–P discrepancies because the Verbal items, much more so than Performance items, are geared to mainstream American culture.

In her study of Puerto Rican children, Shellenberger (1977) speculated that the verbal deficit may be partially due to the difficulties encountered in learning two languages simultaneously. This explanation may not be adequate, in view of San Diego, Foley, and Walker's (1970) findings with 30 highly educated Filipino adults whose native language was Tagalog. This sample scored higher on the WAIS Verbal Scale by 6 points; this V > P discrepancy was half as large as the difference found for a matched sample of Americans, but it was far different from the consistent P > V profile found for Hispanic or American Indian adults, even those with college educations (Whitworth & Gibbons, 1986).

McShane and Cook (1985) provided an intelligent and insightful discussion of the P > V pattern in Hispanics; they urged the systematic study of the impact of new variables, such as previous experience with working under time pressure, the degree to which directions are understood, the degree of understanding of the test-taking format, social desirability, the extent to which the subject is giving responses perceived to be desirable, and the tendency for people in certain cultures to endorse extreme responses.

In their review of American Indian studies, McShane and Plas (1984a) offered numerous potential explanations of the typical P > V pattern; these include physiological variables (e.g., otitis media and fetal alcohol syndrome), sociocultural factors (which emphasize nonverbal communication), and neurological considerations regarding lateralization of cerebral function. Brandt (1984) has criticized many of the premises and conclusions of McShane and Plas (1984a); however, I agree wholeheartedly with McShane and Plas's (1984b) response to Brandt, and especially with their stress on treating their statements as hypotheses that need to be tested scientifically to help foster better understanding of the cognitive strengths and weaknesses of American Indians.

Clinical Implications of Research Results

Even without clear understanding of the cause of P > V profiles for some bilingual cultures within the United States, there is ample reason to believe that the verbal deficit is not merely a reflection of low intellectual functioning. As I have maintained for the WISC-R regarding the assessment of a bilingual child (Kaufman, 1979b), I reiterate for the WAIS-R as it pertains to bilingual adult assessment: "[I]t is quite clear that Verbal IQs or other indexes of verbal ability—although they may be meaningful for understanding the [individuals] better—do not reflect their intellectual potential. . . . When the WISC-R [or WAIS-R] is deemed an appropriate instrument for use with a bilingual [individual] . . ., *the examiner is advised not to compute or interpret the Full Scale IQ.* (p. 33)." Although I know of no data indicating that the FS-IQ is invalid for bilingual samples, I still encourage clinicians to focus on the separate V- and P-IQs, rather than on an amalgam of the two, to avoid merging what research data suggest are two quite distinct constructs for bilingual people.

Autism

Infantile autism, a pervasive developmental disorder, is accompanied by the following set of symptoms: early onset, inability to use speech and language to communicate normally, social aloofness and impaired social relations in general, and bizarre motor behavior such as ritualistic and obsessive movements (Rutter, 1978). Autistic children, adolescents, and adults tend to score higher on tests of rote memory and nonverbal intelligence than on verbal measures (Bartak & Rutter, 1976; DeMyer, 1975).

However, true understanding of cognitive functioning in autistic individuals is often hampered by the presence of multiple pathologies, most notably mental retardation (Rutter, 1979). Consequently, Lincoln, Courchesne, Kilman, Elmasian, and Allen (1988) identified a carefully diagnosed sample of 33 individuals between 8½ and 29 years (mean age = 17½), all of whom were diagnosed independently by a psychiatrist and clinical psychologist as meeting strict DSM III criteria for a primary diagnosis of infantile autism; subjects with moderate to severe retardation, cerebral palsy, seizure disorders, or other psychiatric disorders were excluded.

The autistic subjects were tested on either the WISC-R or WAIS-R, and scored 12 points higher on the Performance Scale (mean = 83) than on the Verbal Scale (mean = 71); of the 33 subjects, 27 had P > V (Lincoln et al., 1988). These results, even the mean subtest profiles, were extremely similar to the Wechsler results for the subjects from two studies of less purely autistic individuals summarized by Rutter (1979). Hence, it seems reasonable to conclude that autistic individuals do indeed evidence a predictable P > V profile and that this pattern is primarily due to autism, not to the other pathologies that often occur concurrently in those diagnosed as autistic.

The causes of autism are a subject for conjecture and debate, with some researchers favoring a more environmental, psychodynamic approach, and others favoring psychobiological factors (Lincoln et al., 1988; Rutter, 1979). This lack of concurrence in etiology has led to reliance on historical and behavioral criteria for diagnosis, resulting in a heterogeneous group of individuals receiving the diagnosis of infantile autism. According to Springer and Deutsch (1985): "Newer findings have suggested, however, that the psychodynamic approach is too limited. For example, parents of an autistic child do not have an increased chance of having a second autistic child, compared with those without an autistic child. . . . Current approaches to autism focus on its origins in brain dysfunction[;] . . . the disorder may differentially involve the left hemisphere" (p. 225).

Evidence for the left hemisphere deficiency hypothesis comes from several sources (Springer & Deutsch, 1985):

- The well-known language deficits of autistic individuals

- The right-brain strengths in art and music displayed by many autistic people

- The fact that an unusually high 65% of autistic children are left-handed or mixed dominant (Colby & Parkinson, 1977)

- An EEG study showing greater right hemisphere activity for autistics than for normals during linguistic tasks (Dawson, Warrenburg, & Fuller, 1982)

- A much stronger preference by autistic children than control children for listening to songs with their left ear (Blackstock, 1978)

Also supporting a left hemisphere involvement in autism is the extent of the problems in language development that autistics display; they seem to be deficient in the essential capacity of associating meaning with symbols, words, and actions (Hermelin & O'Connor, 1970; Wing, 1971).

The left hemisphere explanation remains hypothetical, lacking hard evidence. Also, a left-brain deficiency may explain the autism in some, but not all, autistics. Regardless of controversies over etiologies, Wechsler examiners need to be aware of a likely P > V profile for people with infantile autism. As with bilingual individuals, the Full Scale IQ may not be very meaningful for autistics; if it is computed for an autistic individual with a large P > V discrepancy, it should be interpreted primarily as the midpoint of two very different skill areas. The case report of Chester P. on pages 372–376 concerns an adolescent with suspected autism.

Learning Disabilities and Illiteracy

Learning-disabled children often display P > V profiles on the WISC or WISC-R (Kaufman, 1979b), and several studies show that learning-disabled adolescents and adults, excluding those in college (Blalock, 1987; Vogel, 1986), tend to score higher on the Performance Scale. Learning-disabled college students fail to demonstrate the P > V profile, perhaps because they have managed to achieve despite their learning disability. In fact, they typically evidence the opposite pattern of V > P by as much as 10 points, or they may display no V–P difference at all (Blalock, 1987; Gajar, Murphy, & Hunt, 1982; Gregg & Hoy, 1985; Rogan & Hartman, 1976; Salvia, Gajar, Gajria, & Salvia, 1988; Vogel, 1986). Consequently, the following discussion excludes learning-disabled students attending college.

Review of Research Findings on the P > V Profile

Learning-disabled adolescents (ages 13–18) tested on the relevant Wechsler scale displayed P > V profiles whether they were classified as delinquent ($N = 25$) or nondelinquent ($N = 25$); they outperformed the matched normal control group on the Performance Scale (Sobotowicz, Evans, & Laughlin, 1987). Similarly, McCue, Shelly,

and Goldstein (1986) evaluated 75 male and 25 female learning-disabled adults (mean age = 24 years) referred for assessment by a state vocational rehabilitation agency and found a WAIS P-IQ superiority of 5 points (V-IQ = 87, P-IQ = 92).

Frauenheim and Heckerl (1983) tested 11 severely dyslexic adults on the WAIS-R at ages 25–30 (mean = 27) who had been previously diagnosed at age 10½. As children, they scored 21 points higher on the Performance Scale (WISC V-IQ = 84, P-IQ = 105); more than 15 years later, they earned almost identical mean scores on the WAIS-R (V-IQ = 85, P-IQ = 104) for a P > V discrepancy of 19 points.

Thirty learning disabled adolescents, ages 16–17, had a P > V profile on both the WAIS-R (V-IQ = 91, P-IQ = 102) and WISC-R (V-IQ = 90, P-IQ = 105), but these discrepancies of 11 and 15 points, respectively (Sandoval, Sassenrath, & Penaloza, 1988), may have been inflated to some extent by the fact that 60% of the sample was Hispanic.

Gold and Horn (1983) administered the WAIS to male inmates identified as illiterates. They divided their sample into low, medium, and high groups (mean FS-IQs of 70, 78, and 86, respectively), with sample sizes of about 13 per subsample. Each IQ group had P > V profiles ranging from 7 to 11 points. A small P > V discrepancy of only 3 points was found for 319 inmates identified as underachieving readers (Kender, Greenwood, & Conard, 1985), but this sample was neither illiterate nor learning-disabled.

Although the various studies have generally included small samples, the available data indeed suggest that learning-disabled adolescents and adults have a decided P > V profile of substantial magnitude. Deficiencies on the Verbal Scale are sensible since the WAIS-R and WISC-R Verbal tasks are heavily achievement oriented, and learning-disabled or illiterate adults are, by definition, poor achievers in reading and related subject areas. Consequently, for learning-disabled individuals of any age, "It is conceivable that P > V . . . may be related to a discrepancy between their fluid and crystallized abilities" (Kaufman, 1979b, p. 29).

Yet the consistent ACID profile (low scores on Arithmetic, Coding, Information, Digit Span) shown by reading- and learning-disabled children and adolescents on the WISC and WISC-R (Kaufman, 1979b; Rugel, 1974; see also chapter 13) suggests a deficiency in left hemisphere sequential processing as well. Whereas poor scores on Arithmetic and Information are consistent with a crystallized intelligence/school achievement deficit, the low scores on Coding and Digit Span are more compatible with a left-brain processing deficit.

Clinical Implications of Research Findings

The implications of Wechsler research on LD children and adults are that the obtained IQs may be misleading. Low Verbal IQs are likely to reflect, at least to some extent, the poor school achievement of these individuals, and are also impaired by unusually low scores on Verbal tasks that are more associated with the third factor. Whereas the Performance IQ is often the best estimate of LD children and adults' intellectual ability (except for those who attend or graduate from college despite their disability), this nonverbal estimate of intelligence is likely to be depressed (at least for males; see pp. 450–451) by a poor score on Coding/Digit Symbol.

The best solution is to group the tasks in accordance with the three factors from factor analysis, or to apply Bannatyne's four groupings of subtests (see pages 381–382): Spatial (Picture Completion, Block Design, Object Assembly), Verbal Conceptualization (Vocabulary, Comprehension, Similarities), Sequential (Arithmetic, Digit Span, Digit Symbol), and Acquired Knowledge (Information, Arithmetic, Vocabulary). For many LD individuals, the best evidence for intellectual potential will come from the Perceptual Organization factor or Banna-

tyne's Spatial category. The Distractibility factor or Sequential category reveals a possible attentional or processing deficit, and the Acquired Knowledge grouping indicates a more specific achievement-related deficiency.

Delinquency and Psychopathic Behavior

Wechsler (1944) noted the P > V profile for delinquents, sociopaths, and psychopaths about a half-century ago on the Wechsler-Bellevue. He considered this pattern to be a "sign" of psychopathic behavior, and a half-generation later Wechsler (1958) stated in regard to *male* adolescents and adults: "The most outstanding feature of the sociopath's test profile is his systematic high score on the Performance as compared to the Verbal part of the Scale. Occasional exceptions occur but these generally reflect some special ability or disability" (p. 176).

Validation of Wechsler's P > V Sign

Wechsler's general assertion about a P > V profile for male delinquents and psychopaths has generally been supported by group means on the Verbal and Performance Scales of the Wechsler-Bellevue, WISC, WISC-R, WAIS, and WAIS-R (Andrew, 1974; Grace & Sweeney, 1986; Kaufman, 1979b; Matarazzo, 1972).

For example, Matarazzo (1972, Table 14.1) summarizes mean IQ scores on several Wechsler scales for 29 samples from a variety of studies of adolescent and adult delinquents and psychopaths; the mean P > V profile ranged from 0.1 to 16.0 points for these numerous, variously defined, samples, with a median discrepancy of 6.0 points. However, Wechsler's strong statement about the power of the P > V sign for delinquents and psychopaths for *individual* cases is not supported by the moderate P > V discrepancies found in most studies of groups or in those investigations that explored the V–P patterns for specific individuals (Matarazzo, 1972).

Interactions With Age, Race, Wechsler Battery, and Reading Ability

The P > V sign seems to be more characteristic of adolescent delinquents aged 12½ to 15 years tested on the WISC or WISC-R than those aged 16 and above tested on the WAIS or WAIS-R (Andrew, 1974; Grace & Sweeney, 1986; Henning & Levy, 1967; Matarazzo, 1972, Table 14.1). The pattern also seems to be more characteristic of whites than blacks (Grace & Sweeney, 1986; Henning & Levy, 1967) and may even be an artifact of other variables related to psychopathic behavior such as reading disabilities (Henning & Levy, 1967; Matarazzo, 1972; Zinkus & Gottlieb, 1979). Also, Groff and Hubble (1981) found larger P > V differences on the WISC-R for male delinquents with relatively high IQs (either V- or P-IQ ≥ 89) than for those with low IQs (6.7 versus 2.6 points).

Regarding age and race, Henning and Levy (1967) found P > V profiles ranging from 3 to 10 points on the WISC (median = 5½) for 10 subsamples of white male delinquents aged 12 to 15 years, but found trivial V–P discrepancies of ± 2 points for five subsamples of 16- to 17-year-old white male delinquents tested on the WAIS (total sample = 1,250). For black male delinquents (total sample = 1,111) in Henning and Levy's (1967) large-scale study, grouped into the same 15 age-samples, the WISC produced slight P > V profiles for 12- to 15-year-olds (median difference = 2½ points), but the WAIS yielded small V > P discrepancies for each of five subsamples aged 16–17 years (median difference = 1 point).

Grace and Sweeney (1986), using the WISC-R and WAIS-R with 40 black and 40 white male delinquents averaging about 16 years of age, also found age and race differences regarding the P > V sign. They found larger P > V patterns for 14½-year-olds tested on the WISC-R than for 17-year-olds tested on the WAIS-R (11.1 versus 5.3 points), and they also identified greater P > V differences for whites

(9.0 points) than for blacks (6.3 points) when data for both instruments were combined. Similarly, DeWolfe and Ryan (1984) administered the WAIS-R to 70 male felons or suspected felons (39 white and 31 black, ranging from 16 to 73 years of age with a mean of 29 years) and found a race difference that reached significance at the .10 level: 59% of the whites, versus 39% of the blacks, showed a P > V profile.

Grace (1986) reaffirmed the interaction with race, showing a more substantial P > V profile for white than black 16-year-old male delinquents. But the results of his study raised the possibility of an *instrument*-related difference in the profiles rather than an *age*-related difference. Grace (1986) tested only 16-year-olds, assigning them randomly to be administered the WISC-R or WAIS-R. Whites given the WISC-R showed P > V of 13 points, but whites given the WAIS-R had P > V of only 4 points. Similarly, blacks displayed a P > V profile of 7 points on the WISC-R but had a V–P discrepancy of 0 points on the WAIS-R. As noted previously, Sandoval et al. (1988) also observed a more substantial P > V profile on the WISC-R (15 points) than on the WAIS-R (11 points) for their sample of learning-disabled adolescents. Also, Hispanics have obtained larger P > V differences on Wechsler's children scales than on his adult scales (see pp. 281–283), and 16-year-old EMRs had a larger P > V discrepancy on the WISC-R than on the WAIS (3.7 points; Nagle & Lazarus, 1979).

Adult prison inmates tested on the WAIS-R have also evidenced relatively small P > V differences. Kender et al. (1985) found a difference of 3½ points for 565 incarcerated males and females ranging from 16 to 65 years (average age = 30). Although the P > V profile was almost identical for underachieving readers (*N* = 319) and adequate readers (*N* = 246) in Kender et al.'s investigation, Zinkus and Gottlieb (1979) did find a difference between adolescent males in the 13- to 18-year age range when this group was divided into those with adequate educational achievement and those with severe academic deficiencies: The former group had a slight (1-point) V > P profile, whereas the group with school learning problems had P > V by about 4 points. DeWolfe and Ryan (1984) also found a significant relationship between the P > V sign and reading ability for their sample of adult male felons and suspected felons; among reading-disabled inmates, 62% had P > V patterns compared to only 36% of nonreading–disabled inmates.

As indicated previously, Gold and Horn (1983) found substantial mean WAIS IQ differences in favor of Performance IQ (7 to 11 points) for male illiterate prison inmates (82% black) aged 16 to 51 with an average education level of 7.5. However, the P > V discrepancy might have been related to their psychopathic behavior, reading problem, low level of formal education, or some combination of these three variables. Indeed, the type of crime might have been a factor as well. DeWolfe and Ryan (1984) found the P > V pattern in 87% of the male inmates convicted of sex crimes, compared to 33% of those incarcerated for murder or attempted murder.

Overview of Research Results

The compilation of data during the past half-century on delinquents and those demonstrating sociopathic behavior suggests that the P > V sign may be associated to some extent with the Wechsler profiles of younger adolescents tested on the WISC or WISC-R. The P > V pattern is occasionally found in older adolescent and adult populations of delinquents and psychopaths. For example, Lueger and Cadman (1982) found higher Performance IQs than Verbal IQs for 89 male delinquents aged 14–17 tested on the WISC, WISC-R, or WAIS. They discovered that 92% of the boys classified as recidivists (those who were convicted of a felony or lesser offense within 15 months after release from a residential treatment program) had higher Performance than Verbal IQ profiles, and they

reported mean P > V profiles of 5½ to 9½ points for their groups of recidivists, nonrecidivists, and program-terminated delinquents.

In general, male delinquents who are recidivists seem to display significantly larger P > V mean differences on the WISC-R than delinquents with just one official adjudication (Bleker, 1983; Haynes & Bensch, 1981). There is also evidence that the WISC-R IQs of young delinquents were stable over a span of nearly 2½ years (coefficients of .86–.93); the group displayed P > V of 4.2 points on the first test and 7.6 points on the retest (Haynes & Howard, 1986).

In contrast to the typical WISC or WISC-R results, the P > V pattern on the WAIS and WAIS-R is *not* usually associated with delinquent or sociopathic behavior. When the mean profile does emerge for samples of older adolescents or adults, the likelihood is that the discrepancy is due to a confounding variable such as a reading disability or low level of education rather than to the delinquent behavior per se. It seems that Wechsler (1944, 1958) was incorrect to place so much faith in the P > V sign for delinquents and psychopaths, at least concerning his tests for older adolescents and adults.

Mental Retardation

Zimmerman and Woo-Sam (1973) summarized numerous correlational studies involving the WAIS and other tests. Included in the 14 tables in their chapter 2 are 14 samples of mentally retarded adolescents and adults from 11 investigations for which they provide mean Verbal and Performance IQs. These samples included a total of 863 individuals—males and females and blacks and whites—whose mean chronological ages ranged from 16 to 47. Of the 14 samples, 10 had a P > V profile of 1 to 7 points, while four groups had V > P of 1 to 3 points. Overall, the weighted mean P > V discrepancy for the 14 samples equaled 2.7

points, suggesting a slight tendency for samples of mentally retarded adolescents and adults to score higher on the Performance than Verbal Scale. However, three of the four samples showing the strongest P > V profiles (mean discrepancies of 7 points) had mean P-IQs of 84 to 86, suggesting that the definitions of retardation may be a bit lax in some investigations. For those appropriately diagnosed as mentally retarded, a P > V profile may be nonexistent.

Calvert and Crozier (1978) have offered some support for the previous supposition. They tested 3 low-functioning adult males admitted for assessment in a hospital in England. This group included 22–23 males in each of five Full Scale IQ categories ranging from 40–49 to 80–89 (mean chronological age for each subsample was 23 to 28). Calvert and Crozier (1978) observed a P > V profile only for those individuals who scored above an IQ of 69, the cut-off typically used to denote retarded intellectual functioning. Of the 44 males with IQs in the 70–89 range, 59% earned higher P-IQs, 34% had higher V-IQs, and 7% scored equally on the two IQ scales; 68% of those with IQs clearly above the retarded level (80–89) earned P > V patterns.

In marked contrast, males with IQs below 70 tended to earn the opposite profile of higher Verbal IQs: 91% of those with mean IQs in the 40–49 range had higher Verbal IQs; for individuals with FS-IQs from 50–69, 57% had higher Verbal IQs, 30% had higher Performance IQs, and 13% had equal IQs. Thus, the P > V profile does not seem to be characteristic of mentally retarded adolescents and adults, and the opposite profile may well characterize individuals with IQs in the moderately or severely retarded range.

Possibly, Wechsler's scales may differ in producing V–P discrepancies, as noted on page 287. Nagle and Lazarus (1979) evaluated 16-year-old EMRs in counterbalanced order on both the WISC-R and WAIS. The 30 adolescents had an 8.2-point superiority in P-IQ on the WISC-R compared with a 3.7 advantage on the WAIS.

Skilled, Semiskilled, and Unskilled Work

Adults engaged in occupations that are generally classified as semiskilled or unskilled show a slight tendency to earn higher Performance than Verbal IQs (Reynolds, Chastain, Kaufman, & McLean, 1987). For adults aged 20–54 who were tested as part of the WAIS-R standardization program, those in skilled, semiskilled, and unskilled occupations earned mean P-IQs that were about 2 to 3 points higher than their mean V-IQs (Reynolds et al., 1987, Table 4). For ages 55–74 there were too few people in the unskilled category, but elderly individuals in skilled and semiskilled occupations displayed a mean P > V profile of 1½ to 4 points.

These P > V patterns may be education related since people in semiskilled and unskilled jobs, especially, average less than a high school education. Regardless of the reason for the small but consistent pattern of high Performance IQs in adults engaged in skilled, semiskilled, and unskilled occupations, clinicians need to be aware of these findings. In contrast to the slightly higher Performance than Verbal IQs of adults actively engaged in the aforementioned set of occupations, children and adolescents whose *parents* are engaged in skilled, semiskilled, or unskilled occupations do *not* tend to have P > V profiles. Extremely similar V- and P-IQs are earned by children, ages 6–16, on the WISC-R and by older adolescents, ages 16–19, on the WAIS-R whose parents are employed in unskilled, semiskilled, or skilled jobs (Kaufman & Doppelt, 1976; Reynolds et al., 1987).

CORRELATES OF HIGH VERBAL IQ

Adolescent and adult samples that tend to earn higher Verbal than Performance IQs on the WAIS or WAIS-R are those with at least some college education, psychiatric disorders (e.g., schizophrenia, depression), motor coordination problems, Alzheimer's-type dementia, Full Scale IQs of 110 or above, or those employed in professional or technical occupations. The V > P profiles for people who have attended, or graduated from, college have been amply documented (see Table 6.11, Table 10.3, and pages 337–339), although it is worth noting that the V > P profile for adults with 13 or more years of education characterizes abnormal as well as normal populations: Loro and Woodward (1976) reported a 22-point Verbal superiority for psychiatric patients having 12+ years of formal schooling versus V–P discrepancies of 0–2 points for patients with less education (total sample = 214). Variables associated with V > P profiles, other than high levels of education, are discussed in the sections that follow.

Psychiatric Disorders

Depression, schizophrenia, manic-depression, and a variety of other psychiatric disorders are often associated with a V > P profile.

Depression

Depression is often accompanied by lowered Performance IQ (Gregory, 1987; Zimmerman & Woo-Sam, 1973), perhaps because of psychomotor retardation due to impaired concentration, anxiety, or low motivation. This V > P pattern may be small, such as the 2.3-point difference on the WAIS for 21 depressed patients studied by Loro and Woodward (1976), or it may average more than 15 points as it did for Pernicano's (1986) sample of 12 male veterans hospitalized for depression who were administered the WAIS-R.

Schizophrenia

Pernicano (1986) also observed a V > P profile on the WAIS-R for his sample of 15 hospitalized schizophrenics, although the value of the difference was 6½ points rather than the 16 points observed for the depressed patients. (Per-

nicano did find the expected P > V pattern, by 7½ points, for his group of 7 patients with personality disorders, so a high Verbal profile was not simply characteristic of Pernicano's entire sample of male hospitalized veterans.) The 117 schizophrenics assessed on the WAIS by Page and Steffy (1984) showed a similar 6-point V > P pattern, with the high Verbal profile observed for the 65 male (+7.3 points) and 52 female (+4.6 points) schizophrenics. Loro and Woodward (1976) found a higher mean Verbal IQ for their sample of schizophrenics with well-defined disorders, but the discrepancy was only about 2 points.

In contrast, Gruzelier and Hammond (1976) found a substantial reduction in *verbal* ability on the WAIS compared to visual-spatial performance ability in a group of 19 chronic patients "diagnosed as unambiguously schizophrenic by the hospital psychiatrists" (p. 39). These authors interpreted the WAIS profile as supporting their hypothesized explanation of schizophrenia as being associated with left hemisphere dysfunction, especially within the temporal-limbic system. Gruzelier and Hammond found further support for their hypothesis from the results of other measures administered to their sample of 19 chronic schizophrenics, such as auditory temporal discrimination and skin conductance, and from previous research findings including WISC results for children at genetic risk for schizophrenia (Gruzelier & Mednick, 1976).

Although Gruzelier's hypothesis is interesting, and is supported by other researchers as well (Flor-Henry, 1976; Gur, 1978; Tucker, 1981), he seems to have overinterpreted the Wechsler data. Other studies have tended to show small V > P differences, not P > V profiles, for schizophrenic samples. Further, 21 psychotics were significantly discriminated from 25 patients with borderline disorders on the WAIS V–P discrepancy, with the former group showing a more depressed Performance IQ (Hymowitz, Hunt, Carr, Hurt, & Spear, 1983).

Finally, Gruzelier and Hammond (1976) did not report mean Verbal and Performance IQs for their sample, opting to present only age-corrected scaled scores for the separate subtests; the means for the 6 Verbal subtests (7.4) and 5 Performance subtests (7.9), estimated from a bar graph of the 11 scaled scores, were not strikingly different.

Manic-Depression

A sample of 21 manic-depressive outpatients (38% male, mean age = 50), all on lithium therapy, obtained an 11-point V > P profile (WAIS V-IQ = 97.7, P-IQ = 86.9; Nair, Muller, Gutbrodt, Buffet, & Schwartz, 1979). The sample's worst performance was in Digit Symbol, although the most interesting finding was the significant negative correlation between Performance IQ and duration of lithium therapy ($r = -.52$). The lowest P-IQs were earned by manic-depressive patients who had been on lithium therapy for the longest time. Those on lithium for the longest time also tended to be characterized by mental slowness. This slowness, rather than diminished accuracy, may account for the depressed P-IQ (Judd, Hubbard, Janowsky, Huey, & Takashi, 1977). Nonetheless, evidence from animal behavior studies (Johnson & Barker, 1972) suggests that lithium's effects may emerge by "impairing central analysis of stimulus input whereby significance is attached to sensory information" (p. 666). Consistent with both proposed explanations are the significant negative correlations between length of lithium therapy and the manic-depressive patients' success on Picture Arrangement and Digit Symbol (Nair et al., 1979).

Generalized Psychiatric Samples

Apart from Gruzelier and Hammond's (1976) investigation, most Wechsler studies of previously defined psychiatric populations seem to produce V > P profiles. Todd, Coolidge, and Satz (1977), who found V > P patterns for their various samples of brain-lesioned adults

regardless of the location of the lesion (see p. 279), also identified a 4½-point V > P profile for their psychiatric control group ($N = 78$, including 17 with depression and 15 with some form of psychosis). Page and Steffy (1984) likewise found high Verbal–low Performance patterns to characterize their sample of 429 adult psychiatric inpatients, which earned a mean V-IQ = 94.3 and a mean P-IQ = 88.9 (+5.4 discrepancy). The 6-point Verbal superiority for Page and Steffy's (1984) group of schizophrenics was reported previously; but these investigators also observed a 7½-point V > P profile for 46 neurotics, although they found a V–P difference of less than 1 point for 108 inpatients with personality disorders.

Is V > P for Psychiatric Patients an Artifact?

Kljajcic and Berry (1984) administered the WAIS to 33 male and 22 female admissions to a psychiatric hospital and identified an 11-point V > P profile for those with Full Scale IQs less than 90 ($N = 30$), a 2-point difference in favor of V-IQ for individuals with average intelligence ($N = 16$), and a 7-point V > P pattern for psychiatric patients with IQs of 110+. These authors join with the interpretation of Pickering, Johnson, and Starey (1977), who obtained their own data and reviewed additional studies, in arguing that the WAIS produces an *artifactual* depression in Performance IQ due to normative inadequacies. Pickering et al. (1977) went so far as to recommend making a +5-point correction in Performance IQ!

I find this interpretation so untenable that it hardly merits discussion. Suffice it to say that the WAIS and WAIS-R normative procedures (except for ages 16–19 on the WAIS-R, as explained on pages 83–85) are exemplary. Any consistent V > P profiles found for any particular subsamples, such as psychiatric populations, are undoubtedly a function of some characteristics of those samples; for psychiatric inpatients, the V > P pattern is probably due to variables such as depressed behavior, psychomotor retardation, lack of concentration, anxiety, low motivation, and the like, which tend to affect success differentially on the Wechsler Performance subtests.

Kljajcic (1984) conducted an additional study with the WAIS, comparing inpatients with 15+ V > P profiles (N = 35) to a matched control group of inpatients (N = 35) earning V- and P-IQs within 5 points of each other. He found that these groups did not differ significantly in psychiatric diagnosis, EEG, CT scan, memory, visual-motor integration, or severity of problem and concluded: "The WAIS VIQ > PIQ proved to be of remarkably little predictive utility. . . . It appears unjustified to administer as expensive a procedure as the WAIS for the purpose of VIQ > PIQ analysis with psychiatric inpatients" (p. 576). Similarly McEchron (1980) found small relationships between V–P discrepancies and variables on the MMPI and Behavior Problem Checklist and concluded that the discrepancies have little practical value for understanding individual behaviors and personality variables. Based on the bulk of research reported in this chapter, I disagree with the aforementioned negative conclusions about the utility of the V–P discrepancy as a tool for clinical interpretation.

Motor Coordination Problems

Success on Wechsler's Performance Scale requires good nonverbal reasoning and concept formation, as well as the ability to demonstrate this nonverbal intelligence via well-coordinated motor behavior. The presumption is that individuals have adequate coordination to convey the level of their nonverbal thinking capacities, and P-IQ is intended to primarily reflect a person's nonverbal intelligence, *not* his or her ability to perform coordinated fine motor activities. When this assumption is violated during an administration of the WAIS-R because of a neurological disorder or a related reason, then,

as with the scores earned by children on the WISC-R, noncognitive coordination difficulties "may serve to reduce the Performance IQ to an underestimate of nonverbal thinking" (Kaufman, 1979b, p. 36).

Investigation of the Performance Subtest Profile

By coincidence, the five Performance subtests on the WAIS-R are ordered in their sequence of administration from the one that demands the least motor coordination (Picture Completion) to the one requiring the most pure fine motor ability (Digit Symbol). In fact, the amount of motor coordination required for each successively administered Performance subtest gradually increases from the first task to the fifth one, just as it does with the five regularly administered WISC-R Performance subtests (Kaufman, 1979b). Picture Arrangement, administered directly after Picture Completion, demands some motor coordination to move the pictures appropriately within the time limit; however, the pictures do not have to be spaced equally or arranged in a particularly straight line, and no bonus points are allotted on this WAIS-R for quick, perfect performance. Block task Design and Object Assembly both place a premium on well-coordinated motor activity to arrange the blocks or puzzle pieces in their proper, precise alignment, and to earn bonus points for rapid solutions to the problems. WAIS-R Object Assembly probably places a greater premium on good motor coordination than does WAIS-R Block Design, because bonus points undoubtedly contribute more to an adolescent's or adult's scaled score on the former subtest than on the latter one; this result was observed for preadolescents and adolescents on the WISC-R (Kaufman, 1979b), but comparable WAIS-R data are unavailable.

The greater emphasis on speed for Object Assembly is probably related to the relative ease of solving the four puzzles on both the WISC-R and WAIS-R within the generous time limits; since most people tend to solve three or all four puzzles correctly, the main discriminator between high and low scorers is the rapidity of the response. For Block Design, even well-coordinated individuals of average or below average intelligence fail several of the nine-block items within the relatively short time limits because of conceptual, not coordination, problems. Nonetheless, both Block Design and Object Assembly demand both nonverbal reasoning and coordination for successful performance. Digit Symbol is almost completely a psycho-motor, clerical task because its cognitive component is small and the amount of actual conceptualization demanded of the person is limited.

The ordering of the WAIS-R Performance subtests from the one requiring the least motor coordination to the one demanding the most coordination is convenient for examiners. As with the WISC-R, whenever a person's Performance scaled scores decrease fairly steadily from the first one to the last one given, the examiner should immediately consider the possibility that the trend is due to a motor difficulty. As with the assessment of children on the WISC-R (Kaufman, 1979b), it is important to find behavioral support for hypotheses derived from subtest patterns, such as poor fine motor coordination: "If no coordination difficulty was apparent during the examination, particularly during the Performance subtests, the hypothesis probably requires quick rejection" (p. 37). Other explanations are then needed for the decline in Performance scores from Picture Completion to Digit Symbol. Fatigue is always a possibility, especially if the Verbal subtests showed the same declining trend and the person seemed to tire noticeably as the testing proceeded. Another potential explanation, at least for a person who earned a high Verbal IQ, is the application of verbal skills to Performance tasks. Such verbal compensation is most helpful on Picture Completion, because of verbal responding, and on Picture Arrangement, because of verbal mediation; verbalization of nonverbal strategies can sometimes be beneficial on Block Design and Object Assembly, but it is not very helpful on Digit Symbol. If behavioral observations suggest a notable motor problem, the person should probably be administered a thorough neuropsychological battery to assess his or her motor skills more fully.

Coordination Difficulties for Multiple Sclerosis Patients

One especially pertinent study of adults with motor difficulties was conducted by Heaton, Nelson, Thompson, Burks, and Franklin (1985), who administered the WAIS and Halstead-Reitan Battery to 100 patients with multiple sclerosis (MS). Of this sample, 57 MS patients had a relapsing-remitting disease course, and had been in remission for one month or longer when assessed; 43 patients had a chronic-progressive form of MS, never experiencing significant remission. Both patient groups displayed the predicted V > P profile. As expected, however, the discrepancy was larger for the chronic-progressive sample (V-IQ = 110, P-IQ = 98, discrepancy = +12 points) than for the MS patients with remission (V-IQ = 111, P-IQ = 106, discrepancy = +5 points).

The subtest profile on the Performance Scale was not revealing for the relapsing-remitting patients, but for the chronic patients it conformed closely to the hypothesized pattern based on the supposed amount of motor coordination demanded by each WAIS-R Performance subtest: The chronic-progressive MS patients earned their highest mean Performance scaled score on Picture Completion (9.8) and their lowest on Object Assembly (8.4) and Digit Symbol (8.5). The motor coordination difficulties of the MS patients were clearly documented by their performance on the Halstead-Reitan neuropsychological battery and by clinicians' ratings. Five of the neuropsychological subtests administered measure sensory-motor functioning without a clear-cut cognitive component. The total group of MS patients performed significantly more poorly than did 100 matched normal controls on all five sensory-motor tests, and the chronic-progressive MS patients scored significantly lower than the relapsing-remitting patients on three of the five tasks. Further, the clinicians' motor ratings classified 100% of the chronic patients as having motor impairment, compared to 77% of the patients in remission and 3% of the controls (Heaton et al., 1985).

Performance Deficits in Huntington's Disease

Huntington's disease is associated with progressive motor deficits as well as symptoms of dementia and tends to be accompanied by V > P Wechsler profiles (Brandt et al., 1984; Butters, Sax, Montgomery, & Tarlow, 1978; Fedio, Cox, Neophytides, Canal-Frederick, & Chase, 1979; Josiassen, Curry, Roemer, DeBease, & Mancall, 1982). Whereas the motor symptoms in this genetically transmitted disease involve "involuntary, spasmodic, often tortuous movements that ultimately become profoundly disabling" (Lezak, 1983, p. 188), the V > P profile emerges in the very early stages of the disease (Butters et al., 1978) and for patients suffering only minor movement disorders (Josiassen et al., 1982). In the Josiassen study, for example, the 13 Huntington's patients (mean age = 45.5 years, mean education = 12.7 years) scored 9.4 IQ points lower on the WAIS Performance Scale. Brandt et al.'s (1984) 13 patients with recent onset of chorea (abnormal movements) had V > P of 5.5 WAIS IQ points compared to a 9.4-point discrepancy for 44 patients with advanced chorea. The patients with advanced Huntington's disease showed significant decrements on the Performance, but not the Verbal, subtests; nonetheless, intellectual differences between the recent and advanced patients were far more moderate in magnitude than differences in adaptive and social functioning (Brandt et al., 1984).

In the studies by Butters et al. and Josiassen et al., the Huntington's patients earned their highest Performance scaled score on the non-motoric Picture Completion subtest, while generally scoring low on visual-motor and timed tasks (including Arithmetic). Their deficiency on the Performance Scale was matched by a clear-cut weakness on sequential subtests (see pp. 512–513). Good performance on Picture Completion compared to the other nonverbal tasks may not only be related to the motor demands of Wechsler's subtests, however; Huntington's patients generally seem to have difficulty with tasks that lack familiarity and structure, are perceptually complex, or require a complex response (Aminoff, Marshall, Smith, & Wyke, 1975; Fedio et al., 1979; Lezak, 1983). Yet the motor component cannot be minimized. Brandt et al.'s (1984) advanced Huntington's patients showed their greatest disabilities (and their biggest decrements relative to the patients with recent onset of chorea) on the two subtests requiring the most motor coordination—Digit Symbol and Object Assembly. Regardless of the patients' difficulties with nonverbal and sequential tasks, they clearly do best on skills that have been overlearned, like reading, writing, and Wechsler's Verbal Comprehension subtests (Lezak, 1983).

Alzheimer's-Type Dementia

Although the cognitive deficiencies of patients with Alzheimer's-type dementia are complex, there is evidence that these patients tend to display V > P patterns on the WAIS. Fuld (1984) was able to obtain valid WAIS data for 46 Alzheimer's patients; based on IQs prorated from four Verbal and three Performance subtests, she observed V > P profiles of 15 or more points in 24 (52%) of these patients. Intriguingly, Fuld (1984) also obtained dramatic V > P findings for 20 normal graduate and undergraduate students who were given drugs to induce experimentally the impaired cholinergic neurotransmitter functioning believed to characterize Alzheimer's patients. All 20 subjects demonstrated V > P patterns, with 15 (75%) showing differences of at least 15 points.

To ensure that the V > P profile did not merely reflect the high educational attainment of the sample, Fuld (1984) administered placebos to a control group of 22 medical and undergraduate students. This group also tended to have higher Verbal IQs (16 individuals, or 73%, had V > P), but only 18% of the control subjects had a Verbal superiority by 15 or more points.

Brinkman and Braun (1984) also identified a WAIS V > P pattern in their sample of 23 adults suspected of Alzheimer's-type dementia. This group scored 7 points higher on the Verbal Scale (IQs of 97 and 90). However, it is unclear whether the V > P pattern that seems to be associated with Alzheimer's disease is useful in differentiating Alzheimer's patients from those with other types of dementia. In Brinkman and Braun's (1984) investigation, the 39 patients with multi-infarct dementia clearly did not evidence a substantial V > P pattern (V-IQ = 95, P-IQ = 94). However, Fuld (1984) found that 7 of her 11 multi-infarct dementia patients (64%) showed a V > P profile of 15+ points, very similar to the value of 52% obtained for the patients with Alzheimer's-type dementia. There is evidence that a subtest profile derived by Fuld for Alzheimer's patients may be effective in distinguishing these patients from others with similar disorders even if the V–P discrepancy is not diagnostic.

Full Scale IQ of 110 or Above

Consistent with the finding that highly educated adults display higher scores on the Verbal than Performance Scale is the finding that adolescents and adults with IQs in the High Average (Bright), Superior, and Very Superior ranges earn V > P profiles. Matarazzo and Herman (1985) combined data for the 1,880 individuals aged 16–74 in the WAIS-R standardization sample and grouped them into five IQ categories. Of the 177 people earning Full Scale IQs of 120 or more, about one-fourth had V–P IQ discrepancies, in either direction, of 15+ points.

Of this group with sizable discrepancies between their verbal and nonverbal abilities, 62% evidenced V > P profiles. A similar result emerged for the 312 people scoring 110–119 on the WAIS-R Full Scale; of the portion of this sample earning V–P differences of at least 15 points, 57% had V > P profiles. Using other criteria for determining large differences between V- and P-IQ (10, 13, or 22 points), Matarazzo and Herman (1985, Table 5) showed that people in the 110–119 and 120+ IQ ranges consistently demonstrated V > P patterns more so than P > V profiles. None of the other IQ categories displayed characteristic V–P differences.

Professional and Technical Occupations

In view of the V > P patterns observed for highly educated and intelligent adults, it is axiomatic that the occupations chosen by bright, educated individuals will evidence high Verbal patterns; that is precisely what occurs. In their analysis of WAIS-R standardization data, Reynolds, Chastain, Kaufman, & McLean (1987) observed small mean differences in favor of Verbal IQ for 124 professional and technical workers, ages 20–54 (V-IQ = 113, P-IQ = 110, discrepancy = 3 points), and for 20 elderly adults, ages 55–74, in similar occupations (V-IQ = 115½, P-IQ = 109½, discrepancy = 5 points). Similar differences even emerged for 62 older adolescents, ages 16–19, whose parents were in professional or technical occupations (V-IQ = 108, P-IQ = 105, discrepancy = 3 points).

WHEN V–P IQ DISCREPANCIES ARE MEANINGLESS

There are several circumstances when the difference between a person's Verbal and Performance IQs is of little interpretive value, and may even be misleading. Four such factors have been discussed in some depth for the WISC-R (Kaufman, 1979b, pp. 43–50); since they apply as well to the WAIS-R, they are summarized here.

IQs Do Not Correspond to Factor Scores

When examiners look at the V–P IQ difference, they are interested in the person's underlying abilities within the verbal and nonverbal spheres, not the obtained scores *per se.* The discussion of the WAIS-R factor analysis in chapter 8 indicates that two Verbal subtests are not always good measures of the Verbal Comprehension factor, and that two Performance subtests do not measure Perceptual Organization very well. The WAIS-R tasks that are often mavericks are Arithmetic, Digit Span, Picture Arrangement, and Digit Symbol. The two Verbal subtests are more associated with the third, or distractibility, factor than with Verbal Comprehension across the entire 16- to 74-year age range. The two Performance subtests simply do not measure nonverbal intelligence, except for elderly individuals; Picture Arrangement does not seem to measure any WAIS-R factor consistently at ages 16–54, and Digit Symbol is mostly a measure of Freedom from Distractibility for the 16- to 54-year age range.

Consequently, clinicians need to be aware of fluctuations in the subtest profile that relate to the factor structure of the WAIS-R. An immediate clue is the splitting of the Verbal scaled scores into two groups, with the Arithmetic/Digit Span dyad emerging as either much lower or higher than the clustering of scores on the remaining strongly Verbal subtests. For example, a person may earn scaled scores of 6 to 8 on Arithmetic and Digit Span, versus scores in the 10 to 14 range on the four Verbal Comprehension subtests. Whenever an examiner discerns this particular pattern, or finds an unusually discrepant score within the Performance profile on either Picture Arrangement or Digit

Symbol, he or she should consider such findings as red flags that suggest the possible meaninglessness of the V–P discrepancy.

The examiner should then group the subtests in accordance with the three-factor WAIS-R solutions (see Table 8.9 on page 251) and compute the person's mean scaled score on the Verbal Comprehension, Perceptual Organization, and Freedom from Distractibility factors. These mean scaled scores can then be converted to their equivalent percentile rank (Wechsler, 1981, p. 151); the difference between the percentile ranks for the verbal and perceptual factors then provides a better estimate of that person's verbal–nonverbal discrepancy than any comparisons derived from the actual Verbal and Performance IQs. Whereas it is feasible for examiners to compute prorated IQs or factor scores based on the recategorized groupings of subtests (see p. 434), some examiners should be wary when computing extra standard scores; too many IQs and "IQ equivalents" in a case report may confuse the reader, and the additional computations increase the chance of clerical errors.

Verbal Compensation of Performance Deficit

As discussed previously, some verbally bright individuals can score well on Wechsler's nonverbal tasks by using their well-developed verbal skills. Verbal responding on Picture Completion, verbal mediation on Picture Arrangement, and "thinking aloud" on Block Design and Object Assembly may be used as compensatory techniques for people with high verbal intelligence coupled with visual-motor deficits. Individuals who are particularly adept at this compensation can inflate their Performance IQs substantially, far beyond the level of their "true" nonverbal intelligence. Such individuals will conceivably still earn significantly higher Verbal than Performance IQs, but the discrepancy may be a "normal" 14 points instead of an extraordinary 25 points.

Obviously, the person who can spontaneously compensate for a nonverbal deficiency, especially in a highly structured, timed situation, has strong integrities and well-integrated brain functioning. That is the upside of the finding. The downside is that the person may truly have a visual-motor deficit requiring rehabilitation or remediation, such as a patient who has suffered a stroke in the right hemisphere; the failure for a sizable V > P pattern to emerge may mask the real underlying deficits in the person's cognitive functioning. The alert clinician will be able to infer significant, and perhaps substantial, verbal–nonverbal discrepancies for a person who otherwise does not score remarkably differently on the Verbal and Performance Scales. The things to look for are scaled scores on the first two Performance subtests administered, Picture Completion and Picture Arrangement, that are clearly above the scores on the remaining nonverbal tasks (and similar in magnitude to most Verbal scaled scores), coupled with clear-cut behavioral observations of the use of verbal mediation when solving items on tasks like Picture Arrangement and Block Design.

Scatter in Verbal or Performance Subtest Profile

The use of summary scores such as IQs are based on the assumption that a unitary ability is being measured by the IQ scale. When a Verbal IQ is reported for a person, one assumes that the six Verbal subtests are primarily measuring verbal intelligence for that person. However, if a person was raised in a different culture, his or her low scores on Information and Comprehension may reflect that cultural difference rather than a verbal deficit, especially if the person performed at a much higher level on Similarities and Arithmetic. Analogous assumptions hold for the computation of Performance IQ; a highly anxious person who performs poorly on tasks like Digit Symbol and Object Assembly, which place great emphasis on quick performance, may be exhibiting the negative impact

of that anxiety rather than a deficiency in nonverbal intelligence.

The role of scatter in the Verbal or Performance Scale was discussed implicitly in both of the preceding sections concerning factor analysis and verbal compensation. Scatter in the Verbal Scale often occurs when the Arithmetic/ Digit Span dyad splits off from the Verbal Comprehension subtests; variability in the Performance Scale is common when scores on Picture Completion and Picture Arrangement are elevated due to a verbal compensation for a visual-motor deficit. What I am adding here is the notion that *whenever* there is significant scatter among a person's subtest scores on either the Verbal or Performance Scale, *for whatever reason*, the IQ on that scale is less meaningful than if the scores were more unitary. If an individual's scaled scores on the Verbal Scale range from a low of 2 to a high of 14, how meaningful is V-IQ as a summative statistic of the person's verbal intelligence? The same reasoning holds for wide scatter within the Performance Scale. When the obtained IQ is merely the midpoint of two or more different set of skills, that IQ is not very meaningful.

When the Verbal and/or Performance IQ can be shown to be nothing more than a midpoint of distinct abilities, any comparisons involving the IQs (such as the V–P discrepancy) are usually meaningless. The examiner's goal then becomes the regrouping of subtests into alternative categories (see chapters 12–14) to discern the person's specific areas of integrity and deficit. To enable the examiner to determine when the amount of profile variability within the Verbal or Performance Scale is significant or "marked," consult the discussion of this issue in chapter 13.

Effects of Retesting

There are few good intelligence tests for adolescents and adults, and the WAIS-R (or its predecessors) has been the test of choice whenever intellectual assessment is required. Thus, when a person requires a retest for whatever reason, the same test battery is typically given. Since clinical and neurological patients are frequently assessed repeatedly to evaluate their current status, issues concerning retesting assume an important practical role. As discussed at length in chapter 4, gains on the Performance Scale are considerably larger than gains on the Verbal Scale. Gains for normal people on the WAIS-R over a 1- to 2-month interval average 3 points in V-IQ, 8½ points in P-IQ, and 6 points in FS-IQ. Similar practice effects have been observed for clinical populations (Matarazzo, Carmody, & Jacobs, 1980) and for children as well as adults (Kaufman, 1979b).

Consequently, the average person will show a *relative* gain of 5 to 6 points on the Performance Scale when retested on the WAIS-R because P-IQ improves by 5½ points more than does V-IQ as a result of the practice effect. Catron (1978; Catron & Thompson, 1979) retested college students on the WAIS using five time intervals (5 minutes, 1 week, 1 month, 2 months, and 4 months). The relative gains in P-IQ, compared to V-IQ, going from the shortest to the longest interval were the following: 11, 6½, 8, 6½, and 7 points. When retested immediately, the relative Performance gain was huge; it dropped substantially when a 1-week interval was used, but remained a fairly constant 7 points for the groups of college students tested by Catron (1978; Catron & Thompson, 1979), even for intervals as long as 4 months. Even though the *absolute* gains in IQ were smaller the longer the time interval (Full Scale IQ gained 8 points after 1 week, but 4 points after 4 months), Performance IQ continued to gain relatively more than Verbal IQ by a rather constant amount.

Impact of Retesting for Individual Assessment

The net result of this practice effect is to produce relatively higher Performance than Verbal IQs in individuals who are retested on a Wechsler Scale over an interval of a few months (perhaps as long as a year or more). A person who earns a P > V pattern by a nonsignificant 8 points on an initial testing of the WAIS-R would be expected to show a significant P > V profile by about 14 points upon a retest, *simply due to the predictable practice effect that leads to greater improvement in P-IQ than V-IQ.* Similarly, a person with P > V of 15 points on the first administration is likely to have a striking discrepancy of more than 20 points on the retest due to the practice effect. The practice effect works in reverse for people who initially show significant superiority on the Verbal Scale. A significant V > P profile of 12 points on the first test is likely to decline to a trivial 5 or 6 points on the retest, and so forth.

The overall conclusion is that V–P differences on a retest of the WAIS-R are likely to be meaningless in most circumstances unless the initial test was invalid (e. g., because of the person's low motivation), or if at least 1 year has elapsed between administrations. V–P IQ discrepancies on a retest can only be interpreted in the context of the V–P differences observed on the first test. If the V–P discrepancies follow a lawful pattern—i.e., they show a shift upon retesting in the direction of a relatively higher P-IQ, by perhaps 5 to 10 points—the V–P IQ difference on the retest should be considered *artifactual.* The V–P IQ discrepancy on the first testing probably gives a truer picture of the person's underlying verbal and nonverbal abilities than does the IQ difference on the second administration.

Impact of Retesting for Research

The practice effect can have a significant impact on the interpretation of group data as well. For example, Juolasmaa et al. (1981) tested 60 cardiac patients pre– and post–open heart surgery on the WAIS (10-month interval) to evaluate the impact of heart surgery on intellectual performance. They observed a 4-point gain in P-IQ after surgery compared to a ½-point improvement in V-IQ, concluding: "In general, the rates of improvement exceeded those of impairment, the tests of visual functions showing the highest rise" (p. 186). What they really observed was probably the practice effect in action. Similarly, Seidenberg et al. (1981) attempted to distinguish between practice effects and real cognitive changes in their group of epileptics by showing that those with reduced seizure frequency demonstrated the biggest intellectual gains. Nonetheless, the practice effect was clearly in evidence for patients who had improved in their seizures and for those who had not. Both samples showed V > P profiles on the initial WAIS administration of about 6 points; the relative Performance versus Verbal gain due to practice reduced the V–P IQ discrepancy on the retest to about zero for both subsamples of patients.

CHAPTER 9 SUMMARY

This chapter is the first of three on V–P IQ discrepancies and covers the following topics: (a) the distinction between statistical significance and statistical abnormality, (b) an overview of the studies exploring V–P differences in patients with unilateral brain damage, (c) discussions of research pertaining to groups of individuals allegedly showing characteristic V > P or P > V profiles, and (d) illustrations of instances when V–P IQ discrepancies are meaningless.

WAIS-R V- and P-IQs for adults aged 25–74 years need to differ by only 9 points to be significantly discrepant at the 5% level, a smaller value than is needed for the WISC-R (12 points), and for adolescents and 20- to 24-year-olds on the WAIS-R (10–12 points). However, differences between WAIS-R Verbal and Performance IQs must typically be at least *twice* as large as the significance values to be abnormal or unusual. In general, the higher the person's Full Scale IQ category, the larger the discrepancy needed to infer abnormality. Statistically *significant* V–P differences are those that are

repeatable upon retesting, i.e., not due to chance factors. Statistically *abnormal* discrepancies are those that occur infrequently within a normal population. It is essential that clinicians consider base rates of abnormality before inferring that an individual's V–P difference is abnormal.

The results of over 40 studies involving the testing of patients with unilateral brain damage on the W-B I, WAIS, and WAIS-R give basic support to the long-held contention that left-lesion patients have characteristic P > V profiles, while right-lesion patients show V > P discrepancies. However, the support is far more impressive for patients with right hemisphere damage. Across all studies, the latter group averaged a 9-point Verbal IQ superiority compared to about a 4-point Performance advantage for left-lesion patients. WAIS and WAIS-R studies were generally less impressive regarding the predicted V–P profiles than were the studies conducted with the W-B I. Most notably, left-lesion patients showed an average P > V difference of about 2½ points on the WAIS or WAIS-R compared to a 7½-point discrepancy on the older battery. In addition, patients with bilateral brain damage earned mean W-B I V- and P-IQs that are about equal, whereas their mean WAIS/WAIS-R IQs showed about a 6-point Verbal superiority.

The following variables are often associated with characteristically high P-IQs: bilingualism, autism, learning disabilities or illiteracy, delinquency or psychopathic behavior, mental retardation, and blue-collar occupations. Numerous investigations have shown that bilingual Hispanic and American Indian children, adolescents, and adults earn substantially higher Performance than Verbal IQs. Although studies with adults are relatively uncommon, the findings agree generally with the bulk of WISC-R literature showing an average P-IQ superiority of about 7–10 points for Hispanics and a more substantial 15–30 points for American Indians. The reasons for these P > V profiles are related to language differences and the difficulty in learning two languages simultaneously, but the following variables are also potentially crucial: cultural and subcultural differences, experience in working under time pressure, the degree of understanding of the test-taking format, physiological variables (e.g., otitis media in American Indians), and lateralization of brain functions.

Research on autistic individuals is complicated by the presence of mental retardation in many of the subjects. Evidence from various studies, including one that eliminated retarded subjects from consideration, indicates a typical pattern of high Performance–low Verbal on Wechsler's scales and related tasks. Left hemisphere dysfunction has been implicated by several researchers, although disagreements regarding etiologies and definitions of autism are prevalent.

Learning-disabled, illiterate, and dyslexic adolescents and adults display a characteristic P > V profile of about 5 to 15 points. However, learning-disabled college students are an exception; they usually evidence the opposite profile, by about 10 points, or have no V–P difference at all. The P > V sign for delinquents and psychopaths was advocated by Wechsler over a half-century ago. Whereas groups of delinquents and psychopaths average about 6 points higher on P-IQ than V-IQ, supporting Wechsler's generalization, his claim that the sign is useful for individual diagnosis has not been supported. Further, among delinquents and psychopaths, the P > V discrepancy tends to be larger for younger adolescents than for older adolescents and adults; larger on the WISC/WISC-R than on the WAIS/WAIS-R; larger for whites than blacks; and sometimes explainable by intervening variables like reading disabilities or number of criminal offenses.

Mental retardation has sometimes been associated with P > V profiles; most studies with adolescents and adults, however, suggest only a slight profile (2–3 points), with the possibility that individuals with very low IQs may even display a high Verbal profile. A slight 2–3 point superiority in P-IQ has also been demonstrated by adults engaged in semiskilled or unskilled occupations.

The following variables have been associated with V > P profiles: high educational attainment, psychiatric disorders, motor coordination problems, Alzheimer's-type dementia, high IQs, and professional or technical occupations. Individuals with college backgrounds earn higher V-IQs, even if they are abnormal. Psychiatric patients, in general, display V > P profiles; this finding has been observed for schizophrenics (although some have argued for low V-IQ in schizophrenia), depressives, manic-depressives, and generalized psychiatric samples. The consistent finding of about a 5- to 6-point V > P profile in diverse psychiatric samples has impelled some researchers (erroneously) to suggestion a "correction" for this "artifact."

Performance subtests range from one requiring little or no motor coordination (Picture Completion) to a test of psychomotor speed (Digit Symbol), with most of Wechsler's nonverbal tasks requiring good coordination for success. Groups with known motor problems (patients with multiple sclerosis or Huntington's disease) earn substantially higher V- than P-IQs. Among multiple sclerosis patients, discrepancies were larger for chronic than relapsing-remitting patients (12 versus 5 points); the chronic patients performed worst on the tasks most dependent on motor coordination. Analogous results were obtained when patients with advanced Huntington's disease were compared to those with a recent onset. Alzheimer's patients show a stronger V- than P-IQ, and slight V > P profiles typify groups of normal individuals with Full Scale IQs of 110 or above and those employed in professional or technical occupations.

Clinicians need to be able to go beyond the computed Verbal and Performance IQs to determine when the discrepancy between the two may be misleading or meaningless. Illustrations include instances when the IQs do not correspond to the factor scores, when a person uses a verbal strength to compensate for a Performance deficit, when scatter exists in the subtest profiles, and when a person is retested on the WAIS-R.

V–P IQ Discrepancies in Brain-Damaged Adults: Interactions With Gender, Race, and Other Patient Variables

Chapter 9 discussed V–P IQ discrepancies in relation to brain damage and numerous other variables, and presented both empirical and clinical approaches to interpretation of Wechsler's important dichotomy. Although the investigations of patients with unilateral brain damage were treated in some depth (see pages 271–281), the interactions between the V–P discrepancy and patient variables like gender or type of lesion have been saved for thorough analysis in this chapter. Chapter 11 continues the discussion of V–P IQ discrepancies in brain-damaged adults, focusing on subtest patterns of left lesion and right lesion patients and other clinical issues regarding interpretation of the discrepancies.

The goal of this chapter is to answer questions regarding the relationship of V–P IQ discrepancies in these patients to the following variables: (a) gender, (b) race, (c) nature of the brain damage, (d) acuteness versus chronicity of the lesion, (e) inclusion of aphasics in the samples, (f) age of onset, and (g) education level.

GENDER OF PATIENTS WITH LATERALIZED LESIONS

Males and females are believed to differ in various aspects of brain functioning (Witelson, 1976), and they have demonstrated differences in cerebral organization in experiments with normal individuals using techniques such as dichotic listening and assessment of the superiority of the left or right visual fields for verbal versus visual-spatial stimuli (Bryden, 1979). Lezak (1983) concludes: "Lateralization of verbal and visuospatial functions to the left and right hemispheres, respectively, tends to be greater for males than for females" (p. 220). Yet this variable has been ignored by many researchers despite the likelihood, or at least the conceivability, of gender differences in the relationship between the localization of a lesion to the left or right hemisphere and the direction of the V–P discrepancy.

Lansdell's Initial Observations

Over a quarter of a century ago, Lansdell (1962) observed gender differences concerning the impact of temporal lobe neurosurgery on epileptic patients' verbal and nonverbal behavior. Removal of the right temporal lobe affected the visual perception of males, who demonstrated a significant reduction in their artistic aptitude following the surgery; similarly, removal of the left temporal lobe, as predicted by lateralization research on brain function, resulted in men scoring significantly lower on a test of proverbs after surgery than before. In marked contrast, these hypothesized reductions in visual-spatial and verbal performance following right and left temporal lobe surgeries, respectively, failed to occur for women. Lansdell (1968) subsequently obtained similar findings with the Wechsler-Bellevue, concluding that "the results suggest that perceptual abilities are to some extent represented differently in the brains of men and women" (p. 266).

Regardless of Lansdell's (1962, 1968) suggestions of gender differences in cerebral lateralization and the similar sentiments of other neuropsychologists (Buffery & Gray, 1972), the issue of male–female differences in Wechsler studies of patients with unilateral lesions was mostly ignored until McGlone's (1977, 1978) research was published, including a literature review that she claimed supported the existence of these differences (McGlone, 1980).

Dennerll (1964), following Lansdell's (1962) lead, found that he was better able to classify males than females according to location of lesion when using subtest scores as "predictors" in regression analyses. But researchers largely ignored his early cross-validation of Lansdell's preliminary work. Samples of males and females were simply combined in most studies, and it was common for investigators not to bother to even tell the reader how many men and women comprised the left-lesion and right-lesion samples (e.g., Doehring, Reitan, & Kløve, 1961;

Leli & Filskov, 1981a; Satz, 1966). As recently as 1985, Reitan failed to give the gender breakdown of his 56 patients with left or right hemisphere lesions.

McGlone's Research

McGlone's (1977, 1978) clear demonstration of gender differences gave new impetus to this line of investigation. In her first study, males and females with right lesions both showed the expected pattern, but the V > P difference of 15.8 points for males far exceeded the value of 5.1 for females. McGlone (1977) did not provide enough data to compute V–P differences for her left-lesion patients (Verbal IQs were provided only for half of her male sample and three-fourths of her female sample—the nonaphasics—but Performance IQs were presented only for the total left-lesion samples); nevertheless, she gave evidence that a low V-IQ characterized the male nonaphasics (mean = 87) but *not* the female nonaphasics (mean = 99).

McGlone (1978) then reported the following results in her second study: Males with left lesions had P > V of 11.2 points, and males with right lesions had V > P of 13.5 points; females with left hemisphere lesions had a V–P IQ discrepancy of approximately zero (−0.1), and females with right-brain lesions had a V–P difference of +4.2. These findings were rather compelling, but they were also misleading because McGlone failed to inform readers that the samples in her two studies were "largely overlapping," a fact that Bornstein & Matarazzo (1984, p. 707) uncovered in a personal communication from McGlone in 1983. Thus, rather than providing an independent cross-validation of her first set of results, McGlone's (1978) follow-up investigation was just a restatement of her initial findings.

However, McGlone's (1980) review helped ignite interest in the gender-difference topic. Her review was handicapped by a relative paucity of pertinent data because "the sex composition of neurological patient samples has traditionally been biased by the inclusion of a greater proportion of males" (p. 216); nonetheless, McGlone helped place the issue of neuropsychologically meaningful gender differences before the professional forum; commentary from 37 of her peers appeared in response to her review in the same 1980 issue of *Behavioral and Brain Sciences*. Many contributors were skeptical of her findings (e.g., Kinsbourne, 1980; Sherman, 1980), but significant research efforts followed.

Basically, McGlone's lead was pursued by researchers who investigated the gender difference issue either by (a) reviewing numerous previous investigations of patients with unilateral brain damage who were tested on the Wechsler scales (Bornstein & Matarazzo, 1982, 1984; Inglis & Lawson, 1982; Lawson & Inglis, 1983), or (b) systematically investigating gender differences with new samples of brain-damaged adults that included groups of men and women matched on key variables like age, education, and severity of lesion (Bornstein, 1984; Herring & Reitan, 1986; Inglis, Ruckman, Lawson, McLean, & Monga, 1982; Snow & Sheese, 1985; Whelan & Walker, 1988).

Recent Well-Controlled Investigations

The new, well-controlled studies differed in their findings. Inglis et al. (1982) confirmed the dramatic gender differences reported by McGlone (1977, 1978). The remaining four investigations, however, failed to find significant interactions between gender and V–P IQ discrepancy for patients with left lesions and right lesions tested on the Wechsler-Bellevue (Herring & Reitan, 1986), the WAIS (Snow & Sheese, 1985; Whelan & Walker, 1988), and the WAIS-R (Bornstein, 1984).

Bornstein (1984) and Whelan and Walker (1988) truly found identical results for male and female patients, but the results of the other two

studies were less decisive. Herring and Reitan (1986) did indeed observe the predictable V–P differences for patients of both sexes with lateralized lesions, but they failed to stress that the *magnitude* of the discrepancies was about *twice* as large for males than females. Further, Snow and Sheese (1985) found no gender difference of consequence, but they neglected to point out just how atypical their findings were in comparison to previous brain lateralization research: They found V > P for *all* samples (even left lesion), with the discrepancies equal to about 1 standard deviation or more for three of the groups (males and females with right lesions, and males with left lesions).

Reanalysis of Old Data

Meyer and Jones (1957) presented data for a group of 31 temporal lobe epileptics who were tested on Wechsler-Bellevue, Form I, about 1 week prior to a temporal lobectomy, and on Form II about 1 month following surgery. Meyer and Jones ignored potential gender differences, even though they systematically evaluated the impact of other key variables (age, age of onset, duration of seizures) on the size of the observed "verbal deficit" for patients with left and right temporal lobectomies. Fortunately, they did give enough information about each member of the sample to permit other researchers to compute gender differences.

Table 9.6 presented separate results for males and females based on their postoperative IQs on Wechsler-Bellevue, Form II, which I computed from the raw data in one of Meyer and Jones's (1957) tables. Although sample sizes were quite small for the separate groups of men and women with left- or right-brain lesions (ranging from 5 to 11), the data support a gender-related trend: Among patients with left temporal lobectomies, males showed a sizable P > V discrepancy (about 11 points), but females did not; in contrast, V > P differences for patients with right-brain lesions were larger for females (about 7 points) than for males (3 points).

These findings are clouded by the fact that some patients demonstrated bilateral EEG foci. Whereas Bornstein and Matarazzo (1984) chose to eliminate these bilateral cases in their review of gender differences, I do not agree. Meyer and Jones (1957) indicated that each bilateral patient had a "marked predominance of one focus" (p. 761); postoperative IQs were analyzed, and quite obviously all patients in the "left lesion" group had their left temporal lobe removed while every right-lesion patient had his or her right lobe removed; the elimination of 13 out of 31 patients leaves samples of only 2 to 8 patients for examining gender-related differences.

Inglis and Lawson (1981) conducted a more ingenious analysis of Meyer and Jones's (1957) data. They used regression equations developed from the relationship between the two forms of the Wechsler-Bellevue to predict each patient's expected postoperative V- and P-IQ on Form II based on his or her preoperative score on Form I. They predicted from the hypothesized asymmetry of the brain that patients who underwent a left temporal lobectomy would obtain significantly lower Verbal IQs on Form II than would be expected from their preoperative score, and that those who had their right temporal lobe surgically removed would have a significantly lower than expected postoperative Performance IQ.

This pattern was found quite clearly for males, but *not at all* for females. Inglis and Lawson's (1981) valuable finding of an interaction with sex, coupled with their interest in McGlone's (1977, 1978) research, impelled them to conduct an extremely well-designed, controlled comparison of the V–P discrepancies of 20 male and 20 female adults with unilateral brain damage (Inglis et al., 1982), and to evaluate the variable of gender in a carefully thought-out meta-analysis of numerous studies of V–P discrepancy and left- versus right-brain lesions (Inglis & Lawson, 1982).

Inglis and Lawson's Study of Gender Differences

As noted previously, Inglis et al. (1982) found results that closely paralleled McGlone's (1977, 1978) dramatic gender-related interaction. They controlled for type of brain damage by including in their sample only right-handed, nonaphasic patients who had experienced a single thrombotic cerebrovascular accident (stroke); whose medical condition had stabilized; and who had experienced no other neurological disorder. Each group (i.e., males with right-brain lesions, females with left-brain lesions, etc.) was equally divided among new patients (the stroke occurred within the last 6 months) and old patients (the stroke occurred 1 to 12 years prior to testing). The groups were matched with each other and with a control group of 20 medical patients (10 males and 10 females with no symptoms or signs of neurological disorders) on the variables of age, education, and familial history of lefthandedness. Further, the brain-damaged samples were matched almost exactly on an index of severity.

The well-matched groups of stroke victims yielded striking gender differences. For males, V–P discrepancies exceeded 1 standard deviation for the left- and right-damaged samples, in the precise directions predicted by cerebral organization research. Females with left hemisphere lesions showed no V–P discrepancy, while those with right hemisphere lesions displayed only a small (4½ point) V > P difference. The interaction involving scale (V versus P), gender, and side of lesion proved to be highly significant ($p < .0001$). As expected, the control group had V–P discrepancies of approximately zero.

Meta-Analyses of Gender Difference Studies

In their meta-analysis of gender differences, Inglis and Lawson (1982) identified numerous Wechsler-Bellevue and WAIS studies of patients with unilateral brain damage that reported the proportions of males and females constituting the samples. They identified 15 such publications, including 3 that provided separate data for males and females. The authors then studied the 22 samples reported on in the 15 studies, computing the percentage of males in each group. These percentages ranged from zero for the all female samples to 100 for the all male samples and were spread fairly well across the entire range.

Inglis and Lawson (1982) hypothesized that P > V for left-damaged patients would be higher for males than females, and that V > P for right-damaged patients would likewise be higher for males than females. Consequently, they predicted significant positive correlations between the percentage of males in left-lesioned samples and the mean P > V discrepancies for those samples. Analogously, they anticipated significant positive correlation between the percentage of males in right-lesioned samples and the mean V > P discrepancies for those samples. Their reasoning was sensible: If males tend to show the predicted relationship between V–P IQ difference and left- versus right-brain damage, but females do not, the samples with many females should evidence smaller V–P differences in the predicted direction than the samples with few females.

Inglis and Lawson's (1982) meta-analysis supported their hypotheses. For left brain–damaged adults, mean P > V discrepancies correlated .53 with percentage of males in the samples; for right brain–damaged patients, mean V > P difference scores correlated .46 with percentage of males. When the patient samples are combined, V–P differences correlated .48 with the percentage of males. All of these correlations are statistically significant. The results indicate that gender of the brain-damaged patients accounts for about 25% of the variance in the V–P IQ discrepancy scores. In view of the impact of other variables on the size of V–P discrepancy for adults with unilateral brain damage (e.g., age, precise location of lesion,

cause of damage), the relationships found by Inglis and Lawson (1982) for the variable of gender are substantial, noteworthy, and clinically valuable.

Bornstein and Matarazzo (1982) reviewed a large number of Wechsler-Bellevue and WAIS studies with patients having unilateral brain damage, paying particular attention to Inglis and Lawson's (1982) conclusions about gender differences, but also addressing other variables like location of the lesion and diagnostic etiology. They concluded that there is support for lowered V-IQ in patients with left damage, and a corresponding lower P-IQ for right-damaged adults. However, they conceded that "these laterality findings will more likely be seen in male patients than in female patients" (p. 329).

Bornstein and Matarazzo (1982) pointed out that two of the major negative studies regarding laterality of brain damage and V–P difference, the large-scale investigations conducted by Smith (1966a, 1966b) and by Todd et al. (1977), had proportions of females that were in the 35–40 range. They hypothesized that the high percentages of females in these studies may have been partially responsible for the negative findings, although they noted that data provided by Todd et al. (1977) make the "gender" explanation for that study unlikely. Indeed, Todd et al. conducted an analysis of variance using gender as an independent variable and found a nonsignificant interaction between gender and discrepancy score.

Bornstein and Matarazzo's (1984) second review of Wechsler studies of brain-damaged adults replicated Inglis and Lawson's (1982) methodology and computed correlations between the percentage of males and mean V–P IQ discrepancies. They also included additional samples not identified by Inglis and Lawson and made some decisions different from those of Inglis and Lawson regarding the elimination of overlapping data and the exclusion of patients with evidence of bilateral damage.

Overall, Bornstein and Matarazzo computed coefficients based on 28 samples of patients with unilateral brain damage. They obtained significant coefficients, but their values were lower than the correlations of about .50 reported by Inglis and Lawson. They found a coefficient of .42 between the percentage of males and mean P > V for left-damage samples and a correlation of .39 for the right-lesion groups.

Bornstein and Matarazzo concluded from their results that only about 15% of the variance in the V–P discrepancies of adults with unilateral brain damage can be attributed to the patient's gender, rather than the estimate of 25% that emerged from Inglis and Lawson's (1982) meta-analysis. Bornstein and Matarazzo (1984) stood by their earlier statement that lateralization of brain lesion is more associated with predictable V–P differences in men than women, but they cautioned against overinterpretation of the significant correlations found in the retrospective studies conducted by them and by Inglis and Lawson (1982).

They noted that the percentage of men in each sample is but one of numerous variables on which the samples differ; they also vary on the etiology of the lesions (with most samples composed of heterogeneous groups of patients), acuteness versus chronicity of lesions, inclusion or exclusion of dysphasic patients, and nature of the neurodiagnostic criteria for selecting patients. Regarding the latter point, Bornstein and Matarazzo (1984) stress that the more recent studies have had the benefit of modern technology, such as application of computerized axial tomography (CAT) scans, which has cast some doubt on the accuracy of the classification of patients as "purely" right or left damaged in some of the earlier investigations.

Snow, Freedman, and Ford (1986) entered into the debate over gender differences, concluding that such differences tended to characterize Wechsler-Bellevue but *not* WAIS studies. They reported a nonsignificant .37 correlation between the percentage of males and the size of V–P IQ discrepancy for 16 samples tested on the WAIS, compared to a significant

(.05 level) correlation of .58 for 12 samples tested on the Wechsler-Bellevue. However, their conclusion is unwarranted. Appropriate methodology does not depend on one coefficient falling just short of statistical significance and the other one emerging as significant. *The coefficients must be shown to be significantly different from each other to support their conclusion.* The values do not differ sufficiently to justify Snow et al.'s interpretation of the data.

Nonetheless, Snow et al. are correct in trying to understand variables that might interact with gender to account for the male–female differences observed in the literature. These authors also showed that the percentage of males correlated about .90 with age, education, and chronicity in Wechsler-Bellevue studies, although these findings were not replicated in the WAIS investigations. The ultimate impact of Snow et al.'s (1986) results is to remind researchers and clinicians that the best way to study the relationship of *any* variable to the impact of unilateral brain damage is to hold as many other variables constant as is reasonably possible, given the practical constraints on neuropsychological research.

Research Issues in the Investigation of Gender Differences

I concur with Bornstein and Matarazzo's (1984) plea for "a comprehensive prospective study that, at the very least, controls for a number of potentially important lesion-related variables" (p. 709) as a means of delineating the role of gender in V–P discrepancies in patients with unilateral brain damage. However, in the absence of such a landmark study and of "a large scale retrospective study with enough patients in the sample to permit statistical control of such potentially relevant variables . . . by involving a number of large medical centers in a single, coordinated effort" (Bornstein & Matarazzo, 1984, p. 709), we must try to understand the variable of gender as best we can based on the considerable data base available. I disagree emphatically with Jacklin's (1989) strong suggestion to stop conducting research on gender-related cognitive differences, a point discussed on pages 157–158.

Meta-analysis (Bornstein & Matarazzo, 1984; Inglis & Lawson, 1982; Snow et al., 1986) provides one useful research technique. Another is to compare the V–P differences of males and females only from those reasonably well-controlled investigations that included both sexes in approximately equal numbers. Inglis and Lawson (1982) did compare V–P discrepancies for separate groups of male and female patients, combining data from several studies. However, they failed to match the male and female samples on any pertinent variables. For example, their aggregated sample of male patients included data from studies comprising only males. Consequently, the sample of 170 males included a group like Black's (1974a) 21-year-old veterans with missile wounds; no similar group was included among the 55 female patients. The latter sample was composed only of temporal lobe epileptics (spanning a wide age range) or elderly stroke victims. Inglis and Lawson's (1982) male–female comparisons were therefore contaminated by nearly all the intervening variables noted by Bornstein and Matarazzo (1984).

Aggregated Data From Gender Difference Studies

Table 10.1 presents data from eight studies that included males and females in approximately equal proportions. Most of these studies were extremely well designed, controlling for differences between the sexes on variables like age, education, nature of lesion, and recency of lesion. Despite Snow et al.'s (1986) cautions to the contrary, data were combined across instruments, as the Wechsler-Bellevue, WAIS, and WAIS-R were all used for one or more studies. The instrument given has, nonetheless, been held constant since the same Wechsler test was administered to men and women in each separate study.

To a reasonable degree, the variables of concern to Bornstein and Matarazzo (1984) and Snow et al. (1986) were controlled in the male–female comparisons presented in Table 10.1. The neurodiagnostic criteria that were used in each study, whether primitive or high-tech, were applied equally to males and females. Similarly, variables such as age, education, recency of lesion, and etiology were not appreciably different for the men and women within each separate investigation. Therefore, the data shown in Table 10.1 come as close as is presently feasible to the type of coordinated effort that Bornstein and Matarazzo have urged.

As shown in the table, each gender is represented by more than 115 patients with left hemisphere lesions and more than 125 patients with right hemisphere lesions; data are based on 245 women and 263 men with unilateral brain damage. Taken separately, five of the eight studies showed apparent gender differences in the V–P discrepancies for patients with lesions in each hemisphere; only the investigations by Snow and Sheese (1985), Bornstein (1984), and Whelan and Walker (1988) failed to discern meaningful gender-related findings.

Taken together, P > V was 6.2 points for males with left lesions but only 1.6 points for females with left lesions. Similarly, patients with lesions in the right hemisphere evidenced larger V > P differences if they were males (11.8 points) than if they were females (6.7 points).

I believe that the accumulated data in Table 10.1 show strong support for the alleged gender-related interaction between side of lesion and direction of V–P difference. For both sexes, damage to the right hemisphere produced more striking V–P discrepancies than damage to the left hemisphere. But for males, the V > P of about 12 points for right-lesioned patients is nearly twice the value of 6½ points for females.

The 6-point P > V difference for left-damaged adult males does not measure up to the opposite discrepancy for right-damaged adult males, but the observed difference still gives good support to the predicted hypothesis of depressed Verbal IQs for patients with lesions in their left hemispheres. For females, however, the P > V discrepancy of less than 2 points for those with left hemisphere lesions does *not* support the age-old hypothesis.

In sum, women apparently have a different cerebral organization than men, and may differ in the asymmetry of their brains. However, the reason for the interaction with gender is far less obvious than the fact of it.

TABLE 10.1   V-P IQ discrepancies for separate groups of males and females displaying lesions localized in the left or right hemispheres

| | FEMALES | | | | MALES | | | |
| | LEFT LESIONS | | RIGHT LESIONS | | LEFT LESIONS | | RIGHT LESIONS | |
Study	N	V–P	N	V–P	N	V–P	N	V–P
Wechsler-Bellevue								
Meyer & Jones (1957)								
Temporal lobe epileptics (postoperative)	9	–2.0	6	+7.0	11	–11.0	5	+3.0
Herring & Reitan (1986)								
Tumor (2/3) and Stroke (1/3)	24	–4.1	24	+3.2	24	–8.0	24	+8.8
Lansdell (1968)								
Temporal lobe epileptics (postoperative)	8	–4.9	20	–3.4	11	–8.8	13	+2.2
WAIS								
McGlone (1978)								
Stroke (2/3) and Tumor (1/3)	20	–0.1	17	+4.2	23	–11.2	17	+13.5
Inglis et al. (1982)								
Stroke	20	0.0	20	+5.0	20	–15.0	20	+19.0
Snow & Sheese (1985)								
Stroke	5	+8.0	12	+22.7	14	+13.9	14	+19.8
Whelan & Walker (1988)								
Tumor	16	+0.8	14	+13.9	13	+2.7	21	+10.5
WAIS-R								
Bornstein (1984)	15	–5.5	15	+11.1	17	–4.9	16	+10.6
Weighted Mean	**117**	**–1.6**	**128**	**+6.7**	**133**	**–6.2**	**130**	**+11.8**

NOTE: V–P equals mean V-IQ minus mean P-IQ.

Proposed Explanations of the Interaction With Gender

McGlone's Asymmetry Hypothesis

McGlone (1977) found a much greater proportion of aphasics among her male than female patients with left hemisphere damage (48% versus 13%), a result that characterized both her tumor and stroke patients; she also found greater verbal intelligence deficits and verbal memory loss in her male than female patients following left-brain lesions. Further, McGlone discovered that females with left lesions and females with right lesions performed about equally well on visual-spatial and perceptual tasks usually associated with right hemisphere function: Block Design, Thurstone's (1938) Spatial Relations test requiring mental rotations, and a test of immediate memory of photographed faces.

In marked contrast, males with right-brain damage were far outstripped on these spatial tasks by nonaphasic males with left hemisphere lesions. McGlone (1978) concluded: "For the women, cognitive deficits tended to be less severe and less specific compared to men" (p. 126). Her proposed explanations for the gender-related findings in her investigations (McGlone, 1977) are (a) a "greater degree of bilateral speech representation in women" (p. 787) than in men, (b) "sex differences in the underlying neural organization of speech processes within the left hemisphere" (p. 789), and (c) greater control of the right hemisphere in women (compared to men) over certain verbal functions.

McGlone's (1977) conclusion is "that asymmetrical specialization of the two cerebral hemispheres is less characteristic of adult female right-handers than adult male right-handers" (p. 790). She reiterated this conclusion in her review and analysis of pertinent investigations (McGlone, 1980), although a number of her peers disputed predictions that follow logically from her explanation of the gender differences in brain-damaged patients (e.g., Hier & Kaplan, 1980; Kinsbourne, 1980).

Inglis and Lawson's Emphasis on Female Processing of Performance Tasks

Inglis and Lawson (1982) disagree with McGlone's (1977, 1978, 1980) explanations of the gender differences based on the results of empirical analyses that they conducted as part of their meta-analysis of pertinent Wechsler studies. They developed regression equations to predict the V- and P-IQs of male and female adults with left or right lesions, based on the association of the percentage of men in each study to the magnitude of the separate IQs. Table 10.2 presents the results of these analyses.

As shown in Table 10.2, the predicted Verbal IQs of men and women with right hemisphere damage are about equal, as are the predicted Verbal IQs of men and women with left hemisphere damage. In striking contrast are the predicted Performance IQs of the neurological patients: Among left-lesion cases, men outscored women by 6 points on the Performance Scale; among right-lesion cases, women outscored men by the same amount.

Inglis and Lawson (1982) then attempted to cross-validate these findings by comparing the V- and P-IQs of all-female samples with unilateral brain damage to the V- and P-IQs of all-male samples with unilateral brain damage; the results of this second type of analysis fully supported the results of the regression analysis. They interpreted their double-barreled findings as contradicting McGlone's assertions, and instead favor a quite different explanation of the gender differences observed in the Wechsler V–P studies of patients with lesions to the left or right hemisphere.

Inglis and Lawson (1982) cite the equal Verbal IQs of males and females having the same localization of brain damage (i.e., left or right hemisphere) as providing strong support for the *similarity* of how the two sexes process information when solving Wechsler's Verbal subtests. Males and females differ, according to these researchers, in how they apply strategies to Wechsler's Performance tasks. They believe

TABLE 10.2   Results of Inglis and Lawson's (1982) regression analyses for male and female subjects with left and right brain lesions

	Predicted Verbal IQ		Predicted Performance IQ	
	Left Lesion	*Right Lesion*	*Left Lesion*	*Right Lesion*
Males	84	98	94	87
Females	86	97	88	93
Difference	−2	+1	+6	−6

that their analyses suggest "that the functional organization of the cerebral hemispheres in women may *not* be more symmetrical than it is in men" (p. 679). Inglis and Lawson (1982) offer the following model to explain the gender differences in the Wechsler V–P/lesion studies:

The Verbal Scale items are left hemisphere, verbal problems for both men and women. The Performance Scale items, however, tend to be processed as left hemisphere tasks (i.e., more verbally) by women, whereas men use mainly right hemisphere (i.e., more spatial, nonverbal) processing in their solution. Because women may solve the items in the Performance Scale through the use of a more verbal strategy than men, left lesion women show a greater deficit on this scale. As right brain-damaged women also process these items verbally, and because their verbal skills remain relatively intact, they thus show a lesser impairment on the Performance Scale (p. 680).

Inglis and Lawson (1982) further argued against McGlone's (1977) "less asymmetry for women" hypothesis by refuting her finding of more aphasics among male than female patients with left-brain damage. They cited evidence from Hier and Kaplan (1980), who claim that McGlone's (1977) findings with a small sample are inconsistent with the clinical experience of most neurologists or speech pathologists. Hier and Kaplan also presented data from three large-scale studies (total $N = 767$) that showed male aphasics to outnumber female aphasics only

slightly. Inglis and Lawson also believed that McGlone's stress on the gender-related nature of aphasia should lead to clear-cut male–female differences on the Verbal Scale for patients with left hemisphere lesions. As indicated in the previous summary of Inglis and Lawson's data, this does not seem to be the case.

Inglis and Lawson's Failure to Focus on V–P Discrepancies

Regardless of Inglis and Lawson's (1982) careful, intelligent analyses and the cogent arguments put forth by them and other respected researchers (Bryden, 1979, 1980; Harris, 1980; Sherman, 1978, 1980) in support of the "different strategies" used by men and women, I disagree with their conclusions. First, I do not believe that it is particularly meaningful or appropriate to compare *just* the Verbal IQs (or Performance IQs) of males and females having brain damage lateralized to one hemisphere. We have no knowledge of premorbid intelligence and therefore cannot evaluate how much the Verbal or Performance IQ has fallen as a result of the brain lesion. The males and females with left hemisphere damage may have equal Verbal IQs, but that tells us little about the specific impact of the neurological impairment on verbal intelligence for men and women.

I believe that it is essential to consider *both* the Verbal and Performance Scales when estimating the deleterious effects of brain lesions on intellectual functioning. The use of both scales provides a built-in control regarding a patient's relative loss of mental function. In effect, the V–P IQ comparison allows each patient to serve as his or her own control. We simply begin with the assumption that the mean premorbid difference between the Verbal and Performance IQs equals zero for any particular patient group. The mean V–P discrepancy for a sample then provides a simple index of loss of function in verbal or nonverbal intelligence, a loss that is presumably due to the brain damage.

This index measures *relative loss,* since it is possible (indeed likely) that brain damage to either hemisphere will affect intellectual performance, at least to some extent, on both of Wechsler's scales. Yet in the absence of good estimates of premorbid intelligence, and in view of the great difficulty in applying ideal experimental design to these studies (you can't exactly "assign" patients to undergo left or right brain lesions, and finding good nonneurological controls is almost impossible), the V–P IQ index of relative loss of function becomes quite valuable.

Looking at Verbal and Performance IQs separately has too many experimental pitfalls to merit much interpretive generalization. Also, Inglis and Lawson (1982) compared the Verbal IQs of males and females with left lesions using two questionable techniques: (a) one set of data used *estimates* of these IQs, via regression equations, where the predictor (percentage of males) accounted for much less than 50% of the variance in the criterion; and (b) the second set of data compared unequal samples of men and women, samples that differed in key variables besides gender, such as age and type of lesion (see p. 307).

Premorbid V–P IQ Differences of Brain-Damaged Samples

There is a legitimate question regarding my assertions of the value of comparisons based on the V–P discrepancy: Is it reasonable to assume that the mean premorbid V–P difference of any given sample equals zero? Certainly that assumption would not hold for any particular *individual.* As discussed at length previously (see pp. 265–269), it is quite common for normal individuals to have substantial differences in their V- and P-IQs. But it's a different story for *groups.* The entire WAIS-R normative sample of 1,880 individuals had mean V- and P-IQs that were virtually equal (99.8 and 99.9, respectively). That equality is predictable because the test was normed to have mean Verbal IQs and mean Performance IQs of 100.

However, the equal V- and P-IQs also hold for separate groups of males and females in the standardization sample (Matarazzo et al., 1986): Males (mean V-IQ = 100.9, mean P-IQ = 100.6, mean V–P discrepancy = +0.3); females (means of 98.7, 99.2, and −0.5, respectively). Further, separate groups of men and women do not have sizable V–P discrepancies even when grouped by education level. Years of education completed is related more closely to V–P differences than any other background variable, as discussed in chapter 6. Matarazzo et al. (1986) provide the data in Table 10.3 on Verbal–Performance IQ differences for men and women with different educational levels.

These data show that the mean V–P IQ discrepancy is clearly related to education level; adults with lower education levels score a bit higher on the Performance Scale, whereas more

TABLE 10.3 Verbal–Performance IQ differences for men and women as a function of education

Years of Education	V Minus P Males	V Minus P Females
0–7	−2.5	−2.3
8	−2.3	−3.6
9–11	−1.5	−2.0
12	+0.3	−0.4
13–15	+2.3	+1.8
16+	+5.0	+3.7

NOTE: Data are from Matarazzo et al. (1986).

highly educated adults tend to do better on the Verbal Scale (see pp. 337–342 for a more thorough discussion of this topic). However, these differences are most notable for the extremes of educational background, i.e., 0–8 or 16+ years of schooling, reaching as high as +5 points. As indicated in Tables 9.6 and 9.7, very few samples of brain-damaged patients come from either educational extreme. Most samples had a mean number of years completed within the 10 to 12 range.

As shown above, the expected V–P IQ difference for such samples is, at most, 2 points in favor of Performance IQ. But since values are presented for a combination of grades 9, 10, and 11, it is reasonable to assume that the largest differences are for grade 9 and that the expected differences for samples with 10–12 years of education are between zero and 1 point. Therefore, it is a most logical and empirically defensible assumption to expect brain-damaged samples with a moderate amount of education to have had a mean premorbid V–P IQ discrepancy of about zero; the V–P difference for patients with left or right damage is thus an excellent estimate of a group's relative loss of function following neurological impairment.

The Inglis/Lawson Hypothesis and Subtest Profiles

Even if one grants that the V–P difference, not a simple comparison of one IQ at a time, is the essential unit of study, it is still necessary to refute Inglis and Lawson's contention that the Performance Scale alone accounts for the different V–P findings for men and women with lateralized lesions. Some evidence against their notion comes from subtest data that they presented for male and female stroke victims (Inglis et al., 1982). These data are presented in Table 10.4, which compares the scaled-score profiles of males and females with left lesions, and of males and females with right lesions.

As indicated, men and women with left lesions differed consistently and systematically on

Verbal as well as Performance subtests: Women with left hemisphere damage scored about 1 scaled-score point *higher* than men with the same type of damage on Verbal tasks, but scored about 1½ points *lower* than the men on Performance subtests. The identical pattern of identical magnitude—only in reverse—occurred for men and women with right-brain lesions. Thus, men and women differed a bit more on Performance than Verbal subtests, but only slightly more. Table 10.4 clearly shows that subtests on *both* of Wechsler's scales are instrumental in leading to smaller than predicted P > V IQ discrepancies for females with left lesions, and smaller than predicted V > P differences for females with right lesions.

These findings are more in agreement with McGlone's (1977, 1978, 1980) interpretation that female brains are organized with less cerebral asymmetry than are the brains of males than with Inglis and Lawson's (1982) conclusions that women depend on verbal strategies to solve Performance subtests. Also inconsistent with Inglis and Lawson's reasoning are the results of some analyses conducted with the normal standardization sample.

Evidence from Correlational and Factor Analyses, by Gender

If Inglis and Lawson (1982) are correct in their hypothesis that women and men solve nonverbal problems differently, with women demonstrating "a preference for verbal, left hemisphere approaches to problem solving . . ., even when these problems are intended, by the examiner, to be nonverbal, right hemisphere tasks" (p. 681), then other logical hypotheses would follow. First, the Inglis/Lawson hypothesis suggests that Verbal and Performance IQs should be more correlated in women than men, since women presumably apply similar strategies for tasks on both scales. A higher correlation for women would mean that V–P discrepancies should tend to be smaller for women; their base

TABLE 10.4 Mean scaled scores on the WAIS earned by males and females with unilateral brain damage due to stroke

Subtest	LEFT LESION			RIGHT LESION		
	Males (N=20)	Females (N=20)	Mean Diff.	Males (N=20)	Females (N=20)	Mean Diff.
Verbal						
I	8.0	8.2	−0.2	11.4	10.3	+1.1
C	6.8	7.6	−0.8	10.8	10.3	+0.5
A	7.8	8.2	−0.4	11.0	9.1	+1.9
S	7.4	9.5	−2.1	11.0	9.8	+1.2
DSp	7.2	8.4	−1.2	11.4	10.4	+1.0
V	7.5	8.2	−0.7	11.8	11.0	+0.8
Peformance						
PC	10.8	9.2	+1.6	9.8	10.8	−1.0
BD	9.6	7.4	+2.2	7.3	9.4	−2.1
PA	10.2	8.7	+1.5	8.0	8.6	−0.6
OA	9.0	8.2	+0.8	7.0	9.0	−2.0
Mean						
Verbal	7.4	8.4	−1.0	11.2	10.2	+1.0
Performance	9.9	8.4	+1.5	8.0	9.4	−1.4

NOTE: Mean Diff. = mean for males minus mean for females. Data are from Inglis et al. (1982). Digit Symbol was not administered to any of the patients.

rates of occurrence should be substantially different than for men.

Second, it follows from Inglis and Lawson's speculations that the factor structure for males and females should differ markedly. Clear-cut, separate verbal and nonverbal dimensions should emerge for men, but the distinction should be cloudy for women; in particular, Performance subtests would have far higher loadings on the Verbal Comprehension factor for women than men.

To address the Inglis/Lawson hypothesis by correlational techniques, Kaufman, McLean, and Reynolds (in press *b*) computed coefficients of correlation between V- and P-IQs for separate groups of men and women from the standard-ization sample. They divided the normative group into four age levels and discovered that V-IQ and P-IQ correlated about equally well for men (average *r* = .72) and women (average *r* = .73). Coefficients ranged from .69 to .77 for males and from .68 to .77 for females; none of the comparisons at the four age groups reached statistical significance. These findings clearly contradicted Inglis and Lawson's hypothesis that women tend to use verbal processing to solve nonverbal problems.

Table 10.5 summarizes base-rate data for V–P IQ discrepancies separately for men and women, based on comprehensive tables provided by Matarazzo et al. (1986) for the total stan-dardization sample. As indicated, the base rates

TABLE 10.5   Verbal–Performance IQ discrepancies of a given magnitude or greater, for separate groups of males and females

Size of V–P Discrepancy (Regardless of Direction)	MALES (N=940)		FEMALES (N=940)	
	N	%	N	%
5	631	67.1	615	65.4
10	368	39.1	343	36.5
15	176	18.7	156	16.6
20	89	9.5	82	8.7
25	28	3.0	27	2.9

NOTE: Data are based on tables presented by Matarazzo, Bornstein, McDermott, and Noonan (1986).

for males and females are rather similar. For example, about 19% of males and 17% of females have V–P differences (regardless of direction) of 15 points or more; about 3% of each sex have discrepancies of 25 or more points. Although the small differences in percentages for men and women are all in the direction predicted by Inglis and Lawson's (1982) hypothesis, the similarities in the distributions far outweigh the slight differences. The results in Table 10.5 are contrary to Inglis and Lawson's suggestion that women, more so than men, use verbal strategies to solve nonverbal problems.

In chapter 8 (pages 241–242 and Table 8.2) separate factor analyses for men and women suggested that females (more so than males) *do* tend to apply verbal strategies to tasks intended by Wechsler to be nonverbal. Such a finding would support Inglis and Lawson's claims. But those factor analyses were based on a wide age range (16–74 years), perhaps masking age-related trends in the data.

Table 10.6 shows the results of WAIS-R factor analyses conducted for separate groups of men and women at four age levels: 16–19, 20–34, 35–54, and 55–74 (Kaufman, McLean, & Reynolds, in press *a*). Overall, the factor

structures for men and women across the age range are extremely similar. Coefficients of congruence for males and females across the four age groups ranged from .972 to .995 for the Verbal Comprehension and Perceptual Organization factors (Kaufman et al., in press *a*), astonishingly high values.

The most pertinent test of the Inglis/Lawson hypothesis concerns the loadings of the Performance subtests on the Verbal Comprehension factors. Their hypothesis predicts that nonverbal tasks should have higher Verbal loadings for females than males, since women purportedly use verbal strategies to solve nonverbal problems. These crucial loadings (shown in boxes in Table 10.6) are, indeed, higher for females at ages 16–19 and 20–34. For women in this age range Picture Arrangement is decidedly a *verbal* task, and Picture Completion has a strong verbal component.

However, women at ages 16–34 do *not* differ from men in the application of verbal strategies during Block Design, Object Assembly, and Digit Symbol. Furthermore, an *opposite* trend is observed at ages 35–54: Men use verbal strategies far more than women when solving nonverbal items. (Three of the five Performance subtests loaded in the .50s on Verbal Compre-

TABLE 10.6 Varimax rotated two-factor WAIS-R solutions for males and females at four age groups

| | AGES 16–19 | | | | AGES 20–34 | | | | AGES 35–54 | | | | AGES 55–74 | | | |
| | Males | | Females | | Males | | Females | | Males | | Females | | Males | | Females | |
Subtest	VC	PO	VC	PO	VC	PO	VC	PO	VC	PO	VC	PO	VC	PO	VC	PO
Verbal																
I	81*	32	84*	20	80*	33	80*	27	74*	36	80*	36	80*	26	78*	38
DSp	35	48*	48*	23	50*	25	51*	34	57*	29	52*	42*	52*	36	41*	50*
V	82*	37	85*	28	85*	30	88*	31	89*	28	87*	31	90*	25	82*	36
A	54*	51*	64*	39	64*	37	59*	46*	59*	43*	54*	57*	61*	37	55*	53*
C	72*	32	71*	36	72*	34	73*	33	70*	26	80*	32	75*	33	78*	36
S	72*	33	76*	30	57*	46*	70*	36	68*	39	76*	35	71*	42*	67*	49*
Performance																
PC	34	47*	43*	44*	34	66*	48*	62*	52*	52*	49*	53*	39	62*	45*	65*
PA	31	37	49*	26	35	55*	61*	34	52*	41*	51*	50*	44*	60*	36	53*
BD	22	76*	28	85*	36	72*	29	80*	42*	73*	30	78*	30	76*	34	79*
OA	23	62*	18	58*	21	69*	25	72*	26	87*	21	67*	17	78*	23	65*
DSy	39	52*	42*	45*	38	37	34	37	56*	38	33	58*	39	63*	40*	52*

NOTE: VC = Verbal Comprehension; PO = Perceptual Organization. Decimal points are omitted. Asterisks mark loadings of .40 and above. Data are from Kaufman et al. (in press *a*). The loadings shown in boxes indicate the degree to which each performance subtest has a verbal component for males and females across the 16- to 74-year range.

hension for these middle-aged men.) In addition, at ages 55–74, *neither sex* applied verbal strategies to Performance tasks to any marked degree.

Thus, an overview of the WAIS-R factor structures for males and females attests to the *similarity* of these patterns. Where differences occur, they are as likely to disagree as to agree with predictions made on the basis of Inglis and Lawson's (1982) hypothesis. In fact, only one instance gives the Inglis/Lawson hypothesis good support: *black* females, compared to black males, a topic that is treated in the section on race differences in brain-damage studies (see pages 317–322 and Table 10.9).

McGlone Hypothesis Versus Inglis/Lawson Hypothesis

The results of empirical analyses discussed in the preceding section and shown in Tables 10.4, 10.5, and 10.6 generally contradict the Inglis/Lawson hypothesis and give more support to McGlone's (1977, 1978, 1980) notion of less asymmetry in the cerebral organization of female versus male brains; Lezak (1983) also concludes from her review of pertinent studies that "[l]ateralization of verbal and visuospatial functions to the left and right hemispheres, respectively, tends to be greater for males than for females" (p. 220).

The present results likewise do not support Sherman's (1978) "bent-twig" hypothesis, which posits that the quicker maturation of females leads to a verbal precocity that "bends the twig" towards a female preference for using verbal cognitive strategies to solve either verbal, or supposedly nonverbal, intellectual problems.

Support for greater lateralization among males than females comes from a variety of sources, although the results of the studies are certainly not unanimous (Springer & Deutsch, 1985). Witelson (1976) studied laterality in children by administering a haptic test to children aged 6 to 13 years. She had the children try to identify objects by touch, using their right or

left hands. Brain asymmetry would predict that a nonverbal skill like identification of an object is largely in the domain of the right hemisphere; consequently, children's left (contralateral) hand should be significantly better than their right hand at object identification. This hypothesis was borne out for boys but not for girls, suggesting that the supposed greater laterality of males than females is present in childhood.

Several studies using techniques like verbal dichotic listening or tachistoscopic presentation of stimuli to the left or right visual field have found gender differences in cerebral organization, usually favoring the greater asymmetry of males. To Springer and Deutsch (1985): "The strength of the case . . . rests on the diversity of methodologies (clinical studies, dichotic listening, tachistoscopic presentation, and electrophysiology) that point to the same conclusion: females are less lateralized than males" (p. 183). They conclude: "A review of the studies that do not support this conclusion shows that most report no differences between the sexes. It is a rare study that reports sex differences in the direction of greater lateralization in females. This consistency suggests that there are true differences that are small in magnitude" (p. 183).

One reason for the failure of researchers to consistently find gender differences in cerebral organization may be that the difference resides in a *potential* for females to compensate for damage or dysfunction. Perhaps women tend to solve problems in a manner similar to men under ordinary circumstances. However, when the circumstances are extraordinary, such as having the type of brain dysfunction that might cause a learning disability or having a lateralized brain lesion associated with depressed Verbal or Performance IQ, females may be better equipped to spontaneously compensate for the deficit.

Many more boys than girls are learning disabled. Possibly girls respond better to the brain dysfunction; conceivably, girls may be able to compensate for a kind of brain dysfunction that in boys would lead to a learning disability. Even LD females may have better compensatory strategies than LD males. Indirect evidence for this hypothesis comes from an examination of subtest profiles of LD children, adolescents, and young adults. Some research (discussed in some depth on pages 450–451) suggests that the so-called ACID profile associated with learning disabilities holds only for males; females perform poorly on three of the four ACID subtests, but tend to do quite well on Coding/Digit Symbol. The latter task has elements of both left hemisphere and right hemisphere processing and may be amenable to compensation from an intact part of the brain. Similarly, females with left hemisphere lesions may show a smaller deficit in V-IQ than males with left lesions (and, analogously, females with right lesions may show a smaller deficit in P-IQ) because *subsequent* to the damage they may use their capacity for compensation when solving verbal (or nonverbal) problems.

This greater flexibility and capacity for compensation may result from a superior ability of females to demonstrate interhemispheric integration. Denckla (1974) has speculated that dyslexics may have faulty interhemispheric integration, and Witelson (1976, 1977) has also stressed the value of good integration for success in school-oriented activities. Since girls are far less likely than boys to be dyslexic, and women with lateralized lesions evidence less predictable V-P profiles than men with right versus left lesions, it may be that females surpass males in the ability to integrate the two cerebral hemispheres. Certainly cerebral integration is an important aspect of a complex psychomotor task like Digit Symbol.

Greater interhemispheric integration would be a plausible mechanism to explain McGlone's (1977, 1978, 1980) suggestion that females have more lateralization of speech functions than males, and it also may relate to Inglis and Lawson's (1982) claim that women have a greater capacity than men to solve nonverbal problems via verbal mediation. Certainly, if females really do have a more efficient system for integrating strategies from the two hemispheres, one would

expect women to demonstrate less cerebral asymmetry than men, at least under a circumstance (like an acute brain lesion) that prevents the application of an optimal problem-solving strategy.

Despite the evidence presented here, the support for McGlone's position in preference to the Inglis/Lawson hypothesis is speculative and tentative. Most of the evidence is indirect, and it is unwise either to discount the criticisms of McGlone's (1980) conclusions (Hier & Kaplan, 1980; Inglis & Lawson, 1982; Kinsbourne, 1980) or to ignore the "verbal strategy" hypothesis advanced by Inglis and Lawson and by others (Bryden, 1980; Harris, 1980; Sherman, 1978). What is needed is a series of investigations of normal and brain-damaged males and females that evaluate directly and systematically possible gender differences in the application of verbal mediation to nonverbal problem solving (Kaufman et al., in press *b*).

RACE OF PATIENTS WITH LATERALIZED LESIONS

Researchers were slow to realize that gender differences among patients with unilateral lesions was a topic worthy of consideration. They have virtually ignored the issue of race differences. To my knowledge, only one study has addressed this important issue, the doctoral dissertation investigation conducted by Munder (1976). Even though this study was executed quite well, included a substantial number of patients, and yielded provocative results, Munder's work has not been included in summaries of Wechsler research involving brain-damaged patients (Bornstein & Matarazzo, 1982, 1984; Inglis & Lawson, 1982; Matarazzo & Herman, 1985).

It is unusual, in fact, for investigators to indicate the racial breakdown of their samples, even for groups that are likely to include representative numbers of blacks such as war veterans with missile wounds (e.g., Black, 1973, 1976). Even Lansdell, perhaps the earliest investigator to identify the importance of the variable of *gender* in brain lesion studies, failed to give the proportions of whites and blacks in his study of 150 men, many of whom had penetrating missile wounds (Lansdell & Smith, 1975).

Munder's Careful Investigation of V–P Differences by Race

Munder (1976) obtained her data by searching through psychological and medical records from a number of hospitals, selecting all brain-damaged males tested with a complete WAIS. Neurological diagnosis was arrived at independently of psychological test results for all patients based on some or all of the following criteria: EEG, brain scan, surgery, autopsy. Patients with vision problems or incapacitating physical anomalies were not used in the study. Multiple analysis of covariance was used to control for age, years of education, and time interval between brain damage and date of testing.

The following numbers of male patients were investigated by Munder (1976): 25 whites and 25 blacks with left hemisphere lesions, 25 whites and 25 blacks with right hemisphere lesions, and 25 whites and 25 blacks with diffuse lesions (total sample size of 150). All patients were aged 18 or above, and no patient had known brain damage prior to age 18; Munder (1976) did not, however, provide the mean age or age range for the groups. There was no attempt made to control for type of lesion, either by etiology or specific location.

Table 10.7 summarizes the results of Munder's study, using Verbal and Performance IQs that have been adjusted for the covariates. As indicated, the white men demonstrated the expected patterns of P > V and V > P for lesions to the left and right hemispheres, respectively. As was true for most studies in

Tables 9.6 and 9.7, the mean V–P discrepancy was larger for white patients with right-brain damage (+15.1 points) than for those with left damage (−5.2 points). Black male patients with right damage showed the expected pattern of V > P (by +10.4 points), but blacks with left lesions did not. Instead, the latter sample of adults evidenced a V–P IQ difference of +5.7 points.

Regardless of race, patients with diffuse brain damage obtained a mean difference of about 5 points favoring the Verbal Scale. Thus, adult black male patients with brain damage displayed a V > P profile regardless of the location of the lesion, the same result reported for the patients studied by Todd et al. (1977). Differences shown between blacks and whites in Table 10.7 were found by Munder (1976) to be statistically significant. Her analysis of covariance uncovered a significant interaction effect (.001 level) between race and location of brain damage on V- and P-IQs.

Subtest Patterns for Brain-Damaged Males by Race

Table 10.8 looks at the 11 WAIS subtests by race, comparing the mean scaled scores earned by patients with left lesions with the mean scaled scores earned by patients with right lesions. It was not meaningful to compare white patients with left lesions to black patients with left lesions because the white patients scored significantly and substantially higher than black patients on all WAIS IQs (Munder, 1976).

In Table 10.8, the scaled scores are different from the scores shown for the same groups in Table 11.1. The Table 11.1 scaled scores are the actual, observed values, which are appropriate to report for an accumulation of data across studies. For the present analysis, however, which aims to clarify to the degree possible an understanding of the interaction with race, it made more sense to control for extraneous variables; hence the scaled scores shown in

TABLE 10.7 V–P IQ discrepancies on the WAIS for separate groups of black and white patients displaying localized or diffuse lesions

Group	LEFT LESIONS			RIGHT LESIONS			DIFFUSE LESIONS		
	Mean V-IQ	*Mean P-IQ*	*V–P Diff.*	*Mean V-IQ*	*Mean P-IQ*	*V–P Diff.*	*Mean V-IQ*	*Mean P-IQ*	*V–P Diff.*
Blacks	87.4	81.7	+5.7	91.5	81.1	+10.4	90.8	86.3	+4.5
Whites	92.5	97.7	−5.2	101.6	86.5	+15.1	97.5	91.2	+6.3
Total group	90.0	89.7	+0.3	96.5	83.8	+12.7	94.1	88.7	+5.4

NOTE: Data are from Munder (1976). The sample is composed of 150 adult males: 25 from each race in each brain-damage category. The mean IQs are adjusted values, based on a multiple analysis of covariance in which the following variables were covaried: chronological age, years of education, and time interval between the onset of the brain damage and the psychological testing.

Table 10.8 have been adjusted for three covariates—age, education, and interval between brain damage and date of testing.

The comparisons shown in Table 10.8 indicate that 9 of the 11 subtests behaved as predicted for whites, but only four subtests (all Verbal) behaved as hypothesized for blacks. That is to say, one would anticipate patients with left lesions to outscore patients with right lesions on Performance subtests, but to perform more poorly on Verbal subtests.

For whites, substantial differences in the predicted directions were observed between the two patient groups on all tasks except Information and Digit Symbol. For blacks, none of the Performance subtests distinguished between patients with left- or right-brain damage; left-lesion subjects did, however, outscore right-lesion subjects by about 1 scaled-score point on Comprehension, Vocabulary, Arithmetic, and Digit Span. Note that the latter two tasks are more associated with the Freedom from Distractibility factor than with the Verbal Comprehension factor.

Munder's (1976) covariance analyses with the separate subtests identified only three that produced significant interactions between race and location of brain damage (i.e., left, right, diffuse): Block Design, Picture Completion, Object Assembly. In her discriminant function analyses, the subtests with the highest coefficient weights for the race × location interaction were Picture Completion, Block Design, and Similarities. Therefore, Munder's statistical treatment of the data obtained on male brain-damaged patients suggests that blacks and whites may differ in the cerebral organization of their brains, with the biggest differences occurring for Similarities and the three most spatial or simultaneous subtests (the ones grouped together by Bannatyne, 1971, to form his Spatial Ability category, and the ones that have been most closely identified with the field independent/field dependent cognitive style; see Goodenough and Karp, 1961).

Bogen, DeZure, Tenhouten, and Marsh (1972) have speculated that within our culture, blacks may develop their right hemispheres more completely than their left hemispheres, a pattern opposite to that of whites. Munder (1976) has cited the research of Bogen et al. (1972) and also of Levy (1972) to infer that blacks are more bilateralized for language than whites, and that blacks have less asymmetry than whites regarding verbal and spatial abilities. Interestingly, these are the same hypotheses advanced by McGlone (1977) regarding gender differences.

Evidence From Factor Analysis

Inglis and Lawson (1982) argued that females tend to use verbal strategies on some of Wechsler's nonverbal tasks, accounting for the gender differences associated with V–P IQ discrepancies in the studies of adults with unilateral brain damage. I argued against this hypothesis

for a number of empirical reasons, preferring McGlone's explanation of greater cerebral asymmetry for males than females (see pages 308–317). However, Inglis and Lawson's hypothesis is legitimate to invoke as a potential explanation for the race differences found by Munder (1976) in her investigation of brain-damaged males, despite the evidence advanced here in support of a cerebral asymmetry argument. Indeed, the factor structure for blacks reported in chapter 8 (pages 241–242 and

TABLE 10.8 Mean scaled scores on the WAIS earned by black males and white males with unilateral brain damage

	BLACKS			WHITES		
Subtest	Left Lesion (N=25)	Right Lesion (N=25)	Mean Diff.	Left Lesion (N=25)	Right Lesion (N=25)	Mean Diff.
Verbal						
I	8.3	8.7	−0.4	9.5	9.9	−0.4
DSp	7.2	8.5	−1.3	7.4	8.6	−1.2
V	7.3	8.4	−1.1	8.6	10.3	−1.7
A	6.8	8.0	−1.2	8.5	9.7	−1.2
C	7.9	9.0	−1.1	8.3	10.9	−2.6
S	7.8	7.7	+0.1	8.7	10.4	−1.7
Performance						
PC	7.5	8.0	−0.5	10.4	8.0	+2.4
PA	6.7	6.7	0.0	8.8	6.9	+1.9
BD	5.7	5.8	−0.1	9.3	7.5	+1.8
OA	5.7	6.0	−0.3	8.9	6.4	+2.5
DSy	5.0	5.0	0.0	6.1	5.8	+0.3
Mean						
Verbal	7.6	8.4	−0.8	8.5	10.0	−1.5
Performance	6.1	6.3	−0.2	8.7	6.9	+1.8

NOTE: Mean Diff. = mean for left lesion minus mean for right lesion. Data are from Munder (1976). Mean scaled scores in this table are values that have been adjusted for three covariates: age, education, and interval between brain damage and date of testing. These values differ, therefore, from the unadjusted values presented in Table 11.1.

247–248, Tables 8.2 and 8.5) suggests that blacks and whites have different processing styles.

Whether examining two-factor or three-factor solutions, blacks (but not whites) tend to use *both* verbal and nonverbal problem-solving styles for Arithmetic, Picture Completion, and Picture Arrangement. The factor loadings for these three subtests were nearly as high on the Verbal as the Perceptual factor for black adolescents and adults, ages 16–74. However, those analyses combined males and females. Since Munder studied only males, separate race × gender analyses were evaluated (Kaufman, McLean, & Reynolds, in press *a*) to determine

whether the findings for the total black sample generalized to both sexes.

Table 10.9 presents two-factor solutions of the WAIS-R for black males and black females, ages 16–74. For comparison purposes, analogous factor patterns are presented in Table 10.9 for white males and white females. The results for blacks are intriguing, as substantial gender differences emerged. For black *males*, Digit Span, Arithmetic, and Similarities were about equally associated with both the Verbal Comprehension and Perceptual Organization factors. (For black females, they behaved as verbal subtests, as Wechsler intended.) Importantly, the Perfor-

TABLE 10.9 Varimax rotated two-factor solutions of the WAIS-R for black males and females and for white males and females

| | BLACKS NORMAL STANDARDIZATION SAMPLE (AGES 16–74) | | | | WHITES NORMAL STANDARDIZATION SAMPLE (AGES 16–74) | | | |
| | Male (N=93) | | Female (N=99) | | Male (N=836) | | Female (N=828) | |
Subtest	VC	PO	VC	PO	VC	PO	VC	PO
Verbal								
I	86*	23	85*	21	80*	26	83*	25
DSp	46*	50*	63*	24	47*	36	46*	41*
V	90*	24	89*	24	90*	23	89*	23
A	55*	57*	66*	45*	62*	36	59*	45*
C	72*	38	78*	32	74*	24	76*	32
S	61*	57*	80*	39	61*	47*	68*	43*
Performance								
PC	38	69*	55*	52*	33	66*	38	67*
PA	32	75*	57*	53*	33	61*	38	57*
BD	21	74*	20	74*	26	81*	27	80*
OA	19	80*	23	63*	19	76*	19	69*
DSy	33	69*	26	69*	27	64*	23	63*

NOTE: Decimal points are omitted. Loadings of .40 or above are asterisked. Data are from Kaufman, McLean, and Reynolds in press a. The number of whites and blacks totals 1,856 rather than 1,880 because 24 individuals in the standardization sample whose race was classified as "other" (e.g., American Indian, Asian American) were excluded.

mance subtests showed no special tendency to load substantially on the Verbal dimension for black males.

In contrast, for black *females,* Picture Completion and Picture Arrangement were related about equally to the Verbal and Perceptual factors. Therefore, black males and females seem to process information in distinctly different ways. Black males tend to use *nonverbal* or *simultaneous* strategies (along with verbal-sequential strategies) when faced with Wechsler's Verbal tasks. In contrast, black females apply *verbal* problem-solving approaches (in conjunction with the preferred nonverbal strategies) when executing some of Wechsler's Performance subtests. Consequently, Inglis and Lawson's (1982) hypothesis that females use verbal strategies for nonverbal tasks holds only for black females, a group that has probably not been included very frequently in Wechsler studies of brain-damaged adults.

The results presented for whites across the broad 16–74 year range in Table 10.9 reinforce the findings summarized in Table 10.6 for four age groups: White males and females do not seem to differ systematically in how they solve nonverbal tasks, contrary to Inglis and Lawson's (1982) proposed explanation of gender differences in brain-damage studies.

The findings for black males are provocative, since they are wholly consistent with the race differences observed by Munder (1976) in her investigation of male neurological patients. Both races showed predicted V > P patterns for patients with right hemisphere lesions; based on the factor loadings summarized in Table 10.9, males (regardless of race) use Perceptual Organization abilities almost exclusively to solve Wechsler's Performance subtests. Since right-brain damage impairs perceptual, simultaneous processing, both black men and white men would be expected to have depressed P-IQs.

Only white men, however, showed characteristic P > V patterns for patients with unilateral damage to the left hemisphere. Black men, who seem to apply both nonverbal and verbal processes to several Verbal tasks, did not display the predicted P > V pattern. A sensible hypothesis is that the black males were able to use their intact nonverbal strategies (there was no brain damage in the right hemisphere) to solve verbal items, thereby avoiding a lowered Verbal IQ. This hypothesis must remain tentative, pending systematic investigation of the issue, since the WAIS-R factor analysis that generated the hypothesis was based on fewer than 100 black men.

Future Directions

Regardless of causation, Munder's (1976) investigation of race differences produced provocative findings, particularly since the research topic of significant race differences in IQ has produced so few meaningful explanatory hypotheses. It would be useful if other neuropsychological researchers attempted to replicate Munder's results. For now, there is no other evidence to suggest black–white differences in the V–P patterns of patients with unilateral lesions; the race difference finding is, thus, far more equivocal than the gender difference hypothesis. Also, Munder limited her samples to males, so it is not even appropriate to generalize her results to female black patients with unilateral lesions.

NATURE OF BRAIN DAMAGE

When Smith (1966a, 1966b) reported the first major negative findings regarding left- versus right-brain damage and direction of V–P IQ discrepancy, he also speculated on the intervening variables that may have led to the contradictory findings. He pointed to methodological problems in most studies, including his own, stressing that "lumping together younger and older patients with different types of lesions in various parts of the two hemispheres obscures possible significant differences in effects as a function of the nature, age, extent, dynamics, and specific locus of the lesion within arbitrarily defined cortical and subcortical gross structures" (Smith, 1966a, p. 121).

Bornstein and Matarazzo (1984) also tried to reconcile McGlone's (1977, 1978) negative findings for females with the bulk of positive findings for other patient samples by focusing on the nature of the brain damage in her samples. They note: "[R]eview by us of McGlone's actual data in her published studies reveals that *right* lesion females did demonstrate the expected pattern of VIQ greater than PIQ; and that, among the *left* lesion women, patients with vascular symptoms did demonstrate the expected pattern of VIQ less than PIQ, but women patients with tumor did not" (p. 707).

Bornstein and Matarazzo (1984) went one step further in this "sub-analysis" to emphasize that "[a]mong the left tumor females . . ., more than 50 per cent had meningiomas . . . which tend to be slowly progressive [and] may allow the brain to compensate" (pp. 707–708). Herring and Reitan (1986) further noted that the males in McGlone's (1977) samples of tumor patients had more intrinsic tumors than did the females (who had more extrinsic tumors), at least raising to Herring and Reitan (1986) "the possibility that the men had more malignant, destructive, and extensive lesions" (p. 537).

The issue of whether V–P discrepancies and side of lesion are more or less related for different types of brain lesion is crucial and is commonly discussed; I have not, however, seen a systematic treatment of this topic in the literature. Most investigators have combined a variety of etiologies to form their "left-lesion" and "right-lesion" samples, and even then they usually come up with groups that are small by research standards. It is impractical to expect researchers to identify samples whose lesions are due to tumors or stroke and are restricted to the anterior left or right parietal lobes.

Such control would be useful, since much clinical experience by neuropsychologists like Reitan has led to detailed understanding of brain-behavior relationships. For example, Reitan (1974) states that "Block Design is especially sensitive to posterior right hemisphere involvement and especially to right parietal and occipital damage whereas Picture Arrangement is more sensitive to anterior right temporal lesions" (p. 45); other researchers have verified these findings (e.g., Black & Strub, 1976; Long & Brown, 1979). But that degree of control is not feasible in research. Even if it were, other variables would impinge on the interpretation of the findings of a very specific type of brain damage: severity of the lesion, cause of the brain damage, acuteness or chronicity of the lesion, age at onset, education of patient, and so forth.

In the absence of the ideal, I have accumulated findings from the available studies that used reasonably homogeneous samples. Table 10.10 summarizes the results of 18 studies, comprising eight samples of stroke victims, five patient groups with generalized or posterior tumors, ten samples with temporal lobe epilepsy, one group with head injuries, one with missile wounds, and three samples whose injuries were confined to the frontal lobes. The results are interesting.

Lesions Caused by Stroke, Head Injury, and Tumors

Stroke victims show substantial V–P discrepancies. Because the composite samples are relatively large (about 125 with lesions in each hemisphere), we can have confidence in the generalizability of the results: P > V by 6½ points for left-lesion patients, and V > P by 13½ points for patients with right hemisphere lesions. These hypothesized findings are even more dramatic for male stroke victims—V–P differences of about −10 and +17 points for patients with left and right lesions, respectively. For females, however, only strokes to the right hemisphere produced the predictable V > P pattern (by a substantial 9½ points); for left lesion female stroke patients, the V–P discrepancy was zero.

TABLE 10.10 Mean V-P IQ discrepancies on various Wechsler scales for adults having different types of brain lesions

Type of Lesion/Study	LEFT LESIONS					RIGHT LESIONS				
	N	Mean V-IQ	Mean P-IQ	V-P Diff.		N	Mean V-IQ	Mean P-IQ	V-P Diff.	
Stroke										
Reitan & Fitzhugh (1971/W-B)										
Male	15	—	—	−19.8		15	—	—	+10.8	
McGlone (1978/WAIS)										
Males	15	—	—	−16.0		11	—	—	+16.0	
Females	13	—	—	−3.0		11	—	—	+4.0	
Haaland & Delaney (1981/WAIS)	26	87	94	−7.0		17	111	99	+12.0	
Inglis et al. (1982/WAIS)										
Males	20	84	99	−15.3		20	107	88	+19.6	
Females	20	90	90	+0.2		20	101	96	+4.5	
Snow & Sheese (1985/WAIS)										
Males	14	104	90	+13.9		14	104	84	+19.8	
Females	5	97	89	+8.0		12	102	79	+22.7	
Tumors (Generalized or Posterior)										
Smith (1966b/W-B)	48	94	94	0.0		51	98	92	+6.8	
McGlone (1978/WAIS)										
Males	8	—	—	−7.5		6	—	—	+14.0	
Females	7	—	—	+3.5		6	—	—	+5.0	
Haaland & Delaney (1981/WAIS)	14	94	94	0.0		15	100	97	+3.0	
Whelan & Walker (1988/WAIS)										
Posterior	21	93	90	+2.4		24	103	88	+14.7	
Temporal Lobe (Epileptics)										
Meyer & Jones (1957/W-B)										
Males	11	87	98	−10.8		5	97	94	+3.2	
Females	9	80	82	−1.9		6	110	103	+7.0	
Dennerll (1964/W-B)	29	86	96	−10.3		31	106	94	+12.5	

TABLE 10.10 (Continued)

	LEFT LESIONS				RIGHT LESIONS			
Type of Lesion/Study	N	Mean V-IQ	Mean P-IQ	V-P Diff.	N	Mean V-IQ	Mean P-IQ	V-P Diff.
Meier & French (1966/W-B) Sample I	14	92	101	−8.7	16	102	99	+2.7
Lansdell (1968/W-B)								
Males	11	—	—	−8.8	13	—	—	+2.2
Females	8	—	—	−4.9	20	—	—	−3.4
Meier & French (1966/WAIS) Sample II	15	90	94	−3.7	25	100	91	+8.4
Buffery (1974/WAIS)	13	89	93	−4.6	17	103	95	+7.4
Ivnik et al. (1987/WAIS)	28	94	102	−7.6	35	103	101	+1.9
Fedio & Mirsky (1969/WISC) Children (age 10½)	15	96	98	−2.4	15	104	100	+4.0
Head Injury								
Uzzell et al. (1979/WAIS)	8	72	81	−8.7	13	96	79	+17.5
Missile Wounds								
Black (1974b/WAIS)	50	95	98	−3.4	36	98	94	+4.5
Frontal Lobe Lesions								
Smith (1966b/W-B) Tumors	18	90	91	−1.4	23	103	99	+3.8
Black (1976/WAIS) Missile wounds	28	99	102	−3.3	16	99	100	−1.1
Whelan & Walker (1988/WAIS) Tumors	8	90	90	−0.4	11	105	99	+5.6

(Continues)

TABLE 10.10 (Continued)

Type of Lesion/Study	LEFT LESIONS				RIGHT LESIONS			
	N	Mean V-IQ	Mean P-IQ	V-P Diff.	N	Mean V-IQ	Mean P-IQ	V-P Diff.
Totals								
Stroke	128			−6.4	120			+13.5
Males	64			−10.1	60			+16.8
Females	38			+0.1	43			+9.5
Tumors (Generalized or Posterior)	98			+0.2	102			+8.4
Temporal Lobe Epilepsy								
Including children	153			−6.9	183			+5.0
Excluding children	138			−7.4	168			+5.1
Males	22			−9.8	18			+2.5
Females	17			−3.3	26			−1.0
Head Injury	8			−8.7	13			+17.5
Missile Wounds	50			−3.4	36			+4.5
Frontal Lobe Lesions	54			−2.2	50			+2.6

NOTE: Sample sizes for McGlone's (1978) groups of male and female adults with strokes or tumors are estimates, based on the ratio of 2/3 to 1/3 characterizing the proportion of patients in the total sample with strokes versus tumors. The mean V–P differences for McGlone's (1978) male and female stroke and tumor patients with localized lesions were determined by visual inspection of her graph. Mean differences for some samples in the table were computed from mean IQs rounded to the nearest tenth.

The direct impact of stroke on differential V–P performance, more so than other lesions, follows logically from the nature of cerebrovascular accidents: They feature "the disruption of the supply of nutrients—primarily oxygen and glucose—to the brain as a result of disrupted blood flow. The inability of the nervous tissue of the brain to survive more than several minutes of oxygen deprivation accounts for the rapidity with which irreversible brain damage takes place" (Lezak, 1983, pp. 175–176). Further, "[s]ince each carotid artery supplies blood to one cerebral hemisphere, lateralized deficits are common among stroke victims" (Brown, Baird, & Shatz, 1986, p. 387).

The only type of lesion, besides stroke, to show such dramatic results was head injury (V–P differences of −8½ and +17½ for left and right damage, respectively). However, these results, for an almost all-male sample of patients with hematomas, hemorrhagic contusions, or cerebral swelling, are derived from a single study with small patient samples (Uzzell et al., 1979).

Patients with tumors do not demonstrate clear-cut laterality findings. As shown in Table 10.10, tumors to the left hemisphere produced no V–P difference for the composite sample of 98 patients; right-brain tumors for about an equal number of patients produced V > P, as predicted, but the mean value of about 8½ points is substantially less than the sizable discrepancy found for stroke patients.

Temporal Lobe Epilepsy

The most frequent group of homogeneously defined patients with lateralized lesions has been temporal lobe epileptics. Data are presented for 10 separate samples in Table 10.10, most of whom were tested postoperatively following removal of the afflicted temporal lobe. For three of these samples, data were presented that permitted evaluation of V–P discrepancies both before and after the lobectomy.

Basic Findings for More Than 300 Epileptics

Temporal lobe epileptics are the only group who displayed predictable V–P differences of about equal magnitude based on the side that the lesion was located. Since one sample comprised only children with epilepsy (Fedio & Mirsky, 1969), aggregated data are presented both with and without this young sample. For adult temporal lobe epileptics, patients with left lesions had P > V by 7½ points, and those with right lesions had V > P by 5 points. Since these composite values are based on over 300 patients, the results are probably generalizable to other samples of temporal lobe epileptics.

These studies have the advantage of being confined to a reasonably specific part of each hemisphere, and most of the samples were tested following the surgical removal of the affected temporal lobe. Consequently, it is sensible to conclude from Table 10.10 that the left temporal lobe has a clear impact on verbal ability, as measured by Wechsler's Verbal Scale, and the right temporal lobe has a decided impact on a person's success on Wechsler's Performance Scale. Data for separate groups of temporal lobe epileptics suggest that the findings may hold true for males but not females; however, the small samples of men and women prevent anything other than tentative hypotheses.

Preoperative Versus Postoperative V–P Discrepancies

Table 10.11 shows the results of two studies (comprising three samples) of temporal lobe epileptics that permitted a comparison of preoperative and postoperative scores on the Wechsler Verbal and Performance Scales. The samples differed greatly in the mean interval between the temporal lobectomy surgery and the posttest (means of about 1 month, 1 year, and 3 years). Nevertheless, one finding characterized all three samples: V–P differences *prior* to surgery were in the predictable directions

TABLE 10.11 V–P IQ discrepancies obtained by temporal lobe epileptics both before and after temporal lobectomies

Study	Postoperative Interval	Preoperative			Postoperative			Change	
		V-IQ	P-IQ	V-P	V-IQ	P-IQ	V-P	V-IQ	P-IQ
Meyer & Jones (1957; W-B)									
Left Lesion (N=20)	1 mo.	94	99	−5.1	84	91	−6.8	−9.8	−8.1
Right Lesion (N=11)	1 mo.	102	100	+2.4	104	99	+5.3	+1.8	−1.2
Meier & French (1966)									
Sample I (W-B, pre and post)									
Left Lesion (N=14)	10 mo.	94	95	−1.6	92	101	−8.7	−1.5	+5.6
Right Lesion (N=16)	11 mo.	100	98	+1.8	102	99	+2.7	+2.6	+1.7
Sample II (W-B, pre; WAIS, post)									
Left Lesion (N=15)	3.2 yr.	91	93	−1.7	90	94	−3.7	−0.9	+1.1
Right Lesion (N=25)	3.6 yr.	100	97	+2.7	100	91	+8.4	−0.3	−6.0
Weighted Means									
Left Lesion (N=49)				−3.1			−6.4	−4.7	−1.4
Right Lesion (N=52)				+2.4			+6.0	+1.0	−2.6

NOTE: V–P stands for Verbal IQ minus Performance IQ. "Change" refers to the change in Verbal IQ and Performance IQ preoperatively to postoperatively. It equals postoperative IQ minus preoperative IQ; therefore, negative signs refer to lower postoperative IQs. Mean differences between V- and P-IQs, and between preoperative and postoperative IQs, were computed from mean IQs rounded to the nearest tenth. Buffery's (1974) and Ivnik et al.'s (1987) preoperative and postoperative data for temporal lobe epileptics are excluded from this table because their pre and post samples did not contain the same patients.

based on the side of the lesion, but these discrepancies were small; *subsequent* to surgery, V-P differences were still in the predicted directions, but the removal of the left or right temporal lobe apparently led to a substantial increase in mean V-P discrepancies.

Across the three samples, with about 50 subjects in each group (left and right lobectomies), the V-P differences changed from about 3 points before surgery to about 6 points after surgery. Following the lobectomies, left-brain patients dropped most in their Verbal IQs and right-brain patients evidenced a slight decrease in their Performance IQs.

Meier and French (1966) noted that Picture Arrangement scores were especially depressed due to right temporal lobectomy. Lezak (1983) and Milner (1954) observed the opposite in their clinical observations—namely, that patients with temporal lobe lesions did poorly on Picture Arrangement but that this poor performance was present prior to surgery and did not worsen from the lobectomy.

Lezak (1983) seemed to support Milner's (1954) conclusion that abnormally functioning tissue may lead to greater deterioration of test performance than the absence of the tissue. The data in Table 10.11, however, provide an empirical contradiction to Milner's inference, at least regarding the relationship of V-P discrepancies to the removal of the left or right temporal lobe in epileptics.

Temporal Lobe Versus Parietal Lobe Lesions

Warrington and James (1967) divided their 36 right-lesion and 29 left-lesion patients into the following groups, each composed of 16 or 17 patients: right temporal, right parietal, left temporal, left parietal. The two right-damage groups overlapped by two patients who had damage to both areas, and the two left-damage groups overlapped by three patients; 62% of the patients had tumors.

Warrington and James found no difference between the right temporal and right parietal groups regarding V-P discrepancy, with both showing a substantial 15-point difference favoring Verbal IQ. However, left temporal damage seemed more sensitive than left parietal damage to a verbal deficit; the former group had P > V by 6½ points, compared to P > V of 3 points for the latter sample. The P > V pattern of nearly 7 points for the patients with left temporal damage (composed of 10 with tumors, 3 with strokes, 2 with abscesses, and 1 each with a missile wound and lobectomy) is similar to the P > V discrepancy reported in Table 10.10 for patients with left temporal lobe epilepsy.

Frontal Lobe Lesions

In contrast to the temporal lobe's relationship to the differential cognitive functioning of the two hemispheres, the frontal lobe seems to be external to the cerebral asymmetry. Combining data from Smith's (1966c) and Whelan and Walker's (1988) studies of tumors confined to the frontal lobes, and Black's (1976) study of missile wounds that were similarly confined, Table 10.10 reveals very slight V-P differences for patients with left- or right-brain lesions. Although the differences are both in the predicted direction, they are too small (2 to 2½ points) to be of consequence.

Frontal Versus Posterior Lesions

When WAIS scores of missile wound patients with frontal lesions are compared to the scores of missile wound patients with posterior lesions, the frontal lobe sample earned IQs of about 100, significantly higher than the mean IQs of about 90 earned by patients with posterior lesions (Black, 1976). Also, Lansdell and Smith (1975) found that nonverbal factor scores were significantly related to side of lesion in the predicted direction; however: "Scores for patients with damage limited to the frontal lobes showed small side differences, suggesting that damage other than to the frontal lobe on the right caused the impairment shown by the non-verbal scores" (p. 923).

All of these results are consistent with Teuber's (1964) conclusions from a review of pertinent literature that (a) lesions in the frontal lobes affect cognitive performance less than lesions in other parts of the brain, and (b) there are no apparent differences between the effects of right and left lesions of the frontal lobes on higher intellectual functions. The present results are also consistent with the findings of other investigations of missile wounds to the frontal lobes (Newcombe, 1969; Schiller, 1947) and of frontal lobe tumors (Battersby, Krieger, & Bender, 1956; Pollack, 1955).

Although Smith (1966c) did not detect a laterality pattern in the V–P differences of patients with left versus right frontal tumors, he did observe two findings that are at variance with Black's (1976) results with missile wound patients and with Teuber's (1964) conclusions. First, he found that patients with left frontal tumors had lower Full Scale IQs than those with right frontal tumors (90 versus 101); second, he found that patients with frontal lobe tumors in one of his subsamples (but not in the other) earned similar mean Full Scale IQs to patients with lesions in nonfrontal regions of the brain. Smith (1966c) attributed these aberrant findings to differences in his samples from many previous samples on variables such as age (his group was older than most samples with a mean age of 46) and the acuteness of the lesions in his samples (they were tested immediately before or just after surgery).

Interestingly, Whelan and Walker (1988) replicated Smith's (1966c) results almost exactly with their male and female tumor patients. Like Smith's group, Whelan and Walker's patients had an average age of 47 and were tested within 1 month of surgery (48 presurgery, 16 post-surgery). In Whelan and Walker's investigation, men and women with *right* frontal lobe tumors achieved WAIS IQs of about 100, but those

with *left* frontal lobe tumors had depressed Verbal and Performance IQs of 90—paralleling the lowered IQs of patients with *left posterior* tumors.

Whelan and Walker (1988) further demonstrated that tumors in the *right* hemisphere are more likely to produce the expected, large V > P discrepancy if they are located in the posterior regions of the brain (14.7 points) than in the anterior, frontal regions (5.6 points). This finding held true for separate samples of men and women. Patients with lesions in the *left* hemisphere, however, failed to produce P > V patterns regardless of the location of the tumors.

Table 10.10 shows that patients with missile wounds in various portions of the brain (Black, 1974b) showed predictable V–P discrepancies depending upon which side the wound was on, but that the differences were a rather small 4 points. Black (1974b) noted, however, that most (about 85%) of the patients with missile wounds in his sample had frontal lobe injuries, although the injuries often affected other regions as well. Hence, the V–P discrepancies that he found for missile wound patients were probably attenuated by the preponderance of frontal lobe lesions. By way of contrast, only about 20% of his right- and left-lesion samples had temporal lobe lesions, about 35% had lesions of the occipital lobe, and about 10% had parietal wounds. (The percentages exceed 100 because many patients had damage to multiple areas.)

ACUTE VERSUS CHRONIC LESIONS

The impact of the recency of the lesion on cognitive impairment has been discussed by early researchers of V–P differences in patients with unilateral lesions as a likely intervening variable in many studies (Fitzhugh, Fitzhugh, & Reitan, 1961; Kløve & Fitzhugh, 1962). These investigators felt that failure to control for the acuteness versus the chronicity of the left or right lesions probably accounted for the negative findings in the literature. Specifically, they hypothesized that acute (new) lesions are more likely than chronic (long-standing) lesions to lead to predictable V–P discrepancies for patients with unilateral brain damage.

This hypothesis is consistent with a bulk of clinical and research findings (Lezak, 1983) that stress that "the recency of the insult may be the most critical factor determining the patient's psychological status" (p. 210). Lezak stated further: "Even patients with less severe damage are likely to experience confusion to some degree for days, weeks, and sometimes months following a head injury or stroke. . . . This confusion is often accompanied by disorientation, difficulty in concentration, poor memory and recall for recent experiences, fatigability, irritability, and labile affect" (p. 210). Furthermore: "The greatest cognitive gains will be achieved within the first six months after onset" (p. 210).

Fitzhugh et al.'s Study

Fitzhugh et al. (1962) systematically evaluated the acute–chronic dimension and found significant V–P discrepancies in the predicted direction only for their sample of patients with acute lesions; the differences for the chronic patients, though in the anticipated direction, were just 2 to 4 points.

Although Fitzhugh et al.'s study is often cited as evidence for the impact of the recency of brain damage on Wechsler test patterns, their samples of acute and chronic patients differed on numerous other variables as well: institution (acute patients were at a university medical center, chronic patients at a state hospital); gender (acute patients were predominantly male, chronic patients included a majority of females); nature of brain damage (acute injuries were almost all strokes, tumors, or head injuries, whereas chronic patients had convulsive disorders due to a wide variety of causes); education level (acute patients had an average of 8

years of education; chronic patients had an average of 5½ to 6 years); and IQ level (acute patients had mean FS-IQs of about 85; chronic patients had mean FS-IQs of about 70). Based on the previous discussion of gender differences, that variable alone might have accounted for the different V–P findings for the acute and chronic patients.

Aggregated Data From Several Samples

Table 10.12 was compiled from Fitzhugh et al.'s (1962) investigation and two additional studies (comprising four samples in all) that examined acuteness versus chronicity as an independent variable. The combination of data from these diverse samples should give more insight into the importance of this variable than is provided by Fitzhugh et al.'s unmatched samples. The data from the two samples of stroke patients investigated by Inglis et al. (1982) are of particular value because the samples of acute and chronic patients were carefully matched on the variables of gender (by treating males and females separately), age, education (exception: chronic males with left lesions were much more educated than acute males with left lesions), familial lefthandedness, and severity of lesion.

Fitzhugh et al. (1962) did not specify how soon after the brain lesion the group with "recently developed symptoms of cerebral dysfunction" (p. 306) were tested, but they noted that the chronic sample was tested about 25 years following the first noted seizure. Todd et al. (1977) used a 1-year cut-off to determine acuteness and chronicity; all patients who were tested on the WAIS within 1 year of brain damage were designated as acute, while those tested 13 or more months following damage were classified as chronic. In Inglis et al.'s (1982) study, the acute samples had suffered a stroke within 6 months of testing (mean = 3 months), and the chronic groups had had a stroke 1–12 years prior to testing (mean = 4 years).

TABLE 10.12   V–P IQ discrepancies for patients with acute and chronic lesions lateralized to the left or right hemisphere

| | ACUTE LESIONS | | | | CHRONIC LESIONS | | | |
| | Left | | Right | | Left | | Right | |
Study	N	V–P	N	V–P	N	V–P	N	V–P
Fitzhugh et al. (1962)	18	−9.1	25	+15.0	20	−3.9	25	+2.1
Todd et al. (1977)	15	+12.7	11	+10.5	26	+2.2	20	+6.3
Inglis et al. (1982)								
Males	10	−10.2	10	+24.0	10	−20.3	10	+15.2
Females	10	−5.3	10	+6.6	10	+5.8	10	+2.4
Weighted Mean	53	−2.4	56	+14.2	66	−2.5	65	+5.5

As indicated in Table 10.12 for the composite samples, left brain–damaged patients with acute lesions and with chronic lesions *both* had a P > V difference of about 2½ points. Among right hemisphere patients, however, acute subjects showed a far more substantial V > P discrepancy than chronic patients (14 versus 5½ points). Both right-lesion groups showed the predicted pattern, but only the acute group showed a sizable discrepancy. Thus, the data in Table 10.12 suggest that left-lesion patients do not vary in their V–P differences as a function of the recency of the lesion, but that acuteness–chronicity is a key variable for patients with right hemisphere damage.

The relative improvement, over time, in right-brain cognitive functioning by patients with damage to that side of the brain attests to the recuperative powers of brain-injured people. Lezak (1983) states: "Intellectual functions, particularly those involving immediate memory, attention and concentration, and specific disabilities associated with the site of the lesion generally continue to improve markedly during the first six months or year, and improvement at an increasingly slower rate may go on for a decade or more following a stroke or other single-event injury to the brain" (pp. 210–211).

Nonetheless, it is still consistent with previous research and clinical experience to find a V > P discrepancy of 5½ points in chronic right-lesion patients because full recovery is rare, even for apparently slight injuries (Brodal, 1973; Schachter & Crovitz, 1977).

A Correlational Study

Snow, Freedman, and Ford (1986) correlated the absolute value of the V–P differences for several samples of left- and right-lesion patients with the number of months following the onset of the damage. They obtained a strong *negative* relationship (−.83) based on data from Wechsler-Bellevue investigations, showing once again that larger V–P IQ discrepancies are more likely to emerge for patients who recently became brain injured than for those with long-standing injuries. Since Snow et al. (1986) grouped the left-lesion and right-lesion samples together for their correlational analysis, it was possible neither to deny nor confirm the hypothesis proposed here that acuteness versus chronicity is a more important variable for lesions to the right hemisphere.

INCLUSION OF APHASICS

Another potentially contaminating variable in the Wechsler V–P studies with brain-damaged patients is the inclusion of severe dysphasics or aphasics among the left-lesion samples.

Smith Versus Inglis and Lawson

Smith (1966a, 1966b) believed that the failure of Reitan and his colleagues to report the proportion of aphasics in their samples of left-lesion patients in most of their studies confirming the predicted relationship between V–P discrepancy and side of lesion may have contributed to the positive findings. Smith (1966b) stated emphatically: "Reports of lower verbal than performance scores by groups of aphasics with left-sided lesions are no more surprising than lower performance scores would be for any groups of patients with or without brain lesions but with severe visual impairment or total blindness (p. 518)."

However, Smith's strong claims lead to a gray area regarding who should be included in or excluded from samples of brain-lesioned patients. If aphasics are excluded, what about apraxics or patients with constructional disorders who have an analogous type of right-brain lesion? What about patients whose neurological dysfunction leads to impaired motor functioning; is it fair to assess such patients on Wechsler's timed Performance subtests even if their lesions are clearly documented as intrinsic to the right hemisphere?

Inglis and Lawson (1982) recognized the complexity of the aphasia issue and took a position quite opposite Smith's concerning sample selection for Wechsler studies of patients with unilateral brain damage: "The argument in favour of excluding aphasic patients from this kind of study usually depends upon a reference to their 'untestability' on some verbal items. This is, however, essentially an inability to return correct responses on these tasks, and is in itself a direct consequence of cerebral insult. It therefore constitutes part of the phenomenon under investigation and should probably not be a ground for excluding patients from consideration" (p. 679).

Unsystematic Empirical Investigation of the Aphasia Issue

Smith (1966b) evaluated data for left brain–damaged samples both with and without the aphasics. Of his entire sample of patients with tumors in the left hemisphere ($N = 48$), 21 (or 44%) demonstrated a $P > V$ profile; excluding the 12 aphasics from the sample reduced the percentage to 31. In Smith's (1966a) larger sample of 92 adults with left hemisphere lesions, the percent with $P > V$ profiles was approximately cut in half (36% to 19%) when the 28 aphasics were excluded. However, Smith's (1966a, 1966b) data on V–P differences (apart from the issue of including aphasics) are at variance with results from most studies of patients with unilateral brain damage, as has been noted previously. Generalization is therefore tenuous.

Satz, Richard, and Daniels (1967) disagreed with Smith's contentions about the impact of including aphasics in brain-damaged samples. They found a deficiency in Wechsler verbal ability for their left-lesion sample ($N = 23$) and concluded that "the impairment in verbal performance was not simply a function of aphasia in that only two Ss in the left-sided group had a clinical history of language disorder" (p. 370).

Like Smith's study, however, Satz et al.'s findings and method of reporting data differed from the mainstream of studies in this area.

First, they found an unusually large (12.6 point) P > V pattern for left-lesion adults. Second, they did not present the actual mean V- and P-IQs obtained by their patients but only values adjusted for several covariates. Since one of the covariates in the V-IQ analysis was the patient's *Performance IQ* (and, conversely, one of the covariates in the P-IQ analysis was V-IQ), the reported mean values for each separate IQ scale are made experimentally dependent. The actual mean V-P differences for the patient samples may be quite a bit smaller.

Nonetheless, some other investigators have agreed with Satz et al.'s basic conclusions regarding the minor impact of aphasia on the V-P results of brain-damage studies. McGlone (1977) found prominent verbal deficits in her sample of left-lesion males, even when aphasics were eliminated. Meyer and Jones (1957) pointed out that aphasia is also likely to affect success on most Performance tests, not just on Verbal tasks, because of the verbal instructions and verbal mediation associated with the supposed "nonverbal" subtests.

Inglis et al.'s Investigation of the Aphasia Issue

Inglis et al. (1982) systematically studied the impact on V-P IQ discrepancies of eliminating aphasics from their samples of left-lesion men and women. They excluded 12 left-lesion patients who scored relatively high on the Orzeck Aphasia Evaluation Test (Orzeck, 1964)—three patients from each of their four left-lesion samples (acute and chronic males and females). Inglis et al. then randomly eliminated three patients from each right-lesion group and reconducted their analyses.

The V-P differences with and without aphasics are shown in Table 10.13. The discrepancies for right-lesion patients changed by 1 to 2 points when the data were reanalyzed with reduced samples; since the right-lesion groups were reduced to 7 patients by arbitrary deletions, the 1–2 point changes are due to chance and reflect a baseline for comparison when evaluating the left-lesion samples.

As indicated in Table 10.13, elimination of the three aphasic patients from each left-damaged group produced a change in V-P discrepancy of about 4 to 8 points. All changes were in the expected direction: P > V became smaller (more positive) due to a relative group improvement in verbal ability. For females with acute left lesions, the elimination of the aphasics totally took away the "predicted" P > V pattern; for females with chronic lesions, the "opposite to prediction" pattern simply became more extreme when aphasics were eliminated.

The male left-lesion samples, even without aphasics, demonstrated the predicted P > V profile. The V-P differences of −6.3 points (acute) and −12.7 points (chronic) for non-aphasic samples were not as impressive as the original values of −10.2 and −20.3, respectively. Nevertheless, Inglis et al.'s (1982) well-controlled study supports the notion that a verbal deficit is characteristic of left-lesion males even when aphasics are eliminated from the analysis.

The available data suggest that excluding aphasics from samples of left-lesion patients serves to raise the mean Verbal IQs of the samples and, hence, to reduce the magnitude of P > V patterns. For males, at least, this reduction does not eliminate the predicted profile of a verbal deficit for left-lesion patients; it just reduces the effect.

Recent Research Trends

It seems that more recent investigators of V-P differences in unilateral brain-lesioned adults have strived to reduce the impact of aphasia on the left brain–damaged samples (e.g., Bornstein, 1984; Snow & Sheese, 1985). If this has been a goal of many investigators, that might partly account for the much smaller P > V discrepancy found for left-lesion patients than the corresponding V > P difference found for right-lesion patients. As mentioned briefly in chapter 11 (see pp. 364–365), this possible difference in experimental design may be related to the larger P > V profile found for left brain–damaged subjects with the Wechsler-Bellevue than with the WAIS or WAIS-R; most of the Wechsler-Bellevue studies were conducted a number of years ago, as opposed to the more recent WAIS and WAIS-R investigations.

Personally, I am more in agreement with Inglis and Lawson (1982) than with Smith (1966a, 1966b) regarding the inclusion or exclusion of aphasics from left-lesion samples. I don't equate aphasia with blindness, although I

certainly favor eliminating severe aphasics from left hemisphere samples, especially if they are unable to respond to virtually any Wechsler verbal items. Similarly, I cannot imagine including in any unilateral brain-damage sample anyone who has a visual-motor defect due to the brain lesion that makes it impossible to assess them meaningfully on timed, manipulative tasks.

But, these extremes aside, I agree in principle with Inglis and Lawson's (1982) assertion that "[t]he exclusion of aphasic patients must, in fact, impose a bias on patient samples. The subsequent projection of results thus obtained from such selected samples to characterize focally damaged neurological patients in general is therefore of doubtful validity" (p. 679).

TABLE 10.13   V–P differences for stroke patients, with and without those identified as aphasic

Group	V–P IQ Discrepancy Including Aphasics	V–P IQ Discrepancy Excluding Aphasics	V–P Change
Males			
Acute			
Left Lesion	−10.2	−6.3	+3.9
Right Lesion	+24.0	+23.1	−0.9
Chronic			
Left Lesion	−20.3	−12.7	+7.6
Right Lesion	+15.2	+13.5	−1.7
Females			
Acute			
Left Lesion	−5.3	+2.9	+8.2
Right Lesion	+6.6	+8.8	+2.2
Chronic			
Left Lesion	+5.8	+12.5	+6.7
Right Lesion	+2.4	+3.9	+1.5

NOTE: Data are from Inglis et al. (1982). Each subsample including aphasics comprises 10 subjects; each sample excluding aphasics comprises 7 subjects.

AGE OF PATIENT SAMPLES

Brain Damage in Children and in Adults

Brain damage in children is different from brain damage in adults. The impact of lesions in early childhood on intelligence and neuropsychological functioning is often more profound and more generalized than lesions occurring during adulthood (Crockett, Clark, & Klonoff, 1981). However: "The consistent findings since the last century indicate not only significantly greater recovery from comparable brain insults in infants and children than in adults but also more severe and persisting sequalae in adults with advancing age" (Smith, 1983, p. 770). Also, adults with recent neurological problems tend to have more difficulty with immediate problem-solving ability than with memory, whereas children evidence the opposite pattern (Reed & Reitan, 1969).

Although V–P discrepancies in adults have generally been shown to relate predictably to the side of the lesion, particularly for patients with right lesions, such findings have not usually held for children (e.g., Fedio & Mirsky, 1969; Lewandowski & DeRienzo, 1985; Reed & Reitan, 1969). These differences may be due to developmental trends in cerebral lateralization (Krashen, 1972), qualitatively different types of brain injuries in children and adults (Klonoff & Thompson, 1969), less rigorous criteria for determining locus of injury or type of pathology for children than adults (Fedio & Mirsky, 1969), greater plasticity in younger than older brains (Smith, 1983), or some combination of these and other reasons.

The nature of the discrepancies between studies of neurological injuries in children versus adults is a topic of some controversy (Satz & Fletcher, 1981; Smith, 1983); Satz and Fletcher, for example, disputed the notion of greater plasticity in children's brains. The pur-pose of this section is not to try to resolve or even articulate these issues, but to examine the role of age as an intervening variable in *adult* studies of Wechsler V–P IQ discrepancies and side of lesion.

Empirical Analysis With Samples of Adolescents and Adults

Meyer and Jones (1957) correlated chronological age to the magnitude of verbal deficit for epileptics who had their left temporal lobe removed. The correlation for this group, which ranged in age from 12 to 46 years (mean = 27.7), was a trivial and nonsignificant .10. Snow, Freedman, and Ford (1986) also observed small, chance relationships between mean V–P IQ discrepancy and mean chronological age for numerous samples of left- or right-lesion patients tested on the WAIS ($r = .23$) or Wechsler-Bellevue ($r = .02$).

Other systematic investigations of age as an intervening variable in Wechsler/unilateral damage studies are apparently lacking in the literature. Consequently, I have explored this variable by grouping the data from the various studies on the Wechsler-Bellevue (Table 9.6) and WAIS/WAIS-R (Table 9.7) according to the mean age of the sample (whenever this information was provided). This is a crude but useful type of meta-analysis; the results are summarized in Table 10.14. The five groups thus assembled are based on substantial numbers of left- and right-lesion patients; only the samples of elderly people had fewer than 100 patients, with the other groups ranging from 140 to 315 patients. There are clear-cut fluctuations with age.

Left-lesion patients showed the smallest P > V differences at the extremes, with the largest discrepancy occurring at ages 25–34. Elderly patients with right hemisphere damage showed the largest V > P pattern, while the

TABLE 10.14 The relationship of mean age of brain-damaged sample to size of V–P IQ discrepancy for patients with left hemisphere and right hemisphere lesions

| | LEFT LESIONS | | RIGHT LESIONS | |
Mean Age of Sample	N	V–P Diff.	N	V–P Diff.
20–24	177	−3.0	164	+9.3
25–34	140	−7.5	183	+4.5
35–44	305	−4.3	308	+10.0
45–54	315	−3.6	307	+9.2
55+	85	−2.9	83	+14.9

NOTE: These data are from all studies in Tables 9.6 and 9.7 that indicated mean age of the sample. However, like Tables 9.6 and 9.7, overlapping samples are excluded. V–P Diff. equals V–IQ minus P–IQ.

group of 25–34 year olds demonstrated the smallest V–P discrepancy. The reasons for these particular findings are not apparent to me, and the groups undoubtedly differ unsystematically on other variables; also, the mean age of each sample does not take into account the variability in age that characterized the patient groups.

Yet the apparent age-related differences evident in Table 10.14 at the least suggest the need for systematic, controlled investigation of chronological age as a key variable in influencing the magnitude of the V–P differences displayed by patients with unilateral lesions. Further, Herring and Reitan (1986) report the *identical finding* for elderly patients with right lesions, based on unpublished studies in their laboratory, that emerged as a meaningful result in Table 10.14: "Older persons with right cerebral hemisphere lesions . . . showed a striking intraindividual lowering of PIQ compared with VIQ" (p. 540).

Whereas elderly people, in general, show a decline in nonverbal ability (see chapter 7), this decreased level of functioning is evident in lowered scaled scores and sums of scaled scores on the Performance Scale. It does not show up in the mean Performance IQ. The WAIS or WAIS-R scaled scores are obtained from a ref-

erence group of adults aged 20–34, but the IQs are normed to have a mean of 100 (and *SD* of 15) based on the person's own age group. Consequently, groups of non–brain-damaged adults at every age level would be expected to have a V–P IQ discrepancy of zero points. Although some investigators have maintained that elderly people, in general, have characteristic V > P profiles (Rust, Barnard, & Oster, 1979), the method used by Wechsler to norm his adult scales makes this an untenable hypothesis.

EDUCATION LEVEL OF PATIENT SAMPLES

More than other background variables, a person's level of education relates to his or her Verbal–Performance difference. This variable was previously discussed in chapter 6 and was also treated in this chapter in the section on gender differences. This section looks at the mean V–P differences for normal adolescents and adults who differ in years of education across various other background variables and then tries to determine the impact of the brain-damaged sample's education level on the observed mean V–P discrepancy.

Relationship of V–P to Years of Education for Normal Adults

Reynolds, Chastain, Kaufman, and McLean (1987, Table 1) provided data for six educational categories for the total standardization sample of 1,880, spanning ages 16–74. Mean V–P discrepancies for each educational group (V-IQ minus P-IQ) are shown in Table 10.15.

Another interesting approach to the relationship of V–P discrepancies to education level was explored by Bornstein, Suga, and Prifitera (1987). They reported the proportions of people in the standardization sample who had V > P and P > V by a given number of points at each of four educational levels. Using a criterion of 10 or more points between the IQs, they found that for individuals with 0–8 and 9–11 years of education, about *twice* as many had P > V as compared to V > P (about 22% versus 11%); for people with 13+ years of education, the pattern was exactly reversed (31% versus 14%). Using the more familiar criterion of 15 or more points between Verbal and Performance IQs, Bornstein et al. (1987) found similar results, as shown in Table 10.16.

TABLE 10.15   Mean WAIS-R V–P discrepancies (V minus P) by educational group for the total standardization sample (ages 16–74)

Years of Education	Mean V–P Difference
0–7	−2.3
8	−2.8
9–11	−1.7
12	0.0
13–15	+2.2
16+	+4.7

NOTE: Data are from Reynolds et al. (1987).

TABLE 10.16   Meaningful WAIS-R V > P and P > V discrepancies by education group for the total standardization sample (ages 16–74)

Years of Education	Percent with V > P	Percent with P > V
0–8	3.1	10.7
9–11	5.9	9.7
12	9.0	9.5
13+	14.4	6.4

NOTE: V–P discrepancies are based on the 15-point criterion. Data are from Bornstein et al. (1987).

Table 10.17 presents data from the standardization sample for separate age, gender and race groups (Reynolds et al., 1987), using the same four categories reported by Bornstein et al. (1987). The data reported previously for the six educational groups, Bornstein et al.'s percentages of individuals with significant V > P and P > V differences, and the analyses presented in Table 10.17 generally support the pattern of high Performance IQ for people with less than a high school education, and high Verbal IQ for people with at least some college. Since Hispanics traditionally have lower levels of education than the mainstream culture, the education variable likely accounts for a part of their characteristic P > V Wechsler profiles (see pp. 281–284).

However, Table 10.17 reveals some interesting interactions between education level and the background variables of age and race:

- For individuals with *low education* (8 years or less), P > V is larger for ages 16–44 (4–5 points) than for ages 45–74 (0–3 points).
- For individuals with *high education* (13 years or more) V > P is smaller for ages 16–44 (2–3 points) than for ages 45–74 (5–7 points).

TABLE 10.17 Mean WAIS-R V–P IQ differences for normal people differing in education level, separately by age, gender, and race

Group	YEARS OF EDUCATION			
	0–8	9–11	12	13+
Age				
16–19	−4.7	−0.6	+1.7	+3.0
20–34	−4.1	−3.1	−1.1	+1.9
35–44	−3.7	−3.6	−1.2	+2.4
45–54	−0.7	−3.7	−0.2	+5.7
55–64	−0.4	−1.3	−0.9	+4.8
65–74	−3.0	−2.2	+2.9	+7.2
Gender				
Male	−2.3	−1.4	+0.4	+3.8
Female	−2.9	−2.0	−0.4	+2.9
Race				
White	−3.1	−2.1	−0.1	+3.6
Black	−0.1	+1.4	+1.0	−1.7
Total Sample	−2.6	−1.7	0.0	+3.4

NOTE: Data are for the WAIS-R standardization sample, computed from Table 7 in an article by Reynolds, Chastain, Kaufman, and McLean (1987). V–P IQ difference equals mean Verbal IQ minus mean Performance IQ.

- The V–P IQ discrepancies for blacks do not bear any relationship to education level; they average about zero regardless of years of schooling.

Clinical Implications of Base-Rate Education Data

Clinicians and researchers should use Table 10.17 as a base-rate table of expected V–P differences for brain-damaged patients, in the absence of premorbid intelligence data. In most cases, the mean V–P differences are small in magnitude for various education levels, usually 4 points or less. However, even an adjustment of a few points can be revealing in a clinical sense.

For example, suppose a 60-year-old college-educated white man suffers a stroke that damages his left hemisphere, and he is subsequently found to have P > V of 6 points. From Table 10.17, we see that educated people aged 55–64 average V > P by 4.8 points. Hence, our best guess is that the brain-damaged man had a premorbid V–P difference of +5 points. Therefore, he probably went from +5 points before the stroke to −6 points after the cerebral lesion, a net shift of 11 points. This relative loss in nonverbal-spatial ability is thus far greater than the loss suggested by P > V of 6 points.

The data in Table 10.17 provide a rough estimate of a neurological patient's premorbid intelligence based on the background variable (educational level) that is most related to IQ. For a better estimate of premorbid V-, P-, or FS-IQ, examiners may wish to use regression tables developed for the WAIS-R by Barona, Reynolds, and Chastain (1984). These equations take into account several background variables in addition to education. However, note that even the most sophisticated equations for estimating premorbid intelligence on the Wechsler scales misclassify a person's intellectual category more than half the time (Silverstein, 1987a).

Research Implications of Base-Rate Education Data

The values shown in Table 10.17 are even more valuable for research purposes (applied to group data) than for clinical evaluation of a single patient, because there is great variability in the V–P discrepancies observed for the separate individuals within a sample—even a homogeneous one such as elderly, college-educated, white males; group data are far more stable and predictable.

The impact of education on the overall data presented for the numerous Wechsler studies of patients with unilateral brain damage summarized in Tables 9.6 and 9.7 is likely to be minimal. The reason, as noted previously (pp. 311–312), is that nearly all the samples had a mean education level of 10 to 12 years. The mean or expected V–P discrepancy for individuals with a moderate amount of education is close to zero, as shown in Table 10.17.

However, the role of years of education is more sizable for samples with extremely high or low levels of education. Fitzhugh and Fitzhugh's (1964b) sample of 52 patients (about half male, half female) with chronic seizure activity (see Table 9.7) had a mean education level of about 5½ years and an average age of 37. From Table 10.17, we find out that normal groups aged 35–44 with 8 or less years of education have a mean P > V profile of 3.7 points. Thus, our presumption is that Fitzhugh and Fitzhugh's (1964b) left- and right-lesion samples each had a mean *premorbid* V–P discrepancy of −3.7 points.

Subsequent to their brain damage, the left-lesion sample had a V–P difference of −4.8 and their right-lesion sample had a corresponding discrepancy of +4.5. However, if we take into account that the group likely had P > V of about 4 points *before* the lesion, then a P > V discrepancy of about 5 points *after* the lesion is really no change—i.e., no meaningful discrepancy—at all! (If they had P > V of 3.7 points prior to the lesion, and 4.8 points following the lesion, then the net "increase" in the V–P discrepancy is only 1.1 point.)

In contrast, the V > P profile for the right-lesion patients is quite impressive considering that, as a group, they probably started with the *opposite* profile (P > V). Adjusting their mean V–P difference of +4.5 by the probable initial difference of −3.7 indicates a relative decrease in their nonverbal ability by about 8 points.

Thus, evaluating the data from Fitzhugh and Fitzhugh's (1964b) study without consideration of their sample's low education level leads to the erroneous conclusion that the patterns for left- and right-lesion patients are equal and opposite in magnitude, mildly supporting predictions from the cerebral asymmetry literature. However, when the values are corrected for the likely premorbid V–P discrepancy, strong support for functional asymmetry is given for lesions to the right hemisphere, and no support is obtained for left lesions. The latter conclusion is consistent with the overview of all research on this topic using the WAIS or WAIS-R.

As early as the mid-1960s, Smith (1966a) was aware that Wechsler researchers investigating brain damage were remiss in ignoring the education level of the patients:

In addition to numerous ambiguities inherent in psychological studies of the effects of undifferentiated "brain lesions," comparisons of the mean education of the patients with lower verbal than performance aggregate weighted scores clearly illustrate one that has been consistently overlooked in such studies of effects of lateralized brain lesions. Wechsler (1944, p. 126) presented data for large samples showing that as mean [Wechsler-Bellevue] Full Scale IQ's decreased from 120 and above to 75 and below, the proportion of patients with higher performance than verbal IQ's increased from 21.0 percent to 74.3 percent. (p. 118).

Education Level and V–P for Brain-Damaged Samples

Table 10.18 summarizes all of the studies in Tables 9.6 and 9.7 that provided education information for their unilateral brain-damaged samples. The studies are grouped by mean education levels, cutting across other variables such as type of lesion, instrument used for assessment, gender, and so forth. The resultant composite samples range in size from 119 to 288, encompassing four levels of education: less than 10 years, 10 years, 11 years, and 12+ years. (The latter category is essentially 12 years since only the study by Ivnik et al., 1987, had a mean number of years above 12.)

These data show that the mean P > V profile for left-lesion patients is systematically related

TABLE 10.18   The relationship of mean education of brain-damaged sample to size of V–P IQ discrepancy for patients with left hemisphere and right hemisphere lesions

Mean Education Level of Sample (Years of School Completed)	Left Lesions		Right Lesions	
	N	V–P Diff.	N	V–P Diff.
Less than 10 years	119	−7.2	130	+9.1
10 years	184	−5.6	199	+11.1
11 years	288	−4.9	288	+9.5
12+ years	210	−1.5	167	+7.1

NOTE: These data are from all studies in Tables 9.6 and 9.7 that indicated mean education level of the sample. However, like Tables 9.6 and 9.7, overlapping samples are excluded. V–P Diff. equals V–IQ minus P–IQ.

to the years of education of the sample; it is larger for those with low education than for those with relatively high education, ranging from 7.2 points for patients with less than 10 years of schooling to 1.5 points for patients with 12 or more years of formal education. These results are predictable from the data shown in Table 10.17 for normal individuals with varying numbers of years of education. Basically, the results summarized in chapter 9 (see especially Tables 9.6 and 9.7) suggest that low V-IQ is barely characteristic of patients with left lesions. Many samples do not show a P > V profile, and the mean discrepancy is only a few points. The present education analysis suggests that a portion of the small P > V discrepancy for patients with left hemispheric lesions may be an artifact of their education level because many samples averaged less than 12 years of formal education.

The data in Table 10.18 for right-lesion patients do not show the same predictable relationship evidenced for left-lesion samples, as differences of about 9 points (± 2) characterized each sample. However, if the group with the lowest amount of education is not considered, the descending means for the samples with 10, 11, and 12+ years of education do accord well with predictions based on the known relation-

ship between years of education and mean V–P discrepancy for a group. Certainly for patients with left hemisphere damage, the overview shown in Table 10.18 indicates the importance of interpreting the results of a V–P IQ comparison in the context of the person's (or group's) level of formal education.

Herring and Reitan (1986) also noted the same type of relationship between level of education and V–P discrepancy indicated in Table 10.18 for patients with *left* lesions, based on unpublished studies in their laboratory: "[P]ersons with lower educational levels and left cerebral hemisphere lesions had relatively low VIQ compared with PIQ, whereas VIQs were only slightly lower than PIQs for persons with left cerebral hemisphere lesions when educational levels were higher" (p. 540).

Education as a Variable for Normal Vs. Brain-Damaged People

Finlayson, Johnson, and Reitan (1977) systematically investigated the role of education level on the psychological and neuropsychological test performance of 51 brain-damaged and 51 control subjects (all males) who were matched on age (34–35 years) and handedness. Although Finlayson et al. (1977) used the old Wechsler-Bellevue and did not examine the side of the lesion as a variable (nor did they limit the study to those with unilateral damage), the results are instructive.

These investigators compared normal and neurological subjects from three educational backgrounds: grade school (mean of 8 years of education), high school, and university (mean of 17 years). Finlayson et al. (1977) obtained the mean V–P differences in Table 10.19 for their samples. These results show the tendency for people with much education to be more "verbal-minded" than those with little education. The 10-point Verbal superiority for brain-damaged college-educated adults is far more than the trivial V–P differences for patients with less formal schooling.

Similarly, although the highly educated controls demonstrated only a 1-point superiority in Verbal IQ, it contrasted with the opposite pattern of P > V by 8 points for grade school controls. For both the brain-lesion and control samples, the university groups had a *relative* verbal superiority of about 8–9 points when compared to the grade school cohorts.

Munder (1976) also gave empirical support to the notion that the relationship between education level and IQ is comparable for brain-damaged patients and normal individuals. Chapter 6 reported that years of education correlates higher with Verbal IQ (mean $r = .60$) than with Performance IQ (mean $r = .44$), based on

TABLE 10.19   V–P differences on the Wechsler-Bellevue for normal and brain-damaged people from three educational backgrounds

	Brain-Damaged	Normal Control
Grade school	+2.6	−8.1
High school	−1.7	−3.0
University	+10.4	+0.8

NOTE: V–P differences equal V–IQ minus P–IQ. Data are from Finlayson et al. (1977).

data provided by Reynolds et al. (1987). Munder obtained highly similar values for her brain-damaged group composed of 150 patients (75 white, 75 black): V-IQ ($r = .67$) and P-IQ ($r = .43$). She also obtained correlations between education level and Verbal subtests for her large neurological population that resembled closely the corresponding values for normal individuals (Kaufman, McLean, & Reynolds, 1988b).

CHAPTER 10 SUMMARY

This chapter integrates the literature on V–P discrepancies in patients with lateralized brain lesions, attending specifically to the following interacting variables: gender, race, nature of the brain damage, acuteness versus chronicity of the lesion, inclusion of aphasics in the sample, age of patients, and education level. Gender differences have been reported in some studies but not others. The predicted patterns of low Verbal IQ for left-lesion patients and low Performance IQ for right-lesion patients seem to be more characteristic of male than female patients. The cause of these apparent gender differences has been attributed by McGlone to greater cerebral asymmetry for males; Inglis and Lawson attribute the gender difference to the application by females of verbal strategies to solve nonverbal problems. Several analyses of WAIS and WAIS-R data argue against the Inglis/Lawson verbal mediation hypothesis.

One well-designed study found race differences in whether male brain-damaged individuals display the predicted V–P patterns; white patients tended to evidence the predicted IQ relationships more so than black patients. Although some interesting discrepancies in the WAIS-R factor structure for blacks and whites may be related to the possible race differences in patients with lateralized lesions, the latter finding requires cross-validation.

The degree to which predicted V–P discrepancies accompany left or right lesions depends upon the type of lesion. Strokes tend to produce dramatic V–P differences in the predicted direction, especially for males. Patients with tumors in the right hemisphere display V > P profiles, but those with left hemisphere tumors evidence no V–P difference. Temporal lobe epileptics show the predicted pattern for patients having lesions in the left as well as right hemisphere, although the mean discrepancies are modest in magnitude. Lateralized frontal lobe lesions, whether caused by missile wounds or tumors, have little impact on V–P discrepancies. Posterior lesions, especially in the right hemisphere, are more likely than frontal lesions to yield predictable profiles. Comparisons of temporal lobe epileptics have been made before surgery (when they have documented, lateralized lesions) and following surgery (after the lobe with the lesion has been removed). V–P differences were in the predicted directions for the left- and right-lesion samples of epileptics, but these differences were *larger* following the surgical removal of the temporal lobe.

Acuteness versus chronicity of lesions has long been considered a key variable in determining the magnitude of V–P discrepancies; however, the major study on which generalizations were based (i.e., acute patients have larger V–P differences in the predicted direction than do chronic patients) failed to match the patient groups on any variables. A compilation of research on this topic suggests that acute patients with right hemisphere lesions display larger V > P profiles than chronic patients with right lesions. However, the acuteness–chronicity variable may not be meaningful for left-lesion patients.

Researchers differ on the advisability of including aphasics in studies of patients with unilateral brain damage. Some claim that including this group introduces bias into the analysis, while others insist that exclusion constitutes bias. Systematic analysis of left-lesion samples both with and without aphasics reveals that V–P differences are in the predicted direction in either instance. However, for samples of both acute and chronic patients, the discrepancies are notably smaller when aphasics are excluded.

Age as a variable in brain damage research has usually been approached by comparing lesions in children versus adults. Lateralized lesions in children are less likely than unilateral lesions in adults to produce predictable V–P discrepancies, although the possible reasons for this age-related difference are many, and disagreements abound among experts in the field. Few investigations have systematically examined the relationship of chronological age to the V–P discrepancies observed for patients with lateralized lesions. When the samples of patients in the various pertinent studies are grouped by mean age, the largest V > P profile for right-lesion patients was observed for the oldest sample (ages 55+ years); this same age group evidenced the *smallest* P > V discrepancy among left-lesion patients. The age analysis findings are difficult to interpret, but suggest that careful research in this area is needed.

Educational attainment relates systematically to the size of a person's V–P IQ discrepancy. Those with less than a high school education, on the average, score 2–3 points higher on the Performance Scale; college graduates score nearly 5 points higher on the Verbal Scale. These relationships have important clinical implications for individual neuropsychological assessment, and provide valuable base-rate data for interpreting the results of V–P analyses in neuropsychological research studies. When the samples of patients with left hemisphere lesions are grouped by their mean education level, the P > V profile is a direct function of education; the mean discrepancy is largest for those with the least education. In addition, there is evidence to support the conclusion that the relative verbal superiority of college-educated adults applies to brain-damaged as well as normal individuals.

V–P IQ Discrepancies in Brain-Damaged Adults: Subtest Patterns, the Laterality Index, Clinical Issues, and Illustrative Case Reports

This is the third in a series of three chapters on WAIS-R V–P IQ discrepancies. Chapter 9 explored numerous variables associated with high V-IQs or high P-IQs, including brain damage, and provided some empirical and clinical guidelines for interpretation of an individual's discrepancy. Chapter 10 was devoted to the relationship between patient variables and V–P discrepancy in brain-damaged adults. This chapter continues the focus on brain-damaged adults, dealing with the following general topics: (a) the subtest patterns obtained by patients with left versus right lesions, to see if these patterns provide insight into the greater sensitivity of the V–P IQ difference for patients with right damage (V > P of 9 points) compared to those with left damage (P > V of only 4 points); (b) the Laterality Index proposed by Lawson and Inglis (1983), which is integrally related to the subtest patterns of brain-damaged individuals, to delineate its potential clinical value; and (c) the interpretation of V–P IQ discrepancies for individuals with lateralized lesions, a de-

parture from the stress that has been given to group findings. The latter goal is accomplished by studying the emotional disturbance that often accompanies unilateral brain damage, by considering clinical suggestions for dealing with behaviors such as fatigue and coordination difficulties, and by integrating research on pertinent topics.

SUBTEST PATTERNS FOR LEFT- AND RIGHT-LESION PATIENTS

The diverse studies of brain-damaged patients suggest that the WAIS and WAIS-R V–P discrepancy seems to be a better indicator for those with right lesions than for those with left focal damage. This section examines the separate Wechsler subtests to see if observable patterns are evident that help make sense of the accumulating data on brain damage.

Mean Scaled Scores for Patients With Focal Brain Damage

Table 11.1 presents mean scaled or weighted scores on the 11 Wechsler subtests for all of the unilateral brain-damaged patient samples that provided these data for all or most subtests. The table includes five samples tested on the Wechsler-Bellevue and eight assessed with the WAIS. Basically, the right-lesion samples demonstrated their highest scores on Verbal subtests and their lowest scores on Performance tasks, as predicted.

Typically, the mean scores for right-lesion samples on the tests of verbal ability were in the average range (9–11); exceptions were for the two tasks that are more associated with the Freedom from Distractibility factor than the Verbal Comprehension factor (Arithmetic, Digit Span) and for the two groups (samples 12 and 13 in the table) with low overall functioning. Mean scores for right-lesion patients were in the average range for four samples (samples 1, 3, 7, 8) on Block Design, and for three samples on Object Assembly (samples 1, 3, 7). However, samples 1, 3, and 8 are limited to temporal lobe epileptics; lesions to the temporal lobe are not associated with poor performance on Block Design and Object Assembly, both of which are sensitive to lesions in the more posterior regions of the right hemisphere (Lezak, 1983; Reitan, 1986).

Left-lesion samples generally scored higher on Performance than Verbal tasks, as many hypothesize. However, they usually scored below the average range on *all* subtests.

Discrimination Between Right- and Left-Lesion Patients

Table 11.2 summarizes the data in Table 11.1 by presenting mean scaled scores for left- and right-lesion patients tested on the Wechsler-Bellevue and the WAIS. The Wechsler-Bellevue and WAIS produced differences in the subtest profiles for left-lesion patients, and they produced essentially the same differences in the profiles for right-lesion patients. It is interesting that right-lesion patients exhibit essentially the same differences. For example, left-lesion patients scored substantially higher on the WAIS than the Wechsler-Bellevue on Digit Span, but they demonstrated the reverse pattern on Digit Symbol; likewise, right-lesion patients displayed these exact results.

Overall comparison of the subtest performance of left- and right-lesion patients on the Wechsler-Bellevue and WAIS produces highly similar findings: Right-lesion patients outscored left-lesion patients by an average of 1½ to 2½ points on all Verbal subtests; left-lesion patients outperformed right-lesion patients on all Performance subtests except Digit Symbol by 1 to 1½ points; and the two patient samples did not differ in their scores on Digit Symbol.

Only two subtests functioned markedly differently on the Wechsler-Bellevue and WAIS—Picture Completion and Arithmetic. Whereas Picture Completion discriminated effectively between left- and right-lesion samples on the Wechsler-Bellevue, it did not do so on the WAIS. Arithmetic discriminated adequately for both test batteries, but it did a better job on the Wechsler-Bellevue.

When subtest data were combined for all 13 samples, only Digit Symbol failed to discriminate between left- and right-lesion patient groups. The four remaining Performance tasks all discriminated in the predicted direction between the two patient samples, and they all discriminated about equally well. The six Verbal subtests discriminated effectively between left- and right-lesion samples in the predicted fashion, and five of the tasks (all but Arithmetic) were about equally good at it.

If the subtest means are examined for only left-lesion patients and only for right-lesion patients to determine which tasks produce the largest differences *within* each group, the following results emerge. On the Wechsler-Bellevue, left-lesion patients did best on Object Assembly and Block Design and worst on Digit

TABLE 11.1 Mean scaled or weighted scores on the Wechsler-Bellevue and WAIS subtests by patients with lesions localized in the left or right hemisphere

Subtest	WECHSLER-BELLEVUE STUDY					WAIS STUDY							
	1	2	3	4	5	6	7	8	9	10	11	12	13
Left Lesion													
I	7.0	8.1	8.3	8.0	7.7	8.0	8.2	8.1	—	9.2	9.3	7.8	6.8
C	8.4	8.5	8.6	6.7	7.5	6.8	7.6	8.8	—	8.6	8.2	7.4	6.6
A	7.4	5.8	7.7	5.0	5.0	7.8	8.2	9.1	9.6	8.8	8.7	6.6	6.3
S	6.7	7.8	9.2	5.0	8.1	7.4	9.5	8.8	8.9	6.7	8.9	7.5	4.9
DSp	7.8	5.0	6.4	2.8	5.5	7.2	8.4	8.5	8.1	7.5	7.8	7.1	5.2
V	7.2	7.6	7.0	6.5	8.0	7.5	8.2	7.0	9.1	8.1	8.6	6.8	6.5
DSy	8.5	6.7	8.0	5.8	5.8	—	—	8.1	—	5.5	6.6	4.9	2.5
PC	8.7	8.5	10.4	9.0	8.8	10.8	9.2	10.1	10.6	8.9	10.8	7.4	6.8
BD	9.6	9.0	10.2	8.7	7.6	9.6	7.4	10.3	10.4	8.0	9.8	5.6	5.8
PA	8.9	7.9	9.4	7.3	8.5	10.2	8.7	8.9	8.9	8.0	9.4	6.7	5.9
OA	9.9	9.5	10.6	8.1	8.2	9.0	8.2	8.5	8.6	7.3	9.3	5.7	5.7
Right Lesion													
I	10.6	10.2	9.8	10.3	9.4	11.4	10.3	9.6	—	9.9	10.4	8.0	8.4
C	11.4	10.1	11.8	10.1	10.5	10.8	10.3	10.9	—	11.0	11.4	8.2	9.1
A	10.2	8.3	7.1	7.1	7.8	11.0	9.1	9.9	9.3	9.2	10.2	7.4	7.8
S	10.5	9.5	10.8	8.2	10.5	11.0	9.8	10.6	9.7	8.9	11.3	6.6	7.5
DSp	10.5	7.4	8.5	5.1	7.5	11.4	10.4	9.0	10.9	8.9	9.3	7.7	7.6
V	10.6	9.6	9.1	10.1	10.0	11.8	11.0	9.6	10.4	9.7	11.0	7.4	8.7
DSy	8.2	6.0	9.6	4.8	6.5	—	—	8.2	—	6.6	6.8	4.0	3.8
PC	8.8	8.1	9.8	8.5	6.4	9.8	10.8	9.1	9.2	9.3	8.8	7.0	7.3
BD	9.1	6.2	9.9	5.8	5.8	7.3	9.4	9.8	7.5	8.0	8.4	5.0	5.5
PA	8.9	6.5	7.5	6.0	6.5	8.0	8.6	6.9	6.9	7.6	8.0	5.6	5.7
OA	9.2	7.8	10.2	7.0	6.0	7.0	9.0	7.9	6.3	7.3	7.2	5.2	4.7

NOTE: The numbers in the heading correspond to the following studies: 1. Denneril (1964); 2. Kløve (1959); 3. Meier & French (1966, Sample 1); 4. Reitan (1955c); 5. Doehring et al. (1961); 6. Inglis et al. (1982, Males); 7. Inglis et al. (1982, Females); 8. Meier & French (1966, Sample II); 9. Warrington & James (1967); 10. Zimmerman et al. (1970); 11. Munder (1976, Whites); 12. Munder (1976, Blacks); 13. Simpson & Vega (1971). Sample sizes for the patients with left and right lesions are presented in Table 9.6 for studies 1–5, and in Table 9.7 for studies 6–13.

TABLE 11.2 Differences between the weighted means earned on the 11 Wechsler-Bellevue and WAIS subtests by patients with left and right lesions

Subtest	WECHSLER-BELLEVUE			WAIS			TOTAL		
	Left Lesion N=118	Right Lesion N=120	Mean Diff.	Left Lesion N=178	Right Lesion N=205	Mean Diff.	Left Lesion N=296	Right Lesion N=325	Mean Diff.
C	8.1	10.7	−2.6	7.7	10.3	−2.6	7.9	10.5	−2.6
V	7.4	9.9	−2.5	7.8	9.9	−2.1	7.6	9.9	−2.3
DSp	5.7	8.0	−2.3	7.5	9.4	−1.9	6.8	8.9	−2.1
I	7.8	10.1	−2.3	8.2	9.7	−1.5	8.0	9.9	−1.9
S	7.4	9.9	−2.5	7.8	9.4	−1.6	7.7	9.6	−1.9
A	6.2	8.4	−2.2	8.2	9.2	−1.0	7.4	8.9	−1.5
DSy	7.0	7.0	0.0	5.4	5.9	−0.5	6.3	6.4	−0.1
PC	8.9	7.3	+1.6	9.3	8.9	+0.4	9.2	8.3	+0.9
BD	9.0	7.3	+1.7	8.4	7.6	+0.8	8.6	7.5	+1.1
OA	9.4	8.1	+1.3	7.8	6.8	+1.0	8.4	7.3	+1.1
PA	8.3	7.2	+1.1	8.3	7.1	+1.2	8.3	7.1	+1.2

NOTE: Mean Diff. = mean for patients with left lesions minus the mean for patients with right lesions. Subtests are listed in the order of their mean differences for the total sample, going from the most negative to the most positive.

These weighted means are based on data presented in Table 11.1 for five Wechsler-Bellevue and eight WAIS studies. Sample sizes shown are for all subtests except Information, Comprehension, and Digit Symbol, which had missing data for some samples tested on the WAIS. The sample sizes for Information and Comprehension were as follows: WAIS—left lesions = 149, right lesions = 169; Total—left lesions = 267, right lesions = 289. For Digit Symbol, the corresponding WAIS and Total sample sizes were 109, 129, 227, and 249, respectively.

Span and Arithmetic; on the WAIS, they did best on Picture Completion and Block Design and worst on Digit Symbol and Digit Span.

For patients with right hemisphere lesions, the following dyads are highest and lowest: on the Wechsler-Bellevue, Comprehension/Information versus Digit Symbol/Picture Arrangement; on the WAIS, Comprehension/Vocabulary versus Digit Symbol/Object Assembly.

Hemispheric Functioning: Process Versus Content

The results summarized in Table 11.2 are quite revealing and may relate to the reason why patients with left hemisphere lesions do not display the predicted P > V profile in most

studies. For both the Wechsler-Bellevue and WAIS, the deficiencies shown by left-lesion patients are on the third or distractibility factor, *not on the Verbal Comprehension dimension.* The Freedom from Distractibility factor has been interpreted as sequential or successive processing (Bannatyne, 1971, 1974; Kaufman, 1979b; Kaufman & Kaufman, 1983b), the type of mental processing that has been associated with the *left* hemisphere by cerebral specialization researchers (Levy, 1972; Sperry, 1968). Hence, damage to the left hemisphere may disrupt a person's ability to *process* sequentially, not necessarily his or her ability to handle verbal *content.*

Conversely, left-lesion patients performed best on the three Wechsler-Bellevue and WAIS subtests that are the best measures of the Perceptual Organization factor: Picture Completion, Object Assembly, Block Design. These are precisely the Wechsler subtests that provide measurement of simultaneous or holistic processing, the problem-solving style associated with the *right* hemisphere.

Left-lesion patients are able to process relatively well with their right hemispheres, and they score adequately on the Wechsler Performance subtests that are excellent measures of simultaneous processing. However, they have more difficulty with the Performance subtests that have a decided sequential component: Digit Symbol and Picture Arrangement. Just as their weakness may be sequential processing, so too their strength may be simultaneous processing; this process distinction is different from the content distinction that is examined whenever the Verbal and Performance IQs are compared.

Sequential Components of the Verbal Scale

The implication is that left-lesion patients may not manifest a P > V pattern, but they may evidence significant discrepancies between factor scores on Perceptual Organization (akin to simultaneous processing) and Freedom from Distractibility (akin to sequential processing). In chapters 3 and 8, a review of Wechsler factor analyses indicates that the best WAIS-R measures of Perceptual Organization are Picture Completion, Object Assembly, and Block Design, and that the best measures of Freedom from Distractibility are generally Digit Span and Arithmetic. These combinations of subtests, as well as the familiar quartet of Verbal Comprehension subtests, are used here to evaluate the *left*-lesion patients' profiles.

On both the Wechsler-Bellevue and WAIS, the samples with left hemisphere damage earned a mean scaled score of 8.7 on Perceptual Organization subtests. This value is nearly 1 scaled-score point higher than their Verbal Comprehension mean (7.8), but it exceeds their distractibility/sequential mean (7.1) by a greater margin. Further, there is some evidence that

Digit Symbol may belong with the third WAIS-R dimension. If the performance of the left-lesion sample on Digit Symbol is considered, the mean discrepancy between Perceptual Organization (8.7) and Freedom from Distractibility (6.8) is nearly 2 points.

Process Differences for Specific Samples

These data, which suggest that left-lesion adults performed markedly better on the Perceptual Organization (simultaneous processing) factor than on the distractibility (sequential processing) factor, also held for 11 of the 13 left-lesion groups shown in Table 11.1. The only groups that did not show a deficit on the Freedom from Distractibility dyad or triad were samples 7 and 12, the samples of females (Inglis et al., 1982) and blacks (Munder, 1976), respectively. Each of these groups displayed no difference between mean subtest scores on the Perceptual Organization and distractibility dimensions, supporting the conclusions reached earlier regarding gender and race differences in the impact of unilateral brain damage on test performance.

For the remaining 11 samples, differences in favor of Perceptual Organization were sizable, suggesting that examination of V–P IQ differences in left-damage patients has masked a real deficit in these patients' ability to process information sequentially as a consequence of their brain lesions.

These comparisons indicate that the left-lesion patients may evidence a considerably greater deficit in sequential processing/distractibility than in Verbal Comprehension when contrasted to nonverbal intelligence. The differences in mean scaled scores were nearly *twice* as big for the Freedom from Distractibility factor as for the Verbal Comprehension dimension. More to the point, the patients with left cerebral lesions performed at considerably different levels on the two factors that virtually compose the Verbal Scale; this result makes it essential to explore a patient's subtest profile before drawing any inferences from a simple V–P comparison.

Several studies have reported factor scores for their groups of left- and right-lesion patients, and all but one study has supported the conclusions presented here. Dennerll (1964) found that his left-lesion temporal lobe patients had a large difference between the perceptual and distractibility factor scores, in favor of the former; the difference between the perceptual and verbal dimensions was considerably smaller.

Black (1974b) found only a 3.4-point P > V discrepancy for his missile wound patients with left hemisphere damage; this difference is in striking contrast to the 11.4-point discrepancy that results when subtracting the distractibility factor score from the perceptual factor score. Black (1976) even found a meaningful relationship among factor scores for his sample with lesions to the left *frontal* lobe; although this sample had a V–P discrepancy of only −3.3 points, they had a difference of 7.6 points in favor of the Perceptual Organization factor score when compared to the distractibility factor score.

The one negative finding was by Ivnik et al. (1987) from his sample of left hemisphere temporal lobe epileptics. This group had a postoperative P > V difference of 7.6 points, but had a slightly higher distractibility than perceptual factor score.

Practical Inferences From Studies of Factor Scores

Of the 13 separate studies reported in Table 11.1, eight had sizable differences (about ½ scaled score point or more) in the left lesion patients' mean scores on the Verbal Comprehension versus Freedom from Distractibility factors. Of these eight discrepancies, *seven* indicated greater deficits on the distractibility dyad than on the verbal ability dimension. This finding, coupled with the analyses described in the previous section, challenges the utility of the V–P IQ discrepancy for patients with left hemisphere damage.

For patients with right hemisphere lesions, however, the conventional V–P IQ difference seems an adequate statistic. Damage to the right cerebral hemisphere should not have a particularly adverse effect on either the Verbal Comprehension or the Freedom from Distractibility dimensions; hence, there is no negative consequence of combining them, which is the net effect of computing a Verbal IQ. It is also sensible to examine the Performance IQ as a whole, instead of just the three subtests that are most associated with the Perceptual Organization factor, because (a) Picture Arrangement has a decided simultaneous as well as sequential component and is known to be sensitive to right temporal lesions (Reitan, 1986), and (b) Digit Symbol tends to be low regardless of location of lesion, so it will not artificially elevate the P-IQ of patients with deficits in visual-spatial-simultaneous functioning.

Verbal Components of the Performance Scale

Most of the arguments that clinicians and researchers have advanced for the inadequacy of exploring V–P differences in patients with unilateral brain damage have focused on the Performance Scale. Benton (1962), Heilbrun (1956), Parsons, Vega, and Burn (1969), and others have stressed the verbal components of the Performance subtests such as the ability to follow verbal directions, give verbal responses, and use verbal mediation during "nonverbal" problem solving.

Parsons et al. (1969) suggested that "patients with verbal-symbolic deficits might perform poorly [on the Performance Scale] whether or not they are displaying visual-constructive deficits" (p. 552). They noted that "the Performance scale is comprised of a more heterogeneous group of subtests than the Verbal scale . . . [and] is not as good a criterion measure for testing the hypothesis of differential hemispheric control of psychological functions" (p. 552). Lezak (1983) pointed out that lesions to the left hemisphere can affect success on non-verbal subtests in ways that are unrelated to verbal skills: "Patients with left hemisphere damage may make defective constructions because of tendencies toward simplification. . . . Their ability to perform complex manual—as well as oral—motor sequences may also be impaired" (p. 56).

Despite the obvious truth in the claims of a verbal-saturated Performance Scale and the sense of Lezak's statements, the data seem to support the Verbal Scale as the primary culprit in sabotaging the V–P discrepancy in brain-lesion studies. Benton (1962) felt that depressed Verbal IQs in left-lesion patients are almost axiomatic in view of decades of research and clinical knowledge, but that lowered Performance IQs in right-lesion patients are not sensible and should not be anticipated. In fact, the accumulation of research in this area has confirmed the *opposite* of Benton's predictions. Further, the Performance IQs of patients with right lesions have been uniformly low in most studies, compared to Verbal IQs, and *all* nonverbal subtests have been depressed.

As shown in Table 11.2, the mean scores on the five Performance subtests are in the 6½ to 8 range for both the Wechsler-Bellevue and WAIS, compared to means in the 8 to 10½ range on the Verbal subtests. For left-lesion patients, the Performance Scale again "hangs together" quite well. Excluding Digit Symbol, these samples averaged 8 to 9 on the Performance subtests on both the Wechsler-Bellevue and WAIS. Perhaps their problems with verbal tasks did affect their success on the Performance tasks. Nonetheless, the left-lesion patients still outstripped the right-lesion patients on all Performance tasks except Digit Symbol. In addition, the left-lesion patients' low scores on Digit Symbol are conceivably related primarily to their sequential deficit.

Overall, the verbal aspects of Wechsler's supposedly nonverbal tasks may have reduced the P > V discrepancies in many studies of left-lesion patients. However, I feel that there is more empirical support for the argument that

the two hemispheres differ more in how they *process* information than in the *content* that is being processed. Thus, damage to the right hemisphere would produce a deficit in simultaneous processing (measured by the Perceptual Organization factor), and damage to the left hemisphere would produce a deficit in linear, sequential processing (hypothesized to be measured by the Freedom from Distractibility factor).

Some Pertinent Research

Whereas left lesions *may* impair functioning on tests of verbal factual knowledge and reasoning, a more reliable occurrence is that such lesions will certainly depress scores on the verbal-sequential tests of Arithmetic and Digit Span. Black (1986b), in an investigation of patients with unilateral lesions stemming from a variety of causes (average age = 36, average years of education = 12), found that the left-lesion patients ($N = 40$) performed more poorly than the right-lesion patients ($N = 47$) both in their forward span and in their backward span.

Support for a process approach to brain functioning also comes from an investigation of the reading achievement of 86 left-lesion and 76 right-lesion patients averaging 40 years of age and 13 years of education (Heaton, Schmitz, Avitable, & Lehman, 1987). Both groups were deficient, compared to a control group of 100 normal adults, in Reading Recognition and Reading Comprehension on the Peabody Individual Achievement Test (PIAT). However, the left-lesion group performed significantly worse than the right-lesion sample only on the recognition (oral reading) task. Consequently, the two brain-damaged groups did not differ significantly in reading per se but in the subtest requiring sequential, linear analysis of letters and syllables.

The emphasis on process rather than on content or the nature of the stimulus has been articulated by Lezak (1983), based on her clinical experience and review of much neuropsychological literature:

[E]ach hemisphere mediates stimuli entering through all sensory channels. Hemisphere specialization is supramodal *in that it is organized on the basis of the capacity to process verbal or configurational material rather than in terms of sensory modalities. . . . Time-bound relationships of sequence and order characterize many of the functions that are vulnerable to left hemisphere lesions. . . . These differences in hemisphere functioning reflect very basic processing differences between the hemispheres. . . . The left hemisphere best handles time-related material that comes in linear sequences, such as verbal statements, mathematical propositions, and the programming of rapid motor sequences. The right hemisphere is superior when the material cannot be described adequately in words or strings of symbols (pp. 54–57).*

Should V–P Discrepancies Be Used for Assessing Brain Damage?

Some neuropsychologists are opposed to the use of the V-IQs and P-IQs because they are too heterogeneous and global. Smith (1966a) felt that "[t]he arbitrary lumping together of all WB verbal subtests into a hypothesized dimension of 'verbal' intelligence, and of all Performance subtests into another hypothesized dimension . . . confounds efforts to define the specific effects of specific brain lesions" (p. 121). Lezak (1983) echoes these sentiments: "Both Verbal and Performance Scale IQ scores . . . are based on averages of some quite dissimilar functions that have relatively low intercorrelations and bear no regular neuroanatomical or neuropsychological relationship to one another. . . . There is also considerable functional overlap between these two scales" (p. 242).

I respect the message conveyed by these clinicians, but I feel that it is unwise to take such an extreme stance. Wechsler's combination of tasks into two scales was not "arbitrary," and the results of factor analysis point to impressive commonalities among Verbal Comprehension subtests and among Perceptual Organization subtests, not to their "dissimilar functions." Table 11.2, summarizing subtest

patterns from 13 studies, shows that the six Verbal subtests are about equally good at discriminating right-lesion from left-lesion patients, and the same can be said for most Performance tasks (Digit Symbol is the main exception).

The use of a regrouping of the 11 subtests into three categories, corresponding to the three factors, is a wise adjunct to interpretation, particularly for left-lesion patients. However, this recategorization is a refinement of the Verbal and Performance Scales; it should be conducted alongside the examination of a patient's V–P differences as a possible explanation of any observed discrepancies (or failure to find meaningful discrepancies).

The V–P differences remain important because of the bulk of clinical and neuropsychological research that has been conducted with these IQs. However, as stressed throughout this book and elsewhere (Kaufman, 1979b; Kaufman & Kaufman, 1983b), the global IQs are merely the starting point of profile analysis. The next stages involve systematic, empirical evaluation of subtest profiles, a process that should help pinpoint the specific cognitive deficits that accompany specific localized brain lesions to either hemisphere.

But Wechsler's V- and P-IQs should not be dismissed as being useless for neurological patients, and the IQ concept should not be told to "rest in peace" (Lezak, 1988a; see chapter 2). The WAIS-R, even more so than the WISC-R, can be arguably thought of as a two-factor rather than a three-factor test battery (see chapter 8), with the two factors corresponding quite nicely to Wechsler's division of subtests into Verbal and Performance scales.

And the research results with right-lesion patients, even if not with left-lesion patients, have shown a consistent V > P pattern for a multitude of samples, spanning diagnostic etiologies, test batteries, various adult age ranges, and educational levels. Even though females and blacks seem to differ from males and whites in the nature and magnitude of V–P discrepancies, females and blacks with right hemisphere damage nonetheless displayed V > P patterns.

The V–P difference has great utility for understanding the cognitive assets and deficiencies of adults with unilateral brain damage. Examiners should almost always go beyond the IQs and incorporate the distractibility factor into their interpretation of these strengths and weaknesses, especially with left-lesion patients. But I consider the reliance on global scores, whether IQs or scores derived by regrouping the subtests into three factors, a far more sensible procedure than relying on just a few isolated subtests or on a set of "signs" such as Picture Completion > Arithmetic or Information > Object Assembly (Simpson & Vega, 1971) to assess lateralized brain damage.

THE LATERALITY INDEX

Lawson and Inglis (1983) and their colleagues (Inglis & Lawson, 1986; Lawson & Inglis, 1984, 1985; Lawson, Inglis, & Stroud, 1983; Tittemore, Lawson, & Inglis, 1985) have introduced a novel use of factor analysis to facilitate better understanding of the cognitive impairments associated with learning disabilities and lesions to the left or right hemisphere. Like Benton (1962) and others concerned with the "impurity" of Wechsler's Verbal and Performance Scales, these researchers tried to identify a method of quantifying the degree of "verbalness" and "nonverbalness" in each separate subtest.

A Verbal–Nonverbal Bipolar Factor

Lawson and Inglis's solution was to study the *unrotated* factor patterns of various Wechsler batteries and of the K-ABC, rather than the rotated solutions that have been stressed by other investigators. Whereas the *first* unrotated factor has frequently been identified as a *g* or general intelligence factor, and used as a means of comparing the degree to which each subtest is saturated with *g* (see pp. 251–255), Lawson and Inglis were perhaps the first researchers to focus on the *second* unrotated factor in principal components analysis.

They observed that this dimension is bipolar, composed of negative factor loadings by Verbal tasks and positive loadings by Performance tasks. Lawson and Inglis (1983) interpret this unrotated bipolar factor "as relating to a verbal-nonverbal continuum of test material" (p. 834). They report correlations of .90 and above between factor scores on this dimension and V–P IQ discrepancies for the WAIS and WAIS-R standardization samples (Lawson & Inglis, 1983; Lawson et al., 1983). They reason further that subtests with the most negative loadings are the most verbal, while the tasks with the most positive loadings are the most heavily saturated with nonverbal ability.

The results of the WAIS analysis showed Comprehension and Vocabulary to have the most extreme negative loadings, with Block Design and Object Assembly emerging as the most positively loaded. Lawson and Inglis (1983) see these findings as consistent with intuitive expectations about the degree of verbalness required by each task, and therefore as supporting their interpretation of the dimension. For example, the two Performance tasks with the most positive loadings "appear to involve the ability to visualize configurations in space and hence would not, on the face of it, seem to depend greatly on verbal processing" (p. 834).

Relationship of Index to Profiles of Brain-Damaged Patients

To make the verbal–nonverbal dimension functional, Lawson and Inglis computed factor score coefficients (almost identical to the unrotated factor loadings for the second dimension) for each test battery they and their colleagues have studied; then they provided formulas to allow clinicians to compute factor scores on this dimension for any person that they assess.

For the children's tests (WISC-R, K-ABC), the researchers have named this factor score the Learning Disabilities Index because it correlated in the low .90s with the mean subtest profiles of learning-disabled children and adolescents on the WISC and WISC-R (Inglis & Lawson, 1986; Lawson & Inglis, 1985). (Research with learning-disabled children and adults has revealed a characteristic profile that parallels the factor loadings of the unrotated factor 2: high scores on Wechsler's visual-spatial tasks and low scores on subtests like Information and Arithmetic; see Kaufman, 1979b, and pp. 448–455.)

For the WAIS and WAIS-R, Inglis and Lawson (1983) have labeled the factor score the Laterality Index because its factor score coefficients correlated an astonishing .97 with the size of the differences produced by each subtest when comparing the means earned by patients with left versus right lesions, summarized from nine Wechsler-Bellevue and WAIS studies reported in the literature.

Table 11.3 presents the factor score coefficients for the Wechsler subtests on the WAIS-R, WAIS, and WISC-R. The subtests are listed in the same order as in Table 11.2, going from the Verbal task on which the right-lesion patients most outscored the left-lesion patients to the Performance task on which the reverse was true. The coefficients for the WAIS show a remarkable relationship to the mean differences between brain-damaged samples, going from $-.32$ on Comprehension, and gradually becoming more positive until peaking at $+.57$ for Object Assembly.

The relationship is just as astounding as the virtually perfect correlation reported by Lawson and Inglis (1983) based on data for a similar, and overlapping, set of studies. Only Similarities and Picture Arrangement are misplaced; the rank-order correlation between the WAIS factor coefficients and the relative ability of the WAIS

subtests to discriminate between patients with left and right brain lesions equals .96 ($p < .01$).

Coefficients for the WAIS-R resemble closely the WAIS coefficients (the unrotated factors correlate .98, according to Lawson and Inglis, 1983), although the two verbal-sequential tasks have coefficients that are less negative for the WAIS-R than the WAIS. Like the WAIS Laterality Index, the WAIS-R Laterality Index, based on the pattern of its factor coefficients, is legitimately termed a verbal–nonverbal dimension. The same cannot be said for the WISC-R Learning Disability Index.

Challenging the Interpretation of the Learning Disabilities Index

Although Lawson and Inglis (1984) have chosen to interpret the second WISC-R unrotated dimension as reflecting a verbal–nonverbal continuum, their arguments are specious. The three most negative coefficients are by Digit Span, Arithmetic, and Coding—the sequential/distractibility triad—and the two most positive coefficients are by Object Assembly and Picture Completion, the tasks that are arguably the best measure of simultaneous, holistic, right-brain processing (Kaufman, 1979b).

The Verbal Comprehension subtests have mild negative values between $-.04$ and $-.15$. These coefficients are too low to consider the dimension on the verbal–nonverbal continuum; so is the correlation of only .75 between this second unrotated factor and V–P IQ discrepancy for the WISC-R standardization sample (Lawson & Inglis, 1984). (Contrast the 56% overlap in variance for the WISC-R with the values of 90% and 81% for the WAIS and WAIS-R, respectively.) Quite clearly, the WISC-R Learning Disabilities Index appears to be on the sequential–simultaneous continuum, not the verbal–nonverbal continuum.

Inglis and Lawson (1986) also interpret the second unrotated factor for the K-ABC as a

TABLE 11.3 Factor score coefficients of Wechsler's subtests on the verbal–nonverbal dimension identified by Lawson and Inglis as the Laterality Index or Learning Disabilities Index

Subtest	WAIS	WAIS-R	WISC-R
Comprehension	−.32	−.29	−.04
Vocabulary	−.31	−.33	−.15
Digit Span	−.24	−.12	−.47
Information	−.24	−.32	−.14
Similarities	−.12	−.20	−.05
Arithmetic	−.20	−.08	−.33
Digit Symbol/Coding	+.15	+.14	−.25
Picture Completion	+.15	+.26	+.37
Block Design	+.47	+.45	+.26
Object Assembly	+.57	+.62	+.45
Picture Arrangement	+.25	+.10	+.27

NOTE: Subtests are listed in the same order as they are listed in Table 11.2—i.e., in order of "mean difference" is based on data from all Wechsler-Bellevue and WAIS studies (mean for left-lesion patients minus mean for right-lesion patients), going from the most negative difference to the most positive difference. Data are from Lawson and Inglis (1983, 1984) and Lawson, Inglis, and Stroud (1983).

bipolar verbal–nonverbal dimension, even though a sequential–simultaneous interpretation is more consistent with the theory underlying the K-ABC and with the pattern of factor score coefficients: The most negative coefficients were obtained for Number Recall and Word Order (the best measures of sequential processing), and the most positive coefficients were for Gestalt Closure and Triangles (among the best measures of simultaneous processing); the highly verbal Riddles subtest had a factor score coefficient of only −.06.

Data presented by Inglis and Lawson indicate that the WISC-R and K-ABC Learning Disabilities Indexes are quite valuable for distinguishing learning-disabled children from normal children. Similarly, WAIS data provided by these authors and their colleagues show the potential value of the Laterality Index for discriminating left-lesion patients from right-lesion patients. However, despite the use of the same methodology for children as for adults, I dispute

these investigators' interpretation of these indexes as measuring the same psychological trait. The Learning Disabilities Index and the Laterality Index are measuring decidedly different constructs.

Psychometric Properties of the Laterality Index

The findings for the Laterality Index are quite provocative in view of the preceding discussions and analyses in this chapter. Lawson and Inglis (1983) and Lawson et al. (1983) provided guidelines for computing the Laterality Indexes for the WAIS and WAIS-R based on the age-corrected scaled scores, *not* the regular scaled scores used to generate IQs. The resultant index has a population mean of 0 (since the mean V–P IQ discrepancy for the normal population is designed to be 0) and a standard deviation of approximately 300.

For the WAIS-R, the split-half reliability of the index averages .78, and the test–retest coefficient is .79 (Lawson et al., 1983). To compute the index, enter the person's WAIS-R *age-corrected* scaled scores into Examiner's Form 11.1 on page 379. Patients with *left* damage are hypothesized to have strongly *positive* indexes; patients with *right* damage are expected to have highly *negative* indexes.

Clinical Value of the Laterality Index

Is it worth computing the Laterality Index for patients with suspected or known brain damage? On the positive side, the index does relate closely to the degree to which the separate subtests discriminate between left- and right-lesion samples. Also, Lawson and Inglis (1983) present some interesting additional data for the sample of 40 male and 40 female stroke patients with unilateral brain damage tested on the WAIS by Inglis et al. (1982); this group has been discussed in chapter 10 and in earlier sections of this chapter and is described in Table 9.7.

In accordance with the hypothesized indexes anticipated for left- and right-lesion patients, the male stroke patients with left lesions earned a mean Laterality Index of +315.4 (slightly more than 1 *SD* from the mean) and the males with right lesions had a mean index of −526.4 (about 1¾ *SD* from the normative mean). Data for females were not so impressive—mean Indexes of −15.5 for left-lesion patients and −146.8 for right-lesion patients. These values support the finding observed previously for Inglis et al.'s (1982) sample and for a composite of male versus female samples with unilateral brain damage: Males show the predicted pattern based on side of brain lesion; females demonstrate a moderate relationship, but only for right-lesion samples.

Interestingly, a similar gender difference was observed for the WISC-R Learning Disabilities Index, as boys with learning disabilities obtained a much higher Index (i.e., more in the predicted direction) than girls with learning disabilities

(Tittemore et al., 1985). This gender difference was not observed, however, for 211 learning-disabled applicants for a special college program who were tested on either the WAIS or WAIS-R; males and females each earned mean Laterality Indexes of about zero (Ackerman, McGrew, & Dykman, 1987).

I believe that the disadvantages of using the Laterality Index outweigh its advantages at this time:

(a) The Laterality Index is cumbersome for examiners to compute and is defined by confusing parameters (a standard deviation of 301 on the WAIS and 302 on the WAIS-R).

(b) The reliability coefficients below .80 fall below most standards of desirable consistency.

(c) The indexes presented for males and females in Inglis et al.'s (1982) investigation seem to provide the identical information and conclusions that were provided by a simple examination of the V–P IQ differences.

(d) The correlations between V–P discrepancy and factor score coefficients are so high for the WAIS (.95) and WAIS-R (.90) that one has to wonder whether or not they are measuring precisely the same thing.

(e) There is no evidence that the Laterality Index represents a better application of factor analysis to neuropsychological research than the use of factor scores from the rotated solutions, especially the combination of the two or three distractibility/sequential tasks that seemed to facilitate interpretation of the data in Table 11.2 (see pp. 347–351).

The main value of the Laterality Index lies in its *potential* for distinguishing between patients with left and right lesions. It is a creative idea, and Lawson and Inglis are to be commended for introducing an exciting, new line of investigation to the field. However, research with the index is essential, particularly in comparison to the results of analyses involving both the V–P IQ discrepancy and comparisons of success on the Perceptual Organization subtests versus success on both the Verbal Comprehension and Freedom from Distractibility factors. If the Laterality Index proves to be useful over and above the other comparisons, then it will truly be a valuable asset for examiners to compute indexes routinely in their clinical and neuropsychological practices.

CLINICAL ISSUES IN THE INTERPRETATION OF A PATIENT'S V–P DIFFERENCE

The preceding sections have focused primarily on research findings for groups of patients. Sometimes too much attention on group differences can obscure the interpretation of a given brain-damaged patient's discrepancy between his or her V- and P-IQs.

Individual Versus Group Data

Matarazzo and his colleagues have consistently warned examiners to be aware of the huge difference between mean values obtained for *groups* and a set of scores earned by any particular *individual;* along with this wise and essential warning is Matarazzo's vital reminder to pay careful attention to base rates of differences that characterize a normal population, and always to compare the magnitude of observed differences (such as V–P discrepancies) to the normal or expected differences (Bornstein & Matarazzo, 1982, 1984; Matarazzo, 1972; Matarazzo & Herman, 1985).

Consequently, the significant and persistent V > P pattern of 9 or 10 points for right-lesion patients tested with the Wechsler-Bellevue or WAIS or WAIS-R is statistically meaningful, and tells us much about *groups* of patients with right-brain damage; they do have a deficiency in the skill measured by Wechsler's

Performance Scale, and that deficit is causally linked to the specific location of their brain lesion.

Grouped data, however, are much more reliable than the data for any one person in that sample. A 9-point V–P discrepancy is unusually large for a group, but for an individual aged 16–24 that difference is not reliably different from zero at the .05 level, and it barely reaches statistical significance for adults aged 25–74 (see pages 264–265). Further, even a V–P difference as large as 15 points is highly significant in a statistical sense, but it occurs fairly commonly in the normal population. As shown in Table 9.3, discrepancies of 15 or more points occur in about 18% of normal adults, far too common an occurrence to infer the presence of an abnormality such as brain damage.

Subsequent to their review of numerous unilateral brain damage studies, Bornstein and Matarazzo (1982) emphasized: "These findings suggest that groups of subjects with lateralized cerebral dysfunction tend to have greater discrepancies between VIQ and PIQ scores than would occur in a nonneurological population. Nevertheless it is important to stress that the evaluation of these Verbal-Performance differences must be determined for each *individual* patient in the context of base rates and also with respect to other neuropsychological measures" (p. 329).

For any individual patient, then, the precise V–P IQ difference obtained needs to be compared to the base rates provided for the WAIS-R in Tables 9.3 and 9.4. As a general rule of thumb, a difference of at least 20 points occurs in less than 10% of normal people, and is unusual enough to consider that the discrepancy may be related to the specific lesion, pending integration of the findings with other neurological data and pertinent background information (e.g., education level). From Table 9.4, though, the size of an abnormal difference, occurring less than 10% of the time, may be as little as 12 points for adults with Full Scale

IQs below 80, or as much as 22 points for adults with superior ability.

Consideration of base rates or explanations of V–P differences other than brain damage is often lacking in the literature and, undoubtedly, in clinical practice as well. Balthazar and Morrison (1961), for example, investigated the hypothesis that "a difference of seven points or greater between Wechsler Verbal and Performance Subtest scales would be of diagnostic value in determining left-right and indeterminately unilateralized brain damage" (p. 161), and subsequently supported the experimental hypothesis. Whiddon (1978) states: "Study I revealed that a VIQ-PIQ difference of more than 10 points could serve as a sign of brain damage" (p. 5051-B).

Fortunately, there are also researchers like Black (1974a), who used base-rate tables to select a criterion of 20 or more points to reflect possible neurological dysfunction and concluded that "seven per cent of the bilateral lesion Ss, 28 per cent of the right-hemisphere lesion Ss, and 14 per cent of left-hemisphere lesion Ss demonstrated such dysfunction" (p. 816).

Emotional Disturbance and Lateralized Lesions

Lezak (1983) and others (e.g., Heilman, Bowers, & Valenstein, 1985) have pointed out that lesions in the left versus right hemisphere are accompanied by different types of emotional reactions. Clinicians need to understand these differences to facilitate their interactions with patients having unilateral brain damage, especially when assessing these patients shortly after the damage has occurred.

Left-Lesion Patients

Damage to the left hemisphere is often accompanied by anxiety, undue cautiousness, oversensitivity to the impairment, and depression (Buck, 1968; Galin, 1974; Jones-Gotman & Milner, 1977; Lezak, 1983). Lezak (1983) notes:

"Patients with left hemispheric lesions are more likely than those with right-sided brain damage to exhibit a catastrophic reaction (extreme and disruptive emotional disturbance). The catastrophic reaction may appear as acute, often disorganizing anxiety, agitation, or tearfulness disrupting the activity that provoked it. Typically, it occurs when patients are confronted with their limitations, as when taking a test" (p. 61). Goldstein (1948) first used the term *catastrophic reaction* to describe the profound depression accompanying left hemisphere lesions; subsequent empirical investigations have supported the tendency for catastrophic reactions and depression to be more associated with left than right hemispheric damage (e.g., Gainotti, 1972; Gasparrini, Satz, Heilman, & Coolidge, 1977).

Depression, a common side effect of left hemisphere damage, is often accompanied by numerous clinical presenting symptoms. These include "depressed mood and agitation; . . . psychomotor retardation; impaired immediate memory and learning abilities; defective attention, concentration, and tracking; impaired orientation; an overall shoddy quality to cognitive products; and listlessness with loss of interest in one's surroundings. . . . [T]he performance of depressed patients on drawing and construction tasks may be careless, shabby, or incomplete due to apathy, low energy level, and poor motivation but, if given enough time and encouragement, . . . may make a recognizable and often fully adequate response" (Lezak, 1983, p. 235).

Caine (1986), in summarizing literature on depressed patients, stressed their impairments in sustaining attention, memory, learning ability, mental control, and motor performance. Based on these presenting clinical symptoms, it is not surprising that "[d]epressed people often have distinctly higher Verbal [than Performance] IQs" (Gregory, 1987, p. 72).

Gass and Russell (1985) studied the relationship of emotional adjustment (MMPI profile) to functional loss (WAIS Verbal IQ) in a study of 31 white male patients with carefully documented left hemisphere damage. These investigators were critical of previous investigations of the emotional behavior in patients with left-brain lesions because of failure to control for premorbid status, to exclude aphasics, to exclude patients with right hemisphere pathology, and to screen for inconsistent MMPI profiles.

Gass and Russell (1985) used state-of-the-art neurodiagnostic techniques to ensure that the patients' lesions were confined to the left hemisphere; they also controlled for education level in their multivariate data analysis. Their results showed that regardless of the degree of impairment in verbal intelligence, the patients with right lesions consistently had MMPI profiles suggestive of the following emotional symptoms: "mild dysphoria, worry, and concerns or preoccupations with regard to one's physical condition" (p. 669). The implications of the left-lesion patients' MMPI emotional profiles are quite consistent with the stereotypical behaviors described previously for these patients.

Right-Lesion Patients

Patients with right hemisphere damage typically have different emotional reactions than those with left lesions. The depression that accompanies left lesions can be simulated by inactivating the left hemisphere via the Wada technique, i.e., intracarotid injections of sodium amytal; in contrast, inactivation of the right hemisphere by this technique is likely to produce euphoria (Nebes, 1978). Thus,

> [P]atients with right hemisphere damage tend to experience relative difficulty in discerning the emotional characteristics of stimuli with corresponding diminution in their emotional responsivity . . . [and] difficulty comprehending the affective quality of speech. . . . [They] are less likely to be dissatisfied with themselves or their performance than are those with left hemisphere lesions, and they are less likely to be

> aware of their mistakes. . . . At least in the acute or early stages of their condition, they may display an indifference reaction, tending to deny or make light of the extent of their disabilities. . . . Relatively few patients with right hemisphere lesions are depressed during their hospitalization. . . . However, a number become depressed later. . . .

When [depression] does develop it is apt to be more chronic, more debilitating, and more resistive to intervention (Lezak, 1983, pp. 60–62).

The inappropriate indifference of right-lesion patients was first stressed in the early 1950s (Denny-Brown, Meyer, & Horenstein, 1952; Hecaen, Ajuriaguerra, & Massonet, 1951). This indifference was observed by Gainotti (1972) in right-damaged patients, just as the catastrophic reaction was observed in left-damaged patients, in a study of 160 individuals with lateralized lesions. Whereas Gainotti considered the profound depression of left-lesion patients to be a normal response to severe cognitive deficits, "he felt the indifference reaction was an abnormal mood associated with denial of illness" (Valenstein & Heilman, 1979, p. 425).

In a study of 50 white male patients with right hemisphere damage, Gass and Russell (1987) studied the relationship of emotional adjustment (MMPI profile) to functional loss (WAIS Performance IQ); this investigation was analogous to these authors' similar study, described previously, of left-lesion patients (Gass & Russell, 1985). Gass and Russell (1987) used sophisticated neurodiagnostic techniques to ensure that the patients' lesions were confined to the right hemisphere; they also controlled for age and education level in their multivariate data analysis. Their results showed that regardless of the degree of impairment in nonverbal intelligence, the patients with right lesions consistently had MMPI profiles suggestive of the following emotional symptoms: mildly depressed, pessimistic, and worried; discouraged and lacking initiative; somatic preoccupation; denial; and limited emotional insight. This profile sounds fairly consistent with clinical observations of right-lesion patients, but interpretation is hampered by the investigators' failure to report the degree of chronicity of the subjects' lesions, or to control for this important variable.

Even more consistent with the indifference and denial of right-lesion patients were the results of a creative study conducted by Anderson and Tranel (1989). They investigated 100 brain–damaged patients' *awareness* of their own cognitive deficits, as measured by a neuropsychological battery that included the WAIS-R. This sample included 32 acute stroke victims with lesions lateralized to the left ($N = 12$) or right ($N = 20$) hemisphere. Nearly all (90%) of the right-lesion patients demonstrated unawareness of cognitive deficits in intelligence, memory, or other areas, and five right-lesion patients with substantial paralysis even denied having motor problems. Significantly fewer of the left-lesion patients (41%) evidenced unawareness of a cognitive deficit; none of these patients with partial paralysis denied having motor difficulties.

Clinical Applications of the Emotional Component of Brain Damage

The generally different, predictable affective responses to damage to the left or right hemispheres must be taken into account when interpreting the V–P discrepancy studies involving patients with unilateral brain damage. The emotional behaviors accompanying left lesions, most notably anxiety, depression, carelessness, and low energy level, are likely to have their most significant impact on Wechsler's Performance IQ. Attention to detail is important to performance on Wechsler's nonverbal tasks such as Picture Arrangement, yet impaired and disordered attention in signal detection tasks has been documented in several investigations of depressed patients (Caine, 1986). Indeed, the V > P that often characterizes the profiles of depressed patients (Gregory, 1987), is *opposite* to the P > V that is anticipated for people with left hemisphere lesions. This antagonistic

influence on V–P differences *may* be a primary reason why left-lesion patients have demonstrated such trivial P > V profiles in so many studies of unilateral brain damage on the WAIS and WAIS-R. This hypothesis, however, is mere speculation; there are no data to support the contention that depression systematically lowers the P-IQs of left-lesion patients.

The emotional limitations of right hemisphere patients may also affect their relative success on the Verbal and Performance Scales. Their difficulties with recognizing emotional tone in facial expressions, for example, may lead to lowered scores on Picture Arrangement, a social awareness task that measures this skill to some extent. Consequently, low scores on Picture Arrangement, for some right-lesion patients, may have an emotional, rather than a visual-spatial, causality. Similarly, the indifference and lack of awareness of their mistakes that many right hemisphere subjects display may lead to low scores on the Block Design, Object Assembly, and Picture Arrangement subtests, which are dependent on the person's ability to benefit from visual, sensory-motor feedback.

Also, lack of awareness of mistakes and difficulty in comprehending the affective quality of speech can have a negative influence on a right-damaged person's success on the *Verbal* Scale, most notably in the patient's ability to improve ambiguous or incomplete responses after querying by the examiner. Finally, the possibility of a resistant-to-change depression in chronic (but not acute) right-lesion patients may lead to sizable V > P profiles in patients with long-standing right-brain damage. Although this discrepancy may have been absent during acute stages of the illness, its later appearance may be primarily a function of the depression than of any visual-spatial degeneration.

Although these potential emotional influences on the V–P discrepancies of patients with unilateral brain damage are speculative, they are quite important because of the consistency of the clinical observations across patients with diverse types of right- or left-brain lesions.

When the right hemisphere lesion response of indifference appears in a left-lesion patient, this occurrence is so uncharacteristic that probably the most likely explanation is bilateral involvement of either a temporary or permanent nature; Lezak (1983) states that "damage that is actually bilateral damage may be classified as unilateral" (p. 61). In addition, Lezak (1983) reminds us that "descriptions of differences in the emotional behavior of right and left hemisphere damaged patients reflect observed tendencies that are not necessary consequences of unilateral brain disease" (p. 62).

Therefore, we need to be aware that some portion of the observed V > P differences in right-lesion patients may be due to emotional, not physiological or anatomical, characteristics associated with the location of the lesion; and the same explanation may be partly at the root of the failure of many studies to display the predicted P > V profile for patients with left hemisphere damage.

V–P Interpretation in the Context of Patients' Behaviors

Merely identifying an abnormally large V–P IQ difference in a patient with unilateral brain damage is just the beginning of the interpretive procedure, as Bornstein and Matarazzo (1982) implied. The difference must next be evaluated in the context of other neurological data, behavioral observations, research findings, and background variables that interact with V–P differences such as age, gender, race, education level, and Full Scale IQ.

Observation is especially pertinent for neurologically impaired individuals because they are often characterized by sensory deficits, motor deficits, distractibility, depression (particularly those with left damage or chronic right damage), poor frustration tolerance, motivational defects, and a tendency to fatigue easily (Lezak, 1983, pp. 124–127).

Fatigue

The problem with fatigue is often best handled by testing neurological patients in the early morning when they "are most apt to be rested and energized" (Lezak, 1983, p. 126). With the Wechsler-Bellevue or WAIS, failure to respond to a patient's fatigue would likely have led to a depressed Performance IQ, since all Performance tasks were administered last. This occurrence might have produced V > P profiles for right-lesion patients that would have been interpreted wrongly as a visual-spatial deficit, but it is not a concern for current examiners because the WAIS-R adopted the WISC-R administration procedure of alternating Verbal and Performance subtests.

Since fatigue is a potential problem for elderly people as well as brain-damaged examinees, data from Rust, Barnard, and Oster's (1979) WAIS investigation are perhaps pertinent here. They administered the Performance tasks before the Verbal subtests to half of their sample of 44 normal adults, ages 65 and above, and used the conventional order for the other half. The order of presentation was *not* related significantly to V–P discrepancy.

Sensory Problems

Reduced vision and/or hearing on the side opposite to the lesion occurs commonly for patients with unilateral lesions (Lezak, 1983); "[p]atients with right-sided lesions, in particular, may have reduced awareness of stimuli in the left half of space" (p. 124). The Boston process approach (Milberg, Hebben, & Kaplan, 1986) focuses on observation of strategies and qualitative features of a patient's performance: "[B]y observing the strategy used by a disabled patient on verbal and visuo-spatial tasks one can distinguish the defects due to peripheral injury from those due to cognitive dysfunction" (pp. 83–84).

Reitan and Fitzhugh (1971) administered a battery of tests that included several measures of somatosensory functioning that focused on tactile, visual, and auditory imperception of simple stimuli under conditions of bilateral simultaneous stimulation: "In every instance, groups with left cerebral lesions performed more poorly on the right than left side of the body, and the reverse was true for groups with right cerebral lesions. The magnitude of these differences appeared to be smaller for auditory than tactile or visual deficits. . . . Lateralized deficiencies in perception of simultaneous tactile stimuli were more reliable in the group with left cerebral lesions, whereas the lateralized differences in the visual modality were more significant for the group with right cerebral damage" (pp. 220–221). Goldstein and Shelly (1973) likewise identified significant sensory impairments (auditory, visual, and tactile) in the hypothesized directions for their samples of left- and right-lesion patients.

Unfortunately, subtle sensory deficits are difficult to spot immediately. Lezak (1983) made the following clinical suggestions for examiners to heed when testing a patient with a lateralized lesion: (a) position yourself either across from the person, or at the side that is most likely intact; (b) be certain that the person can see all visually presented stimuli; and (c) speak to the ear on the same side as the damaged hemisphere.

Motor Coordination Problems

Reitan and Fitzhugh (1971) found the most striking differences between left- and right-lesion patients to be on tests of motor coordination; deficiencies on tests like motor strength and motor speed for the upper extremity contralateral (opposite) to the side of the lesion were far more pronounced than deficiencies on the somatosensory tests discussed above, or on the verbal and performance aspects of the Wechsler-Bellevue.

Haaland and Delaney (1981) noted the same pattern of contralateral deficiency on all motor tests in the battery they administered to their stroke and tumor patients with unilateral lesions, but they also observed deficiencies in the ip-silateral hand and arm on those tasks requiring sensory-motor interaction for both the right- and left-lesion groups. Goldstein and Shelly (1973) were able to discriminate right- from left-lesion patients with some of the motor tests they administered (measures of tactile recognition), but tests of complex psychomotor problem solving, grip strength, and tapping discrepancy did not discriminate.

Despite these findings of motor deficits, both contralateral and ipsilateral, in patients with lateralized lesions, Lezak (1983) concluded that motor coordination difficulties present less of a problem to clinical examiners than do sensory deficits. She argued that valid assessment is still quite feasible, although she cautioned that it is common for patients to "have use of only one hand and that may not be the preferred hand" (p. 125).

The key issue is whether the motor problems of patients with unilateral brain damage will affect P-IQ. If so, then the V > P profiles of right-lesion patients may be partly due to their coordination difficulties rather than a visual-spatial disorder; similarly, the lack of P > V patterns in left-lesion adults may be due to a depressed P-IQ, concomitant to defective motor ability. The latter possibility is especially conceivable since left damage primarily affects motor coordination of the right arm and hand.

Research suggests that motor coordination problems may not have an adverse effect on Performance IQ. Reed and Reitan (1963c) compared the Wechsler-Bellevue performance of right-lesion and left-lesion patients with motor involvement (hemiplegia or hemiparesis) to brain-damaged adults with no lateralized motor deficits. They found no significant differences in the Performance or Verbal weighted scores of the patients with and without lateralized motor problems and concluded that patients with left and right motor deficits have different V–P profiles on the Wechsler-Bellevue, but "[t]he differential impairment of these groups of subjects is attributable to lateralization of cerebral dysfunction and seems to be unrelated to lateralization of the motor deficit per se. These findings support the research of Briggs (1960), who found that subjects performed nearly as well with either hand as with both hands on the performance subtests of the Wechsler Adult Intelligence Scale" (p. 106).

The detection of motor coordination problems in a patient with unilateral brain damage is an essential clinical observation for every examiner. A patient's success on a visual-motor subtest may be impaired when the patient is able to use only one hand, and the problem may be exacerbated if the nonpreferred hand must be used for Digit Symbol, Block Design, and Object Assembly.

Regardless of group data from research investigations, examiners must determine for every patient tested the degree to which Performance IQ is affected by a subtle or obvious motor impairment. This clinical observation must be coordinated with the actual V–P difference to discern the patient's relative abilities in the constructs that underlie the Verbal and Performance Scales.

Distractibility

Astute clinical observations are also necessary when testing patients who are distractible, "a common concomitant of brain damage" (Lezak, 1983, p. 125). The inability to shut out irrelevant stimulation can be minimized by testing in what Lezak (1983) calls a *sterile environment:* "The examining room should be relatively soundproof and decorated in quiet colors, with no bright or distracting objects in sight. . . . Drab colors and quiet patterns or a lab coat are recommended apparel for testing" (p. 125).

However, some patients will be distractible regardless of the examiner or testing environment, and the subtests composing the Freedom from Distractibility factor are likely to be the ones most affected. Poor performance on these tasks due to distractibility leads to a very different interpretation from poor scores due to a verbal-sequential deficit. The latter cause of

low scores reflects a deficit associated with the left hemisphere, whereas the former cause is not limited to either side of the brain.

Examiners must be alert to distractible behavior, and they need to assess its probable impact on test performance. Since the two WAIS-R distractibility subtests are on the Verbal Scale, it is V-IQ that will most likely be artificially depressed for a distractible patient. Hence, examiners of left-lesion patients must be especially aware that some large P > V discrepancies, or some large differences between scores on the Perceptual Organization versus Freedom from Distractibility factors, may be a deficit in distractible behavior rather than in left hemisphere verbal/sequential/linear processing.

Compensatory Mechanisms

In addition to the keen observational skills needed to determine the validity and meaning of V–P discrepancies, examiners should be aware of unusual phenomena associated with unilateral brain damage that may affect the size of the difference. For example, Lezak (1983) noted that sometimes the intact hemisphere will solve problems normally handled by the damaged hemisphere, which may mask the deficits caused by the lesion.

Smith (1981, 1983) has offered useful discussions of the nature of compensatory mechanisms and has also treated another type of masking that may occur as a result of the principle of *diaschisis:* "[T]he radiation of pathologic influences of focal lateralized lesions disrupting the functions of remote, anatomically intact structures not only in the damaged hemisphere, but also in the opposite healthy hemisphere as well" (Smith, 1981, p. 180). This loss of function in the intact hemisphere, which is sometimes a temporary phenomenon, can depress both the V- and P-IQs, and thereby hide the specific impact of the focal lesion—at least in patients tested when the lesion is acute.

An occurrence opposite in effect to diaschisis is described by Lezak (1983): "[A] diminished functional capacity in one hemisphere may be accompanied by augmented or exaggerated activity of the intact hemisphere" (p. 58). Some research suggests that left hemisphere functioning is occasionally improved following right hemisphere damage, e.g., by the verbosity and overwriting of many right-lesion adults (Lezak & Newman, 1979); similarly, right-brain processing tasks such as visual closure are sometimes performed better by left-lesion than by neurologically intact people (Wasserstein, 1980). This type of augmentation leads to a *larger* V–P IQ difference than one would anticipate solely from the specific deficits due to the lateralized lesion.

Should Neuropsychologists Still Use the Wechsler-Bellevue?

Some neuropsychologists continue to use the Wechsler-Bellevue as part of their comprehensive batteries, bypassing both the WAIS and WAIS-R (Herring & Reitan, 1986). Chapter 9 presented data suggesting the greater sensitivity of the Wechsler-Bellevue V–P discrepancy, compared to the corresponding discrepancy in the WAIS or WAIS-R, for patients with *left* hemisphere lesions (see Tables 9.6 and 9.7). The mean P > V profile for these patients averaged 7.5 points for the W-B versus 2.4 points for the WAIS/WAIS-R investigations. The difference in results is intriguing, raising the question of whether Reitan and other neuropsychologists are correct to persist in administering the W-B to patients with brain damage. The goal of this section is to answer this practical clinical question.

Some Negative Wechsler-Bellevue Data

Wechsler-Bellevue data have some negative aspects that deserve mention. First, the median V–P difference for patients with *bilateral* lesions in a number of studies was about zero for the W-B, compared to 6 to 7 points in favor of V-IQ for the WAIS and WAIS-R. This difference suggests that the W-B may be more sensitive in distinguishing patients with right lesions from those with bilateral lesions. But more important, the difference indicates that the V–P discrepancy on the WAIS or WAIS-R is more sensitive in distinguishing patients with bilateral lesions from normal adults. The failure of patients with damage to both hemispheres to demonstrate any V–P difference on the W-B may hinder diagnosis of neurological impairment when such a diagnosis is suspected but unconfirmed. Table 9.6 reveals that 7 of the 18 samples of patients with left-brain lesions displayed very small mean P > V discrepancies on the W-B (0.0 to 4.9 points).

Further, Smith's (1966a) large-scale study of nearly 100 patients with lesions lateralized to each hemisphere (see pp. 279–280) is not included in Table 9.6 because he provided only percentages of individuals with P > V. About half of those nearly 200 patients, those with acute tumors (Smith, 1966b), are included in Table 9.6. However, data provided in the two studies suggest that his larger, heterogeneous sample of left-lesion patients (Smith, 1966a) displayed the uncharacteristic V > P profile, as compared to the V = P profile that characterized his smaller sample of patients with acute tumors (Smith, 1966b). If the atypical data for Smith's larger sample had been included in the table, the mean Wechsler-Bellevue V–P difference for patients with left damage would have been closer in magnitude to the smaller discrepancies noted for the WAIS and WAIS-R.

Research by Reitan and the Fitzhughs

Nonetheless, even with these "modifications" of Wechsler-Bellevue data, there are still distinct differences between the Wechsler-Bellevue and its successors regarding the sensitivity to left lesions that require exploration. As discussed in chapter 3, Fitzhugh and Fitzhugh

(1964a) tested 179 brain-damaged adults suffering from epilepsy or related convulsive disorders on the Wechsler-Bellevue and then, two years later, retested them on the WAIS. This large sample was not further broken down by lateralization of lesion, but the heterogeneous sample as a whole had a mean V–P discrepancy of −5.3 points on the Wechsler-Bellevue (V-IQ = 74.6, P-IQ = 79.9) compared to a mean V–P IQ discrepancy of −0.1 points on the WAIS (V- and P-IQs of 73.7 and 73.8, respectively). The investigators were quite impressed by the different mean Performance IQs yielded by the two instruments for the same sample (mean V-IQs did not differ significantly), and concluded that research results obtained for the Wechsler-Bellevue are not directly applicable to the WAIS.

The different findings for the Wechsler-Bellevue and WAIS/WAIS-R regarding V–P IQ differences and location of brain lesion seem to reinforce Fitzhugh and Fitzhugh's (1964a) conclusions, at least concerning discrepancies between the Verbal and Performance IQs. However, Fitzhugh and Fitzhughs' concerns are still based on patients who were tested 2 years apart, not concurrently. Real changes in the group's verbal and nonverbal abilities possibly occurred in that interval. This possibility is not so unlikely considering the differences in V–P IQ discrepancies that may characterize recent versus chronic neurological impairment (see pp. 330–332); even though the group was not "acute" during the first testing, they were still about 2 years more chronic upon the WAIS retest than upon the prior Wechsler-Bellevue administration.

In addition, their sample of 179 brain-damaged adults had mean IQs in the mid-70s, about 20 points lower than most samples of brain-lesioned patients reported in the literature. Hence, their findings may not generalize to other brain-damaged populations. Also, the differences may be related to the newer (and much better) norms for the WAIS than Wechsler-Bellevue. Sometimes updated norms (which in-variably produce lower scores than older norms) affect verbal and nonverbal abilities differently; this was precisely the case for adolescents when the 1949 WISC was revised in 1974 (Doppelt & Kaufman, 1977), and it characterized the generational changes in the IQs of 14 nations reported by Flynn (1987; see pp. 50–52).

Reitan (1985) has resisted switching from the Wechsler-Bellevue to the WAIS or WAIS-R, and has continually "discouraged efforts of some psychologists to pool W-B I and WAIS data, or to substitute the WAIS for the W-B I when utilizing his (Reitan's) or their own normative data" (Matarazzo, 1972, p. 397). I do not support this practice. I grant that the data in Tables 9.6 and 9.7 suggest greater sensitivity of V–P discrepancies on the Wechsler-Bellevue than on the WAIS or WAIS-R to the specific localization of brain lesions. However, there are so many other variables that affect V–P differences (see chapter 10 and the discussion in this chapter), that vary unsystematically from Wechsler study to Wechsler study, that it is impossible to focus on just one variable (such as the specific test instrument used) and reach any firm conclusions.

Further, the Wechsler-Bellevue findings are based on almost half the number of patients conducted with the WAIS or WAIS-R; a total of 761 patients participated in Wechsler-Bellevue studies, compared to 1,438 patients assessed with either the WAIS or WAIS-R. The Wechsler-Bellevue findings might conceivably resemble the WAIS/WAIS-R results more closely if another 15 studies had been conducted with the older scale. The discussion presented previously for Smith's (1966a) large sample, a group that had to be excluded from Table 9.6, reinforces this notion. The Wechsler-Bellevue tended to be the instrument used for the first group of studies on brain localization and V–P discrepancy. Probably the early studies included a number of aphasic or severely dysphasic patients; although such patients certainly have damage to the left hemisphere, their inclusion in Wechsler studies is questionable since they are handicapped on any measure of verbal ability (see pp. 332–335). Careful reading of the numerous studies summarized in Tables 9.6 and 9.7 suggests that WAIS studies, more commonly than Wechsler-Bellevue investigations, have eliminated or limited the number of aphasics and dysphasics in the left-lesioned samples. Researchers attending to this variable (e.g., Bornstein, 1984; Inglis, Ruckman, Lawson, McLean, & Monga, 1982; McGlone, 1977; Satz, Richard, & Daniels, 1967) invariably used the WAIS or WAIS-R; the one major exception was Smith (1966a, 1966b), whose results on the Wechsler-Bellevue for left-damaged patients differed from the results of most other researchers. The control for aphasia in numerous WAIS/WAIS-R investigations may partially explain why the P > V discrepancies found for patients with left hemisphere lesions are much larger on the Wechsler-Bellevue than on the WAIS or WAIS-R. The difference may have little to do with the instrument per se.

Two studies of patients with lesions localized to the right or left hemisphere—one using the Wechsler-Bellevue and one using the WAIS—had substantially overlapping samples. These patients are among the 179 brain-damaged adults tested on both Wechsler tests over an interval of 2 years (Fitzhugh & Fitzhugh, 1964a). Fitzhugh and Fitzhugh (1964b) included in their WAIS study as many patients as possible from the chronic samples in their previous Wechsler-Bellevue study (Fitzhugh, Fitzhugh, & Reitan, 1962). They were able to include 70% of their 20 left-damaged patients and 68% of their 25 right-damaged patients in their follow-up study with the WAIS. These overlapping samples produced the V–P IQ discrepancies in Table 11.4 (data from Tables 9.6 and 9.7). The Fitzhugh and Fitzhugh data have the same limitations discussed previously. Nonetheless, the results on the Wechsler-Bellevue and the WAIS for the overlapping samples are not all that different; further, the differences in the results between the two studies favor the WAIS regarding theoretical predictions.

Conclusion: Do Not Use the Wechsler-Bellevue

Certainly, there are no rational reasons to assume that the Verbal and Performance constructs on the Wechsler-Bellevue are measuring different skill areas in adults than the constructs of the same name on the WAIS or WAIS-R; indeed, a plethora of rational and empirical reasons justify concluding the opposite (see chapter 3). More important, many changes were made from the Wechsler-Bellevue to the subsequent editions of the adult scale, and these modifications led to decreased ambiguity in administration and scoring, updated content, improved quality of the illustrations on Performance items, increased reliability of the separate subtests and the IQ scales, updated and more representative norms, and so forth.

The IQs yielded by the Wechsler-Bellevue are so out of date, and most subtests are so much less reliable than the current, modified subtests, that one cannot reasonably have confidence in the Verbal, Performance, and Full Scale IQs yielded by the adult test, which is now more than a half-century old. If the accuracy of the obtained Wechsler-Bellevue IQs is so open to doubt, how can anyone truly have confidence in the difference between the Verbal and Performance IQs yielded by that outdated instrument with antequated norms—norms that were never representative of the U.S. on the

TABLE 11.4 V–P IQ discrepancies on the W-B and WAIS for overlapping samples of patients

Test	Left Lesion	Right Lesion
Wechsler-Bellevue	−3.9	+2.1
WAIS	−4.6	+4.5

NOTE: Data are from Fitzhugh et al. (1962) and Fitzhugh and Fitzhugh (1964b). Discrepancy equals V–IQ minus P–IQ.

key variables of occupation, geographic region, and race?

I would urge anyone who is still administering the Wechsler-Bellevue (or the WAIS) to abandon the practice at once and begin to use the WAIS-R for all assessments, neuropsychological or otherwise.

ILLUSTRATIVE CASE REPORTS

Two sample psychological case reports follow: Walt H., a white 21-year-old male who suffered brain damage following a car accident at age 14; and Chester P., a black adolescent male suspected of autism. Walt has a striking V > P pattern, suggestive of damage that is exclusively or primarily confined to the right cerebral hemisphere. Chester displays the anticipated P > V profile characteristic of individuals with autism or related language disorders. (Both are actual cases, although their names and other identifying information have been altered to preserve anonymity.) I have modified the test interpretation sections of these reports (and of the single reports that follow chapters 14, 15, and 16) to conform to the specific interpretive procedures advocated in this book; however, these modifications affect only how the test results are communicated, not the basic findings themselves.

As is evident from these two reports, and from the other case reports in this book (including the two that Hynd and Semrud-Clikeman included at the end of chapter 17 on neuropsychological assessment), report writing is as individual an endeavor as test administration. Competent interpretation of the WAIS-R depends upon the examiner's ability to integrate the test data with data from other relevant tests, cognitive and otherwise. Further, test scores are interpretable only in the context of the person's specific background and clinically observed behaviors. The interpretive rules and guidelines elaborated throughout this text are useful to a

point; however, competent interpretation often demands modifying the suggested procedures to fit a specific case.

Consequently, I am opposed to the computerized case reports that are so prevalent and easily available to clinicians. Some computerized techniques are available that simplify clerical procedures, such as determining significant strengths and weaknesses; I see no problem with that type of short cut. However, I strongly oppose those computerized techniques that offer specific interpretations of WAIS-R IQ and subtest profiles and that generate canned reports. Nothing is more individual than the report that communicates the results of a psychological, neuropsychological, or psychoeducational evaluation to those who will potentially use the results for the person's benefit.

Walt H., Age 21, Head Injury

Referral and Background Information

Walt H. was referred to determine current levels of abilities and to make appropriate vocational suggestions for him. Walt is currently unemployed and lives at home with his mother and one younger sister. He has one older sister who no longer lives at home. He enjoys a good relationship with his stepfather, who is currently separated from his mother. Walt was involved in a car accident a few months before his 15th birthday. The accident resulted in partial paralysis of his left side and in a significant loss of vision. Vision in his right eye is limited to gross form discrimination peripherally and to light/dark awareness in his central vision. Central vision in his left eye is normal but peripheral vision is severely limited. Difficulties with both short-term and long-term memory were noted after the accident.

Prior to his accident, Walt was enrolled in public school and was placed in a learning-disabilities resource room. Difficulties were noted in reading, spelling and behavior. Both before and after the accident, Walt was taking

Cylert for diagnosed hyperactivity. He is currently taking no medications.

Subsequent to the accident, Walt enrolled in a new public high school following his family's move to another state. Placement in a learning-disabilities resource room was continued. During this period, presenting problems included severe motor deficits and limited vision. Partial paralysis continued to affect his left side, and his balance was tenuous. Walt was naturally left-handed and consequently was forced to learn to use his right hand for writing activities. His remaining vision permitted him to do most academic tasks; however, he experienced significant difficulties in tracking across a page or across the blackboard.

Cognitively, Walt evidenced similar deficits to those noted prior to the accident. In addition, short-term memory was inconsistent and periods of confusion and disorientation were noted.

Walt progressed steadily and was able to graduate from high school at age 19. During high school and subsequent to graduation, he received training through state vocational rehabilitation services. Training included job skills and a period of training at a nearby school for the deaf and blind.

He was administered a WISC-R at age 12, prior to his accident, and obtained a Full Scale IQ of 101 (Verbal and Performance IQs were not available). After his accident, Walt was administered a WAIS-R at age 17. That testing yielded a Verbal IQ of 91, a Performance IQ of 66, and a Full Scale IQ of 77. The large difference in favor of Verbal IQ over Performance IQ (25 points), the motor damage to the left side of Walt's body, and the precise nature of his visual problems all suggest that he suffered right cerebral damage—either primarily or exclusively—from his accident.

This current testing was initiated in an effort to establish Walt's level of functioning and to isolate specific skill abilities and deficits. Walt has expressed a desire to determine career areas for which he is best suited.

Appearance and Behavioral Characteristics

Walt is a 21-year, 7-month-old white male with blond curly hair; he is heavyset and below average height. Walt was tested over the course of three sessions. The first session was in a psychologist's office at a high school; testing conditions were good. Subsequent sessions were at the University of Alabama under adequate testing conditions. Walt appeared to be at ease with all examiners and rapport was easily established and maintained throughout the testing. It is felt that these results represent a valid and reliable indication of his current level of functioning.

The effects of the accident were noted in his measured, somewhat rigid movement patterns. Physical posturing was used as an apparently effective accommodation to his limited vision.

Walt presented himself as a friendly, highly verbal young man. He conversed freely with the examiners and did not seem to be intimidated by the situation. At times he seemed to "search for words," but he nonetheless communicated his thoughts and feelings effectively. He appeared to be relaxed and frequently demonstrated a good sense of humor. When discussing the progress he had made, Walt appeared to be self-confident and seemed genuinely proud of what he had accomplished. He expressed a strong determination to continue his progress and indicated that he hoped some day to be able to help other people.

During the initial portions of the testing at the university, Walt evidenced a degree of disorientation. When asked to name the current date (April 15th), his response was delayed. After some thought, he responded, "I'm not sure. It's not January, . . . April?". He was also uncertain as to what city or university he was in, even though this had been a frequent topic of conversation.

In general, Walt experienced difficulty on tasks that were abstract. When he encountered difficulty, he tended to persist and did not frus-

TABLE 11.5   Walt H.: Tests Administered

Wechsler Adult Intelligence Scale—Revised (WAIS-R)

Verbal	Scaled Score	Age-Corrected Scaled Score	Performance	Scaled Score	Age-Corrected Scaled Score
Information	8	(8)	Picture Completion	7	(7)
Digit Span	8	(8)	Picture Arrangement	5	(5)
Vocabulary	7	(8)	Block Design	5	(5)
Arithmetic	7	(7)	Object Assembly	5	(5)
Comprehension	14	(14)—S	Digit Symbol	2	(2)—W
Similarities	9	(10)			

Age-Corrected Verbal Mean = 9   Age-Corrected Performance Mean = 5

   IQ (±95% confidence)
   Verbal = 93 ± 4
   Performance = 66 ± 6
   Full Scale = 79 ± 4

Woodcock-Johnson Psycho-Educational Battery (1977 edition)

	Standard Score	Percentile
Cognitive Ability		
Broad Cognitive Scale	81	10th

Subtest	Approximate Grade Equivalent
Visual Matching	1.8
Spatial Relations	1.3
Blending	1.4
Memory for Sentences	9.5
Visual-Auditory Learning	1.3
Numbers Reversed	5.5
Analysis-Synthesis	3.5
Concept Formation	3.0
Picture Vocabulary	7.0
Quantitative Concepts	7.0
Antonyms-Synonyms	8.0
Analogies	8.0

TABLE 11.5 (Continued)

Tests of Achievement

Subtest	Approximate Grade Equivalent
Letter-Word Identification	7.0
Word Attack	4.0
Passage Comprehension	10.0
Calculation	7.0
Applied Problems	5.0

	Standard Score	Percentile Rank

Aptitude-Achievement Comparisons

	Standard Score	Percentile Rank
Reading		
Aptitude	87	19th
Achievement	79	8th
Mathematics		
Aptitude	74	4th
Achievement	75	5th

Peabody Picture Vocabulary Test—Revised (PPVT-R), Form L

Standard Score	Percentile	Stanine	Age Equivalent
82	13	3	14-7

Vineland Adaptive Behavior Scales (Expanded Form)

Domain	Standard Score (±95% confidence)	Percentile Rank	Adaptive Level
Communication	84 ± 10	14	Moderately low
Daily Living Skills	108 ± 8	68	Adequate
Socialization	106 ± 8	66	Adequate
Motor (estimated)	61 ± 12	0.5	Low (mild deficit)
Fine Motor (est.)			Moderately High
Gross Motor (est.)			Low
Adaptive Behavior			
Composite	98 ± 6	45	Adequate

Bender-Gestalt Test of Visual-Motor Integration (B-G)

Koppitz scoring errors: 5

Developmental age equivalent: 6.0 to 6.5 years

trate easily. Walt evidenced the ability to learn on tasks that were initially difficult for him. He tended to approach such problems with a trial-and-error method of problem solving and was most successful when accompanying instructions were ordered and step-by-step. Throughout the testing, Walt's processing skills appeared to be slow, and his answers tended to be measured and deliberate.

Test Results and Interpretation

Walt H. earned a Full Scale IQ of 79 ± 4 on the WAIS-R, which classifies him in the Borderline range of intellectual functioning, ranking him at about the 8th percentile when compared to individuals his age. On the Woodcock-Johnson, Walt earned a standard score of 81, ranking him at about the 10th percentile when compared to individuals his own age. On the Peabody Picture Vocabulary Test—Revised (PPVT-R) Walt earned a standard score of 82, which ranks him at about the 13th percentile. All of these scores are consistent in categorizing Walt's cognitive functioning at the juncture of the Borderline and Low Average classifications of intelligence.

While the differences among the three global scores are not significant, it should be noted that a significant difference exists between the WAIS-R Verbal IQ, 93 ± 4 (Average) and Performance IQ, 66 ± 6 (Educable Mentally Retarded). This 27-point difference is significant at the .01 level and is abnormal, occurring very rarely (less than 1% of the time) among adults with IQs comparable to Walt's. The Verbal IQ, when compared to the other global scores, is less affected by Walt's brain damage since his accident seems to have primarily affected his right cerebral hemisphere. As such, it is felt that Walt's Verbal IQ of 93 (32nd percentile), is more representative of Walt's true intellectual functioning than other obtained scores. His low Performance IQ (2nd percentile) undoubtedly reflects the impact of right cerebral damage suffered in the car accident. His high Verbal-

low Performance profile was evident on the Woodcock-Johnson as well: Good performance on tests of verbal memory, concept formation, and reasoning; very deficient performance on visual-spatial, nonverbal reasoning, and timed tests.

Throughout the entire testing, Walt approached tasks in an ordered, sequential manner. He experienced difficulties on tasks that required him to view stimuli as a whole rather than in parts. His strategy seemed to be a function of both his limited vision and his preferred mode of cognitive processing. On Picture Arrangement, Walt's restricted vision forced him to view each picture individually rather than scanning them as a whole. However, on tasks such as Block Design and Object Assembly Walt was able to view the stimuli as a whole, but his solutions remained sequential in nature. When presented with a Woodcock-Johnson task that involved reading sentences of symbolic figures, Walt again approached the task sequentially. He read figure by figure and was thus unable to make use of contextual clues. Woodcock-Johnson Concept Formation required Walt to view a series of geometric figures of varying sizes, shapes, and colors. The task involved determining rules that governed relationships among the figures. Walt tended to view each figure separately and evidenced difficulty in formulating global rules. Design reproduction on the Bender-Gestalt further evidenced an inability to maintain the gestalt and a reliance on sequential solutions.

Walt's performance further demonstrated a preference for concrete tasks and difficulties on items involving abstractions. Walt tended to do well on tasks that involved concrete solutions; this was noted on Similarities, Vocabulary, and Comprehension, which all measure verbal conceptualization. Social awareness (measured by Comprehension) was Walt's highest score on the WAIS-R (91st percentile). He received maximum credit on all items on the Comprehension subtest with the exception of two, which involved interpretation of abstract proverbs. On the Woodcock-Johnson Visual-Auditory Learning subtest, Walt generally was able to recall figures that were more concrete in nature. The figure for "And" was an abstract grouping of 3 circles, and Walt was consistently unable to match the word to the symbol as he read. On the Arithmetic tasks on both the WAIS-R and the Woodcock-Johnson, Walt tended to subvocalize. He appeared to have difficulty visualizing solutions and relied on concrete manipulation of his fingers.

As noted previously, Walt was forced to switch to his right hand for writing tasks as a result of the accident. While generally slow and deliberate, Walt's writing and fine motor skills tend to be adequate. He did experience difficulties on tasks involving visual-motor integration, particularly when those items were timed. This timed visual-motor coordination deficit was most notable on Digit Symbol (less than 1st percentile), a test of psychomotor speed.

Evidence was noted of a degree of disorientation and of poor organizational skills. As noted previously, Walt was unable to easily recall the current month and the city that he was in. Walt has apparently developed strategies to assist in orientation. While trying to recall the month, Walt stated that he typically relied on his watch, but that the battery was dead and he had forgotten to replace it. Disorganization was noted on the overall order of his Bender-Gestalt performance.

Academically, Walt performed somewhat below the level to be expected when viewing his Verbal IQ as the best estimate of his potential. He did, however, achieve at a level commensurate with his scholastic aptitude in both reading and mathematics, as assessed by the relevant clusters on the Woodcock-Johnson. Indicated skill deficits in the areas of Word Attack (4.0 grade equivalent) and Letter-Word Identification (7.0 grade equivalent) may be a reflection of reading disabilities evidenced prior to his accident.

While Walt's physical limitations severely restrict his mobility, he appears to be functioning within an average range of adaptive behavior. He appears to possess adequate social skills and is generally able to care for personal needs independently.

Summary and Recommendations

Walt, a 21-year, 7-month-old white male of heavy build and below average height, was referred in an effort to obtain an evaluation of his current level of abilities and to make vocational recommendations. Walt earned a Full Scale IQ of 79 on the WAIS-R, placing him in the Borderline range of intellectual functioning. Similar scores were noted on the Woodcock-Johnson Tests of Cognitive Ability and the PPVT-R, as he scored 81 and 82, respectively, on these measures. A significant and striking discrepancy was noted on the WAIS-R between his Verbal IQ of 93 and the Performance IQ of 66. This discrepancy, significant at the .01 level and abnormal in its magnitude, appears to indicate that the Verbal IQ is a more representative reflection of Walt's intellectual abilities than are the three global scores or his Performance IQ. The WAIS-R IQs obtained in this evaluation are nearly identical to the values obtained 2 years after his car accident. Hence, whatever improvement in Walt's visual perceptual functioning that one might expect to occur spontaneously was already completed 5 years ago. At this point, Walt's intellectual abilities, both verbal and nonverbal, are stable and not likely to change very much in the future.

Walt evidenced a preference for sequential problem solving rather than simultaneous problem solving and appeared to be more at ease on concrete tasks than on tasks involving abstractions. While Walt's vision is severely limited, he appears to have developed effective compensatory skills.

On this battery of tests, Walt demonstrated a relatively high level of verbal skill; his score was about average for his age of 21. He evidenced good learning ability and persistence and flexibility in problem solving. He demonstrated good social skills and appeared to have a good self-concept. Walt presented himself as a very determined young man and expressed an interest in helping others.

Deficits were noted in visual-motor skills and in his ability to function efficiently in timed situations. A degree of disorientation was also observed. Walt's academic achievement appears to be somewhat below the level to be expected from his evidenced Verbal IQ.

Walt's demonstrated skills and expressed desires would appear to be commensurate with jobs involving helping others. He is able to learn effectively when training procedures reflect step-by-step, organized instruction and patience. Problems involving transportation to and from work might be addressed by provision of an on-site residence. Therefore, possible job areas might include nursing homes, hospitals, residential treatment facilities, or facilities such as the Boys' Ranch. Vocational Rehabilitation services should be utilized in an effort to facilitate these recommendations.

Examiners and Report Writers: Graduate students in Drs. Nadeen and Alan Kaufman's advanced assessment course at the University of Alabama: Buddy (James) Allen, Sandy Bennett, Jean Dalton, Susan Ervin, Bill Gilchrist, Debra Nix, Ella Shamblin, Margaret Webster, and Louise White.

Five-Month Follow-up Report: Walt

The results of Walt's evaluation were communicated to his mother and to Vocational Rehabilitation Services. Walt's file was activated by Vocational Rehabilitation, and he received a complete physical evaluation. Efforts were begun to locate appropriate employment. In the ensuing period Walt was hired as a night manager in a small convenience store. While he was able to handle most tasks individually, the complexity and need for rapid response proved to be too difficult.

Three months ago, Walt was hired in the housekeeping department of a local nursing home. His employers have proven to be patient and flexible. Walt needed time to orient himself to the physical plant, but his supervisor reports that Walt is currently performing well as a full-time employee. Walt says that he is comfortable with his duties and enjoys interacting with the residents.

Transportation continues to be problematic but Walt is currently able to ride with a fellow employee. Schedules have been rearranged by his employers to assist Walt in this area. While Walt is happy with his present position, he is anxious to move beyond his current duties. Possible alternative placements are currently being explored with his case worker at Vocational Rehabilitation Services.

Chester P., Age 17, Possible Autism

Reason For Referral

Chester P., a black male who just turned 17, was seen for reevaluation because his father has requested assistance with future planning for his son.

Background and Observations

Chester was last assessed at age 14. Psychological testing indicated a highly discrepant Verbal–Performance difference on the WISC-R, i.e., Verbal IQ of 65, Performance IQ of 101, and Full Scale IQ of 80. Errors on the Bender-Gestalt were not significant. He lives at home and continues to attend a therapeutic school. Mr. P. feels that his son is in a "caring situation" at the school, but they do not have a prevocational program and his concern is "where does he move from there." Chester's family is not interested in residential placement for him unless it could provide special benefits they could not provide at home. Most of Chester's social activities are with his family. His father voiced concern over Chester's poor socialization skills and the fact that he has no friends of his age where he lives.

Early developmental history, as reported by Mr. P., is sketchy and thus cannot support or rule out a possible diagnosis of primary autism. Chester was adopted when he was "less than 6 months old" through the Department of Children and Family Services. Nothing unusual was recalled in his birth or perinatal history. Problems were first noted when he was 2 years old or perhaps 4 years old as he exhibited delayed language development. Whether other areas of functioning were delayed could not be recalled by his father.

At the time of the present evaluation, Chester was quite cooperative despite a rather lengthy testing session. He exhibited delayed and immediate echolalia. Frequently, he would read from the examiner's manual at a distance of 3 to 5 feet (looking at the printed words upside down) and attempt to anticipate the next question and answer.

His answers were often verbal associations or functional descriptions rather than definitions or scorable responses. Tasks that appeared more difficult for him, e.g., verbal questions about social situations, resulted in much agitated movement and irrelevant noises, e.g., teeth clicking. He was quite anxious to do the psychomotor tasks, e.g., WAIS-R Block Design, and he insisted on taking the test materials from the examiner so that he could set up the task himself. Several times when Chester could not answer, he would turn to the wall and in a booming, almost theatrical voice ask the question to a nonexistent person—for example, "Hey mister, could you tell me three kinds of blood vessels?" Chester did not respond when asked if there was really someone there; however, this examiner felt that Chester was playfully diverting attention away from his own lack of knowledge rather than hallucinating. Later he reportedly paced in the waiting room, repetitively saying, e.g., "to be or not to be, that is the question . . . to be or not to be that's the

construction," etc. He had begun this kind of behavior earlier during testing when asked to name United States presidents. Despite these bizarre verbalizations and his tendency toward aloofness, Chester did not appear to be exhibiting hallucinatory behavior and did not exhibit any systematized delusions.

During the evaluation, Chester complied with the examiner's request to draw a picture of himself; however, he first drew a full figure of himself standing next to a female figure, which he identified as the examiner. Later he drew another full figure of himself standing alone, and separate pictures of his face and the examiner's face. Chester seemed to accomplish these drawings with ease, and while they did not exhibit a great deal of detail, they were well proportioned, accurate, and without pathognomonic features.

Chester remained rather aloof during the evaluation, unable to respond to normal conversation with the examiner. Most responses were short phrases; however, his noncommunicative speech was more complex.

Test Results and Interpretation

In contrast to the 36-point Verbal deficit that Chester displayed on the WISC-R at age 14 (P-IQ = 101, V-IQ = 65), he performed at a normal level of functioning on both WAIS-R scales at the present evaluation. His WAIS-R Performance IQ of 113 ± 9 (High Average intelligence, 81st percentile) was still a significant 24 points greater than his Verbal IQ; further, differences as large as 24 points are abnormal, occurring less than 5% of the time in adolescents or adults with average intelligence. Yet his WAIS-R Verbal IQ of 89 ± 5 (23rd percentile) placed him at the juncture of the Low Average and Average categories, not within the deficient range of mental ability.

Based on the large V–P discrepancy, Chester's Average WAIS-R Full Scale IQ of 99 ± 5 (47th percentile) is meaningless; he clearly expresses his intellect far better nonverbally, with

TABLE 11.6   Chester P.: Tests Administered

Wechsler Adult Intelligence Scale—Revised (WAIS-R)

Verbal	Scaled Score	Age-Corrected Scaled Score	Performance	Scaled Score	Age-Corrected Scaled Score
Information	6	(8)	Picture Completion	9	(9)—W
Digit Span	15	(17)—S	Picture Arrangement	5	(5)—W
Vocabulary	4	(5)—W	Block Design	17	(18)—S
Arithmetic	3	(4)—W	Object Assembly	16	(18)—S
Comprehension	2	(3)—W	Digit Symbol	8	(8)—W
Similarities	12	(14)—S			

Age-Corrected Verbal Mean = 8   Age-Corrected Performance Mean = 12

   IQ (± 90% confidence)

   Verbal = 89 ± 5

   Performance = 113 ± 9

   Full Scale = 99 ± 5

Peabody Picture Vocabulary Test—Revised (PPVT-R), Form L

Receptive vocabulary standard score = 79 (8th percentile)

Age equivalent = 12-7

Bender-Gestalt Test of Visual-Motor Integration

Normal performance according to Koppitz scoring system

concrete materials, than via verbal comprehension and expression. However, the enormous scatter characterizing his subtest profile, within *both* the Verbal and Performance Scales, even reduces the meaningfulness of his high Performance–low Verbal pattern. Other explanations fit Chester's profile fluctuations better than Wechsler's verbal–nonverbal dichotomy.

Basically, Chester's WAIS-R profile is one of extremes, with scaled scores ranging from well below the 1st percentile (responding verbally to socially relevant problems) to the 99th percentile (rapidly constructing abstract designs out of blocks), when compared to other 17-year-olds. The degree of Verbal scatter, Performance scatter, and scatter among all 11 subtests is huge and striking, occurring less than 1% of the time in the normal population. Ches-

ter's greatest strength is in visual-constructive ability (above the 99th percentile), as he excelled in assembling cut-up picture puzzles as well as designs. His most deficient area is his ability to express his ideas with spontaneous verbalizations, whether defining words or solving questions of social relevance (2nd percentile). He displayed striking weakness, in general, with school-related, fact-oriented tasks (4th percentile) compared to his very superior visual-spatial skills (98th percentile). The latter strength was reinforced by his normal Bender-Gestalt performance (one minor error based on Koppitz's scoring system), indicating intact visual-motor integration.

All of these results are consistent with Chester's behaviors and possible diagnosis of autism. However, no comparison explains his assets and

TABLE 11.6   (Continued)

Kaufman Test of Educational Achievement (K-TEA), Brief Form

	Standard Score (± 90%)	Percentile Rank	Grade Equivalent
Reading	96 ± 10	39th	10.8
Spelling	96 ± 11	39th	11.1
Mathematics	73 ± 10	4th	6.4
Battery Composite	85 ± 7	16th	8.8

Vineland Adaptive Behavior Scales (Expanded Form)
(Based on interview with Mr. P., Chester's father)

Domain	Standard Score[a]	Adaptive Level[a]	Age Equivalent	Percentile[a]
Communication	85 ± 9	Adequate	14-0	16th
Daily Living Skills	61 ± 7	Low (Mild Deficit)	9-4	<1st
Socialization	47 ± 7	Low (Moderate Deficit)	5-10	<0.1st
Adaptive Behavior Composite	59 ± 5	Low (Mild Deficit)	9-9	<1st

[a]Based on norms for ages 17-0 through 17-3 (standard scores are banded by 90% confidence interval).

deficits better than a contrast of his success on tests of abstract thought (a verbal test of similarities, telling how two things are alike, plus the nonverbal abstract design test) versus tests of social comprehension (the verbal test of social problem solving, and a nonverbal task of arranging pictures to tell a meaningful story). Each category spans verbal and nonverbal content, and each involves high-level reasoning ability. Yet Chester performed at the 98th percentile on the abstract thought tests, compared to the 2nd percentile on the measures of social understanding. Overall, Chester displayed a more broadly defined strength in fluid intelligence, the ability to solve novel problems with flexibility. This asset spanned verbal reasoning and short-term memory tests as well as a variety of nonverbal visual-spatial tests. Excluding the one

fluid task with social content, Chester performed better than 96 out of 100 adolescents his age on measures of fluid intelligence.

On the PPVT-R, Chester earned a standard score of 79 (8th percentile), basically consistent with his Verbal IQ, but better than his WAIS-R scores on tasks requiring much verbal expression. When he is allowed to respond to school-related items nonverbally (as on the PPVT-R), or with just one or two words (as on a WAIS-R task of general information) he performs much better than when extra verbalization is required.

He evidenced this relative strength on an achievement battery as well, the K-TEA Brief Form. He earned Average standard scores of 96 (39th percentile) on both the Reading and Spelling tests, performing about as well as one might expect from his WAIS-R IQs. The Reading test assesses word recognition as well as comprehension, but requires little verbalization; the Spelling test requires a written response. His Mathematics score of 73 (4th percentile) indicates a poor level of arithmetic concepts, reasoning, and computation skills (sixth-grade level), a finding that was underscored by his very low score on the WAIS-R Arithmetic subtest. He evidenced inadequate arithmetic performance with oral presentation (WAIS-R), with visual presentation and written response (the first half of the K-TEA), and with combined oral and visual presentation (the second half of the K-TEA).

On the Vineland Adaptive Behavior Scales (Expanded Form), based on Mr. P.'s report, Chester performed at about a 10-year level, demonstrating a mild deficit in his overall adaptive behavior. Despite his difficulty with WAIS-R verbal expressive tasks, Chester has a relative asset in communication, notably receptive and written; he also has all of the basic self-help skills. He reads on his own initiative, makes phone calls, and follows current events. Areas of relative deficit are in self-direction, socialization (interpersonal relationships, play and leisure time, coping skills), and expressive communication. Chester cannot make change for minor purchases nor does he go out unsupervised during the day. Most of his social activities are with the family, and he has few friends who are his peers in age and ability level. He helps around the house by cleaning his room, taking out the garbage, and assisting with the lawn chores.

Diagnostic Impression

Chester is a 17-year-old black male who exhibits atypical patterns of development in terms of language and social skills. Currently his tested verbal abilities are much improved over his last evaluation; however, he still exhibits significantly poorer verbal than performance abilities. Interpretation of social situations on test ma-

terials and socialization skills in general continue to be areas of extreme difficulty for Chester. He exhibits loose associative verbalizations, which may not be predicted on the basis of his language disorder alone; however, no clear-cut mental illness appears evident to this examiner. He does display striking strengths in abstract thought, visual-spatial skills, and fluid intelligence (even within the verbal sphere) and has adequate reading and spelling abilities; arithmetic skills are poor, while adaptive behavior is inconsistent.

The unavailability of a clear developmental history makes a diagnosis of Infantile Autism impossible; however, Chester appears to be exhibiting an amelioration in left hemisphere deficits, characteristic of autistic adolescents. The following diagnosis, found in the Diagnostic and Statistical Manual of Mental Disorders III, appears to best reflect Chester as this examiner sees him at this time: 299.8x Atypical Pervasive Developmental Disorder: distortions in the development of multiple basic psychological functions that are involved in the development of social skills and language, and that cannot be classified as either Infantile Autism or Childhood onset Pervasive Developmental Disorder.

Recommendations

Family conference with the father to discuss our recommendations for programming with Chester to include the following:

(a) Socialization activities: Getting involved in organized activities such as Art classes, or working with younger children as a volunteer, might be appropriate social activities.

(b) Prevocational training.

(c) Independent living training.

(d) Encouragement of independent living activities by his family.

The above recommendations may be most effectively carried out in a milieu therapy setting, such as The Group Home run by Mrs. H., which has been discussed with Mr. P. However, if the P. family wishes to keep Chester at home on a full-time basis, other arrangements may be sought to provide these same programmatic needs.

Examiner: Judith Ivins, Psychologist III

CHAPTER 11 SUMMARY

This chapter, the third of three on V–P IQ discrepancies, again focuses on brain-damaged individuals. The following topics are covered: (a) subtest patterns obtained by patients with lateralized lesions, (b) Lawson and Inglis's Laterality Index, and (c) clinical issues pertaining to individual assessment (as opposed to interpretation of group research findings). Based on subtest data for 13 samples of patients with unilateral lesions, right-lesion patients outscored left-lesion patients on all six Verbal subtests, while left-lesion subjects performed better on four of five Performance subtests. Digit Symbol was the only Wechsler subtest to fail to discriminate between the patient samples; both left-damage and right-damage patients earned low scores on Digit Symbol. Across the 13 studies (five Wechsler-Bellevue, eight WAIS), all Verbal subtests, with the slight exception of Arithmetic, were about equally effective in discriminating between right- and left-lesion samples. Similarly, Picture Completion, Picture Arrangement, Block Design, and Object Assembly distinguished about equally well between the lateralized patient groups.

An evaluation of the subtest fluctuations *within* each sample revealed that the area of greatest relative deficit for patients with left hemispheric damage was reflected in the Freedom from Distractibility factor rather than the Verbal Comprehension dimension. Since the distractibility factor (whether defined by the Arithmetic-Digit Span dyad or the familiar triad that includes Digit Symbol as well) is also potentially a measure of sequential or successive processing, the

left-lesion patients seemed to display well-developed simultaneous processing contrasted with weak sequential processing. This *processing* hypothesis (as opposed to a verbal–nonverbal *content* hypothesis) was supported not just for aggregated data, but for most of the individual samples as well. Despite these results, the overall findings suggest the advisability of continuing to rely on V–P IQ discrepancies when assessing patients with brain damage.

Lawson and Inglis and their colleagues propose the use of a Laterality Index, derived from the second *unrotated* factor in principal components analysis, for the assessment of brain damage in patients. They interpret the unrotated dimension as a bipolar verbal–nonverbal factor that can be converted to an index producing positive values for left-lesion patients and negative values for right-lesion patients. The factor score coefficients correlated in the high .90s with the size of the mean differences produced by each Wechsler subtest when comparing the scores of patients with left- versus right-brain damage. When the WISC-R and K-ABC are analyzed, Lawson and Inglis identified a Learning Disabilities Index that they interpret as an analog of the Laterality Index for adults. However, the children's index seems to measure a different construct, a sequential–simultaneous, rather than a verbal–nonverbal, dimension. Despite potential advantages of the Laterality Index, it is of questionable clinical value because it is cumbersome to compute, has unusual metrics and substandard reliability, and has not been demonstrated to provide more diagnostic information than is obtainable from a simple V–P discrepancy.

When evaluating V–P differences for individuals instead of groups, extreme caution must be exercised. What are large differences between groups of patients may not even be statistically significant for a given individual. In addition, individual interpretation demands understanding of clinical phenomena associated with lateralized lesions. For example, left-lesion patients prototypically demonstrate a profound depression known as a catastrophic reaction, while right-lesion patients are more prone to euphoria or indifference. These opposite reactions are likely to affect the observed V–P discrepancy in different ways.

Other behavioral observations must also be considered when evaluating V–P differences. Fatigue, on the Wechsler-Bellevue or WAIS, may lead to a depressed P-IQ because the six Verbal subtests are given first on those tests; the alternation of Verbal and Performance subtests on the WAIS-R makes fatigue less of a problem for V–P interpretation. Clinicians need to understand sensory, motor coordination, and attentional deficits associated with lesions in the left or right hemisphere to facilitate V–P analysis. Although there is some evidence that motor coordination problems may not markedly depress a person's P-IQ, individual observations are more important than group data for this determination. Examiners must also be alert to compensatory mechanisms employed by patients because the use of an alternative strategy for solving verbal or nonverbal tasks can sometimes mask a real brain-related deficiency.

Wechsler-Bellevue studies of patients with unilateral brain damage suggest that this outdated instrument is more sensitive than the WAIS or WAIS-R to left hemisphere lesions, raising the question of whether examiners should continue to use the Wechsler-Bellevue. Although some neuropsychologists continue to use this 1930s battery, the answer is a resounding no. There are considerable negative Wechsler-Bellevue data that do not lend themselves to V–P IQ discrepancy analysis because of the way the data were reported. Also, differences in defining patient samples have occurred over the years that may account for changes in the V–P discrepancies observed for patient samples in the 1950s and 1960s versus the more recent past. Finally, the extremely outdated Wechsler-Bellevue norms and the inferior psychometric properties of the old battery compared to its successors make it inadvisable to persist in using a relic of the past.

EXAMINER'S FORM 11.1   Computation of the Inglis-Lawson Laterality Index for the WAIS-R (Developed by A. S. Kaufman)

Worksheet for: *Examinee's Name* _____   *Date* _____

Step 1. Enter the person's *age-corrected* scaled scores for each subtest in column A.

Step 2. For each subtest, multiply the person's age-corrected scaled score by that subtest's weight (indicated in column W), and enter each product in the column headed A × W. *Be sure to retain the minus signs for the Verbal subtests.*

Step 3. Sum columns A and A × W. Substitute these sums in the formula given below the worksheet.

Step 4. Divide the Laterality Index by 302 to convert it to a *z* score.

WAIS-R SUBTEST	*AGE-CORRECTED* SCALED SCORE (A)	*WEIGHT* (W)	A × W
Verbal			
Information		−32	
Digit Span		−12	
Vocabulary		−33	
Arithmetic		−08	
Comprehension		−29	
Similarities		−20	
Performance			
Picture Completion		26	
Picture Arrangement		10	
Block Design		45	
Object Assembly		62	
Digit Symbol		14	
	Sum (A) = ☐	Sum (A × W) = ☐	

Laterality Index (LI) = Sum (A × W) − 2.1 × Sum (A)

LI = _____ − 2.1 × _____

LI = _____

To interpret the LI, see pages 352–356. To convert the LI to a *z* score, use the formula shown below.

$$z_{LI} = LI \div 302 = \text{_____} \div 302 = \text{_____}$$

Profile Interpretation: What the Subtests Measure

Chapters 12, 13, and 14 treat the crucial topic of WAIS-R profile interpretation by trying to integrate and explain the fluctuations that occur in each individual's subtest profile. Chapter 12 sets the foundation for this type of test interpretation by delineating the abilities and traits that each task measures and by indicating clinical, developmental, neuropsychological, and empirical aspects of each of the 11 separate subtests. Chapter 13 presents empirical methods to facilitate the identification of significant strengths and weaknesses in the WAIS-R profile, to assess the unusualness of the person's degree of subtest scatter, and to examine the results of empirical studies suggesting characteristic profiles for learning-disabled individuals and for adults with Alzheimer's-type dementia. Chapter 14 offers several rational and clinical approaches for generating meaningful hypotheses from the examinee's WAIS-R profile. Both chapter 13 and chapter 14 make full use of the raw materials presented in this chapter.

At the end of chapter 12 are four *Examiner's Forms* to facilitate the clinician's task of evaluating the testing conditions and recording observations of the examinee's behaviors. Like the Examiner's Forms at the end of chapters 11, 13 and 14, *these forms may be xeroxed without permission of the author or publisher.*

WAYS OF GROUPING THE WAIS-R SUBTESTS

Wechsler (1939) opted for a two-pronged categorization of his Wechsler-Bellevue subtests into Verbal and Performance Scales. He maintained this organizational system for each succeeding version of his scales, although he readily admitted: "Of course, the abilities represented in the tests may also be meaningfully classified in other ways. But the Verbal vs. Performance subdivision remains a concurrent dichotomy regardless of other ways in which the tests are classified" (Wechsler, 1974, p. 9).

Some of the more clinically useful methods of recategorizing the WAIS-R subtests are covered briefly in the following sections to serve as a basis for understanding some of the terms and categories used later in the chapter in the subtest-by-subtest analysis of each task.

Factor Analysis

In chapter 8, the WAIS-R factor structure was explored in detail for normal and abnormal samples, and for groups classified by age, gender, and race.

Two Factors

When *two* factors are rotated, the dimensions correspond precisely to Wechsler's Verbal and Performance Scales. All six Verbal tasks load highest on the Verbal Comprehension factor, while all five Performance tasks relate closest to the Perceptual Organization dimension (see Table 8.1). *These WAIS-R factor-analytic findings represent the strongest evidence for the construct validity of Wechsler's Verbal and Performance Scales that has appeared in a half-century of empirical literature.*

Three Factors

When three factors are rotated, based on a wealth of data with numerous samples (see pages 247–250), the WAIS-R factors are best defined as shown in Table 12.1. Picture Arrangement and Digit Symbol are excluded from the three-factor structure because each is inconsistently or weakly related to the factors, based on studies of separate normal, abnormal, racial, gender, and age groups. When three factors are interpreted, these two subtests are usually best interpreted as measures of unique abilities, or as a dyad that shares elements of sequencing and convergent-production. Chapter 8 discusses when

to interpret two or three factors for a given individual. Chapter 13 permits computation of standard scores on the three factors and describes an interpretive system.

Bannatyne's Categories

The four-pronged division of WISC subtests proposed by Bannatyne (1968, 1971) and subsequently modified (Bannatyne, 1974) has achieved widespread use for the assessment of children (Kaufman, 1979b). Numerous WISC and WISC-R investigations of reading and learning-disabled children have revealed characteristic profiles for groups of children with learning difficulties; they perform relatively well on the Spatial triad, but demonstrate weaknesses in the Sequential and Acquired Knowledge areas (Kaufman, Harrison, & Ittenbach, in press; Rugel, 1974). This categorization system has also been applied to adults (e.g., Cordoni, O'Donnell, Ramaniah, Kurtz, & Rosenshein, 1981; Salvia, Gajar, Gajria, & Salvia, 1988) and is a useful way of organizing their profiles as well. Indeed, some evidence suggests that learning-disabled adults also perform poorly on the subtests composing Bannatyne's Sequential and Acquired Knowledge groupings (see pp. 448–455).

Bannatyne's recategorization of Wechsler tasks, as applied to the WAIS-R, is shown in Table 12.2.

All WAIS-R tasks except Picture Arrangement are included in Bannatyne's system, and two tasks (Vocabulary, Arithmetic) appear on two different scales. Picture Arrangement ap-

TABLE 12.1   A three-factor structure for the WAIS-R

Verbal Comprehension	Perceptual Organization	Freedom from Distractibility
Information	Picture Completion	Arithmetic
Vocabulary	Block Design	Digit Span
Comprehension	Object Assembly	
Similarities		

TABLE 12.2 Bannatyne's categorization of WAIS-R tasks

Verbal Conceptualization Ability	Spatial Ability	Sequential Ability	Acquired Knowledge
Vocabulary	Picture Completion	Arithmetic	Information
Comprehension	Block Design	Digit Span	Vocabulary
Similarities	Object Assembly	Digit Symbol	Arithmetic

pears to measure skills akin to both Sequential and Spatial abilities; its exclusion from Bannatyne's approach again reinforces its maverick, subtest-specific nature. The Spatial Ability category corresponds to the Perceptual Organization factor in the WAIS-R three-factor solutions, to the subtests most associated with Witkin's field dependence/field independence cognitive style (Goodenough & Karp, 1961), and to the tasks most associated with the simultaneous processing of stimuli (Das, Kirby, & Jarman, 1979; Kaufman, 1979b; Kaufman & Kaufman, 1983a, 1983b).

The Sequential Ability grouping corresponds to the familiar Freedom from Distractibility triad, although for the WAIS-R the Arithmetic-Digit Span dyad seems like the best representation of this factor. As Bannatyne's name for the category implies, it also reflects what I have referred to as the sequential processing of stimuli, and to what the Das-Luria model calls successive processing. Consequently, a comparison of Bannatyne's Spatial and Sequential categories for a given individual may give insight into that person's mental processing preference, whether sequential or simultaneous. If the Luria (1980) model is extended one step further, the person's Picture Arrangement scaled score may give some clues to his or her planning ability.

The two categories composed only of Verbal subtests are also quite useful for profile analysis. The Acquired Knowledge grouping, in particular, often separates out from the remainder of the Verbal Scale for bright individuals who are dyslexic or who have completed only a little

formal education; and for people of average or above average intelligence who have made the most of their ability through intellectual striving. The Acquired Knowledge grouping will be uncharacteristically low in the first case, and unusually high in the second.

A method for converting a person's scaled scores on the four different triads of WAIS-R tasks to standard scores (mean = 100, SD = 15) is given in chapter 13, as is a simple empirical technique for computing strengths and weaknesses on the four Bannatyne categories (see pp. 432–438).

Horn's Modified Fluid–Crystallized Model

Chapter 7 on aging revealed the importance of the Cattell-Horn model of fluid and crystallized intelligence for interpreting age-related changes in intelligence across the adult lifespan. In general, Wechsler's Verbal Scale measures the kind of education-related abilities associated with crystallized thinking, while the Performance tasks assess the novel problem solving that characterizes fluid thinking. This distinction is maintained generally—but not completely—when grouping WAIS-R subtests by the Cattell-Horn model.

Horn (1985) reports that four categories, not two, are required to group Wechsler's adult subtests, and that a modified fluid–crystallized model is needed for the WAIS (and, hence, WAIS-R). The model shown in Table 12.3 is taken from Horn's (1985) Figure 3, based on analyses that he did with a colleague, J. J. McArdle, using more than 100 different samples of subjects tested on the WAIS. In Horn and McArdle's (1980) initial WAIS model, five abilities were hypothesized: Crystallized Intelligence, Fluid Intelligence, Short-Term Acquisition and Retrieval, Long-Term Storage and Retrieval, and Broad Speediness. Table 12.3 represents their final synthesis of data, in which the two retrieval categories were merged into one.

By this division, only the four Verbal Comprehension tasks are considered measures of crystallized intelligence, with Similarities considered a measure of fluid intelligence as well. The fluid category cuts across content areas by comprising four Performance and two Verbal subtests, including one (Digit Span) with symbolic content. The Retention category includes measures of short-term retention as well as long-term retrieval; Arithmetic is included only in this category, while Information (crystallized) and Digit Span (fluid) have a dual loading. Digit Symbol's strong subtest-specific variance is evidenced by its status as the only member of the Speed category.

See pages 432–438 for a method for converting Horn's three major categories to standard scores and for identifying a person's strengths and weaknesses on the three categories.

Osgood's Psycholinguistic Approach

Kirk, McCarthy, and Kirk (1968) developed the Illinois Test of Psycholinguistic Abilities (ITPA) based on Osgood's theory of communication. Although the ITPA was constructed to measure a child's language abilities, most of its component tasks are quite similar to the kinds of subtests that are included in Wechsler's intelligence batteries. Despite the ITPA's focus on children and language, the Osgood approach represents a useful way of regrouping WAIS-R subtests for adolescents and adults.

The model has three dimensions of cognitive abilities: channels of communication, levels of organization, and psycholinguistic processes. The major channels of communication, "the routes through which the content of communication flows" (Kirk et al., 1968, p. 7), are auditory-vocal and visual-motor. These are assessed quite well on the WAIS-R; all Verbal subtests are processed within the auditory-vocal channel, and all Performance tasks (with the possible exception of Picture Completion) are processed within the visual-motor channel. Picture Completion, for a person who verbalizes the response, is best categorized as a visual-vocal subtest. Interpreting the WAIS-R from the vantage point of channels of communication recognizes that all WAIS-R tasks are a measure of communication ability as well as intelligence. If a person

TABLE 12.3   Horn and McArdle's model of WAIS-R tasks

Crystallized	Fluid	Retrieval	Speed
Information	Picture Completion	Information	Digit Symbol
Vocabulary	Picture Arrangement	Arithmetic	
Comprehension	Block Design	Digit Span	
Similarities	Object Assembly		
	Similarities		
	Digit Span		

has a defective channel, perhaps because of a brain-related sensory-motor deficiency, either the Verbal or the Performance IQ will not be a valid measure of intelligence for that individual.

Osgood's levels of organization, the "degree to which habits of communication are organized within the individual" (Kirk et al., 1968, p. 7), include *representational* and *automatic*. The former requires high-level, complex thinking, demanding the utilization of symbols and their meaning; in contrast, the automatic level requires less voluntary behavior and involves over-learned, highly organized habits. Automatic processing "is involved in such activities as visual and auditory closure, speed of perception, ability to reproduce a sequence seen or heard, rote learning, synthesizing isolated sounds into a word, and utilizing the redundancies of experience" (Kirk et al., 1968, p. 7).

Whereas one might immediately assume that any task included on a test of intelligence would, by definition, be at the representational level of organization, that is not quite the case. Certainly, most subtests are representational in nature. However, Digits Forward is clearly an automatic task, even though Digits Backward is representational. In addition, both Picture Completion and Digit Symbol have components of both automatic and representational tasks, and are best categorized as being at *both* levels of organization. Not infrequently, an individual will earn relatively high scores on Picture Completion and Digit Symbol while the remainder of the Performance Scale is depressed. This pattern may well be associated with a person who, despite limited intelligence, has highly developed "automatic processing" skills. One might anticipate that person to have an average to good forward span (6 digits or more) as well.

Within each channel of communication, regardless of the level of organization, an individual must apply certain processes to the acquisition and use of the language: *reception* (recognizing and comprehending what is seen or heard); *association* (also called *organization;*

mediating the information received by interpreting, organizing, or otherwise mentally manipulating the symbols); and *expression* (making a response, either vocally, gesturally, or manipulatively). All cognitive tasks have aspects of all three processes, although automatic-level tasks have little association or mediation. The ITPA includes representational subtests that stress a *single* process within either the auditory-vocal or visual-motor channel. In fact, their names reflect this goal: auditory reception, visual association, manual expression, and so forth.

Some WAIS-R subtests, most notably Comprehension and Block Design, are strong measures of all three psycholinguistic processes. Within the auditory-vocal channel, Comprehension requires excellent reception (because the questions are long and often complex), association (it is a high-level reasoning task), and expression (complex verbal responses are typically needed for 2-point answers). Similarly, the visual-motor Block Design subtest makes heavy demands on all three processes. However, six of the WAIS-R subtests can be categorized as measures of *primarily* one psycholinguistic process within each major channel of communication. Table 12.4 shows this categorization.

Within the auditory-vocal channel, Information is a good measure of reception. The individual must interpret a fairly long oral question with a minimal amount of association (simply remembering a fact, not problem solving) and expression (most responses require a single word). Similarly, Picture Completion assesses visual reception—interpreting the pictures—while making virtually no associative or expressive demands.

Similarities is mainly a test of relating or associating two concepts; the receptive demands are limited to the understanding of two words per item (e.g., DOG-LION) and even a person with unimpressive expressive abilities can earn 2 points on many items with just a single word. Picture Arrangement makes few expressive de-

TABLE 12.4   WAIS-R subtests categorized by Osgood's psycholinguistic model

	Psycholinguistic Process		
Channel	*Reception*	*Association*	*Expression*
Auditory-vocal	Information	Similarities	Vocabulary
Visual-motor	Picture Completion	Picture Arrangement	Digit Symbol

mands on the subject because there are no time bonuses for perfect performance, and the line of pictures need not be perfectly aligned. It is an excellent measure of visual association, but it falls short of being primarily a measure of this single process because of its major receptive demands (interpreting the pictures). Nonetheless, I have included this subtest as a measure of association within the visual-motor channel because the ITPA Visual Association subtest (solving visual analogies) has the identical flaw.

Vocabulary is a good measure of verbal expression; the individual has to understand just a single spoken word, and knowledge of each word must be retrieved from long-term storage, not figured out. The person's score depends heavily on how well he or she can spontaneously express the concept in words. Similarly, Digit Symbol makes minimal receptive demands (the symbols to be processed are quite simple) and requires little thinking. When operating from the Osgood model, it is essentially a test of psychomotor speed, or manual expression. In this respect, expression within the visual-motor channel requires excellent motor coordination, in contrast to the gestural communication necessary for success on the ITPA Manual Expression subtest (e.g., demonstrating gesturally the way to brush one's teeth).

Examiners who apply the Osgood model, especially for brain-injured or learning-disabled adolescents and adults, should be able to pinpoint the channel or level of organization that is defective, as well as the specific process that is deficient (reception, association, expression).

Rapaport's Pioneering Clinical Model

The first generation of Wechsler clinicians grew up on Wechsler's own interpretations of the tests (his pattern analysis), along with Cohen's (1952a, 1952b) factor-analytic inferences and Rapaport's clinical model, which tried to bridge the gap between intellectual functioning and personality development (Mayman, Schafer, & Rapaport, 1951; Rapaport, Gill, & Schafer, 1945–46). From these sources, and perhaps especially from the clinical interpretive approach advocated by Rapaport and his colleagues, came the wealth of conventional clinical wisdom that has survived to the present day.

Rapaport preceded Hunt's (1961) important declaration that the IQ was neither fixed nor constant, and stressed the influence of personality, environmental stimulation, emotional stimulation, defensive styles, cultural predilections, psychopathology, and brain injury on the maturation and expression of intelligence. He predated modern approaches to systematic profile interpretation (for example, by urging examiners to evaluate deviations of each Wechsler-Bellevue subtest from the person's average of all subtests), and ensured that future generations of clinicians would interpret Wechsler intelligence profiles in the context of personality development and environmental influences.

I do not generally agree with a number of Rapaport's assertions, such as the notion that *cognitive* tests like Arithmetic or Picture Completion are primarily measures of the *behavior* of concentration. I also disagree with the pertinence of many of the Rapaport-Schafer hypotheses regarding the clinical interpretation of specific findings in individuals' profiles being associated with a variety of pathological conditions: for example, misses on easy Comprehension items conceivably reflecting schizophrenia or psychotic depression; decrements in Information, contrasted with adequate Comprehension, indicating a hysteric reaction; or increments in Picture Completion suggesting a possible paranoid trend (Gilbert, 1978). As Matarazzo (1972) notes: "Little evidence in the way of validation for these or related hypotheses emerged" (p. 467).

Particularly indefensible, from the standpoint of psychometrics, are some of the inferences made by psychoanalytically oriented clinicians who have carried Rapaport's ideas to an extreme. For example, Allison, Blatt, and Zimet (1968) inferred from high Digit Symbol and low Digit Span a person "who seems to be controlling strong and pressing anxiety by excessive activity. . . . When we find the reverse pattern, a high Digit Span and a low Digit Symbol, we are usually confronted with an essentially depressed person who is attempting to ward off recognition of depressive affect perhaps in a hypomanic way, usually via denial, but not necessarily through activity and acting out behavior" (p. 32).

Nonetheless, the Rapaport approach occupies a unique place in clinical history; it depended heavily on Wechsler's clinical insights and on considerable empirical data and has been influential in the clinical lore that has been passed on from generation to generation of clinicians. Further, Rapaport's analysis of Wechsler tasks in terms of the abilities and traits they measure represents a useful contemporary supplement for interpreting WAIS-R subtest profiles.

Basically, Mayman et al. (1951) posit five thought functions that affect differential performance on the Wechsler subtests: memory, concept formation, visual organization, visual-

motor coordination, and orienting responses. Memory and Concept Formation facilitate the accumulation of experiences and memories, while visual organization (without essential motor activity) and visual-motor coordination deal with the key role of visual-perceptual processes in directing motor behavior and manipulations. The orienting category includes attention, concentration, and anticipation, each a crucial behavior that guides the selective orientation of each person in every reality situation. This category relates to Luria's (1980) Block 1 (attentional) and Block 3 (planning) operations, with attention and concentration considered a Block 1 function and anticipation a Block 3 function. In contrast, the remaining four Mayman-Schafer-Rapaport categories pertain primarily to Luria's Block 2, or coding, functions.

Each Wechsler task is considered to assess many functions, but one or two are considered primary for virtually every subtest. Comprehension does not fit directly into the five-pronged system. It measures the concept of judgment, which straddles the intellectual and emotional domains. Judgment is not quite concept formation, and not quite an orienting response, although it requires conceptual understanding and an "emotional-attitudinal orientation" that enables the individual to automatically select the relevant, appropriate aspects of each social situation. Table 12.5 shows how the remaining 10 WAIS-R tasks fit into Rapaport's scheme.

Rapaport's system has a number of benefits:

- It provides a sensible rationale for a common split that occurs in individuals' Performance profile (visual organization without essential motor activity versus visual-motor coordination).

- It provides a behavior-related explanation for the frequent split of Arithmetic and Digit Span from the remaining Verbal subtests.

- It provides possible behavioral explanations for low or high scores of many on the WAIS-R subtests.

TABLE 12.5 Rapaport's categorization of WAIS-R tasks

Memory	Concept Formation	Visual Organization	Visual-Motor Coordination	Orienting Responses
Information				
				Digit Span (attention)
Vocabulary	Vocabulary (verbal)			
				Arithmetic (concentration)
	Similarities (verbal)			
		Picture Completion		Picture Completion (concentration)
		Picture Arrangement		Picture Arrangement (anticipation)
	Block Design (nonverbal)		Block Design	
			Object Assembly	Object Assembly (anticipation)
			Digit Symbol	Digit Symbol (concentration)

- It shows the combination of the important cognitive and behavioral components of most Performance subtests.

- It offers behavioral hypotheses for two pairs of nonverbal tasks that may be uncharacteristically high or low for a given individual (anticipation—Picture Arrangement and Object Assembly; concentration—Picture Completion and Digit Symbol).

- It provides a rationale for a person's performance on Arithmetic or Block Design to be similar to his or her performance on tasks included in the *opposite* scale (concentration and concept formation, respectively).

Dean's Individual Ability Profile

Dean (1983) presented a system for regrouping WAIS-R subtests into 12 categories, which he referred to as his individual Ability Profile. Some of his categories overlap groupings discussed previously for other systems (most notably the factor-analytic trichotomy and Bannatyne's four-category system). Most of his remaining groupings augment profile interpretation in unique ways, and these are considered here:

General Ability—composed of the subtests that are the best measures of *g*, or general ability; except for people of limited formal education, for which this grouping must be interpreted cautiously, "[a] subject who performs poorly on this factor is seen as cognitively less able to compete within the dominant culture . . . [;] performance here presents the best single measure of the subject's cognitive ability to deal with the daily requirements of a technical, industrialized society" (Dean, 1983, p. 6). Dean included six tasks in this category, but I have added a seventh (Arithmetic) because WAIS-R data clearly show it to rank with the Verbal Comprehension subtests and to surpass the two nonverbal members of this grouping: Information, Vocabulary, Arithmetic, Comprehension, Similarities, Picture Completion, and Block Design.

Dean (1983) also groups several dyads together in ways that should aid WAIS-R interpretation (see Table 12.6); he provided the following definitions of these six two-subtest categories:

Abstract Thought—"[t]he ability to go beyond the concrete to the manipulation of concepts without a readily available referent in the environment . . . the abstraction and manipulation of components" (p. 6).

Remote Memory—"the recall or recognition of elements encoded greater than a month or two in the past . . . information which is assumed to have been overlearned in the remote past" (p. 7).

Visual Memory—"a compilation of long-term and short-term non-verbal memory components" (p. 8).

Auditory Memory—"reception and recall of information presented in the auditory mode . . . short-term auditory memory as a prerequisite to more complex processing . . . these subtests require not only auditory memory, but more specifically, verbal auditory memory" (p. 10). (The two tasks in this category are identical to the ones that define the WAIS-R Freedom from Distractibility factor, but Dean's grouping offers an alternative interpretation of this dyad.)

Social Comprehension—"a measure of the individual's social understanding . . . the client's ability to apply customs, social knowledge, and mores to specific situations. . . . Clients who score high on this factor are able to interpret and act upon environmental cues in a socially acceptable manner" (p. 12).

Visual-Motor Speed—"visual organization and continuous feedback in the motor execution of spatial tasks . . . the execution of these tasks [Digit Symbol and Object Assembly] requires significantly greater control over motor production than that required in either

TABLE 12.6   Dyads of WAIS-R subtests based on Dean's Individual Ability Profile

Abstract Thought	Remote Memory	Visual Memory	Auditory Memory	Social Comprehension	Visual-Motor Speed
Similarities	Information	Picture Completion	Digit Span	Comprehension	Object Assembly
Block Design	Picture Completion	Digit Symbol	Arithmetic	Picture Arrangement	Digit Symbol

the Block Design or Picture Arrangement subtests" (p. 14).

The latter category, Visual-Motor Speed, was actually named Visual-Motor Coordination by Dean (1983). In addition, Dean included another grouping that he labeled Psychomotor Speed, composed of four Performance subtests (all but Picture Completion). I do not like Dean's Visual-Motor Coordination label for the Digit Symbol–Object Assembly dyad because it is the *speed* component that distinguishes this particular pair of Performance subtests; Digit Symbol is almost a pure test of speed (see Horn's classification of it), and perfect construction of the four Object Assembly items, without any bonus points, yields a scaled score of 8 (25th percentile!). Similarly, the Psychomotor Speed label does not really fit the four WAIS-R Performance subtests because (a) it is an ability that is usually considered Digit Symbol's (and Coding's) uniqueness, and (b) WAIS-R Picture Arrangement does not merit inclusion because, unlike its WAIS counterpart, bonus points are *not* given for quick, perfect performance. If Picture Arrangement is deleted from Dean's category, then the remaining triad is identical to Rapaport's Visual-Motor Coordination category. For simplicity and clarity, I have thus merged the names of Dean's two categories to produce Visual-Motor Speed.

Guilford's Structure-of-Intellect Model

Guilford's (1967) popular three-dimensional structure-of-intellect model has been applied to Wechsler's scales for years (Meeker, 1969). Although it has been invaluable in a theoretical sense, clinicians have generally found it to be of limited value for profile interpretation. Nonetheless, I include it here because it sometimes represents the only way to make sense out of fluctuations in an individual's subtest profile. Table 12.7 shows brief definitions of the four Guilford operations, and the three types of Guilford content, that are measured by the WAIS-R. (The operations of "divergent-production" and "behavioral" content are excluded

TABLE 12.7   Guilford's operations and contents measured by the WAIS-R

Operations (intellectual processes)	
Cognition	immediate awareness, recognition, or comprehension of stimuli
Memory	retention of information in the same form in which it was stored
Evaluation	making judgments about information in terms of a known standard
Convergent-production	responding to stimuli with the unique or "best" answer
Contents (nature of the stimuli)	
Semantic	words and ideas that convey meaning
Figural	shapes or concrete objects
Symbolic	numerals, single letters, or any coded symbol

because the WAIS-R does not assess these aspects of Guilford's system.).

The third dimension of the model, the products (how the stimuli are organized), are of less general importance to WAIS-R interpretation and are not considered here; however, in the subtest-by-subtest analysis that follows, the products are indicated (except for Information, which includes several). Meeker (1969) classified Wechsler subtests according to the *major* abilities that each measures; obviously, all tasks involve cognition to some extent, but this operation is only listed for a task when it is of primary importance.

The organization of WAIS-R subtests by operation and content is shown in Table 12.8; only the major ability (semantic memory) is listed for Information, although scattered items assess other abilities as well.

Meeker's (1969) regrouping of Wechsler's subtests according to Guilford's structure-of-intellect model has several valuable features:

• External verification for the emergence of the Picture Completion-Block Design-Object

Assembly triad as the best reduction of the Perceptual Organization factor (they are the only WAIS-R tasks with *figural* content).

• A rational explanation for Picture Arrangement's and Digit Symbol's failure to load consistently on any of the three factors (their Guilford classifications differ greatly from all other subtests).

• An alternative explanation of the Freedom from Distractibility factor and Bannatyne Sequential category in terms of *symbolic content* (number ability).

• A rationale for Picture Arrangement's frequent concordance with a person's verbal rather than nonverbal abilities (according to Meeker, despite its use of pictures, it is the *semantic* meaning of the pictures that is manipulated mentally).

• An explanation for those profiles in which Comprehension is more in agreement with Performance than Verbal scores (a strength or weakness in the operation of *evaluation*).

• A sensible reason for Arithmetic's substantial loadings on both the verbal and the distrac-

TABLE 12.8   Meeker's classification of Wechsler's subtests according to Guilford's structure-of-intellect model

WAIS-R Subtest	Cognition	Memory	Evaluation	Convergent-Production
Verbal				
Information		Semantic		
Digit Span		Symbolic		
Vocabulary	Semantic			
Arithmetic	Semantic	Symbolic		
Comprehension			Semantic	
Similarities	Semantic			
Performance				
Picture Completion	Figural		Figural	
Picture Arrangement			Semantic	Semantic
Block Design	Figural		Figural	
Object Assembly	Figural		Figural	
Digit Symbol			Symbolic	Symbolic

tibility factors (it measures *both* semantic cognition and symbolic memory).

ABILITIES MEASURED BY THE 11 WAIS-R SUBTESTS

Each of the 11 WAIS-R subtests is dissected in the pages that follow in terms of several analyses: Cognitive and Behavioral, Empirical, Aging, Clinical, and Neuropsychological. The six Verbal subtests are listed first in their order of administration, followed by the five Performance tasks, also in their order of administration.

Sources and Methods for Analyzing Each Subtest

Cognitive and Behavioral Analysis

Cognitive and behavioral analysis begins with a delineation of the abilities and traits assessed by each subtest in accordance with the various models discussed in the preceding sections of this chapter. These approaches include factor analysis, Bannatyne's categorizations, Horn's modification of the fluid–crystallized dichotomy, Osgood's psycholinguistic interpretation of cognitive tasks, Rapaport's clinical analysis, Dean's Individual Ability Profile, and Guilford's structure-of-intellect model. Next, other skills measured by each subtest, and the behavioral and background influences affecting test performance, are indicated. Finally, each subtest's specific contribution to the WAIS-R is shown.

The major sources for developing the lists of shared and unique abilities and traits for the 11 WAIS-R subtests (apart from the ones associated directly with Bannatyne, Horn, and so forth) were Kaufman (1979b), Matarazzo (1972), Sattler (1988), and Zimmerman and Woo-Sam (1973).

Aging, Clinical, and Neuropsychological Analyses

The *aging analysis* was based on data presented by McLean, Kaufman, and Reynolds (in press b) for the separate subtests, a study that was treated in depth in chapter 7. This analysis presents adjusted mean scaled scores on each subtest for seven adult age groups (ages 20–24 through 70–74), after first equating for education level. The *clinical analysis* contains points stressed by Zimmerman and Woo-Sam (1973), Matarazzo (1972), and by Mayman, Schafer, and Rapaport (1951), as well as clinical inferences from my own experiences as a trainer; Zimmerman and Woo-Sam's thorough analyses of each subtest were, however, the most important single source. For the *neuropsychological analysis,* I relied very heavily on Lezak's (1983) research and clinical approach to the practical and brain-related aspects of each WAIS-R subtest; on the Boston process approach (Milberg, Hebben, & Kaplan, 1986); on Reitan's (1986) work; and on numerous articles in neuropsychological journals, including the many that I discussed in chapters 9, 10, and 11 on Verbal–Performance IQ discrepancies and brain damage.

Empirical Analysis

The *empirical analysis* includes thumbnail capsules of each subtest's *g* loadings (from Table 8.11); reliability and stability coefficients (from the WAIS-R Manual, Wechsler, 1981, Tables 10 and 11); subtest specificities (from Table 8.12); a partitioning of the total variance of each subtest into its component parts, such as the proportion attributed to each of the three WAIS-R factors (derived from Table 8.4); and the subtest or subtests that each task is most and least related to (from the WAIS-R Manual, Wechsler, 1981, Table 16). The analyses report values for the total standardization sample, ages 16–74 ($N = 1,880$); however, important, systematic differences due to chronological age are noted.

The partitioning of each subtest's variance into separate components was derived from the three-factor rotated solution for the total WAIS-R sample, presented by Parker (1983) and reported in Table 8.4. The *square* of a subtest's loading on a given factor equals the proportion of variance for the subtest that is accounted for by that factor. For example, Information loaded .75, on average, on the Verbal Comprehension factor for normal individuals; consequently, 56% of Information's variability (.75 squared) is accounted for by a person's Verbal Comprehension ability.

The sum of a subtest's variance on the three factors equals that task's *common factor variance,* the proportion of the subtest's variability that can be accounted for by the three major factors associated with the WAIS-R. The amount of a subtest's variance due to *error* (unreliable variance) equals 1 minus the subtest's reliability coefficient. If the common factor variance and error variance are summed, the amount that is left over (when subtracted from 100) equals the task's reliable variance that is not associated with any of the three factors. Other terms for this portion of the variance are *subtest specificity* and *reliable unique variance.* However, I have avoided these terms in the empirical analysis for each subtest to avoid confusion; that is, the values thus obtained do not correspond precisely to the subtest specificities reported by Parker (1983) and summarized in Table 8.12. The lack of correspondence stems from the fact that there are several equally defensible methods for computing a subtest's unique variance. I have opted for Parker's approach (which is based on the multiple squared correlation of each subtest with the remaining 10 subtests) because it is the most objective; it is independent of the number of factors that one chooses to interpret.

For the empirical analysis that I present for each subtest, however, I had to use an alternative definition of subtest specificity (one dependent on the rotation of three factors). Otherwise, the percentage of variance would not have totaled 100. For most subtests, the two different estimates of specificity are relatively small: ±6% for six subtests; ±9% for eight subtests. The largest differences are for the two tasks most associated with the third factor, Digit Span and Arithmetic. Digit Span's huge specificity of 45% using Parker's (1983) method drops to 28% when the variance common to the three factors is used to determine uniqueness. For Arithmetic, the value decreases from 30% (above the 25% cut-off used to infer "ample" specificity) to 18%.

What these results mean is that much of the so-called unique variance for Digit Span and Arithmetic is really not subtest-specific variance at all; rather it reflects a chunk of variance that these two tasks share with each other, as reflected in the predominantly two-task distractibility factor. This type of shared variance does not show up in the multiple squared correlations that Parker used to compute specificities, but it is still a "real" portion of common variance whenever examiners choose to interpret the small, but often important, third factor.

Which estimates of specificity should examiners use when interpreting WAIS-R profiles? I suggest using Parker's values, because these are the more objective uniqueness estimates. However, clinicians should be aware that the specificities are a good deal less for Digit Span and Arithmetic whenever they interpret the third factor for a given person. But in that circumstance the examiner has already made the decision to interpret Digit Span and Arithmetic *jointly,* based on the ability these two tasks share (whether it is seen as Freedom from Distractibility, sequential ability, auditory memory, or the like); hence, there would be no need to make any inferences about either task's uniqueness.

The values that I present in the Empirical Analysis section for each subtest regarding its "Abilities Other Than the Three Factors" are, nonetheless, meaningful. Picture Arrangement and Digit Symbol are the only two subtests for which the percentage attributable to these other abilities *exceeds* the percentage for any of the three factors. This finding validates the decision to omit these two tasks (and only these two) from the regrouping of the WAIS-R subtests into three factors.

Information

Cognitive and Behavioral Analysis

Abilities Shared With Other Subtests

Factor Analysis: Two- and three-factor solutions: Verbal Comprehension

Bannatyne: Acquired Knowledge

Horn: Crystallized intelligence

Retrieval

Osgood: Auditory-vocal channel of communication

Representational level of organization

Auditory reception

Rapaport: Memory

Dean: General ability

Remote memory

Guilford: Memory (primarily) of semantic content

Other skills: Fund of information

Long-term memory

Influences Affecting Subtest Scores

- Alertness to the environment
- Cultural opportunities
- Foreign language background
- Intellectual curiosity and striving
- Interests
- Learning disabilities ("ACID" profile)
- Outside reading
- Richness of early environment
- School learning

Uniqueness (subtest specific abilities or traits)

- Range of general factual knowledge

Empirical Analysis

g loadings: $r = .81$ (2nd best)

Reliability: split-half $= .89$, test–retest $= .91$

Subtest specificity/error variance: 20% vs. 11% (adequate specificity)

Proportion of Variance Attributed to:

Verbal Comprehension factor:	56%
Perceptual Organization factor:	7%
Freedom from Distractibility factor:	9%
Abilities other than the 3 factors:	17%
Error:	11%

Most related to: Vocabulary ($r = .81$)

Least related to: Object Assembly ($r = .39$)

Aging Analysis

Mean scaled score across the adult age range (controlling for education):

AGE GROUP	INFORMATION MEAN
20–24	9.9
25–34	10.4
35–44	10.0
45–54	10.8
55–64	10.9
65–69	10.9
70–74	10.4

Clinical Analysis

- Items are emotionally neutral and nonthreatening.
- Easy to rationalize failures as due to limited experience or specialized knowledge.
- Those with chronic anxiety may suffer early failures and depressed scores in general; effortless, automatic responding facilitates good performance.
- Failure on easy items, coupled with success on harder items, suggests retrieval difficulties.

- Mentally retarded score especially low, but relatively high scores are sometimes obtained by individuals who have overlearned facts without true understanding.

- Bizarre responses are quite rare, hence noteworthy when they do occur (Illustrations of bizarre responses from Matarazzo, 1972, p. 486: a) an adolescent psychopath, asked for the distance from Paris to New York, replied, "I don't know, I never walked that far"; b) a schizophrenic responded that the Koran is "like a chorus or a piece of cord"; c) a manic depressive responded that the capital of Italy is "Rome, but it could have changed").

- Responses given with trivial, unnecessary detail suggest obsessiveness.

- Those with repressive defensive styles may perform poorly by pushing out of consciousness any facts that are even mildly associated with conflict; repression impairs both the acquisition of the facts and the recall of known facts; Information well below both Vocabulary and Comprehension may suggest repression.

- High scores often reflect intellectual ambitiousness, and may be associated with the defensive style of intellectualization.

- Low scores may sometimes reflect a tendency to give up easily, hostility toward a "schoolish" task, or a perfectionistic approach where no response is preferred to an imperfect answer.

Neuropsychological Analysis

- Generally resistant to psychopathology and cerebral damage, so it serves as a good estimate of premorbid functioning.

- Limits should be tested with those having known or suspected brain damage to determine if failures reflect ignorance, loss of previously learned facts, or inability to retrieve the information.

- A markedly low score in the absence of a rational explanation (e.g., low education, cul-

tural deprivation, foreign background), particularly in the context of relatively low scores on the other Verbal tests, suggests left hemisphere involvement.

- "[T]emporal lobe epilepsy may result in specific impairment of this subtest" (Milberg, Hebben, & Kaplan, 1986, p. 70).

Digit Span

Cognitive and Behavioral Analysis

Abilities Shared With Other Subtests

Factor Analysis:	Two-factor solutions: Verbal Comprehension
	Three-factor solutions: Freedom from Distractibility
Bannatyne:	Sequential
Horn:	Fluid intelligence
	Retrieval
Osgood:	Auditory-vocal channel of communication
	Automatic level of organization (Digits Forward)
	Representational level of organization (Digits Backward)
Rapaport:	Attention
Dean:	Auditory memory
Guilford:	Memory of symbolic content (units and systems)
Other skills:	Auditory sequencing
	Encoding information for further cognitive processing (Digits Backward)
	Facility with numbers
	Mental alertness
	Sequential (linear, left-brain) processing

Influences Affecting Subtest Scores

- Ability to receive stimuli passively
- Attention span

- Anxiety
- Distractibility
- Flexibility (when switching from forward to backward span)
- Learning disabilities ("ACID" profile)
- Negativism (refusal to try to reverse digits, refusal to exert effort until the more challenging reversal task, or refusal to take a "meaningless" test)

Uniqueness (Subtest specific abilities or traits)
- Immediate rote recall
- Reversibility (Digits Backward)

Empirical Analysis

g loadings: $r = .62$ (3rd worst; only .57–.58 at ages 16–34, but .64–.65 at ages 35–74; a good measure for blacks, .71)

Reliability: test–retest = .83

Subtest specificity/Error variance: 45% vs. 17% (ample specificity)

Proportion of Variance Attributed to:

Verbal Comprehension factor:	9%
Perceptual Organization factor:	5%
Freedom from Distractibility factor:	41%
Abilities other than the 3 factors:	28%
Error:	17%

Most related to: Arithmetic ($r = .56$)

Least related to: Object Assembly ($r = .33$)

Aging Analysis

Mean scaled score across the adult age range (controlling for education):

AGE GROUP	DIGIT SPAN MEAN
20–24	10.1
25–34	10.0
35–44	9.9

AGE GROUP	DIGIT SPAN MEAN
45–54	10.1
55–64	9.9
65–69	9.4
70–74	9.4

Clinical Analysis

- Testing the limits and recording responses are important to help discern whether failure is due to poor memory, sequencing problems, anxiety, inattention (perhaps caused by intrusions into consciousness of anxieties or emotionally laden ideas), distractibility, negativism, low motivation, inability to develop a strategy (such as "chunking"), or low intelligence in general.

- Although the average child and adolescent has a forward span that is two digits longer than the backward span (Kaufman, 1979b, p. 151), the average adult has a forward span that exceeds his or her backward span by one digit (on the WAIS, for example, adults aged 25–34 have a forward span of six digits and a backward span of five digits; Wechsler, 1958); deviations from this norm—much longer forward than backward spans, or shorter forward than backward spans—are therefore clinically meaningful.

- Sensitive to testing conditions that fall short of the ideal.

- Good performance by a person whose psychopathology has disrupted success on other WAIS-R tasks may be demonstrating the "ability to rally to a simple task" (Zimmerman & Woo-Sam, 1973, p. 105).

- Hearing-impaired individuals and those with auditory discrimination problems are often unduly handicapped on this subtest.

- *State* anxiety (e.g., test anxiety), rather than *trait* or chronic anxiety, seems to disrupt the repetition of digits.

- Impulsivity may be noted by an individual who starts to respond before the examiner has completed the item or by one who repeats the digits very rapidly.

Neuropsychological Analysis

- The combination of forward and backward span into a single score reduces the task's neuropsychological value because brain injury often affects the two skills differently.

- Large differences (five or more digits) in favor of forward span occur rarely in normal people, but are more common in brain-damaged individuals; "[m]oreover, a Digits Backward [span] of 3 in a young adult, in itself is indicative of brain dysfunction" (Lezak, 1983, p. 267).

- For neuropsychological purposes, the WAIS-R *span*, rather than the *score* (based on 1 point for each trial), is more diagnostic of possible brain damage; a person can achieve a *low* scaled score by passing only one trial per item yet display "an *average* span for both digit span forward and the reversed digit span" (Lezak, 1983, p. 267).

- Digits Forward is more sensitive to left-brain lesions than to diffuse or right-brain lesions.

- Digits Backward is sensitive to left hemisphere damage, but it also may be impaired in patients with right lesions with visual field defects.

- Digits Forward is a fairly stable skill that is generally resistant to most types of dementia, but Digits Backward "is very vulnerable to the kind of diffuse damage that occurs with many dementing processes" (Lezak, 1983, p. 270); also, "[d]igit span backward is more sensitive to brain dysfunction than digit span forward" (Milberg et al., 1987, p. 72).

- "Unlike Digits Forward, Digits Backward shows little improvement over time following trauma . . . or psychosurgery" (Lezak, 1983, p. 270).

Vocabulary

Cognitive and Behavioral Analysis

Abilities Shared With Other Subtests

Factor Analysis: Two- and three-factor solutions: Verbal Comprehension

Bannatyne: Verbal Conceptualization
Acquired Knowledge

Horn: Crystallized intelligence

Osgood: Auditory-vocal channel of communication
Representational level of organization
Verbal expression

Rapaport: Memory
Concept formation (verbal)

Dean: General ability

Guilford: Cognition of semantic units

Other skills: Fund of information
Handling abstract verbal concepts
Long-term memory
Learning ability

Influences Affecting Subtest Scores

- Cultural opportunities
- Foreign language background
- Intellectual curiosity and striving
- Interests
- Outside reading
- Reading ability (since a word list is presented to the examinee)
- Richness of early environment
- School learning

Uniqueness (subtest specific abilities or traits)

- Language development
- Word knowledge

Empirical Analysis

g loadings: $r = .86$ (best measure)

Reliability: split-half $= .96$, test–retest $= .92$

Subtest specificity/Error variance: 19% vs. 4% (adequate specificity)

Proportion of Variance Attributed to:

Verbal Comprehension factor:	66%
Perceptual Organization factor:	7%
Freedom from Distractibility factor:	12%
Abilities other than the 3 factors:	11%
Error:	4%

Most related to: Information ($r = .81$)

Least related to: Object Assembly ($r = .42$)

Aging Analysis

Mean scaled score across the adult age range (controlling for education):

AGE GROUP	VOCABULARY MEAN
20–24	9.7
25–34	10.3
35–44	10.3
45–54	10.6
55–64	11.0
65–69	10.7
70–74	11.1

Clinical Analysis

- Those with repressive defensive styles may perform poorly by pushing out of consciousness any word meanings that are even mildly associated with conflict; repression impairs both the acquisition of the word knowledge and the recall of specific words that the person knows.
- High scores often reflect intellectual ambitiousness and striving, and may be associated with the defensive style of intellectualization.
- Content of responses lends itself to clinical analysis regarding the person's fears, preoccupations, feelings, interests, background, status, and possible bizarre thought processes; perseveration, clang associations (ponder–yonder, assemble–resemble), and incoherent strings of words are also observable.
- Responses need not be wrong to be clinically rich; of special clinical value are correct or partially correct responses that suffer from overelaboration (often containing trivial detail), ellipsis (omitting words, such as defining breakfast as "eggs and toast"), and self-reference (a sanctuary is "a safe place, far away from the ones who want to hurt you").
- Responses should be evaluated to distinguish between individuals who give overlearned, almost rote and mindless, answers, and those with intellectual striving who approach the task with refreshing vigor by infusing responses with current experiences.
- Perseveration is sometimes evidenced when patients "give the same introduction to each response" (Milberg et al., 1986, p. 72).

Neuropsychological Analysis

- Relatively insensitive to most types of psychopathology and even to many recent cerebral injuries, so it serves as a good estimate of premorbid intelligence.
- Sensitive to left hemisphere lesions, but less so than most Verbal subtests; not very sensitive to diffuse or bilateral lesions.
- Long administration time, compared to the unique information it yields, makes its cost-effectiveness questionable for known brain-damaged patients who may fatigue easily.
- The most likely WAIS-R subtest to distinguish between the diagnoses of brain damage and thought disorder because patients with the latter diagnosis "occasionally let down their guard on this innocuous-appearing verbal skill test to reveal a thinking problem in

'clangy' expressions, idiosyncratic associations, or personalized or confabulatory responses" (Lezak, 1983, p. 270).

Arithmetic

Cognitive and Behavioral Analysis

Abilities Shared With Other Subtests

Factor Analysis:	Two-factor solutions: Verbal Comprehension
	Three-factor solutions: Freedom from Distractibility (primarily); Verbal Comprehension (secondarily)
Bannatyne:	Sequential
	Acquired Knowledge
Horn:	Retrieval
Osgood:	Auditory-vocal channel of communication
	Representational level of organization
Rapaport:	Concentration
Dean:	General ability (excluded from Dean's grouping, but merits inclusion)
	Auditory memory
Guilford:	Memory of symbolic implications
	Cognition of a semantic system
Other skills:	Auditory sequencing
	Encoding information for further cognitive processing
	Facility with numbers
	Mental alertness
	Sequential (linear, left-brain) processing
	Long-term memory
	Reasoning (numerical)

Influences Affecting Subtest Scores

- Attention span
- Anxiety
- Concentration
- Distractibility
- Learning disabilities ("ACID" profile)
- School learning
- Working under time pressure

Uniqueness (subtest specific abilities or traits)

- Computational skill

Empirical Analysis

g loadings: $r = .75$ (5th best)

Reliability: split-half = .84, test–retest = .85

Subtest specificity/Error variance: 30% vs. 16% (ample specificity at ages 20–74, adequate at ages 16–19)

Proportion of Variance Attributed to:

Verbal Comprehension factor:	19%
Perceptual Organization factor:	12%
Freedom from Distractibility factor:	30%
Abilities other than the 3 factors:	23%
Error:	16%

Most related to: Vocabulary ($r = .63$) and Information ($r = .61$)

Least related to: Object Assembly ($r = .42$)

Aging Analysis

Mean scaled score across the adult age range (controlling for education):

AGE GROUP	ARITHMETIC MEAN
20–24	9.9
25–34	10.2
35–44	10.0
45–54	10.4
55–64	10.4

AGE GROUP	ARITHMETIC MEAN
65–69	10.0
70–74	10.3

Clinical Analysis

- Since actual computational skills required for success are learned in elementary school and are, at most, seventh-grade level, failure is frequently due to temporary inability to attend or concentrate, "blocking" on mathematics items, nervousness at taking a school-like task without paper and pencil, a negativistic or defeatist attitude, and so forth.

- Wrong responses should be analyzed to infer whether the error was in computation, selection of the wrong operation, or failure to understand or attend to the question; for example, in response to the question about the number of hours it takes to walk 24 miles at the rate of 3 miles per hour, the answer "9" suggests an error in computational skill, while "27" reflects a reasoning mistake, and "1,000" is bizarre.

- Testing the limits without time pressure and with paper and pencil is often advised to help assess the roles of anxiety and concentration on test performance.

- Poor performance should be interpreted as a deficit in mathematical ability only after ruling out the wide range of behavioral and cognitive (e.g., short-term memory, sequencing) hypotheses that are known to have a strong impact on WAIS-R Arithmetic scores.

- For retarded individuals, the subtest measures a skill akin to social intelligence or adaptive behavior because the early items involve counting and handling money.

- The nature of the Arithmetic items commonly arouses anxiety in examinees; how they respond to the anxiety and possible frustration (by rejecting the test, by composing themselves and doing well, by acting agitated and distressed) is of clinical interest.

- Reflective, compulsive, obsessive, or neurologically impaired individuals with excellent arithmetic skills may perform relatively poorly compared to other Verbal subtests because of failure to respond within some time limits, and failure to earn any of the five possible bonus points (maximum scaled score with no bonus points is only 11!).

Neuropsychological Analysis

- Routinely administer Item 1 (block counting) to all individuals with known or suspected right hemisphere lesions because they may have difficulty with the visual stimuli despite succeeding on much harder oral questions.

- Patients with immediate memory and related problems are not likely to display their true mathematical ability because of the oral nature of the task, and will conceivably experience great difficulty with the more complex, multistep items.

- The oral format prevents identification of the difficulties of patients whose spatial problems would be revealed on a paper-and-pencil test; also, "the examiner may remain ignorant of a figure or number alexia that would show up if the patient had to look at arithmetic symbols" (Lezak, 1983, p. 264).

- Patients with damage to the left temporal or left parietal lobe have been reported to perform poorly on Arithmetic; so have some patients with right hemisphere lesions due to memory, attentional, or organizational difficulties.

Comprehension

Cognitive and Behavioral Analysis

Abilities Shared With Other Subtests

Factor Analysis: Two- and three-factor solutions: Verbal Comprehension

Bannatyne: Verbal Conceptualization

Horn: Crystallized intelligence

Osgood:	Auditory-vocal channel of communication
	Representational level of organization
Rapaport:	Judgment
Dean:	General ability
	Social comprehension (social intelligence)
Guilford:	Evaluation of semantic implications
Other Skills:	Common sense (cause-effect relationships)
	Reasoning (verbal)
	Verbal expression

Influences Affecting Subtest Scores

• Cultural opportunities
• Development of conscience or moral sense
• Negativism ("People shouldn't pay taxes," "You don't need a marriage license")
• Overly concrete thinking

Uniqueness (subtest specific abilities or traits)

• Demonstration of practical information
• Evaluation and use of past experiences
• Generalization (proverbs items)
• Knowledge of conventional standards of behavior
• Social maturity
• Judgment

Empirical Analysis

g loadings: $r = .78$ (4th best)

Reliability: split-half = .84, test–retest = .80

Subtest specificity/Error variance: 23% vs. 16% (adequate specificity)

Proportion of Variance Attributed to:

Verbal Comprehension factor:	50%
Perceptual Organization factor:	9%
Freedom from Distractibility factor:	7%

Abilities other than the 3 factors:	18%
Error:	16%

Most related to: Vocabulary ($r = .74$)

Least related to: Object Assembly ($r = .40$)

Aging Analysis

Mean scaled scores across the adult age range (controlling for education):

AGE GROUP	COMPREHENSION MEAN
20–24	9.9
25–34	10.2
35–44	10.4
45–54	10.6
55–64	11.0
65–69	11.0
70–74	10.4

Clinical Analysis

• Selecting the appropriate information needed to make relevant judgments demands a stable and balanced emotional-attitudinal orientation; hence, maladjustment of any sort often depresses scores.
• More than any other Wechsler subtest, Comprehension straddles the intellectual and emotional arenas.
• Conventional, rather than creative, problem-solving approaches are rewarded.
• Foreign-born subjects who have not assimilated U.S. culture are handicapped by many items, as are those from nonmainstream U.S. subcultures.
• The content of the responses is extremely valuable for indicating areas of current emotional conflict or concern; the following illustrations are taken from Zimmerman and Woo-Sam (1973, Table 4.1):

Passive, dependent—"Wait until found" if lost in forest; "My mother says to" wash clothes.

Phobic—wash clothes because "Germs kill you"; regarding deaf people, "It's a disease, from sex."

Delinquent—"Open it up and take the money," or "Throw it away," if find envelope.

Unreflective—"Yell fire" in movie theater; "Go back the same way" if lost in forest.

Alogical—deaf people have "No tongue"; shallow brooks proverb means "Women talk a lot."

Naive—"Country land is better, pretty" compared to city land; hot iron proverb means "Hit somebody"; marriage license "So no adultery."

Contentious—pay taxes to "Pay off politicians, graft"; "I prefer the country" to city land.

- To a much lesser extent than Vocabulary, the intrusion of emotional problems and conflicts on Comprehension responses is likely to lead to scores of zero.

- Routinely test the limits to infer the degree of real understanding when individuals (especially retarded or emotionally disturbed) give overlearned responses; stereotypes, bizarre thought processes, mere parroting, and coaching in socialization may underlie such answers.

- Provides "a rich sampling of the subject's coping ability. Active mastery versus passive dependency may be highlighted; the same applies to socialized versus antisocial behavior" (Zimmerman & Woo-Sam, 1973, p. 73).

- Responses offer clues regarding the disturbed patient's practicality and ability to behave appropriately in social situations; however, be cautious about generalizing from responses to single-issue questions since real-life adjustment is complex and multidimensional.

- Determine if pattern of successes and failures conforms to the types of questions that com-

pose Comprehension: "personal and social behavior, general knowledge, and social obligations" (Milberg et al., 1986, p. 70).

- Obsessive individuals frequently give responses that are overlong and detailed.

Neuropsychological Analysis

- Patients with right hemisphere damage may score high, yet behave impractically and unreasonably.

- The most sensitive of any Wechsler Verbal subtest to left hemisphere lesions.

- A good measure of premorbid intelligence for patients with right, bilateral, or diffuse lesions.

- Brain-related impulsivity in formerly bright individuals may evoke very different responses to various items: impulsive responses to the emotional movie and forest items; carefully reasoned answers to the city land or child labor item.

Similarities

Cognitive and Behavioral Analysis

Abilities Shared With Other Subtests

Factor Analysis:	Two- and three-factor solutions: Verbal Comprehension
Bannatyne:	Verbal Conceptualization
Horn:	Crystallized intelligence
	Fluid intelligence
Osgood:	Auditory-vocal channel of communication
	Representational level of organization
	Auditory association
Rapaport:	Concept formation (verbal)
Dean:	General ability
	Abstract thought
Guilford:	Cognition of semantic content (relations and transformations)

Other skills: Handling abstract verbal concepts
                Distinguishing essential from nonessential details
                Reasoning (verbal)
                Verbal expression

Influences Affecting Subtest Scores
- Flexibility
- Interests
- Negativism ("They're not alike")
- Overly concrete thinking
- Outside reading

Uniqueness (subtest specific abilities or traits)
- Logical abstractive (categorical) thinking

Empirical Analysis

g loadings: $r = .79$ (3rd best; the best measure for blacks, .86)

Reliability: split-half = .84, test–retest = .84

Subtest specificity/Error variance: 24% vs. 16% (adequate specificity)

Proportion of Variance Attributed to:

Verbal Comprehension factor:	45%
Perceptual Organization factor:	13%
Freedom from Distractibility factor:	7%
Abilities other than the 3 factors:	19%
Error:	16%

Most related to: Vocabulary ($r = .72$)

Least related to: Object Assembly ($r = .43$) and Digit Span ($r = .45$)

Aging Analysis

Mean scaled score across the adult age range (controlling for education):

AGE GROUP	SIMILARITIES MEAN
20–24	10.0
25–34	10.2
35–44	9.6
45–54	9.9
55–64	9.6
65–69	9.5
70–74	9.0

Clinical Analysis

- Responses should be evaluated to determine if they are *abstract* (table and chair are "furniture"), *concrete* (coat and suit are "made of cloth"), or *functional* (north and west "tell you where you are going").

- Like Vocabulary responses, Similarities responses need not be wrong to be clinically rich; of special clinical value are correct or partially correct responses that suffer from overelaboration, ellipsis, and self-reference; also interesting are *overinclusive* wrong responses (dog and lion both consist of cells or molecules, praise and punishment both start with the letter *p* and are both words; Matarazzo, 1972, p. 490).

- Among Verbal Comprehension subtests, Similarities is the least affected by specific learning, formal education, background, and experience (hence, its fluid as well as crystallized classification in Horn's system); the emphasis is on finding the relationship (preferably abstract) between two concepts, but the actual concepts tend to be well known, even to retarded individuals (two of the hardest items are work–play and fly–tree).

- Two-point responses to the first few items (fruits, animals, clothing) often reflect overlearned, everyday associations rather than true abstract thought.

- How a raw score is obtained tells much about a person's potential: A string of 1s suggests concretistic thinking and relatively limited potential, probably not due to maladjustment; a mixture of 2s and 0s implies the possibility of greater capacity for superior performance.

- "Personal preoccupations are rarely expressed and, therefore, are diagnostically meaningful when they invade this subtest" (Zimmerman & Woo-Sam, 1973, p. 93).

- Searching for relationships between the pairs of concepts sometimes evokes creative thinking and visual imagery; unlike Comprehension, the creativity does not invariably mean a wrong response.

- Responses "may reveal character trends: meticulousness, ostentation, sophistication" (Zimmerman & Woo-Sam, 1973, p. 94).

- Obsessive individuals may earn unusually high scores by giving numerous responses since a 2-point response is counted even if it is embedded in 1-point and 0-point answers (as long as the total response is not spoiled).

- Performance on this highly conceptual subtest is quite vulnerable to psychopathology.

Neuropsychological Analysis

- Unlike Comprehension, Similarities is not affected by the impulsive behavior and lack of social appropriateness that are associated with some brain injuries.

- Brain-damaged patients often have difficulty giving abstract, conceptual responses that are worth 2 points.

- Similarities scores are very sensitive to left hemisphere lesions, especially in the left temporal and frontal lobes.

- Depressed Similarities scores are associated with bilateral damage to the frontal lobes, but not to damage to the right frontal lobe.

Picture Completion

Cognitive and Behavioral Analysis

Abilities Shared With Other Subtests

Factor Analysis:	Two- and three-factor solutions: Perceptual Organization (primarily); Verbal Comprehension (secondarily)
Bannatyne:	Spatial
Horn:	Fluid intelligence
Osgood:	Visual-motor (or vocal) channel of communication
	Automatic and representational levels of organization
	Visual reception
Rapaport:	Visual organization (without essential motor activity)
	Concentration
Dean:	General ability
	Remote memory
	Visual memory
Guilford:	Cognition of figural units
	Evaluation of a figural system
Other skills:	Simultaneous (holistic, right-brain) processing
	Distinguishing essential from nonessential details
	Visual closure
	Visual perception/processing of meaningful stimuli (people–things)

Influences Affecting Subtest Scores

- Ability to respond when uncertain
- Alertness to the environment
- Cognitive style (field dependence/field independence)
- Concentration
- Negativism ("Nothing's missing")
- Working under time pressure

Uniqueness (subtest specific abilities or traits)

- Visual alertness
- Visual recognition and identification (long-term visual memory)

Empirical Analysis

g loadings: $r = .70$ (7th best overall, 2nd best on Performance Scale; only .60 at ages 16–19, but .72–.74 for adults)

Reliability: split-half = .81, test–retest = .88

Subtest specificity/Error variance: 34% vs. 19% (ample specificity)

Proportion of Variance Attributed to:

Verbal Comprehension factor:	19%
Perceptual Organization factor:	31%
Freedom from Distractibility factor:	3%
Abilities other than the 3 factors:	28%
Error:	19%

Most related to: Vocabulary ($r = .55$), Similarities ($r = .54$), and Block Design ($r = .54$)

Least related to: Digit Span ($r = .37$)

Aging Analysis

Mean scaled score across the adult age range (controlling for education):

AGE GROUP	PICTURE COMPLETION MEAN
20–24	10.3
25–34	10.2
35–44	9.7
45–54	9.0
55–64	9.0
65–69	8.1
70–74	7.4

Clinical Analysis

- Personality integration is sometimes revealed by Picture Completion performance: "The pointing out of tiny gaps in the lines of the sketch, the inability to identify simple objects, or the tendency to designate them in some bizarre scheme, all suggest distortion of reality" (Zimmerman & Woo-Sam, 1973, p. 134).

- The basically simple task of finding missing parts of common pictures is usually considered enjoyable and nonthreatening.

- The 20-second time limit is ample for most nonretarded and nonbrain-damaged individuals.

- A person's response rate is worth noting; quick, incorrect answers suggest impulsivity, while failure to respond within the limit (especially to easy items) is of potential diagnostic value.

- Confabulatory responses (stating that something not in the picture is missing, e.g., "the person" in the car without door handles) are diagnostic of psychopathology when they occur several times during the subtest or are bizarre ("His wife is missing" for the man without a finger; Matarazzo, 1972, p. 493).

- People who insist "Nothing is missing" for several items may be negative, hostile, or even phobic.

- Success "reflects not only alertness and attention to details but an aspect of reality testing that may figure only marginally in other subtests . . . [,] the kind of reality testing with which psychotic patients have so much difficulty" (Hymowitz, Hunt, Carr, Hurt, & Spear, 1983, p. 594); consistent with this clinical hypothesis is schizophrenics' relatively weak Picture Completion score (Crookes, 1984; Wechsler, 1944), a decrement not found for patients suffering from depression or personality disorders (Crookes, 1984).

Neuropsychological Analysis

- Extremely resilient to the impact of brain damage.

- Good indicator of premorbid intelligence, especially for patients with left hemisphere lesions with limited "ability to formulate the kinds of complex spoken responses needed for the Verbal subtests" (Lezak, 1983, p. 275).

- Patients with visual agnosia may completely fail to identify the stimulus.

- Note whether individuals consistently fail items where the missing part is embedded within the figure, but have "no difficulty when the important feature belongs to the contour" (Milberg et al., 1986, p. 73).

Picture Arrangement

Cognitive and Behavioral Analysis

Abilities Shared With Other Subtests

Factor Analysis: Two-factor solutions: Perceptual Organization
Three-factor solutions: Inconsistent

Bannatyne: Uncategorized; has both a sequential and spatial component

Horn: Fluid intelligence

Osgood: Visual-motor channel of communication
Representational level of organization
Visual association

Rapaport: Visual organization (without essential motor activity)
Anticipation

Dean: Social comprehension (social intelligence)

Guilford: Convergent-production of a semantic system
Evaluation of semantic relations

Other skills: Common sense (cause-effect relationships)
Distinguishing essential from nonessential details
Reasoning (nonverbal)
Synthesis
Visual perception/processing of meaningful stimuli (people-things)
Visual sequencing

Influences Affecting Subtest Scores

- Creativity
- Cultural opportunities
- Exposure to comic strips
- Working under time pressure

Uniqueness (subtest specific abilities or traits)

- Anticipation of consequences
- Planning ability (comprehending and sizing up a total situation)
- Temporal sequencing and time concepts

Empirical Analysis

g loadings: $r = .63$ (4th worst; only .52 at ages 16–19, but .65–.70 for adults; excellent measure for blacks, .79)

Reliability: split-half = .74, test–retest = .72

Subtest specificity/Error variance: 35% vs. 26% (ample specificity)

Proportion of Variance Attributed to:

Verbal Comprehension factor:	18%
Perceptual Organization factor:	18%
Freedom from Distractibility factor:	5%
Abilities other than the 3 factors:	33%
Error:	26%

Most related to: Picture Completion ($r = .51$), Vocabulary ($r = .51$), Information ($r = .50$), and Similarities ($r = .50$)

Least related to: Digit Span ($r = .37$) and Digit Symbol ($r = .39$)

Aging Analysis

Mean scaled score across the adult age range (controlling for education):

AGE GROUP	PICTURE ARRANGEMENT MEAN
20–24	10.2
25–34	10.0

AGE GROUP	PICTURE ARRANGEMENT MEAN
35–44	9.4
45–54	9.0
55–64	8.8
65–69	7.4
70–74	6.6

Clinical Analysis

- Having the individual verbalize the stories, of both correct and incorrect sequences, is quite valuable for clinical understanding of the responses; however, the examiner should reconstruct the person's arrangements and request the verbalizations *after* completing the subtest to avoid violation of the norms and possibly giving the person a strategy for solving the harder items.

- Observing the person's process of handling the cards tells much about thought processes: trial-and-error versus insightful approach, reliance on visual feedback, impulsivity versus reflectivity, poor strategy generation.

- Examining thought processes via verbalizations "may reveal important aspects of the subject's cognition—precise or confused and tangential, socially oriented or self-oriented, realistic or bizarre, the ability or inability to relate verbal to visual-motor tasks" (Zimmerman & Woo-Sam, 1973, p. 156).

- Illustrations of verbalizations from Matarazzo (1972, pp. 492–493): FLIRT (Item 2), person charged with homicide: "A guy walks down the street with the head of a woman; he might have killed her"; FISH (Item 8), alcoholic with severe depression: "This guy didn't catch anything—he is cursing the water—he jumps in"; TAXI (Item 10), patient with a schizophrenic process: "The man carries a dummy—she changes into a woman in the taxi and he gets very hot and excited."

- Failure may be due to poor visual acuity or visual perception; adequate performance on Picture Completion will frequently rule out these factors as causes of a low Picture Arrangement score.

- The WAIS had two simple (three-card) items to ease the person into an unfamiliar task and ensure early success; the WAIS-R has only one such item, followed by four fairly complex five- or six-card items, causing some low-functioning individuals to "fall off a cliff" and fail miserably at this task.

- Failure on occasional items may be related to the individual's cultural background, which may teach interpretations of social situations that are different from American customs; surprisingly, however, this is *not* a pervasive problem.

- Performance on this logical, temporal task is impaired by serious psychopathology and bizarre thinking.

Neuropsychological Analysis

- Item 5 (ENTER), whether passed or failed, is a good one for requesting verbalizations from brain-damaged patients "because it can be misinterpreted in ways that may show patients' preoccupations along with their difficulties comprehending visual information or integrating sequential material" (Lezak, 1983, pp. 282–283).

- Picture Arrangement scores are vulnerable to brain damage in general, but are "specifically sensitive to the status of the right anterior temporal lobe" (Reitan, 1986, p. 21).

- Patients with frontal lobe damage have been reported "to shift the cards only a little if at all and to present this response (or nonresponse) as a solution" (Lezak, 1983, p. 284).

- Cards may need to be placed in a *vertical* column, instead of horizontally, for patients with "visual field and visual-spatial neglect deficits" (Milberg et al., 1986, pp. 73–74).

Block Design

Cognitive and Behavioral Analysis

Abilities Shared With Other Subtests

Factor Analysis: Two- and three-factor solutions: Perceptual Organization

Bannatyne: Spatial

Horn: Fluid intelligence

Osgood: Visual-motor channel of communication

Representational level of organization

Rapaport: Visual-motor coordination

Concept formation (visual analysis and synthesis)

Dean: General ability

Abstract thought

Guilford: Cognition of figural relations

Evaluation of figural relations

Other skills: Reproduction of models

Simultaneous (holistic, right-brain) processing

Synthesis

Trial-and-error learning

Visual perception/processing of abstract stimuli (designs-symbols)

Influences Affecting Subtest Scores

- Cognitive style (field dependence/field independence)
- Visual-perceptual problems
- Working under time pressure

Uniqueness (subtest specific abilities or traits)

- Analysis of whole into component parts
- Nonverbal concept formation
- Spatial visualization

Empirical Analysis

g loadings: $r = .72$ (6th best overall, best measure on Performance Scale; only a fair measure for blacks, .67, 2nd lowest)

Reliability: split-half = .87, test–retest = .86

Subtest specificity/Error variance: 32% vs. 13% (ample specificity)

Proportion of Variance Attributed to:

Verbal Comprehension factor:	7%
Perceptual Organization factor:	48%
Freedom from Distractibility factor:	11%
Abilities other than the 3 factors:	21%
Error:	13%

Most related to: Object Assembly ($r = .63$)

Least related to: Digit Span ($r = .43$)

Aging Analysis

Mean scaled score across the adult age range (controlling for education):

AGE GROUP	BLOCK DESIGN MEAN
20–24	10.3
25–34	9.8
35–44	9.3
45–54	9.1
55–64	8.4
65–69	7.8
70–74	7.2

Clinical Analysis

- Reflectivity or compulsivity can lower scores substantially because of 19 possible bonus points for quick, perfect responses; maximum scaled score for solving every item correctly while earning no bonus points is only 10.
- Observations of problem-solving approach may reveal a wide variety of behaviors: trial-

and-error behavior versus a holistic and in-sightful attack, ability to establish and implement a learning set, persistence, motor coordination, hand preference, concentration, distractibility, anxiety (to stopwatch and time pressure), frustration tolerance, rigidity, perseveration, speed of processing, impulsiveness, carelessness, work habits, self-attitudes, ability to benefit from feedback, and cautiousness.

- Some individuals feel that the task is too much like a child's game and become defensive or negative when asked to put the blocks together.

- Visual-perceptual problems (e.g., figure-ground) can be detected during Block Design, especially with limit testing (recognizing, rather than constructing, correct and incorrect responses).

- Some individuals refuse to try and instead give up easily; others learn while taking the items and sometimes "catch on" just when they discontinue (additional testing beyond that point is advised with such individuals, who may pass several items that do not "count" in the score, but are of great clinical value); reasons for catching on after early failures may be "aging, a dementing process, frontal lobe disease, or head injury" (Lezak, 1983, p. 280).

- "Bizarre solutions (design constructed on top of the card, or made vertically) can indicate poor reality ties. Suspiciousness ('Not enough blocks,' 'Can't be done') might reflect a projection of failure onto the material" (Zimmerman & Woo-Sam, 1973, p. 151); the so-called bizarre solutions may also indicate what Lezak (1983) refers to as the "stickiness" associated with the performance of some organic patients, like those with severe frontal lobe damage, or like Alzheimer's patients and others with "diffuse loss of cortical neurons" (p. 279).

Neuropsychologial Analysis

- Brain-damaged patients (especially right hemisphere) with visual-spatial impairment have special difficulty with those items having extensive diagonals in the designs.

- Brain-damaged patients who are excessively slow in responding should be allowed to complete at least one design beyond the time limit to evaluate their persistence, frustration tolerance, ability to solve complex items with time constraints removed, and satisfaction with their possible success.

- Vulnerable to any kind of cerebral brain damage; it is "least affected when the lesion is confined to the left hemisphere, except when the left parietal lobe is involved" (Lezak, 1983, p. 279).

- Block Design scores are very sensitive to posterior lesions in the right hemisphere, especially the parietal lobes.

- Both hemispheres are essential for good Block Design performance because of both the analytic and synthetic nature of the task.

- Patients with *right* hemisphere damage and concomitant visual-spatial deficits do best on designs that can be analyzed through verbalization; their errors are likely to be "disorientation, design distortions, and misperceptions . . . [and they may] lose sight of the squared or self-contained format of the design altogether" (Lezak, 1983, p. 281).

- Patients with *left* hemisphere damage are able to maintain the gestalt of the designs, but may make errors in the smaller details, such as the orientation of a single block; left-lesion patients, especially parietal lobe, "tend to show confusion, simpification, and concrete handling of the design" (Lezak, 1983, p. 280).

- "Both right and left hemisphere damaged patients make many more errors on the side of the design contralateral to the side of the lesion" (Lezak, 1983, p. 281).

- Note "whether the patient worked in the normally favored directions for a right hander (left to right and top to bottom)" (Milberg et al., 1986, p. 73).

Object Assembly

Cognitive and Behavioral Analysis

Abilities Shared With Other Subtests

Factor Analysis: Two- and three-factor solutions: Perceptual Organization

Bannatyne:	Spatial
Horn:	Fluid intelligence
Osgood:	Visual-motor channel of communication
	Representational level of organization
Rapaport:	Visual-motor coordination
	Anticipation
Dean:	Visual-motor speed
Guilford:	Cognition of figural content (systems and transformations)
	Evaluation of figural relations
Other skills:	Synthesis
	Simultaneous (holistic, right-brain) processing
	Trial-and-error learning
	Visual closure

Influences Affecting Subtest Scores

- Ability to respond when uncertain
- Cognitive style (field dependence/field independence)
- Experience with puzzles
- Flexibility
- Persistence
- Working under time pressure

Uniqueness (subtest specific abilities or traits)

- Ability to benefit from sensory-motor feedback
- Anticipation of relationships among parts

Empirical Analysis

g loadings: $r = .61$ (2nd worst; only .53 at ages 16–19)

Reliability: split-half $= .68$, test–retest $= .70$

Subtest specificity/Error variance: 23% vs. 32% (inadequate specificity)

Proportion of Variance Attributed to:

Verbal Comprehension factor:	4%
Perceptual Organization factor:	53%
Freedom from Distractibility factor:	3%
Abilities other than the 3 factors:	8%
Error:	32%

Most related to: Block Design ($r = .63$)

Least related to: Digit Span ($r = .33$)

Aging Analysis

Mean scaled score across the adult age range (controlling for education):

AGE GROUP	OBJECT ASSEMBLY MEAN
20–24	10.3
25–34	10.0
35–44	9.4
45–54	8.7
55–64	8.4
65–69	7.4
70–74	7.1

Clinical Analysis

- Reflectivity or compulsivity can lower scores substantially because of 12 possible bonus points for quick, perfect responses; maximum scaled score for solving every item correctly while earning no bonus points is only 8 (even earning 1 bonus point per item yields a scaled score of only 10).

- As on Block Design, observations of problem-solving approach may reveal a wide variety of behaviors: trial-and-error behavior versus a holistic and insightful attack, persistence, motor coordination, hand preference, concentration, distractibility, anxiety (to stopwatch and time pressure), frustration tolerance, rigidity, perseveration, speed of processing, impulsiveness, work habits, self-attitudes, ability to benefit from feedback, and cautiousness; also of interest is *when*, during the problem-solving process, the individual realizes what object he or she is trying to assemble.

- Some individuals feel that the task is too much like a child's game and become defensive or negative when asked to solve the puzzles; others become frustrated on the Hand and Elephant because of the virtual elimination of clues (i.e., the drawn-in cues on all puzzle pieces of the Manikin and Profile).

- Intense bodily concerns may lower scores on this task (Blatt's hypothesis, which is considered to be more valid for adults than children, e.g., Blatt, Baker, & Weiss, 1970; this hypothesis has been challenged, e.g., Turner & Horn, 1976).

- Individuals who try to "peek" behind the screen while the examiner is positioning the pieces may be revealing insecurity, impulsivity, or low moral development.

- "When the subject piles pieces one on top of another, reality ties can be questioned" (Zimmerman & Woo-Sam, 1973, p. 173).

Neuropsychological Analysis

- Because bonus points affect greatly a person's scaled score, performance is particularly vulnerable to cerebral damage, most notably to posterior lesions, especially in the right hemisphere; lowered scores for frontal lobe pa-

tients probably relate to the highly speeded nature of the task.

- Patients with damage to the right posterior cortex have difficulty with visual-spatial concepts; they are likely to accept as correct very wrong responses, and to assemble the puzzles "in piecemeal fashion by matching lines and edges in a methodical manner although, typically, they do not recognize what they are making until the puzzle is almost completely assembled" (Lezak, 1983, p. 285).

- Patients with left hemisphere damage may make errors on the details although they are able to maintain the overall contour and gestalt of the total puzzle.

- The concrete approaches of some brain-damaged patients may not affect Object Assembly performance (because of the construction of meaningful pictures), although it is likely to impair Block Design performance, notably when copying the abstract designs from the cards; in general, though, when brain damage hinders the patient's ability to construct the designs in Block Design, it also impairs his or her performance on Object Assembly.

- Individuals who consistently ignore puzzle pieces placed on one side or the other may have impairment in their visual fields.

- As on Picture Completion items, note whether errors occur more on details embedded within the object or on information provided by the contour.

Digit Symbol

Cognitive and Behavioral Analysis

Abilities Shared With Other Subtests

Factor Analysis: Two-factor solutions: Perceptual Organization
Three-factor solutions: Inconsistent (Freedom from Distractibility at ages 16–54, but weak)

Bannatyne: Sequential

Horn: Speed

Osgood: Visual-motor channel of communication

Automatic and representational levels of organization

Manual expression

Rapaport: Visual-motor coordination

Concentration

Dean: Visual-motor speed

Visual memory

Guilford: Convergent-production of symbolic content (units and implications)

Evaluation of symbolic units

Other skills: Encoding information for further cognitive processing

Facility with numbers

Learning ability

Reproduction of models

Sequential (linear, left-brain) processing

Visual perception of abstract stimuli (designs-symbols)

Visual sequencing

Influences Affecting Subtest Scores

- Anxiety
- Compulsive concern for accuracy and detail
- Distractibility
- Learning disabilities ("ACID" profile)
- Persistence
- Working under time pressure

Uniqueness (subtest specific abilities or traits)

- Ability to follow directions
- Clerical speed and accuracy
- Paper-and-pencil skill
- Psychomotor speed
- Visual short-term memory

Empirical Analysis

g loadings: $r = .59$ (worst measure; only .49 at ages 20–34; a good measure for blacks, .70)

Reliability: test–retest = .82

Subtest specificity/Error variance: 48% vs. 18% (ample specificity)

Proportion of Variance Attributed to:

Verbal Comprehension factor:	10%
Perceptual Organization factor:	14%
Freedom from Distractibility factor:	13%
Abilities other than the 3 factors:	45%
Error:	18%

Most related to: Block Design ($r = .47$), Vocabulary ($r = .47$), Similarities ($r = .46$), and Arithmetic ($r = .45$)

Least related to: Object Assembly ($r = .38$) and Picture Arrangement ($r = .39$)

Aging Analysis

Mean scaled score across the adult age range (controlling for education):

AGE GROUP	DIGIT SYMBOL MEAN
20–24	10.5
25–34	9.9
35–44	9.4
45–54	8.5
55–64	7.7
65–69	6.6
70–74	5.5

Clinical Analysis

- Visual impairment must be ruled out before interpreting a low score.
- Testing the limits by determining how many symbol pairs were committed to memory (either directly following the task or after

administering Similarities, the last subtest given) provides useful information about a person's incidental learning and efficient application of an intelligent problem-solving strategy.

- Illiterates may be at a disadvantage since four of the symbols are letters (L, O, U, X); so may people who rarely write because of the pencil-and-paper aspect of the task.

- "The most common errors tend to be perseverative runs in the first line, the only place where sequences of any kind occur" (Zimmerman & Woo-Sam, 1973, p. 124).

- Individuals who have demonstrated perfectionistic or compulsive tendencies prior to Digit Symbol should be told *during the sample items* that they need to copy the symbols legibly, but not perfectly.

- Be attentive to changes in the person's response rate during the subtest (perhaps by noting progress at the end of each 30-second interval; Milberg et al., 1986) because such changes may relate to motivation, distractibility, fatigue, memorizing some or all of the symbols, boredom, and so forth.

- Scores are likely to be impaired for depressed individuals.

- Verbally encoding the symbols may facilitate performance; testing the limits (by asking the person about his or her strategy at the end of the subtest) should uncover this intelligent use of verbal mediation.

Neuropsychological Analysis

- Digit Symbol scores are extremely sensitive to cerebral damage, regardless of its localization in the right or left hemisphere; hence, it is of great use for indicating the presence of damage but useless for inferring lateralization of the lesion.

- Reitan (1986): Digit Symbol calls upon functions of the left hemisphere when dealing with symbols, and on the right hemisphere "by the requirement of drawing various

shapes" (p. 20); the task's various components, including the timed element "combine to produce a test that is generally sensitive to the condition of the cerebral cortex" (p. 20).

- Patients with "right hemispheric damage, particularly if it is right frontal, . . . are most likely to make orientation errors, usually reversals" (Lezak, 1983, p. 273).

- Digit Symbol is the WAIS-R task that is *most* sensitive to brain injury "in that its score is most likely to be depressed even when damage is minimal, and to be the most depressed when other subtests are affected as well" (Lezak, 1983, p. 273).

- Examine the symbols that are drawn: "Are they rotated, flipped upside down, or transformed into perceptually similar letters? . . . Does the patient use the box as part of the symbol, . . . consistently make incorrect substitutions, or skip spaces or lines of the task?" (Milberg et al., pp. 72–73).

CHAPTER 12 SUMMARY

This chapter, the first of three on subtest profile interpretation, "sets the table" for profile analysis by providing specific information about each of the 11 subtests regarding the abilities it assesses and its clinical and neuropsychological significance. First, several methods of grouping Wechsler's subtests are described; then, each task is analyzed from the various perspectives. From factor analysis, two-factor solutions conform to Wechsler's division of the subtests into Verbal and Performance Scales; three-factor solutions produce the familiar four-task Verbal Comprehension factor (Information, Vocabulary, Comprehension, Similarities), a three-subtest Perceptual Organization dimension (Picture Completion, Block Design, Object Assembly), and a Freedom from Distractibility dyad (Arithmetic–Digit Span).

Bannatyne's system, commonly used with the WISC-R for learning disabilities assessment, applies to the WAIS-R as well. The four Bannatyne categories, which overlap with each other, are Verbal Conceptualization (Vocabulary, Comprehension, Similarities), Spatial Ability (the Perceptual Organization triad indicated previously), Sequential Ability (Arithmetic, Digit Span, Digit Symbol), and Acquired Knowledge (Information, Vocabulary, Arithmetic).

Horn's extended fluid–crystallized model of intelligence also adds to clinicians' understanding of the major dimensions assessed by the WAIS-R. His crystallized grouping is identical to the Verbal Comprehension quartet, while his fluid category merges two Verbal subtests (Digit Span, Similarities) with four Performance tasks (Similarities is included in both groupings, Digit Symbol in neither). In addition, Horn's system comprises a Retention category (Information, Digit Span, Arithmetic) and a one-subtest (Digit Symbol) measure of Speed.

Osgood's theory of communication offers several ways of categorizing the WAIS-R subtests: auditory-vocal (Verbal) versus visual-motor (Performance) channels of communication; representational versus automatic levels of organization; and receptive, associative, and expressive psycholinguistic processes. Whereas all WAIS-R subtests are categorized at the representational (high-level, complex) level of organization, three tasks have automatic (overlearned) components: Digit Span, Picture Completion, Digit Symbol. Similarly, although all subtests assess at least two of the three psycholinguistic processes, some (e.g., Vocabulary as a measure of verbal expression and Picture Completion as a measure of visual reception) typify a single process.

Rapaport's clinical model stretches back nearly a half-century, yet it still retains much that is useful for contemporary test interpretation. Some psychoanalytic interpretive techniques take Rap-

aport's methods to an extreme, but his basic division of subtests into five areas of cognition and behavior is valuable. Rapaport's categories include memory, concept formation (verbal and nonverbal), visual organization (without essential motor activity), visual-motor coordination, and orienting responses (attention, concentration, and anticipation).

Dean has assembled an eclectic approach to WAIS-R interpretation that subsumes many of the categories from other interpretive systems while adding some additional and interesting groupings. One category, General Ability, includes numerous tasks, while the others are dyads such as Abstract Thought (Similarities, Block Design), Remote Memory (Information, Picture Completion), and Social Comprehension (Comprehension, Picture Arrangement). Finally, Guilford's three-dimensional model of intelligence (operations or processes, contents, and products) offers novel ways of categorizing WAIS-R subtests that sometimes hold the key for competent profile analysis.

In the subtest-by-subtest analysis of each of the 11 WAIS-R tasks, the cognitive components and behavioral influences affecting test performance are derived primarily from the various systems just described. In addition, the following analyses are conducted systematically for the 11 subtests: (a) *Aging,* based on mean scaled scores earned by different adult age groups, controlled for differences in educational attainment; (b) *Clinical,* with inferences derived primarily from leading authorities on the clinical assessment of intelligence; (c) *Neuropsychological,* based on leading authorities on neuropsychological assessment; and (d) *Empirical,* involving traditional considerations (e.g., reliability), plus the partitioning of each subtest's variance into the portions accounted for by each of the three factors, the portion that is separate from the major factors, and the portion that is due to errors.

EXAMINER'S FORM 12.1   Evaluation of Testing Conditions (Developed by A. S. Kaufman)

Name: _____   Date of Evaluation: _____

Age: _____   Gender: M F   Medication (and dosage): _____

Ethnic Background: _____   Special Conditions (e.g., hearing-impaired

Reason for Referral: _____.   or bilingual): _____

Tests Administered: _____   Examiner: _____

Instructions: Place a check mark (✓) under the appropriate number for each testing condition. Omit any items that are irrelevant, inappropriate, or not observed. Use margins for comments and illustrative examples.

DESCRIPTION OF TESTING CONDITIONS DURING EVALUATION

TEST CONDITION	*Optimal* 1	2	*Adequate* 3	4	*Threat to Test's Validity* 5
Physical Environment					
Noise Level	____	____	____	____	____
Room Temperature	____	____	____	____	____
Lighting	____	____	____	____	____
Size of Furniture	____	____	____	____	____
Privacy of Room	____	____	____	____	____
Unexpected Interruptions (e.g., ambulance outside, telephone call, door knock)	____	____	____	____	____
Examiner–Examinee Interaction					
Separation Problem (from therapist, relative, caretaker, teacher)	____	____	____	____	____
Establishment of Rapport	____	____	____	____	____
Maintenance of Rapport	____	____	____	____	____
Evidence of Power Struggle	____	____	____	____	____
Communication Problems (e.g., examiner's inability to speak examinee's primary language)	____	____	____	____	____

EXAMINER'S FORM 12.1   (Continued)

	DESCRIPTION OF TESTING CONDITIONS DURING EVALUATION				
TEST CONDITION	Optimal 1	2	Adequate 3	4	Threat to Test's Validity 5
Physical Condition of Examinee					
Off Required Medication	_____	_____	_____	_____	_____
Unusual Fatigue	_____	_____	_____	_____	_____
Boredom (e.g., on retest)	_____	_____	_____	_____	_____
Apparent Illness	_____	_____	_____	_____	_____
Possible Visual Problem	_____	_____	_____	_____	_____
Possible Hearing Problem	_____	_____	_____	_____	_____
Missing Glasses/Hearing Aid	_____	_____	_____	_____	_____

EXAMINER'S FORM 12.2   Observations of Test Behaviors I: General Demeanor and Response to Items (Developed by A. S. Kaufman)

Name: _____   Date of Evaluation: _____

Instructions: Place a check mark (✓) under the appropriate number for each behavior. Omit any items that are irrelevant, inappropriate, or not observed. Use margins for comments and illustrative examples.

	DESCRIPTION OF PERSON'S BEHAVIOR DURING TESTING				
BEHAVIOR	*Optimal (Not a Problem)* 1	2	*Occasional Problem* 3	4	*Frequent Problem* 5
General Demeanor					
Anxiety Level	____	____	____	____	____
Restlessness	____	____	____	____	____
Degree of Self-confidence	____	____	____	____	____
Motivation Level	____	____	____	____	____
Alertness	____	____	____	____	____
Hostility	____	____	____	____	____
Immaturity	____	____	____	____	____
Insecurity	____	____	____	____	____
Fearfulness	____	____	____	____	____
Risk-taking	____	____	____	____	____
Perseverance	____	____	____	____	____
Resistance (vs. Cooperation)	____	____	____	____	____
Affect	____	____	____	____	____
Response to Test Items					
Attention Span	____	____	____	____	____
Distractibility	____	____	____	____	____
Concentration	____	____	____	____	____
Frustration Tolerance	____	____	____	____	____
Impulsivity	____	____	____	____	____
Perseveration	____	____	____	____	____
Carelessness	____	____	____	____	____
Interest Level	____	____	____	____	____
Flexibility	____	____	____	____	____
Need for Repetition	____	____	____	____	____
Compulsivity	____	____	____	____	____
Ability to Follow Directions	____	____	____	____	____

EXAMINER'S FORM 12.3   Observations of Test Behaviors II: Socialization, Language, Cognitive & Motor (Developed by A. S. Kaufman)

Name: _____   Date of Evaluation: _____

Instructions: Place a check mark (✓) under the appropriate number for each behavior. Omit any items that are irrelevant, inappropriate, or not observed. Use margins for comments and illustrative examples.

BEHAVIOR	Optimal (Not a Problem) 1	2	Occasional Problem 3	4	Frequent Problem 5
Socialization					
Aggressiveness (toward examiner)	____	____	____	____	____
Aggressiveness (toward objects)	____	____	____	____	____
Eye Contact	____	____	____	____	____
Manipulativeness	____	____	____	____	____
Response to Nonverbal Communication	____	____	____	____	____
Response to Praise	____	____	____	____	____
Boastfulness	____	____	____	____	____
Appropriate Expression of Feelings	____	____	____	____	____
Suspiciousness	____	____	____	____	____
Bizarre/Unusual Behaviors	____	____	____	____	____
Language					
Articulation	____	____	____	____	____
Grammar	____	____	____	____	____
Fluency of Speech	____	____	____	____	____
Spontaneous Verbalizations	____	____	____	____	____
Elaborations (when questioned)	____	____	____	____	____
Excessive Talking	____	____	____	____	____
Understanding Directions and Conversation	____	____	____	____	____
Use of Unusual Language (Bizarre, Ritualistic)	____	____	____	____	____
Use of Obscene Language	____	____	____	____	____

(Continues)

EXAMINER'S FORM 12.3 (Continued)

	DESCRIPTION OF PERSON'S BEHAVIOR DURING TESTING				
BEHAVIOR	Optimal (Not a Problem) 1	2	Occasional Problem 3	4	Frequent Problem 5
Cognitive and Motor					
Fine Motor Coordination	____	____	____	____	____
Gross Motor Coordination	____	____	____	____	____
Excessive Movement	____	____	____	____	____
Speed of Motor Response	____	____	____	____	____
Legibility of Handwriting	____	____	____	____	____
Problem-solving Approach (efficient vs. inefficient)	____	____	____	____	____
Ability to Benefit from Feedback	____	____	____	____	____
Creativity	____	____	____	____	____
Attention to Visual Detail	____	____	____	____	____
Visual-Perceptual Ability	____	____	____	____	____

EXAMINER'S FORM 12.4 Observations of Test Behaviors III: Summary (Developed by A. S. Kaufman)

Name: _____ Date of Evaluation: _____

1. List any threats to test validity based on the *testing conditions* (ratings of 4 or 5 on Form 12–1) _____

_____

_____

2. List any threats to test validity based on the *test behaviors* (ratings of 4 or 5 on Forms 12–2 and 12–3):

General Demeanor: _____

_____

Response to Test Items: _____

_____

Socialization: _____

_____

Language: _____

_____

Cognitive and Motor: _____

_____

Additional Observations and Comments: _____

_____

In view of the ratings of the testing conditions and the test behaviors, evaluate the overall validity of the obtained scores (circle one):

Excellent   *Very Good*   *Good*   *Fair*   *Poor*

List *specific subtests,* if any, invalidated due to testing conditions, test behaviors, or other factors. _____

_____

Profile Interpretation: Empirical Approaches

This chapter, the second of three on WAIS-R profile interpretation, is divided into three parts: WAIS-R IQs and scaled scores; empirical analysis of the subtest profile (to determine statistically significant strengths and weaknesses and the presence or absence of marked subtest scatter); and presentation of empirical research regarding so-called characteristic profile patterns associated with learning disabilities (e.g., the ACID grouping) and with Alzheimer's-type dementia (Fuld profile).

WAIS-R IQS AND SCALED SCORES

Before engaging in comprehensive analyses of WAIS-R profile fluctuations, it is almost always advisable to begin with systematic statistical treatment of the IQs and scores. My preferred approach is to start with the most global score,

Full Scale IQ, and proceed in stages to the 11 specific subtests. The sections that follow deal with the Full Scale IQ and the "curious" WAIS-R scaled scores.

WAIS-R Full Scale IQ

The logical starting point in Wechsler profile interpretation is the Full Scale IQ, the most reliable score in the battery (.96 for ages 16–19 and .97–.98 for the adult age groups; Wechsler, 1981, Table 10). This score should be assigned an intellectual category, using Wechsler's (1981, Table 9) classification system or any other system of the examiner's choice. The purpose of the verbal label is to facilitate communication, not to pigeonhole the subject, and most terms in Wechsler's system (e.g., Superior for IQs of 120–129 or Low Average for IQs in the 80s) communicate quite well to the professional and layperson alike. However, the terms used for IQs below 80 can be misleading. The 70–79 range is called Borderline by Wechsler, and IQs of 69 and below are considered Mentally Retarded. The former term is indecisive, and may be confused with the DSM III psychiatric label of the same name; the latter term implies a diagnosis, even though an intelligence test may not be used to determine mental retardation without systematic assessment of the individual's adaptive behavior (see chapter 15). Examiners who are accustomed to Wechsler's classification system may wish to use it with a slight amendment: substituting Well Below Average for Borderline and Lower Extreme for Mentally Retarded.

Statistical Treatment of Full Scale IQ

Next, FS-IQ should be converted to a percentile rank, using either Wechsler's (1981) Table 8, which includes only selected IQ values, or more comprehensive tables that give percentile ranks for virtually every IQ (Kaufman & Kaufman, 1983a, Table 4; Sattler, 1988, Table BC-1). Finally, surrounding the Full Scale IQ with a band of error is essential to ensure that the IQ is perceived as a *range* rather than a specific number. Table 13.1 presents bands of errors for FS-IQ (and also for V-IQ and P-IQ) at five levels of confidence between 68% ($\pm$ 1 SE_M) and 99%, based on data provided by Wechsler (1981, Table 12) and Naglieri (1982, Table 1).

Although technically the confidence intervals presented in Table 13.1 are not "precise" and require modification to account for regression effects and other statistical concerns (Brophy, 1986; Knight, 1983), I believe that they are appropriate for clinical use. For theoretical purposes, one must be aware that "the predicted value of the true score is not the observed score itself" (Dudek, 1979, p. 336), and that "the standard error of a set of test scores can be calculated in at least three ways and has a different interpretation depending on the formula used" (Knight, 1983, p. 671). For clinical evaluations, banding the obtained IQs with the confidence intervals shown in Table 13.1 and

stating that one can have 90% (or 95%, etc.) confidence that the true score is contained in the interval is an acceptable practice. Such interpretive explanations are not perfectly accurate, but they avoid the potential clerical errors of computing regressed true scores, working with decimals, and choosing the appropriate formula for the appropriate occasion (as advocated by Knight, 1983). The simple whole-number intervals, when placed around obtained IQs, communicate even to the novice that scores on intelligence tests have a certain amount of built-in error.

The Role of Full Scale IQ in Profile Interpretation

The careful statistical treatment and categorization of the Full Scale IQ as the first interpretive step does not mean that it is holy, or even the most important result of the evaluation. As the most global score, it becomes the *baseline* of the individual's performance, the midpoint that establishes the person's average level of functioning. This overall score then becomes the fulcrum for allowing the examiner to determine areas of strength and weakness within the total profile. The IQs are *normative* scores that rank the individual against a representative reference group and establish whether he or she is deficient or average or bright or superior in overall functioning. But the crux of profile interpretation is *ipsative,* the evaluation of strong and weak areas relative to the person's own midpoint. Ipsative and normative interpretations are one and the same only in those instances where the person's mean score equals the population mean.

FS-IQ is that midpoint and, as such, becomes the target for the astute clinician, a target at which to take careful aim in the search for both integrities and deficiencies within the cognitive and behavioral domains. The individual tested makes an unspoken plea to the examiner not to summarize his or her intelligence in a single, cold number; the goal of profile interpretation

TABLE 13.1 Bands of error surrounding the WAIS-R V-, P-, and FS-IQs at five levels of confidence for separate groups of adolescents and adults

Level of Confidence	ADOLESCENTS (AGES 16–19)			ADULTS (AGES 20–74)		
	V-IQ	*P-IQ*	*FS-IQ*	*V-IQ*	*P-IQ*	*FS-IQ*
68%	± 3	± 5	± 3	± 3	± 4	± 3
85%	± 4	± 7	± 4	± 4	± 5	± 4
90%	± 5	± 9	± 5	± 4	± 6	± 4
95%	± 7	± 10	± 6	± 5	± 8	± 5
99%	± 8	± 13	± 8	± 7	± 10	± 7

NOTE: Data for 68% interval are based on Wechsler's (1981) Table 12; data for the other four levels of confidence are based on Naglieri's (1982) Table 1. Values in this table have been rounded *up* to provide more conservative estimates of the confidence intervals, even if the actual decimal was a little less than .5 (e.g., the FS-IQ's 68% confidence interval for adults, reported as ± 3, was actually 2.4).

should be to respond to that plea by identifying hypothesized strengths and weaknesses that extend well beyond the limited information provided by the FS-IQ and that will conceivably lead to practical recommendations that help answer the referral questions.

Examining Verbal–Performance IQ Discrepancies

The first challenge to the sanctity of the FS-IQ in profile interpretation comes from the V–P IQ discrepancy. If it is found to be significant, FS-IQ immediately becomes less important than the distinction between the person's verbal and nonverbal intelligence in describing his or her cognitive functioning. Tables 9.1 and 9.2 permit computation of the significance of the difference between V-IQ and P-IQ; pages 264–270 address the statistical issues of significance and abnormality regarding the V–P discrepancy; and chapters 9, 10, and 11 interpret this difference clinically and neuropsychologically.

The tables of statistical significance and abnormality presented in chapter 9, and the more detailed tables presented by Matarazzo and Herman (1984a, 1985) of the frequency of occur-

rence of V–P discrepancies within the normal population, will, I hope, discourage psychoanalytically oriented clinicians from making unfounded inferences from differences between the Verbal and Performance Scales. For example, Allison, Blatt, and Zimet (1968) claimed: "An eight to ten point difference between Verbal and Performance IQs . . . indicates only a highly verbal subject with possible obsessive-compulsive tendencies. When the Verbal IQ begins to have a marked imbalance over the Performance IQ (by greater than 15 points), more serious pathological trends may be considered" (p. 34). Even more outrageous in view of data for normal adults is Allison et al.'s (1968) proclamation that "a Performance IQ greater than a Verbal IQ in individuals of at least average intelligence is atypical. Three major diagnostic trends, all of which have acting out as a primary feature, are suggested by such a pattern: hysteric, narcissistic, and psychopathic character disorders" (p. 35).

Psychometric treatment of a V–P discrepancy must precede its clinical interpretation. If the V–P difference is statistically significant, each of these IQs should be assigned an intellectual category, converted to a percentile rank, and banded with error. The same tables recommended for determining the category and percentile rank of FS-IQ apply as well to both V-IQ and P-IQ because each has the same parameters (mean = 100, SD = 15). In addition, Table 13.1 presents confidence intervals for Verbal and Performance IQ along with Full Scale IQ. If, however, the V–P IQ discrepancy is *not* significant, it is usually unnecessary to give each IQ full statistical treatment. Sometimes such treatment will actually confuse the reader of a report because it seems contradictory; for example, explaining that a P-IQ of 94 is *not* significantly higher than a V-IQ of 87 will make little sense if the former is called Average and the latter Low Average.

The importance of base-rate data for assessing the abnormality of V–P differences, presented in chapter 9, is revealed in two of the illustrative case reports: Robert N., a mildly retarded man (pp. 579–584), and Clara S., a brain-damaged woman (pp. 629–636). Each displayed an identical V > P discrepancy of 14 points. However, such discrepancies occur infrequently (less than 5% of the time) only for individuals earning FS-IQs below 70 (see Table 9.4). Consequently, the difference was abnormal for Robert but not for Clara.

Regardless of the significance, abnormality, or interpretation of the V–P discrepancy, the next step in WAIS-R profile analysis involves investigation of the fluctuations among the 11 subtests. Unfortunately, the peculiar method used to obtain each person's set of scaled scores makes this task harder for the WAIS-R (and the WAIS before it) than for Wechsler's children's scales.

The Curious Nature of WAIS-R Scaled Scores

Wechsler's scaled scores have a mean of 10, a standard deviation of 3, and a range of 1 to 19. These simple parameters have allowed cli-

nicians to easily compare a person's performance from one subtest to another; to evaluate fluctuations in a person's scores on the same subtest from one time to another; and to relate the subtest scores of different people, regardless of their ages. The beauty of the scaled score for the WISC-R and WPPSI-R (and for their successors) is that it always has the same meaning for an individual. No matter what the child's or adolescent's age, or the particular subtest in question, the examiner has the interpretive luxury of knowing that 10 is average, 7 is 1 SD below the mean, 16 is 2 SDs above the mean, and so forth.

The examiner never had this luxury with the WAIS, and, much to my surprise and chagrin (Kaufman, 1985a), this problem was not solved with the WAIS-R. The WISC-R and WPPSI-R determine a child's scaled scores based on norms for his or her age peers, so that the child is compared directly to others of comparable chronological age. Scaled scores of 10 are average at each age on every subtest, a statistical necessity for proper profile interpretation. On the WAIS and WAIS-R, however, all scaled scores are based on a reference group aged 20–34. What sense is it to obtain a profile of scaled scores for a 17-year-old or a 70-year-old using data for young adults? None that I could ever see. Development on each subtest follows its own unique pattern, as shown in chapter 7, based on its timed versus untimed nature, its fluid versus crystallized aspects, and so forth. Forcing a comparison of an adolescent's or elderly person's scores on each separate task to the performance of a reference group of 20- to 34-year-old adults makes a mockery of developmental changes and robs the scaled score of the very advantages that make it so useful for Wechsler's children's batteries.

A table in the WAIS-R Manual (Wechsler, 1981, Table 18) illustrates my point. This table shows the mean scores earned by 80 adolescents, age 16, tested on both the WISC-R and

WAIS-R. The group had average, and nearly identical, V-IQs of about 99.5 on both instruments. The WISC-R scaled scores reflected this average intelligence, ranging from 9.7 to 10.4 (mean = 9.9); the WAIS-R scaled scores did not (they ranged from 7.5 on Vocabulary to 9.5 on Digit Span, with a mean of 8.4). The differential changes of selected subtests across the age range are further illustrated in Table 13.2 for two Verbal and two Performance subtests (mean scores are taken from Wechsler, 1981, Table 15).

Clearly, the subtests average 10 only at ages 20–24, one of the samples included in the reference group used to develop scaled-score norms. The mean is about 9 for ages 16–17 and 35–44, about 8 for ages 55–64, and a mere 7 (!) for the oldest group in the WAIS-R standardization sample. In addition, within three of the five samples shown there is a substantial range in the mean scores for the selected subtests. These data are not adjusted for education level or other cohort effects, and cannot be interpreted to infer a decline of intelligence with age (see chapter 7). However, they do indicate how inadequate the WAIS-R scaled scores are for depicting the average performance at each separate age group and for making comparisons among scaled scores within each age sample.

Proponents of the reference-group method (e.g., Binder, 1987) might argue that the use of a single scaled-score table permits comparison of adults to each other regardless of their age by providing a common referent. They might also add that the IQ tables are developed for each of the nine separate WAIS-R age groups, a procedure that effectively controls for age in the scores that count most—the three reliable IQs. Further, the proponents will point out that the WAIS-R Manual does indeed offer scaled-score tables for each of the nine age groups (in Appendix D) as supplements to interpretation.

None of these arguments is viable. Comparison of adults on a common referent is occasionally important, such as for disability claims (Binder, 1987), but it is not generally a prime goal of *individual* clinical assessment; in any case, Wechsler's (1958, Appendix 2) tables of Efficiency Quotients, which compare a person's Full Scale score with the average score earned by the "peak" age group, could have been developed as a supplement to allow direct comparison of adults at different ages. The fact that the IQs are based on separate age groups makes the use of a young adult reference group even more ludicrous. The major scores yielded by the WAIS-R are derived from different nor-

TABLE 13.2   Differential changes in mean WAIS-R scaled scores across the age range for selected Verbal and Performance subtests

	AGE GROUP				
Subtest	*16–17*	*20–24*	*35–44*	*55–64*	*70–74*
Information	8.0	9.7	9.6	9.6	8.9
Similarities	8.7	9.9	9.2	8.4	7.3
Picture Completion	9.5	10.2	9.1	8.1	6.6
Digit Symbol	10.0	10.4	9.0	6.9	4.9
Mean	9.0	10.0	9.2	8.2	6.9

NOTE: Data are from Weschler (1981, Table 15).

mative samples, which produces some silly profiles. At age 70, for example, an adult earning Superior IQs in the 120s will display a Performance scaled score profile filled with 7s, 8s, and 9s. If his or her V- and P-IQs are about the same, this equality will be revealed by Verbal scaled scores averaging 12 or 13, contrasted with Performance scaled scores of 8 to 9. The IQs and scaled scores just don't match, except in a bizarre way.

Ultimately, the age-corrected scaled scores in Appendix D of the WAIS-R Manual solve the interpretive problem, but not without cost. Sensible interpretation of WAIS-R profiles demands that examiners compute this second set of age-based scores to gain the benefits possible from Wechsler's scaled scores: possessing a mean of 10 and *SD* of 3 for all subtests at each age; controlling for differential change in the various skill areas, and permitting easy comparisons from task to task, from one testing to another, and from person to person. The cost? Examiners are forced to enter a new set of tables producing a profile having an unwieldy 25 standard scores (3 IQs and 22 scaled scores). They double the chance of clerical and computation errors, and must remember that the reference group scaled scores *must* be used to generate the IQs; examiners who unwittingly or misguidedly use the age-corrected scaled scores to compute the IQs are making an error of *mammoth* proportion.

But regardless of the risks involved, a second profile of age-corrected scaled scores should almost always be computed for each individual (it is desirable, but not essential, for adults aged 20–34) before beginning empirical and clinical interpretive procedures. Most of the methods that follow are all based on the *age-corrected* scaled score profile, even if that fact is not always specifically mentioned. The principal exception concerns the evaluation of an individual's *subtest scatter,* since the only tables available for this analysis (McLean, Kaufman, & Reynolds, in press) were derived from the "reg-

ular" scaled scores (data for the age-corrected scaled scores were unavailable for analysis).

EMPIRICAL ANALYSIS OF THE SUBTEST PROFILE

The next few sections detail systematic ways of empirically attacking WAIS-R subtest profiles: determining significant strengths and weaknesses among the 11 separate subtests; computing standard scores for the WAIS-R factors, Bannatyne categories, and Horn groupings, and determining strong and weak areas within each system; and determining whether subtest scatter is normal or unusual. All but the scatter analysis require the use of age-corrected scaled scores.

Determining Significant Subtest Strengths and Weaknesses

I have previously endorsed a systematic, empirical system for determining significant strengths and weaknesses in the WISC-R profile (Kaufman, 1979b). The method avoids a comparison of myriad pairs of Wechsler subtests (e.g., Information versus Vocabulary, Comprehension versus Picture Arrangement) in favor of a more global approach to the problem: computing the significance of the difference between each Verbal subtest and a person's mean Verbal scaled score and then repeating the process for each Performance scaled score compared to the person's Performance mean. This method involves five or six comparisons per scale instead of an indeterminate number and invokes order in the process; the pairwise method exploits chance fluctuations, makes Type I errors likely (Knight & Godfrey, 1984), and produces a series of statements about pairs of specific tasks instead of a crisp overview of the person's strengths and weaknesses.

Modifications in the WISC-R Interpretive Rules

Silverstein (1982d) pointed out that even the method I was advocating took a little too much advantage of chance, and he employed the "Bonferroni" correction to ensure that significant fluctuations do not merely reflect the results of making about a dozen comparisons. For the WISC-R, I urged examiners to compute the child's mean Verbal scale score and to consider as a significant strength ($p < .05$) all Verbal scores that were 3 points or more above the mean; significant weaknesses were revealed by specific scaled scores that were at least 3 points below the mean. Similarly, I applied the same ± 3 rule for inferring strong and weak subtest scores on the Performance Scale (Kaufman, 1979b). The data that I analyzed suggested that 3 points was a good approximation of the actual values produced for each Verbal and Performance subtest, which ranged from 2.3 to 3.3 (Kaufman, 1979b, Table 2-2).

Silverstein's (1982d, Table 2) corrected values make my simple rule untenable for WISC-R profiles. Instead, strengths and weaknesses may be identified by ± 3 points from the relevant mean for all six Verbal subtests and for Block Design; a ± 4 rule is required for the remaining four WISC-R subtests. When comparing each subtest to the mean of *all* WISC-R subtests (see p. 428), ± 4 works well for all subtests except Object Assembly, Coding, and Mazes. These three subtests require ± 5 points.

A WAIS-R Rule of Thumb

For the WAIS-R, however, a ± 3 rule still works rather well as a quick guideline for computing significant strengths and weaknesses within the Verbal and Performance Scales. Table 13.3, taken from Silverstein's (1982d) Table 3, shows the precise magnitudes of the differences needed for significance at the .05 and .01 levels for each subtest when compared to the person's own mean score on the WAIS-R Verbal, Performance, and Full Scales. Most values at the .05 level are within about a half-point of 3.0. The exceptions are minor, mainly Vocabulary and Object Assembly, which require ± 2 and ± 4 points, respectively; of the 22 comparisons between subtest and global scale shown in Table 13.3, 18 (82%) range between 2.4 and 3.5.

Hence, I suggest the following rule of thumb for interpreting significant ($p < .05$) strengths and weaknesses on WAIS-R subtests, whether the scaled scores are compared to the person's own mean score on the Verbal, Performance, or Full Scale: Interpret as a significant *strength* each scaled score that is 3 or more points *above* the mean, and interpret as a significant *weakness* each scaled score that is 3 or more points *below* the mean.

I believe that 95% confidence is ample for nearly all assessment situations inasmuch as the reasons for identifying the strong and weak areas are to help generate hypotheses to explain a person's cognitive assets and liabilities, and to ensure some statistical order during the interpretive process, preventing examiners from declaring trivial differences to be meaningful. More stringent rules than the one suggested would limit the generation of useful hypotheses and betray the purpose for giving the test battery in the first place.

Should Rules of Thumb Be Used?

For the K-ABC, I present tables of specific values for each subtest at each age and encourage examiners to enter these tables to determine significance (Kaufman & Kaufman, 1983a); in my Wechsler texts, I encourage the application of simple rules of thumb. Why? Because the computation of strengths and weaknesses on the K-ABC is part of the interpretive process presented in the manual; the tables for making these determinations appear in sequence to allow the examiner to go from raw scores to standard scores to significant profile fluctuations as part of the total scoring process. Columns appear

TABLE 13.3   Differences required for statistical significance when comparing a person's age-corrected scaled score on each WAIS-R subtest to his or her own mean scaled score on the relevant global scales

WAIS-R Subtest	Mean of the Person's 6 Verbal Tasks		Mean of the Person's 5 Performance Tasks		Mean of the Person's 11 WAIS-R Tasks	
	$p<.05$	$p<.01$	$p<.05$	$p<.01$	$p<.05$	$p<.01$
Verbal						
Information	2.4	2.8	—	—	2.6	3.1
Digit Span	2.9	3.5	—	—	3.4	3.9
Vocabulary	1.8	2.1	—	—	1.9	2.2
Arithmetic	2.8	3.3	—	—	3.1	3.7
Comprehension	2.9	3.4	—	—	3.3	3.8
Similarities	3.0	3.5	—	—	3.4	4.0
Performance						
Picture Completion	—	—	3.0	3.5	3.4	4.0
Picture Arrangement	—	—	3.2	3.9	3.8	4.4
Block Design	—	—	2.5	3.0	2.8	3.2
Object Assembly	—	—	3.5	4.2	4.1	4.8
Digit Symbol	—	—	3.0	3.6	3.5	4.0

NOTE: Data are from Silverstein's (1982d) Table 3. All values have been corrected for multiple comparison errors.

on the front of the record form for entering the subtests that are significant "S"s and "W"s. For the WISC-R and WAIS-R, this interpretive procedure is not included in the manual and has instead been "tacked on." Consequently, I feel that a simple rule of thumb, one that does not force examiners to search out extra tables, will motivate them to employ empirical procedures for interpreting Wechsler subtest profiles.

Some researchers have opposed these rules of thumb, preferring to use precise tabled values to compute strengths and weaknesses (Campbell & Wilson, 1986). To me, these arguments are as weak as Knight's (1983) efforts to persuade examiners to compute regressed IQs and use several different formulas to determine standard errors of measurement. Using precise values (rounded to the nearest tenth or hundredth!) to

determine strengths and weaknesses, as proposed by Campbell and Wilson (1986), ignores the realities of a clinician's task in making sense out of a subtest profile, as well as the problems encountered in scoring several of Wechsler's subtests. Apart from the administration and scoring errors that are a built-in part of the Wechsler evaluation process (see pp. 101–105), even conscientious examiners disagree about the distinction between 0-, 1-, and 2-point responses on several Verbal subtests (I worked closely with Wechsler in designing these systems for the WISC-R, and I still have difficulty in evaluating some responses); examiners also differ in determining exactly when an individual has completed a Picture Arrangement or Block Design—possibly affecting the number of bonus points given—and in questioning ambiguous verbal responses.

Intriguingly, Gregory (1987) cited one of his research studies in which five different graduate student testers obtained quite different mean IQs for their respective, quasi-random subsamples of 5- to 10-year-old children (whose means ranged from 90 to 104). "The tester whose subjects had an average IQ of 90 was very formal, precise, cold, and hurried. . . . [T]he tester whose subjects had an average IQ of 104 . . . went beyond good rapport to offer support and encouragement that bordered on leading the subjects to the correct answer" (p. 154).

Consequently, I can find no rational defense for encouraging clinicians to use empirical rules that not only encourage additional clerical errors but that suggest a kind of psychometric precision that is just not obtainable in the clinical setting. Empirical rules and guidelines are needed to prevent interpretive chaos, but they should be simple and easily internalized. Further, they should not be so conservative that they impede the formulation of hypotheses about the person's cognitive and behavioral functioning.

Identifying Significant Strengths and Weaknesses on the WAIS-R

For the WAIS-R, I depart a bit from the interpretive technique that I proposed for the WISC-R (Kaufman, 1979b). Previously, I encouraged examiners to compare Verbal subtests to the child's Verbal mean and Performance subtests to the child's Performance mean. This technique treats each scale separately, in deference to the strong Verbal Comprehension and Perceptual Organization factors that emerged in a plethora of WISC-R investigations. Certainly the same two factors are just as robust for the WAIS-R, but I now believe that it makes more sense to use the separate Verbal and Performance means *only* when the V–P IQ discrepancy is significant; if it is due to chance, then the Full Scale mean should be used as the point of comparison for each scaled score. This approach ought to be used for the WISC-R as well (see p. 426 for the values required for significance).

The steps listed below should be followed to interpret strengths and weaknesses in the 11-subtest WAIS-R profile. Examiner's Form 13.1 (pp. 460–461) should simplify the process.

1. Enter supplementary Table 21 in Appendix D of the WAIS-R Manual (Wechsler, 1981) to compute *age-corrected* scaled scores based on the person's chronological age.

2. Compute the difference between WAIS-R V-IQ and P-IQ and enter Table 9.1 or 9.2 to determine its significance.

3. If the V–P IQ discrepancy is significant at whatever level the examiner chooses to interpret as meaningful (85%, 90%, 95%, 99%), the examiner should compare each age-corrected Verbal scaled score to the person's *Verbal* mean (based on all six age-corrected scaled scores) and each age-corrected Performance scaled score to the person's *Performance* mean. Round each mean to the nearest *whole* number. If the V–P IQ discrepancy is *not* significant, the examiner should compare each of the 11 WAIS-R age-corrected subtest scores to the Full Scale mean (based on all 11 subtests). Round the mean to the nearest whole number.

4. Systematically compare each age-corrected scaled score to the relevant mean. The ± 3 rule may be used for all comparisons to determine significant strengths and weaknesses at the .05 level. Scaled scores 3 or more points *above* the mean denote significant *strengths*; scaled scores 3 or more points *below* the mean denote significant *weaknesses*. These should be indicated directly on the front page of the Record Form with "S" or "W" next to the pertinent scores.

   Alternative Step 4: Examiners who prefer greater precision may choose to use the mean or means rounded to the nearest tenth, and to use the exact values (for the .05 or .01 level) reported for each separate subtest in Table 13.3.

5. The identification of significant fluctuations in the WAIS-R subtest profile is just the

beginning of test interpretation. Making sense of these fluctuations is the crux of the task, and is treated in depth from several perspectives later in this chapter.

Illustrations of the Strength and Weakness Method

Example of Ben G. (see Table 13.4).

1. Age-corrected scaled scores were computed for Ben G., a stroke victim, using Table 21 in the WAIS-R Manual (Wechsler, 1981, p. 148). These values are shown in parentheses in the column to the right of the "regular" scaled scores.

2. The V–P IQ discrepancy of 35 points in favor of Verbal IQ is statistically significant, exceeding by far the value of 12 points that is required for significance at the .01 level (see Table 9.1). From Table 9.4, it is also evident that differences greater than 30 points are *abnormal* or *unusual* for adults with Average Full Scale IQs, occurring less than 1% of the time in the normal population.

3. Since the V–P discrepancy is significant, *separate* means were computed for the Verbal subtests and the Performance subtests, using the *age-corrected* scaled scores for this analysis. The fact that the V-P discrepancy is abnormal is important clinically and diagnostically; however, for subtest profile analysis, the difference need only be *significant* (even barely) to warrant the computation of separate mean values. As indicated below Ben's profile, his Verbal mean scaled score equals 11.8, which rounds to 12. His Performance mean is exactly 6.

4. Each of Ben's age-corrected Verbal scaled scores was compared, in turn, to his mean Verbal scaled score of 12. Using the ± 3 rule to determine significant strengths and weaknesses in the Verbal profile reveals relative strengths in Vocabulary (4 points above his Verbal mean of 12) and Similarities (3 points above his mean). His single relative

weakness was the 8 he earned in Digit Span. Fluctuations in his other Verbal scores may be attributed to chance.

This procedure was repeated for the five Performance subtests. A relative strength was observed in Picture Arrangement (his scaled score of 9 exceeded his Performance mean by 3 points), and a weakness was observed in Digit Symbol. Fluctuations in the Picture Completion, Block Design, and Object Assembly scaled scores are probably due to chance. Note that Ben's *strength* in Picture Arrangement is only relative to his generally poor nonverbal ability. His Picture Arrangement score is actually *below* his Verbal mean, highlighting the truly ipsative nature of this type of profile analysis.

Alternative Step 4. A similar pattern emerges if a more statistically rigorous technique of profile interpretation is applied, using the exact mean of 11.8 for the Verbal scale and the precise subtest-by-subtest values required for significance (see Table 13.3). On the Verbal Scale, the same two strengths and one weakness are obtained. Within the Performance domain, the 2 in Digit Symbol remains a significant weakness, but the 9 in Picture Arrangement falls just short of significance (a strength would need to be 9.2— i.e., 3.2 points above the mean of 6.0). The differences in the patterns are slight, but I prefer less conservatism and more opportunities to identify meaningful hypotheses. If the .01 level is used instead of .05 (see Table 13.3), only three significant fluctuations remain: Digit Span, Vocabulary, and Digit Symbol. Again, I find the more conservative approach inhibiting for clinical purposes.

5. Uniting the strengths and weaknesses into a meaningful whole is essential to understanding Ben's profile. The key finding, naturally, is the severe right hemisphere lesion-related depression on P-IQ. Specific areas of relative strength seem to be in verbal concept formation (Vocabulary, Similarities)

TABLE 13.4   WAIS–R profile of Ben G.

White male, age 63, high school graduate, business executive
Reason for evaluation: Recent stroke, right hemisphere

Subtest	Raw Score	Scaled Score	Age-Corrected (ages 55–64) Scaled Score
Verbal			
Information	20	10	(11)
Digit Span	11	7	(8)—W
Vocabulary	67	16	(16)—S
Arithmetic	11	9	(10)
Comprehension	23	11	(11)
Similarities	25	14	(15)—S
Performance			
Picture Completion	12	6	(8)
Picture Arrangement	7	6	(9)—S
Block Design	4	4	(5)
Object Assembly	14	4	(6)
Digit Symbol	6	1	(2)—W

V-IQ = 112   *Age-Corrected Scaled Scores*
P-IQ = 77   Verbal mean = 11.8, rounds to 12
FS-IQ = 95   Performance mean = 6.0
V > P discrepancy of 35 points is statistically significant ($p < .01$).

and visual organization (Picture Completion, Picture Arrangement), while relative weaknesses appear on three subtests (Digit Span, Arithmetic, Digit Symbol) that have numerous interpretations. Systematic, step-by-step interpretation of Ben's scaled-score fluctuations appear in chapter 14.

Example of Gwen W. (see Table 13.5).

1. Gwen's age-corrected scaled scores were computed, and are shown in parentheses in Table 13.5.

2 and 3. The 7-point advantage in favor of P-IQ is not statistically significant at the .05 level, the level that I consider appropriate for most assessment purposes. Whereas 7 points is significant at $p < .15$ for all adults, and at $p < .10$ for adults of Gwen's approximate age (45–54; see Table 9.1), I chose to treat the discrepancy as due to chance. Consequently, I computed the mean of Gwen's 11 age-corrected scaled scores to serve as the comparison point for her scaled scores on all subtests constituting the Full Scale. As indicated beneath her WAIS–R profile, this value equals 13.4, which rounds to 13.

Examiners who feel comfortable with the 85% or 90% level of confidence for V–P discrepancies should interpret the 7-point

TABLE 13.5   WAIS-R profile of Gwen W.

Black female, age 46, Associate Degree (attending college part-time), middle school paraprofessional
Reason for evaluation: Career counseling

Subtest	Raw Score	Scaled Score	Age-Corrected (ages 45–54) Scaled Score
Verbal			
Information	23	12	(12)
Digit Span	25	16	(17)—S
Vocabulary	54	11	(12)
Arithmetic	12	10	(10)—W
Comprehension	24	11	(11)
Similarities	25	14	(15)
Performance			
Picture Completion	19	14	(15)
Picture Arrangement	11	8	(10)—W
Block Design	46	14	(16)—S
Object Assembly	36	12	(15)
Digit Symbol	69	12	(14)

V-IQ = 118   *Age-Corrected Scaled Scores*

P-IQ = 125   Full Scale mean = 13.4, rounds to 13

FS-IQ = 124

V–P discrepancy of 7 points is *not* statistically significant at the .05 level.

discrepancy as significant, and therefore should compare each Verbal scaled score to Gwen's Verbal mean (12.8, or 13), and each Performance scaled score to her Performance mean (14.0).

There are no "right" or "wrong" decisions regarding levels of significance or the degree of liberalness or conservatism in one's interpretive approach. Examiners need to select decision rules they feel comfortable with, apply them systematically, and interpret the profiles accordingly. The only wrong decision, I believe, is to use no empirical guidelines at all, leaving the way open to incon-

sistent interpretation and the likely overinterpretation of chance fluctuations.

4. Gwen scored 3 or more points above her overall mean of 13 on two subtests (Digit Span, Block Design), suggesting relative strength on these tasks. Relative weaknesses were indicated by her age-corrected scaled scores of 10 on both Arithmetic and Picture Arrangement.

Alternative Step 4. Using Gwen's precise overall mean of 13.4 and the exact deviations required for significance at $p < .05$ (see Table 13.3) produced three significant fluctuations: Digit Span and Arithmetic. Picture Arrangement was not significantly weak since it technically requires a 3.8 deviation from a person's overall Full Scale mean. The 16 on Block Design fell just short of the value of 16.2 required for a strength.

If the .01 level of significance is used, *none* of the 11 subtests deviates significantly from Gwen's mean score of 13.4.

5. Gwen's patterns of strengths and weaknesses lend themselves to interpretation using Bannatyne's four-category system, Horn's distinction between fluid and crystallized intelligence, and Dean's interpretive system; these approaches were discussed in chapter 12. Applying Bannatyne's method, Gwen seems to perform much better on Spatial (Block Design, Picture Completion, Object Assembly) than Acquired Knowledge (Arithmetic, Information, Vocabulary) tasks. However, the three Spatial subtests are also measures of fluid intelligence, as are the two Verbal subtests on which Gwen excelled: Digit Span and Similarities. Consequently, according to Horn's system she has very strong fluid ability and relatively weak crystallized ability. Two of Dean's categories help complete the picture: Gwen performed well on tests of Abstract Thought (Similarities, Block Design) and relatively poorly on measures of Social Comprehension (Picture Arrangement, Comprehension).

The guidelines for coming up with these or similar interpretations are presented later in the chapter, and also in chapter 14. However, no significant deviations would have emerged had the .01 level of significance been selected. That criterion would have attributed all subtest fluctuations to chance, preventing the generation of the aforementioned interesting hypotheses about Gwen's cognitive ability spectrum. The findings regarding her fluid versus crystallized abilities, abstract thought, and so forth will be just as important as her Superior level of mental

functioning in providing this intelligent paraprofessional with valuable recommendations regarding her selection of a new vocation.

Interpreting the Factors, Bannatyne Categories, and Fluid–Crystallized Intelligence

Three of the interpretive systems presented in chapter 12—the factors, Bannatyne categories, and Cattell-Horn fluid–crystallized approach—are so popular and potentially valuable for generating meaningful hypotheses about an individual's cognitive functioning that my colleagues and I (Ishikuma, Applegate, & Kaufman, 1989) have developed tables to facilitate their analysis. The factor-analytic trichotomy has been used for nearly 40 years by Wechsler clinicians with children, adolescents, and adults; it reflects the persistent finding that *three* (not Wechsler's proposed two) distinct aspects of intellect underlie the Wechsler-Bellevue and its descendants. The Bannatyne categories came on the scene more recently, reaching the crest of their popularity during the past 10 or 15 years. They have been shown in research study after research study to yield characteristic WISC and WISC-R profiles for reading- and learning-disabled children (Kaufman, 1979b; Rugel, 1974); more recently, the value of Bannatyne's system for adolescent and adult learning-disabled individuals (Salvia, Gajar, Gajria, & Salvia, 1988) has convinced me of its contributions to the WAIS-R as well as the WISC-R. Finally, Cattell and Horn's distinction between fluid and crystallized intelligence has received wide attention in both clinical and theoretical circles, and is especially important for the assessment of intelligence across the adult lifespan using the WAIS-R (see chapter 7).

Assessment of Verbal Skills by the Three Approaches

The three interpretive approaches are similar. The empirical factors and rational Bannatyne categories each include two scales that assess, in "pure" form, the verbal and nonverbal dimensions of intelligence that Wechsler intended to measure when he first developed the Wechsler-Bellevue. The Verbal Scale measures a person's ability to understand the spoken word and to respond orally. However, only four of the six WAIS-R tasks (the ones composing the Verbal Comprehension factor that, incidentally, are the same tasks that constitute Horn's crystallized intelligence grouping) assess the essence of verbal intelligence: the ability to comprehend verbalizations, verbally mediate during the problem-solving or retrieval process, and express one's thoughts in words. In Bannatyne's system, only three subtests constitute his Verbal Conceptualization factor (Vocabulary, Comprehension, Similarities), since he legitimately considers Information to be more of a memory and achievement-oriented test than a measure of concept formation.

Assessment of Nonverbal Skills by the Three Approaches

Within the Performance domain, both the factor-analytic and Bannatyne systems abbreviate the five-subtest Performance Scale by deleting the factorially complex Picture Arrangement and Digit Symbol tasks, while retaining the same three tasks that cluster together conceptually and empirically: Picture Completion, Block Design, and Object Assembly. This combination has variously been labeled Perceptual Organization (factor analysis) Spatial Ability (Bannatyne), simultaneous processing (Kaufman, 1979b), and analytic thinking (field dependence/field independence cognitive style; Goodenough & Karp, 1961). Regardless of label, the combination reflects the blend of visual-perceptual skills, visual-motor coordination, and nonverbal reasoning that Wechsler probably intended to measure when he first sought to elevate nonverbal intelligence to the same exalted plateau as verbal intelligence.

The Horn model does not have a nonverbal component, but it does yield a scale with a distinct nonverbal flavor: fluid intelligence. This category intends to measure the kind of learning that is not specifically dependent on schooling and formal training, but one that is acquirable in less structured ways. To some extent, Wechsler considered Performance IQ to measure this type of fluid thinking, but Horn focused more on the process than the content of Wechsler's tasks when assigning them to the fluid or crystallized domains. Consequently, four of the Performance subtests are measures of fluid intelligence, but so are the two Verbal tasks that are the least related to formal education: Similarities and Digit Span. Similarities is included in the crystallized grouping as well because of the verbal concepts that must be learned before one can uncover their relationships; Digit Symbol is excluded from the fluid category because it is more a measure of speed than intellectual functioning.

The Spatial-Perceptual Simultaneous-Analytic triad might legitimately be labeled Fluid Intelligence because all three tasks are prime components of Horn's dimension; despite the various skill areas tapped by Picture Completion, Block Design, and Object Assembly, each subtest assesses a person's flexibility and adaptability when faced with new problem-solving situations.

Assessment of Additional Skills by the Three Approaches

All three interpretive systems include a third component that involves memory to some extent and that diverges from Wechsler's two-pronged division of his tasks. WAIS-R factor-analytic results suggest a two-subtest scale composed of Arithmetic and Digit Span, labeled Freedom from Distractibility or Auditory Memory (Dean, 1983). Bannatyne added Digit Symbol to this dyad to form his Sequential Ability category, and Horn included Information with the distractibility duo to yield his Retention grouping.

Both Bannatyne's and Horn's systems have a fourth category. Horn's is a speed factor, composed only of Digit Symbol; it is excluded from the interpretive approach developed by Ishikuma et al. (1989) and described here because of its dependency on a single (relatively unreliable) subtest. Bannatyne's fourth category, Acquired Knowledge, represents a subgrouping of Verbal subtests, the ones that are most like achievement tests on other batteries (e.g., the Peabody Individual Achievement Test—Revised; see chapter 16). The combination of these three subtests (Information, Arithmetic, Vocabulary) does *not* emerge as a separate dimension in factor analysis (Matheson, Mueller, & Short, 1984; Naglieri & Kaufman, 1983), but it is nonetheless included in the Bannatyne interpretive system because it seems to be especially valuable in identifying an area of weakness in dyslexic adults and in learning-disabled individuals, including females and those attending college (see pp. 448–455).

Computing Standard Scores for the Factors, Bannatyne Categories, and Horn Groupings

To be optimally meaningful, it is desirable to convert a person's scores on the subtests in each category to a standard score having the familiar mean of 100 and standard deviation of 15. Ishikuma et al. (1989) developed such formulas for each factor from factor analysis, each Bannatyne category, and each Horn grouping. The formulas within each category were so similar from age group to age group across the entire 16- to 74-year age range that Ishikuma et al. concluded that a single formula per category (derived for the total standardization sample of 1,880) would suffice for everyone between ages 16 and 74. These simple formulas are presented for each factor, Bannatyne category, and Horn grouping in Table 13.6. To use these formulas, *it is necessary to compute the age-corrected scaled scores* for all component subtests.

For example, the formula to compute the Verbal Comprehension factor score is $1.4\ X_{ss} + 44$.

X_{ss} equals the person's sum of age-corrected scaled scores on the subtests that make up each category. For Verbal Comprehension, these subtests are Information, Vocabulary, Comprehension, and Similarities. For example, Ben G. earned the following age-corrected scaled scores on these four tasks: 11, 16, 11, and 15, respectively. The sum of these scores equals 53; hence, substitute 53 for X_{ss} in the formula. $1.4\ (53) + 44 = 74.2 + 44 = 118.2$. This value rounds off to 118, which becomes Ben's Verbal Comprehension standard score (also called a factor score).

Examiners who do not wish to perform these computations should consult Ishikuma et al. (1989), who present conversion tables for all factors, Bannatyne categories, and Horn groupings for the total sample of 16- to 74-year-olds in the WAIS-R age range.

Reliability of Factors, Bannatyne Categories, and Horn Groupings

Table 13.7 presents reliability coefficients and standard errors of measurement for the three factors, four Bannatyne categories, and three Horn groupings. These data are presented for separate groups of adolescents (ages 16–19) and adults (ages 20–74); Ishikuma et al. (1989) present coefficients and SE_M's for each of the nine age groups. I have combined data for adolescents since the values for ages 16–17 were not markedly different from those for ages 18–19. Similarly, the fluctuations for the seven adult age groups between ages 20–24 and 70–74 were minor, so data are shown for adults as a whole.

For all separate categories in the three interpretive systems, reliabilities are excellent for adults, never falling below .90 and sometimes exceeding .95. The values are generally lower for adolescents, although still quite good. Several coefficients are less than .90, most notably the

TABLE 13.6 Formulas for converting WAIS-R sums of age-corrected scaled scores of subtests composing various groupings to standard scores having a mean of 100 and *SD* of 15

Grouping	Formula	Component Subtests
Factors		I + V + C + S
Verbal Comprehension	$1.4\ X_{ss} + 44$	
Perceptual Organization	$2.0\ X_{ss} + 40$	PC + BD + OA
Freedom from Distractibility	$2.8\ X_{ss} + 44$	DSp + A
Bannatyne Categories		
Verbal Conceptualization	$1.9\ X_{ss} + 43$	V + C + S
Spatial	$2.0\ X_{ss} + 40$	PC + BD + OA
Sequential	$2.1\ X_{ss} + 37$	DSp + A + DSy
Acquired Knowledge	$1.9\ X_{ss} + 43$	I + V + A
Horn Groupings		
Fluid Intelligence	$1.1\ X_{ss} + 34$	DSp + S + PC + PA + BD + OA
Crystallized Intelligence	$1.4\ X_{ss} + 44$	I + V + C + S
Retention	$2.0\ X_{ss} + 40$	I + DSp + A

NOTE: Each formula applies to the entire 16- to 74-year age range, and each one must be used with *age-corrected* scaled scores. X_{ss} equals the *sum of the age-corrected scaled scores for the subtests in each grouping*. Data are from Ishikuma, Applegate, and Kaufman (1989).

.82 for the Freedom from Distractibility factor score.

Determining Strengths and Weaknesses Within Each System

Table 13.7 allows examiners to compute significant strengths and weaknesses among the three factor scores, four Bannatyne categories, or three Horn groupings. In addition to reliability information, this table presents the size of the difference required for statistical significance when comparing a person's standard score on each factor to his or her own mean score on the three factors (Verbal Comprehension, Perceptual Organization, Freedom from Distractibility). Table 13.7 provides analogous data for the Bannatyne categories and the Horn groupings. Hence, the interpretive system presented here is exactly like the one described previously for computing strengths and weaknesses on the 11 subtests: The person's average performance defines the baseline against which each separate cluster is compared. Standard scores significantly above the person's mean are relative strengths; scores below the mean are relative weaknesses. Examiner's Forms 13.2, 13.3, and 13.4 (pp. 462–467) are intended to facilitate these computations.

The method of determining strengths and weaknesses is illustrated below using the profile of Ben G. (see Table 13.4). Cursory examination of his scaled scores suggested strength in Verbal Conceptualization and weakness in

TABLE 13.7   Factor scores, Bannatyne clusters, and Horn groupings: Reliability coefficients and determining strengths and weaknesses

Cluster	Reliability Coefficients and Standard Errors[a]				Size of Difference Required for Significance When Comparing Each Score to the Person's Own Mean Score on Relevant Clusters[b]			
	Teens (16–19)		Adults (20–74)		Teens (16–19)		Adults (20–74)	
	r_{xx}	SE_M	r_{xx}	SE_M	p<.05	p<.01	p<.05	p<.01
Factor Analysis								
Verbal Comprehension (I + V + C + S)	.96	3.1	.96	2.9	± 8	±10	± 7	± 9
Perceptual Organization (PC + BD +OA)	.87	5.5	.91	4.6	±11	±13	± 9	±11
Freedom from Distractibility (DSp + A)	.82	6.3	.90	4.6	±11	±14	± 9	±11
Bannatyne								
Verbal Conceptualization (V + C + S)	.94	3.7	.95	3.3	± 9	±11	± 8	± 9
Spatial (PC + BD + OA)	.87	5.5	.91	4.6	±11	±14	±10	±11
Sequential (DSp + A + DSy)	.87	5.6	.92	4.2	±11	±14	± 9	±11
Acquired Knowledge (I + A + V)	.95	3.4	.96	3.1	± 8	±10	± 7	± 9
Horn								
Fluid Intelligence (DSp + S + PC + PA + BD + OA)	.91	4.6	.94	3.6	± 9	±11	± 7	± 8
Crystallized Intelligence (I + V + C + S)	.96	3.1	.96	2.9	± 7	± 9	± 6	± 8
Retention (I + DSp + A)	.90	4.8	.94	3.8	± 9	±11	± 7	± 9

[a]SE_M's are in standard score units ($SD = 15$).

[b]Each factor or category score, after being converted to a standard score having a mean of 100 and SD of 15 (using the formulas in Table 13.6), is compared to the person's own mean on all categories in that particular system; for example, a person's standard score on Verbal Conceptualization Ability is compared to his or her mean on the four Bannatyne categories; the score on Perceptual Organization is compared to his or her mean score on the three factors; and so forth. All values for significant deviations have been corrected by the Bonferroni technique.

NOTE: Data are from Ishikuma, Applegate, and Kaufman (1989).

Sequencing. A more systematic investigation of these general hypotheses follows.

1. Compute Ben's *age-corrected* scaled scores; this has already been done in Table 13.4.

2. Sum Ben's three age-corrected scaled scores for the subtests constituting the Verbal Conceptualization cluster. Ben earned scores of 16 on Vocabulary, 11 on Comprehension, and 15 on Similarities. His sum equals 42. Repeat this procedure for the other three Bannatyne categories. (Ben's sums are 19 for Spatial, 20 for Sequential, and 37 for Acquired Knowledge.)

3. Enter each of Ben's sums into the relevant formula (from Table 13.6), as the value of X_{ss}.

   Verbal Conceptualization = 1.9 X_{ss} + 43 = 1.9 (42) + 43 = 79.8 + 43 = 122.8, which rounds to 123.

   Spatial = 2.0 X_{ss} + 40 = 2.0 (19) + 40 = 38 + 40 = 78

   Sequential = 2.1 X_{ss} + 37 = 2.1 (20) + 37 = 42 + 37 = 79

   Acquired Knowledge = 1.9 X_{ss} + 43 = 1.9 (37) + 43 = 70.3 + 43 = 113.3, which rounds to 113.

4. Sum Ben's standard scores (mean = 100, *SD* = 15 for the population at large) on the four Bannatyne categories, and divide by 4 to compute his average category score.

Verbal Conceptualization	123
Spatial	78
Sequential	79
Acquired Knowledge	113
Sum =	393
Mean =	98.2,

   which rounds to 98

5. Subtract Ben's mean from each of the four standard scores.

Verbal Conceptualization 123 − 98 = +25

Spatial   78 − 98 = −20

Sequential   79 − 98 = −19

Acquired Knowledge 113 − 98 = +15

6. Compare these deviations to the size of the discrepancies required for statistical significance shown in Table 13.7. At the $p < .05$ level, deviations of 7 to 10 points are needed for significance for adults, depending on the category; at the .01 level, 9 to 11 points are necessary. All of the deviations are significant at the .01 level, although the .05 level provides ample significance for most interpretive purposes. Thus, Ben (who had suffered right hemisphere damage due to a stroke) displays *relative strengths* in both Verbal Conceptualization Ability and Acquired Knowledge, and *relative weaknesses* in Spatial Ability and Sequential Ability. As indicated in the thorough interpretation given to Ben's subtest profile in chapter 14, his low score on the Sequential triad may not reflect a weakness in sequential ability; it probably indicates a deficiency in processing symbolic stimuli. Analogous steps to the six shown here are used to determine a person's relative strengths and weaknesses among the three factor scores or the three Horn groupings.

Selecting a System

Ordinarily, an examiner will select only *one* of the three interpretive approaches for a thorough empirical analysis. The systems overlap so much with each other that it is not worthwhile to perform all of the computations for all three systems. Further, the mound of data that will accumulate from such an effort may easily overwhelm examiners, causing confusion and clerical errors.

If examiners have a particular orientation toward one system or another, they may routinely employ it with each person they test. Clinicians who feel comfortable with the three factor scores may compute the scores as a matter of course for everyone. Similarly, examiners who find the fluid–crystallized model to be especially valuable from either a theoretical or practical standpoint, or who consider Bannatyne's four categories to offer a useful regrouping of Wechsler's tasks, may give preference to one of these approaches.

The nature of the referral problem may also dictate the system of choice. A person believed or known to be learning-disabled may be best served by the Bannatyne system, inasmuch as his four categories have produced meaningful results in countless studies of learning disabled children, adolescents, and adults (see pp. 448–455). Someone who may have dementia or other age-related diseases involving deterioration of cognitive abilities may display quite different functioning whether assessed by fluid or crystallized tasks in view of their different characteristic aging patterns (see chapter 7); for these individuals, Horn's model may be ideal. Finally, the three factor scores may offer the best analysis of a WAIS-R profile for a person who has suffered recent brain damage. The Perceptual Organization factor score measures the type of process associated with right hemisphere functioning, while both the Verbal Comprehension and Freedom from Distractibility factor scores assess abilities tapped by the left cerebral hemisphere (see pp. 347–351).

The individual's particular pattern of scaled scores is another determinant of the best interpretive methodology. The factor-analytic approach adds *one* major component to the V–P dichotomy already incorporated in Wechsler's IQ scales: the Freedom from Distractibility factor (the Arithmetic-Digit Span dyad), variously defined as sequential processing, auditory memory, number ability, attention-concentration, and so forth. *In order to consider application of the three factor scores, it is essential for the distractibility dyad to form a meaningful unit.* In the example of Gwen W. (Table 13.5), for example,

a strength was observed in Digit Span and a weakness was found in Arithmetic. Quite obviously, the dyad is not measuring a unitary ability for Gwen, so any computed standard score will be the meaningless midpoint of two very different skills. Although Bannatyne's Sequential category and Horn's Retention grouping will likewise be meaningless for Gwen (each one includes both Arithmetic and Digit Span), that fact does not impair the value of these systems. In Horn's approach, the primary distinction is between fluid and crystallized intelligence; in Bannatyne's system, the subdivision of the Verbal Scale into Verbal Conceptualization and Acquired Knowledge components frequently yields insight into the person's abilities that is *not* provided by the global Verbal IQ, by the Verbal Comprehension/crystallized intelligence cluster, or by the split of the Verbal Scale into components corresponding to Factor I (Verbal Comprehension) and Factor III (Freedom from Distractibility).

More specific guidelines for computing and interpreting the Freedom from Distractibility factor appear in the next chapter, as do informal recommendations for choosing among the factor-analytic, Bannatyne, Horn, and other approaches.

Interpreting Subtest Scatter on the WAIS-R

Interpretation of subtest scatter, like interpretation of Verbal–Performance IQ discrepancies, must go beyond the presence or absence of statistically significant differences. The existence of a significant V–P difference is important, but it does not assume potential diagnostic significance unless that discrepancy is also shown to be *abnormal,* that is, to occur relatively infrequently among the normal population of adolescents and adults. Analogously, identifying significant strengths and weaknesses within an individual's subtest profile does not achieve possible diagnostic relevance unless the fluctuations in the scaled scores are so large that they occur rarely within the total population. Normal scatter was found to be surprisingly large for the WISC-R (Kaufman, 1976a) and WPPSI (Reynolds & Gutkin, 1981); the average scaled score range (highest minus lowest scaled score) was found to equal 7 points—more than 2 standard deviations—for both instruments. In this section, I examine normal and abnormal subtest scatter on the WAIS-R.

Scaled-Score Ranges on the WAIS-R

McLean, Kaufman, and Reynolds (in press) essentially replicated for the WAIS-R the subtest scatter studies that had previously been conducted for the Wechsler children's batteries; scatter data were never made available for the WAIS. Data for these analyses were available only for the regular scaled scores, the ones derived from the 20- to 34-year-old reference group that are used to compute IQs. Ideally, the scatter indexes should have been based on the age-corrected scaled scores, the units that I have focused on in this chapter, but that was not possible. *Consequently, when evaluating subtest scatter in an individual's profile, examiners must remember to base all computations on the regular scaled scores, not the age-corrected values.*

McLean et al. (in press) computed scaled-score ranges on the Verbal (six subtests), Performance (five subtests), and Full Scales (11 subtests) for each of the 1,880 adolescents and adults in the WAIS-R standardization sample and then conducted analyses of variance to determine if these ranges were significantly related to the variables of age, gender, race, urban–rural residence, and educational attainment. For the total group, the average Full Scale range was 6.7 points ($SD = 2.1$), not substantially different from the values found for the WISC-R (7.0; Kaufman, 1976a) and WPPSI (6.9; Reynolds & Gutkin, 1981). For the WAIS-R Verbal and Performance Scales, identical mean ranges of 4.7 were obtained.

The WAIS-R sample was divided into four large age groups (16–19, 20–34, 35–54, 55–74)

to determine if the size of the ranges was significantly related to chronological age. Fortunately, age proved to be a nonsignificant variable (mean Full Scale ranges were 6.7 ± 0.2 for the four age groups). Had the mean scaled score ranges fluctuated significantly from age to age, lack of scatter data on the age-corrected scaled scores would have created serious problems in interpretation. However, the lack of age-related changes in subtest scatter permitted McLean et al. to combine data across the entire 16- to 74-year age span and affords examiners the luxury of applying these data with confidence to any individual they test, regardless of the person's age.

The variables of gender and urban–rural residence, like chronological age, were generally not significantly related to the size of the scaled-score range. However, significant differences emerged fairly consistently for race (blacks versus whites; subjects from "other" nonwhite races were excluded from the analyses), and they emerged strikingly for education level. Full Scale range, for example, averaged 6.8 for whites and 6.0 for blacks; for education level, the range was considerably greater for individuals with much education than for those with little formal education, especially on the Verbal and Full Scales. This relationship is shown in Table 13.8 (from McLean et al., in press, Table 1).

Inferring Significant Scatter in a WAIS-R Profile

Because of the substantial relationship between subtest scatter and educational level, it is apparent that a single base-rate table for significant scatter will not suffice. McLean et al. (in press) opted for a table that presented scatter "norms" for individuals at different levels of Full Scale IQ. We chose IQ level rather than the highly correlated variable of education because it is not always possible to get honest answers from clients regarding their educational attainment. We also found that the changes in mean scaled-score ranges from the higher IQ levels (120

TABLE 13.8 Years of education in relation to scaled-score range on the WAIS-R IQ scales

Years of Education	SCALED-SCORE RANGE		
	Verbal	Performance	Full Scale
16+	5.5	4.9	7.6
13–15	5.2	5.0	7.2
12	4.7	4.7	6.6
9–11	4.4	4.9	6.4
8	4.3	4.4	6.3
0–7	4.0	4.0	5.9

NOTE: Data are from McLean et al. (in press).

and above) to the lower levels (80 and below) were even more dramatic for IQ than for education. Further, unlike the differences in the way the Verbal and Performance scaled score ranges behaved from education level to education level (evident in the data shown in Table 13.8), the two WAIS-R IQ scales showed almost identical decreases in magnitude with decreasing Full Scale IQ (see the mean values shown in Table 13.9).

A final justification for using IQ level as a means of developing separate base-rate tables for scatter comes from a very similar study of WAIS-R scatter conducted independently of the McLean et al. investigation (Matarazzo, Daniel, Prifitera, & Herman, 1988); both sets of authors were unaware of the other's investigation. Matarazzo et al. (1988) used correlational techniques to relate scaled-score range to background variables and found that the significant correlations between scatter and diverse variables reduced to about *zero* (even for educational attainment) after partialing out Full Scale IQ from the coefficient.

Table 13.9 presents the base-rate data for subtest scatter when scatter is defined as the size of a person's scaled-score range on the Verbal, Performance, and Full Scales (McLean

et al., in press). As indicated above, this table provides separate "scatter norms" for individuals within the 16- to 74-year range who obtain WAIS-R Full Scale IQs of 120 and above, 110–119, 90–109, 80–89, and below 80. In this respect, the subtest scatter table is organized identically to the V–P IQ discrepancy "norms" table in chapter 9 (Table 9.4).

To use the base-line subtest scatter table, first compute the person's ranges of scaled scores (highest score minus lowest score) using only the regular scaled scores based on the 20- to 34-year-old reference group. Then enter Table 13.9 with these values. Suppose a man with a WAIS-R Full Scale IQ of 61 had a Verbal scaled-score range of 4 points, a Performance range of 8 points, and a Full Scale range of 9 points. Enter the columns in Table 13.9 corresponding to Full Scale IQs "Below 80" to determine if any of these ranges are unusual or abnormal. First enter with the Verbal range of 4 points. Note that a Verbal range for low IQ people must be a least 5 points to qualify as abnormal using the most liberal criterion of < 15%. The Verbal range of 4 points is therefore too small to be considered abnormal by any reasonable standard. However, the man's Performance range of 8 points is between the values of 7 and 9 that correspond to frequencies of occurrence of < 5% and < 1%, respectively. His range, therefore, occurs less that 5% of the time among normal people. So does his Full Scale range of 9 points, which equals the tabled value for < 5%.

In a case report, the examiner might report that this low-functioning man displayed a normal amount of subtest scatter on the Verbal Scale, but that his degree of scatter within the Performance Scale, and across his total WAIS-R profile, was unusual or abnormal in that less than 5% of people in the normal population display a comparable amount of subtest variability. Of course, the precise cut-off used to determine marked or abnormal scatter in a profile depends on the examiner's personal preference. Examiners should be aware of one in-

TABLE 13.9 Subtest scatter "norms" table: Size of Verbal, Performance, and Full Scale scaled-score range required for abnormality at various levels of occurrence in the normal population, by IQ category

Frequency of Occurrence	FULL SCALE IQ CATEGORY					Total Sample
	Below 80	80–89	90–109	110–119	120 and Above	
Verbal Scale						
<15%	5	6	7	8	8	7
<10%	6	7	8	9	9	8
<05%	7	8	9	10	10	9
<01%	8	10	11	11	11	11
Mean	3.5	4.2	4.8	5.1	5.4	4.7
SD	1.3	1.8	1.8	2.0	1.9	1.9
Performance Scale						
<15%	5	6	7	8	8	7
<10%	6	7	8	9	9	8
<05%	7	8	9	10	10	9
<01%	9	10	12	12	12	12
Mean	3.5	4.2	4.9	5.0	5.1	4.7
SD	1.6	1.7	2.2	2.1	1.9	2.1
Full Scale						
<15%	7	8	9	10	10	9
<10%	8	9	10	11	11	10
<05%	9	10	11	12	12	11
<01%	10	12	13	14	14	13
Mean	5.0	6.0	6.8	7.2	7.6	6.7
SD	1.6	1.8	2.0	2.1	2.1	2.1

NOTE: Data are from McLean, Kaufman, and Reynolds (in press). All distributions are based on data for the total norms sample of 1,880, as are the means and SDs for the total sample. Means and SDs for the separate IQ groups are for a slightly reduced sample of 1,856 (excluding 24 individuals from other "nonwhite" groups). The values for the 15% level were obtained from unpublished data; all values in the table are smoothed slightly (McLean et al., in press).

teresting finding from Matarazzo et al.'s (1988) investigation of WAIS-R scatter. *The amount of Verbal scatter in a person's WAIS-R profile is essentially independent of the amount of Performance scatter in that same person's profile.* Matarazzo et al. used three different scatter indexes and found that a person's Verbal index and

Performance index consistently correlated only .08–.09 with each other, regardless of the index used.

Another potentially interesting finding in the Matarazzo investigation concerns the reliability of scatter indexes; however, this result is not really interpretable because of flawed methodology. Matarazzo et al. (1988) computed the split-half reliability of Full Scale scatter indexes by assigning each subtest to a "half-WAIS-R." They obtained low reliability coefficients for the three scatter indices that they studied (the value of .41 for scaled-score range was the highest), but there is no justification for computing split-half reliability, for assuming that a homogeneity model is appropriate for scatter, or for selecting any particular two-way division of the WAIS-R tasks. Test–retest reliability is an ideal way of assessing the reliability of the scatter indices; however, even though Matarazzo and Herman (1984a) conducted thorough analyses of the test–retest data (see chapter 4), they opted not to assess the stability of WAIS-R scatter.

In general, whenever a person evidences a significant V–P IQ discrepancy, examiners should focus on the separate scaled-score ranges for the Verbal and Performance Scales. The Full Scale range will ordinarily not be too meaningful. The existence of marked scatter on the Full Scale for a person with a statistically significant V–P IQ difference is usually just another manifestation of the verbal–nonverbal distinction, offering no new information. Indeed, if a person has a large V–P difference coupled with little scatter *within* each separate scale, the finding of an abnormal range of scores on the Full Scale will mislead the examiner to infer considerable subtest scatter when, in fact, the only real scatter in the WAIS-R profile is between the two global scales.

Illustrations of the Range Method of Determining Significant Scatter

The examples of Ben G. and Gwen W. are used here to further illustrate the application of Table 13.9. Using the regular scaled scores, rather than the age-corrected values that were used in the earlier illustrations, Ben is found to have the following scaled score ranges: Verbal (16 minus 7 = 9) and Performance (6 minus 1 = 5). Since his Full Scale IQ is 95, the column headed "90–109" in Table 13.9 is entered. The Verbal range of 9 occurs less than 5% of the time among normal people, which, based on my personal sense of what is unusual, constitutes marked Verbal scatter. In contrast, his Performance range of 5 points is not at all unusual, occurring more than 15% of the time. I didn't compute his Full Scale range, but if I did it would have been huge (his scaled scores ranged from 1 on Digit Symbol to 16 on Vocabulary, for a range of 15). Ranges this large are quite rare, occurring less than 1% of the time. Yet this enormous range is a mere reflection of his striking V > P profile of 35 points and adds nothing to the interpretation of this right-lesion patient's WAIS-R profile.

Gwen W., with a Full Scale IQ of 124 and a nonsignificant V–P discrepancy of 7 points, displayed a Verbal range of 6 points (16 minus 10), a Performance range of 6 points (14 minus 8), and a Full Scale range of 8 points (16 on Digit Span minus 8 on Picture Arrangement). Entering Table 13.9 using the columns labeled "120 and Above" indicates that all of these ranges reveal normal subtest scatter, falling well short of the values of 8 (V-range, P-range) and 10 (FS-range) required for abnormality at the 15% level of occurrence. Her significant profile fluctuations are important, telling the examiner that she has meaningful differences in several skill areas; these differences are potentially valuable for addressing the referral issue of vocational guidance. Integration of her profile fluctuations suggests relative strengths in fluid intelligence and abstract thought, coupled with relative weaknesses in crystallized intelligence and social comprehension. Such a profile, if consistent with her pattern of interests on a test like the Strong-Campbell Interest Inventory, might lead her toward professions that capitalize on fluid and abstract skills (e.g., computer programming) and away from socially and academically oriented positions (e.g., teacher).

Note, however, that her profile fluctuations are of no diagnostic significance. They are valuable for making practical recommendations, but since her subtest scatter is normal, no abnormality in her cognitive functioning should be inferred—even if she had been referred for a possible abnormality such as emotional disturbance. Note, too, that the magnitude of Gwen's scaled-score ranges (6–8 points) is normal for very intelligent individuals. These identical ranges, if they occur in a person of low average, borderline, or deficient functioning, are large enough to be rare. Each of Gwen's ranges occurs less than 15% of the time for individuals with FS-IQs of 80–89, and less than 10% of the time for those scoring below 80 on the WAIS-R Full Scale.

Number of Significantly Deviating Subtest Scores

In addition to scaled-score range, another common index of subtest scatter is the number of subtests that deviate significantly from the person's own mean. McLean et al. (in press) present base-line data for this index as well, although I've always preferred the simplicity of the scaled-score range. For the WAIS-R, the use of the number of significant deviant scores greatly increases the examiner's clerical work because the whole process of determining significant strengths and weaknesses, described previously, is based on age-corrected scaled scores. Since all scatter data are derived from the regular "reference group" scaled scores, examiners who prefer the number-of-deviant-scores method must recompute the significantly deviating subtests by using the regular scaled scores.

Matarazzo et al. (1988) also preferred the scaled-score range method because of its ease of computation, but they provide excellent *empirical* support for its use. Some investigators (e.g., Plake, Reynolds, & Gutkin, 1981) have criticized the range technique for focusing only on extreme scores, and have opted for methods that account for *every* profile fluctuation (e.g., the standard deviation or variance of the subtest deviations). Although this criticism is logical, Matarazzo et al. (1988) have shown that the

scaled-score range method provides the same information as the more thorough "standard deviation" (*SD*) method: The Verbal scaled-score range correlated .97 with the Verbal *SD* index; the two Performance scatter indices correlated .98; and the Full Scale indices correlated .93. Interestingly, the number of significant deviations correlated less impressively than did the scaled-score range with the *SD* index (.80–.84) (Matarazzo et al., 1988).

Table 13.10, derived from McLean et al's. (in press) data, shows the number of subtests that deviated significantly from the person's mean V, P, and FS scaled-score at four levels of "frequency of occurrence." To determine the number of significantly deviating subtests, McLean et al. (in press) used a constant value of ± 3 points from the relevant mean. Hence, examiners who wish to apply this index of scatter should likewise use ± 3 points as the criterion of significance.

Illustrations of the Number of Significant Deviations Method

Ben G.'s mean of his "reference group" scaled scores equals 11.2, or 11, on the Verbal Scale and 4.2, or 4, on the Performance Scale. Applying the ± 3 rule reveals *three* significantly deviating subtests on the Verbal Scale (Digit Span is weak; Vocabulary and Similarities are strong), and *one* on the Performance Scale (Digit Symbol is weak). The results of this analysis are the same as those of the previous analysis with age-corrected scaled scores for the Verbal Scale but *not* the Performance Scale. The previous Performance analysis revealed two significant deviates: Picture Arrangement (strength) and Digit Symbol (weakness).

Entering Table 13.10 in the column headed "90–109" (Ben's FS-IQ equals 95) indicates that Ben's having three significantly deviating Verbal subtests is unusual, occurring less than 10% of the time in the normal population. However, it is common to have one Performance deviate; three are needed to be unusual at the < 15%

TABLE 13.10   Subtest scatter "norms" table: Number of significantly deviating WAIS-R subtest scores (± 3 points) from a person's own mean required for abnormality at various levels of occurrence in the normal population, by IQ category

Frequency of Occurrence	FULL SCALE IQ CATEGORY					Total Sample
	Below 80	80–89	90–109	110–119	120 and Above	
Verbal Scale						
<15%	2	2	2	3	3	3
<10%	2	2	3	3	3	3
<05%	3	3	4	4	4	4
<01%	5	5	5	5	5	5
Performance Scale						
<15%	3	3	3	3	3	3
<10%	3	3	4	4	4	4
<05%	4	4	4	4	4	4
<01%	5	5	5	5	5	5
Full Scale						
<15%	3	3	3	4	4	3
<10%	4	4	4	5	6	4
<05%	5	5	5	6	7	5
<01%	7	7	7	8	8	7

NOTE: Data are from McLean, Kaufman, and Reynolds (in press). All distributions are based on data for the total norms sample of 1,880. The values for the 15% level were obtained from unpublished data; all values in the table are smoothed slightly (McLean et al., in press).

level. These results indicate Verbal scatter, but not Performance scatter, within Ben's WAIS-R profile, yielding complete agreement with the scatter analysis using scaled-score ranges. However, agreement will not always be unanimous because the "number of significant deviations" index only correlates about .80 (.77–.81) with the corresponding scaled-score range index (Matarazzo et al., 1988).

As with the range method, it is not advisable to compute the number of significantly deviating subtests from the Full Scale mean for a person who has a significant V–P IQ discrepancy. For Ben, whose overall mean on the 11 regular scaled scores equals 8.0, this procedure produces

three significant strengths (all Verbal) and three significant weaknesses (all Performance). The six significant deviates are unusual, occurring less than 5% of the time in the normal population, but this finding is just a reflection of Ben's substantial V > P profile.

Gwen W.'s mean scaled score rounds to 12 for all three scales, producing *one* significant Verbal deviation (a strength in Digit Span), *one* significant Performance deviation (a weakness in Picture Arrangement), and *two* significant deviations from the Full Scale mean (the same two tasks). (Note that the use of the regular scaled scores fails to yield the additional weakness in Arithmetic and strength in Block Design that emerged from the analysis based on age-corrected scaled scores.) The values of 1 to 2 significant subtests fall well short of abnormality when entering Table 13.10, reinforcing the finding of the scaled-score range method of determining subtest scatter, namely that Gwen has a flat WAIS-R profile.

Selz and Reitan's Scatter Index

Selz and Reitan (1979) proposed a scatter index for use with Wechsler's batteries that is closely related to the scaled-score range method. These neuropsychologists suggested computing the Full Scale range by subtracting the lowest from the highest scaled score and then dividing the range by the person's mean scaled score on all subtests. The resulting index is considered normal to superior if it is less than 1.00; values between 1.00 to 1.40 are slightly below normal; values of 1.41 to 1.75 are "probably below normal limits, yet not considered to be definitive of brain damage" (p. 261); and values of 1.76 and above indicate "definite impairment" (p. 261).

Gutkin and Reynolds (1981a) evaluated the Selz-Reitan scatter index for the WISC-R and found only the 1.76 criterion to be useful because it did, indeed, occur rarely within the normal population of children aged 6 to 16. Although the 1.4 cut-off was generally useful, it did not function very well for low IQ children (< 85). Of more immediate interest here is Willson and Reynolds' (1985) similar investigation of the Selz-Reitan index for adolescents and adults based on data from the WAIS-R standardization sample.

The cut-off points for abnormality developed by Selz and Reitan (1979) simply do not apply to the WAIS-R. Willson and Reynolds (1985) computed the Selz-Reitan scatter index for the entire WAIS-R normative sample and reported a mean value of 1.26; this value is well above the mean for the WISC-R (.76 for 12 subtests; Gutkin & Reynolds, 1981a), as well as the 1.00 cut-off suggested by Selz and Reitan to denote "normality." The value of 1.40, the second cut-off used to distinguish between "slightly below normal" and "probably below normal," corresponded to the 70th percentile, indicating that this value, too, is completely normal. The final cut-off point of 1.76 (rounded to 1.80) equaled the 92nd percentile. Values as high as 1.80, therefore, are relatively rare in that they are obtained by about 8% of normal adolescents and adults; they are *not* so rare, however, that they should be used in any way as an indicator of "definite impairment."

Willson and Reynolds (1985) also observed a significant and substantial relationship between the Selz-Reitan scatter index and educational attainment, occupational group, and Full Scale IQ. For example, 105 individuals engaged in semiskilled occupations earned FS-IQs below 85; among this group, 28% earned indices exceeding 1.80. Consequently, indices above the "definite" impairment level are common for adolescents and adults of low occupational status, limited education, and/or low IQ.

Examiners who wish to use the Selz-Reitan scatter index for the WAIS-R may find useful the following table, derived and estimated from Willson and Reynolds (1985, Table 1):

FREQUENCY OF OCCURRENCE	VALUE OF INDEX
<15%	1.7
<10%	1.8
<5%	2.0
<1%	2.5

Although Willson and Reynolds did not provide enough data to develop separate abnormality tables by IQ or socioeconomic level, the above table for the total sample should be useful for examiners who prefer to follow Selz and Reitan's suggestion to divide the scaled-score range by the person's mean scaled score as the best estimate of Wechsler scatter.

Using the cases of Ben G. and Gwen W. as illustrations, we find that Ben's Selz-Reitan scatter index equals 1.88 (range = 15, mean scaled score = 8.00) and Gwen's index equals 0.66 (range = 8, mean = 12.18). Ben's index occurs infrequently (less than 10% of the time among normals), and Gwen's is well within the normal range. Although Ben is known to have brain damage, the abnormal index should in my opinion be used as corroborative evidence, not as a pathognomonic indicator of impairment. Further, Willson and Reynolds' (1985) important research with the Selz-Reitan index should be a reminder to examiners *not* to take anyone's scatter index on faith or trust, no matter how impressive their clinical or neuropsychological reputation; such indexes require data from large representative samples and are evidently not generalizable from one Wechsler scale to another.

Overview

Ultimately, examiners need to exercise clinical judgment when they choose one type of scatter index or the other, and whether they define abnormal scatter as occurring less than 15% of the time—or less than 1% of the time—in the normal population. The use of scatter tables is more important than precisely *how* they are used. Clinicians should always use some type of empirical, base-rate, normative approach to the assessment of scatter in a WAIS-R profile; this mandate refers to scatter *between* the Verbal and Performance Scales as well as to scatter *within* each scale. What has been interpreted as marked scatter in the profiles of exceptional individuals in the past has been shown by research in the 1970s and 1980s to be not so unusual after all. Numerous studies of the WISC-R have shown that learning-disabled and emotionally disturbed populations, more often than not and despite stereotypes to the contrary, reveal V–P discrepancies and subtest profiles that are normal by any reasonable definition of normality (Kaufman, Harrison & Ittenbach, 1989).

Even when WISC-R scatter indexes between normal and abnormal samples differ statistically, they don't usually differ meaningfully. Exceptions occur for some groups; for example, notably greater than normal V–P differences and subtest scatter have been observed for learning-disabled children with superior intelligence (Schiff, Kaufman, & Kaufman, 1981) and for American Indians classified as nonhandicapped, learning-disabled, or educationally disadvantaged (Teeter & Moore, 1982). But for most abnormal groups of children and adolescents, the distributions of scatter indexes overlap greatly with the distributions for normal youngsters. Similar results are likely to emerge in future WAIS-R studies.

Such a finding did, indeed, occur in one study conducted by Salvia et al. (1988) with a group of 74 learning-disabled college students. Table 13.11 shows their mean scaled-score ranges on the WAIS-R (data for their control group of 74 nondisabled college students, and for WAIS-R normative data based on individuals with 13–15 years of education, are shown for comparison purposes).

The values for the LD college students were significantly higher than the values for the nonhandicapped college students (Salvia et al., 1988), but the means are not strikingly different, and, on a case-by-case basis, subsequent examination of the ranges for the two samples "revealed considerable overlap" (p. 634). Quite obviously, the same results would hold when comparing the means for the LD college students to the normative means for people with 13–15 years of education; these data were unavailable to Salvia et al. (1988). Salvia et al. also found a larger V–P IQ discrepancy (the absolute magnitude, regardless of direction) for their LD college students compared to their control sample, but the difference (11.9 versus 9.8) did not reach statistical significance.

McLean et al. (in press) warn:

[I]t is essential that clinicians make use of the base-rate tables . . . before inferring that someone has

TABLE 13.11 Mean scaled-score ranges on the WAIS-R for learning-disabled college students and for normal control groups

| | Scaled Score Range | | |
Sample	*Verbal*	*Performance*	*Full Scale*
LD college students	6.0	5.9	8.0
Normal college students	5.2	5.5	7.2
Standardization sample (13–15 years of education)	5.2	5.0	7.2

"marked" scatter in his or her WAIS-R subtest profile. . . . Depressed individuals "may have difficulty with timed subtests due to psychomotor retardation" (Pernicano, 1986, p. 542); schizophrenics may experience relative difficulty with spatial-performance tasks on the Wechsler scales; . . . and individuals with Alzheimer-type dementia may perform better on Information/Vocabulary than on Similarities/Digit Span or Digit Symbol/Block Design (Fuld, 1984). However, no inferences about the meaningfulness of hypothesized profile scatter should be made without first demonstrating empirically that the amount of variability in the profiles of abnormal individuals is unusual or atypical. . . . The base-rate tables . . . should be used by clinicians for individuals, but also by researchers for data obtained by groups with identified pathologies.

Matarazzo et al. (1988) further warned that "[e]ven when one has identified a range between highest and lowest subtest scores that is unusually large, it is not necessarily true that the high and low scores indicate premorbid IQ on the one hand and impairment on the other" (p. 948). In a more extensive treatment of this important neuropsychological issue, Matarazzo and Prifitera (in press) present some compelling empirical arguments against the fairly common practice (e.g., Gregory, 1987) of inferring a brain-damaged patient's premorbid IQ from his or her highest scaled scores and inferring cognitive loss from the lowest scores. As Matarazzo and Prifitera remind neuropsychologists who engage in this unsupported practice, peaks and

valleys occur commonly in the scaled score profiles of normal individuals; hence, the low scores may easily have characterized any given patient's profile even before the brain injury.

Matarazzo et al. (1988) have offered clinicians additional sound advice: "Scatter is never interpreted in isolation. Rather, it is best interpreted in light of other objective information . . . such as previous intelligence test scores from school or occupational records, job history, socioeconomic indices, and hospital and other diagnostic information. . . . [W]ide clinical experience and good judgment continue to play an irreplaceable role" (pp. 948–949).

CHARACTERISTIC WAIS-R PROFILES

Clinicians have long searched for characteristic subtest profiles associated with brain dysfunction and psychopathology with the same zeal that medical researchers apply to the search for biochemical patterns of cancer or AIDS patients, or that psychiatrists apply to the behavioral patterns of mass murderers. Mostly, these quests have not been fruitful—not unlike the quests of other scientists. Unforeseen and often unknown complexities have frustrated Wechsler's search for a subtest profile associated with organic brain syndrome or the search of others for patterns that would be pathognomonic of schizophrenia, psychotic depression, and countless other disorders.

Two profiles, however, have gained some research support as being reasonably characteristic of their target populations, and these are treated in this section: the ACID profile for learning-disabled and dyslexic adolescents and adults, and the Fuld profile for patients with Alzheimer's-type dementia.

The ACID Profile in Learning-Disabled Individuals

A large body of research, mainly with the WISC or WISC-R, has explored subtest profiles of reading- and learning-disabled individuals and has identified consistency from study to study: Mean scores are highest for Bannatyne's Spatial category and lowest for his Sequential and Acquired Knowledge groupings (Kaufman, 1979b; Rugel, 1974; Kaufman, Harrison, & Ittenbach, in press). Further, a pattern of low scaled scores on four of the subtests that define the Sequential and Acquired Knowledge categories has particularly shown resilience from one LD sample to another. This quartet makes up the ACID grouping because of the first initials of the four tasks—*A*rithmetic, *C*oding, *I*nformation, *D*igit Span. Even though Coding is called Digit Symbol on the WAIS-R, I will continue to refer to the profile as the ACID pattern inasmuch as that nickname has become entrenched in the literature and has been used by WAIS and WAIS-R researchers (Salvia et al., 1988; Vogel, 1986).

ACID and Bannatyne Patterns on the WAIS-R for LD Individuals

Table 13.12 summarizes the results of six samples of adolescents and young adults tested on the WAIS-R; three samples are learning-disabled, and three are included for comparison purposes. The table presents mean standard scores on the Bannatyne categories, the ACID profile, and the WAIS-R IQ scales. I computed

the standard scores for the Bannatyne categories, entering the formulas presented in Table 13.6 with the relevant sum of scaled scores derived from group means. For the ACID profile, I derived a new conversion formula using Tellegen and Briggs's (1967) simple method (ACID standard score = $1.6 X_{ss} + 36$) and substituted group means into the formula. Although these formulas are intended for use only with age-corrected scaled scores, I entered them with the regular scaled scores (the only ones provided) for the four samples having mean chronological ages within the 20- to 34-year age range encompassed by the WAIS-R reference group.

It would have been inappropriate to enter the formulas with the regular scaled scores for the LD sample of 16-year-olds (Sandoval, Sassenrath, & Penaloza, 1988) or for Salvia et al.'s (1988) 18.4-year-old control group of nonhandicapped college students. Scaled scores for these groups are simply not comparable to the regular scaled scores because of developmental factors as well as the questionable nature of the WAIS-R norms for adolescents. Consequently, I opted to estimate the age-corrected scaled scores for these two samples by using the mean values presented in the articles (mean subtest scores in the Sandoval article; mean Bannatyne and ACID clusters in the Salvia paper), along with scaled-score Tables 19 and 21 in the WAIS-R Manual (Wechsler, 1981). Although the precise standard scores for the ACID profile and Bannatyne clusters shown in Table 13.12 for the two adolescents samples are estimated values, I believe that they are fairly accurate and that the overall profiles depict each group's relative strengths and weaknesses.

As indicated in the table, Salvia et al.'s (1988) group of 74 LD college students earned an ACID standard score of 101.6, about ½ standard deviation below their mean FS-IQ of 108.9. Also, the 11 dyslexic adults evaluated by Frauenheim and Heckerl (1983) scored 76.3 on the ACID profile compared to their FS-IQ of 92 (a difference of more than 1 standard deviation). Despite the small sample of dyslexics, this result is given credence by previous test data: When

TABLE 13.12 Mean Bannatyne, "ACID," and IQ scores of groups of learning-disabled adolescents and adults on the WAIS-R

| | LEARNING-DISABLED SAMPLES | | | COMPARISON SAMPLES | | |
| | | | | Prisoners[d] | | Normal |
Category	College Students[a] (N=74)	Dyslexic Adults[b] (N=11)	16 Year Olds[c] (N=30)	Poor Readers (N=319)	Adequate Readers (N=246)	College Students[a] (N=74)
Bannatyne						
Verbal Conceptualization	111.9	94.3	96.3	86.5	87.2	126.0
Spatial	105.3	111.4	108.3	91.9	92.1	117.0
Sequential	100.0	75.4	86.5	88.4	88.2	116.5
Acquired Knowledge	105.2	83.8	93.8	85.9	86.5	124.5
"ACID"	101.6	76.3	87.7	86.9	86.9	119.5
WAIS-R IQ						
Verbal	110.1	85	90.6	86.7	86.1	122.9
Performance	103.5	104	101.8	90.0	89.8	119.4
Full Scale	108.9	92	95.4	87.4	86.5	124.5

[a]Data from Salvia et al. (1988). Mean age = 22.2 years for LD college students and 18.4 years for the normal college students.

[b]Data from Frauenheim and Heckerl (1983). Mean age = 27 years.

[c]Data from Sandoval et al. (1988). Mean age = 16½ years.

[d]Data from Kender et al. (1985). Mean ages equal 31.5 years (poor readers) and 29.0 (adequate readers).

NOTE: Mean standard scores on Bannatyne categories were computed by entering the group mean sum of scaled scores on pertinent subtests into the appropriate formula from Table 13.6. Mean ACID standard scores were computed in the same way using the formula: $ACID = 1.6 X_{ss} + 36$. Mean age-corrected scaled scores were estimated from the regular scaled scores for Sandoval et al.'s (1988) 16-year-olds, and from the mean regular scaled scores on the Bannatyne and ACID groupings for Salvia et al.'s (1988) 18-year-old control group. For all other samples, the regular scaled scores were entered into the relevant formulas because their mean ages were within the 20- to 34-year range of the WAIS-R reference group.

tested on the WISC more than 15 years previously, they obtained virtually identical IQs and mean scaled scores on the Bannatyne groupings and ACID subtests.

Sandoval et al.'s sample of 30 learning-disabled 16-year-olds scored about ½ standard deviation lower on the ACID subtests than on the Full Scale. Like the data for the tiny sample of dyslexic adults, the results for the small group of 16-year-olds are given additional support by the appearance of a highly similar ACID profile on the WISC-R (the group was tested in counterbalanced order on both instruments). Further,

comparable patterns were observed on the WAIS in McCue, Shelly, and Goldstein's (1986) investigation of 100 learning-disabled adults (mean age = 24.4); like the learning-disabled samples shown in Table 13.12, McCue et al.'s group performed relatively poorly on the ACID subtests (an estimated ½ SD below their Full Scale IQ of 88.6).

The dyslexic group (Frauenheim & Heckerl, 1983), the 16-year-old LD sample (Sandoval et al., 1988), and McCue et al.'s (1986) 100 LD adults tested on the old WAIS each obtained highly similar Bannatyne patterns of Spatial >

Verbal Conceptualization > Acquired Knowledge *and* Sequential. Such patterning accords well with much previous research on the WISC-R (Kaufman, Harrison, & Ittenbach, in press). The poor performance by each of these groups on the ACID subtests actually reflects a merger of their consistent weaknesses in Sequential Ability and Acquired Knowledge. The Spatial superiority of Sandoval et al.'s LD adolescents must be interpreted cautiously, however, since 40% of the sample was Hispanic, a group characterized by P > V profiles (see chapter 9).

Despite the persistence of the Bannatyne and ACID patterns from childhood to adulthood for Frauenheim and Heckerl's (1983) *group* of dyslexics and the occurrence of discrepancies of ½ to 1 *SD* between FS-IQ and ACID standard score, there is reason for caution: Spreen and Haaf (1986), in their investigation of LD subtypes of people followed up longitudinally, gave some evidence that in *individual* cases the ACID profile does not persist from childhood to adulthood.

Exceptions Among LD College Students, Especially Females

Salvia et al.'s (1988) LD college students performed relatively low on Bannatyne's Sequential grouping but, unlike samples of LD children and LD adults without college educations, their greatest strength was *not* the Spatial category. This college sample did best on WAIS-R Verbal Conceptualization, probably reflecting the fact that LD students attending college are the elite among LD samples and have achieved far more than others with a similar disability. Blalock's (1987) 91 LD adults (36 either in college or college graduates) and Vogel's 31 female LD college students also scored higher on Bannatyne's WAIS Verbal Conceptualization than Spatial category; a third sample of 57 LD college students scored about equally well on both WAIS groupings (Cordoni, O'Donnell, Ramaniah, Kurtz, & Rosenshein, 1981). In addition, 211

applicants for a special college program for LD students (161 given the WAIS, 50 given the WAIS-R) performed about equally well on the Verbal Conceptualization and Spatial categories, a finding that held for female as well as male applicants (Ackerman, McGrew, & Dykman, 1987). Both Cordoni et al.'s (1981) and Ackerman et al.'s (1987) samples performed extremely poorly on Bannatyne's Sequential and Acquired Knowledge categories and on the ACID profile; Blalock's (1987) group scored especially low on the Sequential category and ACID subtests; and Vogel's (1986) female LD sample had decided weaknesses on Acquired Knowledge and the ACID profile.

With striking consistency in study after study of LD samples of adolescents and adults tested on the WISC, WISC-R, WAIS, or WAIS-R, the group means reflect substantial and occasionally striking decrements on the ACID profile and on Bannatyne's Sequential grouping. Deficits on Acquired Knowledge occur frequently but are less predictable, especially for college students with learning disabilities; again better performance on verbal tasks, whether conceptual or achievement oriented, is not overly surprising for LD individuals who have managed to compensate for their disabilities sufficiently to aspire to higher education.

The one slightly maverick study is Vogel's (1986) sample of female college students with learning disabilities (mean age = 20), tested on the WAIS, who showed a marked weakness in Acquired Knowledge, a moderate weakness on the ACID profile, but only a small decrement on the Sequential category. Analysis of the separate subtests indicated that they obtained their three lowest mean scaled scores on Arithmetic, Information, and Digit Span (8.1–9.6), but earned their top scaled score in the fourth member of the ACID quartet: Digit Symbol (11.5). Females traditionally outperform males by a substantial amount on Coding and Digit Symbol (see pages 354–356), and Vogel's group composed of all female LD students is a rarity; indeed, a huge majority of LD groups are predominantly male.

Could the consistently low scores on Coding/ Digit Symbol be partly a function of the *maleness* of most previous LD samples of children and adults and partly a function of their learning problems?

Fischer, Wenck, Schurr, and Ellen (1985) investigated this question for the WISC-R for 254 boys and 73 girls aged 9–14 years and found results that paralleled Vogel's. The boys earned mean scaled scores below 8.0 on the four ACID subtests while scoring about 9 or 10 on all other tasks except Vocabulary (mean = 8.3). The girls earned their three lowest scaled scores on Information, Arithmetic, and Digit Span (6.5–7.2), but did well on Digit Symbol (9.5). Comparing the Bannatyne profiles of LD and emotionally disturbed individuals, Fischer et al. found gender to be a more influential moderating variable than IQ or type of achievement discrepancy. Additionally, Vogel (1990), in a review of the literature for children, supported a clear gender difference on Coding for LD students; this subtest was typically the second-lowest for males with LD (Digit Span was lowest), but for LD females Coding "never fell into the lower third of the hierarchy" (p. 45).

Gender differences were not so apparent in Ackerman et al.'s (1987) investigation of 211 applicants to a special LD college program, of whom nearly one-quarter were given the WAIS-R and the rest the WAIS. The authors tested about 150 males (38 on the WAIS-R) and 60 females (12 on the WAIS-R). They combined scores across instruments, despite observing the typical mean IQ difference of 5 to 6½ points in favor of the WAIS (see chapter 3). Nonetheless, from their graph of WAIS/ WAIS-R scaled scores for separate groups of male and female LD applicants (Ackerman et al. 1987, Figure 1), it is evident that females did not do particularly well on Digit Symbol. The ACID profile was not quite as pronounced for females as for males, but Digit Symbol was only the *seventh* highest scaled score for females. Further studies, using only the WAIS-R, are

needed to determine if the ACID profile characterizes the profiles of both male and female LD individuals.

Comparison of LDs to Other Samples

Table 13.12 presents data on three samples that might loosely be considered control populations. The most meaningful comparison group is the large sample of incarcerated adults who were grouped on the basis of their reading ability by Kender, Greenwood, and Conard (1985). These samples demonstrated a slight elevation in Spatial Ability but performed about equally well on the other three Bannatyne categories and on the ACID profile. Both samples earned FS-IQs that approximately equaled their ACID standard scores (means of 86–87). These results were in marked contrast to the difference of at least ½ standard deviation in favor of FS-IQ that characterized the profiles of several LD samples on the WAIS-R (see Table 3.12) and the WAIS (Cordoni et al., 1981; McCue et al., 1986).

The lack of deficiencies on Sequential and ACID groupings for the incarcerated adults suggests that these profiles may be more characteristic of LD samples than of behavior disordered populations. In the WISC-R literature, differential diagnosis between these two exceptional groups has typically been unsuccessful (Clarizio & Bernard, 1981; Henry & Wittman, 1981); a review of many WISC-R studies reveals good performance on Spatial subtests and poor performance on Sequential and Acquired Knowledge subtests by *both* LD *and* emotionally disturbed samples (Fischer et al., 1985; Kaufman et al., in press, Tables 7 and 8). Kender et al.'s (1985) results with such large samples suggests that differential diagnosis may be possible with the WAIS-R, especially for LD students *without* college educations. The group of poor ("underachieving") readers provides a particularly good comparison group for the LD samples because this group does *not* qualify as learning- or reading-disabled. Whereas most reading- and learning-disabled samples of children and adults have been shown to perform relatively poorly on Bannatyne's Sequential category, Kender's sample of underachieving readers earned their *highest* two Verbal scaled scores on Digit Span and Arithmetic, and their Digit Symbol scaled score (though lower than other Performance subtests) surpassed their performance on *all* Verbal subtests.

Table 13.12 shows the WAIS-R profile of another comparison group, Salvia et al.'s (1988) nonhandicapped college students. Like most of the various samples of LD college students discussed previously, this nonhandicapped sample scored highest on the Verbal Conceptualization category. However, their FS-IQ exceeded the ACID standard score by 5 points, not very different from the 7-point discrepancy observed for Salvia et al.'s LD college students. The normal college students did perform about equally on the Spatial and Sequential groupings, though, in contrast to the Spatial > Sequential pattern observed consistently for all other samples of LD college students tested on the WAIS or WAIS-R.

Salvia et al. (1988) compared the LD and normal college samples statistically and found that the normals performed significantly higher on three of the four Bannatyne categories (all but Verbal Conceptualization), on the ACID subtests, and (as discussed on pp. 446–447) on several scatter indexes. The scatter comparisons are legitimate, because scatter indexes have been shown to be independent of chronological age (McLean, Kaufman, & Reynolds, in press). Unfortunately, the Bannatyne and ACID comparisons are meaningless because the control group was substantially younger than the LD students (22.2 versus 18.4 years). Contrasting the mean scaled scores (or their sums) is of little value because they are not comparable; the scaled scores for adolescents on the WAIS-R are especially questionable. Salvia et al. should have used age-corrected scaled scores for their Bannatyne and ACID analyses, and they should also have controlled for FS-IQ since the control

group scored substantially higher than the LDs (124.5 versus 108.9).

The ACID Profile Versus Bannatyne System

The ACID pattern represents a deficient area for LD adolescents and adults, but the three LD samples shown in Table 13.12 scored even lower on the WAIS-R Sequential standard score than on the ACID score. On the WAIS, the same finding occurred for Blalock's (1987) LD adults, whereas McCue et al.'s (1986), Cordoni et al.'s (1981), and Ackerman et al.'s (1987) LD samples earned closely similar means on the Sequential and ACID standard scores. Only Vogel's (1986) all-female sample of LD college students scored lower on the ACID than Sequential score. (I computed standard scores for the WAIS studies as well, but preferred to report only WAIS-R data in Table 13.12. Using correlational data in the WAIS Manual for ages 25–34, I discovered that all formulas for the WAIS were identical to the ones for the WAIS-R.) I believe that the best way to look for a "characteristic" WAIS-R profile for LD adolescents and adults is to use the Bannatyne system. The ACID system does not seem to contribute anything over and above the Bannatyne groupings, so I suggest that it be dropped from consideration, except for research purposes. The Bannatyne approach permits systematic analysis of a person's strengths and weaknesses on the relevant categories (see pp. 432–438), and is therefore preferable for the interpretation of *individual* profiles. All of the previous discussions have been on group data, but clinical interpretation requires analysis of individual data, which are more unstable than group means.

Overreliance on the ACID profile also may impel examiners to overlook the value of an Acquired Knowledge subtest, Vocabulary, for LD adolescents and adults. In Ackerman et al.'s (1987) study of applicants to a special LD college program, WAIS subtest scores were entered in a step-wise regression analysis to predict WRAT Reading, Spelling, and Arithmetic for separate groups of LD males and females. Vocabulary and Digit Span were the only two significant predictors of Reading for *both* males and females. The same two subtests were the only significant predictors of Spelling for females. Vocabulary and Digit Symbol (a dyad that assesses learning ability; see Table 14.3) proved to be the two best predictors of WRAT Arithmetic (excluding WAIS Arithmetic) for males, again showing the value of the Vocabulary subtest for LD adolescents and young adults.

Should Acquired Knowledge Be Included in Bannatyne's Approach?

Matheson, Mueller, and Short (1984) analyzed WISC-R data and concluded that a separate Acquired Knowledge factor does not emerge. From rotations of varied numbers of WAIS-R factors (Naglieri & Kaufman, 1983), it is quite evident that the same finding holds for the WAIS-R. Matheson et al. (1984) concluded: "Bannatyne's Acquired Knowledge category has no validity as a construct separate from his Conceptualization category. . . . [Other analyses] do not inspire confidence in Acquired Knowledge as a factor that may usefully be compared to Sequencing" (p. 289). The large overlap between Acquired Knowledge and other Bannatyne categories stems, in part, from the fact that this grouping shares one subtest with both Verbal Conceptualization (Vocabulary) and Sequential (Arithmetic). They suggested eliminating Acquired Knowledge and interpreting either the remaining three Bannatyne groupings or "Kaufman's three factors" (p. 289).

I disagree with this suggestion. Matheson et al. (1984) appropriately pointed out the small reliability of the difference between Acquired Knowledge and either Verbal Conceptualization or Sequential, but I do not advocate pairwise comparisons. The method I suggest is based on Davis's (1959) formulas for comparing one subtest score to the person's mean score on several subtests. This approach is applicable for scales or categories as well as subtests and has an important feature: It fully takes into account any overlap between the categories. (I discovered this fact when I wanted to apply Davis's formulas to the overlapping scales that constitute the McCarthy Scales. I telephoned my former professor, Fred Davis, who described to me the robustness of his formulas.) Consequently, the method of comparing each category to the person's mean standard score on all categories circumvents some of the problems associated with pairwise comparisons involving Acquired Knowledge. In addition, the lack of factor-analytic evidence for normal individuals, or even for groups of LD individuals, does not address the fact that the achievement-oriented triad often splits apart some for individuals, notably from the rest of the Verbal Scale the mentally retarded (see pp. 547–549) and learning disabled. Also, the inclusion of Acquired Knowledge as a Bannatyne category allows examiners to study two important subdivisions of the Verbal Scale simultaneously—concept formation/reasoning versus school achievement, and a split akin to the Factor I versus Factor III division.

High Spatial Versus Low Sequential

For virtually all adolescents or adults believed to be learning disabled, one might anticipate relatively good performance in Spatial Ability versus relatively poor performance in Sequential Ability. In Table 13.12 the LD college students scored 5 points higher on Spatial than Sequential; the dyslexic adults scored 36 points higher, and the 16-year-olds scored 22 points higher. The WAIS investigations produced similar findings: McCue et al.'s (1986) LD adults scored 11 points higher on Spatial than Sequential; Blalock's (1987) LD adults (40% with college experience) scored 7 points higher; and Cordoni et al.'s (1981) LD college students scored 14 points higher. In the study that merged WAIS and WAIS-R data (Ackerman et al., 1987), males had a 15-point Spatial > Sequential differential, while the female applicants to a special LD college program had a 10-point discrepancy. Only Vogel's (1986) sample of female college LD students showed a trivial difference in favor of Spatial Ability (2 points).

Among the comparison samples, the two groups of incarcerated adults scored 3½ to 4 points higher, while the normal college students earned virtually identical scores on the Spatial and Sequential categories. Cordoni et al.'s (1981) normal control group of 17 normal college students scored 1 point lower on Spatial Ability. Thus, high Spatial–low Sequential profiles are far more associated with LD adolescents and adults (median discrepancy of 11 points for eight samples) than with pertinent comparison samples (median of 2 points for four samples).

High Spatial Versus Low Acquired Knowledge

Vogel's (1986) sample of female college LD students did show a more substantial 6-point difference when comparing Spatial Ability to Acquired Knowledge. Of the samples in Table 13.12, large discrepancies of about 15 or more points favoring Spatial Ability over Acquired Knowledge were observed for all LD samples except Salvia et al.'s (1987) college students, who performed equally on the two categories. Among samples tested on the WAIS or on both the WAIS and WAIS-R, Spatial > Acquired Knowledge differences of at least 10 points were found for McCue et al.'s (1966) LD adults, Cordoni et al.'s (1981) LD college students, Ackerman et al.'s (1987) males, and Ackerman et al.'s females. However, Blalock's (1987) LD adults, many with college backgrounds, joined Salvia et al.'s LD college students in demonstrating a trivial Spatial-Acquired Knowledge difference. Note, however, that Salvia et al.'s (1987) college control group evidenced an 8-point *superiority* in Acquired Knowledge over Spatial Ability; other comparison samples had small (3- to 6-point) differences in favor of Spatial Ability.

Overall, a deficiency in Acquired Knowledge is to be anticipated for LD adolescents and adults, with the occasional exception of those in college. The median discrepancy in favor of Spatial Ability was 11 points for nine LD samples, compared to 4.5 points for four comparison groups.

Implications for Examiners

When clinicians examine WAIS-R Bannatyne profiles for LD referrals, research suggests that they should anticipate strength in Spatial Ability contrasted with weakness in Sequential Ability and Acquired Knowledge. For college students, Verbal Conceptualization Ability may conceivably join Spatial Ability as an area of relative strength, and Acquired Knowledge may fail to emerge as a weakness. For female LD referrals, Sequential Ability may not emerge as a striking weakness because of good performance on Digit Symbol.

For all LD adolescents and adults, clinicians should routinely determine each individual's strengths and weaknesses on the Bannatyne categories, using the method outlined on pages 432–438. Ideally, each person should have a significant strength on Spatial and significant weaknesses in Sequential and/or Acquired Knowledge to be strongly suggestive of a learning-disabilities profile. However, the ideal is not essential to reach the conclusion of probable learning disabilities. Based on the values for significance shown in Table 13.7, a person who simultaneously has a strength in one Bannatyne category and a weakness in another will necessarily score at least *20* points higher on the strength than the weakness; it is unreasonable to insist on a discrepancy of that magnitude. Consequently, I believe that an LD profile is supported when at least *one* of the proposed categories reaches statistical significance and the others are in the right direction. For example, the LD profile is supported for a referral who (a) earns a significant weakness in Sequential, (b) scores *above* his or her own mean Bannatyne score on Spatial, and (c) scores *below* his or her own Bannatyne score on Acquired Knowledge.

For a female subject, examiners should examine the Digit Symbol scaled score. If it is one of her best scores, the Freedom from Distractibility factor score (which excludes Digit Symbol) might give the best clue to her area of deficiency. The Bannatyne approach may still prove to be an effective method of profile attack, but examiners might choose instead to conduct an analogous analysis based on the three-factor scores. A key point in making the decision is whether the Verbal Scale seems to split into high Verbal Conceptualization and low Acquired Knowledge. If they select the factor-analytic approach, examiners should expect above average performance in Perceptual Organization and relatively weak performance in Freedom from Distractibility, with a significant deviation emerging in at least one of these areas. For LD college students, a strength in Verbal Comprehension may emerge as well.

As noted in chapter 9, LD individuals (except those with college backgrounds) tend to have P > V patterns. Apparently, the low Verbal IQs obtained by learning-disabled children, adolescents, and adults are related both to their failure to achieve appropriately in school subjects and to a deficiency in whatever the third factor measures—sequential processing, distractibility, the ability to manipulate symbols, and so forth. On the WAIS-R, as opposed to the WISC-R, examiners should be aware that these deficient areas will have a greater impact on Verbal IQ *because Digit Span contributes directly to V-IQ* but is excluded from the IQ computations for the WISC-R.

The Fuld Profile for Alzheimer's-Type Dementia

The Fuld profile (Fuld, 1983, 1984) has generated a growing amount of interest with a WAIS/WAIS-R profile that she believes to be characteristic of adults with Alzheimer's-type dementia (DAT). Most of the research has been quite positive, particularly in discriminating DAT

patients from patients with other types of dementia.

The Fuld Profile

Fuld derived her WAIS profile from an earlier study (Drachman & Leavitt, 1974) and initially reported that an estimated 50% of DAT patients, compared to less than 1% of normal elderly adults, displayed the characteristic profile (Fuld, 1983). She and other investigators subsequently conducted careful research studies to systematically confirm or deny these clinical estimates.

The profile makes use of only seven WAIS-R subtests (actually, Fuld and most other researchers have used the WAIS), eliminating the four tasks "which are most likely to reflect cultural bias or difficulties in visual acuity" (Fuld, 1984, p. 382): Arithmetic, Comprehension, Picture Completion, Picture Arrangement. The seven tasks are grouped as follows:

A = [Information + Vocabulary] divided by 2

B = [Similarities + Digit Span] divided by 2

C = [Digit Symbol + Block Design] divided by 2

D = Object Assembly

The Fuld profile, which is computed using *age-corrected* scaled scores, is shown below.

$$A > B > C \le D \text{ and } A > D$$
$$\text{or}$$
$$\frac{I + V}{2} > \frac{(S + DSp)}{2} > \frac{(DSy + BD)}{2} \le (OA)$$
$$\text{and } \frac{(I + V)}{2} > (OA)$$

The profile has a neuro*pharmacological* basis rather than a neuro*anatomic* basis and is related to neurotransmitter changes noted in DAT; Fuld (1984) noted that "a dramatic deficiency of the cholinergic system is the most severe neurochemical change known to occur in DAT" (p. 381). Fuld's WAIS-R profile indicated previously is believed to show the patterning of abilities that results from cholinergic dysfunction. In a systematic investigation of the Wechsler profile, Fuld (1984) studied normal college students, about half of whom had a chemically induced cholinergic deficiency that mimicked the chemically related dysfunction of Alzheimer's patients. Of the 19 drug subjects, 53% displayed the characteristic Fuld profile; in contrast, only 18% of the 22 college students receiving an injection of a placebo drug evidenced the profile. The difference was statistically significant.

Fuld (1984) investigated the WAIS profiles of a variety of dementia patients as well, studying only those who could be assessed validly on the seven WAIS tasks of interest. Of 138 eligible patients, only 77 usable protocols were obtained: 33 with a research diagnosis of DAT, 11 with probable DAT, 6 with a combination of DAT and multi-infarct dementia (MID), 12 with MID, and 15 with other types of dementia.

For data analysis, the 33 "pure" DAT patients were contrasted with the 12 MID patients; 45% of the DAT patients displayed the Fuld profile compared to 8% of the MID patients, a significant discrepancy. In fact, the percentage of Alzheimer's patients evidencing the profiles is about the same (44%) when the definition is expanded to include all 50 patients who manifested DAT to some extent (diagnosed DAT, probable DAT, and a combination of DAT and MID). This percentage is significantly greater than the 4% found in the 27 patients with MID or other dementias. Data from Fuld's (1984) study are presented in Table 13.13, along with data from the several attempts at cross-validation of the Fuld profile.

Validity of the Fuld Profile

Fuld's (1984) initial research showed strong validity of her profile, demonstrating significant and substantial differences between college students with and without a drug-induced cholinergic dysfunction, and between DAT patients and those with other types of dementia. The data from cross-validation studies generally support that validity. Brinkman and Braun (1984)

replicated Fuld's finding, observing the characteristic WAIS profile in 13 of 23 DAT patients, but in only 2 of 39 MID patients, an impressive, statistically significant result. Tuokko and Crockett (1987) searched for instances of the Fuld profile in the WAIS protocols of 74 healthy, elderly men and women (ages 50–90 years, mean age = 70.1; mean education = 13.3 years), and found only 1 such occurrence. Heinrichs and Celinski (1987) identified the Fuld profile in just 5 of 50 male head-injured patients with a mean age of 40.6 years and a mean educational level of 9.9 years.

The most negative finding was reported by Filley, Kobayashi, and Heaton (1987). Whereas they observed the Fuld pattern in only 1 of their 42 normal controls (mean age = 64 years), confirming its rare occurrence in the population at large, they found a relatively small percentage of their 41 DAT patients to manifest the profile (21.9%). A second control group, composed of 30 patients referred for dementia but diagnosed as having other disorders (see footnote a to Table 13.13), displayed the Fuld profile in 16.7% of the protocols. This percentage did not differ significantly from the DAT percent. Although the DAT patients in Filley et al.'s study may have been less impaired than the DAT patients in other studies (a larger proportion were testable, and all lived in the community as opposed to nursing homes or institutions), their diagnostic criteria were extremely similar to Fuld's (1984) and Brinkman and Braun's (1984).

The negative findings by Filley et al. (1987) are thus not easily explainable. Of their 41 DAT patients, 21 were tested on the WAIS and 20 on the WAIS-R. Fuld profiles were evidenced by 14.3% of those taking the WAIS and 30% taking the WAIS-R, but the difference was not statistically significant. Satz, Van Gorp, Soper, and Mitrushina (1987) administered only the WAIS-R in their investigation of the Fuld profile, but they tested only normal adults, not dementia patients. Their sample of 149 healthy adults aged 60–94 (mean age = 71.1; mean

TABLE 13.13 Frequency of occurrence of the Fuld Profile for groups having Alzheimer's-type dementia and for control populations

Study	PERCENTAGE OF VARIOUS SAMPLES EVIDENCING THE FULD PROFILE					
	Alzheimer's-Type Dementia	Multi-Infarct Dementia	Other Dementias	Head Injury	Nondementia Patients[a]	Normal Elderly[b]
Fuld (1984)	44% (N=50)	8% (N=12)	0% (N=15)			
Brinkman & Braun (1984)	57% (N=23)	5% (N=39)				
Tuokko & Crockett (1987)						1% (N=74)
Heinrichs & Celinski (1987)				10% (N=50)		
Filley et al. (1987)	22% (N=42)				17% (N=30)	2% (N=42)
Satz et at. (1987)						13% (N=149)
Satz et al. (1989) Ages:						
55–64						6% (N=160)
65–69						6% (N=160)
70–74						7% (N=160)
Totals	38% (N=115)	6% (N=51)	0% (N=15)	10% (N=50)	17% (N=30)	7% (N=745)

[a]The 30 nondementia patients include 13 with depression, 4 alcoholics, and 1–3 with a variety of disorders such as schizophrenia and stroke.

[b]The percentage of normal adolescents and adults (ages 16–74 years) in the WAIS-R standardization sample displaying the Fuld profile is 6.2 (Satz et al., 1989); no significant differences were observed for chronological age.

NOTE: Satz et al. (1987) and Satz et al. (1989) used the WAIS-R; Filley et al. (1987) used the WAIS-R or WAIS; all other studies used the WAIS. All profiles are based on *age-corrected* scaled scores.

education = 14.0 years) produced 19 instances of the Fuld profile (12.8%). However, since these authors administered the Satz-Mogel short form of the WAIS-R, I question the validity of individual subtest profiles (see pp. 138–140).

Nonetheless, their normal percentage is well below the percentage found among DAT patients in other studies. Further, in a subsequent study, Satz et al. (1989) explored the percentage of individuals in the WAIS-R standardization sample displaying the Fuld profile and found only 6% to 7% at ages 55–64, 65–69, and 70–74 (see Table 13.13). Across the entire 16- to 74-year age range, 6.2% of the sample evidenced the Fuld profile; the occurrence of the profile was *not* significantly related to age. The profile showed no relationship to race, but was significantly related to gender and, for ages 25–74, to educational attainment. Males displayed the profile more so than females (7.3% versus 5.1%); in addition, educated adults were far more likely than less educated people to evidence the Fuld profile (Satz et al., 1989). Adults with some college (8.9%) and college graduates (11.9%) displayed the Fuld profile more commonly than adults from other educational groups (3.6%–5.6%).

In another interesting additional analysis, Satz et al. (1989) explored the Fuld profile using *regular* scaled scores, not just the age-corrected scaled scores advocated by Fuld. Fuld's decision to use age-corrected scaled scores was given strong support by these results. Satz et al. observed a striking increase in the percentage demonstrating Fuld profiles with increasing age when the regular (uncorrected) scaled scores were used. The proportions increased from < 1% at ages 16–17 to 9.3% at ages 25–34 to 36.6% at ages 70–74. To Satz et al. this finding implied that Alzheimer's patients differ from elderly people without the disease in the same way that normal older adults differ from normal younger adults. This intriguing finding is treated again in chapter 17.

Overview of the Fuld Profile

The data shown in Table 13.13 across all studies support the use of the Fuld profile for differential diagnosis of DAT. Even taking into account the disappointing results of Filley et al.'s (1987) investigation, 38% of the 115 Alzheimer's patients displayed the Fuld profile compared to 9% of adults with other disorders (MID, other dementias, head injury, nondementia patients) and 7% of normal elderly peo-

ple. The ability of the profile to discriminate between DAT patients and those with MID or other dementias (38% versus 4½%) is especially noteworthy. When the Fuld pattern is observed, the differences tend to be sizable for DAT patients. The 22 DAT patients (out of 50) who demonstrated the profile in Fuld's (1984) investigation earned the following age-corrected scaled scores on the WAIS.

A (Information, Vocabulary) ÷ 2 =	9.6
B (Similarities, Digit Span) ÷ 2 =	6.9
C (Digit Symbol, Block Design) ÷ 2 =	1.5
D (Object Assembly) ÷ 2 =	3.4

The problems with the Fuld formulas are: (a) more than half of the DAT patients do *not* display the Fuld profile, so its failure to emerge does not rule out DAT as a plausible diagnosis; (b) virtually all data have been obtained with the old WAIS, so its generalization to the WAIS-R remains speculative; (c) the formula places too much emphasis on Object Assembly, the least reliable (.68) and stable (.70) WAIS-R subtest, and the only task with inadequate subtest specificity; (d) the profile will conceivably emerge for patients without DAT (e.g., those with Parkinson's disease) who are on anticholinergic medication (Fuld, 1984); and (e) the accuracy of the clinical diagnosis of DAT may not be enhanced very much by the formula because diagnostic accuracy is contingent on population base-rates, and there is a "high incidence of DAT in comparison to other causes of dementia" (Fuld, 1984, p. 388).

Filley et al. (1987) and Satz et al. (1987) have each discussed the importance of base-rates on diagnostic accuracy. Satz et al. (1987) concluded that the results of their analysis of the value of the Fuld pattern, within the context of different base-rates, "provide cautious optimism for the potential application of the WAIS-R pattern . . . as a conditional marker of DAT. . . . If these results can be replicated on larger samples, they offer special promise in the use of [the Fuld profile] in the early detection and/or differential diagnosis of DAT" (p. 772).

The research results to date are compelling despite the caveats that I raised above regarding the application of Fuld's formula and a piecemeal treatment of data derived from a fragmented WAIS-R. I certainly agree with Satz et al.'s (1987) "cautious optimism" and see the Fuld approach as far more promising than other attempts to discriminate between Alzheimer's patients and other elderly individuals (e.g., Leli & Filskov, 1979; Leli & Scott, 1982). Examiner's Form 13.5 (pp. 467–468) facilitates the use of Fuld's formula.

CHAPTER 13 SUMMARY

This chapter, the second of three on profile interpretation, stresses *empirical* treatment of the data, beginning with the most global score, the Full Scale IQ, and proceeding to subtest interpretation. The FS-IQ should be banded with error and converted to an intelligence category and percentile rank, but it mostly serves as the midpoint of a person's ability spectrum—the fulcrum for inferring relative areas of strength and weakness. Next is the interpretation of V–P discrepancies, a topic covered in some detail in previous chapters, followed by computation of statistically significant strengths and weaknesses in the subtest profile.

The analysis of subtest fluctuations is made unnecessarily difficult by the method used to derive scaled scores, namely the application of subtest norms for ages 20–34 years to *everyone* within the 16- to 74-year age range. This range robs the scaled score of one of its principal benefits, its constant parameters (mean = 10, SD = 3) from subtest to subtest and from age to age. To remedy this built-in flaw, it is important for examiners to compute *age-corrected* scaled scores in addition to the regular set of scaled scores, to permit systematic profile analysis.

After computing the age-corrected scaled scores, examiners determine significant strengths and weaknesses within the subtest profile relative to the person's own mean scores. When the person has a significant V–P IQ discrepancy, examiners are advised to compute Verbal strengths and weaknesses relative to the person's Verbal mean, and to compute Performance strengths and weaknesses relative to his or her Performance mean. In contrast, if the V–P difference is not significant the midpoint should be the person's mean of all 11 subtests. As a rule of thumb, significant strengths must be at least 3 points above the individual's mean score (V, P, or FS), while significant weaknesses must be at least 3 points below the pertinent mean. A series of five steps is presented, and illustrated with two WAIS-R profiles, regarding the statistical computations necessary to determine significant fluctuations within the age-corrected scaled score profile, and the logical approach needed to interpret the deviating scores.

In addition to an empirical system for inferring significant deviations from a person's mean on single subtests, comparable systems are offered to determine significant strengths and weaknesses in a person's profile of standard scores (mean = 100, SD = 15) regarding (a) the three factor scores, (b) the four Bannatyne categories, and (c) three of Horn's categories from his fluid–crystallized analysis of the WAIS-R. Formulas are also provided to permit examiners to convert scaled scores on the component subtests in each category to standard scores, and the reliabilities of each cluster for adolescents and adults is likewise reported. Since the three interpretive approaches overlap to some extent, guidelines are discussed to help clinicians select the most appropriate system.

Subtest scatter interpretation requires the use of the regular scaled scores because data on the age-corrected scaled scores were unavailable for analysis. Tables are provided to allow examiners to determine whether a person has an unusual amount of scatter in his or her subtest profile on the Verbal, Performance, or Full Scales, as defined by (a) scaled score range (highest minus lowest scaled score), and (b) number of subtests deviating significantly from the person's own mean score. In addition, Selz and Reitan's scatter index is evaluated and interpreted as an alternative method of inferring significant subtest scatter in WAIS-R profiles.

The last section of the chapter deals with characteristic profiles that have come to be associated with the assessment of learning disabilities and Alzheimer's disease. The LD profile is often called the ACID profile because it is defined by low WISC-R scores on *A*rithmetic, *C*oding, *I*nformation, and *D*igit Span. This profile also occurs for the WAIS-R with LD adults, as does a similar profile associated with the Bannatyne category system: high Spatial Ability coupled with low Sequential Ability and low Acquired Knowledge. These profiles, however, do not hold particularly well for LD college students, who often do as well on Verbal Conceptualization as on Spatial, and who sometimes perform adequately on the Acquired Knowledge triad. Nonetheless, virtually all LD students, including those in college, evidence weakness

on Sequential Ability and on the ACID profile. The only possible exception to this finding concerns female LD adolescents and college students, who perform adequately on Digit Symbol, a component of both the Sequential and ACID groupings. Overall, the Bannatyne approach seems like the best method for evaluating WAIS-R profiles for LD adolescents and adults; the ACID grouping does not seem as efficient as a comparison among the individual's scores on the four Bannatyne categories.

The Fuld profile, which involves relationships among seven WAIS-R subtests, shows great promise for the diagnosis of Alzheimer's-type dementia (DAT). This profile has been found in about 40% of patients with DAT and has even emerged for normal college students with a chemically induced cholinergic deficiency (mimicking the chemical dysfunction of DAT patients). In contrast, this profile has been observed relatively infrequently among normal elderly individuals (7%), and it clearly does not characterize types of dementia other than DAT, such as multi-infarct dementia.

EXAMINER'S FORM 13.1   Determining strengths and weaknesses on the 11 WAIS-R subtests (Developed by A. S. Kaufman)

Instructions for Worksheet

Step 1. Determine whether the person's Verbal–Performance IQ discrepancy is statistically significant before using this form.

Step 2. • If the V–P discrepancy is *not* significant, enter the person's *age-corrected* scaled scores in the column headed Full Scale.
   • If the V–P discrepancy *is* significant, enter the person's *age-corrected* Verbal scaled scores in the column headed Verbal and enter the person's *age-corrected* Performance scaled scores in the column headed Performance.

Step 3. Compute the relevant mean or means of the age-corrected scaled scores, depending on the columns used. Round the mean(s) to the nearest whole number.

Step 4. Subtract the person's mean score from each age-corrected scaled score. If scores were entered in the Verbal and Performance columns, compare each Verbal subtest to the Verbal mean, and each Performance subtest to the Performance mean. Enter the difference scores in the column headed D. Use negative signs to denote scores below the person's mean.

Step 5. Differences that are 3 or more points *above* the person's mean score are relative *strengths*. Enter an S in the S or W column next to each difference of at least 3 points. Differences that are 3 or more

EXAMINER'S FORM 13.1   (Continued)

points *below* the person's mean score are relative *weaknesses*. Enter a *W* in the S or W column next to each difference of at least −3 points. (Alternative method: Use the precise significance values for each subtest in Table 13.3 to determine strengths or weaknesses. For this method, do not round means to the nearest whole number in Step 3.)

Worksheet for: Examinee's Name _____ Date _____

	AGE-CORRECTED SCALED SCORES				
WAIS-R SUBTEST	VERBAL	PERFORMANCE	FULL SCALE	(D)	(S OR W)
Verbal					
Information	I _____		I _____	_____	_____
Digit Span	Dsp _____		Dsp _____	_____	_____
Vocabulary	V _____		V _____	_____	_____
Arithmetic	A _____		A _____	_____	_____
Comprehension	C _____		C _____	_____	_____
Similarities	S _____		S _____	_____	_____
Performance					
Picture Completion		PC _____	PC _____	_____	_____
Picture Arrangement		PA _____	PA _____	_____	_____
Block Design		BD _____	BD _____	_____	_____
Object Assembly		OA _____	OA _____	_____	_____
Digit Symbol		DSy _____	DSy _____	_____	_____
Sum =	_____	_____	_____		
Divide by	6	5	11		
Mean =	_____	_____	_____		
Rounded Mean =	_____	_____	_____		

EXAMINER'S FORM 13.2 Computing WAIS-R factor scores and determining significant strengths and weaknesses on the three factors (Developed by A. S. Kaufman)

Instructions for Worksheet A

Step 1. Enter the person's *age-corrected* scaled score for each subtest in the appropriate column of Worksheet A. (Note that Picture Arrangement and Digit Symbol are not included on any of the factors.)

Step 2. Sum the three columns, entering each sum on the relevant line.

Step 3. Multiply each sum by the value indicated for each factor. Enter each product (to the nearest tenth) on the relevant line.

Step 4. Add the product to the constant indicated for each factor. Enter this sum on the relevant line. These values equal the person's *standard scores* (mean = 100, SD = 15) on the three WAIS-R factors.

Step 5. Round each standard score to the nearest whole number and enter each value on the relevant line.

Worksheet A for: Examinee's Name _____ Date _____

WAIS-R SUBTEST	VERBAL COMPREHENSION	PERCEPTUAL ORGANIZATION	FREEDOM FROM DISTRACTIBILITY
Verbal			
Information	I _____		
Digit Span			DSp _____
Vocabulary	V _____		
Arithmetic			A _____
Comprehension	C _____		
Similarities	S _____		
Performance			
Picture Competion		PC _____	
Block Design		BD _____	
Object Assembly		OA _____	
Sum =	_____	_____	_____
Multiply Sum by	(1.4)	(2.0)	(2.8)
Product =	_____	_____	_____
Add the Constant	+44	+40	+44
Sum = Standard Score =	_____	_____	_____
Rounded Standard Score =	_____	_____	_____

EXAMINER'S FORM 13.2 (Continued)

Instructions for Worksheet B

Step 1. Enter the rounded standard scores on the three factors in the spaces provided.

Step 2. Compute the mean of the three standard scores, rounding the mean to the nearest whole number.

Step 3. Subtract the person's mean score from each of the three standard scores. Enter the difference scores in the column headed D. Use negative signs to denote scores below the person's mean.

Step 4. Determine whether each difference is significant at the .05 level using the values provided. Differences that equal or exceed these values are significant strengths or weaknesses for the person. Enter an S or W in the column provided to denote significance.

Worksheet B for: Examinee's Name _____ Date _____

WAIS-R FACTOR	STANDARD SCORE	(D)	SIZE OF SIGNIFICANT DIFFERENCE ($p<.05$) AGES 16–19	AGES 20–74	(S OR W)
Verbal Comprehension	_____	_____	± 8	±7	_____
Perceptual Organization	_____	_____	±11	±9	_____
Freedom from Distractibility	_____	_____	±11	±9	_____

Sum =	_____
Divide by	3
Mean =	_____
Rounded Mean =	_____

EXAMINER'S FORM 13.3   Computing standard scores on Bannatyne's WAIS-R categories and determining significant strengths and weaknesses on the four categories (Developed by A. S. Kaufman)

Instructions for Worksheet A

Step 1. Enter the person's *age-corrected* scaled score for each subtest in the appropriate column(s) of Worksheet A. (Note that Picture Arrangement is not included in any of the categories.)

Step 2. Sum the four columns, entering each sum on the relevant line.

Step 3. Multiply each sum by the value indicated for each category. Enter each product (to the nearest tenth) on the relevant line.

Step 4. Add the product to the constant indicated for each category. Enter this sum on the relevant line. These values equal the person's *standard scores* (mean = 100, *SD* = 15) on the four categories.

Step 5. Round each standard score to the nearest whole number and enter each value on the relevant line.

Worksheet A for: Examinee's Name _____   Date _____

WAIS-R SUBTEST	VERBAL CONCEPTUALIZATION	SPATIAL	SEQUENTIAL	ACQUIRED KNOWLEDGE
Verbal				
Information				I _____
Digit Span			DSp _____	
Vocabulary	V _____			V _____
Arithmetic			A _____	A _____
Comprehension	C _____			
Similarities	S _____			
Performance				
Picture Completion		PC _____		
Block Design		BD _____		
Object Assembly		OA _____		
Digit Symbol			DSy _____	
Sum =	_____	_____	_____	_____
Multiply Sum by	(1.9)	(2.0)	(2.1)	(1.9)
Product =	_____	_____	_____	_____
Add the Constant	+43	+40	+37	+43
Sum = Standard Score =	_____	_____	_____	_____
Rounded Standard Score =	_____	_____	_____	_____

EXAMINER'S FORM 13.3 (Continued)

Instructions for Worksheet B

Step 1. Enter the rounded standard scores on the four Bannatyne categories in the spaces provided.

Step 2. Compute the mean of the four standard scores, rounding the mean to the nearest whole number.

Step 3. Subtract the person's mean score from each of the four standard scores. Enter the difference scores in the column headed D. Use negative signs to denote scores below the person's mean.

Step 4. Determine whether each difference is significant at the .05 level using the values provided. Differences that equal or exceed these values are significant strengths or weaknesses for the person. Enter an S or W in the column provided to denote significance.

Worksheet B for: Examinee's Name _____ Date _____

BANNATYNE CATEGORY	STANDARD SCORE	(D)	SIZE OF SIGNIFICANT DIFFERENCE ($p<.05$) AGES 16–19	AGES 20–74	(S OR W)
Verbal Conceptualization	_____	_____	± 9	± 8	_____
Spatial	_____	_____	±11	±10	_____
Sequential	_____	_____	±11	± 9	_____
Acquired Knowledge	_____ ↓	_____	± 8	± 7	_____
Sum =	_____				
Divide by	4				
Mean =	_____				
Rounded Mean =	_____				

EXAMINER'S FORM 13.4   Computing standard scores on Horn's WAIS-R groupings and determining significant strengths and weaknesses on the three groupings (Developed by A. S. Kaufman)

Instructions for Worksheet A

Step 1. Enter the person's *age-corrected* scaled score for each subtest in the appropriate column(s) of Worksheet A. (Note that Digit Symbol is not included in any of the groupings.)

Step 2. Sum the three columns, entering each sum on the relevant line.

Step 3. Multiply each sum by the value indicated for each grouping. Enter each product (to the nearest tenth) on the relevant line.

Step 4. Add the product to the constant indicated for each grouping. Enter this sum on the relevant line. These values equal the person's *standard scores* (mean = 100, *SD* = 15) on the three Horn groupings.

Step 5. Round each standard score to the nearest whole number and enter each value on the relevant line.

Worksheet A for: Examinee's Name _____   Date _____

WAIS-R SUBTEST	FLUID INTELLIGENCE	CRYSTALLIZED INTELLIGENCE	RETENTION
Verbal			
Information		I _____	I _____
Digit Span	DSp _____		DSp _____
Vocabulary		V _____	
Arithmetic			A _____
Comprehension		C _____	
Similarities	S _____	S _____	
Performance			
Picture Completion	PC _____		
Picture Arrangement	PA _____		
Block Design	BD _____		
Object Assembly	OA _____		
Sum =	_____	_____	_____
Multiply Sum by	(1.1)	(1.4)	(2.0)
Product =	_____	_____	_____
Add the Constant	+34	+44	+40
Sum = Standard Score =	_____	_____	_____
Rounded Standard Score =	_____	_____	_____

EXAMINER'S FORM 13.4 (Continued)

Instructions for Worksheet B

Step 1. Enter the rounded standard scores on the three Horn groupings in the spaces provided.

Step 2. Compute the mean of the three standard scores, rounding the mean to the nearest whole number.

Step 3. Subtract the person's mean score from each of the three standard scores. Enter the difference scores in the column headed D. Use negative signs to denote scores below the person's mean.

Step 4. Determine whether each difference is significant at the .05 level using the values provided. Differences that equal or exceed these values are significant strengths or weaknesses for the person. Enter an S or W in the column provided to denote significance.

Worksheet B for: Examinee's Name _____ Date _____

HORN GROUPING	STANDARD SCORE	(D)	SIZE OF SIGNIFICANT DIFFERENCE ($p<.05$) AGES 16–19	AGES 20–74	(S OR W)
Fluid Intelligence	_____	_____	±9	±7	_____
Crystallized Intelligence	_____	_____	±7	±6	_____
Retention	_____	_____	±9	±7	_____
Sum =	_____				
Divide by	3				
Mean =	_____				
Rounded Mean =	_____				

EXAMINER'S FORM 13.5   Determining the presence or absence of the Fuld profile for assessing patients with suspected Alzheimer's-type dementia (Developed by A. S. Kaufman)

Instructions for Worksheet

Step 1. Enter the person's *age-corrected* scaled score for each subtest in the appropriate column of the Worksheet. (Note that only seven WAIS-R subtests are used.)

Step 2. Sum the four columns (labeled A, B, C, and D), entering each sum on the relevant line.

Step 3. Compute the mean for each column. Some means may include a decimal of .5. Retain the decimal point; do not round. Note that column D is not actually a mean, but is the person's score on a single subtest, Object Assembly. The Object Assembly score can simply be entered on the "D line" at the bottom of the column.

Step 4. Answer the four questions at the bottom of the Worksheet. Answer Yes to a question if the difference is in the right direction, even if the difference is very small (e.g., 1/2 point).

Step 5. If all four questions are answered Yes, then the Fuld profile for Alzheimer's-type dementia is *confirmed*. A "No" to any one of the four questions means that the profile is *not* confirmed. See the discussion of the Fuld profile on pages 455–459.

Fuld Profile: $A > B > C \leq D$ and $A > D$

Worksheet for: Examinee's Name _____ Date _____

WAIS-R SUBTEST	A	B	C	D
Verbal				
Information	I _____			
Digit Span		DSp _____		
Vocabulary	V _____			
Similarities		S _____		
Performance				
Block Design			BD _____	
Object Assembly				OA _____
Digit Symbol			DSy _____	
Sum =	_____	_____	_____	_____
Divide by	2	2	2	1
Mean =	_____	_____	_____	_____
	A	B	C	D

Answer the following four questions. Circle either Yes or No. All four questions *must* be answered YES.

1. Is A greater than B?   YES   NO   3. Is C less than or equal to D?   YES   NO
2. Is B greater than C?   YES   NO   4. Is A greater than D?   YES   NO

CHAPTER 14

Profile Interpretation: Generating WAIS-R Hypotheses

This chapter integrates the logical analysis of each WAIS-R subtest (chapter 12) with the empirical treatment of the subtest profile (chapter 13) to convert an individual's array of WAIS-R age-corrected scaled scores into clinically meaningful hypotheses about his or her cognitive functioning. I have inferred relationships of the various hypothesized strengths and weaknesses to personality variables whenever possible, although I have been singularly unimpressed with the plethora of articles over the past four decades searching for the intersection of personality (often defined as MMPI profile) and intellect (WAIS profile).

When defined broadly, intelligence has been shown to relate significantly to personality variables such as ego functioning (Allen, Coyne, & David, 1986). When treated separately, global measures of intelligence and personality are each able to distinguish among neuropsychiatric samples, and the best discrimination seems to occur when both measures are combined (Holland & Watson, 1980). But the results become muddy when the mental and personality measures are fragmented into their component parts, and interrelationships are sought between this Wechsler subtest and that MMPI, Rorschach, or 16 PF scale. Findings from one study often are not replicated due to the idiosyncrasies of any given sample; cross-validation of findings is essential, even though the outcome of such experimental rigor is frequently depressing (Turner & Horn, 1977). Even when results are replicated, the magnitude of the relationships may change substantially (Bolton, 1980).

Consequently, my goal in this chapter is to structure the examiner's task of identifying meaningful cognitive hypotheses that may be embedded in a person's WAIS-R profile by restructuring and regrouping the component subtests. Where these hypotheses have reasonably consistent research support regarding their clinical, behavioral, or neuropsychological meaning, that support is indicated. Mostly, however, personality-based interpretations of subtest profiles (Allison, Blatt, & Zimet, 1968) do not seem to generalize, and I have therefore down-played them. Profile attack is featured in the sections that follow, with emphasis on the iden-tification—and not necessarily the clinical inter-pretation—of diverse strengths and weaknesses within the adolescent's and adult's cognitive and behavioral spectrum.

This chapter is organized in four sections, two of which reflect different approaches to WAIS-R profile attack, depending on the ex-aminer's preferred processing style: (a) intro-duction to profile interpretation; (b) a sequential approach to profile attack; (c) a simultaneous approach to profile attack; and (d) illustrative case reports, which demonstrate the outcome of the various hypothesis generation methods and the integration of WAIS-R data with back-ground information, test behaviors, and data from other tests.

INTRODUCTION TO PROFILE INTERPRETATION

Before discussion of WAIS-R profiles begins, the raw materials for interpretation, presented in chapters 12 and 13, require systematic organi-zation. Next the section describes the basic tenets that underlie my philosophy of profile interpretation and hypothesis generation.

Rational and Empirical Raw Materials for Profile Interpretation

The abilities that each WAIS-R subtest is be-lieved to assess, and the behaviors and back-ground variables that are generally believed to influence a person's subtest performance, are organized in Tables 14.1 through 14.4. Tables 14.5 and 14.6 offer empirical treatment of var-ious groupings of WAIS-R subtests to help examiners make objective decisions about a per-son's areas of relative strength and weakness.

Clusters of Abilities or Traits on the WAIS-R

One of the main goals of profile attack, as described in this chapter, is to regroup a per-son's subtest scores to infer global areas of integrity and deficit. This goal is facilitated by organizing the abilities and traits that each WAIS-R subtest measures. Table 14.1 presents cognitive hypotheses associated with two or more of the six WAIS-R Verbal subtests; Table 14.2 does the same for the five Performance subtests. The remaining two tables deal with all 11 tasks regarding the cognitive abilities (Table 14.3) and influences on test performance (Table 14.4) that are believed to affect success on two or more WAIS-R subtests.

These tables are quite similar to tables that I presented for the WISC-R (Kaufman, 1979b), with one major exception: The WAIS-R tables include the average reliability of each grouping of subtests for adolescents (ages 16–19) and adults (ages 20–74). I added these data in re-sponse to appropriate criticism of my WISC-R tables (Piotrowski & Siegel, 1984). Tables 14.1 to 14.4 present averages rather than data for each separate age group for simplicity's sake, and also because analyses of the nine standardization age groups revealed consistency *within* the two adolescent groups, and *within* the seven adult samples, despite frequent sub-stantial differences between adolescents and adults. In general, the WAIS-R subtests, IQs, and subtest clusters are more reliable for adults than adolescents.

As Piotrowski and Siegel (1984) indicated: "By subscribing to Kaufman's method of [WISC-R] profile analysis, the practitioner as-sumes that the psychometric properties of the various composites are approximately equivalent and that they are at least powerful enough to justify analysis" (p. 184). For the WAIS-R, those implicit assumptions are not made; the examiner can use the reliability of the various composites presented in the four tables to de-termine which clusters have sufficient reliability to warrant interpretation.

TABLE 14.1 Abilities shared by two or more WAIS-R Verbal subtests

| Ability | VERBAL SUBTEST | | | | | | RELIABILITY | |
	Information (I)	Digit Span (DSp)	Vocabulary (V)	Arithmetic (A)	Comprehension (C)	Similarities (S)	Teens (16–19) r_{xx}	Adults (20–74) r_{xx}
Factor Analysis								
Verbal Comprehension	I		V		C	S	.96	.96
Freedom from Distractibility		DSp		A			.82	.90
Bannatyne								
Verbal Conceptualization			V		C	S	.94	.95
Acquired Knowledge	I		V	A			.95	.96
Horn								
Crystallized Intelligence	I		V		C	S	.96	.96
Retrieval	I	DSp		A			.90	.94
Osgood								
Auditory-Vocal Channel	I	DSp	V	A	C	S	.96	.97
Rapaport								
Verbal Concept Formation			V			S	.93	.94
Memory	I		V				.96	.96
Dean								
Auditory Memory		DSp		A			.82	.90

(Continues)

TABLE 14.1 (Continued)

| Ability | VERBAL SUBTEST | | | | | | RELIABILITY | |
	Information (I)	Digit Span (DSp)	Vocabulary (V)	Arithmetic (A)	Comprehension (C)	Similarities (S)	Teens (16–19) r_{xx}	Adults (20–74) r_{xx}
Guilford								
Memory	I	DSp		A			.90	.94
Semantic Cognition			V	A		S	.93	.95
Symbolic Memory		DSp		A			.82	.90
Other Skills								
Auditory sequencing		DSp		A			.82	.90
Fund of information	I		V				.96	.96
Handling abstract verbal concepts			V			S	.93	.94
Long-term memory	I		V	A			.95	.96
Mental alertness		DSp		A			.82	.90
Verbal expression			V		C	S	.94	.95
Verbal reasoning					C	S	.88	.91

NOTE: Thanks are due Toshinori Ishikuma and Harue Ishikuma for computing the reliability coefficients shown in this table.

TABLE 14.2 Abilities shared by two or more WAIS-R Performance subtests

| | PERFORMANCE SUBTEST | | | | | RELIABILITY | |
Ability	Picture Completion (PC)	Picture Arrangement (PA)	Block Design (BD)	Object Assembly (OA)	Digit Symbol (DSy)	Teens (16–19) r_{xx}	Adults (20–74) r_{xx}
Factor Analysis							
Perceptual Organization	PC		BD	OA		.87	.91
Bannatyne							
Spatial	PC		BD	OA		.87	.91
Osgood							
Visual-Motor Channel	PC	PA	BD	OA	DSy	.89	.93
Rapaport							
Anticipation		PA		OA		.72	.80
Visual Organization	PC	PA		OA		.79	.86
Visual-Motor Coordination			BD	OA	DSy	.86	.90
Dean							
Visual Memory	PC			OA	DSy	.80	.88
Visual-Motor Speed				OA	DSy	.74	.83
Guilford							
Figural Cognition	PC		BD	OA		.87	.91
Figural Evaluation	PC		BD	OA		.87	.91
Convergent-production		PA			DSy	.76	.85

(Continues)

TABLE 14.2 (Continued)

| | PERFORMANCE SUBTEST | | | | | RELIABILITY | |
| | Picture Completion (PC) | Picture Arrangement (PA) | Block Design (BD) | Object Assembly (OA) | Digit Symbol (DSy) | Teens (16–19) r_{xx} | Adults (20–74) r_{xx} |
Ability							
Other Skills							
Nonverbal reasoning		PA		OA		.72	.80
Reproduction of models			BD		DSy	.86	.90
Simultaneous processing	PC		BD	OA		.87	.91
Synthesis		PA	BD	OA		.84	.89
Trial-and-error learning			BD	OA		.84	.86
Visual closure	PC			OA		.76	.85
Visual perception/ processing abstract stimuli			BD		DSy	.86	.90
Visual perception/ processing meaningful stimuli	PC	PA				.79	.86
Visual sequencing		PA			DSy	.76	.85

NOTE: Thanks are due Toshinori Ishikuma and Harue Ishikuma for computing the reliability coefficients shown in this table.

TABLE 14.3 Abilities shared by two or more WAIS-R Verbal or Performance subtests

Ability	Verbal subtest						Performance subtest					Reliability	
	I	DSp	V	A	C	S	PC	PA	BD	OA	DSy	Teens (16–19) r_{xx}	Adults (20–74) r_{xx}
Bannatyne													
Sequential		DSp		A							DSy	.87	.92
Horn													
Fluid Intelligence		DSp				S	PC	PA	BD	OA		.91	.94
Osgood													
Automatic Level of Organization		DSp					PC				DSy	.83	.91
Rapaport													
Attention–Concentration		DSp	V	A			PC				DSy	.88	.93
Concept Formation			V			S			BD			.94	.95
Dean													
General Ability	I		V	A	C	S	PC		BD			.96	.97
Abstract Thought						S			BD			.89	.90
Remote Memory	I						PC					.86	.89
Social Comprehension					C			PA				.81	.86
Guilford													
Cognition			V	A		S	PC		BD	OA		.94	.96
Evaluation				A	C		PC	PA	BD	OA		.91	.94
Semantic Content	I		V	A		S		PA			DSy	.95	.96
Symbolic Content		DSp		A							DSy	.87	.92

(Continues)

TABLE 14.3   (Continued)

| Ability | VERBAL SUBTEST | | | | | | PERFORMANCE SUBTEST | | | | | RELIABILITY | |
	I	DSp	V	A	C	S	PC	PA	BD	OA	DSy	Teens (16–19) r_{xx}	Adults (20–74) r_{xx}
Other Skills													
Common sense (cause–effect)					C			PA				.81	.86
Distinguishing essential from nonessential detail						S	PC	PA				.86	.91
Encoding further information for processing		DSp		A							DSy	.87	.92
Facility with numbers		DSp		A							DSy	.87	.92
Learning ability			V								DSy	.89	.93
Reasoning				A	C	S		PA		OA		.90	.93
Sequential processing		DSp		A							DSy	.87	.92

NOTE: All WAIS-R subtests, at least to some extent, reflect Osgood's Representational level of organization. Thanks are due Toshinori Ishikuma and Harue Ishikuma for computing the reliability coefficients shown in this table.

TABLE 14.4 Influences likely to affect scores on two or more WAIS-R Verbal or Performance subtests

Influence	Verbal subtest						Performance subtest					Reliability	
	I	DSp	V	A	C	S	PC	PA	BD	OA	DSy	Teens (16–19) r_{xx}	Adults (20–74) r_{xx}
Ability to respond when uncertain							PC			OA		.76	.85
Alertness to environment	I						PC					.86	.89
Anxiety		DSp		A							DSy	.87	.92
Attention span		DSp		A								.82	.90
Cognitive style (field dependence/field independence)							PC		BD	OA		.87	.91
Concentration				A			PC				DSy	.86	.92
Cultural opportunities	I		V		C			PA				.94	.95
Distractibility		DSp		A							DSy	.87	.92
Flexibility		DSp				S				OA		.83	.89
Foreign language background	I		V									.96	.96
Intellectual curiosity and striving	I		V									.96	.96
Interests	I		V			S						.96	.96
Learning disabilities	I	DSp		A		S					DSy	.91	.94
Negativism	I	DSp			C	S	PC					.89	.94
Outside reading	I		V		C	S						.96	.96
Overly concrete thinking					C	S						.88	.91
Persistence										OA	DSy	.74	.83

(Continues)

TABLE 14.4 (Continued)

| Influence | VERBAL SUBTEST | | | | | | PERFORMANCE SUBTEST | | | | | RELIABILITY | |
	I	DSp	V	A	C	S	PC	PA	BD	OA	DSy	Teens (16–19) r_{xx}	Adults (20–74) r_{xx}
Richness of early environment	I		V									.96	.96
School learning	I		V	A								.95	.96
Working under time pressure				A			PC	PA	BD	OA	DSy	.91	.94

NOTE: Examiners should never infer a person's background or behaviors from the pattern of subtest scores. Background information must be verified by reliable sources, and behaviors must be observed or inferred by the examiner during the testing session. The subtests listed in this table are the ones most likely to be affected by each influence (background or behavioral variable). However, it is unlikely that *all* subtests listed for a given influence will be affected, and it is conceivable that tasks not listed may be affected. For example, a person with a poor attention span is likely to perform poorly on whatever subtests failed to attract his or her interest (not just on Arithmetic and Digit Span). Thanks are due Toshinori Ishikuma and Harue Ishikuma for computing the reliability coefficients shown in this table.

In general, clusters with reliability coefficients above .85 represent stable enough abilities or traits to support confident interpretation; coefficients of .75 to .85 require more cautious interpretation, and the infrequent values below .75 suggest clusters that probably should not be interpreted. Two groupings produced reliabilities below .75 for adolescents: Picture Arrangement-Object Assembly (.72) and Object Assembly-Digit Symbol (.74). These same composites yielded the lowest coefficients for adults as well, but the values were more respectable (.80 and .83, respectively). However, the reliability coefficients for most subtest combinations in Tables 14.1 through 14.4 are quite outstanding, especially for adults aged 20–74, with numerous coefficients in the .90s. Whereas six different combinations of subtests produced reliability coefficients of .80 or below for adolescents (all of which were pairs of Performance subtests), the values for adults dipped below .85 only for the two Performance dyads mentioned previously.

Examiner's Forms 14.1, 14.2 and 14.3 (see pp. 526–532) were developed from Tables 14.1 through 14.4 to aid the clinician in identifying significant strengths and weaknesses in the examinee's WAIS-R profile.

Banding the Cluster Scores With Error

Tables 14.5 and 14.6 are provided to further objectify interpretation of the various clusters and the differences between them. Standard errors of measurement (SE_M) and 90% confidence intervals (C. I.) are presented in Table 14.5; Table 14.6 shows the size of the difference required for statistical significance ($p < .05$) when comparing a person's scores on any two clusters. These tables permit the examiner to interpret the psychometric properties of each composite that is hypothesized as an area of asset or liability for an individual, using any of the profile attack procedures outlined in depth in later sections of this chapter.

TABLE 14.5 Standard errors of measurement and 90% confidence intervals for WAIS-R subtest clusters having differing degrees of reliability

Reliability of Cluster	STANDARD DEVIATION = 3		STANDARD DEVIATION = 15	
	SE_M	90% C. I.	SE_M	90% C. I.
.72–.73	±1.6	±2.6	±8.0	±13.0
.74–.76	±1.5	±2.5	±7.5	±12.5
.77–.79	±1.4	±2.3	±7.0	±11.5
.80–.82	±1.3	±2.1	±6.5	±10.5
.83–.85	±1.2	±2.0	±6.0	±10.0
.86–.88	±1.1	±1.8	±5.5	±9.0
.89–.90	±1.0	±1.6	±5.0	±8.0
.91–.92	±0.9	±1.4	±4.5	±7.0
.93–.94	±0.8	±1.2	±4.0	±6.5
.95	±0.7	±1.1	±3.5	±5.5
.96	±0.6	±1.0	±3.0	±5.0
.97	±0.5	±0.9	±2.5	±4.5

NOTE: SE_M = Standard error of measurement; C. I. = Confidence Interval. Values for SD = 15 are rounded to the nearest half-point.

The SE_Ms and C. I.s in Table 14.5 are based on the *reliability* of each composite of WAIS-R subtests; they are not provided separately for the voluminous number of specific groupings presented in the four tables. Simply select any cluster of subtests in Tables 14.1 through 14.4 that is believed to be strong or weak for a person; note its reliability coefficient, being careful to select the value for adolescents or adults, whichever is appropriate; and then enter Table 14.5 with the coefficient to determine the cluster's SE_M or 90% confidence interval.

The table lists these values in two ways: to correspond to a standard deviation of 3, and to correspond to a standard deviation of 15. The appropriate value depends on how the examiner chooses to combine the scaled scores on the subtests constituting the clusters. Examiners who compute the average of the age-corrected scaled scores (which have a mean of 10 and $SD = 3$ for each age group) should band this mean score with a SE_M or C. I. based on a standard deviation of 3. If examiners convert the sum of the age-corrected scaled scores to a standard score having a mean of 100 and SD of 15, they must use the bands of error that correspond to a standard deviation of 15. Formulas for converting sums of subtest scores to standard scores are given in chapter 13 (Table 13.6) for each factor score, Bannatyne category, and Horn grouping. Additional formulas for various other subtest combinations are presented in Table 14.5.

Determining Significant Differences Between Scores on Clusters

Table 14.6 should help determine whether a person performed significantly differently on any two clusters that the examiner wishes to

TABLE 14.6 Size of difference between two WAIS-R subtest clusters required for significance ($p < .05$), based on their average reliability coefficient

	SIGNIFICANT DIFFERENCE BETWEEN CLUSTER SCORES	
Average Reliability of Clusters	*Standard Deviation = 3*	*Standard Deviation = 15*
.72–.73	4.4	22.0
.74–.76	4.2	21.0
.77–.79	3.9	19.5
.80–.82	3.6	18.0
.83–.85	3.3	16.5
.86–.88	3.0	15.0
.89–.90	2.7	13.5
.91–.92	2.4	12.0
.93–.94	2.1	10.5
.95	1.9	9.5
.96	1.7	8.5
.97	1.4	7.0

NOTE: Values for $SD = 15$ are rounded to the nearest half-point.

compare. First determine the reliability of each pertinent composite in Tables 14.1 through 14.4; then compute the average reliability of the two clusters; finally, enter Table 14.6 with the average coefficient to determine the size of the difference between the two clusters that is needed to be statistically significant at the .05 level. Again, values are provided for both $SD = 3$ and $SD = 15$, whichever is appropriate. The values shown in Table 14.6 are based on the assumption that examiners will compare a person's scores only on that particular pair of clusters. If several comparisons are made for the same person, slightly larger differences are required for significance. However, if examiners are judicious and limit the number of comparisons to two or three for any particular individual, the values in Table 14.6 offer good guidelines for assessing whether a person performed differently on any two WAIS-R clusters.

Several illustrations of how to use Table 14.6 are given throughout this chapter—for example, on pp. 507–508 to determine whether Ben G. performed at significantly different levels on the two Rapaport categories of visual organization and visual-motor coordination.

A Rule of Thumb

The following rule of thumb is useful for examiners who do *not* wish to do the elaborate computations to determine significant differences between composites, or to enter formulas to compute standard scores:

When comparing a person's performance on two groupings of subtests, compute his or her mean age-corrected scaled score for each grouping. Differences of 1 standard deviation (3 points) may be considered significant. [Exception: If the composites are relatively unreliable (coefficients in the high .70s or low .80s), differences of 4 points are needed for significance.]

A Note for the Mathematically Insecure

Examiners who prefer to avoid mathematics, except for the minimal level required to determine a person's strengths and weaknesses on the subtests (using the $\pm$ 3 method), should not be chagrined by the numbers, formulas, and empirical guidelines that are presented here. Even the preceding rule of thumb can be ignored by those who do not wish to be overwhelmed by numbers. These empirical steps and tables are provided for examiners who are comfortable with that sort of thing. It is the *rational* approach to hypothesis generation that is the crux of profile attack and that should be absorbed by all examiners; empirical treatment of the data is only useful when it facilitates, not impedes, hypothesis generation. The next section spells out the rational postulates and axioms of the philosophy of profile interpretation inherent in "intelligent testing" that I have advocated for numerous multiscore test batteries. These tenets are far more important for competent WAIS-R interpretation than any combination of tables or formulas.

Basic Tenets of the Philosophy of Hypothesis Generation

1. Examiners must be detectives, actively attacking subtest profiles in systematic fashion. They need to regroup the subtests in new ways to best explain each individual's subtest-to-subtest fluctuations. Different theories of intelligence as well as practical and clinical approaches to assessment must be integrated to find the one best synthesis for each person tested.

2. As many subtests as possible should be grouped together to denote a person's areas of strength and weakness. Hypotheses generated from three subtests, for example, are usually more potent than hypotheses generated from two subtests. The more reliable the hypothesized strength or weakness, the more valuable it is for practical recommendations.

3. A corollary of the previous postulate is that subtest-specific hypotheses are usually to be

avoided. A strength or weakness in a single subtest reflects a narrow area of asset or deficit, one that will not likely generalize to the real world. Some subtests have a considerable amount of reliable unique variance (e.g., Digit Symbol) and frequently do not pair up with any other WAIS-R task. In such instances, interpret the specific ability as the person's strength or weakness; however, such interpretations should be used only as a last resort.

4. A person who scores significantly high on a subtest does not have a strength in all of the abilities and traits measured by that subtest; a person scoring very low does not have a weakness in every test component. The person is likely to be especially strong or weak in one or two abilities that the task assesses; the examiner's job is to determine the specific asset or liability by carefully evaluating the person's performance on other WAIS-R tasks that measure similar abilities.

5. The empirical determination of significant strengths and weaknesses is the starting point of test interpretation, not the end point. In essence, the existence of at least one significant fluctuation in the WAIS-R profile gives the examiner his or her "detective's license"—sanction to enter the profile to make sense out of the significant fluctuation. Without significant deviations, differences in the scaled scores are usually best interpreted as due to chance. When one or more scores deviate significantly from the person's mean, the other (nonsignificant) scaled scores become useful interpretive adjuncts for hypothesis testing, depending on whether they are above or below the individual's mean score.

6. When generating hypotheses, examiners should aggregate tasks. Just as subtest-specific interpretations are discouraged, so too are hypotheses that are derived by pitting one subtest against another. Some psychologists (e.g., Sattler, 1988) encourage this

type of interpretation: "High Comprehension and low Arithmetic may suggest that reasoning ability is adequate in social situations but not in situations involving numbers" (p. 176). "High Object Assembly and low Picture Arrangement may suggest that visual inductive reasoning skills are better developed than visual sequencing skills" (p. 178). Most WAIS-R subtests, especially unstable tasks like Object Assembly and Picture Arrangement, are just not reliable enough to permit interpretation of differences between subtests. In fact, the reliability of the difference between these two Performance subtests is only .52 (Feingold, 1984).

Even reliable subtests like Information and Comprehension cannot support the kinds of diagnostic inferences that are sometimes attributed to them: "High Comprehension, especially coupled with lower Information, . . . is characteristic for hysterics. The reverse pattern . . . is generally seen in the obsessive-compulsive" (Allison, Blatt, & Zimet, 1968, p. 25). At the worst, such analyses can promote test abuse because of inadequate validation; at the best, they encourage overinterpretation of chance error. The substantial correlation between Information and Comprehension (.68, on the average) attenuates the reliability of the difference between these two tasks, producing a value of only .58 (Feingold, 1984).

When an approach stressing differences between single subtests is applied, it must be done by an examiner with considerable expertise, usually in neuropsychology, to answer specific referral questions; in addition, differences between the subtests must be substantial (at least 2 standard deviations) to warrant a statement such as Reitan's (1986): "Picture Arrangement seems to be specifically sensitive to the status of the right anterior temporal lobe . . . and Block Design to more posteriorly located right hemispheric disturbances. . . . Localization of involvement within the posterior part of the right cerebral hemisphere is sometimes possible through evaluation of differential scores obtained on Picture Arrangement and Block Design" (p. 21). Yet Reitan (1986) is still cautious, reminding clinicians, "[o]f course, judgment of deficiencies on these tests must be made within the context of other scores earned by the subject on the performance subtests of the Wechsler Scale" (p. 21).

Psychometric considerations should also apply when comparing pairs of tasks. Feingold (1984, Table 1) presents the reliability of the difference between all possible pairs of WAIS-R (and WAIS, and WISC-R) subtests. The values range from .39 to .82 for the WAIS-R, with a median coefficient of .65; two-thirds of the values are below .70. The lowest reliability, ironically, is for a pair of subtests that clinicians commonly evaluate to compare a person's constructional ability with abstract versus meaningful stimuli—Block Design-Object Assembly. If .75 is arbitrarily set as a minimum coefficient to permit meaningful comparisons of one WAIS-R subtest with another, the following pairs may legitimately be compared: Vocabulary-Block Design (.82), Vocabulary-Digit Symbol (.79), Vocabulary-Digit Span (.78), and Information-Block Design (.76). Five other pairs fell just short of the cut-off, producing values of .73–.74: Information-Digit Span, Vocabulary-Arithmetic, Vocabulary-Picture Completion, Block Design-Digit Span, and Information-Digit Symbol.

7. Hypotheses generated from reorganization of a WAIS-R profile are just that—hypotheses. They are not facts but ideas about a person's cognitive and behavioral functioning that require external verification to be optimally meaningful. This type of cross-validation can come from background information (e.g., knowledge about the individual's cultural opportunities, behavioral descriptions by others who know the patient, nature of a head injury), clinical observations of the person's test-taking behavior, and scores on other pertinent subtests. This intelligent, scientific attitude toward hypothesis validation is also characteristic of clinicians such as Allison et al. (1968) and Sattler (1988) who advocate interpretation of differences between specific subtests.

Never infer a behavioral or background hypothesis about a person based simply on a grouping of subtest scores. One should neither hypothesize distractibility because of low scores on Digit Span and Arithmetic nor suggest a poor early environment because of deficits in Information and Vocabulary. Behavioral hypotheses require external support from the clinician's observations of test behavior, from behavioral rating scales filled out by others, and so forth. Background hypotheses demand reliable verification about the individual's environment as a child, adolescent, and adult. The use of other tests and subtests to check out WAIS-R generated hypotheses is dealt with in depth in chapter 16, which discusses a variety of cognitive and achievement tests that are useful WAIS-R supplements.

8. The interpretive guidelines presented in chapters 12–14, both empirical and rational, are not inviolable. They are intended as aids to interpretation and should not serve to cripple clinical inferences from a WAIS-R administration. Rules, no matter what their empirical foundation, cannot replace good judgment and must not supersede clinical, neuropsychological, or psychoeducational insights. Rules are meant to be broken; however, violation of guidelines and principles should occur with full knowledge of "proper" interpretive procedures, not out of ignorance.

Consider the following WAIS-R Verbal profile of age-corrected scaled scores for a depressed female adult patient, Margaret H., who had difficulty sustaining attention and concentration during the evaluation, and manifested a significant V > P discrepancy:

Information:	10
Digit Span:	6
Vocabulary:	9
Arithmetic:	6
Comprehension:	10
Similarities:	9

Using the strict empirical rules from chapter 13, Margaret's Verbal mean equals 8.3, which rounds to 8. None of the six scaled scores deviates significantly from her mean, implying that all fluctuations are due to chance. However, the examiner has the right to ignore the empirical rules for Margaret because of (a) clinical observations of difficulties with attention and concentration, (b) the knowledge that Digit Span and Arithmetic are the two Verbal tasks that are most likely to be affected by such difficulties, and (c) awareness of the bulk of empirical research showing that Digit Span and Arithmetic frequently split off from the other four subtests, the Verbal Comprehension tetrad.

The examiner might compare Margaret's mean scaled score on the four Verbal Comprehension subtests (9.5) to her mean on the two "distractibility" tasks (6.0). The difference of 3.5 points is significant based either on the "rule of thumb" of 3 points or on the value of 2.1 points shown in Table 14.6 for a comparison of composites having an average reliability coefficient of .93 (see Table 14.1). However, even the latter empirical justification is not necessary when an examiner can support a decision with clinical observations, clinical knowledge, and/or awareness of research results.

9. Don't flood case reports with scaled scores and standard scores. The various empirical guidelines for interpretation and formulas for obtaining standard scores for selected clusters should be used by the mathematically comfortable examiner to organize the WAIS-R profile systematically and to generate logical hypotheses. When serving this "tool" function, the standard scores and statistical comparisons bring order to the interpretive process. However, these extra standard scores and statistical contrasts should be included sparingly in psychological or neuropsychological case reports.

The results of the empirical analyses must be included in the report, but the additional statistics are more likely to overwhelm and confuse than to impress and elucidate. WAIS-R examiners are already operating under the handicap of having to report, in some way, two complete sets of scaled scores on the 11 subtests along with three IQs. Those 25 scores, plus a mandatory V–P IQ comparison, do not need augmentation with extra standard scores and statistical contrasts. A few won't hurt (e.g., if a factorial, Bannatyne, or Horn analysis helps clarify the profile, following the empirical procedures in chapter 13), but, in general, the fewer the numbers in a report, the greater the likelihood of crisp communication to the reader.

Interpreting Specific Abilities and Traits

As stated previously, hypothesis generation should focus on generating viable hypotheses about an individual's strengths and weaknesses by combining subtests, two, three, four, and five at a time. Subtest-specific interpretations are the last resort because of their relative instability and limited generalizability. However, sometimes subtest-specific interpretations are warranted because no hypothesis involving an aggregation of two or more subtests makes any sense. To facilitate subtest-specific interpretation of the 11 WAIS-R subtests, Table 14.7 presents a list of the unique abilities and traits that each task is believed to assess. This list has been compiled from the subtest-by-subtest analysis presented in chapter 12. Table 14.7 also offers summary information about each subtest's reliable specific variance and error variance (see chapter 8, pp. 255–257, and Table 8.12), and it indicates whether the amount of specific variance, relative to its error variance, is "ample," "adequate," or "inadequate."

Only Object Assembly has an inadequate rating, suggesting that under ordinary circumstances a significantly high or low score on this subtest should *not* be interpreted in isolation from other WAIS-R tasks. As with any rule, exceptions may be made depending on circumstances. For example, a very low score on Ob-

ject Assembly (perhaps 6 points or more below the mean) might be used to help localize a suspected focal lesion caused by a tumor within the posterior region of the right hemisphere.

Distributions of Subtest Variance

In chapter 12, the amount of variance accounted for by each of the three major factors is indicated for each subtest in the section labeled Empirical Analysis. Table 14.8 summarizes these proportions for all 11 subtests. For each subtest, the total variance equals 100%; based on factor analysis and knowledge of a task's reliability coefficient it is possible to apportion this total variance into components. Table 14.8 shows

TABLE 14.7 Specific abilities and traits associated with each WAIS-R subtest and the subtest specificity of each subtest

WAIS-R Subtest	Specific Abilities and Traits	Subtest Specificity[a]
Verbal		
Information	Range of general factual knowledge	Adequate (20%–11%)
Digit Span	Immediate rote recall Reversibility (Digits Backward)	Ample (45%–17%)
Vocabulary	Language development Word knowledge	Adequate (19%–4%)
Arithmetic	Computational skill	Adequate (ages 16–19) Ample (ages 20–74) (30%–16%)
Comprehension	Demonstration of practical information Evaluation and use of past experience Generalization (proverbs) Knowledge of conventional standards of behavior Social maturity Judgment	Adequate (23%–16%)
Similarities	Logical abstractive (categorical) thinking	Adequate (24%–16%)

(Continues)

TABLE 14.7   (Continued)

WAIS-R Subtest	Specific Abilities and Traits	Subtest Specificity[a]
Performance		
Picture Completion	Visual alertness Visual recognition and identification (long-term visual memory)	Ample (34%–19%)
Picture Arrangement	Anticipation of consequences Planning ability (comprehending and sizing up a total situation) Temporal sequencing and time concepts	Ample (35%–26%)
Block Design	Analysis of whole into component parts Nonverbal concept formation Spatial visualization	Ample (32%–13%)
Object Assembly	Ability to benefit from sensory-motor feedback Anticipation of relationships among parts	Inadequate (23%–32%)
Digit Symbol	Ability to follow directions Clerical speed and accuracy Paper-and-pencil skill Psychomotor speed Visual short-term memory	Ample (48%–18%)

[a]The percentages in parentheses indicate the percentage of reliable unique variance followed by the percentage of error variance. Values are the averages for the total WAIS-R standardization sample (ages 16–74). See chapter 8 for a discussion of Ample, Adequate, and Inadequate subtest specificities and a more thorough subtest-by-subtest treatment (Table 8.12).

the percentage of variance for each of the 11 WAIS-R subtests that is accounted for by the Verbal Comprehension factor, Perceptual Organization factor, and Freedom from Distractibility factor; by abilities other than these three factors; and by error. The methodology involved and the relationship of subtest specificity to the variance accounted for by abilities other than the three factors has been explained in chapter 12 (pp. 391–393).

Table 14.8 helps examiners set expectations for what each subtest is most likely to measure for an individual. All four Verbal Comprehension subtests are predominantly measures of that factor, i.e., of what Wechsler conceived of as verbal intelligence. About half to two-thirds of

TABLE 14.8 Proportions of the variance of each subtest attributed to each of the three factors, to other abilities, and to error (ages 16–74)

WAIS-R Subtest	PERCENTAGE OF TOTAL VARIANCE ATTRIBUTED TO:				
	Verbal Comprehension	Perceptual Organization	Freedom from Distractibility	Other Abilities	Error
Verbal Comprehension					
Information	56	7	9	17	11
Vocabulary	66	7	12	11	04
Comprehension	50	9	7	18	16
Similarities	45	13	7	19	16
Perceptual Organization					
Picture Completion	19	31	3	28	19
Block Design	7	48	11	21	13
Object Assembly	4	53	3	8	32
Freedom from Distractibility					
Digit Span	9	5	41	28	17
Arithmetic	19	12	30	23	16
Not Consistently Associated With Any Factor					
Picture Arrangement	18	18	5	33	26
Digit Symbol	10	14	13	45	18

each of these tasks' total variance is accounted for by the Verbal Comprehension factor. Block Design and Object Assembly each bear a similar overlap with the Perceptual Organization factor, and are therefore first and foremost measures of the essence of Wechsler's conception of nonverbal intelligence. Two other WAIS-R subtests, Digit Span and Arithmetic, are also primarily related to a factor, but one that Wechsler did not hypothesize: the third, smaller, dimension that is associated with distractibility, number ability, attention-concentration, sequential ability, anxiety, auditory memory, and mental alertness. In essence, Digit Span and Arithmetic are most likely to be associated with *each other,* to pair up and form a small but psychologically meaningful factor that is separate from

the global constructs of verbal and nonverbal intelligence.

Of the three remaining WAIS-R subtests, Picture Completion is about equally associated with Perceptual Organization and abilities other than the three factors, and Picture Arrangement and Digit Symbol are not closely related to any of the three factors. The latter two tasks might be expected, on a probability basis, to split off from the rest of the Performance Scale. They might cluster together, since they are the only nonverbal subtests to measure Guilford's operation of convergent-production, or to have strong visual-sequential (rather than visual-spatial) components. They might just as easily split apart from each other and, perhaps, assess a subtest-specific ability. Picture Arrangement and Digit Symbol correlate very poorly with each other (.39) and modestly with other subtests, and each has a large proportion of reliable unique variance.

Consequently, examiners should begin profile attack with certain anticipations: The four Verbal Comprehension subtests are most likely to cluster together as a solid unit; Block Design and Object Assembly—either with or without their frequent companion, Picture Completion—are likely to form the crux of a small but reliable measure of the person's nonverbal intelligence; Arithmetic and Digit Span will probably pair off as a measure of either a behavior or ability that was not in Wechsler's game plan; and Picture Arrangement, Digit Symbol, and perhaps Picture Completion are the tasks most likely to deviate significantly from the Performance or Full Scale mean. The latter three subtests might pair up with each other or with another WAIS-R subtest, or be interpreted as a unique area of strength or weakness.

A Sequential Step-by-Step Approach to Hypothesis Generation

Hypothesis generation can be performed in a linear, sequential, "left-brained," scientific manner, analogous to the step-by-step technique that I have advocated for the WISC-R (Kaufman, 1979b) and K-ABC (Kaufman & Kaufman, 1983b); this section details such an approach. I will illustrate this sequential method using the WAIS-R age-corrected scaled score profile of Ben G., the 63-year-old white male with right hemisphere brain damage following a stroke who was used for illustrative purposes in chapter 13. This high school graduate, a successful business executive prior to his cerebrovascular accident, was described by his examiner as attentive, surprisingly nondistractible, highly verbal and articulate, and possessing a good sense of humor. He displayed poor frustration tol-

erance, particularly on Block Design and Object Assembly, but the examiner did not believe that his frustration with his own lack of ability contributed to his low scores on several Performance subtests. His fine-motor coordination was poor, contributing both to his frustration and his low scores on timed motor tasks. He earned a WAIS-R V-IQ of 112, P-IQ of 77, and FS-IQ of 95; the 35-point V > P discrepancy is both significant and highly unusual in the normal population.

Step 1. Determine Significant Subtest Strengths and Weaknesses

This first step is the empirical procedure for determining significant deviations from the person's own mean, as described in chapter 13. The appropriate methodology has already been applied to Ben's WAIS-R profile; his age-corrected scaled scores, with strengths and weaknesses indicated, are repeated here for convenience.

Verbal	
Information	11
Digit Span	8—W
Vocabulary	16—S
Arithmetic	10
Comprehension	11
Similarities	15—S
Verbal mean = 12	

Performance	
Picture Completion	8
Picture Arrangement	9—S
Block Design	5
Object Assembly	6
Digit Symbol	2—W
Performance mean = 6	

Thus, Ben displayed five significant profile fluctuations: three strengths (Vocabulary, Similarities, Picture Arrangement) and two weaknesses (Digit Span, Digit Symbol). The goal of the remainder of hypothesis generation is to understand *exactly* where Ben's areas of asset and deficit lie. What abilities or traits can best explain his exceptional success in Vocabulary and Similarities or his deficiencies in Digit Span and Digit Symbol? What integrity enabled him to score near-average in Picture Arrangement (and in Picture Completion, a "near-strength"), despite his Borderline Performance IQ?

Step 2. Select One Significant Subtest (S or W) for Study

Select any one significant strength or weakness in the person's subtest profile for in-depth evaluation. Locate this subtest in Tables 14.1 to 14.4 and write down all shared abilities (and influences affecting test performance) that pertain to this subtest.

For Ben, I arbitrarily selected Vocabulary, one of his Verbal strengths. All abilities and "influences" that include Vocabulary, taken from Tables 14.1, 14.3, and 14.4, appear in Table 14.9. (Abbreviations of all subtests that measure a given "shared" ability, or are subject to a particular influence, are shown.)

Guidelines for Accepting and Rejecting Potential Hypotheses

In order to consider any particular ability or influence an area of strength, it is desirable for the person to have a significant strength in at least one of the subtests composing the composite, and for scores on all other component tasks to be above the person's mean (the Verbal or Performance mean, as relevant, for individuals with a significant V–P discrepancy; the Full Scale mean for those with V-IQ approximately equal to P-IQ).

If a person scores *below* his or her mean score on a subtest included in a cluster, that cluster is ordinarily not an area of strength. *Exception:* If a composite comprises five or more subtests (e.g., Guilford's cognition and semantic content composites shown in Table 14.9), it is

permissible for one task to be below the mean (even significantly below).

If a person scores *precisely at his or her mean* on any subtests included in a cluster, *do not reject* that cluster as a possible area of strength. *Exceptions:* For composites composed of two subtests, the person must score above his or her mean on both tasks (and significantly high on one); for composites composed of three subtests, no more than one scaled score should equal the person's mean.

The interpretation of *weaknesses* follows the identical logic and rules described above for strengths. Instead of scoring above the mean on relevant subtests, to depict areas of strength, individuals must score *below* the mean, to depict areas of weakness. All rules, and exceptions to these rules, indicated previously for strengths (e.g., the treatment of scores equal to the mean), apply as well for weaknesses.

Hypotheses based on the *influences* affecting test performance (listed in Table 14.4) do not demand the rigor necessary for hypotheses involving *abilities*. These lists are composed of the subtests most likely to be affected by each behavioral or background influence. However, there is no guarantee that a person who has completed an advanced graduate degree will do well in all WAIS-R subtests affected by school learning (the person may have a math block, for example). Similarly, "negative" individuals may display this negativism on only one or two of the four subtests that are most affected by this behavior; or they may be negative on several subtests not listed in Table 14.4. The major reasons for accepting or rejecting any hypotheses regarding influences are clinical observations of test behavior and reliable knowledge about a person's background or behavioral tendencies.

Some of these rules for hypothesis generation are different from the more rigid rules for the WISC-R (Kaufman, 1979b) and K-ABC (Kaufman & Kaufman, 1983b). However, the modifications indicated here regarding scores equal to the mean, clusters with five or more subtests,

TABLE 14.9 Shared abilities and influences related to Ben G.'s significant strength in Vocabulary

					Subtest						
	I	DSp	V	A	C	S	PC	PA	BD	OA	DSy
Abilities (Tables 14.1 and 14.3)											
Verbal Comprehension (factor analysis)	I		V		C	S					
Verbal Conceptualization (Bannatyne)	I		V		C	S					
Acquired Knowledge (Bannatyne)	I		V	A		S					
Crystallized intelligence (Horn)	I		V		C	S					
Auditory-vocal channel (Osgood)	I	DSp	V	A	C	S					
Verbal concept formation (Rapaport)	I		V			S					
Memory (Rapaport)	I		V								
Semantic cognition (Guilford)	I		V	A	C	S					
Fund of information	I		V								
Handling abstract verbal concepts	I		V			S					
Long-term memory	I		V	A							
Verbal expression			V		C	S					
Concept formation (Rapaport)			V			S			BD		
General ability (Dean)	I		V	A	C	S	PC		BD		
Cognition (Guilford)			V	A	C	S	PC		BD	OA	
Semantic content (Guilford)	I		V	A	C	S		PA			
Learning ability			V								DSy
Influences (Table 14.4)											
Cultural opportunities	I		V		C	S		PA			
Foreign language background	I		V								
Intellectual curiosity and striving	I		V								
Interests	I		V			S					
Outside reading	I		V			S					
Richness of early environment	I		V								
School learning	I		V	A							

and different approaches for influences versus abilities represent my current thinking about profile interpretation on *any* multiscore test battery.

Verbal Strengths in Ben's Profile

Note in Ben G.'s subtest profile that only one other Verbal subtest yielded an age-corrected scaled score above his Verbal mean of 12: the 15 he earned in Similarities, also a significant strength. Consequently, most of the composites listed in Table 14.9 must be rejected as areas of possible strength for Ben due to the presence of one or more scaled scores below his Verbal mean.

The only hypotheses that cannot be immediately rejected because of below average performance on Information, Arithmetic, and Comprehension are listed in Table 14.10.

Of these four, two must be rejected because of limited success on Performance subtests: concept formation (Ben scored below his Performance mean of 6 on Block Design) and learning ability (Ben had a significant weakness in Digit Symbol). Consequently, Ben's area of strength concerns the abilities measured by *both* of his high Verbal scaled scores, obtained on Vocabulary and Similarities. He is strong in Rapaport's *verbal concept formation* (his ability to organize memories and experiences) and in *ability to deal with abstract verbal (but not nonverbal) concepts.*

By uniting his strong performance in two Verbal subtests, even though subsequent analysis did not permit the aggregation of any other WAIS-R tasks, one comes to a more powerful and useful conclusion about Ben's area of asset (the generalized ability to deal with verbal concepts) than is possible by considering the unique abilities measured by each subtest in isolation.

Step 3. Follow the Same Procedures for Other S's and W's

The same type of detective work should be applied to the other significant strengths and weaknesses in Ben's profile. The Vocabulary analysis has mostly accounted for Similarities. The only abilities and influences to investigate regarding Similarities are the ones that exclude Vocabulary; see Table 14.11.

Of these eight hypotheses, the three influences are immediately eliminated as areas of strength: He was not negative; overly concrete thinking pertains only to weaknesses, not strengths; and flexibility is ruled out by his significant weakness in Digit Span. Verbal reasoning is ruled out by his below-the-mean score on Comprehension; his Comprehension score, coupled with a similarly low score on Arithmetic, eliminates a hypothesis of good reasoning ability. Similarly, the hypothesis of strong fluid intelligence is ruled out by his weakness in Digit Span and his scaled score of 5 (below his Performance mean of 6) on Block Design. For reasoning and fluid intelligence (both defined by five or more subtests), two low scores were required to reject the hypotheses.

Although Ben does not have a strength in abstract thought (because of his low Block De-

TABLE 14.10 Ben G.: Possible strengths based on peaks and valleys in his Verbal profile

	Subtest			
Verbal concept formation (Rapaport)	V	S		
Handling abstract verbal concepts	V	S		
Concept formation (Rapaport)	V	S	BD	
Learning ability	V			DSy

TABLE 14.11   Additional shared abilities and influences related to Ben G.'s significant strength in similarities

					Subtest			
Abilities (Tables 14.1 and 14.3)								
Verbal reasoning			C	S				
Fluid intelligence (Horn)	DSp			S	PC	PA	BD	OA
Abstract thought (Dean)				S			BD	
Distinguishing essential from nonessential detail				S	PC	PA		
Reasoning		A	C	S		PA		OA
Influences (Table 14.4)								
Flexibility	DSp			S				OA
Negativism	DSp		C	S	PC			
Overly concrete thinking			C	S				

sign), the hypothesis of *distinguishing essential from nonessential detail* is viable; his significant strength in Similarities is joined by scores of 8 to 9 on the other two tasks (both above Ben's Performance mean of 6).

Verbal Weaknesses in Ben's Profile

Next, consider Ben's significant Verbal weakness, an 8 in Digit Span. Table 14.12 lists some hypotheses to consider as areas of potential weakness. I have eliminated from the list any clusters that include Vocabulary or Similarities (unless they are composed of five or more subtests) because these are his areas of *strength*.

Of this list, only three hypotheses can be eliminated by the step-wise procedure: Ben does not have a weakness in fluid intelligence because of above average scaled scores on Similarities, Picture Completion, and Picture Arrangement; and he is not weak in Osgood's automatic level of organization, or in Rapaport's attention-concentration, because his score of 8 on Picture Completion is above his Performance mean. (I have listed attention-concentration in Table 14.3 as an "ability" because in Rapaport's model the

behaviors he refers to as orienting responses seem to bridge the gap between emotional attitude and cognitive aptitude.)

All of the remaining hypotheses are viable. The Digit Span-Arithmetic dyad represents an area of weakness because he scored below his Verbal mean in Arithmetic. So do the triads that add Digit Symbol or Information to the distractibility dyad because Ben evidenced a significant weakness in Digit Symbol and below-the-mean performance in Information. He even revealed a significant ACID profile, the characteristic pattern associated with learning disabilities. Consequently, the examiner's task is to select from among all of the various interpretations given to these combinations of subtests to identify the hypotheses that best apply to Ben.

All of the influences can be eliminated quickly. He demonstrated a good attention span and no apparent distractibility during the evaluation. Despite the presence of a significant ACID profile, any suggestion of minimal brain dysfunction and learning problems for an elderly person whose V–P profile reflects his known, massive right hemisphere damage is irrelevant.

TABLE 14.12 Shared abilities and influences related to Ben G.'s significant weakness in Digit Span

				Subtest					
Abilities (Tables 14.1 and 14.3)									
Freedom from Distractibility (factor analysis)		DSp	A						
Auditory memory (Dean)		DSp	A						
Memory (Guilford)	I	DSp	A						
Retention (Horn)	I	DSp	A						
Symbolic memory (Guilford)		DSp	A						
Auditory sequencing		DSp	A						
Mental alertness		DSp	A						
Sequential (Bannatyne)		DSp	A						Dsy
Fluid intelligence (Horn)		DSp		S	PC	PA	BD	OA	
Automatic level of organization (Osgood)		DSp			PC				DSy
Attention-concentration (Rapaport)		DSp	A		PC				DSy
Symbolic content (Guilford)		DSp	A						Dsy
Encoding information for further processing		DSp	A						DSy
Facility with numbers		DSp	A						DSy
Sequential processing		DSp	A						DSy
Influences (Table 14.4)									
Anxiety		DSp	A						DSy
Attention span		DSp	A						
Distractibility		DSp	A						DSy
Learning disabilities ("ACID")	I	DSp	A						DSy

All hypotheses pertaining to the Digit Span-Arithmetic dyad can likewise be ignored. When more generalized hypotheses emerge involving a dyad coupled with a third subtest (in this case either Digit Symbol or Information), the two-subtest hypotheses are too limited in scope to be of much value. Thus, Ben's areas of weakness may be associated with a memory deficit (whether looked at from Guilford's or Horn's perspective), a sequencing problem (from Bannatyne's or a cognitive-processing approach), or a difficulty in handling numbers and symbols. He may also have difficulty encoding information in storage for further processing. These competing, but not necessarily mutually exclusive, hypotheses are dealt with in Step 4 of the interpretive process.

Weaknesses in Ben's Performance Profile

On the Performance Scale, Ben's significant weakness in Digit Symbol is already included in several hypotheses, but this task must now be evaluated for additional hypotheses that are separate from Digit Span and Arithmetic. Table 14.13 lists Ben G.'s potential weaknesses, excluding ones that are immediately eliminated because of strengths in Vocabulary or Similarities.

Ben's significant strength in Picture Arrangement, and/or his relatively good score in Picture Completion, rule out the following potential areas of weakness: visual-motor channel of communication, evaluation, visual memory, convergent-production, visual sequencing, concentration, and working under time pressure. Visual-motor speed and persistence are eliminated because Ben scored at his Performance mean of 6 on Object Assembly. (For dyads, both scaled scores must be above the mean.) In fact, Ben did lack persistence when facing frustration, but the examiner believed that this was a consequence of his relatively weak performance on several visual-motor tasks, not a cause of it.

Ben scored below his Performance mean on Block Design, suggesting the following areas as possible cognitive weaknesses: visual perception/processing of abstract stimuli and reproduction of models. Visual-motor coordination is also a potential weakness for Ben since he scored precisely at his Performance mean of 6 on Object Assembly. However, the motor triad does not trivialize eliminate the two hypotheses involving just Digit Symbol and Block Design because each hypothesis may generalize to the Verbal Scale; Ben's difficulty with models might relate to a verbal memory problem, and his low scores on tasks using abstract stimuli may reflect a more generalized deficiency with symbols, including numbers.

Strengths in Ben's Performance Profile

The only remaining significantly deviating subtest not yet treated is Ben's relative strength

TABLE 14.13   Additional shared abilities and influences related to Ben G.'s significant weakness in Digit Symbol

	Subtest					
Abilities (Tables 14.2 and 14.3)						
Visual-motor channel (Osgood)		PC	PA	BD	OA	DSy
Visual-motor coordination (Rapaport)				BD	OA	DSy
Visual memory (Dean)		PC				DSy
Visual-motor speed (Dean)					OA	DSy
Convergent-production (Guilford)			PA			DSy
Reproduction of models				BD		DSy
Visual perception/processing of abstract stimuli				BD		DSy
Visual sequencing			PA			DSy
Evaluation (Guilford)	C	PC	PA	BD	OA	DSy
Influences (Table 14.4)						
Concentration	A	PC				DSy
Persistence					OA	DSy
Working under time pressure	A	PC	PA	BD	OA	DSy

on Picture Arrangement. Table 14.14 lists the hypotheses involving this subtest, excluding the ones that have previously been accepted or rejected.

All but two of the hypothesized strengths listed in Table 14.14 must be ruled out. The two viable hypotheses are visual organization (without essential motor activity) and visual perception/processing of meaningful stimuli (people and things). The others are eliminated either because of his below-the-relevant-mean performance on Block Design or Comprehension or because of his score of 6 on Object Assembly.

Step 4. Integrate Hypotheses With Behaviors and Background Knowledge

The hypothesis generation procedures must now be integrated. The potential strengths and weaknesses need to be related to each other to detect consistencies, and they have to be juxtaposed with information known or observed regarding the person tested. To some extent, this integration has already been done. Based on observations of Ben's test behaviors, a variety of influences (e.g., anxiety, distractibility) have been ruled out as explanations of Ben's low scores.

Potential Areas of Asset and Liability

The previous detective work has uncovered the following viable hypotheses.

POSSIBLE STRENGTHS	POSSIBLE WEAKNESSES
1. Visual organization	1. Visual-motor coordination
2. Visual-perception/processing of meaningful stimuli	2. Visual-perception/processing of abstract stimuli
3. Verbal concept formation (handling abstract verbal concepts)	3. Reproduction of models
4. Distinguishing essential from nonessential details	4. Memory (retention)
	5. Sequencing (sequential processing)
	6. Symbolic content (number facility)
	7. Encoding information for further processing

TABLE 14.14 Shared abilities related to Ben G.'s significant strength in Picture Arrangement

		Subtest		
Abilities (Tables 14.2 and 14.3)				
Anticipation (Rapaport)			PA	OA
Visual organization (Rapaport)		PC	PA	
Common sense (cause-effect)	C		PA	
Nonverbal reasoning			PA	OA
Synthesis			PA	BD	OA
Visual perception/processing of meaningful stimuli		PC	PA	
Social comprehension (Dean)	C		PA	

Rapaport's Model

Ben was observed to have poor motor coordination. His relatively low scores on the three nonverbal tasks requiring good coordination is in agreement with the behavioral observation, and the hypothesis is accepted. His success on the two Performance subtests that do not have essential motor activity indicates that he can be relatively successful within the visual-motor channel when he can bypass coordination in favor of thinking. Consequently, the Rapaport model provides a good interpretation of the fluctuations in Ben's Performance profile. Despite his massively lowered P-IQ, presumably due to the stroke he suffered, Ben has an integrity in visual organization coupled with a deficiency in visual-motor coordination.

Abstract Versus Meaningful Stimuli

Ben's near-average scores in Picture Completion and Picture Arrangement were probably influenced as well by a few other variables: He does seem to display a strength in distinguishing essential from nonessential details, and he apparently does differ in his ability to process meaningful versus abstract stimuli. His perception of abstract stimuli is intact. This finding was verified by testing the limits on Block Design; he was consistently able to recognize when his productions were incorrect and to select the correct "match" for an abstract design from an array of choices. However, he has difficulty processing abstract stimuli, whether they are simple designs (Digit Symbol), complex designs (Block Design), or numbers (Digit Symbol, Digit Span, Arithmetic).

Numerical Stimuli, Memory, and Sequential Ability

Ben's problems in manipulating numbers were evident in comparing his forward and backward spans in Digit Span. He was able to repeat 7 digits forward, but only 2 backward, a noteworthy differential. His normal forward span, along with his relative strength in Picture Ar-

rangement, indicates that hypotheses involving weak sequencing ability are less tenable. His short-term auditory memory seems intact, although his verbal concept formation still far outstrips his verbal memory.

During Digit Symbol, Ben was observed constantly referring to the matched pairs of digits and symbols, sometimes twice before copying a single symbol. This observation suggests a problem with short-term visual memory, a deficiency that might be exacerbated by the abstract and symbolic nature of the stimuli and by difficulty in encoding information for further processing. His virtual lack of ability to reverse digits is also consistent with these suggested deficiencies.

Differences in the cognitive requirements for Digits Forward and Digits Backward have been widely chronicled (Banken, 1985; Griffin & Heffernan, 1983), with the reversal of digits requiring more complex and higher level mental processing (Jensen & Figueroa, 1975) and demonstrating greater sensitivity to brain dysfunction (Milberg, Hebben, & Kaplan, 1986). Even severe amnesia patients may evidence normal or above average forward spans (Butters & Cermak, 1980). Ben's failure to reverse digits, despite an excellent forward span, conforms to some research findings with patients having right brain damage (Costa, 1975; Weinberg, Diller, Gerstman, & Schulman, 1972), although the hypothesized spatial component associated with digit reversal is equivocal (Black & Strub, 1978; Richardson, 1977).

Black (1986a), in an investigation of 162 adult brain-damaged patients (47 right-lesion, 40 left-lesion, 75 bilateral, averaging about 40 years of age and a little more than 12 years of education), found that both forward and backward digit repetition was "significantly impaired in patients with brain damage . . . [especially] for those patients with left lesions" (pp. 778–779). Subsequent analysis, however, showed that regardless of localization, patients with a visual spatial deficit (like Ben) had a significant depression in "[b]ackward, but not forward, digit repetition" (Black, 1986a, p. 779). Further, although the difference did not reach significance, the occurrence of large differences in favor of forward span over backward span (3 or more digits) was relatively common for brain-damaged patients evidencing visual spatial dysfunction (Black, 1986a).

Verbal Compensation of Performance Deficit

One possible explanation for Ben's relatively high scores on Picture Completion and Picture Arrangement that is not evident from the tables of shared abilities concerns the fact that these are the two nonverbal tasks that most benefit from verbalization and verbal mediation. Ben's High Average V-IQ makes this a viable explanation. However, he was not observed to verbalize spontaneously during any Performance subtest (except to curse loudly when faced with failure), and he responded to nearly all Picture Completion items by pointing to the missing part or saying a crisp "don't know."

Overview of Ben's Strengths and Weaknesses

Overall, Ben has excellent verbal intelligence, highlighted by a special strength in handling abstract verbal concepts. This asset in dealing with abstract concepts does not generalize to abstract stimuli; he has a deficiency in processing abstract and symbolic stimuli (designs, numbers), compared to a relative strength in processing meaningful stimuli (people, things). Ben does poorly on mental tasks that depend on much visual-motor coordination, but performs considerably better within the visual-motor channel when coordination is deemphasized or eliminated. His good visual organization ability is facilitated by his relative ease at distinguishing essential from nonessential detail. His inability to process abstract and numerical stimuli may be due, in part, to great difficulty in encoding information for further processing and in reproducing a visual model,

both of which relate to a more generalized memory problem.

Ben's profile, although perhaps best interpreted from Rapaport's model, still lends itself to subsequent analysis by the step-by-step Bannatyne approach described in chapter 13 (in fact, his profile was subjected to this analysis; see pp. 435–437). His strength in verbal concept formation or Verbal Conceptualization relates to Bannatyne's Category System, as does his weakness on the Digit Span-Arithmetic-Digit Symbol triad. The fact that a sequential interpretation of this triad was rejected in favor of a deficiency in symbolic content is irrelevant. One does not have to ascribe to Bannatyne's interpretations of his categories in order to apply his system meaningfully.

Step 5. If No Viable Hypotheses Emerge, Interpret Unique Skills

When the preceding steps yield no fruitful hypotheses involving two or more subtests, interpret specific abilities measured by significant strengths and weaknesses; use Table 14.7 as an interpretive guide. Sometimes one or two significantly deviating subtests will be left out of the more global hypotheses that are formulated; in that case, interpret these unique strengths or weaknesses in conjunction with the more generalizable explanations of the person's WAIS-R profile.

A SIMULTANEOUS APPROACH TO HYPOTHESIS GENERATION

My work with the K-ABC regarding its development and application has made me sensitive to individual differences in the way children or adults approach the same problem. For some people, the sequential, rule-governed methodology described previously conforms well to their typical processing approach; for others, it is a nightmare. Consequently, I am including an alternative method of hypothesis generation, one that might be preferable to individuals who prefer to rely more on simultaneous, holistic ("right-brained") problem-solving strategies. This approach also has sequential components, but it emphasizes configurations of subtests and the simultaneous treatment of two or three tasks at a time while deemphasizing mathematical computations and comparisons. Examiners who wish to apply mathematical rigor to the simultaneous methodology may do so, but it is optional. Even the empirical determination of significant strengths and weaknesses in the subtest profile, using the simple ± 3 method, is optional.

Only one statistical application is mandatory: *After* the examiner reaches conclusions about contrasting strengths and weaknesses (e.g., high on Verbal Comprehension—low on distractibility; high on visual-sequential—low on visual-spatial), *determine whether the difference is statistically significant.* The easiest way to make this comparison is to average the scaled scores for the subtests constituting the strength, and also average the scores for the subtests composing the weakness. If they differ by 3 points or more (using the rule of thumb given on p. 481), the hypothesis is confirmed. Alternatively, use the more specific values for determining significant differences between clusters given in Table 14.6.

For examiners who wish to compute standard scores for some clusters, I have provided Table 14.15. This table gives formulas for various combinations of WAIS-R subtests that are discussed in the following sections on configurations, and should be used in conjunction with the similar formulas provided in chapter 13 (Table 13.6) for the factor score, Bannatyne, and Horn categories. Examiners who want to determine whether standard scores on two related WAIS-R clusters are significantly different should consult Table 14.6; the average reliability of each pertinent pair of clusters is presented

in Table 14.15 to facilitate its joint use with Table 14.6. Those examiners who wish to avoid mathematics as much as possible can simply ignore these tables of formulas and significant differences and rely solely on the simple rule of thumb for assessing significant assets and deficits.

Basically, examiners who interpret the WAIS-R in a simultaneous, holistic fashion will focus on *configurations* among the subtests, usually within each separate scale. They will first look for each scale to split into two recognizable halves; they will then see whether the profile reveals a split between pairs of subtests that differ in an important way (e.g., the distinction evident in Ben's profile between abstract and meaningful stimuli); finally, if necessary, they will look for the coupling of subtests that often go together (e.g., the social comprehension dyad of Comprehension and Picture Arrangement).

The next several sections discuss common configurations of subtests within the Verbal and Performance Scales and a variety of WAIS-R dyads spanning both scales that frequently "pair up" in an individual's profile. The configurations indicated here are similar to the ones discussed for the WISC-R (Kaufman, 1979b, Chapter 5).

Common Configurations of the WAIS-R Verbal Scale

Several global configurations involving five or all six WAIS-R Verbal subtests occur frequently enough to warrant their internalization by examiners, especially those who prefer a holistic hypothesis generation strategy: Factor I versus Factor III; memory versus conceptualization; the amount of verbal expression required for successful performance; and fluid versus crystallized intelligence.

Factor I Versus Factor III

The factor-analytic division, which defines the pattern of scores earned by Nicole H. in the

TABLE 14.15 Formulas for converting selected composites of WAIS-R subtests to standard scores having a mean of 100 and *SD* of 15

Composite[a]	Formula	Component Subtests
Verbal Configurations		
Memory/Little verbal expression	$2.0\ X_{ss} + 40$	I + DSp + A
Conceptualization/Much verbal expression (mean reliability = .92/.94)	$1.9\ X_{ss} + 43$	V + C + S
Performance Configurations		
Visual organization	$2.9\ X_{ss} + 42$	PC + PA
Visual-motor coordination (mean reliability = .82/.88)	$2.0\ X_{ss} + 40$	BD + OA + DSy
Visual perception/processing of abstract stimuli	$2.9\ X_{ss} + 42$	BD + DSy
Visual perception/processing of meaningful stimuli (mean reliability = .82/.88)	$2.9\ X_{ss} + 42$	PC + PA
Nonverbal reasoning	$3.0\ X_{ss} + 40$	PA + OA
Reproduction of models (mean reliability = .79/.85)	$2.9\ X_{ss} + 42$	BD + DSy
Visual-Spatial (Simultaneous)	$2.0\ X_{ss} + 40$	PC + BD + OA
Visual-Sequential (mean reliability = .82/.88)	$3.0\ X_{ss} + 40$	PA + DSy
Visual closure	$2.9\ X_{ss} + 42$	PC + OA
Visual sequencing (mean reliability = .76/.85)	$3.0\ X_{ss} + 40$	PA + DSy
Visual memory	$3.0\ X_{ss} + 40$	PC + DSy
Synthesis (mean reliability = .82/.88)	$2.0\ X_{ss} + 40$	PA + BD + OA
Both Scales		
Social comprehension	$2.9\ X_{ss} + 42$	C + PA
Abstract thought (mean reliability = .85/.88)	$2.9\ X_{ss} + 42$	S + BD
Fund of information	$2.6\ X_{ss} + 48$	I + V
Trial-and-error learning (mean reliability = .90/.91)	$2.8\ X_{ss} + 44$	BD + OA
Verbal reasoning	$2.7\ X_{ss} + 46$	C + S
Nonverbal reasoning (mean reliability = .80/.86)	$3.0\ X_{ss} + 40$	PA + OA

(Continues)

TABLE 14.15   (Continued)

Composite[a]	Formula	Component Subtests
Auditory memory	$2.8\ X_{ss} + 44$	DSp + A
Visual memory		
(mean reliability = .81/.89)	$3.0\ X_{ss} + 40$	PC + DSy
Auditory memory	$2.8\ X_{ss} + 44$	DSp + A
Reproduction of models		
(mean reliability = .84/.90)	$2.9\ X_{ss} + 42$	BD + DSy
Auditory sequencing	$2.8\ X_{ss} + 44$	DSp + A
Visual sequencing		
(mean reliability = .79/.88)	$3.0\ X_{ss} + 40$	PA + DSy

[a]Mean reliability coefficients for the two preceding clusters are shown in parentheses. The first value is the mean for adolescents (ages 16–19); the second value is the mean for adults (ages 20–74).

NOTE: X_{ss} equals the sum of a person's age-corrected scaled scores on each subtest included in a composite. Substitute the relevant sum into the formula to compute the person's standard score (mean = 100, SD = 15). Table 13.6 provides formulas for factor scores and for composites based on Bannatyne's and Horn's interpretive systems.

case report at the end of this chapter, probably occurs more often than any other within WAIS-R Verbal or Performance profiles. A quick glance at the Verbal subtests commonly indicates that an individual's subtest fluctuations conform precisely to the results of countless factor structures: The four so-called Verbal Comprehension subtests (Information, Vocabulary, Comprehension, Similarities) cluster together, with the person performing either substantially higher or lower on the Freedom from Distractibility dyad of Digit Span and Arithmetic. Ideally, the person's age-corrected scaled scores on Digit Span and Arithmetic will *both* be above (or below) all four Verbal Comprehension scores to confirm a Factor I–Factor III split in the Verbal profile. However, it is still the *difference* between the factor scores that determines the meaningfulness of the dichotomization. When this difference is significant, examiners who are not offended by sequential strategies may wish to apply the systematic

assessment of strengths and weaknesses on the three WAIS-R factors detailed in chapter 13.

Sometimes Information joins the distractibility dyad in splitting off from the rest of the Verbal Scale. When this division of the six Verbal subtests into two halves occurs, the factor-related split must yield to a different interpretation: either the amount of verbal expression required for optimal task performance (pp. 503–505) or memory versus conceptualization (pp. 502–503).

When a bonafide Factor I–Factor III split occurs, the person's scaled score on Digit Symbol should immediately be related to his or her level of performance on the Factor III dyad. Is the Digit Symbol score fairly consistent in magnitude to the depressed or elevated scores on Digit Span and Arithmetic? If so, that finding further reinforces the importance of the Freedom from Distractibility factor for understanding the profile fluctuations. Even though Digit Symbol is not so closely associated with the

WAIS-R distractibility triad that it merits automatic inclusion on the dimension, there is still some factor-analytic support for its relationship, especially for adolescents and adults ages 20–54 (see chapter 8). Yet, whether Factor III is composed of just two subtests or the familiar WISC-R triad is of less concern than the interpretation given to the dimension. As evident by scanning Tables 14.1, 14.3, and 14.4, an impressive variety of interpretations may be assigned to a strength or weakness on the distractibility dyad or triad. The examiner's task is to narrow down the hypotheses to the degree possible.

This task was illustrated earlier for Ben G. to assess whether his Factor III weakness was in sequencing, memory, or number ability. Other illustrations are elaborated elsewhere (Kaufman, 1979b, chapter 3). The main points to consider are these: Is there crisp behavioral support, or reliable clinical reports, to justify distractibility, anxiety, or poor attention span as an explanation of poor performance? If memory is a plausible explanation of the dimension, is there evidence to support a strength (no longer having to check the "code" halfway through Digit Symbol) or weakness (needing frequent repetition of questions)? Is a sequencing problem evident on Picture Arrangement, and are any referral problems consistent with a sequential deficit ("Has difficulty following directions")? Is a strength or weakness in number ability consistent with background information about the person (works as an accountant; had a math block in school)?

Arithmetic, Digit Span, and sometimes Digit Symbol may be interpreted from the factor-analytic model (Freedom from Distractibility), Bannatyne's approach (Sequencing Ability), the K-ABC neuropsychological model (Sequential Processing), a Jensen (1982) Level I–Level II theory (Memory) or a Guilford structure-of-intellect framework (Symbolic Content). The theory doesn't matter; neither does the name given to the dyad or triad by the theorists. Only the *interpretation* of the factor for a given individual is of concern, and that task depends entirely on the clinician's acumen as an observer of behavior and integrator of data from numerous sources.

Scores on the WAIS Verbal Comprehension subtests have been shown to correlate significantly and occasionally substantially with the personality trait Temperamental Independence, a second-order factor on the 16 PF scale. Relationships in the .40s were obtained for middle-aged men and women with High Average IQs (Turner, Willerman, & Horn, 1976), while significant correlations of about .25–.30 were obtained for males and females aged 16 to 61 (median age = 29) with a mean FS-IQ of 94 (Bolton, 1980). Those with higher abilities on the Verbal Comprehension factor thus tend to be characterized by temperamental independence: "general criticalness, low rigidity, self-assurance, and self-control" (Turner et al., 1976, p. 349).

Low scores on both Factor I and Factor III are associated with damage lateralized to the left hemisphere, although there is some evidence that the distractibility dyad and triad are even more depressed than Verbal Comprehension for these patients (see chapter 11). Patients with Huntington's disease perform especially poorly on Arithmetic, Digit Span, Digit Symbol, and Picture Arrangement (e.g., Josiassen, Curry, Roemer, DeBease, & Mancall, 1982; see pp. 512–513), suggesting that their Factor III deficiency may reflect a sequential weakness. A similar pattern was observed in a case study of a 34-year-old male with a head injury primarily affecting the right hemisphere, causing the investigators to hypothesize a potential role of that hemisphere for serial ordering (Milberg, Cummings, Goodglass, & Kaplan, 1979).

The sensitivity of the third factor to generalized brain impairment, regardless of localization, was shown by Bowers, Washburn, and Livesay's (1986) investigation of the WAIS with 44 neuropsychological referrals (ages 16–48, mean age = 35). These investigators conducted a multiple regression analysis using the Halstead Impairment Index as the criterion. Factor III correlated −.54 with the Halstead Index (Factor

I correlated a nonsignificant −.21), and was the first predictor selected in the regression analysis; pairing Factor III with errors on the Benton Visual Retention Test (the only other significant predictor) produced a multiple correlation of .62 with the Impairment Index.

Bowers et al. (1986) basically interpreted Factor III as a measure of attentional processes. In contrast, Roszkowski (1983) rejected an attentional/distractibility interpretation after studying the pattern of correlations between Factor III and subscales on an adaptive behavior inventory for 111 mentally retarded males and females (ages 16–43, mean age = 24; mean WAIS FS-IQ = 63). Ownby and Mathews (1985), in a WISC-R factor-analytic study incorporating several neuropsychological measures, rejected the distractibility label as simplistic and favored an interpretation of Factor III as a measure of complex cognitive processes, suggesting the label *executive processes* (p. 534).

I feel that analyses based on group data cannot adequately address the meaning of the third Wechsler factor because I believe that the factor measures different abilities or behaviors for different individuals. More important than arriving at a universally accepted label is the realization that research has shown this small factor to be a powerful correlate of learning disabilities, brain damage, and dementia-related conditions such as Huntington's disease. It is crucial to consider this factor for virtually anyone assessed on the WAIS-R; when it seems to be significant as a strength or weakness for a person, it is equally essential to interpret the factor specifically for that individual.

Memory Versus Conceptualization

Each of the six WAIS-R Verbal subtests makes demands on a person's memory and concept formation, although they differ considerably in the relative role assigned to each function. At one extreme is Digit Span, a test of short-term memory with a small conceptual component, the ability to reverse digits. Similarities occupies the opposite extreme of high conceptual–low memory. The ability to find the common, preferably abstract, element that unites two verbal concepts is perhaps a prototypical conceptual task. Memory is required to remember the examiner's question (short-term) and to retrieve the two concepts from storage (long-term), but the demands are minimal on both counts. The questions are short, and reduce to just two words—the concepts to be compared; further, the concepts themselves are simple, common, and usually overlearned.

Whereas dividing the Verbal Scale into memory and conceptual halves is neither pure nor unequivocal, there has been some consensus on this type of dichotomy within the literature. To both Guilford and Horn, the following subtests have a clear-cut memory component: Information, Digit Span, and Arithmetic. In contrast, Vocabulary, Comprehension, and Similarities are considered good measures of one or more of the following by Bannatyne, Guilford, Rapaport, or Dean: concept formation, judgment, cognition, evaluation, abstract thought, and social comprehension. Indeed, this triad of subtests composes Bannatyne's Verbal Conceptualization category. Nonetheless, Arithmetic is classified by Guilford as a measure of cognition as well as memory, and Vocabulary is categorized by Rapaport as a dual measure of concept formation and memory. Hence, when examiners search for a memory–conceptualization split within the WAIS-R Verbal Scale, they must do so with flexibility and with the awareness that most Verbal subtests are complex.

Ben's Verbal profile (repeated below) provides a good example of a clear-cut memory–reasoning split (conceptual subtests are in boldface).

VERBAL SUBTEST	AGE-CORRECTED SCALED SCORE
Information	11
Digit Span	8
Vocabulary	**16**

Arithmetic	10
Comprehension	**11**
Similarities	**15**

Without computing significant strengths and weaknesses, and without following a systematic, sequential method of hypothesis generation, simultaneous processors should immediately detect a strength in conceptualization, contrasted with a generalized weakness in short- and long-term memory. Ben's highest memory score equalled his lowest conceptualization score. To ensure that this configuration is significant, compute his mean score in each category (14.0 in conceptualization, 9.7 in memory) and subtract them (4.3 points, or 4 points after rounding the means to whole numbers). This value exceeds the rule of thumb of 3 points, and is also significant when entering Table 14.6 with the average reliability of Horn's Retention cluster and Bannatyne Verbal Conceptualization category (.94, computed from values for adults given in Table 14.1; this mean coefficient is also presented in Table 14.15).

Examiners who want to compute standard scores for Ben on the two halves of the Verbal Scale may enter the relevant formulas shown in Table 14.15 for memory and conceptualization. His sum of scaled scores on the three memory tasks equals 29, while his conceptualization sum equals 42. Entering these values into the formulas produces a conceptualization standard score of 123, strikingly larger than his memory standard score of 98.

Of the six Verbal subtests, Digit Span and Information are generally the best measure of memory, while Comprehension and Similarities are the "purest" tests of verbal conceptualization. Sometimes these two competing dyads will be considerably different from each other, in either direction, suggesting a possible difference in the person's memory and conceptual abilities; in this instance, examiners relying on a configuration approach to hypothesis generation need to be prepared to ignore the complex Arithmetic and Vocabulary subtests and focus on the best

measures of each ability. Reliabilities are sometimes not provided for a given combination of tasks in Tables 14.1 to 14.4 (such as Digit Span and Information, in the preceding example); and examiners will often find no standard score conversion formula to correspond to their clinically derived (perhaps unique) combination of subtests resulting from their profile attack. Even so, whenever examiners use the configuration approach to subdivide a person's WAIS-R subtests into strong and weak areas, they should routinely confirm the significance of the finding by the simple procedure of verifying that the mean age-corrected scaled scores differ by at least 3 points.

Further, the fact that the triads discussed in this section have been labeled "memory" and "conceptualization" is no guarantee that an obvious split of a Verbal profile into these two halves reflects differences in these skill areas. The interpretation of the person's strength and weakness must be verified with behavioral and background data, inasmuch as other explanations are possible, even conceivable. This point becomes apparent in the next section, which deals with a competing interpretation of the same Verbal Scale dichotomy.

Amount of Verbal Expression Required

Three WAIS-R subtests demand individuals to put their ideas into words, to express their thoughts spontaneously via several well-chosen words. Each of these tasks has its own 2-1-0, somewhat subjective, scoring system in the appendixes of the WAIS-R Manual, is quite prone to examiner error, and makes up the category that Bannatyne calls Verbal Conceptualization Ability: Vocabulary, Comprehension, and Similarities. The remaining three Verbal subtests, composing the memory triad discussed in the previous section, are similar to each other apart from the memory component: Each requires the individual to give a brief verbal response, just a word or two, a number, or a series of numbers. People who have good ideas but who lack the facility to express them directly will be penalized on the three WAIS-R tasks that make the greatest demands on verbal expression.

Suppose that a person scores relatively high (or low) on Bannatyne's conceptual category. How does an examiner know whether to interpret the strength (or weakness) in terms of the conceptual or the expressive component of the triad? First, consider the person's verbal behavior during the test and the type of responses recorded on the record form. Poor expressive abilities are revealed by people who continually have difficulty explaining themselves, even during casual conversation or spontaneous verbalizations, or when they clearly understand the concepts being tested. In contrast, individuals with facility in verbal expression often demonstrate this skill by their directness in communication, use of pertinent and high-level vocabulary, and by responding to queries with appropriate elaboration. Frequently, good verbal expression and concept formation go hand in hand; the person who is able to communicate insightfully and directly has also mastered the concepts as well.

Sometimes, however, the strength is clearly conceptualization *or* expression. Good concept formation, in the absence of facile expressive skill, is evidenced by a person who responds tersely to items, gaining credit by use of pertinent abstractions and generalizations. The reverse pattern is demonstrated by someone who is extremely verbose (whose responses are written in the margins and all over the record form page), who consistently piles up 2-point responses on Similarities by giving several responses of varying quality, and who earns 2 points on Vocabulary and Comprehension items by an aggregation of 1-point answers, not by abstract thinking.

Low scores on Vocabulary, Similarities, and Comprehension are commonly due *either* to poor conceptualization or poor expressive abilities. Again, many clues are found from behavioral observation and evaluation of the type of responses given. Usually Similarities provides

the best clue to the nature of the deficiency. Whereas Comprehension often involves explaining, and Vocabulary frequently demands elaboration, most Similarities items can be answered at a 2-point level by a single, well-chosen word or two ("Clothing," "Senses," "Have life"). An extremely low score on Similarities compared to the other two conceptual tasks and/or a set of virtually all 1-point responses to Similarities items implicates poor conceptualization rather than expression as the primary cause of the failure. Analogously, extremely high Similarities for a person who does generally well on the other two tasks implies strong concept formation rather than verbal expressive abilities. The simple pattern of scores is not enough, though; corroboration is necessary from clinical observation of behaviors and background information.

Autistic children and adults, for example, are known to have poor verbal expression and, in fact, earn by far their lowest Wechsler scaled scores on Vocabulary and Comprehension (see the case report of Chester P. on pp. 372–376; also see Lincoln, Courchesne, Kilman, Elmasian, & Allen, 1988; Rutter, 1978). In addition, Henrichs and his colleagues have conducted considerable research on a profile pattern in male psychiatric patients that they term Cluster IV, characterized by relatively high scores on Vocabulary and Comprehension, coupled with low scores on visual-motor coordination subtests (Amolsch & Henrichs, 1975; Henrichs & Amolsch, 1978; Henrichs, Krauskopf, & Amolsch, 1982). Patients whose WAIS pattern matched this particular cluster had similar backgrounds and behaviors, depending on their age; older patients were best characterized as belligerent alcoholics and younger ones as schizoid (Amolsch & Henrichs, 1975). Many Cluster IV male patients had poor work adjustment, were withdrawn, and presented as depressed and anxious (Henrichs et al., 1982). The investigators generally interpreted the WAIS clusters from Gittinger's Personality Assessment System (PAS; Winne & Gittinger, 1973). Examiners who find the PAS useful for clinical assessment (not me) might find Henrichs's actuarial approach a useful adjunct for making behavioral and psychological inferences about male psychiatric patients who evidence strong verbal expressive abilities (versus weak coordination) in their WAIS-R profiles.

Regardless of the interpretation given to a split between the low expression (memory) and high expression (conceptual) subtests on the Verbal Scale, the occurrence of this configuration has some implications: (a) V-IQ becomes an inefficient summary of the person's verbal intelligence; (b) the Verbal Comprehension factor loses meaning, because Information splits off to join the distractibility dyad; and (c) systematic evaluation based on Bannatyne's system (which includes the Verbal Conceptualization category) or Horn's system (which includes the Retention grouping) is advised.

Fluid Versus Crystallized Intelligence

Although Digit Span and Similarities were described previously as falling at opposite ends of the memory–conceptual continuum, these two Verbal subtests are united by their deemphasis of formal education. Although Horn considered Similarities a member of his crystallized intelligence grouping, he also included it and Digit Span in the fluid intelligence category along with most of the Performance tasks. The remaining four Verbal subtests are very dependent on specific learning, whether primarily at home (Comprehension) or at school (Information, Arithmetic, Vocabulary). Horn (1985) excluded Arithmetic from his crystallized category based on his numerous research studies. Nonetheless, this task is included in Bannatyne's Acquired Knowledge grouping and is quite clearly related to formal school achievement. However, clinicians who prefer to operate consistently within the Horn system should eliminate Arithmetic from consideration in this analysis.

Sometimes an individual's total Verbal profile will dichotomize in the aforementioned manner,

as Gwen W.'s WAIS-R scores did in the interpretive example presented in chapter 13 (also see pp. 372–376 for the dramatic split obtained by Chester P). Table 14.16 repeats Gwen's entire set of age-corrected scaled scores for convenience (fluid subtests are shown in boldface).

Gwen's peaks in Digit Span and Similarities should be evident to anyone with a configuration orientation. Quick computation indicates that her mean score on the Digit Span/Similarities dyad (16) is at least 3 points higher than her mean on the remaining Verbal subtests (about 11). However, the hypothesis of fluid ability accounting for Gwen's Verbal profile elevations cannot be treated in isolation from the other WAIS-R tasks known to assess fluid intelligence. If she is especially strong in fluid ability, she would be expected to demonstrate this strength on at least some of the nonverbal subtests as well; if not, an alternative explanation of high Similarities and high Digit Span is needed.

In fact, Gwen's V–P discrepancy (V-IQ = 118, P-IQ = 125) is consistent with a hypothesis of good fluid intelligence. The P > V of 7 points is not significant at the .05 level, but it is in the predicted direction. She scored high on three of the four nonverbal fluid tasks (15–16, in the same ballpark as her Digit Span and Similarities scores), supporting an initial hypothesis of strong fluid ability. The configuration approach, when applied only to Gwen's Performance scores, leads to a new set of hypotheses (regarding visual-spatial versus visual-sequential abilities, discussed on p. 512). These additional hypotheses, however, are not contradictory to a fluid intelligence interpretation of Gwen's mental functioning. Neither is her low score on Picture Arrangement, since one cannot expect unanimity for a six-subtest category.

Examiners who wish to conduct a systematic reorganization of Gwen's WAIS-R profile, one that rejects a V–P approach in favor of a fluid–crystallized model, should conduct a Horn

TABLE 14.16   Gwen W.'s age-corrected scaled scores

Verbal Subtest	Age-Corrected Scaled Scores	Performance Subtest	Age-Corrected Scaled Scores
Information	12	**Picture Completion**	15
Digit Span	17	**Picture Arrangement**	10
Vocabulary	12	**Block Design**	16
Arithmetic	10	**Object Assembly**	15
Comprehension	11	Digit Symbol	14
Similarities	15		

analysis of the data. First, compute her sums of scaled scores on the six fluid subtests (X_{ss} = 88), the four crystallized tasks (X_{ss} = 50), and the three retention subtests (X_{ss} = 39). Next, enter these sums into the relevant conversion formulas in Table 13.6 and round her obtained standard scores to the nearest whole number. The results of these computations follow:

Fluid intelligence =   131

Crystallized intelligence = 114

Retention =   118

Gwen's mean on the three Horn categories equals 121.0. At the .05 level for adults, the Fluid intelligence and Retention standard scores must each deviate from the mean by 7 points to be significant; the Crystallized score requires a 6-point deviation (see Table 13.7). Consequently, Gwen's deviation of +10 on Fluid intelligence is a significant strength (also surpassing the 8-point difference required for the .01 level); her deficit of 7 points is a significant weakness (but falls short of the 8 points needed for the .01 level); and Retention does not differ significantly from her mean. This analysis confirms the hypothesis that Gwen has well-developed fluid ability accounting for her high scores on Digit Span and Similarities in her dichotomized Verbal profile.

Some evidence supports a deficit in fluid intelligence for alcoholics with cirrhosis of the liver. Smith and Smith (1977) administered the WAIS to 20 cirrhotic alcoholics; 20 alcoholics without the liver disease, and to 20 control (nonalcoholic, noncirrhotic) medical patients. The groups were matched on age (mean = 51.1 years), education (mean = 11.2 years), and other variables. Each sample had small V–P differences (5 points or less), although both alcoholic samples displayed subtest profiles showing depressed scaled scores on the Performance subtests and on the Digit Span-Similarities dyad. A decrement in fluid intelligence was suggested, although the age of the sample necessitated converting the regular scaled scores to estimated age-corrected scaled scores before checking the hypothesis.

Estimating the age-corrected scaled scores and substituting the pertinent sums into the WAIS-R formulas for obtaining standard scores on fluid and crystallized intelligence (from Table 13.6) produced the mean scores shown in Table 14.17.

Although the apparent weakness in fluid ability for noncirrhotic alcoholics was illusory, an artifact of the age of the sample, Smith and Smith's (1977) findings suggest a fluid intelligence deficiency for alcoholics with cirrhosis of the liver. Such deficits, as well as the visual-motor coordination deficiencies displayed by

TABLE 14.17   Mean standard scores for fluid and crystallized intelligence for alcoholics and controls

	Cirrhotic Alcoholics	Noncirrhotic Alcoholics	Control Patients
Crystallized intelligence	98	101	110
Fluid intelligence	91	101	114
Difference	+7	0	−4

NOTE: Based on data presented by Smith and Smith (1977).

these cirrhotic alcoholics (see pp. 508–509), are consistent with the cortical and subcortical brain damage that has been documented to accompany excessive alcohol use, based on autopsy (Courville, 1966), pneumoencephalography (Haug, 1968), and EEG analysis (Burdick, Johnson, & Smith, 1970). Further, the damage to the liver caused by alcohol and resulting in atrophic cirrhosis relates directly to brain dysfunction (Thienes & Haley, 1972); also, in a discriminant function analysis conducted with 12 neuropsychiatric subsamples (Overall, Hoffmann, & Levin, 1978), alcoholics "ranked next to the organic brain syndromes on both . . . dimensions of deficit" (p. 1320).

Common Configurations of the WAIS-R Performance Scale

Wechsler Performance subtests correlate lower with each other than do the Verbal subtests, and some argue that the WAIS-R Perceptual Organization factor is best defined by only two of the five Performance subtests: Block Design and Object Assembly (see chapter 8). Consequently, fluctuations among the Performance tasks are frequent, and the scale commonly splits in a number of ways. Most Performance subtests have long been known to be particularly sensitive to brain damage (see chapters 9–11), tend to be lowered relative to Verbal subtests for psychiatric patients (see pp. 290–292), and are commonly the best discriminators among neuropsychiatric patients with diverse pathologies (Overall et al., 1978). The specific divisions of

Performance subtests and the interpretations assigned to the clusters therefore assume importance for clinical and neuropsychological evaluations.

The following configurations among four, or all five, Performance subtests are discussed in the next sections: (a) Rapaport's distinction between visual organization and visual-motor coordination, (b) the meaningfulness of the visual stimuli, (c) sequential versus simultaneous processing strategies, and (d) visual memory versus nonverbal thinking (synthesis).

Visual Organization Versus Visual-Motor Coordination

A frequent Performance dichotomy, easy to spot, conforms to Rapaport's distinction between visual organization (without essential motor activity) and visual-motor coordination. The subtests are administered in a sequence that begins with the task least dependent on motor coordination (Picture Completion) and ends with the most motor-oriented subtest (Digit Symbol). The Rapaport dichotomy produces a configuration that splits the first two subtests listed on the record form from the remainder of the scale. This division was easily in evidence in Ben's profile; he earned age-corrected scaled scores of 8 or 9 on Picture Completion-Picture Arrangement (mean = 8.5) compared to scores of only 2 to 6 on the visual-motor triad (mean = 4.3). Substituting Ben's sums of age-corrected scaled scores into the pertinent Table 14.15 formulas yields a visual organization standard score of

91 versus a visual-motor coordination standard score of 66; the 25-point discrepancy is statistically significant (see Table 14.6).

The Rapaport nonverbal subdivision is especially important for neuropsychological assessment because the two visual organization subtests are far more impervious to cerebral damage than are the tasks dependent on motor coordination. Picture Completion is one of the most resilient subtests on the WAIS-R, whereas a Picture Arrangement deficiency is associated with a fairly specific type of brain lesion: damage to the right anterior temporal lobe. In contrast, the ability to perform well on Block Design and Object Assembly can be disrupted by right hemisphere (especially posterior) lesions in the occipital or parietal lobes, by lesions to the right posterior temporal lobe, by frontal lobe lesions, and by lesions in the left hemisphere (Lezak, 1983; Reitan, 1986). Digit Symbol seems sensitive to almost any type of brain damage, regardless of localization (Reitan, 1986; see Tables 11.1 and 11.2).

Because so many variables affect a person's success on the visual-motor triad in addition to coordination, any deficiency in this area must be corroborated with other test scores, behaviors, and information before concluding that the person has a visual-motor deficit. High visual organization–low visual-motor coordination implies that the individual has adequate or better nonverbal intelligence, but is unable to express it on tasks that make heavy demands on motor coordination and motor speed. That interpretation suggests that the obtained P-IQ underestimates nonverbal intelligence. Yet coordination may not be the culprit; as discussed in the next section, the person with poor visual-motor performance may be handicapped by an inability to process abstract stimuli. Alternatively, the person may simply be a slow problem solver, truly denoting limited nonverbal intelligence. Such slowness will tend to depress scores on the highly speeded Block Design, Object Assembly, and Digit Symbol subtests. Less affected are scores on Picture Completion

and Picture Arrangement, neither of which offers bonus points for rapid solutions.

If the speed component, rather than the motor element, leads to low visual-motor coordination scores, the examiner must try to discern whether the slowness is due to a cognitive limitation or a behavioral trait such as apathy, compulsiveness, or anxiety. If the low scores are related either to the affective domain or the psychomotor domain, the visual organization cluster may offer the best estimate of the individual's nonverbal intelligence. Good clinical skills are essential.

The cirrhotic alcoholics studied by Smith and Smith (1977) evidenced a substantial deficit on the visual-motor triad as well as their fluid intelligence. After converting their mean regular scaled scores into estimated age-corrected scaled scores and entering the relevant cluster sums into the appropriate equations (Table 14.15), I discovered that alcoholics with cirrhosis of the liver scored substantially higher on the two visual organization subtests (mean standard score = 96) than on the visual-motor triad (mean = 86). The noncirrhotic alcoholics and the control medical patients had small differences (1–3 points) between their standard scores on the two Rapaport categories. In Overall et al.'s (1978) WAIS study of 29 alcoholics (one of 12 subsamples investigated), this group also evidenced a profile split that conformed to Rapaport's division of nonverbal subtests. Since these investigators adjusted their scaled scores for age, I entered the sums of scaled scores into the relevant formulas (Table 14.15); these alcoholics earned a standard score of 84 on visual organization, compared to 74 on visual-motor coordination. In a WAIS study of 20 young alcoholics with a mean age of 33 years (Blusewicz, Schenkenberg, Dustman, & Beck, 1977), the portion of the sample designated as severe alcoholics ($N = 13$) demonstrated a 6-point discrepancy in favor of visual organization (102 versus 96) when I applied the formulas in Table 14.15; in contrast, the seven subjects categorized as nonsevere scored 4 points *lower* on visual organization (100 versus 104).

Low visual-motor coordination is also associated with the Cluster IV male psychiatric patients studied by Amolsch and Henrichs (1975), a topic discussed previously (pp. 504–505).

Meaningful Versus Abstract Stimuli

Picture Completion and Picture Arrangement use pictures of people and things, whereas Block Design and Digit Symbol require the perception and processing of abstractions—complex designs, simple designs, and numbers. Object Assembly doesn't fit neatly into either category. For the WISC-R, I classified Object Assembly with the two "Picture" subtests because the final product to be assembled is meaningful (Kaufman, 1979b). However, the first two WISC-R puzzles are named for the child, and all four puzzles have at least one large piece that makes the object to be constructed obvious to all but the severely impaired. For the WAIS-R, none of the puzzles is named, and some individuals are unaware of the nature of what they are constructing for the Elephant and, especially, the Hand. Consequently, I have eliminated Object Assembly from consideration when evaluating the Performance Scale configuration from the vantage point of the type of stimuli to be processed; the puzzle pieces may be seen as meaningful by many people, but are likely to be processed as abstractions by others—for example, by some neurological patients.

As indicated previously, Block Design and Digit Symbol are among the most sensitive WAIS-R subtests to brain damage, so low scores on this dyad are quite meaningful. These two tasks represent the most striking weakness demonstrated by Alzheimer's-type dementia patients, with the dyad forming an integral part of Fuld's (1984) characteristic profile.

In Overall et al.'s (1978) investigation of the WAIS profiles of 414 adults classified into 12

neuropsychiatric categories, the abstract stimuli dyad proved meaningful for psychopathological as well as organic groups; either Digit Symbol or Block Design produced the lowest mean scaled score for 11 of the 12 subgroups. The remaining group, nonparanoid schizophrenics, scored lowest on Object Assembly, followed closely by both Digit Symbol and Block Design. (These scaled scores were adjusted to hold age, gender, race, and socioeconomic status constant.) Using data provided in Overall et al.'s (1978) Table 4, I entered the WAIS-R conversion formulas (Table 14.15) and discovered that all 12 clinical samples earned mean scores on the processing of meaningful stimuli that were higher by 2 to 10 points than scores on abstract stimuli. The groups with the following defining characteristics displayed discrepancies of at least 5 standard score points: organic brain syndrome, drug abuse, alcoholism, schizoaffective depressed, psychotic depression, depressive reaction, and situational reaction. All five Performance subtests discriminated significantly among the 12 samples (compared to three of six Verbal tasks), but Digit Symbol emerged as the *best* discriminator on the WAIS.

Of all of Wechsler's subtests, Digit Symbol and Block Design have probably been the subject of the most investigations by experimental psychologists. Specific block placement strategies and other components of successful and unsuccessful Block Design performance have been dissected for samples of children (Jones & Torgesen, 1981) and adults (Schorr, Bower, & Kiernan, 1982; Royer, 1977), with some of the key issues centered on the application of analytic or synthetic problem-solving styles; this issue is treated in the next section, which deals with mental processing. The information-processing components of Digit Symbol have also been investigated extensively (Laux & Lane, 1985), with many researchers trying to explain the consistent gender differences favoring females (Majeres, 1983; see pp. 154–156), the dramatic age decline in test performance (Gilmore, Royer, & Gruehn, 1983; see chapter 7), and the role of this task in clinical evaluation (Hart, Kwentus, Wade, & Hamer, 1987) and neuropsychological diagnosis (Bauer, Schlottmann, Kane, & Johnson, 1984). The experimental research on Block Design and Digit Symbol affirms the psychological and theoretical meaningfulness of this dyad, and the clinical and brain-related research reinforces its potential value for differential diagnosis.

Because of the complexity of the Performance tasks in general, and the Block Design-Digit Symbol dyad in particular, it is necessary to cross-validate any hypothesis regarding an individual's discrepancy between perceiving or processing meaningful versus abstract stimuli. More likely than not, the person will evidence better performance in meaningful than abstract stimuli; the reverse pattern is not as explainable from a neuropsychological framework and is less valuable in a diagnostic sense. When Digit Symbol and Block Design are high relative to the "Picture" dyad, other explanations may be necessary. Possibly the person is threatened by the social stimuli, especially in Picture Arrangement, and feels more comfortable with neutral stimuli. Or the difference may be more related to the *imitative* aspect of Digit Symbol and Block Design (both involve reproduction of models), a skill that may be better developed than problem solving without a model.

The latter hypothesis requires consideration of Object Assembly rather than Picture Completion performance. Picture Arrangement and Object Assembly are each nonverbal-reasoning, problem-solving tasks; unlike the Block Design-Digit Symbol dyad, neither reasoning subtest provides the individual with a model to copy. Some individuals perform better when a model is provided, and others do better without one. When Picture Arrangement pairs with Object Assembly, in contrast to a different level of performance on the two nonverbal imitative tasks, the examiner should entertain a reasoning versus imitation hypothesis. Table 14.15 includes these clusters, permitting examiners to compute and compare a person's standard scores

on each dyad. Additional support for this hypothesis may reside within the configuration of the Verbal profile. An individual with better imitative than reasoning skills within the visual-motor sphere, for example, might well display a comparable profile of high memory–low reasoning within the auditory-vocal channel (see pp. 502–503).

But when the pattern does not involve Object Assembly, and the nonverbal configuration clearly implies a deficiency in perceiving or processing abstract stimuli compared to meaningful stimuli, verification of the hypothesis can take several forms. Is there any evidence of brain damage, either diffuse or in the posterior regions of the right cerebral hemisphere? Did the individual have difficulty on Verbal subtests that use numerical symbols (Digit Span, Arithmetic)? Did he or she do better on the more meaningful, context-related Verbal subtests (Information, Comprehension) than on the ones that require responses to isolated verbal concepts (Vocabulary, Similarities)? It is advisable to administer a supplementary test that employs abstract stimuli but has no time limits and does not depend on motor coordination. Tests of matrix analogies are especially valuable for this purpose, such as Raven's (Raven, Court, & Raven, 1983), Naglieri's (1985a, 1985b), or the nonverbal portion of the forthcoming Kaufman Brief Intelligence Test (Kaufman & Kaufman, in press *b*). If a person is able to reason effectively with abstract stimuli on an analogies test, the cause of poor performance on Block Design and Digit Symbol is obviously related to some other variable (speed, coordination, imitation), but *not* to the abstractness of the stimuli.

Simultaneous Versus Sequential Processing

The three subtests that make up Bannatyne's Spatial Ability category and that compose the Perceptual Organization factor are also measures of simultaneous processing, the kind of gestalt-holistic problem-solving approach that cerebral specialization researchers associate with the right hemisphere and Luria adherents attribute to the occipital-parietal regions of the brain. Although not clear-cut measures of analytic, linear, left-brain processing, the remaining Performance subtests (Picture Arrangement, Digit Symbol) have a decided *sequential* component. Consequently, a common configuration of the Performance Scale is for the three simultaneous processing subtests to split off as a cluster, with the individual performing about equally well on Digit Symbol and Picture Arrangement (either substantially higher or lower than on Picture Completion-Block Design-Object Assembly).

The occurrence of this dichotomy may reflect a Guilford-like division of the nonverbal scale into "cognition" and "convergent-production" components; the visual-spatial triad measures the former operation, the visual-sequential subtests assess the latter. This hypothesis can be checked by investigating the individual's level of performance on the Verbal tasks that measure cognition, especially Vocabulary and Similarities. Alternatively, a sequential-simultaneous hypothesis can be verified or rejected by examining performance on the two Verbal subtests that are believed to assess sequential processing: Digit Span and Arithmetic. Do not accept a processing explanation as viable for an apparent visual-spatial versus visual-sequential dichotomy of the Performance Scale unless the person evidenced a similar level of functioning (either high or low) on the verbal-sequential dyad. Further, examiners should not conclude that the individual has a simultaneous strength or weakness unless there is behavioral support for that contention. For example, did the person use a trial-and-error, sequential method of constructing puzzles and designs and placing pictures, or was an insightful, reflective, holistic problem-solving approach evident?

If verification of a processing interpretation of the Performance Scale is lacking (from Verbal Scale scores or from clinical observations), one should explore other options. Even if Digit Symbol and Picture Arrangement pair up, this occurrence may be coincidental. Remember that

each of these subtests is *primarily* a measure of unique abilities or of skills that are not measured by the three major factors; each of these subtests *secondarily* measures *error* variance more so than any of the factors (see Tables 14.7 and 14.8). Hence, assigning unique or chance interpretations to fluctuations on Digit Symbol or Picture Arrangement is always defensible (an exception to my bias against subtest-specific inferences).

One aspect of each subtest's uniqueness pertains directly to a processing interpretation stemming from the Luria model. He posits the existence of three "blocks" or "functional units" in the brain; Block 1 concerns arousal or attention, Block 2 deals with successive and simultaneous coding functions, and Block 3 involves higher level planning processes (Luria, 1980; Naglieri & Das, 1988). Digit Symbol, apart from its sequential component, is for Rapaport a measure of concentration and is often a member of the distractibility triad; therefore, it may be thought of as a measure of arousal, a Block 1 function that "maintains a proper state of arousal or cortical tone . . . [which] is also important for effective performance because too much or too little interferes with proper processing of information" (Naglieri & Das, 1988, p. 36). In addition, Picture Arrangement has long been considered a measure of planning ability, of anticipation of consequences, and, by inference, of Luria's third functional unit.

From this perspective, an individual's performance on Digit Symbol (and perhaps Digit Span, a measure of attention according to Rapaport) may reflect arousal or orientation toward the tasks in general; scores on Arithmetic and Digit Span may denote successive or sequential processing; success or failure on the Spatial triad may indicate simultaneous processing; and Picture Arrangement performance may denote planning, the ability to develop strategies, to generate hypotheses, and generally to program, regulate, and verify activity (Naglieri & Das, 1988).

From Naglieri and Das's (1988) research, one might be tempted to treat *both* Picture Arrangement and Digit Symbol as measures of Block 3. Naglieri and Das interpret as planning ability a factor that includes tests of number matching and trail-making, tests that incorporate the same type of clerical and psychomotor skills that define Digit Symbol. However, I do not agree with their interpretation of the factor as indicative of Luria's third block. The seemingly low-level clerical and time-sensitive skills that compose this dimension contradict Naglieri and Das's (1987) description of Block 3 characteristics: "Planning entails the aptitude for asking new questions, solving problems, and self-monitoring, which . . . may represent one of the most complex forms of human behavior" (p. 355). This description applies to Picture Arrangement and to the WISC-R Mazes subtest, but it does not define Digit Symbol or some of the tasks that Naglieri and Das (1987, 1988) have used to define their planning dimension.

The profile of Gwen W. offers a good example of Performance Scale patterning that conforms to a visual-spatial/visual-sequential processing dichotomy (age-corrected scaled scores follow, with simultaneous subtests in bold print):

Picture Completion	**15**
Picture Arrangement	10
Block Design	**16**
Object Assembly	**15**
Digit Symbol	14

Gwen's mean score on the three simultaneous subtests (15.3) is significantly higher than her mean on the visual-sequential tasks (12.0; see Table 14.6). The formulas for converting her scores to standard scores (Table 14.15) produce standard scores of 132 (simultaneous) and 112 (visual-sequential), respectively. However, this significant differential does not reflect a discrepancy in Gwen's processing style.

Observations of her problem-solving style gave strong evidence of a holistic, simultaneous, efficient approach. But her profile offered no support for weak sequential abilities. Her scaled score of 17 in Digit Span suggested that her reflected sequential skills were as well developed as her simultaneous skills. Her relatively low score on Arithmetic (10) was consistent with an overall mathematical weakness that was evidenced throughout her school record and on the Graduate Record Examination. Her low score in Picture Arrangement may indicate poor planning ability, although it may indicate relatively weak social comprehension (she performed comparably on Comprehension). Probably, Gwen's strength on the three simultaneous-spatial-perceptual organization tasks is merely a manifestation of her excellent *fluid* intelligence, an explanation discussed previously (pp. 505–506).

Relatively high scores on visual-spatial compared to visual-sequential tasks characterize autistic individuals. Lincoln et al.'s (1988) 33 nonretarded autistic children, adolescents, and adults (age range 8½ to 29, mean age = 17½ years), tested on the WISC-R or WAIS-R, had a mean scaled score of close to 9 on the spatial triad, versus a mean of about 6 on Picture Arrangement and Digit Symbol-Coding. The differential was similar in Rutter's (1978) autistic sample (means of about 6⅔ and 3⅓, respectively). In Rutter's sample, the deficiency on visual-sequential tasks was comparable to the group's deficit in verbal expression, although the nonretarded autistic group studied by Lincoln et al. showed its most striking weakness in expressive skills.

A group of 21 manic-depressives on lithium therapy performed poorly on WAIS visual-sequential tasks, especially Digit Symbol; the lowest scores on Picture Arrangement and Digit Symbol were obtained by patients who had been on lithium the longest (Nair, Muller, Gutbrodt, Buffet, & Schwartz, 1979), a finding discussed previously (p. 291). In addition, high simultaneous–low sequential Performance profiles have been found fairly consistently for patients with Huntington's disease (see p. 294). Consistencies among several samples of patients with this genetic disease imply that they truly have a strength in simultaneous processing coupled with a weakness in sequential processing. Huntington's patients typically earn their highest Performance scaled score on Picture Completion, while evidencing depressions in Digit Symbol, Picture Arrangement, Arithmetic, and Digit Span (Brandt et al., 1984; Butters, Sax, Montgomery, & Tarlow, 1978; Josiassen, Curry, Roemer, DeBease, & Mancall, 1982).

The spatial-simultaneous triad has also been found to be of clinical significance for a different sample with motor coordination problems: patients with multiple sclerosis (Heaton, Nelson, Thompson, Burks, & Franklin, 1985; see pp. 293–294). All five Performance subtests (versus only two of six Verbal tasks) discriminated significantly between normal adults and patients having multiple sclerosis. But only Block Design, Object Assembly, and Picture Completion significantly discriminated between two samples of multiple sclerosis patients, one with relapsing-remitting symptoms, the other having chronic-progressive multiple sclerosis.

Interpretation of the three simultaneous subtests requires some caution. Although performance on the tasks has been positively associated with a field-independent cognitive style (Goodenough & Karp, 1961), there is some evidence, based partly on WAIS Block Design data, that the two constructs (spatial ability, field-independent cognitive style) are indistinguishable from one another (MacLeod, Jackson, & Palmer, 1986). Further, as discussed in chapter 6 on the WAIS-R stratification variables, all three tasks produce significant gender differences favoring *males* at two or three of the age groups studied. Object Assembly correlated poorest with educational attainment among all 11 WAIS-R subtests, and the spatial triad ranked at the bottom (with Picture Arrangement) as the worst correlates of education (Kaufman, McLean, & Reynolds, 1988b).

Block Design is often a maverick subtest regarding its processing demands. Picture Completion and Object Assembly stress the synthetic, visual closure skills that are so closely associated with a simultaneous processing approach to problem solving. Block Design demands this synthetic ability as well, but it also makes heavy demands on analytic ability. Especially when constructing the designs from the two-dimensional cards with the guidelines removed, individuals must first effectively analyze the design into its component blocks before they can synthesize a solution. The relevance of both processing styles has been demonstrated both in neuropsychological research and practice (cf. Lezak, 1983, pp. 276–281). Matarazzo (1972) noted: "Oddly enough, individuals who do best on the test are not necessarily those who see, or at least follow, the pattern as a whole, but more often those who are able to break it up into small portions" (p. 212).

Support for Block Design's analytic component comes from experimental psychology research conducted by Schorr, Bower, and Kiernan (1982) with 10 undergraduate students from Stanford included in each of three studies. These authors distinguished between two types of strategies, one more simultaneous (synthetic), the other more sequential (analytic). The synthetic style involves holistic pattern matching; the analytic style demands mentally segmenting each block in the design. Results of each study indicated the predominant application of *analytic* problem-solving strategies. Although Royer (1984) challenged the use of the analytic-synthetic typology by Schorr et al. (1982), these investigators responded cogently to Royer's criticisms (Kiernan, Bower, & Schorr, 1984). Although one cannot generalize much from data obtained on a group of undergraduate students at a highly rated university, it is clear that Block Design items can be solved efficiently by sequential approaches, simultaneous approaches, or a combination of the two.

Sometimes, therefore, Block Design must be deleted when conducting a processing analysis of the Performance Scale. Like Picture Arrangement and Digit Symbol, Block Design may be solved sequentially or by an integration of processes; and like the two visual-sequential subtests, Block Design demands good verbal comprehension of lengthy verbal directions read by the examiner. Picture Completion and Object Assembly, by contrast, depend more heavily on the gestalt function with minimal emphasis on analysis or on the so-called left-brain function of interpreting lengthy verbalizations. Examiners should be alert for the emergence of the Picture Completion-Object Assembly dyad in Performance profiles. Should the appropriate configuration be detected, this visual closure dyad should be contrasted to the visual-sequencing dyad. Pertinent formulas are provided in Table 14.15 to permit this processing comparison.

Visual Memory Versus Nonverbal Thinking

One other configuration involving the entire Performance Scale is easily and immediately recognizable: the "book-end" pattern, with elevations on the first and last Performance subtests administered (see case report of Clara S. on pp. 629–636). High scores on Picture Completion and Digit Symbol conceivably indicate a good visual memory, since the former tests long-term visual memory, and the latter assesses short-term visual memory (although to a lesser extent than perceptual speed; Laux & Lane, 1985). The other three Performance subtests measure nonverbal thinking and problem solving, as opposed to memory; Block Design assesses nonverbal concept formation, and Picture Arrangement and Object Assembly are good measures of nonverbal reasoning. Together, the latter three tasks measure synthesis, assembling parts into a whole, either temporally (Picture Arrangement) or spatially.

According to Osgood's communication theory, the visual memory dyad assesses skills that are at least partially at the automatic, overlearned level of organization. In contrast, the thinking triad comprises high-level, representational measures of adult intelligence. Some subjects who are low in nonverbal thinking will be able to perform adequately, or even exceptionally, on the two more automatic, visual memory subtests that make fewer demands on higher intellectual processes. Although some individuals have the reverse pattern of high thinking–low memory, I suspect that alternative hypotheses are necessary to explain the profile. For example, Rapaport classifies both Picture Completion and Digit Symbol as measures of concentration. Individuals with low scores on these tasks may have difficulty concentrating, a hypothesis that may be confirmed or rejected by behavioral observation.

Regardless of the direction of the "book-end" configuration, the formulas provided in Table 14.15 allow the computation of standard scores on the components, while Table 14.6 permits determination of the significance of the discrepancy.

Dyad Configurations on Both Scales

Clinicians who apply the configuration method of generating hypotheses should be alert to a few patterns that involve dyads on both the Verbal and Performance Scales. Several comparisons involve cross-validation of a finding from one scale to the other regarding memory, imitation, sequencing ability, and reasoning. If a person reasons well or poorly on the Verbal Scale (Similarities, Comprehension), does this strength or weakness maintain on the Performance Scale (Picture Arrangement, Object Assembly)? A number of these comparisons are included in Table 14.15 to allow examiners to compute standard scores on categories that are assessed in similar fashion both verbally and nonverbally. Table 14.6 then permits determination of the significance of the discrepancy on these contrasts.

In addition, two specific comparisons involving the Verbal and Performance Scale are of sufficient importance to warrant separate discussion: social comprehension versus abstract thought and fund of information versus trial-and-error learning.

Social Comprehension Versus Abstract Thought

Two of Dean's (1983) clusters provide an interesting contrast for WAIS-R examiners to consider: Social Comprehension (Comprehension-Picture Arrangement) and Abstract Thought (Similarities-Block Design). Each category holds fairly constant the content to be processed (by including one Verbal and one Performance subtest); all four tasks assess high-level reasoning or conceptual processes.

The Social Comprehension dyad combines the two subtests that have interpersonal themes, socially oriented items, and real-world problem-solving situations. They are believed to measure social judgment and common sense and may tentatively be thought of as a crude measure of social intelligence. As Dean (1983) stated: "Both subtests examine the client's ability to apply customs, social knowledge, and mores to specific situations" (p. 12). Some psychologists (e.g., Sattler, 1988) explore *differences* between the two subtests to infer specific modes of social functioning: "High Picture Arrangement coupled with low Comprehension may suggest sensitivity to interpersonal nuances, but a disregard for social conventions" (p. 177). I find little validity in such interpretations, but consider it useful to *combine* an individual's performance on the two socially oriented WAIS-R tasks to get a more reliable estimate of social understanding. (The reliability of the difference between Comprehension and Picture Arrangement is only .60; see Feingold, 1984.)

The Abstract Thought dyad represents an ideal point of comparison. Similarities presents verbal concepts totally out of social context (even Arithmetic incorporates a social setting for each item), requiring abstract reasoning with each pair of concepts. Further, the abstract designs that constitute the Block Design items are about as far removed as possible from the so-

cially relevant stimuli in Picture Arrangement. "Although basic concrete knowledge may be required, each subtest requires the subject to go beyond that knowledge level to the abstraction and manipulation of components" (Dean, 1983, p. 6). How well a person solves problems in an abstract setting versus a social setting is therefore of considerable clinical value regarding inferences about a person's personality, intellectual potential in quite different circumstances, and neuropsychological integrity.

Configuration analysis of Chester P.'s profile (Table 11.6) reveals a dramatic strength in Abstract Thought coupled with a striking Social Comprehension weakness. Gwen W.'s profile also suggests a strength in Abstract Thought and a weakness in Social Comprehension. Two of her highest age-corrected scaled scores were in Similarities and Block Design. Although her exceptional fluid abilities contributed to her success, it is also evident that she is especially adept at Abstract Thought. This finding assumes more meaning in view of her significant weakness in Picture Arrangement (scaled score of 10) and comparable score in Comprehension (11). The differences in her mean scaled score on the two categories (15.5 versus 10.5) is far greater than the rule of thumb of 3 points. When standard scores are computed for Gwen using the formulas in Table 14.15, the 29-point difference (Abstract Thought = 132; Social Comprehension = 103) is striking and significant (see Table 14.6). Gwen's relative deficiency in social understanding is consistent with her self-report of not getting along with several teachers at the middle school where she worked as a paraprofessional, and with her stated desire "to find a job where she can just do her thing and not be hassled."

The best validation of the Abstract Thought–Social Comprehension differential comes from Browning and Quinlan's (1985) study of the Wechsler profiles of 91 adolescent and young adult psychiatric patients (45 females, 46 males) ranging in age from 13 to 30 years (mean = 19). These patients were administered

Loevinger's Sentence Completion Test (SCT) for measuring ego development (Loevinger & Wessler, 1970), along with either the WISC-R (N = 16), WAIS (N = 46), or the WAIS-R (N = 29). The SCT is meant to measure an aspect of personality functioning akin to social intelligence: "The exercise of social judgment and the capacity for anticipation and planning may be compared to Loevinger's description of ego development as a 'complexly interwoven fabric of impulse control, character, interpersonal relations, conscious preoccupations and cognitive complexity'" (Browning & Quinlan, 1985, p. 261).

These investigators grouped the patients into three ego development categories based on the SCT—preconformist (the lowest level), protoconformist, and postconformist (the highest level). I entered each group's mean sum of scaled scores on the two pertinent categories into the Table 14.15 formulas to produce standard scores. The results require cautious interpretation because of the merger of data from three Wechsler batteries and the inability to convert the values to age-corrected scaled scores; nonetheless, the findings in Table 14.18 are intriguing. The largest deficiency in Social Comprehension was evidenced by the group with the lowest level of ego development, with the discrepancy narrowing with increased ego functioning.

Browning and Quinlan (1985) also found that Comprehension correlated highest with the SCT among the 11 subtests (.44), and that the correlation remained a significant .34 after partialling out FS-IQ. Although Picture Arrangement failed to correlate significantly with

Loevinger's ego development test, according to Browning and Quinlan, "[t]he hypothesis of some association was partially supported" (p. 262).

In general, studies of the social intelligence hypothesis pertaining to the two Social Comprehension tasks have produced mixed findings. (Because of the relatively low correlations between WAIS and WAIS-R Picture Arrangement, any findings with the WAIS subtest must be treated cautiously; see pp. 86–87.) Schill (1966) and his associates (Schill, Kahn, & Muehleman, 1968a, 1968b) showed that WAIS Picture Arrangement related positively to measures of extraversion, such as the MMPI Social Introversion scale, for three samples of college students; Johnson (1969) found the opposite pattern in psychiatric patients. Terry and Berg (1984) reconciled these discrepant findings by demonstrating a significant interaction with the MMPI Psychopathic Deviance (P_D) scale. High WAIS Picture Arrangement was related to high extraversion only in psychiatric patients with high P_D.

Turner and Horn (1976) failed to find any support for a social intelligence hypothesis in their MMPI-WAIS correlational study, using data from 400 adoptive parents (mean age = 37 for mothers, 40 for fathers). Picture Arrangement did not consistently relate to MMPI items on the Social Introversion scale or to other socially relevant items for males or females; and the MMPI items that consistently correlated with Comprehension were no more socially pertinent than the items that were significant correlates of Vocabulary. In contrast to

TABLE 14.18 Abstract Thought–Social Comprehension comparisons and ego development

	Preconformist	Protoconformist	Postconformist
Abstract Thought	105.0	105.6	114.2
Social Comprehension	96.5	99.4	110.6
Difference	+8.5	+6.2	+3.6

NOTE: Based on data from Browning and Quinlan (1985).

Turner and Horn's (1976) negative findings, Edinger's (1976) investigation of 15 male process schizophrenics (mean age = 21.5 years) yielded positive results: WAIS Picture Arrangement correlated significantly with the Phillips Premorbid Adjustment Scale, even after partialling out FS-IQ.

WAIS-R investigations have been just as contradictory as the WAIS studies. Nobo and Evans (1986) found trivial, nonsignificant correlations involving the two Social Comprehension subtests and any of the five measures of social behavior (including the MMPI Social Introversion scale) for 37 college students. In contrast, Sipps, Berry, and Lynch (1987) used the California Psychological Inventory (CPI) scales to predict raw scores on WAIS-R Comprehension and Picture Arrangement for 85 normal adults (mean age = 29) and obtained positive results. The CPI scales of Capacity for Status and Flexibility (in thinking and social behavior) were significant predictors for both subtests. Both subtests were significantly related to CPI measures of social behavior, even after partialling out Vocabulary score; Sipps et al. (1987) concluded that there is "substantial evidence in support of the notion that Comprehension and Picture Arrangement are to some degree measures of social intelligence" (p. 503).

Despite the optimism of the latter team of researchers, the construct validity of the WAIS-R Social Comprehension category remains speculative: The studies have reported mixed results; the samples vary widely, are too dependent on college student populations, and are sometimes haphazard; the criteria are often dubious at best. (Are socially intelligent people necessarily extraverted?) I also question whether the correlational approach is the best methodology for investigating the issue. I find the Browning and Quinlan (1985) criterion of ego development the most compelling, and their methodology the most direct. But despite their generally favorable findings, the validity of Social Comprehension is primarily *face* validity (the test items *seem* to measure the intended

aptitude) rather than criterion-related or construct validity.

Far less pertinent research has been conducted with the Abstract Thought dyad. Psychosurgery (frontal lobe or limbic-hypothalmic regions) has reportedly led to deficient abstract thinking, as measured by Wechsler's Block Design and Similarities (Jurko & Andy, 1973) and Kohs's Block Design test (Walsh, 1977). But a summary of pertinent research has led Joschko (1986) to conclude that "deficits in abstract thinking following psychosurgery either are not permanent or cannot be dissociated from factors related to long-term psychiatric illness" (p. 310).

From the perspective of the Personality Assessment System (Krauskopf & Davis, 1973; Winne and Gittinger, 1973), [i]ndividuals who achieve relatively low Block Design and Similarities scores are termed 'flexible, compensated' and considered as someone who . . . 'denies and punishes sensitivity'; rejects the subtle . . . [and is] *[e]xplosively emotional under stress*'" (Kunce, Ryan, & Eckelman, 1976, p. 44). The PAS might predict violent behavior from some individuals low in Abstract Thought, and some evidence to support the association of low Similarities scores with violent behavior was provided by Kunce et al. (1976) for white males court-committed as criminally insane. Kunce et al. cross-validated their finding with a second sample of white males from the same institution, and Hays and Solway (1977) obtained comparable results with the WISC for a racially mixed group of violent and nonviolent juvenile delinquents. Yet the generalizability of this theory-supported relationship was challenged when the *opposite* finding (relatively high Similarities) was observed on the WAIS with young *black* offenders (Lira, Fagan, & White, 1979).

Fund of Information Versus Trial-and-Error Learning

Information and Vocabulary are so correlated with each other (.81) that exploring differences between them is a feeble exercise. As a team, however, this "fund of information" dyad reflects a formidable combination for evaluating a person's intellectual accomplishments in culturally relevant verbal arenas. This pair of subtests was proposed as a psychometrically powerful short form (Feingold, 1982; see pp. 137–138) and, indeed, has much to recommend it: Information and Vocabulary are the most reliable WAIS-R subtests, both in terms of internal consistency and stability; they typically emerge as the best measures of *g* and of the Verbal Comprehension factor; they are the highest correlates of educational attainment among the 11 WAIS-R tasks; they are resilient to the impact of aging (see chapter 7); and they often remain as intact strengths for patients with organic or functional disorders such as Huntington's disease (Josiassen et al., 1982), multiple sclerosis (Heaton et al., 1985), Alzheimer's-type dementia (Fuld, 1984), cirrhotic and noncirrhotic alcoholism (Smith & Smith, 1977), schizophrenia and other psychoses (Holland & Watson, 1980; Overall et al., 1978), and diffuse or bilateral brain damage (Gonen & Brown, 1968; Lezak, 1983).

An individual's fund of information has been shown empirically to have a definite cultural component (Cernovsky, 1986; Holland & Watson, 1980), in contrast to the Performance dyad of Block Design-Object Assembly, which relates closely to the Cattell-Horn notion of fluid intelligence (Horn, 1985). Just as Information and Vocabulary are the best exemplars of the Verbal Comprehension factor, the nonverbal dyad captures the essence of Perceptual Organization (see Table 14.8); some have argued that the nonverbal factor should be composed *only* of Block Design and Object Assembly (Gutkin et al., 1983). Both tasks involve a visual synthesis or construction ability and are susceptible to the impact of trial-and-error learning. One can learn how to combine pairs of blocks on the early designs via trial and error and apply this learning to the more complex designs that come later; a similar type of learning set can affect performance on the more difficult Object As-

sembly items. By contrast, learning sets or trial-and-error learning have no place in the Information-Vocabulary dyad; solving early items does not influence performance on later items—except, perhaps, as confidence builders. Consequently, test–retest gains over an interval of several weeks on the Verbal dyad are very small, while the practice effect on the Performance dyad is generally much larger (Wechsler, 1981, Table 11).

The psychometric properties of Block Design-Object Assembly do not match those of the Verbal dyad, but, largely because of Block Design, the nonverbal dyad is both reliable and valid. Unlike the Verbal dyad, the Performance tasks relate relatively weakly to education level, they decrease dramatically with age (even after controlling for education), and they are typically among the subtests *most* likely to reveal deficits in individuals with a wide variety of neuropsychiatric disorders (as evidenced by research citations throughout this chapter). Consequently, the comparison of the "fund of information" dyad with the "trial-and-error" dyad affords examiners a crisp overview of a person's verbal and nonverbal skills (or crystallized versus fluid intelligence; or acquired knowledge versus spatial ability); the difference may be related to the referral problem and may help pinpoint areas of asset and deficit that might otherwise be obscured by other fluctuations within the Verbal and Performance Scales.

Clinicians may also wish to compare performance on Information-Vocabulary with the person's success on either the Social Comprehension or Abstract Thought dyad. Some tentative WAIS research suggests that such comparisons may be made cautiously in certain diagnostic circumstances. McMullen and Rogers (1984) examined the traditional clinical hypothesis that obsessive personality styles are associated with a high score on the fund of information dyad and low Comprehension, whereas the reverse cognitive pattern is associated with hysteric personality styles. They found a significant interaction in the predicted direction, in support of the clinical hypothesis, for the 16 most extreme scorers among their sample of 65 college students.

For the Abstract Thought category, evidence was provided, and then cross-validated, in support of the notion that scores on the fund of information dyad and on Similarities may distinguish among temporal lobe and generalized epileptic patients (Milberg, Greiffenstein, Lewis, & Rourke, 1980). These investigators postulated that generalized seizure patients would have high scores on WAIS Information + Vocabulary, contrasted with a relatively low Similarities score, and that temporal lobe seizure patients would display good Similarities performance and a poor fund of information. Milberg et al. (1980) applied discriminant function analysis and reported excellent "hit" rates of 77% (initial sample of 39 patients) and 79% (for a cross-validation sample of 39 patients). A second experiment with the WAIS (Bolter, Veneklasen, & Long, 1981), however, found considerably lower hit rates (a median of about 54% for several comparisons); Bolter et al. concluded that "the WAIS seizure index may be of limited diagnostic utility in the assessment of seizure patients" (p. 552).

ILLUSTRATIVE CASE REPORT

The following case report for Nicole H., a 34-year-old college student experiencing learning problems, illustrates the methods and procedures for WAIS-R interpretation described in chapters 13 and 14. These techniques are also exemplified in the two case reports at the end of chapter 11 and the single case reports included at the end of chapters 15 and 16.

Nicole H., Age 34, Learning Problem

Referral and Background Information

Nicole (Nikki) volunteered for testing and evaluation available through the psychoeducational assessment class, as she has been concerned about her poor performance on tests in a college-level statistics course, inconsistent performance in her college coursework, test anxiety, and a possible learning disability. She is interested in finding out if she has the ability to complete a degree from the University of Alabama. Nikki has been aware of a problem since grade school (she repeated the 7th grade). Her particular problems are with numbers and details. She has noticed that she reverses numbers (as well as some letters, but to a lesser extent). She knows number concepts but makes mistakes with her checkbook, for example, despite good concentration. She took only one math course in high school; she took college algebra at the University of Alabama and failed it. She indicates that she is frustrated because she knows something is wrong, but she does not know what it is. She wants to know what the problem is and how to deal with it.

Nikki reports that she was diagnosed 8 years ago as having Grave's disease (hyperthyroidism with one or more of the following: goiter, exophthalmos, pretibial myxedema). The disease is not controlled at the present time, although she has had isotope therapy, which resulted in the reverse condition (hypothyroidism). Side effects of the disease and/or treatment, according to Nikki, include memory problems and emotional side effects such as nervousness and irritability.

Nikki is married and has two daughters (aged 2 and 11). Her husband is about to finish his Ph.D. program in physical education. She returned to school after more than 10 years and is now a junior in home economics at the University of Alabama, majoring in food and nutrition. One of her stated reasons for returning to school was to be a good mother to her older child, who is "gifted." Nikki is currently taking Introductory Statistics, Economics, and two classes in nutrition. While doing well in nutrition courses, she is having great difficulty with statistics and economics. Nikki works part-time at a local child development center. Although she is undertaking a great deal, she does not report a great deal of support from either her husband or parents.

Nikki says that she wants to be a county health counselor and work with pregnant teenagers regarding their prenatal care. She likes to read and play the piano.

Appearance and Behavioral Characteristics

Nikki, a 34-year-old Caucasian female, wears glasses and is of medium height and weight. She was cooperative and a willing worker throughout the testing session, although she was shy at the beginning.

It was evident throughout the session that Nikki was highly motivated. On a task requiring her to define a word she gave a string of responses until she felt comfortable with her answer. On a task of immediate recall of digits she closed her eyes and tried to concentrate on the task.

One of Nikki's outstanding characteristics was her excellent verbal ability (rich vocabulary and expressions). On a task requiring her to define words she frequently gave a few synonyms (e.g. "terminate" is "to end," "complete," and "finish") or long elaborations. Nikki successfully used trial-and-error strategy to solve verbal questions. Asked to explain the meaning of the saying, "One swallow doesn't make a summer," on a task testing her commonsense understanding of social situations, she was puzzled at first, asking, "One swallow?" She did not seem to be familiar with the saying. She began to describe the migration of swallows. While giving trial responses, she was able to find the proper answer. It should be noted that when she faced a hard question, she often laughed, saying, "Oh, boy," before trying. Laughing seemed to be her strategy for coping with anxiety.

Nikki exhibited her poor facility with numbers and her fear of them. On a test of general information, her responses to two questions requiring numerical answers (e.g., the population of the U.S.) were not even "in the ballpark." She also had extreme difficulty in re-

peating digits in their reverse order. When solving oral arithmetic problems, she was so nervous that she could not correct her responses even when she was aware that she was giving wrong answers. After the task she gave a sigh of relief.

Nikki showed her poor short-term memory, having to check with the key very often on a task requiring her to copy symbols that are paired with numbers. Though she tried to be careful, she made several mistakes, for example, copying the symbol for the number 3 in the box for the number 4.

Test Results and Interpretation

On the WAIS-R Nikki earned a Verbal IQ of 103, a Performance IQ of 98, and Full Scale IQ of 100, scores that place her in the Average classification of intelligence and rank her at about the 50th percentile for people her age. Her true Full Scale IQ has a 90% likelihood of falling in the 96–104 range. Her similar Verbal and Performance IQs indicate that she performed as well with tasks requiring verbal comprehension and expression as she did with manipulation of concrete materials and visual-motor activities.

Nikki's highly consistent scores on the three IQs mask the high degree of scatter that characterized her subtest profile. Within the Verbal Scale, her regular scaled scores ranged from 6 to 15, and four of the six subtests were significantly discrepant from her own average scaled score on the WAIS-R. Fluctuations of this magnitude are rare, occurring in less than 5% of adults with Average IQs. In contrast, there was little variability in Nikki's nonverbal subtests, as she displayed a single relative strength in a test of nonverbal concept formation and spatial visualization (84th percentile). Her best score, however, was on the Verbal Scale in a task of general information (91st percentile), reflecting her generally superior performance in tests of acquired verbal knowledge and verbal expression ("Who wrote Faust?" "Why should people pay taxes?")

TABLE 14.19   Nicole H.: Tests administered

Wechsler Adult Intelligence Scale-Revised (WAIS-R)

Verbal	Scaled Score	Age-Corrected Scaled Score	Performance	Scaled Score	Age-Corrected Scaled Score
Information	15	(14)—S	Picture Completion	9	(9)
Digit Span	6	(6)—W	Picture Arrangement	10	(10)
Vocabulary	14	(13)—S	Block Design	13	(13)—S
Arithmetic	8	(8)	Object Assembly	9	(9)
Comprehension	14	(13)—S	Digit Symbol	8	(8)
Similarities	9	(9)			

Age-Corrected Mean of 11 Subtests = 10

   Verbal IQ = 103 ± 4

   Performance IQ = 98 ± 6

   Full Scale IQ = 100 ± 4

Selected clusters from the Woodcock-Johnson Psycho-Educational Battery (1977 ed.)

	Percentile
Mathematics Aptitude	90th
Mathematics Achievement	21st
Written Language Aptitude	46th
Written Language Achievement	21st

Strong-Campbell Interest Inventory

Highest Rated Occupations:
   Occupational Therapist
   Physical Therapist
   Registered Nurse

Nikki's assets and deficits are better understood by departing from a strict Wechsler Verbal–Performance model and regrouping the WAIS-R subtests in other ways. She earned the following standard scores on the three factors that underlie the WAIS-R: Verbal Comprehension (113), Perceptual Organization (102), and Freedom from Distractibility (83). Analysis of these scores reveals that Nikki has a significant strength (80th percentile) in Verbal Comprehension and a significant weakness (13th percentile) in the so-called distractibility factor. Nikki's attention and concentration during the test were optimal, so her poor performance cannot be explained by distractibility. Rather, both tasks in this cluster (oral arithmetic and memory for digits) require auditory short-term memory and number manipulation. Her weaknesses seem to be primarily in these two areas.

It should be noted that her incorrect responses on the Arithmetic task were frequently very close to correct ones (e.g., 38¢ in place of 36¢, $1.85 in place of $1.86), implying that Nikki has weaknesses in the mental manipulation of numbers and computation rather than in quantitative reasoning. This finding accords well with her statement that she knows number concepts but still makes mistakes. As noted previously, her weakness with numbers was observed even on a test of general information;

Nikki failed some quantitative factual items (e.g., "How far is it from Paris to New York?") despite responding correctly to all of the more difficult nonnumerical items. Further, she performed at a relatively low level in a task requiring the rapid copying of abstract symbols that are paired with numbers. Performance on this task is influenced by short-term memory and number ability (plus other variables). As stated previously, Nikki clearly exhibited poor short-term memory on the task. Therefore, one may infer that her relative weaknesses in both the Verbal and Performance Scales were in tasks dependent on number ability and short-term memory.

Compared to her strength in verbal comprehension and expression, Nikki also evidenced significant relative weakness (45th percentile) in her "fluid" abilities. Fluid abilities reflect adaptability and flexibility when confronted with novel problems; Nikki had relative difficulty with such tasks within both the Verbal Scale (telling how two "things" are alike) and the Performance Scale (assembling cut-up picture puzzles).

In order to assess Nikki's aptitude and achievement in mathematics and written language, the appropriate clusters were administered from the Woodcock-Johnson Psycho-Educational Battery. In Mathematics Aptitude, Nikki ranked at the 90th percentile for people her age. In striking contrast, Nikki surpassed only 21% in Mathematics Achievement, which is consistent with her performance on the oral arithmetic test on the WAIS-R (25th percentile). She did poorly in calculation with paper and pencil and in practical problem solving. She demonstrated only 53% mastery on mathematics tasks that others having her aptitude score perform with 90% mastery. We see a person who has superior aptitude in mathematics but has not been able to apply it to acquire computational and problem-solving skills.

In Written Language Aptitude, Nikki ranked at the 46th percentile for people her age. In contrast, her scores in Written Language Achievement exceeded only 21% of the people her age. She did poorly on a task requiring her to respond in writing to a variety of questions demanding knowledge of punctuation, spelling, and usage. She demonstrated just 55% mastery on written language tasks that others having her aptitude score perform with 90% mastery. These results, coupled with the finding that Nikki has excellent verbal comprehension and oral expression, suggest that she has the potential to do better than she currently does in written language.

On the separate cognitive tasks in the Woodcock-Johnson Mathematics Aptitude and Written Language Aptitude scales, Nikki's performance was generally consistent with her WAIS-R performance. She was most successful on a test requiring her to give antonyms and synonyms (e.g., she knew the synonym of "munificent"), and was least successful in repeating numbers in reverse order.

Nikki was given the Strong-Campbell Interest Inventory (SCII), a measure of interests (not aptitudes) that provides general prediction of occupations in which she may find satisfaction. The results of the SCII suggest that Nikki may be happiest when she works with people for the welfare of others in less structured settings and gets many opportunities for self-expression. The areas she is most interested in are music/drama, art, domestic arts, and nature. The occupations she may enjoy most include occupational therapist, physical therapist, and registered nurse. Her goal of becoming a county health counselor and working with pregnant adolescents seems to fit her interests very well; so does her choice of college major (food and nutrition).

Summary and Conclusion

Concerned about her poor performance on tests and a possible learning disability, Nikki, a 34-year-old female, volunteered for evaluation to find out whether she can graduate from the University of Alabama, what her learning problems are, and how she can deal with them. She was a hard worker, using trial-and-error strategies to solve verbal items successfully. Nikki performed in the Average range, earning a Verbal IQ of 103, a Performance IQ of 98, and a Full Scale IQ of 100 on the WAIS-R. Further examination of the test results showed that she has strengths in verbal comprehension and expression and relative weaknesses in numbers, short-term memory, and "fluid" ability (solving novel problems). The test results of selected clusters from the Woodcock-Johnson Psycho-Educational Battery revealed that Nikki has average aptitude in written language and superior aptitude in mathematics but has not been able to apply these aptitudes to acquire writing skills and computational skills. Nikki's Strong-Campbell Interest Inventory results conform well with her college major and her choice of occupation.

It is apparent from the evaluation that Nikki has the ability to complete her college degree. Although the discrepancy between her ability and achievement in mathematics is fairly large, it is not sufficient to suggest a learning disability. Instead, her poor performance in mathematics seems to stem in part from the quality of math education she has received and in part from her being away from school for more than 10 years.

Nikki seems to try to accomplish too much at once: taking four courses, working part-time, and taking care of her family as a wife and mother of two children. This overload, in the face of little support from her husband and parents, seems to be making her extremely anxious and may be related to her inconsistent performance in her college courses. She needs to learn that she doesn't have to be perfect. Nikki's goal of becoming a county health counselor to help deliver prenatal care to pregnant teenagers is consistent with her interests and abilities.

Recommendations

1. Nikki should cut back on her workload. She should take fewer university courses each semester and should take more time to complete her college education.

2. Nikki should find time to get away from the house to concentrate on studying.

3. Nikki should take remedial math courses or go to the Learning Skills and Tutorial Center, where she can get tutorial service for free. Her tutor needs to help with the specific subject matter.

4. Nikki should take remedial grammar courses (such as Basic Writing) or go to the Writing Center, where she can get tutorial service on grammar and writing for free. The center has many returning students who are able to learn in a nonthreatening atmosphere.

5. In an effort to accommodate her memory difficulties, Nikki should study over several short periods of time, rather than in a block of, say, 3 straight hours. Nikki should also use a tape recorder, taping classes and talking into the tape recorder so that she can listen again and again to what she is trying to learn.

6. She should make learning more active to study effectively. The following suggestions are recommended.

    (a) Make a test for herself and practice it under no pressure

    (b) Make fact sheets and quiz herself

    (c) Try to teach her gifted daughter the subject matter of her courses and have her daughter try to teach her or quiz her

    (d) Make every effort to make her studying game-like and challenging.

Examiners and Report Writers: Graduate students in Drs. Nadeen and Alan Kaufman's advanced assessment course at the University of Alabama; Peggy Connell, Ellen Dossett, Elizabeth Eller, Toshinori Ishikuma, Marcia O'Neal, and Gwen Wilson.

CHAPTER 14 SUMMARY

Chapter 14, the third of three profile interpretation chapters, focuses on the generation of valid hypotheses for explaining significant fluctuations in WAIS-R subtest profiles. The raw ingredients for this combined rational and empirical endeavor are the abilities measured by two or more subtests and the influences that affect performance on several tasks. For convenience, these "shared" abilities and influences are organized into four tables that constitute the raw materials for hypothesis generation. The reliability of these clusters appears in the tables; additional tables are provided to permit converting different groupings of tasks to standard scores, banding the standard scores with error, and determining whether the difference between two cluster scores is large enough to be statistically significant. As a rule of thumb, a difference of 1 standard deviation is required for significance when comparing a person's standard scores on any two clusters of WAIS-R subtests.

The following basic rules for examiners apply for the generation of hypotheses: (a) work like a detective, regrouping tasks in different ways; (b) group as many tasks as possible together when forming hypotheses; (c) avoid subtest-specific hypotheses, if possible; (d) identify the specific aspect of a task that is strong or weak; (e) recognize that finding significant profile fluctuations is the starting point, not the goal, of interpretation; (f) aggregate tasks when forming hypotheses rather than pitting one subtest against another; (g) cross-validate hypotheses with data from other tests, background information, and clinical observations of behavior; (h) apply interpretive rules as guidelines, but use clinical inferences liberally; (i) include only the most essential scores in case reports. Empirical analysis indicates that the Verbal Comprehension tetrad is likely to band together in a person's profile; Block Design and Object Assembly may conceivably cluster together, perhaps with Picture Completion, to form an estimate of the person's nonverbal intelligence; Arithmetic and Digit Span are likely to band together; and Picture Arrangement and Digit Symbol are the tasks most likely to splinter off alone.

Two methods of hypothesis generation are offered, one sequential and one simultaneous.

The sequential, step-by-step approach is quite similar to the linear interpretive systems I have presented elsewhere for the WISC-R and other tests. The simultaneous method affords examiners with a holistic processing orientation the chance to develop hypotheses by observing various configurations within the subtest profile. After detecting meaningful configurations, simple empirical checks are advised to ensure that the apparent differences in skill areas are real. Illustrations of both the sequential and simultaneous interpretive techniques are presented, along with a discussion of common configurations to anticipate within the Verbal Scale, within the Performance Scale, and across both scales.

Common Verbal configurations include Factor I versus Factor III, memory versus conceptualization, the amount of verbal expression required, and fluid versus crystallized intelligence. Factor III deficits have been associated with brain impairment, Huntington's disease, and learning disabilities, although research has failed to pinpoint precisely what this third Wechsler factor assesses. The subtests requiring much verbal expression are also the ones demanding good conceptualization skills. Some groups, such as autistic individuals, characteristically do not perform well on these tasks; good clinical skills are needed to infer the reason for a person's high or low scores on the pertinent subtests. Low fluid intelligence has been observed in alcoholics with cirrhosis of the liver.

Common Performance Scale configurations are as follows: (a) visual organization versus visual-motor coordination, (b) meaningful versus abstract stimuli, (c) simultaneous versus sequential processing, and (d) visual memory versus nonverbal thinking. Visual-motor coordination deficits have been found in severe alcoholics, while a deficiency in the processing of abstract stimuli has been associated with alcoholism, brain damage, Alzheimer's-type dementia, psychopathology, and other disorders. The pair of Performance subtests with a sequential component (Picture Arrangement, Digit

Symbol) represents a deficiency for patients with Huntington's disease, autism, multiple sclerosis, and manic-depression. These subtests, along with the trio of spatial-simultaneous tasks, permit WAIS-R interpretation from the vantage point of Luria's Blocks 1, 2, and 3. Block Design, though primarily a simultaneous task, is quite complex and has important analytic components as well.

Two configurations that comprise both the Verbal and Performance Scales are Social Comprehension versus Abstract Thought and fund of information versus trial-and-error learning. Deficits in Social Comprehension have been observed for individuals low in ego development, although research results have been mixed regarding the validity of the so-called social intelligence dyad of Comprehension and Picture Arrangement. Fund of information (Information + Vocabulary) emerges as an intact strength for a variety of clinical samples such as patients with Alzheimer's-type dementia, schizophrenia, and multiple sclerosis.

EXAMINER'S FORM 14.1 Determining relative strengths and weaknesses on the WAIS-R Verbal Scale (Developed by A. S. Kaufman)

Instructions for Worksheet:

(1) For this Worksheet, examiners indicate whether a person's scaled score on each Verbal subtest is *above, equal to, or below his or her own mean score*. The goal is to generate hypotheses about strengths and weaknesses, using the method described on pages 488–497. *No numbers are entered on this Worksheet, only +'s, –'s, and 0's.*

(2) Use the person's mean *Verbal* scaled score if he or she had a significant V–P IQ discrepancy. Otherwise, use the mean of all 11 subtests. Round the relevant mean to the nearest whole number. *Only age-corrected scaled scores should be used.*

(3) Determine if the person's age-corrected scaled score on each subtest is above, below, or equal to his or her own mean score.

(4) If a scaled score for a subtest is *above* the mean (by at least 1 point) put a "+" in all boxes in that subtest's column. If it is at least 3 points above, put "++" in all boxes.

(5) If a scaled score for a subtest is *below* the mean (by at least 1 point) put a "–" in all boxes in that subtest's column. If it is at least 3 points below, put "—" in all boxes.

(6) If a scaled score for a subtest is *equal to* the mean, put a 0 in all boxes in that subtest's column.

(7) Determine whether there are enough "+" or "—" signs in each row to denote a possible *strength* or *weakness* in the relevant abilities; *follow the rules on page 489.* Circle the S for all abilities identified as possible strengths. Circle the W for all abilities identified as possible weaknesses. See Chapter 14 to aid in interpretation.

Worksheet for: Examinee's Name _____ Date _____

| | | | | VERBAL SUBTEST | | | |
Ability	Information (I)	Digit Span (DSp)	Vocabulary (V)	Arithmetic (A)	Comprehension (C)	Similarities (S)	S or W
Verbal Comprehension; Crystallized Intelligence (Horn)	☐		☐		☐	☐	S W
Verbal Conceptualization (Bannatyne); Verbal expression			☐		☐	☐	S W
Acquired Knowledge (Bannatyne)	☐		☐	☐			S W
Long-term Memory (Influenced by school learning)							

Retrieval (Horn); □

Memory (Guilford)
(Influenced by learning disabilities)   □   S □   W □

Semantic Cognition
(Guilford)   □   □   S □   W □

Freedom from Distractibility;

Auditory Memory (Dean);   □

Symbolic Memory (Guilford);   □   S □   W □

Auditory Sequencing;

Mental Alertness
(Influenced by attention span, anxiety, and distractibility)   □

Verbal Concept Formation
(Rapaport);   □

Handling Abstract
Verbal Concepts
(Influenced by interests and outside reading)   □   S □   W □

Verbal Reasoning
(Influenced by negativism and overly concrete thinking)   □   □   S □   W □

Memory (Rapaport);   □

Fund of Information
(Influenced by cultural opportunities, foreign language background, intellectual curiosity and striving, outside reading, interests, early environment, and school learning)   □   S □   W □

EXAMINER'S FORM 14.2 Determining relative strengths and weaknesses on the WAIS-R Performance Scale (Developed by A. S. Kaufman)

Instructions for Worksheet:

(1) For this Worksheet, examiners indicate whether a person's scaled score on each Performance subtest is *above, equal to, or below his or her own mean score.* The goal is to generate hypotheses about strengths and weaknesses, using the method described on pages 488–497. *No numbers are entered on this Worksheet, only +'s, −'s, and 0's.*

(2) Use the person's mean *Performance* scaled score if he or she had a significant V–P IQ discrepancy. Otherwise, use the mean of all 11 subtests. Round the relevant mean to the nearest whole number. *Only age-corrected scaled scores should be used.*

(3) Determine if the person's age-corrected scaled score on each subtest is above, below, or equal to his or her own mean score.

(4) If a scaled score for a subtest is *above* the mean (by at least 1 point) put a "+" in all boxes in that subtest's column. If it is at least 3 points above, put "++" in all boxes.

(5) If a scaled score for a subtest is *below* the mean (by at least 1 point) put a "−" in all boxes in that subtest's column. If it is at least 3 points below, put "−−" in all boxes.

(6) If a scaled score for a subtest is *equal to* the mean, put a 0 in all boxes in that subtest's column.

(7) Determine whether there are enough "+" or "−" signs in each row to denote a possible *strength* or *weakness* in the relevant abilities; *follow the rules on page 489.* Circle the S for all abilities identified as possible strengths. Circle the W for all abilities identified as possible weaknesses. See Chapter 14 to aid in interpretation.

Worksheet for: Examinee's Name _____ Date _____

	PERFORMANCE SUBTEST					
Ability	*Picture Completion (PC)*	*Picture Arrangement (PA)*	*Block Design (BD)*	*Object Assembly (OA)*	*Digit Symbol (DSy)*	*S or W*
Perceptual Organization; Spatial (Bannatyne);	☐					S W
Figural Cognition and Evaluation (Guilford);		☐	☐	☐		S
Simultaneous Processing (Influenced by field-dependent cognitive style)						

		S	W
Visual-Motor Coordination (Rapaport)	☐	☐	☐
Synthesis	☐	☐	☐ S W
Visual Organization (Rapaport);	☐		
Visual Perception/Processing of Meaningful Stimuli	☐		S W
Anticipation (Rapaport);	☐		
Nonverbal Reasoning		☐	S W
Visual Memory (Dean) (Influenced by concentration)	☐	☐	S W
Visual-Motor Speed (Dean) (Influenced by persistence)		☐	☐ S W
Convergent-production (Guilford);	☐		☐ S W
Visual Sequencing			
Visual Closure (Influenced by ability to respond when uncertain)	☐	☐	S W
Reproduction of Models;			
Visual Perception/Processing of Abstract Stimuli		☐	☐ S W
Trial-and-Error Learning		☐	S W

EXAMINER'S FORM 14.3   Determining relative strengths and weaknesses on both the WAIS-R Verbal and Performance Scales (Developed by A. S. Kaufman)

Instructions for Worksheet:

(1) For this Worksheet, examiners indicate whether a person's scaled score on each WAIS-R subtest is *above, equal to, or below his or her own mean score*. The goal is to generate hypotheses about strengths and weaknesses, using the method described on pages 488–497. *No numbers are entered on this Worksheet, only +'s, −'s, and 0's.*

(2) Use the person's mean *Verbal* scaled score for each Verbal subtest, and the person's mean *Performance* scaled score for each Performance subtest, if he or she had a significant V–P IQ discrepancy. Otherwise, use the mean of all 11 subtests. Round the relevant mean to the nearest whole number. *Only age-corrected scaled scores should be used.*

(3) Determine if the person's age-corrected scaled score on each subtest is above, below, or equal to his or her own mean score.

(4) If a scaled score for a subtest is *above* the mean (by at least 1 point) put a "+" in all boxes in that subtest's column. If it is at least 3 points above, put "++" in all boxes.

(5) If a scaled score for a subtest is *below* the mean (by at least 1 point) put a "−" in all boxes in that subtest's column. If it is at least 3 points below, put "—" in all boxes.

(6) If a scaled score for a subtest is *equal* to the mean, put a 0 in all boxes in that subtest's column.

(7) Determine whether there are enough "+" or "−" signs in each row to denote a possible *strength* or *weakness* in the relevant abilities; *follow the rules on page 489.* Circle the S for all abilities identified as possible strengths. Circle the W for all abilities identified as possible weaknesses. See Chapter 14 to aid in interpretation.

Worksheet for: Examinee's Name _____   Date _____

Ability	I	DSp	V	A	C	S	PC	PA	BD	OA	DSy	S or W
	VERBAL SUBTEST						PERFORMANCE SUBTEST					
General Ability (Dean)	☐		☐	☐	☐	☐	☐	☐	☐	☐	☐	S W
Fluid Intelligence (Horn)		☐				☐	☐	☐	☐	☐	☐	S W
Cognition (Guilford)			☐			☐	☐	☐	☐	☐		S W
Evaluation (Guilford)				☐	☐		☐	☐	☐		☐	S W
Semantic Content (Guilford)	☐			☐	☐	☐		☐				S W

							S	W
Reasoning	□	□	□	□	□	□	□	
Attention/Concentration (Rapaport) (Influenced by attention span, anxiety, concentration, distractibility)	□			□	□	□	□	
Sequential (Bannatyne);								
Symbolic Content (Guilford);								
Encoding Information for Further Processing;	□					□	□	
Facility with Numbers;								
Sequential Processing (Influenced by attention span, anxiety, distractibility, and learning disabilities)								
Automatic Level of Organization (Osgood)	□			□	□	□	□	
Concept Formation (Rapaport)		□	□	□	□	□	□	
Distinguishing Essential from Nonessential Detail			□	□	□		□	
Abstract Thought (Dean)				□	□		□	

(Continues)

EXAMINER'S FORM 14.3 (Continued)

Ability	VERBAL SUBTEST						PERFORMANCE SUBTEST					S or W
	I	DSp	V	A	C	S	PC	PA	BD	OA	DSy	
Remote Memory (Dean) (Influenced by alertness to environment)	☐						☐					S W
Social Comprehension (Dean); Common Sense (cause-effect) (Influenced by cultural opportunities)					☐			☐				S W
Learning Ability			☐								☐	S W

Chapter 15

Mental Retardation,
Adaptive Behavior Assessment,
and Giftedness

Patti L. Harrison, *The University of Alabama*

Patti L. Harrison is Associate Professor and Chair of the School Psychology training program at The University of Alabama. While earning her Ph.D. in school psychology at The University of Georgia, she assisted in the development of the K-ABC. As a research associate with American Guidance Service, Dr. Harrison was closely involved in the development and standardization of the K-ABC and was project director of the Vineland Adaptive Behavior Scales. She is author of the Vineland Classroom Edition Manual and senior author of the upcoming Early Screening Profiles, and has published numerous articles and chapters on intelligence, adaptive behavior, and preschool assessment. A member of three editorial boards of professional journals, Dr. Harrison is also the Alabama delegate to NASP and the President-elect of the Alabama Association of School Psychologists.

Adolescents and adults at the two extremes of the intellectual continuum, the mentally retarded at one end and those with superior intelligence at the other, may appear to be so diverse that inclusion of both groups in the same chapter seems unwarranted. The two groups have many obvious differences, of course. Yet individuals in both groups require special consideration during assessment, considerations that are elaborated in this chapter. Individuals within the two groups vary widely in functioning, and assessment of that functioning serves similar purposes. Outcomes of assessment for both mentally retarded and gifted individuals include diagnosis of special abilities and development of vocational plans that take these special abilities into account. This chapter focuses primarily on the low end of the ability spectrum because assessment of mentally retarded adolescents and adults is a more frequent practice than assessment of gifted individuals, but topics related to giftedness are covered at the end of the chapter. Although the pages that follow address numerous concerns, the largest portion of the chapter is devoted to a topic of vital importance, particularly for the mentally retarded: the concept of *adaptive behavior* and major tests for assessing it.

MENTAL RETARDATION: DEFINITIONS, RESEARCH, AND INTELLECTUAL ASSESSMENT

Mentally retarded adolescents and adults represent a challenge to psychologists who assess intelligence. There are many known causes of mental retardation, and mentally retarded individuals form a very heterogeneous group. Indeed, the term *mental retardation* is itself rather vague, representing a variety of psychological and other deficits (Gregory, 1987; Zigler & Balla, 1981). Mentally retarded individuals have differing capacities for independent living, employment, and other activities, and differing needs for services from psychologists and other professionals; assessment of these individuals is therefore conducted for a variety of purposes. This section of the chapter describes characteristics of mentally retarded adolescents and adults, offers guidelines for assessing their intelligence and adaptive behavior, and discusses uses of assessment for planning interventions and vocational programs.

Defining Mental Retardation

Prior to the development of intelligence tests, mental retardation was primarily seen as a medical disorder; medical professionals were easily able to diagnose those individuals with extremely low levels of intellectual functioning and with associated severe physical and psychological disabilities (Horn & Fuchs, 1987; Matarazzo, 1972). People with less severe handicaps were not recognized as being mentally retarded or were diagnosed as mentally ill. Re-

forms in public education and new methods of treatment for individuals with mental disorders underscored the need for more objective standards of diagnosing mental retardation, for methods to distinguish mild to severe levels of retardation, and for ways to distinguish between mental retardation and mental illness. With the development of their first intelligence test, Binet and Simon found an objective way for measuring intelligence and diagnosing mental retardation.

The development of the Binet-Simon scales and their American translations in the first part of the twentieth century led to a reliance on intelligence test scores as the single method for diagnosing mental retardation. However, in the early 1960s the American Association on Mental Deficiency (AAMD) defined *three* necessary components for a diagnosis of mental retardation (Heber, 1959, 1961), components that continue to be emphasized in the current AAMD definition: "Mental retardation refers to significantly subaverage general intellectual functioning existing concurrently with deficits in adaptive behavior and manifested during the developmental period" (Grossman, 1983, p. 1). Similar definitions of mental retardation may be found in Section 504 of the Vocational Rehabilitation Act; Public Law 94-142, the Education of All Handicapped Children Act; and Public Law 94-602, Developmental Disabilities Amendment. Further, a survey of state departments of mental retardation and developmental disabilities indicated that the majority use the AAMD definition of mental retardation (Lowitzer, Utley, & Baumeister, 1987).

Intellectual Functioning

"General intellectual functioning" is defined by the AAMD as the result of individual assessment with one or more standardized, general intelligence tests, with "subaverage intellectual functioning" defined as an intelligence test score of approximately 70 or below (Grossman, 1983). The upper limit of 70 is intended as a guideline by the AAMD and can be extended to 75 or more, depending on errors in measurement associated with the particular instrument used. The AAMD specifies that professional judgment in diagnosing mental retardation must be flexible: Some individuals with intelligence test scores higher than 70 may truly need special education or rehabilitation programs for the mentally retarded, while others with scores below 70 may not.

Setting a criterion IQ of 70 or below for classification of mental retardation is an arbitrary designation (Gregory, 1987). The earliest versions of the AAMD definition set a higher upper limit for intelligence test scores (e.g., 80 or 85). Practically, higher limits resulted in a larger percentage of the population being classified as mentally retarded, creating greater demand for educational and community services. For humanistic reasons, a lower intelligence score criterion removed the stigma of a label of mental retardation for many individuals.

Adaptive Behavior

According to the AAMD, [A]daptive behavior is defined as the effectiveness or degree with which individuals meet the standards of personal independence and social responsibility expected for age and culture group (Grossman, 1983, p. 1). Deficits in adaptive behavior are identified as significant limitations in meeting standards of learning, maturation, personal independence, and social responsibility and are determined through clinical assessment and standardized scales. An individual with significantly subaverage intelligence but no deficits in adaptive behavior and an individual with deficits in adaptive behavior but intelligence above the subaverage range cannot be classified as mentally retarded. No "upper limits" for scores on adaptive behavior scales are given by the AAMD, as they are for intelligence test scores, making it difficult to operationalize the adaptive behavior deficits required for a classification of mental retardation. At the time the AAMD manual was written, there was less experience with the use of adaptive behavior scales than with intelligence tests, and differences in the scoring systems of different adaptive behavior scales hampered development of a criterion.

Developmental Period

The AAMD defines the developmental period as "the period of time between conception and the 18th birthday" (Grossman, 1983, p. 1). Deficits in the developmental period may result from factors such as brain damage, degenerative process in the central nervous system, or psychosocial factors. Although retardation may result from central nervous system trauma after the developmental period, these manifestations are properly classified as dementia and not mental retardation.

Levels and Prevalence of Mental Retardation

Mentally retarded adolescents and adults display a wide range of deficits in functioning. Some are totally dependent on caregivers, while others are able to maintain almost complete independence. Although there are large numbers of mentally retarded persons in the United States, prevalence rates indicate that about 75% of retarded persons are mildly or moderately retarded and 25% are severely or profoundly retarded.

Four Levels of Mental Retardation

Four levels of mental retardation are defined by the AAMD (see Table 15.1). In public schools, the mild and moderate categories are usually labeled as educable (EMR) and trainable mental retardation (TMR), respectively. The AAMD specifies a five-step procedure for determining the level of retardation. The first step is to determine that a problem exists—for example, to determine that a person is experiencing developmental delays; the second step is to determine that deficits in adaptive behavior exist.

TABLE 15.1   The AAMD's four levels of mental retardation

Level	IQ Range
Mild	50–55 to approximately 70
Moderate	35–40 to 50–55
Severe	20–25 to 35–40
Profound	less than 20–25

SOURCE: Adapted from Grossman, H. J. (1983). *Classification in mental retardation.* Washington, DC: American Association on Mental Deficiency.

The third step is to measure general intelligence and the fourth is to decide whether the person exhibits retardation in intellectual functioning. The fifth step is to determine the level of retardation according to the level of intellectual functioning.

Individuals with mild to moderate levels of retardation can be distinguished from those with severe to profound levels of retardation by several characteristics other than intelligence test scores (Landesman-Dwyer & Butterfield, 1983). Severely to profoundly retarded individuals have at least three times the rate of mortality during childhood than do the mildly to moderately retarded. The severely to profoundly retarded are diagnosed during the preschool years or infancy. Mildly to moderately retarded individuals are usually diagnosed during their school years. The duration of retardation is lifelong for severely to profoundly retarded individuals. Some mildly and moderately retarded individuals may improve their functioning as a result of intervention or may function adequately in a new environment and no longer meet the criteria for a classification of mental retardation. Severely to profoundly retarded people are usually placed in settings outside the home, such as institutions or community residential facilities; mildly to moderately retarded individuals more often live in the home. Severely to profoundly retarded individuals often have apparent medical or neurological problems; these problems are not typically associated with mild or moderate retardation. The parents and siblings of the severely to profoundly retarded usually have normal intelligence; family members of mild to moderately mentally retarded people often have below-average intelligence. Finally, all social classes are represented in cases of severe to profound retardation, while lower social classes are overrepresented in mild and moderate levels.

Expected Versus Actual Prevalence

Grossman (1983) reported that the incidence of mental retardation in the United States is about 125,000 births each year, with a prevalence of about 3% of the population, or more than 6 million people. However, prevalence rates for mental retardation are difficult to determine and vary by age, ethnicity, and geographic location (Fryers, 1984; Landesman-Dwyer & Butterfield, 1983; Reschly & Jipson, 1976). The expected prevalence of intelligence test scores below 70, using the normal curve, is 2.3%. Since the AAMD definition of mental retardation specifies *both* subaverage intelligence and deficits in adaptive behavior, expected prevalence when both criteria are used varies according to the correlation between the intelligence test and adaptive behavior measure (Silverstein, 1983). For example, if the correlation between the adaptive behavior scale and intelligence test is 1.0, the expected prevalence of individuals with adaptive behavior *and* intelligence test scores below 70 (more than 2 standard deviations below the mean) is 2.3%. If the correlation between the adaptive behavior and intelligence measures is .6, the expected prevalence is 0.5%. If the correlation between the two types of measures is 0, the expected prevalence is 0.05%. Studies have demonstrated that large percentages of individuals who have been classified as mentally retarded because of subaverage intelligence would be declassified if both intelligence and adaptive behavior scores are used as criteria (Childs, 1982; Fischer, 1978; Reschly, 1981).

Age and Prevalence

Different prevalence rates of mental retardation have been reported for different age groups. Landesman-Dwyer and Butterfield (1983) indicated that about 0.2% of the population is classified as mentally retarded at age 5, 2% at age 15, and 0.5% at age 30, with a dramatic eak in prevalence at 10 to 15 years of age. It has been suggested that this peak occurs because most mildly retarded children are identified after they enter school and are not noticed by the community once they leave school (Landesman-Dwyer & Butterfield, 1983; Scheerenberger, 1987; Sattler, 1988). Although many cases of mild retardation seem to "disappear" after the school years, mildly retarded adults often use coping mechanisms and other strategies to blend into the community; some evidence suggests that IQs continue to fall in the retarded range and that the everyday lives of these individuals never completely parallel the lives of their non-retarded peers (Baroff, 1986). Note, however, that competing evidence suggests a possible real increase in the IQs of retarded individuals over time, a topic discussed on pages 119–121.

Schuster and Butler (1986) conducted a follow-up study of a group of individuals eligible for classification as mentally retarded during their school years. Some of these individuals *were* classified as mentally retarded and received special education services, and some were not classified as mentally retarded, although there were no differences in intelligence between the two groups. Twenty years later, it was found that the group of individuals classified as mentally retarded in school did *not* differ from those who were not classified in terms of anxiety, self-concept, interactions with others, occupation, income, and education. Thus, being classified as mentally retarded during the school years had no apparent detrimental effects nor did special education services provide benefits, relative to the qualities assessed in the study.

Two Distinct Groups of Mental Retardation

A well-documented observation about the prevalence of mental retardation is that it does not correspond to the normal curve for intellectual functioning in the population (Haskins, 1986; Roberts, 1952; Scheerenberger, 1987; Vandenberg & Vogler, 1985; Zigler & Balla, 1981). Although the prevalence of mental retardation at intelligence test score levels between 50 and 70 appears to correspond to the normal curve in that range, there is a greater prevalence of mental retardation in IQ ranges below 50 than would be expected from the normal curve, as seen in Figure 15.1.

Two distinct groups of mentally retarded individuals seem to be represented by IQs above and below 50 (Grossman, 1983; Zigler & Balla, 1981). The group of individuals with IQs between 50 and 70, or about 75% of all retarded individuals, is hypothesized to represent simple genetic variation; these individuals are usually neurologically intact (although current technology may be unable to detect neurological problems in these individuals); many are from low socioeconomic groups, have no physical abnormalities, and are diagnosed during the school years. The group of individuals with IQs below

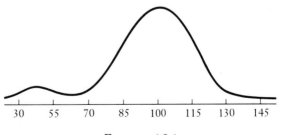

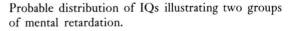

FIGURE 15.1

Probable distribution of IQs illustrating two groups of mental retardation.

50, about 25% of all retarded individuals, often have known organic causes for the retardation, central nervous system pathology, and associated physical abnormalities, and can usually be identified during infancy. Fryers (1986) predicted that the future will see an increase in the prevalence of individuals with IQs below 50 because modern medical technology has reduced perinatal and infant mortality for infants with severe handicaps.

Roberts (1952) provided evidence to support the two distinct groups of mentally retarded individuals, one group representing genetic variation and the other group retardation due to detectable organic causes. He hypothesized that if mild retardation is due to simple genetic variation in the human species, siblings of these mildly retarded individuals would have below average intelligence test scores. On the other hand, IQs of siblings of the more severely retarded group would be in the average range, if genetic factors are not at work. His findings supported his hypothesis: The average IQ of siblings of mildly retarded individuals was about 80, while the average IQ of siblings of the more severely retarded was about 100.

Nichols (1984), in a replication of Roberts's study, found similar results for white retarded children. The siblings of the mildly retarded had a mean IQ of about 85 and of the more severely retarded, about 103. Different results were obtained for black children; siblings of mildly retarded black children had a mean IQ of about 78, and siblings of more severely retarded black children also had a mean IQ of about 78. Nichols suggested that the lack of a difference between siblings of black mildly retarded and severely retarded children may have been due to the downward shift in the IQ distribution of the black population. According to Nichols, black children with IQs in the severely retarded range are similar to the mildly retarded in terms of familial patterns, central nervous system pathology, and socioeconomic status.

Factors Associated With Mental Retardation

Mental retardation has many known causes, often grouped into biological/organic factors and social-environmental factors. Terdal (1981) reported that about 200 syndromes associated with mental retardation have been identified. Grossman (1983) specified numerous factors associated with mental retardation, as indicated in Table 15.2. This section includes a discussion of several of the factors that may be associated with many of the mentally retarded adolescents and adults assessed by psychologists.

Fetal Alcohol Syndrome

The cognitive impairment associated with fetal alcohol syndrome is so compelling that this syndrome is becoming one of the most commonly recognized biological causes of mental retardation (Abel, 1980). In addition to impaired mental functioning, physical features associated with fetal alcohol syndrome include microcephaly, small midface, short nose, and joint abnormalities, and behavioral features such as visual-motor deficits, irritability, and hyperactivity (Bloom, Hersh, Podruch, Weisskopp, Topinka, & Reese, 1986). Fetal alcohol syndrome is caused by consumption of alcoholic beverages by the mother during the prenatal period. Scheerenberger (1987) reported average IQs of individuals with fetal alcohol syndrome to be 70 in France, 85 in Germany, and 65 in the United States. Broman, Nichols, and Kennedy (1975) compared a group of children with fetal alcohol syndrome to a group of matched controls. Of the fetal alcohol syndrome group, 44% had IQs below 79 compared to only 9% for the controls.

Phenylketonuria

Phenylketonuria (PKU) is a recessive genetic disorder that results in an inability to metabolize the protein phenylalanine, found in milk and other foods (Hetherington & Parke, 1986).

Phenylpyruvic acid accumulates in the body, gradually damaging the central nervous system, usually resulting in mental deficits, irritability, poor coordination, hyperactivity, and convulsions. Most hospitals now routinely test infants for PKU, and children with the disorder are put on a restricted diet in the first few weeks of life. If dietary therapy is started early, the damage can be restricted. Baumeister (1967) reported that average IQs of individuals who started dietary treatment in the first 2 months of life were in the normal range, compared to an average IQ of about 50 when treatment was started later than 7 months and an average IQ of about 25 when treatment was started later than 3 years of age. Jackson (1981) indicated that 96% of individuals with untreated PKU have IQs below 60, with many in the severely and profoundly retarded range.

Chromosomal Anomalies

The most common chromosomal anomaly associated with mental retardation is Down syndrome, or a triplet instead of a pair of the 21st chromosome. Individuals with Down syndrome have a unique appearance, usually almond eyes with eyelid fold, round heads, small noses, and protruding tongues. They often have other characteristics such as webbed fingers, an awkward walk, dental anomalies, and increased incidence of heart disorders and respiratory infections. Down syndrome results in variable degrees of mental retardation, with most individuals falling in the severe to profound levels (Bloom et al., 1986; Smith, 1982). Other chromosomal anomalies associated with mental retardation, which occur with less frequency than Trisomy 21, include Trisomy 13 and 18 and structural deletion of Chromosome 5 (Cri-du-chat syndrome) and Chromosome 4.

Some anomalies of the sex chromosomes are associated with mental retardation, although individuals with triple instead of pairs of sex chromosomes most typically experience only mild cognitive deficits that do not fall in the mentally retarded range. Additional chromosomes beyond a triplet are associated with increasing degrees of retardation (Matarazzo, 1972; Smith, 1982). Bloom et al. (1986), Smith (1982), and Jackson (1981) reported that males with Klinefelter's syndrome (XXY) are not usually retarded, but that larger percentages than normal have IQs below average and their Performance IQs are typically higher than their Verbal IQs. Females with Turner's syndrome (only one X chromosome) also are seldom mentally retarded, but often have Verbal IQs that are higher than Performance IQs, and deficits in visual memory, right-left orientation, digits backward, and word fluency. About one-third of females with Triple X syndrome have normal intelligence and two-thirds have some cognitive deficits, with a few falling in the mentally retarded range. The XYY pattern is associated with IQs that are 10–15 points below normal, on the average. The average IQ of individuals with the XXXX pattern is about 55. The XXXXX and XXXXY patterns are associated with moderate to severe mental retardation. Robinson et al. (1982) reported average WISC-R IQs for samples of children 8 to 10 years of age with sex chromosome anomalies: Triple X syndrome—IQs of 87–91; Turner's syndrome—IQs of 87–88; Klinefelter's syndrome—IQs of 98–100. Mean Verbal and Performance IQs were fairly equal, the biggest discrepancy being 4 points in favor of P-IQ for children with Triple X syndrome.

A sex chromosomal anomaly *frequently* associated with mental retardation is Fragile X syndrome, or a malformation or fragile site on an X chromosome. Female carriers with a fragile site on one of their X chromosomes usually have normal intelligence or only mild cognitive deficits, but males who have a fragile site on their X chromosome usually have severe retardation (Bloom et al., 1986). Rogers and Simenson (1987), in a study of males with Fragile X syndrome, reported that this syndrome is second only to Down syndrome in chromosomal

TABLE 15.2   Factors associated with mental retardation

Infections and Intoxications
    Prenatal infection (e.g., congenital rubella, congenital syphilis)
    Postnatal cerebral infection (e.g., viral or bacterial infections)
    Intoxication (e.g., toxemia of pregnancy, lead, fetal alcohol syndrome)

Trauma or physical agents (e.g., prenatal or postnatal injury, prenatal or postnatal hypoxia)

Metabolism or Nutrition
    Neuronal lipid storage diseases
    Carbohydrate disorders (e.g., galactosemia, hypoglycemia)
    Amino acid disorders (e.g, phenylketonuria)
    Other disorders of metabolism
    Mineral disorders
    Endocrine disorders
    Nutritional disorders
    Other (e.g., postnatal failure to thrive)

Gross brain disease (postnatal)
    Neurocutaneous dysplasia
    Tumors
    Cerebral white matter, degenerative
    Specific fiber tracts or neural groups, degenerative
    Cerebrovascular system
    Other

Unknown Prenatal Influence
    Cerebral malformation (e.g., anencephaly)
    Craniofacial anomaly (e.g., microcephaly)
    Status dysraphicus (e.g., hydrocephaly, congenital)

anomalies associated with mental retardation. They found that the mean IQs of those individuals in their sample with Fragile X syndrome who resided in institutions was 23 and that the mean IQ of those residing in community settings was 38.

Birth Factors and Growth Factors

Birth factors and physical growth factors have traditionally been associated with mental retardation, but their influence may be smaller than assumed. Some birth factors are associated with mental retardation; however, they may interact with low socioeconomic status as causes of mental retardation, and research suggests that birth factors by themselves must be severe to result in mental retardation. Werner (1986), in a longitudinal study of 698 children who had none or some perinatal complications, found that the most retarded of these children had both severe perinatal complications and lived in the poorest homes. Bouchard and Segal (1985), in a comprehensive review of factors associated with intelligence, found that factors such as birth weight do not correlate very highly with intelligence and that any correlation was due more to differences between families than birth factors. Further, only very low birth weights were associated with low IQ. (See Table 2.3 for a summary of Bouchard and Segal's literature review.) Scheerenberger (1987) reported that the lower the birth weight, the greater the probability of neurological deficits. About 1.5%

TABLE 15.2 (Continued)

Chromosomal anomalies
   Down syndrome (Trisomy 21)
   Patua syndrome
   Edwards syndrome
   Autosomal deletion syndromes (e.g., Cri-du-chat syndrome)
   Balanced autosomal translocation in normal individual
   Other conditions due to autosomal anomalies
   Donadal syngenesis, ovarian dysgenesis, Turner syndrome, XO syndrome
   Klinefelter's syndrome
   Other conditions due to sex chromosome anomalies (e.g., additional sex chromosome, Fragile X syndrome,
      Trisomy 13, Trisomy 18, Triple X syndrome, XYY syndrome)
   Conditions due to anomaly of unspecified chromosome

Other Conditions Originating in the Prenatal Period
   Disorders relating to short gestation and unspecified low birthweight
   Slow fetal growth and fetal malnutrition
   Disorders relating to long gestation and high birthweight
   Maternal nutritional disorders

Psychiatric Disorders

Environmental influences
   Psychosocial disadvantage
   Sensory deprivation
   Other

Other Conditions
   Defects of special senses

SOURCE: Primarily Grossman (1983).

of infants who weigh more than 2,500 grams at birth have neurological deficits, compared to 4.5% for those who weigh 2,000 to 2,500 grams, 10% for those who weigh from 1,000 to 1,999 grams, and 25%–30% for those weighing less than 1,000 grams.

Maternal age is another birth factor often associated with mental retardation (Scheerenberger, 1987). The incidence of retardation is greater in children of younger mothers, but is also associated with inadequate prenatal care, premature birth, and poverty. The risk of retardation due to chromosomal anomalies is greater for children of older mothers: There is a 1 in 1,550 chance of chromosomal anomalies when maternal age is under 30, compared to a 1 in 700 chance for maternal ages 30–34, a 1

in 250 chance for maternal ages 35–39, and a 1 in 85 chance when maternal age is 40–42. Overall, there is a 1 in 40 chance of chromosomal anomalies in children of mothers older than 40 years.

Physical growth measures seem to have a small relationship to intelligence. Fisch, Bilek, Horrobin, and Chang (1976) divided a large sample of 7-year-old children into superior, average, and low intelligence groups and determined differences between the three groups according to weight, height, and head circumference at ages 1, 4, and 7. The only consistent difference occurred with head circumference. Children with superior intelligence had larger head circumference, on the average, than children with average and low intelligence, although there were no significant differences between the average and low groups.

Social-Environmental Factors

The division of factors associated with mental retardation into biological/organic factors and social-environmental factors is not distinct because many biological causes of retardation are associated with social-environmental factors (Campbell & Ramey, 1986). For example, Scott and Carran (1987) reported that maternal education and ethnicity predict both low birthweight and school failure and that many environmental risks in low social classes (e.g., exposure to toxic substances, stress, poor prenatal care, neglect, lack of cognitive stimulation) can result in retardation due to an interaction of organic and social-environmental causes. In any event, approximately 75% of mentally retarded individuals have no detectable organic cause for the retardation, which is attributed somewhat vaguely to social-environmental factors, familial retardation, or psychosocial disadvantage (Grossman, 1983; Sattler, 1988).

The majority of individuals with mild to moderate levels of mental retardation are thought to be retarded due to psychosocial disadvantage. Many of these individuals are of lower socioeconomic background; there is still the question of whether the retardation is more related to inadequate cultural nourishment and poverty or some factor that is genetic in nature and cannot be detected with present technology (Wolman, 1985). Further, the specific etiology of familial retardation is difficult to isolate because several sets of factors interact and no one factor in itself accounts for the mental retardation (Grossman, 1983; Scott & Carran, 1987).

Many studies investigating relationships between specific social-environmental factors and intelligence have been conducted, with the general conclusion that some social-environmental factors are indeed related to intelligence to some degree (Bouchard & Segal, 1985; see Table 2.3). For example, Steelman and Doby (1983), with a sample of over 3,500 children aged 6 to 11, found no relationship between birth order and scores on the Vocabulary and Block Design subtests of the WISC-R. A significant relationship between family size and Vocabulary, but not Block Design, was found for both black and white children. Children who had six or more siblings scored ⅔ to 1 standard deviation lower on Vocabulary than did children with one sibling, while children who had six or more siblings scored only ¼ to ½ standard deviation lower on Block Design than did children with one sibling.

Elardo, Bradley, and Caldwell (1977) found that the emotional and verbal responsiveness of the mother, provision of appropriate play materials, and maternal involvement with children during the first 2 years of life were significantly related to later language development. McGowan and Johnson (1984) reported that the mother's education, maternal attitudes encouraging children's independence, and reciprocal parent–child interactions were significant factors in an investigation of a causal model between environmental factors and intelligence for Mexican American children. Bradley and Caldwell (1981) found significant correlations between academic achievement and environmental factors such as provision of toys, games, and reading materials, physical environment, parental pride, affection and warmth, and variety of stimulation, even when maternal education and children's intelligence were controlled.

Intellectual Assessment

Individual intellectual assessment, in addition to adaptive behavior assessment, is a key component in diagnosing and classifying mental retardation and developing plans for programming. Although intelligence test scores alone are never supposed to be used to classify a person as mentally retarded, they possess more structure and objectivity than most adaptive behavior scales; professionals who work with mentally retarded people thus tend to rely on intelligence tests when classifying a person as mentally retarded (Grossman, 1983; Smith & Knoff, 1981). Intelligence tests can be extremely useful in the general assessment of mentally retarded individuals as well as in the determination of areas of strength around which they can achieve their potential and experience fulfilling lives (Lindemann & Matarazzo, 1984).

The most common use of intellectual assessment for mentally retarded adolescents in school is to determine the need for placement in special education classes. For mentally retarded adults and older adolescents, intelligence is assessed to determine eligibility for benefits, to determine competence or incompetence in handling themselves, to monitor functioning, and to assess employability or unemployability (Lindemann & Matarazzo, 1984). Intelligence tests are useful as part of vocational planning for mentally retarded adolescents and adults (Capps, Levinson, & Hohenshil, 1985). Overall intellectual functioning is assessed to determine the level to which a mentally retarded person might progress in an occupation. Specific intellectual strengths and weaknesses are evaluated to determine the potential to meet the various demands of a job (e.g., visual-spatial skills, verbal skills, memory).

The intelligence tests most widely used with mildly and moderately mentally retarded adolescents and adults are the WISC-R and WAIS-R; this section discusses the use of these two instruments. The Wechsler scales, however, can seldom be used with severely and profoundly mentally retarded individuals. The WISC-R has a minimum Full Scale IQ of 40 and the WAIS-R a minimum of 45. In addition, the WAIS-R has few simple items that are appropriate for mentally retarded adults (Kaufman, 1985a).

The third edition of the Stanford-Binet was also commonly used for this purpose until the publication of its fourth edition in 1985. The degree to which either the old or new Binet is currently used for the assessment of mental retardation is unknown.

Several types of measures can be used to assess the functioning of severely and profoundly mentally retarded adults. Gregory (1987) and Sattler (1988) recommend informal assessment procedures to estimate mental age. Some adaptive behavior instruments, because they often have more floor than do intelligence tests and can be administered through observation or third-party interview, are used to gain an estimate of a severely or profoundly retarded person's everyday functioning (Durham, 1983; Gregory, 1987). The Functional Intelligence Scale of the forthcoming KAIT (Kaufman & Kaufman, in press a) should also be quite useful for assessing the intelligence of very low functioning individuals.

Factor Analytic Studies of the Wechsler Scales for the Retarded

Kaufman, Harrison, and Ittenbach (in press) reviewed 31 factor analytic studies of the WISC-R for samples of children of different ages, ethnicity, and normal and exceptional classifications. Robust Verbal Comprehension and Perceptual Organization factors were consistently reported for these samples. Many of the investigations found a third factor, labeled Freedom from Distractibility, which includes the Digit Span, Arithmetic, and Coding subtests. Three investigations explored the factor structure of the WISC-R for mentally retarded adolescents; the results are summarized in Table 15.3. (Note that the sample for Van Hagen and Kaufman's 1975 study included individuals aged 6–16 years although the other two samples were adolescents.) The results of these investigations are similar to those found with normal children and children with other handicaps. The Verbal Comprehension and Perceptual Organization factors are supported for mentally retarded adolescents. A third factor, Freedom from Distractibility, is present, but consists of Arithmetic and Coding and does not include Digit Span, as did most of the factor analyses with normal children. In Van Hagen and Kaufman's (1975)

TABLE 15.3   Factor loadings on the WISC-R for three samples of mentally retarded adolescents

WISC-R Subtest	Verbal Comprehension			Perceptual Organization			Freedom from Distractibility		
	1	2	3	1	2	3	1	2	3
Verbal									
Information	69*	72*	73*	−05	03	12	33	−05	24
Similarities	73*	56*	67*	−06	01	08	24	03	23
Arithmetic	34	35	41*	−05	13	16	75*	58*	54*
Vocabulary	80*	87*	57*	16	02	27	13	−10	02
Comprehension	67*	56*	53*	33	09	48*	−25	04	12
Digit Span	—	12	46*	—	41*	06	—	20	29
Performance									
Picture Completion	22	21	16	64*	66*	83*	07	−27	12
Picture Arrangement	05	37	46*	62*	50*	41*	32	−18	45*
Block Design	−11	−25	27	78*	71*	62*	12	10	05
Object Assembly	10	−03	04	85*	63*	70*	−13	10	09
Coding	06	−17	26	30	−01	45*	74*	42*	43*
Mazes	—	—	10	—	—	67*			

NOTE: Decimal points are omitted. Loadings of .40 and above are asterisked.
NOTE: The samples were as follows: 1. Educable mentally retarded children, ages 12–15 (*N*=95) (Cummins and Das, 1980). 2. Low IQ children, ages 14–16 (*N*=78) (Groff and Hubble, 1982). 3. Mentally retarded children, ages 6–16½ (*N*=80) (Van Hagen and Kaufman, 1975).

study, Picture Arrangement also had a significant loading on the Freedom from Distractability factor, consistent with the findings of several factor analyses of retarded samples with the 1949 WISC. The study by Groff and Hubble (1982) included a separate factor analysis for mentally retarded children aged 9–11 years, and Digit Span did have a significant loading on Freedom from Distractibility for this age group. Although only three investigations using mentally retarded adolescents are reported, the three-factor structure of the WISC-R is supported. However, practitioners must be cautious about including Digit Span with the third factor. For some clients, Picture Arrangement may be included when interpreting the Freedom from Distractibility factor if its scaled score is similar

in magnitude to the Arithmetic and Coding scores.

Atkinson and Cyr (1988) conducted factor analyses of the WAIS-R for a sample of 204 adults with Full Scale IQs below 80. A two-factor solution yielded factors corresponding to the Verbal and Performance Scales. A three-factor solution yielded Verbal Comprehension, Perceptual Organization, and Freedom from Distractibility factors. The Arithmetic and Digit Span subtests had primary loadings on the Freedom from Distractibility factor; Information, Comprehension, and Block Design had secondary loadings on this factor. The results of the factor analyses with low IQ adults were compared to factor analyses conducted by the researchers with the WAIS-R normative sample.

For the two-factor solution, coefficients of congruence were .99 for the Verbal factor and .99 for the Performance factor. For the three-factor solution, coefficients of congruence were .97 for the Verbal Comprehension factor, .98 for the Perceptual Organization factor, and .91 for the Freedom from Distractibility factor.

WISC Versus WISC-R
for Retarded Individuals

Berry and Sherrets (1975) reported that the WISC-R FS-IQ was about 3½ points lower than the WISC FS-IQ for a group of educable mentally retarded adolescents. Hamm, Wheeler, McCallum, Herrin, Hunter, and Catoe (1976) found that the WISC-R was 7.5 points lower than the WISC for a group of EMR adolescents, and Catron and Catron (1977) found that the WISC-R Full Scale IQ was 5.6 points lower than the WISC for EMR adolescents. Quattrocchi and Sherret (1980) in a review of many studies comparing the WISC and WISC-R for children, mostly educable mentally retarded, reported that WISC-R Verbal IQs were on the average 1 to 7 points lower than WISC IQs. WISC-R Performance IQs were 0 to 3 points lower, and WISC-R Full Scale IQs were 3 to 4 points lower.

Although the WISC-R is the instrument of choice because of its more recent norms, clinicians on a few isolated occasions may conduct a reevaluation with the WISC-R after a child was previously evaluated with the WISC; lower WISC-R scores can be expected in such cases. Granted, the WISC-R norms, based on standardization data from the early 1970s, are becoming out of date themselves, and the publication of the third edition of the WISC is likely to yield an instrument with lower scores than the WISC-R.

WAIS Versus WAIS-R
for Retarded Individuals

Because the WAIS-R was published in 1981, practitioners are still likely to encounter a situation where a mentally retarded person had been administered the WAIS in a previous evaluation and then administered the newer WAIS-R for reevaluation. As noted in chapter 3, the WAIS-R produces lower IQs than the WAIS by about 6 to 6½ points, with smaller differences or differences in the opposite direction observed for low-functioning (and high IQ) people (see pp. 90–92 and Table 3.13). Simon and Clopton (1984), for example, administered the WAIS and WAIS-R to a group of mildly and moderately retarded adults in counterbalanced order and found that WAIS-R Full Scale and Verbal IQs were significantly higher than WAIS IQs by about 2 and 4 points, respectively. Goldman (1987) compared the two instruments with a group of adults who had been given the WAIS first and the WAIS-R several years later, as would be the case in a typical reevaluation. For adults with average intelligence, the WAIS-R Full Scale IQ was significantly lower by 4.8 points; for adults with borderline intelligence, the WAIS-R was significantly lower by 3.5 points. There was no difference between WAIS and WAIS-R scores for mildly retarded individuals and the WAIS-R was significantly higher by 6.3 points for moderately retarded individuals.

These two studies indicate that the WAIS-R, unlike the WISC-R, may yield slightly higher IQs than the WAIS for mentally retarded adults. When a client has been classified as mentally retarded using the WAIS, a clinician may find that he or she scores in the borderline range on the WAIS-R. A clinician may find that a client who was previously classified as moderately retarded with the WAIS may later score in the mildly retarded range on the WAIS-R. Practical consequences such as these may sometimes present dilemmas for the practitioner. However, the AAMD guidelines for classifying mental retardation purposefully allow professional judgment about a person's need for special education or rehabilitation programs to play a role in decision making about diagnosing retardation. Such professional judgments should be exercised when a mentally retarded person obtains a higher or lower score during reevaluation with the WAIS-R.

WISC-R Versus WAIS or WAIS-R for Retarded Adolescents

Comparisons between the WISC-R and WAIS-R are particularly important for two reasons. First, the initial evaluation of a mentally retarded client younger than 16 may use the WISC-R and reevaluation after his or her 16th birthday may use the WAIS-R, requiring psychologists to compare the scores from two different evaluations. Second, either the WISC-R or WAIS-R may be administered to 16-year-old mentally retarded adolescents. With the WAIS, Zimmerman and Woo-Sam (1982), Craft and Kronenberger (1979), and Nagle and Lazarus (1979) found IQs to be consistently higher by 8 to 14 points than WISC-R IQs when the WAIS was administered several years after the WISC-R to mentally retarded individuals. Because these studies were longitudinal, it is unclear whether differences between WAIS and WISC-R were due to differences in test content and scoring or the time period between administration of the two tests.

Similar findings have been reported for the WAIS-R when administered a few years after the WISC-R, as discussed in depth in chapter 4 (see pp. 119–123 and Table 4.10). For example, Zimmerman, Covin, and Woo-Sam (1986), using a sample of EMR students, found that WAIS-R scores were significantly higher than WISC-R scores obtained 3 years earlier, by 3 to 5 points on the average. Further, Zimmerman et al. (1986) found the greatest difference between WISC-R and WAIS-R for subjects with lower IQs; scores from the two measures became more similar as IQs approached 100. For example, 19 of the 34 subjects in the study who had WISC-R IQs below 70 obtained WAIS-R IQs above 70. Rubin, Goldman, and Rosenfeld (1985) conducted a comparable study with mentally retarded clients at a residential institution and reported results similar to Zimmerman's findings: Moderately retarded clients had an average difference of about 14 points and mildly retarded clients an average difference of 7 points. Consequently, clinicians should anticipate higher WAIS-R IQs for retarded adolescents or young adults who were tested a few years earlier on the WISC-R. Whether this IQ gain reflects a "true" gain in intelligence is discussed on pp. 119–123.

Verbal–Performance Differences and Subtest Scatter on the Wechsler Scales

Kaufman (1976b) reported that the average Verbal–Performance discrepancy, regardless of direction, for children in the WISC-R standardization sample was 9.7 points. These findings indicate that it is not unusual for nonhandicapped children to have a significant difference between their verbal and nonverbal abilities, and that Verbal–Performance differences by themselves cannot be used to diagnose exceptionalities such as learning disabilities, emotional disturbance, or mental retardation.

Mentally retarded children obtain average Verbal–Performance discrepancies on the WISC-R comparable to those of nonhandicapped children. According to several studies (Gutkin, 1979a; Naglieri, 1979; Schmidt & Saklofske, 1983; Thompson, 1980), average Verbal–Performance differences of mentally retarded children range from 7½ to 10 points. The results of this research suggest that the magnitudes of the Verbal–Performance differences for mentally retarded children are not usually atypical in comparison to those for nonhandicapped children.

Kaufman (1976a) also reported that children in the WISC-R standardization sample typically exhibited much scatter in their subtest performance, as seen by the average difference of 7 points between the highest and lowest subtest scores. Similar findings have been reported for mentally retarded children, refuting the myth that mentally retarded individuals have flat profiles. Average ranges of subtest scores of mentally retarded students in studies by Gutkin (1979), Naglieri (1979), Schmidt and Saklofske (1983), and Thompson (1980) were from about 6 to 7½ points.

Comparable studies of mentally retarded adolescents and adults on the WAIS-R are not available to determine if their V–P and subtest scatter indexes are substantially different from the values reported for normal individuals (see chapter 9 and chapter 13). However, data for members of the WAIS-R standardization sample with IQs below 80 indicated smaller than average V–P discrepancies (see Table 9.4) and subtest scatter (see Table 13.9). For example, Matarazzo and Herman (1985) indicated that a V–P discrepancy of at least 10 points was obtained by 40% of the WAIS-R normative sample. However, they found that individuals with IQs below 80 had fewer significant V–P discrepancies than individuals with higher IQs. For example, 47.5% of adults with IQs 120 or above had a 10-point discrepancy, compared with only 15.8% of adults with IQs below 80.

Characteristic Wechsler Profiles for Mentally Retarded

Research with the WISC-R and WAIS-R has explored typical subtest profiles for mentally retarded individuals (for a discussion of their V–P profiles, see pp. 288–289). Table 15.4 shows mean IQs and the rank order of subtest means from a number of studies involving mentally retarded individuals. A rank of 1 signifies the easiest subtest and a rank of 10 indicates the most difficult subtest. (Digit Span and Mazes were not always given, and Digit Span was only given in one of the two WAIS-R studies, so these two subtests are not included in Table 15.4.) The consensus rankings in Table 15.4 were obtained by computing the mean ranking for each subtest and rank ordering the means.

The results summarized in Table 15.4 indicate that, on the WISC-R, Picture Completion and Object Assembly were the easiest subtests, and Vocabulary, Information, Similarities, and Arithmetic were the most difficult. Although

only two studies were reported for the WAIS-R and consensus rankings from these should be interpreted with caution (e.g., there were fairly large discrepancies between the rankings for Similarities and Digit Symbol for the two studies), Block Design, Object Assembly, and Picture Completion were the easiest subtests and Arithmetic and Vocabulary the most difficult. Although the easiest and most difficult subtests are fairly similar for the WISC-R and WAIS-R, some discrepancies should be noted. Block Design was the easiest subtest on the WAIS-R, yet received a consensus ranking of 6 on the WISC-R. Comprehension was the third easiest subtest on the WISC-R, but received a consensus ranking of 7.5 on the WAIS-R.

The consensus rankings with the WAIS-R are also quite different from results of studies using the WAIS with mentally retarded adults in institutions. Barclay, Giray, and Altkin (1977) and Hill (1978) analyzed data using five large samples of subjects (Ns = 51 to 509) from the East, Midwest, and West. Mean subtest scores across all five samples indicated that Object Assembly, Picture Completion, and Comprehension were the easiest subtests, and Picture Arrangement, Digit Span, and Arithmetic were the most difficult.

One approach to interpreting the findings in Table 15.4 is to use Bannatynes's category system (see pp. 381–382). According to this system, mentally retarded individuals have a characteristic strength in Spatial Ability and a weakness in Acquired Knowledge. Kaufman (1979b) suggested that the weakness in Acquired Knowledge reflects poor long-term memory or inadequate school-related skills. For some mentally retarded individuals, this characteristic pattern may be associated with limited cultural opportunities or low scholastic achievement. This information may be used to generate hypotheses, conduct supplementary assessment or observations, or plan programs. For example, Kaufman (1979b) suggested that if a culturally disadvantaged, mentally retarded individual ob-

TABLE 15.4 Rank ordering of WISC-R and WAIS-R subtest means for mentally retarded samples

Source	N	Information	Similarities	Arithmetic	Vocabulary	Comprehension	Picture Completion	Picture Arrangement	Block Design	Object Assembly	Coding[a]	Mean V-IQ	Mean P-IQ	Mean FS-IQ
WISC-R														
Catron & Catron (1977)	62	10	9	6	8	3	1	4.5	7	2	4.5	62	64	60
Clarizio & Bernard (1981)	141	8.5	8.5	7	10	5	1	3	4	2	6	68	74	68
Henry & Wittman (1981)	40	9	4	8	5	3	1	10	7	2	6	66	66	63
Kaufman & Van Hagen (1977)	80	6	4.5	9	10	4.5	1	7	2.5	2.5	8	54	56	51
Law, Box, & Moracco (1980)	30	10	6	5	8	2.5	1	7	9	4	2.5	68	71	66
Nagle & Lazarus (1979)	30	9	6	7	10	8	2	3.5	5	1	3.5	—	—	63
Reilly, Wheeler, & Ettinger (1985)	20	7	8	6	9	5	1	2.5	10	2.5	4	59	63	58
Rubin, Goldman, & Rosenfeld (1985)	41	5	3	9	8	7	1	2	6	4	10	59	61	56
Schooler, Beebe, & Koepke (1978)	127	8	10	7	9	4	1	3	5	2	6	68	74	68
Vance, Hankins, Wallbrown, Engin, & McGee (1978)	238	10	9	4	7	1	2	8	6	3	5	64	64	62
WISC-R Consensus Rankings		9	7.5	7.5	10	3	1	4	6	2	5			
WAIS-R														
Rubin, Goldman, & Rosenfeld (1985)	41	5	1	9	6.5	8	2	6.5	3	4	10	70	66	66
Simon & Clopton (1984)	29	7	9	10	8	6	3	5	1	2	4	62	66	62
WAIS-R Consensus Rankings		6	4	10	9	7.5	2	5	1	3	7.5			

[a]Coding is replaced by Digit Symbol on the WAIS-R.

NOTE: Digit Span was not administered in all studies and so has been excluded.

tains low scores on the Acquired Knowledge subtests (Information, Arithmetic, and Vocabulary) but relatively better scores on the other verbal subtests (Similarities, Comprehension, and Digit Span), success in an educational or training program may be possible. A finding that the mentally retarded obtain a characteristic profile should *not* be used for differential diagnosis of mental retardation or discrimination of mental retardation from other handicaps. Research summarized by Kaufman et al. (in press) indicates that characteristic profiles do not effectively discriminate among normal individuals or individuals with different exceptionalities. For example, emotionally disturbed and learning-disabled children also appear to have a strength in Spatial Ability and a weakness in Acquired Knowledge as well as in Sequencing Ability.

MENTAL RETARDATION: ADAPTIVE BEHAVIOR ASSESSMENT

Adaptive behavior assessment is an integral part of the assessment of mentally retarded adolescents and adults. As indicated, deficits in adaptive behavior and subaverage intellectual functioning must be substantiated before a person can be classified as mentally retarded. Adaptive behavior assessment is also an important part of planning for vocational and treatment programs. This section explores adaptive behavior assessment with mentally retarded adolescents and adults and reviews the major adaptive behavior instruments. Guidelines are given for the clinical assessment of mentally retarded individuals using adaptive behavior measures in conjunction with intelligence tests.

Characteristics of Adaptive Behavior

Adaptive behavior has been incorporated into the broader concept of social competence. Greenspan (1979, 1981) suggested that social competence consists of physical competence, adaptive intelligence, and socio-emotional adaptation. Adaptive intelligence includes conceptual, practical, and social intelligence; practical and social intelligence are similar to the AAMD's concept of adaptive behavior. Gresham and Elliot (1987) suggested that social competence includes two interrelated dimensions, adaptive behavior and social skills, and that social competence deficits may be classified as skill deficits, performance deficits, self-control skill deficits, and self-control performance deficits.

It has been argued that adaptive behavior is not as clearly defined as other constructs that are typically assessed for mentally retarded individuals—for example, intelligence and achievement (e.g., Clausen, 1972; Gresham & Elliot, 1987; Zigler, Balla, & Hodapp, 1984). Others have pointed out the consistencies among definitions of adaptive behavior and the structure of adaptive behavior scales (e.g., Holman & Bruininks, 1985; Kamphaus, 1987; Meyers, Nihira, & Zetlin, 1979; Reschly, 1982). The AAMD definition of adaptive behavior has tended to influence other definitions of the construct, while other constructs, such as intelligence, do not have a broad, unifying definition (Kamphaus, 1987). The following common elements are found in definitions of adaptive behavior: the developmental nature of the behaviors; common dimensions of adaptive behavior; recognition of cultural influences and situational specificity; and emphasis on performance rather than skills or ability (Bruininks, Thurlow, & Gilman, 1987; Holman & Bruininks, 1985; Horn & Fuchs, 1987; Kamphaus, 1987; Meyers et al., 1979; Nihira, 1982; Reschly, 1982; Sparrow, Cicchetti, & Balla, 1984a, 1984b; Witt & Martens, 1984).

Developmental Nature

Adaptive behavior is recognized as being developmental, increasing in complexity as normally developing individuals grow older. Most adaptive behavior scales emphasize the developmental qualities of the construct by providing age-based norms and items that cover a wide range of developmental activities. Grossman (1983) identified particular adaptive behavior skills that are necessary for different developmental periods. Sensorimotor, communication, self-help, and socialization skills are important during infancy and early childhood. These skills continue to be important throughout life. Academic, reasoning and judgment, environmental mastery, and social skills are additional adaptive behaviors for childhood and early adolescence. Older adolescents and adults add vocational and social performance and responsibility to their repertoire of adaptive behaviors.

Basic Dimensions

Two major dimensions of adaptive behavior are typically reflected in definitions and measures of adaptive behavior: independence (or personal functioning) and social responsibility. Common domains within these dimensions are found in definitions of adaptive behavior and in the items of most adaptive behavior scales:

Self-help skills (eating, dressing, toilet training, grooming, personal hygiene, etc.)

Interpersonal/socialization skills (interacting with others, playing, group activities, cooperating, etc.)

Physical and motor skills (coordination, control, sensory abilities, etc.)

Communication skills (verbal expression, verbal understanding, articulation, etc.)

Applied cognitive skills (using money, telling time, reading signs and other basic written material, writing name and address, etc.)

Domestic skills (food preparation, cleaning, washing clothes, etc.)

Vocational/occupational skills (operating machinery and equipment, being on time for work, job-search skills, etc.)

Responsibility (taking care of belongings, following directions, taking initiative, responding to the needs of others, etc.)

Grossman (1983) suggested that performance of self-help, social, motor, and communication skills is the focus of assessment in infancy and early childhood, and delays in these areas may indicate delays in the maturation process. Delays may suggest the need for medical services, early childhood education, and family intervention. Adaptive behavior assessment in later childhood and adolescence is related more to the learning process rather than maturation process. Performance of basic cognitive/academic skills such as reading and writing is important, but the focus is on skills necessary for coping with the environment, including applying concepts of time, number, and money, responsibility, and interpersonal relationships. Deficits in these skills may indicate the need for specialized educational programs. Adaptive behavior assessment for older adolescents and adults focuses on the occupational skills needed for gainful employment and on the ability to take responsibility for living independently, in addition to the skills required for younger individuals. Deficits may indicate a need for vocational training, job behavior training, and support from agencies for living arrangements, depending on the severity of the deficits.

Cultural Influences

Adaptive behavior is related to the various cultural or ethnic expectations that individuals must meet. Anthropologists have documented the diverse expectations placed on individuals in different cultures around the world and the influences that factors such as climate, geography, and financial resources have on these expectations. Differences in the expectations of various cultures within the United States may be more subtle but they undoubtedly exist. Norms concerning dress, communication, and other factors vary across geographic regions and subcultures of the United States. It is impossible to develop an adaptive behavior scale that measures all possible expected behaviors of all cultures, so most adaptive behavior scales sample basic adaptive behavior skills that are common to most cultures. Skills that are specific to certain cultures, communities, or other groups (e.g., using public transportation, dressing for snowy weather) must usually be assessed on an informal basis.

Situational Specificity

Adaptive behavior is very much influenced by the demands of specific situations (Horn & Fuchs, 1987). Different adaptive behaviors are required in the home, school, community, workplace, and other settings. A child in a one-child family may not be expected to take turns at home, but this is an expected behavior in school. An adolescent leaving the school to go into the workplace may find different expectations for dress and conduct. An adult who changes jobs may find that the new employer has different expectations for work behavior. Adaptation to new situations is an ongoing process, occurring through experience with the new environment and interactions with the significant people in that environment. Adaptive behavior requires recognition of different expectations and an ability to change behavior to meet them. Horn and Fuchs (1987) provided an excellent description of the situational specificity of adaptive behavior:

> Thus, adaptive behavior is a construct influenced by considerations of place and time. A person judged as "adaptive" in one setting may not necessarily be evaluated similarly in another place; adaptive behaviors at one developmental level are qualitatively different from those at another level. In short, adaptive behavior is relative and dynamic, rather than absolute and static. (p. 11)

Performance Versus Ability

An implicit assumption in the definition of adaptive behavior is that people must have the ability or skills to perform activities required for personal and social self-sufficiency. However, the definition emphasizes the *observable* performance of the activities, and adaptive behavior measures typically focus on what people *do,* rather than on what they *can* do to take care of themselves. One's adaptive behavior is considered to be deficient if one has skills but does not routinely use them—if a person is able to tie his or her own shoes but does not do it. It is important in adaptive behavior assessment and intervention to distinguish between skill deficits and performance deficits (Gresham & Elliott, 1987). If a person does not have a skill, informal assessment may suggest why he or she does not have it (for example, if he or she has no experience with the activity or if physical or cognitive limitations prevent its acquisition) and whether he or she can learn it. If a person does have a skill but does not perform it, informal assessment may suggest why (for example, because of anxiety, fear, lack of motivation) and provide information for the development of an intervention program.

History of Adaptive Behavior Assessment

Present concepts of adaptive behavior can be traced to the idea of social competency. Historically, the concept of social competency was expanded by early scholars attempting to describe those who could not cope with their environment, the mentally retarded or the "idiots," "fools," or "dullards." During the years of the Renaissance and Reformation, language and law defined mental retardation in social terms related to current concepts of adaptive behavior (Kagin, 1968). In the nineteenth century, writers dealt with the question of social competency and the relationship of adaptive behavior to the acceptance and understanding of the retarded person and his or her relationship with others in the community. Definitions of mental retardation in the 1800s usually described those factors that are now called adaptive behavior. Itard and Haslan in 1819, Sequin in 1837, and Voisin in 1843 spoke essentially about adaptive behavior, using phrases such as *skills training, social norms,* and *adaptability to environment* (Lambert, Windmiller, Cole, & Figueroa, 1975). Voisin made one of the earliest attempts to measure adaptive behavior in 1843 (Leland, Shellhaas, Nihira, & Foster, 1967).

The Impact of Intelligence Tests

Definitions of mental retardation continued to emphasize social adequacy until the development of intelligence tests (Nihira, 1985). The introduction of the Binet scales in the early 1900s led to the practice in the United States of using IQ scores to classify people as mentally retarded. The reliance on IQ as the chief means of diagnosing mental retardation continued for many years, despite increasing concerns about using a single measure and about bias in intelligence tests (Meyers et al., 1979).

Although Binet and Simon provided the instrument that led to the practice of using low IQ as the major criterion of mental retardation in the United States, their suggestions for classifying mental retardation stressed that such a classification required more than a particular score on their scale (Matarazzo, 1972). Great Britain incorporated the concept of social adequacy into its definition of mental retardation in 1913. Great Britain's practice was not followed in the United States for some time, and Goddard and others promoted the use of the Binet scales and the IQ as the index for measuring retardation.

Contributions of Edgar Doll

Edgar Doll (1940, 1941, 1953, 1966), the pioneer in the objective assessment of adaptive behavior and author of the Vineland Social Maturity Scale (Doll, 1935, 1965), disagreed with the emphasis on IQ as the only criterion for classifying mental retardation in the United States. He suggested that in focusing on intelligence, socially adequate and socially inadequate people were combined into one category and treated in similar ways. His six criteria defining mental deficiency listed social incompetence first, followed by subaverage intelligence. Thus, the

identification of mentally retarded persons, according to Doll, must first be based on their inability to take care of themselves and to get along with others. Intelligence should be assessed once a deficit in social adequacy is identified. A classification of mental retardation, rather than some other handicap, is supported if a socially inadequate person exhibits subaverage intelligence. Doll also emphasized the necessity of interventions to treat social inadequacy; he wrote that no mental diagnosis should begin without an assessment of social adequacy and end without a prediction of social adequacy following treatment.

It was not until 1959 that the AAMD published its first official manual, which included deficits in adaptive behavior, in addition to low intelligence, in the definition of mental retardation (Heber, 1959, 1961). Subsequent revisions of the AAMD manual (Grossman, 1973, 1977, 1983) have continued to emphasize adaptive behavior. Although modified somewhat, the basic premises of Doll's work are evident in current AAMD manuals.

The Parsons Project

Because there were no adequate adaptive behavior instruments available when the first AAMD manual was published, the AAMD sponsored a project to develop an understanding of adaptive behavior and a useful technique for its measurement at Parsons State Hospital in Kansas during the 1960s (Leland, Shellhaas, Nihira, & Foster, 1967). The focus of the Parsons project was remediation, rehabilitation, and placement of the mentally retarded. The participants in the project suggested that the use of objective adaptive behavior instruments would clarify many problems confronting those working with the mentally retarded and would improve evaluation and treatment. They emphasized that to understand an individual's adaptive behavior, specific behaviors that limit the individual's ability to survive as a member of society must be evaluated. The AAMD Adaptive Behavior Scale

(Nihira, Foster, Shellhaas, & Leland, 1969) and an increased recognition of the need to assess and provide interventions for adaptive behavior were two key products of the project.

Adaptive Behavior Assessment in the 1970s and 1980s

Since the Parsons project, adaptive behavior assessment has become a standard practice in evaluations of the mentally retarded. The expansion of adaptive behavior assessment has occurred for two primary reasons (Meyers et al., 1979; Witt & Martens, 1984). The first is the need for unbiased assessment. Several lawsuits in the 1970s (e.g., the *Diana* and *Larry P.* cases) dealt with the use of intelligence tests as the only criterion for placing minority children into the special education programs for the mentally retarded and the disproportionate number of minority children in these programs. Many of the children, often called "six-hour retarded children," exhibited adequate adaptive behavior outside of school, and a primary issue was whether the children were "really retarded." Mercer (1973) was influential in bringing attention to the six-hour retarded child and promoting adaptive behavior assessment. In a comprehensive study in Riverside, California, she found that many minority children who were classified as retarded exhibited adequate functioning outside of school.

A second reason for increased use of adaptive behavior scales was the need for training skills that would enable mentally retarded individuals to live more independently and to function in the community. The 1960s and 1970s were the beginning of a period of "deinstitutionalization," or movement of mentally retarded people from large, residential facilities to more normal settings such as group homes and sheltered workshops. The focus on deinstitutionalization continues today. In public schools, adaptive behavior training is seen as a way to help place mentally retarded children into less restrictive settings and classes with normal children and

as a way to promote the transition from school to the community and jobs.

Adaptive behavior assessment has received further emphasis from federal legislation, including Section 504 of the Vocational Rehabilitation Act of 1973; Public Law 94-142, the Education for All Handicapped Children Act of 1975; and Public Law 94-602, the Developmental Disabilities Amendment of 1978. These laws promote the education, employment, and training of the handicapped and enforce stringent guidelines for assessment, classification, education, and treatment practices. Public Law 94-142, for instance, requires that states seeking financial assistance from the federal government provide free and appropriate public education to all handicapped children. The definition of mental retardation in the law is basically the same as the AAMD definition, and adaptive behavior deficits must be determined before a child can be classified as mentally retarded. Public Law 99-457, a reauthorization of Public Law 94-142, focuses on early intervention for handicapped preschool children as well as secondary education and transition services for handicapped adolescents who are leaving school.

Purposes for Assessing Adaptive Behavior

The ability to take care of one's self and the ability to get along with others are important goals for everyone, regardless of age or handicapping condition. Four specific developmental goals for mentally retarded adolescents and adults highlight the necessity of assessing adaptive behavior and using the results to develop intervention plans (Baroff, 1986). The first is the need for *self-management* in order to achieve independence and personal responsibility. Many mentally retarded adolescents and adults, particularly the mildly retarded, can be expected to achieve an independent adjustment and acquire self-help, domestic, and community skills. The second goal is *employment*. Mentally retarded adolescents and adults can be trained for many levels of employability. The mildly retarded typically are employed in unskilled jobs, primarily service positions, and the more severely retarded in sheltered workshops. A third goal is the *fulfillment of adult social roles.* The mildly retarded can carry on social roles including friendships with the opposite sex, marriage, and parenthood. The moderately retarded have friends of the opposite sex, although they do not often marry. They are more socially isolated than the mildly retarded and may spend more time in solitary activities such as playing cards and watching television. Severely and profoundly retarded individuals are usually not expected to enter many adult social roles. The final goal is *community adjustment,* including using the services of community agencies, participating in recreational activities, and, unfortunately, staying out of trouble with law enforcement agencies. Baroff indicated that there are disproportionate numbers of mentally retarded people in prisons, not because of criminal tendencies, but due to factors such as proneness to confess crimes they have not committed and, once in prison, lack of rehabilitation services.

Classification

The adaptive behavior of mentally retarded adolescents and adults is assessed for the purpose of classification of the handicap and development of intervention and treatment plans (Coulter, 1980; Meyers et al., 1979; Witt & Martens, 1984). The AAMD and most federal and state laws concerning mental retardation require that deficits in adaptive behavior be documented before a person is classified as mentally retarded. According to Horn and Fuchs (1987), individuals who have IQs in the severely or profoundly retarded range usually demonstrate obvious deficits in adaptive behavior, and although adaptive behavior must be assessed to meet guidelines, there is seldom a question about whether these people are mentally retarded. Individuals with milder handicaps may not always exhibit concurrent deficits in intelligence and adaptive be-

havior, and adaptive behavior assessment plays an important role in the classification of mental retardation for these people. Adaptive behavior assessment, along with intellectual assessment, is unfortunately used only for identification of mild mental retardation in many cases; there is a need for more use of adaptive behavior assessment to plan intervention programs for these individuals (Horn & Fuchs, 1987).

The assessment of adaptive behavior for individuals with other handicapping conditions may be equally important, but is beyond the scope of this chapter. See Mercer (1973), Mealor (1984), and Sparrow and Cicchetti (1987) for discussions of assessing the adaptive behavior of emotionally and behaviorally disturbed individuals; Meacham, Kline, Stovall, and Sands (1987) and Pollingue (1987) for individuals with sensory and physical handicaps; and Weller and Strawser (1987) for learning-disabled students.

Program Planning

A second general purpose of adaptive behavior assessment is to aid in planning treatment and interventions to achieve the goals of self-management, employment, fulfilling adult social roles, and community adjustment, discussed earlier. Horn and Fuchs (1987) suggested that interventions for the mildly retarded should be geared to meet the requirements of home, school, work, and community settings. For the moderately to profoundly retarded, intervention programs should emphasize functional skills necessary to achieve at least partial functioning in as many settings as possible. Although adaptive behavior measures provide useful information for planning intervention programs, there has been little research concerning their treatment validity (Holman & Bruininks, 1985). However, numerous investigations have supported the success of training in self-help and social skills, such as those found in items of adaptive behavior scales.

Adaptive behavior assessment is a major component of an ecological approach to assessment of and intervention for handicapped individuals (Horn & Fuchs, 1987). Adaptive behavior assessment is necessary to determine skills and coping strategies demonstrated by individuals in their current setting and those demanded by any setting in which individuals hope to participate. Interventions can be planned to "fill in the gaps" between the demands of current and new settings. For example, a mildly retarded adolescent may plan to seek employment following completion of high school, and his or her last few years in school can be geared to acquiring the skills necessary to succeed in the work setting. A severely retarded individual in an institution may participate in a program geared to the acquisition of skills he or she will need in a community group home.

Major Adaptive Behavior Scales for Adolescents and Adults

Many adaptive behavior scales are used with adolescents and adults, with some sources reporting well over 100 instruments (Meyers et al., 1979). This section reviews major adaptive behavior scales that can be used with adolescents and adults. The scales selected are those that are standardized or readily available. Many other adaptive behavior scales have been developed for "in house" use and are not discussed.

Vineland Adaptive Behavior Scales

The Vineland Adaptive Behavior Scales (Harrison, 1985; Sparrow, Balla, & Cicchetti, 1984a, 1984b) are a revision of the Vineland Social Maturity Scale (Doll, 1935, 1965); three versions have a wide range of uses with mentally retarded adolescents and adults. The Interview Edition, Survey Form, for children from birth through 18 years of age and low-functioning adults, is administered to parents or caregivers during a semistructured, open-ended interview and provides a norm-referenced assessment of adaptive behavior. The Interview Edition, Expanded Form, with twice as many items as the

Survey Form, provides a norm-referenced assessment for infants through adults from an interview with parents and caregivers, but its primary purpose is to provide detailed information about adaptive behavior deficits and a sequential guide for planning intervention programs. The Classroom Edition is a questionnaire completed by teachers. Normative data for the Classroom Edition were collected for ages 3 through 12 years; age equivalents may be obtained for low-functioning adolescents older than 12, but due to the technical limitations of age equivalents and lack of age-appropriate items, the Classroom Edition has limited use with adolescents and adults.

The Vineland measures 4 domains and 11 subdomains of adaptive behavior, and 1 domain of maladaptive behavior, as seen in Table 15.5. (The Motor domain, and its Gross and Fine subdomains, is optional for individuals 6 years of age and older and is given only when motor deficits are suspected.) A global score, the Adaptive Behavior Composite, is formed from the adaptive behavior domains.

TECHNICAL QUALITIES   The Vineland Survey Form was standardized with a national sample of 3,000 individuals from birth through 18 years of age. The standardization sample was stratified in order to match U.S. Census data on race or ethnic group, community size, sex, region of the country, and parents' level of education. Supplementary samples of handicapped individuals were also included in the standardization to provide special norms. These included ambulatory mentally retarded adults in residential facilities, nonambulatory mentally retarded adults in residential facilities, mentally retarded adults in nonresidential or community facilities, emotionally disturbed adolescents in residential facilities, and hearing-impaired and visually handicapped children in residential facilities. The Expanded Form was not used during standardization; an equating study allowed the generation of norms using standardization data from the Survey Form. The Classroom Edition was stan-

TABLE 15.5   Content of the Vineland Adaptive Behavior Scales

Domain	Subdomains
Communication	Receptive Expressive Written
Daily Living Skills	Personal Domestic Community
Socialization	Interpersonal Relationships Play and Leisure Time Coping Skills
Motor Skills	Gross Fine
Adaptive Behavior Composite	
Maladaptive Behavior	

dardized with a sample of 2,984 children selected to match U.S. Census data, according to the same stratification variables used with the Survey Form.

Median internal consistency estimates, across age groups, for the Survey Form domains and Adaptive Behavior Composite range from .83 to .94 (median = .89), for the Expanded Form .86 to .97 (median = .93), and for the Classroom Edition .80 to .98 (median = .94). Interrater reliability coefficients for the Survey Form range from .62 to .78 (median = .74), and test–retest reliability coefficients for the Survey Form range from .81 to .88 (median = .85). The manuals for the Vineland report validity data including developmental progression of scores, factor analyses, correlations with other adaptive behavior scales and intelligence tests, and differences between the scores of handicapped and nonhandicapped individuals.

SCORING AND INTERPRETATION   Several types of norm-referenced information may be obtained from the Vineland. Age-based standard scores, with a mean of 100 and standard deviation of 15 and ranging from 20 to 160, are available for the domains and the Adaptive Behavior Composite. National percentile ranks, stanines, age equivalents, adaptive levels, and bands of error may also be determined. Age equivalents and adaptive levels (descriptive categories of high, moderately high, adequate, moderately low, and low) are used for the subdomains. The Maladaptive Behavior domain of the Survey Form and Expanded Form yields maladaptive levels (nonsignificant, intermediate, and significant). The supplementary norm groups of handicapped individuals used for the Survey Form and Expanded Form provide percentile ranks that allow a comparison between a handicapped person and others with the same handicap.

The Vineland provides several types of information for planning treatment and interventions. The profiles of normative scores and strengths and weaknesses in adaptive behavior can be used to select areas that may need to be addressed in intervention programs. The Expanded Form was specifically designed to yield systematic and comprehensive information for planning intervention programs. Items on the Expanded form are arranged in clusters of two to eight items listed in developmental order. The items in the clusters represent sequential skills needed to master the highest level, or target, of the cluster.

CONCLUSIONS   The Vineland is a flexible instrument, is well normed, and has good evidence to support validity (Anastasi, 1988; Taylor, 1989), although some domains and subdomains have relatively low internal consistency and interrater reliability (Oakland & Houchins, 1985; Salvia & Ysseldyke, 1988). The supplementary norms are especially useful for mentally retarded adults (Campbell, 1985).

Criticisms of the Vineland include the finding that standard score means and standard deviations vary from age group to age group (Silverstein, 1986b); the Vineland authors attribute this finding to sampling variability (Cicchetti & Sparrow, 1986). Oakland and Houchins (1986) noted that the semistructured interview format is difficult for novice examiners and that informants may not have the necessary knowledge to respond to some items (e.g. using plurals, attending school or public lectures).

Scales of Independent Behavior

The Scales of Independent Behavior (SIB) (Bruininks, Woodcock, Weatherman, & Hill, 1984, 1985) is a norm-referenced measure used for infants through mature adults. Four adaptive behavior skill clusters encompass 14 subscales, as seen in Table 15.6. The four clusters are combined to form the Broad Independence Scale. A problem behavior scale measures eight areas and yields four maladaptive indexes. Administration of the SIB occurs through an interview with a third party who knows the client well, such as a parent or teacher; when possible, the SIB can be administered to the client. An easel is used during the interview; the informant is shown possible responses to items on the easel pages.

TECHNICAL QUALITIES   The SIB was standardized with a sample of 1,764 individuals,

ages birth to 44 years, stratified according to race, sex, community size, geographic location, and socioeconomic status. Median internal consistency estimates across age levels for clusters range from .83 to .97 (median = .92). Test–retest reliability estimates range from .78 to .91 (median = .87) for adaptive behavior clusters, and interrater reliability estimates range from .74 to .86 (median = .81). The technical manual reports a respectable amount of validity evidence, including differences between scores of handicapped and nonhandicapped individuals, developmental progression of scores, and correlations with other adaptive behavior scales and intelligence tests.

SCORING AND INTERPRETATION   A variety of norm-referenced scores are obtained with the SIB, including standard scores with a mean of 100 and standard deviation of 15, age equivalents, percentile ranks, and normal curve equivalents. Additional scores provide useful information for assessment and planning intervention programs. Training or instructional ranges indicate the adaptive behavior skill levels that would be perceived as easy for the client through the level perceived as difficult or frustrating for the client. Relative performance indexes provide a prediction of the client's expected quality of performance on tasks similar to those evaluated with the SIB. For example, a relative performance index of 50/90 indicates that the client can be expected to perform with 50% independence the tasks that others the same age usually perform with 90% independence. Functioning levels describe performance in descriptive terms ranging from severe deficit to very superior. Adjusted adaptive behavior scores compare a client's independence with others of the same intellectual level, using the Woodcock-Johnson Broad Cognitive Ability (1977 ed.) cluster score as the measure of intelligence. For example, the adjusted scores may indicate that, although the person performs at the 5th percentile when compared to his or her age peers,

TABLE 15.6   Content of the Scales of Independent Behavior

Clusters	Subscales
Motor Skills	Gross Motor
	Fine Motor
Social Interaction and Communication Skills	Social Interaction
	Language Comprehension
	Language Expression
Personal Living Skills	Eating and Meal Preparation
	Toileting
	Dressing
	Personal Self-Care
	Domestic Skills
Community Living Skills	Time and Punctuality
	Money and Value
	Work Skills
	Home/Community Orientation
Broad Independence (Full Scale)	
Internalized Maladaptive Behavior	Hurtful to Self
	Unusual or Repetitive Habits
	Withdrawal or Inattentive Behavior
Asocial Maladaptive Behavior	Socially Offensive Behavior
	Uncooperative Behavior

he or she is performing at the 75th percentile when compared to others of the same intellectual level.

Intervention planning is accomplished on the SIB in several ways. The observed profile of strengths and weaknesses can be used to determine goals of training programs. Training or instructional ranges allow program plans to focus on tasks appropriate for the client's level of functioning. In addition, at the end of administration of each scale of the SIB, respondents are asked to identify individual skill areas in need of improvement. This informal information provides objectives for training programs.

CONCLUSIONS   The SIB, like the Vineland, is a psychometrically sound instrument with a representative norm sample and adequate support for validity (Cummings & Simon, 1988; Gregory, 1987), although the reliability of some scales and subscales is relatively low (Salvia &

Ysseldyke, 1988). A feature in the evaluation of mentally retarded adolescents and adults is the SIB's tie with the Woodcock-Johnson and interpretation of adaptive behavior using others of the same intelligence as a comparison (Sattler, 1988). Criticism of the SIB is directed at its complicated myriad of specialized scores (Sattler, 1988). In addition, Cummings and Simon (1988) noted that the highly structured, closed-end interview used for administration may result in a respondent's overestimation of a client's skills.

AAMD Adaptive Behavior Scale

CLINICAL VERSION   There are two versions of the AAMD Adaptive Behavior Scale. The "clinical version" was designed for use with mentally retarded individuals, ages 3 to 69 years, who reside in institutions (Nihira, Foster, Shellhaas, & Leland, 1974). This version measures adaptive behavior in 10 domains and maladaptive behavior in 14 domains, shown in Table 15.7. The items are contained in a questionnaire that can be completed by a person familiar with the client, or the items can be administered to parents, teachers, or caregivers during an interview.

The clinical version was standardized with about 4,000 individuals in residential facilities across the country. No attempts were made to stratify the sample or determine the level of retardation. The manual reports median interrater reliability estimates of .86 for adaptive domains and .57 for maladaptive domains, but no test–retest or internal consistency reliability estimates are reported. The manual reports some evidence to support validity, such as differences between adaptive behavior scores of individuals who participate in different placements within an institution or who are at different levels of adaptive behavior, according to clinical judgment.

Norm-referenced information obtained from the clinical version of the AAMD scale consists of age-based percentile ranks for each of the domains. These data can be used to assist in determining the focus of intervention programs. Comprehensive guidelines for planning intervention programs are not provided, but items on the scale are arranged in clusters, similar to those found on the Vineland Expanded Form, and may be informally reviewed to obtain objectives for programs.

SCHOOL EDITION The AAMD Adaptive Behavior Scale—School Edition (Lambert, 1981; Lambert & Windmiller, 1981) was designed for children aged 3 to 17 years. The instrument measures 21 domains and 5 factors of adaptive behavior, reported in Table 15.8. It is administered by interviewing an informant or having an informant complete the questionnaire booklet.

The School Edition was standardized with about 6,500 children in California and Florida. No stratification variables were used to select the sample, but the children and adolescents were classified as normal, educable mentally

TABLE 15.7 Content of the AAMD Adaptive Behavior Scale—Clinical Version

Part 1: Adaptive Domains	Part 2: Maladaptive Domains
Independent Functioning	Violent and Destructive Behavior
Physical Development	Antisocial Behavior
Economic Activity	Rebellious Behavior
Language Development	Untrustworthy Behavior
Numbers and Time	Withdrawal
Domestic Activity	Stereotyped Behavior and Odd Mannerisms
Vocational Activity	Inappropriate Interpersonal Manners
Self-Direction	Unacceptable Vocal Habits
Responsibility	Unacceptable or Eccentric Habits
Socialization	Self-Abusive Behavior
	Hyperactive Tendencies
	Sexually Aberrant Behavior
	Psychological Disturbances
	Use of Medications

NOTE: The domain "Use of Medications" is not included on any factor.

TABLE 15.8 Content of the AAMD Adaptive Behavior Scale—School Edition

Factors	Domains
Personal Self-Sufficiency	Independent Functioning Physical Development
Community Self-Sufficiency	Economic Activity Language Development Numbers and Time Pre-vocational Activity
Personal-Social Responsibility	Withdrawal Self-Direction Responsibility Socialization
Comparison Score (total of first three factors)	
Social Adjustment	Aggressiveness Antisocial versus Social Behavior Rebelliousness Trustworthiness Habits Activity Level Symptomatic Behavior
Personal Adjustment	Mannerisms Appropriateness of Interpersonal Manners Vocal Habits

NOTE: The domain "Use of Medications" is not included on any factor.

retarded, or trainable mentally retarded. The manual reports internal consistency reliability estimates ranging from .27 to .97. Validity data, including correlations with intelligence and achievement tests, factor analyses, and comparison of handicapped and nonhandicapped children, are also reported.

Percentile ranks for the 21 domains are obtained using normal, educable, or trainable mentally retarded children and adolescents as reference groups. Factor scores are reported as scaled scores with a mean of 10 and standard deviation of 3. The manual provides criterion-referenced techniques for determining detailed information about adaptive behavior deficits and for program planning.

CONCLUSIONS Both versions of the AAMD Adaptive Behavior Scale offer comprehensive

assessment of adaptive behavior in many domains and information concerning areas of strength and weakness (Elliott, 1985; Sattler, 1988). However, their psychometric properties are not as well defined as the Vineland and SIB. Norms are not representative of the U.S. population and some domains do not demonstrate adequate reliability (Salvia & Ysseldyke, 1988; Sattler, 1988; Taylor, 1989). The recommended use of these two instruments is for clinical or criterion-referenced assessment of deficits; their use in making important diagnostic decisions is not recommended (Sattler, 1988; Taylor, 1989).

Normative Behavior Checklist and Comprehensive Test of Adaptive Behavior

The Normative Adaptive Behavior Scale (NABC) and Comprehensive Test of Adaptive Behavior

(CTAB) (Adams, 1984a, 1984b, 1986), for individuals ranging in age from birth to 21 years, both measure six categories; the CTAB includes several more specific subcategories of adaptive behavior, listed in Table 15.9. Both instruments yield a total adaptive behavior score. The NABC provides a brief norm-referenced assessment of adaptive behavior and includes a sample of CTAB items. The longer CTAB provides both norm- and criterion-referenced information. The NABC is administered in a questionnaire completed by a third-party informant. The CTAB uses direct observations and testing of the client, along with reports by informants, to assess adaptive behavior.

TECHNICAL QUALITIES The NABC was normed with 6,130 individuals from all regions of the country, stratified only according to sex. The CTAB was not standardized with normal subjects, but normative data for normal subjects were determined through an equating study with the NABC. The CTAB was standardized with two samples of mentally retarded individuals, one sample of about 4,500 non-school retarded subjects from three regions of the United States and another sample of about 2,000 in-school retarded subjects in Florida. Internal consistency reliability estimates for the NABC categories range from .96 to .99 and, for the CTAB subcategories, .78 to .99 (all but one estimate

TABLE 15.9 Content of the Normative Adaptive Behavior Checklist and Comprehensive Test of Adaptive Behavior

Categories	Subcategories
Self-Help Skills	Toileting Grooming Dressing Eating
Home Living Skills	Living Room Kitchen-Utensil Use and Cooking Kitchen-Cleaning Bedroom Bath and Utility Room Yard Care
Independent Living Skills	Health Skills Telephone Skills Travel Skills Time-Telling Skills Economic Skills Vocational Skills
Social Skills	Self-Awareness Interaction Skills Leisure Skills
Sensory and Motor Skills	Sensory Awareness and Discrimination Motor Skills
Language Concepts and Academic Skills	Language Concepts Math Skills Reading and Writing Skills

is above .90). NABC test–retest reliability estimates for categories range from .79 to .99 (median = .98). CTAB test–retest reliability estimates range from .95 to .99 (median = .97). The manual reports limited validity information, consisting of correlations with the WISC-R and Vineland Social Maturity Scale.

SCORING AND INTERPRETATION   Scores for both instruments include standard scores with a mean of 100 and standard deviation of 15, percentile ranks, performance rankings, and age equivalents. The manual indicates that the NABC should not be used for program planning. The comprehensive assessment provided by the subcategories of the CTAB is useful for planning an intervention program; the items in the categories form a sequential list of adaptive behavior activities, and the manual includes a detailed description for preparing a "scope and sequence chart" to be used in intervention plans.

CONCLUSIONS   The CTAB provides useful clinical information, and the guidelines for planning interventions are excellent, but the psychometric properties of the NABC and CTAB limit their use as norm-referenced instruments. The standardization samples were not representative of the United States population and validity data are limited. Taylor (1989) recommends use of the NABC as a screening instrument only.

Pyramid Scales

The Pyramid Scales (Cone, 1984) are somewhat different from the previously discussed instruments. There are 20 scales, designed for infants through adults, which are tied to three sensory areas, as shown in Table 15.10. The scales are criterion-referenced and are tied to 5,000 specific objectives and a complete training curriculum (Cone, 1986). The scales are administered though a questionnaire or a structured interview with an informant. The Pyramid Scales can be very useful when norm-referenced scores are not needed for an individual.

TABLE 15.10   Content of the Pyramid Scales

Zone	Area
Sensory Zone	Tactile Responsiveness
	Auditory Responsiveness
	Visual Responsiveness
Primary Zone	Gross Motor
	Eating
	Fine Motor
	Toileting
	Dressing
	Social Interaction
	Washing/Grooming
	Receptive Language
	Expressive Language
Secondary Zone	Recreation/Leisure
	Writing
	Domestic Behavior
	Reading
	Vocational
	Time
	Numbers
	Money

Clinical Assessment of Adaptive Behavior with Mentally Retarded Adolescents and Adults

As indicated throughout this book, intelligence testing of adolescents and adults provides a wealth of information about skills, strengths and weaknesses, as well as hypotheses for predicting behavior. However, intelligence tests offer only one source of information about a client (Anastasi, 1988). Adaptive behavior assessment is another source of potentially valuable information for making decisions and plans concerning mentally retarded and other handicapped adolescents and adults.

Adaptive behavior assessment is an important component of the flexible, multidimensional process recommended for evaluation of handicapped individuals. Most adaptive behavior scales sample skills in multiple domains, including self-help, interpersonal, cognitive, communication, and motor skills. They typically allow multiple informants (e.g., parents, caregivers, teachers) to be used in the assessment process and do not rely only on structured testing of the client. Adaptive behavior scales sample many behaviors important in the various environments (home, school, community, job) in which mentally retarded clients must function. Adaptive behavior assessment can assist in planning intervention programs geared to the acquisition and performance of everyday self-help and social skills. Deficits in adaptive behavior may be related to home, family, school, or work conditions, and these conditions may also be amenable to organizational or environmental interventions.

Comprehensive clinical assessment of adaptive behavior must incorporate several factors. The relationship between intelligence and adaptive behavior must be considered and results from both types of assessment must be integrated in the evaluation of a mentally retarded person. A related topic is declassification, which may occur when scores from both intelligence and adaptive behavior scales are used to determine eligibility for a classification of mental retardation. A third factor in adaptive behavior assessment is the type of informant used. Informants such as parents, teachers, and caregivers base their ratings on adaptive behavior in different settings, and their scores are not interchangeable. Finally, informal assessment of adaptive behavior is a useful supplement to an adaptive behavior scale.

Relationship Between Cognitive Measures and Adaptive Behavior

One of the more common misconceptions about adaptive behavior is that it is equivalent to cognitive functioning (Coulter, 1980). Many professionals who work with mentally retarded adolescents and adults often expect those with low intelligence to have low adaptive behavior and vice versa. Although adaptive behavior and cognitive functioning are obviously related, the conceptualization and measurement of the two constructs differ in several respects (Meyers et al., 1979). Cognitive functioning is usually conceptualized as a thought process, while adaptive behavior emphasizes everyday behavior. Tests of cognitive functioning measure optimal maximum performance, or potential, while adaptive behavior scales measure typical performance. Intelligence is assumed to be stable, while adaptive behavior is assumed to be modifiable.

RESEARCH RESULTS Many studies have investigated the relationship between measures of intelligence and adaptive behavior and moderate correlations between the two are typically found (Harrison, 1987b). For example, Roszkowski and Bean (1980) reported a correlation of .66 between the AAMD Adaptive Behavior Scale and intelligence for institutionalized mentally retarded individuals. Bruininks et al. (1985) found correlations ranging from .20 to .39 between SIB clusters and the Woodcock-Johnson for nonhandicapped adolescents and adults and .61 to .85 for handicapped adolescents and adults. Sparrow et al. (1984a) reported correlations of .09 to .51 between the Vineland Survey Form and several intelligence scales administered for mentally retarded adults in residential facilities and .37 to .49 for mentally retarded adults in community facilities. Meyers et al. (1979) summarized correlations between adaptive behavior and intelligence measures for mentally retarded adults and indicated that low to moderate correlations are typically found for the mildly retarded and that moderate to high correlations are found for residential clients. Nihira (1985) reported that correlations between adaptive behavior domains and intelligence are usually higher for the cognitive and communication domains of adaptive behavior scales.

Some research has been specifically conducted to investigate the independence of adaptive behavior and intelligence. Keith, Fehrmann, Harrison, and Pottebaum (1987) used Vineland Survey Form and Kaufman Assessment Battery for Children scores for normal children in a confirmatory factor analysis and supported the hypothesis that adaptive behavior and intelligence are two separate but related constructs. Bruininks and McGrew (1987) and Connor, Kamphaus, and Harrison (1988) reached similar conclusions using canonical correlation analyses with adaptive behavior and intelligence scores of normal individuals. Bruininks and McGrew found adaptive behavior and intelligence to be independent regardless of age or whether the subjects were mentally retarded or normal.

Research has also supported the hypothesis that the relationship between school achievement and adaptive behavior is low to moderate (Harrison & Kamphaus, 1984; Lambert, 1981; Oakland, 1980; Stinson, 1988). For example, Christian and Malone (1973) reported correlations of −.18 to .11 between AAMD Adaptive Behavior Scale and WRAT scores for mentally retarded individuals in residential treatment. Perhaps a more appropriate criterion than school achievement for adaptive behavior scales is *life* achievement (Kamphaus, 1987). Several studies have found a positive relationship between scores from adaptive behavior scales and measures of life achievement, such as work success and productivity (e.g., Irvin, Halpern, & Reynolds, 1977; Malgady, Barcher, Davis, & Towner, 1980).

SUGGESTIONS FOR ASSESSMENT The most obvious practical implication of the moderate relationships between adaptive behavior and cognitive functioning is that mentally retarded individuals may have different scores on measures of adaptive behavior and cognitive ability, two distinct but related areas of functioning. An adolescent or adult may have low intelligence and school achievement and adequate adaptive behavior, while another client may exhibit the opposite pattern of functioning. The case of Jessica illustrates the former pattern.

Jessica is 18 years, 8 months of age and has participated in a program for EMR students for 10 years. Her current psychological evaluation yielded a WAIS-R Full Scale IQ of 63, stan-dardized achievement scores in the low 60s, and the Vineland Survey Form scores found in Table 15.11. Jessica's intelligence and achievement scores are in the low extreme and, according to AAMD guidelines, are in the mildly retarded range. Her Vineland adaptive behavior scores are in the moderately low to adequate range. Thus, Jessica's functioning is quite different in these two distinct areas.

Her performance on the Vineland Survey Form domains is also consistent with research findings. The Communication domain represents a significant weakness for Jessica, compared to her own average level of functioning. Her adaptive levels on the three Communication subdomains indicate that, although her receptive and expressive skills are in the adequate range, her written skills are low. Research suggests that communication and cognitive skills, such as those found in the Vineland Written subdomain, are more related to scores from intelligence and achievement tests than are other areas of adaptive behavior.

Declassification

Declassification occurs when individuals no longer meet the requirements for classification as handicapped or when they meet some but not all requirements (Reschly, 1982). The issue of declassification is particularly important for the classification of mild mental retardation. Until fairly recently, people were categorized as mildly mentally retarded based solely on their intelligence test scores. Because emphasis has shifted to documenting deficits in adaptive behavior in addition to subaverage intellectual functioning, individuals with low intelligence who exhibit adequate adaptive behavior should no longer be classified as mentally retarded.

Ineligibility for services for the mentally retarded is usually an issue with individuals with mild intellectual deficits only. Many individuals with moderate to profound intellectual deficits usually have concurrent deficits in adaptive be-

TABLE 15.11   Results of the Vineland Adaptive Behavior Scales Survey Form for Jessica, age 18 years, 8 months

Domain Standard Scores	Subdomain Adaptive Levels
Communication: 51 ± 11	Receptive: Adequate Expressive: Adequate Written: Low
Daily Living Skills: 100 ± 9	Personal: Adequate Domestic: Adequate Community: Adequate
Socialization: 90 ± 9	Interpersonal Relationships: Adequate Play and Leisure Time: Adequate Coping Skills: Low
Adaptive Behavior Composite: 74 ± 7	

NOTE: Standard scores are reported with bands of error at the 90% confidence level.

havior, and there is no question that they are mentally retarded.

RESEARCH RESULTS   Several studies have investigated outcomes of using adaptive behavior and intelligence measures jointly in the classification of mental retardation. Childs (1982) and Reschly (1981) found that large percentages of individuals would have been declassified as mentally retarded if the criteria of both low intelligence and adaptive behavior had been applied. These studies dealt with *possible* outcomes of using dual criteria; they did not investigate the actual frequency of declassification for the mildly retarded. Fisher (1978) found that 60% to 75% of a sample of EMR students were declassified when adaptive behavior scores were used for classification in addition to IQ.

SUGGESTIONS FOR ASSESSMENT   Frequency of declassification of mentally retarded adults and adolescents may be affected by the operational definition of *adaptive behavior deficits*. Definitions of mild mental retardation usually give specific ranges of intelligence test scores (e.g., 55 to 70) but there are usually no similar cutoff scores for adaptive behavior measures. Some

agencies may require strict adaptive behavior cut-off scores that are comparable to requirements for intelligence (e.g., below 70, or 2 or more standard deviations below the mean) while others may have less strict or more subjective criteria (e.g., below 85, or deficits in some subdomains of adaptive behavior).

For mentally retarded adolescents attending public school, the frequency of declassification may be affected by the way in which adaptive behavior is viewed. Reschly (1982, 1985) suggested two components of adaptive behavior, school-based and out-of-school. School-based adaptive behavior focuses on behaviors exhibited in the school setting with an emphasis on basic academic skills. Out-of-school adaptive behavior focuses on the self-help and social skills performed in the home and community. A student who exhibits low intelligence and low school-based and out-of-school adaptive behavior can be classified as mentally retarded. A student with low intelligence and school-based adaptive behavior, but adequate out-of-school adaptive behavior (i.e., the "six-hour retarded student"), cannot be classified as mentally retarded, according to most requirements for this classification, but might be classified as "educationally handicapped." Most school districts, however, do not have a special education category for Reschly's second group, though they may have other remedial services available for these students.

Declassification may pose a real dilemma for professionals working with mildly retarded adolescents and adults. For example, an adult may lose special services and financial assistance if he or she is declassified. A high school student who has participated in an EMR program for several years may become ineligible to receive specialized vocational training available for many EMR students in high school. Once again, the AAMD suggestion for flexible professional judgment in diagnosing mental retardation should be followed when dealing with possible cases of declassification.

In Jessica's case (see Table 15.11), her intelligence, achievement, and adaptive behavior scores could result in declassification. If a strict cut-off score below 70 is used to define adaptive behavior deficits, Jessica's Adaptive Behavior Composite of 74 would declassify her. If a cut-off of below 85 is used, she would not be declassified. She could also be declassified if it is noted that she exhibits average functioning in the self-help and social areas of adaptive behavior and deficits in areas that are related to cognitive abilities.

Informants for Adaptive Behavior Assessment

Most adaptive behavior instruments are rating scales administered to an informant who is familiar with the person being assessed. Although adaptive behavior rating scales administered to third-party informants should be interpreted cautiously, due to factors such as informant bias or lack of knowledge about the behaviors being assessed, use of informants can provide an ecologically valid means of assessing the adaptive behavior of mentally retarded adolescents and adults. Asking an informant to describe the daily activities of the client provides an assessment of "real world" behaviors exhibited in a variety

of settings and is not based on information gathered from a rather artificial testing situation (Holman & Bruininks, 1985). The informant method also allows significant others in the mentally retarded person's environment, such as parents, teachers, caregivers, and supervisors, to be involved in the assessment process.

RESEARCH RESULTS   The different types of informants for adaptive behavior scales are not interchangeable. The two primary types of informants for mentally retarded adolescents are parents and teachers. Mealor and Richmond (1980), Bailey (1979), Heath and Obrzut (1984), and Spivack (1980) found significantly higher scores for parents when their adaptive behavior ratings were compared to those of teachers. Harrison and Kamphaus (1984) and Mayfield, Forman, and Nagle (1984) reported low to moderate correlations between the scores of teachers and parents on adaptive behavior scales. In fact, Harrison and Kamphaus (1984) found that teachers' adaptive behavior scores correlated higher with cognitive measures than they did with parents' adaptive behavior scores. Findings such as these prompted Bracken and Barnett's (1987) suggestion that adaptive behavior scales lack convergent validity and interrater reliability.

Bracken and Barnett's suggestion deserves consideration, but the low correlations and lack of agreement between parents and teachers scores may reflect an *expected* outcome of adaptive behavior assessment related to the definition of the construct. As indicated earlier in this chapter, the definition of adaptive behavior emphasizes cultural influences and the expectation of various settings and significant others in the client's environment. Parents and teachers observe mentally retarded adolescents in different settings and may have different expectations for behavior. Further, for mentally retarded minority adolescents, school may represent a white, middle-class environment to which they have difficulty adjusting (Hetherington & Parke, 1986). Given these factors, it may be feasible to assume that parents and teachers should not necessarily agree about their ratings of adaptive behavior.

SUGGESTIONS FOR ASSESSMENT The research concerning the type of informant used with adaptive behavior scales has several practical implications. First, it may be necessary to assess a mentally retarded client's adaptive behavior by using several informants to obtain ratings of the client's adaptive behavior in several settings. For example, assessments with both parents and teachers are recommended for a mentally retarded adolescent in a school setting. For a mentally retarded adult who resides in a group home and works in a sheltered workshop, assessment with supervisors in both settings is recommended. Second, different informants may not demonstrate agreement in their assessments of adaptive behavior. If differences do exist, the accuracy of the informants' ratings may not necessarily be in question. Instead, disagreement between informants may lead to informal assessment, designed to gain important information about the person's adaptive behavior and the demands of settings and significant others in those settings. Questions such as the following can be answered through informal assessment: Is the person's behavior different in different settings? Do significant others have different expectations for the person? What implications do the different expectations have for the person's development? What changes can be made to promote growth in adaptive behavior in the different settings?

Differences between adaptive behavior scores from two or more informants may complicate the classification of mental retardation. The case of John illustrates this problem. John is a 12-year-old adolescent boy being considered for the EMR program in his school. He has a WISC-R Full Scale IQ of 68, a Vineland Survey Form Adaptive Behavior Composite of 84, and a Vineland Classroom Edition Adaptive Behavior Composite of 65. Is John eligible for the EMR program? His IQ and Vineland Classroom Edition score are in the deficient range, but his

Vineland Survey Form score is only below average. Consistent with research, the adaptive behavior rating obtained from his teacher is more comparable to his intelligence than it is to his parent's rating of adaptive behavior. The question of whether John is eligible for his school's EMR program must be determined by his eligibility committee according to the emphasis that it places on teachers' and parents' ratings and the criterion they use for adaptive behavior deficits.

Another option in adaptive behavior assessment of mentally retarded adolescents and adults is to use the client himself or herself as the informant. Indeed, it is more practical to use mentally retarded adolescents and adults themselves, rather than teachers, parents, or caregivers, as the informant. The clients may have more information about their own activities than other informants.

Several studies have found that adaptive behavior measures obtained from mildly retarded clients were comparable to caregiver ratings, but that measures from moderately to severely retarded persons were questionable (Nathan, Millhand, Chilcutt, & Atkinson, 1980; Sigelman et al., 1981). Voelker et al. (1987) and Voelker, Shore, and Miller (in press) compared Vineland Survey Form results obtained from moderately and severely retarded adults living in group homes and from their counselors and found no significant differences, with a few exceptions. The Maladaptive Behavior domain scores were significantly different for caregivers and self-informants. Lower functioning clients reported fewer maladaptive behaviors than counselors and higher functioning clients reported more maladaptive behaviors than their counselors. Lower scores were obtained on the Communication domain for higher functioning self-informants than for counselors. Clearly, valuable clinical information may be obtained by using mentally retarded clients as their own informants for adaptive behavior scales. Norms for most adaptive behavior scales are based on third-party informants, however, and scores based on information from self-informants should be interpreted with caution. The best practice is to use self-informant measures in conjunction with parent, supervisor, or other third party informants.

Informal Adaptive Behavior Assessment

Adaptive behavior scales are an integral part of the adaptive behavior assessment of mentally retarded adolescents and adults but, as with any type of assessment, structured scales fail to take into account a variety of factors about a person's functioning. For example, informants for adaptive behavior scales may not have sufficient knowledge of a person's behavior in all situations or may present biased information. The information obtained from an informant in one setting may not generalize to other settings. Some adaptive behaviors may be fostered and maintained in highly structured, nurturing settings; in other settings, the person may not exhibit the adaptive behaviors. Adaptive behavior instruments measure behavior up to a given point in time, and results from the instrument may ignore rapid developmental or behavioral changes. Adaptive behavior scales provide only a *sample* of behavior and may not adequately assess all behaviors important for a specific individual. For these reasons, informal assessment should always be conducted to supplement and expand the information obtained from standardized scales.

One way to informally assess adaptive behavior is to observe the client. Informal observations of adaptive behavior should be conducted in a variety of settings and situations. Adaptive behavior scales often require informants to give generalized responses to items or, in other words, to describe what the mentally retarded client does across all situations in that environment. Informal observation of the client's behavior in specific situations can be conducted; for example, the person's interactions with younger versus older peers, normal versus handicapped peers, and parents versus teachers, and in stressful versus relaxed situations. The sit-

uation itself as well as the behavior of significant others can be assessed. For example, what characteristics of one setting versus another setting foster the behavior or prevent the client from exhibiting the behavior? What interactions motivate or threaten the person? How does the person's adaptive behavior change as he or she gains more experience with the situation? Additional informal assessment with informants during the administration of an adaptive behavior scale presents a means of discussing issues related to adaptive behavior. These include behaviors that caregivers or supervisors find worrisome, current adaptive behavior interventions they are using, and specific environmental factors that affect the person's adaptive behavior.

Feuersten's (1979) model of dynamic assessment can be applied to informal assessment of adaptive behavior. His model, typically applied to intelligence testing, uses a test-teach-retest approach in which the client's level of functioning is determined, training is provided, and the client's response to the training is evaluated. For informal assessment of adaptive behavior, the person's current performance of an activity can be determined, either through use of an adaptive behavior scale, direct testing, or informal assessment. Training of the activity can be given. Then generalization of the training to other settings can be assessed, and the training itself can be evaluated to determine successful techniques.

Adaptive Behavior Interventions for Mentally Retarded Adolescents and Adults

Assessment has three major purposes when the results are to be used to plan interventions (Verhaaren & Conner, 1981). Assessment results should lead to *education,* or training in skills that allow people to achieve their potential. They should lead to *prevention* of further problems from occurring and to the *reduction* of negative effects from any handicapping condition.

Adaptive behavior assessment has several features that enable the planning of interventions to achieve these purposes. Most instruments yield scores in several domains, and strengths and weaknesses in adaptive behavior can be determined to indicate the client's specific intervention needs (Witt & Martens, 1984). Informal assessment of adaptive behavior can yield additional information about possible objectives of intervention, and can be useful in monitoring the effectiveness of the program. Some adaptive behavior scales, for example, the AAMD Adaptive Behavior Scale, Vineland Expanded Form, and Pyramid Scales, list adaptive behavior items in hierarchical sequences that can be used in the carefully designed, sequential training suggested for improving adaptive behavior (Langone & Burton, 1987).

Training in adaptive behavior should be an ongoing process that occurs in the environments where the person is expected to exhibit the behavior, in addition to more structured, classroom-type settings (Langone & Burton, 1987). Efforts should also be made to generalize structured teaching of skills to out-of-classroom settings. Training should be conducted by all significant others in the person's environment, including parents, teachers, and supervisors.

Steps for Training

Cone's (1987) series of steps for training adaptive behavior can easily be incorporated into a mentally retarded person's educational or habilitation plan. These steps combine the requirements of different settings with an assessment of a person's current functioning. Step 1 is to determine long-range goals for the person; these are the behaviors required for a specific situation, such as entry into a job or transfer to a nonresidential setting. Step 2 is to determine the person's *current* performance of the behaviors required to achieve step 1. The assessment of current performance should include

the results of adaptive behavior assessment, as well as intellectual, vocational, and other types of assessment. Step 3 requires a comprehensive assessment of the skills the person needs to acquire to achieve the long-range goals, including an evaluation of the difference between the client's current functioning and the demands of the new setting. The demands of the new setting may be determined by observing behavior in these settings and by interviewing counselors, employers, and others with an adaptive behavior instrument about a successful, "fictional" client in the setting. The final steps are to estimate the amount of time needed to achieve the long-range goals and to develop annual, monthly, and weekly goals and immediate instructional objectives.

Training for Community Living and Jobs

Two specific types of training are particularly important for mentally retarded adolescents and adults: training in skills necessary for functioning in a community living setting, such as a group home or supervised or unsupervised apartment or other residence, and training in vocational skills. Much research supports the importance of adaptive behavior in these two types of training. Bruininks, Thurlow, and Gilman (1987) have suggested that problem behavior and antisocial acts are among the primary reasons that mentally retarded people are placed in institutions instead of community settings. For example, samples of institutionalized and noninstitutionalized mentally retarded clients matched on intelligence and other variables exhibited significant differences on the AAMD Adaptive Behavior Scale, primarily on the Maladaptive Behavior domains (Campbell, Smith, & Wool, 1982). Adaptive and maladaptive behavior has been shown to be a factor in the successful and unsuccessful placement of mentally retarded individuals in community settings (Bruininks et al., 1987; Sutter, Mayeda, Call, Yanagi, & Yee, 1980; Taylor, 1976; Thiel, 1981).

Other research has shown a marked improvement in adaptive and maladaptive behavior when mentally retarded individuals are placed in more normal settings. Thompson and Carey (1980) found that severely and profoundly mentally retarded individuals showed significant improvements in adaptive behavior when placed in structured group homes. Conroy, Efthimiou, and Lemanowicz (1982) compared a sample of mentally retarded clients who left an institution with a group who remained in the institution. The two groups were matched on intelligence. Although there were no differences in adaptive behavior between the two groups at initial testing, the deinstitutionalized individuals had higher adaptive behavior after leaving the institution. Eyman, Demaine, and Lei (1970) investigated factors related to improvement of adaptive behavior in group homes and found that improvement of older, less retarded individuals was associated with positive ratings of comfort and deployment of staff, access to the home, local proximity of services, and blending with the neighborhood. Research has also shown improvement in adaptive behavior within institutions when residents are placed in more normal, less traditional buildings (MacEachron, 1983; Witt, 1981).

Adaptive behavior has importance in work settings as well. Bruininks et al. (1987) indicated that deficiencies in social and interpersonal skills are the primary factors involved in the failure of mentally retarded individuals to find and retain jobs and be integrated into vocational settings. Further, social and interpersonal skills are important factors in making the transition from school to work. Malgady, Barcher, Davis, and Towner (1980) found adaptive behavior successfully predicted sheltered workshop placement and follow-up placement 1 year later for a group of mentally retarded adolescents. Other researchers have found that scores from adaptive behavior measures were significantly related to later ratings by vocational rehabilitation counselors, to work competency, and to sheltered workshop productivity (Carsrud,

Carsrud, Dodd, Thompson, & Gray, 1981; Cunningham & Presnall, 1978; Halpern, Raffeld, Irvin, & Link, 1975).

Given the ample evidence for the importance of adaptive behavior in community and vocational settings, adaptive behavior must be considered in the prediction of successful placement of mentally retarded individuals in these settings and in the interventions designed to achieve successful placement. When planning interventions, special attention must be given to the client's motor, communication, cognitive/academic skills, and social skills and any problem behaviors, and to behavioral expectations on the job or in the community. For example, in the area of motor skills, does the client have the necessary gross motor skills required, including ambulation, strength for lifting, and coordination? The fine motor skills demanded for many types of employment requiring activities such as assembly work and packing may represent intervention objectives. Communication skills are often a relative weakness for mentally retarded adolescents and adults, compared with skills in other areas (Sparrow et al. 1984a). Many work and community settings do not place as much emphasis on mentally retarded clients' communication skills, particularly written communication skills, as they do other adaptive behaviors, but it should be determined to what extent communication skills are emphasized in a particular setting. Poor social skills and problem behaviors are two of the major reasons mentally retarded clients are unsuccessful in work and community settings (Bruininks et al., 1987). It should also be determined to what extent a person is required to work or interact with others and if there are any problem behaviors that may interfere with successful placement. Self-help skills such as personal hygiene, dressing, grooming, and domestic skills are necessary for most work and community settings. Finally, using transportation, telling time, and using the telephone may be objectives for a new placement.

GIFTEDNESS

The first section of this chapter discussed the assessment of adolescent and adults in the lower extreme of intellectual functioning. Like the mentally retarded, adolescents and adults with superior intellectual abilities represent a heterogeneous group of individuals who may be assessed by psychologists for a variety of purposes. Bright adolescents may be evaluated for possible placement in gifted or honors programs or advanced placement in high school or college. Adults with exceptionally high intelligence may be assessed for occupational placement and planning. Although psychologists evaluate mentally retarded adolescents and adults more often than those with superior abilities (Harrison, Kaufman, Hickman, & Kaufman, 1988), the number of adults, particularly older adults, in our society is steadily growing and with this change in the population more emphasis is being placed on lifelong intellectual development and education beyond formal schooling (Burnham, 1982). More older adults are entering college and considering mid-life career changes. Psychologists are likely to see more clients of average or superior intelligence who face occupational concerns, in addition to mental health concerns, and intellectual assessment of these individuals can be an important facet in assisting them in decision making.

Superior intellectual functioning is only one aspect of "gifted" functioning and, although most definitions of gifted functioning emphasize cognitive abilities, above average intelligence and giftedness are not interchangeable concepts. Tannenbaum (1983) reported that the target population for gifted programs in schools includes those individuals with exceptional intellectual skills, as well as those with exceptional academic ability in specific areas, creativity, leadership skills, and skills in the arts and psychomotor areas. Gifted individuals, whether they are adolescents being considered for placement in a school's gifted program or adults being

considered for job placement, may demonstrate exceptional abilities in only one or in several areas.

This section discusses the intellectual assessment of adolescents and adults with superior intelligence and reviews controversial aspects of using intelligence test scores as a criterion for gifted functioning. Supplements to traditional intelligence tests, which provide additional information about exceptional abilities, are described. There are many supplemental procedures used in assessment of gifted adolescent and adults, but this section focuses on tests of critical thinking and higher mental processes and on tests of creativity.

Intellectual Assessment

Individual intelligence tests have many positive features that promote competent assessment of superior abilities (Kaufman & Harrison, 1986). Although intelligence should never be the sole criterion for determination of gifted functioning and multifaceted assessment should always be used to obtain a complete picture of any person's abilities, intelligence tests meet the practical needs of predicting success in academic and other settings, yield information about a variety of cognitive skills, and have exemplary psychometric properties. Intelligence tests, when used appropriately, supply the single best method for assessing outstanding cognitive abilities and provide information unavailable from any other source (Sattler, 1988). The following pages discuss the usefulness of intelligence tests in predicting academic and adult accomplishments, research on the use of the Wechsler scales with individuals in the upper intellectual ranges and implications for test interpretation, and guidelines for intellectual assessment.

Prediction of Academic
Achievement and Adult Accomplishment

Intelligence tests were originally designed to predict academic functioning and there is little doubt that they have succeeded in this purpose (Anastasi, 1988; Robinson & Chamrad, 1986; Whitmore, 1980). Research on the value of intelligence tests in predicting school achievement (see pp. 18–19) has consistently found that intelligence tests are excellent predictors and that they predict academic achievement significantly better than measures of any other single type of functioning, such as social skills and motor ability. Most intelligence tests measure abilities that are prerequisites for school learning and can be thought of as measures of academic potential or scholastic aptitude (Anastasi, 1988).

To a lesser but significant degree, intelligence tests also predict behavior beyond that required for school activities, because many academic skills are also required for everyday life in modern technological society (Anastasi, 1988). For gifted individuals, no other single measure is as predictive of future accomplishment as intelligence tests (Brody & Brody, 1976). Cronbach (1976) stated, "The ultimate justification for collecting test scores is that they indicate (with some margin of error) what can be expected in the practical world" (p. 242).

Terman's Study of the Gifted

Terman's longitudinal study of gifted children and the extensive follow-up of these individuals through their adult years represent the best-known and most persuasive evidence for the validity of intelligence tests in predicting superior academic and life accomplishments (Oden, 1968; Sears, 1977; Sears & Barbee, 1977; Terman, 1925, 1954; Terman & Oden, 1947, 1959). In the 1920s a large number of gifted children with Stanford-Binet IQs above 135 were identified in California schools. The children were followed into their late adult years and a variety of data were collected concerning school history, occupation, marriage and family, distinctions and awards, general mental health, and other attributes. Over the years, these gifted individuals had more accomplishments than their normal counterparts. The group, in general, had

exceptional academic records and many awards and honors; as adults they were represented by a long list of publications, patents, and scholarly distinctions. The majority of individuals went to graduate school and had jobs in the highest occupational categories. They rated themselves higher than average on physical and mental health and satisfaction with jobs and life. They had lower suicide and divorce rates than the general population. However, the sample was characterized by a group of individuals who began to pull ahead of another group during high school, although the two groups had equivalent IQs and achievement in elementary school. The group that pulled ahead was more likely than the other group to enter and graduate from college and to give higher ratings for life accomplishments.

Differences were noted between males and females in Terman's gifted group. Men were typically more satisfied than women with their occupations. Women, of whom 45% were housewives, generally rated themselves as more satisfied than men with friends and cultural activities. Both men and women reported greater satisfaction with family life than did controls, although there were no differences between the two sexes on this rating.

Although it appears from Terman's study that these gifted children grew up to be gifted adults, Matarazzo (1972) cautioned against generalizing the findings to all gifted individuals and pointed out that some of the individuals in Terman's study did *not* exhibit exceptional accomplishments as adults. Hughes and Converse (1962) and Laycock (1979) criticized Terman's study on several methodological grounds that must be taken into account when interpreting the results. One criticism concerns the initial selection of children for possible participation in the study. Children were selected based on teacher's nominations, and a disproportionate number of economically advantaged children were included. Further, the single IQ from the Stanford-Binet, with its emphasis on academic potential, was used to predict accomplishments; the study thus did not assess many talents of the gifted children.

Meeker (1985), using a more contemporary sample than Terman's, followed 69 gifted individuals identified in the early 1960s until they were in their early 30s. Like the individuals in Terman's sample, these gifted individuals were performing successfully in their jobs. However, Meeker found that the gifted individuals were less likely to marry and had fewer children.

Relationship Between Intelligence Tests and Occupation

Matarazzo (1972) reviewed research concerning relationships between intelligence test scores and occupational characteristics. The studies used data from the Army Alpha (Army General Classification Test) administered during World Wars I and II and from the WAIS and found that there were high correlations between test scores and occupational responsibility in the army, success in pilot training, preinduction occupations, occupations 12 years after entering the service, and educational attainment. Matarazzo concluded that, on the average, adults in professional or executive occupations had superior intelligence, those in trades and skilled occupations had average intelligence, and those in semiskilled occupations had below average intelligence. Matarazzo stressed that this conclusion represented *average* findings and that the range of intelligence scores at each occupational position was quite large. This result is illustrated clearly in Figure 6.1 and Table 6.10, and the relationship of IQ to occupation level is discussed in more depth on pages 21–23 and pages 166–172.

Research With the Wechsler Scales for Individuals With Superior Intelligence

Although research concerning the use of the Wechsler scales with adolescents and adults in the upper ranges of intelligence is not as extensive as that with the mentally retarded, several research studies have explored exceptionally high performance on the scales.

Factor Analysis of the WISC-R

Factor analysis of the WISC-R for gifted children, including adolescents, has supported the Verbal Comprehension and Perceptual Organization factors but offers less support for interpretation of the Freedom from Distractibility dimension for these individuals. Karnes and Brown (1980), using a sample of 946 gifted children and adolescents aged 6 to 16 years, found Verbal Comprehension and Perceptual Organization factors, but the third factor received high loadings from the Arithmetic and Picture Completion subtests instead of the Arithmetic-Digit Span-Coding triad found with many samples of normal children (Kaufman et al., in press).

Characteristic Profiles on the WISC-R

Investigations of average Verbal and Performance WISC-R IQs for gifted children and adolescents indicate that mean Verbal IQs are typically greater than mean Performance IQs, as seen in Table 15.12. Table 15.12 also summarizes the rank ordering of subtest mean scores for five samples of gifted children and adolescents. The subtests on which children did their best are Comprehension and Similarities, and the subtests on which they did their worst appear to be Coding, Picture Completion, and Arithmetic. It should be noted that Coding was the most difficult subtest in each of the five studies, a sensible result in view of its low *g* loading for the WISC-R (Kaufman, 1979b). Arithmetic, on the other hand, was the second most difficult subtest in three of the five studies. Arithmetic received higher rankings in the two studies with the largest samples (Karnes & Brown, 1981; Sapp et al., 1985), but was the most difficult *Verbal* subtest in these two studies.

According to Bannatyne's system for categorizing Wechsler profiles (see pp. 381–382),

TABLE 15.12 Rank ordering of WISC-R subtest means for gifted samples

		WISC-R Subtest												
Source	N	Information	Similarities	Arithmetic	Vocabulary	Comprehension	Picture Completion	Picture Arrangement	Block Design	Object Assembly	Coding[a]	Mean V-IQ	Mean P-IQ	Mean FS-IQ
Henry & Wittman (1981)	40	4	3	9	2	1	8	7	5.5	5.5	10	—	—	130
Karnes & Brown (1981)	946	4	2.5	5	1	2.5	7.5	6	9	7.5	10	126	121	126
Sapp, Chissom, & Graham (1985)	371	4	2	6	3	1	9	7	5	8	10	130	121	129
Schiff, Kaufman & Kaufman (1981)	30	3	1	9	2	4	8	5	6	7	10	128	113	123
Wheaton & Vandergriff (1981)	26	3	2	9	5	1	8	7	6	4	10	138	133	140
Consensus Rankings		4	2	8	3	1	9	6.5	5	6.5	10			

NOTE: The study by Schiff et al. (1981) consisted of learning-disabled gifted children.

a characteristic profile on the WISC-R for gifted children and adolescents appears to be the Verbal Conceptualization > Acquired Knowledge > Spatial > Sequential pattern. Although many gifted individuals have higher Verbal than Performance IQs, the Verbal subtests appear to split into the two distinct and somewhat unexpected categories of Verbal Conceptualization and Acquired Knowledge. McGee and Brown (1984) also found that Comprehension scores were significantly higher than Information and Vocabulary scores on the WISC-R for children being considered for gifted placement and on the WAIS for bright college students, even though Comprehension scores are less dependent on formal education and other skills in which gifted individuals typically excel.

It should be noted that the subjects for the Schiff, Kaufman, and Kaufman (1981) study were gifted learning-disabled children. The subtest rankings in Table 15.12 do not include Digit Span because this optional subtest was not administered in most studies. For the subjects studied by Schiff et al., Digit Span was administered and was the second most difficult subtest, providing support for a relative weakness in sequencing ability for these children, similar to that found with nongifted learning-disabled children (Kaufman et al., in press). However, a weakness in sequencing ability is found in most studies of gifted children regardless of the presence of a learning disability, as seen in Table 15.12, so low scores on Coding, Digit Span, and Arithmetic will not necessarily contribute to the differential diagnosis of a learning disability in gifted children.

WAIS-R Verbal–Performance Differences

Little research has been conducted with the WAIS or WAIS-R for adults with superior intelligence, probably because of the difficulty in locating subjects for such research. Matarazzo and Herman (1985) analyzed V–P discrepancies for different ranges of IQ groups in the WAIS-R standardization sample; these results are summarized in Table 9.3. Compared to adults with below average intelligence, many adults with Full Scale IQs of 120 and above exhibited Verbal–Performance IQ differences of greater than 10 points. These data indicate a positive relationship between Full Scale IQ and the percentage of subjects who exhibited significant Verbal–Performance differences. A total of 47.5% of adults with IQs 120 and above had significant Verbal–Performance differences, 44.6% at IQs 110–120, 40.9% at IQs 90–109, 27.8% at IQs 80–89, and 15.8% at IQs 79 and below. Compared to findings with the WISC-R supporting a greater Verbal than Performance IQ for many gifted children, adults in the highest IQ groups had a less pronounced tendency to have greater verbal than performance skills. A total of 26% of adults with IQs 120 and above had significantly greater Verbal than Performance IQs, while 21.5% exhibited the opposite pattern (Matarazzo & Herman, 1985). This topic is also treated in chapter 9 (p. 295).

The IQ Controversy: Guidelines for Gifted Assessment

The traditional use of intelligence test scores as the sole criterion for gifted functioning has been highly criticized. In the public schools, rigid criterion scores are frequently used to enable students with IQs of 131 to enter a gifted program but deny entrance to those with IQs of 129. Similar rigid cut-offs for cognitive test scores may be used for entrance to honors classes, advanced placement, or other activities for exceptional adolescents and adults. Cognitive test scores may be emphasized while other evidence, such as outstanding school achievement or creative accomplishment, is ignored.

Opposition to Intelligence Testing

Abusive practices such as these have led some professionals who work with the gifted to argue that identification of gifted individuals by using intelligence test scores is a serious mistake (e.g.,

Sternberg, 1986; Treffinger & Renzulli, 1986). They argue that intelligence tests measure only one aspect of giftedness, academic giftedness, rather than other aspects, such as creative giftedness. They suggest that intelligence, as measured by traditional intelligence tests, is an abstract, poorly defined concept, and that intelligence test scores represent only a limited sample of the dynamic, multifaceted functioning described in contemporary theories of intelligence.

Arguments for Intelligence Testing

Proponents of using intelligence tests with gifted individuals agree with the arguments of the opponents and do not promote the sole use of intelligence tests to identify gifted functioning (e.g., Kaufman & Harrison, 1986; Robinson & Chamrad, 1986). They suggest, however, that intelligence tests have many positive characteristics that enhance gifted assessment, provide the most objective measure of gifted ability, and can be used intelligently with gifted individuals. They point out that intelligence tests have the best psychometric properties of any measure used with gifted individuals, are excellent predictors of academic achievement and success, and yield scores in several areas for a multifaceted interpretation of mental abilities. Psychologists who administer individual intelligence tests obtain qualitative information, in addition to scores, through careful administration and interpretation and clinical observation of the test taker. Some characteristics that may be observed by the acute examiner include problem-solving approach, language usage, self-concept, attention span, adaptation to change, anxiety, and reaction to novel tasks (see Examiner's Forms 12.2 and 12.3).

Intelligence tests can be used to identify gifted individuals who don't correspond to the stereotypical "gifted pattern" of extensive verbal ability and academic achievement and high motivation. Less objective methods of identifying gifted students, such as parent and teacher nominations, may result in a failure to identify gifted individuals with undeveloped potentials, handicapping conditions, low verbal ability, and lack of motivation who do not fit the "good student" pattern of striving, conforming, high achievers. Whitmore (1979, 1980, 1981) supplied evidence that underachieving and handicapped students often have talents that are not recognized until they are administered an individual intelligence test.

Guidelines for Best Practice

Kaufman and Harrison (1986, pp. 158–159) offered the following guidelines for the appropriate use of intelligence tests in gifted assessment.

1. Intelligence test scores should never be the only basis for determining gifted abilities. Gifted individuals may have many characteristics that intelligence tests were never designed or have attempted to measure—for example, social maturity, creative skills, and many types of specialized aptitudes.

2. Criterion scores (e.g., IQs of 130 or 140) should not be used to exclude individuals from programs for the gifted. If an individual has exceptional specialized skills that are not assessed by an intelligence test or is nonverbal, handicapped, or an underachiever, he or she should be considered for gifted placement even if his or her IQ falls short of the cut-off.

3. The bands of error associated with test scores should be taken into account when determining if an individual has gifted abilities. The scores on any psychological test are never free from errors in measurement, and a person's obtained score should always be considered an estimate of his or her "true" ability. Bands of error should be used to provide a more accurate representation of a range of scores that have a high probability of including a person's true ability.

4. Intelligence test scores should be used not only for determination of gifted ability, but

to plan educational, occupational, and other program plans as well. The identification of gifted adolescents and adults is not conducted simply to see if they have exceptional abilities. The individuals usually require specialized planning for achieving their potential and capitalizing on their strengths.

5. Intelligence test scores should not be used to make decisions about people. A simple, important, but often forgotten principle in psychological assessment is that tests cannot make decisions; *people* make decisions and tests are just one source of information that assist in the decision making.

Supplements to Traditional Intelligence Tests

The preceding arguments in favor of using intelligence tests to assess the abilities of superior adolescents and adults distinctly support the use of other types of assessments to supplement the IQ and to obtain a more complete picture of functioning. Many types of tests may be used in a supplemental battery, depending on the reason the person is being assessed, the types of decisions that must be made, and the types of programs or activities in which the person may participate. For example, an assessment battery for a high school student being considered for gifted placement or for an honors or advanced placement program may consist of achievement tests, creativity tests, and tests of special aptitude, in addition to an intelligence test. An assessment battery for an adult wishing to consider a new career or advanced vocational training may consist of aptitude tests, measures of critical thinking and problem-solving ability, vocational aptitude and interest tests, and measures of motivation and other personality characteristics, in addition to an intelligence test.

In this section, two of the many types of supplemental measures are reviewed. Specialized cognitive tests, which measure the higher level mental processes and critical thinking skills expected of gifted individuals in many programs and activities, represent an important and useful

supplement. So do tests of creativity, which have been a traditional part of gifted assessment and which emphasize skills that are related to, but relatively distinct from, cognitive skills.

Tests of Higher Mental Processes and Critical Thinking

The Watson-Glaser Critical Thinking Appraisal (Watson & Glaser, 1980) is a widely used group-administered, paper-and-pencil test for individuals in grades 9 through college and for adults. The test may be used to assist in making a variety of educational and occupational decisions and includes problems that may be encountered daily in real life. Six scores are available from the scale: Inference, Recognition of Assumptions, Deduction, Interpretation, Evaluation of Arguments, and Total. Norms based on high school and college students and on business and civic service employees are available. The instrument is well constructed, but has several limitations (Berger, 1985; Helmstadter, 1985). The test has relatively low reliability coefficients, and the skills measured by the tests may not be generalizable to actual activities in schoolwork. Critical decisions about individuals should therefore not be made using only Watson-Glaser scores.

The Structure of Intellect Learning Abilities Test (Meeker & Meeker, 1981) is an instrument used with children and adolescents through grade 12, although its psychometric qualities have been questioned (Coffman, 1985; Leton, 1985). A psychologist may elect to use several of the subtests to supplement an intellectual assessment, however. Based on Guilford's Structure of Intellect model (see pp. 389–390), the basic test offers 26 subtests in five areas for preschoolers through adolescents: comprehension, memory, evaluation, convergent production, and divergent production. Additional forms that may be used with adolescents include a reading form, arithmetic-math form, developmental vision form, and career and vocation form.

The Ross Test of Higher Cognitive Processes (Ross & Ross, 1979) has norms for grades

4–6, but some subtests may provide useful clinical information for students in higher grades. Subtests include analogies, deductive reasoning, missing premises, abstract relations, sequential synthesis, questioning strategies, analysis of relevant and irrelevant information, and analysis of attributes.

Tests of Creative Ability

Creative thinking is defined as fluency, readiness to change items of perception and thought, and flexible and elaborative thinking (Guilford, 1985). The concept of creative thinking is not synonymous with intelligence; all levels of creativity may be found at high levels of intelligence, and creative thinking is seldom measured on traditional tests of intelligence (Anastasi, 1988).

Guilford (1985) and Meeker (1985) suggested that creative thinking can be classified as divergent-production according to the structure-of-intellect model; according to this model, creatively gifted individuals excel in divergent-production while academically gifted individuals excel in convergent-production. Guilford (1985) defines divergent-production as "producing a number of alternative items of information from memory storage, either verbatim or in modified form, to satisfy a given need, such as naming objects that are both hard and edible, or suggesting a number of different titles for a given story" (p. 232). Convergent-production, on the other hand, requires producing a specific, single, correct solution.

PREDICTION OF CREATIVE PERFORMANCE Creative thinking appears to be predictive of creative performance in everyday life (Guilford, 1985). Torrance (1980, 1981) conducted a longitudinal study of children who were administered a test of creativity in grades 1–6. Test scores were used to predict a variety of later creative achievements, including number of high school and post–high school creative products, the quality of the products, and future career image. Correlations between creative thinking scores and later achievements ranged from .38 to .58 with a multiple correlation of .62.

PSYCHOMETRIC PROPERTIES OF CREATIVITY TESTS There are several widely used tests of creativity, but they are not typically characterized by the sound norming and reliability and validity studies of most individual intelligence tests (Kaufman & Harrison, 1986). Evidence suggests that intelligence and creativity tests have relatively small correlations with each other, as would be expected for two types of instruments that measure different constructs. However, different tests of creativity do not exhibit correlations with each other that are any higher than their correlations with intelligence tests. Ausubel and Sullivan (1970) suggested that people who have made major impacts in creative fields such as art are more intelligent than those who have not made contributions. In spite of the questionable psychometric properties of creativity tests and the difficulty in developing a good, operational definition of creativity for use in measuring the construct, creativity tests are potentially valuable adjuncts to intelligence tests for individuals who do not fit the pattern of academic giftedness.

INFORMAL ASSESSMENT Sattler (1988) provided a list of creative thinking tasks that can be used in informal assessment. These include asking individuals to list novel ways in which objects can be used, ways to improve objects, the effects of new or unusual events, ways objects or ideas are similar or different, words that begin with a specified letter, and synonyms and antonyms for words. In addition, biographical sketches and creative achievements can be reviewed to informally assess creativity.

STRUCTURE OF INTELLECT TESTS Guilford and his colleagues at the Aptitudes Research Project developed several tests of divergent-production in their research on the structure-of-intellect model (Christensen, Guilford, Merrifield, & Wilson, 1978). The tests include fluency for words, ideas, associations, and expressions, listing alternative uses of objects, providing possible titles for short stories, listing consequences of events, drawing objects and sketches, and drawing decorations on designs. The Structure of Intellect Learning Abilities Test (Meeker & Meeker, 1981) also includes subtests measuring divergent production.

TORRANCE TESTS The Torrance Tests of Creative Thinking (Torrance, 1984) are the most well-researched and analyzed instruments for measuring creativity (Kaufman & Harrison; 1986; Treffinger, 1985). Two tests are included in this battery for use with individuals in kindergarten through college: Thinking Creatively with Words and Thinking Creatively with Pictures. Each test may be scored on fluency, flexibility, originality, and elaboration. The seven verbal subtests are Asking, Guessing Causes, Guessing Consequences, Product Improvement, Unusual Uses, Unusual Questions, and Just Suppose. The three figural subtests are Picture Construction, Picture Completion, and Parallel Lines.

An additional Torrance test is Thinking Creatively with Sounds and Words (Torrance, Khatena, & Cunningham, 1973). The test is recommended for research use only and measures the ability of individuals in third grade through adulthood to generate novel associations for auditory stimuli.

The Khatena-Torrance Creative Perception Inventory (Khatena & Torrance, 1976), designed for adolescents and adults, is useful for assessing emotional factors in creativity. The scale, a paper-and-pencil self-rating inventory, includes two tests of creative self-perceptions: What Kind of Person Are You? and Something About Myself. The subscales are environmental sensitivity, initiative, self-strength, intellectuality, self-confidence, inquisitiveness, awareness of others, and disciplined imagination.

ILLUSTRATIVE CASE REPORT

The case study of Robert N. illustrates the integration of scores on intelligence tests and adaptive behavior measures as part of the as-

sessment process for an individual with suspected or known mental retardation. The use of the Vineland Adaptive Behavior Scales in conjunction with the WAIS-R is also demonstrated for illustrative case studies of individuals with brain damage (Walt H. on pp. 366–372 and Clara S. on pp. 629–636) and suspected autism (Chester P. on pp. 372–376).

Robert N., Age 36, Mild Retardation

Reason for Referral

Robert N. was referred for a psychological evaluation by the Area Services for Work and Rehabilitation (ASWR). An assessment of Robert's current level of functioning is needed to update his record. There is also some question as to whether neurological abnormalities may be present. Staff at the workshop feel that Robert is not working at his potential.

Background Information

Robert was born in a displaced persons camp in West Germany. The pregnancy and delivery were uncomplicated. Soon after his birth, an epidemic swept through the camp, affecting all who were living there. In addition to this, Robert had an upper respiratory ailment (possibly pneumonia) during infancy. His mother describes his development as normal during his first 2 years. At age 2, he reportedly began having temper tantrums and became increasingly active and unpredictable. When Robert was 5 years old, he and his family moved from Europe to a Ukrainian neighborhood in the Midwest, making it possible for them to maintain close cultural ties. Robert has two brothers (one of whom is retarded) and a sister.

Robert attended the local school for exceptional children from age 9 to 16. He was finally asked to leave the school because of unverified problems. He attended the local state school from age 17 to 24, and the Center for Developmentally Disabled (CDD) from age 25 to 33, before moving to the residential apartment facility where he currently resides. There is little information regarding his educational history; his work history is reportedly good. Robert was in a variety of vocational programs at CDD, where he received training in food and janitorial services. His work skills and attitude were described as good.

Psychological evaluations conducted through the years have consistently found Robert to function in the mildly retarded range of intelligence. A psychologist at the state school also diagnosed him as having a passive-aggressive personality disorder with "some indication of a schizophrenic type attitude." Robert recently began therapy at a mental health clinic, focusing on increasing his ability to express emotion appropriately, as well as on social skills and assertiveness training. Ms. K., his therapist, feels that he is depressed and may also have some paranoid ideation.

Robert has a history of seizure-like activity and a chronic gastro-intestinal disorder. His current medications are Tagamet, Gaviscon, and Colace. He lives in a workshop setting. No significant disturbances are currently being reported, but staff at the workshop feel that he is not working at a level consistent with his potential. Robert is described as withdrawn and as being somewhat of a loner. His father is deceased, and Robert has limited contact with family members. He reports that one of his brothers recently had a heart attack but is recovering nicely. This report could not be verified by Mr. R., on-site coordinator of the residential apartment facility.

Observations and Impressions

Robert is an attractive 36-year-old Caucasian male of average height. He was neatly dressed in casual clothing and seemed adequately groomed, although some body odor was noticeable. His speech was clear and easily intelligible. He seemed somewhat clumsy (e.g., he had some difficulty seating himself). Robert avoided eye contact by gazing downward, and he seemed distant during much of the session. He would speak only when spoken to and then tended to answer in single words, although he was capable of formulating complete sentences. Although he was generally cooperative, he displayed occasional flashes of hostility when his responses were questioned by the examiner. Robert was wearing glasses but complained of having difficulty seeing some of the more detailed stimuli.

Test Results and Interpretation

Robert's performance on a standard measure of cognitive functioning (WAIS-R) places him within the mildly retarded range of intelligence (estimated at the 9½ year level). His Full Scale IQ of 66 (± 4 with 90% confidence) indicates that he surpassed the mental functioning of only about 1% of the adults his age. Moreover, there was a significant difference between his Verbal IQ of 73 (4th percentile) and Performance IQ of 59 (< 1st percentile). The 14-point discrepancy is not only significant but unusual; differences of that magnitude or greater occur less than 5% of the time in adults with IQs below 80. Robert thus displayed far better mental skills in the domain of verbal comprehension and expression than in nonverbal reasoning and visual-motor coordination. In the latter areas, he performed better than only 3 out of 1000 adults his age. His Verbal–Performance split is consistent with the results of previous testing and may indicate the existence of a learning disorder related to nonverbal abilities. However, given that performance tasks generally require a greater expenditure of energy than do verbal tasks, his poor performance on such tasks may also reflect his depressed emotional state. Robert's highest score, which was in the below-average range, was on a verbal test of short-term auditory memory. Particular deficits were noted on a verbal test of arithmetic and on nonverbal measures involving the visual analysis and integration of social stimuli. Robert's approach to tasks calling for integration seemed to be to work piece-by-piece. He was unable to conceptualize a whole, and he earned a raw score of zero on a task requiring him to put pictures in the correct order to tell a story. Consistent with this difficulty in visual analysis and integration, Robert scored significantly below mental age expectancy on a separate measure of visual-motor integration (Bender-Gestalt). His drawings were characterized by distortions of shape, rotations, and an inability to integrate the designs, all of which are signs of possible organic involvement.

Robert's academic skills are also fairly consistent with what would be expected of someone at his mental age. He is reading (recognition only) at a third-grade level, spelling at a fourth-grade level, and doing arithmetic at a fifth-grade level. He can, for example, recognize several common words and spell some three-letter words and words representing something he is interested in (e.g., soccer). He is able to count and recognize written numbers but was unable to perform even the simplest computations in either verbal (Arithmetic, WAIS-R) or written (WRAT-R) form.

According to self and supervisor reports on the Vineland Adaptive Behavior Scales, Robert's social adaptive functioning, while still generally in the mild mentally retarded range (composite standard score = 69, with Domain scores ranging from 65 to 80), is notably above his cognitive functioning. Overall, Robert functioned at the approximate level of a 13-year-old in the adaptive domains of Communication, Daily Living Skills, and Socialization. His standard scores are just estimates, because norms are not available for those above the age of 18 years. Adaptive behavior strengths are in self-direction, independence, and use of leisure time. For example, Robert goes out unsupervised both during the day and at night, travels to distant points alone, and is fairly responsible about letting others know his whereabouts. Both Robert and his supervisor report that he is able to make change, manage his own spending money of $20 per week, buy his own clothing, and make major expenditures with assistance, but it should be noted that he was unable to make even the most basic computations in the current testing. Weaknesses were also evident in some aspects of his Written, Communication, Domestic, and Community skills (e.g., he does not communicate by letter or follow current events and is unable to use tools or utensils). When compared to other mentally retarded adults in nonresidential facilities, his adaptive behavior was exceptional, surpassing 95% of the individuals in this supplementary reference group in overall adaptive behavior.

In projective personality measures as well as in his general demeanor, Robert conveyed feelings of sadness and general lack of energy. He also seemed preoccupied with thoughts of death. These thoughts may stem from his feelings of sadness and anger regarding the loss of his father. He also seems concerned about his brother, whom he reported had recently suffered a heart attack. Whether or not the heart attack actually occurred, his mentioning it reflects his fear of potential losses. His fear of others breaking into his apartment, reported by his therapist, is consistent with this theme. Robert also seems to fear that he might die. In addition to these issues, he feels that he has failed to obtain competitive employment and this perceived failure seems to affect his self-esteem. His desire to make more money and his considerable appetite may reflect, at least in part, his emotional neediness. Staff at the residential apartments describe him as solemn and as somewhat of a loner. He tends to display resistance when demands are placed upon him (e.g., at the workshop), which implies that there may be some complicity in his failure to obtain competitive employment. Robert is reportedly verbally aggressive and boastful with the few friends he does have, but is quiet and shy with people he doesn't know. He seems to have an appropriate level of sexual interest and reports socializing with women and having had a girlfriend in the past.

Summary

Robert is an attractive 36-year-old Caucasian male of average stature. He has a history of seizure-like activity and a chronic gastro-intestinal disorder, which is being treated with medication. He is currently functioning in the mildly retarded range of intelligence (at about the 9½ year level overall; WAIS-R Full Scale IQ = 66), with significantly better verbal (V-IQ = 73) than nonverbal (P-IQ = 59) skills. Deficits displayed on various measures of visual-motor integration are consistent with possible organic involvement. Robert's academic skills are fairly congruent with mental age expectancy. According to self and supervisor reports, his social adaptive functioning (13-1 year level), though deficient, is notably higher than his cognitive-functioning. Strengths in this area are in self-direction, independence, and use of leisure time; weaknesses seemed present in some aspects of communication, domestic, and community skills. Personality assessment indicated feelings of sadness, lack of energy, preoccupation with death and loss in general, and insubstantial social relationships.

Diagnostic Impression

DSM III

Axis I: 300.40 Dysthymic Disorder
317.00 Mild Mental Retardation

Axis II: 301.84 Passive-Aggressive Personality Disorder

TABLE 15.13   Robert N.: Tests administered

Wechsler Adult Intelligence Scale—Revised (WAIS-R)

Verbal	Scaled Score	Age-Corrected Scaled Score	Performance	Scaled Score	Age-Corrected Scaled Score
Information	5	(4)	Picture Completion	1	(2)
Digit Span	8	(8)—S	Picture Arrangement	1	(2)
Vocabulary	5	(5)	Block Design	3	(4)
Arithmetic	2	(2)—W	Object Assembly	2	(2)
Comprehension	5	(5)	Digit Symbol	3	(4)
Similarities	5	(6)			

Age-Corrected Verbal Mean = 5

Verbal IQ = 73±4

Performance IQ = 59±6

Full Scale IQ = 66±4

Age-Corrected Performance Mean = 3

Wide Range Achievement Test—Revised (WRAT-R)

	Grade Equivalent	Standard Score
Reading	end of *third* grade	60
Spelling	beginning of *fourth* grade	66
Arithmetic	beginning of *fifth* grade	68

TABLE 15.13 (Continued)

Bender-Gestalt Test of Visual-Motor Integration (B-G)

19 errors (total)—well below mean for a 5-year-old boy (Koppitz scoring)

Vineland Adaptive Behavior Scales (Expanded Form) (Self-report, corroborated by Mr. R., supervisor at residential apartment facility)

Domain	Standard Score[a]	Adaptive Level[a]	Age Equivalent	National Percentile[a]	Supplementary Percentile[b]
Communication	80 ± 9	Moderately Low	13-9	9th	99th
Daily Living Skills	65 ± 7	Low (Mild Deficit)	10-10	1st	70th
Socialization	79 ± 7	Moderately Low	14-9	8th	90th
Adaptive Behavior Composite	69 ± 5	Low (Mild Deficit)	13-1	2nd	95th

[a]Based on norms for ages 18-8 through 18-11 and older (standard scores are banded by 90% confidence interval).
[b]Based on supplementary norms for mentally retarded adults, ages 18 and older, in nonresidential facilities.

Adaptive Level of Subdomains

Adequate: Communication (Receptive, Expressive); Daily Living Skills (Personal); Socialization (Interpersonal Relationships, Play and Leisure Time, Coping Skills)

Moderately Low: Communication (Written); Daily Living Skills (Domestic)

Low: Daily Living Skills (Community)

Thematic Apperception Test (TAT)

Rotter Incomplete Sentences Blank

Axis III: History of seizure-like behavior, chronic gastro-intestinal disorder (by medical report)

Axis IV: Psychosocial stressors: Brother's heart attack, 4 - Moderate

Axis V: Highest level of adaptive functioning in past year: 4 - Fair

Recommendations

• Robert should continue therapy at the mental health clinic to deal with his emotional problems and build social skills. The therapist should be in touch with staff at the workshop to devise a program aimed at increasing his productivity.

• It is recommended that Robert take courses in functional academic skills (e.g., reading, writing, arithmetic) at one of the area community colleges. Improved skills in these areas should increase his chances of obtaining competitive employment.

Examiner: Maria Nucci
Supervisor: Judith Ivins, Psychologist III

CHAPTER 15 SUMMARY

This chapter addresses the two extremes of the intellectual continuum, the mentally retarded and individuals with superior intelligence. The chapter focuses primarily on assessment of mentally retarded adolescents and adults because such assessment typically assumes more primacy than assessment of the gifted. An important topic in the chapter is adaptive behavior assessment, an area of pertinence for the mentally retarded.

The American Association on Mental Deficiency (AAMD) defines three components of mental retardation: subaverage intelligence, deficits in adaptive behavior, and manifestation of the retardation during the developmental period. The AAMD further specifies four levels of retardation based on intellectual functioning: mild, moderate, severe, and profound. Mild and moderate levels can be distinguished from severe and profound levels in several ways, as discussed in the chapter, including typical age of diagnosis, duration, placement facility, associated medical problems, and social class. Data indicate a greater prevalence of mental retardation in the severe and profound range than would be expected from the normal curve of intellectual functioning. These findings suggest the existence of two distinct groups of mentally retarded individuals: Individuals with IQs between 50 and 70 are hypothesized to represent simple genetic variation, while individuals with IQs below 50 typically have recognizable organic causes for the retardation.

Numerous factors associated with mental retardation are discussed in the chapter. Organic factors, including fetal alcohol syndrome, phenylketonuria, Down syndrome, and Fragile X syndrome, account for about 25% of the individuals with mental retardation. Retardation of the other 75% is likely due to social-environmental factors.

The WISC-R and WAIS-R are the most widely used intelligence tests with mildly and moderately mentally retarded adolescents and adults, and the chapter includes a summary of research on this population using these two scales. Factor analytic studies of the WISC-R support a factor structure for the mentally retarded that is similar to that found with normal

samples. Research indicates that the WAIS-R may yield slightly higher IQs than either the WAIS or WISC-R for mentally retarded adolescents and adults, contrary to findings with normal samples. Mentally retarded children obtain WISC-R subtest scatter and average Verbal–Performance discrepancies comparable to those of normal children. However, WAIS-R standardization data indicate that adults with lower IQs had fewer significant Verbal–Performance discrepancies than those with higher IQs. Characteristic profiles on the Wechsler scales for the mentally retarded include a relative strength in Spatial Ability and a relative weakness in Acquired Knowledge.

The chapter discusses in detail many topics related to the assessment of adaptive behavior, which is a major component in the diagnosis of mental retardation and in planning vocational and treatment programs. Intelligence test scores were used for many years as the sole criterion for mental retardation. However, the 1970s and 1980s saw increased use of adaptive behavior instruments due to legislation and litigation concerning unbiased assessment and the need for training that would enable mentally retarded individuals to live and function in mainstream society.

Adaptive behavior includes several key elements: developmental nature, the dimensions of personal and social responsibility, cultural influences, situational specificity, and emphasis on performance versus ability. There are two general purposes of adaptive behavior assessment, classification and program planning. The chapter includes a description of how adaptive behavior assessment can be used to assist mentally retarded adolescents and adults in meeting goals of self-management, employment, fulfillment of adult social roles, and community adjustment.

Clinical assessment of adaptive behavior is an important component of the flexible, multidimensional process recommended for evaluation of mentally retarded individuals. Adaptive behavior assessment should incorporate an analysis of the relationship between adaptive behavior and intelligence, the use of multiple informants who observe the individual in several settings, and the use of standardized as well as informal assessment. The chapter includes reviews of several of the major standardized adaptive behavior scales. Both the Vineland Adaptive Behavior Scales and Scales of Independent Behavior have outstanding psychometric properties and are excellent for classification of mental retardation and planning intervention programs. Other scales reviewed in the chapter that are less psychometrically sound but may be useful for clinical purposes are the AAMD Adaptive Behavior Scale, Normative Adaptive Behavior Checklist, Comprehensive Test of Adaptive Behavior, and Pyramid Scales.

The discussion of gifted assessment focuses on superior intellectual functioning. The use of intelligence tests with gifted individuals is reviewed, including research supporting the prediction of academic achievement, adult accomplishment, and occupation with intelligence test scores; the controversy about using intelligence tests as the sole criterion for gifted ability; and guidelines for the appropriate use of intelligence tests. Research with the WISC-R for gifted individuals indicates a factor structure similar to that found with normal individuals and a relative strength in Verbal Comprehension. WAIS-R standardization data reflect a slight tendency for adults with high IQs to have greater verbal skills. The chapter concludes with a review of supplements to intelligence tests that are useful during gifted assessment: tests of higher mental processes and critical thinking and tests of creativity.

Memory, Cognitive, and Achievement Supplements to the WAIS-R

The WAIS-R is the king of adult assessment; any other instrument currently in use for adult assessment (excluding noncognitive domains) is, by virtue of the WAIS-R's status and popularity (Harrison, Kaufman, Hickman, & Kaufman, 1988; Sprandel, 1985), a supplement to the WAIS-R. Tests of memory and achievement are commonly given during psychoeducational, clinical, and neuropsychological evaluations, but rarely without accompanying the WAIS-R. Such tests are thus truly supplements. So too are measures of adaptive behavior for the assessment of retardation (see chapter 15), creativity tests for the assessment of giftedness (see chapter 15), and neuropsychological batteries (see chapter 17).

Cognitive batteries, however, need not be subordinate to the WAIS-R. The Woodcock-Johnson Psycho-Educational Battery (Woodcock & Johnson, 1977) was normed from preschool age through old age; the cognitive portion includes several novel and interesting tasks and has excellent psychometric properties. The only problem is that clinicians have not adopted it for clinical assessment (Harrison et al., 1988), so for all practical purposes, the Woodcock-Johnson may best be thought of as a supplement to the WAIS-R—namely, as a source of different tasks for testing WAIS-R–generated hypotheses. Unless the new Woodcock-Johnson Psycho-Educational Battery—Revised (WJ-R; Woodcock & Johnson, 1989) is able to succeed where its predecessor failed, this new theory-based battery will likewise assume the role of WAIS-R supplement. Similarly, regardless of how successful we are in developing the forthcoming Kaufman Adolescent and Adult Intelligence Test (Kaufman & Kaufman, in press *a*) —a battery for ages 11 to 75+, derived from neuropsychological and Cattell-Horn theory, that was being carefully normed on a large, representative sample as this book went to press— it must be adopted for clinical use to become an alternative to the WAIS-R. Otherwise, it will merely join the ranks as a WAIS-R supplement.

This chapter discusses three types of WAIS-R supplements, focusing on measures with national standardization samples: (a) tests to assess *memory,* which are basically the component subtests of the Wechsler Memory Scale—Revised (Wechsler, 1987); (b) tests of *cognitive ability,* and (c) individually administered *achievement* tests, either for quick individual screening of global academic areas, or for a comprehensive, in-depth understanding of the person's strengths and weaknesses in academic areas. The cognitive tests include one measure of a homogeneous skill, the Peabody Picture Vocabulary Test—Revised, and several multisubtest batteries for adolescents and/or adults: the Cognitive portion of the WJ-R, the Stanford-Binet IV, and the revision of the Detroit Tests of Learning Aptitude (DTLA-2). The individually administered achievement batteries discussed are the popular standard, the Wide Range Achievement Test—Revised (WRAT-R), and four additional (and psychometrically far better) instruments: the Kaufman Test of Educational Achievement (K-TEA), Brief and Comprehensive Forms; the Achievement portion of the WJ-R; the Peabody Individual Achievement Test—Revised; and the Woodcock Reading Mastery Test—Revised (WRMT-R).

MEMORY ASSESSMENT: THE WECHSLER MEMORY SCALE— REVISED

The assessment of the diverse aspects of memory functioning is an essential part of clinical and neuropsychological evaluation, especially for adults. Since many adult neuropsychiatric disorders involve disruption of certain memory functions (Poon, 1986), as does the normal aging process (see chapter 7), comprehensive measurement of short- and long-term memory cannot be relegated to secondary status. The topic of adult memory assessment has been treated in considerable depth from a clinical

vantage point (Gregory, 1987) and a neuropsychological perspective (Grant & Adams, 1986), with much attention given to memory disorders of the elderly within both of these disciplines (Poon, 1985, 1986). Research on memory has been summarized and integrated (e.g., Estes, 1982; Squire, 1986), including research on the first edition of the Wechsler Memory Scale (Wechsler, 1987, Chapter 5) and on Russell's (1975, 1988) "revision" of Wechsler's (1945) original memory battery (Gregory, 1987).

Consequently, this section focuses on the almost brand-new, recently restandardized Wechsler Memory Scale—Revised (WMS-R), a test that "David Wechsler began work on . . . in the late 1970s, and [for which he] was able to complete the major changes before his death in 1981" (Wechsler, 1987, p. *iii*).

Various Editions of the Wechsler Memory Scale

The original Wechsler Memory Scale (Wechsler, 1945) was composed of seven tasks, came in two forms, and yielded a global Memory Quotient. Its emphasis was on short-term memory of verbal material, and it failed to offer distinctions between verbal and visual memory or between short- and long-term memory-contrasts of diagnostic relevance for clinical and neuropsychological assessment. In addition, the global treatment of memory was antithetical to the results of laboratory experiments with normal individuals and the findings from brain-related studies of disordered adults. The "norms" for the WMS were poor, based on 200 patients at Bellevue Hospital in New York, ages 25–50, with norms extrapolated for younger and older individuals; Wechsler intended these norms to be "provisional," but they lasted for 40 years (Piersma, 1986). The WMS was sometimes found to be diagnostically useful (e.g., Gilleard, 1980), but was typically blasted by critics (Erickson & Scott, 1977; Prigitano, 1978). Still, it persisted as one of the most popular clinical assessment tools (Brinkman, Largen, Gerganoff, & Pomara, 1983).

Russell (1975, 1988) attempted to remove some of the difficulties with the WMS by adapting and renorming Wechsler's scale: He selected two of Wechsler's subtests, one verbal (Logical Memory) and one figural (Visual Reproduction); these tasks are administered, with the subject responding twice—immediately, and following a 30-minute delay that is filled with interference activities. Russell (1975) called this adaptation the Wechsler Memory Scale—Revised (WMS-R), an instrument that became "the first choice of a growing number of clinicians for general, all-purpose memory assessment" (Gregory, 1987, pp. 27–28).

Like the original Wechsler Memory Scale, Russell's WMS-R was weak psychometrically, in that it was poorly standardized by any reasonable criterion, and had been developed in an unsystematic manner. Russell's battery came closer than the original to meeting practical diagnostic needs by permitting so-called left hemisphere/right hemisphere comparisons and short-term/long-term contrasts, but it nonetheless was a weak link in the clinical evaluation process.

Wechsler (1987) and The Psychological Corporation, by systematically revising and re-standardizing the old scale, have created an instrument that comes closer than the previous tests to meeting assessment needs in a psychometrically defensible manner. Unfortunately, the name chosen for the battery, though a sensible choice, is identical to the name assigned by Russell (1975, 1988) to his popular clinical tool: the Wechsler Memory Scale—Revised (WMS-R). The result will be confusion for anyone examining the clinical literature in memory or reading integrations of research findings, since the name WMS-R refers to two entirely different instruments. For the sake of clarity in this text, whenever I refer to the WMS-R, I am referring only to Wechsler's (1987) revision of his original Wechsler Memory Scale.

Overview of the WMS-R

The individually administered WMS-R was normed in 1985–1986 on adolescents and adults aged 16–74, matching the WAIS-R age range. The battery contains nine subtests, of which one (Information and Orientation Questions) is a brief test of mental status to determine a person's general alertness to the environment and ability to be tested validly on cognitive tests. Whereas this 14-item screening test (composed of two WMS tasks plus new items) does not enter into any of the WMS-R composite scores, the remaining eight subtests are grouped in various ways to provide the following standard scores, known as Indexes, having a mean of 100 and *SD* of 15: Verbal Memory, Visual Memory, General Memory (Verbal + Visual), Attention/Concentration, Delayed Recall.

Organization of the WMS-R

These eight subtests require an average administration time of 30 minutes and compose the "short form" of the WMS-R. The regular WMS-R also includes 30-minute delayed recall of the stimuli presented previously for two verbal and two visual subtests, along with the Information and Orientation questions; it takes a reported 45 minutes to 1 hour to administer. The battery was developed "as a diagnostic and screening device for use as part of a general neuropsychological examination, or any other clinical examination requiring the assessment of memory functions. . . . [It] is intended principally for detecting poor memory functioning, and most of its subtests therefore have relatively low 'ceilings' " (Wechsler, 1987, pp. 1, 7).

Changes from the old to the new WMS include stratified norms; replacement of the single Memory Quotient with a profile of composite scores; addition of three new visual memory subtests (Figural Memory, Visual Paired Associates, Visual Memory Span); addition of delayed recall measures; and revision of scoring guidelines for several tasks to improve scoring accuracy (Herman, 1988; Wechsler, 1987, p.

2). The new "scoring criteria for the Logical Memory (Stories) and Visual Reproduction (Designs) subtests are outstanding" (Powel, 1988, p. 400), far superior to the old guidelines.

The eight subtests are organized into the five scales. Although the WMS-R Manual is well written and impressively thorough, including intelligent integrations of research on the original memory scale plus considerable validation of the revised battery, it is remiss in failing to provide a simple overview of the scale composition. Table 16.1 provides such an overview.

Mental Status Screener

INFORMATION AND ORIENTATION QUESTIONS Items are given that are intended for impaired populations and are answered correctly by most normal adolescents and adults; topics covered include personal information (your mother's first name), orientation (the day of the week), and common stored information (name of the president of United States).

Verbal Memory Subtests

LOGICAL MEMORY Two brief stories are read to the individual, who then must try to retell them from memory.

VERBAL PAIRED ASSOCIATES The examinee tries to learn eight word pairs, some easy (baby-cries) and some hard (obey-inch), within six trials. (Only the first three trials are scored; the criterion of a perfect repetition within six trials is needed for the delayed recall presentation.)

Visual Memory Subtests

FIGURAL MEMORY One or more abstract designs is exposed for five seconds; the examinee has to select these stimulus designs from an array of correct and incorrect designs.

VISUAL PAIRED ASSOCIATES The examinee tries to learn six associations, which pair an abstract line drawing with a color, within six trials. (Only the first three trials are scored; the criterion of a perfect repetition within six trials is needed for the delayed recall presentation.)

VISUAL REPRODUCTION Abstract designs, each exposed for 10 seconds, must be drawn from memory.

Attention/Concentration Subtests

MENTAL CONTROL Examinees are asked to perform three overlearned tasks that most normal individuals can easily pass: counting back-

TABLE 16.1 Composition of the Wechsler Memory Scale—Revised

WMS-R Subtest	Verbal Memory	Visual Memory	General Memory	Attention/ Concentration	Delayed Recall[a]
Logical Memory	X		X		X
Verbal Paired Associates	X		X		X
Figural Memory		X	X		
Visual Paired Associates		X	X		X
Visual Reproduction		X	X		X
Mental Control				X	
Digit Span				X	
Visual Memory Span				X	

[a]Delayed Recall scores are based on a second request for recall of stimuli, 30 minutes after the original presentation of stimuli.

wards from 20, rapidly saying the alphabet, counting by 3s.

DIGIT SPAN   Digits Forward and Digits Backward.

VISUAL MEMORY SPAN Touching randomly placed colored squares on a page in the same order that they were touched by the examiner; like Digit Span, the number of squares touched increases with each item, and there is both a forward and backward span.

Delayed Recall

After a 30-minute interval, the examinee is asked to retell the stories from Logical Memory; to remember the paired associates from Visual Paired Associates and Verbal Paired Associates; and to redraw the designs exposed previously during Visual Reproduction.

Standardization of the WMS-R

Unfortunately, the care that was so evident in the construction of the revised battery, in the preparation of an excellent manual, and in the collection of validation data was absent in the collection of standardization data. The stratification variables of gender, race, geographic region, and education were matched with reasonable precision, *but only 316 individuals were tested across the vast 16- to 74-year age span.* Approximately 50 adolescents and adults were tested at each of six age groups: 16–17, 20–24, 35–44, 55–64, 65–69, and 70–74. Norms for ages 18–19, 25–34, and 45–54 were obtained by interpolation. Even though the mean WAIS-R Full Scale or short form IQs for the standardization sample were found to be a bit high (mean of about 104), the publisher chose to develop norms "at a slightly higher level than would be ideal" (Wechsler, 1987, p. 49) rather than apply a simple adjustment to the data. The WMS-R norms are clearly superior to any of the so-called normative data collected for the

original WMS or for Russell's (1975, 1988) adaptation of that battery, but they nonetheless fall far short of good psychometric practice.

Reliability and Stability of the WMS-R

Reliability and stability data are provided for all of the WMS-R scales and subtests (Wechsler, 1987, pp. 59–63). The five-subtest General Memory scale had a disappointingly low mean reliability coefficient of .81 (ranging from .74 to .87), as did its component scales of Verbal Memory (mean = .77, range of .69–.83) and Visual Memory (mean = .70, range of .59–.76). Delayed Recall produced a mean coefficient of .77 (range of .68–.85), with the Attention/Concentration scale emerging as the only cluster with very good reliability (mean = .90, range of .88–.93). Stability coefficients were of similar magnitude, based on test–retest studies conducted at ages 20–24, 55–64, and 70–74 for about 50 adults per group (total N = 151). Mean coefficients were as follows: General Memory (.80), Verbal Memory (.73), Visual Memory (.71), Attention/Concentration (.86), and Delayed Recall (.79).

Whereas the reliability coefficients (composed mostly of split-half and coefficient alpha values) showed no particular age trend, the WMS-R Indexes were clearly *more stable* for ages 70–74 (mean coefficient across the five scales of .85) than for the other two age groups (means = .73–.74). The latter finding is important because memory assessment is so essential for evaluations of elderly adults, but the overall trend is for disappointing reliability and stability coefficients for all WMS-R Indexes except Attention/Concentration. Unfortunately, the latter scale, which includes Digit Span, offers the *least* new information when the WMS-R is used as a WAIS-R supplement.

Reliabilities and stabilities represent a significant problem for the separate subtests. Only Digit Span and Visual Memory Span emerged unscathed, as each had mean reliability coefficients in excess of .80 and stability coefficients in the .64 to .84 range. Five of the eight subtests composing the various scales had mean reliability coefficients between .44 and .60; if the Delayed Recall tasks are considered separate subtests, 8 of 12 subtests had coefficients between .41 and .60. The stability data were even worse: Excluding Information and Orientation questions (which produced very low coefficients, mostly because of the highly restricted range of scores earned by normal adults), the mean stability coefficients for the 12 subtests that compose the scales (eight regular subtests plus four Delayed Recall tasks) were .58 for ages 20–24 (range of .30–.80), .59 for ages 55–64 (range of .19–.84), and .69 for ages 70–74 (range of .45–.84).

Basically, these results cast doubt on the meaningfulness of a person's memory profile on the WMS-R. Alternate forms reliability was rather poor for the WMS (Bloom, 1959) and for Russell's WMS revision (McCarty, Logue, Power, Ziesat, & Rosenstiel, 1980); WMS-R reliability, though improved over its earlier versions, has unfortunately followed suit. Fluctuations among the five WMS-R composite Indexes must be interpreted with extreme caution, while interpretation of the separate subtests should be avoided, period. The most meaningful comparison is between the Attention/Concentration and General Memory Indexes, because they are the most reliable and stable; they are also the only Indexes with factor analytic support, as discussed in a later section. However, regardless of the brain-related implications of the Verbal Memory-Visual Memory dichotomy, these Indexes are generally neither reliable nor stable enough to permit reliable interpretation of their differences. Similarly, although a General Memory versus Delayed Recall comparison yields potentially important data, the reliability of the difference score is questionable.

The WMS-R Manual provides the size of the differences required for statistical significance for these three comparisons (Wechsler,

1987, Table 14); the differences of about 20–22 points needed at the .05 level for the verbal-visual and general-delayed comparisons reinforce the relative unreliability of the respective scales. Because of this reliability deficit, the only way a person can display a meaningful difference between most pairs of Indexes is by having a huge discrepancy. Powel (1988) criticized the WMS-R for not breaking down Delayed Recall into verbal and visual components; however, the entire Delayed Recall Scale—much less two "half-scales"—is far too unreliable to support such a dichotomy.

Validity of the WMS-R

The publisher of the WMS-R is to be commended for conducting and arranging for numerous validity studies on the revised memory scale, reported in Chapter 5 of the Manual and in a special issue of *The Clinical Neuropsychologist* (Rourke & Adams, 1988) devoted to the WMS-R. These various analyses and investigations are discussed in this section.

Factor Analysis

The factor structure of the WMS-R was quite similar to the structure observed for the first edition of the battery (Wechsler, 1987, pp. 65–68, 75–77). The original battery often produced three factors, one a mental status dimension, and the other two closely resembling the General Memory and Attention/Concentration scales described previously for the WMS-R (e.g., Dye, 1982). For the WMS-R, the subtest that screens for mental status was eliminated from the analysis; the remaining eight subtests clustered into two factors that formed the basis of the General Memory and Attention/Concentration scales.

Analyses conducted for the entire standardization sample aged 16–74 ($N = 316$) and for a mixed clinical sample ($N = 346$) produced extremely similar solutions. In both analyses, three subtests had very high loadings (.70s) on

General Memory, coupled with negligible loadings on the other factor: Visual Paired Associates, Verbal Paired Associates, and Visual Reproduction. Similarly, analyses for both normal and clinical samples revealed that Digit Span and Mental Control loaded substantially (.70s and .80s) on Attention/Concentration and poorly on the other dimension. The placement of the remaining subtests on one WMS-R scale or the other was given strong support from either the normal analysis or the clinical analysis, but not both. In addition, the publisher conducted factor analyses separately for ages 16–44 and 55–74, noting that "factor structures were comparable across the two age groups" (Wechsler, 1987, p. 77).

The publisher reported exploratory, or traditional, principal factor analyses in the WMS-R Manual. Roid, Prifitera, and Ledbetter (1988) conducted confirmatory factor analyses with essentially the same normal and clinical samples cited in the Manual to compare whether a one-factor, two-factor, or three-factor model provided the best fit to the data. For both samples, a two-factor General Memory and Attention/Concentration model was by far superior. The three-factor model, which examined the existence of separate Verbal Memory and Visual Memory factors underlying the eight subtests, did not receive empirical support.

Bornstein and Chelune (1988) cross-validated the principal factor results presented in the Manual, using a sample of 434 patients (56% male; mean age = 44.7 years) referred for neuropsychological evaluations at two medical centers. Their factor patterns conformed almost identically to placement of the subtests on the two factor-derived scales. Seven of the eight subtests loaded much higher on their designated factor, with the eighth (Visual Memory Span) showing a slight preference for Attention/Concentration.

Interestingly, when Bornstein and Chelune (1988) entered WAIS-R V-IQ and P-IQ as variables in the factor analysis, both scales loaded higher on the Attention/Concentration than on the General Memory factor, the differential for V-IQ being quite substantial (.84 to .21). Coupled with the finding that FS-IQ loaded higher on the Attention/Concentration dimension for the normal and clinical samples cited in the WMS-R Manual (Wechsler, 1987), these results imply that the General Memory factor measures an ability that is quite separate from general intellectual functioning. In addition, the close association of WAIS-R IQ with the Attention/Concentration scale presents a strong challenge to the *behavioral* label assigned to this cluster. More likely, the scale is a measure of a *cognitive* ability such as Bannatyne's sequential ability, sequential processing, numerical ability, or primary memory.

One additional analysis by Bornstein and Chelune is intriguing. When they included the four Delayed Recall tasks in the analyses, they obtained three factors, one of Verbal Memory and one of Visual Memory, along with the familiar Attention/Concentration dimension. When the same procedure was applied by the test publisher, a delayed retention factor again failed to emerge: "Each delayed-recall subtest loaded on the same factor with its immediate-recall counterpart" (Wechsler, 1987, p. 76). No mention was made, however, regarding the emergence of a third factor. The failure of a verbal-visual split to emerge without the inclusion of the Delayed Recall tests, via both exploratory (Bornstein & Chelune, 1988) and confirmatory (Roid et al., 1988) factor analytic techniques, renders the construct validation support for Verbal Memory and Visual Memory tenuous at best.

A fascinating sidelight occurred when WAIS-R V-IQ and P-IQ were entered in an expanded matrix that included the Delayed Recall tasks: The two IQs continued to load with the Attention/Concentration dimension; V-IQ did *not* load with the Verbal Memory subtests nor did P-IQ align itself with the Visual Memory factor. A similar separation of verbal and nonverbal constructs on Wechsler's intelligence versus memory scales was observed when Larrabee, Kane, and Schuck (1983) factor analyzed WAIS subtests along with WMS tasks.

In all, the factor analyses give strong support to the construct validity of two of the five WMS-R composites and weak support to Verbal Memory and Visual Memory. The immediate/delayed distinction failed to receive any factor analytic support. Empirical support is therefore mild for the verbal-visual distinction and nonexistent for the immediate-delayed split. The combination of low reliability, low stability, and little or no factor support conspires to turn the WMS-R into a two-scale battery, not the five-scale test that was intended. One of the robust factors (Attention/Concentration) seems to measure the same construct as the Freedom from Distractibility dimension isolated in so many investigations of Wechsler's intelligence scales (Herman, 1988; also see chapters 3 and 8). Empirical support for this relationship was provided by Larrabee et al. (1983) in their factor analytic study of the WAIS and WMS.

Memory and Education, Gender, and Age

Another aspect of construct validity lies in demonstrating that groups that logically should differ on the construct in question do, in fact, differ in their mean scores. Educational level, for example, should relate significantly to memory ability, as it does to all cognitive abilities. The publisher of the WMS-R divided the entire standardization sample into three educational groups: less than 12 years of education, high school graduate, and more than 12 years of education (Wechsler, 1987, Table 17). On all five Indexes, a significant relationship (.001 level) was obtained with education. Those with more than 12 years of education earned mean Indexes of about 107–108, compared to means of 99–100 for the high school graduates and means of 94–95 for those with less than 12 years of formal education.

Based on the literature, one would *not* anticipate gender differences in memory, but one would expect memory to decline with increasing age, especially as assessed on tests of secondary memory (e.g., as measured by paired associate tasks; Poon, 1985). Gender differences did, in fact, prove nonsignificant for the set of Indexes and for the Information and Orientation Questions as well, whereas age was significantly related to the set of five Indexes (Wechsler, 1987, p. 77). Examination of mean raw scores on the five Indexes and various subtests (Wechsler, 1987, Tables 7, 8) indicates peak performance at ages 16–17 on General Memory, Verbal Memory, Visual Memory, and Delayed Recall, with ages 20–24 scoring highest on Attention/Concentration. In almost every instance, lower mean scores were earned on each scale and subtest with increasing age. Since weighted raw score composites on the five scales do not communicate very well, I have converted each mean raw score from Wechsler's (1987) Table 8 to Indexes based on a common reference group (rounded to the nearest whole number). For the purposes of this analysis, I used the norms for ages 35–44 as the reference sample. The results are presented in Table 16.2.

These results show the decrements in mean scores earned by adults in each successive age group. No developmental inferences are possible because of uncontrolled cohort effects such as education, but it is noteworthy that the Visual Memory scale has the largest decrease in mean score. This scale includes figural and abstract stimuli; as discussed in chapter 7, declines in intelligence with age are greatest for fluid subtests, especially those with abstract and figural content. In contrast, decreases in Verbal Memory mean scores with increasing age are much less for Verbal Memory than Visual Memory, mirroring the age changes observed for the WAIS-R V-IQ and P-IQ (see Figures 7.1 and 7.2).

Poon (1985) has summarized findings from numerous research investigations, showing that age-related declines in secondary memory tasks like paired associate tests are far greater than declines in tests of primary memory (like Digit Span). The mean decreases across the age range

TABLE 16.2   Scores on the WMS-R by age group

Scale	AGE GROUP					
	16–17	*20–24*	*35–44*	*55–64*	*65–69*	*70–74*
General Memory	106	98	97	88	86	82
Attention/Concentration	105	107	100	97	92	91
Verbal Memory	106	100	99	91	90	88
Visual Memory	104	99	97	85	80	73
Delayed Recall	111	99	97	88	83	78

NOTE: All scores are standard scores (mean = 100, SD = 15), using ages 35–44 as the reference norms for all six ages.

were clearly more substantial for the scales that include tests of secondary memory than for Attention/Concentration, which is composed of primary memory tests. Analyses of mean scores earned by the different age groups on the various WMS-R subtests (Wechsler, 1987, Table 7) is consistent with Poon's conclusions from the memory literature, although the decrease in mean scores seems much greater for the secondary memory tasks with abstract content (Visual Paired Associates, immediate and delayed) than for the Verbal secondary memory subtests.

The greater WMS-R age-related changes for fluid, nonverbal, and secondary memory tasks, as compared to verbal and primary tasks, was also supported in large-scale developmental studies of the WMS (Bak & Greene, 1981; Margolis & Scialfa, 1984; Zagar, Arbit, Stuckey, & Wengel, 1984).

Discrimination of Abnormal and Normal Groups

The preceding analyses provide evidence of the construct validity of the WMS-R, as do analyses of *abnormal* samples that are known to have extremely deficient memories, such as Alzheimer's patients, other dementia patients, and individuals with alcoholic Korsakoff's syndrome. The WMS-R Manual (Wechsler, 1987, Table 19) and the special issue of *The Clinical Neuropsychologist* (Rourke & Adams, 1988) include data on a variety of clinical samples. The mixed

sample of clinical patients whose factor structure was found to be so similar to the structure for normal adults performed significantly below the standardization sample (.001 level) on all five Indexes, earning means in the low to mid-80s (Wechsler, 1987, Table 18).

Table 19 of the WMS-R Manual presents the mean Indexes for 14 discrete groups of clinical patients, most with sample sizes below 20; presumably these samples, totalling 341, constituted most of the mixed clinical sample whose data were factor analyzed. Overall, not one mean Index for any group was as high as 100. Indexes were in the low to mid-90s for alcoholics, depression patients, and adults with multiple sclerosis; generally in the 80s for those with brain cancer, posttraumatic stress syndrome, seizure disorders, and environmentally induced worksite neurotoxins; in the 70s and low 80s for patients with closed head injury, undifferentiated dementia, schizophrenia, and stroke; and typically in the 60s (1st to 2nd percentile) for Alzheimer's patients, adults with Huntington's disease, and those with Korsakoff's syndrome.

These results support the validity of the five WMS-R Indexes. Support is also provided in the Manual for the validity of the mental status screener, which significantly and meaningfully discriminated normals from adults with Alzheimer's disease, Huntington's disease, and Korsakoff's syndrome. Normal adults scored significantly higher on the Information and

Orientation questions than most of the 14 small clinical samples reported in the Manual, but most differences were within 1 point of the mean for normals (about 13½ out of 14).

Several interesting validation studies were reported in the special issue of *The Clinical Neuropsychologist,* and these findings are summarized here. Butters et al. (1988) examined the WMS-R's discrimination ability among patients with dementia (20 with Alzheimer's-type, 24 with Huntington's disease) and amnesia (16 patients, 11 with alcoholic Korsakoff's syndrome, 5 with presumed damage to the hippocampus). These abnormal groups were easily distinguishable from younger and older normal controls, and they displayed distinctive differences in their WMS-R Indexes, as shown in Table 16.3.

The amnesia patients had normal Attention/ Concentration scores, with deficient performance in General Memory (both Verbal and Visual) and strikingly weak ability in Delayed Recall, consistent with their severe anterograde memory problems. Whereas the Huntington's patients displayed a flat, deficient memory profile, the patients with Alzheimer's-type dementia had more variability: They performed significantly better in Attention/Concentration than in General Memory. A similar relationship of better primary memory than other types of memory was shown for the mildly demented Alzheimer's patients studied by Storandt, Botwinick, and Danziger (1986). Mohs, Kim, Johns, Dunn, and Davis (1986) also noted substantial variability in the memory performance of Alzheimer's patients, who evidenced the greatest

impairment on the most complex memory and language tests.

The comparison of the two factor-based WMS-R scales had diagnostic significance; the mean difference for amnesia patients (31 points) was significantly larger than the mean discrepancy for Alzheimer's patients (17 points), which was in turn significantly greater than the 6-point difference for Huntington's patients. The difference between General Memory and Delayed Recall was also significantly larger for amnesia patients (12 points) than for either group of dementia patients. Because of its close relationship to IQ, the high mean Attention/ Concentration score of amnesia patients "probably reflects the relative intactness of the amnesics' intellectual capacities" (Butters et al., 1988, p. 144) compared with the cognitive deficits that characterize dementia patients. The investigators concluded that the revised battery was far superior to the original, one-score WMS. Indeed, the scale structure of the WMS-R permits differential diagnosis of dementia and amnesia patients; the global index yielded by the WMS was not nearly as effective because amnesia patients "tend to perform within the normal range on tests of attention and concentration while demented patients do not" (Powel, 1988, p. 402). The latter contention was given good support by the WMS-R data gathered by Butters et al. (1988).

Ryan and Lewis (1988) compared the performance of 40 recently detoxified chronic male alcoholics with that of 40 normal controls matched on the variables of age (means of about 50 years), gender, and education (close to 13

TABLE 16.3   Mean WMS-R Indexes for patients with Alzheimer's-type dementia, Huntington's disease, and amnesia

Abnormality	Verbal Memory	Visual Memory	General Memory	Attention/ Concentration	Delayed Recall
Alzheimer's	62	70	59	76	61
Huntington's	68	62	61	67	64
Amnesia	72	78	69	100	57

NOTE: Data are from Butters et al. (1988).

years of education). The normals scored significantly higher than the alcoholics on all five Indexes, although the mean scores for the 40 alcoholics, like those of a group of 62 alcoholics reported in the WMS-R Manual, tended to be in the 90s. The strong deficit observed for the alcoholics in Visual Reproduction (immediate and delayed recall), relative to the normal controls, is consistent with the hypothesized deficits for alcoholics on the WAIS-R in visual-motor coordination and the ability to process abstract stimuli (see pp. 508–509). It is also in agreement with several investigations of alcoholics showing that generally, "nonverbal memory has been found to be more impaired than verbal, and this difference has been interpreted in terms of lateralized cerebral hemisphere dysfunction" (Hightower & Anderson, 1986, p. 1000).

In a study of memory deficits in 45 patients with multiple sclerosis, matched with normal controls on age (means of about 39 years), gender (60%–75% female), and education (over 14 years of education), Fischer (1988) found significant deficiencies for the multiple sclerosis patients on all five WMS-R Indexes. Nonetheless, like the groups of alcoholics, these patients earned mean Indexes in the 90s. Just as multiple sclerosis patients achieve higher WAIS-R V-IQs than P-IQs (see pp. 293–294), Fischer's sample scored almost ½ SD higher on the Verbal Memory than the Visual Memory Index (means of 98.8 and 92.4, respectively). The deficits shown by Fischer's patient sample in learning new verbal and nonverbal material on the paired associate tasks is consistent with a body of research on multiple sclerosis patients (e.g., Heaton, Nelson, Thompson, Burks, & Franklin, 1985; Huber et al., 1987); so is the group's relative deficit (mean of 91.7) on Delayed Recall, the WMS-R's measure of long-term retention memory (Caine, Bamford, Schiffer, Shoulson, & Levy, 1986; Heaton et al., 1985).

Chelune and Bornstein (1988) conducted an important investigation of WMS-R profiles in patients with unilateral lesions to the left ($N = 59$) or right ($N = 56$) hemisphere. The brain-damaged samples were well matched on age (means of about 37 years), gender (about 60% male), education (high school graduates), WAIS-R FS-IQs (about 87), handedness (87% righthanded), and type of lesion). Their mean Indexes are shown in Table 16.4.

These findings mirror the results of the Wechsler IQ analyses (see Tables 9.6 and 9.7): The right-lesion patients showed a substantial, predicted deficit in Visual Memory relative to Verbal Memory (12 points), while the left-lesion patients evidenced a trivial discrepancy. However, when the two patient groups were compared with each other on the verbal and visual tasks (as opposed to intraindividual comparisons), a significant interaction was obtained supporting the cerebral specialization of the brain. Right-lesion patients outscored their left-lesion counterparts on Verbal Memory subtests, while the reverse pattern was obtained for Visual Memory tasks. This predicted interaction is consistent with findings with earlier versions of the WMS (Bornstein, 1982; Snow & Sheese, 1985) and with laboratory results (Kimura, 1963).

In general, the results of WMS-R validation studies support the validity of the revised battery for a variety of clinical samples that are known or suspected of memory impairment. The results generally show the superiority of the WMS-R over its predecessors, the WMS and Russell (1975) revision of the WMS, and are in basic agreement with the findings from diverse clinical samples on the WMS and other memory tests (Gregory, 1987; Poon, 1986).

Evaluation of the WMS-R

That the WMS-R is a great improvement over Wechsler's (1945) original test or Russell's (1975, 1988) modification is axiomatic. It is strengthened by the addition of visual memory tasks, measures of delayed recall, and a better scoring system; further, its profile of composite Indexes allows for impressive evidence of the

TABLE 16.4 WMS-R profiles for patients with unilateral brain lesions

Lesion Site	Verbal Memory	Visual Memory	General Memory	Attention/ Concentration	Delayed Recall
Left hemisphere	84	85	82	89	79
Right hemisphere	93	81	86	83	82

NOTE: Data are from Chelune and Bornstein (1988).

scale's validity with numerous clinical samples. Also, the test Manual is generally well written and comprehensive. Even though the test has psychometric flaws, the Manual is nonetheless sophisticated, both psychometrically and clinically, and is replete with a set of validity studies. The Manual "represents a tremendous improvement on the scanty few pages available to guide the user of its predecessor" (Powel, 1988, p. 400).

The biggest negatives of the battery are the small standardization sample, necessitating the generation of norms for entire age groups via interpolation, and the low reliability and stability of most scales and virtually all subtests. The two factor-derived scales are sufficiently reliable and stable to permit meaningful comparisons between two types of memory functioning. The limited empirical support for the meaningfulness of the other scales, and their unimpressive reliability and stability coefficients, render them almost useless for individual diagnosis. Group means are much more reliable than any one individual's scores, allowing meaningful interpretation of *group* differences in the various clinical studies of abnormal samples. However, *individual* profiles, even for members of groups with extreme scale variability such as those with Korsakoff's syndrome, are likely to produce nonsignificant scale discrepancies because of the lack of reliable measurement of the presumed constructs. *Quite clearly, the assets of the WMS-R for clinical research do not translate into individual assessment and diagnosis, a most unfortunate outcome.*

Other liabilities of the WMS-R concern the fact that it was not developed from a unified

theoretical base, some ambiguities in the Manual (what type of activities, if any, are supposed to be conducted during the 30-minute interval prior to the administration of the Delayed Recall subtests?), limited floors for some scales, and the limited coverage of memory abilities. Regarding the latter two shortcomings, Butters et al. (1988) stated: Indexes are not awarded below 50, yet "more than 25% of the amnesic and demented patients earned scores below 50 on the General and Delayed Memory Indices. . . . [Also,] the absence of recognition tests for the verbal tasks and the Visual Reproduction test prevents direct comparisons between recall and recognition memory" (p. 146).

Powel (1988) criticized the WMS-R for failing to measure information decay (the Delayed Recall score does not indicate what proportion of the original material was forgotten by each examinee), for having a summary page on the record form that promotes clerical errors, and for requiring "a 1 hour administration time, [and] up to a half hour of scoring time" (p. 402). To C. R. Reynolds (personal communication, 1989), the WMS-R is a hassle to use. Nonetheless, Powel (1988) concluded that the WMS-R offers "more promise than any other comprehensive test of memory on the market and [I] strongly endorse its use" (p. 403).

The WMS-R as a WAIS-R Supplement

Since the WAIS-R includes but a single short-term memory subtest among its 11 tasks (Digit Span), the WMS-R as a whole offers examiners much valuable supplementary information.

Interpretation should generally be limited to the two factor-oriented scales, unless the referral question or hypotheses derived from WAIS-R profile analysis suggest specific strengths and weaknesses within the person's cognitive or memory profile. For example, when testing a patient with suspected Korsakoff's syndrome or dementia, the General Memory versus Delayed Recall comparison is essential to facilitate differential diagnosis. Similarly, when testing a person suspected of a brain injury, the Verbal Memory-Visual Memory comparison is essential to aid in localization of the presumed lesion.

Because of the unreliability of most subtests, only two WMS-R subtests merit interpretation on their own—Digit Span and Visual Memory Span. Digit Span represents a good alternate form for WAIS-R Digit Span if the examiner wants a retest because performance on the WAIS-R task was impaired by distractibility or anxiety. Visual Memory Span is a wonderful supplement to the WAIS-R because it measures forward and backward span in the visual-motor modality, an important check on the specificity or generality of hypotheses derived regarding WAIS-R Digit Span performance. Percentile ranks may be computed for these WMS-R subtests from tables in Appendix C of the Manual (Wechsler, 1987).

The entire Attention/Concentration scale is a valuable supplement to the WAIS-R for any individual for whom the third factor represents an important contributor to profile interpretation. This scale is reliable and construct valid and affords a different look at the person's skill on whatever ability or trait is presumed to underlie the third factor for any particular individual; the readministration of Digit Span provides a check on the stability of the person's auditory short-term memory, and is a small price to pay to get the other dividends. In addition, the General Memory scale, although not as reliable as desired, becomes a useful WAIS-R supplement for any referral whose memory or learning ability is suspect in any way. Factor analyses of the WMS-R and WAIS-R IQs reveal that the General Memory scale is, for practical purposes, independent of intelligence; hence, its administration alongside the WAIS-R is guaranteed to offer nonoverlapping, and potentially crucial, psychometric and clinical information.

Whenever specific WMS-R tasks are desired for following up on WAIS-R–derived hypotheses, it is important to administer them in twos and threes. For example, suppose an examiner wants to check the extent of a person's apparent deficit in the perception or processing of abstract stimuli (based on low Block Design and Digit Symbol scores; see pp. 509–511). The most pertinent WMS-R subtest to administer is Visual Reproduction (both immediate and delayed). Because of the low reliability of each task separately, be sure to administer it in both formats; compute the percentile rank for each task using the appropriate table (Wechsler, 1987, Appendix C), but *only interpret the mean of the two percentile ranks.* No empirical evidence of the validity of the mean of the two percentiles exists, but the magnitude of a person's average performance on the immediate and delayed recall of abstract designs has considerable face validity for following up hypotheses of a deficit in the perception or processing of abstract visual stimuli.

Although the Information and Orientation questions subtest is brief, does not have demonstrated stability because of the lack of variability in normal adults, and does not measure the numerous areas desired for a complete mental status exam (see Gregory, 1987, Chapter 1), it is nonetheless an important WAIS-R supplement. Mental status measurement is important for anyone suspected of dementia or related disorders; low scores hinder interpretation of any scores obtained on a cognitive test like the WAIS-R and are of potential diagnostic relevance. Despite the disappointing standardization sample for the WMS-R, its norms are still representative of the U.S. and are far superior to the slightly normed or unnormed variety of mental status tests that are in use in clinics and hospitals throughout the country. The distributions of Information and Orientation total scores by age and the percentages passing each of the 14 items by age (Wechsler, 1987, Tables C-2 and C-3) are extremely valuable data for the use of Wechsler's mental status test as a WAIS-R supplement in preference to the other available screeners (Gregory, 1987).

One final note about the WMS-R as a WAIS-R supplement. As stated by the author and publisher, the memory battery was developed to detect impairment, and most subtests have a limited "top." Consequently, the use of the WMS-R or any of its component parts as WAIS-R supplements is advised primarily for testing hypotheses regarding low functioning, not high functioning.

ASSESSMENT OF COGNITIVE ABILITIES

This section describes, evaluates, and discusses four cognitive tests in terms of their value as WAIS-R supplements: the Woodcock-Johnson Psycho-Educational Battery—Revised, Cognitive portion (WJ-R/C), the Peabody Picture Vocabulary Test—Revised (PPVT-R), the Stanford-Binet Fourth Edition (S-B IV), and the revised Detroit Tests of Learning Aptitude (DTLA-2). Except for the DTLA-2, all of these tests are administered in easel format.

Although the Differential Ability Scales (DAS; Elliott, in press) for ages 2½ to 17 years was recently standardized, decisions about the composites were not finalized as this book went to press, which prevented a thorough description of the instrument in this text (M. H. Daniel, personal communication, 1989). Upon its publication, this United States adaptation and restandardized version of the British Ability Scales will make an excellent supplement to Wechsler's scales for adolescent assessment. The DAS was normed on a superb sample of 3,475 children and adolescents that closely matched recent U.S. Census figures on key stratification variables (Daniels, 1989).

Although some of the cleverest of the British Ability Scales subtests were excluded from the DAS, such as the Piaget-based Formal Operational Thinking task, the 13 school-age subtests (10 cognitive, 3 achievement) in the new battery are well constructed, have had biased items removed, and are generally reliable (M. H. Daniel, personal communication, 1989); also, Elliott (in press) offers separate reliability coefficients by *ability level* for each age, a novel feature. Probably the most valuable Wechsler supplements among the DAS subtests are Sequential and Quantitative Reasoning (a nonverbal test requiring hypothesis generation and flexibility), Matrices, and Speed of Information Processing.

Woodcock-Johnson Psycho-Educational Battery—Revised: Cognitive

The 1977 version of the Woodcock-Johnson (Woodcock & Johnson, 1977) and its 1989 revision (Woodcock & Johnson, 1989a) are the only cognitive tests normed on representative samples of adults spanning young adulthood through old age. The WJ-R was normed from ages 2 to 90+ years on 6,359 individuals selected to provide a cross-section of the U.S. population. (Woodcock & Mather, 1989a). The sample contained 705 preschool children, 3,245 students in grades K–12, 916 college/university students, and 1,493 individuals aged 14 to 90+ years who were not enrolled in school. Representation on important background variables was adequate but not excellent, necessitating the use of a weighting procedure. Whereas the cognitive portion of the 1977 WJ lacked a theoretical base, and was developed from a practical, psychoeducational model, the WJ-R is rooted in the Cattell-Horn fluid–crystallized theoretical distinction and, more specifically, in Horn's expansion of the models.

Overview of the Theoretical Model

The WJ-R is composed of two major portions, Cognitive and Achievement; the Interest Scales included in the 1977 WJ have been eliminated. The focus of this discussion is the Cognitive portion of the WJ-R (WJ-R/C). The Achievement battery is treated later in the chapter with other measures of academic achievement (pp. 620–622).

The WJ-R/C comprises 21 subtests—11 of the original 12, with generally slight modifications, plus 10 new tasks. Two of the new tasks are actually Delayed Recall versions of memory subtests (one new, one old), using a format similar to Wechsler's (1987) Delayed Recall scale in the WMS-R. The 21 subtests measure seven cognitive factors from Horn's (1985) model; they are grouped into a Standard Scale, composed of 7 subtests (1 task per factor), an Extended Scale, composed of seven additional subtests for a total of 14 (2 subtests per factor), and a "third level" Supplementary Battery, composed of all 21 tasks (2 to 4 per factor). Two of the supplementary cognitive subtests are each on two of the Horn factors.

The subtest eliminated from the 1977 version of the WJ/C, Quantitative Concepts, was among the most achievement-oriented; the WJ was soundly criticized for including several tasks that belonged more logically on the Achievement rather than the Cognitive portion of the batteries (e.g., Shinn, Algozzine, Marston, & Ysseldyke, 1982). Indeed, there was empirical support for that contention (Kaufman & O'Neal, 1988a). Quantitative Concepts is now a supplementary subtest on the Achievement portion of the WJ-R. The seven factors are listed in Table 16.5 along with Horn's label for the factor and the name assigned to it by Woodcock and Johnson (1989a).

Thus, the WJ-R/C measures fluid intelligence (adaptability and flexibility when solving novel problems), crystallized intelligence (formally acquired verbal-educational skills), and five additional factors. From the Wechsler model,

Verbal IQ is a combination of Comprehension-Knowledge and Short-term Memory; and Performance IQ reflects a blend of Fluid Reasoning, Visual Processing, and Processing Speed. Long-term Retrieval is measured by the WMS-R, not the WAIS-R, while Auditory Processing is more of a perceptual than mental task and, therefore, outside the Wechsler domain. From the point of view of the K-ABC/Luria/cerebral processing model, Short-term Memory is akin to Sequential Processing and Comprehension-Knowledge to left hemisphere verbal abilities; Visual Processing and Fluid Reasoning represent different aspects of Simultaneous Processing; and Processing Speed is either a measure of attention-arousal (Luria's, 1980, Block 1) or planning ability (Luria's Block 3), depending on one's theoretical orientation.

Description of the Subtests

The subtests are listed according to the factor or factors they are intended to measure. The first subtest listed for each factor is double-asterisked (**), indicating that it is part of the 7-subtest Standard Scale; the second subtest listed is single-asterisked (*), indicating its inclusion on the 14-subtest Extended Scale. Following the subtest name are parentheses that indicate: (a) whether the subtest is Old, i.e., from the 1977 battery, or New; (b) its median reliability coefficient for the five adolescent and adult age groups for which Woodcock and Mather (1989a, Table 7.5) provided data (ages 13, 18, 30–39, 50–59, and 70–79); and (b) the magnitude of its loading on the particular factor based on a confirmatory factor analysis reported by Woodcock (1988), using data from 422 members of the standardization sample from tenth grade to adult.

Factor 1: Long-term Retrieval (G$_{lr}$). The subject retrieves information stored minutes or days earlier.

   **Memory for Names (New, .91 reliability, .95 factor loading). The subject

TABLE 16.5   Horn factors and their corresponding cognitive factors making up the Woodcock-Johnson Psycho-Educational Battery—Revised, cognitive portion

Horn Factor	WJ-R/C Cognitive Factor
1. Long-term Storage and Retrieval (TSR)	Long-term Retrieval (G_{lr})
2. Short-term Apprehension and Retrieval (SAR)	Short-term Memory (G_{sm})
3. Clerical Perceptual Speed (G_s)	Processing Speed (G_s)
4. Auditory General Ability (G_a)	Auditory Processing (G_a)
5. Visual General Ability (G_v)	Visual Processing (G_v)
6. Crystallized Intellect (G_c)	Comprehension-Knowledge (G_c)
7. Fluid Intellect (G_f)	Fluid Reasoning (G_f)

learns the names of "space creatures" in a paired-associate learning task.

*Visual-Auditory Learning (Old, .92 reliability, .93 factor loading). The subject is taught visual symbols that stand for words and has to "read" sentences composed of the symbols.

Delayed Recall/Memory for Names (New, .93 reliability, .93 factor loading). The subject is asked, several days later (without advanced notice of the retest) to name the space creatures learned in the Memory for Names subtest.

Delayed Recall/Visual-Auditory Learning (New, .92 reliability, .77 factor loading). The subject is asked, several days later (without advanced notice of the retest) to name the symbols learned in the Visual-Auditory Learning subtest.

Factor 2: Short-term Memory (G_{sm}). The subject stores information and retrieves it immediately or within a few seconds.

**Memory for Sentences (Old, .84 reliability, .62 factor loading). The subject tries to repeat phrases and sentences presented on a tape.

*Memory for Words (New, .75 reliability, .77 factor loading). The subject tries to repeat, in the correct sequence, lists of unrelated words presented on a tape.

Numbers Reversed (Old, .88 reliability, .75 factor loading). The subject hears series of numbers presented on tape and has to repeat them in the reverse order.

Factor 3: Processing Speed (G_s). The subject works quickly, particularly under pressure to maintain focused attention.

**Visual Matching (Old, .78 reliability, .84 factor loading). The subject has to rapidly identify and circle two identical numbers in a row of six numbers.

*Cross Out (New, .75 reliability, .83 factor loading). The subject has to rapidly mark the 5 identical drawings in a row of 20 that match the first drawing in the row.

Factor 4: Auditory Processing (G_a). The subject fluently perceives patterns among auditory stimuli.

**Incomplete Words (New, .82 reliability, .55 factor loading). The subject hears, on a tape, a series of words missing one or more phonemes and has to identify each complete word.

*Sound Blending (Old, .87 reliability, .63 factor loading). The subject hears, on a tape, words broken up into their components (syllables and/or phonemes) and has to identify each complete word.

(This subtest was formerly called Blending.)

Sound Patterns (New, .88 reliability, .49 factor loading). The subject hears, on a tape, pairs of complex sounds (differing in pitch, rhythm, or sound content) and has to indicate whether each pair is the same or different.

Factor 5: Visual Processing (G$_v$). The subject fluently manipulates stimuli that are usually visual in the "mind's eye."

**Visual Closure (New, .69 reliability, .33 factor loading). The subject has to identify a picture or drawing that is "obscured" by missing lines or areas, distortions, or superimposed patterns.

*Picture Recognition (New, .84 reliability, .54 factor loading). The subject is presented with pictures and then has to recognize them from an array of similar pictures.

Spatial Relations (Old, .83 reliability, substantially modified, .01 factor loading). The subject has to select shapes from an array of stimuli that can be combined to construct a target figure. (On the 1977 WJ, but not the revision, this task was highly speeded.)

Factor 6: Comprehension-Knowledge (G$_c$). The subject demonstrates the breadth and depth of his or her knowledge of a culture.

**Picture Vocabulary (Old, .90 reliability, .87 factor loading). The subject has to name pictured objects or actions.

*Oral Vocabulary (Old, .90 reliability, 1.00 factor loading). The subject is presented words orally and has to give either the antonym or synonym. (This subtest was formerly called Antonyms-Synonyms.)

Listening Comprehension (New, .78 reliability, .76 factor loading). The subject listens to brief passages presented on a tape and has to name, via the "cloze" technique, the word that is missing at the end of each passage.

Verbal Analogies (Old, .91 reliability, .65 factor loading). The subject has to complete phrases with words that provide appropriate verbal analogies. (This subtest was formerly called Analogies.)

Factor 7: Fluid Reasoning (G$_f$). The subject reasons in a novel situation.

**Analysis-Synthesis (Old, .89 reliability, .63 factor loading). The subject learns to apply a given set of rules (e.g., a *black* square with a *blue* square is the same as a *yellow* square) to solve novel equivalency problems.

*Concept Formation (Old, .93 reliability, .68 factor loading). The subject tries to identify rules governing concepts when presented with positive and negative instances of the concepts.

Spatial Relations (Old, .83 reliability, substantially modified, .74 factor loading). (Also on Factor 5/Visual Processing.)

Verbal Analogies (Old, .91 reliability, .39 factor loading). (Also on Factor 6/Comprehension-Knowledge.)

Evaluation

In my Buros review of the 1977 WJ (Kaufman, 1985b), I concluded that the battery "is a mixture of extremes, possessing some outstanding qualities, yet hampered by glaring liabilities. . . . [The WJ] represents a monumental and creative effort by its authors. . . . [I] urge examiners, especially those from a Wechsler/Binet orientation, to take the time and trouble to master it. The effort will be well worth it" (pp. 1762, 1765). Cummings (1985) and Hager (1986) agreed that the WJ is a "significant addition" to the available psychometric instruments. These comments apply as well to the WJ-R.

The new battery is incredibly comprehensive. Woodcock's tests invariably possess excellent psychometric properties, the data are treated with statistical sophistication, and the subtests include a huge dose of originality. The WJ-R is no exception. The standardization sample is large and adequate. The factor loadings shown in parentheses by the subtest names indicate generally strong factor analytic support for the construct validity of the battery for adolescents and adults; comparable support was provided by Woodcock (1988; Woodcock & Mather, 1989a) for large samples of children and adults. In addition, reliability coefficients are excellent; for adolescent and adult samples, the seven subtests in the Standard Scale have reliabilities ranging from .69 to .91 (median = .84). For all 21 subtests, the range is .69 to .93 with a median value of .88. Coefficients for the Broad Cognitive Scale—Standard and Broad Cognitive Scale—Extended each average .95 for the adolescent and adult groups (Woodcock & Mather, 1989a, Tables 7.5 and 7.6).

However, Woodcock's converted scores are invariably complex, creating "clerical havoc" for examiners, and the WJ-R/C is no exception here either. The extensive scores and profiles, composed of aptitude/achievement discrepancy scores, W-scores, standard scores, relative mastery indexes, and the like, present a time-consuming and error-prone burden for examiners. Woodcock and Johnson (1989a) have come much closer to meeting the needs of psychologists than they did with the first edition of the battery by incorporating familiar standard scores (mean = 100, SD 15) directly into the interpretive system and by providing standard scores for each separate subtest. The authors also offer a comprehensive interpretive system for the WJ-R/C profile. Unfortunately, the end result is still a clerical nightmare for examiners, especially those who are uncomfortable dealing with numbers.

The fact that the total battery is composed of Cognitive and Achievement portions is a big plus for learning disabilities assessment. The aptitude clusters in the areas of reading, math, written language, knowledge, and oral language are useful for comparing aptitude and achievement in very specific domauns. However, the achievement loading of several cognitive sub-

tests, though addressed mildly by the transfer of Quantitative Concepts to the Achievement portion of the battery, remains a significant problem for WJ-R/C users. In the 1977 WJ, Picture Vocabulary and Antonyms-Synonyms (now Oral Vocabulary) joined Quantitative Concepts as subtests with considerable loadings on Achievement factors (Kaufman & O'Neal, 1988a), but only the mathematical task was reassigned. Further, in his confirmatory factor analyses of the WJ-R, Woodcock (1988) included numerous Achievement subtests: Science, Social Studies, Humanities, Word Attack, and Writing Fluency. These subtests were closely associated with a Cognitive factor. The first three tasks had strong loadings on the Comprehension-Knowledge factor, Word Attack was one of the best measures of Auditory Processing, and Writing Fluency was related about equally to Auditory Processing and Processing Speed.

A second concern with the WJ-R/C is its usefulness for adult assessment. The 1977 WJ/C attained some measure of utility for childhood and adolescent evaluations, but never was able to crack the adult market. Most of the research generated on the battery has been with children (McGrew, 1986). Occasional studies were conducted with adolescents (e.g., Phelps, Rosso, & Falasco, 1984, 1985) and adults (e.g., Buchanan & Wolf, 1986; Gregg & Hoy, 1985), but these were few in number. Indeed, the evidence suggested that the WJ has a different factor structure for adults than for children and adolescents (Kaufman & O'Neal, 1988a, 1988b; McGrew, 1987). Further, although the WJ Achievement scale earned some popularity for adult assessment, and was highly regarded by its users, the Cognitive scale did not (Harrison, Kaufman, Hickman, & Kaufman, 1988; see p. 13).

The negative history of the WJ/C for adult assessment does not mean that the WJ-R/C is a poor candidate to serve as an alternative to the WAIS-R for some assessment purposes; it just means that it will have to accomplish what the WJ/C was unable to in the course of about 12 years, despite possessing adequate norms for adults aged 18–65+. In addition, the battery may not relate too directly to the IQs yielded by the WAIS-R. The WJ-R Broad Cognitive Ability Scale, both Standard and Extended versions, correlated only .63–.64 with WAIS-R FS-IQ for 51 adolescents aged 17 (Woodcock & Mather, 1989a, Table 7.9). Further, *both* the Fluid Reasoning and Comprehension-Knowledge scales correlated higher with WAIS-R V-IQ than with P-IQ; indeed the seven WJ-R/C factors correlated only .20 to .44 with WAIS-R P-IQ, suggesting that the WJ-R Broad Cognitive subtests do not assess Perceptual Organization very effectively. In fact the Fluid Reasoning tasks, although nonverbal to some extent, tend to rely on verbal responding, labeling, and mediation for success.

The new theoretical structure of the WJ-R/C seems to give the battery a good deal to overcome if it is to achieve wide application as a tool for the clinical assessment of adults (and perhaps children, as well). The idea of a widely respected theoretical base is excellent, and the Horn-Cattell system certainly fills the bill. But I question the practicality of using a seven-scale system for clinical evaluations. Focusing on crystallized and fluid intelligence would have been a fine idea, particularly in view of the relevance of this dichotomy for research on aging (see chapter 7), but dwarfing these two scales among a total of seven seems ill-advised. The Standard Scale measures each of the seven scales with one subtest apiece. That is not enough. Is it sensible to think of complex, multifaceted intelligence tasks as measures of only one cognitive factor? The approach used for developing the WJ-R/C Standard Scale depends on assigning a *unique* interpretation to each subtest, a practice that represents a backward step—at least regarding the history of clinical assessment with Wechsler's scales.

The Standard Scale purportedly takes about 40 minutes to administer. But all the clinician will obtain from that time spent is a measure

of *g*, and perhaps not a very good measure in view of the inclusion of subtests like Visual Matching and Incomplete Words. Administering a second set of seven tasks from the Supplemental battery (the Extended Scale) doubles administration time while affording interpretation of each of the seven factors via a dyad. If dyads afforded thorough measurement of a construct, then all the developers of four-subtest Wechsler short forms could have advocated two-subtest estimates of V-IQ and P-IQ based on an administration of a short form. Fortunately, this has not been the practice. Is it sensible or practical to administer the entire 21-subtest Cognitive battery? I doubt it. Four of the scales are still assessed by only two or three tasks. Further, of the three scales that comprise four subtests, two overlap (Comprehension-Knowledge and Fluid Reasoning each contain Verbal Analogies), and the other presents practical problems for many clinicians: Will the subject be available for retesting a few days later on the two delayed recall tasks that form half of the Long-term Retrieval Cognitive Factor?

The WJ-R/C seems better suited for research purposes and for psychoeducational assessment (taking advantage of the co-normed Cognitive and Achievement batteries and the discrepancy norms for making aptitude/achievement comparisons) than for conventional neuropsychological and clinical evaluations. As such, its new format renders the WJ-R/C as an excellent WAIS-R *supplement* for adult assessment, which may be its major contribution. Since the WJ-R/C offers reliable and valid measurement of each of seven Horn factors, any one or two or three of these scales can be used to follow up hypotheses generated by an administration of the WAIS-R or a thorough neuropsychological battery.

The WJ-R/C as a WAIS-R Supplement

The 19 WJ-R/C subtests (excluding the impractical delayed recall tasks) represent a veritable gold mine of tasks for supplementary assessment. Two of the Long-term Retrieval tasks (Memory for Names, Visual-Auditory Learning), and two of the Fluid Reasoning tasks (Analysis-Synthesis, Concept Formation) are true controlled learning subtests, affording assessment of a person's learning ability—a skill that unfortunately is not measured very well by conventional intelligence tests. These subtests are all novel in format and represent excellent WAIS-R supplements whenever learning ability, fluid intelligence, and/or long-term memory are in question. The two Fluid Reasoning learning tasks are especially valuable for following up WAIS-R–generated hypotheses regarding a possible age- or brain-related decline in fluid intelligence. Whereas the WAIS-R Performance subtests place a premium on visual-motor coordination and speed of response, Analysis-Synthesis and Concept Formation involve no motor coordination at all and speed of response is not a major variable in determining a person's performance level. Spatial Relations, now that the 3-minute time limit has been removed, is also a good test of the type of spatial visualization that is demanded by Block Design (except that the WJ-R task requires no imposition of motor speed).

Note, however, that the WJ-R/C, despite its plethora of subtests, does not provide adequate follow-up of hypotheses regarding Perceptual Organization, Wechsler's construct of nonverbal intelligence. If an examiner speculates that an asset or deficit on the WAIS-R reflects *fluid* intelligence, then the WJ-R/C has much to offer. But if good or, more typically, deficient *nonverbal visual-spatial* ability requires verification, then only Spatial Relations, among the entire Cognitive battery, is a useful supplement. As mentioned previously, the other Fluid Reasoning subtests have a heavy verbal component; and despite the use of figural material, they do not assess visual-spatial skills. Indeed, like the old Binet and its predecessor, the WJ-R/C is extremely steeped in the tradition of measuring intelligence through predominantly verbal means.

The WAIS-R assesses short-term memory with Digit Span and remote memory with Picture Completion and Information, but fails to assess long-term memory over a few minutes. This important skill is assessed well by the WJ-R/C Long-term Retrieval subtests, as it is by the WMS-R General Memory scale. Both of these sets of tasks are good WAIS-R supplements. In addition, the measures of Auditory Processing and Visual Processing, which might be called low-level cognitive tasks with strong perceptual components, allow evaluation in areas that are not measured by tests of high-level intelligence. Yet, neuropsychological evaluation often calls for assessment of such perceptual processes, rendering these WJ-R Cognitive Factors of special value. In all, the breadth and underlying theoretical model of the WJ-R detract from its utility as a WAIS-R rival, but render it the best WAIS-R supplement available.

Peabody Picture Vocabulary Test—Revised

The PPVT-R (Dunn & Dunn, 1981) is a measure of receptive vocabulary that yields "standard score equivalents" having the familiar IQ mean of 100 and standard deviation of 15. In its previous incarnation as the PPVT (Dunn, 1959) it yielded an IQ; because of its brief administration time of 10 to 20 minutes, the old PPVT became a source of test abuse for examiners who wanted a quick measure of IQ for school children or clients. The PPVT-R, still brief to administer, discourages that type of interpretation by removing the terms mental age and IQ from the record form, although some forms of test abuse die hard.

For the purposes of adolescent and adult clinical assessment, the PPVT-R is considered a WAIS-R supplement, to be used as a check on verbal ability, especially for individuals with depressed WAIS-R Verbal IQs suspected of having deficiencies in expressing their answers verbally. The PPVT-R has the advantage of being normed for adults (through age 40), coming in two alternate forms (L and M), and of measuring a verbal skill via a nonverbal format: pointing to the one picture out of four that corresponds to the object (e.g., drum, tusk), concept (e.g., cooperation, emaciated), or action (e.g., stretching, pilfering) named by the examiner.

The brevity of the PPVT-R makes it a natural for research investigations as well as clinical assessment, and it is a "regular" in the *Journal of Clinical Psychology, Psychology in the Schools,* and the *Journal of Psychoeducational Assessment.* Whereas a great majority of the investigations reflect its predominant use with children and youth, a growing number of studies with adults have been appearing (Mangiaracina & Simon, 1986; Prout & Schwartz, 1984; Stevenson, 1986). The PPVT-R *Technical Supplement* (Robertson & Eisenberg, 1981) provides an excellent summary of a wealth of studies on the old PPVT and of some PPVT-R investigations as well.

Technical Qualities

The PPVT-R was standardized on a nationally representative sample of children and adults aged 2–6 to 40 years (Dunn & Dunn, 1981). Two separate standardizations were conducted, one for ages 2–6 to 18–11, and one for ages 19 to 40. The former sample was larger (100 males and 100 females per age group for a total sample of 4,200), and more representative; it matched Census data closely on the variables of geographic region, occupation of father, ethnic background, and community size. The adult sample was composed of 201 to 216 people, about equally divided by sex, in each of four age groups: 19–24, 25–29, 30–34, and 35–40 (total of 828 adults). Whereas the total sample matched Census data closely on the key variable of occupational status, it was decidedly *not* representative of the U. S. on the variable of geographic region (more than half the sample came from the North Central region), and no data were gathered on community size or on

the essential variable of ethnic background. Of even more concern is the fact that virtually the entire adult normative group was tested in a *group* format. Further, both Form L and Form M were administered randomly to the sample of children and adolescents; only Form L was given to the adults.

The median split-half reliability coefficient for 21 age groups between 2–6 and 18 years was .80 for Form L and .81 for Form M (Dunn & Dunn, 1981). The values for adolescents aged 12–18 were a bit higher: Form L (.78–.88, median = .86) and Form M (.79–.86, median = .84). For adults the coefficients for Form L ranged from .80 to .83 for the four age groups, with a median of .82. Alternate forms reliability coefficients were slightly lower for PPVT-R standard scores, averaging .79 for ages 2–6 to 18 and .85 for adolescents; no alternate forms data are reported in the Manual for adults. Stevenson (1986) examined the alternate forms reliability of the PPVT-R for adults, based on counterbalanced administration of Forms L and M to 60 referrals for suspected learning disorders (ages 18–37, mean = 25). The obtained coefficient was good (.88). Alternate forms reliability over a retest interval of 9–31 days produced median stability coefficients of .77 for ages 2–6 to 18 years and of .80 for just the samples of 12- to 18-year-olds. However, stability coefficients ranged widely from the mid- to high- .50s for ages 2–6, 5, and 18 to values of about .90 for ages 11 and 12.

The PPVT typically correlated in the .60–.70 range with expressive vocabulary tests and with global measures of verbal intelligence such as the old Binet and Wechsler's Verbal Scale (Dunn & Dunn, 1981; Robertson & Eisenberg, 1981). Values reported for the PPVT-R for children have sometimes been nonsignificant and trivial (e.g., Vance, Kitson, & Singer, 1983), although most studies of the PPVT-R and WISC-R, for example, seem to have found results for the revised battery that are quite similar to the PPVT findings (e.g., Candler, Maddux, & Johnson, 1986; Hollinger & Sarvis, 1984).

The PPVT correlated with WAIS V-IQ .71, on the average, based on the results of seven investigations (Dunn & Dunn, 1981). Results of studies using the revisions of each of these tests have produced similar coefficients: (a) .80 for Form L and .78 for Form M with WAIS-R V-IQ for the 60 referrals described previously (Stevenson, 1986); (b) .59 with WAIS-R V-IQ for 21 mildly retarded adults aged 18 to 63, mean equal to 32 years (Prout & Schwartz, 1984); (c) .90 with WAIS-R V-IQ for 40 psychiatric inpatients, aged 18 to 40 with a mean of 28 years (Mangiaracina & Simon, 1986); and (d) .64 with WAIS-R V-IQ for 29 male inmates in a maximum security penitentiary, mean age = 30 years (Carvajal, Shaffer, & Weaver, 1989). The coefficient of .90 for the psychiatric inpatients was inflated substantially by the extreme heterogeneity of the sample (PPVT-R SD was an atypical 23.6), whereas the value of .64 for the inmates was attenuated by restricted range (corrected coefficient = .79). The PPVT-R also correlated .69 with composite score on the Stanford-Binet, Fourth Edition, for 32 undergraduate psychology students, ages 18–20 years (Carvajal, Gerber, & Smith, 1987).

Overall, I agree with McCallum's (1985) contention that the PPVT-R's "[p]sychometric characteristics appear adequate to excellent" (p. 1127). The Manual is excellent and thorough, and "provides guidelines and cautions for the interpretation of converted PPVT-R scores" (Wiig, 1985, p. 1128).

Evaluation

The PPVT-R is reliable for a brief test, but it is not as reliable as one would expect for a test composed of 175 items. The biggest hindrance to the reliability of the obtained scores is the huge role played by chance: Each item is a four-option multiple-choice question, meaning that guessers will be correct one out of four times. A person on a "roll" can mask a receptive vocabulary deficiency, while a person experiencing a run of bad luck can exaggerate a mild deficit. Probably the best solution to this problem is one that is rarely used, namely, administering both forms of the PPVT-R and relying solely on the average of the two standard scores. Certainly chance guessing can be tolerated as a necessary evil in group-administered tests, but it defies the purpose of individual administration.

It is unfortunate that the PPVT-R norms stop at 40 and that the adult norms are so far inferior to the superb norms for children and adolescents. This psychometric handicap limits the usefulness of the test, especially for older adults. When the test is used with individuals above age 40, simply use the norms for ages 35-0 to 40-11 and indicate that the standard score is an estimate. If only one form is given instead of the preferred two, use Form L because all adult norms are based on that form. Currently, data on the PPVT-R for adolescents and adults are being collected during the standardization program of the Kaufman Adolescent and Adult Intelligence Test (Kaufman & Kaufman, in press a).

Use of the PPVT-R as a WAIS-R Supplement

The PPVT-R's reliability and validity data for adolescents and adults are generally good, and the revision was done thoroughly and with extreme care. Consequently, despite the test's shortcomings for adult assessment, clinicians are nonetheless advised to administer the PPVT-R more or less routinely as a WAIS-R supplement. Much information is gained in a short time, the task is simple to administer, and the numerous easy items make the test a good ice-breaker for developmentally disabled adults. Nothing on the WAIS-R is quite like the PPVT-R, which permits a nice contrast to the expression-dependent V-IQ. Naturally, the PPVT-R standard score is a more valuable supplement for individuals who evidence difficulty with verbal expression, but it represents an interesting "extra" WAIS-R subtest for every examinee when it comes time to investigate hypotheses to explain profile fluctuations.

Clinicians who administer the PPVT-R should keep several points in mind:

- Remember that the subtest measures a homogeneous ability involving receptive vocabulary, and is not to be thought of as an overall measure of intelligence (according to language expert Elisabeth Wiig, 1985, it is "an up-to-date, well standardized, norm-referenced test of standard receptive, American English vocabulary" [p. 1128])

- Try to administer both forms of the PPVT-R to counteract the built-in error associated with chance guessing. (Form M should routinely be given whenever Form L produces a standard score that seems out of line with other information or data about the person.)

- Remember to interpret the obtained score with some caution because the norms for adults stop at age 40, are not representative of the U.S. on some important variables, and were obtained in a group format.

- Realize that success on the PPVT-R depends on the ability to integrate "right-brain" visual stimuli with "left-brain" word knowledge, which is therefore a complex skill that may be related to a person's neurological integrity or specific dysfunction.

Stanford-Binet Intelligence Scale, Fourth Edition

The new edition of the Binet, a drastic revision of the old test of the same name, got off to a bad start. The test kit was mailed out prematurely, well before the administration and scoring manual arrived; it was like getting a complex toy for Christmas or a large applicance, minus the assembly instructions. When the Manual arrived months later, it contained insufficient reliability information to permit meaningful interpretation; soon some of its norms tables were discovered to contain serious errors. Had it not been for its venerated name, the new battery probably would have died a quick death, following at least one reviewer's proposal to heed a eulogy proposed previously for the old Binet: "To the S-B IV, *Requiescat in pace:* and so it should have stayed" (Reynolds, 1987a, p. 141). Although the new battery does not seem to be used too frequently as the primary measure of intelligence by school psychologists (Obringer, 1988), only yields norms for adults as old as 23, and has seriously flawed norms, it does provide the clinician with some excellent, novel, and reliable tasks to supplement the WAIS-R.

Overview of the Battery

The S-B IV (Thorndike, Hagen, & Sattler, 1986a, 1986b) was developed to conform to a three-level hierarchical model: The first level is general ability or *g;* the second level is composed of three factors, two from the Horn-Cattell model (crystallized and fluid-analytic abilities) and one labeled Short-Term Memory; and the third level is composed of three reasoning factors, Verbal, Quantitative, and Abstract/Visual. In confusing fashion, the battery yields four area scores plus a Test Composite, where the three areas at the third level of the hierarchy are joined by one of the three second-level factors (Short-Term Memory). Each of the five composites produces a Standard Age Score (SAS), *not* an IQ (a bit of an irony for a Binet scale), having the familiar Binet mean of 100 and *SD* of 16. The four separate areas closely resemble the four cognitive scales that McCarthy (1972) developed for the McCarthy Scales of Children's Abilities. Together, the Verbal Reasoning and Quantitative Reasoning areas reflect Wechsler's notion of verbal intelligence, while Abstract/Visual Reasoning is akin to Perceptual Organization, and Short-Term Memory resembles the skill underlying the Freedom from Distractibility factor. From the point of view of a simultaneous-sequential processing model, Abstract/Visual Reasoning assesses gestalt-like, holistic, "right-brain" processing, and Short-Term Memory (except for the visual-spatial Bead Memory subtest) measures "left-brain," linear, successive processing.

Each area is composed of three or four subtests, for a battery total of 15 tasks, although only a few of the subtests span the entire 2- to 23-year age span for which S-B IV norms are provided. Thirteen of the subtests (excluding Absurdities from the Verbal Reasoning area and Copying from the Abstract/Visual Reasoning area) are intended for adults. The specific tasks to administer to a given person are a function of that person's chronological age and his or her score on the Vocabulary subtest (a "routing" task). However, even within the set of tasks that might be given to each individual, the examiner can choose a tailor-made battery to suit the clinician's predilections. An infinite number of abbreviations are feasible, affording the examiner with a kind of unstructured flexibility that might promote test abuse ("nothing short of IQ roulette," according to Reynolds, 1987a, p. 141); further, the SAS scores are based on the *number* of tasks administered per area, not on the *type* of subtests given, an unacceptable psychometric procedure (Reynolds, 1987a).

Validation of the Model

The model underlying the S-B IV has received little empirical support. Even though books and articles about S-B IV profile interpretation feature the area scores (Hopkins & Delaney, 1987; Naglieri, 1988b; Rosenthal & Kamphaus, 1988; Spruill, 1988), I am not convinced of their meaningfulness or reality as psychological constructs. Confirmatory factor analysis has offered mild support for the four factors (Keith, Cook, Novak, White, & Pottebaum, 1988; Ownby & Carmin, 1988), while the more traditional exploratory methods (e.g., principal factor analysis with varimax rotation) have offered *no* support (Reynolds, Kamphaus, & Rosenthal, 1988). Even the confirmatory analyses were not consistently

supportive from age group to age group (Ownby & Carmin, 1988), were considerably less supportive of the fluid–crystallized split characterizing the second level in the hierarchy (Keith et al., 1988), and offered overall "mixed support for the construct validity of the new Binet" (Keith et al., 1988, p. 272).

The exploratory factor analyses suggested only one to three significant factors underlying the S-B IV, with little apparent relationship between the obtained factors and either level 2 or level 3 of the Binet model (Reynolds et al., 1988). Two factors emerged for ages 18–23 years, but the rotated dimensions were not even remotely "pure," as nearly half the subtests had loadings of .40 or above on *both* factors. At age 12, 9 of the 12 tasks in that analysis had loadings of .50 or more on both dimensions. These data, as well as the confirmatory analysis data, attest that the new Binet, like the old Binet, is a strong measure of *g*. Although the confirmatory data disagree with the claims of some (Sandoval & Irvin, 1988; Slate, 1986) that the Binet measures nothing but *g*, I'm not sure that such claims are very far from the truth. To me, models underlying a test need verification by *both* the confirmatory and exploratory approaches, not just one or the other. All the confirmatory support in the world for Wechsler's Verbal and Performance scales would have provided little interpretive consolation to clinicians if the exploratory analyses had not shown the existence of robust Verbal Comprehension and Perceptual Organization dimensions for any test battery that Wechsler assembled.

The mild confirmatory analysis support, in the wake of other conflicting evidence against the validity of the Binet model, impels me to agree with the warning of one of the Binet authors (Sattler, 1988) that "routine use of area scores is not recommended" (p. 289). I believe it is best to think of the S-B IV as an overall scale of general intelligence that offers reliable measurement in the abilities assessed by 15 separate subtests, but that offers area composites of questionable psychological meaning.

Description of the Subtests

The 15 subtests are described here, grouped by the area in which they are included. This grouping is more for organizational purposes than any other reason because of the inconsistent and questionable empirical support for the S-B IV model. Each subtest name is followed in parentheses by the median Kuder-Richardson 20 (alpha) reliability coefficient and g loading for adolescents (ages 12–17), and the precise reliability and g values obtained for the 18- to 23-year-old adult sample. Reliability data are from Thorndike et al. (1986b, Table 5.1); data for g loadings are from Reynolds et al. (1988, Table 1). The subtest reliability coefficients are outstanding, although it is conceivable that stability coefficients could be quite a bit lower. Test–retest data are not presented for adolescents or adults, but such data are provided for preschool and elementary school children (Thorndike et al., 1986b, Tables 5.4 and 5.5). The values were low for these groups; for example, for 55 elementary school children, the coefficients ranged from .28 to .86 for the 12 subtests given (median = .64), much lower than the K-R 20 reliability coefficients.

Verbal Reasoning

Vocabulary (ages 12–17—reliability = .88, g loading = .83; ages 18–23—reliability = .94, g loading = .89). The subject demonstrates word knowledge by naming pictures (easier items) and responding verbally to words that are spoken by the examiner and read by the person (WAIS-R Vocabulary analog).

Comprehension (ages 12–17—reliability = .91, g loading = .80; ages 18–23—reliability = .96, g loading = .85). The subject points to body parts (easier items) and responds verbally to items having social relevance (WAIS-R Comprehension analog).

Absurdities (ages 12–14—reliability = .93, g loading = .71). The subject has to state what is incongruous, or absurd, about pictures (e.g., a calendar with 32 days).

Verbal Relations (ages 14–17—reliability = .91, g loading = .65; ages 18–23—reliability = .91, g loading = .71). The subject has to state how three objects or concepts are alike, but different from a fourth (e.g., "How are bread, hamburgers, and apples alike, but different from milk?").

Abstract/Visual Reasoning

Pattern Analysis (ages 12–17—reliability = .94, g loading = .68; ages 18–23—reliability = .96, g loading = .80). The subject has to put shapes in a formboard (easier items) and then has to use between two and nine black-and-white patterned blocks to copy pictures of abstract designs (WAIS-R Block Design analog).

Copying (ages 12–13—reliability = .86, g loading = .72). The subject has to use green cube "blocks" to copy block patterns constructed by the examiner (easier items) and then has to copy geometric designs with pencil and paper.

Matrices (ages 12–17—reliability = .90, g loading = .76; ages 18–23—reliability = .92, g loading = .77). The subject has to choose the object, abstract design, or letter that best completes a matrix analogy.

Paper Folding and Cutting (ages 14–17—reliability = .94, g loading = .69; ages 18–23—reliability = .93, g loading = .72). The subject has to select from among five options the abstract picture that shows how a folded and cut piece of paper would look (where it is creased and where there are holes of different shapes) after it is unfolded (scissors are used to help demonstrate the task).

Quantitative Reasoning

Quantitative (ages 12–17—reliability = .92, g loading = .82; ages 18–23—reliability = .95, g loading = .91). The subject demonstrates mathematical knowledge on items measuring skills such as counting, solving arithmetic reasoning problems, and knowledge of quantitative concepts (WAIS-R Arithmetic analog).

Number Series (ages 12–17—reliability = .91, g loading = .80; ages 18–23—reliability = .93, g loading = .82). The subject is presented with a series of numbers and must figure out what two numbers come next in the series (e.g., 8, 12, 16, 20, 24,—,—).

Equation Building (ages 14–17—reliability = .91, g loading = .62; ages 18–23—reliability = .91, g loading = .69). The subject is presented with a row of numbers and mathematical signs and has to rearrange them to construct a correct equation (e.g., 1 3 4 6 + − = can be transformed into 6 − 3 + 1 = 4).

Short-Term Memory

Bead Memory (ages 12–17—reliability = .90, g loading = .72; ages 18–23—reliability = .95, g loading = .80). The subject is presented with colorful beads of different shapes and has to construct, on a plastic stick, bead patterns identical to patterns presented briefly (in pictures) by the examiner.

Memory for Sentences (ages 12–17—reliability = .90, g loading = .71; ages 18–23—reliability = .94, g loading = .81). The subject tries to repeat phrases and sentences of increasing length and complexity.

Memory for Digits (ages 12–17—reliability = .84, g loading = .62; ages 18–23—reliability = .88, g loading = .72). The subject has to repeat digits spoken by the examiner, with items covering both forward and backward series (WAIS-R Digit Span analog).

Memory for Objects (ages 12–17—reliability = .72, g loading = .58; ages 18–23—reliability = .78, g loading = .56). The subject is shown pictures one at a time and then must point to them in the correct sequence when shown an array of pictures that includes the same pictures plus distractors.

Evaluation

The S-B IV authors constructed some novel and interesting tasks, most with superb reliability and superior g loadings; the materials tend to be quite attractive. The Technical Manual (Thorndike et al., 1986b) is also replete with an impressive array of validity studies encompassing a variety of normal and exceptional samples and numerous instruments. The S-B IV Test Composite, for example, correlated .91 with WAIS-R FS-IQ for 47 normal adults (mean age = 19-5) and .79 with WAIS-R FS-IQ for 21 mentally retarded adults (mean age = 19-5). The coefficient for the normal group was inflated because of the heterogeneity of the sample, and the coefficient for the retarded group was attenuated by range restriction. The Binet composite was 9.3 points lower than the FS-IQ for the retarded sample. In a study of 32 college students reported by Carvajal, Gerber, Hewes, and Weaver (1987), a coefficient of .91 was obtained between the most global Binet and WAIS-R scores, despite restriction of range in the test scores.

Reliable subtests often translate to "long" subtests, and that is true for the new Binet. A four-hour administration time can be anticipated if the entire battery of 15 subtests is given (Walker, 1987). The logical solution is to offer shortened versions, which the Binet people do, but their practice of allowing unlimited flexibility in the choice of subtests represents a testing hazard. Certainly the weak construct validation support for the Binet model reflects a serious shortcoming for clinicians who want scores in domains having the logical appeal of labels like "fluid," "crystallized," "verbal," "memory," and so forth. However, the worst problem with the S-B IV is the normative sample. The single most important stratification variable for an intelligence test is socioeconomic status, and the test publisher did little or nothing to ensure that representative proportions of individuals were tested on this key variable.

Consequently, 43.7% of the Binet sample graduated from college compared to only 16.0% in the U. S. population. Only 15.0% of the sample had parents in occupations like precision production, operators, and fabricators, in contrast to 32.5% in the U. S. as a whole. The disparity "is due to the fact that only children whose parents returned a Permission Form could be tested, and the parents of higher SES tended to return the forms more frequently than those of lower SES" (Thorndike et al., 1986b, p. 24). This is a lame excuse. All publishers face the same problem; the solution is to beat the bushes to find willing participants at all SES levels until you succeed. Just testing the easy-to-get cases does not produce a representative sample, even if it is large ($N = 5,013$ between ages 2 and 23 years). Nor does applying a weighting procedure, as employed by the Binet authors, solve the problem. Such an approach forces the data from a few individuals in certain "cells" to go an awfully long way.

Although some consider the weighting technique an adequate solution to the problem (Glutting & Kaplan, in press; Keith et al., 1988), I do not. Neither do a number of reviewers of the battery (Reynolds, 1987a; Sandoval & Irvin, 1988; Slate, 1986). It is well documented that the easiest cases to obtain for any type of research or assessment study are the ones who, for whatever reason, tend to earn the highest scores (Horn & Donaldson, 1976). This tendency was shown dramatically in chapter 7 regarding the ability level of those individuals who keep returning for follow-up testing (see especially Figure 7.6). By not spending the effort

necessary to secure a representative sample, even the weighting procedure cannot compensate for what probably is a serious bias in the representativeness of the volunteers for the Binet standardization. The publishers made a half-hearted attempt at norming the S-B IV above age 23 by requesting that the 24- to 32-year-old parents of school-age children volunteer for testing (Thorndike et al., 1986b), but "it was determined that the obtained sample was not representative" (p. 20).

I am also concerned by the norms generated for a number of subtests based on a relatively small number of subjects. Norms are generated at age 13 on Copying, for example, based on a sample of 124 individuals (at younger ages, for whom the subtest was intended, sample sizes were in the 300–400 range). The only 13-year-olds who were given Copying are the least able ones, the ones who performed poorly on the routing test and began testing at a low entry level. Hence, the samples for "extended" norms are atypical and unrepresentative. Even though the authors (Thorndike et al., 1986b, p. 30) were aware of this problem and made statistical "adjustments," I feel uneasy with age norms developed from data on the least able older individuals or the smartest young ones.

These problems lead me to believe that the Binet should be used as a supplement to other major tests for children, adolescents, and adults, and not as the primary measure of intelligence for anyone. The difficulty is especially acute for adult assessment, which includes a single age group spanning ages 18–23 composed of only 194 individuals. The sample is not only the smallest of all Binet age groups, but there is some question about the advisability of merging older adolescents and young adults into a single adult sample in view of the considerable differences in mean sums of scaled scores earned by ages 18–19 and 20–24 on the WAIS-R (Wechsler, 1981, Table 7). Even though the adolescent norms for the WAIS-R are suspect (see pp. 83–85), substantial differences in ability level for individuals ages 18–19 and 20–24 characterized the WAIS data as well (Wechsler, 1955, Table 7).

The S-B IV as a WAIS-R Supplement

The S-B IV is a poor choice as the main intelligence test for adolescent or adult assessment but, like the WJ-R/C, it provides a wealth of interesting supplementary tasks for the WAIS-R. Each of the 15 Binet subtests yields standard scores having a mean of 50 and *SD* of 8. The unusual choice of 8 for the standard deviation was intended to simplify the conversion to the metric used for the area and test composites (just multiply the subtest score by 2, since 50 ± 8 is half of 100 ± 16), but the net result is unnecessary confusion for the examiner. Many clinicians are accustomed to *T*-scores (mean = 50, *SD* = 10), a factor that impairs easy interpretation of the Binet subtest scores. I suggest converting the subtest standard scores to percentile ranks (Thorndike et al., 1986b, Table D.1) and interpreting only these percentile ranks when using Binet tasks to follow up WAIS-R hypotheses.

Because of the questionable accuracy of the S-B IV norms, these percentiles should be interpreted as *estimates* of the person's level of functioning. When testing someone above the age of 23 years, use the norms for ages 18–23 and treat the obtained score as an even rougher estimate of performance level. For middle-aged and elderly adults, the obtained percentile ranks should be contrasted with percentile ranks earned by the subjects on the *regular* WAIS-R scaled scores, *not* the age-corrected scaled scores; like the WAIS-R regular scaled scores, the Binet subtest scores for older adults are based on a reference group of younger adults.

One of the key advantages of the S-B IV as a WAIS-R supplement is its suitability for children, with the norms for some tasks extending as low as age 2. Consequently, the Binet allows supplementary assessment of the verbal and nonverbal abilities of mentally retarded and other low-functioning individuals who earn raw scores

of 0, 1, 2, or 3 points on the WAIS-R subtests. In particular, it is advisable to administer the Binet subtests that are direct analogs of WAIS-R tasks: Vocabulary, Comprehension, Quantitative, and Pattern Analysis. Each of these four Binet tasks is normed for children as young as 2 years, yet is normed for adults as well; there is plenty of "bottom" for assessing the functioning of people scoring below the WAIS-R norms on any or all of the comparable WAIS-R tasks.

Pattern Analysis, for example, allows the measurement of a person's nonverbal concept formation, even if he or she earned a raw score of zero on WAIS-R Block Design. Pattern Analysis includes some items composed of two-block designs, some involving matching just a *single* block, and some requiring placement of simple shapes in a formboard. Although the items have time limits, there are no bonus points, greatly reducing the role played by speed in determining a person's score. Similarly, Vocabulary has easy picture vocabulary items for retarded adults who cannot define words orally, Comprehension has simple social awareness items, and Quantitative has preschool-level number concept items. A word of caution, however: Pattern Analysis, like a few other Binet tasks (notably Paper Folding and Cutting), can become quite complicated to administer if the examinee fails to catch on quickly. The Binet requires heavy verbiage from the examiner, has many specific administrative rules to follow, and can result in confusion regarding whether or not to administer some of the sample items.

An individual's response time is generally unimportant for success on Binet subtests; Pattern Analysis is the only task that enforces time limits for most of its items. Hence, the S-B IV is ideal for checking out WAIS-R hypotheses regarding the cause of low scores on Performance subtests. Is poor fluid intelligence suspected? Administer Pattern Analysis, Paper Folding and Cutting, Matrices, and Number Series. Does the person possibly possess good nonverbal reasoning and Perceptual Organization ability, despite a general slowness in response time and a possible visual-motor deficit? Administer Paper Folding and Cutting and Matrices. Does a deficit in Perceptual Organization generalize to nonverbal skills not measured by the WAIS-R? Administer Matrices and Bead Memory. Does a patient with suspected or known right hemisphere damage have difficulty maintaining the gestalt of a 2 × 2 or 3 × 3 square on Block Design items? Administer Pattern Analysis to see if the patient can solve the "linear" items.

The novel tasks with high *g* saturation afford an excellent opportunity to explore the reasoning abilities of anyone given the WAIS-R, whether the goal is to follow up a deficit or a strength in reasoning capacity. The Matrices subtest is ideal for this purpose, especially the clever high-level items that appear directly on the record form involving relationships among letters of the alphabet; so is the ingenious Equation Building subtest, the familiar Number Series task, and the interesting quasi-analog to WAIS-R Similiarieis: Verbal Relations.

Although the Short-Term Memory scale offers several interesting subtests for following up WAIS-R hypotheses pertaining to high or low Digit Span performance, Memory for Objects is not sufficiently reliable to interpret in isolation, Memory for Digits is virtually identical to Digit Span, and the scale as a whole does not have construct validity support. A better choice is the Attention/Concentration and/or General Memory scales on the WMS-R, or the memory tasks on the WJ-R/C.

Detroit Tests of Learning Aptitude

The revision of the old 19-subtest Detroit Tests of Learning Aptitude by Hammill (1985) reflects a substantial degree of modification, both in terms of content and concept, of the battery that was developed originally in 1935 (Baker & Leland, 1967). Hammill retained 7 subtests,

developed 4 novel ones, and then grouped all 11 component tasks into four different domains, each composed of an aptitude dichotomy: Linguistic (Verbal vs. Nonverbal), Cognitive (Conceptual vs. Structural), Attentional (Attention-Enhanced vs. Attention-Reduced), and Motoric (Motor-Enhanced vs. Motor-Reduced). The DTLA-2 presents norms tables for ages 6 to 17 years.

Overview of the DTLA-2 Model

Hammill's (1985) model recognizes the complexity of the kinds of tasks used to measure mental ability and reflects a learning disabilities orientation (although Hammill was influenced strongly by Spearman and Wechsler). It is shown in Table 16.6 to indicate the placement of each subtest within each domain.

These dichotomies are defined in the following ways:

- Verbal Aptitude involves knowledge of words and their use; Nonverbal Aptitude does *not* involve reading, writing, or verbalization
- Conceptual Aptitude involves language, problem solving, abstraction, and conceptualization; Structural Aptitude involves knowledge about shapes, sequences, patterns.
- Attention-Enhanced stresses concentration and short-term memory; Attention-Reduced stresses long-term memory.
- Motor-Enhanced requires complex manual dexterity; Motor-Reduced requires oral or pointing responses and is relatively motor-free.

The complexity of the DTLA-2 Composites makes it difficult to say precisely what factor structure to expect; nonetheless, one would anticipate that exploratory analysis would be congruent with at least one of the four domains. In view of the strong factor analytic support for Wechsler's Verbal–Performance dichotomy, and Hammill's (1985) claim that "Wechsler was definitely the role model" (p. 10) in constructing the DTLA-2, one would expect validation of the Linguistic domain, the Verbal–Nonverbal

TABLE 16.6 Hammill's model of the Detroit Tests of Learning Aptitude (DTLA-2)

DTLA Subtest	Linguistic		Cognitive		Attentional		Motoric	
	V	NV	Con	Str	Enh	Red	Enh	Red
Word Opposites	V		Con			Red		Red
Sentence Imitation	V		Con		Enh			Red
Oral Directions	V		Con		Enh		Enh	
Word Sequences	V			Str	Enh			Red
Story Construction	V		Con			Red		Red
Word Fragments	V		Con			Red		Red
Design Reproduction		NV		Str	Enh		Enh	
Object Sequences		NV		Str	Enh		Enh	
Symbolic Relations		NV	Con			Red		Red
Conceptual Matching		NV	Con			Red		Red
Letter Sequences		NV		Str	Enh		Enh	

V = Verbal, NV = Nonverbal, Con = Conceptual, Str = Structural, Enh = Enhanced, Red = Reduced

dichotomy. Aiken (1987) did not find such support for the Linguisitic domain, or any other domain, in his principal factor analysis with varimax rotation. Instead, he identified a large general reasoning dimension (loadings of .40 or higher by seven subtests), and factors he considered to measure auditory attention span and visual attention span.

The large general factor is consistent with Hammill's (1985) approach to test construction: "Since the development of the DTLA-2 was strongly influenced by Spearman, subtests were selected for their contribution to *g* rather than as representatives of particular special abilities" (p. 10). Like the S-B IV, the DTLA-2 seems to be primarily a measure of general intelligence, at least for clinical assessment purposes. As such, I consider its greatest value for adolescent and adult assessment to be as a source of interesting supplementary tasks to the WISC-R and WAIS-R.

Description of the Subtests

The 11 DTLA-2 subtests, normed for ages 6–17, are described here. The parentheses fol-

lowing each test name indicate whether the task was on the old DTLA, or was developed new for the DTLA-2; additionally, the means of three coefficient alpha reliability estimates (presented by Hammill, 1985, Table 8) for ages 12–13, 14–15, and 16–17) are provided.

Word Opposites (Old, previously called Verbal Opposites; reliability for ages 12–17 = .91). The subject responds verbally with the opposite of the word spoken by the examiner.

Sentence Imitation (Old, previously called Auditory Attention Span for Related Syllables; reliability for ages 12–17 = .89). The subject tries to repeat the exact sentence spoken by the examiner.

Oral Directions (Old; reliability for ages 12–17 = .86). The subject uses pencil and paper to execute varies commands spoken by the examiner.

Word Sequences (Old, previously called Auditory Attention Span for Unrelated Words; reliability for ages 12–17 = .89). The subject tries to repeat, in the same order, a series of unrelated words spoken by the examiner.

Story Construction (New; reliability for ages 12–17 = .88). The subject is shown three pictures and is asked to make up a story about each one.

Word Fragments (New; reliability for ages 12–17 = .95). The subject is asked to read words that are printed with various parts of the letters missing (a gestalt closure task).

Design Reproduction (Old; reliability for ages 12–17 = .91). The subject is briefly shown complex abstract designs and tries to reproduce them from memory with paper and pencil.

Object Sequences (Old, previously called Visual Attention span for Objects; reliability for ages 12–17 = .93). The subject is briefly shown a row of pictures on a card; then he or she is shown another card with the pictures in a different order and must try to write the numbers that indicate the original order.

Symbolic Relations (New; reliability for ages 12–17 = .86). The subject is shown a visual "problem" (an abstract matrix analogy), and has to select the solution from among a row of six designs.

Conceptual Matching (New; reliability for ages 12–17 = .75). The subject is shown a stimulus picture and must select from among 10 pictures (each representing a concept, e.g., a guitar represents music, a hammer represents tools) the one that goes conceptually with the stimulus.

Letter Sequences (Old, previously called Visual Attention span for Letters; reliability for ages 12–17 = .92). The subject is briefly shown a card containing a row of letters and must then write the letters in the same order they were shown.

Evaluation

The reliability coefficients for the subtests, with the exception of Conceptual Matching, were generally quite good; stability coefficients were lower (four coefficients were below .80, even after correction for range restriction), but the retest sample was composed of only 33 children spanning the whole DTLA-2 age range. The biggest problem, however, is the DTLA-2's normative sample, which, like the sample for the S-B IV, does not match the U. S. Census data on the crucial variable of socio-economic status. The sample is composed of 1,532 individuals (91–184 at each year of age between 6 and 17 years), about equally divided by gender, and representative of the U. S. on the variables of race, geographic region, and urban–rural residence. However, only 12% of the sample had parents who did not graduate from high school, compared to an approximate 29% in the U. S. (Thorndike et al., 1986b, Table 3.8). Similarly, 52% of the DTLA-2 sample had at least some college, versus 34% within the U. S. Unlike the S-B IV, no weighting procedure was applied, indicating that the normative sample is of a higher SES classification than the nation as a whole. The net result is an unfairly "steep" set of norms that will make the average person earn lower scores than his or her true ability level would warrant.

The Manual provides limited empirical evidence of validity. The composite score (General IQ) derived from all 11 subtests (mean = 100, SD = 15) correlated .83 with WISC-R FS-IQ for 76 special education students. Correlations with achievement are also provided, but only for three small samples (20 to 32) in grades 2, 6 and 11. The literature seems to have added little to our knowledge of the DTLA-2; Silverstein (1986a) presented tables to facilitate interpretation of the various composites, while Coleman, Jorgenson, and Evans (1988) reported a correlation of .86 between DTLA-2 General IQ and WISC-R FS-IQ for 55 children, ages 6–12 years, referred for learning problems.

Other concerns with the DTLA-2 Manual are (a) its failure to indicate examiner qualifications; (b) long and intricate subtest directions, often presented without concrete aids; (c) ambiguous directions to examiners; and (d) problems with the design of specific subtests, such as the scoring system for Story Construction and the use of words as stimuli for the Word Fragments subtest (Radencich, 1986).

Use of the DTLA-2 as a WAIS-R Supplement

The limitations noted for the DTLA-2 make it useful primarily as a source of supplementary subtests rather than as the main instrument of choice for an evaluation. The subtests yield scaled scores having Wechsler parameters (mean = 10, SD = 3), although the absence of norms for adults forces examiners to use the norms for 17-year-olds for all older adolescents and adults. The obtained scaled scores should be considered rough estimates of the person's ability level because of the problems with the norms. For individuals above age 17, the estimates become even rougher; as with the Binet subtests, the DTLA-2 subtest scores should be compared to an adult's *regular* scaled scores, not the age-corrected ones. For an adolescent, however, the age-corrected scaled scores offer the most relevant comparison.

Three of the DTLA-2 subtests (Word Opposites, Sentence Imitation, Word Sequences) have direct analogs on the WJ-R/C; the far better norms and psychometric properties of the WJ-R/C make its subtests the logical choices as supplements. The clever Binet Matrices subtest is likewise to be preferred to the DTLA-2 Symbolic Relations task, and the WMS-R and WJ-R/C offer more accurate assessment of memory than any of the DTLA-2 memory subtests. Conceptual Matching would have made a nice WAIS-R supplement, but its reliability is too low to support its specific interpretation.

The three tasks that provide unique supplementary value are Story Construction, Word Fragments, and Oral Directions. The first two tasks have been soundly criticized by Radencich (1986), but I still consider them valuable. Story Construction measures verbal expression in a very unstructured situation (telling a story about

a picture), which affords a good follow-up for a person suspected of having poor verbal intelligence primarily due to an inability to express ideas in his or her own words. Word Fragments is a clever test. Before administering it, the examiner must make sure that the individual can read adequately. If so, this task allows clinicians to assess Perceptual Organization and simultaneous processing via the desirable medium of *verbal* stimuli. Finally, the Oral Directions subtest provides a direct measure of the hypothesis that a person has difficulty with auditory processing or otherwise comprehending spoken directions. This DTLA-2 task is a good one to give for individuals who evidenced difficulty with the Wechsler Verbal tasks having long stimuli (Information, Arithmetic, Comprehension), and who had trouble understanding what to do on the Performance subtests with lengthy oral directions (Picture Arrangement, Block Design, and Digit Symbol/Coding).

INDIVIDUAL ACHIEVEMENT BATTERIES

No clinician would have difficulty with the following analogy: "The most popular adult *intelligence* test is the WAIS-R, just as the most popular adult *achievement* test is the _____? _____." Nor would he or she have difficulty with an analog of an old Binet item: "In what way are the WAIS-R and WRAT-R the same, and how are they different?" Both instruments are far and away the most used tests in their respective categories for clinical assessment of adults (Harrison, Kaufman, Hickman, & Kaufman, 1988); however, the WAIS-R has excellent psychometric properties, but the WRAT-R—to be polite—does not. Yet the WRAT-R, like its predecessor the WRAT, is clearly the king of clinical assessment of achievement for children, adolescents, and adults. As Witt (1986) summed up succinctly: The WRAT "has the distinction of being perhaps the most maligned, yet most often used, individually administered test in existence" (p. 87). Regarding the descriptions of the WRAT's psychometric properties, Thorndike (1972) once proclaimed that "the procedure is apparently known only to the authors and God, and He may have some uncertainty" (p. 68). The WRAT-R's statistical techniques and explanations of them are no less obscure, and Thorndike's comments apply to the new battery as well. For example, the method used to determine reliability may as well have been written in Latin. ("The failure to report traditional reliability estimates is inexcusable," according to Reynolds, 1986b, p. 540.) The test authors also failed to supply the proportions of the standardization sample corresponding to each supposed stratification variable (Harrison, 1987b).

In this section, I first describe and review the WRAT-R and then discuss four fine alternatives to the WRAT-R. Each one is statistically sophisticated and was developed with care between the mid- to late 1980s, has outstanding psychometric properties, and is suitable for testing adolescents and adults at a wide range of ability levels. Two of the tests were normed through old age (WJ-R, Achievement portion; Woodcock Reading Mastery Tests—Revised, or WRMT-R), while the K-TEA—Brief and Comprehensive Forms and PIAT-R were normed through ages 18–19. The WRMT offers in-depth diagnostic analysis of a person's reading ability; the other three provide detailed measurement of academic achievement in a variety of areas. The K-TEA Brief Form is a screening test, like the WRAT-R; the PIAT-R is midway between a screener and a thorough assessment tool; and the other batteries offer comprehensive measurement of academic achievement. Each has its own special features and occasional problems, but all are outstanding candidates for administration as WAIS-R supplements (either the complete battery or the scales of special relevance); the biggest difficulty with any of these tests is the multiple-choice format, and hence the role of the "guessing" factor, for three PIAT-R subtests. The WJ-R/A, K-TEA Comprehensive, and WRMT-R are

especially useful whenever thorough educational evaluation is warranted and specific educational implications regarding diagnosis and remediation are highly desirable outcomes of the assessment.

Since the K-TEA and PIAT-R are normed through older adolescence, and provide no adult norms, clinicians who choose these tests for adults will need to use the norms for the oldest available reference group to obtain standard scores (age 18 or grade 12 for the K-TEA Brief and Comprehensive Forms, and also for the PIAT-R). This circumstance is far from ideal, although it is not as big a problem for achievement tests as it is for cognitive batteries like the S-B IV or DTLA-2. As indicated in chapter 7, crystallized, school-related skills tend to maintain through old age, whereas the more fluid intellectual abilities decline early and steadily.

Data provided for the original WJ (Woodcock, 1978, Table C) show the changing mean scores of the Achievement clusters across the broad range from grade 1 through age 65+. These mean scores are plotted (see Figure 16.1) for each of the four WJ Achievement clusters and also for the Broad Cognitive Scale, composed of 12 Cognitive subtests, both fluid and crystallized. (W-scores are shown in this graph, in which a score of 500 corresponds to the mean performance of a beginning fifth grader. Standard deviations for adolescents and adults are about 15 for the Broad Cognitive Scale, about 20 for Reading, Mathematics, and Knowledge, and about 25 for Written Language.) As shown, mean scores on Reading and Mathematics are fairly stable between grade 12 and old age (65+), whereas Written Language and Knowledge show little fluctuation between grade 12 and age 64, before declining notably for the older sample.

The WRAT-R does offer norms through age 74, but that is not a good reason to select the test. Harrison (1987b) points out: "The characteristics of the adult sample are so vague and confusing that the use of the WRAT-R with individuals above age 18 is probably not advis-

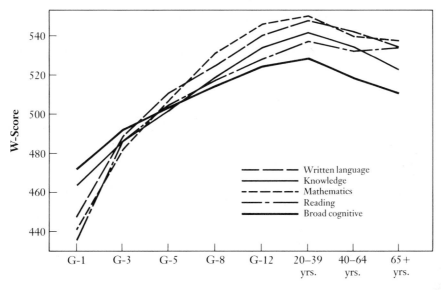

FIGURE 16.1

Mean Weighted W-Scores on the 1977 WJ Achievement clusters and Broad Cognitive Ability Scale between grade 1 and ages 65+ years (data from Woodcock, 1978, Table C).

able." And Reynolds (1986b) noted that the WRAT-R authors did not follow randomization in selecting the adult sample; Jastak and Wilkinson (1984) indicated that they had to make "involved corrections" of the norms "with the adult sample because of some idiosyncrasies in the sample selections" (p. 26). Thus, the adult WRAT-R norms seem no better or no worse than using the age 18 or grade 12 norms for adults when giving the PIAT-R or K-TEA. All achievement tests discussed in the pages that follow, except for the WRAT-R, are administered in easel format.

Wide Range Achievement Test—Revised

The WRAT-R (Jastak & Wilkinson, 1984), first "standardized" in 1936, is composed of Level 1 (ages 5 to 11 years) and Level 2 (ages 12 through adulthood) and takes about 30 min-

utes to administer. It yields standard scores (mean = 100, SD = 15) for each of three subtests, Reading, Spelling, and Arithmetic.

Description of the Subtests

Reading: Naming letters and pronouncing words out of context.

Spelling: Copying abstract marks resembling letters and writing or printing one's name (easier items); writing or printing words dictated, and used in a sentence, by the examiner.

Arithmetic: Counting, reading numbers, and solving simple oral number problems (easier items); using paper and pencil to perform written computations.

Technical Qualities and Evaluation

The WRAT has long been criticized for excluding reading comprehension from the Reading subtest; so has the use of written computation as essentially the sole means of evaluating arithmetic skills. Of greater concern for the WRAT-R are its psychometric properties. As indicated, conventional reliability coefficients have not been provided by the test authors. Test–retest coefficients were provided, "but are virtually useless" because Jastak and Wilkinson (1984) failed to indicate the time interval and because they based the analyses on small samples of a few school-age groups (Harrison, 1987b). "The standard error of measurement is treated skimpily" (Reid, 1986, p. 539). Content validity of the WRAT-R has also been soundly criticized. For example, Witt (1986) indicated that "the authors state: 'The content validity of the WRAT-R is apparent.' Apparent to whom? Not to me. Saying the content validity of the reading test is apparent . . . is like saying a needle is quite apparent in the proverbial haystack" (p. 89). Reynolds (1986b) added that Jastak and Wilkinson "apparently mistake face validity for real validity" (p. 540).

The WRAT-R norms are based on a large sample ($N = 5,600$; 200 in each of 28 age groups from 5 to 74 years) but are nonetheless poor. The norms are terrible for adults, as noted, and are bad for children as well. Harrison (1987b) pointed out the major problems: "Socioeconomic status was not used as a stratification variable, although research clearly shows that [SES] has a stronger relationship with achievement than does race. . . . Perhaps the greatest concern is the failure to describe the actual composition of the sample." In addition, Reynolds (1986b) stated that "[c]ollapsing all non-White racial groups into one category makes no sense either" (p. 540). The sample is alleged to be representative of the U.S. on variables such as geographic region; however, "whereas the North Central region, consisting of 12 states, is shown to have 26% of the population, individuals from only one state, Illinois, were included in the standardization" (Reid, 1986, p. 539).

The reviewers conclude:

- "In summary, the WRAT-R presents the same perplexing enigma for users as did its predecessor. . . . Primarily because of unresolved questions of validity and shortcomings in the standardization procedures, in its present form the WRAT-R must be considered unsuitable for general use" (Reid, 1986).

- "The WRAT-R is no real advance over previous editions and, although it is popular (due almost entirely to its brevity), there is no justification for continued use of the scale until much more is known about it. . . . Continued support and purchase of such poor tests will only encourage their continued development" (Reynolds, 1986b, pp. 540–541).

- "The general uses of the WRAT-R given in the manual are not supported by the test's psychometric qualities. . . . Some practitioners justify their use of the WRAT-R by saying, 'I use it for screening purposes only.' There is no support for this use, either. Using the WRAT-R for screening may result in a great disservice to students" (Harrison, 1987b).

- "Clearly the time saved in using the WRAT-R is not worth the potential cost in diagnostic errors which are likely (in fact probable) when using this threadbare test. . . . Unless one is in need of a quick and dirty assessment of achievement, there is absolutely no reason to ever use the WRAT-R. A number of tests exist which provide information which is more comprehensive, more accurate, more diagnostically useful, and more relevant for planning instruction. In fact, one is far better off using informal testing procedures than to use the WRAT-R" (Witt, 1986, pp. 89–90).

Will these scathing reviews of the WRAT-R curtail its widespread use in clinical practice? Naaaaah!

Woodcock-Johnson Psycho-Educational Battery—Revised: Achievement

The 1977 edition of the Woodcock-Johnson, Achievement portion (Woodcock & Johnson, 1977), provided a thorough 10-subtest measure of academic achievement that yielded reliable clusters (mid-.90s) in the areas of Reading, Mathematics, Written Language, and Knowledge. The achievement battery was among the three most popular tests of achievement used for adults in the survey conducted by Harrison et al. (1988). Although it trailed the WRAT (or WRAT-R) and PIAT by a substantial margin (see pp. 13–14), users of the WJ/A were quite satisfied with it, much more so than WRAT or PIAT users were with their choice of batteries; it was also considered an exceptional achievement test by WJ reviewers (Cummings, 1985; Hager, 1986; Kaufman, 1985b).

The 1989 revision of the Woodcock-Johnson Achievement battery (WJ-R/A; Woodcock & Johnson, 1989b) is expanded to 14 subtests, 9 of which compose the Standard Battery, and 5 supplementary tests. The instrument was standardized on the same large sample of 6,359 individuals aged 2 to 90+ years described on page 599. Like the 1977 WJ/A, the revised achievement battery includes subtests and clusters that are quite reliable. Median cluster reliabilities for adolescents and adults ranged from .93 (Broad Written Language) to .96 (Broad Mathematics, Skills) for the five areas of achievement assessed by the Standard Battery. Median reliabilities for adolescents and adults ranged from .88 to .94 for the 9 Standard subtests and from .76 (Writing Fluency) to .94 (Calculation) for all 14 tasks (Woodcock & Mather, 1989b, Tables 6-5 and 6-6).

Description of the Subtests

The 14 WJ-R/A subtests are listed below by curricular area. The nine subtests in the Standard battery (two to three per Achievement cluster) are listed first in each curricular area and asterisked. Parentheses following the test name indicate (a) whether the subtest is old, i.e., from the 1977 WJ with little modification, or new to the 1989 edition; and (b) its median reliability coefficient for the five adolescent and adult age groups for which Woodcock and Mather (1989b, Table 6-5) provided data (ages 13, 18, 30–39, 50–59, and 70–79). The Written Language Supplemental battery includes separate scores in Punctuation and Capitalization (P), Spelling (S), Usage (U), and Handwriting (H), in addition to the two supplementary subtests. The P, S, U, and H scores are derived from the various Achievement subtests composing the Written Language cluster.

Reading

*Letter-Word Identification (old, .90 reliability). The subject recognizes letters and reads words of increasing difficulty.

*Passage Comprehension (old, .89 reliability). The subject identifies and states the missing word in passages that are read silently.

Word Attack (old, .90 reliability). The subject reads nonsense words or uncommon real words by applying phonetic rules.

Reading Vocabulary (new, .92 reliability). The subject reads words and demonstrates understanding by stating either the word's synonym (Part A) or antonym (Part B).

Mathematics

*Calculation (old, .94 reliability). The subject performs mathematical calculations ranging from simple arithmetic operations to complex computations.

*Applied Problems (old, .93 reliability). The subject solves practical mathematical problems presented orally, many with pictorial stimuli.

Quantitative Concepts (old, .89 reliability; formerly part of the WJ Cognitive, not

Achievement, Battery). The subject demonstrates knowledge of mathematical concepts, symbols, and vocabulary.

Written Language

*Dictation (old, .92 reliability). The subject responds in writing to demonstrate knowledge of spelling, punctuation, capitalization, and language usage.

*Writing Samples (new, .89 reliability). The subject writes responses to a variety of demands to demonstrate the quality of his or her written expression.

Proofing (old, .91 reliability). The subject identifies and corrects errors in typewritten sentences.

Writing Fluency (new, .76 reliability). The subject formulates and writes simple sentences as rapidly as possible.

Knowledge

*Science (old, .88 reliability). The subject demonstrates factual knowledge in the areas of the biological and physical sciences.

*Social Studies (old, .89 reliability). The subject demonstrates factual knowledge in domains of social studies such as geography, government, and economics.

*Humanities (old, .90 reliability). The subject demonstrates factual knowledge related to art, music, and literature.

Special Features and Evaluation

The authors of the WJ-R/A (Woodcock & Johnson, 1989b) have improved their battery considerably to make it even more appealing to practitioners who are able to devote much administration time to tests of achievement. The revised battery comes in alternate forms A and B, comprises 14 subtests (9 in the Standard Battery and 5 in the Supplemental Battery), and includes expanded measures of writing ability. Moreover, the WJ-R/A is co-normed with a complete Cognitive battery on a large (over 6,300 people), fairly representative national sample across the wide age range of 2 to 90+ years (see page 599). Tables are provided to permit computation of discrepancy scores for aptitude/achievement comparisons, and profile data include relative mastery indexes (RMIs), complex cluster difference scores (DIFFs), and a variety of converted scores to facilitate learning disabilities assessment.

The WJ-R/A's normative sample is good and its technical qualities are excellent. It is truly a wide-range, state-of-the-art, updated, and comprehensive measure of academic achievement that has the advantage of being standardized across the entire childhood, adolescent, and adult age span. As with the WJ/A and the WJ and WJ-R Cognitive batteries, however, the relative complexity of the scores and the sophisticated interpretive system will confuse some examiners and result in clerical errors. The scoring system for the new Writing Samples subtest is time-consuming and subjective; it makes the scoring systems for Wechsler's Vocabulary and Comprehension subtests, long sources of complaint to clinicians, seem objective by comparison.

Kaufman Test of Educational Achievement: Brief and Comprehensive Forms

The K-TEA (Kaufman & Kaufman, 1985a, 1985b) is an individually administered achievement battery normed for grades 1–12 (ages 6–18) that offers two forms, a Brief Form for quick screening of academic achievement, and a Comprehensive Form for in-depth measurement of achievement, including the assessment of strengths and weaknesses in very specific skills, operations, and processes. The Brief Form yields scores in Reading, Mathematics, and Spelling; the five-subtest Comprehensive Form provides assessment of Reading Decoding,

Reading Comprehension, Mathematics Applications, Mathematics Computation, and Spelling. The Brief Form offers a Battery Composite, and the Comprehensive Form provides three global composites: Reading, Mathematics, Total Battery. The two forms do not overlap in item content, and have separate manuals. All subtest and composite scores for both forms are standard scores (mean = 100, SD = 15), derivable from either grade-based norms or age-based norms. The Brief Form requires about 30 minutes to administer and the Comprehensive Form about 55–75 minutes, although testing times are considerably less for young school-age children.

Description of K-TEA Brief Subtests

Reading: The subject identifies letters and pronounces a steeply graded list of words (the easier half of test) and then demonstrates reading comprehension by responding orally or by gesture to commands appearing in printed statements (the harder half of test).

Mathematics: The subject solves written computational problems using paper and pencil (the easier half of test) and then demonstrates knowledge of basic concepts and the ability both to reason numerically and to apply mathematical principles to real-life problems, via oral and visual stimuli (the harder half of test).

Spelling: The subject writes or prints (or spells orally if writing is difficult) a steeply graded list of words said aloud and used in a sentence by the examiner.

Description of K-TEA Comprehensive Subtests

Reading Decoding: The subject identifies letters and pronounces words of gradually increasing difficulty.

Reading Comprehension: For most items, the subject reads short paragraphs and then responds orally to one or two questions at the end of each paragraph that he or she must also read; the easiest and most difficult items require the subject to respond orally or by gesture to commands appearing in printed statements.

Mathematics Applications: The subject demonstrates knowledge of basic concepts and the ability both to reason numerically and to apply mathematical principles to real-life problems, via oral and visual stimuli.

Mathematics Computation: The subject solves written computational problems using paper and pencil, showing knowledge of the four basic operations and complex operations such as algebra.

Spelling: The subject writes or prints (or spells orally if writing is difficult) a list of words of gradually increasing difficulty said aloud and used in a sentence by the examiner.

Technical Qualities

Brief Form subtests had an average split-half reliability coefficient of .85–.87 for adolescents (ages 12–18 years), along with stability coefficients of similar magnitude. Comprehensive Form subtests had average split-half coefficients of .92–.95 for adolescents, and also had closely similar stability coefficients. The Brief Form Battery Composite had split-half and stability coefficients in the low to mid-.90s for adolescents; the three Comprehensive Form composites produced values invariably in the .96–.98 range. Reliability and stability estimates for children (ages 6–11) were a little higher than the values observed for adolescents on the Brief Form, but were virtually identical to adolescent values on the Comprehensive Form.

The Comprehensive Form was normed twice, permitting the development of separate norms for the fall (N = 1,067) and spring (N = 1,409). The Brief Form was standardized in the fall on 589 individuals who were also tested on the Comprehensive Form to allow for the application of the "equipercentile equating" technique; i.e., the Brief Form was equated to the

Comprehensive Form to permit construction of fall and spring norms for both versions of the K-TEA. Normative samples for the Brief and Comprehensive Forms matched Census figures quite closely on the stratification variables of grade level, sex, geographic region, socio-economic status (parental occupation), and race or ethnic group; age and educational placement (regular or special education classes) were secondary stratification variables. Dickinson (1986) pointed out that for the Brief Form, "[t]he grade level samples were quite small" (p. 334), averaging about 50 per group.

The K-TEA manuals provide considerable evidence of content, construct, and concurrent validity. Test reviewers (e.g., Henson & Bennett, 1985) have praised the K-TEA as being "technically strong and . . . designed with the needs of the practitioner in mind" (p. 326); the test authors heeded well the "necessary precautions for controlling for reliability and construct and content validity" (p. 374). Lewandowski (1986) noted that the "construction, standardization, and statistical characteristics of the K-TEA are all exceptional" (p. 260), but warned: "[T]he only available information on validity is presented in the test manual. This is clearly a limitation and one that will require time and future research to resolve" (p. 260).

Special Features and Evaluation

The availability of two forms of the K-TEA, one for quick screening and one for in-depth assessment, is a special feature of the K-TEA, as are the separate fall and spring norms and the systematic, empirical system for interpreting strengths and weaknesses within both the Brief and Comprehensive profiles. The Brief Form measures both decoding and comprehension on its Reading subtest, and assesses quantitative concepts, arithmetic reasoning, and computational skills on its Mathematics subtest. The Comprehensive Form provides an error analysis to allow examiners to determine a person's specific assets and deficits on finite skills, pro-

cesses, and operations within each academic area. Figure 16.2 illustrates this norm- and criterion-referenced technique, showing the different pattern of errors displayed in Mathematics Computation for two children earning the identical raw score.

Based on the error analysis, "[t]eachers can use the results from the K-TEA to address accurately the specific areas for remediation" (Roberts, 1988, p. 30). "The Comprehensive Form, with its breakdown of skills, offers the practitioner a very effective tool for helping teachers improve instructional programs for individual students" (Worthington, 1987, p. 326). In addition, the "Brief Form offers a number of advantages over other brief form tests" (Dickinson, 1986, p. 336); to Worthington (1987), it's "an instrument far superior to most on the market for quick assessment of skills (p. 326), and "is an excellent alternative to the WRAT-R" (Reynolds, 1986a, p. 1).

Like the WJ/A, the K-TEA has been reviewed very favorably. According to Lewandowski (1986), for example: "The K-TEA is a state of the art test in several ways. . . . The test is simple in format and easy to administer. . . . It has several advantages over similar achievement tests, primarily its two forms, actuarial approach, conceptual framework, and method for error analysis. . . . The weaknesses of the K-TEA are not major or glaring ones" (pp. 260–261). The major disadvantages of the K-TEA are (a) a limited floor for young school-age children, and a limited ceiling for high-functioning adults (Lewandowski, 1986; Reynolds, 1986a); (b) the separate norms for fall and spring and extensive interpretive system have a downside, namely potential confusion in selecting the right norms table (Roberts, 1988), insufficient cautions regarding the interpretation of abnormal scatter (Dickinson, 1986), questionable classification of two math items (Radencich, 1986), and the need for a sophisticated practitioner to interpret the profiles (Henson & Bennett, 1985; Worthington, 1987); and (c) lack of coverage of all seven areas needed for LD assessment, e.g., listening comprehension (Wor-

Error Analysis Summary

Mathematics Computation	Number of Items Attempted	Average Number of Errors	Student's Number of Errors	Skill Status		
				Weak[a]	Average[b]	Strong[c]
SKILL CATEGORY	Table 22	Table 22	Page 11			
Basic Addition	6	0	0	W	(A)	S
Regrouping Addition	5	0 - 1	2	(W)	A	S
Basic Subtraction	6	0	0	W	(A)	S
Regrouping Subtraction	4	1 - 3	4	(W)	A	S
Multiplication	6	1 - 2	0	W	A	(S)
Division	2	—	1	W	A	S
Fractions	1	—	1	W	A	S
Advanced Addition	1	—	1	W	A	S
Advanced Subtraction	0	—	0	W	A	S
Algebraic Equations	0	—	0	W	A	S
Square Roots & Exponents	0	—	0	W	A	S

Mathematics Computation	Number of Items Attempted	Average Number of Errors	Student's Number of Errors	Skill Status		
				Weak[a]	Average[b]	Strong[c]
SKILL CATEGORY	Table 22	Table 22	Page 11			
Basic Addition	6	0	0	W	(A)	S
Regrouping Addition	5	0	0	W	(A)	S
Basic Subtraction	6	0	0	W	(A)	S
Regrouping Subtraction	4	1 - 2	0	W	A	(S)
Multiplication	7	1 - 2	6	(W)	A	S
Division	4	3	4	(W)	A	S
Fractions	2	—	2	W	A	S
Advanced Addition	1	—	1	W	A	S
Advanced Subtraction	0	—	0	W	A	S
Algebraic Equations	2	—	1	W	A	S
Square Roots & Exponents	0	—	0	W	A	S

[a]Student's Number of Errors is greater than the Average Number of Errors
[b]Student's Number of Errors is equal to (or within the range of) the Average Number of Errors
[c]Student's Number of Errors is less than the Average Number of Errors

FIGURE 16.2

The Mathematics Computation Error Analysis Summary on the K-TEA Comprehensive Form, completed for two students who obtained the same Mathematics Computation standard score. (Reprinted with permission of American Guidance Service.)

thington, 1987). For the purpose of adult assessment, a clear shortcoming is the lack of adult norms. Currently, adult data are being gathered for the K-TEA Brief Form during the standardization program for the Kaufman Adolescent and Adult Intelligence Test (KAIT; Kaufman & Kaufman, in press a).

Peabody Individual Achievement Test—Revised

The original PIAT enjoyed fairly widespread use for children and adults (see pp. 13–14), although in a survey of tests used for adolescents and adults (Harrison et al., 1988), PIAT users were even less satisfied than WRAT-R users with their achievement test. The updated, revised, and restandardized battery (PIAT-R; Markwardt, 1989) includes six subtests, five from the old PIAT and a new Written Expression subtest. There are numerous new items in the PIAT-R subtests, although the format of each retained subtest is the same. Like the PPVT-R, Mathematics, Spelling, and Reading Comprehension are still composed of four-choice multiple-choice items, introducing errors of measurement due to chance when subjects guess. When used with the WAIS-R, clinicians must be aware of the substantial overlap between Markwardt's construct of achievement and Wechsler's construct of verbal intelligence; both include measures of arithmetic and general information.

The PIAT-R is normed from grades K through 12 and ages 5 through 18 years, with norms provided by both age and grade. The PIAT-R yields standard scores (mean = 100, SD = 15) for each of the five old subtests, General Information, Reading Recognition, Reading Comprehension, Mathematics, and Spelling, and for three composites: Reading, Written Language (combining scores on Spelling and Written Expression), and Total Test (excluding Written Expression, however). Two levels of Written Expression are provided, Level I, which assesses prewriting skills for grades K and 1, and Level II for grades 2 through 12. Scores for Written Expression are stanines for both levels, and norm-based developmental scaled scores for Level II. Estimated administration time of the PIAT-R is 60 minutes.

Description of Subtests

General Information: The subject responds to questions of general factual information presented orally.

Reading Recognition: The subject demonstrates understanding of the shapes and sounds of letters and pronounces words of gradually increasing difficulty.

Reading Comprehension: The subject reads a sentence silently, and on the next page (with the sentence no longer in view) selects the one picture out of four that best illustrates that sentence.

Mathematics: The subject demonstrates knowledge and application of mathematical concepts and facts, ranging from number recognition to geometry and trigonometry, via a four-choice multiple-choice format.

Spelling: The subject shows letter recognition and then must select the one word out of four that is spelled correctly.

Written Expression: The subject demonstrates prewriting skills such as copying letters and words from dictation (Level I), or writes a story in response to a picture prompt (Level II).

Technical Qualities

The 60-minute estimate of administration time seems low in view of the length of the subtests, each of which was lengthened by exactly 16 items: The Reading Comprehension subtest is now composed of 82 items, while the other four regular subtests each comprise 100 items; the 20%–25% increase in test length may have been done, in part, to offset the chance factors associated with the four-choice multiple-choice format of three PIAT-R subtests. (By contrast, the K-TEA Comprehensive Form includes 50–60 items in each of its five subtests.) That Markwardt (1989) was indeed successful is indicated by the outstanding split-half reliability coefficients obtained for the five subtests: Medians of .93 to .96 were obtained for adolescents (ages 12–18 years), with similar results observed for children aged 5–11 years. Coefficients for the composites were phenomenal, ranging as high as .99 for Total Test. Nonetheless, I am troubled by the chance factors at work in the three multiple-choice subtests. An individual on a hot streak, or a person with rotten luck, can produce distorted estimates of their ability level.

This hunch was upheld by the test–retest reliability data. Even though the median stability coefficients for the five regular subtests were good, averaging .90–.96 for eight age groups between 6 and 16 years (sample sizes of 23 to 39), they were erratic for Mathematics and Reading Comprehension. Values for these subtests dipped as low as .65, with three of the eight coefficients for Mathematics falling below .80. This type of wild inconsistency did not occur for the other three PIAT-R tasks, but one value for Spelling (also a multiple-choice test) was below .80.

Reliability coefficients for the Written Expression subtest are presented in a number of ways, and none of the results are very encouraging. Interrater reliabilities ranged from .30 to .81 (median of .58) for one Level II picture used to prompt a story, and from .53 to .77 (median of .67) for the other picture prompt. Alternate "form" reliability coefficients ranged from .44 to .61. Although values of coefficient alpha were higher, this technique is inappropriate when items are not experimentally independent.

The standardization sample was composed of 1,563 individuals, 97–148 at each grade level between K and 12. Sample characteristics provided a close match to Census data on the variables of sex, geographic region, socioeconomic status (parental education), and race or ethnic group. The only questionable procedure is offering norms for 5-year-olds based on a total sample of 45 children.

Special Features and Evaluation

The new Written Expression subtest is a special feature of the PIAT-R, as is the Written Language composite composed of the Spelling and Written Expression subtests. In view of the extreme unreliability of the latter task, it is difficult to imagine that its score will prove especially valuable. The Written Language composite is reliable, mostly because of the contribution of Spelling, and may be useful for diagnosis of learning disabilities. I have always been concerned about the PIAT Reading Comprehension task because its format depends on short-term memory (the printed sentence is removed from view when the subject selects the picture that illustrates the sentence) as well as visual perception skills. Similarly, the multiple-choice format for three of the subtests has always troubled me. The superb split-half reliability coefficients suggest that the problem may not be as severe as I have feared, but the stability coefficients indicate that there is indeed a problem. The new Reading composite standard score is good, and its reliability (averaging .97) is outstanding.

The PIAT-R is easy to administer and, except for the new Written Expression subtest, easy to score. The standardization sample, like the reliability coefficients, is excellent. The Manual's lack of criterion-related validity coefficients with other reading tests, however, is regrettable. The content of the PIAT-R is much updated (only 35% of the PIAT items were retained), and the Manual offers good evidence of content validity (Markwardt, 1989, Part IV). The factor analysis reported in the Manual fails to support the construct underlying the new Reading composite, as each Reading task loaded highest on a different factor. Markwardt did offer an informative chapter on proper interpretation of test scores and of the resultant profile (Markwardt, 1989, Part III). Overall, the PIAT-R does not measure up to the WJ-R/A or K-TEA as a measure of achievement, although it is far superior to the WRAT-R.

Woodcock Reading Mastery Test—Revised

The WRMT-R (Woodcock, 1987) provides in-depth assessment of diverse aspects of the reading process. It contains a readiness section, a cluster of basic skills, and several measures of reading comprehension, both of separate words and sentences. The WRMT-R (pronounced "Worm-Tar" by the publisher's staff, but probably most often called "Woodcock Reading" by practitioners) comes in two forms, G and H, although only Form G includes all subtests; Form H contains only the Basic Skills and Reading Comprehension clusters. The WRMT-R is normed from age 5 to 75+ years, and averages about 45 minutes of administration time for the complete battery (Form G); the Readiness cluster takes about 15 minutes to give. In addition to cluster scores in Readiness, Basic Skills, and Reading Comprehension, the WRMT-R offers scores labeled Total Reading—Full Scale (Basic Skills + Reading Comprehension clusters), and Total Reading—Short Scale (Word Identification + Passage Comprehension subtests).

The battery offers age-based and grade-based scores and bears a strong resemblance to the WJ and WJ-R, both Cognitive and Achievement portions. Like the WJ, the WRMT-R offers W-scores (the Rasch model–based standard scores depicted in Figure 16.1) and Relative Performance Indexes, an interpretive approach that sometimes baffles clinicians from the Wechsler mold. The WRMT-R actually borrows a WJ subtest (Visual-Auditory Learning) for its Readiness cluster, uses reading analogs of WJ Cognitive subtests on the Word Comprehension subtest, contains extremely similar reading subtests (e.g., Passage Comprehension), and uses items closely resembling those on the WJ (or WJ-R) specialized tests of knowledge in areas like social studies and science. The addition of subtests like Reading Vocabulary to the WJ-R/A makes the overlap between WRMT-R and WJ even greater.

Description of the Subtests

Readiness Cluster
Visual-Auditory Learning: This is the same task appearing in the WJ-R, Cognitive portion.
Letter Identification: The subject identifies uppercase and lowercase letters presented in various styles of type (there is also a criterion-referenced Supplementary Letter Checklist).

Basic Skills Cluster
Word Identification: The subject reads words presented in isolation.
Word Attack: The subject reads nonsense words or uncommon real words by applying phonetic rules.

Reading Comprehension Cluster
Word Comprehension: Composed of three tasks. The subject responds to written words by providing the opposite (Antonyms), the synonym (Synonyms), or the answer to an incomplete analogy (Analogies). (Items may also be grouped across the three subtests to provide scores in General Reading, Science-Mathematics, Social Studies, and Humanities).
Passage Comprehension: The subject identifies and states the missing word in passages (typically one or two sentences in length) that are read silently.

Technical Qualities

Reliability coefficients are generally good for the subtests and excellent for the clusters. Median split-half reliability coefficients on the subtests for adolescents and adults (grade 8, grade 11, college students, and adults) ranged from .86 for Word Attack to .96 on Word Identification; only the values for Passage Comprehension displayed wide variability (.68–.92). Cluster reliabilities for adolescents and adults averaged .94–.96. Reliabilities for children tended to be a bit higher. Unfortunately, no stability data are provided. Evidence of content validity is satisfactory, but the key issue of construct validity is ignored, and criterion-related validity for the revised battery is meager (correlations with WJ/A Reading cluster for four grade levels).

The WRMT-R standardization sample includes 4,201 individuals from grades K through 12, plus 1,023 college students (to produce separate college norms), and 865 subjects aged

20 to over 75 who were not enrolled in college. The three samples matched Census data reasonably well on the stratification variables of sex, race, origin (Hispanic, non-Hispanic), and geographic region. The school-age sample matched Census data on community size, but the percentages were a bit off for the adult sample. This variable was not used for the college population, but instead matched Census proportions on type of institution (public/private, university/other 4-year/2-year). The adult sample matched Census data on educational attainment, occupational status (employed, unemployed, not in labor force), and occupational type (white collar/blue collar and farm/service). Weighting procedures were applied to improve the match of sample to Census. However, a serious shortcoming of the norms is the failure to stratify grades K–12 and college samples on the crucial variable of socio-economic status. Another problem is the failure to present normative data separately by grade level for the K–12 sample, or by age level for the adult sample.

Special Features and Evaluation

The WRMT-R has several features that distinguish it: Thorough coverage of many aspects of the reading process; alternate forms; designated places on the Test Record to record errors, facilitating informal error analysis; a comprehensive Manual, replete with guidelines for test interpretation on many levels, sophisticated empirical procedures, instructional suggestions, and case studies; and well-stratified norms for adults across the entire lifespan. Although the adult norms are an excellent feature, reading comprehension is only measured one word at a time or in passages that do not exceed three sentences, a serious problem that Radencich (1988) described as "severely limiting at the intermediate level and above" (pp. 171–172). She further criticized the WRMT-R for its incomplete evaluation of reading because it "does not adequately consider many of the factors that

recent research has pointed to as critical to reading assessment—interest level . . ., level of prior knowledge . . . , ability to read narrative vs. different patterns of expository writing" (p. 172), and so forth. Nonetheless, Radencich conceded that no available test takes all the pertinent factors into account, and the "WRMT-R is one of the most carefully constructed reading tests on the market" (p. 173).

Failure to stratify the grade K–12 and college norms groups on socio-economic status is a great liability, as is the Manual's lack of stability data and virtual lack of concurrent and construct validity data. In addition, examiners need to be quite sophisticated with numbers to benefit from the numerous helpful interpretive guidelines provided (and even to interpret the yielded profiles of scores.) The new WJ-R/A regular and supplementary Reading cluster is probably a better choice than the WRMT-R for thorough measurement of an individual's reading ability, although both of these batteries—along with the K-TEA Comprehensive Form Reading Composite, with its systematic approach to error analysis—are excellent WAIS-R supplements when detailed understanding of reading ability is called for.

ILLUSTRATIVE CASE REPORT

The report that follows of Clara S., a 52-year-old woman who suffered brain damage following meningitis at age 40, demonstrates the integration of the WAIS-R with the Vineland Adaptive Behavior Scales (discussed in chapter 15) and with several of the instruments treated in the present chapter: Woodcock-Johnson, Cognitive portion (1977 ed.); PPVT-R; and K-TEA, Brief Form. See also the two illustrative reports at the end of chapter 11 and the single case reports at the end of chapter 14 and chapter 15 for further examples of the integration of WAIS-R scores with data yielded by supplementary instruments.

Clara S., Age 52, Brain Damage (Meningitis)

Referral and Background Information

Clara S., a 52-year-old married Caucasian woman who is the mother of three children, was referred for post-illness psychometric evaluation. She suffered damage to the right hemisphere, and possibly to the frontal lobes of her brain, as a result of a prolonged episode of cryptococci meningitis at age 40. The purpose of this evaluation was to establish Clara's current level of functioning and to provide guidance by evaluating her present capabilities.

Prior to the onset of Clara's illness, she was involved in numerous community activities and was employed as a bookkeeper in a professional office. She reportedly exhibited particularly good typing skills and was adept at mathematics. She had a high energy level and generally optimistic outlook.

The incubation period for cryptococci meningitis is unknown; however, Clara and her husband report having noticed personality and behavioral changes approximately 1 year before the critical phase of her illness. She began a period of time in which she suffered from depression, severe headaches, and general malaise in addition to flattened affect and a decline in social judgment. By the time a spinal tap provided the clinical data that resulted in an appropriate diagnosis, her brain had been subjected to intense pressure from acquired hydrocephalus, and she required surgery. Following surgery, Clara remained in a coma for 30 to 40 days; for several weeks after regaining consciousness, she experienced delusions accompanied by visual and auditory hallucinations. Clara has no memory of the time in which she was so critically ill; however, when she regained consciousness it became apparent to those around her that significant cognitive and motor damage had resulted.

Clara and her family stated that she has made slow but steady progress during her postoper-ative years in terms of her ability to function independently. However, she continues to suffer from deficits in fine motor skills, equilibrium, and spatial orientation, and her social skills and planning abilities reportedly continue to be deficient.

A neuropsychological evaluation using the Wechsler Adult Intelligence Scale—Revised (WAIS-R) was conducted 3 years ago (9 years following her illness). At that time she achieved a Verbal IQ of 100 (50th percentile), a Performance IQ of 75 (5th percentile), and a Full Scale IQ of 88 (21st percentile). In addition, based on her scores on specific subtests, her intellectual ability before her illness was estimated to have been in the Superior range.

Though the difficulties Clara has encountered have adversely affected her self-esteem and self-confidence, she has in recent years begun developing compensatory strategies that have enabled her to resume driving a car and acquire the skills required for independent living.

Appearance and Behavioral Characteristics

Clara is a tall, slim, well-groomed lady who exhibited remarkable poise throughout the evaluation. The only outward manifestations of impairment were her use of a cane and her lack of bilateral hand movement. She relied almost exclusively on the use of her right hand, though she did use her left to provide stability on some of the drawing tests. Her handwriting was neat.

Clara's conversational skills were good, and she spoke without problems in articulation. She responded appropriately on a variety of topics, and demonstrated adequate fluency. Her verbal responses tended to be concrete. For instance, she defined winter as "cold weather," said that "dog" and "lion" were alike because "they have four legs," and that a "coat" and "suit" "both have sleeves." Seldom did she respond with an abstract idea such as an overall category (i.e., seasons, animals, clothing).

Throughout the tests, Clara demonstrated better receptive than expressive skills. She was able to see errors in her work when copying drawings even when she was not able to execute the task correctly. She often understood concepts that she found difficult to express or for which she was unable to immediately retrieve the needed vocabulary.

She tolerated frustration well, often responding to it with humor. On one occasion, an examiner told Clara that the items on a particular subtest would not be as difficult as ones she had attempted previously. When the task became more complex, Clara laughingly stated, "You lied."

She appeared to appraise her own strengths and weaknesses realistically—conceding, for example, that she was not good at puzzles or at tasks involving directionality. She acknowledged and accepted matter-of-factly both success and failure. At no time did she make an effort to apologize for deficiencies; however, she appeared to give good effort, consistently working until the end of time limits.

Numerous compensatory strategies were noted. Among these were talking herself through her motor tasks or ones that involved perception of spatial orientation; posturing with her left hand to improve her stability and balance; and counting dots or rotating cards of abstract designs in order to "see" more accurately. When working one of the puzzle items, Clara commented on the absence of lines, indicating that she was seeking and depending on additional visual cues to solve the puzzle.

The tempo of Clara's work was somewhat reflective. She demonstrated adequate stamina and virtually no distractibility.

Good rapport was easily established, and the results of this evaluation may be considered a valid assessment of Clara's current level of functioning.

Test Results and Interpretation

On the WAIS-R Clara obtained a Full Scale IQ of 84, which classifies her in the Low Average range of intelligence and ranks her at the 14th percentile for people her age. The chances are 9 out of 10 that her true Full Scale IQ falls within the range of 80 to 88. Her Performance IQ of 78 (7th percentile) is significantly lower than her Verbal IQ of 92 (30th percentile) at the .01 level of confidence. This indicates that Clara functions better when expressing her intelligence verbally than when manipulating concrete nonverbal materials.

A high Verbal, low Performance profile is typical of an individual who has sustained damage to the right hemisphere, although the magnitude of her V–P discrepancy (14 points) is neither unusual nor abnormal for adults of Low Average intelligence. Clara displayed numerous compensatory strategies that probably helped to minimize her Verbal–Performance difference. For example, when arranging blocks in patterns or looking for missing elements in a picture, she frequently talked her way through the activity, relying on her stronger verbal skills to help compensate for deficits in perceptual abilities.

There was relatively little scatter within the scales; however, it was noted that Clara's relative strength on the Performance Scale related to tasks requiring automatic level responses and visual memory (copying symbols and observing missing elements in a picture, scoring at about the 31st percentile relative to other adults her approximate age).

When presented with nonverbal reasoning tasks, Clara was markedly deficient. She was unable to put together three out of four puzzles of concrete objects (1st percentile) and could not arrange pictures to tell a story (5th percentile). In direct contrast was her good verbal reasoning ability (37th percentile), whether in telling how two objects are alike or responding to socially relevant questions, and her adequate visual memory.

The present WAIS-R global scores are very similar to the data obtained 3 years ago. The change in Clara's Verbal IQ (from 100 to 92) could represent a decline in abilities, but it could also be the result of errors in measurement.

TABLE 16.7   Clara S.: Tests administered

Wechsler Adult Intelligence Scale—Revised (WAIS-R)

Verbal	Scaled Score	Age-Corrected Scaled Score	Performance	Scaled Score	Age-Corrected Scaled Score
Information	8	(8)	Picture Completion	7	(9)—S
Digit Span	7	(8)	Picture Arrangement	4	(5)
Vocabulary	10	(10)	Block Design	5	(6)
Arithmetic	7	(8)	Object Assembly	2	(3)—W
Comprehension	9	(9)	Digit Symbol	6	(8)
Similarities	8	(9)			

Age-Corrected Verbal Mean = 9   Age-Corrected Performance Mean = 6

Verbal IQ = 92 ± 4

Performance IQ = 78 ± 6

Full Scale IQ = 84 ± 4

Woodcock-Johnson Psycho-educational Battery (1977 ed.)

PART I—TESTS OF COGNITIVE ABILITY

Scales	Percentiles
Verbal Ability	54
Perceptual Speed	16
Reasoning	20
Memory	19

Overall Performance (12 subtests) = 18th percentile

Relative Strengths	Relative Weaknesses
Antonyms/Synonyms	Blending
Picture Vocabulary	Visual-Auditory Learning
Memory for Sentences	Spatial Relations
Analogies	Analysis-Synthesis

Peabody Picture Vocabulary Test—Revised (PPVT-R)

Receptive Vocabulary Standard Score: 104 (60th percentile)

Kaufman Assessment Battery for Children (K-ABC)

Gestalt Closure: Scaled Score = 3 (Based on 12-year-olds' norms; mean = 10)

Percentile rank = 1st

TABLE 16.7 (Continued)

Bender-Gestalt Test of Visual-Motor Integration

Koppitz error score = 5

Age equivalent = 7-6 to 7-11

Trail Making

(Based on data obtained by American Guidance Service during a large national tryout of the Kaufman Adolescent and Adult Intelligence Test)

Percentile rank = 6th

McCarthy Scales of Children's Abilities

Verbal Fluency: No deficit

Wechsler Intelligence Scale for Children—Revised (WISC-R)

Mazes: Scaled score = 3 (Based on 16–11 norms; mean = 10)

Percentile rank = Less than 1st

Kaufman—Test of Educational Achievement (K-TEA) Brief Form

	Standard Score	Percentile Rank
(Based on norms for 18-year-olds)		
Reading	99	47
Spelling	91	27
Math	81	10
Total Battery	88	21

Vineland Adaptive Behavior Scales, Expanded Form

(Based on interviews with Clara S. and Mr. S., her husband)

Domain	Adaptive Level
Communication	Low (Mild Deficit)
Daily Living Skills	Adequate
Socialization	Moderately Low
Adaptive Behavior Composite	Moderately Low
Motor (estimated)	Low
Weak Subdomains	
Expressive Communication	Moderately Low
Written Communication	Moderately Low
Socialization/Play and Leisure	Low

Basically the scores indicate that the skills tested are quite stable.

A statistical analysis for calculating approximate premorbid IQ (Barona, Reynolds, & Chastain, 1984) was used to estimate Clara's pre-illness intelligence. This procedure yielded a premorbid Verbal IQ of 104 ± 12, Performance IQ of 103 ± 13, and Full Scale IQ of 104 ± 12, suggesting that her ability level prior to her illness was solidly in the Average range. Based on the previous evaluation, her premorbid IQ was estimated as Superior, but the estimate of Average derived from the Barona/Reynolds formula is probably more accurate.

Clara's overall performance on the Woodcock-Johnson was at the 18th percentile, supporting the WAIS-R assessment of Low Average intellectual functioning. As on the WAIS-R, her verbal abilities emerged as a strength (54th percentile), displayed particularly in her knowledge of vocabulary, synonyms and antonyms, and skill at solving verbal analogies.

Clara had the most difficulty with tasks requiring the integration of abstract or visual-spatial information, as measured by the Perceptual Speed, Reasoning, and Memory scales; her scores ranged from the 16th to the 20th percentile. Reasoning tasks that required Clara to analyze the components of visual-spatial information and use this information to solve a puzzle were especially difficult, reinforcing similar findings on the WAIS-R. Rebus-reading tasks, identifying pictured pieces that fit together to match a given shape, or combining concepts such as round, red, and small to explain inclusion in a group presented problems for Clara. However, when she could use verbal strengths to aid in reasoning tasks (e.g., solving analogies) her success was evident, as it was on the WAIS-R.

Clara demonstrated a relative strength in short-term memory when she was asked to repeat sentences verbatim; however, she experienced difficulty with remembering and reversing a series of digits. This latter deficit is consistent with right hemisphere damage.

Overall strengths and weaknesses can be interpreted in terms of old and new learning efficiency. Her use of previously learned skills, particularly those related to word knowledge, general information, and quantitative concepts, was within normal limits. However, Clara's facility with new learning (learning new visual symbols for familiar words, synthesizing words from disjointed sounds, and learning color equivalency patterns in order to solve puzzles) was markedly deficient.

Difficulty in integrating information was evident throughout testing. On a purely perceptual task of integrative capacity requiring her to identify pictures that were only partially drawn, she performed better than only 1 person out of 100. Even at a very basic level, her planning skills are adversely affected by poor integrative abilities. Clara scored at the 5th percentile on tasks requiring her to place a series of pictures in logical sequence, and at less than the 1st percentile in solving mazes. This weakness was further demonstrated by her performance on Trail Making, a timed "dot to dot" task (6th percentile), a measure of both planning and low-level decision making. Verbal fluency, which was measured in terms of her ability to generate names of members of a particular category, was adequate. This test is noted to be a questionable measure of planning.

Verbal and visual receptive skill strengths were demonstrated by Clara's performance on the PPVT-R, a test of receptive vocabulary (60th percentile), and the Bender-Gestalt test, which assessed her ability to copy designs. She erased several times while working on Bender designs, indicating that her receptive ability in terms of perceiving a correct abstract drawing was better than her ability to carry out or express the task. Here again she displayed her ability to compensate for deficits by counting the dots on one design and rotating the paper to help herself on another.

Achievement as measured by the K-TEA (Brief Form) indicated that Clara's reading ability was at the 47th percentile, spelling at the

27th percentile, and mathematics at the 10th percentile, based on norms for 18-year-olds. Clara's reading scores are commensurate with her verbal intelligence, while her level of achievement in spelling and mathematics is more consistent with her overall intelligence, as displayed on both the WAIS-R and Woodcock-Johnson.

Administration of the Vineland (Expanded Form) yielded information in four domains related to adaptation: Communication, Daily Living Skills, Socialization, and Motor Skills. Since specific age norms are not provided for individuals above the age of 18, the qualitative information rather than emprirical scores appear to be pertinent. Clara and her husband were interviewed on separate occasions; his estimation of her adaptive abilities was notably higher than hers. Based on test data and observations, it appears that Clara more accurately assessed her own abilities.

The Communication domain emerged as Clara's weakest area of adaptation, primarily as a result of her limited use of written material and lack of goal verbalization. Daily Living Skills were in the Adequate category. However, Clara reported the need to plan excursions and projects in advance and difficulties with disorientation in public places. Socialization was viewed as Moderately Low to Adequate by both Clara and her husband, with her main deficit in use of leisure time for hobbies, clubs, or other purposeful activity. Clara's difficulties with equilibrium and fine motor skills have limited her adaptability in the Motor domain.

Summary and Recommendations

Clara is a 52-year-old woman who, as a result of cryptococci meningitis, suffers from reported right hemisphere and frontal lobe brain damage. She demonstrates and reports generally adequate adaptive behavior functioning and her achievement level is commensurate with her ability. Her deficits are initially much less apparent than her strengths because her good language and social skills are both readily perceived. She is a personable individual who demonstrates composure, good attention skills, and a disarming sense of humor.

Results of the WAIS-R testing yielded a Verbal IQ of 92, a Performance IQ of 78, and a Full Scale IQ of 84. Verbal abilities clearly emerged as a strength for Clara, not only in her performance on the WAIS-R, but also in terms of ability she demonstrated on the PPVT-R and the Woodcock-Johnson.

She has good verbal comprehension and recall, an average level of acquired knowledge, and a rather concrete (but adequate) level of verbal concept formation. Her reading ability is good, and neat handwriting was noted.

On nonverbal performance type activities, Clara outperformed only 5 to 10 age-mates out of 100, experiencing difficulty with abstract visual-spatial problem solving, planning, and perception. This Verbal>Performance pattern of abilities is typical of an individual with right hemisphere damage. Clara does demonstrate good ability to compensate, using her stronger verbal skills to facilitate functioning in weaker areas.

Another way of looking at the profile of skills is to view her as having an average level of functioning with old learning (that body of knowledge built up over time), and very weak problem-solving skills with which she can address new learning situations.

Clara has shown courage and perseverance in her recovery from her illness, and there are numerous areas in which she is quite capable of functioning well. It is important for her to be aware of her own strengths and weaknesses so that she can adequately judge the extent to which she is achieving her potential and so that she can establish realistic expectations for herself.

In general, avoidance of activities that would require her to develop complex new skills is recommended. Tasks in this category include operating dangerous or complicated machinery or attempting projects that require a good sense of spatial relations. She should continue to drive only if she feels confident and has access to a car with an automatic transmission.

It was noted that there was a significant discrepancy between Clara's and her husband's evaluation of her adaptive abilities. This is probably due to the very significant progress Clara has made since the onset of her illness and to her husband's understandably hopeful attitude. Clara's strong verbal skills and good grasp of old learning may also to some extent mask her more significant deficits. Clara, however, appears to have a very good understanding of her own abilities, and it will be important for both Clara and her husband to accept the limitations addressed by this report, in that these deficiencies appear to be somewhat stable. Mr. S. may wish to seek counseling with a neuropsychologist or clinical psychologist in order to discuss the findings of this evaluation more fully.

Generally, Clara should seek avenues of endeavor in which she can use her very strong verbal and social skills and in which she can deemphasize those skills that demand other types of abilities.

She might want to investigate working as a volunteer in a school or public library. Here she might read to children and perform other duties related to library work.

In addition, she would appear to be well suited for volunteer work in a convalescent home. She could visit with patients and help with tasks such as letter writing or reading, in addition to serving as a very positive example of an individual who is overcoming physical disabilities. Her identified verbal and social skills would also equip her to work as a tutor in an adult literacy program if this were to become an area of interest.

Should Clara decide to seek employment, her skills could be utilized by a telephone answering service, which would require her to speak with callers and relay messages. Various other telephoning jobs are often available, and Clara's very personable nature would be an asset to her in such a position as long as the situation

was not stressful and did not require excessive levels of physical activity.

Examiners and Report Writers: Graduate students in Drs. Nadeen and Alan Kaufman's advanced assessment course at the University of Alabama: Melinda Adkins, Dorothy Bedsole, Jane Bitgood, Martha Blackwell, Janice Griggs, Betty Moorer, Nancy McGriff, Susanne MacGuire, Ruth Oliver, David Payne, Sidney Quarles, and Penny Rogers.

CHAPTER 16 SUMMARY

This chapter described and evaluated the instruments of potential value as supplements to the WAIS-R for assessing adolescents and adults in the following areas: memory, cognitive skills, and academic achievement. The only clinical instrument of note for the assessment of memory is the Wechsler Memory Scale—Revised (WMS-R), Wechsler's revised and restandardized version of the one-score WMS developed in 1945 and used widely in clinical batteries ever since. The WMS-R is normed for ages 16–74 years, but the small standardization sample and low reliabilities of several composites are serious flaws. Major assets of the WMS-R are the factor analytic support and adequate reliability for two of its scales (Attention/Concentration and General Memory), the valuable supplementary information provided by the General Memory scale, and the impressive evidence of the WMS-R's validity for distinguishing among abnormal samples of adults.

Four cognitive tests were reviewed. The Woodcock-Johnson—Revised, Cognitive portion, normed from age 2 to 90+ years, is a recent revision of the 1977 WJ/C that has been totally overhauled and expanded to conform to Horn's theoretical model. Its division into seven cognitive scales and subsequent expansion into a 21-subtest scale provide a wide array of technically excellent and often novel tasks to serve as superb supplements to the WAIS-R. The various tests of controlled learning and fluid intelligence afford the examiner numerous opportunities to follow up hypotheses generated by a person's WAIS-R profile. However, the attempt by Woodcock and Johnson to measure so many separate abilities, each with few tasks, makes the WJ-R/C a less than desirable choice to serve as the primary measure of intelligence for children, adolescents, or adults.

The PPVT-R is a homogeneous test of a single ability (receptive vocabulary), normed from age 2-6 to 40 years, that provides a useful supplement to the WAIS-R because considerable new information can be obtained about a person's verbal ability in a minimal amount of time. The biggest disadvantages of the PPVT-R are the relatively poor norms available for adults and the role played by chance guessing on this four-choice multiple-choice test.

The fourth edition of the Stanford-Binet, developed from a hierarchical theoretical model that incorporates the Horn-Cattell fluid–crystallized dichotomy, was normed from age 2 to 23 years. The test includes several reliable, novel subtests that make superb supplements to the WAIS-R. However, several key flaws in the test development process, especially an inadequately obtained normative sample and failure to validate the multiscale model that purportedly underlies the battery, make the S-B IV a poor choice as the major intelligence test for child, adolescent, or adult assessment. Similarly, the revision of the Detroit battery (DTLA-2) offers a few interesting and reliable subtests to supplement the WAIS-R profile, but this cognitive battery, normed for ages 6–17 years, is beset by difficulties similar to those of the S-B IV: poor norms and lack of empirical support for the underlying model.

Five achievement batteries are discussed, starting with the much-maligned (and deservedly so) WRAT-R. Various reviews of the widely used WRAT-R are integrated with the technical data to portray an instrument that has inadequate empirical support and an unimpressive standardization sample. Although the test is normed for adults as old as 75+ years, the quality of the adult norms is especially poor. The K-TEA Brief Form is seen as a better choice of screening test because of its superior psychometric properties and its inclusion of comprehension items in the Reading subtest. However, time permitting, the best assessment of academic achievement comes from two thorough test batteries: The Woodcock-Johnson—Revised, Achievement portion, and the K-TEA Comprehensive Form.

The WJ-R/A is an incredibly thorough, state-of-the-art measure of achievement that contains two alternate forms that are well normed through age 75+; it includes reliable measures of subtests in the domains of Reading, Mathematics, Knowledge, and Written Expression. The K-TEA Comprehensive Form, normed for ages 6–18, has separate fall and spring norms, numerous interpretive guidelines in a thorough Manual, and offers a systematic norm- and criterion-referenced error analysis for pinpointing specific assets and deficits in reading, mathematics, and spelling.

The brand-new PIAT-R, a battery that is midway between a screening and comprehensive test, was normed at ages 5–18 years. Its main new feature, a measure of Written Expression, seems too unreliable to be of much diagnostic value. However, the lengthened subtests are quite reliable (despite the questionable use of a multiple-choice format for three subtests), and the standardization sample is excellent. The Manual's interpretive guidelines are good, but its lack of validity data is a notable flaw. The WRMT-R is a battery devoted to diverse aspects of reading ability from readiness skills to comprehension. Its fine norms for adults as old as 75+ years are laudable, although the failure to stratify on socio-economic status for its two other normative samples (grades K–12 and college students) is a problem. The Manual is quite comprehensive, a big plus, and the reliability coefficients are generally good. However, the test only measures comprehension via single words or passages of one to three sentences, provides limited or no evidence of stability and validity, and fails to heed the results of recent research in reading.

Neuropsychological Assessment

George W. Hynd, *University of Georgia and Medical College of Georgia*
Margaret Semrud-Clikeman, *University of Georgia*

George W. Hynd is Research Professor and Chair of the Division for Exceptional Children of Educational Psychology and Psychology at The University of Georgia, where he also directs the Center for Clinical and Developmental Neuropsychology. He is also Assistant Clinical Professor of Neurology at the Medical College of Georgia. Dr. Hynd completed a postdoctoral fellowship in Clinical Neuropsychology at the Minneapolis VA Medical Center with Dr. Francis J. Pirozzolo and was awarded a Fulbright Fellowship in Child Neuropsychology to Finland in 1986. A former editor of School Psychology Review, he is currently on numerous journal editorial boards, is an active consultant to the National Institutes of Health and National Science Foundation, and has authored or edited many books in school psychology and clinical neuropsychology. He has recently published two books, Pediatric Neuropsychology and Neuropsychological Assessment in Clinical Child Psychology.

Margaret Semrud-Clikeman is a psychology intern at Massachusetts General Hospital and is earning her Ph.D. in School Psychology at The University of Georgia. She served as a psychologist in the Wisconsin public schools and completed a predoctoral internship in psy-

chophysiology at the University of Jyvaskyla in Finland. Ms. Semrud-Clikeman's current research focuses on the relationships between deviations in brain morphology and the neurolinguistic difficulties found in dyslexia.

INTRODUCTION

Neuropsychological assessment is a highly specialized approach to the appraisal of individual differences. It is a relatively unique approach in that one of the most basic assumptions held by the qualified examiner is that all behavior is the direct expression to a greater or lesser extent of the integrity of the central nervous system (Heilman, Bowers & Valenstein, 1985). It is also a highly specialized area of clinical expertise in that minimal standards for training exist above and beyond those normally required for practicing psychologists (Bieliauskas & Boll, 1984; Meier, 1981).

It is vital to understand the conceptual and statistical relationship between IQ and the components of ability typically assessed in the neuropsychological evaluation. David Wechsler clearly appreciated these interrelationships, perhaps due to the influence of his brother, Israel S. Wechsler, a respected neurologist. Writing in his brother's *Textbook of Clinical Neurology*, Wechsler (1928) suggested: "Mental measurement and the determination of the level of intelligence are frequently of great help in various conditions characterized by memory, language, and other deficits. Indeed, without a psychologic examination it is occasionally difficult to differentiate between a psychosis and mental defect, while a psychometric test frequently throws light on various types of ill-defined or borderline psychoses" (p. 104).

It might be helpful to conceptualize the relationship between IQ and neuropsychological variables as represented by a large pyramid, with FS-IQ (or g) at the top. Supporting g, the apex of all abilities, are many subcomponents descending vertically on all sides toward the base of the pyramid. The farther one descends toward the base, the more numerous and discrete the blocks or components of ability become. The more discrete the ability (e.g., auditory or visual perception), the higher the correlation with specific neurologic substrata. It is for this reason that IQ is so sensitive to *generalized* impairment (the entire foundation of the conceptual pyramid is compromised) but is relatively insensitive to very focalized lesions of the brain (i.e., one particular block of the foundation).

Within this context, the processes assessed in the neuropsychological evaluation are believed to represent the more compartmentalized subfactors that compose the range of human abilities; this type of assessment, therefore, adds to those more general, higher-order processes measured by the IQ. While there are some conceptual problems represented by these relationships (which are discussed later in the chapter), understanding those factors of ability measured during a neuropsychological assessment should help elucidate the interrelationships at the boundary of brain and mind.

Historical Perspective

Although the exact genesis of this specialty within applied psychology can be debated (Davison, 1974; Gilandas, Touyz, Beumont, & Greenberg, 1984; Heilman et al., 1985; Lezak, 1983; Luria & Majovski, 1977), there is general agreement that the study of brain–behavior relationships had its origins in experimental and clinical neurology. Until the early nineteenth century there existed in neurology no standard nosology for neurological disorders, nor was there a standard approach to the study and documentation of disturbances in brain–behavior relations. Clinicians, in their reports on patients with potentially important focal deficits, often communicated poorly in describing associated symptoms and clinical procedures employed to elicit and document the behavioral consequences of disturbances in the central nervous system. This lack of scientific rigor in the reports of clinical cases proved frustrating for those attempting to develop theoretical formulations of various clinical disorders such as those related to alexia with and without agraphia (Bastian, 1898).

Fortunately, however, more careful clinical descriptions of patients with unilateral brain damage allowed neurologists to test more adequately the theories generated by Gall and his associates. Broca, Jackson, Wernicke, Dejerine, and others carefully collected and reported data on patients with focal brain damage that allowed for the advancement of neurological theory. Important publications by Broca (1863), Wernicke (1874), Bastian (1898), and Mitchell, Morehouse, and Keen (1864) helped advance theory regarding aphasic syndromes, alexia, and hemispatial neglect (Hynd, 1988b).

In response to these "diagram makers" (Head, 1926), a strong antilocalizationist movement arose in which Von Monakow (1911) and later

Lashley (1950) argued that the brain was not an organ divisible into separate compartments and that the effects of focal lesions were both proximal and distal. Lashley's work was particularly important because he applied the techniques of scientific inquiry in psychology to the ablative research paradigms of experimental neurology. His research led him to conclude: "The equivalence of different regions of the cortex for retention of memories points to multiple representation. . . . This means that, within a functional area, the neurons must be sensitized to react in certain combination, perhaps in complex patterns of reverberatory circuits, reduplicated throughout the area" (pp. 478–479).

Despite Lashley's views, a reawakening of localizationist thought occurred, albeit slowly. Factors important in heralding a renewed conceptualization of brain–behavior theory included (1) continued documentation by clinicians that focal brain damage led to predictable alterations in behavior; (2) the development of statistical procedures that allowed researchers to determine which effects on behavioral measures were due to real effects of brain damage and not chance variation; (3) the development of behavioral research paradigms (e.g., dichotic listening, visual half-field techniques) that allowed investigators to examine lateralized cerebral organization in a noninvasive manner; and (4) the development of new cytoarchitectonic and psychophysiological procedures that allowed for a better understanding of the effects of cellular and electrophysiological deviations on observed behavior (Heilman et al., 1985).

Other important factors that helped renew interest in developing a better understanding of brain–behavior relations included a postwar economy that actively encouraged research in the neurosciences and an awareness that patients with once fatal diseases and disorders were surviving longer, thus underscoring the need for identification of strengths, deficits, and appropriate treatment or rehabilitation plans (Hynd, 1988b).

It was in this scientific socio-economic climate that psychologists interested in the study of brain–behavior relations first began to make contributions. Over the past 30 years, the work of Halstead (1947), Reitan (1955b), Luria (1980), and others has contributed to a more comprehensive understanding of how focal lesions affect behavior and to the development of the clinical neuropsychological assessment procedures commonly in use today.

Focus of the Chapter

The major focus of this chapter is on the two most commonly employed neuropsychological assessment batteries. The Halstead-Reitan Neuropsychological Test Battery for Adults (HRNB) and the Luria-Nebraska Neuropsychological Test Battery (LNNTB) will be addressed in some detail since they appear to be the instruments most typically administered. Other, more qualitative approaches based on Luria's (1980) theories (Christensen, 1975), or eclectic approaches, clearly have value but they are not reviewed here for two reasons. First, many of the eclectic approaches employ tests or tasks similar to those found in more traditional batteries. Second, the validation of tests and measures other than these two batteries is generally poor; where adequate validation has occurred (e.g., Benton, Hamsher, Varney, & Spreen, 1983), the studies have failed to document their superiority or uniqueness. This is not to say that other measures, particularly those developed and validated by Benton et al. (1983), are not valuable contributions. Rather, their value beyond that provided by the Halstead-Reitan and Luria batteries has not yet been demonstrated. The Benton tests will therefore be briefly noted but not in as much detail. For descriptions of eclectic neuropsychological approaches in use at major research hospitals, the interested reader is referred to Matthews (1981).

Before reviewing these test batteries, it is appropriate to discuss briefly the general purpose of neuropsychological assessment, discuss some important methodological problems that characterize this literature, and point out some relevant issues with regard to training in the administration and interpretation of these clinical procedures.

Purposes of Neuropsychological Assessment

In a general sense, the purpose of neuropsychological assessment is not significantly different from more traditional clinical assessment. Both types of assessment have as a primary goal the characterization of an individual's current psychological status. In this sense, both more traditional clinical assessment and neuropsychological assessment aim to provide an accurate description of an individual's mental status, intellectual level, personality, and overall adjustment. Identifying patterns of strength and weakness in a person's profile is often desired. Further, both traditional clinical assessment and neuropsychological assessment have as goals an accurate diagnosis and the formulation of attainable treatment objectives. Despite these similarities, neuropsychological assessment differs from traditional clinical assessment in important ways.

Additional objectives of neuropsychological assessment include (1) differentiation of functional versus organically based disorders; (2) documentation of a patient's current mental status and, in cases of trauma or injury, an estimate of the premorbid level of functioning; (3) documentation of the rate or recovery after injury or the rate of deterioration in degenerative neurological disease; (4) recommendations for appropriate rehabilitation after traumatic brain injury; and (5) compilation of data that may be useful in evaluating neuropsychological theory. Neuropsychological evaluation thus requires knowledge and skills beyond those typically required of the applied clinician.

Approaches to Neuropsychological Assessment

Although the ultimate objectives of the clinician conducting a neuropsychological examination may be consistent with those of other clinicians, there are vastly different approaches one might employ in conducting the neuropsychological assessment. Neuropsychological approaches to assessment employ basically two approaches: the test battery approach and the qualitative syndrome analysis approach.

The Test Battery Approach

The test battery approach is best represented by the Halstead-Reitan Neuropsychological Test Battery and, perhaps, by the Luria-Nebraska Neuropsychological Test Battery. Test batteries have some advantages in that they generally have been developed over a number of years and have been the subject of many validity studies, are comprehensive and assess abilities across a broad range of human performance, are standardized and provide norms for assessing performance, and are widely taught and frequently administered. Underscoring this last point, Golden and Kuperman (1980) surveyed clinical psychology programs throughout the United States and found that over 50% of graduate programs in clinical psychology taught the Halstead-Reitan procedures to their students.

The test battery approach to neuropsychological assessment is not without its problems, however. Disadvantages are several: (1) they are generally lengthy (the Halstead-Reitan battery, for example, may take 6 to 8 hours to administer); (2) the information they provide is often redundant; (3) the norms provided with these batteries are not adequate by contemporary standards of psychometric test construction; and (4) comparison of a person's performance to a normative sample does not provide much information about his or her intraindividual variability, particularly in relation to impaired brain–behavior relations. Further, and perhaps most serious, these battery approaches, particularly the Halstead-Reitan battery, have been criticized for being atheoretical (Luria & Majovski, 1977).

The Qualitative Syndrome Analysis Approach

A second approach, often referred to as Luria's (1980) qualitative syndrome analysis, based on Christensen's (1979) summary of Luria's evaluation procedures, is dynamic in nature and responsive to the patient's individual deficits. The assessment itself focuses specifically on the deficits evidenced by the patient. A detailed and accurate clinical picture emerges through a careful evaluation of the components of the behaviors that comprise the deficit. Such a dynamic and clinically guided approach puts extreme emphasis on the abilities of the examiner and demands a comprehensive understanding of neurological and neuropsychological organization. Such an approach has advantages: (1) it is a more efficient use of clinical time as nonessential test procedures are not administered, as they may be in the battery approach; (2) it has the advantage, according to Luria and Majovski (1977), of being rooted in a long tradition of neuropsychological research; and (3) since the evaluation focuses primarily on articulating the nature of the patient's disabilities, a much clearer view emerges of how behavior disassembles through neurological trauma.

Despite its appeal, however, there are some significant problems with qualitative syndrome analysis: (1) because such emphasis is placed on the expertise and judgment of the examiner, reliability of diagnosis has yet to be documented empirically using such an approach; (2) the validity of these assessment procedures has not been established or researched to the extent of those composing the batteries; and (3) since there are no norms for these procedures, it is impossible to judge empirically the exact nature of differences between individuals on these measures (Gilandas et al., 1984). Further, the failure

to investigate a broad band of behaviors in the assessment and to employ a standard set of tests makes the data generated through these procedures inadequate in research settings. In other words, because not every patient is administered the same set of tests, it is nearly impossible to compare performance across subject groups.

To dichotomize assessment into the battery approach and a more qualitative approach best represented by Luria (1980) is perhaps unfair. As Harlow (1938) suggested, "[i]f it's a dichotomy, it's wrong." In fact, many neuropsychologists employ an eclectic, norm-based standardized battery that allows a qualitative appraisal of a patient's performance. The neuropsychological approach and measures outlined by Lezak (1983), Gilandas et al. (1984), Filskov and Leli (1981), and others represent such an integrated conceptualization. As noted previously, however, these eclectic approaches often employ procedures from the major batteries and vary so widely in orientation that a productive review of them is not realistically possible. One should be aware, nonetheless, that there are many different approaches to neuropsychological assessment other than the batteries and procedures reviewed in this chapter.

METHODOLOGICAL PROBLEMS AND ISSUES IN NEUROPSYCHOLOGICAL ASSESSMENT

As a specialized discipline within applied psychology, clinical neuropsychology faces a number of unique challenges (Boll, 1985). Some of the important problems relevant to neuropsychology include the persistent notion of organicity, factors that affect neuropsychological test performance, the status of brain–behavior relations, and the fact that many variables affect reliability and validity studies in this area. Issues that have particular relevance include those related to what constitutes appropriate professional preparation in clinical neuropsychology and, in a related vein, what specialized training is necessary to administer and interpret neuropsychological tests. It may be helpful to briefly address each of these important methodological problems and issues.

The Concept of Organicity

Central to the concept of organicity is the idea that any damage to the outer cortex or subcortical brain results in a unitary constellation of signs that represent the effects of damage. Basically, the concept of organicity has as its central construct the assumption that damage to the brain produces reliable and consistent pathologic symptoms or, in relation to neuropsychological assessment, a constellation of observable behaviors that indicate brain damage. By selecting those assessment procedures that are most sensitive to or best elicit these pathologic signs, the neuropsychologist can presumably diagnose accurately whether brain impairment exists.

These assumptions have a long history, and the notion of organicity persists despite evidence to the contrary. Davison (1974) suggested that four factors led to and maintained such a perspective as the effects of brain damage. First, the work of Lashley (1929) suggested that the location of a lesion was not so important as the size of a lesion. Supporting a mass actionist perspective reflective of the earlier work of Goltz (Hynd, 1988b), Lashley's work on the effects of brain damage in the rat was uncritically applied to the presumed effects of brain damage in humans. Such a view led to the assumption that minor head damage had predictable minor effects and that major damage had predictable (and additive) major effects.

Second, the early work of Goldstein (1952) on the effects of brain damage suggested to other psychologists that specific "organic" effects resulted from brain damage. His views supported the unitary construct of organic ef-

fects and suggested that patients differed only in *severity* of effects, having little relation to the location of a lesion.

Third, the psychometric approach that has so characterized American psychology, particularly neuropsychology (Luria & Majovski, 1977), has led to a search for the best single indicator of brain damage. Davison (1974) noted that the undue attention that Wechsler's hold/don't hold dichotomy has received reflects this focus on identifying tests that best discriminate between normality and pathology. A fascination with this notion continues today, and studies are still being published on the discriminant validity of Wechsler's hold/don't hold formulation (e.g., Larrabee, Largen, & Levin, 1985), or the value of specific tests as indicators of organicity (e.g., Crookes, 1983). Perhaps the best example of studies reflecting this unidimensional view of organicity is the overwhelming body of literature regarding the use of the Bender-Gestalt test in identifying brain impairment. Studies have consistently shown that this test is the most frequently administered psychometric instrument in neuropsychology (Craig, 1979) and in other settings. The popularity of this test is most likely due to its short administration time and the belief that poor performance reflects "organic" factors.

Finally, the influence of dynamic and Gestalt psychology had a profound effect on how brain–behavior relations were viewed. In terms of diagnosis and treatment, both perspectives emphasized the clinical identification of "organicity" so that patients could be dichotomized into those with functional (nonorganic) disorders or those with organic (brain-damaged) personalities; the former were considered more responsive to Gestalt or dynamic therapy procedures, and the latter more refractive to such intervention. The development of indicators of organicity on the Rorschach illustrates this point (e.g., Piotrowski, 1937).

A more prismatic view of assessment has emerged with the advent of a more comprehensive and interactive understanding of how neurological trauma affects alterations in behavior, accompanied by a more sophisticated and psychometrically sensitive approach to the highly variable effects of brain trauma. Clearly the work of Reitan, Luria, and many others has led away from such a unitary conceptualization and has fostered an even greater appreciation of the very often subtle effects of generalized or lateralized neurological impairment (Boll, 1983, 1985; Ross, 1981, 1985).

Factors That Affect Neuropsychological Test Performance

Test performance is affected to a greater or lesser extent by a host of variables including motivation; arousal and attention; socioeconomic status; developmental, educational, and medical history; age; and the conditions under which the tests are administered. In neuropsychological assessment the effects of these variables may be exaggerated, and variably so, having a significant effect on the reliability and validity of the measures administered. This is indeed a very significant problem.

Age

Age, for example, has an expected and well-documented effect on the level and kind of performance evidenced by children on neuropsychological measures (Hynd & Willis, 1988), and the effects of early brain injury on the cognitive development of children is well documented (Dennis, 1985a, 1985b). With adults, the age-related changes on neuropsychological performance are more subtle. However, with advancing age there are documented decrements in processing speed, sensory acuity, and memory, and in components of intelligence (Boll & Reitan, 1973; Botwinick, 1981; Prigatano & Parsons, 1976; Read, 1988). The relationship between aging and loss of intellectual function was treated in depth in chapter 7; see also pages 335–337 for a discussion of age as an interacting

variable regarding the relationship of V–P IQ discrepancy and lateralization of brain lesions.

Since age-related changes typically are subtle in normal adults, it is difficult to judge in some cases whether observed deficits on neuropsychological tasks are related to normal aging or represent the early manifestations of some disease process. Norms are clearly of importance in making this determination; but because the norms for the batteries are not adequate by today's standards and because tests employed on eclectic batteries were normed differently and on different populations, the subtle differences between normality and pathology are difficult to detect.

Age also exerts an effect on the kinds of disorders that may manifest clinically. Closed head injury is often associated with adolescence and young, primarily male, adults, while multiple sclerosis has an average age of onset during early to middle adulthood (Merritt, 1979). Cerebrovascular problems and Alzheimer's disease generally manifest later in adult development. Thus, in cases of questionable etiology and diagnosis, there are age-related disease processes that might be expected and correlated to the patient's history and neuropsychological findings.

The fact that age exerts such a significant effect on neuropsychological test performance and particularly intelligence test performance has clinical utility in the diagnosis of age-related disorders. For example, Fuld (1984) has reported on a WAIS-R marker that may be helpful in the differential diagnosis of dementia of the Alzheimer's type (DAT); this marker profile and associated research were treated in detail on pages 455–459. As noted in the earlier chapter, Fuld examined the incidence of this marker in several populations and found that about half the patients with DAT had the marker, whereas less than 10% of the non-DAT subjects did. Among normal elderly adults, Satz, Van Gorp, Soper, and Mitrushina (1988) found that only 12% of 149 healthy aged adults (ages 60–94) displayed the Fuld profile. Satz, Hynd, D'Elia, Van Gorp, Ledbetter and Connor (1989) extended the latter findings by examining the incidence of this marker in the WAIS-R standardization sample across ages 16–74 (see Table 13.13). With the use of regular, *non-age-corrected,* scaled scores, the incidence increased very significantly across development; by age 70–74, fully 36% of normal aged adults showed the marker. However, when *age-corrected* scores are employed, the incidence of the marker showed a nonsignificant change across ages 16–74 (6.2%). These results strongly support Fuld's (1984) decision to use *age-corrected* scaled scores to detect the presence or absence of her marker profile. The findings with the WAIS-R data also suggest that some clear age-related changes occur across normal development, as reflected on Wechsler's subtests (see chapter 7). However, the base rate *within* age domains for the Fuld marker profile is very low. DAT patients show the same type of decline, but it seems to represent an acceleration of normal age-related changes. These findings need to be interpreted cautiously, but they do provide evidence that age-related changes do occur and that certain tests may be useful in diagnosing accelerated deterioration of cognitive processes as found in DAT (Berg, 1985).

Attention

Patients with closed head trauma, in addition to other difficulties, often have severe deficits in focusing and regulating attentional resources. In traditional clinical appraisal, efforts are made to ensure that patients maximize their performance by putting forth good effort. With the head-injured patient, however, attention may be variable across tasks depending on the difficulty encountered as well as on the level and effects of fatigue on the existing attention deficits. Thus, the validity of profile analysis is affected to a relatively unknown extent, so that it is difficult to determine without additional correlated evidence if a singular deficit performance

indicates focal or general pathology or results from variable attention. Clinical judgment is required to make such a determination, a factor that underscores the importance of employing both quantitative and qualitative methods of test interpretation.

Gender

There also appear to be important gender differences in terms of the effects of lateralized brain damage. A series of studies by McGlone suggested that when left or right hemispheric damage occurs in males there is the typical reduction in verbal or performance IQ, respectively. However, these effects were not consistently found in females with left or right focal hemispheric damage (McGlone & Davidson, 1973; McGlone & Kertesz, 1973; McGlone, 1977, 1978). Some investigations (e.g., Bornstein, 1984) have failed to find meaningful gender differences, although the bulk of research on this topic (which is treated in considerable depth in chapter 10) does support McGlone's hypothesis of gender differences.

While some studies of aphasic patients do not necessarily support the view that important gender effects exist (e.g., De Renzi, Faglioni, & Ferrari, 1980; Kertesz & Shepard, 1981), other, better controlled studies do (Basso, Capitani, & Maraschini, 1982). Such investigations have important theoretical implications: The existence of such gender differences may suggest that females are more bilaterally represented for verbal and visual-spatial abilities and may be less affected than males by unilateral damage (see pp. 301–317). If so, one might expect not only that unilateral damage would have a less significant impact on females, but that they would recover more rapidly than males. Clinically, then, one might expect to find a better correlation between unilateral brain damage and test performance in males than in females. However it is clearly inappropriate to use verbal–performance IQ dichotomies as the only diagnostic indicators of unilateral impairment (Bornstein, 1983a; 1984).

Socio-economic Factors

Socio-economic factors also affect neuropsychological test results. For example, one often finds that the higher the educational level prior to head injury, the better the outcome. Depending on the specific nature of the neurological impairment (e.g., trauma, degenerative disease, tumor), there may be differential effects on the ability to perform that are independent of the person's level of intelligence or adaptive behavior. For example, Waber and her colleagues examined the effect of socio-economic status on aspects of neuropsychological performance. Using a high and low SES dichotomy, they hypothesized that high SES children tended to process stimuli analytically, reflecting left hemispheric processes, while low SES children tended to rely on global gestalt processes of the right hemisphere. Employing a visual-field paradigm and spatially arranged words as stimuli, they found evidence that lateralized hemispheric effects did exist in relation to SES independent of the effects of intelligence (Waber, Carlson, Mann, Merola, & Moylan, 1984). Thus, the effects of SES may manifest themselves in a relatively poorly understood fashion on brain organization, particularly in the early years of development. The effect of SES independent of IQ in adults has been less well studied.

However, knowing that these factors can and do affect neuropsychological test performance has certain advantages. The fact that educational level and intellectual level are highly correlated allows one to predict premorbid levels of functioning in cases where brain damage has affected ability level (Leli & Filskov, 1978; Matarazzo, 1972). (The interactive role played by the patient's education level in the relationship between V–P IQ discrepancy and laterality of brain lesions is treated on pages 337–342.)

Neurological Factors

The results of neuropsychological assessment can reflect not only the focal effects of brain damage or impairment but may also suggest those functions impaired through more distal effects. In 1911, Von Monakow observed that in cases of brain damage there are immediate effects that result from the destruction of tissue, and that, in addition, there may be a depression of behaviors that are functionally related to the behaviors directly affected by the damage. He termed this phenomena *diaschisis*. Thus, when they encounter depressed performance on specific measures of neuropsychological ability soon after trauma, inexperienced clinicians find it difficult to differentiate primary deficits directly related to the focal damage from those that may reflect distal suppression of correlated regions. Further, to some extent early recovery of function after trauma may reflect not reorganization or the plasticity of function, but the reemergence of the regions suppressed through diaschisis. Although neural changes may explain or reflect this process (Kolb & Whishaw, 1980), the true extent of brain damage immediately after the insult is often very difficult to assess accurately because of these effects. The topic of diaschisis was discussed earlier regarding lateralized lesions and V–P IQ discrepancies (see pp. 362–363).

Research investigating the hypothesized effects of diaschisis suggests that this phenomenon exists (Reivich, Jones, Castano, Crowe, Ginsberg, & Greenberg, 1977; Waltz, 1972) and that the effects may not be just temporary, but may persist over time (Ghannam, Javornisky, & Smith, 1979). Consequently, it may be inappropriate to expect that the effects of focal damage affect only those behaviors subserved by the damaged tissue.

Further, the effects of brain damage may evolve significantly over time not only because of the normal course of recovery but also because cytoarchitectonic changes may take place over time. For example, epilepsy is not infrequently encountered in patients with head trauma; while the course of seizure activity may evolve over years, so too may correlated neuropathological changes. Some have suggested that in epilepsy of traumatic origin, scarring changes may occur progressively for perhaps 20 to 30 years after the initial insult (Harris, 1980). Thus, in some cases it is not unreasonable to expect possible correlated behavioral changes years after the initial insult.

Relation of IQ to Neuropsychological Performance

The previous section has shown that there exists a very significant relationship between intelligence and nearly all measures of neuropsychological ability. Wechsler (1958) and Luria (1980) both agreed that there was no "center" for intellectual processes, but they also agreed that there may very well be differentiated sensory and motor systems in the brain that are correlated to intellectual processes. Wechsler (1958) suggested:

> One cannot expect anything like [a] fixed center of intelligence for purely logical reasons. Intelligence deals not with mental representations but with relations that may exist between them, and relations cannot be localized. . . . [F]or effective functioning intelligence may depend more upon the intactness of some rather than other portions of the brain, but in no sense can it be said to be mediated by any single part of it (p. 20).

Early studies of large samples of undifferentiated brain-damaged patients using the Wechsler scales supported his views. Some abilities, typically those assessed by subtests requiring memory, timed performance, and abstract concept formation, were impaired in the presence of brain trauma, while other abilities seemed more refractive to damage. The similarity between those subtests that showed age-related effects, as discussed above, and those

that showed effects due to trauma did not go unnoticed (Lezak, 1983). Wechsler (1958) developed a Deterioration Index (DI) (or DQ, for Deterioration Quotient), which allowed one to use scores from subtests that showed little or no change from brain damage (*Hold* tests) and from those that did show change (*Don't Hold* tests) in order to identify patients with an organic disorder.

Those subtests that were considered to "Hold" were Vocabulary, Information, Object Assembly, and Picture Completion, while those that "Don't Hold" were Digit Span, Similarities, Digit Symbol, and Block Design. The DI was calculated using the formula

$$ DI = \frac{Hold - Don't\ Hold}{Hold} $$

Wechsler (1958) recommended that .10 or .20 should be considered the criterion for possible deterioration. Many studies have examined the usefulness of the DI or other ratios (e.g., Hewson, 1949); generally, the results adequately classify normal subjects but misclassify as many as half of the neurologically impaired populations (e.g., Smith, 1962). Research addressing the DI has suggested, however, that it may be useful in evaluating the severity of dementia in Alzheimer's patients (Larrabee, Largen, & Levin, 1985).

Pattern analysis was for a time also believed useful in differentiating organic patients from those with no sign of organicity. Basically, brain damage tended to produce deficits in abstract reasoning, so that one might expect Similarities, Block Design, and perhaps Picture Completion to be depressed in relation to other subtest scores (Russell, 1972).

Dissatisfaction with the ability of IQ tests, particularly the Wechsler scales, to distinguish between brain damage and impairment has more recently led Lezak (1988a) to suggest that neuropsychologists abandon the use of the IQ concept in neuropsychological assessment. Lezak suggested that IQ scores can obscure important aspects of a patient's profile on neuropsychological measures and, in fact, totally misrepresent ability. (Lezak's position and arguments against it are treated extensively in chapter 2.)

A significant problem exists with this position, however: There is a very strong relationship between IQ and performance on neuropsychological tests. In fact, some factor analytic studies suggest that the neuropsychological measures (which in some cases may take 4 to 6 hours to collect after the IQ measure) contribute very little additional data beyond that variance explained by the IQ test. In other words, neuropsychologists often administer measures that are so highly correlated with components of IQ that they provide little additional data. Considering Luria's (1980) notions regarding the interactions of components of functional systems (discussed below), it may not be conceptually inconsistent to collect these data. Considerable redundancy results when neuropsychological assessment coincides with tests of IQ; but because IQ tests are still our best single predictor of academic achievement, they retain their value in clinical appraisal (Hynd, 1988a).

In fact, there exists evidence that WAIS IQ scores discriminate between normality and brain damage as effectively as summary scores from both the Halstead-Reitan and Luria-Nebraska batteries (Kane, Parsons, & Goldstein, 1985). This study provides evidence that the summary scores of these three instruments are so highly correlated with general ability that if any of the subprocesses composing general ability are affected through neurological damage, g will most likely be similarly depressed. In this context, Lezak (1988a) is correct in her suggestion that neuropsychologists should be developing and validating new and more meaningful measures beyond that expressed in measures of general ability, particularly if they want to make statements beyond whether brain damage or impairment exists.

Training in Neuropsychological Assessment

It would be ideal if the skills learned in graduate training programs were sufficient so one were equipped to perform a competent neuropsychological assessment upon the completion of formal education and an internship. Despite the fact that many clinical training programs offer coursework and perhaps even some supervised practicum experience in neuropsychological assessment (Golden & Kuperman, 1980), graduate students typically lack basic knowledge in neuroscience. Worse, there is some evidence that neuropsychological assessment skills are often obtained through short-term workshop experiences that offer no supervision in administering the batteries or in their interpretation (Craig, 1979).

Meier (1981) recognized that neuropsychology had gained sufficient status to warrant professional training models and guidelines. He also recognized that such training was not generally available within the curricula of most applied psychology programs. Further, other applied and academic psychologists wanted recognition of their area's contributions to human neuropsychology.

Guidelines for doctoral training in clinical neuropsychology have been published (Beiliauskas & Boll, 1984), based largely on the models provided by Meier and his efforts to encourage cooperation between Division 40 of the American Psychological Association (Clinical Neuropsychology) and the International Neuropsychological Society (INS). While no formal accreditation mechanism of doctoral programs yet exists, more formal standards for training may eventually be reinforced through program accreditation. At present, however, psychologists receive no standard training in neuropsychological assessment techniques.

The development of the applied specialty of clinical neuropsychology has reached the point where neuropsychology has its own unique set of problems and issues. It even has its own areas of subspecialization: There are those who are primarily interested in pediatric neuropsychology (Hynd & Willis, 1988), developmental neuropsychology (Spreen, Tupper, Risser, Tuokko, & Edgell, 1984), geriatric neuropsychology (Botwinick, 1981), and so on.

THE HALSTEAD-REITAN NEUROPSYCHOLOGICAL BATTERY

The Halstead-Reitan Neuropsychological Battery was developed initially from the work of Halstead at the University of Chicago and from the efforts of Reitan at Indiana University Medical Center. The HRNB is the most frequently administered neuropsychological test battery, and many of the eclectic assessment batteries use procedures from it (Matthews, 1981).

Halstead was trained in experimental psychology and from 1939 to 1969 was very interested in developing a model of biological intelligence through his work with brain-injured patients. He developed a series of tests that covered abstract reasoning, analysis and synthesis, visual-motor skills, visual memory (simple and complex), and measures of motor abilities. Using these measures, he sought to refine his concept of biological intelligence, which he defined as the basic coping and adaptive behaviors of the individual that are not tapped by traditional psychometric measures (Boll, 1981). His basic premise was that an index could be developed to provide insight into the functioning of the central nervous system (Halstead, 1947).

Halstead's battery included the following tasks: Tactual Performance Test (Time, Memory, Localization), Seashore Rhythm Test, Speech Sounds Perception Test, Finger Oscillation, Time Sense Test, Critical Flicker Test, and Critical Flicker Duration. Based on data

from these tasks, Halstead used factor analysis to provide supportive evidence for the constructs of biological intelligence. Although the analysis employed too many tests with too few subjects, Halstead nonetheless concluded that there were four important factors (Reed, 1985). These factors included Factor C, a Central integrative field factor representing the connection between the previously organized experiences of the individual and novel stimuli (the shared variance between intelligence and adaptive behavior); Factor A, Abstraction, involving the processing of similarities and differences; Factor P, Power, the capability of the brain for further growth, lessening the impact of affective forces; and Factor D, a factor allowing for the medium through which stimuli are interpreted (the final common pathway) (Boll, 1981).

Reitan worked with Halstead from 1944 to 1950 as his first doctoral student, and he continued to refine the tests and measures when he left Chicago to establish the first neuropsychology laboratory at Indiana University Medical Center in 1951. In constructing their battery, both Reitan and Halstead attempted to use tasks that would reflect a full range of human abilities. They agreed that not all deficits in brain-injured patients could be observed. Consequently, they decided to construct the battery on an empirical basis, so that the battery that volved would represent an empirical validation of tests sensitive to different types of brain lesions (Reitan, 1986). Reitan made several contributions to the battery, not the least of which were many validation studies. He also added ten measures to the original battery, including measures of symbolic and expressive language, motor coordination, concept formation, and general intelligence (Small, 1980). Consequently, the final battery had tasks that were sensitive in assessing the behavioral correlates of aphasia, apraxia, sensoriperceptual deficits, and acalculia. These symptoms had not been adequately addressed on Halstead's battery.

Conceptual Model of the HRNB

The major goal of the HRNB is to assess the central processing ability of the brain. Input and output measures were represented, as were measures of global functioning. Reitan and Wolfson (1985) noted six categories of measures included in the battery: input; attention/concentration/memory; verbal abilities; spatial abilities; spatial/sequential/manipulatory; abstraction/reasoning/logical analysis; output. Tasks range from simple to complex with the attention/concentration variable cutting across the entire battery. Some tasks require retrieval of previously learned material, while others include novel problem-solving abilities; still others require simple perceptual processing. Reitan and Wolfson (1985) provided the flow chart shown in Figure 17.1 depicting the behavioral correlates of brain function.

Goodglass and Kaplan (1979) have suggested that specific and global measures be incorporated into a neuropsychological battery. Reitan's battery seems to meet this suggestion in that both specific measures (sensory imperception tests, finger oscillation) and general measures (Category Test, Trails B) are included. Halstead took into account Goldstein and Sheerer's (1941) finding that abstraction abilities are most sensitive to the effects of brain lesions because they seem to be affected by damage to nearly any part of the brain. This, of course, is consistent with Wechsler's (1958) conceptual framework regarding the relationship between intelligence and brain functioning.

Assessment Strategies and Procedures

Strategies for analysis of data are helpful due to the wealth of information provided by the HRNB. The overall level of performance is most often used in neuropsychological assessment to judge the presence or absence of impairment. Reitan and Wolfson (1985) have sug-

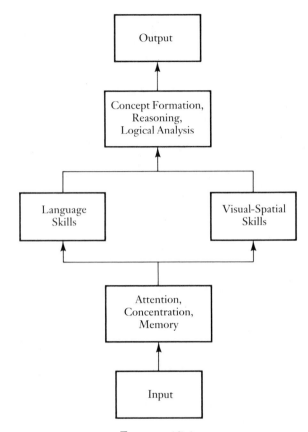

FIGURE 17.1

A conceptual model of the behavioral correlates of brain function.

gested three other assessment strategies. First, data can be analyzed in terms of whether the results show abnormal signs as contrasted with the normal population. Second, test results can be interpreted by comparison between tests. Third, comparisons between the left and right side of the body are possible.

The administration time of the HRNB depends on the subject's age, medical condition, motivation, and other related variables that always potentially affect neuropsychological assessment. The complete battery, including the WAIS-R and WRAT-R, can take about 5 hours or longer to complete. A technician with 4 to 6 weeks of intensive training can be employed to administer the HRNB if so desired (Boll, 1986). The following section provides an overview of the HRNB, followed by a discussion of the validity of these assessment procedures.

The Battery

The HRNB can be administered to individuals 15 years and older; it is recommended that the MMPI and WAIS-R be administered concurrently. The HRNB is divided into two parts. The first part consists of five subtests: Category, Tactual Performance Test—Time, Memory, and Localization, Seashore Rhythm Test, Speech Sounds Test, and Finger Oscillation. Scores on these tests are used to compute the Impairment Index. This Impairment Index is calculated by counting the number of tests out of the seven contributing scales on which the subject's scores fall into the range characteristic of brain-damaged individuals (Reitan, 1955a).

The second part of the battery consists of an additional three parts: Reitan's modification of the Halstead-Wepman Aphasia Screening Test, the Trail Making Test, and various procedures of sensorimotor functions (bilateral simultaneous stimulation through auditory, tactile, and verbal modalities—Finger Localization, Finger-Tip Number Writing Perception, and Tactile Form Recognition). The following brief description of each test outlines what it is believed to measure and how it is scored. Unlike the Luria-Nebraska Neuropsychological Battery, the HRNB is not consistent in how tests are scored across scales or measures.

Description of the Tasks

CATEGORY TEST The Category Test employs a slide projector and a small screen. Subjects sit in front of the screen, which has four levers labeled 1–4 placed below it. Subjects are told they will see seven groups of pictures, each of which has a single principle. The task is to inspect the figure and choose the lever that represents the given principle. When the response is correct, a bell sounds; if it is incorrect,

a buzzer sounds. The first two groups of figures are generally solved by all subjects. The succeeding groups are noticeably more difficult, with the last group being a review of all of the previous groupings.

This test is thought to be a measure of complex concept formation, which involves adapting and/or shifting responses as a consequence of positive or negative feedback. The score on the Category Test is the total number of errors on all seven tests. The criterion score on this test is more than 50 errors.

TACTUAL PERFORMANCE TEST The Tactual Performance Test (Time, Memory, and Localization) is a modification of the Seguin-Goddard Form Board. The subject is blindfolded before the materials are presented. The task involves fitting the wood blocks into their correct slots, first with the preferred hand, then with the nonpreferred hand, and finally with both hands. Each attempt is timed, and the total time needed to complete all three parts is used as the Time score. Not until the blocks and board are removed is the subject's blindfold removed. At that time the subject is asked to draw a representation of the blocks in their proper places. The drawing provides the score of the Memory (how many blocks are correctly recalled) and Localization (the number of blocks in correct juxtaposition) components.

This test is believed to tap the ability for form discrimination, kinesthesis, coordination and efficiency of hand and arm usage, manual dexterity, and memory and visualization. The three scores (Time, Memory, and Localization) each contribute to the Halstead Impairment Index. The criterion score for the total time is 15.6 minutes. A memory score of 6 and a localization score of 5 are also criterion scores.

RHYTHM TEST The Rhythm Test is a subtest of the Seashore Tests of Musical talent. The subject listens to a cassette tape of 30 pairs of rhythmic beats that are varied between same and different. The test is thought to measure alertness, ability to sustain attention, and the ability to differentiate between same and different with auditory stimuli. The score on this test is the number of correct choices made. This score is then transformed into a rank score with the criterion score > 5.

SPEECH-SOUNDS PERCEPTION TEST This scale consists of 60 spoken nonsense words that are variations of the "ee" sound. Each choice is presented in a multiple-choice format. The subject listens to the recording and underlines the correct selection on a printed form. This test requires the subject to maintain attention and to relate what is heard to a visual representation. The score is the number of errors or omissions. Although the criterion level is more than 7 errors, Reitan's (1955b) data revealed that normal controls may score 7 errors, and subjects with documented cerebral lesions may show 14 or more errors.

FINGER OSCILLATION TEST This scale measures finger-tapping speed. The subject taps with the index finger of the preferred hand first and then with the index finger of the nonpreferred hand. Performance is based on five consecutive 10-second trials for each hand. The score is the mean of five trials for each hand. The cut-off for impairment is 50 to 51 taps for the preferred hand. Of clinical importance is the difference between the two hands—generally 10% or less, with the nonpreferred hand being slower.

TIME SENSE TEST, CRITICAL FLICKER FREQUENCY, AND CRITICAL FLICKER FREQUENCY DEVIATION As Reitan recommended that these tests not be a part of the regular battery, they will only be noted in passing. Reitan's (1955b) research has shown that the results obtained from these tests have been found to be statistically non-significant in distinguishing between normal and brain-injured groups. Thus, these tests are rarely given.

The following measures do not contribute to the computation of the Impairment Index, but are used as additional clinical assessment procedures of the patient's functioning.

APHASIA SCREENING TEST This test is a modification of the Halstead-Wepman Aphasia Screening Test (Halstead & Wepman, 1947). The test seeks to determine the possible existence of a deficit in receptive or expressive processing. Items on this test sample naming abilities, spelling, reading, calculation, copying of simple designs, pronunciation, expressive and receptive language, identification of body parts, and right-left discrimination. Scoring of performance is either correct or incorrect. The items on this test are simple enough that most intact adults can perform all items correctly. Although there is no cut-off score for judging performance on this test, qualitative analysis of performance can be revealing.

TRAIL MAKING TEST This test consists of two parts, A and B. Part A is always administered first and consists of 25 numbered circles in altered order. The subject's task is to connect the circles in order as quickly as possible. Part B requires the subject to connect 25 circles numbered 1–13 and lettered A–L in alternating sequence (1-A-2-B-3-C, etc.). The score is the amount of time required to complete each part, A and B.

This test is thought to measure the ability to quickly scan the page, to sequence stimuli, to shift rapidly between number and letter concepts, and to perform under time constraints. Cut-off scores are 30–40 for Part A and 91–92 on Part B. However, Reitan (1955b) reported that when these criteria were used, 23% of subjects were misclassified with Part A and 15% with Part B. There is some evidence that Trail Making is a measure of planning ability (Naglieri & Das, 1987, 1988).

SENSORY IMPERCEPTION TESTS These tasks are designed to determine how accurately a subject can perceive unilateral stimulation. Tactile functions are assessed by touching either hand alone and both hands. Unilateral and bilateral simultaneous stimulation procedures are used alternatively, with hand and contralateral face stimulation also assessed. Auditory imperception is assessed by rubbing fingers lightly together behind each ear and asking the subject to indicate his or her perception of the stimuli. Visual imperception is measured by the examiner moving the index finger slightly in the peripheral visual field while the subject stares at the examiner's nose. The subject must indicate when unilateral or bilateral stimulation occurs.

TACTILE FINGER RECOGNITION On this test the subject is required to identify which finger was touched by the examiner. The subject wears a blindfold during the test, and the score totals 20 correct for each hand (four trials per finger). Finger localization is thought to be a very sensitive measure of somatosensory dysfunction. A score for the left hand and right hand also aids in clinical interpretation.

FINGERTIP NUMBER WRITING PERCEPTION This task is similar to Tactile Finger Recognition. The subject is blindfolded and the numbers 3, 4, 5, and 6 are written on each hand four times. The score is a total of 20 per hand and allows for a comparison of right and left performance.

TACTILE FORM RECOGNITION This test requires the subject to identify four plastic shapes (triangle, square, cross, and circle), which are placed in the subject's hand. The subject must use the other hand to indicate which shape it is. The score is the number of errors per hand and the total response time.

GRIP STRENGTH Subjects are asked twice to demonstrate their strength, using a hand dynamometer, alternating between hands. The task measures grip strength and the score, the average of two trials per hand, allows for both level of performance and right-left comparisons.

Validation Studies

The broad-based effectiveness of the HRNB has been repeatedly evaluated by many different investigators. The battery has been evaluated in terms of its effectiveness in discriminating brain damage from normal functioning, how it localizes focal deficits, and how it reflects lateralized dysfunction. Importantly, and to some extent different from the studies examining the validity of the Luria-Nebraska, the HRNB has been researched by many different groups other than Reitan and his colleagues. Table 17.1 summarizes some of these early studies.

Brain-Damaged Versus Normal and Psychiatric Subjects

The initial validation study was conducted by Reitan (1955b). Two groups of patients, heterogeneous brain-damaged patients and non–brain-damaged hospital controls, were compared and all measures except the Flicker Fusion Test significantly discriminated between the groups. A further study by Reitan (1958) achieved statistically significant group separation employing Trails A and B. Reitan's early studies were promising; for example, using the Trails A Test he could correctly classify 70% of the non–brain-damaged population and 78.5% of the brain-damaged subjects. The performance on Trails B was even better at achieving accurate group classification in that 81% of the non–brain-damaged patients were correctly identified and 88.5% of the brain-injured patients were identified.

An independent study by Vega and Parsons (1967) attempted to cross-validate the HRNB. This study used similar procedures but produced somewhat lower levels of performance, with the brain-damaged patients showing significantly poorer performance than the controls. Other studies by Matthews, Shaw, and Kløve (1966), Alvarez (1962), Boll (1974), Goldstein and Shelley (1972), and Shreiber, Goldman, Kleinman, Goldfader, and Snow (1976) have provided good evidence that the measures composing the full

TABLE 17.1   Chronological summary of studies examining the validity and reliability of the Halstead-Reitan Neuropsychological Test Battery

Author	Population	N	Gender M/F	Mean Age
Reitan (1955b)	Brain Damaged (BD)	50	35/15	32.74 (10.61)[a]
	Controls (C)	50	35/15	32.36 (10.78)
Ross & Reitan (1955)	BD	13	NR[c]	34.15 (8.46)
	MS	13	10/3	33.61 (6.70)
	Controls	13	NR	33.54 (8.33)
Shure & Halstead (1958)	Left posterior-small (LPS)	12	NR	32.5
	Right posterior-small (RPS)	11		31.8
	LP-large (LPL)	7		32.1
	RP-large (RPL)	9		40.1
	L frontal large (LFL)	10		36.8
	R frontal large (RFL)	10		39.7
	RF-small (RFS)	6		34.7
	LF-small (LFS)	7		32.4
Chapman & Wolff (1959)	Frontal-small	9	NR	45.2
	Frontal-large	12		42.5
	Posterior-small	14		35.3
	Posterior-large	10		46.0
	All frontal	21		43.7
	All posterior	24		39.8
	All small	23		39.2
	All large	22		49.1
Reitan (1959)	BD	50	35/15	32.42
	Controls (C)	50	35/15	32.36
Reitan (1960)	Dysphasic	32	30/2	37.00 (11.23)
	Nondysphasic	32	30/2	36.69 (10.38)
	Control	32	30/2	35.47 (10.78)
Doehring & Reitan (1961)	BD: Right homonymous visual field defect (R-VFD)	19	NR	39.37 (13.86)
	BD: L-VFD	19		36.42 (16.82)
	BD: No VFD	19		39.37 (15.72)
	Chronic illness controls	19		40.47 (9.32)

[a]Denotes standard deviation.
[b]Halstead-Reitan Neuropsychological Test Battery.
[c]NR = Not reported.

Tests Employed	Type of Study	Results
HRNB[b]	Differential diagnosis	Significant differences between groups on all measures except critical flicker frequency = BD < C
HRNB	Differential diagnosis	Impairment Index discriminates between controls and other 2 groups at $p < .002$
HRNB	Localization	Frontal patients were significantly more impaired on tests of abstraction ($p < .05$); hemisphere not significantly related to abstraction Impairment Index significantly discriminated frontal from nonfrontal ($p < .001$) Frontal cases: Size of lesion significantly related to impairment ($p < .001$)—size not related to severity for posterior lesions
HRNB W-B IQ Scale	Localization	Mass of tissue loss correlated significantly with Impairment Index (.77, $p < .01$) Mass of frontal tissue loss correlated significantly with Impairment Index (.35, $p < .05$) Lg. posterior poorer than lg. frontal ($F = 4.89$; $p < .05$)
HRNB W-B IQ Scale	Differential diagnosis/ validity	Significant differences between groups using Impairment Index ($p < .001$) Impairment Index more sensitive a discriminator than V-IQ, P-IQ, FS-IQ, hold/don't hold tests ($p < .001$)
W-B IQ Scale HRNB Aphasia Screening	Differential diagnosis	Control better than both BD groups (significant test NR) BD groups similar on tests except nondysphasic better on speech perception and Trails B (significance test NR)
WAIS HRNB	Differential diagnosis	Group means significantly differed at the .01 level on all measures but finger tapping and time sense memory Control significantly superior ($p < .01$) on all measures except time sense memory L-VFD significantly lower than R-VFD ($p < .01$) on category and TPT-time and memory components

(Continues)

TABLE 17.1   (Continued)

Author	Population	N	Gender M/F	Mean Age	
Reed & Reitan (1963a)	BD	40	NR	28.00 (5.91)	
	Controls	40		28.00 (5.91)	
	Old Control I	46		44.74 (2.75)	
	Old Control II	29		55.35 (4.30)	
Reed & Reitan (1963b)	Young	36	NR	28.05 (5.07)	
	Old	29		52.96 (6.27)	
Wheeler, Burke, & Reitan (1963)	Left Hemisphere (LH)	25	20/5	35.00 (11.48)	
	Right Hemisphere (RH)	31	25/6	33.39 (10.94)	
	Diffuse BD	23	22/1	35.43 (10.71)	
	Controls	61	60/1	32.00 (11.38)	

Author	Population	N	Gender M/F	1st grp	2nd grp
Wheeler & Reitan (1963)					
	LH	53	NR	41.3	38.9
	RH	61		34.7	38.6
	Diffuse BD	76		36.5	46.2
	Controls	114		31.1	36.6

Author	Population	N	Gender M/F	Mean Age	
Fitzhugh, Fitzhugh, & Reitan (1965)	Alcoholics	35	35/0	40.57 (9.75)	
	Young	18		32.54 (3.24)	
	Old	17		49.18 (6.37)	
	BD	35	35/0	40.23 (9.94)	
	Young	18		32.06 (3.27)	
	Old	17		49.06 (6.58)	
	Controls	35	35/0	39.77 (10.27)	
	Young	18		31.06 (3.31)	
	Old	17		49.18 (6.05)	
Shaw (1966)	MS	44	NR	NR	
	Epileptics	113			
	Migraine	11			
	Neoplastic brain disease	9			
	Infectious brain disease	35			
	Cerebrovascular	65			
	Parkinson's	23			
	Head injury	71			
	Undiagnosed BD	71			
	MR	7			
	Nonbrain disease	52			
	Psychopathology (No BD)	98			

Tests Employed	Type of Study	Results
HRNB W-B IQ Scale Trails A & B	Differential diagnosis	Rank-order comparisons (old vs. young) were significant (rho = .49) Impairment Index discriminated significantly between BD and Controls ($p < .001$) and Group I vs. II ($p < .01$)
HRNB W-B IQ Scale	Differential diagnosis	Rho difference between groups significant ($p < .01$)
W-B IQ Scale HRNB Trails A & B	Differential diagnosis	Impairment Index: 87% hit rate for C vs. All BD; 94.5% hit rate for C vs. BD-diffuse; 90.5% hit rate for C vs. LH; 87.9% hit rate for C vs. RH; Full Battery hit rate: 90.7% for C vs. All BD 98.8% for C vs. BD-diffuse 93.0% for C vs. L 92.4% for C vs. R
W-B IQ Scale HRNB Trails A & B	Differential diagnosis/ cross-validation	Full Battery hit rate: 85% for C vs. All BD groups 87% for C vs. Diffuse BD 89% for C vs. LH 87% for C vs. RH 88% for LH vs. RH 80% for Diffuse BD vs. LH 71% for Diffuse BD vs. RH
W-B IQ Scale HRNB Trails A & B	Differential diagnosis	Alcoholics > BD on TPT-time and location, Rhythm, Impairment Index C > BD on all measures C > alcoholics on category, TPT-time and location, speech, and Impairment Index Age not significant as variable
HRNB	Reliability and validity of Category test	Reliability of Category test = .98 Correlation between Category test and Impairment Index = .64

(Continues)

TABLE 17.1   (Continued)

Author	Population	N	Gender M/F	Mean Age
Matthews, Shaw, & Kløve (1966)	BD	32	NR	31.19 (11.32)
	Psychiatric	32		31.25 (11.73)
Vega & Parsons (1967)	Moderate BD	50	44/6	41.7 (14.8)
	Psychiatric	50	37/13	40.8 (13.1)
Watson, Thomas, Anderson, & Felling (1968)	Schizophrenics	50	50/0	43.1 (9.5)
	Organics	50	50/0	
Klonoff, Fibiger, & Hutton (1970)	Schizophrenics	42	NR	47.44 (4.32)
Reitan, Reed, & Dyken (1971)	MS	30	25/5	36.43 (9.57)
	Controls	30	25/5	36.43 (9.46)
DeWolfe, Barrell, Becker, & Spaner (1971)	Old schizophrenics (OS)	25	NR	73 (6.2)
	Young schizophrenics (YS)	25		45 (5.7)
	Old brain-damaged (OBD)	25		70 (7.0)
	Young BD (YBD)	25		44 (10.6)
Reitan & Boll (1971)	Parkinson's	25	20/5	50.92 (8.57)
	Controls	25	20/5	50.84 (8.78)
Goldstein, Deysach, & Kleinknecht (1973)	BD	10	6/4	46.1 (5.6)
	Normals	10	6/4	

Tests Employed	Type of Study	Results
HRNB WAIS Trails A & B MMPI	Differential diagnosis	All HRNB measures significantly discriminated ($p < .05$) P-IQ and FS-IQ significant differences ($p < .01$) between groups 91% hit rate of BD 66% of psychiatric misclassified
HRNB WAIS	Validation	All tests significantly discriminated the groups ($p < .001$) Education significantly related to control performance but not BD
HRNB-6 tests	Differential diagnosis Clinician vs. actuarial approach	Misclassified 76%–92% of schizophrenics as organics; 54% correctly classified by the Impairment Index, while 53% correctly classified by clinicians
HRNB W-B IQ Scale	Test–retest reliability (12 months)	All scored above cutoff for significant impairment (mean = .7) Reliabilities ranged from .49 (TPT-location) to .83 (Impairment Index)
HRNB Trails A & B	Differential diagnosis	All MS subjects showed significant deficient performance on all tasks ($p < .05$) Impairment Index was significantly discriminative ($p < .001$)
WAIS HRNB-9 subtests	Differential diagnosis	Category test significantly discriminated YS from YBD ($p < .01$) Speech sounds, WAIS Picture Completion and Block Design significantly discriminated OS from OBD Impairment Index not significant for any diagnosis
W-B IQ Scale HRNB Trails A & B	Differential diagnosis	Significant group differences on all HRNB measures except time sense memory ($p < .001$)
HRNB-8 subtests Bender-Gestalt WAIS, MMPI	Differential diagnosis Clinical vs. novice HRNB vs. other tests	Impairment Index significantly better than either group of clinicians ($p < .005$) utilizing other measures Impairment Index significantly better than WAIS, Bender, and MMPI ($p < .005$)

(Continues)

TABLE 17.1 (Continued)

Author	Population	N	Gender M/F	Mean Age
Filskov & Goldstein (1974)	BD	89	NR	48.91 (14.71)
Matarazzo, Wiens, Matarazzo, & Goldstein (1974)	Normals	29	29/0	24
Dodrill & Troupin (1975)	Epileptics	17	7/10	27.41 (6.04)
Kiernan & Matthews (1976)	Cerebral lesions (Grp. 1)	81	NR	39.3 (Range 16–73)
	Nonneurological disorders (Grp. 2)	87		32.9 (Range 15–68)
Matarazzo, Matarazzo, Wiens, Gallo, & Klonoff (1976)	BD	16	NR	60
	Schizophrenics	35	NR	47
	Carotid endarterectomy and ischemic	15	13/2	62
	Controls	29	29/0	24
Prigitano & Parsons (1976)	Mild BD	35	32/3	34.6 (13.2)
	Psychiatric	25	18/7	33.2 (15.8)

[d]Number of test administration.

Tests Employed	Type of Study	Results
HRNB	Validity	Validity coefficients with medical procedures (angiography, pneumonoenceph-alography) .93 for laterality .89 for diagnosis 89% hit rate with HRNB
HRNB	Test–retest reliability—4 months	Reliabilities ranged from .44 (Finger Tapping) to .96 (Category test) All but Finger Tapping significantly correlated with retest ($p < .05$)
HRNB	Test–retest 4 administrations 6–12 months apart	Significant differences on Category, TPT-localization, Impairment Index, P-IQ, V-IQ, and FS-IQ between 2nd and 4th administration Impairment Index reliability: I^d vs. II .72 II vs. IV .90 I vs. III .80 III vs. IV .93 I vs. IV .83 II vs. III. 92
HRNB-7 scales	Differential diagnosis	72% overall hit rate using Impairment Index; 84% hit rate for Group 1 39% hit rate for Group 2 77% overall hit rate using statistical averaging: 95% hit rate for Group 1 38% hit rate for Group 2
HRNB	Test–retest reliability	Test–retest correlations for Impairment Index: Controls .08; 100% hit rate Schizophrenics .83*; 71% hit rate carotid/endartectomy .63*; 87% hit rate BD .82*; 100% hit rate *=significant at $p < .01$
HRNB WAIS	Cross-validation of Vega and Parsons (1967)	Education not significantly related for BD but significant for controls All tests except the Category test and Finger Tapping (dominant) discriminated BD from controls Age significantly related to performance on Category, TPT, and Impairment Index for BD and all tests for controls

(Continues)

TABLE 17.1 (Continued)

Author	Population	N	Gender M/F	Mean Age
Schreiber, Goldman, Kleinman, Goldfader, & Snow (1976)	Left Hemisphere (LH)	6	72/2	
	Right Hemisphere (RH)	3		
	Diffuse BD	35		49
	Diffuse LH	7		
	Diffuse RH	11		
	Control	12		41
Golden (1977)	Left BD (LBD)	21	100/16	38.8 (11)
	Right BD (RBD)	31		
	Diffuse BD	34		
	Psychiatric	30		
Finlayson, Johnson, & Reitan (1977)	BD	51	51/0	
	No diploma	17		35.30 (8.19)
	HS	17		34.53 (7.07)
	College	17		34.76 (9.05)
	Control	51	51/0	
	No diploma	17		34.12 (8.72)
	HS	17		34.47 (7.36)
	College	17		35.22 (7.78)
Eckardt & Matarazzo (1981)	Alcoholics	91	91/0	42.2
	Medical controls	20	20/0	45.6
O'Donnell, Kurtz, & Ramanaiah (1983)	Learning disabled (LD)	60	52/8	19.2 (2.0)
	BD	20	15/5	25.0 (3.5)
	Normals	30	21/9	20.0 (1.9)

Tests Employed	Type of Study	Results
HRNB Bender-Gestalt Trails A & B	Validity and localization	All BD significantly poorer on Impairment Index ($p < .01$) Impairment Index not significant discriminator for LH vs. RH TPT time and Rhythm significant discriminator for total RH group
HRNB WAIS	Validity	Full battery hit rate = 95% Localizing hit rate = 90% 90% effective with RBD 40% effective with LBD Block Design, TPT, Trails B, and Impairment Index = 70% overall hit rate 17 of 39 measures = 60% overall hit rate
HRNB WAIS Trails A & B	Differential diagnosis Effect of education	Education had a significant effect on Seashore Rhythm, Speech Sounds, Category, Trails A & B Significant discrimination on each measure between BD and Controls ($p < .001$)
HRNB	Test–retest reliability— 16.8 days (alcoholics), 22.9 days (medical controls)	*For alcoholics:* All tests significantly correlated with first testing ($p < .01$) Ranged from .53 (Trails A, Rhythm, TPT-localization) to .74 (Category test) *For medical controls:* All tests significantly correlated with 1st testing ($p < .05$) Ranged from .48 (Impairment Index) to .93 (TPT-total time)

HRNB	Differential diagnosis	All tests yielded significant differences between controls, LD, and BD groups ($p < .05$) and between LD and BD groups
		Hit rates: 72% overall
		        83% normals
		        63% LD
		        80% BD
		Misclassifications:
		   17% of normals classified LD
		   32% of LD classified normal
		    5% of LD classified as BD
		   20% of BD classified as LD

(Continues)

TABLE 17.1 (Continued)

Author	Population	N	Gender M/F	Mean Age
Goldstein & Shelly (1984)	BD	57	NR	48.61 (11.53)
	Controls	27		43.48 (14.66)
Kane, Parsons, & Goldstein (1985)	BD	46	NR	39.7 (13.5)
	Controls	46		38.9 (11.3)
Kupke & Lewis (1985)	Epileptics I	125	139/111	27.6 (10.2)
	Epileptics II	125		
Bornstein, Baker, & Douglass (1987)	Normals	23	9/14	32.3 (10.3)
Warner, Ernst, Townes, Peel, & Preston (1987)	All psychiatric samples:			
	Harborview	193	115/78	37.1 (15.8)
	Bristol	101	64/37	43.0 (14.5)
	Harborview/WAIS-R	146	80/66	37.4 (14.6)
	WAIS-R	146	70/76	35.8 (14.6)

[c]Wechsler Memory Scale.

Tests Employed	Type of Study	Results
HRNB LNNB WAIS	Discriminative validity	77.4% hit rate for HRNB 79.8% hit rate for LNNB 65.5% hit rate for WAIS 86.9% hit rate for HRNB + WAIS 83.3% hit rate for LNNB + WAIS
HRNB LNNB	Discriminative validity	LNNB discriminated between groups on all scales ($p < .0001$) HRNB discriminated on all subtests, most at $p < .0001$ Hit rates for controls: LNNB = 100%; HRNB = 95.4% Hit rates for BD: LNNB = 93.4%; HRNB = 91.67% Correlation between LNNB and HRNB $r = .83$
WAIS HRNB	Cross-validation	71% of comparisons were significant 52% (P-IQ), 64% (V-IQ), and 66% (FS-IQ) overlap with HRNB Cross-validation range from 14% (Similarities) to 55% (Arithmetic)
HRNB	Test–retest reliability— 3 weeks	Reliability coefficients ranged from .55 on Trails A to .80 on TPT-memory
WAIS or WAIS-R HRNB WMS[c] WRAT	Validation with IQ	IQ correlated significantly with all HRNB measures ($p < .05$) and WMS ($p < .0001$) Ranged from –.62 (Impairment Index) to .60 (Rhythm)

HRNB are successful in differentiating between non–brain-damaged and brain-damaged patients.

However, some studies have not found such positive results (Klonoff, Fibiger & Hutton, 1970; Orgel & McDonald, 1967; Watson, Thomas, Anderson, & Felling, 1968). Golden (1977) cited various methodological issues as possibly explaining the discrepant findings in these studies, including (a) the chronicity of the population used, (b) the selection of the measures used in the studies, (c) the effects of different base rates of different disorders, (d) the effects of various medications the patients might have been taking, (e) the process employed in patient selection, and (f) the method chosen for test analysis.

In an attempt to control for some of these variables, Golden (1977) studied a mixed psychiatric and neurologically impaired population using the HRNB. He found the entire battery of tests was very effective in discriminating between normal and brain-damaged patients. A lower but significant discrimination was found between psychiatric and neurologically impaired subjects. In particular, he found that in using all of the tests in a discriminant analysis to classify subjects, 90.5% of the left-brain injured, 94.1% of the diffuse brain-injured, 93.5% of the right-brain injured, and 100% of the patients in the psychiatric group were correctly classified.

Additional evidence of the effectiveness of the total battery, as well as of the Impairment Index, was reported by Boucher, Dewan, Donnelly, Pandurangi, Bartell, Diamond, and Major (1986). In this study, 20 young male schizophrenics were administered the HRNB. The Halstead Impairment Index, when compared to two alternative, statistically derived indices (percentage of ratings within the Impairment Range, Average Impairment Rating), was found to be the only statistically significant discriminator between the schizophrenics and the normals. O'Donnell, Kurtz, and Ramaniah (1983) also found that the HRNB significantly discriminated between clinic groups, thus lending further sup-

port to the notion that this battery provides adequate clinical information in distinguishing between psychiatric and neurologic populations.

Other investigators have examined the usefulness of the HRNB for patients with brain tumors (Hom & Reitan, 1982; Hom & Reitan, 1984), aphasia (Doehring & Reitan, 1961; Heimburger & Reitan, 1961), Huntington's disease (Boll, Heaton, & Reitan, 1974), and multiple sclerosis (Forsyth, Gaddes, Reitan & Tryk, 1971; Reitan, Reed, & Dyken, 1971), and have used the battery to document the effects of aging (Fitzhugh, Fitzhugh, & Reitan, 1964). While the battery seems to be adequate in distinguishing between normality and pathology, other studies have investigated whether it is useful in the lateralization of dysfunction.

Lateralization of Dysfunction

It will be recalled that Golden (1977) found that the HRNB was effective in classifying patients with right or left brain damage. However, as Golden noted, different types of brain injury differentially affect measures. For example, the Trails Test is equally effective with all groups, while WAIS-R Block Design is more effective in identifying right brain–damaged patients. The Finger Oscillation Test and Tactual Performance Test have also been found useful in reflecting unilateral dysfunction (Boll, 1980). Further, suppression on sensory imperception measures reported on one side of the body can be diagnostic of contralateral impairment (Goldstein & Shelly, 1973; Wheeler & Reitan, 1962). The modified Halstead-Wepman Aphasia Screening Test has been found to be sensitive to both right- and left-sided dysfunction, depending on the items. Items assessing naming, word pronunciation, reading, spelling, and writing were found to be sensitive to left hemisphere damage (Wheeler & Reitan, 1962), and activities such as copying forms were sensitive to right hemisphere dysfunction (Heimburger & Reitan, 1961). The Category Test and Tactual Performance Test (Memory and Localization components) have been documented to be affected by lesions to both cerebral hemispheres (as documented by computerized tomography). Based on her review, Lezak (1983) concluded that the sensory perception tests were most useful in lateralizing lesions but that the measures composing the Impairment Index were not.

Subject-Examiner Variables

Subject-examiner effects on test performance also have been addressed. Subject variables such as age, gender, education, SES, and chronicity vary across studies and all have been reported to have effects on neuropsychological findings. Gilandas, Touzy, Beumont, and Greenberg (1984) found that about three-quarters of the studies with the HRNB focused on 25- to 55-year-olds, while the 16–25 and 55+ groups have not been well studied. Nonetheless, some investigations have demonstrated the importance of some of these variables in terms of their contribution to overall neuropsychological performance. For example, Karzmark, Heaton, Grant, and Matthews (1984) examined the impact of various demographic variables in predicting performance on the HRNB. Using a population of 491 neurologically normal 15- to 81-year-olds, they found that the variables of gender, age, education, race, and occupation accounted for 65% of the variance in the Average Impairment Rating. However, other than gender (in some cases) and age, these variables are not controlled for in most studies.

Educational level in particular is poorly reported in most studies. Generally, the evidence suggests that there is an education effect on the neuropsychological performance of brain-damaged patients (Boll & Reitan, 1973; Finlayson, Johnson, & Reitan, 1977; Prigatano & Parsons, 1976; Reed & Reitan, 1963). Some studies, however, have attempted to address these variables by providing tables to correct for the possible effects of age and education on neuropsychological test performance (e.g., Alekoumbides, Charter, Adkins, & Seacat, 1987). This topic is treated more thoroughly on pages 335–342, including the use of tables to correct for the impact of education on the V-P IQ discrepancies of patients with unilateral lesions.

Reliability

Examining the reliability of neuropsychological measures, particularly test–retest, is fraught with potential problems if one employs a pathological population. Some neurological conditions may show improvement over time (stroke, brain injury), while others may evidence deterioration (dementia). However, most studies that examine individual tests report good split-half reliabilities (e.g., Shaw, 1966) or, in some cases, good test–retest reliabilities (Klonoff, Fibiger, & Hutton, 1970). Matarazzo and his associates found that not only was the Impairment Index reliable with patients with brain damage but that it was also reliable with normal controls (Matarazzo, Matarazzo, Weins, Gallo, & Klonoff, 1976; Matarazzo, Weins, Matarazzo, & Goldstein, 1974).

Overview

The rich history of research focusing on the HRNB is a testament to the fact that it has had a very significant impact on the development of clinical neuropsychology as an applied discipline. Despite the limitations imposed by its lengthy administration time, narrow focus on neurological diagnosis, limited and poorly reported norms, and unrevised format (Dean, 1985; Meier, 1985), it is still the most widely used neuropsychological test battery available today.

LURIA-NEBRASKA NEUROPSYCHOLOGICAL BATTERY

Although the HRNB is still the most frequently administered battery, the Luria-Nebraska has had a significant impact on how clinicians have viewed the assessment process and its results.

Since its introduction a decade ago, the Luria-Nebraska has generated a large and very controversial literature.

In 1966 Luria published his first edition of *Higher Cortical Functions in Man*. This volume had an immediate and profound effect on psychologists and physicians who were involved in assessing the effects of alterations in brain–behavior relations, summarizing as it did a vast literature and introducing to Western readers an integrated overview of a Soviet research tradition. Luria, who was initially trained in psychology and then in neurology, described his own clinical experiences and presented a conceptual framework for individual patient examination. This approach offered a qualitative perspective to the appraisal of individual differences, unlike the empirical approach characterized by the many psychometric measures in use at that time.

In an effort to catalog Luria's (1966) investigative techniques, Christensen visited Luria for a short period of time in 1970 and outlined his clinical procedures. These efforts led to the publication of *Luria's Neuropsychological Investigation* (Christensen, 1975) in which Luria outlined his concept of the neuropsychological examination and described investigative techniques in 10 neuropsychological domains. These domains are listed in Table 17.2.

For Luria, the neuropsychological examination had as its central purpose the study of disturbed higher cortical functions such that a syndrome could be diagnosed accurately. Secondly, the investigation was to assist in the diagnosis of brain lesions. Unique to Luria's conceptualization, particularly in relation to the approach popular in the United States, was the notion that direct localization of function in discrete regions of the cortex was inconsistent with clinical experience. Rather than such a strict localizationist perspective, Luria advanced the notion of "functional systems":

> If "function," defined as the function of a specific tissue, is to be "localized" in a specific area of the secretory system or the nervous system, the "functional system" obviously cannot be "localized" in a specific area of the cerebral tissue, but must be distributed **in a complete system (or in a constellation) of cooperating zones of the cerebral cortex and the subcortical structures.** *By these means—and this is of extreme importance—each of these areas makes a* **highly specific contribution to ensure the operation of the functional system.** *(Luria, 1966 p. 17, emphasis in original)*

Thus, for Luria, the neuropsychological investigation was a highly unique and very individual means of appraisal. It had as its focus the evaluation of the various components of a disturbed functional system such that a decision could be reached as to which cortical area implicated in the functional system was affected. The qualitative nature of this investigation was characteristic of his approach, and he recognized that because of its sharp focus the application of statistical concepts was impossible. Reliability in a statistical sense was not possible, for example, because of the small number of items administered and because of the highly intercorrelated nature of component tasks assessing the integrity of a functional system (Christensen, 1975).

Based on Luria's conceptual framework, Golden sought to merge the advantages of quantitative and qualitative approaches to neuropsychological assessment. The product of his efforts was the Luria-Nebraska Neuropsychological Battery.

Conceptualization

Golden was attracted to Luria's qualitative approach for several reasons. First, the idea that functional behaviors were broken down into their components was attractive because it allowed a more comprehensive assessment of neuropsychological organization. Second, the idea that each investigation was individualized and focused on dysfunction was seen as a major advantage. Luria had suggested, for example, that the competent neuropsychological exami-

TABLE 17.2   Outline of *Luria's Neuropsychological Investigation**

1. The Preliminary Conversation

2. The Determination in Cerebral Dominance

3. Investigation of Motor Functions
   Motor Functions of the Hands
   Oral Praxis
   Speech Regulation of the Motor Act

4. Investigation of Acoustico-Motor Organization
   Perception and Reproduction of Pitch Relationships
   Perception and Regulation of Rhythmic Structures

5. Investigation of the Higher Cutaneous and Kinesthetic Functions
   Cutaneous Sensation
   Muscle and Joint Sensation
   Stereognosis

6. Investigation of Higher Visual Functions
   Visual Perception of Objects and Pictures
   Spatial Orientation
   Intellectual Operations in Space

7. Investigation of Impressive Speech
   Phonemic Hearing
   Word Comprehension
   Understanding of Simple Sentences
   Understanding of Logical Grammatical Structures

8. Investigation of Expressive Speech
   Articulation of Speech Sounds
   Reflected (Repetitive) Speech
   The Nominative Function of Speech
   Narrative Speech

9. Investigation of Writing and Reading
   Phonetic Analysis and Synthesis of Words
   Writing
   Reading

10. Investigation of Arithmetical Skill
    Comprehension of Number Structure
    Arithmetical Operations

11. Investigation of Mnestic Processes
    The Learning Process
    Retention and Retrieval
    Logical Memorizing

12. Investigation of Intellectual Processes
    Understanding of Thematic Pictures and Texts
    Concept Formation
    Discursive Intellectual Activity

*Adapted from Christensen (1975).

nation need not take more than 2 to 3 hours (Christensen, 1975). This was viewed as a great improvement over the 6 to 8 hours the Halstead-Reitan battery took. Further, Luria's investigation was considerably more comprehensive than other eclectic approaches that might involve tests of intelligence or basic sensory or perceptual processes. Finally, Golden saw Luria's investigation as oriented not only toward differential diagnosis, but also aimed at developing rehabilitation plans focused on the specific disability documented (Golden, 1981).

Drawbacks to Luria's approach were also evident. Golden (1981) correctly noted that the tests were not standardized so that one could be assured that two examiners would use the same materials or instructions in administering a similar item found in Christensen's (1975) summary of Luria's approach. Second, no quantification of the test results was offered—or even acknowledged by Luria as important. Thus, the examiner had to rely on clinical intuition in reaching a decision regarding adequate performance on the procedures. Since training with Luria was not possible, and since the opportunity to gain such expertise was not readily available in the United States, some means of formalizing clinical decisions had to be made. Finally, Luria offered no data regarding reliability or validity. This omission was also noted earlier by Reitan (1976).

Based on these perceptions, Golden sought to standardize Luria's investigation within the psychometric tradition prevalent in the United States. Beginning with the published information regarding Luria's investigation, Golden attempted to develop a reliable scoring system. Through multiple tryouts, a battery eventually emerged that took between 2 to 2½ hours to administer. A number of Luria's initial items had been omitted because reliable scoring was not possible, because the items proved difficult for normal controls, or because they proved to be redundant (Golden, 1981).

The Battery

The Luria-Nebraska Neuropsychological Battery is straightforward in that the 11 scales are roughly equivalent to the conceptual scheme outlined by Luria, shown in Table 17.2.

Luria-Nebraska Scales

MOTOR FUNCTIONS   The Motor Functions scale involves a series of test items that are reported to assess both elementary and complex motor abilities. Motor performance using both the right and left hand is assessed through a number of simple timed motor items. In addition to simple drawing tasks, motor movements requiring the mouth and tongue are required.

RHYTHM   This scale assesses the ability to discriminate rhythm and pitch relationships. Also assessed is the ability to produce tonal sequences and a melodic line and to sing a familiar song. The patient also reproduces rhythmic patterns.

TACTILE   For all items on this scale the subject is blindfolded. Using various stimuli, the patient must discriminate the location of tactile stimulation, discriminate between a hard and soft stimulus, and identify common objects by touch. Other items involve matching positional orientation in which one arm is placed in a standard position and perceiving the nature of stimuli written on the wrist.

VISUAL   Visual and spatial skills are assessed by the Visual scale. Simple common objects must be identified by sight; gestalt perception is assessed, as is three-dimensional perception, the ability to tell time, and spatial orientation.

RECEPTIVE SPEECH   The items on the Receptive Speech scale range from those that assess the ability to comprehend simple phonemes to those that require comprehension of words and complex sentences. Other items assess the ability to follow simple instructions, such as instructions involving the use of prepositions and those involving the possessive case.

EXPRESSIVE SPEECH Oral language is appraised on the Expressive Speech scale. Beginning with the simple repetition of phonemes, items progress in difficulty, eventually requiring naming, counting, animated speech, and sentence repetition.

WRITING Basic writing ability is assessed on this scale. Tasks involve simple spelling, copying letters and words and writing them from memory, writing one's name, and spontaneous writing on a predetermined subject.

READING The items on this scale are similar to the items on the Writing scale; the patient must read individual letters, syllables, words, and a short story.

MATH The task includes number identification, writing of numbers from dictation, reading numbers, making comparative numerical judgments, and various addition and subtraction items. Serial subtraction (by 7 and by 13) items are also included.

MEMORY Like the items on the other scales, the items on the Memory scale assess a very wide variety of memory skills. Both verbal and nonverbal memory are assessed. Items assess serial learning, visual memory with interference, memorization of a rhythmic pattern, memorization of serial hand movements, and word and sentence recall. Finally, a word association task is presented.

INTELLIGENCE Items on this scale are similar to other items found on the battery except that they tend to be more difficult and involve abstract reasoning ability. Visual sequential processing is tapped, as are the abilities to abstract thematic information and to reason by analogy. Finally, simple and more difficult arithmetic problems are presented.

Scoring and Interpretation

Item performance on this battery is scored on a 3-point scale derived from earlier studies in the test development stage. A score of 0 indicates normal performance, whereas scores of 1 and 2 indicate increasingly deviant performance. Raw scores are summed within a scale and then converted to T-scores per scale (Golden, Hammeke, & Purisch, 1980). The T-scores have a mean of 50 and standard deviation of 10, where *high* scores denote deviant behavior. Data from 700 persons comprise the norm base, and cut-off scores are provided for differentiating normal from deviant performance.

Special scales were also developed by Golden, Hammeke, and Purisch (1978). The Pathognomonic Scale comprises 32 items that were found to best discriminate between normal functioning and brain impairment. Two further scales, the Right Hemisphere and the Left Hemisphere scales, were derived from those motor and sensory items that best reflect lateralized performance. Age and education corrections exist for the scales as well.

Golden sought to provide a battery that allowed both quantitative and qualitative evaluation of a patient's performance, so a number of steps have been recommended in interpreting a patient's performance. These steps include (1) an analysis of the pattern of performance across the 11 regular and 3 special scales of the battery; (2) an examination of the localization scales, as suggested by McKay and Golden (1979); (3) an inspection of the factor scales that are available to assist in examining more discrete components of the systems investigated (McKay & Golden, 1981); (4) an analysis of test item patterns; and (5) qualitative analysis of the patient's performance (Gilandas et al., 1984).

The development of the Luria-Nebraska Neuropsychological Battery represents a sincere attempt to merge the qualitative approach advocated by Luria and the traditional psychometric-quantitative approach characteristic of present-day practices in the United States. Golden et al. (1982) have emphasized repeatedly that no one scale or factor or item score necessarily reflects the discrete functioning of one specific region of the brain. This view is certainly consistent with Luria's (1980) theory and current concepts (Kupfermann, 1985). Scales and factor scores may at best represent the integrity of the various functional systems addressed by this battery; even the performance on specific items cannot possibly represent the solitary functioning of individual cortical regions. While these cautions and qualifications are consistent with the theoretical formulation of the battery, the validation studies focused on establishing the discriminant validity of the various scales and scores—an approach Luria (1975) had suggested was impossible due to the small number of items per category within the scales or "functional systems." Consequently, the merger between a qualitative and quantitative approach was confronted with a rather important conceptual challenge from the beginning. From the standpoint of differential diagnosis in clinical neuropsychology, this was indeed an important issue. Table 17.3 summarizes representative studies regarding the Luria-Nebraska Neuropsychological Battery.

Validation Studies

The earliest version of the Luria-Nebraska Neuropsychological Battery was referred to as the Luria-South Dakota Neuropsychological Test Battery. This battery was the focus of considerable validation studies. The studies reported by Golden, Hammeke, and Purisch (1978) and Hammeke, Golden, and Purisch (1978) are representative in this regard. These studies most typically examined the effectiveness of the Luria-Nebraska to discriminate between undifferentiated neurological patients and control subjects (usually individuals with other medical problems). As in the Golden et al. (1978) study, t tests were computed between the neurological and control group scores on all 285 items, of

which 253 were significant. Follow-up discriminant analysis using all 285 items resulted in a combination of 30 items that were able to separate the groups with 100% accuracy. The study by Hammeke et al. (1978) examined the ability of the scales to distinguish between groups. They found that t tests between the scores of the controls and neurological patients on the scales all were significantly different. Follow-up discriminant analysis correctly classified 93% of the subjects using the Luria-South Dakota scales. These results in group discrimination were contrasted to that obtained in studies using the Halstead-Reitan battery, which in some studies resulted in a 90% discrimination rate (e.g., Wheeler, Burke, & Reitan, 1962).

Additional studies reported on the ability of the battery to discriminate between brain injured and schizophrenic patients (Golden, Graber, Moses & Zatz, 1980; Lewis, Golden, Purisch, & Hemmeke, 1979a; Purisch, Golden & Hammeke, 1978) and to localize brain lesions (Golden, Moses, Fishburne, Engum, Lewis, Wisniewski, Conley, & Berg, 1981; Lewis, Golden, Moses, Osmon, Purisch, & Hammeke, 1979b; McKay & Golden, 1979a, 1979b; Osmon, Golden, Purisch, Hammeke, & Blume, 1979). Other studies assessed its psychometric properties (Golden & Berg, 1980a, 1980b, 1980c; Golden, Berg, & Graber, 1982; Golden, Fross, & Graber, 1981; Moses & Golden, 1979). Factor analytic studies were also reported (Golden, Hammeke, Osmon, Sweet, Purisch, & Graber, 1981; Golden, Osmon, Sweet, Graber, Purisch, & Hammeke, 1980; Golden, Purisch, Sweet, Graber, Osmon, Hammeke, 1980; Golden, Sweet, Hammeke, Purisch, Graber, & Osmon, 1980).

Brain Injury Versus Schizophrenia

Those studies that examined the usefulness of the battery with schizophrenics reported that scores on the scales adequately discriminated between neurological patients and schizophrenics (Purisch et al. 1978). Using the 14 summary measures, an 83% accuracy rate was achieved in correctly classifying patients. Further, Lewis et al. (1979a) found significant differences when the profile of schizophrenics was compared to that obtained from brain-injured and normal controls. Two subgroups appeared to exist within the schizophrenic population: One group seemed to evidence no signs of brain dysfunction, while the other group of schizophrenics did demonstrate evidence of dysfunction. For schizophrenics in the latter group, poor performance was noted on the Motor, Rhythm, Receptive Speech, Arithmetic, Memory, and Intelligence scales.

Although Lewis et al.'s (1979a) study suggested that subclassifications of schizophrenics may well exist, Purisch et al. (1978) and Golden et al. (1980) employed undifferentiated schizophrenics to further examine the diagnostic accuracy of the battery. In the Purisch et al. (1978) study, multiple *t* tests were again employed using the items of the battery, and it was found that schizophrenics performed better as a group than the brain-damaged patients on 72 items. Golden et al. (1980) examined chronic schizophrenics with and without ventricular enlargement and reported that the battery was 81% correct in determining the presence of ventricular enlargement. Using reliably obtained (.98) ventricular measurements and a diagnostic rule approach, they reported that of the 16 patients diagnosed on the battery as having brain damage, 14 had enlarged ventricles. Of the 26 patients with no evidence of brain dysfunction on the Luria-Nebraska, 24 were found not to have enlarged ventricles or prominent sulci. Golden et al.'s conclusion was that the Luria-Nebraska (as it was now called) was sensitive to the effects of brain damage.

Localization of Dysfunction

However, while the battery might be sensitive to the effects of brain damage, that did not necessarily mean that it was also useful in localizing or in lateralizing focal effects. The re-

sults of studies reported by Golden and his associates addressing this issue have theoretical relevance and are of both practical and clinical importance.

Two studies by McKay and Golden (1979a, 1979b) examined the ability of the battery to lateralize and localize brain lesions. The first study (McKay & Golden, 1979a) focused on developing a left and right hemisphere index. Experimental scales were developed using 15 right and 14 left hemisphere–damaged patients. The resulting items (38 for left and 36 for right hemispheric lesions) that comprised the scales were them employed on a separate validation sample of 40 cases of left hemispheric damage and 31 cases of right hemispheric damage. The use of these separate scales resulted in a correct classification rate of 87%. Lateralization of the lesion was accomplished through computerized tomography, angiogram, or surgical reports. The second study by McKay and Golden (1979b) attempted to derive experimental scales for localization of brain lesions. Using 53 patients with localized brain lesions, seven special scales were empirically derived and included items believed to assess abilities associated with left frontal, left sensorimotor, left parietal-occipital, left temporal, right frontal, right sensorimotor, right partial-occipital, and right temporal regions. The items for these special scales were assigned according to the results of multiple *t* tests on each item between each focal damaged group and that of normal controls. Items that discriminated among more than two groups were eliminated. Plotting the means for these groups, McKay and Golden (1979b) concluded that 47 of the 53 subjects scored poorest on that scale corresponding to their localized lesion.

Both of the above studies evidenced considerable methodological problems, not the least of which was the fact that documentation of lesion localization was not reported in any objective fashion. Studies by Lewis et al. (1979b) and Golden et al. (1981) attempted to address the issues raised in the McKay and Golden (1979a, 1979b) studies.

TABLE 17.3   Chronological summary of studies examining the validity and reliability of the Luria-Nebraska Neuropsychological Battery

Author		Population	N	Gender M/F	Mean Age
Hammeke, Golden, & Purisch (1978)	Study 1	Brain injured	50	27/23	42.0 (14.8)[a]
		Medical controls	50	24/26	43.3 (18.8)
	Study 2	Right Hemisphere (RH)	30	17/13	51.40 (20.5)
		Left Hemisphere (LH)	41	18/23	49.63 (17.5)
Golden, Hammeke, & Purisch (1978)		Brain injured	50	51/49	42 (14.8)
		Medical controls	50		44.3 (18.8)
Purisch, Golden, & Hammeke (1978)		Schizophrenic	50	56/44	44.36 (18.83)
		Brain injured	50		41.32 (14.52)
Osmon, Golden, Purisch, Hammeke, & Blume (1979)		Right Hemisphere (RH)	20	NR	49.11
		Left Hemisphere (LH)	20		(mean for 60 Sa)
		Diffuse brain-damaged (BD)	20		
Lewis, Golden, Moses, Osmon, Purisch, & Hammeke (1979)		RH Frontal	6	3/3	42.5 (13.3)
		Sensorimotor	6	3/3	(mean for 60 Sa)
		Parieto-occipital	6	3/3	
		Temporal	6	4/2	
		LH Frontal	9	5/4	
		Sensorimotor	9	5/4	
		Parieto-occipital	9	4/5	
		Temporal	9	3/6	
		Control	NR	NR	NR
McKay & Golden (1979b)	Study 1	Right Hemisphere (RH)	15	NR	50.3 (22.3)
		Left Hemisphere (LH)	14		49.8 (17.7)
		BD	36		51.3 (21.6)
		Schizophrenic	70		39.6 (22.4)
		Normal	73		48.7 (23.4)
	Study 2	Brain damaged	53	NR	NR
		Medical normals	77		41.3 (16.3)
Lewis, Golden, Purisch, & Hammeke (1979)		Brain damaged	50	27/23	42.0 (14.8)
		Schizophrenics	72	34/38	36.96 (12.98)
Golden (1979)		Multiple sclerosis (MS)	24	NR	36.4
		BD	101		39.0 (12.8)
		Psychiatric	106		Age Range 20–60
		Normals	74		for other groups

[a]Numbers in parentheses are standard deviations.
[b]Luria-Nebraska Neuropsychological Battery.

Tests Employed	Type of Study	Results
LNNB[b]-14 scales	Differential diagnosis	93% hit rate
LNNB-14 scales	Differential diagnosis	87.8% hit rate for LH 86.8% hit rate for RH 87.3% overall hit rate
LNNB-14 scales	Differential diagnosis	90% item hit rate with full battery 100% hit rate for 30 of 285 items
LNNB-14 scales	Differential diagnosis	88% hit rate 100% hit rate on 40 items
LNNB-11 scales	Diagnosis of lateralized BD	Left Hemisphere scale showed only significant group difference
LNNB-14 scales	Localization	78.6% of comparisons were significant 20.2% of nonredundant comparisons were significant
LNNB-14 scales	Experimental lateralizing scales (38 items on LH scale; 36 on RH scale)	60% hit rate on RH scale 71% hit rate on LH scale
LNNB-8 scales	Scale derivation	47 of BD scored highest on scale corresponding to damaged area
LNNB-11 scales	Differential diagnosis	Chronicity and length of hospitalization not related to LNNB performance Schizophrenics performed significantly different on all scales
LNNB-14 scales	Differential diagnosis on MS derived scale	100% hit rate for all groups

(Continues)

TABLE 17.3 (Continued)

Author	Population	N	Gender M/F	Mean Age
Moses & Golden (1979)	BD	50	44/6	43.8
	Medical controls	50	41/9	
Chmielewski & Golden (1980)	Alcoholics	40	40/0	50.24 (9.25)
	Medical controls	40	40/0	47.52 (15.84)
Golden, Sweet, Hammeke, Purisch, Graber, & Osmon (1980)	BD	90	NR	42.1 (15.7)
	Psychiatric	90		39.6 (14.8)
	Normal	90		41.3 (15.3)
Golden, Purisch, Sweet, Graber, Osmon, & Hammeke (1980)	BD	90	NR	42.1 (15.7)
	Psychiatric	90		39.6 (14.8)
	Normal	90		41.3 (15.3)
Golden, Osmon, Sweet, Graber, Purisch, & Hammeke (1980)	BD	90	NR	42.1 (15.7)
	Psychiatric	90		39.6 (14.8)
	Normal	90		41.3 (15.3)
Golden & Berg (1980b)	BD	198	180/158	40.38 (17.2)
	Psychiatric	70		(mean for 338 Sa)
	Normal	70		
Golden & Berg (1980a)	BD	198	180/158	40.38 (17.2)
	Psychiatric	70		(mean for 338 Sa)
	Normal	70		
Golden & Berg (1980c)	BD	198	180/158	40.38 (17.2)
	Psychiatric	70		(mean for 338 Sa)
	Normal	70		
Golden, Graber, Moses, & Zatz (1980)	Schizophrenic with normal CT	26		Age Range 20 to 39
	Schizophrenic with abnormal CT	16	24/18	
Golden, Moses, Graber, & Berg (1981) Study 1	Normals College	20	NR	40.3 (12.8)
	H.S.	20		(mean for 60 Sa)
	No diploma	20		
Study 2	BD College	20	NR	42.1 (15.7)
	H.S.	20		(mean for 60 Sa)
	No diploma	20		
Study 3	BD	60	NR	43.6 (13.8)
	Normals	60		43.2 (15.4)

Tests Employed	Type of Study	Results
LNNB-11 scales	Cross-validation	Hit rate of 96% overall Scales hit rates: 70%–86%
LNNB-14 scales	Differential diagnosis	Significant differences on 6 of 14 scales: Alcoholics had problems in functionally complex tasks
LNNB-Motor, Rhythm, Tactile	Factor analysis	7 factors found on Motor Scales 2 factors on Rhythm and Tactile scales each
LNNB-Visual, Receptive Speech, Expressive Speech, Reading	Factor analysis	3 factors on Visual Scale 2 factors on Receptive Speech 5 factors on Expressive Speech 2 factors on Reading
LNNB-Writing, Arithmetic, Memory, left, & right	Factor analysis	2 factors on Writing Scale, Arithmetic, Memory 1 factor on left and right combined
LNNB-Motor Scale	Item intercorrelation	All items except 9 and 13 were significantly intercorrelated with nonscale items
LNNB-Rhythm Scale	Item intercorrelation	All items except 56, 57, and 61 correlated significantly with nonscale items
LNNB-Writing Scale	Item intercorrelation	All items significantly correlated with nonscale items
LNNB-14 scales	Differential diagnosis	81% hit rate for ventricle enlargement using LNNB 90% hit rate for BD using LNNB
LNNB-12 scales	Validation-effect of level of education	.74 multiple correlation between age, education, and LNNB
LNNB-12 scales	Comparison with above group	91% hit rate
LNNB-12 scales	Differential diagnosis	85% hit rate for BD 83% hit rate for normals 84% total hit rate

(Continues)

TABLE 17.3   (Continued)

Author	Population	N	Gender M/F	Mean Age
Golden, Foss, & Graber (1981)	Neurological	181	NR	NR
	Right Hemisphere (RH)	45		
	Left Hemisphere (LH)	43		
	Psychiatric	83		
	Normal	74		
Golden, Moses, Fishburne, Engum, Lewis, Wisniewski, Conley, & Berg (1981)	Neurological	87	64/23	NR
	Control	30	NR	NR
Golden, Hammeke, Osmon, Sweet, Purisch, & Graber (1981)	BD	90	NR	42.1 (15.7)
	Psychiatric	90		39.6 (14.8)
	Normal	90		41.3 (15.3)
Golden, Kane, Sweet, Moses, Cardellino, Templeton, Vicente, & Graber (1981)	BD	48	40/8	39.8 (19.3)
	Schizophrenic	30	24/6	37.4 (17.6)
	Normal	30	22/8	39.0 (19.8)
Golden, Berg, & Graber (1982)	Stable BD	27	14/13	35.3 (11.2)
Golden, MacInnes, Ariel, Ruedrich, Chu, Coffman, Graber, & Bloch (1982)	Schizophrenics	43	30/13	29.36 (6.3) Age range 20 to 39
Delis & Kaplan (1982)	BD with aphasia	1	1/0	60

Tests Employed	Type of Study	Results
LNNB-11 scales	Split-half reliability and item-scale consistency	All items correlated significantly with scale (shared variance < 10% on 3 cases) Split-half reliability .89 (memory) to .95 (reading)
LNNB-11 scales plus LH, RH, R & L, 8 localization scales	Cross validation for presence, lateralization, and localization of BD	81% hit rate for LH BD 66% hit rate for RH BD 90% hit rate total 75% hit rate for R-L difference 74% hit rate for localization 87% hit rate for normals
LNNB	Factor analysis of Intelligence and Pathognomonic scales	4 factors on Intelligence Scale 4 factors on Pathognomic Scale
LNNB HRNB WAIS CT scans for schizophrenic and BD	Comparison between LNNB and HRNB	LNNB: 87% hit rate for BD 88% hit rate for controls and schizophrenics 88% overall hit rate HRNB: 90% hit rate for BD 84% hit rate for controls and schizophrenics 86% hit rate overall 89% agreement between LNNB & HRNB .69 correlation between HRNB & LNNB
LNNB-13 scales CT scan	Test–retest reliability	Test–retest reliability range = .77 (RH) to .96 (Arithmetic) $\overline{X}$ = .88
LNNB-14 scales CT scan	Differential diagnosis	100% hit rate for enlarged ventricles 36% misdiagnosed as abnormal by LNNB 77% total hit rate Ventricle corr. with LNNB = .76
LNNB-14 scales	Case study	Patient's scores on Expressive Speech Receptive Speech and Motor Scales were not consonant with patient's symptoms nor lesion location

Using a schematic guide, Lewis et al. (1979b) had neurologists or neurological surgeons indicate the focal lesion of 60 patients for whom data were available. An additional criterion was that more than 50% of a lesion had to be localized in only one specified area in each hemisphere. Using these criteria, they examined the performance of patients comprising the same basic groups as noted by McKay and Golden (1979b), whom they did not cite. The performance of the patients in these groups on the 14 scales of the battery was significantly different from that of normals. Post hoc tests revealed that nearly all brain-damaged groups were significantly different from the normals on every scale of the battery; of the 112 possible comparisons between the eight groups, 88 significant differences (78.6%) were obtained. Lewis et al. (1979b) reviewed these differences and concluded that the scales of the battery are differentially sensitive to the focal effects of localized brain damage, consistent with neuropsychological theory. For example, the left frontal lobe–damaged group scored very poorly on the Motor, Expressive Speech, Math, and Pathognomonic scales, whereas the left temporal–damaged group was more than 3 standard deviations from the normal controls on the Receptive Speech scale. In all instances, however, the profiles of the patients in the left hemisphere groups indicated more impairment than did those with right focal hemispheric lesions. One of the conclusions that may be drawn from this finding is that, other than the lateralizing value of the sensory and motor items on this battery, there are very few items that tap components of prosody or other central or anterior processes (Ross, 1981) associated with the right hemisphere.

A follow-up study by Golden et al. (1981), employing the same procedures for localization of a lesion site, found that by using the Right and Left scales good classification (78%) was achieved, but by using the highest localization scale, even higher correct classification of lesion site (84%) was obtained. While this study provided some support for the findings of the Lewis et al. (1979b), a study conducted by Osmon et al. (1979) provided some interesting results. Sixty patients were examined (20 left lesion, 20 right lesion, and 20 diffuse) on the battery. Analysis of variance across the 14 summary scales yielded only one significant difference between these groups. The patients with left hemisphere damage did significantly poorer on the Left Hemisphere scale when compared to the other two groups ($F = 3.17$, $p < .05$). Of considerable interest, though, is the fact that when all scales were used in a discriminant analysis, 59 of the 60 patients (98%) were correctly classified into their appropriate group. What these results mean is that the pattern and level of performance on these scales by the three groups of brain-damaged patients significantly differentiated among the patient groups.

The findings of the Osman et al. (1979) study raised several points. Osman and his colleagues reasoned that the two hemispheres are so interdependent, as predicted by Luria's (1980) theory, that the deficits evidenced by these groups will be very complex. Therefore, the variance examined in the analysis of variance might be expected to be small across the scales. Thus, the discriminant analysis should be employed because it allows the "pattern of deficits to be evaluated" (p. 7). This reasoning is inconsistent with the philosophy that has guided much of the research on this battery, particularly those other studies that did examine very focal effects (e.g., Golden et al., 1981; Lewis et al., 1979b) and reported that most scales distinguished patients with specific and theoretically consistent deficits. A second point to consider is that only one scale evidenced a significant effect in these patients with left, right, or diffuse damage, and that effect was relatively small. In this study the mean scores were not at all *clinically* significant, if the standard deviations reported are taken into account. For example, on the Expressive Speech scale, which in Lewis et al.'s (1979b) report distinguishes left frontal patients, the mean *T*-scores for the left, right, and diffuse patients are 71.40 (SD = 31.67), 65.54 (SD = 12.62), and 73.33 (SD = 20.58), respectively. While the mean T-scores are not very different, the degree of variance is very significant *within* each group, thus ensuring nonsignificant results and drawing into question how clinically useful these scales are. This point is not adequately addressed by these or other authors.

Reliability

Psychometric issues relating to the Luria-Nebraska have also been addressed. Split-half reliability was investigated by Golden, Fross, and Graber (1981) in a population of 338 patients. Across the scales of the Luria-Nebraska, split-half reliabilities (odd-even items) ranged from .89 (Memory) to .95 (Reading). Test–retest reliability (mean interval of 167 days) was examined by Golden, Berg, and Graber (1982) in 27 patients with long-standing neurological disorders. Test–retest correlations ranged from .77 (Right Hemisphere scale) to .96 (Arithmetic) and averaged .88 across the 14 scales.

Factor Analysis

Because Luria (1980) had suggested that neuropsychological ability comprises many different functional systems, Golden and his colleagues conducted a factor analysis of the various scales. The notion was that the resulting factors would reveal those components of the functional system being assessed by that scale. In a series of papers Golden examined the factor structure of the Motor, Rhythm, and Tactile scales (Golden, Sweet, Hammeke, Purisch, Graber, & Osmon, 1980), the Visual, Receptive Speech, Expressive Speech, and Reading scales (Golden, Purisch, Sweet, Graber, Osmon, & Hammeke, 1980), the Writing, Arithmetic, Memory, Left and Right Hemisphere scales (Golden, Osmon, Sweet, Graber, Purisch, & Hammeke, 1980), and the Intelligence and Pathognomonic scales (Golden, Hammeke, Osmon, Sweet, Purisch, & Graber, 1981). Methodologically, these studies

were similar in that 270 subjects were employed, equally divided among normal controls, psychiatric patients, and brain-damaged patients. The number of rotated factors per scale was examined using the scree criteria. While a number of factors were indeed reported per scale, their psychometric and clinical relevance was questioned, as were the results of other studies that examined item intercorrelations for the scales (Golden & Berg, 1980a, 1980b, 1980c).

Controversy

Although additional studies suggested that the Luria-Nebraska correlated well with the results of the Halstead-Reitan battery (Golden, Kane, Sweet, Moses, Cardellino, Templeton, Vicente, & Graber, 1981) and brain ventricular measurements (Golden, MacInnes, Ariel, Ruedrich, Chu, Coffman, Graber, & Bloch, 1981), and also differentiated alcoholics with brain damage (Chmielewski & Golden, 1980), the battery generated a great deal of controversy.

In addition to noting that any standardization of Luria's neuropsychological investigation was a "vulgarization" (Luria, in Christensen, 1975, p. 9) of his clinical approach, Adams (1980) pointed out problems in using ordinal summary measures, particularly for items that were meant to be qualitatively judged. Adams also noted that the subjects employed in these studies have not been well described. Perhaps, however, the two most serious concerns correctly noted by Adams were the overuse of multiple t tests and chi-squares in the search for significant differences and the use of discriminant analysis in which the number of variables not infrequently exceeded the number of subjects. To compound these problems is the fact that the high degree of group classification resulting from the discriminant analysis is not unusual since in the populations examined the patients are so neurologically damaged (and potentially psychiatrically disturbed as well) that they are very likely to perform very poorly on nearly any measure of function. These problems are not necessarily unique to the Luria-Nebraska, and they have been discussed elsewhere (Filskov & Goldstein, 1974; Gordon, 1977).

Other concerns were noted by Spiers (1981, 1982): Not only is it inconsistent with Luria's (1980) theory to employ a scoring system that categorizes qualitative performance (0, 1, and 2), but the studies testifying to the Luria-Nebraska's ability to localize lesion sites did not exclude or control for subcortical involvement in any acceptable fashion.

Delis and Kaplan (1983) further questioned the content validity of the scales, noting that Christensen (1975) organized Luria's investigative techniques into the outline presented in Table 17.2 only for "didactic" purposes. Thus, the resulting heterogeneity of the scales precludes, in Delis and Kaplan's (1983) estimation, any meaningful interpretation of the results.

Golden has attempted to respond to these concerns (Golden, 1980; Golden, Ariel, McKay, Wilkening, Wolf, & MacInnes, 1982), but the controversy generated by the validation research has resulted in unfavorable reviews (e.g., Adams, 1985). Nevertheless, the Luria-Nebraska seems to be one of the more frequently administered batteries in clinical practice, although it is likely that most clinicians administer other measures to assess intelligence, personality, and adaptive functioning. It may well be that the popularity of this battery is related to two factors. First, despite the unfavorable reviews, this battery is efficient in terms of clinical time and, second, studies continue to suggest that the correct classification rate (brain-damaged vs. controls) for the Luria-Nebraska and Halstead-Reitan are nearly identical (Kane et al., 1985). Thus, while there may be serious questions about the validity of the Luria-Nebraska with regard to localization of focal lesions on a case-to-case basis (Delis & Kaplan, 1982), the ability of the battery to discriminate between impaired neuropsychological performance and normality has ensured that it will be employed both clinically and in research/validation studies at some centers where these issues are relevant.

BENTON'S NEUROPSYCHOLOGICAL ASSESSMENT PROCEDURES

Depending on how one defines *neuropsychological*, nearly any test or measure could be construed as a measure of the integrity of the central nervous system. Consequently, there are numerous measures available; most, unfortunately, are poorly validated on small samples of undifferentiated brain-damaged patients. There do exist, however, some valuable contributions; the following brief discussion of some of Benton's instruments highlights those procedures that may have value beyond those measures included in the two batteries reviewed above.

Benton, Hamsher, Varney, and Spreen (1983) have published a collection of tests and procedures developed by Benton and his colleagues over the years. For the most part, adequate data exist validating the use of these procedures with brain-damaged adults with and without localized damage. The norms that are available in some instances for use with children and adolescents are not adequate and suggest an area for further investigation and test validation. Generally, the procedures outlined by Benton et al. (1983) can be conceptualized as tests related to orientation and learning and those related to perceptual and motor abilities.

Tests of Orientation and Learning

Temporal Orientation

This brief quantification of the mental status examination asks three questions: What is today's date?, What day of the week is it?, and What time is it now? Standardized on two independent samples of normal subjects (Benton, Van Allen, & Fogel, 1964; Levin & Benton, 1975), it has been demonstrated to be sensitive to impaired orientation in clinical samples.

Right-Left Orientation

Similar to the test of Temporal Orientation, this measure quantifies in a brief format a means of assessing spatial disorientation, including the patient's orientation to his or her own body and to that of the examiner. Both crossed and uncrossed commands are given to the patient in this 20-item test. Two forms are available. Norms are provided based on a sample of 234 adults aged 16–64. Data on patients with bilateral, right-lesion, left-nonaphasic, and left-aphasic patients are also provided by Benton et al. (1983).

Perceptual and Motor Tests

Serial Digit Learning

As Benton et al. (1983) noted, serial digit learning (learning to repeat a long string of digits correctly for 2 consecutive trials) was first noticed to be deficient in brain-injured patients by Zangwill (1943). Some evidence suggests that digit span, as on the WAIS-R, may not be impaired in brain injury but serial digit learning is (Drachman & Arbit, 1966; Schinka, 1974). Based on this knowledge, Benton and his colleagues developed a serial digit learning task for 8 and 9 digits. "Digits 9" is administered to patients with more than 12 years of education, while "Digits 8" is for those with less than a high school education. Normative data were derived from 500 medically hospitalized patients without neurological disease (Hamsher, Benton, & Digre, 1980) ranging in age from 16 to 74 years. No gender differences were reported. Data from 100 brain-damaged patients were also provided; they demonstrate the sensitivity of this measure in identifying patients with unilateral, and to a greater extent bilateral, disease.

Facial Recognition

It has long recognized that a deficit in facial recognition (facial agnosia or prosopagnosia) may accompany brain damage, particularly in patients with posterior lesions (Benton, 1980; Hecaen & Angelergues, 1962). Benton developed this test to provide a standardized means with which to test the ability to recognize faces. Both a short form of 27 items and a long form of 54 items can be used. There are three parts to the test: matching identical front-view photographs, matching front-view with three-quarter-view photographs, and matching front-view photographs under different lighting conditions. A sample of 286 subjects ranging in age from 16 to 74 years comprised the normative population; smaller but adequate samples of children aged 6–14 years comprised the standardization sample below 16 years of age. A study by Hamsher, Levin, and Benton (1979) provided data on 145 right-handed adults with unilateral focal lesions. As might be expected, patients with right posterior lesions performed inadequately on the test.

Judgment of Line Orientation

Deficits in spatial perception have also been noted in patients with brain damage (Benton, 1982; Critchley, 1953). While many measures of spatial orientation or spatial perception have been devised, such as the Minnesota Paper Form Board Test (Likert & Quasha, 1970) or the Memory for Designs Test (Graham & Kendall, 1960), none had been adequately validated in terms of differentiating the effects of focal lesions. Using a series of spatially oriented lines, the patient must match the orientation of the stimulus line to the array of spatially arranged lines. Two forms are available and good reliability is reported (split-half = .91 for both forms). Divided into six age groups, the test was administered to 137 normal controls and 100 brain-damaged patients (50 with right and 50 with left hemisphere damage). Data are also available for children from 7 to 14 years of age based on a sample of 221 children (Lindgren & Benton, 1980). There was a striking failure rate for patients with posterior, primarily right posterior, lesions (75%).

Visual Form Discrimination

This test was designed to briefly assess visual form discrimination, as ample data suggested that patients with right posterior lesions did poorly on tasks of this sort (Newcombe, 1969). Using a 16-item multiple-choice format, the test was normed on 85 healthy subjects ranging in age from 19 to 74 years. No significant effects were noted for age or sex on this test. Fifty-eight patients with unilateral or bilateral brain damage were also given the test. Of interest is the finding that subjects with both focal unilateral and diffuse brain damage performed poorly. Again, patients with right posterior damage did poorest, with 78% showing defective performance.

Pantomime Recognition

Jackson (1878) and Head (1926) were among the earliest clinicians to recognize that brain damage often affected the ability to engage in symbolic thinking. Evidence especially implicates defective pantomime ability in aphasic patients (Varney, 1982). To test this ability, a videotape was developed in which a person pretends to be using a common object (e.g., spoon, saw, pen). The subject views the pantomime and then, in a response booklet, selects the object from among four choices. This test is not well normed, as it was administered to only 30 hospitalized patients without brain or neurological impairment (age range 38–60). However, 105 aphasic patients were evaluated and 40 patients did poorly on this test, scoring 25 or fewer correct responses out of the 30 items. Most errors in pantomime recognition were of a semantic nature (e.g., correct response is "glass" and the subject indicates "cup").

Tactile Form Perception

This test was designed to assess a patient's ability to recognize tactile stimulation after he or she had already demonstrated deficits on tactile matching or on tactile naming tasks. Two 10-item forms (A and B) are available, each consisting of 10 sandpaper stimulus cards with a 12-choice response card. The subject feels each stimulus card, which is hidden from view, and points to the "match" on the response card. Ninety normal adults comprised the normative population, which ranged in age from 15 to 70 years. With age there is a slight decline in performance. Spreen and Gaddes (1969) have provided norms for children 8 to 14 years of age. The performance of 104 brain-damaged patients indicated that of the 75 patients in whom both hands were tested, only 33 (44%) performed in the normal range. Patients with bilateral brain disease scored very poorly, with fully 83% showing impaired performance. Again, patients with right hemisphere damage performed more poorly than left hemisphere, nonaphasic patients, underscoring the importance of right hemisphere abilities in visual-spatial processing.

Finger Localization

Gerstmann long ago recognized that patients with brain disease had difficulty in naming which finger had received tactile stimulation (Gerstmann, 1924). Others, including Benton (1959) and Ettinger (1963), demonstrated that there were a variety of performance patterns in patients with deficits in finger localization. This 60-item measure consists of three parts: (a) with hands visible; (b) with the hand hidden from view, and (c) with the hand hidden from view with pairs of fingers stimulated. The normative population consisted of 104 hospitalized controls, ranging in age from 16 to 65 years; additional normative data were provided for children 6–12 years. Brain-damaged patients did poorly on this test, with 70% of nonaphasic patients with bilateral disease and 86% of aphasic patients scoring in the impaired range. A study by Gainotti and Tiacci (1973) showed that unilateral deficits in finger localization were much more common in patients with right hemisphere lesions than in those with left hemisphere lesions.

Phoneme Discrimination

Aphasic disorders produce deficits in expressive and receptive language; in many patients, phoneme discrimination seems impaired. This 30-item test is administered using a cassette tape recording, and the patient must discriminate between same or different stimuli. Data from 30 hospitalized controls and 16 nonaphasic right brain–damaged and 100 aphasic left brain–damaged patients provided solid evidence that left brain–damaged patients with aphasia perform very poorly.

Three-Dimensional Block Construction

Visuoconstructive deficits have been variously termed *optic apraxia* and *optic ataxia* by some. Others have preferred the term *constructional apraxia* (Kleist, 1923). Critchley (1953) suggested that performance on two-dimensional paper-and-pencil tasks really did not tap the three-dimensional disability characteristic of constructional apraxia. Based on Critchley's observation, Benton developed this test. Twenty-nine loose blocks are placed before the patient, who then uses them to construct a figure like the model that is presented. One hundred hospital controls, ranging in age from 16 to 63 years, comprised the normative sample. Spreen and Gaddes (1969) provided norms on 259 children, ages 6–12 years. Studies by Benton and Fogel (1962) and Keller (1971) indicated that in brain-damaged subjects poor performance on this test is relatively common, particularly in patients with right hemisphere disease (45% with right brain–damage, 20% with left brain–damage).

Motor Impersistence

The ability to sustain a motor movement is frequently impaired in brain damage; the term *motor impersistence* is used to designate this phenomenon (Fisher, 1956). This test assesses the ability to sustain a motor movement through performance on eight tests, which include keeping the eyes closed, protruding the tongue (eyes

blindfolded), protruding the tongue (eyes open), fixation of gaze in the lateral visual field, keeping the mouth open, central visual fixation, head turning during sensory testing, and saying "ah." Normative data were from 106 hospital controls, of whom 86% performed error-free on all eight measures. Normative data were also provided on 140 children, ages 5–11 years (Garfield, 1963, 1964). In brain-damaged patients, some studies suggest an increased frequency of impaired performance among right hemisphere patients, although motor impersistence clearly occurs in both unilateral and bilateral disease (Joynt, Benton, & Fogel, 1962; Levin, 1963).

The tests provided by Benton and his colleagues are well conceived from a solid theoretical base, and the results of his test development efforts have not only provided clinically useful procedures but have contributed considerably to neuropsychological theory. His tests are particularly useful in assessing singular deficits associated with lateralized dysfunction. In this regard, Benton's data base provides convincing evidence that some functions are indeed more "localized" than others; in diffuse or bilateral brain damage many, if not most, functions are seriously affected, some more than others. Further validation work on these tests by independent researchers is needed, but it seems clear that these measures have a place in the eclectic approach to neuropsychological assessment.

CONCLUSIONS

Neuropsychological assessment encompasses a wide variety of approaches, both theoretical and practical, and requires considerable special expertise beyond that normally possessed by most clinicians. Guidelines for appropriate preparation exist (Meier, 1981, 1985).

This chapter has addressed in some detail the two batteries most frequently employed in clinical assessment. Also presented were Benton's tests, which provide excellent measures of orientation and learning and perceptual and motor processes. The two batteries share many of the advantages and disadvantages that are built into the selection of any neuropsychological battery.

The HRNB has a much longer history of independent validation than does the Luria-Nebraska, but it is considerably less able to assess neurolinguistic processes than is the Luria-based battery. Conversely, the Luria-Nebraska does not provide adequate measures of basic perceptual process in comparison to the HRNB. Both these batteries are thus inadequate in their own fashion. Further, neither battery is adequately normed, and the Benton tests, while impressive in terms of the numbers of brain-damaged patients employed in the validation process, can also be faulted for inconsistent norming practices (e.g., normal versus hospital controls, uneven numbers employed at each age level across tests, inconsistency in whether tests have norms for children).

However, within the theoretical framework provided by each test author, these measures have both clinical and theoretical appeal and practical utility, if employed with knowledge as to the advantages and disadvantages of each. There are some important issues that still need to be addressed with regard to these and other neuropsychological procedures.

One of the most important issues, both clinically and theoretically, concerns the interrelationship between these measures and general ability. These relationships are complex and interactive. For example, Golden et al. (1981) compared the results obtained with the HRNB to those obtained with the Luria-Nebraska, and on the basis of the equally high correct classification rates (86% versus 88%) and significant correlations between the two tests concluded that "the high multiple correlations between the tests suggest that what can be predicted statistically with one test can likely be predicted with the other test as well" (p. 417). Golden et al. concluded that the HRNB and the Luria-Nebraska are "for all practical purposes equivalent" (p. 414).

Chelune (1982) took issue with this conclusion and demonstrated that the high significant correlations between the two neuropsychological batteries were due to the effects of general intelligence. When IQ is partialled out, the average correlation drops to .40, suggesting that only 16% of the variance in the two batteries is shared. Conversely, 67% of the variance shared by these two batteries is due to the high correlation each has with the WAIS IQ scores. Considering Wechsler's original ideas about the neurological basis of IQ, this relationship is not surprising; but, one must wonder, how much extra time should be devoted to assessing skills and abilities that are relatively independent of IQ? This is a very relevant question since it is IQ that often best distinguishes between normality and neurological impairment, as the Hold/Don't Hold dichotomy (despite its severe limitations) and the Fuld formula well illustrate.

The answer to this question depends on the diagnostic issue being addressed. Whether one wishes to distinguish between normality or pathology, localize or lateralize lesions, or describe the cognitive profile and associated changes due to clinical improvement or deterioration are all relevant points to consider. Whether the neuropsychological evaluation provides any additional information over IQ will depend on the skill of the psychologist in further refining the referral questions being asked and in the selection of appropriate and discrete test measures. One must agree with Lezak (1988a), however, that more sophisticated and precise neuropsychological measures need to be developed to answer more sophisticated questions than those addressed by the developers of the HRNB and Luria-Nebraska batteries.

ILLUSTRATIVE CASE REPORTS

The two case reports that follow have been provided by the authors of this chapter to illustrate the neuropsychological approach to evaluation. The report on E.S., a 35-year-old

Case Study: E.S., Age 35, Multiple Sclerosis (Halstead-Reitan Approach)

SEX: Female	HANDEDNESS: Right
EDUCATION: 15 years	OCCUPATION: Student

Relevant Background

E.S., a 35-year-old woman, was referred for a neuropsychological evaluation at her request. She was concerned about difficulties with memory and a reported lack of feeling in her left hand. E.S. was diagnosed with multiple sclerosis 3 years ago. Prior to that time, she described herself as a "straight A" student who had experienced no difficulties in school. However, E.S. began noticing difficulties with her vision and motor skills. Following a full neurological examination she was diagnosed as having multiple sclerosis. She has undergone hyperbaric treatments with some periods of brief remission. Currently, E.S. is very concerned about her memory difficulties, her feelings of depression, her lack of libido, and her anger, which seems to surface as a result of minor irritations. Recently, it was recommended by her adviser that E.S. withdraw from her classes due to difficulties in concentration and the completion of schoolwork. E.S. stated that her goal was to enter medical school in the fall.

Appearance and Behavioral Characteristics

E.S. came to the testing sessions willingly. She was well groomed and polite throughout the session. E.S. is approximately 5 feet 6 inches tall, and has blonde hair and blue eyes. She wore glasses throughout the testing but commented that they really did not help her to see better. Testing materials had to be held close to her face (approximately 6 inches) for her to see them clearly. She stated that she was taking Prednisone for visual problems, but that she had not seen any improvement. She had been on this medication for approximately 6 weeks.

During testing, E.S. required additional time to answer questions. She frequently became impatient with herself when she was either unable to solve the problems or felt that she had arrived at the wrong solution. E.S. did respond well to encouragement, and the examiner found it imperative to provide frequent feedback on her performance; otherwise, E.S. would interpret the examiner's silence as failure. Throughout the two testing sessions E.S.'s hands shook noticeably. She blamed the medication for her motor problems.

E.S. shared her feelings of anger and depression at her diagnosis of multiple sclerosis. She portrayed her life prior to the diagnosis as "great" and with few problems. She has lost a free-lance business due to her inability to function and is presently experiencing marital difficulties.

Examination Procedures

Wechsler Adult Intelligence Scale—Revised (WAIS-R)
Wechsler Memory Scale (Form I)
Halstead-Reitan Neuropsychological Battery
Minnesota Multiphasic Personality Inventory (MMPI)

Test Interpretations

E.S. achieved a Full Scale IQ of 116±4 on the WAIS-R, which places her in the Above Average range of intellectual performance and at the 86th percentile nationally. There is a significant difference of 35 points between her verbal and performance abilities. E.S.'s verbal abilities are in the superior range, while her performance abilities are in the low average range. E.S.'s verbal abilities are fairly uniform and are all in the above average to superior range. In contrast, her performance on perceptual-organizational tasks suggested a relative strength in the area of attention to environmental detail (Picture Completion) with the other subtests being in the low average to average range. The V–P discrepancy is unusually large, occurring less than 1% of the time in the normal adult population.

The Wechsler Memory Scale was also administered. On this test E.S. achieved a memory IQ of 120, which places her in the superior range of functioning on this test. She was able to remember 11 semantic units and

(Continues)

Case Study: E.S., Age 35, Multiple Sclerosis (Halstead-Reitan Approach) (Continued)

9 figural units on the immediate recall test. Perhaps more important, E.S. recalled 9 semantic units and 11 figural units following a 45-minute delay between tests with no prior warning that she would be retested. Moreover, E.S. showed superior skills on the Digit Span test of the WAIS-R by repeating both forward and backward digits to the end of that subtest. Her memory difficulties were not found to be an area of deficit. However, E.S. did score in the significantly impaired range on the MMPI in Depression, which may in fact have had an impact on memory and concentration in everyday life and may have contributed to her relatively low P-IQ.

E.S.'s performance on the MMPI is similar to the performance of many patients with multiple sclerosis (Reitan & Wolfson, 1985). She showed elevations on the neurotic triad; namely, Depression, Hypochondriasis, and Hysteria. Reitan (1955a) suggested that these complaints are legitimate manifestations of multiple sclerosis and should not be viewed in the same manner as those found in other psychiatric patients.

E.S. earned an Impairment Index of .6, which is in the significant range of cerebral impairment (four tests were in the impaired range: Category, TPT-Total Time, Memory, and Localization). She showed no difficulty on the Seashore Rhythm Test, Aphasia Screening Test, or the Speech-Sounds Perception test. However, although E.S.'s score on the Finger Oscillation Test-Dominant Hand is in the normal range, there is a significant difference between hands on time. Generally, more than a 10% difference between hands is considered significant. E.S. showed over a 20% difference between hands. In addition, the slower hand is the left hand, which she has recently complained of losing feeling in. Moreover, E.S. showed errors on the left hand in Fingertip Number Writing (4) and Tactile Form Recognition (3 errors and extended time). She also showed more than a 10% difference between hands on the measure of strength of grip. It is not unusual to see patients with multiple sclerosis evidencing scattered difficulties on the sensory perceptual examination (Reitan & Wolfson, 1985). Her depressed P-IQ is undoubtedly related, to some extent, to her motor problems.

In attempting to lateralize E.S.'s difficulties using Reitan's guidelines, the consistent finding of motor difficulties on the left side on her body implicates the right hemisphere, possibly the sensorimotor areas, as showing involvement in E.S.'s difficulties. Some global dysfunction is seen in her difficulty with complex and abstract material, as evidenced in the Category Test error scores. Reitan (1955a) has suggested that in the earlier stages of MS, abstraction and reasoning abilities may well be spared and that increasing impairment is seen as the disease progresses.

Summary and Recommendations

E.S. possessed above average to superior intellectual abilities with lower performance on tests involving visual and timed performance. She showed adequate memory scores for verbal and figural material but deficits in memory for materials that are tactilely based (TPT-Memory and Localization). Additional areas of deficit are in tactile skills in the left hand as well as measures of tapping speed and grip strength. Global deficits are noted on the Category test and the TPT test-Total Time. Although there is evidence of right hemisphere involvement, particularly of the sensorimotor areas, there is also evidence of global impairment.

Recommendations include:

1. It appears that E.S. is experiencing difficulty in coping with her disabilities, both in her professional and personal life. Therefore, intensive therapy, possible also involving her husband, would be appropriate.

2. Moreover, E.S. requires vocational counseling to help her adjust her aspirations to a more realistic and possibly less stressful level. Medical school may not be a viable option for E.S.

3. E.S. needs to be encouraged to share with her physician her difficulties with recall and memory. Investigation of the effect of Prednisone on her memory should be made.

4. Monitoring of her visual problems appears to be important, particularly given the amount of reading she is currently required to complete.

5. Reevaluation of E.S. in 6 months would be helpful to determine her progress and validate her areas of deficit.

Case Study: E.S., Age 35, Multiple Sclerosis (Halstead-Reitan Approach) (Continued)

E.S.: Psychometric Summary

Wechsler Adult Intelligence Scale—Revised

	Scaled Score	
	Regular	Age-Corrected
Verbal		
Information	12	13
Digit Span	16	16
Vocabulary	14	14
Arithmetic	14	14
Comprehension	14	13
Similarities	16	16
Performance		
Picture Completion	12	13-S
Picture Arrangement	7	8
Block Design	9	10
Object Assembly	6	7
Digit Symbol	8	9

Verbal IQ $= 129 \pm 4$
Performance IQ $= 94 \pm 6$
Full Scale IQ $= 116 \pm 4$

Wechsler Memory Scale (Form I)

Memory Quotient = 120

Minnesota Multiphasic Personality Inventory

Scale	I-Score
?	50
L	43
F	42
K	55
Hs	70*
D	72*
Hy	71*
Pd	55
Mf	52
Pa	53
Pt	56
Sc	57
Ma	43

*Significant

Halstead-Reitan Neuropsychological Battery

Category Test   59*
Tactual Performance Test
  Dominant Hand   10'20"
  Nondominant Hand   8'10"
  Both Hands   3'53"
  Total Time   22'23"*
  Memory   3*
  Localization   4*
Seashore Rhythm Test   28 correct
Speech Sounds Perception   5 errors
Finger Oscillation Test
  Dominant Hand   51.6
  Nondominant Hand   39.6
Impairment Index   .6*
Reitan-Kløve Tactile Form Recognition Test
  Dominant Hand: 15", 0 errors
  Nondominant Hand: 26", 3 errors
Reitan-Kløve Sensory Perception Exam
  No errors
Halstead-Wepman Aphasia Screening Test
  No errors
Tactile Finger Recognition
  No errors
Finger Tip # Writing
  R 1 0 2 0 3 0 4 0 5 0
  L 1 1 2 0 3 2 4 0 5 1
Trail Making Test
  Trails A   34", No errors
  Trails B   72", No errors
Lateral Dominance
  Right hand
  Right foot
  Right eye
Grip Strength
  Dominant   32.0
  Nondominant   27.5

(Continues)

Case Study: P.E., Age 30, Head Injury and Left Temporal Lobectomy (Eclectic Approach)

SEX: Male   HANDEDNESS: Right

EDUCATION: 12 years   OCCUPATION: Truck Driver

Relevant Background

P.E., a 30-year-old man, was referred for a comprehensive neuropsychological examination following a recent motorcycle accident. P.E. experienced a severe closed head injury when the motorcycle he was riding ran into a deer. After he was discharged by Dr. Smith, he attended speech and language as well as occupational therapy services. He is now being considered for reemployment as a truck driver. Thus, the purpose of this evaluation was to assess the extent of P.E.'s recovery and to provide information regarding his present intellectual and social/emotional status.

According to P.E., he was riding his motorcycle down a dirt road after leaving his grandmother's house when a deer jumped in his path and struck him in the chest. He estimates he was traveling 40–50 mph at the time. P.E. was knocked unconscious and remained so until well after his surgery.

Medical records reveal that P.E. suffered an explosive hematoma associated with the left anterior temporal lobe. He was operated on by Dr. Smith, who performed a left subtemporal craniectomy and decompression with an anterior left temporal lobectomy (approx. 5 cm). After some complications, he was taken off the ventilator and returned to the floor from intensive care. P.E. improved rapidly, had good appetite, was ambulatory, was somewhat aphasic, could read, but was emotionally unstable and confused. He improved substantially, it seems, prior to his recent discharge.

Since his discharge P.E. has been unable to return to full-time work. Dr. Smith has continued him on 60 mg. of phenobarbital. P.E. complains of significant memory loss and feels that he has slowed down significantly. Subjectively, P.E. feels ready to go back to work and to rejoin his National Guard unit; he says he is bored remaining around the house. He currently is living with his father and stepmother. Prior to the accident (about 11 months ago), P.E. reports that he drove a truck. As soon as he is permitted, P.E. hopes to drive trucks again.

A speech and language assessment was also recently conducted; it revealed significant improvement yet continued difficulty with verbal abstract reasoning and problem solving. Prior to this, P.E. received an occupational therapy evaluation of his cognitive/perceptual abilities that revealed very serious deficiencies. His memory for digits was 3 x 3, he had seriously impaired short-term memory, and he was not oriented to place or time, although he could recall his name and the names of family members. Spatial relations seemed within normal limits, and his attitude and motivation were good as was his cooperation. Since that time P.E. has continued his therapy sessions and has made considerable progress.

Appearance and Behavioral Characteristics

P.E. appeared for his all-day evaluation appointment early and seemed eager to begin the session. He was appropriately but not well dressed. His general demeanor was slow, friendly, and cooperative. He tried hard on most tasks asked of him and was observed to subvocalize on difficult problems. Consistent with this style, P.E. frequently had long latencies to respond and, surprisingly, this did not on occasion seem to seriously impair his performance. However, it can well be imagined that such a deliberate slow manner of responding would not be appropriate were he in a situation that required rapid rates of response involving cognitive decisions. Overall, these results would appear to be a valid sample of behavior. No obvious vision or hearing deficits were noted.

Evaluation Procedures

   Wechsler Adult Intelligence Scale-Revised (WAIS-R)
   Minnesota Multiphasic Personality Inventory (MMPI)
   Wide Range Achievement Test—Revised (Level 2) (WRAT-R)

Boston Naming Test
Beck Depression Inventory
Benton Visual Retention Test
Benton Facial Recognition Test
Benton Test of Right-Left Orientation
Aphasia Screening Test
Edinburgh Handedness Inventory
Trail Making Test
Grip Strength
Tactile Form Recognition
Rapid Naming Task
Verbal Fluency Task

Test Interpretations

Cognitive-intellectual abilities generally fall within the low average to below average range. He obtained a Full Scale IQ of 82, a Verbal IQ of 82, and a Performance IQ of 85. Thus, there would appear to be no significant differences between P.E.'s verbal-linguistic and perceptual-organizational skills. No particular areas of significant ability or disability emerged on cognitive-intellectual appraisal, and his facilities in the areas assessed by the WAIS-R seem uniformly developed.

Academic attainment suggests that P.E. is able to demonstrate academic competencies at approximately the 7th to 8th grade level. On the Wide Range Achievement Test—Revised, P.E. obtained standard scores in the significantly below average range in Reading (Word Recognition) (78), Spelling (74), and Arithmetic (78). His achievement on this measure is somewhat lower than would be expected based on his cognitive-intellectual results. P.E. was noticeably anxious when faced with unfamiliar math problems and on the spelling task, but was less so on oral reading. In math he was able to correctly add 3-digit numbers, add simple fractions, subtract using borrowing, and divide a 4-place number by a digit number, yet could not successfully multiply fractions or numbers involving decimals. On both oral and silent reading he was very slow.

Neuropsychological processes are surprisingly intact considering the extent of P.E.'s head injury approximately 11 months ago. Linguistic processes are commensurate with his overall estimated level of cognitive performance. On the Boston Naming Test, P.E. scored more than 1 standard deviation below normal but his performance was consistent with his below average Verbal IQ. P.E.'s responses would lead one to believe that naming has been affected by his accident. On a number of occasions he would give a good description for use for the stimulus objects presented and occasionally provided paralexic responses. Verbal fluency was definitely slow but was consistent within expectations of his overall verbal ability. P.E.'s memory for digits has shown substantial improvement. Presently he can recall 6 digits forward and 6 digits backward. Verbal directions are still confusing to P.E., and he frequently asked for clarification. P.E. is strongly right-handed but his grip strength, while favoring his dominant hand, was weak. In fact, his grip strength is approximately equal to that of a 16-year-old male. Perceptual-performance abilities are generally intact. He performed in the average range on a test of facial recognition and his performance was within normal limits on the Benton Visual Retention Test. Even on a memory task P.E. did reasonably well when he was required to draw designs from memory after a 15-second delay. No significant inattention, perseveration, or significant deficits in rote learning were encountered.

Social-emotional adjustment is an area of some concern. Both the results of the Beck Depression Inventory and MMPI suggest the presence of a mild depression. He described himself on the Beck as waking up 1–2 hours early in the morning and having trouble returning to sleep, he has lost more than 10 pounds recently, and he reported that he is so worried about physical problems that it is hard to think of much else. The

(Continues)

Case Study: P.E., Age 30, Head Injury and Left Temporal Lobectomy (Eclectic Approach) (Continued)

results of the MMPI confirm the presence of these self-perceptions, and suggest the presence of a thought disorder. P.E. consistently noted that he hears voices or queer things, often feels that things are not real, and has strange or peculiar thoughts. The results of this appraisal suggest serious concerns regarding P.E.'s mental status, but it should be pointed out that these self-reports stand in contrast to observations made regarding P.E. on the day of the evaluation. Ms. Phillips, his occupational therapist, confirms our observations that P.E.'s behavior is at variance with this finding. His possibly deviant performance on this measure may be inaccurate and reflect more his labored and poor reading comprehension skills. The presence of the mild depression seems an accurate observation, but the presence of the thought disorder appears unconfirmed at present and, it is believed, should not preclude his return to some productive employment.

Summary and Recommendations

P.E. is a 30-year-old single Caucasian male who suffered a severe closed head injury when his motorcycle was struck by a deer. Dr. Smith performed an anterior left temporal lobectomy (approx. 5 cm). He is being followed by Dr. Smith and has received both speech and occupational therapy services. Ms. Phillips referred P.E. for a complete neuropsychological evaluation in order to obtain more information pertaining to readiness to return to full-time employment.

The results of this evaluation reveal that P.E. has experienced a very significant recovery since his accident nearly a year ago and is most likely ready to return to a carefully selected employment setting. It is uncertain as to how significantly impaired P.E. is in relation to his premorbid status. Indications from this evaluation suggest that he suffers residual deficits in language comprehension and possibly short-term auditory memory consistent with the extent of his cerebral trauma. However, it is doubtful that his general level of cognitive ability has been seriously compromised.

The following recommendations are offered:

1. A psychiatric consult may be helpful in determining whether there is a serious disturbance in thought processes with a concurrent depression of significance such that treatment is indicated. The results of this evaluation, particularly observations made of P.E. by us as well as Ms. Phillips, suggest that P.E. may not be as seriously affected as his test results would imply. However, a psychiatric consult may be helpful in determining whether these observations are accurate.

2. P.E. would profit from attending small group sessions in which other head-injured patients participated. A goal of such an experience (or continued work in occupational therapy) would be to continue efforts aimed at helping P.E. cope with socially stressful situations he might encounter upon his return to work. He is highly motivated to return to full-time employment, so he may well profit from these experiences.

3. The results of this evaluation suggest that P.E. may well be ready to return to work in a carefully selected employment environment. Career counseling may be beneficial if P.E. persists in his desire to return to truck driving, which he very much wants to do. His slow response style, somewhat impaired short-term memory, and particularly his occasional difficulty in comprehending oral directions may argue against a return to driving trucks. On the other hand, his persistence, reported responsibility, high level of motivation to work on a full-time basis, and desire to continue working to overcome his accident-induced disabilities argue very positively for some success once he does return to full-time employment. The most appropriate employment setting will need to be carefully considered, however, in light of these observations.

4. While P.E. has indeed made some dramatic progress in his recovery to date, a complete reevaluation of his cognitive and social-emotional status may be helpful in approximately 1 year's time to better chart the extent and eventual course of his recovery. At this time an evaluation of his success in employment may also productively be made.

Case Study: P.E., Age 30, Head Injury and Left Temporal Lobectomy (Eclectic Approach) (Continued)

P.E.: Psychometric Summary

Wechsler Adult Intelligence Scale—Revised

Verbal	Scaled Score Regular	Scaled Score Age-Corrected	Performance	Scaled Score Regular	Scaled Score Age-Corrected
Information	8	7	Picture Completion	7	7
Digit Span	10	10	Picture Arrangement	6	7
Vocabulary	5	5-W	Block Design	8	8
Arithmetic	8	8	Object Assembly	9	9
Comprehension	6	6	Digit Symbol	9	9
Similarities	6	7			

Verbal IQ $= 82 \pm 4$

Performance IQ $= 85 \pm 6$

Full Scale IQ $= 82 \pm 4$

Wide Range Achievement Test—Revised

	(SS)	(Percentile)
Reading	78	7
Spelling	74	4
Arithmetic	78	7

Beck Depression Inventory

Score $= 13$

Minnesota Multiphasic Personality Inventory (K-COR)

Scale	*T*-Score
L	56
F	80
K	11
Hs	57
D	72
Hy	49
Pd	53
Mf	39
Pa	65
Pt	75
Sc	80
Ma	73
Si	62

(Continues)

Case Study: P.E., Age 30, Head Injury and Left Temporal Lobectomy (Eclectic Approach) (Continued)

Boston Naming Test

    Score 49 (< 1 *SD* below average)

Rapid Naming

    Colors: 31 sec.   0 errors

    RAS: 30 sec.   0 errors

Verbal Fluency

    Animals   # 5

    Eat   11

    Wear   6

    Ride   7

    Total Latency 6″

    Total Named   29

Trail Making Test

    Trails A   15″, No errors

    Trails B   46″, 1 error

Benton Revised Visual Retention Test

    Form C—WNL (10 correct)

Edinburgh Handedness Inventory

    LQ = 90% right

Benton Right-Left Orientation

    Score 44 (low average)

Grip Strength

    X R.H. 37.3 kg.

    X L.H. 36.0 kg.

Tactile Form Recognition

    R.H. 8/8 correct

    L.H. 8/8 correct

Aphasia Screening Test

    −3 (2 spelling errors)

woman with multiple sclerosis, demonstrates the Halstead-Reitan method of neuropsychological assessment; the report on P.E., a 30-year-old head-injured man, exemplifies the eclectic approach to neuropsychological evaluation. See pages 293–294 regarding the WAIS or WAIS-R Performance IQ deficits of patients with multiple sclerosis, and page 513 concerning their sequential weakness. See Table 10.10 for a summary of the V-P IQ discrepancies of patients with various types of lateralized lesions (including head injury).

CHAPTER 17 SUMMARY

This chapter provides an overview of two of the most frequently employed standardized batteries for neuropsychological assessment of adults. Discussions of the Halstead-Reitan Neuropsychological Battery and the Luria-Nebraska Neuropsychological Battery, their validation and reliability, tables of representative studies, and illustrative case reports are provided.

The chapter begins with an overview of the historical precedents for present-day neuropsychological practice. Careful documentation of case studies by Broca, Wernicke, Bastian, and Morehouse and colleagues helped advance theories involved with aphasia, alexia, and hemispatial neglect. These clinicians worked on localizing lesions and cerebral dysfunctions. In response to "localizationism," psychologists such as Lashley suggested that damage to any area of the brain can have both proximal and distal effects. Later Luria combined both views in his theory of three different units of brain–behavior functioning that interact as well as act separately. He proposed that damage in one unit not only produces focal difficulties but also affects interactions between units. It was upon these foundations that investigators developed the two major neuropsychological batteries: The Halstead-Reitan Neuropsychological Battery and the Luria-Nebraska Neuropsychological Battery. Benton also developed a series of useful tests.

Inherent advantages and difficulties are present in the battery approach to neuropsychological assessment. Advantages include comprehensiveness, standardization of procedures and norms, history of validation, and widespread use. Disadvantages include long administration time, redundancy of the information provided, inadequate norms, and insufficient theoretical underpinnings. An additional approach utilizes a qualitative assessment of an individual's deficits and strengths. Although this approach has the advantages of a solid theoretical base, efficiency, and a focus on the particular nature of a patient's disabilities, it places great emphasis on subjective, clinical judgment, lacks documentation of validity, and has a dearth of norms.

A number of factors affect test performance on the batteries. Age, attention to task, gender, socio-economic status, neurological factors, intelligence, and education have all been found to interact with test results. Given these cautions, both the HRNB and LNNB are discussed in detail. Tables are provided for both batteries that summarize representative studies investigating the validity and reliability of each battery. Both batteries are able to reliably distinguish brain-damaged adults from normal and/or medical controls. The batteries are less able to

distinguish subjects with severe psychiatric difficulties (e.g., schizophrenia) from brain-damaged subjects or controls.

The Benton neuropsychological procedures are also presented. These measures can be conceptualized as tests of orientation/learning and as tests related to perceptual-motor abilities. The Benton tests are theoretically well conceived and are clinically useful, particularly for diagnosing lateralized dysfunctions. However, further validation of these measures is needed.

Finally, two case studies are provided. One study illustrates the use of the HRNB with a patient diagnosed as having multiple sclerosis. The second case study involves the use of an eclectic approach with a severe closed head injury.

Conclusions from this chapter are that the Benton tests, the HRNB, and the LNNB provide important diagnostic information. However, the HRNB lacks the ability to adequately assess neurolinguistic processes, and the LNNB is deficient in the assessment of perceptual processes. Moreover, norms are inadequate for both batteries and for the Benton tests. The effect of IQ on the results of both test batteries is also unclear and needs further evaluation. In addition, it is not clear that Reitan's procedures for determining the localization and lateralization of damage are supported by empirical data. Recommendations for additional validation of measures as well as the development of more refined assessment procedures are made.

Abel, E. L. (1980). Fetal alcohol syndrome: Behavioral technology. *Psychological Bulletin, 87*, 29–50.

Abrahams, J. P. (1976). Health status as a variable in aging research. *Experimental Aging Research, 2*, 63–71.

Ackerman, P. T., McGrew, M. J., & Dykman, R. A. (1987). A profile of male and female applicants for a special college program for learning-disabled students. *Journal of Clinical Psychology, 43*, 67–78.

Adams, G. L. (1984a). *Comprehensive Test of Adaptive Behavior examiner's manual.* Columbus, OH: Charles E. Merrill.

Adams, G. L. (1984b). *Normative Adaptive Behavior Checklist examiner's manual.* Columbus, OH: Charles E. Merrill.

Adams, K. M. (1980). In search of Luria's battery: A false start. *Journal of Consulting and Clinical Psychology, 48*, 511–516.

Adams, R. L. (1985). Review of the Luria-Nebraska Neuropsychological Battery. In J. V. Mitchell (Ed.), *The ninth mental measurements yearbook* (pp. 878–881). Lincoln, NE: Buros Institute of Mental Measurement, The University of Nebraska Press.

Aiken, L. R. (1987). *Assessment of intellectual functioning.* Boston: Allyn & Bacon.

Albert, M. S., & Kaplan, E. (1980). Organic implications of neuropsychological deficits in the elderly. In L. W. Poon, J. L. Fozard, L. S. Cermak, D. Ehrenberg, & L. W. Thompson (Eds.), *New directions in memory and aging: Proceedings of the George Talland Memorial Conference.* Hillsdale, NJ: Erlbaum.

Alekoumbides, A., Charter, R. A., Adkins, T. G., & Seacat, G. F. (1987). The diagnosis of brain damage by the WAIS, WMS, and Reitan battery utilizing standardized scores corrected for age and education. *International Journal of Clinical Neuropsychology, 9*, 11–28.

Allen, J. G., Coyne, L., & David, E. (1986). Relation of intelligence to ego functioning in an adult psychiatric population. *Journal of Personality Assessment, 50*, 212–221.

Allison, J., Blatt, S. J., & Zimet, C. N. (1968). *The interpretation of psychological tests.* New York: Harper & Row.

Alvarez, E. R. (1962). Comparison of depressive and brain-injured subjects on the trail making test. *Perceptual and Motor Skills, 14*, 91–96.

Aminoff, M. J., Marshall, J., Smith, E. M., & Wyke, M. A. (1975). Pattern of intellectual impairment in Huntington's chorea. *Psychological Medicine, 5*, 169–172.

Amolsch, T. J., & Henrichs, T. F. (1975). Behavioral correlates of WAIS profile patterns: An exploratory study. *Journal of Personality Assessment, 39*, 55–63.

Anastasi, A. (1988). *Psychological testing* (6th ed.). New York: Macmillan.

Andersen, A. L. (1950). The effect of laterality localization of brain damage on Wechsler-Bellevue indices of deterioration. *Journal of Clinical Psychology, 6*, 191–194.

Andersen, A. L. (1951). The effect of laterality localization of focal brain lesions on the Wechsler-Bellevue subtests. *Journal of Clinical Psychology, 7*, 149–153.

Anderson, S. W., & Travel, D. (1989). Awareness of disease states following cerebral infarction, dementia, and head trauma: Standardized assessment. *The Clinical Neuropsychologist, 3*, 327–339.

Andrew, J. M. (1974). Delinquency, the Wechsler P > V sign, and the I-level system. *Journal of Clinical Psychology, 30*, 331–335.

Angoff, W. H. (1988). The nature-nurture debate, aptitudes, and group differences. *American Psychologist, 43*, 713–720.

Armentrout, J. A. (1976). Bender Gestalt recall: Memory measure or intelligence estimate. *Journal of Clinical Psychology, 32*, 832–834.

Armstrong, E. J. (1982). The extent of bias for the WAIS-R for Chicano and white high school students. (Doctoral dissertation, University of North Colorado, 1982, Order No. DA8301133). *Dissertation Abstracts International, 43* (9-A), March 1983, p. 2971.

Atkinson, L., & Cyr, J. J. (1984). Factor analysis of the WAIS-R: Psychiatric and standardization samples. *Journal of Consulting and Clinical Psychology, 52,* 714–716.

Atkinson, L., & Cyr, J. J. (1988). Low IQ samples and WAIS-R factor structure. *American Journal of Mental Deficiency, 93,* 278–282.

Ausubel, D. P., & Sullivan, E. V. (1970). *Theory and problems of child development* (2nd ed.). New York: Grune & Stratton.

Bailey, B. S. (1979). Differential perceptions of children's adaptive behavior. *Dissertation Abstracts International, 40,* 159A.

Bailey, K. G., & Millbrook, J. M. (1984). "Primitiveness" and "advancedness" of pleasures and aversions in relation to WAIS indices. *Journal of Clinical Psychology, 40,* 295–299.

Bajema, C. J. (1968). A note on the interrelations among intellectual ability, educational attainment, and occupational achievement: A follow-up study of a male Kalamazoo public school population. *Sociology of Education, 41,* 317–319.

Bak, J. S., & Greene, R. L. (1981). A review of the performance of aged adults on various Wechsler Memory Scale subtests. *Journal of Clinical Psychology, 37,* 186–188.

Baker, H. J., & Leland, B. (1967). *Detroit Tests of Learning Aptitude: Examiner's handbook.* Indianapolis, IN: Bobbs-Merrill.

Balinsky, B. (1941). An analysis of the mental factors of various age groups from nine to sixty. *Genetic Psychology Monographs, 23,* 191–234.

Baltes, P. B., & Schaie, K. W. (1976). On the plasticity of adult and gerontological intelligence: Where Horn and Donaldson fail. *American Psychologist, 31,* 720–725.

Baltes, P. B., & Willis, S. L. (1982). Enhancement (plasticity) of intellectual functioning in old age: Penn State's Adult Development and Enrichment Project (ADEPT). In F. I. M. Craik & S. E. Trehub (Eds.), *Aging and cognitive processes* (pp. 353–389). New York: Plenum.

Balthazar, E. E., & Morrison, D. H. (1961). The use of Wechsler Intelligence Scales as diagnostic indicators of predominant left-right and indeterminate unilateral brain damage. *Journal of Clinical Psychology, 17,* 161–165.

Banken, J. A. (1985). Clinical utility of considering digits forward and digits backward as separate components of the Wechsler Adult Intelligence Scale—Revised. *Journal of Clinical Psychology, 41,* 686–691.

Banken, J. A., & Banken, C. H. (1987). Investigation of Wechsler Adult Intelligence Scale—Revised short forms in a sample of vocational rehabilitation applicants. *Journal of Psychoeducational Assessment, 5,* 281–286.

Bannatyne, A. (1968). Diagnosing learning disabilities and writing remedial prescriptions. *Journal of Learning Disabilities, 1,* 242–249.

Bannatyne, A. (1971). *Language, reading, and learning disabilities.* Springfield, IL: Charles C. Thomas.

Bannatyne, A. (1974). Diagnosis: A note on recategorization of the WISC scaled scores. *Journal of Learning Disabilities, 7,* 272–274.

Barclay, A. G., Giray, E. F., & Altkin, W. M. (1977). WAIS subtest score distribution of institutionalized retardates. *Perceptual and Motor Skills, 44,* 488–490.

Baroff, G. S. (1986). *Mental retardation: Nature, cause, and management* (2nd ed.). New York: Hemisphere Publishing.

Barona, A., Reynolds, C. R., & Chastain, R. (1984). A demographically based index of premorbid intelligence for the WAIS-R. *Journal of Consulting and Clinical Psychology, 52,* 885–887.

Bartak, L., & Rutter, M. (1976). Differences between mentally retarded and normally intelligent autistic children. *Journal of Autism and Childhood Schizophrenia, 6,* 109–122.

Bartz, W. R., & Loy, D. L. (1970). The Shipley-Hartford as a brief I. Q. screening device. *Journal of Clinical Psychology, 26,* 74–75.

Basso, A., Capitani, E., & Moraschini, S. (1982). Sex differences in recovery from aphasia. *Cortex, 18,* 469–475.

Bastian, H. C. (1898). *Aphasia and other speech deficits.* London: H. K. Lewis.

Battersby, W. S., Bender, M. B., Pollack, M., & Kahn, R. L. (1955). Unilateral "spatial agnosia" ("inattention") in patients with cortical lesions. *Brain, 79,* 68–93.

Bauer, C. A., Schlottmann, R. S., Kane, R. L., & Johnsen, D. E. (1984). An evaluation of the Digit Symbol component of the Russell, Neuringer, and Goldstein average impairment rating. *Journal of Consulting and Clinical Psychology, 52,* 317–318.

Baumeister, A. A. (1967). The effects of dietary control on intelligence in phenylketonuria. *American Journal of Mental Deficiency, 71,* 840–847.

Beck, N. C., Horwitz, E., Seidenberg, M., Parker, G., & Frank, R. (1985). WAIS-R factor structure in psychiatric and general medical patients. *Journal of Consulting and Clinical Psychology, 53,* 402–405.

Benbow, C. P., & Stanley, J. C. (1980). Sex differences in mathematical ability: Fact or artifact? *Science, 210,* 1262–1264.

Benbow, C. P., & Stanley, J. C. (1982). Consequences in high school and college of sex differences in mathematical reasoning ability: A longitudinal perspective. *American Educational Research Journal, 19,* 598–622.

Benbow, C. P., & Stanley, J. C. (1983). Sex differences in mathematical reasoning ability: More facts. *Science, 222,* 1029–1031.

Bengtson, V. L., Reedy, M. N., & Gordon, C. (1985). Aging and self-conceptions: Personality processes and social contexts. In J. E. Birren and K. W. Schaie (Eds.), *Handbook of the psychology of aging* (2nd ed.) (pp. 544–593). New York: Van Nostrand Reinhold.

Benton, A. L. (1959). *Right-left discrimination and finger localization: Development and pathology.* New York: Hoeber.

Benton, A. L. (1962). Clinical symptomatology in right and left hemispheric lesions. In V. B. Mountcastle (Ed.), *Interhemispheric relations and cerebral dominance* (pp. 253–263). Baltimore, MD: Johns Hopkins.

Benton, A. L. (1963). *The Revised Visual Retention Test: Clinical and experimental applications* (3rd ed.). Iowa City, IA: The State University of Iowa.

Benton, A. L. (1980). The neuropsychology of facial recognition. *American Psychologist, 35,* 176–186.

Benton, A. L. (1982). Child neuropsychology: Retrospect and prospect. In J. de Wit & A. L. Benton (Eds.), *Perspectives in child study* (pp. 41–61). Lisse, the Netherlands: Swets and Zeitlinger.

Benton, A. L., & Fogel, M. L. (1962). Three-dimensional constructional praxis: A clinical test. *Archives of Neurology, 7,* 347–354.

Benton, A. L., Hamsher, K., Varney, N. R., & Spreen, O. (1983). *Contributions to neuropsychological assessment: A clinical manual.* New York: Oxford.

Benton, A. L., Van Allen, M. W., & Fogel, M. L. (1964). Temporal orientation in cerebral disease. *Journal of Nervous and Mental Disease, 139,* 110–119. University Press.

Berger, A. (1985). Review of the Watson-Glaser Critical Thinking Appraisal. In J. V. Mitchell (Ed.), *The ninth mental measurements yearbook* (pp. 1692–1693). Lincoln, NE: Buros Institute of Mental Measurements, University of Nebraska Press.

Berger, L., Bernstein, A., Klein, E., Cohen, J., & Lucas, G. (1964). Effects of aging and pathology on the factorial structure of intelligence. *Journal of Consulting Psychology, 28,* 199–207.

Berkowitz, B., & Green, R. F. (1963). Changes in intellect with age: I. Longitudinal study of Wechsler-Bellevue scores. *Journal of Genetic Psychology, 103,* 3–21.

Berry, K. K., & Sherrets, S. A. (1975). A comparison of the WISC and WISC-R scores of special education students. *Pediatric Psychology, 3,* 14.

Bieliauskas, L., & Boll, T. (1984). Division 40/INS Task Force on Education, Accreditation and Credentialing. *APA Newsletter 40.*

Binder, L. M. (1987). Appropriate reporting of Wechsler IQ and subtest scores in assessments for disability. *Journal of Clinical Psychology, 43,* 144–145.

Binet, A. (1890a). Recherches sur les mouvements de quelques jeunes enfants. *La Revue Philosophique, 29,* 297–309.

Binet, A. (1890b). Perceptions d'enfants. *La Revue Philosophique, 30,* 582–611.

Binet, A. (1911). Nouvelle recherches sur la mesure du niveau intellectuel chez les enfants d'école. *L'Année Psychologique, 17,* 145–210.

Binet, A., & Henri, V. (1895). La psychologie individuelle. *L'Année Psychologique, 2,* 411–465.

Binet, A., & Simon, T. (1905). Méthodes nouvelles pour le diagnostic du niveau intellectuel des anormaux. *L'Année Psychologique, 11,* 191–244.

Binet, A., & Simon, T. (1908). Le développement de l'intelligence chez les enfants. *L'Année Psychologique, 14,* 1–94.

Birren, J. E., & Morrison, D. F. (1961). Analysis of the WAIS subtests in relation to age and education. *Journal of Gerontology, 16,* 363–369.

Birren, J. E., & Schaie, K. W. (1985) (Eds.), *Handbook of the psychology of aging* (2nd ed.). New York: Van Nostrand Reinhold.

Black, F. W. (1973). Memory and paired-associate learning of patients with unilateral brain lesions. *Psychological Reports, 33,* 919–922.

Black, F. W. (1974a). Cognitive effects of unilateral brain lesions secondary to penetrating missile wounds. *Perceptual and Motor Skills, 38,* 387–391.

Black, F. W. (1974b). The cognitive sequelae of penetrating missile wounds of the brain. *Military Medicine, 139,* 815–817.

Black, F. W. (1976). Cognitive deficits in patients with unilateral war-related frontal lobe lesions. *Journal of Clinical Psychology, 32,* 366–372.

Black, F. W. (1980). WAIS Verbal–Performance discrepancies as predictors of lateralization in patients with discrete brain lesions. *Perceptual and Motor Skills, 51,* 213–214.

Black, F. W. (1986a). Digit repetition in brain-damaged adults: Clinical and theoretical implications. *Journal of Clinical Psychology, 42,* 770–782.

Black, F. W. (1986b). Neuroanatomic and neuropsychologic correlates of Digit Span performance by brain-damaged adults. *Perceptual and Motor Skills, 63,* 815–822.

Black, F. W., & Strub, R. L. (1978). Digit repetition performance in patients with focal brain damage. *Cortex, 14,* 12–21.

Blackburn, J. A. (1984). The influence of personality, curriculum, and memory correlates on formal reasoning in young adults and elderly persons. *Journal of Gerontology, 39,* 207–209.

Blackstock, G. (1978). Cerebral asymmetry and the development of early infantile autism. *Journal of Autism and Childhood Schizophrenia, 8,* 339–353.

Blaha, J., Mandes, E., & Swisher, C. W. (1987). The hierarchical factor structure of the WAIS-R for learning-disabled adults. *Journal of Clinical Psychology, 43,* 280–286.

Blaha, J., & Vance, H. (1979). The hierarchical factor structure of the WISC-R for learning-disabled children. *Learning Disabilities Quarterly, 2,* 71–75.

Blaha, J., & Wallbrown, F. H. (1982). Hierarchical factor structure of the Wechsler Adult Intelligence Scale—Revised. *Journal of Consulting and Clinical Psychology, 50,* 652–660.

Blakey, W., Fantuzzo, J., Gorsuch, R., & Moon, G. (1987). A peer-mediated, competency-based training package for administering and scoring the WAIS—R. *Professional Psychology: Research and Practice, 18,* 17–20.

Blakey, W., Fantuzzo, J., & Moon, G. (1985). An automated competency-based model for teaching skills in the administration of the WAIS-R. *Professional Psychology: Research and Practice, 16,* 641–647.

Blalock, J. (1987). Intellectual levels and patterns. In D. Johnson & J. Blalock (Eds.), *Young adults with learning disabilities: Clinical studies.* Orlando, FL: Grune & Stratton.

Blatt, S. J., Baker, B. L., & Weiss, J. (1970). Wechsler Object Assembly subtest and bodily concern: A review and replication. *Journal of Consulting and Clinical Psychology, 34,* 269–274.

Blatt, S. J., & Quinlan, P. (1967). Punctual and procrastinating students; A study of temporal parameters. *Journal of Consulting Psychology, 31,* 170–174.

Bleker, E. G. (1983). Cognitive defense style and WISC-R P > V sign in juvenile recidivists. *Journal of Clinical Psychology, 39,* 1030–1032.

Bloom, A. S., Hersh, J. H., Podruch, P. E., Weisskopf, B., Topinka, C. W., & Reese, A. (1986). Developmental characteristics of recognizable patterns of human malformation. In J. M. Berg (Ed.), *Science and service in mental retardation* (pp 34–51). London: Methuen.

Bloom, B. L. (1959). Comparison of the alternate Wechsler Memory Scale forms. *Journal of Clinical Psychology, 15,* 72–74.

Blusewicz, M. J., Schenkenberg, T., Dustman, R. E., & Beck, R. E. (1977). WAIS performance in young normal, young alcoholic, and elderly normal groups: An evaluation of organicity and mental aging indices. *Journal of Clinical Psychology, 33,* 1149–1153.

Bogen, J. E., DeZure, R., Tenhouten, N., & Marsh, J. (1972). The other side of the brain: IV: The A/P ratio. *Bulletin of the Los Angeles Neurological Society, 37,* 49–61.

Boll, T. J. (1974). Right and left cerebral hemisphere damage and tactile perception: Performance of the ipsilateral and contralateral sides of the body. *Neuropsychologia, 12,* 235–238.

Boll, T. J. (1981). The Halstead-Reitan Neuropsychology Battery. In S. B. Filskov & T. J. Boll (Eds.), *Handbook of clinical neuropsychology* (pp. 577–607). New York: Wiley.

Boll, T. J. (1983). Minor head injury in children—out of sight but not out of mind. *Journal of Clinical Child Psychology, 12,* 74–80.

Boll, T. J. (1985). Developing issues in clinical neuropsychology. *Journal of Clinical and Experimental Neuropsychology, 7,* 473–485.

Boll, T. J., Heaton, R. K., & Reitan, R. M. (1974). Neuropsychological and emotional correlates of Huntington's chorea. *Journal of Nervous and Mental Disease, 158,* 61–69.

Boll, T. J., & Reitan, R. M. (1973). Effect of age on performance on the Trail Making Test. *Perceptual and Motor Skills, 36,* 691–694.

Bolter, L., Veneklasen, J., & Long, C. J. (1981). Investigation of WAIS effectiveness in discriminating between temporal and generalized seizure patients. *Journal of Consulting and Clinical Psychology, 49,* 549–553.

Bolton, B. (1980). Personality (16 PF) correlates of WAIS scales: A replication. *Applied Psychological Measurement, 4,* 399–401.

Bornstein, R. A. (1982). Effects of unilateral lesions on the Wechsler Memory Scale. *Journal of Clinical Psychology, 38,* 389–392.

Bornstein, R. A. (1983a). Verbal IQ–Performance IQ discrepancies on the Wechsler Adult Intelligence Scale—Revised in patients with unilateral or bilateral cerebral dysfunction. *Journal of Consulting and Clinical Psychology, 51,* 779–780.

Bornstein, R. A. (1983b). Relationship of age and education to neuropsychological performance in patients with symptomatic carotid artery disease. *Journal of Clinical Psychology, 39,* 470–478.

Bornstein, R. A. (1984). Unilateral lesions and the Wechsler Adult Intelligence Scale—Revised: No sex differences. *Journal of Consulting and Clinical Psychology, 52,* 604–608.

Bornstein, R. A., Baker, G. B., & Douglass, A. B. (1987). Short-term retest reliability of the Halstead-Reitan battery in a normal sample. *Journal of Nervous and Mental Disease, 175,* 229–232.

Bornstein, R. A., & Chelune, G. J. (1988). Factor structure of the Wechsler Memory Scale—Revised. *The Clinical Neuropsychologist, 2,* 107–115.

Bornstein, R. A., & Matarazzo, J. D. (1982). Wechsler VIQ versus PIQ differences in cerebral dysfunction: A literature review with emphasis on sex differences. *Journal of Clinical Neuropsychology, 4,* 319–334.

Bornstein, R. A., & Matarazzo, J. D. (1984). Relationship of sex and the effects of unilateral lesions on the Wechsler Intelligence Scales: Further considerations. *The Journal of Nervous and Mental Disease, 172,* 707–710.

Bornstein, R. A., Suga, L., & Prifitera, A. (1987). Incidence of Verbal IQ–Performance IQ discrepancies at various levels of education. *Journal of Clinical Psychology, 43,* 387–389.

Botwinick, J. (1967). *Cognitive processes in maturity and old age*. New York: Springer.

Botwinick, J. (1977). Intellectual abilities. In J. E. Birren & K. W. Schaie (Eds.), *Handbook of the psychology of aging* (pp. 580–605). New York: Van Nostrand Reinhold.

Botwinick, J. (1981). Neuropsychology of aging. In S. B. Filskov & T. J. Boll (Eds.), *Handbook of Clinical Neuropsychology*. New York: Wiley.

Bouchard, T. J., & McGue, M. (1981). Familial studies of intelligence: A review. *Science, 212,* 1055–1059.

Bouchard, T. J., & Segal, N. L. (1985). Environment and IQ. In B. B. Wolman (Ed.), *Handbook of intelligence* (pp. 391–464). New York: Wiley.

Boucher, M. L., Dewan, M. J., Donnelly, M. P., Pandurangi, A. K., Bartell, K., Diamond, T., & Major, L. F. (1986). Relative utility of three indices of neuropsychological impairment in a young, schizophrenic population. *Journal of Nervous and Mental Disease, 174,* 44–46.

Bowers, T. G., Washburn, S. E., & Livesay, J. R. (1986). Predicting neuropsychological impairment by screening instruments and intellectual evaluation indices: Implications for the meaning of Kaufman's factor III. *Psychological Reports, 59,* 487–493.

Bracken, B., & Barnett, D. (1987). The technical side of preschool assessment: A primer of critical issues. *Preschool Interests, 6–7,* 9.

Braden, J. P., & Paquin, M. M. (1985). A comparison of the WISC-R and WAIS-R Performance scales. *Journal of Psychoeducational Assessment, 3,* 285–290.

Bradley, R. H., & Caldwell, B. M. (1981). The HOME inventory: A validation of the preschool scale for black children. *Child Development, 52,* 708–710.

Bradway, K. P., Thompson, C. W., & Cravens, R. B. (1958). Preschool IQs after twenty-five years. *Journal of Educational Psychology, 49,* 278–281.

Brandt, E. A. (1984). The cognitive functioning of American Indian children: A critique of McShane and Plas. *The School Psychology Review, 13,* 74–82.

Brandt, J., Strauss, M. E., Larus, J., Jensen, B., Folstein, S. E., & Folstein, M. F. (1984). Clinical correlates of dementia and disability in Huntington's disease. *Journal of Clinical Neuropsychology, 6,* 401–412.

Briggs, G. G., Nebes, R. D., & Kinsbourne, M. (1976). Intellectual differences in relation to personal and family handedness. *Quarterly Journal of Experimental Psychology, 28,* 591–601.

Briggs, P. F. (1960). The validity of WAIS performance subtests completed with one hand. *Journal of Clinical Psychology, 16,* 318–320.

Brinkman, S. D., & Braun, P. (1984). Classification of dementia patients by a WAIS profile related to central cholinergic deficiencies. *Journal of Clinical Neuropsychology, 6,* 393–400.

Brinkman, S. D., Largen, J. W., Gerganoff, S., & Pomara, N. (1983). Russell's revised Wechsler Memory Scale in the evaluation of dementia. *Journal of Clinical Psychology, 39,* 989–993.

Broca, P. (1861). Nouvelle observation d'aphemie produite par un elesion de la muite postérieure des deuxième et troisième circonvolutions frontales. *Bulletin de la Société Anatomique de Paris, 36,* 398–407.

Brodal, A. (1973). Self-observations and neuro-anatomical consideration after a stroke. *Brain, 96,* 675–694.

Brody, E. B., & Brody, N. (1976). *Intelligence: Nature, determinants, and consequences.* New York: Academic Press.

Brody, N. (1985). The validity of tests of intelligence. In B. B. Wolman (Ed.), *Handbook of intelligence* (pp. 353–389). New York: Wiley.

Broman, S. H., Nichols, P. L., & Kennedy, W. A. (1975). *Preschool IQ: Prenatal and early developmental correlates.* Hillsdale, NJ: Lawrence Erlbaum.

Brooker, B. H., & Cyr, J. J. (1986). Tables for clinicians to use to convert WAIS-R short forms. *Journal of Clinical Psychology, 42,* 982–986.

Brophy, A. L. (1986). Confidence intervals for true scores and retest scores on clinical tests. *Journal of Clinical Psychology, 42,* 989–991.

Brown, G. G., Baird, A. D., & Shatz, M. W. (1986). The effects of cerebral vascular disease and its treatment on higher cortical functioning. In I. Grant & K. M. Adams (Eds.), *Neuropsychological assessment of neuropsychiatric disorders* (pp. 384–414). New York: Oxford University Press.

Brown, W. R., & McGuire, J. M. (1976). Current psychological assessment practices. *Professional Psychology, 7,* 475–484.

Browning, D. L., & Quinlan, D. M. (1985). Ego development and intelligence in a psychiatric population: Wechsler subtest scores. *Journal of Personality Assessment, 49,* 260–263.

Bruininks, R. H., & McGrew, K. (1987). *Exploring the structure of adaptive behavior* (Report Number 87-1). Minneapolis, MN: The University of Minnesota, Department of Educational Psychology.

Bruininks, R. H., Thurlow, M., & Gilman, C. J. (1987). Adaptive behavior and mental retardation. *Journal of Special Education, 21,* 69–88.

Bruininks, R. H., Woodcock, R. W., Hill, B. K., & Weatherman, R. F. (1984). *Scales of Independent Behavior examiner's manual.* Allen, TX: DLM/Teaching Resources.

Bruininks, R. H., Woodcock, R. W., Hill, B. K., & Weatherman, R. F. (1985). *Development and standardization of the Scales of Independent Behavior.* Allen, TX: DLM/Teaching Resources.

Bruininks, R. H., Woodcock, R. W., Weatherman, R. F., & Hill, B. K. (1984). *Scales of Independent Behavior: Woodcock-Johnson Psycho-Educational Battery: Part Four.* Allen, TX: DLM/Teaching Resources.

Bryden, M. P. (1979). Evidence for sex-related differences in cerebral organization. In M. A. Wittig & A. C. Peterson (Eds.), *Sex related differences in cognitive functioning.* New York: Academic Press.

Bryden, M. P. (1980). Sex differences in brain organization: Different brains or different strategies? *Behavioral and Brain Sciences, 3,* 230–231.

Buchanan, M., & Wolf, J. S. (1986). A comprehensive study of learning disabled adults. *Journal of Learning Disabilities, 19,* 34–38.

Buck, M. W. (1968). *Dysphasia.* Englewood Cliffs, NJ: Prentice-Hall.

Buffery, A. W. H. (1974). Asymmetric lateralization of cerebral functions and the effects of unilateral brain surgery in epileptic patients. In S. J. Dimond & J. G. Beaumont (Eds.), *Hemispheric function in the human brain.* London: Elek Science.

Buffery, A. W. H., & Gray, J. (1972). Sex differences in the development of perceptual and linguistic skills. In C. Ounsted & D. Taylor (Eds.), *Gender differences: Their ontogeny and significance.* London: Churchill.

Burdick, J. A., Johnson, L. C., & Smith, J. W. (1970). Measurements of change during alcohol withdrawal in chronic alcoholics. *British Journal of Addiction, 65,* 273–280.

Burnham, L. B. (1982). Adults: Not grown up children. *Community and Junior College Journal, 53,* 22–26, 46.

Butters, N., & Cermak, L. S. (1980). *The alcoholic Korsakoff's syndrome: An information processing approach to amnesia.* New York: Academic Press.

Butters, N., Salmon, D. P., Cullum, M., Cairns, P., Troster, A. I., Jacobs, D., Moss, M., & Cermak, L. S. (1988). Differentiation of amnestic and demented patients with the Wechsler Memory Scale—Revised. *The Clinical Neuropsychologist, 2,* 133–148.

Butters, N., Sax, D., Montgomery, K., & Tarlow, S. (1978). Comparison of the neuropsychological deficits associated with early and advanced Huntington's disease. *Archives of Neurology, 35,* 585–589.

Caine, E. D. (1986). The neuropsychology of depression: The pseudodementia syndrome. In I. Grant & K. M. Adams (Eds.), *Neuropsychological assessment of neuropsychiatric disorders* (pp. 221–243). New York: Oxford University Press.

Caine, E. D., Bamford, K. A., Schiffer, R. B., Shoulson, I., & Levy, S. (1986). A controlled neuropsychological comparison of Huntington's disease and multiple sclerosis. *Archives of Neurology, 43,* 249–254.

Calvert, E. J., & Crozier, W. R. (1978). An analysis of Verbal–Performance intelligence quotient discrepancies in the Wechsler Adult Intelligence Scale results of mentally subnormal hospital patients. *Journal of Mental Deficiency Research, 22,* 147–153.

Campbell, B., & Wilson, B. J. (1986). An investigation of Kaufman's method for determining scatter on the WISC-R. *Journal of School Psychology, 24,* 373–380.

Campbell, F. A., & Ramey, C. T. (1986). High risk infants: Environmental risk factors. In J. M. Berg (Ed.), *Science and service in mental retardation* (pp. 23–33). London: Methuen.

Campbell, I. A. (1985). Review of Vineland Adaptive Behavior Scales. In J. V. Mitchell, (Ed.), *The ninth mental measurements yearbook* (pp. 1660–1662). Lincoln, NE: Buros Institute of Mental Measurements, University of Nebraska Press.

Campbell, V., Smith, R., & Wool, R. (1981). Adaptive Behavior Scale differences in scores of mentally retarded individuals referred for institutionalization and those never referred. *American Journal of Mental Deficiency, 86,* 425–528.

Candler, A. C., Maddux, C. D., & Johnson, D. L. (1986). Relationship of scores on PPVT-R and WISC-R with special education children and youth. *Perceptual and Motor Skills, 62,* 417–418.

Capps, C. F., Levinson, E. M., & Hohenshil, T. H. (1985). Vocational aspects of psychological assessment: Part III. *NASP Communique, 13*(5), 5–6.

Cargnello, J. C., & Gurekas, R. (1987). The clinical use of a modified WAIS procedure in a geriatric population. *Journal of Clinical Psychology, 43,* 286–290.

Carsrud, A. L., Carsrud, K. B., Dodd, B. G., Thompson, M., & Gray, W. K. (1981). Predicting vocational aptitude of mentally retarded persons: A comparison of assessment systems. *American Journal of Mental Deficiency, 86,* 275–280.

Carvajal, H., Gerber, J., Hewes, P., & Weaver, K. A. (1987). Correlations between scores on the Stanford-Binet IV and Wechsler Adult Intelligence Scale—Revised. *Psychological Reports, 61,* 83–86.

Carvajal, H., Gerber, J., & Smith, P. D. (1987). Relationship between scores of young adults on Stanford-Binet IV and Peabody Picture Vocabulary Test—Revised. *Perceptual and Motor Skills, 65,* 721–722.

Carvajal, H., Shaffer, C., & Weaver, K. A. (1989). Correlations of scores of maximum security inmates on Wechsler Adult Intelligence Scale—Revised. *Psychological Reports, 65,* 268–270.

Carvajal, T. L., Lane, M., & Gay, D. A. (1984). Longitudinal comparisons of Wechsler's scales in educable mentally handicapped children and adults. *Psychology in the Schools, 21,* 137–140.

Catron, D. W. (1978). Immediate test–retest changes in WAIS scores among college males. *Psychological Reports, 43,* 279–290.

Catron, D. W., & Catron, S. S. (1977). WISC-R vs. WISC: A comparison with educable mentally retarded children. *Journal of School Psychology, 15,* 264–266.

Catron, D. W., & Thompson, C. C. (1979). Test–retest gains in WAIS scores after four retest intervals. *Journals of Clinical Psychology, 35,* 352–357.

Cella, D. (1984). The modified WAIS-R: An extension and revision. *Journal of Clinical Psychology, 40,* 801–804.

Cella, D., Jacobsen, P. B., & Hymowitz, P. (1985). A comparison of the intertest accuracy of two short forms of the WAIS-R. *Journal of Clinical Psychology, 41,* 544–546.

Cernovsky, Z. (1986). Masculinity-femininity scale of the MMPI and intellectual functioning of female addicts. *Journal of Clinical Psychology, 42,* 310–312.

Chalke, F., & Ertl, J. (1965). Evoked potentials and intelligence. *Life Sciences, 4,* 1319–1322.

Chance, J., Overcast, T., & Dollinger, S. J. (1978). Aging and cognitive regression: Contrary findings. *Journal of Psychology, 98,* 177–183.

Chapman, L. F., & Wolff, H. G. (1959). The cerebral hemispheres and the highest integrative functions of man. *A.M.A. Archives of Neurology, 1,* 357–424.

Chastain, R., & Joe, G. W. (1987). Multidimensional relations between intellectual abilities and demographic variables. *Journal of Educational Psychology, 79,* 323–325.

Chelune, G. J. (1982). A reexamination of the relationship between the Luria-Nebraska and Halstead-Reitan batteries: Overlap with the WAIS. *Journal of Consulting and Clinical Psychology, 50,* 578–580.

Chelune, G. J., & Bornstein, R. A. (1988). WMS-R patterns among patients with unilateral lesions. *The Clinical Neuropsychologist, 2,* 121–132.

Childs, D. E. (1982). A study of the adaptive behavior of retarded children and the resultant effects of this use in the diagnosis of mental retardation. *Education and Training of the Mentally Retarded, 77,* 109–113.

Chmielewski, C., & Golden, C. (1980). Alcoholism and brain damage: An investigation using the Luria-Nebraska Neuropsychological Battery. *International Journal of Neuroscience, 10,* 99–105.

Christensen, A. L. (1975). *Luria's neuropsychological investigation.* New York: Spectrum.

Christensen, A. L. (1979). *Luria's neuropsychological investigation.* Munkesgaard: Copenhagen.

Christian, W. P., Jr., & Malone, D. R. (1973). Relationships among three measures used in screening mentally retarded for placement in special education. *Psychological Reports, 33,* 415–418.

Cicchetti, D. V., & Sparrow, S. S. (1986). False conclusions about Vineland standard scores: Silverstein's Type I errors and other artifacts. *American Journal of Mental Deficiency, 91,* 5–9.

Clampit, M. K., Adair, J., & Strenio, J. (1983). Frequency of discrepancies between deviation quotients on the WISC-R: A table for clinicians. *Journal of Consulting and Clinical Psychology, 51,* 795–796.

Clarizio, H., & Bernard, R. (1981). Recategorized WISC-R scores of learning disabled children and differential diagnosis. *Psychology in the Schools, 18,* 5–12.

Clark, C., Crockett, D., Klonoff, H., & MacDonald, J. (1983). Cluster analysis of the WAIS on brain-damaged patients. *Journal of Clinical Neuropsychology, 5,* 149–158.

Clausen, J. (1972). The continuing problem of defining mental deficiency. *Journal of Special Education, 6,* 97–106.

Clayton, G. A., Sapp, G. L., O'Sullivan, P., & Hall, L. (1986). Comparative validity of two WAIS-R short forms with vocational rehabilitation clients. *Perceptual and Motor Skills, 63,* 1303–1308.

Coffman, W. E. (1985). Review of Structure of Intellect Learning Abilities Test. In J. V. Mitchell (Ed.), *The ninth mental measurements yearbook* (pp. 1486–1488). Lincoln, NE: Buros Institute of Mental Measurements, University of Nebraska Press.

Cohen, J. (1952a). Factors underlying Wechsler-Bellevue performance of three neuropsychiatric groups. *Journal of Abnormal and Social Psychology, 47,* 359–365.

Cohen, J. (1952b). A factor-analytically based rationale for the Wechsler-Bellevue. *Journal of Consulting Psychology, 16,* 272–277.

Cohen, J. (1957a). A factor-analytically based rationale for the Wechsler-Adult Intelligent Scale. *Journal of Consulting Psychology, 6,* 451–457.

Cohen, J. (1957b). The factorial structure of the WAIS between early adulthood and old age. *Journal of Consulting Psychology, 21,* 283–290.

Cohen, R. J., Montague, P., Nathanson, L. S., & Swerdlik, M. E. (1988). *Psychological testing: An introduction to tests and measurement.* Mountain View, CA: Mayfield Publishing Company.

Colby, K., & Parkinson, C. (1977). Handedness in autistic children. *Journal of Autism and Childhood Schizophrenia, 7,* 3–9.

Coleman, M., Jorgenson, C., & Evans, M. H. (1988). The WISC-R and Detroit Tests of Learning Aptitude: 2. A comparative study. *Journal of Psychoeducational Assessment, 6,* 341–346.

Cone, J. D. (1984). *The pyramid scales.* Austin, TX: PRO-ED.

Cone, J. D. (Ed.). (1986). *The pyramid system: Comprehensive assessment and programming for handicapped persons.* Morgantown, WV: Pyramid Press.

Conley, J. J. (1984). The hierarchy of consistency: A review and model of longitudinal findings on adult individual differences in intelligence, personality and self-opinion. *Personality and Individual Differences, 5,* 11–26.

Connelly, J. B. (1983). Recategorized WISC-R score patterns of older and younger referred Tlingit Indian children. *Psychology in the Schools, 20,* 271–275.

Connor, R., Kamphaus, R. W., & Harrison, P. L. (1988, April). *Testing the independence of intelligence and adaptive behavior constructs.* Paper presented at the meeting of the National Association of School Psychologists, Chicago, IL.

Conroy, J., Efthimiou, J., & Lemanowicz, J. (1982). A matched comparison of the developmental growth of institutionalized and deinstitutionalized mentally retarded clients. *American Journal of Mental Deficiency, 86,* 581–587.

Cordoni, B. K., O'Donnell, J. P., Ramaniah, N. V., Kurtz, J., & Rosenshein, K. (1981). Wechsler Adult Intelligence Scale patterns for learning-disabled young adults. *Journal of Learning Disabilities, 14,* 404–407.

Cornell, E. L., & Coxe, W. W. (1934). *A performance ability scale: Examination manual.* New York: World.

Costa, L. D. (1975). The relation of visuospatial dysfunction to digit span performance in patients with cerebral lesions. *Cortex, 11,* 31–36.

Coulter, W. A. (1980). Adaptive behavior and professional disfavor: Controversies and trends for school psychologists. *The School Psychology Review, 9,* 67–74.

Courville, C. B. (1966). *Effects of alcohol on the nervous system of man.* Los Angeles: San Lucas Press.

Craft, N. P., & Kronenberger, E. J. (1979). Comparability of WISC-R and WAIS IQ scores in educable mentally handicapped adolescents. *Psychology in the Schools, 16,* 502–506.

Craig, D. L. (1979). Neuropsychological assessment in public psychiatric hospitals: The current state of practice. *Journal of Clinical Neuropsychology, 1,* 1–7.

Crandall, F. (1969). *A cross-cultural study of Ahtan Indian and non-Indian high school students in Alaska on selected value orientations and measured intellectual ability.* Unpublished doctoral dissertation, Clark University, Worcester, MA.

Critchley, M. (1953). *The parietal lobes.* London: Edward Arnold.

Crockett, D., Clark, C., & Klonoff, H. (1981). Introduction: An overview of neuropsychology. In S. B. Filskov & T. J. Boll (Eds.), *Handbook of clinical neuropsychology* (pp. 1–37). New York: Wiley.

Cronbach, L. J. (1970). *Essentials of psychological testing* (3rd ed.). New York: Harper & Row.

Cronbach, L. J. (1984). *Essentials of psychological testing* (4th ed.). New York: Harper & Row.

Crookes, T. G. (1984). A cognitive peculiarity specific to schizophrenia. *Journal of Clinical Psychology, 40,* 893–896.

Cummings, J. A. (1985). Review of the Woodcock-Johnson Psycho-Educational Battery. In J. V. Mitchell (Ed.), *The ninth mental measurements yearbook,* (pp. 1759–1762). Lincoln, NE: Buros Institute of Mental Measurements, University of Nebraska Press.

Cummings, J. A., & Simon, M. S. (1988). Review of the Scales of Independent Behavior. *Journal of Psychoeducational Assessment, 6,* 315–320.

Cummins, J. P., & Das, J. P. (1980). Cognitive processing, academic achievement, and WISC-R performance in EMR children. *Journal of Consulting and Clinical Psychology, 48,* 777–779.

Cunningham, T., & Presnall, D. (1978). Relationship between dimensions of adaptive behavior and sheltered workshop productivity, *American Journal of Mental Deficiency, 82,* 386–393.

Cunningham, W. R., Clayton, Z. & Overton, W. (1975). Fluid and crystallized intelligence in young adulthood and old age. *Journal of Gerontology, 30,* 53–55.

Cunningham, W. R., & Owens, W. A. (1983). The Iowa State study of the adult development of intellectual abilities. In K. W. Schaie (Ed.), *Longitudinal studies of adult psychological development* (pp. 20–39). New York: Guilford.

Cyr, J. J., & Brooker, B. H. (1984). Use of appropriate formulas for selecting WAIS-R short forms. *Journal of Consulting and Clinical Psychology, 52,* 903–905.

Dalton, J. E., Pederson, S. L., & McEntyre, W. L. (1987). A comparison of the Shipley vs. WAIS-R subtests in predicting WAIS-R Full Scale IQs. *Journal of Clinical Psychology, 43,* 278–280.

Daniel, M. H. (1989). Differential Ability Scales. *Research Notes.* San Antonio, TX: The Psychological Corporation.

Das, J. P., Kirby, J., & Jarman, R. F. (1979). *Simultaneous and successive cognitive processes.* New York: Academic Press.

Davis, F. B. (1959). Interpretation of differences among averages and individual test scores. *Journal of Educational Psychology, 50,* 162–170.

Davis, F. B. (1971). The measurement of mental ability through evoked potential recording. *Educational Record Research Bulletin, No. 1.*

Davison, L. A. (1974). Current status of clinical neuropsychology. In R. M. Reitan & L. A. Davison (Eds.), *Clinical neuropsychology: Current status and applications* (pp. 325–362). Washington, DC: V. H. Winston & Sons.

Dawson, G., Warrenburg, S., & Fuller, P. (1982). Cerebral lateralization in individuals diagnosed as autistic in early childhood. *Brain and Language, 15,* 353–368.

Dean, J. (1985). A multivariant assessment and treatment technique for alcohol problems. *International Journal of the Addictions, 20,* 1281–1290.

Dean, R. S. (1983). *Manual: Report of individual evaluation for use with WAIS/WAIS-R.* Orlando, FL: Psychological Assessment Resources.

Dean, R. S. (1988). Comment on "IQ: R. I. P." *NASP Communique, 17*(4), 4.

Deaux, K. (1984). From individual differences to social categories: Analysis of a decade's research on gender. *American Psychologist, 39,* 105–116.

Delaney, H. D., Norman, R. D., & Miller, D. A. (1981). An exploration of the verbal encodability hypothesis for sex differences in the Digit-Symbol (symbol–digit) test. *Intelligence, 5,* 199–208.

Delis, D. C., & Kaplan, E. (1982). The assessment of aphasia with the Luria-Nebraska Neuropsychological Battery: A case critique. *Journal of Consulting and Clinical Psychology, 50,* 32–39.

Delis, D. C., & Kaplan, E. (1983). Hazards of a standardized neuropsychological test with low content validity: Comment on the Luria-Nebraska Neuropsychological Battery. *Journal of Consulting and Clinical Psychology, 51,* 396–398.

DeMyer, M. K. (1975). The nature of neuropsychological disability in autistic children. *Journal of Autism and Childhood Schizophrenia, 5,* 109–128.

Denckla, M. B. (1974). Development of motor coordination in normal children. *Developmental Medicine and Child Neurology, 16,* 729–741.

Dennerll, R. D. (1964). Prediction of unilateral brain dysfunction using Wechsler test scores. *Journal of Consulting Psychology, 28,* 278–284.

Denney, N. W. (1982). Aging and Cognitive Changes. In B. B. Wolman (Ed.) *Handbook of Developmental Psychology,* (pp. 807–827). Englewood Cliffs, NJ: Prentice-Hall.

Dennis, M. (1985a). Intelligence after early brain injury: I. Predicting IQ scores from medical variables. *Journal of Clinical and Experimental Neuropsychology, 7,* 526–554.

Dennis, M. (1985b). Intelligence after early brain injury: II. IQ scores of subjects classified on the basis of medical history variables. *Journal of Clinical and Experimental Neuropsychology, 7,* 555–576.

Denny-Brown, D., Meyer, J. S., & Horenstein, S. (1952). The significance of perceptual rivalry resulting from parietal lesions. *Brain, 75,* 434–471.

DeWolfe, A. S., Barrell, R. P., Becker, B. C., & Spaner, F. E. (1971). Intellectual deficit in chronic schizophrenia and brain damage. *Journal of Consulting and Clinical Psychology, 36,* 197–204.

DeWolfe, A. S., & Ryan, J. J. (1984). Wechsler Performance IQ > Verbal IQ index in a forensic sample: A reconsideration. *Journal of Clinical Psychology, 40,* 291–294.

Dickinson, D. J. (1986). Test review: Kaufman Test of Educational Achievement, Brief Form. *Journal of Psychoeducational Assessment, 4,* 333–336.

Dickstein, L. S., & Blatt, S. J. (1967). The WAIS Picture Arrangement subtest as a measure of anticipation. *Journal of Projective Techniques and Personality Assessment, 31,* 32–38.

Dillon, H. J. (1949). *Early school learners: A major educational problem.* New York: National Child Labor Committee.

Dinning, W. D., & Kraft, W. A. (1983). Validation of the Satz-Mogel short form for the WAIS-R with psychiatric inpatients. *Journal of Consulting and Clinical Psychology, 51,* 781–782.

Dixon, R. A., Kramer, D. A., & Baltes, P. B. (1985). Intelligence: A life-span developmental perspective. In B. B. Wolman (Ed.), *Handbook of intelligence* (pp. 301–350). New York: Wiley.

Dodrill, C. B., & Clemmons, D. (1984). Use of neuropsychological tests to identify high school students with epilepsy who later demonstrate inadequate performances in life. *Journal of Consulting and Clinical Psychology, 52,* 520–527.

Dodrill, C. B., & Troupin, A. S. (1975). Effects of repeated administrations of a comprehensive neuropsychological battery among chronic epileptics. *Journal of Nervous and Mental Disease, 161,* 185–190.

Doehring, D. G., & Reitan, R. M. (1961). Certain language and nonlanguage disorders in brain-damaged patients with homonymous visual field defects. *AMA Archives of Neurological Psychiatry, 132,* 227–233.

Doehring, D. G., Reitan, R. M., & Kløve, H. (1961). Changes in patterns of intelligence test performance associated with homonymous visual field defects. *Journal of Nervous and Mental Disease, 132,* 227–233.

Doll, E. A. (1935). A generic scale of social maturity. *American Journal of Orthopsychiatry, 5,* 180–188.

Doll, E. A. (1940). The social basis of mental diagnosis. *Journal of Applied Psychology, 24,* 160–169.

Doll, E. A. (1941). The essentials of an inclusive concept of mental deficiency. *American Journal of Mental Deficiency, 46,* 214–219.

Doll, E. A. (1953). *Measurement of social competence.* Circle Pines, MN: American Guidance Service.

Doll, E. A. (1965). *Vineland Social Maturity Scale.* Circle Pines, MN: American Guidance Service.

Doll, E. A. (1966). Recognition of mental retardation in the school age child. In I. Phillips (Ed.), *Prevention and treatment of mental retardation.* New York: Basic Books.

Donlon, T. F. (Ed.). (1984). *The College Board technical handbook for the Scholastic Aptitude Test and achievement tests.* New York: College Entrance Examination Board.

Doppelt, J. E. (1956). Estimating the Full Scale score on the Wechsler Adult Intelligence Scale from scores on four subtests. *Journal of Consulting Psychology, 20,* 63–66.

Doppelt, J. E., & Kaufman, A. S. (1977). Estimation of the differences between WISC-R and WISC IQs. *Educational and Psychological Measurement, 37,* 417–424.

Doppelt, J. E., & Wallace, W. L. (1955). Standardization of the Wechsler Adult Intelligence Scale for older persons. *Journal of Abnormal and Social Psychology, 51,* 312–330.

Drachman, D. A., & Arbit, J. (1966). Memory and the hippocampal complex: II. Is memory a multiple process? *Archives of Neurology, 15,* 52–61.

Drachman, D. A., & Leavitt, J. (1974). Human memory and the cholinergic system: A relationship to aging? *Archives of Neurology, 30,* 113–121.

Dubois, P. H. (1970). *A history of psychological testing.* Boston: Allyn & Bacon.

Duckro, P. N., Longstreet, A., & McLaughlin, L. J. (1982). A selection of short forms of the WAIS for use with a low SES psychiatric population. *Journal of Clinical Psychology, 38,* 847–852.

Dudek, F. J. (1979). The continuing misinterpretation of the standard error of measurement. *Psychological Bulletin, 86,* 335–337.

Dukes, L., & Buttery, T. J. (1982). Comparison of two screening tests: Gesell Developmental Test and Meeting Street School Screening Test. *Perceptual and Motor Skills, 54,* 1177–1178.

Duncan, D. R., & Barrett, A. M. (1961). A longitudinal comparison of intelligence involving the Wechsler-Bellevue I and WAIS. *Journal of Clinical Psychology, 17,* 318–319.

Dunn, L. M. (1959). *Peabody Picture Vocabulary Test manual.* Circle Pines, MN: American Guidance Service.

Dunn, L. M., & Dunn, L. (1981). *Manual for the Peabody Picture Vocabulary Test—Revised (PPVT-R).* Circle Pines, MN: American Guidance Service.

Durham, T. W. (1982, August). The relationship of the Vineland Adaptive Behavior Scales to intelligence among the institutionalized mentally retarded. In J. C. Childers (Chair), *Vineland Adaptive Behavior Scales: A measure of adaptive functioning.* Symposium conducted at the meeting of the American Psychological Association, Washington, DC.

Dye, C. J. (1982). Factor structure of the Wechsler Memory Scale in an older population. *Journal of Clinical Psychology, 38,* 163–166.

Eckhardt, M. J., & Matarazzo, J. D. (1981). Test-retest reliability of the Halstead Impairment Index in hospitalized alcoholic and nonalcoholic males with mild to moderate neuropsychological impairment. *Journal of Clinical Neuropsychology, 3,* 257–269.

Edinger, J. D. (1976). WAIS Picture Arrangement and premorbid social competence among process schizophrenics. *Journal of Personality Assessment, 40,* 52–53.

Edinger, J. D., Shipley, R. H., Watkins, C. E., & Hammett, E. B. (1985). Validity of the Wonderlic Personnel Test as a brief IQ measure in psychiatric patients. *Journal of Consulting and Clinical Psychology, 53,* 937–939.

Edwards, B. T., & Klein, M. (1984). Comparison of the WAIS and the WAIS-R with Ss of high intelligence. *Journal of Clinical Psychology, 40,* 300–302.

Eisdorfer, C., Busse, E. W., & Cohen, L. D. (1959). The WAIS performance of an aged sample: The relationship between Verbal and Performance IQs. *Journal of Gerontology, 14,* 197–201.

Eisdorfer, C., & Wilkie, F. (1973). Intellectual changes with advancing age. In L. E. Jarvik, C. Eisdorfer, & J. E. Blum (Eds.), *Intellectual functioning in adults.* New York: Springer.

Ekstrom, R. B., French, J. W., Harman, H. H., & Dermen, D. (1978). *Kit of Factor Referenced Cognitive Tests.* Princeton, NJ: Educational Testing Service.

Elardo, R., Bradley, R., & Caldwell, B. M. (1977). A longitudinal study of the relation of infants' home environments to language development at age three. *Child Development, 48,* 596–603.

Elliott, C. (in press). *Manual for the Differential Ability Scales.* San Antonio, TX: The Psychological Corporation.

Elliott, R. (1987). *Litigating intelligence.* Dover, MA: Auburn House.

Elliott, S. N. (1985). Review of AAMD Adaptive Behavior Scale. In J. V. Mitchell (Ed.), *The ninth mental measurements yearbook* (pp. 2–4). Lincoln, NE: Buros Institute of Mental Measurements, University of Nebraska Press.

Elliott, S. N., Piersol, W. C., Witt, J. C., Argulewicz, E. N., Gutkin, T. B., & Galvin, G. A. (1985). Three-year stability of WISC-R IQs for handicapped children from three racial/ethnic groups. *Journal of Psychoeducational Assessment, 3,* 233–244.

Engel, R., & Henderson, N. B. (1973). Visual evoked responses and I.Q. scores at school age. *Developmental and Medical Child Neurology, 15,* 136–145.

Erickson, R. C., & Scott, M. L. (1977). Clinical memory testing: A review. *Psychological Bulletin, 84,* 1130–1149.

Ertl, J., (1971). Fourier analysis of evoked potentials and human intelligence. *Nature, 230,* 525–526.

Ertl, J., & Schafer, E. (1969). Brain response correlates of psychometric intelligence. *Nature, 223,* 421–422.

Estes, W. K. (1974). Learning theory and intelligence. *American Psychologist, 29,* 740–749.

Estes, W. K. (1982). Learning, memory, and intelligence. In R. J. Sternberg (Ed.), *Handbook of human intelligence* (pp. 170–224). New York: Cambridge.

Ettinger, G. E. (1963). Defective identification of fingers. *Neuropsychologia, 1,* 39–45.

Evans, R. G. (1985). Accuracy of the Satz-Mogel procedure in estimating WAIS-R IQs that are in the normal range. *Journal of Clinical Psychology, 41,* 100–103.

Eyman, R. K., Demaine, G. C., & Lei, T. J. (1979). Relationship between community environments and resident changes in adaptive behavior: A path model. *American Journal of Mental Deficiency, 83,* 330–338.

Eysenck, H. J. (1982). Is intelligence? An epilogue. In H. J. Eysenck (Ed.), *A model for intelligence.* Berlin: Springer-Verlag.

Eysenck, H. J., & Barrett, P. (1985). Psychophysiology and the measurement of intelligence. In C. R. Reynolds & V. L. Willson (Eds.). *Methodological and statistical advances in the study of individual differences* (pp. 1–49). New York: Plenum.

Falconer, D. S. (1960). *Introduction to quantitative genetics.* London: Oliver and Boyd.

Fantuzzo, J., Sisemore, T., & Spradlin, W. (1983). A competency-based model for teaching skills in the administration of intelligence tests. *Professional Psychology, 14,* 224–231.

Faulstich, M., McAnulty, D., Gresham, F., Veitia, M., Moore, J., Bernard, B., Waggoner, C., & Howell, R. (1986). Factor structure of the WAIS-R for an incarcerated population. *Journal of Clinical Psychology, 42,* 369–371.

Fedio, P., Cox, C. S., Neophytides, A., Canal-Frederick, G., & Chase, P. N. (1979). Neuropsychological profile of Huntington's disease: Patients and those at risk. In P. N. Chase, N. S. Wexler, & A. Barbeau (Eds.), *Advances in neurology* (Vol. 23). New York: Raven Press.

Fedio, P., & Mirsky, A. F. (1969). Selective intellectual deficits in children with temporal lobe or centrencephalic epilepsy. *Neuropsychologia, 7,* 287–300.

Feingold, A. (1982). The validity of the Information and Vocabulary subtests of the WAIS. *Journal of Clinical Psychology, 38,* 169–174.

Feingold, A. (1983a). Extracting maximum validity from the WAIS. *Journal of Clinical Psychology, 39,* 994–997.

Feingold, A. (1983b). The validity of the Information and Vocabulary subtests of the WAIS for predicting college achievement. *Educational and Psychological Measurement, 43,* 1127–1131.

Feingold, A. (1984). The reliability of score differences on the WAIS, WISC-R, and WAIS-R. *Journal of Clinical Psychology, 40,* 1060–1063.

Feingold, A. (1988). Cognitive gender differences are disappearing. *American Psychologist, 43,* 95–103.

Feingold, L. (1950). *A psychometric study of senescent twins.* Unpublished doctoral dissertation, Columbia University.

Feuerstein, R. (1979). *The dynamic assessment of retarded performers: The learning potential assessment device, theory, instruments, and techniques.* Baltimore, MD: University Park Press.

Field, D., Schaie, K. W., & Leino, E. Z. (1988). Continuity in intellectual functioning: The role of self-reported health. *Psychology and Aging, 3,* 385–392.

Field, G. E., & Sisley, R. (1986). IQ score differences between the WAIS and the WAIS-R: Confirmation with a New Zealand sample. *Journal of Clinical Psychology, 42,* 986–988.

Fields, F. R. J., & Whitmyre, J. W. (1969). Verbal and Performance relationships with respect to laterality of cerebral involvement. *Diseases of the Nervous System, 30,* 177–179.

Filley, C. M., Kobayashi, J., & Heaton, R. K. (1987). Wechsler intelligence scale profiles, the cholinergic system, and Alzheimer's disease. *Journal of Clinical and Experimental Neuropsychology, 9,* 180–186.

Filskov, S. B., & Goldstein, S. G. (1974). Diagnostic validity of the Halstead-Reitan battery. *Journal of Consulting and Clinical Psychology, 42,* 382–388.

Filskov, S. B., & Leli, D. A. (1981). Assessment of the individual in neuropsychological practice. In S. B. Filskov & T. J. Boll (Eds.), *Handbook of Clinical Neuropsychology.* New York: Wiley.

Finlayson, M. A. J., Johnson, K. A., & Reitan, R. M. (1977). Relationship of level of education to neuropsychological measures in brain-damaged and non-brain-damaged adults. *Journal of Consulting and Clinical Psychology, 45,* 536–543.

Fisch, R. O., Bilek, M. K., Horrobin, J. M., & Chang, P. N. (1976). Children with superior intelligence at 7 years of age. *Archives of American Journal of Diseases of Children, 130,* 481–487.

Fischbein, S. (1980). IQ and social class. *Intelligence, 4,* 51–63.

Fischer, J. S. (1988). Using the Wechsler Memory Scale—Revised to detect and characterize memory deficits in multiple sclerosis. *The Clinical Neuropsychologist, 2,* 149–172.

Fischer, W. E., Wenck, L. S., Schurr, K. T., & Ellen, A. S. (1985). The moderating influence of gender, intelligence, and specific achievement deficiencies on the Bannatyne WISC-R recategorization. *Journal of Psychoeducational Assessment, 3,* 245–255.

Fisher, A. T. (1978, August). *Adaptive behavior in nonbiased assessment: Effects on special education.* Paper presented at the meeting of the American Psychological Association, Toronto.

Fisher, M. (1956). Left hemiplegia and motor impersistence. *Journal of Nervous and Mental Disease, 123,* 201–213.

Fitzhugh, L. C., & Fitzhugh, K. B. (1964a). Relationships between Wechsler-Bellevue Form I and WAIS performances of subjects with long-standing cerebral dysfunction. *Perceptual and Motor Skills, 19,* 539–543.

Fitzhugh, K. B., & Fitzhugh, L. C. (1964b). WAIS results for subjects with longstanding, chronic, lateralized and diffuse cerebral dysfunction. *Perceptual and Motor Skills, 19,* 735–739.

Fitzhugh, K. B., Fitzhugh, L. C., & Reitan, R. M. (1961). Psychological deficits in relation to acuteness of brain dysfunction. *Journal of Consulting Psychology, 25,* 61–66.

Fitzhugh, K. B., Fitzhugh, L. C., & Reitan, R. M. (1962). Wechsler-Bellevue comparisons in groups with "chronic" and "current" lateralized and diffuse brain lesions. *Journal of Consulting Psychology, 26,* 306–310.

Fitzhugh, K. B., Fitzhugh, L. C., & Reitan, R. M. (1964). Influence of age upon measures of problem solving and experiential background in subjects with long-standing cerebral dysfunction. *Journal of Gerontology, 19,* 132–134.

Fitzhugh, L. C., Fitzhugh, K. B., & Reitan, R. M. (1965). Adaptive abilities and intellectual functioning of hospitalized alcoholics. *Quarterly Journal of Studies on Alcohol, 26,* 402–411.

Flaugher, R. L. (1978). The many definitions of test bias. *American Psychologist, 33,* 671–679.

Flor-Henry, P. (1976). Lateralized temporal-limbic dysfunction and psychopathology. *Annals of New York Academy of Sciences, 280,* 777–795.

Flynn, J. R. (1983). Now the great augmentation of the American IQ. *Nature, 301,* 655.

Flynn, J. R. (1984). The mean IQ of Americans: Massive gains 1932 to 1978. *Psychological Bulletin, 95,* 29–51.

Flynn, J. R. (1986). Sociobiology and IQ trends over time. *Behavioral and Brain Sciences, 9,* 192.

Flynn, J. R. (1987). Massive gains in 14 nations: What IQ tests really measure. *Psychological Bulletin, 101,* 171–191.

Fogel, M. L. (1965). The Proverbs Test in the appraisal of cerebral diseases. *Journal of General Psychology, 72,* 169–275.

Forsyth, G. A., Gaddes, W. J., Reitan, R. M., & Tryk, H. E. (1971). *Intellectual deficit in multiple sclerosis as indicated by psychological tests* (Research Monograph No. 23). Victoria, BC, Canada: University of Victoria.

Fowler, P. C., Richards, H. C., & Boll, T. J. (1980). WAIS factor patterns of epileptic and normal adults. *Journal of Clinical Neuropsychology, 2,* 115–123.

Fowles, G. P., & Tunick, R. H. (1986). WAIS-R and Shipley estimated IQ correlations. *Journal of Clinical Psychology, 42,* 647–649.

Fraboni, M., Saltstone, R., Baines, G. H., & Cooper, D. (1988). WAIS-R factor structure in a vocational rehabilitational sample: Additional support for a third factor in special populations. *Psychological Reports, 63,* 819–822.

Franklin, M., Stillman, P., Burpeau, M., & Sabers, D. (1982). Examiner error in intelligence testing: Are you a source? *Psychology in the Schools, 19,* 563–569.

Frauenheim, J. G., & Heckerl, J. R. (1983). A longitudinal study of psychological and achievement test performance in severe dyslexic adults. *Journal of Learning Disabilities, 16,* 339–347.

Frederiksen, N. (1986). Toward a broader conception of human intelligence. *American Psychologist, 41,* 445–452.

Fryers, T. (1984). *The epidemiology of severe intellectual impairment.* London: Academic Press.

Fryers, T. (1986). Factors affecting prevalence of severe mental retardation. In J. M. Berg (Ed.), *Science and service in mental retardation* (pp. 3–14). London: Methuen.

Fuld, P. A. (1983). Psychometric differentiation of the dementias: An overview. In B. Reisberg (Ed.), *Alzheimer's disease: The standard reference* (pp. 201–210). New York: The Free Press.

Fuld, P. A. (1984). Test profile of cholinergic dysfunction and of Alzheimer-type dementia. *Journal of Clinical Neuropsychology, 6,* 380–392.

Gainotti, G. (1972). Emotional behavior and hemispheric side of lesion. *Cortex, 8,* 41–55.

Gianotti, G., & Tiacci, C. (1973). The unilateral forms of finger agnosia. *Confina Neurologica, 35,* 271–284.

Galin, D. (1974). Implications for psychiatry of left and right cerebral specialization. *Archives of General Psychiatry, 31,* 78–82.

Galton, F. (1869). *Hereditary genius: An inquiry into its laws and consequences.* London: Macmillan.

Galton, F. (1883). *Inquiries into human faculty and its development.* London: Macmillan.

Garfield, J. C. (1963). *Motor impersistence in normal and brain-damaged children.* Unpublished doctoral dissertation, University of Iowa.

Garfield, J. C. (1964). Motor impersistence in normal and brain-damaged children. *Neurology, 14,* 623–630.

Garfinkle, A. S. (1982). Genetic and environmental influences on the development of Piagetian logico-mathematical concepts and other specific cognitive abilities: A twin study. *Acta Geneticae Medicae et Gemellologiae, 31,* 10–61.

Gasparrini, W., Satz, P., Heilman, K. M., & Coolidge, F. (1977, February). *Hemispheric asymmetries of affective processing as determined by the Minnesota Multiphasic Personality Inventory.* Paper presented at the meeting of the International Neuropsychological Society, Santa Fe, NM.

Gass, C. S., & Russell, E. W. (1985). MMPI correlates of verbal-intellectual deficits in patients with left hemisphere lesions. *Journal of Clinical Psychology, 41,* 664–670.

Gass, C. S., & Russell, E. W. (1987). MMPI correlates of performance intellectual deficits in patients with right hemisphere lesions. *Journal of Clinical Psychology, 43,* 484–489.

Gass, R. O. (1981). Comparative validity of the Verbal IQ as a short form of the WAIS. *Journal of Clinical Psychology, 37,* 843–846.

Gerstmann, J. (1924). Fingeragnosie: Eine unschriebene storung der orientierung am eigerst korper. *Wein Klin. Wchnschr., 37,* 1010–1012.

Ghannam, J., Javornisky, G., & Smith, A. (1979, February). *Diaschisis in adult chronic aphasics with left hemisphere infraction.* Paper presented at the meeting of the International Neuropsychology Society, San Francisco.

Ghiselli, E. E. (1966). *The validity of occupational aptitude tests.* New York: Wiley.

Ghiselli, E. E. (1973). The validity of aptitude tests in personnel selection. *Personnel Psychology, 26,* 461–477.

Gilandas, A., Touzy, S., Beumont, P. J. V., & Greenberg, H. P. (1984). *Handbook of neuropsychological assessment.* Orlando, FL: Grune & Stratton.

Gilbert, J. (1978). *Interpreting psychological test data: Volume I—Test response antecedent.* New York: Van Nostrand Reinhold.

Gilleard, C. J. (1980). Wechsler Memory Scale performance of elderly psychiatric patients. *Journal of Clinical Psychology, 36,* 958–960.

Gilmore, G. C., Royer, F. L., & Gruhn, J. J. (1983). Age differences in symbol-digit substitution performance. *Journal of Clinical Psychology, 39,* 114–123.

Glutting, J. J., & Kaplan, D. (in press). Stanford-Binet Intelligence Scale: Fourth Edition: Making the case for reasonable interpretations. In C. R. Reynolds & R. W. Kamphaus (Eds.), *Handbook of psychological and educational assessment of children: Volume 1, Intelligence and achievement.* New York: Guilford.

Goddard, H. H. (1911). A revision of the Binet scale. *Training School, 8,* 56–62.

Goh, D. S., Teslow, C. J., & Fuller, G. B. (1981). The practice of psychological assessment among school psychologists. *Professional Psychology, 12,* 696–706.

Gold, P. C., & Horn, P. L. (1983). Intelligence and achievement of adult illiterates in a tutorial project: A preliminary analysis. *Journal of Clinical Psychology, 39,* 107–113.

Golden, C. J. (1977). Validity of the Halstead-Reitan Neuropsychological Battery in mixed psychotic and brain-impaired populations. *Journal of Consulting and Clinical Psychology, 45,* 1043.

Golden, C. J. (1979). Identification of specific neurological disorders using double discrimination scales derived from the standardized Luria neuropsychological battery. *International Journal of Neuroscience, 10,* 51–56.

Golden, C. J. (1981). *Diagnosis and rehabilitation in clinical neuropsychology.* Springfield, IL: Charles C. Thomas.

Golden, C. J., Ariel, R. N., Moses, J. A., Jr., Wilkening, G. N., McKay, S. E., & MacInnes, W. D. (1982). Analytic techniques in the interpretation of the Luria-Nebraska Neuropsychological Battery. *Journal of Consulting and Clinical Psychology, 50,* 40–48.

Golden, C. J., & Berg, R. A. (1980a). Interpretation of the Luria-Nebraska Neuropsychological Battery by item intercorrelation: The rhythm scale. *Journal of Clinical Neuropsychology, 2,* 153–156.

Golden, C. J., & Berg, R. A. (1980b). Interpretation of the Luria-Nebraska Neuropsychological Battery by item

intercorrelation: Items 1–24 of the Motor Scale. *Journal of Clinical Neuropsychology, 2,* 66–71.

Golden, C. J., & Berg, R. A. (1980c). Interpretation of the Luria-Nebraska Neuropsychological Battery by item intercorrelation: The writing scale. *Journal of Clinical Neuropsychology, 2,* 8–12.

Golden, C. J., Berg, R. A., & Graber, B. (1982). Test–retest reliability of the Luria-Nebraska Neuropsychological Battery in stable, chronically impaired patients. *Journal of Consulting and Clinical Psychology, 50,* 452–454.

Golden, C. J., Fross, K. H., & Graber, B. (1981). Split-half reliability and item-scale consistency of the Luria-Nebraska Neuropsychological Battery. *Journal of Consulting and Clinical Psychology, 49,* 304–305.

Golden, C. J., Graber, B., Moses, J. A., Jr., & Zatz, L. M. (1980). Differentiation of chronic schizophrenics with and without ventricular enlargement by the Luria-Nebraska Neuropsychological Battery. *International Journal of Neuroscience, 11,* 131–138.

Golden, C. J., Hammeke, T., Osmon, D., Sweet, J., Purisch, A., & Graber, B. (1981). Factor analysis of the Luria-Nebraska Neuropsychological Battery: IV. Intelligence and pathognomonic scales. *International Journal of Neuroscience, 13,* 87–92.

Golden, C. J., Hammeke, T., & Purisch, A. (1978). Diagnostic validity of a standardized neuropsychological battery derived from Luria's neuropsychological tests. *Journal of Consulting and Clinical Psychology, 46,* 1258–1265.

Golden, C. J., Hammeke, T. A., & Purisch, A. D. (1980). *The Luria-Nebraska Neuropsychological Battery.* Los Angeles: Western Psychological Services.

Golden, C. J., Kane, R., Sweet, J., Moses, J. A., Jr., Cardellino, J. P., Templeton, R., Vicente, P., & Graber, B. (1981). Relationship of the Halstead-Reitan Neuropsychological Battery to the Luria-Nebraska Neuropsychological Battery. *Journal of Consulting and Clinical Psychology, 490,* 410–417.

Golden, C. J., & Kuperman, S. K. (1980). Training opportunities in neuropsychology at APA-approved internship settings. *Professional Psychology, 11,* 907–918.

Golden, C. J., MacInnes, W. D., Ariel, R. N., Ruedrich, S. L., Chu, C. C., Coffman, J. A., Graber, B., & Bloch, S. (1982). Cross-validation of the ability of the Luria-Nebraska Neuropsychological Battery to differentiate chronic schizophrenics with and without ventricular enlargement. *Journal of Consulting and Clinical Psychology, 50,* 87–95.

Golden, C. J., Moses, J. A., Jr., Fishburne, F. J., Engum, E., Lewis, G. P., Wisniewski, A. M., Conley, F. K., Berg, R. A., & Graber, B. (1981). Cross-validation of the Luria-Nebraska Neuropsychological Battery for the presence, lateralization, and localization of brain damage. *Journal of Consulting and Clinical Psychology, 49,* 491–507.

Golden, C. J., Moses, J. A., Jr., Graber, B., & Berg, R. (1981). Objective clinical rules for interpreting the Luria-Nebraska Neuropsychological Battery: Derivation, effectiveness, and validation. *Journal of Consulting and Clinical Psychology, 49,* 616–618.

Golden, C. J., Osmon, D., Sweet, J., Graber, B., Purisch, A., & Hammeke, T. (1980). Factor analysis of the Luria-Nebraska Neuropsychological Battery: III, Arithmetic, memory, left, and right. *International Journal of Neuroscience, 11,* 309–315.

Golden, C. J., Purisch, A., Sweet, J., Graber, B., Osmon, D., & Hammeke, T. (1980). Factor analysis of the Luria-Nebraska Neuropsychological Battery: II, Visual, receptive, expressive, and reading scales. *International Journal of Neuroscience, 11,* 227–236.

Golden, C. J., Sweet, J., Hammeke, T., Purisch, A., Graber, B., & Osmon, D. (1980). Factor analysis of the Luria-Nebraska Neuropsychological Battery: I, Motor, rhythm, and tactile scales. *International Journal of Neuroscience, 11,* 91–99.

Goldman, J. (1987). Differential WAIS/WAIS-R IQ discrepancies among institutionalized mentally retarded persons. *American Journal of Mental Deficiency, 91,* 633–635.

Goldstein, G., & Shelly, C. (1972). Statistical and normative studies of the Halstead-Reitan neuropsychological test battery relative to a neuropsychiatric hospital setting. *Perceptual and Motor Skills, 34,* 603–620.

Goldstein, G., & Shelly, C. (1973). Univariate versus multivariate analysis in neuropsychological test assessment of lateralized brain damage. *Cortex, 9,* 204–216.

Goldstein, G., & Shelly, C. (1984). Discriminative validity of various intelligence and neuropsychological tests. *Journal of Consulting and Clinical Psychology, 52,* 383–389.

Goldstein, K. (1948). *Language and language disturbances.* New York: Grune & Stratton.

Goldstein, K. (1952). The effects of brain damage and personality. *Psychiatry, 15,* 245–260.

Goldstein, K., & Scheerer, M. (1941). Abstract and concrete behavior: An experimental study with special tests. *Psychological Monographs, 53,* Whole No. 239.

Goldstein, S. G., Deysach, R. E., & Kleinknecht, R. A. (1973). Effect of experience and amount of information on identification of cerebral impairment. *Journal of Consulting and Clinical Psychology, 41,* 30–34.

Gonen, J. Y., & Brown, L. (1968). Role of vocabulary in deterioration and restitution of mental functioning. *Proceedings of the 76th Annual Convention of the American Psychological Association, 3,* 469–470. (Summary).

Goodenough, D. R., & Karp, S. A. (1961). Field dependence and intellectual functioning. *Journal of Abnormal and Social Psychology, 63,* 241–246.

Goodglass, H., & Kaplan, E. (1979). Assessment of cognitive deficit in the brain-injured patient. In M. S. Gazzaniga (Ed.), *Handbook of behavioral neuropsychology.* New York: Plenum.

Goolishian, H. A., & Ramsay, R. (1956). The Wechsler-Bellevue Form I and the WAIS: A comparison. *Journal of Clinical Psychology, 12,* 147–151.

Gordon, M., Greenberg, R. P., & Gerton, M. (1983). Wechsler discrepancies and the Rorschach experience balance. *Journal of Clinical Psychology, 39,* 775–779.

Gordon, N. G. (1977). Base rates and the decision-making model in clinical neuropsychology. *Cortex, 13,* 3–10.

Gottfredson, L. S. (1984). *The role of intelligence and education in the division of labor* (Report No. 355). Baltimore, MD: Johns Hopkins University, Center for Social Organization of Schools.

Gottfredson, L. S., & Brown, V. C. (1981). Occupational differentiation among white men in the first decade after high school. *Journal of Vocational Behavior, 19,* 251–289.

Grace, W. C. (1986). Equivalence of the WISC-R and WAIS-R in delinquent males. *Journal of Psychoeducational Assessment, 4,* 257–262.

Grace, W. C., & Sweeney, M. E. (1986). Comparisons of the P > V sign on the WISC-R and WAIS-R in delinquent males. *Journal of Clinical Psychology, 42,* 173–176.

Graham, F. K., & Kendall, B. S. (1960). Memory-for-Designs Test: Revised general manual. *Perceptual and Motor Skills, 11,* 147–188.

Granick, S., Kleban, M. H., & Weiss, A. D. (1976). Relationships between hearing loss and cognition in normally hearing aged persons. *Journal of Gerontology, 31,* 434–440.

Grant, I., & Adams, K. M. (Eds.). (1986). *Neuropsychological assessment of neuropsychiatric disorders.* New York: Oxford University Press.

Green, R. F. (1969). Age-intelligence relationship between ages sixteen and sixty-four: A rising trend. *Developmental Psychology, 1,* 618–627.

Greenspan, S. (1979). Social intelligence in the retarded. In N. R. Ellis (Ed.), *Handbook of mental deficiency: Psychological theory and research* (2nd ed.; pp. 483–531). Hillsdale, NJ: Lawrence Erlbaum.

Greenspan, S. (1981). Social competence and handicapped individuals: Practical implications and a proposed model. *Advances in Special Education, 3,* 41–82.

Gregg, N., & Hoy, C. (1985). A comparison of the WAIS-R and the Woodcock-Johnson tests of cognitive ability with learning-disabled college students. *Journal of Psychoeducational Assessment, 3,* 267–274.

Gregory, R. J. (1987). *Adult intellectual assessment.* Boston: Allyn & Bacon.

Gresham, F. M., & Elliott, S. N. (1987). The relationship between adaptive behavior and social skills: Issues in definition and assessment. *Journal of Special Education, 21,* 167–182.

Gribbin, K., Schaie, K. W., & Parham, I. A. (1980). Complexity of life style and maintenance of intellectual abilities. *Journal of Social Issues, 21,* 47–61.

Griffin, P. T., & Heffernan, A. (1983). Digit Span, forward and backward: Separate and unequal components of the WAIS Digit Span. *Perceptual and Motor Skills, 56,* 335–338.

Groff, M. G., & Hubble, L. M. (1981). Recategorized WISC-R scores of juvenile delinquents. *Journal of Learning Disabilities, 14,* 515–516.

Groff, M. G., & Hubble, L. M. (1982). WISC-R factor structures of younger and older youth with low IQs. *Journal of Consulting and Clinical Psychology, 50,* 148–149.

Grossman, F. M. (1983). Percentage of WAIS-R standardization sample obtaining Verbal-Performance discrepancies. *Journal of Consulting and Clinical Psychology, 51,* 641–642.

Grossman, F. M., Herman, D. O., & Matarazzo, J. D. (1985). Statistically inferred versus empirically observed VIQ–PIQ differences in the WAIS-R. *Journal of Clinical Psychology, 41,* 268–272.

Grossman, H. J. (Ed.) (1973). *Manual on terminology and classification in mental retardation* (1973 revision). Washington, DC: American Association on Mental Deficiency.

Grossman, H. J. (1983). *Classification in mental retardation.* Washington, DC: American Association on Mental Deficiency.

Gruelich, W. W. (1957). A comparison of the physical growth and development of American-born and Japanese children. *American Journal of Physical Anthropology, 15,* 489–515.

Gruzelier, J., & Hammond, N. H. V. (1976). Schizophrenia: A dominant hemisphere temporal-limbic disorder? *Research Communications in Psychology, Psychiatry and Behavior, 1,* 33–72.

Gruzelier, J. H., & Mednick, S. (1976). WISC profiles of children at genetic risk for psychopathology: A neuropsychological interpretation. Unpublished manuscript cited by J. H. Gruzelier & N. V. Hammond (1976). Schizophrenia: A dominant hemisphere temporal-limbic disorder? *Research Communications in Psychology, Psychiatry and Behavior, 1,* 33–72.

Guilford, J. P. (1954). *Psychometric methods.* New York: McGraw-Hill.

Guilford, J. P. (1967). *The nature of human intelligence.* New York: McGraw-Hill.

Guilford, J. P. (1980). Fluid and crystallized intelligences: Two fanciful concepts. *Psychological Bulletin, 88,* 406–412.

Guilford, J. P. (1985). The structure-of-intellect model. In B. B. Wolman (Ed.), *Handbook of intelligence* (pp. 225–266). New York: Wiley.

Gur, R. (1978). Left hemisphere dysfunction and left hemisphere overactivation in schizophrenia. *Journal of Abnormal Psychology, 87,* 226–238.

Gutkin, T. B. (1979a). WISC-R scatter indices: Useful information for differential diagnosis? *Journal of School Psychology, 17,* 368–371.

Gutkin, T. B. (1979b). The WISC-R verbal comprehension, perceptual organization, and freedom from distractibility deviation quotients. Data for practitioners. *Psychology in the Schools, 16,* 356–360.

Gutkin, T. B., & Reynolds, C. R. (1981a). Examination of the Selz and Reitan scatter index of neurological dysfunction with a nationally representative sample of normal children. *Journal of Clinical Neuropsychology, 3,* 38–41.

Gutkin, T. B., & Reynolds, C. R. (1981b). Factorial similarity of the WISC-R for white and black children from the standardization sample. *Journal of Educational Psychology, 73,* 227–231.

Gutkin, T. B., Reynolds, C. R., & Galvin, G. A. (1984). Factor analysis of the Wechsler Adult Intelligence Scale—Revised (WAIS-R): An examination of the standardization sample. *Journal of School Psychology, 22,* 83–93.

Haaland, K. Y., & Delaney, H. D. (1981). Motor deficits after left or right hemisphere damage due to stroke or tumor. *Neuropsychologia, 19,* 17–27.

Hager, P. C. (1985). Woodcock-Johnson Psycho-Educational Battery. In D. J. Keyser & R. C. Sweetland (Eds.), *Test critiques* (Vol. IV, 683–703). Kansas City, MO: Test Corporation of America.

Halpern, A. S., Raffeld, P., Irvin, L., & Link, R. (1975). Measuring social and prevocational awareness in mildly retarded adolescents. *American Journal of Mental Deficiency, 80,* 81–89.

Halstead, W. C. (1947). *Brain and intelligence: A quantitative study of the frontal lobes.* Chicago: University of Chicago Press.

Halstead, W. C., & Wepman, J. M. (1949). The Halstead-Wepman aphasia screening test. *Journal of Speech and Hearing Disorders, 14,* 9–13.

Hamm, H., Wheeler, J., McCallum, S., Herrin, M., Hunter, D., & Catoe, C. (1976). A comparison between the WISC and WISC-R among educable mentally retarded students. *Psychology in the Schools, 13,* 4–8.

Hammeke, T., Golden, C. J., & Purisch, A. (1978). A standardized short and comprehensive neuropsychological test battery based on the Luria neuropsychological evaluation. *International Journal of Neuroscience, 8,* 135–141.

Hammill, D. D. (1985). *Detroit Tests of Learning Aptitude (DTLA-2).* Austin, TX: PRO-ED.

Hamsher, K., Benton, A. L., & Digre, K. (1980). Serial digit learning: Normative and clinical aspects. *Journal of Clinical Neuropsychology, 2,* 39–50.

Hamsher, K., Levin, H. S., & Benton, A. L. (1979). Facial recognition in patients with focal brain lesions. *Archives of Neurology, 36,* 837–839.

Harlow, H. F. (1938). Recovery of pattern discrimination in monkeys following occipital lobe lesions. *Psychological Bulletin, 35,* 686–687.

Harnqvist, K. (1968). Relative changes in intelligence from 13 to 18. *Scandinavian Journal of Psychology, 9,* 50–64.

Harris, A. B. (1980). Structural and chemical changes in experimental epileptic foci. In J. S. Lockard & A. A. Ward, Jr. (Eds.), *Epilepsy: A window to brain mechanisms* (pp. 149–164). New York: Raven Press.

Harris, L. J. (1980). Lateralized sex differences: Substrate and significance. *Behavioral and Brain Sciences, 3,* 236–237.

Harrison, P. L. (1987a). Research with adaptive behavior scales. *Journal of Special Education, 21,* 37–68.

Harrison, P. L. (1987b). Review of the Wide Range Achievement Test—Revised. Accession number AN-10010263, Buros Institute Data Base (Search Label MMYD), BRS Information Technologies.

Harrison, P. L., & Kamphaus, R. W. (1984, April). *Comparison between the K-ABC and Vineland Adaptive Behavior Scales.* Paper presented at the meeting of the National Association of School Psychologists, Philadelphia, PA.

Harrison, P. L., Kaufman, A. S., Hickman, J. A., & Kaufman, N. L. (1988). A survey of tests used for adult assessment. *Journal of Psychoeducational Assessment, 6,* 188–198.

Haskins, R. (1986). Social and cultural factors in risk assessment and mild mental retardation. In D. C. Farran & J. D. McKinney (Eds.), *Risk in intellectual and psychosocial development* (pp. 29–60). Orlando, FL: Academic Press.

Haug, J. O. (1968). Pneumoencephalographic evidence of brain damage in chronic alcoholics. *Acta Psychiatrica Scandinavica* (Supplement), *203,* 135–143.

Haynes, J. P. (1983). Comparative validity of three Wechsler short forms for delinquents. *Journal of Clinical Psychology, 39,* 275–278.

Haynes, J. P. (1985). Comparative validity of two WAIS-R short forms with clients of low IQ. *Journal of Clinical Psychology, 41,* 282–284.

Haynes, J. P., & Bensch, M. (1981). The P > V sign on the WISC-R and recidivism in delinquents. *Journal of Consulting and Clinical Psychology, 49,* 481.

Haynes, J. P., & Howard, R. C. (1986). Stability of WISC-R scores in a juvenile forensic sample. *Journal of Clinical Psychology, 42,* 534–537.

Haynes, J. P., Howard, R. C., & Haynes, S. M. (1987). Internal reliability of the WISC-R with male juvenile delinquents. *Journal of Clinical Psychology, 43,* 496–499.

Hays, J. R., & Solway, K. S. (1977). Violent behavior and differential Wechsler Intelligence Scale for Children char-acteristics. *Journal of Consulting and Clinical Psychology, 45,* 1187.

Hayslip, B., & Sterns, H. L. (1979). Age differences in relationships between crystallized and fluid intelligences and problem solving. *Journal of Gerontology, 34,* 404–414.

Head, H. (1926). *Aphasia and kindred disorders of speech.* London: Cambridge University Press.

Heath, C. P., & Obrzut, J. E. (1986). Adaptive behavior: Concurrent validity. *Journal of Psychoeducational Assessment, 4,* 53–59.

Heaton, R. K., Grant, I., & Matthews, C. G. (1986). Differences in neuropsychological test performance associated with age, education, and sex. In I. Grant & K. M. Adams (Eds.), *Neuropsychological assessment of neuropsychiatric disorders* (pp. 100–120). New York: Oxford University Press.

Heaton, R. K., Nelson, L. M., Thompson, D. S., Burks, J. S., & Franklin, G. M. (1985). Neuropsychological findings in relapsing-remitting and chronic-progressive multiple sclerosis. *Journal of Consulting and Clinical Psychology, 53,* 103–110.

Heaton, R. K., Schmitz, S. P., Avitable, N., & Lehman, R. A. W. (1987). Effects of lateralized cerebral lesions on oral reading, reading comprehension, and spelling. *Journal of Clinical and Experimental Neuropsychology, 9,* 711–722.

Heber, R. F. (1961). A manual on terminology and classification in mental retardation. *American Journal of Mental Deficiency, 1959, 64,* Monogr. Suppl. (Rev. ed.).

Heber, R. F., & Garber, H. (1970). *An experiment in the prevention of cultural-familial retardation.* Paper presented at the Second Congress of the International Association for the Scientific Study of Mental Deficiency, Warsaw, Poland.

Hecaen, H., Ajuriaguerra, J. de, & Massonet, J. (1951). Les troubles visuoconstructifs par lesion parieto-occipitale droit. *Encéphale, 40,* 122–179.

Hecaen, H., & Angelergues, R. (1962). Agnosia for faces (prosopagnosia). *Archives of Neurology, 7,* 92–100.

Heilbrun, A. B. (1956). Psychological test performance as a function of lateral localization of cerebral lesions. *Journal of Comparative and Physiological Psychology, 49,* 10–14.

Heilman, K. M., Bowers, D., & Valenstein, E. (1985). *Clinical neuropsychology* (2nd ed.). New York: Oxford University Press.

Heimburger, R. F., & Reitan, R. M. (1961). Easily administered written test for lateralizing brain lesions. *Journal of Neurosurgery, 18,* 301–312.

Heinemann, A. W., Harper, R. G., Friedman, L. C., & Whitney, J. (1985). The relative utility of the Shipley-Hartford scale: Prediction of WAIS-R IQ. *Journal of Clinical Psychology, 41,* 547–551.

Heinrichs, R. W., & Celinski, M. J. (1987). Frequency of occurrence of a WAIS dementia profile in male head trauma patients. *Journal of Clinical and Experimental Neuropsychology, 9,* 187–190.

Helmstadter, G. C. (1985). Review of Watson-Glaser Critical Thinking Appraisal. In J. V. Mitchell (Ed.), *The ninth mental measurements yearbook* (pp. 1693–1694). Lincoln, NE: Buros Institute of Mental Measurements, University of Nebraska Press.

Henning, J. J., & Levy, R. H. (1967). Verbal–performance IQ differences of white and Negro delinquents on the WISC and WAIS. *Journal of Clinical Psychology, 23,* 164–168.

Henrichs, T. F., Krauskopf, C. J., & Amolsch, T. J. (1982). Personality descriptions from the WAIS: A comparison of systems. *Journal of Personality Assessment, 46,* 544–549.

Henrichs, T. F., & Amolsch, T. J. (1978). A note on the actuarial interpretation of WAIS profile patterns. *Journal of Personality Assessment, 42,* 418–420.

Henry, S. A., & Wittman, R. D. (1981). Diagnostic implications of Bannatyne's recategorized WISC-R scores for learning disabled children. *Journal of Learning Disabilities, 14,* 517–520.

Henson, F. O., & Bennett, L. M. (1985). Kaufman Test of Educational Achievement. In D. J. Keyser & R. C. Sweetland (Eds.), *Test critiques* (Vol. IV; 368–375). Kansas City, MO: Test Corporation of America.

Herman, D. O. (1988). Development of the Wechsler Memory Scale—Revised. *The Clinical Neuropsychologist, 2,* 102–106.

Hermelin, B., & O'Connor, N. (1970). *Psychological experiments with autistic children.* New York: Pergamon.

Herring, S., & Reitan, R. M. (1986). Sex similarities in Verbal and Performance IQ deficits following unilateral cerebral lesions. *Journal of Consulting and Clinical Psychology, 54,* 537–541.

Herring, J. P. (1922). *Herring revision of the Binet-Simon tests: Examination manual—Form A.* London: World Book Co.

Hertzog, C., & Schaie, K. W. (1988). Stability and change in adult intelligence: 2. Simultaneous analysis of longitudinal means and covariance structures. *Psychology and Aging, 3,* 122–130.

Hertzog, C., Schaie, K. W., & Gribbin, K. (1978). Cardiovascular disease and changes in intellectual functional from middle to old age. *Journal of Gerontology, 33,* 872–883.

Hetherington, E. M., & Parke, R. D. (1986). *Child psychology* (3rd ed.). New York: McGraw-Hill.

Hier, D. B., & Kaplan, J. (1980). Are sex differences in cerebral organization clinically significant? *Behavioral and Brain Sciences, 3,* 238–239.

Hightower, M. G., & Anderson, R. P. (1986). Memory evaluation of alcoholics with Russell's revised Wechsler Memory Scale. *Journal of Clinical Psychology, 42,* 1000–1005.

Hill, A. L. (1978). WAIS subtest score characteristics of institutionalized mentally retarded samples. *Perceptual and Motor Skills, 47,* 131–134.

Hill, T. D., Reddon, J. R., & Jackson, D. N. (1985). The factor structure of the Wechsler scales: A brief review. *Clinical Psychology Review, 5,* 287–306.

Hilliard, A. G., III. (1979). Standardization and cultural bias as impediments to the scientific study and validation of "intelligence." *Journal of Research and Development in Education, 12,* 47–58.

Hiltonsmith, R. W., Hayman, P. M., & Kleinman, P. (1984). Predicting WAIS-R scores from the Revised Beta for low functioning minority group offenders. *Journal of Clinical Psychology, 40,* 1063–1066.

Hiltonsmith, R. W., Hayman, P. M., & Ursprung, A. W. (1982). Beta-WAIS comparisons with low functioning minority group offenders: A cautionary note. *Journal of Clinical Psychology, 38,* 864–866.

Himelstein, P. (1983). An additional modification for the rapid calculation of the WAIS Verbal IQ. *Journal of Clinical Psychology, 39,* 259–260.

Holland, T. R., & Watson, C. G. (1980). Multivariate analysis of WAIS-MMPI relationships among brain-damaged, schizophrenic, neurotic, and alcoholic patients. *Journal of Clinical Psychology, 36,* 352–359.

Hollinger, C. L., & Sarvis, P. H. (1984). Interpretation of the PPVT-R: A pure measure of verbal comprehension? *Psychology in the Schools, 21,* 97–102.

Holman, J., & Bruininks, R. (1985). Assessing and training adaptive behaviors. In K. C. Lakin & R. H. Bruininks (Eds.), *Strategies for achieving community integration of developmentally disabled citizens* (pp. 73–104). Baltimore, MD: Paul H. Brookes.

Hom, J., & Reitan, R. M. (1982). Effect of lateralized cerebral damage upon contralateral and ipsilateral performances. *Journal of Clinical Neuropsychology, 4,* 249–268.

Hom, J., & Reitan, R. M. (1984). Neuropsychological correlates of rapidly vs. slowly growing intrinsic neoplasms. *Journal of Clinical Neuropsychology, 6,* 309–324.

Honzik, M. P., Macfarlane, J. W., & Allen, L. (1948). The stability of mental test performance between two and eighteen years. *Journal of Experimental Education, 17,* 309–324.

Hooper, F. H., Fitzgerald, J., & Papalia, D. (1971). Piagetian theory and the aging process: Extensions and expectations. *Human Development, 2,* 3–20.

Hooper, F. H., Hooper, J. O., & Colbert, K. K. (1985). Personality and memory correlates of intellectual functioning in adulthood: Piagetian and psychometric assessments. *Human Development, 28,* 101–107.

Horn, E., & Fuchs, D. (1987). Using adaptive behavior assessment and intervention: An overview. *Journal of Special Education, 21,* 11–26.

Horn, J. L. (1970). Organization of data on life-span development of human abilities. In L. R. Goulet & P. B. Baltes (Eds.), *Life-span developmental psychology: Research and theory* (pp. 424–466). New York: Academic Press.

Horn, J. L. (1978). Human ability systems. In P. B. Baltes (Ed.), *Life-span development and behavior* (Vol. 1; pp. 211–256). New York: Academic Press.

Horn, J. L. (1982). The theory of fluid and crystallized intelligence in relation to concepts of cognitive psychology and aging in adulthood. In F. I. M. Craik & S. Trehub (Eds.), *Advances in the study of communication and affect: Volume 8: Aging and cognitive processes* (pp. 237–278). New York: Plenum.

Horn, J. L. (1985). Remodeling old models of intelligence. In B. B. Wolman (Ed.), *Handbook of intelligence* (pp. 267–300). New York: Wiley.

Horn, J. L., & Cattell, R. B. (1966). Refinement and test of the theory of fluid and crystallized intelligence. *Journal of Educational Psychology, 57,* 253–270.

Horn, J. L., & Cattell, R. B. (1967). Age differences in fluid and crystallized intelligence. *Acta Psychologica, 26,* 107–129.

Horn, J. L., & Donaldson, G. (1976). On the myth of intellectual decline in adulthood. *American Psychologist, 31,* 701–719.

Horn, J. L., & Donaldson, G. (1977). Faith is not enough: A response to the Baltes-Schaie claim that intelligence will not wane. *American Psychologist, 32,* 369–373.

Horn, J. L., & Donaldson, G. (1980). Cognitive development, II. Adulthood development of human abilities. In O. G. Brim & J. Kagan (Eds.), *Constancy and change in human development: A volume of review essays* (pp. 445–529). Cambridge, MA: Harvard University Press.

Horn, J. L., Donaldson, G., & Engstrom, R. (1981). Apprehension, memory, and fluid intelligence decline in adulthood. *Research on Aging, 3,* 33–84.

Horn, J. L., & McArdle, J. J. (1980). Perspectives on mathematical/statistical model building (MASMOB) in research on aging. In L. W. Poon (Ed.), *Aging in the 1980s: Psychological issues* (pp. 503–541). Washington DC: American Psychological Association.

Howell, R. J., Evans, L., & Donning, L. H. (1958). A comparison of test scores for 16- to 17-year-old age group of Navajo Indians with standardization norms for the Wechsler Adult Intelligence Scale (Arizona and New Mexico). *Journal of Social Psychology, 47,* 355–359.

Huber, S. J., Paulsen, G. W., Shuttleworth, E. C., Chakeres, D., Clapp, L. E., Pakalnis, A., Weiss, K., & Rammohan, K. (1987). Magnetic resonance imaging correlates of dementia in multiple sclerosis. *Archives of Neurology, 44,* 732–736.

Hughes, H. H., & Converse, H. D. (1962). Characteristics of the gifted: A case for a sequel to Terman's study. *Exceptional Children, 29,* 179–183.

Humphreys, L. G. (1986). Commentary. *Journal of Vocational Behavior, 29,* 421–427.

Hunt, J. McV. (1961). *Intelligence and experience.* New York: Ronald Press.

Hunter, J. E., (1986). Cognitive ability, cognitive aptitudes, job knowledge, and job performance. *Journal of Vocational Behavior, 29,* 340–362.

Hunter, J. E., & Hunter, R. F. (1984). Validity and utility of alternate predictors of job performance. *Psychological Bulletin, 96,* 72–98.

Husen, T. (1951). The influence of schooling upon IQ. *Theoria, 17,* 61–68.

Hyde, J. S. (1981). How large are cognitive gender differences? A meta-analysis using w^2 and d. *American Psychologist, 36,* 892–901.

Hyde, J. S., & Linn, M. C. (1988). Are there sex differences in verbal abilities? A meta-analysis. *Psychological Bulletin, 104,* 53–69.

Hymowitz, P., Hunt, H. F., Carr, A. C., Hurt, S. W., & Spear, W. E. (1983). The WAIS and Rorschach test in diagnosing borderline personality. *Journal of Personality Assessment, 47,* 588–596.

Hynd, G. W. (1988a). R. I. P. (or ripping) IQ: A reaction. *NASP Communique, 17,* (4), 4–5.

Hynd, G. W. (1988b). *Neuropsychological assessment in clinical child psychology.* Newbury Park, CA: Sage Publications.

Hynd, G. W., & Willis, W. G. (1988). *Pediatric neuropsychology.* Orlando, FL: Grune & Stratton.

Inglis, J., & Lawson, J. S. (1981). Sex differences in the effects of unilateral brain damage on intelligence. *Science, 212,* 693–695.

Inglis, J., & Lawson, J. S. (1982). A meta-analysis of sex differences in the effects of unilateral brain damage on intelligence test results. *Canadian Journal of Psychology, 36,* 670–683.

Inglis, J., & Lawson, J. S. (1986). A principal components analysis of the Kaufman Assessment Battery for Children (K-ABC): Implications for the test results of children with learning disabilities. *Journal of Learning Disabilities, 19,* 80–85.

Inglis, J., Ruckman, M., Lawson, J. S., MacLean, A. W., & Monga, T. N. (1982). Sex differences in the cognitive effects of unilateral brain damage. *Cortex, 18,* 257–276.

Insua, A. M. (1983). WAIS-R factor structures in two cultures. *Journal of Cross-Cultural Psychology, 14,* 427–438.

Irvin, L. K., Halpern, A. S., Reynolds, W. M. (1977). Assessing social and prevocational awareness in mildly and moderately retarded individuals. *American Journal of Mental Deficiency, 82,* 266–272.

Ishikuma, T., Applegate, B., & Kaufman, A. S. (1989). *WAIS-R interpretation from the factor-analytic, Bannatyne, and Horn models.* Unpublished manuscript. University of Alabama, Tuscaloosa.

Ishikuma, T., Moon, S., & Kaufman, A. S. (1988). Sequential-simultaneous analysis of Japanese children's performance on the Japanese McCarthy Scales. *Perceptual and Motor Skills, 66,* 355–362.

Ivnik, R. J., Sharbrough, F. W., & Laws, E. R., Jr. (1987). Effects of anterior temporal lobectomy on cognitive function. *Journal of Clinical Psychology, 43,* 128–137.

Jacklin, C. N. (1989). Female and male: Issues of gender. *American Psychologist, 44,* 127–133.

Jackson, J. H. (1878). On affections of speech from disease of the brain. *Brain, 1,* 304–330.

Jackson, R. H. (1981). Other genetic disorders. In J. E. Lindemann (Ed.), *Psychological and behavioral aspects of physical disability* (pp. 69–116). New York: Plenum Press.

Jaffe, L. S. (1983). *A study of various factors influencing examiner scoring reliability on WAIS-R Vocabulary, Comprehension, and Similarities subtests.* Unpublished doctoral dissertation, California School of Professional Psychology, San Diego.

Jarvik, L. F., & Bank, L. (1983). Aging twins: Longitudinal psychometric data. In K. W. Schaie (Ed.), *Longitudinal studies of adult psychological development* (pp. 40–63). New York: Guilford Press.

Jarvik, L. F., Kallman, F. J., & Falek, A. (1962). Intellectual changes in aged twins. *Journal of Gerontology, 17,* 289–294.

Jastak, S., & Wilkinson, G. S. (1984). *WRAT-R: Wide Range Achievement Test administration manual.* Los Angeles: Western Psychological Services.

Jeffrey, T. B., & Jeffrey, L. K. (1984). The utility of the modified WAIS in a clinical setting. *Journal of Clinical Psychology, 40,* 1067–1069.

Jencks, C., Smith, M., Acland, H., Bane, M. J., Cohen, D., Gintis, H., Heyns, B., & Michelson, S. (1972). *Inequality: A reassessment of the effect of family and schooling in America.* New York: Basic Books.

Jensen, A. R. (1969). How much can we boost IQ and scholastic achievement? *Harvard Educational Review, 39,* 1–123.

Jensen, A. R. (1973). *Educability and group differences.* New York: Harper & Row.

Jensen, A. R. (1980). *Bias in mental testing.* New York: The Free Press.

Jensen, A. R. (1982). The chronometry of intelligence. In R. J. Sternberg (Ed.), *Recent advances in research on intelligence.* Hillsdale, NJ: Laurence Erlbaum.

Jensen, A. R. (1982). Level I/Level II: Factors or categories? *Journal of Educational Psychology, 74,* 868–873.

Jensen, A. R. (1984). The black-white difference on the K-ABC. Implications for future tests. *Journal of Special Education, 18,* 377–408.

Jensen, A. R. (1985a). Methodological and statistical techniques for the chronometric study of mental abilities. In C. R. Reynolds & V. L. Willson (Eds.), *Methodological and statistical advances in the study of individual differences* (pp. 51–116). New York: Plenum.

Jensen, A. R. (1985b). The nature of the black-white difference on various psychometric tests: Spearman's hypothesis. *Behavioral and Brain Sciences, 8,* 193–219.

Jensen, A. R. (1987). The *g* beyond factor analysis. In R. R. Ronning, J. C. Conoley, J. A. Glover, & J. C. Witt (Eds.), *The influence of cognitive psychology on testing: Buros-Nebraska Symposium on Measurement and Testing* (Vol. 3, 87–142). Hillsdale, NJ: Lawrence Erlbaum.

Jensen, A. R., & Reynolds, C. R. (1982). Race, social class and ability patterns on the WISC-R. *Personality and Individual Differences, 3,* 423–438.

Jensen, A. R., & Reynolds, C. R. (1983). Sex differences on the WISC-R. *Personality and Individual Differences, 4,* 223–226.

Jensen, J. A., & Armstrong, R. J. (1985). *Slosson Intelligence Test (SIT) for children and adults: Expanded norms tables application and development.* East Aurora, NY: Slosson Educational Publications.

Johnson, F. N., & Barker, G. J. (1972). Effects of lithium chloride on learned responses. *Diseases of the Nervous System, 33,* 664–666.

Jones, H. E., & Conrad, H. S. (1933). The growth and decline of intelligence: A study of a homogeneous group between the ages of ten and sixty. *Genetic Psychology Monographs, 13,* 223–298.

Jones, R. S., & Torgesen, J. K. (1981). Analysis of behaviors involved in performance of the Block Design subtest of the WISC-R. *Intelligence, 5,* 321–328.

Jones-Gotman, M., & Milner, B. (1977). Design fluency: The invention of nonsense drawings after focal cortical lesions. *Neuropsychologia, 15,* 653–674.

Joschko, M. (1986). Clinical and neuropsychological outcome following psychosurgery. In I. Grant & K. M. Adams (Eds.), *Neuropsychological assessment of neuropsychiatric disorders* (pp. 300–320). New York: Oxford University Press.

Josiassen, R. C., Curry, L., Roemer, R. A., DeBease, C., & Mancall, E. L. (1982). Patterns of intellectual deficit in Huntington's disease. *Journal of Clinical Neuropsychology, 4,* 173–183.

Joynt, R. J., Benton, A. L., & Fogel, M. L. (1962). Behavioral and pathological correlates of motor impersistence. *Neurology, 12,* 876–881.

Judd, L. L., Hubbard, B., Janowsky, D. S., Huey, L. Y., & Takahashi, K. I. (1977). The effect of lithium carbonate on the cognitive functions of normal subjects. *Archives of General Psychiatry, 34*, 355–357.

Juolasmaa, A., Outakoski, J., Hirvenoja, R., Tienari, P., Sotaniemi, K., & Takkunen, J. (1981). Effect of open heart surgery on intellectual performance. *Journal of Clinical Neuropsychology, 3*, 181–197.

Jurko, M. F., & Andy, O. J. (1973). Psychological changes correlated with thalamotomy site. *Journal of Neurology, Neurosurgery, and Psychiatry, 36*, 846–852.

Kagin, E. F. (1968). Adaptive behavior and mental retardation during the Renaissance and Reformation. *Proceedings of the 76th Annual Convention of the American Psychological Association*, 687–688.

Kaiser, S. M. (1986). *Ability patterns of black and white adults on the Wechsler Adult Intelligence Scale—Revised independent of general intelligence and as a function of socioeconomic status*. Unpublished doctoral dissertation, Texas A & M University.

Kalmar, K., Massoth, N. A., Gallagher, D., Westerveld, M., & Lanzi, A. (1985, October). *Wechsler subtest differences and similarities among right-handed torque and non-torque subjects for the WAIS-R, WISC-R and WPPSI intelligence scales*. Paper presented at National Academy of Neuropsychology, Philadelphia, Pa.

Kamphaus, R. W. (1987). Conceptual and psychometric issues in the assessment of adaptive behavior. *Journal of Special Education, 21*, 27–36.

Kamphaus, R. W., & Reynolds, C. R. (1987). *Clinical and research applications of the K-ABC*. Circle Pines, MN: American Guidance Service.

Kandel, E., Mednick, S. A., Kirkegaard-Sorensen, L., Hutchings, B., Knop, J., Rosenberg, R., & Schulsinger, F. (1988). IQ as a protective factor for subjects at high risk for antisocial behavior. *Journal of Consulting and Clinical Psychology, 56*, 224–226.

Kane, R. L., Parsons, O. A., & Goldstein, G. (1985). Statistical relationships and discriminative accuracy of the Halstead-Reitan, Luria-Nebraska, and Wechsler IQ scores in the identification of brain damage. *Journal of Clinical and Experimental Neuropsychology, 7*, 211–223.

Karnes, F. A., & Brown, K. E. (1980). Factor analysis of the WISC-R for the gifted. *Journal of Educational Psychology, 72*, 197–199.

Karson, S., Pool, K. B., & Freund, S. L. (1957). The effects of scale and practice on WAIS and W-B I test scores. *Journal of Consulting Psychology, 21*, 241–245.

Karzmark, P., Heaton, R. K., Grant, I., & Matthews, C. G. (1984). Use of demographic variables to predict Full Scale IQ and level of performance on the Halstead-Reitan battery. *Journal of Consulting and Clinical Psychology, 52*, 663–665.

Kasper, J., Throne, F., & Schulman, J. (1968). A study of the inter-judge reliability in scoring the responses of a group of mentally retarded boys to three WISC subscales. *Educational and Psychological Measurement, 28*, 469–477.

Kaufman, A. S. (1972). A short form of the Wechsler Preschool and Primary Scale of Intelligence. *Journal of Consulting and Clinical Psychology, 39*, 361–369.

Kaufman, A. S. (1973). The relationship of WPPSI IQs to SES and other background variables. *Journal of Clinical Psychology, 29*, 354–357.

Kaufman, A. S. (1975). Factor analysis of the WISC-R at 11 age levels between 6½ and 16½ years. *Journal of Consulting and Clinical Psychology, 43*, 135–147.

Kaufman, A. S. (1976a). A four-test short form of the WISC-R. *Contemporary Educational Psychology, 1*, 180–196.

Kaufman, A. S. (1976b). A new approach to the interpretation of test scatter on the WISC-R. *Journal of Learning Disabilities, 9*, 160–168.

Kaufman, A. S. (1976c). Verbal–Performance IQ discrepancies on the WISC-R. *Journal of Consulting and Clinical Psychology, 44*, 739–744.

Kaufman, A. S. (1977). Should short-form validity coefficients be corrected? *Journal of Consulting and Clinical Psychology, 45*, 1159–1161.

Kaufman, A. S. (1979a). Role of speed on WISC-R performance across the age range. *Journal of Consulting and Clinical Psychology, 47*, 595–597.

Kaufman, A. S. (1979b). *Intelligent testing with the WISC-R*. New York: Wiley.

Kaufman, A. S. (1983a). Comparison of the performance of matched groups of black children and white children on the Wechsler Preschool and Primary Scale of Intelligence. *Journal of Consulting and Clinical Psychology, 41*, 186–191.

Kaufman, A. S. (1983b). Intelligence: Old concepts—new perspectives. In G. W. Hynd (Ed.), *The school psychologist: An introduction* (pp. 95–117). Syracuse, NY: Syracuse University Press.

Kaufman, A. S. (1985a). Review of Wechsler Adult Intelligence Scale—Revised. In J. V. Mitchell (Ed.), *The ninth mental measurements yearbook* (pp. 1699–1703). Lincoln, NE: The Buros Institute of Mental Measurements, University of Nebraska Press.

Kaufman, A. S. (1985b). Review of Woodcock-Johnson Psycho-Educational Battery. In J. V. Mitchell (Ed.), *The ninth mental measurements yearbook* (pp. 1762–1765). Lincoln, NE: Buros Institute of Mental Measurements, University of Nebraska Press.

Kaufman, A. S. (1988). Funeral oration for a long-dead corpse: A reply to Lezak. *NASP Communique, 17* (4), 5.

Kaufman, A. S., & Applegate, B. (1988). Short forms of the K-ABC Mental Processing and Achievement scales at ages 4 to 12-½ years for clinical and screening purposes. *Journal of Clinical Child Psychology, 17,* 359–369.

Kaufman, A. S., & Doppelt, J. E. (1976). Analysis of WISC-R standardization data in terms of the stratification variables. *Child Development, 47,* 165–171.

Kaufman, A. S., & Harrison, P. L. (1986). Intelligence tests and gifted assessment: What are the positives? *Roeper Review, 8,* 154–159.

Kaufman, A. S., Harrison, P. L., & Ittenbach, R. F. (in press). Intelligence testing in the schools. In T. B. Gutkin & C. R. Reynolds (Eds.), *The Handbook of School Psychology* (2nd ed.). New York: Wiley.

Kaufman, A. S., & Ishikuma, T. (1989). *Amazingly short forms of the WAIS-R.* Unpublished manuscript. University of Alabama, Tuscaloosa.

Kaufman, A. S., & Kaufman, N. L. (1975). Social-class differences on the McCarthy Scales for black and white children. *Perceptual and Motor Skills, 41,* 205–206.

Kaufman, A. S., & Kaufman, N. L. (1977). *Clinical evaluation of young children with the McCarthy Scales.* New York: Grune & Stratton.

Kaufman, A. S., & Kaufman, N. L. (1983a). *K-ABC administration and scoring manual.* Circle Pines, MN: American Guidance Service.

Kaufman, A. S., & Kaufman, N. L. (1983b). *K-ABC interpretive manual.* Circle Pines, MN: American Guidance Service.

Kaufman, A. S., & Kaufman, N. L. (1985a). *Manual for the Kaufman Test of Educational Achievement (K-TEA) Brief Form.* Circle Pines, MN: American Guidance Service.

Kaufman, A. S., & Kaufman, N. L. (1985b). *Manual for the Kaufman Test of Educational Achievement (K-TEA) Comprehensive Form.* Circle Pines, MN: American Guidance Service.

Kaufman, A. S., & Kaufman, N. L. (in press a). *Kaufman Adolescent and Adult Intelligence Test (KAIT).* Circle Pines, MN: American Guidance Service.

Kaufman, A. S., & Kaufman, N. L. (in press b). *Manual for the Kaufman Brief Intelligence Test (K-BIT).* Circle Pines, MN: American Guidance Service.

Kaufman, A. S., McLean, J. E., Ishikuma, T., & Moon, S. (1988). Integration of the literature on the intelligence of Japanese children and analysis of the data from a sequential-simultaneous perspective. *School Psychology International, 10,* 173–183.

Kaufman, A. S., McLean, J. E., & Reynolds, C. R. (1988). Sex, race, residence, region, and education differences on the 11 WAIS-R subtests. *Journal of Clinical Psychology, 44,* 231–248.

Kaufman, A. S., McLean, J. E., & Reynolds, C. R. (in press a). WAIS-R factor structure by race and sex. *Journal of Clinical Psychology.*

Kaufman, A. S., McLean, J. E., & Reynolds, C. R. (in press b). Empirical test of the Inglis and Lawson hypothesis about sex differences in WAIS and WAIS-R brain-damage studies. *Journal of Clinical and Experimental Neuropsychology.*

Kaufman, A. S., & O'Neal, M. (1988a). Analysis of the cognitive, achievement, and general factors underlying the Woodcock-Johnson Psycho-Educational Battery. *Journal of Clinical Child Psychology, 17,* 143–151.

Kaufman, A. S., & O'Neal, M. (1988b). Factor structure of the Woodcock-Johnson cognitive subtests from preschool to adulthood. *Journal of Psychoeducational Assessment, 6,* 35–48.

Kaufman, A. S., Reynolds, C. R., & McLean, J. E. (1989). Age and WAIS-R intelligence in a national sample of adults in the 20- to 74-year age range: A cross-sectional analysis with education level controlled. *Intelligence, 13,* 235–253.

Kaufman, A. S., & Van Hagen, J. (1977). Investigation of the WISC-R for use with retarded children: Correlation with the 1972 Stanford-Binet and comparison of WISC and WISC-R profiles. *Psychology in the Schools, 14,* 10–14.

Kausler, D. H. (1982). *Experimental psychology and human aging.* New York: Wiley.

Keith, T. Z., Cool, V. A., Novak, C. G., White, L. J., & Pottebaum, S. M. (1988). Confirmatory factor analysis of the Stanford-Binet fourth edition: Testing the theory-test match. *Journal of School Psychology, 26,* 253–274.

Keith, T. Z., Fehrmann, P. G., Harrison, P. L., & Pottebaum, S. M. (1987). The relationship between adaptive behavior and intelligence: Testing alternative explanations. *Journal of School Psychology, 25,* 31–43.

Keith, T. Z., Harrison, P. L., & Ehly, S. W. (1987). Effects of adaptive behavior on achievement: Path analysis of a national sample. *Professional School Psychology, 2,* 205–216.

Keller, W. K. (1971). *A comparison of two procedures for assessing constructional praxis in patients with unilateral cerebral disease.* Unpublished doctoral dissertation, University of Iowa.

Kelly, M. P., Montgomery, M. L., Felleman, E. S., & Webb, W. W. (1984). Wechsler Adult Intelligence Scale and Wechsler Adult Intelligence Scale—Revised in a neurologically impaired population. *Journal of Clinical Psychology, 40,* 788–791.

Kender, J. P., Greenwood, S., & Conard, E. (1985). WAIS-R performance patterns of 565 incarcerated adults characterized as underachieving readers and adequate readers. *Journal of Learning Disabilities, 18,* 379–383.

Khatena, J., & Torrance, E. P. (1976). *Khatena-Torrance Creative Perception Inventory.* Chicago: Stoelting Co.

Kiernan, R., Bower, G. H., & Schorr, D. (1984). Stimulus variables in the Block Design task revisited: A reply to Royer. *Journal of Consulting and Clinical Psychology, 52,* 705–707.

Kiernan, R. J., & Matthews, C. G. (1976). Impairment index versus *T*-score averaging in neuropsychological assessment. *Journal of Consulting and Clinical Psychology, 44,* 951–957.

Kimura, D. (1963). Right temporal lobe damage. *Archives of Neurology, 8,* 264–271.

King, L. A., & King, D. W. (1982). Wechsler short forms: A brief status report. *Psychology in the Schools, 19,* 433–438.

Kinsbourne, M. (1980). If sex differences in brain lateralization exist, they have yet to be discovered. *Behavioral and Brain Sciences, 3,* 241–242.

Kirk, S. A., McCarthy, J. J., & Kirk, W. D. (1968). *Examiner manual: Illinois Test of Psycholinguistic Abilities.* Urbana, IL: University of Illinois Press.

Kirkpatrick, E. A. (1903). *Fundamentals of child study: A discussion of instincts and other factors in human development with practical applications.* New York: Macmillan.

Kite, E. S. (1916). Translation of A. Binet & T. Simon. *The development of intelligence in children.* Baltimore, MD: Williams and Wilkins.

Kleist, K. (1923). Kriegsverlertzungen des Gehirns in ihrer Bedeutung fur die Hirnlokalisation und Hirnpathologie. In O. von Schjerning (Ed.), *Handbuch der aerztlichen Erfahrung in Weltkriege 1914/1918: Bd. IV, Geistes-und Nervenkrankheiten.* Leipzig: Barth.

Klett, W. G., Watson, C. G., & Hoffman, P. T. (1986). The Henmon-Nelson and Slosson tests as predictors of WAIS-R IQ. *Journal of Clinical Psychology, 42,* 343–347.

Kljajic, I. (1984). The predictive utility of a significantly lower WAIS PIQ with psychiatric inpatients. *Journal of Clinical Psychology, 40,* 571–576.

Kljajic, I., & Berry, D. (1984). Brain syndrome and WAIS PIQ–VIQ difference scores corrected for test artifact. *Journal of Clinical Psychology, 40,* 271–277.

Klonoff, H., & Thompson, G. (1969). Epidemiology of head injuries in adults: A pilot study. *Canadian Medical Association Journal, 100,* 235–241.

Klonoff, H., Fibiger, C. H., & Hutton, G. H. (1970). Neuropsychological pattern in chronic schizophrenia. *Journal of Nervous and Mental Disease, 150,* 291–300.

Kløve, H. (1959). Relationship of differential electroencephalographic patterns to distribution of Wechsler-Bellevue scores. *Neurology, 9,* 871–876.

Kløve, H., & Fitzhugh, K. B. (1962). The relationship of differential EEG patterns to the distribution of Wechsler-Bellevue scores in a chronic epileptic population. *Journal of Clinical Psychology, 18,* 334–337.

Kløve, H., & Reitan, R. M. (1958). Effect of dysphasia and spatial distortion on Wechsler-Bellevue results. *Archives of Neurology and Psychiatry, 80,* 708–713.

Knight, R. G. (1983). On interpreting the several standard errors of the WAIS-R: Some further tables. *Journal of Consulting and Clinical Psychology, 51,* 671–673.

Knight, R. G., & Godfrey, H. P. D. (1984). Assessing the significance of differences between subtests on the Wechsler Adult Intelligence Scale—Revised. *Journal of Clinical Psychology, 40,* 808–810.

Kodama, H., Shinagawa, F., & Motegi, M. (1978). *Manual for the Wechsler Intelligence Scale for Children—Revised* (Standardized in Japan). Tokyo: Nihon Bunka Kagakusha.

Kohs, S. C. (1923). *Intelligence measurement.* New York: Macmillan.

Kolb, D., & Whishaw, I. Q. (1980). *Fundamentals of human neuropsychology.* San Francisco: W. H. Freeman.

Kramer, J. J., Henning-Stout, M., Ullman, D. P., & Schellenberg, R. P. (1987). The viability of scatter analysis on the WISC-R and the SBIS: Examining a vestige. *Journal of Psychoeducational Assessment, 5,* 37–48.

Krashen, S. D. (1973). Lateralization, language learning, and the critical period: Some new evidence. *Language Learning, 23,* 63–74.

Krashen, S. D. (1975). The left hemisphere. *UCLA Educator, 17*–23.

Krauskopf, C. J., & Davis, K. G. (1973). Studies of the normal personality. *JSAS Catalog of Selected Documents in Psychology, 3,* 85 (Ms. No. 415).

Krohn, E. J., & Traxler, A. J. (1979). Relationship of the McCarthy Scales of Children's Abilities to other measures of preschool cognitive, motor, and perceptual development. *Perceptual and Motor Skills, 49,* 783–790.

Kunce, J. T., Ryan, J. J., & Eckelman, C. C. (1976). Violent behavior and differential WAIS characteristics. *Journal of Consulting and Clinical Psychology, 44,* 42–45.

Kunce, J. T., & Schmidt de Vales, E. (1986). Cross-cultural factor analytic similarity of Wechsler intelligence scores for Mexican adults. *Journal of Clinical Psychology, 42,* 165–169.

Kupferman, I. (1985). Genetic determinants of behavior. In E. R. Kandel & J. H. Schwartz (Eds.), *Principles of Neural Science* (2nd ed., pp. 795–804). New York: Elsevier.

Kupke, T., & Lewis, R. (1985). WAIS and neuropsychological tests: Common and unique variance within an epileptic population. *Journal of Clinical and Experimental Neuropsychology, 7,* 353–366.

Labouvie-Vief, G. (1985). Intelligence and cognition. In J. E. Birren & K. W. Schaie (Eds.), *Handbook of the psychology of aging* (2nd ed; pp. 500–530). New York: Van Nostrand Reinhold.

Lambert, N. M. (1981). *AAMD Adaptive Behavior Scale: School edition: Diagnostic and technical manual.* Monterey, CA: Publishers Test Service.

Lambert, N. M., & Windmiller, M. (1981). *AAMD Adaptive Behavior Scale: School edition*. Monterey, CA: Publishers Test Service.

Lambert, N. M., Windmiller, M., Cole, L., & Figueroa, R. (1975). *Manual of the AAMD Adaptive Behavior Scale: Public school version*. Washington, DC: American Association on Mental Deficiency.

Landesman-Dwyer, S., & Butterfield, E. C. (1983). Mental retardation: Developmental issues in cognitive and social adaptation. In M. Lewis (Ed.), *Origins of intelligence* (2nd ed., pp. 479–519). New York: Plenum.

Langone, J., & Burton, T. A. (1987). Teaching adaptive behavior skills to moderately and severely handicapped individuals: Best practices for facilitating independent living. *Journal of Special Education, 21,* 149–166.

Lansdell, H. (1962). A sex difference in effect of temporal-lobe neurosurgery on design preference. *Nature, 194,* 852–854.

Lansdell, H. (1968). The use of factor scores from the Wechsler-Bellevue scale of intelligence in assessing patients with temporal lobe removals. *Cortex, 4,* 257–268.

Lansdell, H., & Smith, F. J. (1975). Asymmetrical cerebral function for two WAIS factors and their recovery after brain injury. *Journal of Consulting and Clinical Psychology, 43,* 923.

Larrabee, G. J., Kane, R. L., & Schuck, J. R. (1983). Factor analysis of the WAIS and Wechsler Memory Scale: An analysis of the construct validity of the Wechsler Memory Scale. *Journal of Clinical Neuropsychology, 5,* 159–168.

Larrabee, G. J., Largen, J. W., & Levin, H. S. (1985). Sensitivity of age-decline resistant ("hold") WAIS subtests to Alzheimer's disease. *Journal of Clinical and Experimental Neuropsychology, 7,* 497–504.

Lashley, K. S. (1929). *Brain mechanisms and intelligence: A quantitative study of injuries to the brain*. Chicago: University of Chicago Press.

Lashley, K. S. (1950). In search of the engram. *Symposia of the Society for Experimental Biology, 4,* 454–482.

Laux, L. F., & Lane, D. M. (1985). Information processing components of substitution test performance. *Intelligence, 9,* 111–136.

Law, J. G., Box, D., & Moracco, J. D. (1980). A validation study of recategorized WISC-R scores of learning disabled children. *Education, 101,* 195–199.

Lawson, J. S., & Inglis, J. (1983). A laterality index of cognitive impairment after hemispheric damage: A measure derived from principal-components analysis of the Wechsler Adult Intelligence Scale. *Journal of Consulting and Clinical Psychology, 51,* 832–840.

Lawson, J. S., & Inglis, J. (1984). The psychometric assessment of children with learning disabilities: An index derived from a principal components analysis of the WISC-R. *Journal of Learning Disabilities, 17,* 513–576.

Lawson, J. S., Inglis, J., & Stroud, T. W. F. (1983). A laterality index of cognitive impairment derived from a principal-components analysis of the WAIS-R. *Journal of Consulting and Clinical Psychology, 51,* 841–847.

Laycock, F. (1979). *Gifted children*. Glencoe, IL: Scott, Foresman.

Leckliter, I. N., Matarazzo, J. D., & Silverstein, A. B. (1986). A literature review of factor analytic studies of the WAIS-R. *Journal of Clinical Psychology, 42,* 332–342.

Lehman, H. C. (1953). *Age and achievement*. Princeton, NJ: Princeton University Press.

Lehman, H. C. (1954). Men's creative production rate at different ages and in different countries. *Scientific Monthly, 78,* 321–326.

Leland, H. (1983). Assessment of adaptive behavior. In K. D. Paget & B. A. Bracken (Eds.), *The psychoeducational assessment of preschool children* (pp. 191–206). New York: Grune & Stratton.

Leland, H., Shellhaas, M., Nihira, K., & Foster, R. (1967). Adaptive behavior: A new dimension on the classification of the mentally retarded. *Mental Retardation Abstracts, 4,* 359–387.

Leli, D. A., & Filskov, S. B. (1979). Relationship of intelligence to education and occupation as signs of intellectual deterioration. *Journal of Consulting and Clinical Psychology, 47,* 702–707.

Leli, D. A., & Filskov, S. B. (1981a). Actuarial detection and description of brain impairment with the W-B Form I. *Journal of Clinical Psychology, 37,* 615–622.

Leli, D. A., & Filskov, S. B. (1981b). Clinical-actuarial detection and description of brain impairment with the W-B Form I. *Journal of Clinical Psychology, 37,* 623–629.

Leli, D. A., & Filskov, S. B. (1981c). Actuarial assessment of Wechsler Verbal-Performance scale differences as signs of lateralized cerebral impairment. *Perceptual and Motor Skills, 53,* 491–496.

Leli, D. A., & Scott, L. H. (1982). Cross-validation of two indexes of intellectual deterioration on patients with Alzheimer's disease. *Journal of Consulting and Clinical Psychology, 50,* 468.

Leton, D. A. (1985). Review of Structure of Intellect Learning Abilities Test. In J. V. Mitchell (Ed.), *The ninth mental measurements yearbook* (pp. 1488–1489). Lincoln, NE: Buros Institute of Mental Measurements, University of Nebraska Press.

Levin, H. (1973a). Motor impersistence in patients with unilateral cerebral disease: A cross-validation study. *Journal of Consulting and Clinical Psychology, 41,* 287–290.

Levin, H. (1973b). Motor impersistence and proprioceptive feedback in patients with unilateral cerebral disease. *Neurology, 23*, 833–841.

Levin, H., & Benton, A. L. (1975). Temporal orientation in patients with brain disease. *Applied Neuropsychology, 38*, 56–60.

Levy, J. (1972). Lateral specialization of the brain: Behavioral manifestations and possible evolutionary basis. In J. A. Kiger, Jr. (Ed.), *The biology of behavior.* Corvallis, OR: Oregon State University Press.

Lewandowski, L. J. (1986). Test review: Kaufman Test of Educational Achievement. *Journal of Reading, 30*, 258–261.

Lewandowski, L. J., & DeRienzo, P. J. (1985). WISC-R and K-ABC performances of hemiplegic children. *Journal of Psychoeducational Assessment, 3*, 215–222.

Lewis, G. P., Golden, C. J., Moses, J. A., Jr., Osmon, D. C., Purisch, A., & Hammeke, T. (1979). Localization of cerebral dysfunction with a standardized version of Luria's neuropsychological battery. *Journal of Consulting and Clinical Psychology, 47*, 1003–1019.

Lewis, G. P., Golden, C. J., Purisch, A., & Hammeke, T. (1979). The effects of chronicity of disorder and length of hospitalization on the standardized version of Luria's neuropsychological battery in a schizophrenic population. *Journal of Clinical Neuropsychology, 1*, 13–18.

Lewis, M. L., & Johnson, J. J. (1985). Comparison of the WAIS and WAIS-R IQs from two equivalent college populations. *Journal of Psychoeducational Assessment, 3*, 55–60.

Lezak, M. D. (1983). *Neuropsychological assessment* (2nd ed.). New York: Oxford University Press.

Lezak, M. D. (1988a). IQ: R. I. P. *Journal of Clinical and Experimental Neuropsychology, 10*, 351–361.

Lezak, M. D. (1988b). The last but hardly final word on the issue. *NASP Communique, 17*(4), 6.

Lezak, M. D., & Newman, S. P. (1979). *Verbosity and right hemisphere damage.* Paper presented at the second European Conference of the International Society, Noordvijkerhout, Holland.

Likert, R., & Quasha, W. (1970). *The Revised Minnesota Paper Form Board Test.* New York: The Psychological Corporation.

Lin, Y. (1979). Note on WAIS Verbal-Performance differences in IQ. *Perceptual and Motor Skills, 79*, 888–890.

Lincoln, A. J., Courchesne, E., Kilman, B. A., Elmasian, R., & Allen, M. (1988). A study of intellectual abilities in high-functioning people with autism. *Journal of Autism and Developmental Disorders, 18*, 505–524.

Lindemann, J. E., & Matarazzo, J. D. (1984). Intellectual assessment of adults. In G. Goldstein & M. Hersen (Eds.), *Handbook of psychological assessment* (pp. 77–99). New York: Pergamon Press.

Lindgren, S. D., & Benton, A. L. (1980). Developmental patterns of visuospatial judgement. *Journal of Pediatric Psychology, 5*, 217–225.

Linn, R. L. (1986). Comments on the *g* factor in employment testing. *Journal of Vocational Behavior, 29*, 438–444.

Lippold, S., & Claiborn, J. M. (1983). Comparison of the Wechsler Adult Intelligence Scale and the Wechsler Adult Intelligence Scale—Revised. *Journal of Consulting and Clinical Psychology, 51*, 315.

Lira, F. T., Fagan, T. J., & White, M. J. (1979). Violent behavior and differential WAIS characteristics among black prison inmates. *Psychological Reports, 45*, 356–358.

Livesay, J. R. (1986). Clinical utility of Wechsler's deterioration index in screening for behavioral impairment. *Perceptual and Motor Skills, 63*, 619–626.

Loevinger, J., & Wessler, R. (1970). *Measuring ego development* (Vol. I). San Francisco: Jossey-Bass.

Long, C. J., & Brown, D. A. (1979, September). *Analysis of temporal cortex dysfunction by neuropsychological techniques.* Paper presented at the meeting of the American Psychological Association, New York City.

Longstreth, L. E. (1984). Jensen's reaction-time investigations of intelligence: A critique. *Intelligence, 8*, 139–160.

Lorge, I. (1936). The influence of test upon the nature of mental decline as a function of age. *Journal of Educational Psychology, 27*, 100–110.

Lorge, I. (1945). Schooling makes a difference. *Teachers College Record, 46*, 483–492.

Loro, B., & Woodward, J. A. (1976). Verbal and Performance IQ for discrimination among psychiatric diagnostic groups. *Journal of Clinical Psychology, 32*, 107–114.

Lowitzer, A. C., Utley, C. A., & Baumeister, A. A. (1987). AAMD's 1983 *Classification in Mental Retardation* as utilized by state mental retardation/developmental disabilities agencies. *Mental Retardation, 25*, 287–291.

Lubin, B., Larsen, R. M., & Matarazzo, J. D. (1984). Patterns of psychological test usage in the United States: 1935–1982. *American Psychologist, 39*, 451–454.

Lubin, B., Larsen, R. M., Matarazzo, J. D., & Seever, M. (1986). Psychological assessment services and psychological test usage in private practice and in military settings. *Psychotherapy in Private Practice, 4*, 19–29.

Lueger, R. J., & Cadman, W. (1982). Variables associated with recidivism and program-termination of delinquent adolescents. *Journal of Clinical Psychology, 38*, 861–863.

Luria, A. R. (1966). *Higher cortical functions in man.* New York: Basic Books.

Luria, A. R. (1973). *The working brain: An introduction to neuropsychology.* New York: Basic Books.

Luria, A. R. (1980). *Higher cortical functions in man* (2nd ed.). New York: Basic Books.

Luria, A. R., & Majovski, L. V. (1977). Basic approaches used in American and Soviet clinical neuropsychology. *American Psychologist, 32,* 959–968.

Lynn, R. (1982). IQ in Japan and the United States shows a growing disparity. *Nature, 297,* 222–223.

Lynn, R. (1983). IQ in Japan and the United States. *Nature, 306,* 292.

Lynn, R. (1987). The intelligence of the Mongoloids: A psychometric, evolutionary and neurological theory. *Personality and Individual Differences, 8,* 813–844.

Lynn, R., & Hampson, S. (1986a). The rise of national intelligence: Evidence from Britain, Japan, and the U.S.A. *Personality and Individual Differences, 7,* 23–32.

Lynn, R., & Hampson, S. (1986b). Intellectual abilities of Japanese children: An assessment of 2-½–8-½-year-olds derived from the McCarthy Scales of Children's Abilities. *Intelligence, 10,* 41–58.

Lynn, R., & Hampson, S. (1986c). The structure of Japanese abilities: An analysis in terms of the hierarchical model of intelligence. *Current Psychological Research and Review, 4,* 309–322.

Maccoby, E. E., & Jacklin, C. N. (1974). *The psychology of sex differences.* Stanford, CA: Stanford University Press.

MacEachron, A. E. (1983). Institutional reform and adaptive functioning of mentally retarded persons: A field experiment. *American Journal of Mental Deficiency, 88,* 2–12.

MacLeod, C. M., Jackson, R. A., & Palmer, J. (1986). On the relation between spatial ability and field dependence. *Intelligence, 10,* 141–151.

Madison, L. S., George, C., & Moeschler, J. B. (1986). Cognitive functioning in the Fragile-X syndrome: A study of intellectual, memory and communication skills. *Journal of Mental Deficiency Research, 30,* 129–148.

Majeres, R. L. (1983). Sex differences in symbol-digit substitution and speeded matching. *Intelligence, 7,* 313–327.

Malgady, R. S., Barcher, P. R., Davis, J., & Towner, G. (1980). Validity of the Vocational Adaptation Rating Scale: Prediction of mentally retarded workers' placement in sheltered workshops. *American Journal of Mental Deficiency, 84,* 633–640.

Malone, D. M. (1985). Comparability of scores earned on the Wechsler Adult Intelligence Scale—Revised and on the Wechsler Adult Intelligence Scale by educable mentally handicapped high school students. *Dissertation Abstracts International, 45,* (8-A), 2453.

Mangiaracina, J., & Simon, M. J. (1986). Comparison of the PPVT-R and WAIS-R in state hospital psychiatric patients. *Journal of Clinical Psychology, 42,* 817–820.

Margolis, R. B., & Scialfa, C. T. (1984). Age differences in Wechsler Memory Scale performance. *Journal of Clinical Psychology, 40,* 1442–1449.

Margolis, R. B., Taylor, J. M., & Greenlief, C. L. (1986). A cross-validation of two short forms of the WAIS-R in a geriatric sample suspected of dementia. *Journal of Clinical Psychology, 42,* 145–146.

Markwardt, F. C. (1989). *Manual for the Peabody Individual Achievement Test—Revised (PIAT-R).* Circle Pines, MN: American Guidance Service.

Matarazzo, J. D. (1972). *Wechsler's measurement and appraisal of adult intelligence* (5th ed.). New York: Oxford University Press.

Matarazzo, J. D. (1985). Review of Wechsler Adult Intelligence Scale—Revised. In J. V. Mitchell (Ed.), *The ninth mental measurements yearbook* (pp. 1703–1705). Lincoln, NE: The Buros Institute of Mental Measurements, University of Nebraska.

Matarazzo, J. D., Bornstein, R. A., McDermott, P. A., & Noonan, J. V. (1986). Verbal IQ versus Performance IQ difference scores in males and females from the WAIS-R standardization sample. *Journal of Clinical Psychology, 42,* 965–974.

Matarazzo, J. D., Carmody, T. P., & Jacobs, L. D. (1980). Test–retest reliability and stability of the WAIS: A literature review with implications for clinical practice. *Journal of Clinical Neuropsychology, 2,* 89–105.

Matarazzo, J. D., Daniel, M. H., Prifitera, A., & Herman, D. O. (1988). Inter-subtest scatter in the WAIS-R standardization sample. *Journal of Clinical Psychology, 44,* 940–950.

Matarazzo, J. D., & Herman, D. O. (1984a). Base rate data for the WAIS-R: Test–retest stability and VIQ–PIQ differences. *Journal of Clinical Neuropsychology, 6,* 351–366.

Matarazzo, J. D., & Herman, D. O. (1984b). Relationship of education and IQ in the WAIS-R standardization sample. *Journal of Consulting and Clinical Psychology, 52,* 631–634.

Matarazzo, J. D., & Herman, D. O. (1985). Clinical uses of the WAIS-R: Base rates of differences between VIQ and PIQ in the WAIS-R standardization sample. In B. B. Wolman (Ed.), *Handbook of intelligence* (pp. 899–932). New York: Wiley.

Matarazzo, J. D., Matarazzo, R. G., Weins, A. N., Gallo, A. E., & Klonoff, H. (1976). Retest reliability of the Halstead Impairment Index in a normal, a schizophrenic, and two samples of organic patients. *Journal of Nervous and Mental Disease, 158,* 37–49.

Matarazzo, J. D., & Prifitera, A. (in press). Subtest scatter and premorbid intelligence: Lessons from the WAIS-R standardization sample. *Psychological Assessment: A Journal of Consulting and Clinical Psychology.*

Matarazzo, J. D., Weins, A. N., Matarazzo, R. G., & Goldstein, S. G. (1974). Psychometric and clinical test–retest reliability of the Halstead Impairment Index in a sample of healthy, young, normal men. *Journal of Nervous and Mental Disease, 158,* 37–49.

Matarazzo, R. G., Matarazzo, J. D., Gallo, A. E., & Wiens, A. N. (1979). IQ and neuropsychological changes following carotid endarterectomy. *Journal of Clinical Neuropsychology, 1,* 97–116.

Matheson, D. W., Mueller, H. M., & Short, R. H. (1984). The validity of Bannatyne's acquired knowledge category as a separate construct. *Journal of Psychoeducational Assessment, 2,* 279–291.

Matthews, C. G. (1981). Neuropsychology practice in a hospital setting. In S. B. Filskov & T. J. Boll (Eds.), *Handbook of clinical neuropsychology* (pp. 645–685). New York: Wiley.

Matthews, C. G., Shaw, D., & Kløve, H. (1966). Psychological test performances in neurological and "pseudoneurologic" subjects. *Cortex, 2,* 244–253.

Mayfield, K. L., Forman, S. G., & Nagle, R. J. (1984). Reliability of the AAMD Adaptive Behavior Scale, Public School Version. *Journal of School Psychology, 22,* 53–61.

Mayman, M., Schafer, R., & Rapaport, D. (1951). Interpretation of the WAIS in personality appraisal. In H. H. Anderson & G. L. Anderson (Eds.), *An introduction to projective techniques* (pp. 541–580). New York: Prentice-Hall.

McCall, R. B. (1977). Childhood IQ's as predictors of adult educational and occupational status. *Science, 197,* 482–483.

McCallum, R. S. (1985). Review of the Peabody Picture Vocabulary Test—Revised. In J. V. Mitchell (Ed.), *The ninth mental measurements yearbook* (pp. 1126–1127). Lincoln, NE: Buros Institute of Mental Measurements, University of Nebraska Press.

McCarthy, D. (1972). *Manual for the McCarthy Scales of Children's Abilities.* New York: The Psychological Corporation.

McCarty, S. M., Logue, P. E., Power, D. G., Ziesat, H. A., & Rosenstiel, A. K. (1980). Alternate-form reliability and age-related scores for Russell's revised Wechsler Memory Scale. *Journal of Consulting and Clinical Psychology, 48,* 296–298.

McCue, P. M., Shelly, C., & Goldstein, G. (1986). Intellectual, academic and neuropsychological performance levels in learning disabled adults. *Journal of Learning Disabilities, 19,* 233–236.

McCullough, C. S., Walker, J. L., Diessner, R. (1985). The use of Wechsler scales in the assessment of Native Americans of the Columbia River Basin. *Psychology in the Schools, 22,* 23–28.

McCusick, V. A. (1986). *Mendelian inheritance in man* (8th ed). Baltimore, MD: Johns Hopkins University Press.

McEchron, W. D. (1980). Interrelationships among discrepancy scores on the Wechsler scales and performance on the MMPI and BPC. *Dissertation Abstracts International, 41* (6-B), 2335.

McGee, S., & Brown, C. (1984). A split in the verbal comprehension factor in WAIS and WISC-R profiles. *Journal of Clinical Psychology, 40,* 580–583.

McGlone, J. (1977). Sex differences in the cerebral organization of verbal functions in patients with unilateral brain lesions. *Brain, 100,* 775–793.

McGlone, J. (1978). Sex differences in functional brain asymmetry. *Cortex, 14,* 122–128.

McGlone, J. (1980). Sex differences in human brain asymmetry: A critical survey. *Behavioral and Brain Sciences, 3,* 215–227.

McGlone, J., & Davidson, W. (1973). The relationship between speech and laterality and spatial ability with special reference to sex and hand preference. *Neuropsychologia, 11,* 105–113.

McGlone, J., & Kertesz, A. (1973). Sex differences in cerebral processing of visuospatial tasks. *Cortex, 9,* 313–320.

McGowan, R. J., & Johnson, D. L. (1984). The mother-child relationship and other antecedents of childhood intelligence: A causal analysis. *Child Development, 55,* 810–820.

McGrew, K. S. (1986). *Clinical interpretation of the Woodcock-Johnson Tests of Cognitive Ability.* Orlando, FL: Grune & Stratton.

McGrew, K. S. (1987). Exploratory factor analysis of the Woodcock-Johnson Tests of Cognitive Ability. *Journal of Psychoeducational Assessment, 5,* 200–216.

McKay, S., & Golden, C. J. (1979a). Empirical derivation of neuropsychological scales for the lateralization of brain damage using the Luria-Nebraska Neuropsychological Test Battery. *Clinical Neuropsychology, 1,* 1–5.

McKay, S., & Golden, C. J. (1979b). Empirical derivation of experimental scales for localizing brain lesions using the Luria-Nebraska Neuropsychological Battery. *Clinical Neuropsychology, 1,* 19–23.

McKay, S., & Golden, C. J. (1981). The assessment of specific neuropsychological skills using scales derived from factor analysis of the Luria-Nebraska Neuropsychological Battery. *International Journal of Neuroscience, 14,* 189–204.

McLean, J. E., Kaufman, A. S., & Reynolds, C. R. (1988a). The canonical relationship between the WAIS-R Verbal and Performance scales. *Perceptual and Motor Skills, 66,* 432–434.

McLean, J. E., Kaufman, A. S., & Reynolds, C. R. (1988b, November). What role does formal education play in the IQ-age relationships across the adult life-span. Paper presented at the meeting of the Mid-South Educational Research Association, Louisville, KY. *Mid-South Educational Researcher, 17*(1), 6–8, 13–18.

McLean, J. E., Kaufman, A. S., & Reynolds, C. R. (in press). Base rates of WAIS-R subtest scatter as a guide for clinical and neuropsychological assessment. *Journal of Clinical Psychology.*

McMullen, L. M., & Rogers, D. L. (1984). WAIS characteristics of non-pathological obsessive and hysteric styles. *Journal of Clinical Psychology, 40,* 577–579.

McNemar, Q. (1942). *The revision of the Stanford-Binet Scale.* Boston: Houghton-Mifflin.

McNemar, Q. (1974). Correction to a correction. *Journal of Consulting and Clinical Psychology, 42,* 145–146.

McQuaid, M. M., & Spreen, O. (1989, February). *Cognitive changes over 15 years in person with a learning disability, as reflected by the Wechsler intelligence scale.* Paper presented at the meeting of the International Neuropsychological Society, Vancouver, British Columbia.

McShane, D., & Cook, V. (1985). Transcultural intellectual assessment: Performance by Hispanics on the Wechsler scales. In B. B. Wolman (Ed.), *Handbook of intelligence* (pp. 737–785). New York: Wiley.

McShane, D. A., & Plas, J. M. (1984a). The cognitive functioning of American Indian children: Moving from the WISC to the WISC-R. *The School Psychology Review, 13,* 61–73.

McShane, D. A., & Plas, J. M. (1984b). Response to a critique of the McShane and Plas review. *The School Psychology Review, 13,* 83–88.

Meacham, F. R. (1985). A comparative study of the WISC-R and WAIS-R Performance IQ scores of 16-year-old hearing impaired students in a residential program. *Dissertation Abstracts International, 45,* (7-A), 2042–2043.

Meacham, F. R., Kline, M. M., Stovall, J. A., & Sands, D. I. (1987). Adaptive behavior and low incidence handicaps: Hearing and visual impairments. *Journal of Special Education, 21,* 183–196.

Mealor, D. J. (1984). *An analysis of intellectual functioning and adaptive behavior of behaviorally disordered students.* Unpublished manuscript, University of Central Florida, Orlando.

Mealor, D. J., & Richmond, B. O. (1980). Adaptive behavior: Teachers and parents disagree. *Exceptional Children, 46,* 386–389.

Meeker, M. N. (1969). *The structure of intellect.* Columbus, OH: Charles E. Merrill.

Meeker, M. N. (1985). Toward a psychology of giftedness: A concept in search of measurement. In B. B. Wolman (Ed.). *Handbook of intelligence* (pp. 787–800). New York: Wiley.

Meeker, M. N., & Meeker, R. (1981). *Structure of Intellect Learning Abilities Test.* Segundo, CA: SOI Institute.

Meier, M. J. (1981). Education for competency assurance in human neuropsychology: Antecedents, models, and directions. In S. B. Filskov & T. J. Boll (Eds.), *Handbook of clinical neuropsychology.* New York: Wiley.

Meier, M. J. (1985). Review of the Halstead-Reitan Neuropsychological Test Battery. In J. V. Mitchell (Ed.), *The ninth mental measurements yearbook.* (pp. 646–649). Lincoln, NE: Buros Institute of Mental Measurements, University of Nebraska Press.

Meier, M. J., & French, L. A. (1966). Longitudinal assessment of intellectual functioning following unilateral temporal lobectomy. *Journal of Clinical Psychology, 22,* 22–27.

Mercer, J. R. (1973). *Labeling the mentally retarded.* Berkeley: University of California Press.

Merritt, H. H. (1979). *Textbook of neurology* (6th ed.). Philadelphia: Lea & Febiger.

Meyer, V., & Jones, H. G. (1957). Patterns of cognitive test performance as functions of the lateral localization of cerebral abnormalities in the temporal lobe. *Journal of Mental Science, 103,* 758–772.

Meyers, C. E., Nihira, K., & Zetlin, A. (1979). The measurement of adaptive behavior. In N. R. Ellis (Ed.), *Handbook of mental deficiency: Psychological theory and research* (2nd ed; pp. 215–253). Hillsdale, NJ: Lawrence Erlbaum.

Milberg, W. P., Cummings, J., Goodglass, H., & Kaplan, E. (1979). Case report: A global sequential processing disorder following head injury: A possible role for the right hemisphere in serial order behavior. *Journal of Clinical Neuropsychology, 1,* 213–225.

Milberg, W. P., Greiffenstein, M., Lewis, R., & Rourke, D. (1980). Differentiation of temporal lobe and generalized seizure patients with the WAIS. *Journal of Consulting and Clinical Psychology, 48,* 39–42.

Milberg, W. P., Hebben, N., & Kaplan, E. (1986). The Boston process approach to neuropsychological assessment. In I. Grant & K. M. Adams (Eds.), *Neuropsychological assessment of neuropsychiatric disorders* (pp. 65–86). New York: Oxford University Press.

Miles, C. C., & Miles, W. R. (1932). The correlation of intelligence scores and chronological age from early to late maturity. *American Journal of Psychology, 44,* 44–78.

Milner, B. (1954). Intellectual function of the temporal lobes. *Psychological Bulletin, 51,* 42–62.

Mishra, S. P., & Brown, K. H. (1983). The comparability of WAIS and WAIS-R IQs and subtest scores. *Journal of Clinical Psychology, 39,* 754–757.

Mitchell, R. E., Grandy, T. G., & Lupo, J. V. (1986). Comparison of the WAIS and the WAIS-R in the upper ranges of IQ. *Professional Psychology: Research and Practice, 17,* 82–83.

Mitchell, S. W., Morehouse, G., & Keen, W. W., Jr. (1864). *Reflex paralysis, article 6.* Washington, DC: Surgeon General's Office.

Mittenberg, W., & Ryan, J. J. (1984). Effects of omitting one to five subtests on WAIS-R Full Scale reliability. *Perceptual and Motor Skills, 58,* 563–565.

Mohs, R. C., Kim, Y., Johns, C. A., Dunn, D. D., & Davis, K. L. (1986). Assessing changes in Alzheimer's disease:

Memory and language. In L. W. Poon (Ed.), *Clinical memory assessment of older adults* (pp. 149–155). Washington, DC: American Psychological Association.

Moon, G., Fantuzzo, J., & Gorsuch, R. (1986). Teaching WAIS-R administration skills: Comparison of the MASTERY model to other existing clinical training modalities. *Professional Psychology: Research and Practice, 17,* 31–35.

Moon, S. (1988). *A cross-cultural validity study of the Kaufman Assessment Battery for Children.* Unpublished doctoral dissertation, University of Alabama.

Moses, J. A., & Golden, C. J. (1979). Cross validation of the discriminative effectiveness of the standardized Luria neuropsychological battery. *International Journal of Neuroscience, 9,* 149–155.

Muhs, P. J., Hooper, F. H., & Papalia-Finlay, D. (1979-80). Cross-sectional analysis of cognitive functioning across the life-span. *International Journal of Aging and Human Development, 10,* 311–333.

Munder, L. (1976). Patterns of deficit in black and white men with brain damage to the left, right and both hemispheres. *Dissertation Abstracts International, 37* (1-B), 442–443 (University Microfilms No. 76–14, 816).

Murphy, G. (1968). Psychological views of personality and contributions to its study. In E. Norbeck, D. Price-Williams, & W. M. McCord (Eds.), *The study of personality* (pp. 15–40). New York: Holt, Rinehart and Winston.

Murray, M. E., Waites, L., Veldman, D. J., & Heatly, M. D. (1973). Differences between WISC and WAIS scores in delinquent boys. *Journal of Experimental Education, 42,* 68–72.

Nagle, R. J., & Lazarus, S. C. (1979). The comparability of the WISC-R and WAIS among 16-year-old EMR children. *Journal of School Psychology, 17,* 362–367.

Naglieri, J. A. (1979). *A comparison of McCarthy GCI and WISC-R IQ scores for educable mentally retarded, learning disabled, and normal children.* Unpublished doctoral dissertation, University of Georgia.

Naglieri, J. A. (1982). Two types of tables for use with the WAIS-R. *Journal of Consulting and Clinical Psychology, 50,* 319–321.

Naglieri, J. A. (1985a). *Matrix Analogies Test—expanded form.* San Antonio, TX: The Psychological Corporation.

Naglieri, J. A. (1985b). *Matrix Analogies Test—short form.* San Antonio, TX: The Psychological Corporation.

Naglieri, J. A. (1988a). Comment on "IQ: R. I. P." *NASP Communique, 17*(4), 4–5.

Naglieri, J. A. (1988b). Interpreting area score variation on the fourth edition of the Stanford-Binet scale of intelligence. *Journal of Clinical Child Psychology, 17,* 225–228.

Naglieri, J. A., & Das, J. P. (1987). Construct and criterion-related validity of planning, simultaneous, and successive cognitive processing tasks. *Journal of Psychoeducational Assessment, 5,* 353–363.

Naglieri, J. A., & Das, J. P. (1988). Planning-Arousal-Simultaneous-Successive (PASS): A model for assessment. *Journal of School Psychology, 26,* 35–48.

Naglieri, J. A., & Kaufman, A. S. (1983). How many factors underlie the WAIS-R? *Journal of Psychoeducational Assessment, 1,* 113–119.

Nair, N. P. V., Muller, H. F., Gutbrodt, E., Buffet, L., & Schwartz, G. (1979). Neurotropic activity of lithium: Relationship to lithium levels in plasma and red blood cells. *Research Communications in Psychology, Psychiatry and Behavior, 4,* 169–180.

Nathan, M., Millham, J., Chilcutt, J., & Atkinson, B. (1980). Mentally retarded individuals as informants for the AAMD Adaptive Behavior Scale. *Mental Retardation, 18,* 82–84.

Nebes, R. D. (1978). Direct examination of cognitive function in the right and left hemispheres. In M. Kinsbourne (Ed.), *Asymmetrical function of the brain.* Cambridge: Cambridge University Press.

Nelson, W. M., Edinger, J. D., & Wallace, J. (1978). The utility of two Wechsler Adult Intelligence Scale short forms with prisoners. *Journal of Personality Assessment, 42,* 302–311.

Nesselroade, J. R., & Labouvie, E. W. (1985). Experimental design in research on aging. In J. E. Birren & K. W. Schaie (Eds.), *Handbook of the psychology of aging* (2nd ed.; pp. 35–60). New York: Van Nostrand Reinhold.

Neuringer, C. (1963). The form equivalence between the Wechsler-Bellevue Intelligence Scale Form I and the Wechsler Adult Intelligence Scale. *Educational and Psychological Measurement, 23,* 755–763.

Newcombe, F. (1969). *Missile wounds of the brain.* London: Oxford University Press.

Newman, H. H., Freeman, F. N., & Holzinger, K. H. (1937). *Twins: A study of heredity and environment.* Chicago: University of Chicago Press.

Nichols, P. L. (1984). Familial mental retardation. *Behavior Genetics, 14,* 161–170.

Nichols, R. (1978). Twin studies of ability, personality, and interests. *Homo, 29,* 158–173.

Nihira, K. (1985). Assessment of mentally retarded individuals. In B. B. Wolman (Ed.), *Handbook of intelligence* (pp. 801–824). New York: Wiley.

Nihira, K., Foster, R., Shellhaas, M., & Leland, H. (1969). *Adaptive Behavior Scales Manual.* Washington, DC: American Association on Mental Deficiency.

Nihira, K., Foster, R., Shellhaas, M., & Leland, H. (1975). *AAMD Adaptive Behavior Scale.* Monterey, CA: Publishers Test Service.

Nobo, J., & Evans, R. G. (1986). The WAIS-R Picture Arrangement and Comprehension subtests as measures of social behavior characteristics. *Journal of Personality Assessment, 50,* 90–92.

Oakland, T. (1980). An evaluation of the ABIC, pluralistic norms, and estimated learning potential. *Journal of School Psychology, 18,* 3–11.

Oakland, T. (1983). Joint use of adaptive behavior and IQ to predict achievement. *Journal of Consulting and Clinical Psychology, 51,* 298–301.

Oakland, T. (1985). Review of Slosson Intelligence Test. In J. V. Mitchell (Ed.), *The ninth mental measurements yearbook* (pp. 1401–1403). Lincoln, NE: Buros Institute of Mental Measurements, University of Nebraska.

Oakland, T., & Houchins, S. (1985). A review of the Vineland Adaptive Behavior Scales, Survey Form. *Journal of Counseling and Development, 63,* 585–586.

Oakland, T., & Parmelee, R. (1985). Mental measurement of minority-group children. In B. B. Wolman (Ed.), *Handbook of intelligence* (pp. 699–736). New York: Wiley.

Oakland, T., & Zimmerman, S. (1986). The course on individual mental assessment: A national survey of course instructors. *Professional School Psychology, 1,* 51–59.

Oakman, S., & Wilson, B. (1988). Stability of WISC-R intelligence scores: Implications for 3-year reevaluations of learning disabled students. *Psychology in the Schools, 25,* 118–120.

Oas, P. (1984). Validity of the Draw-A-Person and Bender Gestalt tests as measures of impulsivity with adolescents. *Journal of Consulting and Clinical Psychology, 52,* 1011–1019.

Obringer, S. J. (1988, November). *A survey of perceptions of the Stanford-Binet IV.* Paper presented at the meeting of the Mid-South Educational Research Association, Louisville, KY.

Oden, M. H. (1968). The fulfillment of promise: 40-year follow-up of the Terman gifted group. *Genetic Psychology Monographs, 77,* 3–93.

O'Donnell, J. P., Kurtz, J., & Ramanaiah, N. V. (1983). Neuropsychological test findings for normal, learning-disabled, and brain-damaged young adults. *Journal of Consulting and Clinical Psychology, 51,* 726–729.

O'Grady, K. E. (1983). A confirmatory maximum likelihood factor analysis of the WAIS-R. *Journal of Consulting and Clinical Psychology, 51,* 826–831.

Okun, M. A. (1976). Adult age and cautiousness in decision: A review of the literature. *Human Development, 19,* 220–233.

Okun, M. A., Siegler, I. C., & George, L. K. (1978). Cautiousness and verbal learning in adulthood. *Journal of Gerontology, 33,* 94–97.

Orgel, S. A., & McDonald, R. D. (1967). An evaluation of the trail making test. *Journal of Consulting Psychology, 31,* 77–79.

Orzeck, A. Z. (1964). *The Orzeck Aphasia Evaluation.* Los Angeles: Western Psychological Services.

Osmon, D., Golden, C. J., Purisch, A., Hammeke, T., & Blume, H. (1979). The use of a standardized battery of Luria's tests in the diagnosis of lateralized cerebral dysfunction. *International Journal of Neuroscience, 9,* 1–9.

Overall, J. E., Hoffmann, N. G., & Levin, H. (1978). Effects of aging, organicity, alcoholism, and functional psychopathology on WAIS subtest profiles. *Journal of Consulting and Clinical Psychology, 46,* 1315–1322.

Owens, W. A. (1953). Age and mental abilities: A longitudinal study. *Genetic Psychology Monographs, 48,* 3–54.

Owens, W. A. (1959). Is age kinder to the initially more able? *Journal of Gerontology, 14,* 334–337.

Owens, W. A. (1966). Age and mental ability: A second adult follow-up. *Journal of Educational Psychology, 57,* 311–325.

Ownby, R. L., & Carmin, C. N. (1988). Confirmatory factor analysis of the Stanford-Binet Intelligence Scale, fourth edition. *Journal of Psychoeducational Assessment, 6,* 331–340.

Ownby, R. L., & Matthews, C. G. (1985). On the meaning of the WISC-R third factor: Relations to selected neuropsychological measures. *Journal of Consulting and Clinical Psychology, 53,* 531–534.

Page, S., & Steffy, R. (1984). WAIS and WISC-R "VP" scores: Sampling characteristics from three psychiatric populations. *Canadian Journal of Behavioral Science, 16,* 99–106.

Papalia, D. E. (1972). The status of several conservation abilities across the life-span. *Human Development, 15,* 229–243.

Parker, J. C., Granberg, B. W., Nichols, W. K., Jones, J. G., & Hewett, J. E. (1983). Mental status outcomes following carotid endarterectomy. *Journal of Clinical Neuropsychology, 5,* 345–353.

Parker, K. C. H. (1983). Factor analysis of the WAIS-R at nine age levels between 16 and 74 years. *Journal of Consulting and Clinical Psychology, 51,* 302–308.

Parker, K. C. H. (1986). Changes with age, year-of-birth cohort, age by year-of-birth interaction, and standardization of the Wechsler adult intelligence tests. *Human Development, 29,* 209–222.

Parsons, O. A., Vega, A., Jr., & Burn, J. (1969). Different psychological effects of lateralized brain damage. *Journal of Consulting and Clinical Psychology, 33,* 551–557.

Paulson, M. J., & Lin, T. (1970). Predicting WAIS IQ from Shipley-Hartford scores. *Journal of Clinical Psychology, 26,* 453–461.

Pederson, N. L., McClearn, G. E., & Friberg, L. (1985). Separated fraternal twins: Resemblance for cognitive abilities. *Behavior Genetics, 15,* 407–419.

Pernicano, K. M. (1986). Score differences in WAIS-R scatter for schizophrenics, depressives, and personality disorders: A preliminary analysis. *Psychological Reports, 59,* 539–543.

Phelps, L., Rosso, M., & Falasco, S. (1984). Correlations between the Woodcock-Johnson and the WISC-R for a behavior disordered population. *Psychology in the Schools, 21,* 442–446.

Phelps, L., Rosso, M., & Falasco, S. (1985). Multiple regression data using the WISC-R and the Woodcock-Johnson Tests of Cognitive Ability. *Psychology in the Schools, 2,* 63–69.

Pickering, J. W., Johnson, D. L., & Stary, J. E. (1977). Systematic VIQ/PIQ differences on the WAIS: An artifact of this instrument? *Journal of Clinical Psychology, 33,* 1060–1064.

Piersma, H. L. (1986). Wechsler Memory Scale performance in geropsychiatric patients. *Journal of Clinical Psychology, 42,* 323–327.

Pieters, H. C., & Sieberhagen, J. J. (1986). Evaluation of two shortened forms of the SAWAIS with three diagnostic groups. *Journal of Clinical Psychology, 42,* 809–815.

Pinneau, S. R. (1961). *Changes in intelligence quotient: Infancy to maturity.* Boston: Houghton-Mifflin.

Pintner, R., & Paterson, D. G. (1925). *A scale of performance tests.* New York: Appleton & Co.

Piotrowski, R. J., & Siegel, D. J. (1984). Interpreting WISC-R profiles: Reliability of subtest composites. *Journal of Psychoeducational Assessment, 2,* 183–190.

Piotrowski, Z. (1937). The Rorschach inkblot method in organic disturbances of the central nervous system. *Journal of Nervous and Mental Disease, 86,* 525–537.

Plake, B. S., Gutkin, T. B., Wise, S. L., & Kroeten, T. (1987). Confirmatory factor analysis of the WAIS-R: Competition of models. *Journal of Psychoeducational Assessment, 3,* 267–272.

Plake, B. S., Reynolds, C. R., & Gutkin, T. B. (1981). A technique for the comparison of the profile variability between independent groups. *Journal of Clinical Psychology, 37,* 142–146.

Plomin, R. (1983). Developmental behavioral genetics. *Child Development, 54,* 253–259.

Plomin, R. (1986). *Development, genetics, and psychology.* Hillsdale, NJ: Lawrence Erlbaum.

Plomin, R. (1988). The nature and nurture of cognitive abilities. In R. J. Sternberg (Ed.), *Advances in the psychology of human intelligence* (Vol. 4; pp. 1–33). Hillsdale, NJ: Lawrence Erlbaum.

Plomin, R. (1989). Environment and genes: Determinants of behavior. *American Psychologist, 43,* 105–111.

Plomin, R., & DeFries, J. C. (1980). Genetics and intelligence: Recent data. *Intelligence, 4,* 15–24.

Plomin, R., Pederson, N. L., McClearn, G. E., Nesselroade, J. R., & Bergeman, C. S. (1988). EAS temperaments during the last half of the life span: Twins reared apart and twins reared together. *Psychology and Aging, 3,* 43–50.

Pollack, M. (1955). *Effect of brain tumour on perception of hidden figures, sorting behavior, and problem solving performance.* Unpublished doctoral dissertation, New York University.

Pollingue, A. (1987). Adaptive behavior and low incidence handicaps: Use of adaptive behavior instruments for persons with physical handicaps. *Journal of Special Education, 21,* 117–126.

Poon, L. W. (Ed.). (1980). *Aging in the 1980s: Psychological issues.* Washington DC: American Psychological Association.

Poon, L. W. (1985). Differences in human memory with aging: Nature, causes, and clinical implications. In J. E. Birren and K. W. Schaie (Eds.), *Handbook of the psychology of aging* (2nd ed.; pp. 427–462). New York: Van Nostrand Reinhold.

Poon, L. W. (Ed.) (1986). *Clinical memory assessment of older adults.* Washington, DC: American Psychological Association.

Powel, J. (1988). Review of the Wechsler Memory Scale—Revised. *Archives of Clinical Neuropsychology, 3,* 397–403.

Prifitera, A., & Ryan, J. J. (1983). WAIS-R/WAIS comparisons in a clinical sample. *Journal of Clinical Neuropsychology, 5,* 97–99.

Prigitano, G. P. (1978). Wechsler Memory Scale: A selective review of the literature. *Journal of Clinical Psychology* [Special Monograph supplement] *34,* 816–832.

Prigitano, G. P., & Parsons, O. A. (1976). Relationship of age and education to Halstead test performance in different patient populations. *Journal of Consulting and Clinical Psychology, 44,* 527–533.

Prout, H. T., & Schwartz, J. F. (1984). Validity of the Peabody Picture Vocabulary Test—Revised with mentally retarded adults. *Journal of Clinical Psychology, 40,* 584–587.

Purisch, A., Golden, C. J., & Hammeke, T. (1978). Discrimination of schizophrenic and brain-injured patients by a standardized version of Luria's neuropsychological tests. *Journal of Consulting and Clinical Psychology, 46,* 1266–1273.

Quattrocchi, M., & Sherrets, S. (1980). WISC-R: The first five years. *Psychology in the Schools, 17,* 297–312.

Radencich, M. C. (1986a). Test review: Detroit Tests of Learning Aptitude (DTLA-2). *Journal of Psychoeducational Assessment, 4,* 173–181.

Radencich, M. C. (1986b). Test update: Kaufman Test of Educational Achievement (K-TEA). *Academic Therapy, 21,* 619–622.

Radencich, M. C. (1988). Test review: Woodcock Reading Mastery Tests—Revised. *Journal of Psychoeducational Assessment, 6,* 168–173.

Ramey, C. T., & Haskins, R. (1981a). The modification of intelligence through early experience. *Intelligence, 5,* 5–19.

Ramey, C. T., & Haskins, R. (1981b). Early education, intellectual development, and school performance: A reply to Arthur Jensen and J. McVicker Hunt. *Intelligence, 5,* 41–48.

Rapaport, D., Gill, M., & Schafer, R. (1945–1946). *Diagnostic psychological testing,* 2 vols. Chicago: Year Book Publishers.

Raven, J. C., Court, J. H., & Raven, J. (1983). *Manual for Raven's Progressive Matrices and Vocabulary Scales (Section 3)—Standard Progressive Matrices.* London: Lewis.

Raybourn, R. E. (1983). The Wechsler Adult Intelligence Scale (WAIS) and the WAIS-Revised: A comparison and a caution. *Professional Psychology: Research and Practice, 14,* 357–361.

Reed, H. B. C., Jr., & Reitan, R. M. (1963a). A comparison of the effects of the normal aging process with the effects of organic brain damage on adaptive abilities. *Journal of Gerontology, 18,* 177–179.

Reed, H. B. C., Jr., & Reitan, R. M. (1963b). Changes in psychological test performance associated with the normal aging process. *Journal of Gerontology, 18,* 271–274.

Reed, H. B. C., Jr., & Reitan, R. M. (1963c). Intelligence test performances of brain damaged subjects with lateralized motor deficits. *Journal of Consulting Psychology, 27,* 102–106.

Reed, J. C. (1985). The contributions of Ward Halstead, Ralph Reitan and their associates. *International Journal of Neuroscience, 25,* 289–293.

Reed, J. C., & Reitan, R. M. (1969). Verbal and Performance differences among brain-injured children with lateralized motor deficits. *Perceptual and Motor Skills, 29,* 747–752.

Reese, H. W., & Rodeheaver, D. (1985). Problem solving and complex decision making. In J. E. Birren and K. W. Schaie (Eds.), *Handbook of the psychology of aging* (2nd ed.; pp. 474–499). New York: Van Nostrand Reinhold.

Reid, N. (1986). Testing the test: Wide Range Achievement Test: 1984 Revised edition. *Journal of Counseling and Development, 64,* 538–539.

Reilly, T. F., Wheeler, L. J., & Ettinger, L. E. (1985). Intelligence versus academic achievement: A comparison of juvenile delinquents and special education classifications. *Criminal Justice and Behavior, 12,* 193–208.

Reinert, G. (1970). Comparative factor analytic studies of intelligence throughout the human life-span. In L. R. Goulet & P. B. Baltes (Eds.), *Life-span developmental psychology: Research and theory* (pp. 467–484). New York: Academic Press.

Reitan, R. M. (1955a). *Instructions and procedures for administering the neuropsychological test battery used at the Neuropsychology Laboratory, Indiana University Medical Center.* Unpublished manuscript.

Reitan, R. M. (1955b). Investigation of the validity of Halstead's measures of biological intelligence. *A.M.A. Archives of Neurology and Psychiatry, 73,* 28–35.

Reitan, R. M. (1955c). Certain differential effects of left and right cerebral lesions in human adults. *Journal of Comparative and Physiological Psychology, 48,* 474–477.

Reitan, R. M. (1958). Validity of the Trail Making Test as an indication of organic brain damage. *Perceptual and Motor Skills, 8,* 271–276.

Reitan, R. M. (1959). The comparative effects of brain damage on the Halstead Impairment Index and the Wechsler-Bellevue Scale. *Journal of Clinical Psychology, 15,* 281–285.

Reitan, R. M. (1960). The significance of dysphasia for the intelligence and adaptive abilities. *Journal of Psychology, 60,* 355–376.

Reitan, R. M. (1966). Diagnostic inferences of brain lesions based on psychological test results. *Canadian Psychologist, 7,* 386–392.

Reitan, R. M. (1974). Methodological problems in clinical neuropsychology. In R. M. Reitan & L. A. Davison (Eds.), *Clinical neuropsychology: Current status and applications* (pp. 19–46). New York: Wiley.

Reitan, R. M. (1976). Neurological and physiological basis of psychopathology. *Annual Review of Psychology, 27,* 189–216.

Reitan, R. M. (1985). Relationships between measures of brain functions and general intelligence. *Journal of Clinical Psychology, 41,* 245–253.

Reitan, R. M. (1986). Theoretical and methodological bases of the Halstead-Reitan Neuropsychological Test Battery. In I. Grant & K. M. Adams (Eds.), *Neuropsychological assessment of neuropsychiatric disorders* (pp. 3–30). New York: Oxford University Press.

Reitan, R. M., & Boll, T. J. (1971). Intellectual and cognitive functions in Parkinson's disease. *Journal of Consulting and Clinical Psychology, 37,* 364–369.

Reitan, R. M., & Fitzhugh, K. B. (1971). Behavioral deficits in groups with cerebral vascular lesions. *Journal of Consulting and Clinical Psychology, 37,* 215–223.

Reitan, R. M., Reed, J. C., & Dyken, M. L. (1971). Cognitive, psychomotor, and motor correlates of multiple sclerosis. *Journal of Nervous and Mental Disease, 153,* 218–224.

Reitan, R. M., & Wolfson, D. (1985). *The Halstead-Reitan Neuropsychological Test Battery: Theory and clinical interpretation.* Tucson, AZ: Neuropsychology Press.

Reivich, M., Jones, S., Castano, T., Crowe, W., Ginsberg, M., & Greenberg, J. (1977). Cerebral function, metabolism, and circulation. In D. H. Ingvar & N. A. Lassen (Eds.), *A model of diaschisis using middle cerebral artery occlusion.* Copenhagen: Munksgaard.

Reschly, D. J. (1981). Evaluation of the effects of SOMPA measures on classification of students as mildly mentally retarded. *American Journal of Mental Deficiency, 86,* 16–20.

Reschly, D. J. (1982). Assessing mild mental retardation: The influence of adaptive behavior, sociocultural status, and prospects for nonbiased assessment. In C. R. Reynolds & T. B. Gutkin (Eds.), *The handbook of school psychology* (pp. 209–242). New York: Wiley.

Reschly, D. J. (1985). Best practices: Adaptive behavior. In A. Thomas & J. Grimes (Eds.), *Best practices in school psychology* (pp. 353–368). Stratford, CT: National Association of School Psychologists.

Reschly, D. J., & Jipson, F. J. (1976). Ethnicity, geographic locale, age, sex, and urban–rural residence as variables in the prevalence of mild retardation. *American Journal of Mental Deficiency, 81,* 154–161.

Resnick, L. B. (1987). The 1987 Presidential Address: Learning in school and out. *Educational Researcher, 16,* 13–20.

Resnick, R. J., & Entin, A. D. (1971). Is an abbreviated form of the WISC valid for Afro-American children? *Journal of Consulting and Clinical Psychology, 36,* 97–99.

Retzlaff, P., Slicner, N., & Gibertini, M. (1986). Predicting WAIS-R scores from the Shipley Institute of Living Scale in a homogeneous sample. *Journal of Clinical Psychology, 39,* 357–359.

Reynolds, C. R. (1982). The problem of bias in psychological assessment. In C. R. Reynolds & T. B. Gutkin (Eds.), *The handbook of school psychology* (pp. 178–208). New York: Wiley.

Reynolds, C. R. (1986a, March). K-TEA terrific! *Information/Edge, 2,*(1), 1, 4. Bensalem, PA: Buttonwood Farms.

Reynolds, C. R. (1986b). Wide Range Achievement Test (WRAT-R), 1984 edition. *Journal of Counseling and Development, 64,* 540–541.

Reynolds, C. R. (1987a). Playing IQ roulette with the Stanford-Binet, 4th edition. *Measurement and Evaluation in Counseling and Development, 20,* 139–141.

Reynolds, C. R. (1987b). Raising intelligence: Clever Hans, Candides, and the miracle in Milwaukee. *Journal of School Psychology, 25,* 309–312.

Reynolds, C. R. (1988). Of straw men and the practice of the ancients: Commentary on Lezak. *NASP Communique, 17,*(4), 6.

Reynolds, C. R., & Brown, R. T. (Eds.) (1984). *Perspectives on bias in mental testing.* New York: Plenum.

Reynolds, C. R., Chastain, R. L., Kaufman, A. S., & McLean, J. E. (1987). Demographic characteristics and IQ among adults: Analysis of the WAIS-R standardization sample as a function of the stratification variables. *Journal of School Psychology, 25,* 323–342.

Reynolds, C. R., & Fletcher-Janzen, E. (1989). *Handbook of clinical child neuropsychology.* New York: Plenum.

Reynolds, C. R., & Gutkin, T. B. (1979). Predicting the premorbid intellectual status of children using demographic data. *Clinical Neuropsychology, 1,* 36–38.

Reynolds, C. R., & Gutkin, T. B. (1981). Test scatter on the WPPSI: Normative analysis of the WPPSI. *Journal of Learning Disabilities, 14,* 460–464.

Reynolds, C. R., Kamphaus, R. W., & Rosenthal, B. L. (1988). Factor analysis of the Stanford-Binet: Fourth edition for ages 2 through 23 years. *Measurement and Evaluation in Counseling and Development, 21,* 52–63.

Reynolds, C. R., Willson, V. L., & Clark, P. L. (1983). A four-test short form of the WAIS-R for clinical screening. *Journal of Clinical Neuropsychology, 5,* 111–116.

Reynolds, W. M. (1979). A caution against the use of the Slosson Intelligence Test in the diagnosis of mental retardation. *Psychology in the Schools, 16,* 77–79.

Reynolds, W. M. (1985). Review of Slosson Intelligence Test. *The ninth mental measurements yearbook* (pp. 1403–1404). Lincoln, NE: Buros Institute of Mental Measurements, University of Nebraska.

Rhudick, P. J., & Gordon, C. (1973). The Age Center of New England Study. In L. F. Jarvik, C. Eisdorfer, & J. E. Blum (Eds.), *Intellectual functioning in adults* (pp. 7–12). New York: Springer.

Roberts, F. (1988, December). Test review: Kaufman Test of Educational Achievement. *NASP Communique, 17,* 30.

Roberts, J. A. F. (1952). The genetics of mental deficiency. *Eugenics Review, 44,* 71–83.

Robertson, G. J., & Eisenberg, J. L. (1981). *Peabody Picture Vocabulary Test—Revised: Technical supplement, Forms L and M.* Circle Pines, MN: American Guidance Service.

Robertson, D. U., Steinmeyer, C. H., & Goff, C. P. (1980). Decision-theoretic approach for WAIS short forms with an inpatient psychiatric population. *Journal of Consulting and Clinical Psychology, 48,* 657–658.

Robinson, A., Bender, B., Borelli, J., Puck, M., Salsenblati, J., & Webber, M. L. (1982). Sex chromosomal abnormalities (SCA): A prospective and longitudinal study of newborns identified in an unbiased manner. *Birth Defects: Original Article Series, 18,*(4), 7–39.

Robinson, N. M., & Chamrad, D. L. (1986). Appropriate uses of intelligence tests with gifted children. *Roeper Review, 8,* 160–162.

Rogan, L., & Hartman, L. (1976). A follow-up study of learning disabled children as adults. Final report. Evanston, IL: Cove School (ERIC Document Reproduction Service No. ED 163 728).

Rogers, D. L., & Osborne, D. (1984). Comparison of the WAIS and WAIS-R at different ages in a clinical population. *Psychological Reports, 54,* 91–95.

Rogers, R. C., & Simensen, R. J. (1987). Fragile X syndrome: A common etiology of mental retardation. *American Journal of Mental Deficiency, 91*, 445–449.

Roid, G. H., Prifitera, A., & Ledbetter, M. (1988). Confirmatory analysis of the factor structure of the Wechsler Memory Scale—Revised. *The Clinical Neuropsychologist, 2*, 116–120.

Rosenthal, B. L., & Kamphaus, R. W. (1988). Interpretive tables for test scatter on the Stanford-Binet Intelligence Scale: Fourth edition. *Journal of Psychoeducational Assessment, 6*, 359–370.

Rosenthal, R., & Ruben, D. B. (1982). Further meta-analytic procedures for assessing cognitive gender differences. *Journal of Educational Psychology, 74*, 708–712.

Ross, A. T., & Reitan, R. M. (1955). Intellectual and affective functions in multiple sclerosis. *A.M.A. Archives of Neurology and Psychiatry, 73*, 663–677.

Ross, E. D. (1981). The Aprosodias: Functional-anatomic organization of the affective components of language in the right hemisphere. *Archives of Neurology, 38*, 561–569.

Ross, E. D. (1984). Right hemisphere's role in language, affective behavior and emotion. *Trends in Neurosciences, 7*, 342–346.

Ross, J. D., & Ross, C. M. (1979). *Ross Test of Higher Cognitive Processes*. Novato, CA: Academic Therapy.

Roszkowski, M. J. (1983). The freedom-from-distractibility factor: An examination of its adaptive behavior correlates. *Journal of Psychoeducational Assessment, 1*, 285–297.

Roszkowski, M. J., & Bean, A. G. (1980). The Adaptive Behavior Scale (ABS) and IQ: How much unshared variance is there? *Psychology in the Schools, 17*, 452–459.

Roth, D. L., Hughes, C. W., Monkowski, P. G., & Crossen, B. (1984). Investigation of validity of WAIS-R short forms for patients suspected to have brain impairment. *Journal of Consulting and Clinical Psychology, 52*, 722–723.

Rourke, B. P., & Adams, K. M. (Eds.). (1988). [Special issue on the Wechsler Memory Scale—Revised]. *The Clinical Neuropsychologist, 2*(2). Lisse, the Netherlands: Swets.

Royer, F. L. (1977). Information processing in the Block Design task. *Intelligence, 1*, 32–50.

Royer, F. L. (1978). Sex differences in symbol-digit substitution task performance. *Intelligence, 2*, 145–151.

Royer, F. L. (1984). Stimulus variables in the Block Design task: A commentary on Schorr, Bower, and Kiernan. *Journal of Consulting and Clinical Psychology, 52*, 700–704.

Rubin, K. H., Attewell, P. W., Tierney, M. C., & Tumolo, P. (1973). Development of spatial egocentrism and conservation across the life span. *Developmental Psychology, 9*, 432.

Rubin, H. H., Goldman, J. J., & Rosenfeld, J. G. (1985). A comparison of WISC-R and WAIS-R IQs in a mentally retarded residential population. *Psychology in the Schools, 22*, 392–397.

Ruchalla, E., Schalt, E., & Vogel, F. (1985). Relations between mental performance and reaction time: New aspects of an old problem. *Intelligence, 9*, 189–205.

Rugel, R. P. (1974). WISC subtest scores of disabled readers: A review with respect to Bannatyne's recategorization. *Journal of Learning Disabilities, 7*, 48–55.

Russell, E. W. (1972). WAIS factor analysis with brain-damaged subjects using criterion measures. *Journal of Consulting and Clinical Psychology, 39*, 133–139.

Russell, E. W. (1975). A multiple scoring method for the assessment of complex memory functions. *Journal of Consulting and Clinical Psychology, 43*, 800–809.

Russell, E. W. (1980). Fluid and crystallized intelligence: Effects of diffuse brain damage on the WAIS. *Perceptual and Motor Skills, 51*, 121–122.

Russell, E. W. (1988). Renorming Russell's version of the Wechsler Memory Scale. *Journal of Clinical and Experimental Neuropsychology, 10*, 235–249.

Rust, J. O., Barnard, D., & Oster, G. D. (1979). WAIS Verbal-Performance differences among elderly when controlling for fatigue. *Psychological Reports, 44*, 489–490.

Rutter, M. (1978). Language disorder and infantile autism. In M. Rutter & E. Schopler (Eds.), *Autism: A reappraisal of concepts and treatment* (pp. 85–104). New York: Plenum.

Rutter, M. (1979). Language, cognition and autism. In R. Katzman (Ed.), *Congenital and acquired cognitive disorders* (pp. 247–264). New York: Raven Press.

Ryan, J. J. (1983). Clinical utility of a WAIS-R short form. *Journal of Clinical Psychology, 39*, 261–262.

Ryan, J. J. (1985). Application of a WAIS-R short form with neurological patients: Validity and correlational findings. *Journal of Psychoeducational Assessment, 3*, 61–64.

Ryan, J. J., Georgemiller, R. J., Geisser, M. E., & Randall, D. M. (1985). Test–retest stability of the WAIS-R in a clinical sample. *Journal of Clinical Psychology, 41*, 552–556.

Ryan, J. J., Georgemiller, R. J., & McKinney, B. E. (1984). *Journal of Clinical Psychology, 40*, 1033–1036. Application of the four-subtest WAIS-R short form with an older clinical sample.

Ryan, J. J., & Lewis, C. V. (1988). Comparison of normal controls and recently detoxified alcoholics on the Wechsler Memory Scale—Revised. *The Clinical Neuropsychologist, 2*, 173–180.

Ryan, J. J., Nowak, T. J., & Geisser, M. E. (1987). On the comparability of the WAIS and the WAIS-R: Review of the research and implications for clinical practice. *Journal of Psychoeducational Assessment, 5*, 15–30.

Ryan, J. J., Prifitera, A., & Larsen, J. (1982). Reliability of the WAIS-R with a mixed patient sample. *Perceptual and Motor Skills, 55*, 1277–1278.

Ryan, J. J., Prifitera, A., & Powers, L. (1983). Scoring reliability on the WAIS-R. *Journal of Consulting and Clinical Psychology, 51,* 149–150.

Ryan, J. J., Prifitera, A., & Rosenberg, S. J. (1983). Interrelationships between factor structures of the WAIS-R and WAIS in a neuropsychological battery. *International Journal of Neuroscience, 21,* 191–196.

Ryan, J. J., & Rosenberg, S. J. (1983). Relationship between WAIS-R and Wide Range Achievement Test in a sample of mixed patients. *Perceptual and Motor Skills, 56,* 623–626.

Ryan, J. J., & Rosenberg, S. J. (1984a). Administration time estimates for WAIS-R subtests and short forms. *Journal of Psycho-educational Assessment, 2,* 125–129.

Ryan, J. J., & Rosenberg, S. J. (1984b). Validity of the Verbal IQ as a short form of the Wechsler Adult Intelligence Scale—Revised. *Journal of Clinical Psychology, 51,* 306–308.

Ryan, J. J., Rosenberg, S. J., & DeWolfe, A. S. (1984). Generalization of the WAIS-R factor structure with a vocational rehabilitation sample. *Journal of Consulting and Clinical Psychology, 52,* 311–312.

Ryan, J. J., Rosenberg, S. J., & Heilbronner, R. L. (1984). Comparative relationships of the Wechsler Adult Intelligence Scale—Revised and the Wechsler Adult Intelligence Scale (WAIS) to the Wechsler Memory Scale (WMS). *Journal of Behavioral Assessment, 6,* 37–43.

Ryan, J. J., Rosenberg, S. J., & Prifitera, A. (1983). On substituting the WAIS-R for the WAIS in neuropsychological assessment: A caution for clinicians. *The Journal of Psychology, 115,* 131–134.

Ryan, J. J., & Schneider, J. A. (1986). Factor analysis of the Wechsler Adult Intelligence Scale—Revised (WAIS-R) in a brain-damaged sample. *Journal of Clinical Psychology, 42,* 962–964.

Salthouse, T. A. (1984, August). *Speculations on the what, when, and why of mental aging.* Paper presented at the meeting of the American Psychological Association, Toronto.

Salthouse, T. A. (1985). Speed of behavior and its implications for cognition. In J. E. Birren and K. W. Schaie (Eds.), *Handbook of the psychology of aging* (2nd ed.; pp. 61–92). New York: Van Nostrand Reinhold.

Salvia, J., Gajar, A., Gajria, M., & Salvia, S. (1988). A comparison of WAIS-R profiles of nondisabled college freshmen and college students with learning disabilities. *Journal of Learning Disabilities, 21,* 632–636.

Salvia, J., & Ysseldyke, J. E. (1988). *Assessment in special and remedial education* (4th ed.). Boston: Houghton Mifflin.

San Diego, E. A., Foley, J. M., & Walker, R. E. (1970). WAIS scores for highly educated young adults from the Philippines and the United States. *Psychological Reports, 27,* 511–515.

Sandoval, J., & Irvin, M. G. (1988). Review of the Stanford-Binet Intelligence Scale: Fourth edition. *Professional School Psychology, 3,* 157–161.

Sandoval, J., Sassenrath, J., & Penaloza, M. (1988). Similarity of WISC-R and WAIS-R scores at age 16. *Psychology in the Schools, 25,* 373–379.

Sapp, G. L., Chissom, B., & Graham, E. (1985). Factor analysis of the WISC-R for gifted students: A replication and comparison. *Psychological Reports, 57,* 947–951.

Sattler, J. M. (1982). Age effects on Wechsler Adult Intelligence Scale—Revised. *Journal of Consulting and Clinical Psychology, 50,* 785–786.

Sattler, J. M. (1988). *Assessment of children.* (3rd ed.) San Diego, CA: Jerome M. Sattler.

Sattler, J. M., & Covin, T. M. (1986). Comparison of the Slosson Intelligence Test, revised norms, and WISC-R for children with learning problems and for gifted children. *Psychology in the Schools, 23,* 259–264.

Sattler, J. M., & Gwynne, J. (1982). White examiners generally do not impede the intelligence test performance of black children: To debunk a myth. *Journal of Consulting and Clinical Psychology, 50,* 196–208.

Sattler, J. M., Polifka, J. C., Polifka, S., & Hilsen, D. E. (1984). A longitudinal study of the WISC-R and WAIS-R with special education students. *Psychology in the Schools, 21,* 294–295.

Sattler, J. M., & Winget, B. M. (1970). Intelligence testing procedures as affected by expectancy and IQ. *Journal of Clinical Psychology, 26,* 446–448.

Satz, P. (1966). Specific and nonspecific effects of brain lesions in man. *Journal of Abnormal Psychology, 71,* 65–70.

Satz, P., & Fletcher, J. M. (1981). Emergent trends in neuropsychology: An overview. *Journal of Consulting and Clinical Psychology, 49,* 851–865.

Satz, P., Hynd, G. W., D'Elia, L., Daniel, M., Van Gorp, W., & Conner, R. (1989). *A WAIS-R marker for accelerated aging and dementia, Alzheimer's type? Base rates of the Fuld Formula in the WAIS-R standardization sample.* Manuscript submitted for publication.

Satz, P., & Mogel, S. (1962). Abbreviation of the WAIS for clinical use. *Journal of Clinical Psychology, 18,* 77–79.

Satz, P., Richard, W., & Daniels, A. (1967). The alteration of intellectual performance after lateralized brain-injury in man. *Psychonomic Science, 7,* 369–370.

Satz, P., Van Gorp, W., Soper, H. V., & Mitrushina, M. (1987). WAIS-R marker for dementia of the Alzheimer type? An empirical and statistical induction test. *Journal of Clinical and Experimental Neuropsychology, 9,* 767–774.

Scarr, S. (1981). Genetics and the development of intelligence. In S. Scarr (Ed.), *Race, social class, and individual differences in IQ* (pp. 3–59). Hillsdale, NJ: Lawrence Erlbaum.

Scarr, S., & Barker, W. (1981). The effects of family background: A study of cognitive differences among black and white twins. In S. Scarr (Ed.), *Race, social class, and individual differences in IQ* (pp. 261–315). Hillsdale, NJ: Lawrence Erlbaum.

Scarr, S., & Carter-Saltzman, L. (1982). Genetics and intelligence. In R. J. Sternberg (Ed.), *Handbook of human intelligence* (pp. 792–896). Cambridge: Cambridge University Press.

Scarr, S., & Grajek, S. (1982). Similarities and differences among siblings. In M. E. Lamb & B. Sutton-Smith (Eds.), *Sibling relationships.* Hillsdale, NJ: Lawrence Erlbaum.

Scarr, S., & Weinberg, R. A. (1976). IQ test performance of black children adopted by white families. *American Psychologist, 31,* 726–739.

Scarr, S., & Weinberg, R. A. (1978). The influence of "family background" on intellectual attainment. *American Sociological Review, 43,* 674–692.

Scarr-Salapatek, S. (1971). Unknowns in the IQ equation. *Science, 174,* 1223–1228.

Schachter, D. L., & Crovitz, H. F. (1977). Memory function after closed head injury: A review of the quantitative research. *Cortex, 13,* 150–176.

Schaie, K. W. (1958). Rigidity-flexibility and intelligence: A cross-sectional study of the adult life-span from 20 to 70. *Psychological Monographs, 72* (9, Whole No. 462).

Schaie, K. W. (Ed.). (1983a). *Longitudinal studies of adult psychological development.* New York: Guilford Press.

Schaie, K. W. (1983b). The Seattle Longitudinal Study: A 21-year exploration of psychometric intelligence in adulthood. In K. W. Schaie (Ed.), *Longitudinal studies of adult psychological development* (pp. 64–135). New York: Guilford Press.

Schaie, K. W. (1983c). What can we learn from the longitudinal study of adult psychological development? In K. W. Schaie (Ed.), *Longitudinal studies of adult psychological development* (pp. 1–19). New York: Guilford Press.

Schaie, K. W., & Hertzog, C. (1983). Fourteen-year cohort-sequential analyses of adult intellectual development. *Developmental Psychology, 19,* 531–543.

Schaie, K. W., & Hertzog, C. (1985). Measurement in the psychology of adulthood and aging. In J. E. Birren & K. W. Schaie (Eds.), *Handbook of the psychology of aging* (2nd ed.; pp. 61–92). New York: Van Nostrand Reinhold.

Schaie, K. W., & Hertzog, C. (1986). Stability and change in adult intelligence: 1. Analysis of longitudinal covariance structures. *Psychology and Aging, 1,* 159–171.

Schaie, K. W., & Labouvie-Vief, G. (1974). Generational vs. ontogenetic components of change in adult cognitive behavior: A fourteen-year cross-sequential study. *Developmental Psychology, 10,* 305–320.

Schaie, K. W., & Schaie, J. P. (1977). Clinical assessment and aging. In J. E. Birren & K. W. Schaie (Eds.), *Handbook of the psychology of aging* (pp. 692–723). New York: Van Nostrand Reinhold.

Schaie, K. W., & Strother, C. R. (1968). The cross-sequential study of age changes in cognitive behavior. *Psychological Bulletin, 70,* 671–680.

Schaie, K. W., & Willis, S. L. (1986). Can decline in intellectual functioning be reversed? *Developmental Psychology, 22,* 223–232.

Scheerenberger, R. C. (1987). *A history of mental retardation.* Baltimore: Paul H. Brookes.

Schiff, M. M., Kaufman, A. S., & Kaufman, N. L. (1981). Scatter analysis of WISC-R profiles for learning disabled children with superior intelligence. *Journal of Learning Disabilities, 14,* 400–404.

Schill, T. (1966). The effect of MMPI social introversion on the WAIS PA performance. *Journal of Clinical Psychology, 22,* 72–74.

Schill, T., Kahn, M., & Muehleman, T. (1968a). WAIS PA performance and participation in extra-curricular activities. *Journal of Clinical Psychology, 24,* 95–96.

Schill, T., Kahn, M., & Muehleman, T. (1968b). Verbal conditionability and Wechsler Picture Arrangement scores. *Journal of Consulting and Clinical Psychology, 32,* 718–721.

Schiller, F. (1947). Aphasia studied in patients with missile wounds. *Journal of Neurology, Neurosurgery, and Psychiatry, 10,* 183–197.

Schinka, J. A. (1974). *Performances of brain damaged patients on tests of short-term and long-term verbal memory.* Unpublished doctoral dissertation, University of Iowa.

Schmidt, H. P. J., & Saklofske, D. H. (1983). Comparison of the WISC-R patterns of children of average and exceptional ability. *Psychological Reports, 53,* 539–544.

Schmitz-Sherzer, R., & Thomae, H. (1983). Constancy and change of behavior in old age: Findings from the Bonn Longitudinal Study on Aging. In K. W. Schaie (Ed.), *Longitudinal studies of adult psychological development* (pp. 191–221). New York: Guilford Press.

Schooler, D. L., Beebe, M. C., & Koepke, T. (1978). Factor analysis of WISC-R scores for children identified as learning disabled, educable mentally impaired, and emotionally impaired. *Psychology in the Schools, 15,* 478–485.

Schorr, D., Bower, G. H., & Kiernan, R. (1982). Stimulus variables in the Block Design task. *Journal of Consulting and Clinical Psychology, 50,* 479–487.

Schreiber, D. J., Goldman, H., Kleinman, K. M., Goldfaber, P. R., & Snow, M. Y. (1976). The relationship between independent neuropsychological detection and localization of cerebral impairment. *Journal of Nervous and Mental Disease, 162,* 360–365.

Schultz, N. R., Jr., Dineen, J. T., Elias, M. F., Pentz, C. A., & Wood, W. G. (1979). WAIS performance for different age groups of hypertensive and control subjects during the administration of a diuretic. *Journal of Gerontology, 34,* 246–253.

Schultz, N. R., Jr., Elias, M. F., Robbins, M. A., Streeten, D. H. P., & Blakeman, N. (1986). A longitudinal comparison of hypertensives and normotensives on the Wechsler Adult Intelligence Scale: Initial findings. *Journal of Gerontology, 41,* 169–175.

Schuster, T. L., & Butler, E. B. (1986). Learning, mild mental retardation, and long-range social adjustment. *Sociological Perspectives, 29,* 461–483.

Scott, K. G., & Carran, D. T. (1987). The epidemiology and prevention of mental retardation. *American Psychologist, 42,* 801–804.

Sears, P. S., & Barbee, A. H. (1977). Career and life satisfaction among Terman's gifted women. In J. C. Stanley, W. C. George, & C. H. Solano (Eds.), *The gifted and the creative: Fifty-year perspective* (pp. 28–65). Baltimore: Johns Hopkins University Press.

Sears, R. R. (1977). Sources of life satisfactions of the Terman gifted men. *American Psychologist, 32,* 119–128.

Seashore, H. G., Wesman, A. G., & Doppelt, J. E. (1950). The standardization of the Wechsler Intelligence Scale for Children. *Journal of Consulting Psychology, 14,* 99–110.

Seidenberg, M., O'Leary, D. S., Giordani, B., Berent, S., & Boll, T. J. (1981). Test–retest IQ changes of epilepsy patients: Assessing the influence of practice effects. *Journal of Clinical Neuropsychology, 3,* 237–255.

Sells, S. B. (1966). *Evaluation of psychological measures used in the health examination survey of children ages 6–11.* U.S. Department of Health, Education, and Welfare, Public Health Service, Vital and Health Statistics, Publication No. 1000 (Series 2, No. 15).

Selz, M., & Reitan, R. M. (1979). Rules for neuropsychological diagnosis: Classification of brain function in older children. *Journal of Consulting and Clinical Psychology, 47,* 258–264.

Shapiro, B. A. (1982). Relation of facial expressions and activities: A study of attensity differences in events. *Perceptual and Motor Skills, 54,* 1199–1211.

Sharp, S. E. (1898-99). Individual psychology: A study in psychological method. *American Journal of Psychology, 10,* 329–391.

Shatz, M. W. (1981). Comment: WAIS practice effects in clinical neuropsychology. *Journal of Clinical Neuropsychology, 3,* 171–179.

Shaw, D. J. (1966). The reliability and validity of the Halstead Category Test. *Journal of Clinical Psychology, 22,* 176–180.

Shellenberger, S. (1977). *A cross-cultural investigation of the Spanish version of the McCarthy Scales of Children's Abilities for Puerto Rican children.* Unpublished doctoral dissertation, University of Georgia, Athens.

Shellenberger, S., & Lachterman, T. (1979). Cognitive and motor functioning on the McCarthy Scales by Spanish-speaking children. *Perceptual and Motor Skills, 49,* 863–866.

Sherman, J. A. (1978). *Sex-related cognitive differences: An essay on theory and evidence.* Springfield, IL: Charles C. Thomas.

Sherman, J. A. (1980). Sex-related differences in human brain asymmetry: Verbal functions—no; spatial functions—maybe. *Behavioral and Brain Sciences, 3,* 248–249.

Shinn, M., Algozzine, B., Marston, D., & Ysseldyke, J. E. (1982). A theoretical analysis of the performance of learning disabled students on the Woodcock-Johnson Psycho-Educational Battery. *Journal of Learning Disabilities, 15,* 221–226.

Shipley, W. C. (1940). A self-administering scale for measuring intellectual impairment and deterioration. *Journal of Psychology, 9,* 371–377.

Shipley, W. C. (1953). The Shipley Institute of Living Scale for measuring intellectual impairment. In A. Weider (Ed.), *Contributions toward medical psychology: Vol. 2. Theory and diagnostic methods* (pp. 751–756). New York: Ronald Press.

Shouksmith, G. (1970). *Intelligence, creativity and cognitive style.* New York: Wiley.

Shuey, A. M. (1966). *The testing of Negro intelligence* (2nd ed.). New York: Social Science Press.

Shure, G. H., & Halstead, W. C. (1958). Cerebral localization of intellectual processes. *Psychological Monographs, 72* (12, Whole No. 465).

Siegler, I. (1983). Psychological aspects of the Duke Longitudinal studies. In K. W. Schaie (Ed.), *Longitudinal studies of adult psychological development* (pp. 136–190). New York: Guilford Press.

Siegler, I., & Botwinick, J. (1979). A long-term longitudinal study of intellectual ability of older adults: The matter of selective subject attrition. *Journal of Gerontology, 34,* 242–245.

Sigelman, C. K., Schoenrock, C. J., Winer, J. L., Spanhel, C. L., Hromas, S. G., Martin, P. W., Budd, E. C., & Bensberg, G. J. (1981). Issues in interviewing mentally retarded persons: An empirical study. In R. H. Bruininks, C. E. Meyers, B. B. Sigford, & K. C. Lakin (Eds.), *Deinstitutionalization and community adjustment of mentally retarded people.* Washington, DC: American Association on Mental Deficiency.

Silverstein, A. B. (1967a). A short short form of the WISC and WAIS for screening purposes. *Psychological Reports, 21,* 682.

Silverstein, A. B. (1967b). A short short form of Wechsler's scales for screening purposes. *Psychological Reports, 21*, 842.

Silverstein, A. B. (1969). An alternative factor analytic solution for Wechsler's Intelligence Scales. *Educational and Psychological Measurement, 29*, 763–776.

Silverstein, A. B. (1971). A corrected formula for assessing the validity of WAIS, WISC, and WPPSI short forms. *Journal of Clinical Psychology, 27*, 212–213.

Silverstein, A. B. (1973). Note on prevalence. *American Journal of Mental Deficiency, 77*, 380–382.

Silverstein, A. B. (1975). A reply to McNemar. *Journal of Consulting and Clinical Psychology, 43*, 423–424.

Silverstein, A. B. (1977a). Comparison of two criteria for determining the number of factors. *Psychological Reports, 41*, 387–390.

Silverstein, A. B. (1977b). Comment on Kaufman's "Should short form validity coefficients be corrected?" *Journal of Consulting and Clinical Psychology, 45*, 1162–1163.

Silverstein, A. B. (1982a). Two- and four-subtest short forms of the Wechsler Adult Intelligence Scale—Revised. *Journal of Consulting and Clinical Psychology, 50*, 415–418.

Silverstein, A. B. (1982b). Validity of random short forms. *Perceptual and Motor Skills, 55*, 411–414.

Silverstein, A. B. (1982c). Validity of Satz-Mogel-Yudin-type short forms. *Journal of Consulting and Clinical Psychology, 50*, 20–21.

Silverstein, A. B. (1982d). Pattern analysis as simultaneous statistical inference. *Journal of Consulting and Clinical Psychology, 50*, 234–240.

Silverstein, A. B. (1982e). Factor structure of the Wechsler Adult Intelligence Scale—Revised. *Journal of Consulting and Clinical Psychology, 50*, 661–664.

Silverstein, A. B. (1982f). Note on the constancy of the IQ. *American Journal of Mental Deficiency, 87*, 227–228.

Silverstein, A. B. (1984a). Estimating Full Scale IQs from short forms of Wechsler's scales: Linear scaling versus linear regression. *Journal of Consulting and Clinical Psychology, 52*, 919.

Silverstein, A. B. (1984b). Standard errors for short forms of Wechsler's intelligence scales with deviant subjects. *Journal of Consulting and Clinical Psychology, 52*, 913–914.

Silverstein, A. B. (1985a). An appraisal of three criteria for evaluating the usefulness of WAIS-R short forms. *Journal of Clinical Psychology, 41*, 676–680.

Silverstein, A. B. (1985b). Two- and four-subtest short forms of the WAIS-R: A closer look at validity and reliability. *Journal of Clinical Psychology, 41*, 95–97.

Silverstein, A. B. (1985c). Cluster analysis of the Wechsler Adult Intelligence Scale—Revised. *Journal of Clinical Psychology, 41*, 98–100.

Silverstein, A. B. (1985d). Verbal–Performance IQ discrepancies on the WAIS-R: Estimated vs. empirical values. *Journal of Clinical Psychology, 41*, 694–697.

Silverstein, A. B. (1986a). Discrepancies between composite quotients on the Detroit Tests of Learning Aptitude. *Journal of Psychoeducational Assessment, 4*, 239–242.

Silverstein, A. B. (1986b). Nonstandard standard scores on the Vineland Adaptive Behavior Scales: A cautionary note. *American Journal of Mental Deficiency, 91*, 1–4.

Silverstein, A. B. (1987a). Accuracy of estimates of premorbid intelligence based on demographic variables. *Journal of Clinical Psychology, 43*, 493–495.

Silverstein, A. B. (1987b). Unusual test score combinations and unusual test score differences. *Journal of Clinical Psychology, 43*, 490–492.

Silverstein, A. B. (1987c). Multidimensional scaling versus factor analysis of Wechsler's intelligence scales. *Journal of Clinical Psychology, 43*, 381–386.

Simon, C. L., & Clopton, J. R. (1984). Comparison of WAIS and WAIS-R scores of mildly and moderately mentally retarded adults. *American Journal of Mental Deficiency, 89*, 301–303.

Simons, M. R., & Goh, D. S. (1982). Relationships between McCarthy Scales of Children's Abilities and teacher's ratings of school achievement. *Perceptual and Motor Skills, 54*, 1159–1162.

Simpson, C. D., & Vega, A. (1971). Unilateral brain damage and patterns of age-corrected WAIS subtest scores. *Journal of Clinical Psychology, 27*, 204–208.

Sipps, G. J., Berry, G. W., & Lynch, E. M. (1987). WAIS-R and social intelligence: A test of established assumptions that uses the CPI. *Journal of Clinical Psychology, 43*, 499–504.

Sisemore, T. A. (1985). A comparison of the WISC-R and WAIS-R in exceptional adolescents. (Fuller Theological Seminary, 1984). *Dissertation Abstracts International, 45* (12-B, Pt. 1), 3962.

Slate, J. R. (1986). A reaction to the revised Stanford-Binet Intelligence Scale: New does not necessarily mean better. *NASP Communique, 15*(1), 3.

Slate, J. R., & Hunnicutt, L. C. (1988). Examiner errors on the Wechsler scales. *Journal of Psychoeducational Assessment, 6*, 280–288.

Slosson, R. L. (1982). *Slosson Intelligence Test* (2nd ed.). East Aurora, NY: Slosson Educational Publications.

Small, L. (1980). *Neuropsychodiagnosis in psychotherapy*. New York: Brunner/Mazel.

Smith, A. (1962). Ambiguities in concepts and studies of "brain damage" and "organicity." *Journal of Nervous and Mental Diseases, 135*, 311–326.

Smith, A. (1966a). Certain hypothesized hemispheric differences in language and visual functions in human adults. *Cortex, 2,* 109–126.

Smith, A. (1966b). Intellectual functions in patients with lateralized frontal tumours. *Journal of Neurology, Neurosurgery and Psychiatry, 29,* 52–59.

Smith, A. (1966c). Verbal and nonverbal test performances of patients with "acute" lateralized brain lesions (tumors). *The Journal of Nervous and Mental Disease, 141,* 517–523.

Smith, A. (1981). Principles underlying human brain functions in neuropsychological sequelae of different neuropathological processes. In S. B. Filskov & T. J. Boll (Eds.), *Handbook of clinical neuropsychology* (pp. 175–226). New York: Wiley.

Smith, A. (1983). Overview or "underview"? Comment on Satz and Fletcher's "Emergent trends in neuropsychology: An overview." *Journal of Consulting and Clinical Psychology, 51,* 768–775.

Smith, C. R., & Knoff, H. M. (1981). School psychology and special education students' placement decisions: IQ still tips the scale. *Journal of Special Education, 15,* 55–63.

Smith, D. W. (1982). *Recognizable patterns of human malformation.* Philadelphia: Saunders.

Smith, H. H., & Smith, L. S. (1977). WAIS functioning of cirrhotic and non-cirrhotic alcoholics. *Journal of Clinical Psychology, 33,* 309–313.

Smith, R. S. (1983). A comparison study of the Wechsler Adult Intelligence Scale and the Wechsler Adult Intelligence Scale—Revised in a college population. *Journal of Consulting and Clinical Psychology, 51,* 414–419.

Snow, W. G., & Sheese, S. (1985). Lateralized brain damage, intelligence, and memory: A failure to find sex differences. *Journal of Consulting and Clinical Psychology, 53,* 940–941.

Snow, J. H., Koller, J. R., & Roberts, D. (1987). Adolescent and adult learning disability subgroups based on WAIS-R performance. *Journal of Psychoeducational Assessment, 5,* 7–14.

Snow, W. G., Freedman, L., & Ford, L. (1986). Lateralized brain damage, sex differences, and the Wechsler intelligence scales: A reexamination of the literature. *Journal of Clinical and Experimental Neuropsychology, 8,* 179–189.

Snyderman, M., & Rothman, S. (1987). Survey of expert opinion on intelligence and aptitude testing. *American Psychologist, 42,* 137–144.

Sobotowicz, W., Evans, J. R., & Laughlin, J. (1987). Neuropsychological function and social support in delinquency and learning disability. *The International Journal of Clinical Neuropsychology, 9,* 178–186.

Sommer, R., & Sommer, B. A. (1983). Mystery in Milwaukee: Early intervention, IQ, and psychology textbooks. *American Psychologist, 38,* 982–985.

Sparrow, S. S., Balla, D. A., & Cicchetti, D. V. (1984a). *Vineland Adaptive Behavior Scales, Expanded Form manual.* Circle Pines, MN: American Guidance Service.

Sparrow, S. S., Balla, D. A., & Cicchetti, D. V. (1984b). *Vineland Adaptive Behavior Scales, Survey Form manual.* Circle Pines, MN: American Guidance Service.

Sparrow, S. S., & Cicchetti, D. V. (1987). Adaptive behavior and the psychologically disturbed child. *Journal of Special Education, 21,* 89–100.

Spearman, C. E. (1927). *The abilities of man.* London: Macmillan.

Sperry, R. W. (1968). Hemisphere deconnection and unity in conscious awareness. *American Psychologist, 23,* 723–733.

Spiers, P. A. (1981). Have they come to praise Luria or to bury him? The Luria-Nebraska Battery controversy. *Journal of Consulting and Clinical Psychology, 49,* 331–431.

Spiers, P. A. (1982). The Luria-Nebraska Neuropsychological Battery revisited: A theory in practice or just practicing? *Journal of Consulting and Clinical Psychology, 50,* 301–306.

Spitz, H. (1986). *The raising of intelligence: A selected history of attempts to raise retarded intelligence.* Hillsdale, NJ: Lawrence Erlbaum.

Spivack, G. M. (1980, April). *The construct of adaptive behavior: Consistency across raters and instruments.* Paper presented at the meeting of the National Association of School Psychologists, Washington, DC.

Sprandel, H. Z. (1985). *The psychoeducational use and interpretation of the Wechsler Adult Intelligence Scale—Revised.* Springfield, IL: Charles C. Thomas.

Spreen, O. (1987). *Learning disabled children growing up: A follow-up into adulthood.* New York: Oxford University Press.

Spreen, O., & Gaddes, W. H. (1969). Developmental norms for 15 neuropsychological tests age 6 to 15. *Cortex, 5,* 171–191.

Spreen, O., & Haaf, R. G. (1986). Empirically derived learning disability subtypes: A replication attempt and longitudinal patterns over 15 years. *Journal of Learning Disabilities, 19,* 170–180.

Spreen, O., Tupper, D., Risser, A., Tuokko, H., & Edgell, D. (1984). *Human developmental neuropsychology.* New York: Oxford University Press.

Springer, S. P., & Deutsch, G. (1985). *Left brain, right brain.* New York: W. H. Freeman.

Spruill, J. (1984). Wechsler Adult Intelligence Scale—Revised. In D. J. Keyser & R. C. Sweetland (Eds.), *Test critiques* (Vol. I; pp. 728–739). Kansas City, MO: Test Corporation of America.

Spruill, J. (1988). Two types of tables for use with the Stanford-Binet Intelligence Scale: Fourth edition. *Journal of Psychoeducational Assessment, 6,* 78–86.

Spruill, J., & Beck, B. (1986). Relationship between the WAIS-R and Wide Range Achievement Test—Revised. *Educational and Psychological Measurement, 46,* 1037–1040.

Squire, L. R. (1986). The neuropsychology of memory dysfunction and its assessment. In I. Grant & K. M. Adams (Eds.), *Neuropsychological assessment of neuropsychiatric disorders* (pp. 268–299). New York: Oxford University Press.

St. John, J., Krichev, A., & Bauman, E. (1976). Northwestern Ontario Indian children and the WISC. *Psychology in the Schools, 13,* 407–411.

Stankov, L. (1988). Aging, attention, and intelligence. *Psychology and Aging, 3,* 59–74.

Steelman, L. C., & Doby, J. T. (1983). Family size and birth order as factors on the IQ performance of black and white children. *Sociology of Education, 56,* 101–109.

Sternberg, R. J. (Ed.). (1982). *Handbook of human intelligence.* Cambridge: Cambridge University Press.

Sternberg, R. J. (1985). *Beyond IQ: A triarchic theory of human intelligence.* Cambridge: Cambridge University Press.

Sternberg, R. J. (1986). Identifying the gifted through IQ: Why a little bit of knowledge is a dangerous thing. *Roeper Review, 8,* 143–147.

Sternberg, R. J. (Ed.). (1988). *Advances in the psychology of human intelligence* (Vol. 4). Hillsdale, NJ: Lawrence Erlbaum.

Stevenson, J. D. (1986). Alternate form reliability and concurrent validity of the PPVT-R for referred rehabilitation agency adults. *Journal of Clinical Psychology, 42,* 650–653.

Stevenson, H. W., & Azuma, H. (1983). IQ in Japan and the United States. *Nature, 306,* 291–292.

Stevenson, H. W., Stigler, J. W., Lee, S., Lucker, G. W., Kitamura, S., & Hsu, C. (1985). Cognitive performance and academic achievement of Japanese, Chinese, and American children. *Child Development, 56,* 718–734.

Stewart, D. D. (1981). Scatter comparability and form equivalence of the verbal scales of the Wechsler-Bellevue, Form I, and the WAIS-R. *Dissertation Abstracts International, 42,* (2-B), 788–789.

Stewart, K. D., & Jones, E. C. (1976). Validity of the Slosson Intelligence Test: A ten-year review. *Psychology in the Schools, 13,* 372–380.

Stinson, M. (1988). *Validity of the adaptive intelligence scale of the Kaufman Adolescent and Adult Intelligence Test for a sample of educable mentally retarded students.* Unpublished doctoral dissertation, University of Alabama, Tuscaloosa.

Storandt, M. (1976). Speed and coding effects in relation to age and ability level. *Developmental Psychology, 12,* 177–178.

Storandt, M. (1977). Age, ability level, and method of administering and scoring the WAIS. *Journal of Gerontology, 32,* 175–178.

Storandt, M., Botwinick, J., & Danziger, W. L. (1986). Longitudinal changes: Patients with mild SDAT and matched healthy controls. In L. W. Poon (Ed.), *Clinical memory assessment of older adults* (pp. 277–284). Washington, DC: American Psychological Association.

Stricker, G., Merbaum, M., & Tangeman, P. (1969). WAIS short forms, information transmission and approximations of Full Scale IQ. *Journal of Clinical Psychology, 25,* 170–172.

Sutter, P., Mayeda, T., Call, T., Yanagi, G., & Yee, S. (1980). Comparison of successful and unsuccessful community-placed mentally retarded persons. *American Journal of Mental Deficiency, 85,* 262–267.

Swenson, W. M., & Lindgren, E. (1952). The use of psychological tests in industry. *Personnel Psychology, 5,* 19–23.

Tambs, K., Sundet, J. M., & Magnus, P. (1984). Heritability analysis of the WAIS subtests: A study of twins. *Intelligence, 8,* 283–293.

Tamkin, A. S., & Jacobsen, R. H. (1987). Age-corrected norms for Shipley Institute of Living Scale scores derived from psychiatric inpatients. *Journal of Clinical Psychology, 43,* 138–142.

Tannenbaum, A. J. (1983). *Gifted children.* New York: Macmillan.

Tanner, J. M. (1962). *Growth at adolescence* (2nd ed.). Oxford: Blackwell Press.

Taylor, J. R. (1976). A comparison of the adaptive behavior of retarded individuals successfully and unsuccessfully placed in group living homes. *Education and Training of the Mentally Retarded, 11,* 56–64.

Taylor, R. L. (1989). *Assessment of exceptional children* (2nd ed.). Englewood Cliffs, NJ: Prentice-Hall.

Teeter, A., & Moore, C. L. (1982). Verbal–Performance IQ discrepancies and subtest scatter on the WISC-R for Native American learning-disabled students. *Educational and Psychological Research, 2,* 1–13.

Teeter, A., Moore, C. L., & Petersen, J. D. (1982). WISC-R Verbal and Performance abilities of Native American students referred for school learning problems. *Psychology in the Schools, 19,* 39–44.

Tellegen, A., & Briggs, P. (1967). Old wine in new skins: Grouping Wechsler subtests into new scales. *Journal of Consulting Psychology, 31,* 499–506.

Telzrow, C. (1988). Summary of "IQ: R. I. P." *NASP Communique, 17*(4), 4.

Terdal, L. G. (1981). Mental retardation. In J. E. Lindemann, *Psychological and behavioral aspects of physical disability* (pp. 179–216). New York: Plenum.

Terman, L. M. (1916). *The measurement of intelligence.* Boston: Houghton-Mifflin.

Terman, L. M. (1925). *Genetic studies of genius* (Vol. 1). Stanford, CA: Stanford University Press.

Terman, L. M. (1954). The discovery and encouragement of exceptional talent. *American Psychologist, 9,* 221–230.

Terman, L. M., & Childs, H. G. (1912). A tentative revision and extension of the Binet-Simon measuring scale of intelligence. *Journal of Educational Psychology, 3,* 61–74; 133–143; 198–208; 277–289.

Terman, L. M., et al. (1925). *Mental and physical traits of a thousand gifted children: Vol. I. Genetic studies of genius.* Stanford, CA: Stanford University Press.

Terman, L. M., & Merrill, M. A. (1937). *Measuring intelligence.* Boston: Houghton-Mifflin.

Terman, L. M., & Merrill, M. A. (1960). *Stanford-Binet Intelligence Scale.* Boston: Houghton-Mifflin.

Terman, L. M., & Merrill, M. A. (1973). *Stanford-Binet Intelligence Scale: 1972 norms edition.* Boston: Houghton-Mifflin.

Terman, L. M., & Oden, M. H. (1947). *The gifted child grows up.* Stanford, CA: Stanford University Press.

Terman, L. M., & Oden, M. H. (1959). *The gifted group at mid-life: Vol. V. Genetic studies of genius.* Stanford, CA: Stanford University Press.

Terry, R. L., & Berg, A. J. (1984). The relationship between WAIS Pa and MMPI Si is mediated by MMPI Pd. *Journal of Clinical Psychology, 40,* 970–971.

Teuber, H. L. (1964). The riddle of frontal lobe function in man. In J. M. Warren & K. Akert (Eds.), *The frontal granular cortex and behavior* (pp. 410–444). New York: McGraw-Hill.

Thiel, G. W. (1981). Relationship of IQ, adaptive behavior, age, and environmental demand to community placement success of mentally retarded adults. *American Journal of Mental Deficiency, 86,* 208–211.

Thienes, C. H., & Haley, T. J. (1972). *Clinical toxicology* (5th ed.). Philadelphia: Lea & Febiger.

Thompson, A. P. (1987). Methodological issues in the clinical evaluation of two- and four-subtest short forms of the WAIS-R. *Journal of Clinical Psychology, 43,* 142–144.

Thompson, A. P., Howard, D., & Anderson, J. (1986). Two- and four-subtest short forms of the WAIS-R: Validity in a psychiatric sample. *Canadian Journal of Behavioral Science, 18,* 287–293.

Thompson, R. J. (1980). The diagnostic utility of WISC-R measures with children referred to a developmental evaluation center. *Journal of Consulting and Clinical Psychology, 48,* 440–447.

Thompson, T., & Carey, A. (1980). Structured normalization: Intellectual and adaptive behavior changes in a residential setting. *Mental Retardation, 18,* 193–197.

Thorndike, R. L. (1972). Review of the Wide Range Achievement Test. In O. K. Buros (Ed.), *The seventh mental measurement yearbook* (pp. 37–38). Highland Park, NJ: Gryphon.

Thorndike, R. L. (1975). Mr. Binet's test 70 years later. *Educational Researcher, 4,* 3–7.

Thorndike, R. L., Hagen, E. P., & Sattler, J. M. (1986a). *Stanford-Binet Intelligence Scale: Fourth Edition.* Chicago: Riverside.

Thorndike, R. L., Hagen, E. P., & Sattler, J. M. (1986b). *Technical manual for the Stanford-Binet Intelligence Scale: Fourth Edition.* Chicago: Riverside.

Thurstone, L. L. (1938). Primary mental abilities. *Psychometric Monographs,* (1).

Thurstone, L. L., & Thurstone, T. G. (1949). *Examiner's manual for the SRA Primary Mental Abilities Test.* Chicago: Science Research Associates.

Tittemore, J. A., Lawson, J. S., & Inglis, J. (1985). Validation of a learning disability index (LDI) derived from a principal components analysis of the WISC-R. *Journal of Learning Disabilities, 18,* 449–454.

Todd, J., Coolidge, F., & Satz, P. (1977). The Wechsler Adult Intelligence Scale Discrepancy Index: A neuropsychological evaluation. *Journal of Consulting and Clinical Psychology, 45,* 450–454.

Torrance, E. P. (1980). Growing up creatively gifted: A 22-year longitudinal study. *The Creative Child and Adult Quarterly, 5,* 148–158.

Torrance, E. P. (1981). Predicting the creativity of elementary school children (1958)—and the teacher "who made a difference." *Gifted Child Quarterly, 25,* 55–61.

Torrance, E. P. (1984). *Torrance Tests of Creative Thinking.* Bensenville, IL: Scholastic Testing Service.

Torrance, E. P., Khatena, J., & Cunningham, B. F. (1973). *Thinking Creatively with Sounds and Words.* Bensenville, IL: Scholastic Testing Service.

Treffinger, D. J. (1985). Review of the Torrance Tests of Creative Thinking. In J. V. Mitchell (Ed.), *The ninth mental measurements yearbook* (pp. 1632–1634). Lincoln, NE: Buros Institute of Mental Measurements, University of Nebraska Press.

Treffinger, D. J., & Renzulli, J. S. (1986). Giftedness as potential for creative productivity: Transcending IQ scores. *Roeper Review, 8,* 150–154.

Tucker, D. (1981). Lateral brain function, emotion, and conceptualization. *Psychological Bulletin, 89,* 19–46.

Tuddenham, R. (1948). Soldier intelligence in World Wars I and II. *American Psychologist, 3,* 54–56.

Tuokko, H., & Crockett, D. (1987). Central cholinergic deficiency WAIS profiles in a nondemented aged sample. *Journal of Clinical and Experimental Neuropsychology, 9,* 225–227.

Turnbull, W. W. (1985). *Student change, program change: Why the SAT scores kept falling* (College Board Rep. 85-2). New York: College Entrance Examination Board.

Turner, R. G., & Horn, J. M. (1976). MMPI item correlates of WAIS subtest performance. *Journal of Clinical Psychology, 32,* 583–594.

Turner, R. G., & Horn, J. M. (1977). Personality scale and item correlates of WAIS abilities. *Intelligence, 1,* 281–297.

Turner, R. G., & Willerman, L. (1977). Sex differences in WAIS item performance. *Journal of Clinical Psychology, 33,* 795–797.

Turner, R. G., Willerman, L., & Horn, J. M. (1976). Personality correlates of WAIS performance. *Journal of Clinical Psychology, 32,* 349–354.

Urbina, S. P., Gooden, C. J., & Ariel, R. N. (1982). WAIS/WAIS-R: Initial comparisons. *Journal of Clinical Neuropsychology, 4,* 145–146.

Uzzell, B. P., Zimmerman, R. A., Dolinskas, C. A., & Obrist, W. D. (1979). Lateralized psychological impairment associated with CT lesions in head injured patients. *Cortex, 15,* 391–401.

Valenstein, E., & Heilman, K. M. (1979). Emotional disorders resulting from lesions of the central nervous system. In K. M. Heilman & E. Valenstein (Eds.), *Clinical neuropsychology* (pp. 413–438). New York: Oxford University Press.

Van Hagen, J., & Kaufman, A. S. (1975). Factor analysis of the WISC-R for a group of mentally retarded children and adolescents. *Journal of Consulting and Clinical Psychology, 43,* 661–667.

Vance, H. R., Brown, W., Hankins, N., & Furgerson, S. C. (1987). A comparison of the WISC-R and the WAIS-R with special education students. *Journal of Clinical Psychology, 43,* 377–380.

Vance, H. R., Hankins, N., Wallbrown, F., Engin, A., & McGee, H. (1978). Analysis of cognitive abilities for mentally retarded children on the WISC-R. *The Psychological Record, 28,* 391–397.

Vance, H. R., Kitson, D., & Singer, M. (1983). Further investigation of comparability of WISC-R and PPVT-R for children and youth referred for psychological services. *Psychology in the Schools, 20,* 307–310.

Vandenberg, S. G., & Vogler, G. P. (1985). Genetic determinants of intelligence. In B. B. Wolman (Ed.), *Handbook of intelligence* (pp. 3–57). New York: Wiley.

Vane, J. R., & Motta, R. W. (1984). Group intelligence tests. In G. Goldstein & M. Hersen (Eds.), *Handbook of psychological assessment* (pp. 100–116). New York: Pergamon.

Varney, N. R. (1982). Pantomime recognition defect in aphasia: Implications for the concept of asymbolia. *Brain and Language, 15,* 32–39.

Vega, A., Jr., & Parsons, O. A. (1967). Cross-validation of the Halstead Reitan tests for brain damage. *Journal of Consulting Psychology, 31,* 619–623.

Vega, A., Jr., & Parsons, O. A. (1969). Relationship between sensory-motor deficits and WAIS Verbal and Performance scores in unilateral brain damage. *Cortex, 5,* 229–241.

Verhaaren, P., & Conner, F. P. (1981). Physical disabilities. In J. M. Kauffman & D. P. Hallahan (Eds.), *Handbook of Special Education.* Englewood Cliffs, NJ: Prentice-Hall.

Vernon, P. A. (1983). Speed of information processing and general intelligence. *Intelligence, 7,* 53–70.

Vernon, P. A., & Kantor, L. (1986). Reaction time correlations with intelligence test scores obtained under either timed or untimed conditions. *Intelligence, 10,* 315–330.

Vernon, P. A., Nador, S., & Kantor, L. (1985). Group differences in intelligence and speed of information-processing. *Intelligence, 9,* 137–148.

Vincent, K. R. (1979). The modified WAIS: An alternative to short forms. *Journal of Clinical Psychology, 35,* 624–625.

Vining, D. R. (1983). Mean IQ differences in Japan and the United States. *Nature, 301,* 738.

Vining, D. R. (1986). Social versus reproductive success: The central theoretical problem of human sociobiology. *Behavioral and Brain Sciences, 9,* 167–187.

Voelker, S. L., Shore, D. L., Brown-More, C., Hill, L. T., & Perry, J. (1987). *Validity of self-report of adaptive behavior skills by mentally retarded adults.* Manuscript submitted for publication.

Voelker, S. L., Shore, D. L., & Miller, L. T. (in press). Vineland Adaptive Behavior Scales with mentally retarded adults: Informant versus self-report. *Mental Retardation and Learning Disabilities Bulletin.*

Vogel, S. A. (1986). Levels and patterns of intellectual functioning among LD college students: Clinical and educational implications. *Journal of Learning Disabilities, 19,* 71–79.

Vogel, S. A. (1990). Gender differences in intelligence, language, visual-motor abilities, and academic achievement in students with learning disabilities: A review of the literature. *Journal of Learning Disabilities, 23,* 44–52.

Von Monakow, C. V. (1911). Lokalization der hirnfunktionen. *Journal für Psychologie und Neurologie, 17,* 185–200.

Waber, D. P., Carlson, D., Mann, M., Merola, J., & Moylan, P. (1984). SES-related aspects of neuropsychological performance. *Child Development, 55,* 1878–1886.

Wagner, E. E., & McCormick, M. K. (1982). Relationships between WAIS Verbal versus Performance decrements and Bender-Gestalt errors. *Perceptual and Motor Skills, 54,* 1259–1263.

Wainer, H. (1988). How accurately can we assess changes in minority performance on the SAT? *American Psychologist, 43,* 774–778.

Walker, N. W. (1987). The Stanford-Binet 4th edition: Haste does seem to make waste. *Measurement and Evaluation in Counseling and Development, 20,* 135–138.

Walsh, K. W. (1977). Neuropsychological aspects of modified leucotomy. In W. H. Sweet (Ed.), *Neuropsychological treatment in psychiatry* (pp. 163–174). Baltimore, MD: University Park Press.

Walton, J. R. (1987). Today's kids, tomorrow's nations. *NASP Communique, 15*(5), 6–7.

Waltz, A. G. (1972). Cortical blood flow of opposite hemisphere after occlusion of the middle cerebral artery. *Transamerican Neurological Association, 92,* 293–294.

Ward, L. C., Selby, R. B., & Clark, B. L. (1987). Subtest administration times and short forms of the Wechsler Adult Intelligence Scale—Revised. *Journal of Clinical Psychology, 43,* 276–278.

Warner, M. H. (1983). *Practice effects, test–retest reliability, and comparability of WAIS and WAIS-R: Issues in the assessment of cognitive recovery in detoxified alcoholics.* Unpublished doctoral dissertation, University of Georgia, Athens.

Warner, M. H., Ernst, J., & Townes, B. D. (1986). Comparison of WAIS and WAIS-R factor structure for neuropsychiatric patients. *Psychological Reports, 59,* 715–720.

Warner, M. H., Ernst, J., Townes, B. D., Peel, J., & Preston, M. (1987). Relationships between IQ and neuropsychological measures in neuropsychiatric populations: Within-laboratory and cross-cultural replications using WAIS and WAIS-R. *Journal of Clinical and Experimental Neuropsychology, 9,* 545–562.

Warrington, E. K., & James, M. (1967). Disorders of visual perception in patients with localized cerebral lesions. *Neuropsychologia, 5,* 253–266.

Wasserstein, J. (1980). *Differentiation of perceptual closure: Implications for right hemisphere functions.* Unpublished doctoral dissertation, City University of New York.

Watson, C. G., Klett, W. G., Kucala, T., Nixon, C., Schaefer, A., & Gasser, B. (1981). Prediction of the WAIS scores from the 1973 Henmon-Nelson revision. *Journal of Clinical Psychology, 37,* 840–842.

Watson, C. G., Thomas, R. W., Anderson, D., & Felling, J. (1968). Differentiation of organics from schizophrenics at two chronicity levels by use of the Reitan-Halstead organic test battery. *Journal of Consulting and Clinical Psychology, 32,* 679–684.

Watson, G., & Glaser, E. M. (1980). *Watson-Glaser Critical Thinking Appraisal.* New York: The Psychological Corporation.

Wechsler, D. (1928). Psychometric tests. In I. S. Wechsler, *A textbook of clinical neurology* (pp. 104–116). Philadelphia: W. B. Saunders.

Wechsler, D. (1939). *Measurement of adult intelligence.* Baltimore: Williams & Wilkins.

Wechsler, D. (1944). *The measurement of adult intelligence* (3rd ed.). Baltimore: Williams & Wilkins.

Wechsler, D. (1945). A standardized memory scale for clinical use. *Journal of Psychology, 19,* 87–95.

Wechsler, D. (1946). *The Wechsler-Bellevue Intelligence Scale, Form II.* New York: The Psychological Corporation.

Wechsler, D. (1949). *Manual for the Wechsler Intelligence Scale for Children (WISC).* New York: The Psychological Corporation.

Wechsler, D. (1955). *Manual for the Wechsler Adult Intelligence Scale (WAIS).* New York: The Psychological Corporation.

Wechsler, D. (1958). *Measurement and appraisal of adult intelligence* (4th ed.). Baltimore: Williams & Wilkens.

Wechsler, D. (1974). *Manual for the Wechsler Intelligence Scale for Children—Revised (WISC-R).* San Antonio, TX: The Psychological Corporation.

Wechsler, D. (1981). *Manual for the Wechsler Adult Intelligence Scale—Revised (WAIS-R).* San Antonio, TX: The Psychological Corporation.

Wechsler, D. (1987). *Manual for the Wechsler Memory Scale—Revised (WMS-R).* San Antonio, TX: The Psychological Corporation.

Wechsler, D. (1989). *WPPSI-R manual: Wechsler Preschool and Primary Scale of Intelligence—Revised.* San Antonio, TX: The Psychological Corporation.

Weinberg, J., Diller, L., Gerstman, L., & Schulman, P. (1972). Digit span in right and left hemiplegics. *Journal of Clinical Psychology, 28,* 361.

Weinberg, R. A. (1989). Intelligence and IQ: Landmark issues and great debates. *American Psychologist, 43,* 98–104.

Weller, C., & Strawser, S. (1987). Adaptive behavior of subtypes of learning disabled individuals. *Journal of Special Education, 21,* 101–116.

Werner, E. E. (1986). A longitudinal study of perinatal risk. In D. C. Farran & J. D. McKinney (Eds.), *Risk in intellectual and psychosocial development* (pp. 3–27). Orlando, FL: Academic Press.

Wernicke, C. (1874). *Der aphasische symptomenkomplex.* Breslau: Cohn and Weigert.

Wesman, A. G. (1968). Intelligent testing. *American Psychologist, 23,* 267–274.

Wheaton, P. J., & Vandergriff, A. F. (1978). Comparison of WISC and WISC-R scores of highly gifted students in public school. *Psychological Reports, 43,* 627–630.

Wheeler, L., Burke, C. J., & Reitan, R. M. (1962). An application of discriminant functions to the problem of predicting brain damage using behavioral variables. *Perceptual and Motor Skills, 16* [Monograph Supplement], 417–440.

Wheeler, L., & Reitan, R. M. (1962). The presence and laterality of brain damage predicted from responses to a short Aphasia Screening Test. *Perceptual and Motor Skills, 15,* 783–799.

Whelan, T. B., & Walker, M. L. (1988). Effects of sex and lesion locus on measures of intelligence. *Journal of Consulting and Clinical Psychology, 56,* 633–635.

Whiddon, M. F., Sr., (1978). Identification and validation of a subtest pattern on the Wechsler Adult Intelligence Scale that will separate brain damaged, schizophrenic, and normal subjects by means of a discriminant function analysis. (University of Southern Mississippi, 1977). *Dissertation Abstracts International, 38,* (10-B), 5051.

Whitmore, J. R. (1979). The etiology of underachievement in highly gifted young children. *Journal for the Education of the Gifted, 3,* 38–51.

Whitmore, J. R. (1980). *Giftedness, conflict, and underachievement.* Boston: Allyn & Bacon.

Whitmore, J. R. (1981). Gifted children with handicapping conditions: A new frontier. *Exceptional Children, 48,* 106–114.

Whitworth, R. H., & Gibbons, R. T. (1986). Cross-racial comparison of the WAIS and WAIS-R. *Educational and Psychological Measurement, 46,* 1041–1049.

Wiig, E. H. (1985). Review of the Peabody Picture Vocabulary Test—Revised. In J. V. Mitchell (Ed.), *The ninth mental measurement yearbook* (pp. 1127–1128). Lincoln, NE: Buros Institute of Mental Measurements, University of Nebraska Press.

Wildman, R. W., & Wildman, R. W. (1977). Validity of Verbal IQ as a short form of the Wechsler Adult Intelligence Scale. *Journal of Consulting and Clinical Psychology, 45,* 171–172.

Williams, R. L. (1974). Scientific racism and IQ: The silent mugging of the black community. *Psychology Today, 7,* 32–41.

Willis, S. L. (1985). Towards an educational psychology of the older adult learner: Intellectual and cognitive bases. In J. E. Birren and K. W. Schaie (Eds.), *Handbook of the psychology of aging* (2nd ed.; pp. 818–847). New York: Van Nostrand Reinhold.

Willoughby, R. R. (1927). Family similarities in mental-test abilities. *Genetic Psychology Monographs, 2,* 239–277.

Willson, V. L., & Reynolds, C. R. (1985). Normative data on the WAIS-R for Selz and Reitan's index of scatter. *Journal of Clinical Psychology, 41,* 254–258.

Wilson, R. S. (1983). The Louisville twin study: Developmental synchronies in behavior. *Child Development, 54,* 298–316.

Wing, L. (1971). Perceptual and language development in autistic children: A comparative study. In M. Rutter (Ed.), *Infantile autism: Concepts, characteristics, and treatment.* London: Churchill-Livingstone.

Winne, J., & Gittinger, J. (1973). An introduction to the Personality Assessment System. *Journal of Clinical Psychology* (Monograph Supplement 38).

Wissler, C. (1901). The correlation of mental and physical tests. *Psychological Review, 3* (Monograph Supplement 16).

Witelson, S. F. (1976). Sex and the single hemisphere: Specialization of the right hemisphere for spatial processing. *Science, 193,* 425–427.

Witelson, S. F. (1977). Developmental dyslexia: Two right hemispheres and none left. *Science, 195,* 309–311.

Witt, J. C. (1986). Review of the Wide Range Achievement Test—Revised. *Journal of Psychoeducational Assessment, 4,* 87–90.

Witt, J. C., & Martens, B. K. (1984). Adaptive behavior: Tests and assessment issues. *The School Psychology Review, 13,* 478–484.

Witt, S. J. (1981). Increase in adaptive behavior level after residence in an intermediate care facility for mentally retarded persons. *Mental Retardation, 19,* 75–79.

Wolman, B. B. (1985). Intelligence and mental health. In B. B. Wolman (Ed.), *Handbook of intelligence* (pp. 849–872). New York: Wiley.

Woodcock, R. (1978). *Development and standardization of the Woodcock-Johnson Psycho-Educational Battery.* Allen, TX: DLM/Teaching Resources.

Woodcock, R. W. (1987). *Woodcock Reading Mastery Tests—Revised: Examiner's manual.* Circle Pines, MN: American Guidance Service.

Woodcock, R. W. (1988, August). *Factor structure of the Tests of Cognitive Ability from the 1977 and 1989 Woodcock-Johnson.* Paper presented at the ACER Seminar on Intelligence, Melbourne, Australia.

Woodcock, R. W., & Johnson, M. (1977). *Woodcock-Johnson Psycho-Educational Battery.* Allen, TX: DLM/Teaching Resources.

Woodcock, R. W., & Johnson, M. B. (1989a). *Woodcock-Johnson Tests of Cognitive Ability: Standard and supplemental batteries.* Allen, TX: DLM/Teaching Resources.

Woodcock, R. W., & Johnson, M. B. (1989b). *Woodcock-Johnson Tests of Achievement: Standard and supplemental batteries.* Allen, TX: DLM/Teaching Resources.

Woodcock, R. W., & Mather, N. (1989a). WJ-R Tests of Cognitive Ability—Standard and Supplemental Batteries: Examiner's manual. In R. W. Woodcock & M. B. Johnson, *Woodcock-Johnson Psycho-Educational Battery—Revised.* Allen, TX: DLM/Teaching Resources.

Woodcock, R. W., & Mather, N. (1989b). WJ-R Tests of Achievement—Standard and Supplemental Batteries: Examiner's manual. In R. W. Woodcock & M. B. Johnson, *Woodcock-Johnson Psycho-Educational Battery—Revised.* Allen, TX: DLM/Teaching Resources.

Worthington, C. F. (1987). Testing the test: Kaufman Test of Educational Achievement, Comprehensive Form and Brief Form. *Journal of Counseling and Development, 65,* 325–327.

Yerkes, R. M. (1917). The Binet versus the point scale method of measuring intelligence. *Journal of Applied Psychology, 1,* 111–122.

Yoakum, C. S., & Yerkes, R. M. (1920). *Army mental tests.* New York: Henry Holt.

Name Index

Subject Index